BLUE GUIDE VICTORIAN ARCHITECTURE

D0663045

Relief of the architect at work, G. J Skipper's office (1896), London Street, Norwich

BLUE GUIDE

VICTORIAN ARCHITECTURE IN BRITAIN

Julian Orbach

A & C Black
London

W W Norton
New York

First edition 1987

Published by A & C Black (Publishers) Limited
35 Bedford Row, London WC1R 4JH

© A & C Black (Publishers) Limited 1987

Published in the United States of America by
W W Norton & Company, Incorporated
500 Fifth Avenue, New York, NY 10110

Published simultaneously in Canada by
Penguin Books Canada Limited
2801 John Street, Markham, Ontario LR3 1BA

British Library Cataloguing in Publication Data

Orbach, Julian
    Victorian architecture in Britain.—
    (Blue guide)
    1. Architecture, Victorian—Great Britain
    I. Title   II. Series
    720'941   NA967

    ISBN 0–7136–2842–1

ISBN 0-393-30070-6   {U.S.A.}

Printed in Great Britain by
Butler & Tanner Ltd, Frome and London

For permission to reproduce illustrations the publishers would like to
thank: the Royal Commission on the Historical Monuments of England,
the Royal Commission on the Ancient and Historical Monuments of
Scotland, the Royal Commission on the Ancient and Historical
Monuments of Wales, the British Architectural Library, University
College of North Wales Library, Nottinghamshire County Council
Leisure Services, Oxford County Libraries, N.S. Mason-Smith (City of
Cambridge Planning Department), A.F. Kersting, P.W.H. Neville, Stefan
Muthesius, Arup Associates, Norwich Union Insurance.

PREFACE

Victorian building in Britain is necessarily a large subject and one that will never be covered adequately to suit all tastes. A guidebook must take the path of the buildings most prominent and most accessible. Victorian church building, for example, will take on a prominence only partly justified while the areas of Victorian terrace housing and suburb that surround every town receive little attention. Discoveries, especially of pioneering industrial buildings, are still being made and many residents of Victorian towns will have a favourite building, whose decoration or interior will have been ignored in this book. Even so, the *aim* has been to include as many significant buildings as possible, rather than restrict the scope to the outstanding. Thus, many entries are brief, but it was felt that the prime purpose of such a guide must be to encourage visits to buildings overlooked in the general guidebooks.

The organisation of the guide is by county, or region in Scotland, subdivided under principal centres, with London subdivided under the boroughs. Within the towns, the buildings are organised to the most convenient pedestrian route, and apologies must be made for those who find themselves attempting to follow a route in reverse. Where possible the routes are circular.

Inclusion of a building in the guide does *not* mean that there is right of access. Where buildings are open to the public this has been mentioned, but otherwise, especially with houses, the privacy of the owner should be respected. Many larger houses are open occasionally or have gardens opened under the various gardens schemes. Local information offices or libraries should have the details, which are too changeable to be included here. Where there is no public access and the building is not visible from a public road or path, requests to visit should be by letter. Churches are increasingly kept locked, and with Victorian churches the number of visitors has been too low in the past for arrangements to be made for obtaining the key. Perseverance can only be recommended, and if enough visitors come perhaps the value of under- loved churches will be appreciated and future users of this guide will find a welcome where now there is only a barred door and blank noticeboard.

There will be many omissions in this guide and errors, though it is hoped not too many. Buildings will have been demolished or mutilated that have been described as if still intact. Every piece of additional information would be more than welcome for inclusion in future editions, especially information on new uses that make access to buildings easier, for example where a country house becomes an hotel or an industrial building a museum or craft centre. In the nature of information on the Victorian world this volume must be treated as a work in progress and its users as explorers.

The author is responsible for writing everything except the parts covering the City of London and the South London boroughs, which were the work of Andrew Derrick, who rescued the enterprise at the eleventh hour. The author's thanks must go to all those in County and City planning offices who read parts of the text for omissions and errors, to the numerous friends who read particular counties, to all those who offered suggestions, especially those in the Victorian Society, whose committee minutes have been invaluable in keeping track of threatened and lost buildings. Much use has been made of reference books, guidebooks, church guides and local history pamphlets too numerous to credit here, but the bedrock for building studies in Britain, the Buildings of England series guided for so long by Sir Nikolaus Pevsner, and its more recent sister series for Wales and Scotland, cannot be too highly praised.

CONTENTS

8   CONTENTS

INTRODUCTION

British architecture, it is sobering to recall, has only rarely had significance outside this island, the natural result of a position peripheral to European culture. The vaulting of Durham Cathedral in 1093 was probably the first in Europe, but the specifically British developments, the Scots tower house, Perpendicular Gothic, the Elizabethan and Jacobean country house or the English Baroque, are offshoots not main stems in European architecture. Between the late 18C and 1914 Britain's role was no longer peripheral, as the exploitation of the colonies gave her the economic strength to challenge the cultural supremacy of continental Europe. The effectiveness of the cultural challenge can be much disputed. It is at least arguable that for the French and German visitor, the sanitary, heating and lighting arrangements of British buildings were more impressive than their outward form, but it is none the less only during the 19C and early 20C that British buildings were discussed, illustrated and imitated widely outside these shores. Colonial ties ensure that the main lines of British architecture have representative examples all over the British Empire, ties of language and trade ensure that the British influence is a strong element in American 'Victorian' architecture, assisted in all these places by the emigration of British-trained architects. A more distant cultural influence built the English style neo-Gothic country houses of Eastern Europe, with their parks on the English model, and—only marginally architectural perhaps—laid out the 'English gardens' in so many continental cities. British engineering influence was universal, most obviously in the building of railways from France to Peru, but also in the construction of glass and iron buildings, of which the 1851 Crystal Palace was the most powerful image of the possibilities in this field.

The analysis of what actually went into that bubbling mixture of Victorian architecture is no easier now than it was at the time, when the single issue most discussed in architectural literature was the absence of, need for, or possibility of, a truly Victorian architecture. At the root of all the discussion was the problem of historicism, one that came upon the 19C architect almost imperceptibly as part of his inheritance from the 18C. During the 18C classical and Renaissance disciplines had been applied gradually so that the early 18C house, classical only in its symmetry and wearing often an eclectic collection of Baroque features adapted from Holland, France and Italy, succumbed to a simplified Renaissance classicism, derived from Palladio, that was steadily modified in the later 18C by admixtures of archaeologically correct classicism, from ancient Roman and Greek remains. By the early 19C archaeological investigation had established a rule-book of Greek classicism that in the nature of such codifications had set a standard of correctness against which freer interpretations could be condemned. The notion of a 'correct' style had arrived and it is significant that rapidly this criterion was applied in condemnation of earlier neo-classicists and of Palladians whose architecture now broke rules of which they had had no knowledge. Those who would challenge the pre-eminence of the Greek found that the ground had changed so that another 'style' with its own codes, rules and historical justification must needs be presented in antithesis. Thus to the Greek could be set up the Roman, or the Palladian, with a justification partly based on heroic ancestry, partly on practicality—the advocates of Renaissance styles could point to the inappropriateness of porticos in a dull climate, or the difficulty of fitting windows to the Parthenon.

The existence of styles in the classical to Renaissance orbit presupposed that styles must exist for codification outside, primarily in the Gothic, already in the late 18C revived for its picturesque (i.e. non-archaeological) qualities. Beyond the Gothic, patrons and architects, inspired by ever-extending travel and romantic illustrated publications, had already by the early 19C begun to dabble in exotic waters that would always be on the fringes of serious architecture, the Indian, the Moorish, the Swiss, the rustic cottage and the Italian villa, none of which could succumb to codification.

By the 1830s the despairing architectural critic could point to the manifest tyranny of the dominant classical style, the Greek, with its ceaseless repetition of the same columns and mouldings, and bewail a national architecture based on copying ancient styles, but would be no longer capable of presenting an alternative that was not itself defined as a style (Gothic, Roman, Italian or Elizabethan) and so subject to the same criticism as the Greek, with the added probability that architects using these other styles would be led by ignorance into absurdities. An antithesis was thus set up between 'copyism' or the slavish imitation, and 'bizarrerie', the reckless combination of details, possibly from historic styles, used in a way that would offend good taste.

The first half of the 19C was a battleground of styles, establishing or failing to establish the limits at which originality slipped into absurdity and equally establishing those styles that might be taken seriously by those of taste, and those that should remain playthings. Thus by 1850 the consensus had been established that Gothic was correct for churches, though its advocates would have its uses universal, that for country houses the English manorial styles, Tudor, Elizabethan and Jacobean, were most apt, Baronial in Scotland, and that the Italian Renaissance form of classicism was more apt than the Greek or Roman buildings of more than one floor, as it was not restrained by giant orders of columns and hence suited best commercial buildings, clubs, hotels and terraced houses. For the occasional major public building the giant porticos of antiquity might be acceptable, but in the main there were few buildings like Birmingham Town Hall where the temple form might be properly adapted without extraneous windows. This is only the roughest of outlines; an eclectic mixture of classic and Italian remained the rule for many Nonconformist churches; attempts were made continuously, without obvious success, to bring the Elizabethan, Tudor and Gothic into street facades, and with much more success into free-standing public buildings where these styles could refer to an antiquity more plausible than the vaguer heroics of classicism. Thus in Scotland, public buildings of the Victorian age with a tower swelling at the top and capped by a pavilion roof are common, though this loosely Franco-Scottish hybrid, referring presumably to the time of James V and Mary Queen of Scots, is a figment of romantic imagination. The Houses of Parliament competition was one of the first to specify Gothic or Elizabethan, on nationalist grounds, to the fury of the classical lobby, and architecture by association remained a staple of the Victorian age thereafter—be it the association of country houses with bogus lineage, the association of bankers and commercial tycoons with the palazzi of Italian merchant princes, or of municipal corporations with the guilds of the Middle Ages.

Thinking architects had always had recourse to discussion of function and structure when faced with the aesthetic arguments of laymen, and in the confusion of the 19C the return to first principles must always have seemed a refreshing alternative. 'Pure taste in architecture has in all past ages been structural', wrote A. Bartholomew in 1839, and many writers followed him bringing also such ideals as 'fitness', 'propriety', 'proportion' and 'pictorial effect', these offered by R. Kerr who concluded an explosive little book against all the established creeds with the observation that 'the principles of Nature and Reason are the very means by which the human mind designs'. More successful in using the functional argument to their ends were the Gothicists. The first half of the 19C established in volume after volume a bank of knowledge of medieval detail, and antiquarian scholars combined with enthusiastic churchmen to settle a canon of taste in the use of medieval detail at least as rigid as that of the Greek Revivalists. The Ecclesiological Society took root in the bosom of the Anglican Church from the 1840s, execrating deviations from current practice, 'correct' having been established, after early deviations into the Perpendicular and Norman styles, as the English Decorated Gothic of the 14C, called Middle Pointed. Their justifications tended towards arcane symbolism just as their churchmanship tended towards the ritualised, but their mentor, and the most influential theorist of the 19C, A.W.N. Pugin, founded his advocacy of the Gothic on functionalism: the theory that 'there shall be no features of a building not necessary for convenience, construction and propriety'. In Pugin's writings are presented, fully formed, two of the most potent arguments of 20C architectural theory, first that form should follow function and secondly that the type of buildings a society produces is a reflection of the spiritual state of that society or, more contentiously, can assist in reforming that spiritual state.

Convenience, construction and propriety in the school of Pugin came to mean the asymmetric plan, where the placing of rooms followed their use, and the exterior elevations, rooflines and chimneys followed the interior plan. Propriety meant that ornament would be appropriate to status, both of a building, greater on a country house than on a parsonage, and of its parts, the dining-room and drawing-room windows more elaborate than those of lesser rooms. To be avoided were artificial symmetries and overplayed variety for the sake of picturesque effect, though the latter was a constant trap. Pugin's theories fitted neatly with house design within the Gothic, manorial and baronial styles whose picturesque tendencies had already encouraged asymmetry and the breaking up of rooflines and wall planes, and it is often a fruitless effort when faced with a rambling Victorian design to say how much picturesqueness is the product of function and how much function has suffered for the sake of the picturesque. None the less the Puginian principle of honesty—the expression of the parts of the building externally, and construction in materials that are not sham (like stucco)—can be detected in innumerable small buildings, especially cottages, schools and parsonages where the trappings of archaeological Gothic have been dispensed with.

The expression of materials advocated by Pugin and bolstered by Ruskin's advocacy in the 1850s of structural colour to unite the divergent twins, structure and decoration, dovetailed perfectly with the passionate mid Victorian interest in geology and natural sciences, seen so clearly in Ruskin's work. The question of the make-up of the world, and no less so the time it took to be made, touched the story of the Creation, whether in the end geology demonstrated the miraculous finger of God or upset the Genesis story completely. The beauties of rocks, which have never been more thoroughly explored, came to be incorporated in the buildings, whether in the marble church fonts that glow like an antique sweet-shop or in the granite and sandstone shafts that enliven many a dull facade. Polychromy, the use of colour in decoration, geology, the exploitation of the beauties of the earth, and naturalistic sculpture, where the artist or self-taught craftsman would take inspiration from the plant forms of nature, combine in the powerful structures of the High Victorian period (c 1855–70) when the Gothic Revival might truly be said to have reached a point where Victorian replaces medieval. The High Victorian was a melange of functional theory, the vigorous Gothic of the Early English, Northern French and North Italian medieval styles, and a delight in solid geometry, sheer wall faces, curves, cones and triangles, that was perhaps the zenith of the attempt to build a new architecture on the bones of the old.

The materials for extravagant polychromy were of course only available thanks to the railway system that in 1840 hardly impinged on the countryside at all, reached Aberdeen and West Cornwall by 1852 and the North tip of Scotland by 1874. Aberdeen granite, Midland red sandstone, Welsh and Cornish slates, Bath stone, Portland stone, and all the products of manufacture, notably terracotta and cast iron, could travel the whole country. The achievements, most notably in the Scottish Highlands, of transporting building materials are astounding, especially when it is remembered that beyond the railway lines the technology of the horse and cart prevailed.

The achievements in engineering remained most spectacular in the bridges and train-sheds of the railway system. The relationship of architects to new technology was diffident—not for them the full structural solutions of the Crystal Palace, that overblown greenhouse, but rather the gradual incorporation of structural iron, fireproof floors, hot-air heating and ventilating systems, and new methods of lighting. In commercial frontages the most readily visible exploitation of iron in architecture can be seen, but those skins of glass held by thin stanchions of metal that so impress our century seem to have passed almost without comment in the age when they were built, not as heroic as the railway sheds, not as architectural as the stone or brick fronts around them. The smaller decorative elements in cast iron, firegrates, railings and gates, and the structures assembled from ready-made components, bandstands and fountains, lamps and benches, remain the most visible products of Victorian iron technology.

The revival of forgotten crafts is one of the most impressive achievements of Victorian architecture, especially church architecture. The specialist firms produced work of the highest technical quality in fields either ignored previously or newly discovered. The sculptural work of Farmer and Brindley, Earp and Nicholls, the stained glass of Clayton and Bell, Powell's, Hardman, Lavers and Barraud, and many others, the metalwork of Skidmore, Hardman, and Singer, the tiles of Minton, Godwin, and Maw and Co., the terracotta and ceramic of Doultons were all products of firms working between the worlds of the artists of the Royal Academy and of industrial mass-production, a meeting of art, architecture and industry on a scale never seen before or since. The role of artist and craftsman in architecture was one constantly discussed, not just in the context of the Ruskinian rejection of the machine age. Decoration in architecture was of paramount importance across the whole field of building and from the time of the Great Exhibition of 1851 the question of art education, the training of craftsmen and the improvement of industrial design was constantly discussed. Architects, painters and sculptors were involved in the design of metalwork, ceramic, stained glass, wallpaper and furniture, and their designs filtered through to influence commercial design on a wider scale.

The mid Victorian notion of progress, and conviction that the 19C could be and would be the climax of human history thus far, shines through contemporary writings of all kinds, nowhere more so than in the encomia written for the opening of great public buildings, where national or municipal chauvinism seems boundless. This meant that the leading artists, and, to a lesser degree, architects and engineers of the day, were held in the highest esteem, knighted, decorated and buried in style. Not coincidentally they began to organise themselves professionally so as to protect the leading practitioners from the jostling mass of builders, surveyors, decorators and jacks of all trades below. The Royal Academy had already gathered together the painters and sculptors, but during the 19C it dominated such areas as the selection of artists for public commissions, while the Institute of British Architects, the Incorporation of Architects in Scotland and the Institute of Civil Engineers established similar positions, all the more important in an era when training was by pupillage not by examination, so that the most obvious check on entry to the professions was not available.

Later Victorian architecture displays a softening in attitudes partly due to exhaustion at the lack of progress in the question of style. The classicists, increasingly eclectic, justified the mélange of elements Italian, French, antique and novel by the argument that the selection of the best details from the past with judicious invention was the best way forward. Certainly the need for multi-storey buildings with generous areas of glass was beyond the resources of historic precedent. The Gothicists, tired after the muscular effects and strong colours of the High Victorian period, succumbed by the 1870s to their own eclecticism, freely selected from the cusp of Gothic and Renaissance in Northern Europe, revelling in that period from c 1550 to 1700 when ignorance of rules classical or Gothic and a delight in surface decoration gave a freedom extremely attractive in an age when the rules had failed. There are obvious parallels between the adoption of these pretty but, to the older generation, 'bastard' styles, and the changes in attitudes in society, the relaxation of the stern and puritan mid Victorian ethic, muscular Christian, self-helping and hard working. The aesthetes of the 1870s and 1880s were a typical second generation, heirs to wealth garnered by unrelenting effort buttressed by unbending morality, and their cult of sensitivity and refinement was in direct opposition to the values of their parents. Their architecture is altogether lighter, conscious of delicate effects and wary of the heroic.

By the end of the century, however, imperialism began to require an appropriate architecture and London, as an imperial capital, particularly failed by comparison with Paris, Berlin or Washington. In the Baroque, that revival of the style of Sir Christopher Wren, a style suited to grand effects in Portland stone but also capable of delicate contrasts of brick and stone, the turn of the century found a comfortable image. That this was not as ponderous and doctrinaire as it sounds was due to the admixture of stylistic freedom inherited from the Aesthetic Movement, a distrust of formal symmetries inherited from the Gothic Revival and a dedication to the Arts and Crafts inherited from Ruskin and Wiliam Morris. Designers in the direct tradition of Morris built and worked in a consciously vernacular manner, taking their technology from rustic craftsmen and seeking to eliminate the distinction of arts and crafts, designer and builder. These in the mainstream employed to great effect the craftsmen as well as the academic painters and sculptors. The architecture of the period around 1900 is of splendid variety, from the formalities of Baroque or Imperial Classicism to the freely handled adaptations of period styles, to the attempts to create a wholly new architecture. A visit to Glasgow, from the Municipal Chambers to the School of Art, demonstrates the widest extremes. It was the period of the small country house, those most instantly likeable of Victorian and Edwardian buildings, of the garden suburb, of the beginnings of humane public housing and of public buildings seemingly designed to encourage the user to come in, for example the libraries scattered over the cities and smaller towns by the generosity of such as Andrew Carnegie and Passmore Edwards.

Between 1837 and 1914 the face of Britain was transformed. Most of the building stock of the country still dates from that period. The architecture of the era is more thoroughly varied than that of any other era, and even the terms Victorian and Edwardian need constant modification if they are to be useful. This guidebook seeks only to be a pointer to what can be skimmed from the surface, and if nothing else, will point up the vitality of the period, that is the bridge to our own age.

EXPLANATIONS AND TERMS

AEDICULE: Window framing of columns or pilasters carrying entablature and pediment. A classical feature that became a common motif of the 'palazzo' style via Renaissance Italy. See Sir Charles Barry's Travellers' and Reform Clubs, Pall Mall, London.

AESTHETIC MOVEMENT: The 'art for art's sake' doctrine of the later 19C associated with Oscar Wilde, J.M. Whistler and the Grosvenor Gallery. A reaction against the stern pieties of the mid 19C, its architectural equivalent was the eclectic prettiness of the 'Queen Anne' style (q.v.).

APSE: Semicircular or polygonal end to a chancel. Not especially common in British medieval architecture but much used in Victorian churches, especially of the 1850s.

ART NOUVEAU: Principally continental movement linked with the arcane interests of the Symbolists and characterised by the use of stylised and sinuous plant and wave motifs. In Britain, C.R. Mackintosh and the Glasgow School approach most nearly, C.H. Townsend and Alfred Gilbert in England.

ARTS AND CRAFTS: Late 19C movement, identified with William Morris and originating with John Ruskin, that elevated craftsmanship and human skill over machine production. Ideologically socialist but in the arts influencing all aspects of design, essentially towards simplicity and freedom from copyism, with a respect for traditional materials and crafts. In architecture, Philip Webb was Morris's closest associate and inspiration to the generation of W.R. Lethaby, C.F.A. Voysey and C.R. Ashbee.

ASYLUMS: The provision of institutions for the insane on a national basis was the result, in England and Wales, of the 1845 Lunacy Act, whereby each county was empowered to build a county asylum. Predecessors of these vast piles, still so prominent outside major cities, were the Bethlehem Hospital ('Bedlam') in London (1674) and the Middlesex County Asylum at Hanwell (1829– 31).

BACK-TO-BACK: A type of economical house construction where two parallel terraces share a single roof and spine wall, hence without rear access, yard or garden.

BALDACCHINO: Altar canopy, generally free-standing on columns.

BANKS: Ornate bank buildings are a corollary of the transition from small private banks to limited companies or joint-stock banks, long the practice in Scotland, only achieved in England through Banking Acts of 1826 and 1833. Savings Banks were established after 1800 to encourage thrift by offering greater interest to very small depositors.

BAPTIST: Nonconformist denomination distinguished by the belief that baptism should be given to believers only. By 1900 there were some half million Baptists in Britain.

BARONIAL: Style developed in Scotland in the 19C from Scots 15C to 17C architecture, characterised by towers, cap-houses and crowstepped gables. David Bryce was the leading practitioner, but it has the character of the Scots national style of the 19C.

BAROQUE: Style of the 17C and early 18C characterised by free variations on classical themes.

Baroque was a term of abuse for much of the 19C, though elements from the English Baroque, the school of Wren, are not unknown in the mixture of Victorian Renaissance styles. The serious revival of Baroque architecture dates from the 1890s, with the English Baroque of Wren, Hawksmoor, Gibbs and Vanbrugh providing a model for public buildings all over Britain. By 1906 superseded by a less exuberant Beaux-Arts (q.v.) classicism.

BEAUX-ARTS: Style of formal classical architecture taught at the École des Beaux Arts in Paris and widespread over Europe and elsewhere in the early 20C. In London, the Ritz Hotel (1903–06; Mewes and Davis) and the British Museum extension (1904–14; J.J. Burnet) show two facets, the Fench 18C manner and monumental classicism, both buildings steel-framed.

CAMPANILE: Strictly a bell tower. In Victorian usage a tower in either Italian Renaissance or Italian Gothic styles.

CASTELLATED: Decorated with battlements. The thin veneer of medievalism applied to late 18C and early 19C country houses.

CEMETERIES: The provision of burial space for expanding towns became a scandal in the early 19C, and was solved in three ways. Private cemetery companies opened 'garden cemeteries', the first, at Kensal Green, London, in 1832; urban parishes purchased land outside the cities for burials; or, under the Burial Act of 1855, urban authorities were empowered to close city centre burial grounds and construct cemeteries outside. The typical post 1855 cemetery had separate Anglican and Nonconformist chapels, decorative lodge and entrances, and well-planted picturesque avenues.

CHURCH OF ENGLAND: The established church in England, revitalised in two principal directions during the 19C. The Evangelical, or Low Church, wing, inspired by John Wesley and the 18C reformers, emphasised personal salvation through conversion and their churches were planned for the hearing of sermons and lessons. The High Church wing, inspired by the Oxford Movement or Tractarians, emphasised sacramental worship and the unbroken connection of the Anglican Church with the medieval church in England. The revival of church architecture on medieval lines and the increasing ritual of their services brought the High Church party close to Roman Catholicism, in externals at least, and led to heated conflict, even riots, in the 1860s. Churches of the two streams are markedly different in arrangement, the one designed for best seeing and hearing of the preacher, the other concentrating ornament on a chancel divided from the congregation.

CHURCH OF SCOTLAND: The established church in Scotland, Presbyterian, more akin to the Nonconformist churches in England, i.e. organised in individual congregations and their ministers without a hierarchy of bishops. The Free Church of Scotland (q.v.) was created by secession in 1843 when some one third of the membership left the Church of Scotland over the issue of appointment of ministers.

CLASSICAL: Classical styles of architecture persisted through the 19C, developing from the stripped neo-classical or neo-Grecian of c 1800–30 through a richer Roman classicism in the 1840s to the eclectic mix of forms antique, Renaissance or modern of the later 19C. Greek classicism had a longer and more distinguished history in Scotland, with Alexander Thomson demonstrating how to think anew in classical terms. C.R. Cockerell was both the most scholarly and original of the English classicists.

COMMISSIONERS' CHURCHES: Churches built under the Church Building Act of 1818 that provided one million pounds for new churches in the expanding towns. Though early examples were in classical styles, the majority were Gothic, but typically a Gothic clothing, either lancet style or Perpendicular (qq.v.), on a plan not different from the classical ones, a large galleried preaching space with short chancel attached. Inevitably the later Gothicists, led by Pugin, abhorred them.

CONGREGATIONAL: Nonconformist denomination, a union of independent congregations with origins in the 16C. The Congregational Union of England and Wales (1832) was the first national focus of all the congregations. By 1900 there were some half million church members in Britain.

CROWSTEPS: A stepped end to a gable wall, a common feature of both Scottish and Dutch architecture revived especially in Scotland.

CUPOLA: A small domed turret crowning a roof, tower or dome in classical buildings. Called a lantern, if glazed.

DECORATED (DEC.): Style of English medieval architecture from the late 13C to mid 14C. Called 'Middle Pointed' in the earlier 19C, it was the style

promoted by the Ecclesiologists (q.v.) to the exclusion of earlier or later Gothic styles, seen as either too primitive or too debased. The heyday of the Ecclesiologists was from the 1840s to 1860, and their essentially Lincolnshire or Northamptonshire detail can be seen all over Britain.

DIAPER: Form of surface decoration in brickwork of patterns, normally lozenges, picked out in black, using over burnt ends or heads of bricks.

EARLY ENGLISH (EE): Style of English medieval architecture from the late 12C to late 13C, notably of Salisbury Cathedral. Popular throughout the 19C, the worst variations being the cheapest, in the form called Lancet (q.v.) Gothic from the plain pointed windows.

EARLY FRENCH: Style of 13C Gothic in Northern France adopted in the 1860s by advanced Gothicists such as W. Burges, H. Clutton and G.E. Street as a more vigorous alternative to Early English (q.v.) or North Italian Gothic.

ECCLESIOLOGISTS: Named from the Ecclesiological Society, founded 1839 as the Cambridge Camden Society to study English Gothic architecture and promote restoration. Through its magazine 'The Ecclesiologist' (1841–68) the Society advanced its own views as to the correct style and ritual arrangements for modern Gothic churches, commenting on new churches and achieving, in the 1840s and 1850s at least, a dictatorial influence on Anglican church builders.

ECLECTIC: Mixed in style. A term particularly used for those mid to later 19C buildings that sought a middle way between Gothic and Classical in some combination of styles, most commonly mixing the round-arched Italian Gothic with more Renaissance inspired, arched details.

EDWARDIAN: Strictly of the years 1901–11, though the roots of most of the major Edwardian styles are in the 1880s and 1890s, and 1914 is a more apt terminal date.

ELEANOR CROSS: A form of Gothic spired memorial, the originals (1291– 94) marking the resting places of the body of Queen Eleanor, wife of Edward I, on the way to London (see Waltham Cross, Essex, and Geddington, Northamptonshire). Much copied in the 19C as a suitable medieval exemplar for public memorials (see Martyrs' Memorial, Oxford).

ELIZABETHAN: The English style of the later 16C, particularly the great country houses, Longleat, Wollaton, Burghley and Hardwick. A favourite throughout the 19C, especially for country houses, but also specified in the 1835 Houses of Parliament competition along with Gothic. The Victorian Elizabethan and Jacobean (q.v.) styles merge often into a loose 'Jacobethan'.

ENCAUSTIC TILES: Type of floor tile of medieval origin where the design is inlaid into the earthenware tile in a contrasting colour. Revived c 1840, encaustic tiles were widely used for church and public building interiors, the partnership of the architect Pugin and the manufacturer Minton producing some of the finest revived Gothic designs, notably for the Houses of Parliament.

EPISCOPAL: Church governed by bishops. The title of the Anglican Church in Scotland, where the Church of Scotland is Presbyterian. Organised in seven dioceses and claiming succession from the medieval church, its churches and cathedrals were mostly 19C, some of the finest Victorian churches in Scotland, and the membership never large, 125,000 in 1900.

EVANGELICAL: Protestant churches emphasising the preaching of the Word of God over sacramental ritual, thus applicable to the 'Low Church' wing of the Anglican Church as well as most of the Nonconformist denominations. The Evangelical Alliance of 1846 had as its aim the combatting of Romanism (Catholicism) and ritualism (High Church Anglicanism).

EXCHANGES: The construction of large halls for the trading of commodities, generally corn, but in appropriate areas coal, wool or cotton, was a Victorian phenomenon. The majority of corn exchanges, common to almost every British town, date from the 1850s consequent on the 1846 repeal of the Corn Laws.

FLÈCHE: Slender spirelet, often of wood, generally rising from the roof ridge of a building.

FREE CHURCH OF SCOTLAND: Church established in the 'Disruption' of 1843 by secession from the Church of Scotland (q.v.) over the issue of patronage and the appointment of ministers. Became the United Free Church in 1900 by union with the United Presbyterian Church.

FREE STYLE: Term applied to the architecture of c 1885–1905 in which traditional motifs and materials were freely reinterpreted often with Arts and Crafts or Art Nouveau (qq.v.) details.

GREEK: see Classical.

HALF-TIMBER: Imitation timber-framing much used in late 19C 'Old English' (q.v.) styles based on vernacular buildings of the 15C to 17C.

HARL: Scots equivalent of roughcast, a finish of aggregate and lime dashed wet against a wall surface.

HIGH VICTORIAN: Term applied to the architecture of the period 1850– 70, mainly of the Gothic Revival, characterised by extreme boldness of forms and detail, sometimes called 'muscularity', the use of simple geometrical forms with wall surfaces left unbroken, and the use of constructional colour. Ruskin's 'Seven Lamps of Architecture' (1849) and 'Stones of Venice' (1851– 53) and Street's 'Brick and Marble in the Middle Ages' (1855) were the influential works for Italian and polychrome architecture (qq.v.), T.H. King's 'Study Book of Medieval Architecture and Art' (1858–68) for Early French (q.v.).

IRON: Constructional iron was used from the late 18C for fireproofing. Cast-iron columns were used right through the 19C, but from c 1850 wrought iron replaced cast iron for beams, making possible the large spans of train- sheds such as St. Pancras, London (1863–65). From the 1880s steel replaced wrought iron for beams. Steel-framing came late, the Ritz Hotel, London (1903–06) being the first major example.

ITALIANATE: General term for two strands of Victorian design, the one derived from Italian Renaissance sources and used for public and commercial buildings in the main, the other, with less specific sources but with a vocabulary of campanile towers, arched windows and deep-eaved roofs, used for picturesque villas and small country houses. See also Palazzo.

JACOBEAN: The English style of the reign of James I. Characteristics are rich wood and plaster decoration and Netherlandish straight or curved gables. Major examples: Hatfield and Audley End. See Elizabethan.

LANCET: Gothic narrow pointed window. Used in early 19C churches for economy and by High Victorians for primitive strength.

LIBRARIES: The provision of free municipal libraries in Britain was made possible by the Library Acts of 1850–53, though the bulk of public library buildings date from after 1887 when Queen Victoria's Jubilee gave encouragement, and after 1900 when Andrew Carnegie gave millions for the building of libraries provided the municipality gave the site and took on the maintenance. Earlier libraries were associated with Mechanics Institutions (q.v.), Literary and Scientific Institutions (q.v.) and other subscription bodies.

LITERARY AND SCIENTIFIC INSTITUTIONS: Subscription clubs, generally with libraries and news-rooms, established fairly widely from c 1815 to c 1860, their educational function gradually taken over by the public libraries in the later 19C.

LOW CHURCH: See Church of England.

MECHANICS INSTITUTIONS: Pioneer education institutions for working people, combining evening lectures with library facilities. The first was established by Dr G. Birkbeck in London in 1823.

METHODIST: Nonconformist churches stemming from the teachings of John Wesley (1703–91), emphasising evangelism and personal religion, but otherwise not radically different from the Church of England on doctrinal matters. The Wesleyan Methodist Church was the central body but there were numerous secessions during the 19C, most notably the Primitive Methodists (1807), Bible Christians (1815) and United Methodists (c 1836). There were some million members in Great Britain by 1900.

NEO-CLASSICISM: Movement of the late 18C to reformulate architecture from first principles, which stimulated a more archaeological approach to classical antiquity. The rationalist intellectual framework made neo-classicism wider than revivalism, as evidenced by the interest in primitivist geometrical forms by revolutionary architects such as Ledoux and Boullée. In the 19C the ideology was abandoned as classicism became one of the various available styles.

NEO-GRECIAN: See Classical.

NEO-GEORGIAN: The revival in the late 19C and early 20C of the domestic architecture of the 18C. Arts and Crafts (q.v.) architects found in the smaller late 17C to mid 18C country houses a suitable vocabulary for recreating a domestic style that had formality without inflexible rules. The style grew from the 'Queen Anne' (q.v.) of the 1870s and 1880s, abandoning the wilder eclecticism and asymmetries for a quiet sobriety.

NONCONFORMIST: Technically denoting all those who did not conform to the forms of the Church of England after the Act of Uniformity of 1662, but generally used to denote Protestant dissenters and not the Roman Catholics.

NORMAN: The style of English architecture over the late 11C and 12C, brought from Normandy at the Conquest. Revived for churches in the 1830s and 1840s, principally as an economic style, and hence in the main with none of the massiveness of the originals.

During the 1840s there were experiments with continental round-arched or Romanesque (q.v.) styles, generally more interesting than the neo-Norman, but after 1850 churches in either style are rare.

OLD ENGLISH: Term used for the vernacular style of the 16C and 17C revived by Norman Shaw and W.E. Nesfield in the 1860s. Its component parts were a picturesque amalgam of motifs, largely from south-east England, principally half-timbering, tile-hanging, tall modelled chimneys and leaded windows. There are precursors in the work of G. Devey in the 1850s and, of all Victorian styles, this had the longest influence, arguably not dead today.

PALAZZO: Italian palace, more strictly town house. In the 19C applied to the Renaissance style adopted by C. Barry for town club-houses (the Travellers' Club 1829, the Reform Club 1838) that rapidly replaced the Greek or other classical styles for imposing urban facades. Initially the sober manner of 16C Rome was influential, gradually in the 1840s superseded by a richer Venetian mode. Used throughout the 19C for town buildings, particularly banks, and with a significant country use for modernising the facades of Georgian country houses.

PAVILION ROOF: Tall slate roof derived from French châteaux, applied to a centre or corner tower. Associated with Paris of the Second Empire (1852–71) (q.v.), particularly the New Louvre, such roofs appear in Britain from the 1850s, generally on eclectic Renaissance inspired buildings (Grosvenor Place, London; 1867) but in Scotland became absorbed into the baronial (q.v.)

vocabulary (Fettes College, Edinburgh; 1862) emphasising the Franco-Scottish connection of the 15C to 16C.

PERPENDICULAR (Perp.): Style of English Gothic architecture from c 1340 to 1600. The first regularly imitated style of the Gothic Revival, because of its easy adaptation to the forms of Georgian architecture, especially the large regularly disposed windows and low-pitched roofs. As a consequence derided by Pugin and the Ecclesiologists (qq.v.) of the 1850s as a debased successor to the Decorated (q.v.) or 'Middle Pointed'.

PICTURESQUE: Late 18C definition of landscape or architectural quality derived initially from the paintings of Claude, but gradually modified to encompass the romantic landscape of untamed nature and appropriately informal architecture. Asymmetrical design and relation to setting were more important to picturesque theory than particular style, but the vernacular cottage amplified into the 'cottage orné', the Italianate villa and the revived Gothic to Tudor (q.v.) styles all have their picturesque component.

PLATE TRACERY: The simplest form of Gothic tracery where the lights appear cut through solid stone. A particular favourite of High Victorian (q.v.) Gothic architects for its muscularity.

POLYCHROMY: The use of varied colours in architecture or decoration. Constructional or permanent polychromy was a feature of High Victorian (q.v.) Gothic architecture answering a desire to combine decoration and structure. Ruskin's 'Stones of Venice' (1851–53) was the inspiration, though polychromy was not restricted to buildings

in the Italian Gothic style.

PORTE-COCHÈRE: A porch wide enough for coaches to pass through.

PORTICO: The columned frontispiece of a temple.

PUGINIAN: The Gothic Revival architecture deriving from the writings and works of A.W.N. Pugin (1812–52). Pugin's passionate advocacy of the Gothic on moral, historical and functional grounds inspired a generation of church builders, the Anglican Ecclesiologists (q.v.) if anything more than Pugin's own Roman Catholics. Puginian churches are Decorated (q.v.). Gothic in style, the various parts clearly differentiated from outside by different roofs, the towers often set asymmetrically and the interiors hierarchically arranged with an intensification of decoration towards the sanctuary. Puginian houses, chiefly vicarages, display a Gothic purified of extraneous decoration, asymmetrical, the elevations following the plan, and the scale and ornament of windows appropriate to the use of the room within.

QUEEN ANNE: Style developed in the 1860s in reaction to High Victorian (q.v.) Gothic by architects such as R. Norman Shaw and J.J. Stevenson that corresponded to the 'Aesthetic Movement' (q.v.) in the other arts. A free eclectic style, seeking after prettiness, its characteristics were the use of red brick with white-painted woodwork, sash windows or leaded lights, steep hipped roofs and curly gables, relief carved panels of festoons, cherubs or sunflowers, and tall chimneys. There was a little of genuine early 18C, but the motifs were freely chosen from 17C artisan mannerism, French, Dutch or Flemish Renaissance, and the school of Wren. The

1870s and 1880s were the heyday, though its influence continued into the more sober neo-Georgian of c 1900.

RENAISSANCE: Catch-all term for both the Italian rediscovery of classical antiquity in the 15C and 16C and the widely different interpretations of Italian motifs in other European countries in the 16C and 17C. In the 19C Renaissance Italian styles (see Italianate and Palazzo) generally superseded the Greek or neo-classical (q.v.) by the 1840s for formal urban facades. In the later 19C, parallel to the eclecticism of the Queen Anne (q.v.) movement, North European Renaissance styles, called Northern Renaissance, English Renaissance, Pont Street Dutch, François Ier, were exploited, especially in towns, for the combination of picturesque gables and ornament capable of endless re-arrangement to fit multi-storeyed and multi-windowed elevations.

REREDOS: Decorated wall or screen behind an altar.

ROCK-FACING: Masonry, squared but the face worked to look naturally rough.

ROMANESQUE: Round-arched style current in Europe before the Gothic, in England called Norman (q.v.).

ROOD: Crucifix set up in churches between the nave and chancel, either hanging, or set on a rood screen or rood beam.

ROUGHCAST: Rough wall coating of aggregate mixed with cement.

RUSKINIAN: Influenced by the writings of John Ruskin. In architecture principally meaning Italian Gothic with structural colour or polychromy (q.v.), unbroken vertical wall surfaces with flush or recessed openings, and massiveness of outline. Ruskin inspired the High Victorian (q.v.) architects of the 1850s and 1860s, though he himself disowned much of their work.

RUSTICATION: Textured finish to masonry in classical architecture in which individual blocks are emphasised by sunk joints or surface modelling.

SADDLEBACK ROOF: Pitched roof of short length, as on a tower.

SCHOOLS: During the 19C educational buildings were built in large numbers. Architecturally the most elaborate were the public schools, private boarding schools for middle-class boys, some of which were of ancient foundation, but all owe their character to the 19C reforms associated with Dr Arnold of Rugby School. Grammar schools were day schools of ancient origin, but mostly remodelled in the 19C as endowed secondary schools providing free or subsidised education. Elementary education on a national scale was provided in the early 19C by two rival systems, the non-denominational British Schools and the Anglican National Schools, both progressively assisted by government grants. The Elementary Education Act of 1870 permitted the construction of schools with public money administered by local school boards, hence the name 'Board Schools' for such schools. After the reform of local government in 1888, local authorities were empowered to build Technical Schools by an act of 1889, the first step to public provision for secondary education, and in 1902 the authorities took control of the Board Schools. Compromises over the question of religious education allowed the denominational schools to remain, parallel to the state-provided schools, supported by state grant and subject to state inspection. In Scotland, a national pattern of parish schools was established early, under an Act of 1696, and in the main these were transferred to the school boards under the 1872 Education Act. Public schools followed English lines, but secondary education was less divided than in England, either on class or religious grounds, the public school having less of a hold on the wealthy classes and the Roman Catholics being the only denomination to have their own schools.

SECOND EMPIRE: The period 1852–70 of Napoleon III's rule in France. Name given to the heavily ornate style of Parisian architecture imitated all over the world from the 1850s to the 1880s, of which the New Louvre (1852–58) and the Opera (1861–74) are the most prominent examples. Eclectic Renaissance detail and tall mansard and pavilion roofs (q.v.) are the most common qualities.

SGRAFFITO: Type of plaster decoration revived in the later 19C where the design is cut through a layer of plaster to a different coloured layer below.

TERRACOTTA: Fired but unglazed clay, extensively used during the 19C for architectural decoration, being cheaper and more durable than most stone. Doultons of Lambeth were the best known firm of many that produced terracotta ornament.

TILE-HANGING: Form of wall covering to timber-frame buildings, especially common in south-east England, where small rectangular roof tiles are hung vertically as a form of weatherproofing. Revived as a common component of later 19C 'Old English' (q.v.) style buildings.

TOWN HALLS: Only gradually during the 19C did town halls become the exclusive seats of municipal government. In the early to mid 19C the administrative function was frequently secondary to a market or a large public concert hall (see Leeds) or law courts, and several cities have council offices quite distinct from town halls (see Birmingham).

TRACTARIAN: Anglican of the High Church reforming wing founded at Oxford in the 1830s by J.H. Newman, John Keble and E.B. Pusey, named after the 'Tracts for the Times' that they published from 1833 to 1841. Their emphasis on the Anglican Church's unbroken succession from the medieval English church, on ritual and the importance of the sacraments provided the ideological foundation for the revival of correct medieval forms in church building.

TUDOR: English architecture of c 1500–50, revived extensively for domestic and collegiate buildings in the 19C, though with little archaeological accuracy, Tudor style meaning essentially the use of the Tudor four-centred or depressed arch. The boundaries between 19C castellated, Tudor and Elizabethan styles are blurred.

UNITARIAN: Nonconformist church believing in a single personality of God, as opposed to the Trinity of Father, Son and Holy Spirit. Known in England from the Reformation, the distinct denomination dates from 1773. Little influence in Scotland.

VENETIAN WINDOW: Triple opening with arched centre, also called a Palladian window.

WAGON ROOF: Curved ceiling, generally achieved by boarding or plaster under close-spaced rafter trusses with collars supported by arched braces.

WORKHOUSE: Institution for the relief of poverty where destitute paupers could be set to work in return for food and lodging. The 1834 Poor Law Amendment Act established in England and Wales a national system whereby unions of parishes were formed to construct and administer workhouses under 'guardians' elected by the ratepayers.

ENGLAND

AVON

BATH. *Bath Abbey* was restored (1864–74; G.G. Scott) with the completion of the fan vaulting, unfinished at the Reformation, the major work. Fittings by Scott throughout and the main E, W and S windows filled with glass by Clayton and Bell, N transept organ case (1913; T.G. Jackson). In abbey churchyard *Concert Room* addition to the 1791–96 Pump Room, English Baroque style (1894–96; J.M. Brydon); to the rear, open colonnade around the Roman Great Bath, discovered 1878–80, with statues of the Roman governors of Britain (G. Lawson). The Concert Room, or Kursaal, was a belated attempt to make Bath a spa town to rival continental spas. To S of Roman Baths, in York St, *arch* and flanking buildings with lively carved animal heads, fragment of the Queen's Bath (1887–89; C.E. Davis), another part of the modernisation. On NE corner of Stall St, *No. 2*, curved fronted pub (1897; C.E. Davis) with very mixed detail. Diagonally opposite, *No. 1 Union St* (1883; C.E. Davis), excellent stone carving. N of the Abbey, High St, with *Guildhall* (1775) on E side. This was extended (1892–97; J.M. Brydon) very successfully in a manner that incorporates later 18C details from the original building with cupolas and other details from the English Baroque. Brydon's competition victory at Bath was an important stage in the late 19C revival of Wrenian styles for public buildings. Curved corners with sculptured friezes (G. Lawson). Inside, fine Council Chamber with ornate plaster ceiling. Brydon continued the building in Bridge St (1898–1900) with a severely handsome *Art Gallery*, the corner entrance the most Baroque part of the whole group. Behind the Guildhall, *Markets* (1863; Hickes and Isaac) circular with cast-iron columns and boarded dome.

S of Guildhall, Orange Grove, the S side a *terrace* of 1707 prettified (1897; C.E. Davis) with shell hoods over all the first-floor windows, the N side with *Magistrates Court* (1865; C.E. Davis) appropriately heavily detailed but dwarfed by the *Empire Hotel* (1900–02; C.E. Davis) an elephantine building, the details lost in five bulky storeys and two floors of variegated roofline culminating in a curved gable irritatingly not quite central. To S, Manvers St, the Jacobean front of *Bath Station* (1841; I.K. Brunel) aligned at the end, but the rest testimony to the failure of the 19C and 20C to honour the formal 18C townscape of Bath. Opposite the station an attempt was made with two handsome curved fronted blocks (1845; ?H.E. Goodridge) but these were not continued, save for one building at the SE corner of Henry St. On E side, *RC church* (1861–65; C.F. Hansom) with 220ft spire, a landmark especially from the railway. Marble arcade columns and late 19C iron screen.

N of the Guildhall, *St. Michael's Church* (1835–37; G. Manners), expensive early 19C Gothic with octagonal spire, the body of the church all smooth ashlar, the details taken from Salisbury Cathedral. At N end of Milsom St, two large banks, *National Westminster* (1865; Wilson and Willcox), richly modelled Italianate towering next to the c 1760 houses of Milsom St, and *Lloyd's* (1875; G.M. Silley).

SW of Queen Square, Chapel Row leads past *Holy Trinity Church* (1874; Wilson, and Willcox and Wilson) towards *Green Park Station* (1869; J.H. Sanders), the former Midland Railway terminus, newly restored. Fine stone facade, designed to fit in with 18C Bath, screening an elegant triple-arched iron train-shed (J.S. Crossley). W of Queen Square, in Charlotte St, N side, *Registry Office* (1840; G. Alexander) in Italian palazzo style, strongly modelled, and *Christian Science Church* (1845; J. Wilson) with Roman Corinthian temple front. Opposite, *Elim Pentecostal Church* (1854; H. and A. Goodridge) N Italian Romanesque, two turrets and a big octagonal centre packed into a cramped site. N of Queen Square, entry to *Royal Victoria Park* (1830; E. Davis), the earliest public park in Britain. Ornate *bandstand* (c 1885; C.E. Davis). Beyond, *obelisk* (1837; G. Manners), oddly three-sided with charming stone lions, commemorating Princess Victoria's eighteenth birthday. Picturesque *cottage*, in Tudor Gothic style and severely neo-classical *archways*, part of the original entrance screen (1831; E. Davis). NW of the park, in Weston Rd, Park Lane and Weston Park, area of large mid 19C villas, Italianate, Tudor and other styles, the best two being in Weston Park, *Vale Lodge* (1859) Gothic, and on E side, *Cranwells* (1850; Wilson and Fuller) early 18C in style, based on Widcombe Manor, Bath.

Lansdown Road leads N from the centre of the town to another area of Victorian villas on a steep slope. *St. Stephen's Church* (1840–45; J. Wilson) picturesquely faces S down the hill with ornate tower of octagonal stages clasped by big corner pinnacles, far from archaeological correctness. Broad nave, chancel added 1883. In Sion Rd, *Glenavon* (1857; J. Wilson) asymmetrical Italianate villa with little octagonal turret, the architect's own house. On E side of Lansdown Rd, *Royal School* (1857; J. Wilson) heavily rock-faced Gothic with off-centre tower and much carved detail. The W side of Lansdown Rd was the site of William Beckford's sadly lost romantic ride from his house in Lansdown Crescent to Lansdown Tower. *Kingswood School* (1851; J. Wilson) occupies part of the site, a Methodist public school, smooth ashlar symmetrical Tudor Gothic, big central tower. The contrast with Royal School is that between early Victorian and High Victorian Gothic.

1m N, *Lansdown Tower* (1825–26; H.E. Goodridge) William Beckford's last folly, built after the collapse of Fonthill Abbey, and a major monument of the picturesque in Britain. 154ft Grecian tower attached to an elementally plain building without Greek detail, indeed pierced by small round-arched windows. The tower became a cemetery chapel after Beckford's death and *Lansdown Cemetery* occupies the grounds. Beckford is buried in fine granite tomb chest (1844; Goodridge). Cemetery gateway and walls (1848; Goodridge) round-arched with Romanesque to Italianate details excellently carved, especially the lettering under the main arch.

E and S of centre: Great Pulteney St leads up to the *Holburne Museum*, a hotel of 1796 cleverly altered (1911; R. Blomfield) with French 18C details. Off Bathwick St, to N, *St. John's Church*, a small High Victorian work (1861; C.E. Giles) now the N aisle of a massive church (1870; A.W. Blomfield). Sanctuary and W windows by Bell and Almond, nave and baptistery windows by Clayton and Bell. S of the museum, *St. Mary's Church* (1814–20; J. Pinch) high quality revived Perp. Chancel (1873–75; G.E. Street), SE chapel (1895; S. Gambier-Parry) with gates by Singer and lovely E window (A. Bell). Baptistery (1906; C. Deacon) with Art-Nouveau silveredmetal gates and hanging corona. Bathwick Hill climbs SE with Regency terraces and villas, giving way to more spacious villas further up. On left side, *Fiesole* (1846; H.E. Goodridge) and *Casa Bianca* (c 1846; Goodridge) Italian style reflecting the period when W.S. Landor compared the hills of Bath to Fiesole, near Florence. Fiesole was Goodridge's own house with a fine front composition of shallow gable over an elemental Venetian window, left open as a balcony. Further up, *Bathwick Grange* (1829; Goodridge) also built for himself, but in the picturesque manner of Lansdown Tower combining Greek elements with a big round-arched loggia. *Bathwick Hill House* (1828; Goodridge) is formally symmetrical with Greek detail. On S side, *Claverton Lodge* (c 1825) altered 1896 (J.M. Brydon) with open attic balcony reminiscent of American 'shingle style' work. In Smallcombe Vale, below, pleasantly rural *Cemetery* (1856) with main chapel (1856; T. Fuller) and octagonal Nonconformist chapel (1861; A.S. Goodridge).

S of Bath Station, off Widcombe Parade, Prior Park Rd leads up to *Abbey Cemetery* laid out 1843 by J.C. Loudon on a steep site with neo-Norman chapel (G. Manners) splendidly at the top. Behind, off Perrymead, *RC Cemetery*, with unusually elaborate chantry chapel (1861; C.F. Hansom), tall, apsed and richly carved. Off Prior Park Rd, *•Prior Park*, the grand Palladian mansion (1735–48) built for Ralph Allen and purchased as a possible RC bishop's palace, seminary and school in 1829. The interior was burnt (1836) and reinstated by H.E. Goodridge, who added the S front stairs and much early 18C carved work from Hunstrete House, Somerset. On the W wing, *•chapel* (1844–82; J.J. Scoles) upsetting the symmetry of the main front, but, inside, a magnificent tunnel-vaulted Corinthian basilica based on French neo-classical precedent. Beyond Prior Park, on the ridge, North Rd runs E. On Shaft Rd, to S, *Lodge Style* (1909; C.F.A. Voysey) stone single- storey house on courtyard plan with Gothic details, a homage perhaps to Pugin and Street. Stumpy entrance tower with bold Gothic doorway, the rest of the house has sweeping stone-tiled roofs and most unusual square stone chimneys. The house is out of the usual Voysey style apparently because the owner wanted a building reminiscent of his Oxford college. To SW, in Church Rd, Combe Down parish *church* (1832–35; Goodridge) with an entertaining filigree spire. The body of the church regularised (1884).

At **Bathampton**, E of Bath, off A36, *Jacaranda*, Bathampton Lane (c 1865), heavily High Victorian former vicarage, rock-faced with plate tracery. Mill Lane leads N from the church to *Toll Bridge* (1872; Hickes and Isaac), stone, Gothic detailed, with pretty Gothic toll-house.

BRISTOL. Central Bristol has suffered from wartime bombing and post-war replanning but much remains of what was one of the great British trading cities. The modern centre, the wide green strip of Colston Avenue and Broad Quay, is the infilled N arm of the harbour. In the centre, *statues* of Edmund Burke (1894; J.H. Thomas) and *E. Colston* (1895; J. Cassidy). On the W side, the *Hippodrome* (1912; F. Matcham), the exterior much reduced but the rich interior intact. Further up, *St. Mary on the Quay* (1839; R.S. Pope) Roman Corinthian porticoed church, originally an Irvingite chapel. At the SW end, overlooking the harbour, *Watershed* (1894; E. Gabriel) a warehouse range now converted to cafes and galleries; its N end, prominent from the centre, is highly decorative in brick and stone with cupola.

E of Colston Ave is the historic centre of Bristol, around Corn St. In Clare St, *No. 2* (1881, C.F. Hansom) on the sharp corner to Baldwin St, *Nos 4–6* (1883; F. Mew: 1896; R.M. Drake) former bank in a most eclectic and heavy-handed classical style. On N side, *No. 15* (1889; E. Edwards) ornately detailed corner building, red sandstone panels varying the Bath stone, with an arched attic gallery—an unusual touch. *Nos 17–19* (1899; A. Waterhouse) bright terracotta Prudential Assurance building in a compressed Loire Château style, effectively using the corner site, and *Nos 25–7* (1903; Oatley and Lawrence) domed Baroque, small but richly inventive in the play of levels and classical orders. In St. Stephen's St to N, *Nos 15–17* (1904; Foster and Wood) charming Arts and Crafts influenced newspaper office with gables, timber oriels and leaded windows. *No. 13* (1878) has glazed brick walls with ornate window surrounds in red moulded brick and three handsome sculpted terracotta heads. *Nos 9–11* (1875; J. Hirst) are exceptionally rich, the lower two floors framed in four giant arches, the upper windows with Florentine tracery and pediment on top.

Clare St leads into Corn St. On S side, *Nos 32–4* (1852–55; R.S. Pope) chastely detailed former head office of Stuckey's Bank contrasting with *No. 36* (1864; W.B. Gingell) an insurance office originally, in the most ornate style, Baroque in its disregard for classical conventions, though the mannerisms are not from Baroque sources. Splendid carved heads of Time and well-equipped firemen. *Nos 38* (c 1850) and *40–2* (c 1830 extended 1925) are quiet Italianate intervals before *No. 44* (1904; E. Gabriel) a lively Baroque front in Portland stone with cupola. Opposite, *No. 47* (1878; J. Weir) and further up *No. 55* (1854–58; Gingell and Lysaght) one of the most splendid 19C banks in Britain, the head office of the West of England and S Wales Bank. In style, the richest Venetian Renaissance, richer than the originals, combining Bath and Portland stone, a subtlety revealed by cleaning. Superimposed orders of columns each carrying a richly carved entablature, the upper one scaled to the proportion of the whole building. Windows arched below and Venetian above with figure sculpture, the carving by J. Thomas. Banking hall like the cortile of an Italian palace. Adjoining, Greek *Magistrates Court* (1828; Pope and Dymond) and larger Greek Ionic *Council House* (1822–27; R. Smirke) with good interiors. Matching Greek building to rear, *No. 5* Broad St (c 1830).

In Broad St, on E side, *Grand Hotel* (1864–69; Foster and Wood) large Early Renaissance style block, crisply carved with powerful upper overhanging cornice above an eaves gallery. *No. 51* (1868; Ponton and Gough) Ruskinian Gothic narrow front, polychrome stone and vigorous carved detail. Further down, *No. 38* (1900; H. Williams) remarkable for the complete decoration of the facade in glazed tile by W.J. Neatby of Doulton's works. The building was Everard's printing works and Everard saw himself as a craftsman printer in the Arts and Crafts tradition, hence the figures of Gutenberg and William Morris working their presses with the Spirit of Knowledge between and the Spirit of Truth in the top gable. Everard's name is in letters designed by him. On the W side, *Guildhall* (1843–45; R.S. Pope), one of the first 19C Gothic town halls, Perp. style but heavily repetitive in detail. Squat central tower. *No. 14* (1844–47; C.R. Cockerell) was the former Bank of England branch, similar to the ones in Manchester and Liverpool in its classical design, fusing Greek and Renaissance principles. A main Greek Doric order to the lower floors with round-arched upper windows under a pediment. The whole front is slightly set back with screen walls up to the street against which stand enclosed porches, giving an effect of depth enhanced by variations in the wall plane of the main front. A masterly design. Adjoining, *No. 12* (1843) prettily detailed narrow front giving access to a charming courtyard of chambers leading through to Small St.

In Small St, E side, *Assize Courts* (1867–70; Pope and Bindon) asymmetrical Gothic with pyramid roofed entrance tower. From Corn St, behind the Exchange, *Covered Market* (1855; R.S. Pope). In St. Nicholas St behind, *Nos 6–10* (1866; Ponton and Gough) stone-faced with arched upper windows and ground-floor iron columns, *No. 18*

Everard's Printing Works (1900; H. Williams and W.J. Neatby), Broad Street, Bristol

(1868; Ponton and Gough) vigorous Italian Gothic, *The Elephant* pub (1867; H. Masters) cheerful front with carved elephant, and *Stock Exchange* (1903; H. Williams) a surprising small-scale temple front in Bath stone with black marble columns. On S side, *Fishmarket* (1873; Pope and Son) with tall red-brick addition to Baldwin St behind (1897; W. Gingell).

The Granary (1869; Ponton and Gough), Welsh Back, Bristol

To S, King St with tall brick warehouse at *No. 35* (c 1870), three floors contained in a Gothic arcade, and *No. 36* (c 1905), warehouse in smooth bright red brick. To S, on corner of Little King St and Welsh Back, •*The Granary* (1869; Ponton and Gough) the finest Bristol warehouse in the arched Romanesque to Gothic style characteristic of mid Victorian Bristol warehouses. Dark red brick with yellow brick, 100ft high, ten floors internally expressed as five main horizontal divisions under a richly corbelled and embattled parapet. Within the arches patterned brick ventilation screens, smaller arches and circular openings of wonderful inventiveness. Across the river, view of the last remaining warehouses on the Redcliffe side, notably the concrete-framed *WCA warehouse* (1896; W.V. Gough) with three great concrete oriels overhanging the water.

In Queen Square on E side, *Port of Bristol Authority* (1889; W.V. Gough) ornate and showy French Renaissance style, wholly inappropriate to the Georgian square. On N side, *Custom House* (1832; S. Smirke) smooth stone with arched windows. This side of Queen

Square was destroyed in riots 1831 and rebuilt in Regency style, *Nos 1–9* (1833; H. Rumley). To SW Prince St leads down to the harbour. On E side stark rubble stone *seed warehouse* (c 1878) and at S end *Bush Warehouse* (1831 and 1837; R.S. Pope), very large tea warehouse, now Arnolfini Arts Centre, crucially sited overlooking the divide of the two arms of the harbour. Grey rubble stone with arcaded elevations, the main S front a generous nine bays wide, the centre broader than the wings. Across *Prince's Bridge* (1879), the Bathurst Basin to E has the polychrome brick facades of *Robinson's Warehouse* (1874; Gingell) almost Moorish in effect with lively patterned brick. Opposite, *General Hospital* (1853–64; Gingell) rubble stone with octagonal corner, formerly domed. Round-arched detail. The massive basement arches were entries to dockside warehousing that helped to finance the hospital. Extensions 1912–15 (Oatley and Lawrence).

Returning to St. Augustine's Parade, Colston St leads N with *Colston Hall* (1864–73; Foster and Wood), round-arched Italian Gothic front spoiled by filling in the upper loggia and by the glazed canopy. Opposite, *Foster's Almshouses* (1861 and 1880; Foster and Wood), delightful three-sided courtyard of brick almshouses with timber details in the Gothic of Burgundy. The Burgundian effects include a patterned tile roof and conical capped timber spiral stair. The S range is 1861, the rest 1880.

SW of St. Augustine's Parade, College Green, triangular space defined by the 20C curved Council House at the top and a plump Queen Victoria *statue* (1888; J.E. Boehm) at the point. On S side, *Cathedral*, the eastern parts early 14C with transepts and tower c 1500, the nave and W towers 1867–88 (G.E. Street). Street had to provide a nave that would harmonise with the remarkable hall-church of the early 14C E end with its unique vaulted choir aisles. This he did with great success, slightly simplifying the complex vaulting patterns and adding capitals to the main shafts, more conventional than the medieval work but appropriate in providing a calm introduction to the intricacies of the E end. French Gothic detail to the twin W towers, the W front too cramped between the towers to achieve cathedral scale. Street's work was completed by J.L. Pearson (1887–95) and his are the choir fittings including screen and tall sculptured reredos. In nave, effigy of Dean Elliott (died 1891; J. Forsyth). The Bishop's Palace and many of the precinct buildings were sacked in the 1831 riots. To W, *Central Library* (1906; C. Holden) attached to the abbey gatehouse. Holden's building ranks among the outstanding public buildings of the Edwardian era, modern in its bold squared massing and minimal stylistic detail, yet wholly harmonious with the medieval gatehouse through the careful alignment of the main lines and the use of stone mullioned oriels each end, echoing the gatehouse oriel as the round-arched entry echoes the Norman arches of the gatehouse. The tower-like end bays frame a central section of three tall arched openings, subtly divided by flat buttresses. In each opening a severe projecting first-floor oriel, like sentry boxes, with figure sculpture above. Above the end bays, open pedimented gables, set back with chequered panelling each side of an arched window. The E and S sides leave period precedent further behind and the play of wall planes dominates. Inside, Byzantinesque entrance hall with green mosaic vaults.

On E side of College Green, *No. 38* (1904; Latrobe and Weston) Art Nouveau fronted former café and *No. 30*, 18C house with fine arched shopfront (1865; Foster and Wood) and Victorian shop interior. Behind the Council House, in St. George's Rd, facade of former *Royal Western*

Hotel (1837; R.S. Pope and I.K. Brunel) the first hotel in Britain designed for railway travellers, part of Brunel's visionary plan to link London and New York via his Great Western Railway to Bristol, his hotel and his Bristol-built transatlantic steamship, the Great Western. It is also the most ambitious of early 19C hotels, of four storeys with giant colonnade across the lower two echoed in attached column frontispieces to the upper two floors.

Park St leads NW from College Green, mostly of late 18C date but *No. 81* with ornate Victorian ground floor. *Nos 17–31* were the former Literary and Philosophical Institute (1820–23; C.R. Cockerell). At the head of the street, the last great Gothic building designed in Britain, the *Wills Tower* of Bristol University (1914–25; Sir G. Oatley) prodigiously scaled Perp. tower built for the tobacco magnates of Bristol, the Wills family. The site, dominating Park St, but setting the tower at an angle, accentuates the four-square strength of the main bulk offset by the filigree effect of tracery and wall panelling, while the corner pinnacles clasping an octagonal top stage complete the unexpectedly delicate effect. Colossal entrance hall, 72ft high and fan-vaulted but with no other purpose than joining the tower to the main range. Great Hall with hammerbeam roof. The university buildings behind are of more conventional Tudor Gothic in red rubble stone (1880; C.F. Hansom) extended to University Rd (1892; F.B. Bond) and to Woodland Rd (1909; G. Oatley). N of the tower, *City Museum* (1899–1904; Sir F. Wills) Edwardian Baroque, another gift of the Wills family as the front proclaims. Good collections of 19C paintings and of furniture by E.W. Godwin. To N, *University Refectory* (1867–71; Foster and Ponton) fully Ruskinian Gothic, built as Library and Philosophical Institution, with polychrome stonework like a N Italian town hall. Sadly much of the carved detail has been stripped off. In University Rd, to rear, *lecture theatre* (1874; S. Colman) idiosyncratic and spiky Gothic, some of it Venetian, with an eye to the main building, some of it not. Beyond *Bristol Grammar School* (1877; Foster and Wood) Tudor Gothic with impressive main hall.

To N, on Queen's Road, *Royal Parade* (1859–68; Foster and Wood) richly Italianate parades of shops, arcaded ground floor surviving or restored on the E side. To N, *Royal West of England Academy* (1857; J.H. Hirst), originally fully Italianate with open first-floor loggia and big external steps, but given a more suave ground-floor and first-floor glazing (1912). Inside, murals by Walter Crane. *Wesleyan Chapel* (1861; Foster and Wood), polychrome Gothic in pink and buff stone, adjoining. Facing down Queen's Rd, *Victoria Rooms* (1839–41; C. Dyer) with eight-column Corinthian portico, the pediment filled with allegorical sculpture, an imposing temple front of Roman richness: Roman being more to early Victorian taste than chaster Greek. In front, Edward VII *statue* (1912; H. Poole) with lively stone and bronze Baroque *fountain* (E. Rickards). To S, in Park Place, derelict remains of former *RC Cathedral*—a sad story—begun 1834 to a grand neo-classical design (H.E. Goodridge) but completed only to the top of the column shafts when a lightweight but inventive timber interior was inserted (1843–49; C. Hansom) and finally refronted (1876; C. Hansom) in a massive Italian Romanesque style, but this also incomplete. To NE, in Wetherell Place, *No. 7* (1860; J.A. Hansom) Puginian Tudor Gothic brick house, built for Hansom himself. Below the Cathedral, Berkeley Place runs behind Brandon Hill. On the side of the hill *Queen Elizabeth's Hospital* (1843–47; Foster and Son) Tudor Gothic school in rubble stone, large and institutionally symmetrical. On Brandon Hill, *Cabot Tower* (1897; W.V. Gough) pink stone tower commemorating the fourth centenary of Cabot's sighting of the Canadian coast, ornate free Gothic stone spire crowded with decoration on top and florid openings with curved balconies below. In Jacob's Wells Rd, *Hill's Almshouses* (1867; C. Hansom) Tudor style with cast-iron access gallery to rear. *Public Baths* (1887; J. Thomas) red brick with big gable, loosely Loire style detailing.

W of the Victoria Rooms Queen's Rd leads into **Clifton**, the late 18C and 19C select suburb of Bristol. *Victoria Square* illustrates the transition from Georgian calm to Victorian richness in three terraces: on E side, *Lansdown Place* (1835; Foster and Son) reticent with pretty first-floor balconies; on N, *Royal Promenade* (1845–49; Foster and Sons) palatially Italianate with heavy stone balconies, much varied window detail, a hefty bracket cornice with low attic of continuous tiny arches, some pierced for windows; and on W, *Nos 15–25* (1855; Foster and Wood) similar but with greater use of round arches, and Florentine tracery added to further enrich the mix. The later Victorian trend against terraces shows in the five villas (c 1865) along the S side. From Lansdown Place, Lansdown Rd runs N with stone villas off in *Royal Park* and *Clifton Park*, the mid 19C villas smooth ashlar-faced, the later ones with heavier detail and rubble facing. On S side of Clifton Park, *Vyvyan Terrace* (c 1842–47; R.S. Pope) 57 bays long, neo-classical with fine Ionic centre colonnade and careful linking of centre and wings to unify the long composition. College Rd leads N with *Worcester Terrace* (1851–53; C. Underwood) to right, finely detailed neo-classical and sharply outlined like 19C terraces in Glasgow. In Worcester Rd, *Nos 1 and 2* (1863; C.F. Hansom) and in College Rd, *Nos 30–4* (c 1884; C.F. Hansom) Gothic gabled villas of the N Oxford type interspersed among the more typical Bristol Italianate villas. *Clifton College* (1862 onwards; C.F. Hansom) makes a picturesque group across the playing fields with pink rubble stone Perp. buildings casually laid out, the main elements Big School (1862) impressively tall with traceried E window, a recessed cloistered range (1869) connected to a gatehouse tower (1889) and, standing forward, chapel (1866). The chapel was transformed (1909; C. Nicholson) by the extraordinary device of pushing out the side walls to create a complex central hexagonal space lit by a top lantern, a small version of the Ely crossing. In front of the chapel, *Boer War Memorial* (1904; A. Drury).

N of the college, Clifton Down, the open space between Clifton and the Avon Gorge, overlooked by the largest of the 19C Clifton villas. *Bristol Zoo*, one of the oldest in the country, has Greek entrance lodges (c 1840) and a Tudor giraffe house (c 1860). Running SW the big Victorian houses, many of them semi-detached despite the prestigious situation. The architectural quality is not high even if the scale impresses. *Glenavon/Eaton* (1853) has Italianate corner towers and a surprising row of curved pediments across the centre, *Avonbank/ Llanfoist* (1853; H. Goodridge) has round-arched detail and side towers, *Elmdale* (1867; G. and H. Godwin) is a colossal single villa, now the Mansion House, singularly graceless with plain canted bays. Beyond, three inflated versions of the standard Bristol villa. On the Down, Gothic *fountain* (1872; G. and H. Godwin). SW of these elephantine houses, earlier 19C ashlar-faced classical villas, *Trafalgar House* (c 1840) with an American looking two-storey portico that breaks most of the classical rules with panache, two villas of c 1845, and *Camp House* (1831; C. Dyer) with two-storey portico and detail closer to Greek, but already showing signs of wandering. On Litfield Place, further round, *Dorset House* (c 1830) an ingenious design with recessed colonnade carrying the second floor across the centre, only the columns are attenuated and spaced unbelievably gauchely. *Christ Church* is Bristol's most impressive Victorian church, the result of a long building history, but surprisingly unified in its EE style. Cruciform church (1841–44; C. Dyer) with fine tower (1844; executed by J. Norton who added the excellent spire in 1859) and aisles (1885).

To W, • *Clifton Suspension Bridge* (1831–64; I.K. Brunel) the noblest and most daring 19C bridge in Britain, vaulting the Avon Gorge between boldly simple battered pylons of rubble stone with smooth top section in pale stone and cast iron. The W pier sits on a huge masonry abutment, particularly dramatic from the A4 below. The wooded W side of the Gorge, Leigh Woods and Nightingale Valley is much associated with the early 19C Bristol school of painters, F. Danby, S. Jackson and S. Colman. Leigh Woods has large late 19C villas in Bridge Rd, Church Rd and North Rd. *The White House*, North Rd (1901; H.D. Bryan) is in the manner of Voysey.

The centre of Clifton: The Mall has terraces of late 18C, extended to W (1840; Foster and Okely) in Regency style with pretty iron balconies. In Regent St, to SE, *Nos 2–14* (c 1883) Italianate. *Clifton Hill House*, below, lovely 18C Palladian villa, was the family house of the poet J.A. Symonds. *Goldney House* of c 1720 was horribly recased (1864; A. Waterhouse). In Clifton Vale to SW, *Nos 1–15* (1843; Foster and Okely) late Regency style stepped terrace with pretty ironwork.

S of the Hotwells Rd, *Cumberland Basin*, complex engineered dock control whereby the old course of the Avon became the Floating Harbour with controlled water levels while the tidal river runs to S in the New Cut. Main works 1803–9, locks 1844–48 (I.K. Brunel) later replaced but one of Brunel's locks survives as does a Brunel tubular girder swing bridge. *Pump House* now converted to a restaurant. To S dominating brick masses of three *tobacco warehouses* (1905, 1908 and 1919). Dark grey brick base and eight storeys of red brick above. Off Cumberland Rd, between the Floating Harbour and the New Cut, Gasferry Rd leads to the restored • *SS Great Britain*, Brunel's second Bristol built steamship, built 1844–45, and as with so much of Brunel's work a leap forward in engineering terms of dazzling virtuosity. She was the first great ship to employ the screw propeller rather than side paddle wheels, the first large iron steamship and the largest ship then afloat. The story of her rescue from wreck in the Falkland Islands and return to the dock where she was built for restoration is one of the triumphs of modern marine archaeology. Open to public. On Prince's Wharf, further E, modern *Industrial Museum* with good collections and *Lifeboat Museum*.

From the roundabout E of the General Hospital, Bedminster Parade leads S into artisan S Bristol. *Zion Chapel* (1830), Gothic *Police Station* (1882; H. Crisp) and classical *bank* (c 1905). In East St the long brick ranges of the Wills *tobacco factories* (F.W. Wills), the first ranges (1884 and 1888) Gothic, the later ranges stripped classical. From the roundabout, to NE, Clarence Rd follows the New Cut to Temple Gate. *Temple Meads Station* is among the most important railway buildings in the country, though the immediate effect is scrappy, the important side buildings half-hidden by the access ramp. The front building (1876; M.D. Wyatt) with its big central Gothic tower (formerly with pyramid roof) was built to join two earlier stations, originally at right angles to each other. That on the left is the original Great Western Railway terminus (1840; I.K. Brunel) through disuse astonishingly intact. Nowhere else does a complete terminus from the earliest days of the railway survive. The sequence of Brunel's buildings begins with the Tudor style offices on Temple Gate, originally symmetrically flanked by carriage gateways. Raised up at first-floor level behind is the train-shed, with an iron columned space where the engines were turned and then the great train-shed with Tudor arched arcades and a 72ft wide roof with mock hammerbeam bracing. All survives just as in the early lithographs. Behind the 1876 front, iron roofed train-shed (F. Fox). On right side, Brunel's second terminus for the Bristol–Exeter line has gone but the Jacobean gabled railway offices (1852; S.C. Fripp) are handsome, if masked by the access ramp.

NW of the station, cut off by ring roads, Victoria St, battered but still with warehouses of c 1875 on N side. In Counterslip, to N, former *Tramway Generating Station* (1899; W.C. Green), splendid Baroque in brick and stone with Venetian window ground-floor motif under recessed Ionic colonnade and top pediment. Handsome arched detailing to sides. To E, over St. Philip's Bridge, the historic Old Market area of the city, devastated by the ring road. In Broad Plain, battered remains of *soap works* complex with massive round-arched detail. In Old Market St at E end, S side, *Trinity Almshouses* (1857–83; Foster and Wood) with cylindrical staircase and timber balconies as at Foster's Almshouses. On corner of Lawford St, *Palace Hotel* (c 1860) full of carved detail. To N, *St. Jude's Church* (1849; S. Gabriel) decent Puginian Gothic with spire. To E, *Trinity Church*, Trinity Rd (1829–32; Rickman and Hutchinson) near derelict ashlar-faced church on the King's College Chapel Cambridge model. To NE, Stapleton Rd with classical *Baptist Chapel* (1885; T.L. Watson) fine ashlar front, the architect from Glasgow. In St. Mark's Rd, to NE, *St. Mark's Church* (1848; Dyer and Gabriel) lively neo-Norman with painted interior. At **Stapleton**, 1m NE, *church* (1857; J. Norton) the spire a landmark from the M32, as, further NE, are the Italianate towers of the former workhouse at Fishponds, *Manor Park Hospital* (1865).

Returning to the inner ring road, the Cheltenham Rd runs N, initially called Stokes Croft. *No. 104*, on E side (1862; E.W. Godwin) good facade arcaded in the Bristol fashion with polychrome touches in the stone, five broad arches below, ten to each of the upper floors in a continuous arcade. E of Cheltenham Rd the densely built early to mid 19C area of Montpelier, to W the large villas of Cotham, prosperous and intact mid 19C suburb. Arley Hill leads NW past *Polish RC church* (1855; Foster and Wood), Italianate former chapel, with curved portico and cupola. In Cotham Brow villas of c 1860–70 continuing to W in Cotham Rd with villas of c 1840–60. At W end of Cotham Rd, *St. Michael's Church*, Butterfield's first work, built as a chapel (1842) extended with tower and apse (1863; E.W. Godwin), Perp. with the random rubble walls that Pugin advocated, odd tiny clerestory windows and a good timber roof. Butterfield never designed another chapel, his religious convictions later allowed him to work only for Anglicans (or episcopalians). Opposite, Arts and Crafts Tudor styled former *Congregational College* (1905; H.D. Bryan) prettily detailed. The *Homoepathic Hospital* (designed 1908; G. Oatley) diagonally opposite, is Elizabethan of a simplified sort, with play of wall planes and plan typically early 20C (not built until 1921). In Woodland Rd, off Tyndalls Park Rd, *Baptist College* (1913; G. Oatley) brick Elizabethan with strong plainly detailed tower. To W, Whiteladies Rd runs N with ashlar villas of c 1850 at S end. To N, in Westbury Park, *St. Alban's Church*, Coldharbour Rd (1908–15; C.F. Dening) with fine interior, the chancel lofty in the manner of Bodley, but the spaces made complex by chancel aisles, on S opening into a side chapel, itself aisled to S. Off North View, *Downs Park*, estate of c 1905–10 Arts and Crafts houses.

1½m NW, at **Henbury**, *Blaise Hamlet* John Nash's super-picturesque cluster of nine cottages, built 1811–12 for J.S. Harford of Blaise Castle, every one varied, with thatch, tall chimneys, wavy walls and all the touches imitated in estate cottages all over Britain in the following few decades.

SE of central Bristol, Bath Rd, A4, leads out from Temple Meads. At Wells Rd Junction, fine cast-iron *signpost*. Off Wells Rd at **Knowle**, ¾m SE, Redcatch Rd runs W with *St. Agnes Retreat House* (1890–94; J.D. Sedding), excellent Arts and Crafts Tudor, partly half-timbered with rear courtyard of stone mullioned windows cleverly divided into bays by recessing alternate sections of the upper wall. Chapel (1900; G.F. Bodley) restrained with good fittings. On Bath Rd, *Arno's Vale Cemetery* (1837), the main Bristol cemetery, now part derelict. Greek Revival Doric lodges, Ionic Nonconformist chapel and Corinthian Anglican chapel, this last more Italianate with lantern tower (all c 1840; C. Underwood). Monuments disappearing into the undergrowth, the happiest and best maintained is one in Hindu style to an Indian scholar who died in Bristol. To E, opposite Arno's Court, former *Transport Depot* (1899; W.C. Green) stone, Baroque with cupola. At **Brislington**, A4, on city outskirts, *Brislington House*, built as a pioneering asylum for the insane by E.L. Fox, originally six houses refronted into a long palazzo-style mansion (1850; C. Underwood) well set over the E approach to Bristol.

4m E of Bristol, on A 420, **Kingswood**, centre of an area known for mining and Methodism, now joined to Bristol. 3m beyond, at **Wick**, *church* (1845–50; C. Dyer: completed W. Butterfield). The sturdy tower, lychgate, roofs and fittings are Butterfield's, note especially the low wooden chancel screen. 4m N of Kingswood, A432, at **Coalpit Heath**, important group of *church, vicarage* and *lychgate* (1844; W. Butterfield), early work in Butterfield's career, showing an approach to the revived Gothic based on Puginian principles but with an economy of decorative detail and functional logic more rigorous than Pugin's. The church has clearly differentiated roofs, slightly more elaborate external treatment of the chancel and Dec. tracery set in walls of local rubble stone, all the elements appropriate to a village church without pretension. The avoidance of ornate detail in favour of sharply outlined walls, buttresses and roofs derives from a hierarchic theory of appropriate display carried further in the *vicarage*, where the Cotswold tradition provides the outline but a gradation of window forms emphasises the more important rooms externally. The exterior asymmetrical form is a masterly composition balancing end gable, porch and large external chimney, the placing arising from the logic of the internal plan and emphasising structure instead of the fancy but redundant detail of earlier revived Gothic work. The *lychgate* is a composition of geometrical solidity, rubble stone, ashlar coping and two deep pointed arches. In the church, good Butterfield fittings and E window by Willement. 2m SW, at **Winterbourne Down**, *church* (1858; G.E. Street) plate traceried with fine round-columned arcade. Lovely rich coloured E window, possibly early Morris work. To N, *Perry Almshouses* (1851) stone Gothic group with fishscale slate roofs.

SW of Bristol, off A370, at **Long Ashton**, *Smyth Almshouses* (1904; E. Gabriel) pretty group with Arts and Crafts details, leaded lights and a big central gable, richly plastered and carrying a clock turret. Harsher Gothic stone *schools* to SW (1860; J. Wilson). At **Barrow Gurney**, 3m SW, off A470, *Barrow Court* (17C: altered c 1880; H. Woodyer) notable for the fine garden buildings (c 1900; Inigo Thomas). Stone Baroque pavilions and curved screen wall with carved heads by A. Drury. The *church* (1889; H. Woodyer) stands right by the house. Rich ironwork to the door, stained glass by Kempe. 5m SE, B3130, at **Chew Magna**, *Chew Manor* (1862–64; J. Norton) Tudor style with angle tower and much carved detail.

CLEVEDON. B3128 14m W of Bristol. Genteel seaside resort developed from the early 19C by the Elton family of Clevedon Court. Modest seafront still of cottage scale with, at N end, *Clevedon Pier* (1869; Ward and Grover) the most attractive of British seaside piers with its delicate arched legs, made from second-hand wrought-iron rails originally intended for Brunel's South Wales Railway. Sadly two sections were destroyed in 1970 leaving the pier-head with its pavilion stranded at sea. Restoration is intended, see exhibition in the toll-house. Clevedon has a spectacular 45ft tide and the unusual structure was designed to give minimum resistance to the water. Behind the seafront, in Alexandra Rd, Albert Rd and Victoria Rd the characterful grey stone houses of the mid 19C that are typical of the town. In Alexandra Rd, delightful *Market Hall* (1869; H. Price) timber on a stone base with hipped roof carrying a top glazed clerestory and central lantern. To N, Hill Rd has buildings of the early 19C, the beginnings of the resort. At SE end, *Christ Church* (1839; Rickman) broad interior and big W tower. In Highdale Rd, to rear, *Claremont* (1865) elaborate Gothic house built to contain the antiquarian collection of G. Braikenridge, Bristol merchant, who endowed Christ Church for his son. *Mount Elton* (1844; S.W. Daukes) is a rubble stone Tudor Gothic villa. S of the pier, large Italianate villas of c 1850 in Elton Rd, ornate *bandstand* (1887) and *St. Brandon's School* (1850; Foster and Wood) large Jacobean style house built for Conrad Finzel, sugar tycoon of Bristol. Off to SW, *old church* where A. Hallam (1811–33) to whom Tennyson dedicated 'In Memoriam' is buried. Tennyson visited Clevedon on his honeymoon in 1850 and supposedly was inspired to write 'Break, break, break, On thy cold grey stones, O sea' here. Old Church Rd leads E to the artisan part of the town. To N, off Queen's Rd, *St. John's Church* (1876–78; W. Butterfield) built for Sir A.H. Elton, in grey stone with red roofs and saddleback tower, the interior sadly whitewashed. At The Triangle, cheerful *Clock Tower* (1897) clad in ceramic by Sir Edmund Elton, an important innovative potter.

At *Clevedon Court* (NT), the 14C to 16C Elton mansion on the E edge of the town, there is good collection of Elton Ware, pottery made c 1880–1920 by Sir E. Elton. NW of the house, *church* (1860; C.E. Giles), All Saint's Lane, High Victorian Gothic with crossing tower, built for the Eltons. Screen and reredos by Comper. Just E of the house Arts and Crafts detailed *waterworks* (1901; H.D. Bryan). Going N from the pier, **Walton Park**, c 1870 suburb. *Church* (1870; J. Norton) with good set of 19C stained glass and painted chancel roof.

3m NE, **Portishead**, 19C seaside resort developed from c 1830. *HMS Formidable* (1904; E. Gabriel) at the Nore Point is a Baroque detailed nautical training school, built to replace the old school housed in the redundant battleship Formidable. 5m E of Clevedon, **Wraxall**, estate village of Tyntesfield, estate of the Gibbs family, merchants and prominent High Church patrons. It was for William Gibbs that Butterfield built Keble College chapel, Oxford. The *Battleaxes Inn* (1880; W. Butterfield) is Butterfield's only pub, with picturesquely varied S front in stone and half-timber with mighty chimney stacks. The interior has been rebuilt. *Tyntesfield* (1862–64; J. Norton) is large and late Gothic in style built to a spreading plan that makes it seem larger than it is. Gothic interiors partly remodelled c 1885 (H. Woodyer). Behind the house, chapel (1875; A. Blomfield) of a size befitting such eminent church builders but surprising attached to a private house. Stone-vaulted, apsed with excellent stained glass by H. Wooldridge.

RADSTOCK. A367 8m SW of Bath. Centre of the defunct Somerset coalfield, a small Victorian town with terraces of miners' houses. At the centre iron *Market Hall* (c 1880). At **Midsomer Norton**, 1m W, High St focussed on round-arched Italian Gothic *Town Hall* (1860). *RC Church* converted from 15C tithe barn (1907–13; Giles G. Scott) most skilfully.

THORNBURY. Off A38 12m N of Bristol. *Thornbury Castle* the 16C prodigy house left unfinished at the execution of Edward Stafford in 1521 was made habitable in the 18C and restored 1854 (A. Salvin). In High St Greek former *Register Office* (1839; S. Daukes). 3m NE, B4509, *Tortworth Court* (1849–52; S.S. Teulon) large and complex Tudor Gothic house building up to a square tower over the stair hall, sadly now without the pyramid roof and lantern that were on top. In the village numerous estate cottages.

WESTON-SUPER-MARE. A370 21m SW of Bristol. Seaside resort from the early 19C. Knightstone Island was developed as a health resort from the 1820s, but Weston's main development was in the mid 19C as a select resort and in the late 19C as a popular resort for day visitors from Bristol or South Wales. The long seafront esplanade was laid out c 1885 with *Grand Pier* (1906) and *Grand Atlantic Hotel* (c 1860 and 1888). The seafront curves round to Knightstone Island with *Pavilion* (1901) and early 19C *bath house*. On the point, *Birnbeck Pier* (1867; E. Birch), decorative iron pier leading out to Birnbeck Island that has a cluster of late Victorian stone buildings.

Inland from the pier and Knightstone Island villas cover the S slope of Worlebury Hill. Large terraces of c 1861 in Atlantic Rd, and earlier terraces lower down around the *parish church* (1826 and 1837) Lower Church St, notably *Oriel Terrace* (1847) Jacobean and *Royal Crescent* (1847) classical with tall arched recesses to each bay, an early Victorian heaviness. S of the church, *School of Science and Art* (1889; H. Price) ornate stone with tile plaques. E of the church, Lower Bristol Rd runs through the principal area of villas. In All Saints Rd, to N, *church* (1899–1902; Bodley) grey stone with triple gabled W end and long light interior typical of Bodley. Off Lower Bristol Rd to E, *Trewartha Park*, row of prettily tile-hung villas (1898; H.D. Bryan). *Trewartha* (c 1870), just to W, is a large Gothic stone house with ornate brick chimneys. To S the present commercial centre on the flat ground, The Boulevard, laid out c 1860, is aligned on the spire of *Christ Church* (1854). In the Boulevard, red brick and stone free Baroque *Library* (1900; H. Price) and *Weston Mercury* offices (1885; H. Price) free Jacobean with tower. To S, off Orchard St, *Museum*, Burlington St in a handsome former Gas Company workshops (1912), excellently adapted. W of the Boulevard, in South Parade, *Royal Hotel* (c 1845) stucco, incorporating the first hotel of 1808. Opposite, handsome stone *bank* (c 1870) in the palazzo style of Bristol, built for a Bristol bank. The entrance to the Italian Gardens, High St, has a 19C sculptured wall moved here (from where?) in 1924. At S end of High St, *Town Hall* (1897; H. Price) and *Board Schools*, Walliscote Rd (1897; H. Price), both ornately detailed in a free Renaissance way. Further S, *Ellenborough Crescent* (1855) surprisingly grand stone-fronted terrace.

1m S, at **Uphill**, *church* (1844; J. Wilson) and *Uphill Castle* castel-

lated early 19C house. 4m E of Weston, at **Banwell**, *Banwell Court* 15C
but much rebuilt c 1870 (H. Price) and *Banwell Castle*, to S, early
Victorian castellated Tudor house. On Banwell Hill, to W, lookout
tower (1840) built for Lord Auckland, Bishop of Bath and Wells. 2m SE,
at **Winscombe**, in *church* stained glass in chancel (E window) by William Burges or his craftsmen Saunders and Weekes (c 1870). Deep rich
colours on a background of blue and white. At **Sidcot**, A38, 1m E,
Quaker *school*, founded 1808, with white Italianate buildings (1838).
2m N, at **Churchill**, pretty Arts and Crafts Gothic *clock tower* (1897;
Silcock and Reay), Wesleyan *chapel* (1881; Foster and Wood), and
brick *almshouses* (1906; Silcock and Reay) arranged around a court
with sundial on a column. At **Lower Langford**, just E, *almshouses*
(1887; Foster and Wood) on an unusually urban scale. Like the Churchill buildings, the gift of Sidney Hill of Longford House, wealthy
Wesleyan philanthropist. At **Blagdon**, A368, 3m E, estate village c
1900 of the Wills, tobacco family of Bristol. *Church* rebuilt except
tower (1907; Sir F. Wills). Coombe Lodge, their house, was rebuilt in
Tudor style in 1930 (G. Oatley).

BEDFORDSHIRE

BEDFORD. County town on the Great Ouse. Over the bridge in St. Paul's Square, statue of *John Howard* (1894; A. Gilbert), the prison reformer. On S side, *Shire Hall* (1878; A. Waterhouse), red brick and terracotta, gabled Elizabethan style with extension to W (1886; B. Champneys) in late 17C style. On N side, former *Corn Exchange* (1871; Ladds and Powell), Italianate.

In Harpur St, to the NW, former *Bedford Modern School* (1829–34: E. Blore), Tudor style, the frontage retained as part of a shopping centre, hence the unfortunate breezeblocked windows. Opposite, *Library* (1834; T. Elger), Greek Doric, stucco fronted. At top of Harpur St, in Dame Alice St, *Prison* (c 1840; J. Brown), Italianate front with governor's house and warders' house flanking entry.

To the W. *Bedford High School* (1878–92; B. Champneys), free 17C style with mullion and bays and centre cupola. Bromham Rd has early 19C villas and *church* (1838; J. Brown), lancet Gothic. To the E, St. Peter's Green with statue of John Bunyan (1874; J. Boehm).

To the N, off De Parys Avenue, *Bedford School* (1889–92; E.C. Robins), Elizabethan style with chapel (1908; G.F. Bodley). To the S, off High Street, *Howard U.R. Church* (1849), stucco fronted, and *Bunyan Meeting House* (1840; Wing and Jackson), on site of barn where Bunyan preached. Bronze doors with scenes from 'Pilgrim's Progress' (F. Thrupp). Bunyan Museum attached. In Castle Close, *Cecil Higgins Art Gallery* with good collection of Victorian decorative arts displayed in Victorian room settings.

2m W of Bedford off A422, **Biddenham**, with a number of c 1900 houses by the Bedford Arts and Crafts architect, C.E. Mallows, rough-cast in the manner of Voysey, notably *Three Gables*, 17 Biddenham Turn. **Bromham** *church*, N of A422, was restored (1868; W. Butterfield) with chancel glass by Lavers and Barraud. Simple and typically Butterfield are the wooden churchyard gates. At **Turvey**, 4m NW on the A428, the *church* has a rich chancel (1852; G.G. Scott) with all the mid 19C fittings, encaustic tiles, painted organ, granite piers.

1½m N of Bedford off A6, *Clapham Park* (1872; J. Usher), red-brick Tudor, for a Bedford ironmaster. 4m N, A6, *****Milton Ernest Hall** (1853–56; W. Butterfield), Butterfield's only large country house, built for his brother-in-law, and one of the finest High Victorian Gothic houses. Built in yellow rubblestone with pale Bath stone window dressings and decorative patterning of red brick to the arches and eaves—the house sparkles in good light. Tall tiled roofs with patterned chimneys, the main roof a strong L shape of uniform height but complicated, especially on the entrance side, by a highly picturesque grouping of descending roof lines and gables in different planes. Openings in a rich variety of Gothic forms, hierarchically ordered so that greater elaboration is given to the main stair lights and principal S front rooms. The S front has the more formal composition of balancing gables, not symmetrically placed, however, and one gable plain stone, the other with hipped roof into which a tall three-sided bay window breaks with timbered top gable. By Butterfield also, the farm buildings behind, two cottages in the village, and the splendid red-brick *mill* with Georgian sash windows and half-hipped gable. Milton Ernest *church* chancel was rebuilt (1858–65; W. Butterfield) with Butterfield fittings and glass by A. Gibbs.

At **Souldrop**, 4m NW, *church* (1861; H. Clutton) with High Victorian detail, stone-vaulted chancel.

6m E of Bedford, A603, at **Moggerhanger**, *church* (1860; W. Slater), severe High Victorian with tall apsed chancel behind pyramid roofed tower.

6m S of Bedford, A6, at **Haynes**, *church*, much elaborated c 1850–65 for the Rev. Lord John Thynne, with glass by O'Connor and Clayton and Bell, tiled floors. Lady Thynne effigy (1868; H.H. Armstead) under alabaster canopy by G.G. Scott.

Biggleswade. A1 12m SE of Bedford. In Market Square, *Town Hall* (1844; J.T. Wing) with Roman Doric upper floor. At **Old Warden**, 3m W, estate village with picturesque cottages of c 1800–40. The *church* is remarkable for all the carved woodwork introduced c 1840 by Lord Ongley, much of it continental, acquired from Belgian convents. Large standing female figure monument to C. Shuttleworth (c 1900) on nave E wall in a genuine Baroque surround. The Shuttleworths, a Lancashire cotton family, built *Old Warden Park* (1872; H. Clutton) in impressive c 1600 style with flat topped bays and an off-centre tower. The picturesque early 19C Swiss garden has been restored by the County Council. At Sandy, 3m N of Biggleswade, to SE, *Sandy Lodge* (1869–77; Clutton), Tudor style in yellow brick.

LEIGHTON BUZZARD. A4146 6m S of Bletchley. In the Market Place *Town Hall* (1851), plain Gothic. Nearby, Barclays Bank (c 1875; A. Waterhouse), Gothic in handsome Bath stone. In High St, *National Westminster Bank* (1856; C.O. Parnell), Italianate in grey brick. Church Square is unexpectedly formal (c 1856; W.C. Reed). In Lake St, brash Renaissance style *Corn Exchange* (1862; Bellamy and Hardy) and small Grecian *Institute* (1845).

WOBURN. A418, 5m NE of Leighton Buzzard. Estate town of the Dukes of Bedford. *Market House* (1830; E. Blore), Gothic in red brick and stone. The old church, now the *cemetery chapel*, has tower rebuilt 1830 (E. Blore). The new *church* (1865–68; H. Clutton) is a far more appropriate estate church, Early French detail strongly handled. Tall tower, originally with spire, stone-vaulted interior with heavy piers, actually paired round columns giving great depth to the arcade. Clutton also designed estate churches at **Apsley Heath** (1868), 2m N, and **Steppingley** (1859–60), 4m E, the latter elaborately carved and with schools by Clutton nearby. At **Ridgmont**, 3m NE, A418, *church* (1854; G.G. Scott), another Bedford estate building in an estate village. Good broach spire.

LUTON. Industrial town developed at turn of the century. The *Museum*, in Wardown Park (1875; T.C. Sorby), has material relating to the older Luton industries: straw hats and pillow lace. 2m S, A6, *Luton Hoo* (open to public), house of 1764 by R. Adam, altered c 1816 and 1843 and then in 1903 recast inside for Sir Julius Wernher, diamond king and friend of Edward VII. Wernher's architects, Mewes and Davis, gave the house a fashionable French tinge with mansard roofs and splendid Beaux Arts staircase hall, gleaming white with iron-railed staircase curving effortlessly up. The house still contains Wernher's art collection. Byzantine style chapel (1875; G.E. Street). 9m N of Luton, A6 at **Silsoe**, *Wrest Park* (1834–36), very much a house out of its period, designed by the owner, Earl de Grey (1781–1859) in an accomplished French Louis XV style with mansard and pavilion roofs. Staircase hall and interiors in similar mode. Orangery (1836) also French in style, but much less disciplined. Earl de Grey also designed Silsoe's successfully Perp. Gothic *church* (1830-31). The

Grey family tombs are in **Flitton** *church*, 1m W: Earl de Grey by Noble (1859), Countess de Grey with weeping husband (c 1853; Sir T. Farrell). 4m W of Luton, A505 at **Dunstable**, *Town Hall* (1879). *Dunstable School* has extensive dark red brick buildings (1887–94; E.R. Robson) in Jacobean style with asymmetrical late Gothic tower.

BERKSHIRE

BRACKNELL. A329 8m SE of Reading. 1m S at **Easthampstead**, *church* (1866; J.W. Hugall) with superb *E window by Burne-Jones (1874). *Easthampstead Park*, to SW, brick Jacobean style (1860). 3m NE at **Winkfield**, *church* with rich chancel decoration, tile work of c 1890 in manner of Botticelli and High Victorian font (1863; J.F. Bentley). 3m E of Bracknell, **Ascot**, red-brick-and-rhododendron late Victorian area. At S Ascot, A330, *church* (1897; J.L. Pearson) red brick with central tower, stone-vaulted E end. By the racecourse, *Ascot Heath House* (1868; R. Kerr) red-brick Jacobean. To NW, *Ascot Priory*, a complex Gothic group built for the Anglican Society of the Holy Trin ity, begun 1861 (C. Buckeridge), continued c 1865–70 (G.G. Scott) and completed 1901 (L. Stokes). The earlier work is severe with plate tracery to Scott's part while Stokes' work is freely detailed with his characteristic horizontal emphasis. Mullion and transom windows with hipped dormers and a fine angle tower capped by a pretty lan tern. The chapel is neo-Norman in the nave extended 1885 (Butterfield) in Early Gothic style. Stone with timber wagon roof, though a vault was apparently intended, and fine polychrome interior of bands of red sandstone, the spacing increased as the wall rises. At **Sunninghill**, to SE, *Cordes Hall* (1902; J. Morris and Son) in the vill age, pretty Arts and Crafts building in brick and roughcast with top lantern. *Silwood Park* (1876; A. Waterhouse), N of A329, very large red-brick Tudor style house. At **Sunningdale**, *church* (1887; J.O. Scott) with crossing spire, chancel of 1860 (G.E. Street). In church carved relief effigy of Prince Victor of Hohenlohe-Langenburg (died 1891) Admiral and relation of Queen Victoria. The effigy is by his daughter Feodora Gleichen.

HUNGERFORD. A338 7m W of Newbury. By the river large Georgian Gothic church in Bath stone (1816; J. Pinch Sr). In the main street cheery polychrome brick and terracotta *Town Hall* (1870; E. Prestwick) with round-arched ground floor and tower with Frenchy bulbous roof. 4m NE, B4000, at **Wickham**, *church* rebuilt (1845–49; B. Ferrey) except tower. Lavish interior carving, but the angels supporting the nave roof are apparently of papier mâché. Far more surprising are the elephants under the aisle roof, also papier mâché, apparently bought at the Paris exhibition of 1862 by Lt.-Col. Nicholson, son of the founder, and intended for the rectory, where they proved too large. Elaborate font and tower screen, the font cover another Nicholson gift, carved by Maoris. At **Lambourn**, 6m N, B4001, the *church* has good E window (1876; Westlake). Nearby Tudor style diapered brick *almshouses* (1852; T.T. Bury) with pretty courtyard. At **Eastbury**, 2m SE, *church* (1852) one of G.E. Street's earliest with big roof sweeping over the aisle. Flint and brick *school* nearby (1859; Street). 8m NE of Hungerford, A338, at **Fawley**, *church* (1865; Street), a very fine work in stone with pyramid roofed tower and apsed chancel rising higher than the nave. Harmonious stone interior carefully and unostentatiously detailed, the chancel beautifully stone-vaulted, the ribs coming low and supported on marble shafts. Mosaic and marble reredos by Earp. E window by Morris and Co (1866).

MAIDENHEAD. A4 13m E of Reading. Battered modest-scale town centre with late 19C brick and half-timbered riverside villas S of the bridge, notably *Oldlands*, Guards Club Rd (c 1895) containing the

Henry Reitlinger art collection (open to public). To S *Maidenhead Railway Bridge* (1839; Brunel). Two shallow elliptical brick arches, the flattest such arches ever built, carry the line across the Thames, the shape allowing maximum height for water traffic and minimum increase in the gradient of the railway. The spans are 128ft but the maximum height only 24ft. Widened 1890. Off A4, to W of the centre, *All Saints' Church*, Boyne Hill (1855–65; G.E. Street), a masterly work, not just the church but a complete group of associated buildings from vicarage to school to stables clustered to the S like a tiny village, all steep tiled roofs and polychrome brick providing a foreground to the church, the tower of brick banded with stone carrying a stone broach spire. Coloured brick interior, with cut brick decoration and excellent fittings by Street, who designed some of the stained glass also. Boyne Hill breathes the high minded spirit of the mid 19C Anglican church, a cloistral group of buildings that provided education for the parish and houses for vicar, curates and schoolmaster all under the shadow of the church, a religious community, but not exclusive of the world outside. To N of centre, Cookham Rd, A4094, leads past *RC church* (1884; L. Stokes) flint and brick, Perp. style. **Cookham** and the Thames nearby is the country of K. Grahame's 'The Wind in the Willows' (1908). Grahame was brought up at **Cookham Dean** on the hill above. Cookham Dean *church* (1844; R.C. Carpenter) has exceptional Pre-Raphaelite glass in the chancel (1863; N.H.J. Westlake).

NEWBURY. A4 18m W of Reading. S of the river, Market Place with red and blue brick Gothic *Town Hall* (1876–81; J. Money) and stone pilastered *Corn Exchange* (1861; J. Dodd). To SW, on Enmore Rd, *St. Nicholas School* (1859; H. Woodyer) large, two-storey red-brick Gothic school, two ranges at right angles linked by a tower and spire in the angle. Acutely pointed details, especially the row of four upper windows with gables breaking into the roofline. 1m S of Newbury, off A34, **Greenham**, *church* (1875; Woodyer) prettily set and remarkable for the complete painted decoration of the interior (c 1888) with patterned roofs and walls, painted scenes and angels in the chancel. *Greenham Lodge* (1879–83; R. Norman Shaw) brick and stone Elizabethan style mansion with tremendous grids of mullioned windows in the wings, lighting a two-storey hall on one side. Now part of the RAF base.

3m N of Newbury, B4494, *Phillip's Hill House* (1907; M. Macartney) late 17C style in red brick. 3m N at **Leckhampstead**, *church* (1859; S.S. Teulon), flint, banded in brick and building up to a cross-gabled centre carrying a lantern turret, all very sharply detailed and no preparation for the polychrome brick interior in yellow, red and black, harsher and sharper by far. E window by Lavers and Barraud. At **Brightwalton**, 2m N, *church* (1862–63; G.E. Street), a lovely design in stone with shingled spire. Low grey stone piers with heavily carved capitals, carved reredos by Earp and bright E window. By the font remarkable deep coloured Pre-Raphaelite window in deep blues, greens and reds by Ford Madox Brown (1863). By Street also, the *school* (1863) brick and stone with Street's favoured half-hipped roofs, a very nice composition, The *Rectory* (1877) completes the group with good play of tall chimneys and some tile-hanging to the wing.

3m NE of Newbury, at **Cold Ash** on the ridge, late 19C villas amid pines. *Thirteover House* (1898; L. Stokes) free Tudor style. Polychrome *church* (1864; C. Beazley) with High Victorian stone and marble fittings. 2m NE, **Marlston**, the church altered 1855 (Butterfield) with W window by Gibbs, chancel 1901. *Marlston House* (1896; E. Burgess) brick and stone Elizabethan, in the manner of Norman Shaw, built for the Palmers, biscuit kings of Reading. Estate cottages E of church in Norman Shaw's more relaxed red-brick and white woodwork manner. 2m N, **Yattendon** was the estate of Alfred Waterhouse, the one Victorian architect to seek and achieve the status of country gentleman. His house has gone but Reading Room and School survive.

Off A4, 5m E of Newbury, **Midgham** church (1869; J. Johnson), the spire a landmark on the hill. Flint with expensive interior, polished granite and marble shafts and much carving. Similar church (1869–72; Johnson) at **Brimpton** 2m S. At **Woolhampton**, A4, the older village stretches up the hill N of the road. To E, *Kennet Orleigh* (c 1909; M. Macartney) late 17C style house built for Macartney himself. Big hipped roof with deliberately placed chimney breaking the careful symmetry. Macartney was a scholarly architect but given to quirky details. Opposite, *The Court* (c 1909; M. Macartney) less definable in style, but with Jacobean shaped gables and mannered late 17C tricks in the brickwork, especially the rusticated chimneys. Further N, *Douai Abbey* established here by the English Benedictine community expelled from England at the Reformation to Douai in France and eventually expelled from France in 1903. *RC church* (1848; G. Wigley) was built for a previous college, E window by Wailes over large marble reredos. College buildings 1884–95 (F. Walters) red brick with gatehouse tower. The buildings for Douai are all post 1918.

PANGBOURNE. A329 5m NW of Reading. Thames-side village much expanded from late 19C with large houses close to the river. In the centre, The Square, with block of shops and, originally, fire station (c 1900; L. Stokes) roughcast and brick gabled group. To W, *Shooter's Hill House*, Shooter's Hill (1898; L. Stokes) Queen Anne style with big roughcast gables and small paned white windows, the style of Norman Shaw. Further on, row of brick riverside houses, following Norman Shaw but with the liveliest excess of white woodwork, balconies, tile-hanging and decorated plaster. Known locally as the Seven Deadly Sins, built c 1890. To SW, *Pangbourne College* (1898; J. Belcher) palatial brick and stone house built for a Scottish shipbuilder in late 17C style. The entrance front has a massive Scots tower. At **Lower Bowden**, 1m W of Pangbourne, *Port Jackson* (1901; A. Mitchell) tile-hung and gabled house. 1m SW, *Buckhold House* (1884; A. Waterhouse) large red brick and terracotta house, now St. Andrew's School built for the Watney family, London brewers. The Watney brewery was by the Lambeth works of Doulton, the tile and terracotta manufacturer, and in the house are painted tile views of Lambeth, Derby, Boston, Mass., and the Marne given by Sir Henry Doulton. The house is prominent N of the M4.

1m S, at **Bradfield**, *Bradfield College* founded 1850 by the rector and squire of Bradfield, T. Stevens. Buildings in red brick and flint with timber framing around the earlier Bradfield Place. The dining hall (1856) has outstanding •glass by Burne-Jones in the W window, made c 1857 by Powell's before Burne-Jones joined William Morris, and hence the earliest pieces of Pre-Raphaelite glass. Strong figure drawing, radiant blues, greens and reds. Timber framed interior with fine tiled chimneypieces. The architect for the school buildings was G.G. Scott, followed by his son, J.O. Scott, but much influenced by Stevens who had strong ideas. Big School (1865–72) and the chapel frame the entrance court, the chapel (1890 and 1901) with low tower and pyramid roof, handsome interior with black marble piers. In the grounds, Greek *theatre* (1890), instituted by the second headmaster, Dr Gray, who rescued the school from the financial ruin that Stevens' ambitious vision had brought about. Greek plays have been performed in Greek at Bradfield regularly since 1890. Bradfield *church* was rebuilt (1847; G.G. Scott) for Stevens with much variety of roof line outside and, inside, long chancel with rib-vaulted apse and severe early Gothic detail. Glass by Wailes.

3m S of Pangbourne, off A340, *Englefield Park*, apparently Victorian Jacobean style with big tower and rich roof line of pointed cupolas all in best Bath stone, save for some flint chequer work on the bays. Actually a house of c 1600 remodelled 1823–29 (T. Hopper) and given the entrance tower and roof line c 1855–65 (R. Armstrong). Splendid Victorian grounds (occasionally open). The *church* (rebuilt 1857; G.G. Scott), with its flint walls and stone broach spire (1868), is the typical estate church. Nearby, *rectory* (1857; P.C. Hardwick) and red-brick estate cottages. 1m SE, at **Theale**, outstanding late Georgian Gothic *church* (1820–22; E. Garbett) in Bath stone to the grandest scale, in the EE style of Salisbury Cathedral. Despite the size of the church the Salisbury mouldings still seem too large but the accuracy is exceptional for 1820. Plaster vaults and genuine medieval chantry chapel removed from Magdalen College, Oxford (the very chantry of the college's founder) as the church was built for the sister of the college president. Tower added 1827 (J. Buckler) and apse 1892.

2m S, at **Sulhamstead**, *Folly Farm* (1906 and 1912; Lutyens) the first part late 17C in style, the extension Arts and Crafts vernacular with sweeping roofs carried down to sloping brick piers around a square pool, like a barn converted to a cloister. 5m SW of Theale, A340, at **Aldermaston**, *Aldermaston Court* (1848–51; P.C. Hardwick) diapered brick Tudor to Elizabethan style house with plentiful stone mullioned windows and bays and ornate chimneys. A garden front tower panelled like E Anglian churches with flushwork but of brick (not flint) and stone and capped by a steep pavilion roof. Extended and some detail toned down in 1893.

READING. The county town, much battered by redevelopment but still with good early 19C houses in stucco and Bath stone built before the onset of the Victorian brick that characterises the town, attractively in some of the smaller terraced streets. *Reading Station* (c 1870) is pleasantly Italianate in yellow brick with a timber lantern, replacing Brunel's odd arrangement of 1840 where there was but one platform with two stations, one for passengers going E, one for those going W. Opposite, stucco *Great Western Hotel* (1844) one of the earliest railway hotels. From Station Rd, Friar St runs E into Market Place. At N end, *Town Hall* (1872–75; A. Waterhouse) Gothic in red and blue brick with corner tower, not monumental but the tower effective from the Market Place. Extensions in Blagrave St for *Museum and Art Gallery*. To NW, The Forbury, with plain neo-Norman *RC church* (1837; A.W.N. Pugin). In Forbury Gardens Berkshire Regiment *Afghan War Memorial* (1886; G. Simonds), an enormous lion, apparently the largest cast-iron sculpture made. N of the gardens Wren style *County Offices* (1904–11; Hall and Warwick). To W, *HM Prison* (1842; Scott and Moffatt) where Oscar Wilde wrote 'De Profundis' during his two years hard labour 1895–97. 'The Ballad of Reading Gaol' (1898) was inspired by the execution at that time of a young soldier, Wooldridge, for the murder of his wife. In the Market Place, W side, former *Corn Exchange* (1854; Clacy and Hawkes) and, on E side,

Gothic shop of Sutton's seeds (1870–73; W. and J. Brown), one of the two most famous 19C Reading firms, the other being Huntley and Palmer's biscuits. At S end, King St, with *Barclays Bank* (1838–39; H. and N. Briant), its palazzo front an early example of the style. In Minster St, to W, *Telephone Exchange* (1908; L. Stokes) and further out, in Castle St, the Grecian portico of *St. Mary's Church* (1840; H. and N. Briant) formerly topped with a square cupola. E of King St, King's Road was developed with villas in stucco and Bath stone (brought up the Kennet and Avon Canal) from 1830. Similar buildings in Queen's Road and London Rd, to S. In Queen's Rd, *Queen's Crescent* (1833) Bath stone fronted. On London Rd, *Eldon Square* with Italianate villas (c 1840) and *Royal Berkshire Hospital* (1839; H. Briant) grandly Greek Ionic fronted. In London St, running N from W end of London Rd, Greek Ionic portico front of *Scientific Institution* (1843; W. Brown) and, by the bridge, *Coroner's Court* (1852; J.B. Clacy) in stucco and stone, still with Grecian pilasters and parapet and Corinthian columns to the first floor, but the windows definitely not Greek with moulded arched panels over.

S of London Rd is the Victorian area now largely taken over by Reading University. On Erleigh Rd, SE of the hospital, *Reading School* (1865–71; W. Woodman) red-brick Tudor with chapel (1873; A. Waterhouse). Reading University acquired the site on London Rd in 1904, endowed by the Palmer family, and in 1947 the Whiteknights Park estate at N end of Redland Rd. On Redland Rd, *St. Andrew's Hall* (1880; Waterhouse) built for one of the Palmers and *Wantage Hall* (1908; C. Steward Smith) Tudor style. Whiteknights Park was broken up for villas with six large houses, four by Waterhouse built 1859–73 of which two survive, *Foxhill* (1868) Waterhouse's own house, and *Whiteknights Park* (1868). In the park, *Museum of English Rural Life.* Further S, on Shinfield Rd, *Leighton Park School* the original building extended by Waterhouse (1890), *Grove House* (1892–94; Waterhouse), *Townson House* and *Peckover Hall* added 1910 (F. Rowntree). To NW, Christ Church Rd, *Christ Church* (1861; H. Woodyer) High Victorian with big EE style steeple. Heavily carved capitals and chancel arch filled at the top with net-like tracery.

3m S of Reading, A33, at **Shinfield**, flint and stone *school* (1861; H. Woodyer) very picturesque. 5m S of Reading, W of A33, at **Beech Hill**, *church* (1866; Butterfield) in flint banded with brick, the interior banded brick and stone with tiled chancel. Glass by Gibbs. *Parsonage* by Butterfield (c 1870 and 1883). At **Stratfield Mortimer**, 2m W, *church* (1869; R. Armstrong) built for the Benyons of Englefield Park expensively in rock-faced stone with spire and lofty interior. Saddleback towered *school* to W (1869).

N of Reading across the Thames the Victorian suburb of **Caversham** with *Caversham Park* (1851; Sir H. Jones) on the hill above, neo-Palladian rebuilt after a fire for W. Crawshay, of the Merthyr Tydfil iron family. Now the BBC External Monitoring Service. Close to the river, Church St turns E into Gosbrook St with Gothic *Baptist church* (1875) and *hall* (1865), both by Waterhouse. 3m W, off A4, at **Sonning**, riverside village, *church* much Victorianised, with restorations by Woodyer (1853 and 1875) and painted chancel roof (1903–06; Bodley). 19C glass including E window (1869; Hardman) and one by Wailes (1853) behind the organ. Marble effigy of Canon Pearson (1883; F. Thrupp). On Thames St, *•Deanery Garden* (1899–1902; Lutyens) built for E. Hudson, the owner of 'Country Life'. Along the street, the old garden wall was kept and the house built right up to it around a tiny court, cloistered on one side. Big tiled roofs, tall chimneys, soft red brick walls and timber-mullion windows, already aged to the patina of the old brick manor houses that Lutyens and his contemporaries admired. Powerful garden front composition of dominant hipped bay window balanced by a dramatic chimney with deep-arched door nestling to one side. The main through axis of the house continues into the garden, laid out by Gertrude Jekyll, with raised terraces by the house and orchard below. To S, *Holme Park* (1881) flint house with brick and terracotta details, now the Reading Bluecoat School.

At **Woodley**, 1m S, *church* (1871; Woodyer) with fine interior and odd acutely pointed bellcote over the porch. *School* by Woodyer. At **Wargrave**, 3m NE, more late Victorian riverside houses. *Woodclyffe Institute and Hall* (1901–05; Cole Adams) gabled with oriel in Norman Shaw style. 1½m E, N of Kiln Green, *Convent*, formerly Yieldhall (1894; J. Belcher) brick and half-timbered house, with entrance tower.

SLOUGH. A4 6m E of Maidenhead. *Railway station* (1886; J. Danks) a single-storey brick station in the style of later GWR works but most surprisingly capped by three bulbous French pavilion roofs with porthole windows. Slough's 19C development dates from the arrival of the railway in 1840. Parish church (1876–1912; J.O. Scott) with remarkable abstract W window (1915). SW of centre, off A355, Chalvey *church* (1861; G.E. Street) flint and brick village church, now fully in Slough. S of the centre, Upton Park, developed from the 1860s with large villas. 2m SE, **Datchet**, with elaborate *church* (1857–60; R. Brandon). Deep coloured glass of 1860s, notably E window by O'Connor. At **Wraysbury**, 2m S, church remodelled by R. Brandon (1862). At **Horton**, 1m N of Wraysbury, the *church* has an E window by Kempe to Milton, who wrote 'Lycidas' near here.

WINDSOR. *Windsor Castle* derives much of its present silhouette from Sir J. Wyatville's expensive works for George IV and William IV (1824–40) mainly to the Upper Ward and the Round Tower in the unpleasing combination of white stone and black mortar with yellow stone dressings. The later Victorian way with castles can be seen at the W end, where the Curfew tower was given a steep pitched roof (1863; A. Salvin) like Carcassonne. In the Lower Ward, residences of the Military Knights of Windsor on S side, heavily restored (1840–47; E. Blore).

Opposite, St. George's Chapel, built 1475–1511 and restored in 1840s under E. Blore, the 1860s under G.G. Scott and the 1880s under J.L. Pearson. Numerous 19C memorials. In the N aisle, effigy of Leopold I of Belgium (1878; Boehm), Queen Victoria's much respected uncle, elected King of Belgium 1831. In NW chapel the spectacular monument (1820–24; M.C. Wyatt) to Princess Charlotte, Leopold's wife who died in childbirth. In S transept effigy of the Prince Imperial (1880; Boehm), the son of Napoleon III killed with the British Army in Zululand, and monument to Christian Victor of Schleswig-Holstein. In the chancel, alabaster reredos (1863; Scott) and tomb of Edward VII and Alexandra (1919; Mackennal). In the choir the stall plates of the Knights of the Garter from the 15C onwards. George III, George IV and William IV are buried beneath the choir. In S chancel aisle coloured marble tomb chest of Duchess of Gloucester (1859; G.G. Scott).

To E, the *Albert Memorial Chapel, intended by Henry VII as a chantry for Henry VI and by Wolsey as his own burial place but ultimately the shrine of Albert, actually his cenotaph as Victoria chose to have him buried in the specially built Royal Mausoleum. The chapel was intended as the public shrine of Albert (whereas the mausoleum was strictly private), though Victoria paid for the work, carried out 1862–75 under G.G. Scott. Scott built the chapel vault, decorated in mosaic by Salviati of Venice to designs by Clayton and Bell. The windows were filled with glass showing Albert's ancestors and the walls elaborately decorated in marble tarsia, a technique invented by Baron H. de Triqueti where pictorial scenes were made up of different coloured marbles, the line decoration incised and filled with coloured mastic. The designs, of Old Testament scenes illustrating Albert's virtues are by Triqueti, executed by J.C. Destréez. Above, charming medallion portraits of the royal family by Susan Durant. Triqueti carved the reredos, in a frame by Scott. Albert's cenotaph (1871–73; Triqueti) is fully medievalising, the prince in the armour of one who has 'fought the good fight' sheathing his sword, his feet resting on his faithful hound. Mourning figures below, including the queen as 'Mourning Royalty' under his feet.

At the W end, marble monument to the Duke of Albany (died 1884; Boehm), Victoria's youngest son who died aged 31 at Cannes, but the overwhelming 'monument of the chapel, between Albany and Albert, is that to the Duke of Clarence, eldest son of the Prince of Wales and his presumed successor who died in 1892 aged 28. If there was an English Art Nouveau, Alfred Gilbert was its star and this his major work, made 1892–99 but the last five figures added 1927. Sculptors of the late 19C New Sculpture school experimented with mixing media, not just the combination of bronze and marble but also with different metals and alloys to achieve polychrome effects. The Clarence monument is masterly in its handling of the materials, bronze and aluminium modelled, etched and coloured to a flickering richness of surface. The tomb chest with the prince laid out in military uniform on his cloak with drawn sword is almost invisible behind a grille of surpassing richness, the caps of the pillars and the canopies over the figure groups like crowns from an underwater fantasy. The figure itself has head and hands of purest white marble, a kneeling angel holds a wreath and thorny crown above, the smooth forms of the angel and the effigy contrasting with the rich folds of the cloak and the nervous intensity of the crown and the surrounding grille.

The Middle Ward of the castle is dominated by Wyatville's crude remodelling of the Round Tower with walled approach road. Beyond, the Upper Ward, with the State Apartments, the quadrangle reworked by Wyatville, quite picturesquely but with unmedieval regularity. The State Apartments have much work by Wyatville overlaying the more interesting work done for Charles II in the late 17C. Grand staircase, Gothic by Salvin (1866). Wyatville's rooms have neo-rococo plasterwork, most notably in the Grand Reception Room. Some half million pounds were spent between 1824 and 1840 on the castle, the most disastrous result being the replacement of the Baroque chapel by the St. George's Hall, designed for Order of the Garter festivities. The Waterloo Chamber (1830 and 1861), the other very large room, was designed to hold Lawrence's portraits of the allied leaders in the Napoleonic Wars.

The *Home Park* stretches S of the castle with, ¾m S, the Royal Mausolea at Frogmore. The *Duchess of Kent Mausoleum* (1859–61; A. Humbert) was built for Queen Victoria's mother, a domed rotunda with granite and bronze details. Statue of the Duchess by Theed and painted interior by L. Gruner. The Duchess died in the same year as Albert, and Victoria decided to build his mausoleum nearby. The

Royal Mausoleum (1862–71; Humbert) enshrines Albert's own tastes in architecture and decoration. The style is Romanesque, similar to the family mausoleum at Coburg which Albert had helped to design, a cross plan with octagonal lantern in smooth ashlar with granite columns. The interior (open to public 11–4 on Whit Monday) is fully High Renaissance, in the manner of Raphael's work at the Vatican. This was Albert's favourite period in art. He had put much effort into the revival of painted decoration in England, taking his lead from the extensive Renaissance revival decorations carried out in contemporary Germany, notably in Dresden and Munich. The interior decoration was largely by German artists under Ludwig Gruner consulting Raphael's work wherever possible. The effect with marble floor, marbled walls, statues and wall-paintings is overpowering. In the centre, the tomb, the largest block of granite ever cut in Britain, flanked by bronze angels with the marble effigies of Albert and Victoria (1861–67; Marochetti). In the chapel also, monuments to the Duke of Kent (1874; Boehm) Victoria's father, to her daughter Princess Alice (1878; Boehm) Grand-Duchess of Hesse, and to her son-in-law the Emperor Frederick III of Germany (1890; Boehm) who reigned only ninety-nine days. His wife, Victoria's elder daugher, conceived the highly sentimental group called 'The Parting' (1862–67; W. Theed) of Victoria and Albert in Anglo-Saxon dress, an allusion to early Anglo-German relations, which is also in the chapel.

Further S, some of the agricultural improvements carried out by Albert, the *Home Farm* (c 1855; G. Dean) with its charming Gothic dairy ornamented with Minton tiles and panels of putti in relief. In the frieze, roundel portraits of the royal children. Carved fountains by John Thomas.

In the town, S of the Castle, *Royal Stables*, Castle Hill (1839–42; Blore). In High St, classical stone *bank* (1910; A.C. Blomfield) and Tudor style *Post Office* (1885). *St. John's Church* (1820; C. Hollis) is Regency Gothic with Victorian chancel (1869; Teulon). In Victoria St to SW, Gothic *almshouses* (1862) and stucco classical *Baptist chapel* (1839). In William St, *chapel* (1832; J. Hollis) yellow brick classical. Off Clarence Rd, *Clarence Crescent* (c 1845; W. Bedborough) late Regency style villa development. Opposite, Trinity Place leads to *Trinity Church* (1842; Blore) formally set in the centre of a square. Yellow brick with spire. Peascod St leads NE back to the centre and the Queen Victoria *statue* on Castle Hill. Set back, *Windsor Central Station* (1897) with its large brick and stone arch across the approach. The old royal waiting-room has been restored by Madame Tussaud's for a 'Royalty and Railways' exhibition. *White Hart Hotel* (1890; R. Robson). Thames St curves down to the river, past *monument* to Prince Christian of Schleswig-Holstein (1903; Goscombe John), to *Windsor and Eton Riverside Station* (1849; W. Tite) Tudor Gothic and quite elaborate. Along Datchet Rd, a long diapered brick wall with twelve Tudor arched doorways, apparently for putting cavalry on trains. At the far end, royal waiting- room.

W of the centre, Clarence Rd leads out with *RC church* (1867; C. Buckler) to S in Alma Rd, ragstone with rich interior, and *St. Stephen's Church* (1874; Woodyer), Vansittart Rd, large economical brick Gothic church with carved reredos. Across A332, **Clewer New Town**, Hatch Lane runs S to *Convent* (1853–90; H. Woodyer) splendid brick Gothic, steep roofed with corbelled-out circular stacks and acutely pointed dormers. Large chapel (1880), polychrome brick with apsed chancel and tall traceried windows, each topped by a sharp gable breaking into the parapet. Lofty interior with stone piers and polychrome walls, full High Church fittings and alabaster effigy of Canon Carter (1901; Bodley), the first warden of the Anglican community of Clewer. 2m W of Windsor, A308, *Oakley Court* (c 1850) highly over-done Tudor Gothic house, all battlements, pinnacles and turrets in red brick and stone, very picturesque.

S of centre of Windsor, Sheet St leads into King's Rd along the edge of the Home Park. To SW, on Frances Rd, polychrome brick *church* (1862; A.W. Blomfield) High Victorian Gothic with plate tracery. On King's Rd, villas from the early 19C onwards including *Queen's Terrace* (1849; S.S. Teulon) in diapered brick with shaped gables. Stucco villas of the 1860s in Osborne Rd, and further out, on King's Rd, brick houses in the style of Norman Shaw (1885). The A332 leads SW across the *Great Park* of 4,800 acres. The Long Walk runs nearly three miles to the George III statue, the '*Copper Horse*' (1824–30; R. West-macott) and, to the W, Queen Anne's Ride runs the same distance towards Ascot from the *estate cottages* (1853; Teulon) on A332 past the *Estate Workshops* (1858–61; Teulon). S of the Copper Horse, *Royal Lodge* with chapel (1863; Teulon). To SW, *Royal School* (1845) pretty brick village school, part of Albert's improvements for the estate workers. On B3022, W of A332, at **Cranbourne**, *church* (1849; Ferrey) with fine early Morris glass (1862) in W window. From King's Rd, A308 runs SE to **Old Windsor**, the riverside *church* rebuilt with shingled spire (1863; G.G. Scott). To SE the former Jesuit *Beaumont College* (1790) with extensions including chapel by J.A. Hansom (1870), the chapel decorated by J.F. Bentley. Just in Surrey, *St. John's*, the prep school (1888; J.F. Bentley) with Northern Renaissance stone fronti-spiece, the rest in the simple red-brick sash-windowed manner of Philip Webb.

North of Windsor, over Windsor Bridge, is **Eton**, the old High Street running up to Eton College. Off to W, *RC church* (1914) splendid S Italian Baroque interior on miniature scale. Parish *church* (1852–54; B. Ferrey). The College buildings begin at Barnes Pool Bridge with the School Yard on right, the great 15C *chapel* on the S side. Most of the 19C fittings have been cleared, but on E wall fine tapestry (1895; Burne-Jones) and at W end screen (1882; Street) carrying the organ with case by Pearson (1885). Effigies of Dr Hawtrey (c 1862, T. Nicholls) and Dr Balston (1892; Farmer and Brindley). The main 19C expansion of the college began with *New Buildings* (1844; J. Shaw) N of School Yard, Tudor style, followed by the Gothic *New Schools* (1861–62; H. Woodyer), at top of the High St, diapered brick with angle tower and additional range behind, facing Slough Rd of 1876, then, down Keate's Lane, *Queen's Schools* and *Lower Chapel* (1889–91; A. Blomfield), big quadrangular group, brick with chapel in stone, Perp. Woodyer's buildings are the most successful, picturesquely grouped and sparely detailed, though the Lower Chapel interior with glass by Kempe is handsome. The most prominent of the later buildings is the *Library and Hall* group (1906–08; L.K. Hall) opposite the Upper School, built as a Boer War Memorial, the library a rotunda in the manner of the Radcliffe Library, Oxford, but in brick and stone Edwardian Baroque, the hall similar style, tunnel-vaulted with giant columns inside. Other turn of the century additions of interest either in neo-Georgian or 17C styles are in Common Lane to NW, *Warre Schools* (1904; T.B. Carter), *Wotton House* (1903; T.E. Collcutt) set back behind and *Caxton Schools* (1903; T.B. Carter), and in Eton Wick Rd, off Keate's Lane, *Walpole House* (1906) on left *Wayneflete* and *Westbury*, both 1899, on right, all by T.E. Collcutt.

52   WOKINGHAM

WOKINGHAM. A329 5m SE of Reading. At the E end, *parish church*
heavily restored (1864; H. Woodyer) with new chancel and E window
by Hardman. In the centre vigorously polychrome brick *Town Hall*
(1860; Poulton and Woodman). At corner of Rectory Rd, Arts and
Crafts Tudor to Baroque *Police Station* (1904; J. Morris). Off Rectory
Rd, *Glebelands* (1897; E. Newton) free style in quiet brick, mullioned
windows but classical cornice. At the W end of town, *St. Paul's Church*
(1862–64; Woodyer) a proud suburban church, paid for by John
Walter, proprietor of 'The Times', dark stone with Bath stone dressings
and highly inventive Gothic details, as in the clerestory tracery. Glass
by Hardman and naturalistically carved font. 1m S, W of the 17C Lucas
Hospital, *Luckley* (1907; E. Newton) the neo-Georgian end of the Arts
and Crafts tradition, broad and symmetrical with wings ending in
copper-clad rounded bays and big hipped roofs, all quietly restrained.
1½m SE at **Holme Green**, *Holme Grange* (1882; R. Norman Shaw)
brick and tile-hung with pleasingly varied front. To S running E to W
is the Nine Mile Ride through the Berkshire heath. At **Heathlands**,
chapel (1864; Butterfield) in brick with fine stone font of the severest
geometry.
    1m S at **Crowthorne**, polychrome brick *church* (1873; Blomfield).
The village was originally to have been called Albertville. Its chief
raisons d'être are the *Broadmoor Asylum* (1863; Maj.-Gen. Jebb) for
the criminally insane, to E, and *Wellington College*, to SW, founded
in the Duke's memory for the orphans of officers. The original buildings (1856–59; J. Shaw) are quite remarkable for their date in being in
an English Baroque style based on Wren, though with florid touches
that seem more French. Rich red brick and stone with white windows,
all small paned as the Queen Anne revivalists of the 1870s liked them,
the composition formally Baroque with low centre and tall wings. The
whole effect is more cheerful than the Gothic equivalent, especially
with the oval windows that appear throughout and the cupolas over
the cross ranges. Gothic chapel (1861–63; G.G. Scott) with thin spire
that groups well with the towers and cupolas from a distance. 1m S of
the college, **Sandhurst**, the edge of the military heathland that stretches over into Surrey (Camberley) and Hampshire (Aldershot). The
settlement is wholly Victorian. *Church* (1853; G.E. Street) with
shingled spire, much 19C glass and wall decoration by Heaton and
Butler. The *Royal Military College* to SE has severe Greek Doric original building (1807). Enormous chapel of which the transepts are the
original round-arched building in the South Kensington style (1879;
Captain Cole) and the rest a war memorial extension of 1922–37 (A.C.
Martin). In the original part, mosaic and marble decoration.
    2m W of Wokingham is *Bearwood, the estate of the Walter family,
founders and owners of 'The Times'. John Walter I founded the paper
in 1785 and suffered the indignity of being pilloried for libelling the
Duke of York in 1789, his son, John II (died 1847), really established
the paper and bought the Bearwood estate in 1832 while his son, John
III (died 1894), built the palatial house. *Church* (1846; J.H. Good Jr) in
Georgian Gothic mode with rich glass by Wailes. *Bear Wood* (1865–
70; R. Kerr) is truly a prodigy among Victorian prodigy houses, built to
the most advanced technological standards of the day. Kerr was the
author of a book on house planning and this house has a horrendously
complex plan, designed to fit but separate all the different functions of
the 19C country house. Main elements of the plan are expressed externally in the beefy Jacobean style, notably of course the staircases,
the main one set in a massive tower. The tiny turret squashed to one
side contained a bachelors' stair, to avoid muddy boots in the hall.

Kerr's planning, for all his writings, seems quite unnecessarily complicated and not especially skilful. Externally the house is impressive for
the long tail of servants' and subsidiary rooms but more so for the
alarming way in which the almost symmetrical main facade crashes
into the massive main tower. Elaborate neo-Jacobean woodwork
inside.

BUCKINGHAMSHIRE

AMERSHAM. A413 10m NW of Uxbridge. In the parish *church* monuments to the Drake family of Shardoloes, including T.T. Drake (1854; H. Weekes) in the Drake chapel. 4m E, A404, at **Chenies**, in the *church*, Bedford Chapel, rebuilt c 1890 (G.F. Bodley) with outstanding monuments to the Russell family, Dukes of Bedford, from the 16C onwards, including the Prime Minister, Earl Russell (died 1878), the 9th Duke (died 1891; G.E. Fox), and Lord A. Russell (1892–1900; A. Gilbert) an encrusted Art Nouveau bronze candelabrum with bronze ideal figures. Glass by Kempe. Much mid 19C Bedford *estate housing* in brick with half-timber and iron lattice glazing. *Woodside House*, N of the church, is a rare work by the glass-painter C.E. Kempe (1897), pretty Queen Anne style with gardens by Lutyens. Just NW, at **Latimer**, Victorian estate village with *church* 1841 (E. Blore), E end 1867 (G.G. Scott), the Scott work richly carved with glass by Clayton and Bell in the apse. *Latimers* (1834–38; E. Blore) is red brick Tudor style, enlarged 1863 (G.G. Scott). 3m N of Amersham, at **Chesham**, *church* restored 1869 (G.G. Scott). At **Ashley Green**, 3m N, *church* (1873; G.E. Street) small-scale and neat design. 3m W of Chesham, at **Pednor**, the lane passes through the farm court of *Little Pednor* (1911; E. Forbes) picturesque group around a circular dovecote. 2m S of Amersham, at **Coleshill**, *church* (1860; G.E. Street), small with timbered bellcote and contemporary glass. 2m W, at **Penn Street**, *church* (1849; B. Ferrey) pleasingly simple cruciform Dec. design with octagonal tower and spire. 5m SE of Amersham, A413, at **Chalfont St. Peter**, *church* mostly rebuilt 1853 (G.E. Street) in fierce polychrome brick, Street's first experiment in the use of structural colour.

AYLESBURY. The county town. In the centre Market Place with Gothic *clock tower* (1876; D. Brandon) and *monuments* to Lord Chesham (1910; J. Tweed) and J. Hampden (1912; H.C. Fehr). At S end, County Hall (1723) and adjoining *Corn Exchange* (1865; D. Brandon) Jacobean. To NE, *Lloyds Bank* (1853 and later) handsome palazzo style corner building. The new shopping centre to E has the slightly surprised looking *tower* of a former chapel (1874; R. Plumbe) providing a High Victorian accent to an inflated vernacular mass behind. The parish *church* to W of Market was heavily restored 1850–69 (G.G. Scott) with much 19C glass, E window by Willement c 1855 based on the 13C glass at Chetwode, Bucks, chancel side windows 1858 (F.W. Oliphant), W window 1856 (O'Connor), exhibited at the 1862 exhibition. Lady Chapel E window an early work of Burlison and Grylls (1870). To NW of centre, *Gaol* (1845; Maj.-Gen. Jebb), Bicester Rd, with typical monumental entrance gate.

5m NW of Aylesbury, A41, **Waddesdon**, estate village for Baron F. de Rothschild, not far from the other Rothschild seats to E of Aylesbury, and perhaps the finest example in the country of a great estate created to display new wealth in emulation of the older landed aristocracy. Rothschild was lavish in his provision for the village, pub, school, hall, almshouses and reading room in half-timbered style lining the main road, the *church* refitted (though the alabaster pulpit c 1851 represents the previous owners, the Dukes of Marlborough) and cottages provided for the tenants. • *Waddesdon Manor* (1874–89; G.H. Destailleur) (NT) itself is an overwhelming French Renaissance style château in red brick and stone, designed by a French architect and finished with all the display that so free-wheeling a style allowed. The grounds were laid out with formal parterres and sculpture close to the house and plantations extending for miles around. Every detail of the estate was similarly expensively arranged from farms to greenhouses. Gladstone's daughter 'felt much oppressed with the extreme gorgeousness and luxury'. Interiors fitted with genuine French woodwork or designed to match and still containing Rothschild's superb collections of French furniture, porcelain and carpets. 2m W, at **Westcott**, *church* (1866; G.E. Street), a beautiful example of Street's pared-down Gothic with mouldings of the simplest profiles set against a pale coloured brick. 3m N of Aylesbury, at **Weedon**, *Lilies* (1869–71; G. Devey) country house, rambling in Devey's manner, but interestingly early example of revived Georgian detail to the main block.

E and NE of Aylesbury was the concentration of Rothschild estates called the 'pays Rothschild', the five country houses, Mentmore, Aston Clinton, Tring, Ascott and Halton built for the children and grandchildren of Baron Nathan de Rothschild who established the London arm of the banking empire. 4m E, at **Aston Clinton**, some estate building survives though Sir Anthony de Rothschild's house has gone. 1½m SW, at Weston Turville, the *rectory* (1838; G.G. Scott) is an example of Scott before his Gothic days, modelled brick and flint symmetrical classical villa. At Halton, to E, *Halton House* (1884; W.R. Rogers), palatial French 18C château style mansion for Baron A. de Rothschild in stone with pavilion roofs, a more sober style than Waddesdon, but expensively finished. French 18C style white and gold interiors. *Mentmore*, the first Rothschild mansion, is some 6m N, built 1852–54 by Sir J. Paxton and G.H. Stokes. Jacobean style, specifically modelled on Wollaton Hall, among the richest of Jacobean houses, and equally ornately treated. Square plan with corner towers and lower, but similar, wings enclosing the entrance court, and all in yellow stone. The house achieves a monumental grandeur relatively rare in Victorian mansions which, even where formally symmetrical, tend to overstressed central accents. Interior arranged like a London club around a full-height arcaded great hall. Other rooms with French 18C woodwork imported. Open to public. The setting on the hilltop is superb. 3m N at **Wing**, *Ascott* (NT), vastly expanded half-timbered house (1874–90; G. Devey) for Baron L. de Rothschild, the style prompted by the c 1606 centre part and by the fiction that this was a country cottage. Rothschild collections of paintings, furniture and Chinese porcelain. Landscaped grounds with ornate bronze fountain (c 1900; T.W. Story) in Roman Baroque style.

5m SE of Aylesbury, A413, **Wendover**, market town with Clock Tower at the crossing and Gothic *Literary Institute* (1862) adjoining. Coombe Hill to W (NT) is the highest point of the Chilterns, crowned by a Boer War memorial *obelisk* (1901).

BEACONSFIELD. A40 7m NW of Uxbridge. The author G.K. Chesterton lived here from 1909 and is buried in the cemetery in Shepherds Lane. 1½m N on Amersham Rd, **Knotty Green**, *Hollymount* (1905–07; C.F.A. Voysey), a small and pleasingly simple example of Voysey's manner, the entrance gable brought low, the front door, arched under an arched moulding, like a child's drawing.

3m E of Beaconsfield, A40, outside **Gerrards Cross**, *Bulstrode Park* (1862; B. Ferrey), heavy brick and stone Tudor style mansion with entrance tower and picturesque quad of outbuildings to one side. In Gerrards Cross, on A40, *church* (1859; Sir W. Tite), an unforgettable exotic in coloured brick, white and yellow with red dressings, Italian round-arched style with domed crossing and a campanile tower.

Gothic touches in the dome and interior capitals. Marbled columns under the dome. To NE of centre, in South Park, large early 20C houses in gabled and half-timbered styles, the best, *The Tudors* (1912; M.H. Baillie Scott) fully timbered with correctly pegged oak framing. 4m S of Gerrards Cross, B416, N of **Stoke Poges**, *Framewood House* (c 1903; G. Horsley) free Tudor style brick entrance front and tile-hanging elsewhere. W of Stoke Poges, at **Farnham Royal**, A355, church rebuilt 1867–69 (W.E. Nesfield), High Victorian Gothic with pyramid roofed tower, shallow relief carving by the clock showing the sunflower motif of the aesthetic movement. Good stained glass by Morris and Co. Nesfield's *Farnham Park* (1865) is much altered. E of Stoke Poges, off A4007, *Langley Park*, c 1760 mansion enlarged (c 1860) with wings in the English Baroque style, relatively unusual at that date. On the garden side, high and plainly detailed orangery. To NE, on Pinewood Rd, **Iver Heath**, *Little Coppice* (c 1905; C.R. Ashbee), miniature Arts and Crafts house in the Voysey manner, roughcast, square plan with a pyramid roof, the essence of Arts and Crafts simplicity. At SE corner of the county, E of Slough, A4, at **Colnbrook**, by the *church* (1849; B. Ferrey) a nice group of Gothic buildings by G.E. Street in polychrome brick, *school* and *master's house* (1858) and red-brick *vicarage* (1853).

SW of Beaconsfield, A4094, at **Wooburn**, *church* restored c 1850 (Butterfield) but notable for the lovely painted Gothic rood screen by Comper (1899) of the utmost delicacy. **Bourne End** to SW is a late 19C Thames-side settlement, **Hedsor**, to S, has full Victorian fittings in the *church* of c 1875. *Rectory* by Street (1861). To S, *Cliveden (NT) the most splendid of Thames-side mansions, rebuilt (1850; Sir C. Barry) for the Duke of Sutherland in Italian palazzo style, perfectly suiting the site dropping steeply away to S, the house standing proudly over the high 17C terrace, evenly and soberly detailed. The entrance front is framed by curved wings, the big porte-cochère an addition (1869; H. Clutton). By Clutton also the extraordinary *clock tower* (1861) to one side, richly modelled French Renaissance style, and the pretty circular *dovecote* on the forecourt. The interiors of the house were much remodelled from 1893 (J.L. Pearson) for the 1st Lord Astor, heir to one of the richest American families. The magnificent gardens, so Italian now, are largely an overlay by the Astor family on the formal bones partly dating back to the 17C. N of the house the main avenue aligns on a splendid Roman Baroque style *fountain* (1897; T.W. Story). Off to left, the Ilex Grove, a romantic mid-Victorian glade with bronze *statue* of Prince Albert (1865; W. Theed) and various other statues and urns. To E of the fountain, Long Garden, Italian Renaissance style formal garden of c 1900. To W of the fountain, Water Garden created by Lord Astor with delightful chinese *pagoda* made for the 1867 Paris exhibition. S of the house, the 17C terrace with central garden room marbled and embellished with gilt iron gates (1895; J.W. Singer) for Lord Astor. Beyond, Italian Renaissance balustrades bought by Astor from the Villa Borghese in Rome, a sale that provoked outrage in Italy. Formal parterre beyond laid out c 1723 with planting beds of 1851–53. Below W side, *Octagon Temple*, 1735, converted by Lord Astor into a memorial chapel (1893; J.L. Pearson), the interior lined in marble and mosaic to dazzling effect. Below the S end of the parterre, *Tortoise Fountain* (1897; T.W. Story) and the beginning of one of the walks leading down to the riverside, the walks and the riverside landing stage embellished with balustrading on the Borghese model. On the riverside, *boathouse* and two *cottages* (1857; G. Devey) in very pretty half-timbered style, showing Devey a pioneer in the return to vernacular styles associated, in the 1860s, with Nesfield and Norman Shaw. One, *Spring Cottage*, incorporates a little spa building of 1813. Steeply above Spring Cottage, *statue* (1866; M. Noble) of the Duke of Sutherland, moved here from the site of the main fountain, N of the house. The wooded valley back from the boathouse is a piece of romantic landscaping of 1869–72. The main entrance *gates* on the Taplow road are elaborate wrought iron (1893; J.W. Singer).

At **Taplow**, 2m S, *Taplow Court* (1855; W. Burn), red-brick and stone recasing of an earlier house, of which a neo-Norman great hall of c 1830 survives inside, the exterior now gabled Elizabethan style. 1m NE of Taplow, *Nashdom Abbey* (1910; Lutyens), built as a private house, in late 18C style to provide a show economically, thus of plain whitened brick enlivened with green shutters. A long garden front is achieved by building virtually two houses separated by a winter garden, the facade running right across, the junction emphasised rather than disguised by a dip in the parapet. Lutyens' handling of period styles is as always subtly original. At **Dropmore**, to N, *church* (1864–66; W. Butterfield), colourful small work in chequered flint and brick with half-timbered W end. Some polychrome brick and tile inside, a massive stone and marble font, tall wooden screen and richly coloured E window (c 1866; A. Gibbs). Just W, an estate *lodge* to Dropmore House encrusted with reused carved woodwork.

BUCKINGHAM. A413 17m N of Aylesbury. The parish *church* is a remodelling of 1862 (G.G. Scott) of a building of 1777, externally now entirely Dec. and the interior impressively timber-vaulted on tall 13C style piers. G.G. Scott was born at **Gawcott**, SW of Buckingham, where his father was curate—and designed the *church* (1827). In Buckingham, the old *workhouse* (1835) Stratford Rd and the S facade of the *Old Gaol* (1839) in High St are early works of G.G. Scott. 3m NW, off A422, at **Shalstone**, *church* rebuilt 1862 (G.G. Scott) in rich Dec. with much naturalistic carving and handsome W tower. 3m N of Buckingham, W of **Akeley**, *Akeley Wood* (c 1868; G. Devey) half-timbered and stone country house, more compact than usual with Devey. To N, at **Lillingstone Dayrell**, *Tilehouse*, (1881; E. Christian), dark red-brick and terracotta Elizabethan style house, now a school.

5m NE of Buckingham, off A422, at **Beachampton**, *church* restored 1873 (G.E. Street) with pretty timber top to the tower and fine stone font. 3m S, at **Nash**, small *church* (1857; G.E. Street) impressively simple with plain lancet windows and contemporary glass. *School* by Street (1857) now village hall. 3m S, at **Little Horwood**, *Horwood House* (1912; D. Blow) Elizabethan style, sensitively handled with thatched stable court and formal gatehouse to the N. 4m SE of Buckingham, A413, at **Addington**, *church* restored 1859 (G.E. Street) with 17C Flemish glass set in the Victorian glazing. Fittings by Street. To S, 3m S of Winslow, at **North Marston**, the *church* has a chancel enriched 1855 (M.D. Wyatt) by Queen Victoria in memory of J.C. Neild, who left his fortune to her. Spectacular colours to the E window (Ward and Nixon). 6m E of Winslow, at **Stewkley**, outstanding Norman *church*, controversially restored 1862 and 1867 (G.E. Street) who added painted decoration to the chancel, a marble and tile reredos and coloured E window, the effect enriching and far from overwhelming.

HIGH WYCOMBE. A40 13m NW of Uxbridge. Market town, furniture making centre from the 18C. Parish *church* heavily restored (1873; G.E. Street) with E window by Hardman, font by Street. In Queen Victoria St, *Town Hall* (1903; J.J. Bateman) pretty Queen Anne style with cupola. On A404, Marlow Hill, to S, *Wycombe Abbey School*, late 18C Gothic mansion with boarding houses up the hill of 1898–1903 (W.D. Caroe), Queen Anne style. W of centre, A40, at **Wycombe Marsh**, small flint *church* by G.E. Street (1859).

1½m N, at **Hughenden**, *Hughenden Manor* (NT), Disraeli's home from 1847 until his death in 1881. A 18C house refaced 1862 (E.B. Lamb) in a curious style that blurs rather than alters the 18C lines, mottled brick with projecting moulded details around the windows and along the parapet, not Gothic, but not obviously anything else. Inside the rooms as Disraeli knew them, pleasantly domestic rather than grand, mildly Gothic in an early Victorian way. Important Disraeli relics. Disraeli set up the *memorial* column (1863; E.B. Lamb) to his father Isaac D'Israeli 1m W of the house. The *church* was largely rebuilt (1874; A. Blomfield) in memory of Disraeli's wife. Painted chancel decoration. Memorial to Disraeli given by Queen Victoria. Outside the E end memorial to Lady Beaconsfield, created viscountess in her own right, Disraeli's earldom coming only at the end of his life when he retired from politics. 4m N, at **Prestwood**, *church* (1849; E.B. Lamb) in flint with Lamb's characteristic angular details and complex roof timbering. 4m NW of Wycombe, A4010, at **Bradenham**, *church* restored 1863 (G.E. Street) with memorial to Isaac D'Israeli (died 1849). 2m N, at **Lacey Green**, *church* (1826) with cast- iron window mullions and rich polychrome brick chancel (1871; J.P. Seddon).

4m S of Wycombe, on the Thames, **Marlow**, with splendid *suspension bridge* (1831–36; W.T. Clark). Parish *church* 1832–35 with chancel and aisles by Street (1875–81) and steeple rebuilt 1898 (J.O. Scott). *Vicarage* 1864 (G.E. Street). In St. Peter's St, *RC church* and *school* (1845–48; A.W.N. Pugin), built for C.R. Scott-Murray of Danesfield as a thank-offering for his conversion in 1844. Relatively modest church with broach spire, but the interior has full range of Pugin fittings, screen, hanging metal lights and stained glass (made by Hardman). The school and house, NE, an excellent composition. 3m W of Marlow, **Medmenham**, with series of Thames-side villas S of the road. *Wittington* (1897 and 1909; R. Blomfield) most attractive of Blomfield's country houses, in late 17C classical style, red brick and stone, the river front pedimented between bay windows. Built for Sir H. Kearley, founder of International Stores. *Danesfield*, to W, (1899–1901; W.H. Romaine Walker) is an exceptionally large recreation of a Tudor courtyard house, all in white chalk with moulded brick chimneys, the river front framed by two four-storey towers, two courtyards behind and a high gatehouse tower. The detail is scholarly, without the harshness of earlier Tudor style work. The building was for R. Hudson, Cheshire soap tycoon who had also had *Medmenham Abbey* adjoining rebuilt (1898; W.H. Romaine Walker) in Gothic style with half- timbered wing of 1911. 2m W, *Greenlands* (1853 and 1871) Italianate large riverside villa with belvedere tower, owned in late 19C by W.H. Smith, the newsagent.

NEWPORT PAGNELL. A422 13m W of Bedford. In the parish *church* bright E window by Street (1860) made by A. Gibbs. 2½m N, B526, at **Tyringham**, *Tyringham House* (1793–97; J. Soane) made unhappily more grandiose in French late 18C style (1909; G. Rees) with dome over the portico and balustraded forecourt. Long classical garden with pools flanked by domed temples 1926 by Lutyens. Opposite, *Gayhurst House*, late 16C mansion, of Victorian interest for the alterations by W. Burges for the 2nd Lord Carrington (1858–60), only a fraction of the intended transformation. Inside one room has walls completely panelled, the frames painted maroon and each panel with lovely paintings of flowers, birds and fruit, the fireplace a richly carved medley of Renaissance themes. In another, two monumental Gothic fireplaces, carved by T. Nicholls, loom in a room seemingly too small by half. Behind the house, a lavatory for male servants; Lord Carrington had an obsession with plumbing much ridiculed at the time. It is circular like a heavily Gothic dovecote, with large stone dormers in the roof and a fierce carved Cerberus, three-headed guardian of hell, on the summit. Burges also designed for Lord Carrington a Gothic enclosure for the Carrington tombs at **Moulsoe**, 3m SE of Newport Pagnell, and rebuilt the chancel of the *church*.

4m W of Newport Pagnell, **Wolverton**, railway town created by the London–Birmingham Railway which opened carriage works here 1838. Some 200 houses were built in the 1840s with parish church (1843; Wyatt and Brandon) before lack of land resulted in a second settlement being built at **New Bradwell**, to E, begun 1854. Much of the housing has gone here but the *church* (1858–60; G.E. Street) survives, a good High Victorian design with some exceptional Arts and Crafts stained glass of 1898 (G. Moira), luminous streaked glass and dramatic composition. *Vicarage* and *schools* by Street (1858), now convent and community centre. N of Wolverton, the railway crosses the Ouse on a six-arch brick *viaduct* (1838; R. Stephenson). At **Old Wolverton**, to W, neo-Norman church of 1815, very early for the revival, good fittings of 1877 (E.S. Harris) and wall-paintings by D. Bell. To SW, B4033, at **Calverton**, *church* (1818–24) with spiky Gothic aisle (c 1855) and richly fitted interior with stained glass by O'Connor, stamped plaster decoration to the chancel walls and painted decoration. The painted work, mosaic reredos and pulpit decoration of 1870 (E.S. Harris).

6m S of Newport Pagnell, A5130, at **Wavendon**, church much restored 1848 (W. Butterfield), the interior richly painted in the chancel, deep colours enhanced by glowing stained glass (1850–52; O'Connor). Excellent Butterfield woodwork, notably the font cover. The very Butterfieldian *parsonage* (1848) is apparently by B. Ferrey. 4m W, where A5 passes under the Birmingham railway, *Denbigh Hall Bridge* (1838; R. Stephenson) with plaque recording this as the temporary N terminus of the line to Birmingham until the Kilsby Tunnel was complete. **Bletchley**, to S, is largely a railway creation. In the *church*, altar by J.N. Comper and E window of 1868 by H. Holiday. Bletchley runs into the older town of **Fenny Stratford** to E, the *church* of 1724–30 extended in polychrome brick (1860; W. White), herring-bone patterned interior.

CAMBRIDGESHIRE

CAMBRIDGE. The Cambridge Colleges, like those of Oxford, employed leading Victorian architects to accommodate the vastly increased number of undergraduates. In the late 19C Alfred Waterhouse had the sort of dominance that T.G. Jackson exercised in Oxford, but his position was far from unrivalled. Cambridge played a central role in the architectural history of 19C church building and the Gothic revival through the Cambridge Camden Society, later the Ecclesiological Society. The Society, founded 1839 by J.M. Neale and B. Webb, had as its goal the study of ecclesiastical architecture and, more important, the promotion of correct Gothic architecture in modern churches, set out in influential pamphlets such as 'A Few Words to Church Builders' (1841). Ceaseless study of ancient churches and ancient church decoration led to a set of principles not merely concerned with building but with the mystical meaning of the forms of the ancient work, so that the correct scale and decoration of the chancel, the use of materials without falsehood (stucco pretending to be stone, or painted wood grain disguising cheap pine) were presented as essential to appropriate Christian worship. The Society's journal 'The Ecclesiologist' (1841–68) was always polemic and constantly attacked for being a first step towards Popery but a whole generation of church architects and church patrons took its advice, to the extent that after 1845 few non-Gothic churches were built and very few of the Gothic ones in the loosely Georgian Gothic manner that had been typical of churches built between 1830 and 1845.

Central Cambridge, the town, rather than the University, is Market Hill. In Market St, *Martyn Hall* (1887; E.S. Prior) flint-faced Gothic mission hall, the flint randomly inset with larger boulders. On S side of Market Hill, modern Guildhall with parts of previous building (1862) behind. To rear, former *Corn Exchange* (1874; R. Rowe) round-arched in polychrome brick with iron and glass interior. St. Mary St leads W to King's Parade, the centre of the university. Behind the Senate House, *Old Schools*, the W court rebuilt on S side (1862–69; G.G. Scott) and since altered, the W range, facing out to Clare College, more inventive (1887–90; J.L. Pearson). On the N side, *Old University Library* (1837–42; C.R. Cockerell) part of a botched scheme to replace the whole Schools in grand neo-classical style with scholarly borrowings from the Italian Renaissance and Wren. The exterior is plain but for the arched E end window as the main front would have screened most of this range. Magnificent tunnel-vaulted library at first-floor level. Senate House Lane leads to *Trinity Hall*, E front rebuilt (1852; A. Salvin) in Italianate style, the range to S (1873; A. Waterhouse) Flemish 16C style gables. To the garden, on N side, brick ranges (1890 and 1909; Grayson and Ould). Beyond, *King's College*, the main 19C addition being the long S side and pretty screen to King's Parade (1824–28; W. Wilkins). The S end of the King's Parade front is of 1873 (G.G. Scott) and, by the river in SW corner, L-plan range 1893 (G.F. Bodley), good neo-Tudor.

To S, on E side of Trumpington St, *Corpus Christi College*, the main court rebuilt in dull Tudor Gothic (1823–27; W. Wilkins). Opposite, behind St. Catharine's College, in Queens' Lane, *Queens' College*. The *Hall interior is very early work by William Morris (1861) with lovely tiles over the fireplace, painted walls and roof, done with G.F. Bodley as architect. Similar painted decoration in the former chapel, now part of the library and not accessible. To N of Front Court, Walnut

Tree Court, with chapel (1890; G.F. Bodley), long, sparely detailed brick Dec. building. Glass by Kempe. To N, facing Queens' Lane, free Tudor range (1912; C. Hare). For W side of the river, see below. In Trumpington St, W side, *University Press* (1831–33; E. Blore), collegiate Tudor front. Opposite, *Pembroke College*, Wren's chapel of 1663 lengthened 1880 by G.G. Scott Jr, who was a fellow of the college and did a tactful job. To S, facing Trumpington St, exuberant red-brick and stone range (1871; A. Waterhouse) in French late Gothic style with elaborate corner tower. Opposite, facing N, Library (1875; Waterhouse). At NE corner, 19C group comprising Master's Lodge (1873; Waterhouse) Tudor style and *New Buildings* (1878; G.G. Scott Jr), excellently detailed stone range in a free 17C style with pretty Dutch gables, carved angels on the end pilasters and first-floor oriel bays, all showing a scholarly understanding of English 17C sources. Link to Master's Lodge and stone screen to Pembroke St 1907 (W. Caroe). On N side of Pembroke St complex group of *science buildings* developed from 1863, the front to Pembroke St (1886–88; J.J. Stevenson) free 17C style, the building to E (1900–04; E.S. Prior) also stone, much more original with Baroque detail. Up Free School Lane, *Cavendish Laboratory* (1876; Fawcett), Gothic, set up under the outstanding scientist, J.C. Maxwell, professor 1871–79, who, Einstein said, changed the axiomatic basis of scientific thought in his electromagnetic theory of light.

To S of Pembroke St another area of university buildings, developed from 1904. Front range (1904–11; T.G. Jackson) in the pretty mixture of Tudor and Renaissance styles that Jackson used at Oxford. In this range are the *Sedgwick Museum of Geology*, founded in memory of the Rev. A. Sedgwick, professor of geology 1818–73, who set out, with Sir R. Murchison, the system of classification and relative ages of the oldest rock strata in Britain, the Cambrian, Devonian and Silurian. At the other end, the *Museum of Archaeology and Ethnology*. Across the court, *Botany School* (1904; W. Marshall) and beyond, *School of Agriculture* (1909; A. Mitchell). At E end of Downing St, *Emmanuel College*. Brick and stone detached library (1909; L. Stokes) to rear, built as lecture rooms, free Arts and Crafts brick and stone range with pretty Gothic lower windows and broad regular mullion and transom windows above and a wavy parapet. Extended in same style 1930. Across Emmanuel St, *North Court* (1910–15; L. Stokes), the most impressive early 20C college building, freely mixing 18C and Tudor Gothic motifs. Typical of Stokes the low, broad arches of the front cloister. Good formal front to Drummer St. Opposite, *No. 30 St. Andrew's St*, Norwich Union offices (1904; G.J. Skipper), Edwardian Baroque, stone-fronted, brick to Downing St. To N, *Christ's College*, the S end of the front a library (1895; G.F. Bodley) and the hall rebuilt (1876–79) by G.G. Scott Jr. At the rear of the site, range (1889; J.J. Stevenson), larger version of the 1640 Fellows' Building. In Sidney St, to N, *Lloyds Bank* (1891; A. Waterhouse) with corner tower and spire and *Sidney Sussex College*, the front cement-faced (1821–32; Sir J. Wyatville). The chapel, in Second Court, has an elaborate English Baroque style interior (1912; T.H. Lyon). On N side of Hall Court, neo-Jacobean range in brick with stone bays and an arcaded cloister (1890; J.L. Pearson).

In Jesus Lane, to NE, *Pitt Club* (c 1865; M.D. Wyatt) late 18C neoclassical in style and *Jesus College* which has important work by the firm of William Morris. The *chapel was restored (1846–49; A.W.N. Pugin) with timber screen, encaustic tiles, stalls (incorporating c 1500 work), altar, lectern and glass, notably the E window (1849) with figures in medallions. From 1864–67 G.F. Bodley restored the roofs with excellent painted decoration by Morris. The ceilings are panelled with armorial and heraldic decoration on foliage backgrounds and the surrounds coved with Pre-Raphaelite angels. From 1873–77 Morris and Co provided stained glass for the rest of the chapel, mostly by Burne-Jones, some scenes by Ford Madox Brown and Morris himself. At the back of Outer Court, to N, range (1869–70; A. Waterhouse), late Gothic with off-centre tower and spire. In Chapel Court, to E, institutional red-brick range (1884; Carpenter and Ingelow). Opposite Jesus College, *All Saints' Church* (1863–70; G.F. Bodley) fine serious Dec. work with spire, a turning-point in Bodley's career in that it returns to the English models favoured by Pugin from the tougher Early French Gothic that had interested most leading church architects, including Bodley, in the previous decade. Interior wholly decorated, mostly by Morris and Co with flowing painted decoration in deep colours, much in need of cleaning. Bodley himself and C.E. Kempe had much to do with the design, so that the patterning is more regular and less naturalistic than Morris and Co.'s usual work. Bodley also influenced Morris in the design of the great E window by demanding the clear glass background to the figures, which are by Burne-Jones, Madox Brown and Morris. *Westcott House*, to W, was an Anglican theological college. Tudor style buildings (1899; Grayson and Ould), extended later. NW of Jesus Lane, *Holy Sepulchre Church*, the famous 12C round church, restored 1841 (A. Salvin) under the eye of the newly formed Cambridge Camden Society. The Society's critics noted with alarm the fixed stone altar, surely a sign of Popery, Anglican churches generally having had a wooden communion table. Behind, *Union Society* (1866; A. Waterhouse).

In St. John's St, running S to King's Parade, *St. John's College*, the dominant 19C element being the towering chapel (1863–66; Sir G.G. Scott). Scott's chapel destroys the scale of First Court, in a way that his chapel at Exeter College, Oxford, though similar in its Sainte Chapelle motifs and scale much larger than the older buildings, does not. The siting of the chapel, as one side of the court, is not picturesque, nor is the contrast of the brown stone and the old red brick. This aside, the chapel is impressive, tall 14C proportions with a bold tower over the W crossing and apsed E end. Fine stone and marble details, fittings by Scott and glass by Clayton and Bell. Across the river, Bridge of Sighs (1831; H. Hutchinson) pretty Gothic access bridge to New Court (1825–31; Rickman and Hutchinson) largest early 19C Gothic college building, classically symmetrical with Tudor Gothic detail, succeeding in being picturesque despite its bulk. Also in St. John's St, *Selwyn Divinity School* (1878; B. Champneys), pretty brick and stone Tudor with vaulted stair hall, and *Trinity College*, the largest college in Cambridge. Notable series of marble figures of famous members in the chapel, Francis Bacon (1845; Weekes), Isaac Barrow (1853; M. Noble), teacher of Newton, Macaulay (1868; T. Woolner), W. Whewell (1872; T. Woolner), conservative master of the college and historian of science, and Tennyson (1909; H. Thornycroft). In Wren's Library a series of busts from the 18C onwards including Woolner's fine bust of the young Tennyson (1857), also Thorwaldsen's statue of Byron (1829), intended for Westminster Abbey. On the opposite side of Trinity St, Whewell's Court (1859–68; A. Salvin) a group of two narrow courts, Tudor style in stone with rear tower to Sidney St. Bay windows added 1908 (W.D. Caroe). *Nos 27–8 Trinity St* (1905; Caroe) free Gothic bank. *Caius College*, Trinity St, front (1870; A. Waterhouse) French 16C style on a large scale, with highly ornamented corner entry capped by a pavilion roof, the very Victorian touch of making most of a corner entry, but here overbearing to the view up King's Parade.

N and W of centre: from St. John's, Bridge St leads towards *Magdalene College* where chapel has E window by Pugin, German 16C style. In Castle St, the *County and Folk Museum*. At end of Northampton St, *Westminster College* (1899; H.T. Hare) very pretty Arts and Crafts Elizabethan style in red brick with battered tower to one side carrying a timber cupola. In Madingley Rd and Grange Rd, running S, good late Victorian houses in the Queen Anne mode. In Madingley Rd, *Balliol Croft* (c 1885; J.J. Stevenson) a pretty composition with segment headed sash windows and first-floor balcony. In Grange Rd, *Nos 60–2* (c 1880; B. Champneys) symmetrical, with timber bay windows and white boarded gables to the garden side, *No. 11* (1913; A. Winter-Rose) free neo-Georgian in variegated yellow brick with handsome early 18C style doorcase and lead-clad front door, and *No. 4* (c 1897; M. Baillie Scott) Voysey style roughcast. In Selwyn Gardens *Nos 4 and 5* (c 1888; J.J. Stevenson) red-brick Queen Anne style. On E side of Grange Rd, *Selwyn College* (1882–89; A.W. Blomfield) Tudor style collegiate buildings, S range added 1908 (Grayson and Ould).

Newnham College, the Pfeiffer Building (1892–93; B. Champneys), Cambridge

On S side of Sidgwick Ave, *Newnham College* with delightful Queen Anne style red-brick buildings (1874–1910; B. Champneys).

The college grew from the efforts of Millicent Fawcett, sister of the pioneering woman doctor Elizabeth G. Anderson and wife of the economist and radical Henry Fawcett, Henry Sidgwick, don at Trinity College, and Anne Clough, sister of the poet. This group of liberally minded radicals set out to found a college for women, open not just to women reading for a degree and not hermetically sealed from the university like Girton College, the first women's college (1871). There was no chapel as Sidgwick did not want to identify with 'every form of institutional Christianity'. The buildings took leave of the Gothic tradition and traditional Cambridge arrangement of rooms on staircases in favour of a cheerful Queen Anne style, with generous white windows and much ornamental moulded brickwork in the artisan mannerist tradition. At the E end ornate Pfeiffer Building (1892–93) with octagonal turrets and lead domes. To S, original Newnham Hall (1874) symmetrical, with Dutch gables. N of the gateway, Sidgwick Hall (1879) with the first of the pretty white bay windows that are a feature of the long range facing S, Clough Hall (1886) especially pretty with a big oriel split by a brick buttress, and the dining hall with copper domed rounded bays. W end additions, neo-Georgian (1905 and 1910). To E, *Ridley Hall* (1871–81; C.S. Luck) Tudor style theological college. Further E, in Silver St, *Darwin College*, with, overlooking the river, *The Old Granary* (c 1890; J.J. Stevenson) built for Darwin's son. Delicate timber balcony and hipped dormers on the river front.

Fitzwilliam Museum (1837–47; G. Basevi), Cambridge

S of centre: from Silver St, Trumpington St with *Peterhouse*, the oldest college. Hall restored 1870 (G.G. Scott Jr) with Morris painted decoration, stained glass and tiles. Morris decoration and glass also to the Combination Room adjoining. In the chapel, Munich glass (1855) one of the earliest importations of Bavarian 19C glass, rich colours, coarse pictorial scenes. Beyond, *Fitzwilliam Museum* (1837–47; G. Basevi) heroic Roman Corinthian facade with eight-columned portico, the columns continued in front of the wings and the composition closed by projecting single bay end pavilions. Pedimental sculpture of the nine muses by W.G. Nicholl to a design by Sir C.L. Eastlake. Interior hall completed 1875 (E.M. Barry), richly coloured. The Fitzwilliam facade in its Roman classicism and vigorous modelling shows the next phase in neo-classicism, from the severe and stylistically limited Greek revival of Smirke's British Museum towards Victorian richness. On Trumpington Rd, to S, *The Leys School* (1875 and later; R. Curwen), Methodist public school. In Bateman St, to left, *Botanic Gardens*, opened 1846, and *Cheshunt College* (1914; P.M. Horder), Congregational training college, successor of the one in Cheshunt, Herts. Lensfield Rd connects Trumpington St to Hills Rd, running SE. On corner, *RC church* (1885–90; Dunn and Hansom), a most expensive work with tall spire and a crossing tower. Dec., heavily carved, especially the W front and lofty interior, apse ended with stone vaulting. Off Hills Rd, *Cambridge Station* (1845; F. Thompson) one of the best surviving early railway stations, a remarkable design, originally simply a tall 15 arched open porte-cochère, a giant Italian loggia adapted to the horse and carriage, now filled in for station offices. On Hills Rd, *Royal Albert Almshouses* (1859; Peck and Stevens) polychrome brick Gothic.

2m NW of Cambridge, A604, *Girton College*, the first college at either Oxford or Cambridge for women, founded 1869 at Hitchin, Herts., and moved to this most secluded site in 1871, as Emily Davies, the first principal, took a cautious line in this radical step, partly to protect the women, partly to ease the opposition of the older colleges. Red-brick and terracotta Tudor style buildings (1871–1902; A. Waterhouse), generously laid out with rooms off corridors rather than the traditional staircase arrangement. 2m W, off A45, *Madingley Hall* 16C mansion restored 1905 (J.A. Gotch), now belonging to Cambridge University. By the lake, lonely statue of *Prince Albert* (1866; J.H. Foley) evicted here from the main hall of the Fitzwilliam Museum. 3m E of Cambridge, off A45, at **Stow-cum-Quy**, *Quy Hall* (1868–70; W. White) yellow brick patterned in red, remodelling a 16C house. Just NE, *Anglesey Abbey* (NT), house of c 1591 incorporating medieval remains and restored 1861 and 1926. 10m E of Cambridge, S of A11, at **Stetchworth**, former *White Horse Inn* (1905; C.F.A. Voysey) low roughcast building with sweeping roof in slate and plain leaded windows. All the details, hipped dormers, sloping buttresses and plain roughcast chimneys characteristic of Voysey.

ELY. A10 16m NE of Cambridge. Ely Cathedral was restored by G.G. Scott from 1847 to 1884, notably the skilful reconstruction of the timber central lantern. Inside, boarded nave roof painted with large medievalising panels (c 1855; S. Le Strange) completed and octagon painting (1858–65) by T. Gambier-Parry. Chancel screen, pulpit, reredos and organ case by Scott (1850–68). Much 19C glass, by Wailes in chancel and octagon, in S transept, S side, by H. Gerente (1847), leading French reviver of medieval glass, and in S aisle 1st, 2nd and 8th windows (1850) by A. Gerente and 10th by Pugin. Good windows by the Rev. A. Moore in N transept, N side, on right. The glass of the 1850s and 60s is characteristically more sharply outlined and in hotter colours than the later work. In the nave effigies to Dr Hodge-Mill (died

1853; J.B. Philip and G.G. Scott) on alabaster and mosaic tomb chest and Bishop Woodford (died 1885; G.F. Bodley). In S chancel aisle effigies of G.A. Selwyn, 1st Bishop of New Zealand (1841–68) (1879; T. Nicholls), and Bishop Allen (died 1845; J. Ternouth) said to incorporate mosaic work intended for Napoleon's tomb in Paris. In N triforium, *Stained Glass Museum*, outstanding pieces of 19C glass. *King's School* occupies monastic buildings to the S and also former Theological College (1881; J. St. Aubyn), brick Gothic, opposite the medieval gatehouse. At **Wilburton**, 5m SW A1123, *Wilburton Manor* (1848–51; A.W. Pugin) red-brick late Gothic style, asymmetrically composed.

HUNTINGDON. A604 15m NW of Cambridge. Former county town of Huntingdonshire. *All Saints' Church*, Market Place, was enlarged 1859 (G.G. Scott). In High St stucco classical *Literary and Scientific Institution* (1843; Pocock and Glover). Along the Ouse mid 19C mills. NW of All Saints, George St, *St. John's Church* (1845; W. Habershon) neo- Norman. George St leads past the *station* (1850; H. Goddard) to *Hinchingbrooke*, 16C and 17C mansion of the Earls of Sandwich remodelled 1833–36 (E. Blore) after a fire. 5m E A1123, **St. Ives**, market town with *statue* (1901; F.W. Pomeroy) of Oliver Cromwell in Market Hill. In *All Saints' Church* painted organ in Bodley manner (1893; J.N. Comper).

MARCH. A141 17m E of Peterborough. Once an important railway junction of the Great Eastern and Great Northern lines. In High St, *church* (1880; T.H. Wyatt) High Victorian still in detail, with spire. In Market Place hefty red-brick *Town Hall* (1900; W. Unwin). At **Doddington**, 5m S, in *church*, N aisle E window c 1865 by Morris and Co.

PETERBOROUGH. *Cathedral* restored 1883–97 (J.L. Pearson), the occasion for a major row, with William Morris leading those opposed to anything but patching repairs. Pearson rebuilt the crossing and part of the West front, in the event with exemplary care. Chancel furnishings including baldacchino by Pearson. In S chancel aisle effigy of Archbishop Magee (died 1891; Pearson, carved Forsyth). In S transept, S window, excellent early Morris glass (1862). N of the Cathedral, in Fitzwilliam St, off Broadway, *RC church* (1896; L. Stokes), small free Gothic church with characteristic turn of the century touches such as the curved line of the battlements and tall, light interior with aisles reduced to wall passages. Park Rd runs N with *All Saints' Church* (1894; Temple Moore) a strong work, with plain SE tower and broad S aisle divided off by a simply moulded arcade.

6m N, A15, at **Northborough**, the poet John Clare lived from 1832–37 in a cottage provided by his friends, a period of relative security broken by bouts of mental illness that led to his being committed to the asylum for the rest of his life. Clare was born and married in **Helpston**, 3m SW, and he was buried (1864) in the churchyard. John Clare *Monument* (1869) opposite the Buttermarket. 2m SW of Peterborough, A605, at **Orton Longueville**, *Orton Hall*, early 19C Elizabethan style house rebuilt for the 9th Marquess of Huntly. Family memorials in the *church*. At **Holme**, 7m S B660, *Holme Wood* (1873; W. Young) red-brick and terracotta Elizabethan style house. At **Ramsey**, B1040, 9m SE of Peterborough, *Ramsey Abbey* was mostly rebuilt (1839; E. Blore) incorporating some parts of the Benedictine abbey, now the Grammar School.

ST. NEOTS. A45 17m W of Cambridge. In *St. Mary's Church* rich

Gothic Rowley monument by T. Earp and effigy of Mrs Walters under a towering Gothic canopy (1893; F. Walters). On corner of High St and South St, former *Corn Exchange* (1863; Bellamy and Hardy), the corner tower truncated. 6m SE, B1040, at **Waresley**, *church* (1856; W. Butterfield) stone with almost detached sheer tower and shingled spire. Splendid interior, the chancel decorated with patterns of inlaid tiles, predominantly green. The effect is delicate. Fine Butterfield woodwork and stone font. E window by O'Connor and N transept window 1865 by Heaton, Butler and Bayne. Adjoining the church, Duncombe *mausoleum* (c 1855; Butterfield). 4m E, B1046, *Long Stowe Hall*, Elizabethan house expensively extended and refronted (c 1900; J.W. Simpson).

WISBECH. A47 20m E of Peterborough. Inland port, its heyday the 18C and early 19C, exporting fenland wheat. In 1847 some 170,000 tons passed through the port but collapsing wheat prices and railway competition set off a rapid decline from c 1855. Extensive works were carried out on the Nene through the later 19C to revive the town allowing ships of up to 18ft draught this far up the river. By the bridge, S side, *Clarkson Memorial* (1881; G.G. Scott) 70ft high Gothic memorial to Thomas Clarkson (1760–1846) leader of the campaign to abolish the slave trade, finally enacted in 1807. On South Brink, early 19C classical *Sessions House*. In Museum Square, *Museum* (1846; G. Buckler) Greek classical. On N side of the bridge, North Brink, with classical *bank* (c 1860) next to *Town Hall* (1810), rear hall 1850 (Bellamy).

CHESHIRE

CHESTER. The county town. Chester *Cathedral* was heavily restored during the 19C by R.C. Hussey from 1844, G.G. Scott from 1868 and A. Blomfield from 1882, partly a consequence of the soft red stone. Scott's work is most visible in the high roof of the Lady Chapel and the extraordinary polygonal roof over the S aisle apse. Inside, nave and aisle roofs by Scott, in N aisle mosaics (1883–86) of scriptural scenes, nave lectern (1876) by Skidmore, ornately Gothic. Crossing screen, organ loft and organ case by Scott (1876). In N transept, effigy of Bishop Pearson (1863; T. Earp). In S transept, effigy of the 1st Duke of Westminster (1902; F.W. Pomeroy), the great S window restored by Blomfield, glass by Heaton, Butler and Bayne (1887). In the choir, reredos and mosaic floor (1876; J.R. Clayton) and bishop's throne, all part of Scott's work. In N choir aisle good mid 19C glass, by Clayton and Bell (1863), Heaton, Butler and Bayne (1863) and four by Wailes, three of 1859, the last of 1853. Brass at W end to the Rev. M.D. Taylor (died 1845) by Hardman, possibly designed by Pugin. In S choir aisle apse decorated in mosaic, fresco and stained glass by Clayton and Bell (1872– 79), adjoining window by Pugin (1850), the two beyond by Wailes (1852). In the Lady Chapel the reconstructed shrine of St. Werburgh and stained glass by Wailes (1859). Attached to the W front, facing Northgate St, former *King's School* (1875–77; A.W. Blomfield), stone, Perp. hiding part of the cathedral but providing a handsome approach. Opposite, • *Town Hall* (1864–69; W.H. Lynn), High Victorian Gothic in stone, symmetrical. Central tower ornately elaborated with cross gables and slate spire. Venetian Gothic in form though English c 1300 and Early French Gothic in detail, the facade displays a noble range of windows to the upper floor and gains in dignity from being elevated on a basement such that the central entry is reached from a double flight of steps.

Shoemakers Row (1897), running S towards The Cross, introduces the revived black and white timbering that contributes so much to the picturesque qualities of the centre, especially in the area of The Rows, the galleried shopping streets around The Cross. At The Cross, the *corner* of Eastgate St and Bridge St is marked by an especially spectacular example (1888; T.M. Lockwood), the already ornate decoration of genuine Cheshire timber-framing inflated both in scale and intensity. *Nos 2–4 Bridge St* (1892) and *9–13 Eastgate St* (1900) both by Lockwood continue the theme. *St. Peter's Church* has a memorial window to Prince Albert (1862; Heaton, Butler and Bayne). Bridge St runs S to *St. Michael's Church*, mostly rebuilt (1849; J. Harrison), now the Chester Heritage Centre. *No. 38* (1897; Douglas and Fordham) on W side is ornately black and white. In Grosvenor St to SW, *Grosvenor Museum* (1885; T.M. Lockwood) high brick and stone Renaissance style front. *RC church* (1874; J. O'Byrne) opposite. To S off Castle St, *Chester Castle* (1788–1822; T. Harrison), major monument of neo-classicism in Britain. Equestrian *statue* of Field Marshal Viscount Combermere (1865; Marochetti) outside, Queen Victoria *statue* (1903; F.W. Pomeroy) in the court. In the Agricola Tower, *Cheshire Military Museum*.

W of The Cross, in Watergate St, the most genuine timber-framing survives, though *God's Providence House* is of 1862 (J. Harrison) reusing parts of the 1652 original. The *Guildhall* is the former Holy Trinity Church (1865–69; J. Harrison) with prominent spire. Eastgate St, E of The Cross, has some of the first revived half-timber work, *Nos*

34–6 (1856; T.M. Penson), and stone Gothic front of *Browns Crypt Buildings* (1858; T.M. Penson) on S side. On N side, *National Westminster Bank* (1859; G. Williams) Corinthian classical, and in St. Werburgh St, the *°E side* is the finest of Chester's late 19C half-timber, built 1895–99 (J. Douglas), in late Gothic style with extremely ornate timbered upper floors, the carved work of great delicacy. To E, *Midland Bank* (1883; Douglas and Fordham) and *Grosvenor Hotel* (1863–66; T.M. Penson) before the *Eastgate*, capped with a scrolly wrought-iron clock turret (1897; J. Douglas). Beyond the arch, on S side, *Old Bank Buildings* (1895; T.M. Lockwood), the best of Lockwood's black and white buildings with row of oriels under the upper jetty and off-centre gables, not excessively patterned, and *Blossoms Hotel* (1896; T.M. Lockwood: extended 1911). In Bath St and Grosvenor Park Rd, S of W end of Foregate St, two good brick rows by J. Douglas, in Bath St (1902–03) relatively modest, in Grosvenor Park Rd (c 1879) larger and varied, the row of gables ending at the *Baptist Chapel*, designed as part of the group. *RC church* beyond (1873–75; E. Kirby). *Grosvenor Park* was laid out 1867 for the 2nd Marquess of Westminster, his *statue* 1869 (T. Thornycroft). To W, *St. John's Church*, heavily restored in the 19C, E window by Clayton and Bell (1863).

NE from the E end of Foregate St, City Rd runs up to *°Chester Station* (1848; F. Thompson), one of the grandest of provincial stations, the exceptionally long front in brick and stone, Italianate style reflecting a single long platform arrangement. Centrepiece flanked by two taller blocks with arcaded ground floors, centre Venetian windows and attic balustrade between arched turrets, these blocks providing enough variety to articulate the whole front. *Queen Hotel* (1861–62; T.M. Penson), Italianate, opposite. E of Foregate St, off Boughton, in Dee Hills Rd, *Uffington House* (1885; E. Ould) built for T. Hughes, author of 'Tom Brown's Schooldays', and named after his home village. Boughton *church* (1876; J. Douglas) is apsed with fine timbered interior. Morris and Co glass of 1881 at E end particularly good, 1887 SE window, the rest later. To SE, in Dee Banks, *Walmoor Hill* (1896; J. Douglas), Douglas' own house, stone, late Gothic to Elizabethan detail, testimony to a successful career. *Nos 31–3* (1869), a Gothic pair, had been Douglas's first house for himself.

2m E of Chester, at **Christleton**, *church* (1874–78; W. Butterfield), retaining the old tower with a new slated cap. Well-proportioned interior in red stone, chequered in white in the chancel which has a prettily panelled roof. Alabaster and mosaic reredos. 5m E, N of A54, at **Ashton**, *church* (1849; E.H. Shellard) cruciform with spire. Art Nouveau pulpit and altar frontal of c 1900 when the chancel was remodelled (J. Douglas). 3m SE, at **Willington**, *Willington Hall* (1829) early example of revived Elizabethan, in diapered brick. 1m E, *°Tirley Garth* (1906–12; C.E. Mallows) Arts and Crafts Elizabethan style mansion in roughcast and stone, on a scale rarely offered to advanced architects of the Voysey school. Built around a central cloister, the elevations rely on massing, and placing of stone mullioned windows and sheer chimney stacks rather than on extensive carved detail for effect. Low and friendly entrance front with broad-arched entry between two canted bays and a plain tower to one side. The garden front more formal, five-gabled, the larger centre gable framed by diagonal stacks. Three large and light mullioned bays alternating with big flush mullioned windows, segmental-arched on the first floor. Galleried great hall inside. Fine gardens by T.H. Mawson, lodges by Mallows. 2m S, NE of **Tarporley**, A49, *Portal* (c 1900–05; W.E. Tower) large and accurate recreation of a timber-framed mansion, exceptionally sympathetically done, reusing genuine woodwork. Full-scale great hall. The accurate recreation of Tudor manor houses was a particular taste of c 1900– 30, assisted by the availability of authentic bits from demolished buildings.

NW of Chester, A540, Parkgate Rd leads out past *Chester College* (1841; J.C. and G. Buckler) Tudor to Elizabethan style with Gothic chapel (1844; J.E. Gregan), all the fittings and E window made by students at the college. 3m NW, at **Great Saughall**, *Shotwick Park*, (1872; J. Douglas: altered 1907) brick Elizabethan style mansion. Bright red *church* (1895; J.M. Taylor) with central spire, quirky in details. 7m NW of Chester, **Neston**, once a port, the *church* rebuilt 1874 (J.F. Doyle) with stained glass by Morris and Co, the earliest (1888) in S aisle. **Parkgate**, just NW, was also formerly a port, now overlooking marshland. On the seafront, *Mostyn House School*, prominent late 19C range, actually remodelled from an inn. Chapel behind (1895; A. Grenfell) designed by the headmaster with good early 20C glass by R.A. Bell each side. 1m E of Neston, on A540, *Hinderton Hall* (1856; A. Waterhouse), Waterhouse's first country house, steep gabled Gothic with a narrow tower over the entry, like an enlarged parsonage. 4m E, at Childer Thornton, on A41, Hooton *church* (1858–62; J.K. Colling), built for the banker R.C. Naylor of Hooton Hall, for whom Colling designed the Albany Building, Liverpool. High Victorian, between Romanesque and Early French Gothic, tough in detail with contrasted texture and colour of the outside stone and octagonal stone lantern over the crossing. Inside the lantern is revealed through the open crown of a stone dome, the dome of Byzantine type with pendentives but the crown ringed with Gothic foliage. Colling was author of works on Gothic ornament and the interior has fine sturdy detail. Heavy green serpentine font, a prizewinner at the 1851 exhibition.

S of central Chester, over the Dee Bridge, in Handbridge, the approach of the estates of the Grosvenor family, Dukes of Westminster, is signalled by the prominent stone spired *church* (1885; F.B. Wade) built for the 1st Duke. Lofty interior with remarkable enamel reredos (1888; C. Heaton) designed by the painter F. Shields. On Grosvenor Rd, A483, *Overleigh Lodge* (c 1893; R.W. Edis), neo-Jacobean lodge to Eaton Hall, the Westminster seat, some three miles S. S of Handbridge, Eaton Rd leads to **Eccleston**, the principal estate village. The Grosvenor estate, notably under the 1st Duke who succeeded in 1869, rebuilt extensively over the whole vast area. Much of the work is by J. Douglas, inventive architect whose styles vary from late Gothic, to domestic revival half-timbering, tile-hanging and ornamental plasterwork and to Jacobean, always with carefully considered brick details. In the village several cottage groups by Douglas, particularly one around a small quadrangle, pumphouse (1874) and pretty school (1878). The *church* (1899; G.F. Bodley), the last commission of the 1st Duke, is an outstanding monument of the late phase of the Gothic Revival, red sandstone, severe and rectangular in outline, aisles and clerestory capped by the plainest horizontal parapet, the clerestory apparently running on into the lowest stage of the tower without a break and the tower rising plain and square above. Bodley's Gothic is here refined to something almost mechanically precise. Inside, arcades and stone vault evenly carried through to the great E window, fastidious detail, colour and ornament coming from the complete set of Bodley furnishings. Stained glass by Burlison and Grylls, the firm Bodley relied on not to overwhelm the architecture. Effigy of

1st Duke (1901; L. Chavalliaud) on canopied tomb chest by Bodley. In the churchyard, in the Grosvenor family plot, tomb of Earl Grosvenor (died 1909; Blow and Billerey) enclosed by an Art Nouveau bronze screen. *Rectory* N of church (c 1896; T.M. Lockwood). S of the village, *The Paddocks* (c 1883; Douglas) built for the Duke's agent with estate office attached. Elaborate brick and stone with Loire château circular corner towers and steep tiled roofs, the outbuildings especially picturesque. *Eccleston Hill* (c 1880) to W, is the substantial house built by Douglas for the Duke's secretary.

On the main drive from Chester, just W of Eccleston, *Eccleston Hill Lodge* (1881; Douglas), the best of the many lodges, a full-scale gatehouse in red brick with steep French pavilion roof and round turrets. The major part of *Eaton Hall* was demolished in 1961 and replaced by a new house, the fifth on the site. Of the monumental Gothic house built (1870–91) by A. Waterhouse for the 1st Duke the *chapel with clock tower and the stable court survive, the 183ft clock tower a slim echo of Manchester Town Hall, visible from miles around. The chapel interior is lofty, rib-vaulted, with stained glass and mosaics by F. Shields, Manchester painter and illustrator. In the forecourt equestrian *statue* (1876–83; G.F. Watts) of Hugh Lupus, medieval ancestor of the Grosvenors, a vigorous example of Watts' work, rough in texture, exaggerated modelling of muscles and drapery. The 1st Duke paid over £600,000 for Waterhouse's works. On the rest of the estate the sum must have been larger, three churches, eight schools, 48 farmhouses and 360 cottages being built for him. The estate, apart from Eccleston village, includes, W of the Dee, **Pulford**, **Dodleston** and **Lower Kinnerton** with smaller hamlets between, one called **Belgrave**, the origin of Belgrave Square, the principal square on the Grosvenor Pimlico estate in London. Notable farmhouses by Douglas off A483, *Green Paddocks Farm* (1872) N of Pulford and *Wrexham Road Farm* (1880) N of the turning to Eccleston.

E of the River Dee **Aldford**, **Bruera**, **Saighton** and **Waverton** are estate villages. At **Aldford**, the *church* (1866) is an early work by Douglas, High Victorian and muscular in the Street or Burges manner. At **Saighton**, *Saighton Grange* c 1500 gatehouse attached to a bleak Tudor style house (1861; E. Hodkinson) built for the 2nd Marquess of Westminster. Between Saighton and Waverton was the Duke's private railway *station* (1897). In **Waverton**, *school* (1873; J. Douglas).

CREWE. A532 15m NW of Stoke on Trent. Railway town formed by the Grand Junction Railway, later LNWR, at the point where lines to Birmingham, Liverpool, Manchester and Chester met, and principal railway works of the LNWR. Very little is left of the original housing laid out 1840. *Christ Church*, (1843; J. Cunningham), Prince Albert Square, was the centrepiece, but almost entirely rebuilt since. *Municipal Buildings* (1902–05; H.T. Hare), Earle St, Edwardian Baroque in stone, *Market Hall* (1854; C. Meason) adjoining in contrasted brick. In West St, *St. Barnabas' Church* (1885; Paley and Austin), simple brick and terracotta well handled with some timber-framing in the aisle cross gables. Good interior fittings.

1m E, A532, **Crewe Green**, estate village of Crewe Hall, the *church* (1857–58; G.G. Scott) in brick outside and in. *Crewe Hall*, the 17C mansion of the Crewe family, was rebuilt 1867–70 (E.M. Barry) after a fire, such that it now appears a Victorian Jacobean house with high off-centre tower. Lavish neo-Jacobean interiors, especially the carved woodwork of hall and staircase, apparently based on the originals. Monumental fireplaces. S of the house, some cottages by W.E.

Nesfield (1865–67), early examples of domestic revival work, tile-hanging and ornamental plaster replacing Gothic motifs. *Stowford Cottages*, E of the Weston Lodge, the most notably picturesque with complicated hipped roofs, overhangs and moulded chimneys. 2m E, at **Barthomley**, Crewe estate village, the church contains Crewe memorials including a highly Gothic one to 1st Lord Crewe (1856) and marble effigy of Lady Houghton (died 1887; J.E. Boehm). 3m NE, at **Alsager**, *St. Mary Magdalene's Church* (1894–98; Austin and Paley) refined and well-detailed late Dec. 3m NE, E of **Rode Heath**, Rode Hall estate with *church* (1864; G.G. Scott) in stone with naturalistic carving to the capitals and richly carved fittings. Good E window. Estate *cottages* by W. White (c 1854) in the simplified style of Butterfield's smallest works, *Nos 182–4 Congleton Rd North* and former *Schoolmaster's house* S of the church.

6m NE of Crewe, A534, **Sandbach**, with parish *church* restored 1847–49 (G.G. Scott), E end glass by Wailes. In High Town Square, *fountain* (1897; T. Bower) and good Gothic group of *Savings Bank* (1854) and *Literary Institute* (1857; G.G. Scott). Gothic *Town Hall* (1889; T. Bower) still in the High Victorian vein. On Crewe Rd, *Sandbach School* (1849–50; G.G. Scott) Gothic with entrance tower. At **Sandbach Heath**, *church* (1861; G.G. Scott), a model example of Scott's work, cruciform, well-composed with central tower and plain recessed spire, the windows in severe EE to early Dec., the rooflines unbroken.

4m SW of Crewe, A534, **Nantwich**, former salt town. In the centre, parish *church* restored 1854–61 (G.G. Scott), with early glass by C.E. Kempe (1876) in porch and N transept W window and one S aisle window (1919) by Harry Clarke of Dublin, the best of early 20C glass designers. N of the church, two Gothic *banks*, one of 1864 (A. Waterhouse), the other 1876 (T. Bower), and *Market* (1868). 1½m NW, at **Beambridge**, *Reaseheath Hall* (1878 and 1892), gabled Tudor to Jacobean mansion, now College of Agriculture. 6m SW of Nantwich, A530, *Combermere Abbey*, 16C, Gothicised in the early 19C. Obelisk across the lake to Viscount Combermere (died 1865), cavalry commander in the Napoleonic Wars. 7m W of Nantwich, A49, *Cholmondeley Castle* (gardens open to public) an early castellated house (1801–04; Marquess of Cholmondeley) made more dramatic with angle turrets and towers (1817–29; R. Smirke). Estate *church* (1892; Douglas and Fordham), 1½m S at **Bickley**, characteristically excellent timber-work inside, hammerbeam roof carried, on N side, on timber posts.

5m N of Cholmondeley Castle, at **Beeston**, *Peckforton Castle* (1844–50; A. Salvin) spectacularly set on the N outcrop of the Peckforton Hills, the finest of all Victorian castles because the most convincingly archaeological with minimal concessions to domestic comfort. Built for the 1st Lord Tollemache, model if feudal landowner, who provided for each tenant, some 250 in all, a cottage and three-acre holding and built some 55 farmhouses, each having 200 acres attached. Salvin's design relies on the careful grouping of massive stone elements disposed around an irregular court, battlements and towers picturesquely on the skyline but the walls left sheer. As befitting such an uncompromising design the windows are severely plain, without mouldings, only the great hall marked by longer lights with transoms and quatrefoil heads. The sequence of towers, lower on the gatehouse and service wing, rises at the E end to a great circular tower on which hinges the right-angled composition of the house, an ingenious plan. Stone-vaulted and stone-walled principal interiors.

Peckforton Castle (1844–50; A. Salvin), Beeston

KNUTSFORD. A50 12m W of Macclesfield. The 'Cranford' of Mrs Gaskell (1810–65) who lived all her life here. In King St, the * *Gaskell Memorial Tower* and former *Coffee House* (1907–08) introduces the remarkable architecture of R.H. Watt, Manchester glove manufacturer and designer of buildings without parallels in Britain, strange syntheses of things seen in the Middle East, Spain and Italy, arranged with an eye for random effects, occasionally and probably fortuitously reminiscent of the work of C.R. Mackintosh. Watt could draw a plan himself but directed a series of architects, usually dismissed for showing signs of independence. The tower and coffee house were to be the social and intellectual centre of the town, a Ruskinian idea, unsuccessful in social terms. The style and stonework echo Jerusalem or Damascus, the severity of line and the curious random placed projecting blocks of stone having a Middle Eastern source, but the small paned curved windows set deep in the base of the towers and the ornamental ironwork have a touch of the Glasgow work of Mackintosh. Elevating quotations, a list of the works of Mrs Gaskell and another of the Kings of England dotted the building. At corner of Drury Lane, *Ruskin Rooms* (1902; R.H. Watt) studded with Mediterranean features, intended as library and recreation room for the employees of the *laundry* he built in Drury Lane (1898), now much altered, but originally a series of minarets, towers and domes that made the view across the town moor one of the oddest in England. W of King St, on the moor, *Swinton Square* (1902; Watt) with domed tower and random projecting blocks, an entrance feature to a row of cottages. At N end of Toft Road, former *Town Hall* (1870; A. Waterhouse) plain brick Gothic. In Legh Rd, S of the centre, Watt had his own house and built or altered a series of others along the W side overlooking the valley. *The Old Croft* (1895), Watt's own house, is relatively ordinary but for the tower added 1907. *Lake House* (1902) in white painted brick has two round towers and an Italian look, but the stable tower is Middle Eastern. *High Morland* (1905), adjoining, is a more extensive Italian villa complete with belvedere tower and matching lodge, where the detail goes more exotic. The *Round House* (1904) has circular corner tower like an acid version of J. Nash's Italian villas of c 1800. *Chantry Dane* and *Aldwarden Brow* (1906) and *The Coach House* (1907) complete the group. *Brae Cottage* (1898; P. Ogden) was built for H. Royce, later of Rolls-Royce. In Toft Rd, to S, *Bexton Croft* (1895; M.H. Baillie Scott) roughcast and half-timbered, Arts and Crafts style.

N of Knutsford, *Tatton Park* (NT), Georgian mansion of the Egerton family. Terraced gardens laid out 1859 (Sir J. Paxton). In the estate *church* at **Rostherne** to N, monument to Lady C. Egerton (died 1845; R. Westmacott Jr), marble sleeping figure with kneeling angel. Just E of Knutsford, B5085, at **Cross Town**, *church* (1880; Paley and Austin) well-detailed Perp. in brick and terracotta. Crossing tower. Inside, Morris and Co. windows to W and S aisle E, c 1894 and 1899. 7m E, at **Wilmslow**, *Pownall Hall*, Gorsey Rd, off A538, villa of c 1830 remodelled from 1886 (W. Ball) for H. Boddington, brewer. Remarkable early Arts and Crafts interiors by the Century Guild, formed 1882 by A.H. Mackmurdo. Much has gone but vigorous metalwork, plasterwork and Renaissance style stained glass (Shrigley and Hunt) survive, together with carved fireplaces and some painted decoration. 1½m N of Wilmslow, B5166, at **Styal**, *Quarry Bank Mill* (NT), silk mill of the Greg family (1784) with complete model village, all now restored, a perfect example of the early Industrial Revolution, still in its rural setting.

7m SW of Knutsford, **Northwich**, salt town transformed in the later 19C by the Brunner and Mond chemical works at Winnington, founded 1873, the predecessor of ICI. 3m N, A559, **Great Budworth**, with estate buildings for the Warburton family of Arley Hall, *George and Dragon* (1875; J. Douglas), and a pretty domestic revival *cottage* (c 1865; W.E. Nesfield) on S side of High St. The use of half-timber and vernacular detail was pioneered by Nesfield and Norman Shaw in the 1860s. W of the village another similar (1868; J. Douglas) showing the leading Chester architect of the later 19C an early follower of the new style. *Arley Hall* (open to public), 3m N, is impressive Jacobean (1833–41; G. Latham) in diapered brick and stone with chapel (1845; Salvin) in stone, formerly attached. Victorian interiors. A hamlet adjoining includes *Chaplain's Cottage* (1854; W. White) a good design in simplified domestic Gothic. 5m NW of Northwich, W of **Acton Bridge**, *Dutton Viaduct* (1837; J. Locke), red sandstone 20-arch railway bridge over the River Weaver.

2m SW of Northwich, A556, at **Hartford**, *church* (1874; J. Douglas), lancet windows and W tower, good interior with rock-faced masonry. Douglas was born at **Sandiway**, just W and built *Sandiway Manor* for himself, the *church* (1902) and *cottages* by the church. By Douglas also, *Oakmere Hall* (1867), W of A49, High Victorian Gothic with pavilion roofed tower and angle turrets. 3m NW, at **Norley**, *church* (1875; J.L. Pearson) in red sandstone with central tower, sturdy EE to Dec. detail. By Pearson also, the *church* (1870) at **Crowton**, 2m N. 2m S of Hartford, at **Whitegate**, *Vale Royal Abbey* (open to public), 16C mansion much altered since for the Cholmondeley family, partly by E. Blore (1833–37), partly by J. Douglas (1860 and 1877), estate *church* (1874; J. Douglas) prettily timbered, and *vicarage* (1877; Douglas). 2m E, off A533, at **Moulton**, *church* (1876; J. Douglas), modest, stone outside, brick within. **Winsford**, 3m S, has the last Cheshire rock-salt mine. Salt is now commonly extracted from brine-springs by evaporation, land subsidence a visible consequence of the pumping out of the briny water. Across the river, to W, in **Over**, *St. John's Church* (1860; J.

Douglas), Douglas's first work, heavily detailed in the High Victorian way.

MACCLESFIELD. A523 12m S of Stockport. Silk manufacturing town since the 18C, on the W edge of the uplands. By the railway, on E side of town, in Commercial Rd, *Arighi, Bianchi Warehouse* (1882), cast-iron and plate- glass front on four storeys, almost wholly glazed. In the centre, Market Place, with *Town Hall* (1823; F. Goodwin and 1869) Greek Ionic, the original portico facing the churchyard, the Market Place front added to match. The parish *church* was mostly rebuilt 1898 (A. Blomfield), to suitable town-church scale. Chestergate runs W to Chester Rd with *RC church* (1838–41; A.W.N. Pugin), one of Pugin's churches where adequate funds were available, as the Earl of Shrewsbury contributed. Perp. with broad E and W windows, tall arcades, and

Arighi, Bianchi Warehouse (1882), Commercial Road, Macclesfield

chancel divided off by a carved timber screen. Stencilled chancel decoration and E window by Warrington. S of Market Place, on Park Green, former *Savings Bank* (1841) Greek Doric and *Library* (1874; J. Stevens) Gothic.

5m W, off A34, *Capesthorne Hall* (open to public), extensive Jacobean style mansion in brick, the recasing of an early 18C house (1837–39; E. Blore), grand scale front with main block framed by turretted gables and enclosed by lower wings. Interiors altered after a fire in 1861 (A. Salvin). Chapel (1720) with terracotta reliefs by G. Tinworth inside. 3m N, at **Nether Alderley**, in the *church* effigies of 1st and 2nd Lords Stanley of Alderley (1856; R. Westmacott Jr and c 1870) the latter with Italian Cosmati-style mosaic to the tomb chest. **Alderley Edge**, to N, the last outcrop of hill towards Manchester, has wealthy manufacturers' houses, notably in Woodbrook Rd and Macclesfield Rd. *Church* (1851; J.S. Crowther) with one S aisle window by Morris and Co. (1873).

8m SW of Macclesfield, **Congleton**, silk and cotton weaving town in 19C. Fine Gothic *Town Hall* (1864–66; E.W. Godwin), similar to but smaller and less ornamented than Godwin's Northampton Town Hall. High central tower. Inside, monumental stone stairway. 2m N, at Hulme Walfield, *church* (1855; G.G. Scott), attractive village church in rock-faced stone. 3m S of Congleton, off A526, *Great Moreton Hall* (1841–43; E. Blore), stone Tudor Gothic mansion, low and rambling, an impressive facade achieved by castellating the service wing and stable court.

RUNCORN. A558 10m SW of Warrington. Mersey estuary port and chemical manufacturing town. The Mersey is crossed by the *Railway Bridge* (1869; W. Baker), lattice girder spans on stone piers with towers each end. In Church St, parish *church* (1847–49; A. Salvin) EE with prominent steeple. Across the river, **Widnes**, the 19C growth based on alkali and chemical industry. By the river, West Bank, later 19C industrial settlement with fine *church* (1908–10; Austin and Paley) on Victoria Promenade. Red stone, Perp. with strong tower. In Widnes, *Town Hall* (1887; F. and G. Holme) brick and terracotta. E of centre, Lugsdale Rd, *RC church* (1864–65; E.W. Pugin) apsed with highly carved capitals. To N, Appleton Rd, *RC church* (1847; Weightman and Hadfield), Pugin-influenced correct Dec. At **Ditton**, to NW, *RC church* (1876–79; H. Clutton) ambitious Early French Gothic with saddleback tower. E of Runcorn, **Halton**, on the rock overlooking the Mersey. *Church* (1851; G.G. Scott) in Main St quite modest but well detailed. S of Runcorn, just N of the expressway, at **Weston**, *church* (1895–98; Douglas and Fordham) in stone with squat tower and spire, chancel roof rising over the nave. Timber arcade inside.

WARRINGTON. A57 18m E of Liverpool. *Parish church*, to E of centre, medieval with fine spire added as part of rebuilding 1859–67 (F. and H. Francis), broad interior, handsomely detailed. Fine late Gothic organ screen (1908; W. and S. Owen). Patten memorials in S transept, among them effigy of Lord Winmarleigh (died 1892; H.H. Armstead). In the Buttermarket, *RC church* (1877; Pugin and Pugin), naturalistic carved capitals, tower with saddleback cap (added 1906). In Market Square, *Market* (1855; J. Stevens) pedimented with Venetian window. In Sankey St, *Woolworths* (1864; J. Douglas), an early work by the leading Chester architect, here still fully Gothic. Next door, *bank* (1847; E. Walters), palazzo style, upper columns and ground floor pilasters. *W.H. Smith* (c 1901; Wright, Garnett and Wright) pretty with plastered gable and oriel windows. In Bold St, to S, *Museum and Art Gallery* (1855–57; J. Dobson) distinguished late classical building. In Museum St *School of Art* (1883; W. Owen). N of centre, Winwick Rd, A49, *St. Anne's Church* (1866–68; J. Douglas), an early work by Douglas, High Victorian in the manner of Street, severely geometrical design with plate tracery. W of centre, on Liverpool Rd, A57, *St. Luke's Church* (1892–93; Bodley), curious double-nave design with central arcade running into the chancel arch.

4m N of Warrington, at **Winwick**, *parish church* with chancel rebuilt 1847–48 (A.W.N. Pugin), a good example of Pugin's work, Dec., steep roofed with all the tracery and buttress details carefully and correctly handled. Fittings and stained glass by Pugin. 2m S of Warrington, at **Higher Walton**, *Walton Hall* (1836–38) Elizabethan style in brick and stone, the house of Sir G. Greenall, brewer, who paid for the *church* (1885; Paley and Austin), notably handsome with crossing tower and spire, the tower with chequer-work patterning. 1½m S of Warrington, A56, at **Stockton Heath**, *church* (1868; E.G. Paley) serious EE style with tile decorated chancel.

CLEVELAND

GUISBOROUGH. A171 7m SE of Middlesbrough. NE of the parish church, *Grammar School* (1887; Waterhouse) gabled Tudor in stone and brick. E of the priory ruins, *Guisborough House* (1857; W.M. Teulon and 1902). 1m SW, *Hutton Hall* (1866; Waterhouse) built for Sir J.W. Pease (cf. Darlington and Saltburn) in a plain gabled red brick with plate tracery.

HARTLEPOOL. A178 12m N of Middlesbrough. West Hartlepool developed as a coal port from 1847 very fast, eclipsing the old town of Hartlepool to N, and the docks, run by the North Eastern Railway, were eventually of an acreage smaller only than Liverpool and London. A new town was laid out from c 1850 on a grid plan with Albert Square and Church Square the main foci, unfortunately cut up by a later railway through Albert Square. Church Square is octagonal with, in the centre, *Christ Church*, (1850–54; E.B. Lamb), rogue Gothic with a heftily detailed tower, especially heavily treated at the top, the parapet curved back to a pierced balustrade, a device typical of Lamb. Also typical of Lamb the low, broad body of the church with massive timber roof, recently damaged by fire. On the W side, *Municipal Buildings* (1886–89; R.K. Freeman) Dutch gabled in bright red brick and terracotta. *Library* (1894; J.W. Brown), Clarence St, similar. Further W, in Victoria Rd, grand *Methodist church* (1871; Hill and Swan) with stone Corinthian portico and large brick and terracotta *Grand Hotel* (1899; J. Garry). In Clarence Rd, large villas of c 1855–60, one of which is the *Art Gallery and Museum*. E of Church Square, Church St, run down but with the *Athenaeum* (1851; R.H. Robson), stone classical, and ornate terracotta *Shades Hotel* (1900). Beyond the railway, the Docks, with some surviving warehouses and *Dock Offices*, Victoria Terrace (1846). S of Church St, in Park Rd and Grange Rd, a few prosperous industrialists' houses. In Grange Rd, free Gothic *Methodist church* (1905; H. Barnes) and *St. Paul's Church* (1885; C.H. Fowler) impressively tall red-brick church with pyramid roofed tower. At **Greatham**, A689 3m SW, *Briarmead* (1883; P. Webb) roughcast and tiled house with characteristic styleless treatment, small paned windows and strong chimneys.

LOFTUS. A174 4m SE of Saltburn. *Town Hall* (1878; E.R. Robson) pretty neo-Tudor, an early date for this sort of free adaptation. *Church* with tower of 1811, the rest mostly of 1901 (Clarke and Moscrop). 2m E at **Easington**, *church* (1888; C.H. Fowler) and 2m S of the village, *Grinkle Park* (1882; Waterhouse) castellated Gothic house built for Sir Charles Palmer, the Jarrow shipbuilder, who had iron mines in the area.

MIDDLESBROUGH. Almost a Victorian New Town and certainly the largest to spring up from almost nothing. There were 25 inhabitants in 1801, 40,000 by 1881 and 90,000 by 1901. The town began modestly as a port developed by the Stockton and Darlington Railway for coal exports after 1830 but its real growth dates from the discovery of iron in the Cleveland Hills behind and its exploitation by the ironmasters H. Bolckow and J. Vaughan followed by I.L. Bell and later Dorman and Long. For most of the period after 1850 the town had a feel more of a gold rush settlement in the USA or Australia with a predominantly male immigrant population. The town has little sense of formal planning, indeed the first town centre around the Market Place N of the railway rapidly declined after the railway cut it off from the later expansion.

In Market Place, *church* (1838; J. Green) and *old Town Hall* (1846; W.L. Moffat) surrounded by new development, and in North St, *Custom House* (1840) handsome Greek Doric, the principal remnants of the early town. Queen's Terrace leads back to the station with some houses of the 1840s and good palazzo style *bank* (1871; J. Gibson). The *station* (1877; W. Peachey) is an uncommonly ornate Gothic building with one arched train-shed surviving behind. The immediate area of the station is blighted for road schemes, the principal victim, in Zetland Rd, being I.L. Bell's *office* (1883; P. Webb), Webb's only commercial building. A most independent design, using motifs familiar from 19C office building, arcaded ground floor, columned upper floor with cornice but the detail with hints of the Gothic and the attic floor in complete contrast, white rendered with Gothic buttresses and a parapet of curving outline. Albert Rd and Corporation Rd are the main axes of the newer centre. Formidable Gothic *Town Hall* (1883–89; G.D. Hoskins) in the manner of Waterhouse, excellently done with asymmetrical tower and hammerbeam roofed hall. Also in Corporation Rd the *Empire Theatre* (1899; Runtz) terracotta-faced with corner cupolas. Good interior. Linthorpe Rd leads S with *All Saints' Church* (1875–78; Street), stone with E rose window, to Albert Park opened 1868. *Dorman Museum* (1903; J.M. Bottomley) domed red-brick building has local history collections. Newport Road leads W with *St. Paul's Church* (1871; R.J. Johnson) in red and yellow brick on S side. To N, off Marsh St, in Cannon St, *St. Columba's* (1902; Temple Moore) severe red-brick church, impressively plain outside, vaulted within. Temple Moore's finest church is *St. Cuthbert's* (1900–02) on Newport Rd, in stone, the road front a fortress-like wall with severely plain angle towers flanking a broad centre rising behind a complex of lower roofs. Interior converted to squash courts. N of the centre, over the Tees, is the *Transporter Bridge* (1911) the largest such bridge in the world. The roadway, or a short section of it, is lifted over the river suspended from an immense steel gantry high enough up to allow free passage to ships below.

Marton Rd leads out SE towards Grove Hill, the wealthiest 19C suburb. *St. John's Church* (1864; J. Norton) is large, in polychrome brick with impressive tower (1883). E of the centre, **North Ormesby** was laid out from c 1860 and further E **South Bank** and **Grangetown** are later 19C. At North Ormesby a formal market place with *church* (1868; W. White). At **Ormesby**, 2m S, *church* (1875; Hicks and Charlewood) with fine tower and spire (1901; Temple Moore). **Eston**, 3m E, was where the ironstone that supported Bolckow and Vaughan's Middlesbrough foundries came from. Red-brick *church* (1883; W. Blessley) with good tower and W front.

SALTBURN-BY-THE-SEA. A174 9m E of Middlesbrough. A railway foundation of the Pease family of Darlington and Middlesbrough. *Station* (1861) in brick with arched porte-cochère and large *Zetland Hotel* (1861; W. Peachey) in yellow brick are the chief survivors of the first phase, together with the Valley Gardens below. In the gardens the *Albert Temple* (1863), actually the resited portico of Barnard Castle railway station. 3m NW, **Marske-by-the-Sea** with *church* (1865; F.P. Cockerell). The seaside development was by the Pease family as at Saltburn. 3m NW is **Redcar**, mostly later 19C seaside town, the wealthier part being Coatham at the W end with large *hotel* (1870). *School* (1869; J.C. Adams), Coatham Rd, red- and blue-brick Gothic.

Red Barns (c 1880; P. Webb), now part of the school, is a minor work of Webb's, built for the son of I.L. Bell of Middlesbrough.

STOCKTON-ON-TEES. 3m W of Middlesbrough. Market town that developed as a port through the 18C and especially after 1825 when the Stockton to Darlington Railway opened bringing coal traffic. After 1860 Middlesbrough became the dominant port. In the High St, *National Westminster Bank* (1874–76; J. Gibson) handsome Italianate characteristic of Gibson's buildings for the former National Provincial Bank. In Nelson St, *Art School* (1892; J. Bottomley), eclectic gabled and towered former school, and Italian Gothic former workhouse offices (1879; E. Clephan). In Major St, *RC church* begun 1841 by Pugin, but only W front original, the rest of 1866–70, the tower broadly to Pugin's design. At the S end of town, *48 Bridge Road*, possibly the original booking-office of the 1825 railway, now set up as a small museum to the world's first passenger line.

3m W at **Elton**, *church* with pretty screen (1907) by J.N. Comper, and 5m W at **Long Newton**, in the churchyard, *mausoleum* (1859; P.C. Hardwick) of the Marquesses of Londonderry. Their main house was the neo-classical *Wynyard Park* E of **Grindon**, A177 5m NW of Stockton, a massive porticoed house of 1822–28, the original design by B.D. Wyatt intended for the Duke of Wellington's unbuilt Waterloo Palace. The fortune came from the marriage of the 3rd Marquess (1778–1854) to the Durham colliery heiress, Lady Vane-Tempest. In the house, Monument Room (1855) commemorating the military career of the 3rd Marquess with his effigy, moved from Long Newton. Adjoining, chapel lavishly decorated in marble and carved wood (1903–10) in Italian Romanesque manner, possibly by Henry Wilson. 5m S, A135, at **Yarm**, brick and stone *railway viaduct* over the Tees (1849; Grainger and Bourne), 43 arches.

CORNWALL

BODMIN. A30 23m NE of Truro. The county town. In the centre, *Assize Court* (1837; H. Burt), granite classical, and nearby, in Fore St, *Market* (1839; W. Harris), Greek Doric. On the hill, S of the town, *obelisk* (1856) to Lt-Gen. Sir W. Gilbert. 2½m SE, *Lanhydrock House* (NT), the grandest 17C house in Cornwall with interiors all rebuilt after a fire in 1881, by R. Coad. It is now a complete surviving example of late Victorian taste, not over ostentatious, with panelled rooms and 17C style plasterwork. Of great interest are the restored service areas with all the equipment for running a Victorian country house, bakehouse, larders, sculleries and dairy, giving a rare view of the 'below stairs' world. 3m S, **Lostwithiel**: on the S side of the town, former *St. Faith's House of Mercy* (1862–64; G.E. Street), a severe grey stone Gothic main building with bay, window broken by a centre buttress rising to an overhanging gable. Plain EE chapel.

5m S of Lostwithiel, at **Par**, *church* (1848; G.E. Street), Street's first church, with his interest in severe geometrical design already apparent in the tower chamfered back in the upper stage to an octagonal base for the spire. Lancet windows without external moulding leaving the line of the wall face unbroken save for plain buttresses. The effect is simple, as appropriate to a country church, the pink local stone laid with none of the harshness of much mid Victorian work. King-post roof and stained glass by Wailes. 4m E, at **Fowey**, by the church, *Place*, 16C house of the Treffry family overhauled in richly carved romantic Gothic by J.T. Treffry (1813–45). 4m W of Par, **St. Austell**, centre of the china clay industry. Parish *church* restored by Street (1872). *Town Hall* (1844; Cope, Eales and Elmslie) in similar palazzo style to Truro Town Hall. At **Carthew**, 2m N, *Wheal Martyn*, open-air museum of the china clay industry based on a restored clay works of c 1880. 1m N, at **Treverbyn**, *church* (1848–50; G.E. Street), Street's second church, simple, well composed work with lancets and some early Dec. style detail.

12m E of Bodmin, A38, **Liskeard**, with early 19C stucco and stone houses on the ridge. On the hill below, *Town Hall* (1859; H. Rice), Italianate with bell-tower. Prominent stone railway *viaduct* S of town, with piers of Brunel timber viaduct adjoining. 12m SE of Liskeard, at **Sheviock**, *church* restored by Street (1850 and 1871), E window by Wailes (1851). 3m S of Sheviock, at **Portwrinkle**, *Whitsand Bay Hotel* (1871), large gabled Tudor style stone house with porch tower, remarkable for having been moved some 6m, from Torpoint, c 1910. Richly coloured stained glass in the stair window. 4m E of Sheviock, by the entry to *Antony House* (NT), fine estate *church* (1863–71; W. White) with spire and exceptional polychrome interior, round marble shafts, red and white arches, painted decoration in chancel and fine contemporary glass, especially the E window. Vicarage behind by White. For *Royal Albert Bridge* (1857–59; Brunel), at Saltash, 13m E of Liskeard, A38, see Plymouth, Devon.

4m N of Bodmin, at **Blisland**, *church* refitted from 1894 (F.C. Eden) with delicate painted screen and Renaissance style reredos. 12m NW of Bodmin, A389, at **Little Petherick**, *church* rebuilt 1858 (W. White) with fine fittings added 1908 (J.N. Comper).

PENZANCE. A30 26m SW of Truro. At the top of Market Jew St, *Market House* (1837; H.J. Whitling), fine Ionic building with portico and dome. In front, *statue* of Sir H. Davy, chemist and inventor of the miners' safety lamp. In Chapel St, *Egyptian House* (c 1830), stucco facade, completely in Egyptian style. Further on, *St. Mary's Church* (1832–35; C. Hutchins), granite, Commissioners' Gothic, with land-mark tower. At foot of Market Jew St, *station* (1852; Brunel). 2m S, **Newlyn**, centre of the late 19C group of outdoor painters called the 'Newlyn School'. Stanhope Forbes, the leading figure, lived at *Higher Faugan*, off Paul Hill, designed for himself (1904). E of Penzance, *St. Michael's Mount*, romantic island monastery rebuilt gradually for the St. Aubyn family, owners from c 1660, the result a miniature Mont St. Michel. The major part of the house (NT) was rebuilt by J.P. St. Aubyn in 1850 and 1875–78, the SE wing rising precipitously from the rock. 5m E of Penzance, B3280, at **St. Hilary**, *church* rebuilt 1854 (W. White). 13m E of Penzance, A394, at **Helston**, granite classical *Market House* (1837; W. Harris). At foot of Coinagehall St, a Tudor Gothic *gateway* (1834; G. Wightwick).

The principal Cornish tin and copper mining areas lay NW and NE of Penzance. Tin and copper were deep-mined from the 18C, and the characteristic surviving feature is the engine-house for the beam-engines that pumped water from the mines. In the early 19C the end of the monopoly on the construction of engines held by Messrs Boulton and Watt led to rapid and competitive development of steam power, Cornish engineers and manufacturers playing the most important role. Camborne was the centre but mines appear all over Cornwall, as do characteristic terraces of miners' houses. The most spectacular mines are those of the far west, around **St. Just**, 6m W of Penzance, *Botallack*, 1½m NW, with its engine-house perched on a ledge half-way down a cliff, and *Levant*, one of the last still with an engine, its workings extending some half-mile out to sea and down to 2000ft below the sea bed. **Hayle**, 9m NE of Penzance, was the main ore port, rock being taken to S Wales for smelting, and also the manufacturing centre for Cornish engines. *Church* (1886; J.D. Sedding), the original parish *church* at Phillack, to NE, was rebuilt 1856 (W. White).

SCILLY ISLES. On **Tresco**, *Tresco Abbey*, the house and garden created by Augustus Smith (1804–72) who bought the lease of the islands in 1834 with the intention of reforming the economy, agricul-ture and education of the islanders, and establishing a model estate on Benthamite principles. The house was built in stages from 1835 onwards, low and picturesque with much mahogany panelling and furniture made from wood salvaged from wrecks. The sub-tropical gardens, with rare plants, were created from the 1850s. In the grounds, Valhalla Museum, built 1871, to house figureheads of ships wrecked on the islands.

TRURO. A39 23m SW of Bodmin. Truro *Cathedral* (1880–1910; J.L. Pearson), the first Anglican cathedral to be built in England since Wren's St. Paul's and with its trinity of spires a building that achieves cathedral scale despite the cramped and low-lying site. The inspira-tion for the soaring outline is Early French, the spires of Caen, com-bined with English features based on the plan of Lincoln Cathedral and the EE style of Salisbury. Externally everything combines to accentuate upward movement, the more impressive for the narrow streets that frame the diverse views of the building. The S transept with its rose window rises up from an ornate porch and curved bap-tistery on the W, and the retained 15C aisle of the former parish church on the E, the lower richness translated into verticality increased by the pyramid-roofed tower between the transept and the old aisle. In all views the gables, turrets and spires compose unexpectedly and harmoniously. Inside, the rib-vaulted roof runs throughout, the lofty height disguising the relative shortness of the cathedral, the mouldings increased in richness in the chancel, where the E transepts and the double aisle on the S side give an added spatial complexity. The interior is completed by an extremely ornate reredos with sanctuary enclosure, the present flat top not originally intended. Rich marble floor. The circular baptistery displays Pearson's vaulting at its finest. *City Hall* (1846–47; Cope and Eales) displays a handsome palazzo

Truro Cathedral (1880–1910; J.L. Pearson)

front in granite with campanile turret. At the top of Lemon St, Doric *column* (1835; P. Sambell) to R. and J. Lander, Truro-born explorers of the Niger. Statue of R. Lander 1853 (N.N. Burnard). *St. Paul's Church* (1848) has a fine chancel of 1882–84 (J.D. Sedding) in free Perp. style.

W of Truro, around Redruth and Camborne, the centre of the Cornish mining area. R. Trivithick, the great Cornish engineer, was born at **Pool**, between the two towns. His father was manager of the Dolcoath mine. At **East Pool**, *Cornish Engines Museum* with two working beam-engines. Engine-houses with their characteristic roofless gables and round chimneys survive at *Wheal Busy mine*, near **Chacewater**, NE of Redruth, at *Wheal Peevor*, near Redruth, with three engine-houses, and near **Porthtowan**, on the coast N of Redruth, where *Wheal Ellen* and *United Hills* engine-houses stand in dramatic relation in the bleak valley. **Portreath** was developed from the 18C by the Basset family of Tehidy, owners of Wheal Basset mine S of Pool, to bring coal for the mines. At **Redruth** was the Mining Exchange, centre of Cornish mining. In centre *clock tower* (1828 and c 1900) in granite. At **St. Agnes**, 8m NW of Truro, further mining remains, notably *Wheal Kitty*, N of the village. Just E, at **Mithian**, *church* (1861; W. White). 14m N of Truro, **Newquay**, fishing port developed as a resort after 1875 when the railway came. *St. Michael's Church* (1909–11; J.N. Comper) is a fine late Gothic work with rood screen and fittings by Comper. *The Tower*, W of the town, is a castellated house of 1835. 7m E of Newquay, at **St. Columb Major**, *Bank House* (1857; W. White), former bank in High Victorian Gothic style, polychrome stone with banded brick and vaulted entry, a fine example of Ruskinian ideas applied to commercial building. Also by White, the *Old Rectory* (1849) and *Penmellyn* (c 1855), good examples of house design by one of the leading Gothicists.

5m SW of Truro, A39, at **Devoran**, *church* (1855–56; J.L. Pearson), surprisingly crudely detailed with short tower overwhelmed by a steep pyramid spire, High Victorian vigour achieved cheaply. 3m SW, **Penryn**, a long main street aligned on the classical steeple (1839) of the Town Hall. 3m SE, **Falmouth**, chief port for the West Indies until c 1840. Good early 19C public buildings, *Custom House*, **Polytechnic**, Church St (1833; G. Wightwick) and *School*, Killigrew Rd (1824). *All Saints' Church* (1887–90; J.D. Sedding), Killigrew St, prominently sited overlooking the town with buttressed W front and broad interior, the nave and chancel ended in large E and W windows, typical of Sedding's work. Interior carving and painted decoration of high quality. *RC church* 1869 (J.A. Hansom), tower and spire 1881. 2m S of Falmouth, at **Maenporth**, *The Crag* (1865; A. Waterhouse), Gothic seaside house, now an hotel. To SW, *Nansidwell Hotel*, **Mawnan Smith** (1910; L. Stokes). On the E side of the Fal estuary, at **St. Anthony-in-Roseland**, opposite St. Mawes, *Place*, symmetrical Gothic (1840), attached to the parish church. **Gerrans** *church*, 2½m N, is a careful rebuilding of 1849 by W. White. By White also the *Old Rectory* (c 1850) at **Ruan Lanihorne** 5m N. To W, between the Fal and Truro rivers, the *Tregothnan* estate of the Boscawen family. *Church* of St. Michael Penkevil, rebuilt 1862–66 (G.E. Street), reusing the elaborate early 14C carved work. Fine Street fittings. The house is a splendid Tudor Gothic mansion of 1816–18 (W. Wilkins) much enlarged 1842–48 (L. Vulliamy). 7m NE of Truro, A39, at **Ladock**, *church* with rich chancel (1862–64; G.E. Street) and E window of 1862 by Morris, among the earliest windows by the Morris firm. Morris glass of 1869 in S aisle E window and 1896 at W end.

CUMBRIA

APPLEBY. A66 13m SE of Penrith. Former county town of Westmorland. The Settle–Carlisle railway (1875; J.S. Crossley), brought with immense difficulty over the Pennines, reached the Eden valley here. On the line to S the great stone viaducts are a feature of the remote valleys, notable examples at **Ormside** S of Appleby and **Smardale** W of Kirkby Stephen. At **Orton**, 10m SW B6260, in the *church* SW window (1880; Campbell, Smith and Co), sentimental angels protecting a little girl against a background sky streaked in turquoise, purple and orange, a striking design.

BARROW-IN-FURNESS. A590 35m SW of Kendal. A new town created by the Furness Railway and its director, Sir James Ramsden, to exploit the iron ore deposits of Furness. H.W. Schneider began the exploitation of the iron in 1840, but development came with Ramsden and the railway in 1846. Ramsden devised the grid plan on which the new town was laid out, set up the municipal government and became the first mayor. The railway company built the town hall, the market, the hotel, shops and offices, owned the seafront and developed the docks. Schneider built the blast furnaces (1856), and from iron the town proceded logically to shipbuilding, the great Vickers yard developing from the Barrow Shipbuilding Co of 1869. In St. George's Square, the centre of the town, the *church* (1859–61; E.G. Paley), the former railway *station* (1863) and the railway *offices* (1864). At the main intersection, Ramsden Square, Ramsden *statue* (1872; M. Noble) and *Library* (1915; J.A. Charles). In Duke St, ambitious Gothic *Town Hall* (1882–27; W.H. Lynn) with central tower, a distinguished follower of Waterhouse's Manchester Town Hall. In front, statue of *Lord Frederick Cavendish* (1885; A.B. Joy), the Cavendish family, Dukes of Devonshire, owning much of the land on which the town was built. *RC church* (1866; E.W. Pugin) ornate with W rose window. On corner of Abbey Rd, *Lloyds Bank* (1873) Italianate. In Abbey Rd, *Institute* (1870; H.A. Darbishire), *Conservative Club* (1899) and *Abbey House* (1913; Lutyens), late Elizabethan style manor house in red sandstone built for the managing director of Vickers and his guests with full great hall inside. In Blake St, *St. James' Church* (1867–69; E.G. Paley) advanced High Victorian Gothic with fine steeple on a gabled tower. The docks are to S and W. On Walney Island, across a narrow channel, **Vickerstown**, begun 1901, garden estate for shipyard workers.

4m NE at **Dalton-in-Furness**, *Castle*, 14C pele tower, restored 1856. *St. Mary's Church* (1882–85; Paley and Austin), excellent example of the firm's work, late Dec. style with much plain walling and bold buttresses. Especially notable the chequer-work on the parapets of tower, perches and E chapels, some flushwork over the bell-openings. Fine interior. 5m NE, **Ulverston**, the parish *church* much rebuilt 1864 (E. Paley). *Station* (1873; Paley and Austin) remarkably large with Italianate detail and tall clock tower. In Union St, *Savings Bank* (1845) classical to Italianate with cupola-topped tower. On Head Hill to NE, *Barrow Monument* (1850; A. Trimen), 100ft replica of the third Eddystone lighthouse built to Sir J. Barrow, Secretary to the Admiralty, founder of the Royal Geographical Society and, with Sir John Banks, promoter of the expeditions to find the NW Passage around Canada. Barrow Point, the N tip of Alaska, was named after him 1826. 3m S, A5087, at **Bardsea**, *church* (1843–53; G. Webster) overlooking Morecambe Bay. Just N, *Conishead Priory* (1821–36; P. Wyatt) very large Gothic mansion, still in the 18C Gothic tradition, wildly asymmetrical and careless of archaeological correctness, picturesque variety being the intention and certainly achieved. 2m W of Bardsea, at **Urswick**, in the *church*, Arts and Crafts woodwork of high quality 1909–12, notably organ case, S door and pulpit tester. At **Aldingham**, 3m S of Bardsea, *Aldingham Hall* (1846–50; M.D. Wyatt) medium-sized Gothic house, quite elaborate in Perp. style.

CARLISLE. The county town, always in a strategic position, became the junction of some seven railways during the 19C. *Citadel Station* (1847; W. Tite) is Tudor Gothic, in stone, designed to blend with the two circular keeps of the *County Buildings and Assize Courts* (1807–12; Telford and Smirke) flanking the entry to English St. Outside, statue of Earl of Lonsdale (1845; M.L. Watson), inside, statue of Major Aglionby MP (1845; M.L. Watson). By the station, *County Hotel* (1856; A. Salvin), mildly Italianate. Off English St, Devonshire St and Lowther St area, c 1820–40 with late Georgian terraces. At head of Devonshire St, *bank* (1840; A. Williams) built as the Athenaeum, pilastered front like contemporary Newcastle buildings. *Victoria Place* (1852) has handsome terraces on each side, without a hint of the Victorian in them. In the Market Place, at top of English St, statue of J. Steel (1846). Castle St leads up to the *Cathedral*, the W front on the stump of the nave, demolished in the Civil War, added 1870 (E. Christian). E window by Hardman with some 14C glass in the head. Reredos and Bishop's Throne part of G.E. Street's restoration (1873–81). In the S chancel aisle marble effigies of Bishop Waldegrave (1872; J. Adams-Acton) and Dean Close (1885; H.H. Armstead), and fine bronze effigy of Bishop Goodwin (1894; H. Thornycroft). Further on, *Tullie House Museum* (1689: extended 1892; C.J. Ferguson), the additions in free Tudor to Elizabethan style. W of Centre, early 19C suburban expansion with Perp. *church* (1828–30; T. Rickman) in Wigton Rd and Greek Doric *Infirmary* (1830–32; R. Tattersall) in Newtown Rd: SW of centre, in Junction St, *Shaddongate Mill* (1836; R. Tattersall), the largest cotton mills then built, seven storeys in stone with 300ft mill chimney. Fireproof construction. In St. James' Rd, *St. James' Church* (1865–67; Andrews and Pepper).

12m SW of Carlisle, A596, at **Wigton**, in the Market Place, *fountain* (1871; J.T. Knowles) to the memory of the wife of G. Moore, Carlisle philanthropist, large square monument on a high base, capped by a pyramid spire with incised naturalistic leaf decoration on each face. Four lovely bronze reliefs by T. Woolner of Acts of Mercy. In West St, former *Mechanics Institute* (1851) classical with carved figures in pediment. *Highmoor House* (1810) has Wigton's most prominent monument, a stone tower, 136ft high, added 1887 as a look-out. 11m NW of Wigton, **Silloth**, developed in the mid 19C as a port for Carlisle. Formal grid layout (1857; Messrs Hay) of three terraces about the *church* (1870; Cory and Ferguson) plate-traceried with spire, apse and brick interior. 4m SW of Carlisle, B5299, at **Dalston**, *Dalston Hall*, c 1500 and 17C fortified house with entrance front of 1899 (C.J. Ferguson). 3m S, *Holm Hill* (c 1840), stone Italianate house with off-centre tower behind, and *Rose Castle*, seat of the Bishops of Carlisle since the 13C, much rebuilt 1829–31 (T. Rickman) in late Gothic style.

3m SE of Carlisle, A6, at **Carleton**, former *County Asylum* (1856; T. Worthington) large and Italianate with Gothic chapel 1875 (J.A. Cory). 3m S, at **Wreay**, *˙church* (1836–42; Sara Losh) without parallel in early Victorian architecture. Sara Losh, daughter of the founder of the Walker Iron Works, Newcastle, designed the church as a memorial to her sister. The style is Romanesque but enriched with carving of the most vivid kind, based on natural forms, animals, plants and fossils, chosen for their symbolic value, a scheme of decoration that in both style and content seems closer to Arts and Crafts work of the late 19C than to the 1830s. The carving is all by a local mason, W. Hindson; beetles and butterflies, lilies and wheat-ears climb the window and door surrounds, the gargoyles ornament the roofline. Inside, broad and stern apse ringed by massive columns with a row of arched openings all around above. Remarkable fittings, two lecterns on trunks of bog-oak, marble altar on back-to-back bronze eagles, alabaster font with symbolic carving, partly by Sara Losh. Outside, mausoleum to Katherine Losh in deliberately primitive or cyclopean, masonry with statue (1850; D. Dunbar) and Anglo-Saxon style cross (1835; S. Losh) based on the Bewcastle cross.

3m E of Carlisle, A69, at **Warwick Bridge**, *bridge* (1837; J. Dobson), neo-Norman *church* (1844; J. Dobson) apsed with broach spire, built for the Dixon family, owners of the great cotton mill at Carlisle. *Holme Eden Hall* (1833; Dobson) was the Dixon seat, Tudor to Elizabethan style with entrance tower and a glorious array of chimneys. The *RC church* (1840; A.W.N. Pugin) is a minor work but wholly correct in its Gothic detail and the simple exterior gives no indication of the bright colour inside with stencilled chancel decoration, gilded nave roof timbers and glass by Hardman (mostly of 1860s). Chancel fittings as Pugin thought appropriate, sedilia, raised altar, screen and recess for the founder's tomb, H. Howard of Corby Castle. Howard is commemorated also in a plaque on the fine railway *viaduct* (1830–34; F. Giles) across the Eden at **Wetheral**, 2m S. At **Crosby**, 3m N of Warwick Bridge, *church* (1854; R. Billings) with the most exaggerated details to the spire. Billings, a noted antiquary, seems always to have pursued a far from conventional course in his own designs. Windows with clear pressed glass stars in the tracery heads. 2m E of Warwick Bridge, *Edmond Castle* (1824–29; R. Smirke) Tudor style with shaped gables the only unusual touch, much extended by Smirke 1844–46. 2m SE, *Gelt Bridge* (1832–35; F. Giles) skew-arched railway viaduct, at the time the largest such arches ever built.

At **Brampton**, A69, to NW, a number of works by Philip Webb for G. Howard of Naworth Castle, important patron of the Pre-Raphaelites. * *Church* (1874–78) Webb's only church, highly individual in detail, as if Webb, a founder of the Society for the Protection of Ancient Buildings wished to suggest the heterogeneous variety of the English parish church over the unified design and style practised by contemporaries such as Bodley or aimed at in the more drastic restorations that the Society was formed to fight. W tower (completed 1906) with saddleback roof and flèche, the bell-openings matching only on opposite faces. N aisle cross-gabled with battlements, S aisle quite different. Inside, nave roof is flat and plastered, like the 18C roofs inserted in so many Victorian churches but removed inevitably by the restorers. Green painted woodwork in the aesthetic movement taste. All the stained glass inevitably by Morris and Co and of superb quality. On the outskirts two houses by Webb. To E, A69, *Four Gables* (1876–78), stone, square plan, gabled on all four sides with sash windows, though the effect is not at all Georgian with dripmoulds over the gable windows and a dripcourse carried right around over the first floor, emphasised at the corners with corbel blocks and stone rainwater spouts. To W, A69, *Green Lanes* (1877) smaller scale, similar in detail. *Naworth Castle*, 3m E, held by the Howards, Earls of Carlisle since the 16C. George Howard, later the 9th Earl, friend of Morris and Burne-Jones, employed Webb and the Morris firm for his London house at Palace Green, Kensington, and Burne-Jones for some decoration at Naworth. The castle, 14C to 17C, was heavily restored after a fire in 1844 (A. Salvin). Just N, *Lanercost Priory*, founded c 1166, its nave, still intact, the parish church. Morris and Co. glass in N aisle and Howard family monuments in N transept, fine bronze tablet to the parents of G. Howard (c 1880; J.E. Boehm) with portrait roundels over two small reliefs from designs by Burne-Jones.

2m N, at **Walton**, *church* (1869; Paley and Austin) severe High Victorian work with W rose window over lancets and NW tower. 5m NW of Brampton, off A6071, *Scaleby Castle*, 14C to 17C border castle given Tudor style S front 1835–40 (T. Rickman). 10m N of Carlisle, off A7, N of **Longtown**, *Netherby Hall* 15C and 18C house given Jacobean trimmings (1835; W. Burn). A pretty suspension *bridge* (1877) crosses the Esk to the *church* at **Kirkandrews** which has gilded and painted screen and reredos of 1893 (Temple Moore).

COCKERMOUTH. A66 31m W of Penrith. Market town, birthplace of Wordsworth (1770). *Wordsworth House* at W end of town is open to public. In Main St, *statue* of the 6th Earl of Mayo (1875), Viceroy of India, assassinated in the Andaman Islands. Off Market Place, *Town Hall*, a converted Methodist chapel of 1841 and parish *church* (1852–54; J. Clarke) with crossing tower and spire. Good E window by Hardman.

13m SE, A66, **Keswick**, centre for the NW lakes. The poet R. Southey lived at *Greta Hall*, part of Keswick School, from 1809 to his death in 1843. In the *Museum*, Station St, Southey relics. Parish *church* (1838; A. Salvin) built for the Leeds manufacturer J. Marshall, dominant tower and spire. Chancel altered 1889 and excellent glass by Holiday added. On Friars Crag, on E side of Derwentwater, *Ruskin Memorial* (NT), bronze by A. Lucchesi. Ruskin was brought here aged five and the view remained his earliest memory. Just W of Keswick, at **Crosthwaite**, Southey is buried in the churchyard. In the *church*, marble effigy of the poet (1846; J.G. Lough). 2m N of Cockermouth, at **Bridekirk**, *church* (1868; Cory and Ferguson), neo-Norman to suit the superb Norman font, interior entirely of brick with vaulted chancel and apse. At **Plumbland**, 5m NE, off B5301, *church* also by Cory and Ferguson (1870), strong detail, cross-gabled tower and spire. 2m W of Cockermouth, A66, at **Brigham**, *church* restored 1863–76 (W. Butterfield) who rebuilt the top of the tower. Inside, delightful stencilled roof decoration and bright glass by A. Gibbs.

To W, the industrialised coastal plain, coal and iron region much decayed. **Workington** had colliery seams extending under the sea. In Washington St, *church* (1823; T. Hardwick) with magnificent Tuscan portico, a larger version of Inigo Jones's Covent Garden portico. Classical steeple with cupola added 1846. **Maryport**, 6m N, was an 18C foundation as a coal port, but developed mostly after 1840. 8m S of Workington, **Whitehaven**, developed as a coal port by the Lowther family as early as 1680 and laid out as a planned town on a grid pattern. In the centre, *St. Nicholas' Church* (1883; Cory and Ferguson), long red sandstone, late Dec. to Perp. style with strong W tower and W transepts. In Duke St, one of the main parallel streets, *Trustee Savings Bank* (1833), classical with Doric porch, and, facing down the street, palazzo style *Town Hall* (1851; W. Barnes). 5m S, at **St. Bees**, medieval nunnery church restored from ruin 1858–87 (W. Butterfield), rebuilt crossing tower, aisles, nave roof and E end wall, the E end a strong composition inside of triple arches with circles over, picked out in coloured inlay. Most remarkable is Butterfield's chancel screen (1887) completely filling the arch in a writhing complexity of wrought iron. **St. Bees School** to E has Tudor style entrance buildings (1842–44; T. Nelson), school-house (1885), chapel and library (1907–10) all added by Paley and Austin. At **Egremont**, 2m E, A595, *church* (1880; T.L. Banks) EE style with NW tower. At **Cleator**, mining village 2m NE, *RC church* (1856; E.W. Pugin) rock-faced stone with E.W. Pugin's characteristic florid carved detail inside.

KENDAL. A6 21m N of Lancaster. In Stricklandgate, *Library* (1908; T.F. Pennington) free Baroque and *St. Thomas' Church* (1837; G. Webster) lancet Gothic. In Highgate, Town Hall (1825–27; G. Webster) classical, much enlarged 1893 (S. Shaw). In Castle St, *St. George's Church* (1839; G. Webster) lancet Gothic with twin towered W front. Chancel 1910 (Austin and Paley). 5m NW, A591, at **Staveley**, in *St. John's Church* (1864; J.S. Crowther) E window by Morris and Co. (c 1875), richly coloured. 2m S of Kendal, at **Natland**, *church* (1909; Austin and Paley) free Perp. with fine W tower and the firm's usual excellent detail. 2m SW, at **Sedgwick**, *Sedgwick House* (1868; Paley and Austin) Tudor Gothic and, at **Crosscrake**, *church* (1875; Paley and Austin). 10m SE of Kendal, B6254, **Kirkby Lonsdale**, the 'Lowton' of Charlotte Bronte's 'Jane Eyre' (cf. Cowan Bridge, Lancaster, Lancs.). *Market House* (1854). Just N, *Underley Hall* (1825; G. Webster) very early example of revived Jacobean style. At **Casterton**, just E, *Casterton School*, the foundation for clergy daughters run by the Rev. W.C. Wilson, originally at Cowan Bridge where the Bronte sisters were pupils. *Church* (1831–33) built for the Rev. Wilson. Chancel glass and wall- paintings 1894 (H. Holiday), late Pre-Raphaelite manner. N of Kirkby Lonsdale, two distinguished *churches* by Paley and Austin, at **Mansergh** (1880) and **Barbon** (1893), another at **Hutton Roof** (1881) to W. 11m E of Kendal, **Sedbergh**, formerly in Yorkshire, *Sedbergh School* founded 1525 with stone buildings by Paley and Austin, fine Perp. chapel (1897), School House (1878) Tudor, Sedgwick House (1879) with free 17C detail and Powell Hall (1906). The Rev. A. Sedgwick (1785–1873), eminent geologist, was educated here.

MILLOM. A5093 25m SW of Ambleside. Iron-working town mostly of later 19C with regular planned layout. In Market Square, *Market House* (c 1890) free Tudor style and three late 19C banks. Imposing *church* (1874–77; Paley and Austin), late Dec. style with crossing tower. 15m N at **Ravenglass**, *Muncaster Castle* (open to public), medieval origins rebuilt 1862–66 (A. Salvin) in convincingly castellated manner, beautifully sited in landscaped grounds. *Church* altered 1874 (Salvin) with good glass by Holiday in chancel and one S window (1882 and 1887). 6m NW, **Seascale**, intended to develop as a seaside resort promoted by the Furness Railway in the later 19C, but unsuccessful. A baronial circular *water tower* in the former goods yard is the chief landmark. 4m NE at **Ponsonby**, in the *church* E window by Morris and Co , W window by Holiday. Another good window by Holiday in *church* (1842; E. Sharpe) at **Calder Bridge** just N.

PENRITH. A6 18m S of Carlisle. Market town and centre for the NW lakes. In Market Place, *clock tower* (1861). 5m W, B5288, at **Greystoke**, *Greystoke Castle*, medieval, much rebuilt in Elizabethan style (1839–48 and 1875–78; A. Salvin) for the Dukes of Norfolk. 5m N of Penrith, A6, at **Plumpton Wall**, *church* (1907; Sir R. Lorimer) handsome Arts and Crafts work with battered profile to the tower and porch, sweeping roof and blank E wall. 1½m NW, *Brackenburgh Tower* mostly of 1903 (Lorimer) in stripped Elizabethan style, emphasis on sheer wall and grid-like windows, picturesque loosely connected plan. 2m W of Plumpton Wall, *Hutton Hall*, medieval and 17C with Tudor style S front and tower (1830 and c 1860–80; A. Salvin). 4m S of Penrith, at **Lowther**, ruins of *Lowther Castle* (1802–14; R. Smirke), monumental castellated house built for the Earl of Lonsdale, the apogee of the late Georgian castle style, wholly symmetrical in smoothest ashlar, the toy fort writ large. In the *church*, monument to the Earl of Lonsdale (died 1844) and outside, Lowther mausoleum (1857; B. Baud) with marble statue inside (1863; E.B. Stephens). 19m NE of Penrith, **Alston**, mining town in 19C, the highest market town in England. Gothic *Town Hall* (1857; A.B. Higham) and parish *church* (1870; J.W. Walton) High Victorian with fine E window (1871; Wooldridge).

WINDERMERE. A591 9m NW of Kendal. Tourist centre for the southern lakes, the railway terminus from Kendal. *St. Mary's Church* begun 1848 has W end, tower and E end by Paley and Austin (1881). By the church, *The Priory*, Gothic villa of c 1860. **Bowness**, to SW, is the older centre on the lake, though mostly now of mid 19C villas and hotels with turn of the century lakeside houses off the main road to S. *Steamboat Museum* with restored steam-powered launches from the late 19C and Edwardian period. S of Bowness, *•Blackwell* (1900; M.H. Baillie Scott), gabled and roughcast house in the manner of Voysey, but much larger than any commission Voysey had without Voysey's compositional skill. The interiors are exceptional Arts and Crafts to Art Nouveau, the drawing-room close to Mackintosh's work, white-painted with thin columns to the inglenook, the hall complex, partly two-storey with half- timbering, while the dining-room has a deep inglenook with Moorish fireplace and lovely peacock frieze. On the lower road, just W, at Gillhead, *•Broadleys* and *Moor Crag*, both by C.F.A. Voysey (1898), two excellent examples of Voysey's mature style, the roughcast walls and massive rendered stacks on sweeping slate roofs so characteristic of his houses here closest to their geographical origins in the Cumberland farmhouses of the 17C. Simplicity of outline with stone-mullion windows flush with the wall face and a total absence of the late 19C effusion of carved work or fancy half-timbering give these houses a clarity exceptional for their date. Broadleys, on a terrace overlooking the lake, has a more formal garden front with three two-storey curved bows breaking into a big hipped roof, the centre bow fully mullioned to light the hall. The entrance front, by contrast, is wholly informal, L-plan with various projecting roofs. Pretty lodge with dry stone walling. Moor Crag, to S, set above the road, in landscaped grounds (T. Mawson) has similar great hipped roof but contained each side by roughcast gables and sweeping right down almost to ground level at the W end and over a low verandah on the garden front. Coach house opposite the drive (1900). To E, S of **Winster**, *Birket Houses* (1904; D. Gibson), larger country house following more closely Cumbrian precedent, especially in the circular chimneys but with something of Voysey in the spare gabled elevations.

4m SE of end of the lake, off A590, at **Field Broughton**, pretty *church* (1892–94; Paley, Austin and Paley) with crossing tower and spire. 2m S, **Cartmel**, with Augustinian *priory* founded 1188. Inside, *effigy* (1885; T. Woolner) of Lord F. Cavendish of Holker Hall, assassinated in Dublin 1882. *•Holker Hall* (open to public), 2m SW, passed to the family of the Dukes of Devonshire in the 18C and the accompanying lands around Barrow-in-Furness were the source of the revival of the family fortunes from the 1850s when the iron ore was exploited and the town of Barrow developed. The house was rebuilt in two phases, the roughcast N wing in plain Tudor style (1838–42; G. Webster) and the far grander red sandstone W wing (1871–75; Paley and Austin) in Elizabethan style with heavily emphatic main elements, a square tower with short lead spire, a tall octagonal turret and a big round angle turret on the garden front. Richly carved Jacobean style staircase. Estate *railway station* at **Cark**, to S, and at **Flookburgh**, *church* (1897; Austin and Paley) built for the Cavendish family, a strong work with wide W tower with saddleback roof and apse raised on an undercroft. Romanesque style. 3m E of Cartmel, **Grange-over-Sands**, resort promoted by Sir J. Ramsden of the Furness Railway who built the *Grange Hotel* (1866). *Station* (c 1877; E.G. Paley) with picturesque half-hipped gables. By the *church* (1853; J. Murray), *clock tower* (1912) free Gothic, slightly Art Nouveau. 8m NW, off A590, at **Finsthwaite**, *church* (1873–74; Paley and Austin), powerful though small-scale Romanesque style building with central tower. Reredos by Salviati. 5m N, at **Near Sawrey**, B5285, *Hill Top* (NT) the home of Beatrix Potter, bought with the royalties of 'The Tale of Peter Rabbit'. The area features in the illustrations of her books, cf. the *Tower Bank Arms* in 'Jemima Puddle-Duck'. At **Hawkshead**, 2m NW, Wordsworth was a pupil at the *Grammar School* (open to public), his name carved on a desk.

5m NE, at head of Windermere, **Ambleside**, resort town, closely connected with William and Dorothy Wordsworth. *Church* (1854; G.G. Scott) with broach spire. NW and SW windows by Holiday (1888–91). Wordsworth memorial chapel. The political economist and reformer Harriet Martineau lived at *The Knoll* (1845), Rydal Rd from 1845–76. Dr Arnold, Headmaster of Rugby, built *Fox How* NE of the town and Matthew Arnold recollected the meeting of Harriet Martineau and Charlotte Bronte at Ambleside in 1850 in his poem 'Haworth Churchyard 1855'. *Rydal Mount* at **Rydal**, just N, was Wordsworth's home from 1813–50. Open to public, collection of Wordsworth relics. **Grasmere**, just W, was where Wordsworth and his sister first settled, at *Dove Cottage* (open to public) 1799–1808, keeping the tenancy of the cottage for T. de Quincey. *Wordsworth Museum* opposite. The Wordsworths are buried in the churchyard. In the *church* Wordsworth memorial (1851; Woolner), a masterly relief portrait with delicate flower panels (including daffodils) each side. A.H. Clough also commemorated in the churchyard. S. of Ambleside, at **Wray**, by the lake, *Wray Castle* (1840–47; H.P. Horner), the most thoroughly castellated of castellated houses, even the porte-cochère fully fortified. Built for J. Dawson, Liverpool surgeon. *Church* (1845). *Pull Woods* (1890; G.F. Armitage), to N, a large gabled and half-timbered house built for Sir W.J. Crossley, engineer. 8m SW of Ambleside, **Coniston**, at head of Coniston Water. Ruskin is buried in the churchyard under a tall Anglo-Saxon style cross (1901; R.G. Collingwood). *Ruskin Museum* with drawings and relics. Ruskin lived at *Brantwood* (open to public), 2m E on the E side of the lake, buying it unseen in 1871. The house was steadily enlarged for Ruskin, who laid out the grounds and built the harbour. 'Fors Clavigera' and 'Praeterita' largely written here. 3m S of Coniston, at **Torver**, small Romanesque style *church* (1884; Paley and Austin) with crossing tower.

DERBYSHIRE

ASHBOURNE. A52 13m NW of Derby. In the market place, stone Italianate *Town Hall* (1861; B. Wilson). In Church St, *Savings Bank* (1843), a neat small palazzo, restrained in the early Victorian way. **Osmaston**, 2m SE, is an estate village of the 1840s and 1850s with thatched *cottages* and *church* (1845; H. Stevens). The manor house has been demolished. At **Ednaston**, 5m SW, *Ednaston Manor* (1912; E. Lutyens) in Lutyens' early Georgian manner with flat stone pilasters on brick and an enveloping roof. Built for one of the Player cigarette family. Excellent gardens.

BAKEWELL. A6 9m NW of Matlock. A spa town promoted not very successfully c 1800 by the Dukes of Rutland of Haddon Hall. In the church, good chancel fittings by G.G. Scott Jr (1879–82). The *vicarage*, further up, is by Waterhouse (1868). At the S edge of town, above the A6, *Burton Closes*, an Elizabethan style house, partly of 1846–48 by Joseph Paxton, extended 1857 and 1888. It looks sad now with the grounds built over, sadder still are the remnants inside of an elaborate decorative scheme by Pugin. 4m S of Bakewell, at **Youlgreave**, the *church* has chancel fittings by Norman Shaw (1869) and an E window by Morris and Co (1876). 4m SE of Bakewell, at **Rowsley**, *church* (1855), built for the Dukes of Rutland, with marble effigy of Lady John Manners and her child (1860; W. Calder Marshall). At **Little Rowsley**, former *station* (1849; J. Paxton), Italianate, the station for Chatsworth originally, and the terminus of the line from Derby for some 18 years while the company and the Duke of Rutland disagreed over the route through to Buxton. On the main road some *cottages* by Paxton (1850). *Chatsworth*, the great estate of the Dukes of Devonshire, is to the N. Joseph Paxton, designer of the Crystal Palace, was successively gardener, greenhouse designer, landscape architect and architect on the estate. His conservatory has gone, but the glazed forcing wall (1848), the planting schemes, arboretum and landscape around the Swiss Lake survive. All around the estate are cottages and lodges designed by Paxton or John Robertson between the 1830s and 1860s. **Beeley**, **Pilsley** and **Baslow** are outliers, but *Edensor*, the village moved by the 6th Duke (1838–42) as it impeded the view from the house, is as complete an early Victorian ensemble as can be found in Britain. Most of the styles available to the student of architecture were employed, neo-Norman, Swiss, Italianate, castellated, all informally grouped regardless of the odd juxtapositions. The detail is worked in best stone, unlike the more ephemeral looking picturesque cottages of the Georgians, and the studied care with which features more usual on churches or castles are put to service on cottages is endlessly surprising, like fancy dress on serious people. The *church* (1867; G.G. Scott) is wholly serious and very handsome. Paxton is buried in the churchyard.

NW of Bakewell, at **Little Longstone**, the railway crossed the Wye Valley on the *Monsal Dale Viaduct* (1863; W. Barlow), denounced by Ruskin at the time, but its five stone arches now an acceptable part of the landscape. S of **Great Longstone**, *Thornbridge Hall*, recased 1897 (C. Hadfield) in stone, Elizabethan style, to a complex silhouette, building-up to a great square tower. Inside some Morris glass of 1876 and 1885 and numerous fittings rescued from other houses. Handsome terraced gardens. 7m N of Bakewell, at **Hathersage**, the *church* has fittings from a restoration by Butterfield (1849–52). Far more impressive, of Butterfield's work, is **Bamford** *church* (1856–60), 3m NW, all in stone with a vigorous simplicity of outline, especially in the way the spire rises straight from the tower. *Vicarage* also by Butterfield (1862).

BUXTON. A6 12m NW of Bakewell. Capital of the Derbyshire Peak District and a spa town from the late 18C, developed by the Dukes of Devonshire. Although the core is Georgian the improvements continued right through the 19C and the town now has very much the feel of a Victorian spa. Behind the Crescent of 1780–90, the former stables (1785) were converted to the *Devonshire Royal Hospital* (1859) and the circular courtyard covered in 1881 by what was then the largest dome in the world at 156ft. The *Park* to the W was laid out by J. Paxton (1852) though the houses around are later. Various 19C *Baths* flank the Crescent and, opposite, is the *Pump Room* (1894; H. Currey). In the Pavilion Gardens, the *Pavilion* (1871; E. Milner) in iron and glass with octagonal Concert Hall added 1875 (R.R. Duke). The *Opera House* (1903; F. Matcham) is one of the best of Edwardian provincial theatres, twin-domed exterior and Baroque plasterwork inside, all recently lovingly restored. The centre of the town is notable for extravagant

The Opera House (1900; F. Matcham), Buxton

cast-iron work, especially the verandahs in front of the shops. In West St, S of centre, *St. Mary's Church* (1914; Currey and Thompson), an advanced Arts and Crafts work, emphatically simple stone exterior with dominant slate roofs and good fittings inside.

CHESTERFIELD. A61 12m S of Sheffield. A battered hilltop town crowned by the famous twisted spire of the parish church. The Market Place, recently saved from redevelopment, has a lumpy *Market Hall* (1857), not beautiful but giving scale to the open space. In Saltergate, *Methodist church* (1870) with big stone classical front. In Marsden St, a disused chapel (1870; J. Simpson) with cast-iron Florentine tracery. In Spencer St, *RC church* (1854 and 1874; J.A. Hansom) with tower-like W end. W of centre, in Ashgate Rd, *The Homestead* (1903–05; Parker and Unwin), Arts and Crafts house, close to the style of Voysey. **Staveley**, to NE of Chesterfield, was an ironworks town with industrial housing at **Barrow Hill**, to N. 5m NE, at **Spinkhill**, *Mount St. Mary's College*, where G.M. Hopkins wrote 'The Loss of the Eurydice' (1878). Buildings from 1842 with spired chapel (1844–46; J.A. Hansom) and large new school of 1876 (H. Clutton). The Derbyshire coalfield stretching down the E border of the county is without notable monuments, but at **Bolsover**, 6m E of Chesterfield, there is an exceptional example of a planned colliery village (1888–93). The colliery at **Clay Cross**, 5m S of Chesterfield, was for a time run by G. Stephenson, the railway engineer. In the *church*, one Burne-Jones window (1879) in the S aisle. George Stephenson designed the castellated N entry to the *Clay Cross Tunnel*.

DERBY. The county town and from 1840 one of the prime railway towns in Britain, junction for several railway lines, headquarters of the Midland Railway, and an important railway engineering centre. The present station is a disappointment, much altered, but opposite, the *Midland Hotel* (1840; F. Thompson) survives, the world's oldest station hotel. Just N of the station, some early railway housing has been restored. Off Railway Terrace, the *engineering works* includes a 16-sided roundhouse of c 1840. The centre of Derby, to NW, is battered by ring roads. London Rd runs in to St. Peter's, past the heavily rebuilt *St. Peter's Church*. Victoria St is the most characteristically 19C street, with an interesting group on the corner of Cornmarket built as *Bank, Hotel and Athenaeum* (1837; R. Wallace), stone and then stucco. Beyond, the *Post Office* (1869), one of several handsome Victorian classical or Italianate buildings in this area. Beyond, in the Strand, *Nos 2–40* (1881) and, in Wardwick, the old *Mechanics Institution* (1882; Sheffield and Hill). Also in Wardwick, the Gothic *Library and Museum* (1876; R.K. Freeman), with *Art Gallery* behind (1883). Cornmarket is the foot of the long spine of central Derby, running N to Market Place, with the *Guildhall*, originally of 1828 (M. Habershon), remodelled with a domed tower in 1842 (Duesbury and Lee). Behind, the covered *Market*, a spectacular iron and glass galleried space (1864). Iron Gate continues N with handsome brick and stone *National Westminster Bank* (1877). The splendid 16C tower of the Cathedral faces down St. Mary's Gate and Queen St continues N beyond. Off to E, in Full St, the *Industrial Museum*. In Queen St, *St. Michael's Church* (1858; H.I. Stevens), its tower a smaller accent between the cathedral and the *RC church* (1839; A.W. Pugin), Pugin's first major church, which is isolated on the far side of the inner ring road. Pugin's tower, even without its intended spire, is a fine work in the Perp. manner, more refined in detail than most of its contemporaries, but still in the style that Pugin soon rejected for the earlier Dec. Tall and light interior with very slim arcades and vaulted apse. The rood stands on a delicate pointed arch, echoing the chancel arch above but not impeding the view as a full screen would.

3m NW of Derby, at **Kedleston**, the great 18C mansion of the Curzon family. The parish *church* was enlarged 1907–13 (G.F. Bodley) for Lord Curzon, the Viceroy of India, to contain the opulent white marble memorial of Lady Curzon (B. Mackennal), her effigy joined by his after his death in 1925. SW of central Derby, in Parliament St, off Uttoxeter New Rd, *St. Luke's Church* (1870–75; Stevens and Robinson), Derby's best High Victorian building, heavily rock-faced with round apse and massive saddleback-roofed tower. 9m W, on A516, *Foston Hall* (1863; T.C. Hine), hard red-brick Jacobean house, now a detention centre. 2m W, at **Sudbury**, the 17C house of the Vernons (National Trust) has a sympathetic wing by G. Devey (1876). In the church, restored 1874 (Devey), numerous Vernon memorials and an E window given by Victoria and Albert in 1850. *Brocksford Hall*, 2m W, is an accomplished neo-Jacobean house (1893; Douglas and Fordham) with picturesque stable court. 7m SW of Derby, off A38, **Repton**, small town, the medieval priory buildings taken over by Repton School in the 16C and much expanded in the 19C. Chapel, originally of 1857 (H.I. Stevens), much enlarged. Memorial Hall (1883–86; A.W. Blomfield), Tudor style. W of the High St, *Easton House* (1907; E. Lutyens), varied with gabled entrance front and Queen Anne garden front. S of central Derby, off Osmaston Rd, the *Arboretum* (1839–40; J.C. Loudon), an early public park laid out by the famous theorist of garden design. Joseph Strutt, mill-owner of Belper and Derby, was the donor. Lodges and gateways in the mixed styles recommended by Loudon in his Encyclopaedia, mostly by E.B. Lamb. 6m S, **Melbourne**, small town dominated by the Norman *church*, restored 1859–62 (G.G. Scott). Chancel glass by Hardman 1869, N transept N window by Powells (1865). *Melbourne Hall* (open to public), the mostly early 18C house of the Coke family, passed by marriage to the Lamb family, Viscounts Melbourne. The second Viscount (1779–1848) was Prime Minister 1834–41, Victoria's early mentor. The estates passed in 1853 to his brother-in-law Lord Palmerston. Thomas Cook the travel agent was born humbly in Melbourne. Opposite his birthplace are the *Thomas Cook Almshouses* (1893; E. Burgess), a delightful courtyard group with Baptist chapel included. One room, reserved for the Cook family on their visits, is inscribed 'Thomas Cook, his family and friends'. 4m SE of Derby, off A6, *Elvaston Castle*, the castellated mansion (1817) of the Earls of Harrington. The 4th Earl (died 1850) enlarged and remo-delled the house 1830–40 (L.N. Cottingham) and laid out the extraor-dinary gardens (open to public), all in a spirit of revived medieval chivalry. The Gothic hall was renamed the 'Hall of the Fair Star' and covered with painted mottoes and symbols. The garden, a strange mixture of romantic influences, has one topiaried enclosure called the 'Garden of Mon Plaisir', another, with a Moorish pavilion, called the 'Alhambra Garden'. All this reputedly carried out for love, the Earl, having married a lady whose past made her unacceptable in society, recreated for her her world of medieval courtly love at Elvaston. 4m NW of Derby, A608, at **Morley**, *Morley Manor* (1900; G.F. Bodley), relatively plain gabled Tudor house, a rare domestic work by the great church architect. To S, *Locko Park*, 18C house of the Drury-Lowe family given an Italian overhaul from 1853 onwards (H.I. Stevens), including the unavoidable belvedere tower. The Italian touches more appropriate than usual as W. Drury-Lowe was a noted collector of

Italian pictures. W of Morley is *Breadsall Priory*, now an hotel, a 17C house that belonged to Charles Darwin's grandfather, the poet and scientist Erasmus Darwin, and was Victorianised (c 1855; R. Scrivener) for his son Sir F. Darwin. Garden front in Jacobean style 1906.

GLOSSOP. A57 13m E of Manchester. Small industrial town on the Manchester edge of the Peak, largely owned by the Dukes of Norfolk in the 19C. Norfolk Square is the centre of the new town, with *Town Hall* (1838; Weightman and Hadfield) and *Market* (1844) behind. The *RC church* (1836; Weightman and Hadfield), Church Terrace, with its Tuscan portico, and the *station* (1847) were part of the Norfolk development, but their house, Glossop Hall, has gone. In the valley bottom various mills of c 1800–50. **New Mills**, 8m S, is another small industrial town, on the Sheffield–Manchester railway, the last of the trans-Pennine railway routes to be built (1894). *Town Hall* (1871), Spring Bank, with clock tower. *St. James's Church* (1878; W.S. Barber), with contemporary almshouses grouped at the W end, has painted decoration inside. **Whaley Bridge**, to the S, has a similar industrial feel. The junction here between the Peak Forest Canal and the Cromford and High Peak Railway is in a unique single building (1832) with boats entering at one end and trains the other.

ILKESTON. A609 8m W of Nottingham. Small industrial town on a hilltop. In the Market Square, red brick *Town Hall* (1867; R.C. Sutton) and *Library* (1904; Hunter and Woodhouse), a good free style building with Baroque touches. Off the Market Place, *Scala Cinema* (1913), a rare unaltered early cinema. Across the valley to the NE of the town, the disused *Bennerley Viaduct* (1878; R. Johnson), lattice-girder construction, one of the last two all-metal viaducts left. In the Shipley country park, NW of the town, the *Home Farm* in one corner is a delightful High Victorian model farm (1860; W.E. Nesfield) with circular tower and pretty roofscape, gradually being rescued from total dereliction. 5m S of Ilkeston, **Long Eaton**, industrial town notable for its tenement *lace factories*, let out in small units and are characterised by curved external staircase towers. The best survivors are on the Erewash canal, W of centre, and at **Sandiacre** and **Draycott**, to N and W. In the Market Place, two very odd buildings, *York Chambers* and *No. 38*, next door, both of 1903 by the local partnership of Gorman and Ross, Arts and Crafts style but with a continental flavour quite unusual in England. Gorman and Ross also designed the *Library* (1906), nearby in Tamworth Rd, with big eaves reminiscent of Frank Lloyd Wright's work and a band of bright tiles beneath.

MATLOCK. A6 18m N of Derby. Victorian spa town spread out along the Derwent valley. Matlock Bank is the modern centre dominated by the *County Hall*, a vast grey pile built as a hydropathic hotel in two parts (1867 and 1885) by John Smedley, local industrialist and spa entrepreneur. Under the French pavilioned tower of 1885, a full-height hall with grand stair, two fine rooms on the ground floor. The scale of the operation can be judged from the size of the covered exercise area, now the County Archives. At the top of the hill, the two turrets of *Rockside* (1903–06; Parker and Unwin), Wellington St, a rival hydro, now College of Education. Further down, *Town Hall* (1899), a late example of the Italianate type. Over the bridge, Matlock Bridge has a later 19C shopping street. The road runs S to Matlock Bath, the original spa, with pretty villas climbing the hillside, picturesque walks, where the Swiss atmosphere so much remarked on by visitors is still discernible, and a late 19C pavilion in the valley. The *station* (c 1885) is decidedly Swiss. On the hillside, *Chapel of St. John* (1897; Guy Dawber), tiny chapel built into the rock, pink stone, simply detailed. High on the cliff-top to the E, dominating many views of Matlock, *Riber Castle* (1862–64), John Smedley's own fantasy castle, stands stark and square like a child's drawing. Ruined now, it houses a zoo and nature reserve.

Cromford Station and Master's House (c 1860; G.H. Stokes)

S of Matlock Bath, **Cromford** is the heartland of the industrial revolution of the late 18C with the first water-powered cotton mill, Arkwright's Mill, founded 1771, in Mill Rd, and, on A6, Arkwright's Masson Mills of 1783. In the village, late 18C industrial housing, notably in North St. At the end of Mill Rd, delightful *station* and station-house (c 1860; G.H. Stokes) with French pavilion roofs. On the steep slopes to the SE, at **Holloway**, *Leahurst* was rebuilt 1825 for Florence Nightingale's father. Her family were mill-owners here. *Christ Church* (1903; P.H. Currey) is Arts and Crafts Gothic with central tower. *Lea Wood* (1874; W.E. Nesfield), to W, is an early work in the Domestic Revival manner pioneered by Shaw and Nesfield, stone with hipped roof and half-timbered full-height bays. At **Crich**, to SE, the *Tramway Museum* has filled a disused quarry with trams from various cities and is gradually rescuing buildings to create an appropriate setting. The facade of the 1752 Derby Assembly Rooms is the most prominent feature. 3m E, at **South Wingfield**, the disused *station* (1840; F. Thompson) is one of the most attractive of early railway designs, in a version of the stripped classical designs then current for gentlemen's lodges. The North Midland Railway from Derby to Chesterfield with bridges by G. Stephenson and stations by Thompson (mostly now gone) was notable for the high quality of its works. Further S, the bridge and tunnel at **Ambergate**, the ten road bridges over the line in Belper, and the *Milford Tunnel*, S of Belper, all of 1839–40 by Stephenson. **Belper**, 10m S of Matlock, was the base of the Strutt family, textile manufacturers from the later 18C. William

Strutt pioneered iron-framed construction c 1800, the forerunner of
19C and modern framed building technology. Most of the original
Strutt mills by the river have been replaced, the dominant building
now the *East Mill* (1912), more typical of Lancashire. *Christ Church*
(1849; H.I. Stevens), Bridge Foot, was built for the mill workers. Hammerbeam roof. In Long Row, some of the least altered workers'
housing of c 1800, the Strutts being pioneers in this respect also. N of
the town, *Cemetery* (1857; E. Holmes), prominent from the railway
and a model of the type with picturesque planting and two chapels
linked by a central spire. 1857 was the year when more cemeteries
were laid out than ever before or since. 3m SW of Cromford,
Wirksworth, a pretty stone town with fine *church* restored by G.G.
Scott (1870–76). The prominent Gothic *Town Hall* (1871; B. Bradley)
was built for the freemasons. In St. John's St, *No. 6* (1842) is a notably
well-detailed small palazzo, originally the Savings Bank. 3m S, *Alton
Manor*, an early domestic work by G.G. Scott (1846) in relatively plain
mullioned-window style.

N of Matlock is **Darley Dale**, built up with villas and hotels as part of
the expansion of Matlock. It had its own hydro, now St. Elphin's
School, but its most prominent buildings are thanks to Sir Joseph
Whitworth, the Manchester armaments manufacturer, who owned
Stancliffe Hall (1872; T.R. Smith: 1879; E.M. Barry), a large gabled
house just N of the town. The *Whitworth Institute and Hotel* (1892; J.
and R. Beaumont), Dale Road, was an expensive social centre in free
Elizabethan style built in memory of Sir Joseph. In the parish *church*,
excellent early Morris glass (1862–63) in the S transept and a late
Burne-Jones design (1892) in the E window.

DEVON

BARNSTAPLE. A361 50m W of Taunton. By the bridge, in the Square, Greek Revival *Bridge Buildings* (c 1840), curved fronted. In the High St, Tuscan-pilastered *N Devon Dispensary* (c 1835) and *Guildhall* (1826; T. Lee) with *Market* and *Butchers Row* added c 1840 (R.D. Gould), the market with iron columns and roof. The parish *church* was restored (1866–82; G.G. Scott) with much 19C glass, E window by Wailes, S aisle E window by Dixon (1879). Good early 19C terraces to SW of the Square, A361. At **Fremington**, A39 3m W, *Fremington House* (c 1900; E. Newton) brick Queen Anne to neo-Georgian style house. *Church* rebuilt 1867 by G.G. Scott. 5m S of Barnstaple, NE of **Chapelton**, A377, *Hall* (1847–50; P. and P.C. Hardwick) Elizabethan style mansion in stone with full-scale great hall.

13m N of Barnstaple, A361, **Ilfracombe**, Victorian seaside resort with attractive terraces of yellow- and red-brick houses climbing up the slope, the 19C town with pleasure gardens running up to the *church* of St. Philip and St. James (1856; J. Hayward), the spire the main landmark of the lower town. *Pavilion* in the gardens (1888; W.H. Gould). Some early 19C terraces on the hillside but most of the 19C building has the attractive bargeboarding and painted timber work of the mid to later 19C. The parish *church*, well inland, is medieval, heavily restored with 19C glass, E window by Hardman, S aisle E by Willement, N aisle E by O'Connor, and one N window W of tower by Lavers and Barraud (1862). Attractive lychgate and vestry added c 1895 (H. Wilson), free Perp. 4m W of Ilfracombe, at **Mortehoe**, *church* with Arts and Crafts mosaic figures on the chancel arch (1903; S. Image). At **Woolacombe**, just S, *church* (1911; W. Caroe), free Gothic simply detailed externally, the chancel with narrow aisles divided off by wooden posts stained green.

21m NE of Barnstaple, A39, **Lynton**, late Victorian seaside resort dramatically sited on the cliff W of Lynmouth bay. Large Victorian hotels, notably the *Valley of the Rocks Hotel* (1888; R. Plumbe) gabled and turretted. Turn of the century *cliff railway* down to Lynmouth. The parish *church* was largely rebuilt (1893–94; J.D. Sedding) with very attractive Art Nouveau leading to the windows. Chancel added 1905 (H. Wilson) in an elemental Byzantine or Early Christian style reminiscent of the work of Lethaby. *Town Hall* (1898; Read and Macdonald) picturesque with half-timber and ornamental balconies. At the W end, *RC church and convent* (1908; L. Stokes), the church tunnel-vaulted and plastered in an Italian Renaissance mode but the window tracery Byzantinesque. E end with lunette window set high over elaborate marble altar. Low marble-panelled walls flanking sanctuary steps. **Lynmouth**, below, was discovered by visitors early in the 19C, Shelley came in 1812. Some Gothic bargeboarded villas and the large rambling *Tors Hotel*.

BIDEFORD. A39 9m SW of Barnstaple. Port on the W side of the Tor-ridge estuary. On the Quay, *Town Hall* (1850; R.D. Gould) Italianate and *Library* (1906; A. Dunn). Across the bridge, *Royal Hotel*, partly 17C, where Charles Kingsley wrote 'Westward Ho!'. 3m N at **Appledore**, pretty seaport with *church* of 1838, plaster-vaulted inside. **Westward Ho!**, 3m SW of Appledore, was a speculative resort founded in the 1860s and named after Kingsley's novel. Principal hotel, church and houses all in yellow brick. The United Services College, now *Kipling Terrace*, was a school mainly for children of parents in colonial service. Rudyard Kipling was educated there and used it as the setting for 'Stalky & Co ' (1899). 2m NE of Bideford, at **Westleigh**, *Tapely Park* (1901; J. Belcher) brick and stone neo-Georgian house of considerable scale. 9m W of Bideford, off A39, **Clovelly**, probably the most picturesque fishing village in Britain, much of the character not fortuitous but the result of careful management through the 19C and 20C by the Hamlyn family of Clovelly Court. Charles Kingsley's father was rector here, and the village described in 'Westward Ho!'. 6m SE of Bideford, **Great Torrington**, with central *Market House* (1842) pedimented with cupola.

EXETER. Exeter *Cathedral* was restored by G.G. Scott (1870– 77), chancel fittings and pulpit by Scott. The *Bishops Palace*, to SE, is largely of 1848 (E. Christian). Central Exeter was devastated by bombs, the principal 19C survivors in the centre are in Queen St, N of High St, the *Higher Market* (1837; G. Dymond and C. Fowler) a long Greek Doric facade in granite. The contemporary *2–8 Queen St* was rebuilt in replica (1985). Further up, *Albert Memorial Museum* (1865; J. Hayward) inspired by Ruskin and by the Oxford Museum. The building is Italian Gothic in emphatically contrasted stone colours with plate-traceried windows and a triple-arched recessed entry. Albert statue inside by E.B. Stephens. Beyond the city walls to N, Northernhay, laid out as a park with 19C statues. From the park can be seen, further N, the *Prison*, New North Road, front of 1790, the main part of 1853 (J. Hayward). W of Queen St, North St leads out over the *Iron Bridge* (1834) to St. David's Hill. *St. David's Church* (1897–1900; W.D. Caroe) is a major work in the free Gothic evolved from English Perp. sources at the turn of the century. Characteristic play of curved details, especially the shallow arches over the windows and curved parapets, giving a slightly Art Nouveau flavour. Broad traceried E and W windows, the W end framed by turrets, reflect the plan with aisles compressed to wall passages. Fine landmark tower. Glass by Kempe and Tower. *St. David's Station* (1864; Lloyd and Fox) has a long classical front screen wall and unusual tall glazed clerestory over the platform behind. S of the High St, in South St, *RC church* (1883; L. Stokes). In Magdalen Rd, *Wynard's Almshouses*, 15C chapel and quadrangle of Gothic cottages (1863). On The 'Quay, by the river, *Maritime Museum* with a collection of some 100 sailing and steam ships. Off Magdalen Rd, SE of the centre, early Victorian development in Wonford Rd with later Victorian villas further E (Victoria Park Rd). In Victoria Park Rd, *Exeter School* (1877–87; W. Butterfield) red-brick Gothic, unusual in plan, a six-storey corner tower for staff accommodation with classrooms, studies and dormitories in a wing running N and dining-hall over kitchen in the W wing. Repetitive simplified Gothic window details and the main mass softened with stone banding. 3m E of Exeter, N of **Clyst St. Mary**, *Bishops Court*, medieval bishops' house remodelled c 1865 (W. White) with plate-traceried Gothic windows, turrets and stencil-decorated interiors. W. White rebuilt the *church* at **Clyst Honiton**, A30, 1m NE.

8m SE of Exeter, A377, **Exmouth**, resort town developed from the late 18C. On Foxhole Hill, *The Barn* (1896; E.S. Prior) highly original butterfly plan Arts and Crafts house in massive stone with slate-hung gables to the centre and splendid circular stone stacks to the wings. Originally thatched. Prior used local materials with conscious naturalism, so that the main sandstone blocks are interspersed with large rounded pebbles and other smaller stones creating an effect something like an ancient and much patched sea-wall. Both fronts are symmetrical dominated by the main gable, the entrance front with a stair tower reaching up into the overhang, the garden front with a verandah roof on granite pillars. 8m S of Exeter, A379, at **Starcross**, by the shore, *Pumping Station* (1846; Brunel), Italianate stone building with truncated campanile, a relic of Brunel's unsuccessful attempt to haul trains by atmospheric propulsion. The pumping stations were to create a vacuum in a continuous iron pipe that sucked a piston attached to the trains. The system worked, drawing trains at up to 60 or 70 miles an hour, but ultimately failed for lack of adequate technology or materials. 3m W of Starcross, B3381, *Mamhead House* (1828; A. Salvin), one of the first Tudor style houses of the 19C to have accurately designed Tudor detail. Ornate chimney stacks, pinnacles and oriels, set in a fine 18C landscaped park. 4m S of Starcross, **Dawlish**, resort laid out in the early 19C with Regency cottages each side of the Dawlish Water. *Stonelands* (1817) W of the centre belonged to Sir J. Rennie, the engineer, Greek Doric villa. *Luscombe Castle*, to W, is picturesque castellated Gothic (1800; J. Nash) with chapel added 1862 (G.G. Scott), banded stone interior. 3m S of Dawlish, **Teignmouth**, resort town, Regency beginnings, with *Den Crescent* (1826; A. Patey) the centrepiece facing the sea. Two curved terraces framing the original Assembly Rooms. Two remarkable Gothic churches, also by A. Patey, *St. Michael's* (1823) neo-Norman and *St. James'* (1820) plaster-vaulted octagon.

9m SW of Exeter, A38, at **Chudleigh Knighton**, *Pitt House* (1845; G.G. Scott) symmetrical neo-Jacobean and *church* (1842; Scott and Moffatt). 2m NW, A382, at **Bovey Tracey**, *St. John's Church* (1852; R.C. Carpenter) S of the river, neat High Church chapel with complete contemporary fittings and glass. Near the parish church, *House of Mercy* (c 1860; Woodyer) Gothic conventual buildings with frescoed chapel. 6m NW of Bovey Tracey, at **North Bovey**, *Manor House Hotel* (1907; D. Blow) very large Jacobean style country house, all in granite, superbly detailed. Built for Lord Hambleden, director of W.H. Smith, but a railway hotel since 1929. To N, 4m N of **Moretonhampstead**, *Castle Drogo* (1910–30; Lutyens) (NT) a twentieth-century castle built for J. Drewe, with a fortune made from the Home and Colonial Stores. Drewe wanted a real castle, chose a site that would suit any medieval baron, overlooking the Teign, and built it in granite. The result is as dramatic a house as any in Britain; the castle crowns the ridge, walls rising sheer with a minimum of carved decoration, the windows not breaking the wall plane so that the whole building appears modelled from the solid. The roofs are flat, behind a battlemented parapet, and the main angles are chamfered, increasing the fortress quality, as each angle suggests a defensible tower in a curtain wall. The interiors are equally splendid, the stair hall granite lit by a huge mullion-and-transom bay window. 7m NW of Exeter, A377, at **Crediton**, in the *church* mosaic memorial at the E end of the nave (1911; W. Caroe) to Redvers Buller, Boer War general.

PLYMOUTH. Naval town heavily damaged by bombing, the centre almost entirely reconstructed. On Royal Parade, *Guildhall* (1870–74; E.W. Godwin with Norman and Hine), High Victorian Gothic with excellent sculpture by H. Hems on the Great Hall. Reconstructed in simpler form after bombing. To W, in Old George St, striped Gothic *clock tower* (1862) and exuberant Bath stone curved-fronted former *bank* (1889), now a pub. To S and SW, remnants of the late Regency stucco terraces of Plymouth, in *The Crescent* (c 1833; G. Wightwick), Athenaeum St and Lockyer St. On corner of Millbay Rd and Citadel

Rd, *Duke of Cornwall Hotel* (1863), Plymouth's finest Victorian Gothic building, highly elaborate with steep roofs, gables, chimneys and a polygonal corner tower. Much carved detail. Built to serve the vanished GWR station and Millbay Docks. S of Citadel Rd, overlooking the Hoe, stucco terraces, *The Esplanade* (1836; G. Wightwick), the much more florid *Elliott Terrace* (c 1860) and the Grand Hotel. On the Hoe, *statue* of Sir Francis Drake (1884; Boehm). W of the centre, in Union St, *The Academy*, former Palace Theatre (1898; Wimperis and Arber), splendid terracotta and tile exterior with two panels of scenes from the Spanish Armada and nautical touches to the rest of the decoration. N of Union St, prominent on the ridge, the tall thin spire of the *RC Cathedral* (1858; J.A. Hansom), Wyndham St, and heavy tower of *St. Peter's Church*, Wyndham Square, with copper roof. Tower added 1906 (G. Fellowes Prynne) to large church of 1880 and 1849. N of Wyndham Square, in North Rd W, *St. Dunstan's Abbey* (1850–60; W. Butterfield), grey stone Gothic, a long range to the street, severe with band of quatrefoil openings, hipped dormers and tall stacks. At the E end a more elaborate gatehouse with tower-like main block behind. Built for an Anglican sisterhood. To E, Patna Place leads S to Harwell St with fine *vicarage* (1887; J.D. Sedding) to the derelict All Saints' Church, roughcast on stone base with leaded windows, freely detailed, the centrepiece framed by half-octagonal turrets carrying an overhanging roof. For this date remarkably free of period detail. NE of centre, at Drake Circus, *Museum and Library* (1907–10; Thornely and Rooke), Edwardian Baroque. To NE, on North Hill, prominent spire of *Sherwell Congregational church* (1862–64; Paull and Ayliffe), High Victorian Gothic with some polychrome touches. Further up, *St. Matthias' Church* (1887; Hine and Rodgers) with landmark Perp. style tower. On Mutley Plain, *Baptist church* (c 1900), eclectic mixture of motifs, Renaissance to Baroque with French pavilion roofs to the twin towers.

W of the centre of Plymouth the naval towns of Stonehouse and Devonport. In **Stonehouse**, on Devil's Point, *Royal William Victualling Yard* (1830–35; Sir J. Rennie), monumental grey granite group in classical to Baroque style built as the principal food stores for the navy. Fine triumphal entry from Cremyll St crowned by a statue of William IV. **Devonport** to W, was severely bombed. The small Greek *Town Hall* and Egyptian former Library (1823–24; Foulston) survive in Ker St of what was a most individual Regency ensemble. In Duke St, to N, grand Italianate former *Mechanics Institute* (1850; A. Norman) stands next to the old *Library* (1844; A. Norman), also palazzo style but shorn of most of its detail. At the foot of Duke St, now within the dockyard, campanile *tower* of the old *Markets* (1852; J.P. St. Aubyn). At the S end of George St, on Mount Wise, overlooking the harbour, heroic monument to Captain Scott (1913; A. Hodge) complete with protecting angel. N of Devonport was the main 19C extension of the dockyard, the *Steam Factory* (1846–48; C. Barry), Keyham Road. Best seen from the Torpoint ferry are the two massive brick chimneys disguised as campanile towers. *Clock tower* feature at S end off Keyham Rd.

Like Portsmouth, Plymouth had an extensive system of fortification built c 1860 during the scare of French invasion. Drake's Island off the Hoe was fortified and a string of *forts* built from the Tamar at Ernesettle to the Plym at Laira across the N side of the town, massive earthworks built up around sunken granite gun emplacements and barracks. To NW of the town, next to the A38 Tamar Bridge, *Royal Albert Bridge* (1857–59; Brunel) carrying the railway some 100ft over the river to give headroom for naval vessels. Brunel's most remarkable

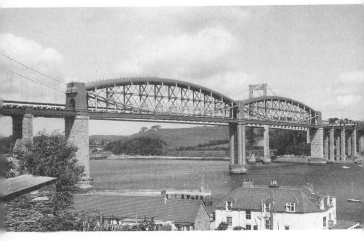

Royal Albert Bridge (1857–59; I.K. Brunel), Plymouth

bridge design, two 461ft curved oval wrought-iron tubes on massive stone piers carry the track suspended beneath. The design thus combines prestressed and prefabricated main members with a suspension bridge. Brunel's name is proudly over the first pier.

6m E of Plymouth, A379, at **Yealmpton**, *church* (1848–49; Butterfield) with Butterfield's first polychrome interior, the arcade piers in alternating grey Devon marbles, the walls with inlaid linear patterns. The complete scheme would have had fresco or tile mosaic decoration, but was not completed as the patron left the Church of England for Rome. Exceptional fittings by Butterfield including font in richly dark marbles, screen wall, pulpit, benches and tiled chancel. E window by Hardman (1857). Uncompleted small village *school* by Butterfield. At **Holbeton**, 2m SE, *church* beautifully restored (1884; J.D. Sedding) with delicate carved woodwork, stained glass by Heywood Sumner, and richly coloured chancel. 1½m NE, *Flete* (1878–83; R. Norman Shaw), castellated house in rock-faced stone grafted onto a 16C to 17C house for one of the partners in Barings Bank, the complex exterior with two big towers unlike Shaw's normal work because this was partly a recasing and carried out piecemeal. Imposing curved three-storey bow overlooking the original range, with service wing running N, a clear predecessor of Lutyens' work at Castle Drogo, Devon, in the shallow oriel, uneven crenellations and windows recessed back from the wall face. Picturesque massive chimney stack with clustered shafts. *Lodge* (1889; J.D. Sedding). At **Ermington**, to N, *church* restored 1889 (Sedding).

SIDMOUTH. B3176 14m E of Exeter. Regency seaside resort with numerous delightful villas, picturesque cottage style, Gothic and castellated with delicate wooden porches and balconies. Esplanade built after 1805. Nowhere else among early 19C resorts is the change in taste from urban terrace house to individual villas more obvious. *Fortfield Terrace* (c 1805) is the most formal terrace, *Coburg Terrace* is Gothic. The *Old Chancel House*, by Coburg Terrace, is exotically picturesque, built 1864 out of fragments of the parish church. The *church* rebuilt 1860 (W. White). Memorial window (1867; Hughes) to Queen Victoria's father, the Duke of Kent, who died at Sidmouth (1820). His house is now the *Royal Glen Hotel*, Glen Rd.

3m N of Sidmouth, A375, **Sidbury**, with large Elizabethan style *Manor House* (1879; D. Brandon), W of the village. Lodges c 1890 (W. Cave). 7m N of Sidbury, **Honiton**, A30, with long High Street on the old London–Exeter road. Parish *church* (1838; C. Fowler) thoroughly neo-Norman in detail, though the shape is the typical preaching house of the early 19C and the interior was originally focused on a massive neo-Norman pulpit. At **Monkton**, 3m NE, A30, the *church* (1863; J. Hayward) restrained Dec. with good E window (1868) by Morris. Later Morris windows in the nave. 4m SW of Honiton, **Alfington** *church* (1849; Butterfield), small brick and roughcast chapel with E window by Pugin. Much more elaborate is the *school* (1850), a delightful building with the most complicated build-up of gables, some hung with patterned tiles, some half-timbered, all in carefully considered relation with the half-hipped roof of the house section rising above. 2m SW, **Ottery St. Mary**, the *church* a version of Exeter Cathedral with transeptal towers. Restoration of the ornate reredos with new figure sculpture 1833 (E. Blore), but the main restoration was in 1849–52 by Butterfield with work by Woodyer in the Lady Chapel. Butterfield picked out the ribs of the vault in red and blue and gold and inserted stained glass by Hardman in the clerestory, E window, Lady Chapel E window and N transept E window, by O'Connor in two S windows of the Lady Chapel, by Warrington in W window and by Wailes. S transept restoration by Butterfield (1878) with glass by Gibbs. The font, in inlaid marbles with a most architectural canopy, is fully High Victorian in the exploitation of massive shapes, a square bowl on a squat round pillar with four small round columns at the angles. Effigy of Lady Coleridge (1879; F. Thrupp). Butterfield restored the church for Lord Coleridge and also altered the *Chanter's House* for him (1880–83) refacing completely the original 18C house and adding the W wing with library, red brick with half-timber and tile-hanging. 2½m SE of Honiton, at **Offwell**, village with picturesque cottages and an Italianate *tower* on Honiton Hill, all built c 1840 by Bishop Copleston of Llandaff, who lived at Offwell House.

5m W of Sidmouth, A376, at **Bicton**, *Bicton House* (1908; W. Tapper) large brick neo-Georgian enlargement of a 18C house with fine gardens open to the public. Early 19C domed glasshouses and orangery. Folly tower (1839) NW of the house. *Church* (1851; J. Hayward) Dec. By the ruins of the previous church, *Rolle Mausoleum* (1850; Pugin), a delightful work with vaulted roof, encaustic tiled floor and highly carved tomb of Lord Rolle against a traceried arch filled with carved leaf scroll, angel figures and armorial devices. Glass by Pugin. 3m S, **Budleigh Salterton**, early 19C resort, much enlarged. On the edge of **Woodbury Common**, *Coxen* (1910; E. Gimson), cottage built for one of Gimson's pupils in Gloucestershire, Basil Young, who trained as a blacksmith, inspired by the Arts and Crafts ideal. Here, true to principles, the house is hand-built of local materials, cob or compressed mud-block walls with thatched roof, though the scale is larger than any normal cob cottage, being three storeys, two within the roof. Simple leaded windows and massive slab of stone over the porch.

13m E of Sidmouth, A3052, *Rousdon* (1874; George and Vaughan), rambling flint and half-timbered mansion built for Sir H. Peek, biscuit magnate, courtyard plan with picturesque pyramid-roofed corner tower and numerous tall brick stacks in the manner of Norman Shaw. Extensive stables in similar style with a tower for a carillon clock over the entry and, beyond, *church* (c 1874; George and Vaughan), small aisleless Early French Gothic, the triple-arched N porch containing Peek's mausoleum. Numerous estate buildings and village hall (1876) probably by the same architects. 5m E, at **Uplyme**, on the Dorset border, A3070, *Woodhouse* (1879; George and Peto), gabled and tile-hung house in the style of Norman Shaw.

TAVISTOCK. A386 14m N of Plymouth. Estate town of the Dukes of Bedford, centre of a tin and lead mining district. In the centre by the Abbey ruins, *Bedford Hotel* with Gothic front of c 1825 (J. Foulston), *Town Hall* (1860) Gothic, and parish *church* with Morris glass (1876) in E window of N aisle. Statue of the 7th Duke of Bedford. Across the top of the town, granite railway *viaduct* (1890), the most prominent monument. W of the centre, *Fitzford House* rebuilt for the Dukes of Bedford (1871) with *statue* of Sir Francis Drake (1883; Boehm) outside. *RC church* (1866–67; H. Clutton), monumental in a tough Norman to Early French Gothic style, very large and elaborately carved, a far-off outrider to the churches by Clutton around Woburn. Vigorous carved arcade capitals and tall SW spire. On the NE edge of the town, *Kelly College* (1877; E. Hansom), heavy Gothic school buildings, the town founded by Admiral Kelly for the education of paupers and his descendants. 5m SW, *Calstock Viaduct* (1908), 12 arches spanning the Tamar, 117ft high, the building material concrete block jointed to look like stone. At **Yelverton**, 5m SE, A386, *church* (1913; Nicholson and Corlette) refined late Gothic with painted roofs. 8m E of Tavistock, at **Princetown**, *Dartmoor Prison*, built 1806 for French prisoners of war but mostly rebuilt as a convict prison 1850.

16m NE of Tavistock, A30, at **Okehampton**, parish *church* (1842–44; J. Hayward), an early work by the leading Exeter church architect. 5m N of Okehampton, at **Jacobstowe**, A3072, *Broomford Manor* (1870; G. Devey), stone-gabled Tudor style house. 11m NW of Okehampton, B3218, at **Halwill**, *Cottage Hospital* (1899; C.F.A. Voysey), low single-storey roughcast building, gabled with windows in stone surrounds.

TIVERTON. A396 14m N of Exeter. Wool and later lace-making town on the Exe. E of the bridge, *Town Hall* (1864; H. Lloyd) High Victorian Gothic with pavilion roofs. Lace-making began W of the river with the establishment of John Heathcoat's lace factory (1816). Terraces of original workers' cottages around and Tudor style *school* (1841). Heathcoat lived at Exleigh, an early 19C villa looking across the Exe to the church. Off Barrington St, former *workhouse* (1837–38; G.G. Scott) classical with octagonal centre. E of the town, *Blundell's School* (1880–82; J. Hayward), Gothic school buildings with chapel. 2m N of Tiverton, *•Knightshayes Court* (1869–73; W. Burges) (NT), fine High Victorian Gothic house in red stone with bold plate-traceried windows and a near symmetrical main front framed by gabled wings with tall bay windows. The design avoids picturesque excess in favour of a strong outline pierced by grid-like openings becoming fanciful only in the roof dormers. Burges' complete romantic scheme of painted decoration and carved woodwork inside was only partly begun before Sir J. Heathcoat-Amory turned to the cheaper firm of J. Crace but the fine great hall, staircase and carved fireplaces survive, while the National Trust have embarked on a programme of uncovering those decorative details later painted out. Stable quadrangle and lodge by Burges. 5m NE of Tiverton, at **Huntsham**, *Huntsham Court* (1869; B. Ferrey), stone gabled mansion, Tudor style. 4m NW of Tiverton, at **Stoodleigh**, *Stoodleigh Court* (1882; George and Peto) free Tudor style.

Knightshayes Court (1869–73; W. Burges), Tiverton

TORQUAY. A379 24m S of Exeter. Resort town developed from the early 19C on the picturesque slopes overlooking Torbay, the pace of development controlled by the Palk family, owners of the manor from 1768. Their architects from the early 19C were the Harveys, J. Harvey and his sons J.T. and W. Harvey. The style of the town developed from early 19C terraces close to the Inner Harbour to richer Victorian terraces and Italianate and Gothic villas, almost all stuccoed, climbing the hills above the bay and spreading over towards Babbacombe to E. At the harbour, *Pavilion* (1911; H. Garrett) with curved copper roof, *Vaughan Parade* (c 1830; J. Harvey) and *Victoria Parade* (c 1850), behind the Strand, *Higher Terrace* (1811; J. Harvey), convex plan. At Meadfoot, E of the harbour, *Hesketh Crescent*, (1846; J.T. and W. Harvey), the grandest Torquay terrace with columned centrepiece and iron first-floor verandah. Italianate villas in semi- tropical gardens on the hill to the E and along the Marine Drive to Babbacombe. On Waldon Hill NW of the harbour villas of the 1850s and 1860s with *St. Luke's Church* (1863; A.W. Blomfield), St. Luke's Rd, at the top, High Victorian with NW turret. The town centre is Union St with *Town Hall* (1911; T. Davison) Edwardian Baroque and former *Library* (1906; Harris and Towse) with domed entry attached. Nearby, *St. Mary Magdalene's Church* (1844–54; A. Salvin) with prominent spire and chancel elaborately refitted after 1878 by G.G. Scott and Temple Moore, by Scott the fine organ case, by Moore the reredos (1889) and marble chancel screens and pulpit (1905). In Market St, *Market Hall* (1852; J.T. Harvey). Torquay's outstanding Victorian church is *St. John's Church* (1861–85; G.E. Street), Montpelier Terrace, with prominent saddleback roofed tower (1885). Interior lavishly fitted in coloured marbles with marble column shafts and finely carved capitals. Wall-paintings in the chancel by Burne-Jones who also designed the E and W windows, mosaic work by Salviati and fine font by Street with ornate ironwork to the font cover. Lady Chapel decorated by Sedding (1890).

At **Torre**, N of centre, *All Saints' Church* (1884–90; J.L. Pearson), Bamfylde Rd, with stone-vaulted aisles and stone transverse arches to the nave, the interior in red sandstone with Bath stone dressings. At **Chalston**, W of the centre, *St. Matthew's Church* (1896; Nicholson and Corlette) late Gothic in the manner of Bodley. At **Babbacombe**, over the headland to NE, some early 19C villas and terraces. **All Saints' Church* (1865–74; W. Butterfield), St. Alban's Rd, Butterfield's most complex exercise in polychrome decoration, one of the masterpieces of Victorian church building. Grey stone exterior with subtle contrasts of colour and texture, elaborately patterned tower and spire. Inside the whole church glows with contrasted stones and marbles. The walls of the nave, over a characteristically sturdy arcade, are patterned with raised stone diagonal lines and sunk foiled panels, the walling banded in red and grey and interspersed with seemingly irregular diagonals of white stone with incised black decoration. The effect is to dissolve the apparent solidity of the walling and carry the eye upward and forward to the richer chancel with its marble floor and painted roof. The font and pulpit are among the richest of Butterfield's marble designs, almost Arabic in the colouring and play of planes. Lectern by Butterfield. Chancel glass by A. Gibbs. In Priory Rd, *RC church* (1865; J.A. Hansom) with tall spire. 7m N of Torquay, A379, **Shaldon** and, across the Teign, Regency **Teignmouth**, with attractive villas. By the bridge, *church* (1893–1902; E. Sedding), free Gothic in banded stone combining Gothic and Renaissance forms. Marble fittings.

9m NW of Torquay, **Newton Abbot**, with early Victorian development in the centre, *Globe Hotel* (c 1840), *Town Hall* (1848), and attractive suburbs laid out from c 1840 by the architect J.W. Rowell around Devon Square and Courtenay Park on the hill S of the town. 2m S of Newton Abbot, at **Abbotskerswell**, E of village, *St. Augustine's Priory* (1863 and later; J.A. Hansom) Gothic conventual buildings with octagonal-towered chapel. S of the village, *Court Grange*, gabled and turretted mansion of 1865 and 1895. 7m W of Newton Abbot, A38, **Ashburton**, market town with Italianate *Market Hall* (1850; A. Norman) in North St and Ionic porticoed *Methodist chapel* (1835) in West St. 3m SW, at **Buckfast**, *Buckfast Abbey*, Benedictine abbey founded from France in 1882 on the site of a Cistercian abbey. Norman to Early French Gothic church (1907–32; F.A. Walters) of considerable size, largely built by the monks. Stone-vaulted interior with triforium and clerestory, impressive though, as in Truro Cathedral, the smooth Bath stone with prominent mortar joints gives a mechanical feel. 3m S of Ashburton, at **Landscove**, *church* (1849–51; J.L. Pearson), an early work, Puginian with a sharp broach spire. *Vicarage* (1851; Pearson). For the Champernowne family Pearson also rebuilt the *church* at **Dartington** 6m S of Ashburton, A384. The original church was restored 1853 but in 1878–80 a new church was built reusing much of the stonework of the old, the tower wholly new.

4m SW of Torquay, **Paignton**, resort town, mostly Victorian, without the gentility of Torquay. The Civic Centre occupies *Oldway* (c 1900), American classical style mansion designed for himself by Paris Singer, son of the sewing-machine magnate I.M. Singer. Monumental marble staircase. 6m S of Paignton, **Brixham**, picturesque former fishing port. *All Saints' Church* by the harbour was practically rebuilt from 1885–1906 (Somers Clarke and Micklethwaite) as a memorial to H.F. Lyte, vicar 1826–47, author of several famous hymns, 'Abide with me' and

'Praise my soul, the King of Heaven' the best remembered. A carillon in the church tower plays the tunes three times a day. Lyte lived at *Berry Head House*, now hotel, and wrote 'Abide with me' there in 1847 watching the sunset over Torbay. 8m S of Paignton, reached by ferry across the Dart, **Dartmouth**, with the *Royal Naval College* hugely red and white on the hilltop behind. The college buildings (1899–1905; Sir A. Webb) are symmetrical with central great hall, chapel and dining-hall terminating the wings lavishly dressed in white Portland stone. The style is freely late 17C mixing Baroque detail with mullion and transom windows, the overwhelming length not satisfactorily balanced by the vertical accents, a domed tower over the centre, cupolas and end towers. Late Gothic tracery to the chapel.

DORSET

BOURNEMOUTH. Resort town developed from early 19C, but predominantly after 1860. Bournemouth's natural attraction is the series of small steep valleys, or chines, running down to the sea, the main one on the line of the Bourne river landscaped as the centre of the resort c 1850, now the Upper, Central and Lower Gardens. At the foot of the Lower Gardens, *pier* (1878; E. Birch). The centre is E of the Gardens in Old Christchurch Rd. Just S, *St. Peter's Church* (1854–79; G.E. Street), first of the series of churches promoted by A.M. Bennett, High Church vicar of St. Peter's to 1880. The church was built piecemeal, W end (1854–59) leaving intact a S aisle of 1851 from the previous church, E end with vaulting and rich alabaster and marble arcades (1860–64), tower (1869) and finally the W transept and spire (1879) rising 202ft. Rich Victorian and early 20C fittings, glass largely by Clayton and Bell, one by Morris (1864) in S chapel. Painted decoration by Clayton and Bell in sanctuary, roof painting by Bodley. Fittings by Street include the pulpit exhibited at the 1862 exhibition. From Gervis Place opposite, *Arcade* (1866–73; H. Joy) to Old Christchurch Rd. From the Square, Richmond Hill runs NW past *RC church* (1872; H. Clutton: 1896; A. Pilkington). St. Stephen's Rd runs W to *St. Stephen's Church* (1881–1908; J.L. Pearson) built as a memorial to the Rev A.M. Bennett, the interior as fine as any Pearson designed. It is fully vaulted with a broad high nave narrowed to an apsed chancel and with double aisles each side, all these also vaulted, the apse vault especially fine with the outer walls and main piers separated by a narrow ambulatory. The spatial effects and technical virtuosity are stunning. Glass by Clayton and Bell. Beyond, *Town Hall* (1880; A. Bedborough), built as an hotel, and *Hospital* (1855; E.B. Lamb), neither particularly distinguished. S of The Square, in Exeter Rd and Bath Rd, some of the earliest buildings, the *Royal Exeter Hotel* the first villa of Bournemouth (1811), much enlarged, and *Royal Bath Hotel*, incorporating a stuccoed building of 1837 (B. Ferrey). In Russell-Cotes Rd, *Russell-Cotes Museum* housed in East Cliff (1894; J. Fogerty) Sir M. Russell-Cotes' villa. Most atmospheric museum, the rooms still much as they were when completed. Outside, a geological terrace of some 200 different sorts of rock. Bath Rd continues E to Lansdowne and *Further Education College and Library* (1911–14; F.W. Lacey) Baroque style. Behind, in Gervis Rd East, *St. Swithun's Church* (1876 and 1891; R. Norman Shaw), the nave of 1891 a single broad space lit by a broad W window on the model of Shaw's Latimer Rd church, Kensington, London.

Christchurch Rd (A35) runs E to **Boscombe**, a separate suburb with villas and hotels over Boscombe Chine, *Chine Hotel* (1873; R.W Edis), Boscombe Spa Rd, and *Burlington Hotel* (1893; T.E. Collcutt), Owls Rd, in good free style. On Christchurch Rd, *St. John's Church* (1893–95; J.O. Scott), flint and stone, and *Hippodrome* (1891–94; Lawson and Donkin), part of a single development with arcade, hotel and shops, florid brick and stone. Interior of music-hall type with balconies on iron columns. To N, Palmerston Rd leads to St. Clement's Rd, *St. Clement's Church* (1871–73; J.D. Sedding), exceptional work for its date, the broad E and W windows with free tracery becoming a hallmark of late 19C Gothic. The tower with its delicate stonework was redesigned by H. Wilson (1890–92). Inside full scheme of decoration, W window by Holiday, E window and Lady Chapel glass by Westlake, lectern by Sedding as also the fine carved stalls. *School* by Sedding.

Adjoining, *Convent of the Sisters of Bethany* (1874 and 1878; R. Norman Shaw) built for an Anglican sisterhood. Two main ranges, the Industrial School (1874) and the sisters' wing (1878) both remarkable for being built in concrete as an economy. The Industrial School is a single rectangle with bold stacks on the outside walls and a great roof that sweeps down to embrace the chimney-breasts, punctuated by large hipped dormers. Tile-hanging disguises the concrete on the first floor. The sisters' wing has exposed concrete to full height on the stair tower. To S, in Knole Rd, *The Knole* (1872–73; Sedding), red brick with gatehouse motif to the entrance.

On Christchurch Rd to E, at **Pokesdown**, *St. James' Church* (1857 and 1870; G.E. Street), a minor work in banded stone with apse, much enlarged 1931. Apse glass by Clayton and Bell. **Southbourne**, to S, was originally a separate resort laid out 1857. By the church, *Vicarage* (1907) and *Parish Hall* (1904) by G. Livesay in free Queen Anne style. By Livesay also, *St. Katharine's Home* (1910) in Church Rd. In Belle Vue Rd, *Foxholes* (1874; F.P. Cockerell) large and bleak stucco villa for H. Reeve, editor of the Edinburgh Review, and *Nos 108 and 257* (c 1900; J. Brewerton) houses in Voysey manner. At **Christchurch** to E, in the Priory, marble monument under tower to Shelley (1854; H. Weekes), romanticised Pietà with the drowned poet resting on the lap of a maiden. The altar table is an early piece of carved furniture by Pugin (1831). His wife (died 1832) is commemorated by a Pugin brass in front of the Berkeley Chantry. E window by O'Connor, NE window by Lavers and Barraud. In the transepts two early paintings by J.E. Millais, 1847. 2m E, at Highcliffe, *Highcliffe Castle* (1830–34; W.J. Donthorn) ruinous romantic Gothic mansion built for Lord Stuart de Rothesay, a folly on the scale of Fonthill with great vaulted porch and stair tower. Incorporated into the building is late French Gothic stonework of superb quality, mostly retrieved by Lord Stuart from Les Andelys in Normandy. In Waterford Rd, *Greystones* (1910–11; E.S. Prior) rubble-stone house in Georgian vernacular manner with great hipped roof and high chimneys, simple leaded casement windows flush with the wall, in the manner of Philip Webb. Less quirky than Prior's earlier houses but details like the diamond shaped windows in the roof and the roof swept forward over an open loggia are quite personal.

NW of Bournemouth, on Wallisdown Rd, *Talbot Village*, model village developed from 1835 with brick cottages, schools (1860; C. Creeke) and *almshouses* (1862; Creeke). *Church* (1868; Evans and Fletcher). W of Bournemouth, A35 runs towards Poole. At beginning of Poole Rd, *St. Michael's Church* (1873; R. Norman Shaw), the best feature the tower (1899; J.O. Scott). Roads run off S to the various chines running down to the sea lined with villas. **Branksome Park** was built up mostly in 1880s. On The Avenue, *Cerne Abbas* (c 1890) red-brick Gothic, very hefty, and some neat c 1900 houses in the roughcast style of Voysey, *No. 23* (c 1905; J. Brewerton), *White House* (1908; R.H. Haslam) and the *Teak House* (1899; A.W. Jarvis and R.H. Haslam), tall flat roughcast tower with stone oriels added 1914. To SW, at **Canford Cliffs**, in Haven Rd, *St. Ann's Hospital* (1910; R.W. Schultz), sanatorium built to suggest a country house, brick with shaped gables and splayed wings. *Compton Acres*, Canford Cliffs Rd, is a villa of 1914 with famous gardens (open to public) laid out from 1919. Off the main A35, at **Branksome**, *St. Aldhelm's Church* (1892; Bodley and Garner), St. Aldhelm's Rd, long three-gabled Perp. style work with the wagon roofs and broad end windows typical of Bodley's late works.

Parkstone, to W, is outer suburb of Poole. On Bournemouth Rd, A35,

* *St. Osmund's Church* (1913–16; E.S. Prior) in Byzantine style following a chancel already built (1904), but Prior's Byzantine is infused with an Arts and Crafts emphasis on texture and wholly inventive delight in pattern-making with the simplest of materials, brick. The brick of the W front is handmade and so varied in colour that the surface ripples unevenly, and the surfaces are all moulded, octagonal towers articulated with rounded shafts, and a main front embossed with diamond patterns surrounding a wheel window with brick arcade over and similar brick balcony strung across a wide segmental arch over the door. The arch, window and doorframe are in terracotta, mechanically hard by contrast. Interior more conventionally basilican with bright terracotta capitals. Reinforced concrete vaults to the aisles. In Church Rd, *St. Peter's Church* (1877–92; J.L. Pearson) tall EE style, the chancel a modification of work begun 1876 (F. Rogers) that proved unsound. Stone vaulting to the aisles, timber to the main roofs. Screen and High Altar by J.L. Pearson, other fittings by F.L. Pearson who completed the W end. S of Bournemouth Rd, in Liliput Rd, *church* with screen, organ case and stalls by Bodley (1906) and Art Nouveau triptych in marble and silver (c 1905; A.G. Walker). In **Poole** itself, early 19C warehouses on The Quay and Georgian Gothic parish *church* (1820). In the harbour, **Brownsea Island**, with *Brownsea Castle* at E tip, much castellated with fragments of a castle of 1547 encased in additions of 1820, 1852 and 1896. The *church* is filled with collected items of sculpture and woodwork brought in by Lord W. Cavendish-Bentinck in late 19C.

BRIDPORT. A35 15m W of Dorchester. In East St, Portland stone fronted *Literary and Scientific Institute* (1834). To S, off road to West Bay, at **Bothenhampton**, * *church* (1887; E.S. Prior), the interior overpowered by the roof, three transverse arches rising almost from the ground to divide the nave like whalebones. The chancel arch is high and narrow, flanked by plain stone wall, the chancel floor itself raised up intensifying the focus. Chancel roof echoing the nave arches but in timber rising from a powerful corbelled arcade under the wall-plate. The side windows are so deeply set as hardly to tell in the massiveness of the walls. E window glass by Prior and altar frontal by Lethaby. At **West Bay**, the little port for Bridport, on the quay, * *Bay House Hotel* (1885; E.S. Prior), terrace of five houses in stone with tile-hung upper floor under a big mansard roof, overhanging first-floor oriels, also tile-hung. A subtle composition of two near identical eight-window ranges, stepped-up slightly to a taller end house of paired but different four-storey bays. 3m E at **Burton Bradstock**, *church* with S aisle added 1897 (E.S. Prior).

1½m NW of Bridport, at **Symondsbury**, remarkable S transept
* window (1885; W. Lethaby), Lethaby's only stained glass design, the four Evangelists with faces full of peasant character, far from the normal pieties, each saint carrying a globe with arcane symbols. The style is closer to woodcut than normal stained glass. 2m W, at **Chideock**, *Chideock Manor*, house of the prominent Catholic Weld family. By the house, *RC church* (1870–72; C. Weld) in basilican style with E end added, converted from a barn (1884), octagonal lantern over the crossing. Painted decoration by Weld and members of his family. Brass to Sir F. Weld. By Chideock *church*, Weld Mausoleum (c 1880; ?C. Weld) with carved crucifix by Weld. 4m W, **Charmouth**, pleasant early 19C resort with stuccoed villas and *church* of 1836 (C. Wallis) lancet Gothic. Just N, at **Catherston Leweston**, *church* (1857; J.L. Pearson) in knapped flint, carefully laid in crazy-paving manner.

Stone-lined interior, well detailed with good stained glass by Clayton
and Bell. *Manor House* adjoining of 1887, Tudor style. 3m W of Charmouth, **Lyme Regis**, fishing port and late 18C resort, the centre partly
rebuilt after a fire in 1844, still in Georgian style. On the Uplyme Road,
RC church (1835; H.E. Goodridge) lancet Gothic, rather overscaled
with octagonal steeple to one side. 3m NW of Charmouth, A35, at
Monkton Wyld, *church* (1848; R.C. Carpenter) the very model of a
Puginian church, Dec. with fine broach spire over the crossing, most
effective in its valley setting. Interior as carefully detailed as the outside with oak screen, very much as Pugin liked, stencil decorated
chancel and fine stained glass of c 1875 by G.E. Cook. Former *Rectory*
also by Carpenter, in stone, handsome Gothic.

St. Andrew's Church (1848; R.C. Carpenter), Monkton Wyld

5m N of Bridport, A3066, at **Melplash**, unusually grand neo-
Norman *church* (1845; B. Ferrey) with central tower and apse. At
Beaminster, 2m N, *vicarage* (1859–61; W. White), to W on Broad-
windsor Rd, good High Victorian Gothic, steeply gabled. Further W,

Horn Park (1911; T.L. Dale), handsome early Georgian style in stone with hipped roof.

DORCHESTER. A35 28m W of Bournemouth. The county town of Dorset and the Casterbridge of Thomas Hardy's novels. Hardy was born at Higher Bockhampton, just NE of the town, educated in Dorchester and returned to the town for the last forty years of his life. In the centre, *St. Peter's Church*, restored by J. Hicks, the Dorchester architect for whom Hardy worked, the plan in the church the only one known signed by Hardy. Rich carved and painted reredos (c 1890; C.E. Ponting), E window by Hardman. In front, *statue* of W. Barnes, Dorset dialect poet (1888; E.R. Mullins). To E, *Town Hall* (1847; B. Ferrey) brick and stone Tudor, the clock turret, so prominent in views down the High St, added 1864. W of the church, *County Museum* (1881; Crickmay and Son) Perp. outside, the main exhibition room a splendid glazed space, the roof carried on tall brightly painted cast-iron columns. Beyond, *Holy Trinity Church* (1875; B. Ferrey) built right by the street with high S aisle, kept narrow to allow light to the nave. Late 19C carved and gilt reredos. E of the Town Hall, High St descends with *All Saints' Church* (1843–45; B. Ferrey), the first built of the buildings by Ferrey that punctuate so effectively the centre of the town, and the best of the three, Dec. in the Pugin mode with fine tower and broach spire on the street line. Contemporary fittings and glass by Wailes in E window. South St and Cornhill run up to the Town Hall. In South St, on E side, hefty pedimented *Methodist church* (1875; W. Allardyce) and *Barclays Bank*, late 18C, supposedly the model for Henchard's house in Hardy's 'The Mayor of Casterbridge'. Opposite, two Baroque *banks*, 1900 and 1901. Further S, on E side, *Congregational church* (1856; Poulton and Woodman) spiky Gothic. On Bridport Rd, W of centre, *Military Museum* housed in The Keep (1876), massive rock-faced gatehouse to the former barracks, a toy castle on a real-life scale. Relics of the Dorset Regiment, Dorset Yeomanry and Militia. In Weymouth Avenue, *Eldridge Pope Brewery* (1880; G.R. Crickmay) appropriately festive in polychrome brick. In Edward Rd, *St. Mary's Church* (1910–12; C.E. Ponting) free Gothic, large and elaborately carved.

1m E of centre, on Wareham road, Alington Ave *Max Gate*, (1885; T. Hardy), Hardy's own house, a rather bleak red-brick villa. At **West Stafford**, to E, *church* with free Gothic chancel (1898; Ponting). *Stafford House* is of 1633 with matching W front (1848–50; B. Ferrey), gabled with arcaded loggia between the wings. E of the village, *Talbothays Lodge* (1894; T. Hardy), plain vaguely neo-Georgian house that Hardy designed for his brother. W of A352 at **Winterborne Came**, *Old Came Rectory* was the house of the poet W. Barnes, rector of Came for 24 years. In the *church* pictorial glass of c 1830–40 and good W window of c 1882. *Came House* (1754) has delicate conservatory with curved roof (c 1840). 5m SW of Dorchester, on **Blackdown Hill**, *Hardy Monument* (1844; A.D. Acland-Troyte) 70ft stone tower to Admiral Hardy, Nelson's flag-captain at Trafalgar.

9m NW of Dorchester, off A356, at **Cattistock**, *church* (1857; G.G. Scott: 1874; G.G. Scott Jr). The older part includes the apsed chancel and W window by Clayton and Bell but the 1874 work is far finer, a great stone tower with extremely long square-headed bell-openings, based on the 16C tower at Charminster, by Dorchester, but stretched, all the features emphasising height. In the base of the tower deep coloured painted decoration and font capped by a 20ft spired canopy. In S aisle one rich Morris window of c 1882. 3m NW at **Rampisham**, *church* with chancel (1845–47) by Pugin and contemporary glass by Powell. *Glebe Farm* (1845–46; Pugin) was the rectory, gabled, neat asymmetrical design.

1m N of Dorchester, on A352, N of **Charminster**, *County Asylum* (1859–63; H. Kendall Jr). 7m N, at **Minterne Magna**, *Minterne* (1904–06; L. Stokes), a house of exceptional quality, stone, freely 16C to 17C, that is with gables, mullion or mullion and transom windows and tracery to the lights of the great hall, but reworked in an idiom wholly personal to Stokes, especially characteristic the square-shouldered outline of the gables, the corners made sturdy by rusticated piers. Similar piers divide the entrance front, the lines of mouldings and parapets strongly defined and simply detailed. The symmetrical garden front is a looser rhythm of broad bays and raised gables with dormers of late 17C type, but the short E side re-emphasises the squared forms with a wide tower strongly contained by square corner piers, vertically incised. The clean lines of the building are most impressive, the carved and moulded work kept in check without harshness. 6m NE of Dorchester, A35, *Athelhampton Manor* 15C to 17C with fine formal gardens laid out 1891 (I. Thomas), open to public. At **Tincleton**, 2m S, *Clyffe House* (1842; B. Ferrey) stark Tudor to Elizabethan style in diapered brick and stone, symmetrical with a roofline of high brick stacks. *Church* 1849 (B. Ferrey). **Tolpuddle**, just E of Athelhampton, is celebrated in the history of trade unionism for the Tolpuddle Martyrs, five labourers sentenced to transportation in 1834 for their part in the formation of a national trades union. What caused the alarm and severity of the Tolpuddle sentences was the prospect of working men uniting across the divides of the separate trades.

SHAFTESBURY. A30 20m W of Salisbury. In the centre plain Tudor style *Town Hall* (1826). In Bimport, *Holy Trinity Church* (1841; G.G. Scott), one of Scott's earliest churches, still in the plain lancet style of the Commissioners' churches. Shaftesbury is the 'Shaston' of Hardy's 'Jude the Obscure'. 3m NW, **Gillingham**, the *church* with attractive tower (1908; C.E. Ponting), Queen St, *vicarage* (1883; E.S. Harris). In Station Rd, Baroque *bank* (1900; G. Oatley). 2m N at **Milton on Stour**, *church* (1868; Slater and Carpenter) well-detailed High Victorian work with broach spire. 3m S of Gillingham, at **East Stour**, *church* (1842; G. Alexander) massive neo-Norman with crossing tower and complete furnishings including galleries inside. 2m N of Shaftesbury, at **Motcombe**, *Motcombe House* (1893–94; George and Peto) large Elizabethan style brick and stone mansion with finely carved detail of an early Renaissance kind, near symmetrical N front with two-storey stone porch, garden front more loosely picturesque. *Church* 1846 (G. Alexander).

S of Shaftesbury, on or just off A350, a group of three quite elaborate *churches* by G. Evans of Wimborne, the quality enhanced by the local greensand stone, **Melbury Abbas** (1851), **Compton Abbas** (1866) and **Fontmell Magna** (1862). In **Sutton Waldron**, just S, *church* (1847; G. Alexander) Tractarian work with all the fittings, but remarkable for having the only complete surviving scheme of decoration by Owen Jones, author of 'The Grammar of Ornament' and responsible for the interior painting of the Crystal Palace. Jones' theories of colour decoration, emphasising the flat use of primary colour and stylisation of ornament, influenced the whole generation of High Victorian designers. Here blues and reds predominate with gold on the chancel roof and stylised patterns around the arches. E window by J. Powell and Sons, the rest with pale glass and patterned leading. To S, at **Iwerne Minster**, *Iwerne Minster House* (1878; A. Waterhouse), stone Gothic mansion for Lord Wolverton, banker, spreading and steep-roofed with high chimneys. Red-brick stables with more lively clock tower. In the *church* vaulted S chapel added 1890 (J.L. Pearson) in memory of Lord Wolverton. Estate cottages in the village.

SHERBORNE. A30 16m W of Shaftesbury. *Sherborne Abbey* was restored from 1850 by R.C. Carpenter and W. Slater, restoration completed in 1880s by R.H. Carpenter. Good glass of c 1851 by Hardman, to Pugin designs in W and S transept windows, choir clerestory glass and painted decoration by Clayton and Bell (1856–58) and large carved reredos (1884; R.H. Carpenter). *Sherborne School* occupies the former monastic buildings, the chapel being the Abbot's Hall, converted 1855 (R.C. Carpenter) and extended 1865 and 1922. The rest of Great Court is a mixed group of Gothic buildings, the gatehouse range to N bland neo-Tudor (1913 and 1923; R. Blomfield), Big School (1877–79; R.H. Carpenter), and School House (1860; Slater and Carpenter), the best of the 19C buildings, severe lancet Gothic. In Carrington Rd, to S, Carrington Building (1909–10; R. Blomfield), late 17C style with shaped gables and cupola. In Trendle St, by the Abbey, *Almshouses*, the 15C original front range intact, restored and extended (1858; W. Slater) with picturesque courtyard and cloister.

At **Trent** 2m NW, *church* altered c 1840–45 for the Rev. W.H. Turner, an atmospheric interior with plaster vaults, tiled chancel walls and floor, and much carved woodwork and stained glass collected by Turner, the medieval glass supplemented with glass by Wailes. Effigy of Turner (1853; W. Theed). Pretty Tudor style *almshouses* (1846) built by Turner. 2m E of Sherborne, A30, at **Oborne**, *church* (1862; W. Slater), small High Victorian work, apsed with marble shafting. Contemporary *vicarage*, admirably spare design, cusped lancets set flush in stone walling. 3m E, at **Purse Caundle**, *Crendle House* (1909; W.H. Brierley) stone, neo-Georgian. 8m SW of Sherborne, off A37, at **Melbury Sampford**, *Melbury House*, remarkable 16C house with hexagonal tower extended late 17C and again, in Tudor style, 1872 (A. Salvin) with bay-windowed library. Much larger additions 1884–85 (G. Devey), picturesquely varied, ending in a great tower. *Church* adjoining altered c 1875 with ornate reredos.

SWANAGE. A351 19m S of Poole. Resort town from the early 19C but most of the development later 19C, notably promoted by G. Burt, quarry owner, contractor and collector of architectural fragments. In the High Street, *Purbeck House* (1875; G. Crickmay) Burt's own house, inflated gabled villa notable for its multi-coloured crazy-paved stone walling. By the house, re-erected former archway from the Hyde Park Corner end of Green Park (1844). The *Town Hall* (1872) has, as frontispiece, the wonderfully rich 1668 front of the Mercers' Hall in the City of London, salvaged by Burt and re-erected 1883. To S, in grounds of Grosvenor Hotel, Peveril Point Road, Gothic *clock tower* (1854), originally set up by London Bridge in memory of the Duke of Wellington. At Durlston Head, to S, Burt built a mock *castle* (c 1890) as a restaurant and put up a Portland stone 40 ton, 10ft wide *globe* to instruct the passer-by. Lighthouse (1881).

3m N of Swanage, B3351, at **Studland**, on the hillside W of the village, *Hill Close* (1896; C.F.A. Voysey), roughcast house under a big hipped roof, mullioned windows in bands and sloping buttresses, all the elements of the Voysey manner, compactly planned as a studio house for A. Sutro, playwright. 5m W of Swanage, B3069, at **Kingston**, on the summit of the Purbeck ridge, *church (1873–80; G.E. Street) built for the 3rd Earl of Eldon, a masterpiece of Victorian church architecture. The scale of the church with its great square central tower is monumental, detailed in stark EE style with Early French Gothic touches, such that nothing detracts from the massive outline, the tower capped-off quite flat, the even lines of nave and transepts unbroken by pinnacles and the apse rising sheer. Nave buttressed by lean-to aisles and W narthex, the W end pierced by a great wheel window of unusual tracery, based on Lausanne Cathedral. Interior of great beauty, white stone and black Purbeck marble, harmoniously proportioned, perfect in detail, the ornament subordinate to the overall lines. Stone vaulting to the E end and fine fittings by Street, understated with delicate iron screen. Glass by Clayton and Bell. Excellent stone *vicarage* (1878–80; Street) now Kingston House. *Encombe House*, to SW, the Eldon seat, is early 18C in the manner of Vanbrugh, altered in similar style 1871–74 (A. Salvin). *Obelisk* (1835) on the hilltop to the 1st Lord Eldon, Lord Chancellor. 5m NW, *Creech Grange* with Tudor to Elizabethan style entrance front (1846). Neo-Norman *church* (1849–68) incorporating genuine Norman arch from Holme Priory. Campanile picturesquely rising through the trees.

WEYMOUTH. A354 8m S of Dorchester. Late Georgian resort town with long esplanade of Georgian terraces interrupted only by the bulk of the *Royal Hotel* (1897; C.O. Law). Towards the N end, *Victoria Terrace* (1855), stone-fronted in contrast to the earlier brick and stucco, and *St. John's Church* (1850–54; T.T. Bury), the spire an effective landmark behind the sweep of terraces. In the narrow centre, *St. Mary's Church* (1815) classical with one Art Nouveau stained glass window by H. Wilson. In Maiden St, Romanesque *Methodist church* (1866; Foster and Wood), and to W, in St. Edmund St, *Guildhall* (1836; T.T. Bury) classical with raised Ionic portico. On Custom House Quay behind, *Fish Market* (1855) and attractive group of warehouses. Facing, across the water, early 19C cottages flanking *Holy Trinity Church* (1834–36; T.T. Bury), the narrow front concealing a spacious interior, enlarged 1887 (Crickmay and Son). S of Weymouth, **Portland Bill**, the stone quarries exploited since the 17C. Convict labour was introduced in 1848, the origin of the famous prison, now occupying *The Verne*, one of Palmerston's forts, built 1860–67 to defend Portland Harbour, itself built with convict labour, the largest harbour in Britain. The original *prison* was at **Grove**, on the E side. The sturdy Romanesque *church* (1870–72) was built by prison labour to the designs of Maj.-Gen. E. Du Cane, Chief Administrator of Prisons, designer of Wandsworth Prison, London, also built by convicts.

WIMBORNE MINSTER. A31 9m NW of Bournemouth. In the *Minster*, W window (1858) a very early work by Heaton and Butler, before R.T. Bayne introduced the strong linear style of the firm's best work. Elaborately carved stone pulpit (1868; T. Earp). Main restoration 1890 (J.L. Pearson) when the roofs were restored to their original pitch and much glass by Clayton and Bell inserted. S of the Minster, *Grammar School* (1849–51; Morris and Henson), diapered brick with towers flanking a main gable. 3m SE, A341, at **Canford Magna**, *Canford Manor*, now Canford School, large and rambling brick and stone Gothic to Tudor mansion originally of 1825–36 (E. Blore) for Lord de Mauley, but vastly enlarged 1846–51 (Sir C. Barry) for the Merthyr Tydfil ironmaster Sir J. Guest and altered later for his son, Lord Wimborne. The entrance front on N is overwhelmed by Barry's tower over the porte-cochère, tall enough to be an accent in all views of the house, Perp. with three square corner turrets and one, taller, octagonal one. A small tower with pretty octagonal lantern provides some balance at the other end of the front. The garden front is mostly by Blore, simpler in detail, building up picturesquely from a two-storey bay on right to a four-storey octagonal tower, but the great roof parallel behind is to Barry's Great Hall, the climax of the interior, with brightly painted hammer-beam roof, stained glass and mosaic decoration. Staircase and screen part of the 1888 alterations for Lord Wimborne (Romaine Walker and Tanner), elaborately carved. The reconstruction of the house was essentially for Lady Charlotte Guest, formidable Victorian, editress of the 'Mabinogion' and influential promoter of interest in Welsh literature, despite which Canford, intended as the family seat, is as far as possible from Wales and the furnaces of Merthyr Tydfil. Guest memorials in the *church* and much Victorian estate building in the village.

1½m NE of Wimborne, **Colehill** *church* (1893–95; W.D. Caroe) in unexpected brick and half-timber, the crossing tower a reminiscence of old Germany with steep roof, dormers and stair turret behind, all tiled and half-timbered. Timber arcade inside. 3m N of Wimborne, at **Stanbridge**, neo-Norman estate *church* (1860; G. Evans), picturesque if unconvincing with its thin tower and spire. Built for Sir R. Glyn of *Gaunt's House*, large brick Tudor style house mostly of 1886–87 (G. Devey), now a school. At **Wimborne St. Giles**, 6m N, *church* restored after a fire in 1908 (J.N. Comper), N aisle rebuilt and a false arcade inserted on S side to balance. Comper gilt and alabaster fittings, splendid Gothic screen and W gallery. Ashley Cooper memorials including one to the philanthropic 7th Earl of Shaftesbury. 3m NW of Wimborne Minster, off B3082, *Kingston Lacy* (NT) the late 17C mansion of the Bankes family, remodelled 1835–46 by C. Barry for W.J. Bankes, collector, friend of Byron and Italophile. Barry recased the house in stone, giving it Italian palazzo details, a rusticated ground floor, loggia on the E front, and S front centrepiece with arched-windowed attic. Inside, Renaissance style stair hall with marble tunnel-vaulted stair and statues by Marochetti, the subsidiary rooms equally Italian, the saloon with painted vault, the Spanish room hung with gilded leather under a rich gilt beamed ceiling removed from the Palazzo Contarini, Venice. The whole house was intended to display Bankes' Italian treasures which he continued to send back from 1841 when he left England, to avoid a homosexual scandal, to his death in 1855. In the park, Egyptian obelisk brought back from Philae by Bankes 1827. *Church* (1907; C.E. Ponting) free Perp., richly fitted.

9m NW of Wimborne, **Blandford Forum**, Georgian town largely rebuilt after a fire in 1731. *Church* (1733) with chancel carefully lengthened (1896; C. Hunt). S of the town, entrance to *Bryanston* (1889–94; R. Norman Shaw), now Bryanston School, the vast red-brick and stone palace built for Viscount Portman on income from London estates. The house cost over £200,000 and replaced a substantial house of 1778. The composition is monumental, a main block flanked by wings embracing the entrance court but set back on the garden front to emphasise the centre. The style, ushering in the Edwardian age, is English Baroque, the style of Wren and the later 17C but with elements from the French 18C. The colour, bright red with banded rustication in Portland stone, extending even to the chimneys and heavy stone dressings to all the windows, is immediately startling, the garden front of the main block benefitting from a relaxation of the frenetic rustication. Inside, the centrepiece is the great hall, stone-

lined and domed, with massive rusticated arches on all four sides,
opening on to the upper passages. The arches can be found again,
more appropriately, in Shaw's Regent Street facade in London.
Church (1895–98; E.P. Warren) well detailed with handsome W tower,
on the site of the original house. 5m W of Blandford, at **Turnworth**,
church (1868–69; J. Hicks and G.R. Crickmay), notable because
Thomas Hardy, who worked for Hicks, designed the foliage capitals.
4m W at **Woolland**, *church* (1857; G.G. Scott), modest exterior with
apse and spired bell turret, but vaulted chancel with Purbeck marble
shafting and rich naturalistic carving to the capitals. 5m SW of Blandford, A354, at **Milton Abbas**, choir and transepts of a great unfinished
14C *church*, restored 1865 (G.G. Scott) for Baron Hambro of Milton
Abbey. S transept S window (1847; Hardman), a richly coloured
design by Pugin. Font (J.A. Jerichau) in the style of Italian cemetery
sculpture, marble angels with cross and palm-frond. Marble effigy of
Baron Hambro (died 1877).

4m SW of Wimborne, A350, at **Lytchett Heath**, *Lytchett Heath
House* (1874–79; D. Brandon), big neo-Jacobean mansion in brick
and stone, built for Lord E. Cecil. *Church* (1898; Crickmay and Son)
free Gothic, rock-faced, breaking into ashlar under the eaves. 2m SW,
at **Lytchett Minster**, *South Lytchett Manor*, refaced 1900–04 (W.D.
Caroe) in yellow stone, the centrepiece a giant Baroque niche pushed
into the core of the house, an uncomfortable effect, like a bite taken
out.

COUNTY DURHAM

BARNARD CASTLE. A67 15m W of Darlington. Dickens stayed at the King's Head, 1838, investigating Yorkshire schools, the background for 'Nicholas Nickleby'. At the end of Newgate, *Bowes Museum* (1869–85; J.A. Pellechet), quite the most remarkable apparition to find in a Durham town, a very large French Second Empire style mansion, designed by a French architect for John Bowes, son of the Earl of Strathmore of Streatlam Castle nearby. Bowes married a French actress with a Spanish title and they collected Spanish painting and French furniture and porcelain. This building, built for the collection, is the most successful example of the style in Britain. Marble entrance hall. The collection itself is a monument to the taste of the period. At **Bowes**, A67 4m SW, Dickens is reputed to have found the original for Dotheboys Hall. To NE, A688, 19C lodges of the demolished Streatlam Castle. At **Staindrop**, 5m NE, in the parish *church* monuments to the Vane family of Raby Castle, including effigy of the 1st Duke of Cleveland (died 1842; Sir R. Westmacott). In the churchyard, mausoleum to the 2nd Duke (1850; W. Burn). *Raby Castle* (open to public) is basically 14C with S front 1843–48 (W. Burn). State rooms by Burn in Jacobean and Rococo styles. At **Whorlton**, 3m E of Barnard Castle, early *suspension bridge* (1829–31; J. and B. Green).

Bowes Museum (1869–85; J.A. Pellechet), Barnard Castle

BISHOP AUCKLAND. A688 10m SW of Durham. Colliery town on the Wear. Ten-arch railway viaduct over the medieval bridge. In Market Place, church (1847; W. Thompson), lancet Gothic, and large mansard roofed *Town Hall* (1860; J.P. Jones). At **Shildon**, 3m SE, A6072, an early railway town, the locomotive works for the Stockton–Darlington railway being set up here in 1833. A very early *railway station* (c 1825–30) survives at **Heighington**, 3m SE, cottage-like with no raised platform. 4m NW of Bishop Auckland, at **Crook**, A689, *RC church* (1853;

E.W. Pugin), Church Hill, with High Altar, now disected, 1864 by J.F.
Bentley, Gothic reredos with painted archangels and alabaster frontal
with painted panels. In the area former iron-making centres at
Witton-le-Wear, **Tow Law** and **Wolsingham** and further up Wear-
dale lead-mining centres at **Westgate**, A689, and **Rookhope**, 4m NW
of Stanhope.

CHESTER-LE-STREET. A167 5m N of Durham. Colliery town, centre
for an extensive mining area. 2m E, *Lambton Castle*, mostly rebuilt
(1796–1828; J. and I. Bonomi) in castellated style. Estate village at
Bournmoor in yellow brick, mid 19C, the *church* (1867; Johnson and
Hicks) much enriched inside (1888; W.S. Hicks). Lambton monuments. The most notable Lambton was the 1st Earl of Durham (1792–
1840), Liberal politician, known in the North as 'Radical Jack', pro-
motor of the 1832 Reform Bill and briefly and influentially Governor-
General of Canada. 4m W of Chester-le-Street, *Beamish Open Air
Museum*, an excellent industrial museum incorporating a recreated
colliery and pit cottages, a transport collection around the re-erected
station (1867) from Rowley and other buildings.

CONSETT. A692 15m SW of Gateshead. Iron and steel town from
1842 to 1980, dominated by the Consett Iron Company works until
their recent clearance. *Hownes Gill Viaduct* (1858; Sir T. Bouch) is the
finest monument, twelve brick arches rising to 150ft. Bouch was the
engineer for the Tay Bridge that collapsed in 1879 and all his bridges
including this one were given extra buttressing. Shotley Bridge was
the fashionable end of Consett, briefly a spa with some Swiss chalet
like houses. 2m N of Consett, A694, at **Ebchester**, R.S. Surtees, author
of the Jorrocks sporting books, is buried. He owned the Hamsterley
Hall estate 2m NW. 10m W of Consett, B6306, **Hunstanworth**, village
rebuilt (1862–63; S.S. Teulon) including *church, school, vicarage*.

DARLINGTON. The heart of the British railway system, where in 1825
Edward Pease, Quaker industrialist, and George Stephenson,
engineer, opened the world's first passenger line, the Stockton and
Darlington Railway. Until 1833 the line used steam for freight only,
passenger trains were horse drawn. The first station *North Road
Station* was built only in 1842, and is now a railway museum housing
Stephenson's locomotion engine of 1825 and other precious early
relics. Plain late Georgian-style buildings with timber train-shed.
Two original bridges of 1825 nearby. The centre of the town is the
Market Place with the former *Town Hall* and *Market* (1861–64; A.
Waterhouse), the Town Hall small, Gothic with steep roof and mullion
and transom windows, the Market iron-framed and terminated by a
fine stone clock tower. *St. Cuthbert's Church* has ornate 19C fittings
and glass. Red-brick classical *Central Hall* (1846; J. Middleton) on S
side. On High Row, *Barclays Bank* (1864; A. Waterhouse) stone,
Gothic with granite shafts and statue of Joseph Pease (1799–1872;
G.A. Lawson) industrialist, philanthropist and the first Quaker MP. In
East St, *Library* (1884; G. Hoskins) rich Flemish Renaissance. Northgate leads up to North Rd station with *Central School* (1893–96; G.
Hoskins) brick and terracotta, free Gothic. *No. 156 High Northgate*
was Edward Pease's house. To W Bondgate leads into Woodland Rd
where *The Woodlands* (1815 and 1860) belonged to Sir J.W. Pease MP.
In Tower Rd the large house of Henry Pease MP, begun c 1830 and
extended massively including ornate gatehouse (1873; Waterhouse).
Further large suburban industrialists' houses S of Woodland Rd

including *Mowden Hall* (1881; Waterhouse) for E.L. Pease, red brick and terracotta, and *Carmel School* (1863; Waterhouse) for A. Pease, brick and sandstone Gothic. In Carmel Rd, *St. Clare's Abbey* (1855–58; J. and C. Hansom), red-brick Gothic conventual buildings. In Coniscliffe Rd further large villas, from late 18C to mid 19C. *The Grange Hotel* was Joseph Pease's house. Further out, extensive *waterworks* begun 1849. E of centre, *Darlington Bank Top* station (1887; W. Bell) with three-span arched iron roof. Red-brick and sandstone front with tall tower. The former *NE Railway offices* (1912; W. Hall), Brinkburn Rd, are grandly Baroque.

DURHAM. The *Cathedral* suffered several restorations in the 19C, none overwhelmingly damaging. The main 19C features are G.G. Scott's ornate marble screen (1870–76) and pulpit (1876). Excellent W window (1867; Clayton and Bell) and, in S transept, S window (1869; Clayton and Bell) and W window (1895; Holiday). In Chapel of the Nine Altars, seated statue of Bishop Van Mildert (1836; J. Gibson). Van Mildert was the founder of Durham University in 1832 and also the last prince bishop, giving up the *castle* and part of the episcopal revenue for the foundation. In Owengate, leading N from the Castle, *almshouses* (1838). Saddler St leads into Market Place. *St. Nicholas' Church* (1857; J.P. Pritchett) with strong spire, *Town Hall* (1851; P.C. Hardwick) Perp. with hammerbeam roof to the hall, and to one side pleasant cast-iron roofed markets. Good 19C commercial buildings, the best the *National Westminster Bank* (1876; J. Gibson), classical. Fine equestrian *statue* (1858; R. Monti) of the 3rd Marquess of Londonderry, cavalry commander in the Peninsular War and diplomat. To SW, over Framwell Gate Bridge, North Rd leads up to the *station* (1857; G. Andrews), Tudor style, set at the end of the great stone *viaduct* (1856) that affords the train passenger such splendid views. Large *RC church* (1865; E.W. Pugin) in Castle Chare, apsed with later tower. Off North Rd, to W, *County Hospital* (1857), Jacobean, and in Red Hills Lane, *Miners Hall* (1913; H.T. Gradon), proud Baroque building with marble hall and council chamber, the Durham miners being one of the most independent and close-knit groups of working men, their traditions established in the earliest days of trade unionism in the 19C. Further out on North Rd, *St. Cuthbert's Church* (1858; E.R. Robson) High Victorian Gothic with saddleback-roofed tower and strong rose window. In Obelisk Lane, opposite, *obelisk* (1840), a marker due N of the University *Observatory* (1840), Elvet Hill Lane. SE of Market Place, over Elvet Bridge, former *Shire Hall* (1896; Barnes and Coates) Old Elvet, bright red brick with Baroque dome and lavish tiled stair hall. In Church St, to S, *St. Oswald's Church* with excellent W window (1864–65; Morris and Co) mostly by Ford Madox Brown. To N, across the river, Leazes Rd leads to *Bede College* (1847) and *St. Hild's College* (1858) Gothic buildings of former training colleges now part of the University.

3m W of Durham, *Ushaw College*, the premier RC seminary in the north of England, successor with the College at Ware, Herts, of the seminary at Douai, disrupted by the French Revolution. Original buildings of 1804–19, classical, but from 1837 much extended in Gothic, initially under A.W. Pugin. Chapel (1884; Dunn and Hansom) replacing Pugin's chapel of 1844 but reusing much of Pugin's stonework and fittings. Rich apsed sanctuary with painted roof and elaborate altar (1890), screen by Pugin. Lady Chapel redecorated by J.F. Bentley reusing Pugin tiles, altar and stained glass. Pugin's High Altar is in the Sacred Heart Chapel. N of the chapel, cloister with chapels begun 1852 by A.W. Pugin and completed by his son, E.W. Pugin, notably stone-vaulted Chapel of St. Carlo Borromeo (1857–59) and mortuary chapel (1858–59). Other Gothic buildings all linked by enclosed corridors include Museum (1856), Infirmary (1858) and Junior College (1857–59) all by E.W. Pugin to N and W, to E of the original buildings Library (1850; J. and C. Hansom) and Ball Court (1850; J. Hansom). To the rear of Junior College, Cemetery (1852; J. Hansom) with cloister walk. 4m SW of Durham, A690, *Brancepeth Castle*, highly romantic silhouette of castle entirely rebuilt 1818–21, following the old outline. To NE of Durham, A690, at **Belmont**, small stone *church* (1855; W. Butterfield) severe plate tracery, and at **West Rainton**, 5m NE, *church* (1864; E.R. Robson) strong High Victorian with landmark spire.

SEAHAM. B1278 5m S of Sunderland. Seaham Harbour was founded 1828 by the 3rd Marquess of Londonderry to ship the coal from his estates. Some early stucco houses and the church (1835–40; T. Prosser) survive from the beginnings. On the seafront, *Londonderry Offices* (c 1860) slightly French with statue of the 6th Marquess (died 1915; J. Tweed), prominent Conservative politician, Viceroy of Ireland 1886–89. In Tempest Rd, *Londonderry Institute* (1853; T. Oliver) with Greek portico. *Seaham Hall*, in the old village to N, was the Londonderry house, stuccoed and unimposing, largely of 1861.

ESSEX

BRAINTREE. A120 12m W of Colchester. Modest town centre with porticoed *Corn Exchange* (1839). At **Bocking**, *RC convent*, Convent Lane, with chapel (1898; J.F. Bentley), half conventual, half parish church with fine fittings especially the marble work in the sanctuary. At **Felsted**, B1417 5m SW, *Felsted School*, small public school for boys with red-brick Gothic buildings (1860–68; F. Chancellor) and chapel (1873). In the village *almshouses* (1878; Chancellor). By Chancellor also the large *church* at **Ford End** on A130 (1871). To NW, at **Greenstead Green**, S of Halstead, *church* (1845; G.G. Scott), an early work, with octagonal tower and spire.

BRENTWOOD. Dominating spire of parish *church* (1882–90; E.C. Lee), flint and stone with strong rounded buttresses. To E, on A129, Hutton *church*, restored 1873 by G.E. Street, good metalwork. To W, **South Weald**, an estate village with *church*, *school* and *almshouses* (1859–68; S.S. Teulon). To S, B186, at **Little Warley**, former regimental *chapel* (1857; Sir M.D. Wyatt) of the Essex Regiment, round arched yellow and red brick with regimental memorials within. At **Great Warley** the **church* (1904; C.H. Townsend) is a jewel of the Art Nouveau side of English Arts and Crafts. Simple roughcast, styleless exterior, the interior low, tunnel-vaulted with marble wall panelling and rich silvered relief plasterwork above culminating in the apse covered in vine tendrils. *Screen* (W. Reynolds Stephens) in bronze, pewter, mother-of- pearl and walnut, the uprights branching out into a thick canopy of intricately carved dog rose over very Art Nouveau angels.

CHELMSFORD. The county town. In Tindal Square, *statue* of Chief Justice Tindal (1847; E.H. Baily), *Corn Exchange* (1857; F. Chancellor) yellow brick round arched, and neo-Georgian Barclays Bank (1905; Sir R. Blomfield). Early Victorian villas on the London road out. To E, A414, *Danbury Place* (1832; T. Hopper), Tudor style apparently largely designed by the owner's wife, Mrs Round. It was later a palace of the Bishops of Rochester. Chapel added c 1860. At **Little Baddow**, 2m N, *rectory* (c 1858; W. White) banded yellow and red brick, a good example of the simplified domestic style developed by Butterfield in the 1850s.

CLACTON-ON-SEA. Early Victorian seaside resort swamped by later developments. Some pretty terraces near the front and an altered late 19C pier. In Tower Rd, a severe, unfinished *church* by Temple Moore (1913). **Frinton-on-Sea**, 4m NE, is mostly turn of the century and later with one exceptional house, *The Homestead* (1905; C.F.A. Voysey), in Second Avenue, roughcast with deep eaves and leaded windows. **Walton-on-the-Naze**, 2m N, was a resort of c 1830 that failed. A stucco terrace remains, the rest is c 1900.

COLCHESTER. Two Victorian monuments dominate the skyline. At the W end a very large *Water Tower* (1882), given a slightly Roman look as befits so ancient a town, and in the centre the improbable 162ft Baroque steeple of the **Town Hall* (1897–1902; J. Belcher), one of the major works of the c 1900 Baroque revival. The main hall is treated with giant columns carrying three Baroque open pediments, Portland stone against red brick, the tower is red brick carrying a stone lantern that suggests Italy, though the motifs, as on the hall, are mostly English Baroque. Good interiors. Behind the water tower, *St. Mary's*

Church (1872; A.W. Blomfield). North Hill leads to the *Royal Eastern Counties Institution* (1843; L. Cubitt), one of the earliest railway hotels, too ambitious as by 1850 it had become a mental hospital. Off High St, Queen St leads to *St. Botolph's Church* (1837; W. Mason), a large neo-Norman building with some good detail but built of white brick. To SE, *Wivenhoe Park* (1846–53; T. Hopper) Jacobean red-brick recasing of an earlier house, now part of Essex University. At **Birch**, B1022 4m SW, expensive estate *church* (1850; S.S. Teulon) of the demolished Birch Hall.

Town Hall (1897–1902; J. Belcher), Colchester

EPPING. A11 5m S of Harlow. Fine *church* (1889; Bodley and Garner) with Bodley fittings, Kempe E window and a very severe broad tower (1908; Bodley). C.E. Kempe, the stained glass artist lived at Copped Hall, 1½m W, now ruinous. Epping Forest, the remains of a royal hunting forest, was saved from clearance by the City of London after lengthy legal battles in 1874 and some six thousand acres were preserved.

HARWICH. A604 15m NE of Colchester. Victorian port created by the

Great Eastern Railway. The *Town Hall* was the railway hotel (1864; T. Allom). **Dovercourt** just to the S was a resort promoted by J. Bagshaw, local MP, who lived at Cliff House (1845) at the end of the seafront. On Marine Parade, *Alexandra Hotel* (1903; G. Sherrin).

HATFIELD BROAD OAK. B183 6m NW of Harlow. Just N, *Barrington House* (1863; E. Browning), Jacobean style brick recasing of a 18C house, determined asymmetry to disguise the original Georgian box shape. At **Sheering**, 3m SW, *Down Hall* (1871–73; F.P. Cockerell), low and rather amorphous but remarkable for being built of mass concrete.

LOUGHTON. A121 4m S of Epping. In Church Lane, neo-Norman brick *church* (1846; S. Smirke) with central tower. *Loughton Hall* (1878; W.E. Nesfield) Queen Anne style country house, an attractive blend of gabled plastered bays, big hipped roof with tall decorated chimneys and top cupola. This was almost Nesfield's last house and shows him as inventive with the mixed blend of 17C and early 18C motifs called 'Queen Anne' as Norman Shaw, his former partner. For comparison, at **Chigwell**, 2m S, *Chigwell Hall* (1876; Norman Shaw), a compact design, brick and tile- hung walls gathered under a hipped roof carried on deep coved eaves, the apparent symmetry ruthlessly broken by an off-centre chimney right on the ridge. Chigwell *church* has rich chancel decoration and fittings by Bodley (c 1900). At **Chigwell Row**, 1½m E, *church* (1867; J.P. Seddon) toughly detailed High Victorian.

MALDON. A414 9m E of Chelmsford. *Maldon East* station (1848), now closed, is a splendid Jacobean building out of all proportion to its status on a branch line, the explanation being that the deputy chairman of the railway wished to be elected MP for Maldon. 5m N at **Little Braxted**, *church* with painted decoration (c 1884) by the architecturally-trained Rev. E. Geldart.

SAFFRON WALDEN. A130 12m N of Bishop's Stortford. In the Market Place, cheerful Italianate former *Corn Exchange* (1847; R. Tress) now the library. Opposite, *Barclays Bank* (1874; W.E. Nesfield), brick and stone with large Elizabethan style windows and subtle interplay between the symmetrical main block and the right-hand side with elaborate Gothic doorway and quite different window levels. Flat parapet with pretty dormer and ornate chimneys. Elaborate High Victorian carved fountain in front. In Abbey Lane, Tudor style *almshouses* (1834). At **Radwinter**, B1053, 5m E, Nesfield rebuilt the *church* (1869), painted chancel roof and metal screen. The tower and spire were added in 1887 (Temple Moore). Nesfield also designed the large gabled *village hall* with Essex style pargetting and cottages by the church, enlarged the *school* (1877) and designed *almshouses* (1887). At **Newport**, A11, 3m S, *Grammar School* (1878; Nesfield). On the main railway to W and NW of Saffron Walden attractive early *railway stations* at **Audley End** and **Great Chesterford** (1845; F. Thompson).

SOUTHEND. Spreading seaside town with the world's longest pier. The resort began in the 1820s but most of the building is late Victorian. Cliff Town, above the pier, was a railway promotion from 1859, white brick houses and a nice bandstand in the clifftop gardens. At the E end of the front Edwardian *Kursaal* (1902; G. Sherrin). At the top of the High St, Victoria Circus, *Technical College* (1900; H.T. Hare) red brick and stone English Baroque. To E, *All Saints' Church* (1889; J. Brooks),

Southchurch Rd, red brick with impressive tall interior. In South-church Avenue, *St. Erkenwald's Church* (1905; W. Tapper), incom-plete half of a noble building, sheer yellow brick walls and bold but-tresses, the windows small and high up.

WALTHAM ABBEY. A121 on the London border. *Waltham Abbey* is the nave of the great Norman church, restored 1859–76 by William Burges such that Victorian and medieval work remain distinct and each masterly. Nave roof painted by E.J. Poynter. At the E end Burges walled across the chancel arch in a muscular Early French Gothic contrasting with the original Norman. Three richly carved lancets below a plate-traceried rose window, a circle surrounded by six equally plain roundels. This powerful architecture recedes behind the glow of the *stained glass*, the very best of early Burne-Jones, before the foundation of Morris and Co. A Tree of Jesse below and Christ surrounded by the Days of Creation in the rose. One other good window at the E end of S aisle, by Holiday (1867). Marble pulpit and alabaster reredos by Burges, carved by Nicholls.

GLOUCESTERSHIRE

CHELTENHAM. A40 9m NE of Gloucester. Cheltenham grew as a spa town from the late 18C, its heyday from about 1800 to the 1840s. The early 19C parts of the town have a spacious dignity echoed in other resort towns of the period, such as Brighton or Leamington, but the quality of the buildings is higher, Bath stone was extensively used and fine ironwork enlivens many an ordinary building. Victorian Cheltenham includes the latter end of the formal terrace developments, mostly still in a Regency mode, and a number of handsome churches.

In the centre, The Promenade, laid out 1818, running S from the old High St to Imperial Square. The *Municipal Offices* occupy a monumental terrace of c 1823. In front, stone Neptune *fountain* (1893; Boulton and Sons). The view down The Promenade is closed by the *Queen's Hotel* (1838; R. and C. Jearrad), stuccoed with tall Corinthian columns across the front breaking forward into a six-column portico. Imperial Square has terraces of c 1834 with the heavy Baroque style *Town Hall* (1901; F.W. Waller) intruding into the central space. Lavish interior hall. S of the Queen's Hotel, is *Montpellier Walk* (c 1840; W. Knight), charming late Regency style terrace of shops with caryatid figures between the shop fronts. *Lloyds Bank* is the former Montpellier Spa (1817 and 1825) overlooking Montpellier Gardens. Parallel with Montpellier St, to NW, is Bayshill Rd, with large villas of c 1830–40, some of the detail going Italianate, the eaves roof replacing the earlier parapet or balustrade. Between Bayshill Rd and Montpellier St, *Cheltenham Ladies College*, pioneering girls boarding school, founded 1854. Buildings from 1873 (J. Middleton), architecturally the most interesting is the *Princess Hall* (1896; E.R. Robson), assembly hall with two tiers of Gothic timber galleries. From Bayshill Rd, St. George's Place runs N to Clarence St. The *Public Library Museum and Art Gallery* (1887; Knight and Chatters) is of Bath stone, free style, more Jacobean than any other, with off-centre tower. In the Museum, excellent collection of Arts and Crafts furniture, particularly of Gimson and the Barnsleys. Adjoining the Museum, quite remarkable red-brick, almost windowless, building on a heavy stone plinth with stone central archway, apparently an *electricity generating station* of c 1890. The heavy Romanesque look has affinities with H.H. Richardson's work in the USA, though the ancestry is more probably in the warehouse styles of Bristol. Opposite, *St. Matthew's Church* (1878; E. Christian), despite the loss of tower and spire, a fascinating church, sternly detailed outside and inside, a very broad nave canted at the E end to a narrow chancel, giving the maximum space for the congregation as the evangelical wing of the Anglican Church liked, but in the High Victorian dress more usual for ritualistic or High Church congregations. Further W, in St. James' Square, *St. Gregory's RC Church* (1854–57; C.F. Hansom) with the finest spire (1864) in Cheltenham, rising 202ft, and good stained glass by Hardman in the E window.

Going N from the top of The Promenade, flanking the Evesham Rd, Pittville, laid out from 1825 with terraces and villas in a park-like setting stretching up to the *Pittville Pump Room* (1825–30; J. Forbes), now a museum of costume, in Pittville Park. Off to SE, past Pittville Circus, *All Saints' Church* (1868; J. Middleton), most elaborate of the several churches that Middleton, a High Victorian architect with a strong personal style, built in the town. Typical of Middleton's work is contrasted stone texture on the outside with elaborate carved detail and interior polychromy. Here the interior is most sumptuous, granite columns, contrasted blue and white stone, tall proportions and a wealth of carved fittings and stained glass. Notable carved pulpit (1872) and font. Chancel screen and font cover, fine ironwork of the 1890s by H.A. Prothero. Returning to Evesham Rd, at 4 Clarence Rd, *G. Holst Birthplace Museum*, the house completely furnished as it might have been in 1874 when the composer was born. Beyond Clarence Square, in St. Paul's St, *St. Paul's College* (1849; S.W. Daukes), attractive and restrained collegiate Gothic buildings. The red-brick and stone late Perp. style chapel was added in 1909 (C.H. Fowler). Fine interior in the manner of Bodley. To S, High St runs NW past *St. Mary's Cemetery*, now gardens, with Greek Doric chapel (c 1830; C. Paul) to the Tewkesbury Rd. On left, *St. Peter's Church* (1847–49; S.W. Daukes), a most striking neo-Norman church, the crossing capped by a circular tower with conical roof, the E end apsed and the W end elaborately detailed with corner square turret. The interior is consistently neo-Norman, though the mouldings are plaster, painted and gilded.

Lypiatt Terrace (c 1840; S.W. Daukes), Cheltenham

Returning to S end of Montpellier Walk, to W, the Lansdown area with large ashlar-fronted Regency style houses in *Lansdown Place* (1825; J.B. Papworth) and *Lansdown Crescent* (1829; Papworth). *Lansdown Terrace* (c 1830–34; R. and C. Jearrad) breaks new ground with projecting first-floor Ionic porticoes on a heavy balcony while *Lansdown Court* (1837) has the early Victorian feature of towers with overhanging roofs. To N, Malvern Rd, *Christ Church* (1838–4; R. and C. Jearrad), archaeologically most incorrect but impressively scaled Bath stone church with W tower and elaborate build-up of pinnacles and gables each side. The interior is a surprise in that it was overhauled from 1888 in Italian basilica style, the original cast-iron columns clad in grey marble and a painted domed apse built on the E end. *St. Mark's Church* (1862–67; J. Middleton), Lansdown Rd, is prominently spired with Middleton's characteristic rich carved detail and rock-faced stonework. S of Lansdown Rd, *St. Stephen's Church* (1873;

J. Middleton), St. Stephen's Rd, rock-faced stone without the intended tower and spire. Inside the effect is rich, with arcade and chancel arch in contrasted Bath stone and blue Forest stone, marble shafting in the chancel and fine carving. The W wall has the original E end carved arcading reset under an arcade filled with statues of the Apostles. To S, *The Park*, laid out from 1833 with Greek revival villas. Tivoli Rd leads N to Lypiatt Rd, across the A40. Here *Lypiatt Terrace* (c 1840; S.W. Daukes), Cheltenham's most handsome Italianate terrace with heavy stone balconies, arched windows and taller pyramid roofed sections breaking up the long elevation. Suffolk Rd (A40) leads E towards Bath Rd. Off to S, *St. Philip's and St. James' Church* (1870; Middleton) in Grafton Rd, with prominent copper saddleback roof to the tower and flèche on top. A richly carved Middleton interior with screen and reredos by H.A. Prothero.

On Bath Rd, *Cheltenham College*, almost the first newly-founded public school of the 19C. Front building (1841–43; J. Wilson), symmetrical ashlar front with central tower. The clasping turrets reappear on other Wilson buildings (cf. St. Stephen, Lansdown, Bath). The grand front contained basically only two large schoolrooms and the back received no architectural treatment at all. A chapel, now the dining-hall, was added (1855; D. Humphris) behind, broad with Perp. detail and some good original stained glass. This was replaced by the present chapel (1896; H.A. Prothero) on a much larger scale, late Perp. style. Carved reredos by Prothero, and around the S side door an exceptionally delicately carved wild rose in sycamore climbs naturalistically, a memorial of c 1901 (H.A. Prothero). At the S end of the main building, additions of c 1865 (J. Middleton). Overlooking the playing fields, *Gymnasium* (1864; F.H. Lockwood), polychrome brick, Gothic. Across the road, *Thirlestaine House* (1823; J.R. Scott), Ionic porticoed with wings added 1840 and 1845 for Lord Northwick's picture collection, hence windowless with classical sculpted relief panels. In Sandford Rd, N of the college playing fields, *General Hospital* (1848; D. Humphris) with giant Ionic portico, the last of Cheltenham's Greek revival buildings. ¾m S of the college, off Leckhampton Rd, *Delancey Hospital* Charlton Lane, (1877; Middleton), plate-traceried Gothic in brick. At **Leckhampton**, to S, parish *church*, Church Rd, rebuilt 1866 (Middleton) with much Victorian stained glass. E. Wilson, who died on Scott's 1912 Antarctic expedition, is commemorated by a cross in the churchyard. On Leckhampton Hill, *Bartlow* (1868; Middleton), large Gothic villa in banded brick and stone. 5m S of Cheltenham, off A435, at **Cowley**, *Cowley Manor*, an Italianate villa (c 1855; G. Somers Clarke) doubled in size c 1900 (R.A. Briggs) with terraced water garden. Stable court of c 1855 with clock tower. In the *church* stained glass of 1872–74 by J. Powell and Sons and elaborate marble reredos with tile mosaic decoration.

3m NE of Cheltenham, A46, at **Southam**, *Southam Delabere*, a substantial 16C house enlarged after 1831 for Lord Ellenborough, Governor General of India 1841–44. Ellenborough added a Gothic NW tower in the 1830s and the big neo-Norman E side tower in the 1840s. In the garden, pretty but decayed Gothic summerhouse with inscriptions commemorating Lord Ellenborough's staff in India. 5m NE, **Winchcombe**, with *church* restored 1872 (J.D. Wyatt), E window 1886 by Hardman. By the church, *School House* (1868; G.G. Scott), built for the Dents of Sudeley Castle, as was the *school* of 1865 behind. S of the church, off Abbey Terrace, Gothic infants *school* (1857) with, to E, *Sudeley Almshouses* (1865; G.G. Scott) Gothic in polychrome stone. At Sudeley, on the hill just S of the town, *Sudeley Castle* (open to the public) 15C and 16C castle much restored from the 1830s, under G.G. Scott from 1854 and J.D. Wyatt 1863–89. The additions are sympathetic to the original. Inside, stained glass by Willement, and Queen Katherine Parr's rooms in the Gothic taste of the 1840s. The Dent family made much of the royal connections of the house, particularly of Queen Katherine, Henry VIII's sixth wife and widow, whose second husband owned the castle from 1547. In the *church*, rebuilt 1859–63 (G.G. Scott), pride of place goes to her lovely white marble effigy (1859; J.B. Philip) on an alabaster tomb chest set in a richly carved recess. The inscription, to 'Quene Kateryn Wife to Kyng Henry' epitomises the slightly overblown archaism of the scheme, but Katherine certainly received a memorial fit for a queen. By J.B. Philip also, the beautifully carved marble and alabaster reredos and font. On the plain, 3m NW of Winchcombe, at **Gretton**, handsome *church* (1868; J.D. Wyatt), apsed with small octagonal tower and spire over the S porch, in the Dec. style favoured by G.G. Scott, whose chief assistant Wyatt had been. 2m NE, off A438, **Toddington**, estate village of *Toddington Manor*, rebuilt 1820–35 by C. Hanbury-Tracy, 1st Lord Sudeley, a distinguished architectural amateur, chairman of the commission that selected the design for the Houses of Parliament. The house is a very large and complex Bath stone building in elaborate Perp. style, broadly symmetrical but to a most extended plan of outer courtyards set diagonally to the main house to create a picturesque effect, something like a large Oxford college with a shorter and stouter version of Magdalen tower as the central accent. The estate *church*, built as a memorial to Lord Sudeley (1873–79; G.E. Street), is a major High Victorian work with S tower and spire and interior in Street's most graceful Dec., the E parts vaulted with dark Purbeck marble shafts, the sanctuary walls elaborated with arcading. E window by Clayton and Bell and complete fittings by Street. Lord Sudeley and his wife have a magnificent tomb-chest memorial with effigies by J.G. Lough 1872.

CHIPPING CAMDEN. B4081 10m NNW of Stow-on-the-Wold. Perfect small Cotswold town to which, in 1902, the architect and designer C.R. Ashbee moved with the Guild of Handicraft which he had set up in East London as a collective of craftsmen working primarily on furniture, metalwork and jewellery, inspired by socialist ideals. The Guild was an offshoot of the ideas of critics of industrial society like Ruskin and Morris who saw in high quality craft work the liberation of the individual workman from the drudgery of machine work. Some 150 people moved from London to set up in the old *Silk Mill* in Sheep Street, an astonishing invasion for a remote Cotswold town, and for some years Arts and Crafts jewellery and furniture was produced. A School of Arts and Crafts was set up to bring in local people, and visitors—socialists, utopians, architects and literary celebrities—came in throngs. Remoteness and the decline in the market for art-work products led to failure in 1908. In the town the Guild initiated a process of careful restoration of old buildings that has persisted ever since. Ashbee restored the 14C *Wool-Staplers Hall* in the High St for himself and the *Norman Chapel House* at Broad Campden for the Singhalese writer, A. Coomaraswamy. **Broad Campden** *church* (1868; J. Prichard) is a small High Victorian work with altar rails by Ashbee (1913).

CIRENCESTER. A417 18m SE of Gloucester. In the Market Place, *Corn Hall* (1862; Medland, Maberly and Medland) ashlar-fronted with good carved detail. The great parish *church* was restored by Scott

(1865) with stone reredos and stained glass by Hardman, mostly late 19C. SW of the Market Place, marooned in the bus station, the former railway *station* (c 1850) in Brunel's Tudor style. On the Tetbury Road, *The Querns* (1825; P.F. Robinson), an early example of picturesque Tudor. At the top of the hill, leafy *cemetery* (1871; Medland and Son) with twin chapels. Further out, off the Tetbury road, *Royal Agricultural College* (1846; Daukes and Hamilton), handsome collegiate Tudor group with central entrance tower and chapel. W of the centre, Cecily Hill, the broad approach street to Cirencester Park with one heavily Victorian accent in the old *Militia Armoury* (1857), embattled and Gothic. SE of the centre, Watermoor, *Holy Trinity* (1850; G.G. Scott), typical Scott early Dec. style church with spire, the windows enlarged by Scott in richer Dec. 1878.

5m N of Cirencester, A435, at **Rendcomb**, *Rendcomb College*, (1864–67; P.C. Hardwick), dramatically sited Italianate house built for Sir F.H. Goldsmid MP, the first Jewish barrister in England and leading patron of causes liberal (University College, London) and Jewish (the Jewish Free School). The house has similarities with the great town houses built in London by Cubitt and his successors, bay windows and the big corner tower providing the characteristically Victorian note. By the village, French Renaissance style *stable court* (1867; Hardwick) with classical arches each side, one capped by a pavilion-roofed tower, opening onto the drive up to the house. Estate cottages in the village and Italianate main lodge. 7m NE of Cirencester, A429, impressive dry stone walls of the *Stowell Park* estate. The house, of c 1600, was enlarged (1886–98; J. Belcher) for the 3rd Earl of Eldon in a free 16C to 17C style. 5m E of Cirencester, A417, at **Poulton**, *church* (1873; Butterfield) stone, stone tiled. Pretty *school*, small and quite vernacular by Butterfield (1873). 3m E **Fairford**, where John Keble (1792–1866), who inspired a whole generation of churchmen towards reform of the Church of England, was born. Keble's 'The Christian Year' (1827) had no rival in 19C religious verse, being reprinted some 160 times before 1872. Memorial in the *church*. 3m N, at **Hatherop**, *Hatherop Castle*, ponderous remodelling (1850–56; H. Clutton) of a c 1600 house for Lord de Mauley. The *church* adjoining was rebuilt for Lord de Mauley by Clutton (1845–55) with saddleback central tower and a quite remarkable SE chapel to Lady de Mauley, apparently designed by W. Burges. The chapel is stone vaulted, the vaulting springing low from a richly carved broad band around. Quirky French Gothic exterior detail. In the chapel effigy of Lady de Mauley (1848; R. Monti), exquisitely carved with extreme naturalism. 2m SE of Fairford, at **Whelford**, pretty village *church* (1864; G.E. Street) apsed with attractive stained glass, some by the Rev H.F. St. John for whom Street restored the nearby *church* of Kempsford. There St. John designed the W window and the rich painted decoration under the crossing tower. 4m E of Fairford, at **Lechlade**, *Lechlade Manor* (1872; J.L. Pearson) off Burford St, stone Jacobean style country house, detailed without the ostentation of much Victorian Jacobean work. Symmetrical S front, with centre rounded bay, more complex asymmetrical W side.

5m SE of Cirencester, off A419, at **Down Ampney**, *church* with complete late Victorian interior decoration (1898; C.E. Ponting), rich carved woodwork by H. Hems, and contemporary metalwork. 4m W of Cirencester, N of A419, **Sapperton**, where the Arts and Crafts workshop of Ernest Gimson and the Barnsley brothers was established in 1894. Their craft work, furniture, metalwork and plasterwork, was made entirely by old methods in reaction both to modern industrialism and to modern design, particularly that type of over-elaborate decoration that obscured both construction and purpose in late Victorian furniture. They moved first to *Pinbury Park*, an isolated part-medieval house overlooking the Frome valley where a fine panelled room with carved fireplace survives from their occupation. Later their workshop was at *Daneway House*, medieval and 16C house W of the village. In the village several cottages by Gimson and the Barnsleys, *Upper Dorvel House*, old cottages extended in local style (1903; E. Barnsley), *Beechanger* (1903; S. Barnsley) and *The Leasowes* (1903; E. Gimson), originally thatched. The *village hall* is by E. Barnsley (1912). All three are buried in the churchyard.

GLOUCESTER. The county town, ravaged by 20C roads. Gloucester *Cathedral* had all the post medieval work removed in 19C restoration under G.G. Scott who designed the elaborate high altar (1873) and many of the choir fittings, notably the tile and marble floor. Much 19C glass, pictorial W window by Wailes (1859), good series of brightly coloured windows in S aisle, of c 1855–65, windows by Kempe in S choir aisle and complete scheme of early 20C glass by C. Whall in the Lady Chapel. St. Andrew's Chapel in S transept has painted decoration in Celtic to Norman style by T. Gambier-Parry. Among the monuments, in the N aisle, Canon Tinling monument (c 1897; H. Wilson), fine kneeling bronze figure before an angel in a green marble surround, high quality Arts and Crafts work. In S transept, small brass and marble memorial to Canon Evans (c 1891; H. Wilson). In S choir aisle, Bishop Ellicott (c 1905; W.S. Frith), alabaster effigy, and in the Lady Chapel plaque (c 1907; A. Drury) to Miss Beale, pioneer of women's education as headmistress of Cheltenham Ladies College. N of the great cloister, former *Bishop's Palace*, rebuilt 1865 (E. Christian). W of the cathedral, in St. Mary's Square, large canopied *monument* (1862; E.W. Thornhill) to Bishop Hooper, burnt on this site. College St, S of the Cathedral has picturesque Tudor-style buildings (1890; F.W. Waller).

In Westgate St, *Shire Hall* (1816; R. Smirke), much enlarged. In Eastgate St, *Guildhall* (1890; G.H. Hunt) Renaissance style. The facade of the 1856 *Market* (Medland and Maberly), pedimented Corinthian with a bell tower, survives in front of rebuilt markets. In Brunswick Rd, *Museum and Library* (1897; F.W. Waller) Gothic, now including the Northern Renaissance style memorial hall (1892; F.W. Waller) next door. From Eastgate St, Barton St leads SE with *All Saints' Church* (1875; G.G. Scott). From the Cross, Northgate St runs NE to London Rd and *St. Peter's RC Church* (1860–68; G. Blount), ambitious stone church with spire. Glass and painted decoration by Clayton and Bell. Further out, between London Rd and Denmark Rd, *Hillfield* (1867; A. Estcourt), elaborate Italianate villa with campanile tower, built for himself by the leading Gloucester builder of the period. Southgate St runs SW from the Cross. At the corner of Commercial Rd, former *Savings Bank* (1850; Hamilton and Medland) palazzo style. In Commercial Rd, the *Custom House* (c 1830; S. Smirke), ashlar classical, and the *Prison*, late 18C enlarged 1845–50. *Gloucester Docks* to S have an impressive group of early 19C brick warehouses built for the Gloucester and Berkeley Canal Company. Off Southgate St, further S, Spa Road leads to the Park, with pleasant early 19C stucco buildings. *Christ Church* (1822; Rickman and Hutchinson), Brunswick Square, was the church for the new suburb, brick and stucco classical, the interior much altered c 1900 (H.A. Prothero) in a Romanesque style with painted decoration to the apse.

2m W of Gloucester, off A40, *Highnam* church (1849–51; H. Woodyer), a major work of the Gothic Revival built for T. Gambier-Parry of Highnam Court. Externally the church is handsome Dec., internally there is a complete and unaltered scheme of painted decoration, mostly by Gambier-Parry, and contemporary stained glass, N aisle by Wailes, S aisle by Hardman to Pugin designs, W window by O'Connor and a later (1859) E window by Clayton and Bell. Gambier-Parry provided also the vicarage, schools and lodge, all by Woodyer, completing this outstanding example of Victorian High Church patronage. Woodyer also designed the *church* (1870) at **Minsterworth**, A48, 2m SW, finely detailed with battlemented tower. 5m W of Highnam, A40, at **Huntley**, *church* (1863; S.S. Teulon) High Victorian Gothic of the most lavish kind, the interior aglow with coloured decoration and ornate carving. The carving, by T. Earp, is richly naturalistic in the arcade capitals and fully polychrome in the pulpit and reredos, exceptional examples of this period of Gothic design. The polychromy extends to coloured banding in the walls and mastic inlay. Teulon's roof woodwork is inventively elaborate and there is contemporary glass by Lavers and Barraud in the chancel and by Teulon in the nave, the Teulon glass quite unusual, like coloured line engraving. *Huntley Manor* (1862; Teulon) is in a mixed style with French tall slate roofs and ponderous detail. 2m S, off A4136, *Blaisdon Hall*, mid Victorian Jacobean style house, now a school. Just SW, at **Flaxley**, *church* (1856; G.G. Scott) with tower and spire and elaborate carved fittings, notably the reredos by J.B. Philip. 12m SW of Huntley, **Coleford**, ironworking centre in the Forest of Dean. *Church* (1880; F.S. Waller). 2m S, at **Clearwell**, expensive *church* (1866; J. Middleton) built by the Countess of Dunraven as a memorial to her son. Heavily polychrome interior like Middleton's Cheltenham churches, marble fittings and painted decoration. 3m W of Coleford, on the Wye, at **Lower Redbrook**, attractive small *church* (1873; J.P. Seddon). At **Bream**, 4m SE of Coleford, *church* rebuilt 1860 (W. White), High Victorian carved capitals and plate tracery, wholly altering the original building of 1823.

7m N of Gloucester, off A417, NW of **Ashleworth**, *Foscombe* (c 1860; T. Fulljames), ornate Gothic house built by the architect for himself, well set on the hillside. 2m N, A417, **Snig's End**, still relatively complete model settlement, set up by the Chartist leader F. O'Connor c 1847 as a smallholding community, one of several around the country. Like the others it eventually failed due to poor finances and muddled administration, but the small single-storey cottages here, and at **Lowbands**, 2m NW, survive, well spaced out in their allotment plots. The *Prince of Wales Inn* on the main road was the largest building, built as the schoolhouse. O'Connor would not have a church. 3m SW of Gloucester, off A38, at **Quedgeley**, *church* much rebuilt 1856 (H. Woodyer) with good glass of c 1857 in the chancel side windows and SE window. 6m SW, on the peninsula created by a bend of the Severn, **Fretherne** *church* (1847; F. Niblett: 1857; J.W. Hugall), spiky Gothic estate church built for the Darell family with much carving and painted decoration. Stained glass by G. Rogers of Worcester.

STOW-ON-THE-WOLD. A429 19m NE of Cirencester. In the centre, *St. Edward's Hall* (1878; Medland) Perp. town hall in the centre of the market place. W of the town, B4077, towards **Upper Swell**, *Abbotswood*, Cotswold style house of 1867 recast from 1902 by Lutyens, the main addition the sweeping entrance gable rising almost from the ground with mannered classical details and the corresponding W gable rising over a water garden, also by Lutyens. Garden occasionally open to public. To SW, 2m W of **Lower Swell**, *Eyford Park* (1910; G. Dawber), handsome early 18C style ashlar-fronted house. In **Upper Slaughter**, to S, terrace of cottages by'the church remodelled 1906 by Lutyens. 1m S of Stow, off A429, *Nether Swell Manor* (1903 and 1911; G. Dawber) rambling in style of c 1600, carefully detailed. 8m SW of Stow, A429, at **Northleach**, the former House of Correction (1790) on the Fosse Way is now museum of agricultural history. At **Hampnett**, just NW of the museum, *church* with a complete scheme of painted decoration in the chancel by the rector, the Rev. W. Wiggin (c 1871). At **Sherborne**, 4m E of Northleach, off A40, *Sherborne House*, 16C mansion with echoes of Longleat rebuilt in similar style (1829–34; L. Wyatt) with the parish *church*, rebuilt c 1845, standing right adjacent.

4m E of Stow, off A436, **Daylesford** *church* (1859–63; J.L. Pearson), an outstanding High Victorian work, the exterior dominated by a sturdy tower and pyramidal stone spire. Early French Gothic in inspiration and conceived like much of the best High Victorian work as an exercise in solid geometry, square and pyramid with steeply pointed gables over the bell-openings cutting up into the pyramid. The bell-openings, richly traceried, are deeply set back so as to emphasise the mass. The church is quite small but the strong lines and sturdy tower give a massive effect. Richly carved interior with banded stone and coloured shafts, the chancel stone vaulted. E and W windows by Wailes, others by Clayton and Bell. 5m N of Stow, A429, **Moreton-in-Marsh**, the High St, along the Fosse Way, dominated by the *Market Hall* (1887; E. George), free-standing in a finely detailed Tudor style with arched ground floor and top clock turret. At the top of the High St, *The White House* (1898; G. Dawber), roughcast and half-timbered Cotswold style house, carefully handled in the Arts and Crafts way. The *church*, off the High St, was thoroughly rebuilt with new tower and spire (1858–60; Poulton and Woodman), E window by N.H.J. Westlake. 1m NW of Moreton, at **Batsford**, *Batsford Park* (1888–92; George and Peto) very large Elizabethan style house elaborately detailed with fine quality carving, built for Lord Redesdale, diplomat in the Far East and author of 'Tales of Old Japan', who created the famous Japanese gardens around the house. Stable court of 1878 (E. George). The *church* was rebuilt (1861; Poulton and Woodman) for the 1st Earl of Redesdale in heavy Romanesque style style. Several Mitford monuments, wall plaque to the 1st Earl (1886; J.E. Boehm) with carved angel and an exceptional white marble low tomb to Frances Mitford (died 1866; W. Burges), the ridged top carved with plant scrolls and birds on a gold mosaic background.

STROUD. A46 28m N of Bath. Important woollen town from the 15C with surviving mills of the late 18C to mid 19C. The parish *church* was rebuilt except the tower and spire (1866–68; Wilson and Willcox), much ornate carving by J. Wall, notably the High Victorian stone and marble pulpit. Carved and painted reredos (1872; G.G. Scott Jr). Some notable stained glass, E window by Clayton and Bell. The Shambles leading up to the church have a pretty 19C cast-iron arcade and the 16C Town Hall has added Victorian stair towers each side. Off Nelson St, in Kendrick St, late 19C brick and terracotta block at entrance to the square in front of the *Stroud Subscription Rooms* (1833; G. Basevi), handsome late classical with an upstairs ballroom. *Congregational Chapel* (1835; C. Baker), in Bedford St, adjoining, unusually fine, pedimented with Ionic columns and centre Venetian window. N of the

High St, in Lansdown, *School of Science and Art* (1890–99; J.P. Seddon and W. Fisher), a very late High Victorian Gothic building, Ruskinian in choice of style and in the splendid carving, notably the band of Gothic leaf scroll with lively animals framing roundels of leading figures scientific and artistic (T.H. Huxley, Lord Kelvin, Turner, Charles Barry). *Library* (1873; W. Clissold) Gothic. On the hill out to the N, A46, former *Convent of St. Rose of Lima* (1867; B. Bucknall), rock- faced stone Gothic buildings with round staircase tower in the entrance recess. Severely detailed with touches reminiscent of work by Burges. Chapel added 1888–95, to the original design, now stripped of fittings.

1m W of Stroud, S of A4096, *Ebley Mills*, large early 19C stone mill with tall tower capped by a slate French roof added c 1862 by G.F. Bodley for the owner, Sir S.S. Marling, whose house on the ridge at Selsley overlooks the mill. At **Selsley**, B4066, SW of Stroud, Marling's house, *Stanley Park*, rebuilt 1850 and 1871 with picturesque turrets, stands next to the *church* (1862; Bodley), one of the finest works of the High Victorian period. The church stands on a bluff overlooking the Frome valley, severely massed with an unbroken ridge line to a steep canted apse, the severe geometry echoed in the square tower with saddleback roof, a landmark from the valley. Fine exterior stone details, a carved buttress marking the nave and chancel division. Within strong carving to the arcade and apse, good fittings and, a milestone in the revival of stained glass work in Britain, the first complete scheme of stained glass by Morris and Co , with apse glass by Morris, Rossetti, Madox Brown and Burne-Jones and a glorious W rose window of the Creation by Philip Webb and Morris. The approach to the church is dignified by a stone lychgate by Bodley following Butterfield's lychgate design at Coalpit Heath, Avon. Bodley later (1876) restored the *church* at **King's Stanley**, 1m W, adding a lovely organ case.

1m S of Selsley, at **North Woodchester**, *St. Mary's Church* (1863; S.S. Teulon) with handsome spire and complex Teulon details in the tracery and the arcading of the S porch. Good stained glass by Saunders, Lavers and Barraud, and Preedy. On the hill to **South Woodchester**, *Franciscan Convent* (1861–69; C.F. Hansom) well set on a sloping site with the chapel built out over a library. Further S, *RC church* (1846– 49; C.F. Hansom), built for William Leigh, a Catholic convert, who founded a Passionist priory here. The priory buildings have gone but the church remains, an excellent example of the manner of Pugin, Dec. with an octagonal spire and contemporary glass by Hardman and Wailes. Alabaster effigy of Leigh (c 1873; R. Boulton) holding a model of the church. W of the church, deep in a valley is *Woodchester Park*, the great unfinished Gothic house built for Leigh c 1854–68 to designs by B. Bucknall, local architect employed by Leigh at the age of 21. Bucknall was the closest English follower of the great French theorist, E. Viollet-le-Duc, translating his works and corresponding with him on the construction of the house which follows Viollet-le-Duc in emphasising Gothic constructional methods over superfluous decoration. Inside it was to have been stone vaulted and the completed parts have superbly constructed vaults and stone arches to support timber floors never inserted. Externally mullion and transom windows fill the main S front, divided by buttresses with carved and practical stone gargoyles. The other fronts are more picturesquely asymmetrical, emphasising the plan and function of the various parts. Deep in its isolated valley, the house, one of the most remarkable of the 19C, remains apparently intact to its stone-tiled roof. Bucknall altered the cottage above the house for Leigh and other Bucknall cottages survive in Nympsfield (Scar Hill and St. Stephens). In **Nympsfield**, off B4066, *almshouses*, now convent, built c 1850 for Leigh. The *church* rebuilt 1861–63 by S.S. Teulon who also enlarged the school. Further SW, B4066, at **Uley**, *church* (1857; Teulon) with ornate tracery and complex timber roofs. W window glass by Teulon.

At **Dursley**, 2m W, A4135, *church* restored 1867 (T.G. Jackson) with E window by Burlison and Grylls. *Chestal House* (1848; L. Vulliamy) is Jacobean style. At **Woodmancote**, just S, small EE style *church* (1844; G. Alexander). 3m W of Dursley, B4060, **Stinchcombe**, with *church* rebuilt 1855 (J.L. Pearson) for Sir G. Prevost, Squire and Vicar. Elaborate reredos and chancel glass by Wailes. *Stinchcombe Manor*, Prevost's house, Tudor style (1837). S of the village, B4060, *Drakestone* (c 1912; O. Milne), long stone house in the manner of Voysey with interior work by Gimson. Beyond, **Stancombe Park** where the Rev. D. Edwards, vicar of Nibley, created a romantic garden in the bottom of the valley, approached by tunnels with a lake, Doric temple, two picturesque cottages, grottoes and cascades, a rare survival. At **North Nibley**, to S, the bluff overlooking the Severn valley is crowned by the *Tyndale Monument* (1866; S.S. Teulon) an 111ft stone rectangular tower tapering up to a top gallery, a monument to W. Tyndale, translator of the Bible into English, born at North Nibley 1484. The *church* has chancel of 1861 (J.L. Pearson) in Early French style with painted decoration throughout and gold mosaic reredos of 1874.

From Stroud, B4070 runs NE towards Slad. At **Uplands**, a suburb of Stroud, N of the road, *church* (1908–10; Temple Moore), fine late Gothic Revival with tower and spire, nave and chancel in one with cross-gabled S aisle and dignified E end with triple arcade and deepset windows under an upper triple window. At **Slad**, described in Laurie Lee's 'Cider with Rosie', *church* of 1831 reconstructed 1869 (B. Bucknall) in a High Victorian manner clearly distinguishable from the ashlar earlier work. E of Stroud, the A419 follows the industrial Frome valley with settlements on the S facing slope and remaining mills below, e.g. at **Brinscombe** where there was a port on the Thames–Severn canal. **Chalford** is the most notable industrial settlement, steeply terraced up the hillside. At **France Lynch**, just E, *church* (1855–57; Bodley), Bodley's first church, exploiting a sloping site for dramatic effect at the E end. Fine carving by Earp and High Victorian polychrome work in marble, lapis lazuli, malachite and tile in the fittings. The exterior is severe with fine tracery and a W end marked by three gabled buttresses framing the W windows. At **Brown's Hill**, W of Chalford, *House of Mercy* (1851; W. White), Tudor style retreat house with lancet Gothic chapel. Further N, at **Bussage**, *church* (1846; J.P. Harrison) built in the first flush of the Oxford Movement by 20 Oxford undergraduates who chose to save £20 a year to build a church in a place where the need was greatest. Bussage was chosen because John Keble's brother was vicar at Bisley. The church is correctly Gothic with E window by O'Connor. S aisle added by Bodley. (1854), his first work, with naturalistic carving. Reredos by Bodley. Bodley also worked on the *church* at **Bisley** for T. Keble, probably designing the pulpit and reredos c 1855, though the main rebuilding of 1862 was by Keble's curate, the Rev. W. Lowder. Village *school* by Bodley (1855) with tilehanging in gable. Keble also provided the pretty Gothic structure around *Bisley Wells*, the village water supply (1863). *Lypiatt Park*, W of Bisley, is a medieval house remodelled 1809 (J. Wyatville) and extended in Gothic style 1876 (T.H. Wyatt). SE of Bisley, at **Waterlane**,

Waterlane House is Regency, given gables and interior fittings in the Arts and Crafts manner by E. Gimson (1907). 3m E of Bisley, *Edgeworth Manor*, early 18C with a gabled Tudor to Elizabethan style W front (1899; E. George). 2m N, *Miserden Park*, early 17C gabled house rebuilt 1875 (A. Waterhouse) and with a wing added 1920 by Lutyens.

TETBURY. A433 10m SW of Cirencester. In the centre, *White Hart Hotel* (1852; L. Vulliamy) Jacobean style. In New Church St, W of the centre, *St. Saviour's Church* (1848; Daukes and Hamilton) built for the poor of Tetbury, then excluded from the parish church, the Tractarian curate C. Lowder, later a renowned High Church priest in E London, raising the money. A good example of the Gothic favoured by the Oxford Tractarians and by Pugin, the elements clearly distinguished with generous roofs and Dec. detail. Glass by O'Connor, original pews and screen, carved stone reredos by Pugin. All the interior fittings appear contemporary making the church an unusually complete survival.

3m SW of Tetbury, A433, at **Westonbirt**, *Westonbirt House* (1863–70; L. Vulliamy) a Victorian prodigy house built at vast expense for R.S. Holford, for whom Vulliamy designed Dorchester House, London, the most splendid of London town houses. The Holfords established at Westonbirt from the 17C, amassed wealth as London lawyers in the 18C and R.S. Holford devoted his inheritance to building, collecting pictures and planting. The tree collection he started in 1829, now *Westonbirt Arboretum*, has become one of the finest in Britain. R.S. Holford employed Vulliamy as architect from c 1840 rebuilding cottages and farms, most of the village houses at Westonbirt and Beverston, restoring Beverston *church* (1844), rebuilding Lasborough *church* (1861) and also building the White Hart at Tetbury. The rebuilding of the house came after the great London palazzo (1851–57). Holford chose Wollaton Hall, Nottingham, as his model and the result is as elaborate a piece of Victorian Elizabethan as any, comparable to and perhaps richer than Mentmore, Beds. The exterior stonework is of the highest quality and the interior, despite some 50 years as a school, survives intact with rooms arranged around a galleried two-storey hall, the grand staircase leading off with walls lined in Spanish leather. Elaborate *lodges* on the main road. Holford memorials in the *church* by the house, alabaster effigy (c 1893) of R.S. Holford. 4m NE of Tetbury, at **Rodmarton**, *Rodmarton Manor* (1906–26; E. Barnsley) Cotswold style house built over a long period to Arts and Crafts principles, all the stone locally quarried and worked, the woodwork and metalwork made by estate workmen and everything done without machinery. The plan of the house is long; the slow process of building is reflected in the big canted bays masking the joins of the side wings and resulting in a slightly incoherent range of gables set off by varied types of tall chimneys. The interiors have fine beamed ceilings and much original Arts and Crafts furniture mostly made on the estate in the manner of Gimson and the Barnsley brothers.

TEWKESBURY. A38 11m N of Gloucester. *Tewkesbury Abbey* was restored 1875–79 (G.G. Scott) relatively carefully, ironic in that this restoration provoked William Morris to set up the Society for the Protection of Ancient Buildings to prevent the type of over-zealous restoration that most British major churches suffered during the 19C. Stalls by Scott and screen by J.O. Scott (1892). Late 19C nave glass by Hardman. In the ambulatory nice portrait plaque to Mrs Craik (1890; H.H.

Armstead). Her 'John Halifax, Gentleman', an immensely popular novel, was set in Tewkesbury (disguised as Nortonbury). In the High St, *Town Hall* with attractive pedimented front of c 1840. E of the High St, *Holy Trinity Church* (1837; E. Trotman), red-brick Gothic with the W front recessed in a giant arch to dramatic effect. 3m W of Tewkesbury, off A438, at **Forthampton**, *church* with work by W. Burges (c 1866), the reredos and very good E window made by Saunders. A window by the pulpit of 1869 by Saunders to designs by H. Holiday. Burges designed the *Yorke Almshouses* (1863–65) by the church, steeply gabled Gothic. *Forthampton Court*, 15C and 18C complex rambling house, has sensitive additions of 1889–91 by P. Webb, especially the white-painted entrance hall and oak stair. At **Apperley**, 4m SW of Tewkesbury, B4213, a surprising Romanesque style *church* (1856; F. Penrose) in brick with terracotta and stone dressings.

HAMPSHIRE

ALDERSHOT. A325 10m W of Guildford. The Military Camp was established in 1855, and the town has grown as an army town ever since. Off the Farnborough Rd, *Wellington Monument* (1838–46; M.C. Wyatt), the ill-fated statue erected in London on top of Constitution Arch at Hyde Park Corner to universal derision as the Duke appeared about to ride off the top of his incongruous pedestal, while the Duke found the imperious arm waving into his upper windows disagreeable. It weighs some 40 tons. Nearby, *All Saints' Church* (1863; P.C. Hardwick) brick, High Victorian with pyramid roofed tower. In the town, attractive *Town Hall* (1904; C. Hutchinson), Grosvenor Rd, and interesting *RC church* (1913; G. Drysdale) in coloured brick, Italian style on a steeply sloped site. 3m N, A325, at **Farnborough**, *Farnborough Abbey*, Benedictine Abbey founded by the Empress Eugenie of France in memory of her husband, the Emperor Napoleon III. The memorial church (1887; G. Destailleur) is in a lavish French Flamboyant Gothic with a surprising Gothic dome. Stone vaulted with complex pendants and ribs. In the crypt, tombs of the Emperor, Eugenie and their son, the Prince Imperial, killed with the British Army in Zululand. Brick Abbey (1887; Destailleur) with incomplete stone additions in Romanesque to early Gothic style (1900–12; Fr B. Williamson). The Empress lived at *Farnborough Hill* (c 1862; H. Kendall Jr), large bargeboarded house with tower the other side of the railway. Now a convent. *Town Hall* (1897; G. Sherrin), Alexandra Rd, free Tudor and late 17C style.

4m NW of Aldershot, A323, at **Fleet**, *All Saints' Church* (1861; W. Burges), a simple brick church, apsed with plate tracery. Painted decoration survives in the nave, but whitewash and later extensions have much altered the original. Splendid Gothic memorial to the founders of the church by Burges, carved by T. Nicholls, two effigies under an overpowering canopy. 2m S, at **Church Crookham**, *church* with chancel by Woodyer (1876) and sgraffito plaster decoration in the nave (1893; H. Sumner). 2m NW of Fleet, *Elvetham Hall* (1859; S.S. Teulon), polychrome brick High Victorian mansion of the most alarming type, not simply for the colouring, deep red banded in black, but more for the extraordinary outlines that Teulon achieved, the house building up to a massive mansard-roofed tower through a variety of roof heights, bay windows, curved gables, dormers and turrets. All this variety and the patterning in the brick succeeds in diffusing the shape into undulating and opposing curves confusing any external reading of the internal plan. Teulon is always a highly individual architect and the desire to avoid period references seems paramount. As an exploitation of the possibilities of brick decoration, Elvetham has few rivals. The porte-cochère is a later addition in the same style. Interiors with much carved wood work and stained glass. Teulon estate buildings around a massive water tower. *Church* (1840; H. Roberts) neo-Norman with elaborate spire, possibly added by Teulon. 2m W, at **West Green**, W of A30, *Fouracre* (1901; E. Newton) symmetrical brick gabled house, quietly detailed in Newton's vernacular Georgian manner. 2m N of Fleet, B3013, *Minley Manor* (1858–60; H. Clutton) another Victorian prodigy house, in the French château style in red brick and stone. Steep pavilion roofs and finely carved stone Gothic detail, all determinedly asymmetrical. Built for a Catholic banker, hence the large chapel and correspondingly small parish *church*, both by Clutton. The house was extended in a freer 17C style by Devey (1886) and orangery, stables and lodge added. A big entrance wing in Clutton's style added 1898. 2m N at **Yateley**, *church* with good E window glass by Morris and Co (1876) and W window by H. Holiday (1885).

ALTON. A31 18m NE of Winchester. A long street on old Winchester road with *Curtis Museum* (1869–80; C. Barry Jr) in the centre, a red-brick courtyard group and spired *church* (1873; F. Dyer) at the SW end. 4m SW, A32, at **East Tisted**, *Rotherfield Park*, early 19C much enlarged in 1860s and 1890s. Gatehouse (1891) and Elizabethan style refacing to main house, large water tower (1860s) and stable tower (1890s). 4m N, N of A31, NE of **Medstead**, *Alton Abbey* founded for seamen (1889) with buildings from 1895 (P. Green) in flint and yellow brick. Fine early 13C style chapel, original in detail. At **Lasham**, 4m NW of Alton, N of A339, *church* (1866; Woodyer) flint with shingled spire. 3m NW, *Moundsmere Manor* (1908; Sir R. Blomfield), large red-brick and stone house, formal reproduction of a country house of c 1700.

ANDOVER. A343 16m SW of Newbury. Hilltop parish *church* (1840–46; A.F. Livesay), imposing flint EE style, all very long lancets. Interior of extremely tall proportions with plaster vaults and an apse closed off by an elongated screen. NW of churchyard, Gothic *Church Institute* (1849) and *almshouses* rebuilt 1872. At **Smannell**, 3m NE, High Victorian small *church* (1857; W. White), in flint and brick with brick interior. Simple mouldings and strong proportions, as in the low piers of the arcade. Similar *church* (1857; W. White) at **Hatherden**, 4m W. 11m NE of Andover, A343, **Highclere**, estate of the Earls of Carnarvon. *Church* (1869; G.G. Scott) in flint with broach spire, built for the ₊4th Earl, a statesman whose career was said to be 'marred by extreme sensitiveness', for he resigned three high offices on matters of principle. *Highclere Castle* (1839–42; Sir C. Barry) was rebuilt for the 3rd Earl, encasing a Georgian house in splendid Elizabethan dress, delicately detailed with symmetrical facades ornamented with narrow corner towers and lacy top balustrading. Like Barry's Houses of Parliament the main symmetry is broken in most views by a very large tower set over the staircase. Exceptionally fine stonework throughout. Interiors mostly of 1861 and later, including a fine stone-vaulted entrance hall and large, less correctly detailed, central hall (1862; T. Allom). In the grounds, *Rotunda* rebuilt by Barry and *church* (1869; G.G. Scott) flint with broach spire. 3m E, at **Ecchinswell**, *church* (1886; Bodley and Garner), tall interior, nave and chancel undivided as Bodley liked, pretty painted decoration to chancel and painted organ case. 11m W of Andover, A338, at **South Tidworth**, *church* (1879; J. Johnson), estate church of Tidworth House. Tall, thin, circular bell turret outside and interior of exceptional richness, marble piers and much carved decoration. Built for Sir John Kelk, London building contractor. *Tidworth House* is of the early 19C much altered after 1850 in classical to Italianate style.

BASINGSTOKE. A30 17m SE of Reading. In the High St, *Town Hall* (1832; L. Wyatt) stucco classical. In Wote St, Italianate *Corn Exchange* (1864) with cast-iron interior. In Victoria St, *All Saints' Church* (1915; Temple Moore), severe ashlar stone building with windows set high and tall light interior. 5m NE, A33, at **Sherfield-on-Loddon**, *North Foreland Lodge* (1898; F.B. Wade), free Tudor to Baroque brick and stone house. Estate cottages on the green. 4m NE, *Stratfield Saye*

House (open to public) bought for the Duke of Wellington by parliament in 1817. Many relics of the Duke's military and political careers. *Wellington Monument* (1863), a column with statue (Marochetti), to E, by A33. 5m E of Basingstoke, S of **Rotherwick**, *Tylney Hall* (1899; R.S. Wornum), large red-brick and stone neo-Jacobean house rebuilt for the South African diamond and gold millionaire, Lionel Phillips. 5m W of Basingstoke, B3400, at **Ashe**, *church* (1877; G.G. Scott Jr) in flint with glass by Kempe (1878) in E window. To SW, *Berrydown* (1897; Lutyens), Tudor to entrance, gabled and tile-hung to the rear. At **Laverstoke**, 3m W, *church* (1896; J.L. Pearson) quite plain with broach spire. *Parsonage* (1858; G.E. Street) with tile-hung gables and bold chimneys, the manner taken up by Norman Shaw and later domestic revival architects from c 1870. *School* by Street (1858).

LYNDHURST. A35 5m W of Southampton. Centre of the New Forest, first popular as a country resort in the late 19C, when many a half-timbered house was built. *Church* (1858–70; W. White), an exceptional High Victorian polychrome brick work, the interior of four colours of brick with very tall notched brick arches. High quality naturalistic stone carving, painted decoration and steep timber roofs carried up from very low aisle walls to a splendid main roof framing large clerestory windows that are the principal source of light. On the wall shafts carved musician angels. No other church in the county shows the angular and hard-edged detail of High Victorian Gothic so well. Excellent Morris glass in the E, and S transept, S windows, one of the earliest commissions by Burne-Jones (1862–63). N transept window by Clayton and Bell. Painted reredos by Lord Leighton (1864) and chancel monument to the founders of the church (1863; G.E. Street). 1m S, *High Coxlease* (1898; Lethaby), W of A337, Arts and Crafts brick house with generous sash windows and triple gabled main front ornamented with strange linear patterns, zigzag under the attic and stepped under the first floor, a sign of Lethaby's interest in elemental decoration. 1m W, off A35, small *church* (1864; Butterfield) at **Emery Down**, in diapered brick. 3m NW at **Minstead**, Sir Arthur Conan Doyle is buried in the *churchyard*, his scale of values nicely indicated by the inscription, 'Patriot, physician, man of letters'. By A31, *Castle Malwood* (1892) and *Malwood* (1883; E. Christian), typical of the late Victorian houses built around the Forest, of which examples can be seen especially at **Burley**, **Boldre** and near **Lymington**. By far the largest is *Rhinefield Lodge*, off A35, 5m SW of Lyndhurst, built 1888–90 (W.H. Romaine Walker) in a lavish Tudor to Elizabethan style. Rock-faced stone with much carved detail and ornate brick chimneys, romantically composed with a long sheet of water on the axis of the central hall bay window. The hall has a hammerbeam roof and minstrels' gallery, originally fitted with an orchestrion or electric organ, and there is elaborate interior carving including a panel of the Armada. The owner's wife inherited a Nottinghamshire colliery fortune. S of **Sway**, B3055, NW of Lymington, *Peterson's Tower* (1879), an extraordinary 218ft concrete folly tower, slightly Mogul in appearance, built by a retired Indian judge who intended to be buried under it. 2m N of Lymington, off A337, *Boldre Grange* (1873; R. Norman Shaw), brick and half-timbered house, a good example of Shaw's 'old English' style with varied silhouette of gables and tall chimneys. In **Lymington**, brick and stone Baroque *Town Hall* (1913) and fine 19C cast-iron shop front on High Street. 5m SW, **Milford on Sea**, developed from 1887 with a good range of late Victorian styles. In Park

Lane, *Westover* (1897; A. Mitchell), late 19C free style, inventively handled.

PETERSFIELD. A272 19m E of Winchester. On NE outskirts, *Churcher's College* (1881; G.R. Crickmay), Gothic school buildings. At **Steep**, 1m N, *By-the-Church*, 17C brick house carefully rebuilt in the Lutyens manner for himself by W. Unsworth (c 1900). To W, *Bedales School*, progressive school founded 1893 with large roughcast main building (1906; E.P. Warren), but remarkable for the Hall and Library block added 1911 (E. Gimson) where a disappointing brick exterior hides a superb timbered interior, the library with massive oak posts supporting a gallery with arched braces to the tie-beams and top-plate, all in best extreme Arts and Crafts manner, hand-shaped and correctly peg-jointed. Oak floor boards of impressive width and library furniture by Gimson and Sidney Barnsley. NE of Steep, *Coldhayes* (1869; A. Waterhouse), Gothic with steep dormered skyline. At **Sheet**, to E, A3, *church* with prominent steeple (1869; A. Blomfield) and, to N, *Adhurst St. Mary* (1858; P.C. Hardwick) gabled Gothic house. 6m W of Petersfield, off A272, at **Privett**, fine estate *church* (1876; A. Blomfield) with tall spire well set on the hillside. Lofty interior with very elaborate fittings. 4m N of Petersfield, W of A325, at **Hawkley**, *church* (1865; S.S. Teulon), neo-Norman with Rhenish-helm tower top. Elaborate interior carving, built as the estate church for *Hawkleyhurst* (c 1860; S.S. Teulon) to N. 3m NE, W of A325, **Blackmoor**, the estate of Sir Roundell Palmer, Lord Selborne, Lord Chancellor under Gladstone, responsible for the 1873 Judicature Act that first established a single Supreme Court. A leading figure in the debates on the Anglican church in the 1880s, he parted with Gladstone over the issue of disestablishment in 1886. *Blackmoor House* (1869–73 and 1882; A. Waterhouse) is Tudor Gothic in stone with a tower, appropriately austere for a strongly religious family. The *church* (1868; Waterhouse) has High Victorian plate tracery and a strong W tower.

PORTSMOUTH. The principal naval base and dockyard since the 16C. The naval dockyard, the harbour and old Portsmouth are on the W side of Portsea Island with the civic and commercial centre just inland and the main residential area, Southsea, on the tip of the island, facing across to Ryde, Isle of Wight. The civic centre around Commercial Rd has been largely rebuilt after bombing. Grand scale *Guildhall* (1886–90; W. Hill), Victorian classical with tall tower, the top rebuilt too simply after the war. Commercial Rd to the S has become Guildhall Walk and has some good late 19C buildings, including the *Prudential offices* (1890; Waterhouse) and the *Theatre Royal* (1884; C.J. Phipps: 1900; F. Matcham). The theatre, proposed for restoration, has splendid interior plasterwork full of nautical mermaids and dolphins, mostly dating from 1900 as does the pretty iron exterior balcony. Behind the Guildhall, *Library* (1903–08; G.E. Smith), freely detailed with Flemish gables, little cupolas and a corner dome. To N, across the railway, Victoria Park, laid out c 1880, and on the N side, Edinburgh Rd, *RC Cathedral* (1877–82; J.S. Crawley: later enlargements), red brick and stone, apsed, with lofty interior. Queen St runs W past the *Royal Naval Barracks* (1900) to Portsea and the main dockyard entry. The 19C dockyard buildings are largely inaccessible, lying beyond HMS Victory and the Royal Naval Museum. Important advances in cast-iron construction were achieved by naval engineers, notably in the recently demolished No. 3 Ship Shop (1849), but iron frame buildings survive elsewhere in the dockyard. Externally most of the 19C buildings are in red brick and stone, imposingly scaled and classical in the tradition of Vanbrugh's military buildings of the early 18C. The Hard and St. George's Rd lead SE to the top of the High St, the centre of Old Portsmouth, much bombed. Former *Cambridge Barracks* (c 1855–60), yellow brick classical, later the Grammar School, on the E side.

Pembroke Rd leads SE from High St towards Southsea. On N side, *Clarence Barracks* (c 1880), red brick with round tourelles and Gothic detail. Opposite, the edge of Southsea Common, stretching round to *Southsea Castle* (open to public), the fort built c 1538 for Henry VIII and later included in the Victorian fortifications of Portsmouth. Offshore can be seen Palmerston's four island forts (see Gosport below) stretching right across the Spithead. Victorian Southsea is behind the Common, stucco for the earlier developments, brick later. Off Kent Rd, W of Palmerston Rd, stucco villas and terraces of c 1840–60 laid out by T.E. Owen, leading figure in the development of 19C Portsmouth. *Sussex Place* (1835), *Sussex Terrace* (1837), *Clifton Terrace* and *Richmond Terrace* (1840s), *Portland Terrace* (1845). Owen designed *St. Jude's Church* (1851), Kent Rd, for his new suburb, spiky rockfaced Gothic with a low church galleried interior. He himself lived in a Gothic villa in Portland Rd, *Dover Court* (1848). Also in Kent Rd, *High School* (1886; J.O. Smith), cheerful gabled brick. To NE, in Albert Rd, *King's Theatre* (1907; F. Matcham) with corner tower and Edwardian Baroque interior. In Lawrence Rd, to N of Albert Rd, *Nazareth House* (c 1900; L. Stokes) free style with cupola-topped tower. In Fawcett Rd, *Holy Spirit Church* (1904–26; J.T. Micklethwaite), tall light interior in the manner of G.F. Bodley, rebuilt after bombing. Furnishings by Temple Moore from the demolished St. Agnes, Kennington, London, including fine Gothic pulpit. The seafront of Southsea runs into Eastney to E, with the *Royal Marine Barracks* (1862–67) the main building of interest, a very large open ended court, in brick except for the stone-faced Officers' Mess. Fine interior now containing the *Royal Marines Museum* (open to public). In Henderson Rd, *Eastney Pumping Station* (open to public), with a pair of massive Boulton and Watt pumping engines of 1887 in working order. From Eastney, Eastney Rd runs N to Milton. W of Milton Rd, *St. Mary's Hospital* (1844; A.F. Livesay), originally the workhouse. St. Mary's Rd runs W from the hospital to *St. Mary's Church* (1887; A.W. Blomfield), Fratton Rd, grandly scaled Perp. style church in flint and stone, on the site of the original parish church for Portsea Island. *Church Institute* (1899; R. Blomfield) neo-Wren.

N of the civic centre, Commercial Rd leads N to the motorway complex of the A3 approach. Off to W, by Charlotte St, the threatened *St. Agatha's Church* (1893–95; J.H. Ball), a basilican church in what was a poor district, hence built in brick and decorated as funds became available. The decoration was the masterpiece of Heywood Sumner executed in sgraffito plasterwork. Sumner decorated the apse with figures of the evangelists and prophets under a Christ in Majesty, the figures separated by bands of vine decoration. Strong lines, with the clarity of wood engraving and fine lettering. Further N, *Charles Dickens Birthplace Museum*, 393 Old Commercial Rd, where Dickens was born in 1812, his father being a clerk to the Navy Pay Office. Portsmouth features in 'Nicholas Nickleby'. Portsmouth was also where Arthur Conan Doyle set up as a doctor and wrote the first Sherlock Holmes story, modelling Dr Watson on his friend Dr James Watson, leading figure in the town's intellectual life.

At **Farlington**, A27, 3m N of Portsmouth, *church* (1872–75; G.E.

Street) exceptionally good, with vaulted chancel rising higher than the nave and subtle interior colouring from two types of stone, set off by marble piers and shafts.

Across the harbour from Portsmouth is **Gosport**, naval town, much damaged by bombs. The principal naval installation at Gosport was from 1828 the Victualling Yard, where all the foodstuffs needed for the navy were purchased, stored and in some cases manufactured. Close to the hard, *Holy Trinity Church* of 1696, given a N Italian exterior look (1887; A. Blomfield), the campanile the principal landmark of old Gosport. At the top of the High St, *Library* (1900; A.W. Cross), Arts and Crafts building of considerable originality. A brick corner tower, tile-hung at the top, pivots two ranges at right angles with roughcast upper floors and deep eaves, in the manner of Voysey. The leading angle of the corner tower has a circular stair turret attached rising to a copper domelet that sits well against the pyramid roof of the tower behind. Clarence Rd leads right, to *St. George's Barracks* (1857–59), handsome with its double range of verandahs, steps to the upper level and the balustrades with good ironwork. A tropical design; according to legend the barracks intended for Gosport are somewhere in the Far East, the plans having been mixed up. The disused *Gosport Station* (1841; W. Tite) has an unexpectedly grand stone colonnade, as this was the terminus for Portsmouth until 1847. After years of dereliction the building has been partly restored. Beyond, the *Royal Clarence Victualling Yard*, Weevil Lane, the largest building, the Granary (1853), where the famous ships' biscuits were made. Brick, late classical in design with iron piers to the ground floor. On Forton Rd, *HMS St. Vincent*, the Royal Marine Barracks (1847; Captain James), brick courtyard of late classical buildings, the entrance arch the only ornate feature. To SW of Gosport, **Alverstoke**, the original settlement with large *church* (1865, 1885; H. Woodyer), the tower added 1906. Tall proportions and Woodyer's characteristic angular tracery. Interior with naturalistic carving. To E on a fine site overlooking the Spithead and Portsmouth, *Haslar Hospital*, the Royal Naval Hospital, 18C but with a prominent pyramid roofed water tower (1885). To W, *Gosport Grammar School* (1844; D. Burton) a Tudor style seaside villa. From here ran the 19C chain of *forts*, part of the extraordinarily elaborate defences of Portsmouth harbour, built in the 1850s and 1860 and known as the Palmerston forts. Lord Palmerston, despite British alliances with France and the two countries' joint involvement in the Crimean War, suspected Napoleon III of Napoleonic ambitions and the Palmerston forts were a response to fears of a landing that would outflank Portsmouth harbour from the W or the N. There were five forts W of Gosport and six along Portsdown Hill, N of the harbour, as well as the island forts in the Spithead and the reconditioned defences on Portsea Island, comprising the most extensive 19C fortifications in Britain, massive complexes of earth embankments protecting sunken gunnery points, barracks, ammunition stores and connecting moats and salients. Of the Gosport forts, *Fort Brockhurst*, off A32, NW of Gosport, is the best survivor and on Portsdown Hill, *Fort Widley*, off A3, has been restored and is open to the public. The scale here is larger than the Gosport forts with masonry and brickwork of the highest quality and a warren of underground chambers of amazing complexity.

RINGWOOD. A31 15m W of Southampton. By the Market Place, parish *church* (1853–55; F. and H. Francis), a good mid 19C town church, large with central tower, strong lines with detail from EE lan-

cets to Dec. tracery carefully handled without excess of carving.
Chancel with glass of 1857 (Ward and Hughes) and wall-painting of
1870. 4m S, B3347, *Avon Tyrrell* (1891; W. Lethaby), Lethaby's first
and largest work, a country house in red brick with tile-hanging in the
manner of Norman Shaw, but with a wilful and sometimes awkward
originality in details. Garden front under a continuous roofline with
strong brick stacks and a fine rhythm of four central gables contained
by a projecting end bay and a huge brick chimney-breast. The
spacing of windows and bays in the centre is an exercise in near
symmetry, only here so close to symmetry that the discordances strike
oddly. The hard red appearance of the house, surprising for an architect later so influential in the Arts and Crafts movement, is partly due
to a later substitution of tile- hanging for plaster on the bay windows
and gables. 3m E, at **Thorney Hill**, *church* (1906; D. Blow) built for
Lord Manners of Avon Tyrrell, Edwardian Baroque with colour-
washed walls and a pretty cupola, looking more Italian than English.

ROMSEY. A27 4m N of Southampton. In the Market Place, *statue* of
Lord Palmerston (1867; M. Noble), who was born at the family home,
Broadlands, in 1784. Palmerston himself is buried in Westminster
Abbey, but there are numerous family memorials in *Romsey Abbey*. In
Cornmarket, to E of Market Place, former *Corn Exchange* (1864), pedimented classical, now a bank. *Broadlands* (open to public) is just S of
the town. Ornate old English style *lodge* (1870; W.E. Nesfield) to
A3057, highly picturesque with half timbering, leaded windows,
moulded plasterwork and an iron sunflower on the main gable. Particularly impressive chimney-stacks. Nesfield also designed a *school*
(1872), Station Rd, for the estate and some cottages at **Pauncefoot**,
A31. 2m W, A27, *Embley Park* was the family home of Florence Nightingale, but mostly rebuilt after it was sold in 1895. She is buried at East
Wellow *church*, to SW. 3m W, A27, **Sherfield English**, estate village of
Melchet Park, 1m W, Jacobean style house built 1863 (H. Clutton) for
the Baring family, bankers, and altered 1911–14 (D. Braddell) for the
Mond family, of ICI chemicals. Village *church* (1902; F. Bath), built for
the Barings, ornate red brick and stone with central tower and spire.

SOUTHAMPTON. An important port since Saxon times but the
modern development dating from the arrival of the railway and construction of the docks 1840–51. The early docks at the S end of the
peninsula have been filled in or altered but the original *station* survives, disused, off Platform Rd, stucco Italianate with a ground-floor
loggia (1839; W. Tite). In Terminus Terrace, *South Western House*
(1871; J. Norton), large red-brick and stone railway hotel with French
roofs. In Canute Rd, former *Custom House* (1847; A. Giles) in yellow
brick and *Cunard Offices*, a railway office building of 1899. To W,
Queen's Park, with a terrace of c 1830–40 along the N edge. Latimer St
leads N towards *St. Mary's Church*, the original parish church, sited
well E of the old town. Rebuilt (1878–84; G.E. Street) and bombed, the
tower and spire remain of Street's design, an impressive landmark. W
of Queen's Park, Town Quay, the waterfront of the medieval town
with High St running N, severely damaged by bombs. W of the High
St, Bugle St, with the former *Yacht Club* (1846; T. Hack), a stucco
palazzo with Tuscan colonnade and detailing in the manner of London
clubs of the period. A belvedere attic rises above the roof, presumably
to survey the harbour. At the N end of Bugle St, on Simnel St, *Council
Buildings* (1900; C.J. Hair), five-storey early council housing with
lower terraces around. On Castle Lane to NE, *County Court* (1851),

heavily Italianate with round-arched centrepiece. On High St, E of the ring road, some good 19C commercial buildings. To S, by Holy Rood Church, *Holy Rood Chambers* (c 1890), red brick and terracotta Gothic, and *bank* (1867; J. Gibson) opposite the church, one of the series of handsome Victorian classical banks Gibson built for the National Provincial Bank from 1864. *Woolwich House* (c 1850–60), N of the church, yellow brick and stone Italianate. Further N, Baroque style *Midland Bank* (1900; T. Whinney) and neo-Elizabethan *Lloyds Bank* (c 1900). N of Bargate, Above Bar, the main commercial street, much bombed. Overlooking Palmerston Park, *Prudential Building* (c 1890; A. Waterhouse), red brick and terracotta. In the park, part of the series of parks created from the old common lands c 1840–50 that are a distinctive feature of the town, *statue* of Lord Palmerston (1868; Sharpe). East Park is the continuation to the N, excellently landscaped with much planting. *Andrews Memorial* statue in the centre, the pedestal engraved with Southampton scenes, and the Baroque *Titanic Memorial* (1912) to the engineers on the liner. To W, West Park, with *statue* of Isaac Watts (1861; R.C. Lucas), theologian and hymn writer, author of 'O God our help in ages past', born in Southampton in 1674. W of the centre, off Shirley Rd, *Christ Church* (1865–66; W. White), Paynes Rd, suburban rubble-stone church with spire and vivid polychrome brick interior. At Millbrook, further W, *church* (1873–80; H. Woodyer), tall proportions and angular tracery.

E of Southampton, across the Itchen, the suburb of **Woolston**. To S, in Weston Grove Rd, *St. Mark's Church* (1863–67; W. White) with High Victorian polychrome brick interior. 2m SE, **Netley**, famous for the now demolished military hospital, built 1856–63 after the Crimean campaign had exposed the scandalous state of military medicine. The hospital was built to a vast scale and a design that ignored all the recommendations on ventilation and planning made by theorists and by those who, like Florence Nightingale, had seen the spread of disease in the older hospitals. The village grew after the hospital was built. N of the village, *Netley Castle*, a 16C fort enlarged and Gothicised c 1850, and much further extended 1885–90 (J.D. Sedding). Picturesque asymmetrical exterior, the skyline mostly Sedding's, notably the principal tower. Sedding also designed *St. Edward's Church* (1886), finely detailed late Dec. with the contrasts of plain surfaces and deep modelling that Arts and Crafts Gothicists liked. Good fittings. 4m N of Southampton, **Eastleigh**, created by the railway at the junction of lines to Portsmouth and Southampton. The original *station* (1839; Tite) survives as a platform building. From 1891 extensive railway workshops were moved to Eastleigh. 1m E at **Bishopstoke**, *church* (1890; E.P Warren) in the late Gothic style of Bodley. Fine iron screen (1903; W. Bainbridge Reynolds) Arts and Crafts Gothic.

WINCHESTER. A33 12m N of Southampton. The county town and 'Wintoncester' of Thomas Hardy's Wessex. From E, Bridge St leads over the Itchen into the High St, with King Alfred statue (1901; H. Thornycroft) and the heavily Gothic *Guildhall* (1871; Jeffery and Skiller), a type uncommon in southern England. Further E, Greek Doric front of former *Market House* (1857; W. Coles). To S, *Winchester Cathedral*, its later history notable for the restoration of 1906–10 when the waterlogged foundations were renewed with divers working actually under the great piers of the crossing. In the nave, alabaster effigy of Bishop Browne (died 1891), choir screen by Sir G.G. Scott (1875). In the choir, reredos of early 16C with statues replaced 1885–99 and E window remade 1852 (D. Evans) with fragments of old glass.

In N transept, monument to Sir R. Buller (1910; Mackennal), General, awarded the Victoria Cross in the Zulu War of 1879, distinguished in the Sudan War of 1884–85, and who in the Boer War of 1900 led three unsuccessful attempts to relieve Ladysmith. In the S transept, splendid Gothic monument (1873; G.G. Scott) to Bishop Wilberforce, energetic High Churchman, known as 'Soapy Sam', celebrated for his clash with T.H. Huxley in Oxford in 1860 over evolutionary theory. Effigy by H.H. Armstead. In the Lady Chapel, set of windows by Kempe, 1897–1900.

S of the Cathedral, in College St, *Winchester College*, founded 1382. Chapel tower carefully restored (1861) by W. Butterfield, whose work in the chapel has mostly been removed. To S of the main buildings, War Memorial Cloister (1922–24) and *Memorial Building*, red brick and stone in a free N Renaissance style, symmetrical front with loggia below and three big oriels above (1898; B. Champneys). Built as Museum and Art School for the quincentenary of the college. To Kingsgate St, *Commoner Gate* (1902; F.L. Pearson) Perp. style. In Romans Rd, W of Kingsgate St, *Music School* (1903; E.S. Prior), idiosyncratic with rounded gables and pyramid roof, in flint and stone, and *Sergeants House* (1869; G.E. Street). St. Cross Rd returns N into Southgate St, where *St. Thomas' Church* (1845–47; E.W. Elmslie) has been converted to County Record Office. An early example of Puginian Dec. with clearly delineated parts, as in the triple roofs of the E end. Broach spire added 1857. From Southgate St, Jewry St leads N. On left, *Library* (1836–38; O.B. Carter), built as a Corn Exchange, a handsome Italianate design in yellow brick and stone with central Tuscan portico, after Inigo Jones's Covent Garden church, flanked by round-arched wings and taller end pavilions with broad pyramid roofs. Romsey Rd leads W from Southgate St with the castle site on left, now only the 13C Great Hall surviving. Inside, Alfred Gilbert's fine bronze statue (1887) of Queen Victoria, imperious with Gilbert's superb drapery and Art Nouveau throne. *County Offices* in Tudor to Elizabethan style, 1895 (A.W. Blomfield) and 1912 (T.G. Jackson) completed 1932. Further W, on right, *Prison* (1848), and on left, *County Hospital* (1863–68; W. Butterfield), red and blue brick Gothic, built in deliberate contrast to the military hospital at Netley, Southampton, without unnecessary expense on ornament and with the external design strictly related to internal function, a design brief that Gothic Revival architects in the 19C were best equipped to fulfil. Florence Nightingale, much consulted, regarded it as a model hospital. Large central block with rooms for nurses and wards running off each side to ensure easy supervision, the decorative elements of the outline provided by a top-level chapel and corner towers off the wards to house bathrooms and lavatories.

5m SW, A3090, at **Hursley**, *church* (1846–48; J.P. Harrison) built for John Keble, leader of the Oxford Tractarian movement, and hence an excellent example of the sort of church that Tractarian vicars thought appropriate for the revived liturgical worship. Dec. style, originally with a spire, and the component parts separately roofed, emphatically different from the Georgian Gothic box-like auditorium. The stained glass by W. Wailes was to an iconographical scheme by Keble later (1858) taken in hand by Butterfield. All this High Church activity in Hursley was directed by Sir W. Heathcote of Hursley Park, pupil of Keble at Oxford, Warden of Winchester College and chairman of the hospital committee in Winchester, a strong-minded and religious landowner who improved the estate and directed the lives of his tenants with mid-Victorian vigour. All tenants were expected in church on Sunday and their children expected to attend the schools. *Hursley*

Park, early 18C and 1902, is largely Edwardian but two lodges survive from Heathcote's day, *Church Lodge* (1866) and *Home Farm Lodge* (1863), both by Butterfield. 7m NW of Winchester, A272, **Stockbridge**. 2m SW, off A3057, *Marsh Court* (1901–04; Lutyens), Elizabethan style house built of off-white chalk with red-tiled hipped roofs and Tudor stacks, very ostentatious with great square bays to the gardens (designed by Jekyll) stepping down towards the river Test. Now a school. At **Longstock**, 1m N of Stockbridge, *church* (1881; W. White) with carved angels to the chancel roof. 7m NE of Winchester, off B3046, at **Northington**, estate *church* (1887–90; T.G. Jackson) built for the Barings of The Grange. Flint and stone with fine W tower and incorporating the neo-classical monument (1846; R. Westmacott Jr) over the Baring vault. The Baring family were bankers with wide American interests, Alexander Baring (1774–1848), Lord Ashburton, being involved in the 1842 treaty for combined action to suppress the slave trade. Another Baring *church* 3m NW, at **East Stratton**, off A33, by Jackson (1885–90), flint with shingled spire. At **Otterbourne**, 4m S of Winchester, A33, the novelist Charlotte M. Yonge was born and lived at *Elderfield* opposite the church. Her father designed the *church* (1837–39) all in blue brick with a steep roof and Charlotte Yonge paid for the apse (1875). She is buried by the S porch. *Brambridge House*, 1m E, is heavily classical with Italianate and French detail.

HEREFORDSHIRE AND WORCESTERSHIRE

EVESHAM. A44 15m SE of Worcester. 5m SE, A44, **Broadway**, outstandingly picturesque Cotswold village that became a centre for late Victorian artists, initially around the Americans, Edwin Abbey and J.S. Sargent. Henry James popularised the village after a stay with Sargent, Abbey and Edmund Gosse in 1886, and the American playwright, Mary Anderson, settled at Court Farm in 1895 to become the leading lady of the colony. The old houses were restored carefully by Arts and Crafts architects, notably G. Dawber and C.E. Bateman, the additions always in keeping and now almost indistinguishable. 3m S of Evesham, A435, at **Sedgebarrow**, *church* restored 1866–68 (Butterfield) with new spire and ornate tile mosaic canopied reredos. Tall timber screen. 5m W, at **Overbury**, late 19C estate building in the village by Norman Shaw for the Martin family of Overbury Court, mostly in stone with some half-timber. By Shaw, the *school* (1875), the *village stores* (1879), the *gates* to the Court (1887) and *village hall* (1895), the stores prettily half- timbered, the hall much grander, in stone, with Baroque porch. At **Kemerton**, to W, *church* rebuilt 1847 (R.C. Carpenter) in Dec. a good example of High Anglican tastes done for B. Webb, Secretary of the Ecclesiological Society. Chancel glass by Willement, fittings by Hardman. 4m W of Evesham, at **Bricklehampton**, *Bricklehampton Hall* (1848; S.W. Daukes), substantial Italianate villa with campanile tower. 3m W of **Pershore**, *Besford Court*, 15C timber-framed houses expanded to a courtyard plan (1912; Randall Wells) in Tudor style with, surprisingly, a completely neo-Romanesque chapel. Good freely handled detail to the main house, curving main stair between stone walls. Great hall with transverse- arched roof. 7m N of Evesham, **Rous Lench**, picturesque, mostly half- timbered estate village of *Rous Lench Court*. Court gardens are romantic Victorian with topiary and much architectural stonework. At the top, late 19C Italian Gothic tower. At **Church Lench**, High Victorian Gothic *school* (1864; F. Preedy).

GREAT MALVERN. A449 7m SW of Worcester. A resort town from the 18C when the medicinal waters were first advertised but the main expansion came after the opening of Dr Wilson's hydro in 1842. Spectacular setting on the E side of the Malvern Hills. Malvern *Priory* was restored 1860 (G.G. Scott), pulpit by Scott, mosaic reredos by Blomfield (1884). On the main road above, c 1810–25 Regency style buildings associated with the *Pump Room* (1819–23; S. and J. Deykes). S of the Priory, Tudor to Jacobean style hotels and lodging houses, *Abbey Hotel* (1848), *Tudor House* (c 1850) and *Holyrood House* (1830) overlooking *Park View* (1845), Dr Wilson's hydro, large and classical. Further large houses in Abbey Rd and Priory Rd which curves back N to *Priory House* (1874; Haddon Bros.), elaborate Gothic. Off Priory Rd, to S, *Malvern College*, (1863; C.F. Hansom), Tudor Gothic open quad with gatehouse tower. Chapel (1897–99; Blomfield) with Kempe glass. Boarding houses around the perimeter, mostly by Hansom 1864–70. From Priory House, Avenue Rd runs E to the *station* (1862; W.E. Elmslie), picturesque Gothic with delightful ironwork on the platforms. The station was linked to the *Imperial Hotel* (1861–62; Elmslie) now Malvern Girls College, massive red-brick and stone Gothic building, originally fully equipped with all the latest water-cure apparatus, including brine baths with salt bought from Droitwich. N of the Priory, in Graham Rd and Victoria Rd, villas of c 1830 onwards. The principal springs were *St. Ann's Well*, on the slope W of the centre, set in a pretty cottage (1815), which early 19C visitors, including Princess Victoria in 1831, reached by donkey, the Chalybeate Spring in Priory Park, and earliest of all, the *Holy Well* at **Malvern Wells**, 2m S, set in a picturesque well-house (1843) said to be based on one at Baden-Baden. Just S at **Little Malvern**, *RC church* (1862; B. Bucknall). The composer, Sir Edward Elgar, is buried in the churchyard. He composed the 'Enigma Variations', 'Sea Pictures' and 'The Dream of Gerontius' at Malvern.

N of the centre, North Malvern and Cowleigh on the NE slopes and Malvern Link below. At **Cowleigh**, *St. Peter's Church* (1863–66; G.E. Street), Cowleigh Bank, a severe small church in dark stone with plate tracery. Fine interior with strong arcade, fittings by Street, E window by Clayton and Bell. Around the N end of the bluff, at **West Malvern**, *church* (1870; G.E. Street) with saddleback tower. Large Italianate house, now *St. James' School* (c 1850 and c 1890), next door. In **Malvern Link**, *Church of the Ascension* (1903; W. Tapper), Albert Park Rd, a most attractive work in the refined and scholarly way of turn of the century Gothicists. Stone cross-gabled tower, white render with stone dressings to the rest, high interior with lancets set deep behind an arcaded wall passage. Transverse-arched nave, rib-vaulted chancel, and fine metal screen by Bainbridge-Reynolds. Art Nouveau font with cover by Bainbridge-Reynolds. On the NE edge of Malvern, off Worcester Rd, *Convent of the Holy Name* with brick chapel (1893; Comper), painted roof and ornate gilt furnishings, especially the reredos. Around are a remarkable group of four houses (1869; G.F. Bodley and P. Webb), built as retreat houses for clergy from St. Peter's, Vauxhall, London, but later taken over by the Anglican sisterhood when they moved from Vauxhall in 1879. Among the earliest Victorian revivals of Georgian architecture, with sash-windows, hipped roofs and classical motifs but used loosely, more in the manner of Georgian farmhouses than the formal politeness of town-houses. 1m NE, A449, at **Newland**, delightful *church and almshouse* group (1862–64; P.C. Hardwick) built for the Beauchamps of Madresfield Court. The church has the most spectacular painted interior (Clayton and Bell) covering all the walls and harmonising with rich marble fittings and superb ironwork. The almshouses are picturesque red brick with tall gate tower, arranged around an open quad. *Madresfield Court*, to SE, is Elizabethan, a romantic moated house much added to 1863–85 (P.C. Hardwick) for the 4th Earl Beauchamp, such that now its romanticism is primarily a 19C creation, with gables, bays, ornate timber flèche and inner court, mostly half-timbered with echoes of medieval Germany, especially in the open gallery along one side. Interiors partly by Hardwick in robust medieval to Jacobean style, but more exotically by C.R. Ashbee and the Guild of Handicrafts (1905–07) for the 7th Earl, sympathetic to the Arts and Crafts ideas of Morris and Ashbee. By the Guild, delicate relief carving on symbolic themes in the library and the complete painted decoration of the chapel in a delicate late Pre-Raphaelite style, the colours especially bright, cheerful angels and flowers predominating. Wall murals in tempera by H. Payne, who also designed the painted decoration that covers the gallery, organ case and roof and the stained glass. Gilt reredos by W.H. Bidlake. Madresfield *church* was rebuilt 1866 (F. Preedy), gloriously coloured E window (c 1906; H.A. Payne). The N Lodge is an ornate half-timbered work by Norman Shaw (1872).

4m SE of Malvern, B4209 at **Hanley Swan**, spired parish *church*

(1872; G.G. Scott) with reredos and tiled E wall by J. Powell and Sons. Just N, *RC church* (1846; C.F. Hansom) with presbytery adjoining, all very much in the manner of Pugin, careful tracery detail, interior with screen, carved reredos, full set of contemporary glass and painted E end. Some of the fittings by Pugin. In the *church* at **Hanley Castle**, 2m SE, fabulous W window by Clayton and Bell. 4m SW, at **Castlemorton**, *Bannut Farm* (1890; C.F.A. Voysey), one of Voysey's first buildings, roughcast and with the long horizontals of his later work, leaded windows and sloping buttresses. Already remarkable for the unmoulded starkness of the walls. 3m E, at **Longdon**, *Eastington Hall*, 13C and 15C timber-framed house expanded into a picturesque open court plan in 1910–11. 3m N, B4424, at **Upton upon Severn**, prominent yellow stone *church* (1878; A. Blomfield) with spire a landmark right across the Severn valley. W window c 1905 by C. Whall. 3m SE, at **Queenhill**, *Pull Court* (1836–46; E. Blore), imposing grey stone Jacobean mansion with shaped gables and an entrance court closed by a monumental gateway and screen walls (now Bredon School).

W of Malvern, on the W slope of the hills, above **Colwall**, *Perrycroft* (1893–94; C.F.A. Voysey), roughcast and slate roof, as became standard for Voysey, but here without gables or dormers to break the long sweep of the hipped roof. Interesting play of planes on the garden front, all under the deep eaves. Oriel bays on the upper floor and the lower floor recessed, the doorway set well back in the centre, and the whole front divided up by sloping buttresses. 5m S, A438, at **Eastnor**, *church* rebuilt 1852 (G.G. Scott) for the Somers family of Eastnor Castle. Reredos 1896 reusing Italian carved fragments. Monument to the 1st Earl Somers (1855; Scott), Gothic shrine, and effigy of the 3rd Earl (died 1883; J.E. Boehm). The *castle* (1812–15; R. Smirke) is one of the outstanding Georgian castellated houses (open to public). The drawing room refurnished in full Victorian Gothic style by Pugin (1851) with chandelier shown at the Crystal Palace. Other rooms richly refitted in the 1870s.

HEREFORD. The *Cathedral* was heavily restored and altered from the late 18C. Crossing and chancel restored by L. Cottingham from 1842, E end rebuilt 1856–63 by G.G. Scott and W front by J.O. Scott 1902–08. The best 19C fitting, the iron screen by Scott, made by Skidmore has been removed. E window by Pugin, made by Hardman (1851), N transept N window by Hardman (1864). Chancel tiling by Scott, reredos (1852) by Cottingham, made by R. Boulton. In N chancel aisle Hunt window by Clayton and Bell. In NE transept, Dean Dawes memorial (1869; M. Noble). In Broad St, W of the cathedral, *Library and Museum* (1872–74; F. Kempson) fully Gothic in a High Victorian way, former *Corn Exchange* (1857; W. Startin) with portico, and *No. 39* (c 1865) polychrome stone warehouse. Further up, *National Westminster Bank* (1863; E.W. Elmslie) palazzo style and *Green Dragon Hotel* with long pilastered front, apparently of 1857. E of High Town, the market place, *Shire Hall* (1817; R. Smirke), with *statue* of Sir G.C. Lewis (1864; Marochetti) outside. Lewis was a man of wide talents, politician, philologist, political theorist, Chancellor of the Exchequer during the Crimean War. In St. Owen's St, beyond, *Town Hall* (1902–04; H.A. Cheers), a crashing Baroque presence clad in yellow terracotta with domed turrets.

W of the centre, in Broomy Hill, *Waterworks Museum* (1880–82), working machinery in elaborate red and yellow brick waterworks with 101ft campanile tower. To N, off A438, *Cider Museum* behind Bulmers Cider Factory. 3m SW, A465, at **Belmont**, *St. Michael's*

Abbey (1854–58; E.W. Pugin). Tall Gothic church with E.W. Pugin's characteristic elaborate tracery and carved detail, crossing tower added 1882. Steep roofed brick monastery adjoining and almshouses with their own chapel (1852). 3m E of Hereford, A438, at **Bartestree**, *RC Convent* (1863; E.W. Pugin), red brick Gothic, much extended. The Perp. chapel re-erected 1869.

KIDDERMINSTER. A449 15m N of Worcester. In the centre, *Town Hall* (1876; J.T. Meredith), *Corn Exchange* (1853; Bidlake and Lovall) and *Library* (1878–92; J.M. Gothing), a civic group in variously Italianate styles. *Statue* of Sir Rowland Hill (1881; T. Brock), reformer of the postal service. Some 19C office buildings and banks along Vicar St. At the foot of Church St, *statue* of Richard Baxter (1875; T. Brock) leading 17C nonconformist, minister at the parish church 1641–66. 3m S, at **Wilden**, *church* (1880) built for A. Baldwin, ironmaster and father of the Prime Minister. Mrs Baldwin was sister-in-law of Burne-Jones and had the whole church filled with stained glass by Morris and Co (1900–14) and herself made the altar frontal, to a Burne-Jones design. To SE, A449, at **Hartlebury**, *church* with nave rebuilt 1836 (T. Rickman), broad light interior, plaster-vaulted with galleries. 6m SE of Kidderminster, off A448, at **Great Dodford**, *church* (1907–09; A. Bartlett), Arts and Crafts Gothic, prettily detailed with small cloistered court tucked in between the nave and tower. 5m NE of Kidderminster, at **Hagley**, estate *church* rebuilt 1858–65 (G.E. Street) for Lord Lyttelton of Hagley Hall, in the grounds of the house. Broach spire, fittings by Street and glass by Holiday in S aisle (1876) and E window (1907).

KINGTON. A44 19m NW of Hereford. In the centre, classical *Town Hall* (1845) and bright red *Market Hall* (1885; F. Kempson). 7m SE, A4112, at **Kinnersley**, *church* with pretty painted decoration (1868) by G.F. Bodley and the Rev. F. Andrews. Organ case by Bodley. Bodley is buried in the churchyard. 8m NE of Kinnersley, A4112, at **Monkland**, *church* rebuilt 1866 (G.E. Street) with shingled spire and Hardman E window. Good Street fittings. **Kingsland** *church*, 3m N, has chancel and decoration of 1866–68 by G.F. Bodley. 12m N of Monkland, off A4110, at **Downton**, *Downton Castle* (1774–78), the first deliberately picturesque house, built by R. Payne Knight in accordance with new Romantic theories of landscape and nature untamed, that is, opposed to the regularised plantations of the school of Capability Brown. The house itself was thus placed on a bluff over the River Teme and approached from the S giving full effect to the romantic qualities of the landscape. The house was castellated, picturesque in outline but only mildly Gothic in detail. Its present Gothic and towered silhouette is Victorian (c 1850; E. Haycock: 1862; S.P. Smith), Victorian values requiring the substance to match the distant appearance, but the substitution of a N drive for the old S approach has lost the effect that so impressed late 18C visitors.

REDDITCH. A441 15m SW of Birmingham. Industrial town built on needle manufacture since the 18C. Parish *church* (1854; H. Woodyer), Church Green, with prominent spire. E end reconstructed 1893 (T. Moore) with plaster vault and mouldings of arches dying into piers. Cast-iron ornamental *fountain* (1883) on the green. Off Plymouth Rd, to SW, *Council offices* (1893; T. Moore), built as a private house. *RC church* (1834; T. Rickman), Beeley Rd, to SE, red sandstone Commissioners' Gothic. 2m NW, at **Tardebigge**, *Hewell Grange* (1884–91;

Bodley and Garner), now a detention centre. Beautifully detailed red stone Jacobean style mansion with symmetrical fronts of shaped gables and mullion and transom windows, based on Montacute House, built for the Earl of Plymouth. Sumptuous two-storey galleried hall with screens each end and delicate carving. 3m N of Redditch, at **Alvechurch**, *church* rebuilt 1859–61 (W. Butterfield) with lovely polychrome interior, walls in red brick diapered in white over sturdy arcades in stone with round piers. Bands of brick are carried across the stone of the original W tower. Richer colour in the chancel with stained glass by Gibbs in E window. S aisle glass by F. Preedy. Large brick and half-timbered *rectory* (1855; Butterfield) and *school* (1856) with school-house (1859–65). 7m SW of Redditch, B4090, at **Hanbury**, *church* restored 1860 (G.E. Street), the E end and Vernon Chapel added in strong EE to a largely 18C church, in heavy contrast. Excellent Street fittings. *School* by Street (1858).

St. Catherine's Church (1874–c 85; J.P. Seddon), Hoarwithy

ROSS-ON-WYE. A40 16m W of Gloucester. 2m SW at **Ham Green**, *church* (1905; G.F. Bodley), one of Bodley's experiments with a double nave, here under a single wagon roof. At **Welsh Bicknor**, 3m S, lavish Norman to EE *church* (1858; T.H. Rushforth) with good contemporary glass. 5m NW of Ross, at **Hoarwithy**, *St. Catherine's Church* (1874, completed after 1885; J.P. Seddon), recasing a building of 1843. A lovely work in Italian Romanesque style with triple apsed E end, campanile tower and cloistered walk. The interior, fitted out over thirty years, has gold mosaic in the apse (G.E. Fox) and marble Byzantinesque columns, excellently carved, mosaic pavements and stained glass by Seddon, mostly of 1906. One good N nave window c 1885 (H.A. Kennedy). *Parsonage and school* (1868; Seddon), altered from an existing schoolroom. 6m N of Ross, off B4224, at **Brockhampton**, *church* (1901–02; W.R. Lethaby) of quite exceptional originality, one of the two or three turn of the century churches that display a rethinking of Gothic forms outside the main stream of tradition. Rubble stone and thatch with square central tower and porch tower weather-boarded and pyramid-roofed, the window details of the most primitive form, reminiscent of Anglo-Saxon work apart from that in the S transept with its novel lattice grid in a square frame. Inside the walls are low, the windows deep-set in a stone band from which spring steep transverse pointed arches carrying a plain plastered roof, actually mass concrete. Massively simple round font with vine tendril carving, stained glass by C. Whall and tapestry by Burne-Jones. *Brockhampton Court* is 18C, extended 1879 (J. Middleton) and 1893 (F. Armitage) in Tudor style with entrance tower. 5m NE of Ross, just in Gloucestershire, at **Kempley**, is a *church* (1903) by Lethaby's pupil, Randall Wells, following Brockhampton in the steep proportions, simplified window detail and lattice tracery, here filling the whole W window. Saddleback tower. The interior, less successful, has good Arts and Crafts fittings.

Church (1901–02; W.R. Lethaby), Brockhampton

TENBURY WELLS. A456 22m NW of Worcester. Briefly a spa from 1839 when the springs were discovered. The Baths, behind the Crow Hotel, were housed in a prefabricated iron structure (1862; J. Cranston) made to Cranston's patent system where the glazing of the roof overlaps in an unusual curved and stepped profile. To be restored after years of dereliction. The parish *church* was mostly rebuilt (1865; H. Woodyer), but the better 19C fittings have gone. 2m SW, *St. Michael's Choir School* (1854; H. Woodyer), church built for the Rev. Sir F. Gore Ouseley together with a college that would assure a full daily choral service in the church, while also educating the sons of clergy and gentlemen 'of moderate means'. The group is one of the finest High Victorian collegiate groups full of characteristic features of

Woodyer's Gothic, steep roofs, broken on the college buildings by acutely pointed dormers, originally separated by tall chimneys. The main block contained the school, the wing Gore Ouseley's house. The church has impressive tall proportions, especially the steep apse. A crossing tower was intended. Inside, spectacularly tall font cover and shrine-like baldacchino over the altar with Gothic gables and flying buttresses. Glass by Hardman, the earliest in the apse. Behind the E end, tomb of Gore Ouseley (died 1889; A. Webb).

5m S of Tenbury, at **Bockleton**, *church* restored 1862 (Woodyer) with fine effigy of W.W. Prescott (1867; Woolner) over a relief of Prescott tending his dying gamekeeper. *Bockleton Court* (1866–69; H. Curzon) is a large gabled brick mansion, Jacobean style. 2m SW, at **Pudlestone**, *church* restored 1851 (Woodyer) with good E window by Hardman (1857). *Pudlestone Court* is mid 19C castellated. 5m W, A44, **Leominster**, with *Town Hall* (1855; J. Cranston), High St, Italianate and *Corn Exchange* (1858; J. Cranston), Corn Square, Gothic. *Clarke Almshouses*, founded 1736, rebuilt 1874. 8m E of Leominster, A44, at **Bredenbury**, *Bredenbury Court* (1873; T.H. Wyatt), rock- faced red stone Italianate mansion with equally rock-faced *church* (1877; T.H. Wyatt). 3m E of Tenbury, at **Lower Rochford**, in the *church*, E window (1863; Morris), an early work of the Morris firm with small Adoration panel. 1m E, A443, at **Newnham Bridge**, *Talbot Hotel* (c 1860; ?H. Curzon), rare example of High Victorian Gothic applied to an inn, canted front with full-height two-light windows actually on the angles and half-hipped dormers.

WORCESTER. Worcester *Cathedral* was restored from 1857 (A. Perkins) including a new E window and from 1864–74 (G.G. Scott) when the W front was remodelled, the N porch rebuilt and much of the structure refaced. Richly painted iron crossing *screen by Scott, made by Hardman, pulpit by Scott. Great W window 1874 (Hardman). Font by Scott with font cover by Bodley. In the N aisle, fine richly coloured window in E bay (1862; Lavers and Barraud). In the Jesus Chapel late 19C screen and reredos, glass by Wailes (1849). In N transept, N window 1866 (Lavers and Barraud), in S transept seated monument to Bishop Philpott (died 1892; Sir T. Brock). In the chancel elaborate carved *reredos by Scott, made by Farmer and Brindley. By Scott also the Bishop's Throne, organ cases, stalls and screens. In the Lady Chapel, painted roof and E window by Hardman, effigies of the Earl of Dudley (1888) and Lord Lyttelton (1878) by Forsyth. Glass in the chancel aisles by Hardman.

The High St runs N, with *statue* of Sir E. Elgar looking across to the cathedral. At the N end, at The Cross, *Lloyds Bank* (1861–62; E.W. Elmslie), proud Bath stone palazzo built as the head office of the Worcester City and County Bank. Next door, looking undersized, Portland stone English Baroque front of *Midland Bank* (c 1904). In Angel St, former *Corn Exchange* (1848; Rowe and Son) and semi-circular portico of *Congregational church* (1858; Poulton and Woodman). N of The Cross, on E side, terracotta *Hop Market Hotel* (1900; A.B. Rowe), then *railway bridge* (1908) and, in Forgate St, Greek Ionic porticoed *Shire Hall* (1834–35; C. Day), set back in a court enclosed by low wings. Queen Victoria statue in forecourt. *Victoria Institute* (1896; Simpson and Allen), red brick and terracotta, with asymmetrical elevations, the Library, to Foregate St, ornamentally decorated with late Tudor style windows and Baroque doorway, the schools, behind, on Sansome Walk, more freely handled. Further up, on The Tything, *Kay and Co. Factory* (1907; Simpson and Ayrton), pared-down detail with gabled front and good lettering. *Royal Grammar School* beyond has front range (1868; A. Perkins) with shaped gables and large neo-Jacobean Hall and Library (1914; A.H. Parker). To N, on Barbourne Rd, *St. George's Church* (1893–95; A. Webb), at E end of the early 19C St. George's Square. Brick front in a free version of King's College Chapel, Cambridge, tall interior, also free Perp. S from the cathedral, factory and *Museum* of the Royal Worcester Porcelain Works, the building of c 1860, on Severn St, in red and yellow brick. The collection includes much heavily ornamented commemorative ware in the taste of the Great Exhibition. E of the centre, *Worcester Shrub Hill station* (1865) in dark engineering brick, Italianate style. On the platform two bay windows prettily covered in glazed tile decoration. By the station *industrial buildings* in red and yellow brick (1864; T. Dickson), built here not because of the railway but for the nearby Worcester and Birmingham Canal which cuts an attractively industrial course down to the river S of the cathedral.

5m NE of Worcester, A38, **Droitwich**, salt-mining town developed as a spa by J. Corbett of the Stoke Prior Salt Works. Most of Corbett's works in the town are of the late 19C in a brick and half-timber style, as in the *Brine Baths* and *Salters Hall*, Victoria Square, the remodelled 16C *Raven Hotel* and the *Worcestershire Hotel*, Corbett Rd. Much the most fantastic of Corbett's buildings is his own house, *Chateau Impney*, just outside the town, built 1869–75 (A. Tronquois) like an industrialist's house from Lille transported to Worcestershire, red brick and stone with the most exaggerated steep-pitched roofs and curly dormers, Louis XIII style. Mrs Corbett was French. The house is now a hotel. 4m W of Droitwich, A449, **Ombersley**, estate village with as much Victorian half-timber as genuine timber-framing. *Church* (1825–29; T. Rickman), plaster vaults and galleries inside.

2m NW of Worcester, at **Upper Broadheath**, *Sir E. Elgar memorial museum* in the cottage where he was born. 1m NE, at **Hallow**, A443, *church* (1867; W.J. Hopkins), good High Victorian interior. 6m NW, A443, at **Great Witley**, *Witley Court* (open to public), the ruins of the great house reconstructed 1855–60 (S.W. Daukes) for the Earl of Dudley and burnt out in 1937, Italianate on the grandest scale incorporating Ionic giant porticoes each side, c 1805 additions by Nash to the original house. Daukes' detail is restrained, characteristically richer than the early 19C would have been, and typical too are the towers rising each side of the garden portico. The vast scale of the house extends to the orangery, attached by a curved wing, and to the Roman Baroque fountains each side, by Forsyth. The fabulous chapel (1735) remains intact, refaced in stone by Daukes and with Victorian fittings in suitable style. 1m N, on the crest of **Abberley Hill**, *clock tower* (1883; J.P. St. Aubyn), 161ft Gothic folly built as a memorial to Joseph Jones of Abberley Hall, a landmark for miles around. *Abberley Hall* (designed 1837, burnt down 1845 and rebuilt to original design 1846–49; S.W. Daukes) is a plain slightly Italianate villa, more Italianate when it had its campanile tower. Estate buildings (c 1885) by J. Douglas of Chester, including the *North Lodge* in brick and half-timber with corner turret and the *Home Farm*. The estate church (1850–52; J.J. Cole) is richly detailed with polished marble and granite columns and naturalistic carving.

4m SW of Worcester, B4244, at **Callow End**, *Stanbrook Abbey*, the only Benedictine nunnery in England, founded in Cambrai 1625 and expelled to England 1808. Monastery buildings by E.W. Pugin, abbey church (1871) with big red and white banded tower and tunnel-vaulted interior, the chancel fittings all removed. Main buildings

(1878–80) bleakly red brick to the entrance, the more attractive cloister front not visible.

HERTFORDSHIRE

BERKHAMSTED. A41 7m NW of Watford. In High St, old *Town Hall* (1859; E.B. Lamb), much Gothic detail crammed into a small lively front. The ground floor was originally open. 3m SE, at **Hemel Hempstead**, in the parish *church*, chancel painted to designs by Bodley (1888). The old *Town Hall* (1851; G. Low), High St, is neo-Jacobean in brick. At **Hunton Bridge**, A41, S of Kings Langley, *church* (1865; Henry Woodyer), richly carved inside (T. Earp) and excellent fittings. Late 19C monuments to the Loyd family, bankers, who paid for the church and the pretty *school* (1858). 5m NW of Berkhamsted, A41, is **Tring**. Part of the Rothschild empire (cf. Mentmore and Waddesdon, Buckinghamshire) in the late 19C. *Tring Park* was recased for Lord Rothschild in the 1870s and various brick and half-timber buildings were built in the town, notably the *Market House* (1899) and *Rose and Crown* (1905). To the E, *Pendley Manor* (c 1874; W.F.C. Ryan), big neo-Jacobean mansion.

BISHOP'S STORTFORD. A11 6m N of Harlow. *Bishop's Stortford College*, original buildings (1867; J. Clarke) in brick, Gothic. At **Furneux Pelham**, 6m NW, the *church has outstanding early Morris glass in the S chapel (1867 and 1874). 5m S of Bishop's Stortford, at **Sawbridgeworth**, the largest group of maltings in Hertfordshire, along the railway. Malting was the principal industry over most of the E part of the country. Characteristic are the cowled drying towers similar to the oast houses of the hop industry. 2m SW, at **High Wych**, a remarkable *church* (1861; G.E. Pritchett), very much in the 'rogue' Gothic vein, mixing flint and red brick and stone outside in a spiky composition while inside is a quite unexpected white brick domed vault to the chancel covered in painted decoration. *Gilston Park* (1852; P.C. Hardwick), 2m SW, is a fanciful stone Tudor style country house, all gables and asymmetry.

HERTFORD. The county town. In Fore St the best Victorian building is the *Corn Exchange* (1857; William Hill), typical giant classical style, also two good late Victorian banks. The parish *church* was rebuilt lavishly in 1895 by Paley and Austin of Lancaster in their best dignified Perp., very impressive if slightly cold in feeling. The church is built in Cheshire red sandstone, a real surprise in Hertfordshire. Now severed from the town centre by an appalling ring road. E of the centre, *Christ's Hospital Girls' School*, the small original schoolroom made the centrepiece of a formal parade of Queen Anne style boarding houses (1901–06; A.R. Stenning). To the SE, off A10, *Haileybury College*, founded for the East India Company with Greek Revival buildings by Wilkins (1805–07) that are now the podium for the massive green dome of the chapel (added 1876; A. Blomfield). R. Blomfield built a series of red-brick school buildings at the end of the 19C including the big Bradby Hall (1887) and the charming Cricket Pavilion in front.

At **Stanstead Abbots**, A414, 4m E, is *Easneye* (1868; Alfred Waterhouse), now *(All Nations College)* built for the Buxton brewing and anti-slavery family, a complex red-brick and terracotta Gothic house with a fine entrance hall. Waterhouse also designed the church and many estate cottages. 2m NE of Hertford, at **Thundridge**, *Poles* (Sir Ernest George), late 19C Jacobethan style brick house with flat-topped bays, now a convent school. At **High Cross**, 1½m further N, the *church* has a remarkable Arts and Crafts W window (c 1893; Selwyn Image) and a S aisle window of c 1895 in similar style by Helen Coombe, wife of Roger Fry. 3m further N, at **Old Hall Green** is *St. Edmund's College*, Catholic training school where A.W.N. Pugin was professor and designed the chapel (1846–53), one of his best works, long and tall with an antechapel like Oxford college chapels, the whole very pure, Gothic without frills. Screen, glass and tiles by Pugin also excellent. Chapel added 1862 (E.W. Pugin). 2m NE of Ware, on the Wareside road, *Fanhams Hall* (1900; W.W. Bethell), very large neo-Elizabethan house, all pebbledash and stone details, richly fitted but dull, more fun is the two-towered entrance lodge and more exotic the Japanese garden complete with tea-house laid out c 1905 by Japanese gardeners.

At **Waterford**, A602, 2m NW of Hertford, *Goldings* (1871–77; G. Devey), large rambling brick house, picturesque if dull in detail. The *church* (1871; H. Woodyer), built for the Smiths of Goldings, is lavishly fitted, the chancel in blue and green mosaic by Powell's (1901– 12), outstanding Morris and Burne- Jones glass. 4m S of Hertford, just W of **Broxbourne**, *Broxbournebury*, an Elizabethan house remodelled c 1878 (E. George), surprisingly harshly for an architect whose later work was carefully detailed. 3m S, at **Cheshunt**, the *church* has painted decoration and organ case by G.F. Bodley (1891). Opposite, *Cheshunt College* (1870; Lander and Bedells), gaunt brick and stone Gothic Nonconformist'college, now council offices.

ST. ALBANS. 10m W of Hertford. The *Cathedral* suffered a brutal restoration from 1879 designed and paid for by the autocratic Lord Grimthorpe. His S transept window was likened to a giant colander. Entirely new W front bears no resemblance to what was there before. The reredos (1890–1903; A. Gilbert) is a masterpiece of Art Nouveau. In the centre, N of the Market Place, *Town Hall* (1829–31; G. Smith), classical. 3m SW at **London Colney**, *All Saints' Convent* (1899; Leonard Stokes), a very original free Tudor work with a powerful blunt entrance tower, brick with stone-carving and stone bands. The cloister has semicircular windows filled with tracery and shallow oriel windows above. 2m E, *North Mymms Park*, a lovely Elizabethan house altered 1893–94 (Ernest George) who gave it the formal garden with little brick and stone summer-houses. A most opulent orangery, the interior entirely marbled in early Renaissance style. 4m E of St. Albans, A414, at **Hatfield**, *Hatfield House* and the *church* bear witness to the Italian tastes of the 3rd Marquess of Salisbury, Prime Minister at the end of the 19C. In the house a rich series of rooms (1870s) in Renaissance style by Italian craftsmen similar to the work done for the Marquess of Bath at Longleat, Wiltshire, and the Duke of Northumberland at Alnwick. Hatfield had its own approach to the railway station complete with viaduct over the cottages of the town. The 3rd Marquess is buried between the church and the house. In the church, a copy of the effigy by Goscombe John (1909) on his memorial in Westminster Abbey. He had the Salisbury chapel embellished in mosaic and alabaster (1871).

4m N of Hatfield, A1, at **Welwyn**, in School Lane, *New Place* (1880), a medium-sized house by Philip Webb, understated with sash windows, generous roofs and tall chimneys and quite without period reference. For a contrast, in Church Street, *Welwyn Hall*, an over-scaled house of similar date where all the elements seem to have crashed together, an uncomfortable tower next to a tall window bay. At **Ayot St. Peter**, 2m SW, polychrome brick *church* (1874; J.P. Seddon) with fully decorated interior, painted chancel, tiles, terracotta chancel arch and stained glass all of c 1880. Vicarage nearby by J.L. Pearson (1866). At **Digswell**, 2m SE of Welwyn, an imposing brick *railway viaduct* (1850; J. Cubitt) of forty arches.

STEVENAGE. A1 9m N of Hatfield. 3m SW, B656, *Knebworth House* (open to public), rebuilt c 1820 and after 1843 for Lord Lytton, the novelist. Dramatic neo-Jacobean staircase and Gothic state drawing-room decorated by Crace. Lutyens, whose wife was a Lytton, designed the formal garden (1907–11) and built *Homewood* (1900) nearby, one of his best early houses with weatherboarded large gables and a contrasting mannerist classical porch. Also by Lutyens, several estate cottages, *St. Martin's Church* (1914), on B197, *Golf Club* (1908) and the gates to the Lytton chapel in the parish church. S of Stevenage, B197, at **Woolmer Green**, a small Arts and Crafts style brick *church* (1899; R.W. Schulz), low and long with a nicely carved screen. At **King's Walden**, 5m W of Stevenage, the *church*, restored 1868 (W.E. Nesfield), has excellent carved High Victorian fittings and one early Morris window (1867). At **Preston** nearby, an Arts and Crafts *church* (1900; T. Carter) in the Voysey manner with an E window by Christopher Whall, among the best of the Arts and Crafts glass designers. *Temple Dinsley* house at Preston is of 1714, enlarged with wings by Lutyens (1908) in matching style.

3m NW of Stevenage, at **Hitchin**, in the Market Square, mixed Italianate *Corn Exchange* (1851; W. Beck). In Broad St, old *Town Hall* (1840; T. Bellamy), handsome Renaissance, and old *Library* (1840), temple fronted. Opposite, new *Town Hall* (1900; E.W. Mountford and G. Lucas), pretty neo-Georgian. In Radcliffe Rd, *Holy Saviour Church* (1865; W. Butterfield) with all Butterfield's rich colour work, inside as well as out, in red, blue and white brick and stone. Church buildings also by Butterfield. 3m NE, **Letchworth**, the world's first garden city founded in 1903 as a result of Ebenezer Howard's 'Tomorrow, the Peaceful Path to Real Reform' (1898). Garden cities were to combine the best of town and country, full of green yet with the industry necessary to support a city, as opposed to a suburb. The vision was of a classless community living a healthy life. Inevitably it was progressive and more notable for middle-class experimentation than for classlessness. Parker and Unwin were the original architects, but many of the best early 20C architects built houses at Letchworth, thus an ideal town to look at the domestic architecture of the period. *Norton Way* is the spine of the earliest housing, *Nos 355–61* (Parker and Unwin; 1905), built for Howard himself, *No. 296*, Parker and Unwin's office, picturesque in roughcast and thatch. Off Norton Way North in Nevells Rd and Icknield Way some 114 houses were built for the 1905 'Cheap Cottages Exhibition'. Larger houses were built S of the centre in Sollershot West, Hitchin Rd and Letchworth Lane. In Barrington Rd is the oddest building, *The Cloisters* (1905; W.H. Cowlishaw), built as a School of Psychology, much given to fresh air and gymnastics. An octagonal tower with open balcony dominates, joined to a great curved wall of windows and two smaller open towers. At **Baldock**, 2m NE, by the church, old *vicarage* by Butterfield (1870–73), red brick with timber to the gables. 8m NE is **Royston**. In Market Hill, the old *Corn Exchange* (c 1830) of patent interlocking bricks with iron columns in the courtyard. *Town Hall* (1855), Melbourne St, yellow brick, originally a Mechanics Institute.

WATFORD. A411 12m NW of London. A battered town. In Market St,

Holy Rood RC Church (1883–90; J.F. Bentley), one of the best late Victorian churches in Britain. A strong design in flint and stone modelled on the local late Gothic. Nearly all the fittings by Bentley, altar rails, reredos, stained glass and wall-painting. The richness is concentrated in the chancel, a space made subtle by the wall passages around that alter the contrast between solid wall and space to something more diffuse. Bentley also designed the little presbytery attached. Watford Junction Station is on the original 1839 line to Birmingham and the *tunnel entrance* to the N still has its imposing classical front (shown in Bourne's lithograph) but visible only from a northbound train. By the station, *Benskins House* (1860; J. Livock), the former station hotel, grandly Italianate. Slightly NW, in Church Rd, *St. Andrew's Church* (1853–57; S.S. Teulon), and the *Salters Company Almshouses* (1863; T.C. Sorby), a pretty red-brick group around a lawn with splendid gates crowned by an arm holding a salt- cellar (the Company crest). At Garston, off the road to St. Albans, *All Saints' Church* (1853; G.G. Scott), a charming small country church not quite swallowed by suburb.

2m E of Watford, A411, is **Bushey**, a popular late Victorian suburb with large houses and schools, now much built over. Three big schools of c 1900, the *Royal Masonic* (1902; Gordon and Gunton), The Avenue, Tudor Gothic around a tall tower, *St. Margaret's* (1898; A. Waterhouse), built for clergy orphans in a hard yellow brick and terracotta, and *Royal Caledonian* (1902; Sir W. Emerson), Aldenham Road, loosely neo-Georgian. At **Aldenham**, to N is *Aldenham School*, a foundation of the Brewers Company of the City of London, buildings from 1825 onwards, mostly mid to late Victorian. *Haberdashers' Aske's School*, another City Company foundation occupies Aldenham House, a c 1700 house much enlarged in the late 19C for H.H. Gibbs, Lord Aldenham, banker. *Home Farm* (1879), Aldenham Rd, by Butterfield for H.H. Gibbs, polychrome brick. In Melbourne Rd, Bushey, is a massively detailed stone doorway, the remnant of *Lululand*, the house of the painter Sir H. von Herkomer built to designs by the great American architect H.H. Richardson from 1886–94. *Bournemead* (1892; J.M. Brydon), next door in Herkomer Rd, a pretty work in the style of Norman Shaw, brick and half-timber. *Tilehurst* (1903), Grange Rd, and *Myholme* (1904), 170 Merry Hill Rd, are small houses by C.F.A. Voysey. From an earlier age, *Haydon Hill*, off Merry Hill Rd, is an Italianate villa of 1842 by Decimus Burton. Off the Elstree Road, *Caldecote Towers* (Rosary Priory School), an elephantine mid Victorian house. In Barnet Lane, **Elstree**, E of Bushey, *The Leys* (1901) by the Glasgow architect George Walton, friend of C.R. Mackintosh. A subtle design, very square under a hipped roof and a curved entrance bay. Inside the hall rises three floors with galleries around.

At **Rickmansworth**, 4m W of Watford, George Eliot lived at The Elms, High St. At **Chorleywood**, 2m NW, *church* (1870; G.E. Street) in flint and stone with fittings all by Street. In Shire Lane, *The Orchard* (1900), C.F.A. Voysey's own house, roughcast with plain stone mullions set flush in the wall and the outer slopes of the two gables swept right down. *Sunnybank*, next door, is also by Voysey (1903). At **Heronsgate**, W of Rickmansworth, was the first Chartist settlement 1847, originally O'Connorville after Fergus O'Connor, the founder. Here the problem of the landless poor was to be solved by a co-operative agricultural community, each household having at least two acres and a cottage. Two-storey paired cottages survive, regularly laid out along narrow lanes, the largest house was the school.

HUMBERSIDE

BEVERLEY. A1097 8m N of Hull. Beverley *Station* (1846; G.T. Andrews) still has the overall roof across the tracks, originally a standard design on this line. *Beverley Minster* was restored from 1863 by G.G. Scott, though the most interesting post-medieval work is the early 18C restoration by Hawksmoor. Hardman glass in nave, W window 1857, crossing screen by Scott c 1875, in S transept Hardman glass on W side (1857) removed from the great S window in 1922. *St. Mary's Church* has W window (1849–50) designed by Pugin and made by Hardman. From a restoration by G.G. Scott (c 1862) dates the very elaborate alabaster and marble pulpit.

5m NW of Beverley, B1248, at **South Dalton**, *church* (1858–61; J.L. Pearson), apparently built by Lord Hotham of Dalton Hall to outshine the church at Scorborough built by his agent. As an estate church this is lavish, the 200ft spire a beacon for miles and the carved work of exceptional richness especially on the upper stage of the tower and on the chancel. Pearson's proportions are masterly, the body of the church a composition of related gables at right angles, building up to the nave roof, and taking the eye up to the tower and spire. More English detail than usual in Pearson's High Victorian works, but inside muscular effects Early French and English are given full rein, the walls shafted up to a florid cornice, compressed columns in the opening over the chancel arch, rich chancel treatment, with complex vistas through to the side chapels. E window by Clayton and Bell. Pretty *almshouses* (1873) adjoining. **Scorborough** *church* (1857–59; J.L. Pearson), 4m E, is far more modest, built at one fifth the cost, but the treatment is very bold, the short tower crowned by a spire seemingly designed for something much larger, because the bell stage is treated as part of the spire rather than the tower. Some polychromy outside, in the single-cell interior stronger colour effects with banded stone and coloured marble wall and window shafts. Vigorous carving, especially the cornice, very similar to South Dalton. Glass by Clayton and Bell. 3m W of Beverley, A1097, at **Bishop Burton**, *church* restored 1864–66 (J.L. Pearson), the chancel largely rebuilt with good glass by Clayton and Bell. 11m W, W of Market Weighton, at **Everingham**, *Everingham Hall* has a splendid Italian style RC chapel attached (1836–39; A. Giorgoli), stuccoed and pedimented outside, inside tunnel vaulted with scagliola columns and pilastered apse. Statues and carved reliefs by L. Bozzoni (1839–44). 5m N, B1246, at **Pocklington**, *station* (1847; G.T. Andrews), Italianate, the overall roof over the tracks imaginatively re-used as a sports hall. *Kilnwick Percy Hall*, just E, is heavily classical with Ionic portico, a recasing of 1845. Matching Ionic lodge and neo-Norman *church* (1865; J.B. and W. Atkinson) in the grounds. 3m E, at **Warter**, the *church* (1862; Habershon and Pite) is remarkable for the early 20C Nunburnholme family memorials by G. Frampton. Fine marble effigy of Isabel Wilson (died 1905), gilded metal memorial to Guy Wilson (died 1908) and marble memorial to the 1st Lord Nunburnholme (died 1907), delicate carving with characteristic early 20C allegorical figures. In the churchyard the graves of Lord Nunburnholme and his son have allegorical figures over (1909–10; G. Bayes) in bronze.

GREAT DRIFFIELD. A164 13m N of Beverley. Market town with parish *church* restored 1880 (G.G. Scott Jr). Rood screen by Temple Moore (1904). Driffield is on the edge of the estates of the Sykes family of Sledmere, notable in the 19C for the huge programme of church building across the Wolds, begun in the 1850s by the 4th baronet, Sir Tatton Sykes, but mostly due to the 5th baronet, also Sir Tatton, who inherited in 1863. For the first Sir Tatton, two fine restorations by J.L. Pearson, also one new church, since demolished. The second Sir Tatton commissioned some 12 churches or restorations from G.E. Street with associated schools and vicarages between 1866 and 1878, then in the 1890s several restorations from Temple Moore and a further four from C.H. Fowler after 1901. Few other Victorian church builders achieved so much, and Sir Tatton's churches, though none of them grandiose, are all of the highest quality, models of sensitive village church architecture. The group N of Sledmere itself are now in N Yorkshire, but described here to maintain their unity.

Church with painted decoration by Clayton and Bell (1872–75), Garton on the Wolds

3m SE of Driffield, B1249, **Wansford** *church* (1868; G.E. Street), small with level roofline and stone spirelet, the windows simple, unified by a string course rising and falling according to the sill levels. Fine interior, the spirelet carried on heavy round piers, very rich marble, alabaster and metal screen, probably of 1870s, grey and white marble pulpit with inlaid patterns and stone reredos. Glass by Clayton and Bell. The approach to the church marked by fine lychgate and cross by Street. By Street also the *parsonage* (c 1872), simply detailed with two parallel roofs. *School* (1877; Street), a good composition of tile-hung gables and bell turret on the roof. 1m NW of Driffield, at **Little Driffield**, *church* (1889; Temple Moore) carefully reusing fragments from the previous church. 2m NW, at **Garton on the Wolds**, *church* altered in two campaigns, chancel rebuilt 1856–57 (J.L. Pearson) in Norman style, following the original, impressively detailed at the E end. Reredos by Pearson (c 1870). The second programme (1871–80; G.E. Street) is most memorable, the entire wall surface covered in frescoes by Clayton and Bell, Gothic drawing style with little of Victorian sentimentality, in colourful patterned borders. Tiled dado below. Clayton and Bell glass. Stone pulpit, possibly by Pearson. Painted roofs. **Wetwang** and **Fridaythorpe** churches, to W, A166, were both restored for Sir Tatton (1901–02; C.H. Fowler). 4m NW of Garton, **Sledmere**, the Sykes estate village, the approach marked by the *Sykes Memorial* (1865; J. Gibbs), Gothic stone tower 120ft high to the 4th baronet, erected by 600 of his friends who 'loved him as a friend and honoured him as a landlord'. Polychrome stone, of tapering outline, square up to the octagonal tip, the change marked by stone oriels on each face, lighting a viewing gallery. Sir Tatton was a notable agricultural pioneer, bringing the Wolds under cultivation, and also a famous breeder of racehorses. *Sledmere House* (open to public) is mostly of 1781–88, but totally reconstructed inside after a fire (1912–17; W. Brierley) following the original plasterwork designs, a most successful recreation of an outstanding Georgian interior. Tiled Turkish room designed c 1912 by Sir Mark Sykes after a room in Istanbul. In the village, *school* (1875; G.E. Street), more Gothic than most of his schools for Sykes, village *well* (1840), a rotunda memorial to Sir C. Sykes, and some elaborate late Victorian estate housing. The *Wagoners' Memorial* (c 1919; Sir M. Sykes) barbaric Romanesque, to the Company raised by Sir Mark on the estate to fight in the Great War, is decorated with carved reliefs of savage Germans and sturdy yeomen. *Eleanor Cross* (1900; Temple Moore), built as the village cross, converted to War Memorial to the 5th Yorkshire Regiment by adding touching and comic scenes on bronze panels. Sledmere *church* (1897–98; Temple Moore) is a serious stone work, Dec., beautifully detailed, the chancel elaborated with inner tracery. Timber wagon roofs.

N of Sledmere, four Street churches for Sir Tatton, **Kirby Grindalythe** *church* (1878) retains medieval tower, good fittings by Street, carved reredos and pulpit. W wall covered in mosaic. Vaulted lychgate. **West Lutton** *church* (1872–75) is unusual for the timbered bell turret. Simple outline under a single roof broken only by coping over the chancel arch but very varied window shapes and buttresses, kept in check by a continuous string course around. Vaulted chancel and fine iron screen. Painted reredos. Excellent lychgate. **Helperthorpe** *church* (1871–73) stands beautifully isolated, approached through a gabled lychgate, the outline memorable for the taller chancel and squat spire, somehow in balance each end of the nave. Plain walls articulated by a continuous string course, nothing in excess. Inside, nave and chancel are continuous, the division marked by steps below and arch high up. N aisle and arcade added 1893 (Temple Moore). Good fittings by Street, N aisle reredos by Moore. Stained glass of 1893 (Burlison and Grylls). *Parsonage* by Street (1876). **Weaverthorpe** *church* was restored by Street (1870–72), the alterations suiting the severe Norman structure. Painted barrel roof, iron pulpit and tower screen, brass chancel screen. Painted reredos and stained glass by Clayton and Bell. 7m N, at **East Heslerton**, A64, *church* (1874–77; Street), one of the last for Sir Tatton Sykes, but with a High Victorian bluntness not present in the earlier works. Lancet windows, W end with lean-to loggia, chancel roof higher than the nave and apsed E end, ringed with buttresses. The tower has a slim octagonal bell stage and spire above. Inside, vaulted E end, good fittings by Street including iron screen. Churchyard cross and lychgate, as at the other Sykes churches, completing the picture. *Parsonage* by Street (1875). 3m SW of Sledmere, B1251, at **Fimber**, *church* (1869–71; Street) under a single roof with a sheer pyramid-roofed tower, reminiscent of Butterfield. Simple interior enriched with brass screen, marble reredos and glass by Clayton and Bell. Lychgate by Street. 4m W, at **Thixendale**, a complete group of *church* in its walled enclosure with lychgate and cross (1868–70), *vicarage* (1873) and *school* (1874), the church well set in the valley with bellcote between nave and chancel. Street fittings. **Kirby Underdale** *church*, 3m SW, was restored by Street 1871. **Bishop Wilton** *church*, S of A166, is Norman with restoration work by three of the Sykes' architects, by Pearson the hammerbeam roof (1858), E window and memorial window to Sir Tatton Sykes Sr (1864), by Street (1873–76) the metal screen, and by Temple Moore (1902) the black and white floor and the font. 3m SW of Driffield, at **Kirkburn**, the Norman *church* was restored for Sir Tatton Sykes Sr 1856–57 (J.L. Pearson), the chancel rebuilt, reredos and screen by Street (1872).

12m NE of Driffield, **Bridlington**, resort town on Bridlington Bay. On the sea front, *Alexandra Hotel* (1863), North Beach, large Italianate. On Quay Rd, *Christ Church* (1840; G.G. Scott), among Scott's first churches, he called it his 'first and worst', being built before he saw the light of archaeological Gothic. Scott later restored *Bridlington Priory* in the Old Town, adding the contrasting Norman and Perp. style W towers (1876). Glass by Wailes in E and W windows. At **Bessingby**, 2m SW, *church* (1893; Temple Moore), handsome Dec. with central tower, carefully detailed. Just NE of Bridlington, at **Sewerby**, neo-Norman *church* (1848; G.G. Scott and Moffatt), the style usually dismissed by advanced architects at this date, unless there were historical reasons for its use. *Sewerby Hall*, the Bridlington Art Gallery and Museum, is 18C and early 19C with early Victorian stables, conservatory and gatehouse (H.F. Lockwood).

GRIMSBY. A46 37m NE of Lincoln. Fishing port developed in the 19C by the Manchester, Sheffield and Lincolnshire Railway, Royal Dock built 1849–52. By Royal Dock, *Victoria Flour Mill* (1906). On Cleethorpe Rd, also the *Royal Hotel* (1863–65; M.E. Hadfield), Gothic, the *Dock Offices* (1885) with *statue* of Prince Albert (1879; Theed) holding a plan of the docks, for which he laid the foundation stone in 1849, and *Custom House* (1874). Much the most prominent dock structure is the *Hydraulic Tower* (1852; J.W. Wild), Italian Gothic modelled on Siena Town Hall. In the centre, *Town Hall* (1863; Bellamy and Hardy), palazzo style, and Italianate *Yarborough Hotel* (1851; A. and G. Williams). **Cleethorpes**, just E, was developed and owned by the railway. The main expansion came from 1880 when the Promenade was built and the *station* remodelled with an iron and glass refreshment room. *Church* (1866; J. Fowler). At **Little Coates**, A1136, just W of Grimsby, *church* (1913; W. Tapper) built alongside the medieval church. Fine vaulted chancel.

HULL. One of the leading English ports since the Middle Ages, with important 19C dock developments, unfortunately the English city worst affected by post-war planning and neglect especially in the old town between the docks and the river Hull. Recently some restoration has begun. Queen Victoria Square is the centre of Victorian Hull. Queen Victoria *statue* (1903; H. C. Fehr) and the former *Docks Office* (1867–71; C.G. Wray), an ornate Renaissance style building in Portland stone on a triangular site dominant with its three domed cupolas.

This has now been converted to an excellent Docks Museum. On S side, *Ferens Art Gallery* (1924) and, to W, *City Hall* (1903–09; J.H. Hirst), domed Baroque. To NE, Queen's Gardens occupies the site of the infilled Queen's Dock (1775), first of the three docks that ringed the old town from the river Hull to the river Humber. At E end, *Wilberforce Column* (1834), 90ft Greek Doric column to the abolitionist of the slave trade, born in Hull. *Princes Dock* (1827–29) and *Humber Dock* (1803–09), S of the Docks Office, have survived repeated plans to fill them in and the waterside is the most attractive part of central Hull. On Princes Dock, E side, stuccoed Ionic classical gateway (1842) and one refurbished warehouse further down. The Inner Ring road cuts between the two docks. Off Humber Dock, on *Railway Dock* (1846; J.B. Hartley), *No. 13 warehouse* (c 1851) survives, seven storeys, plain brick with three shallow gables, the end block of an immensely long similar range, now gone.

From the Princes Dock gateway into the old town via Posterngate. *Trinity House chapel* (1839–44; H.F. Lockwood), classical with Corinthian portico to the courtyard and fine interior, the *Trinity Almshouse* (1828) and *Trinity House offices* (1844) are all part of Trinity House, founded in 14C and later devoted to the control of shipping, training of seamen and relief of distressed sailors. *Holy Trinity Church*, the largest of English parish churches, was restored 1841–45 (H.F. Lockwood) and 1859–72 (G.G. Scott). In S aisle two stained glass windows (1897 and c 1907) by Walter Crane, made by J.S. Sparrow in distinctive thick and darkly coloured glass. To E, Market Place with *Market Hall* (1902–04; H. Baines) to N, freely detailed with attached tower. In Lowgate, stone-fronted *Midland Bank* (1869–70; W. Botterill), in Silver St, *Hepworth's Arcade* (1894; W.H. Kitching), glass-roofed with Art Nouveau detail. *St. Mary's Church* was heavily restored 1861 (G.G. Scott) when the pavement was cut through the tower. On corner of Alfred Gelder St, *Post Office* (1908; J. Williams), Imperial classical, facing the far more monumental *Guildhall* (1906– 14; Sir E. Cooper), the long street elevation Corinthian-columned between centre and end pavilions, the ends topped with heroic sculpture (A. Hodge). On the front, pedimented upper portico and centre tower, all to an overwhelming scale, civic pride made manifest in Portland stone. In High St, to E, the decayed main street of the old town, *Transport and Archaeology Museum* housed in the former Corn Exchange (1856; Bellamy and Hardy), stone-fronted classical, and *Wilberforce House*, now a museum, Wilberforce's birthplace. *No. 17*, a gabled brick warehouse (c 1870), impressively plain, is restored together with the 18C Pease warehouse on the Hull.

NW of Queen Victoria Square, in Prospect St, Baroque style *Library* (1900; J.S. Gibson) on corner of Albion St. To E, in Kingston Square, *New Theatre* (1830–34; R.H. Sharp), classical, built as Assembly Rooms, and former *School of Medicine* (1833; H.R. Abraham). *RC church* (1829), Jarratt St, is stucco classical with Baroque decoration over the altar (1894). W of Queen Victoria St, on Anlaby Rd, *College of Art* (1902; E.A. Rickards), an excellent design by one of the least pompous Baroque revival designers, brick and stone, banded in the pedimented centre with an exuberantly sculpted two-storey curved porch bay. Lively ironwork in the balcony. To N, *Hull Paragon Station* (1848; G.T. Andrews), the S side Italian palazzo style in fine stone, the central range with balustraded porte-cochère, now enclosed, the coupled columns echoed in pilasters on the main block behind, wings each side and end pavilions. *Royal Station Hotel* (1851; G.T. Andrews) in matching style at SE corner, extended 1904–05.

Large tiled booking hall, glazed concourse and train-shed of 1904–05 (W. Bell). Built for George Hudson, the 'Railway King', the first railway millionaire and controller of some half of the railways in England before his bankruptcy in 1855. NW of centre, Spring Bank runs up to *Hull General Cemetery* (1847) with *Hymer's College* (1889–93; Botterill, Son and Bilson) to S, free 17C style combining mullioned windows and cupola. Prince's Avenue runs N to *Pearson Park* with statues (1863 and 1868) of Victoria and Albert (T. Earle). To W, in Westbourne Avenue and Salisbury St, *Westbourne Park* estate laid out with ornate fountains at the two crossings and with early Queen Anne revival houses (1876; G.G. Scott Jr) in red-brick and white cement panels, a cheerful combination but unattractive if neglected. Dutch gables, hipped roofs and tall chimneys survive but not the timber cupolas that some of the houses had. In Northumberland Avenue, *almshouses* (1884; Smith and Brodrick), pretty domestic revival courtyard group. To E, off Beverley Rd, in Sculcoates Lane, *St. Mary's Church* (1916; Temple Moore), brick, interior impressively severe.

5m W of Hull, A63, at **North Ferriby**, *church* (1846–48; J.L. Pearson), Pearson's first large church, completely modelled on the work of Pugin, Pearson not yet showing a personal touch, but with good proportions and prominent broach spire. 4m NW, A63, at **Brantingham**, *War Memorial* made up of bits of the demolished 1862 Hull Town Hall. *Brantingham Thorpe* (1868–82; G. Devey) is a rambling Jacobean mansion built for C. Sykes, friend of Edward VII when Prince of Wales. The *church* was restored for Sykes by G.E. Street (1872).

SCUNTHORPE. A18 24m E of Doncaster. Iron and steel town, mostly late 19C brick. Parish *church* (1891; J. Crowther), High St, stately Perp. style with high W tower, the gift of Lord St. Oswald of the steel company. 4m N, *Normanby Hall* (1825–30; R. Smirke), Regency style stone mansion, now a museum. 4m SW, at **Burringham**, on the Trent, *church* (1857; S.S. Teulon), polychrome brick, apsed with heavy plate tracery. 6m NW, on the edge of the marshes, at **Eastoft**, *church* (1855; J.L. Pearson), a neat severe design, steep roofed with lancets and minimal ornament. 7m NW of Eastoft, A161, **Goole**, seaport 47 miles from the sea, founded 1826 by the Aire and Calder Navigation Company at the outlet of their Knottingley Canal. Handsome *church* (1843–48; Hurst and Moffatt) in Perp. style with tall crossing spire, built by the Company. 8m W, at **Snaith**, in the *church* marble statue (1837; F. Chantrey) to Viscount Downe. Just S, at **Cowick**, small brick church (1853–54; W. Butterfield), steep roofed, the little bell turret projecting and carried on a high narrow arch. *School* and *vicarage* by Butterfield, all three good examples of his simplest manner, where funds were short, variety coming from roofline and chimneys rather than carved window detail. Similarly simple *church* (1854) at **Pollington**, to SW, with school and vicarage. A third contemporary group by Butterfield nearby, at **Hensall**, is just in N Yorkshire.

ISLE OF WIGHT

COWES. A3020 5m N of Newport. A yachting centre since the 18C, headquarters of the Royal Yacht Squadron, founded 1812 as the Yacht Club. J.C. Stevens bought the yacht 'America' over in the Great Exhibition year, 1851, and successfully raced fifteen boats around the island, taking home the 'America's Cup'. The Squadron club house is Henry VIII's *Castle* reconditioned for the Squadron in 1856 (A. Salvin). Pretty, early 19C houses on the hill, larger and later in Queens Rd. On top of the hill, *St. Mary's Church* with its extraordinary neo-Grecian tower (1816; J. Nash), the rest of 1867. Behind, *Northwood House* remodelled 1838–43 (G. Mair) for George Ward who built the church tower as a mausoleum. Neo-classical with Egyptian and Etrurian painted interiors. Early 19C lodge by Nash. Across the Medina river, East Cowes, residential suburb with *church* 1868 (T. Hellyer) except for the tower (1831; J. Nash). Nash lived at East Cowes Castle, demolished, and is buried in the churchyard. To NE, *Norris Castle* (1799; J. Wyatt) romantically set over the Solent. Princess Victoria stayed here in 1831 and 1833.

Osborne House (1845–51; T. Cubitt), near Cowes

In 1845 Victoria and Albert bought the *Osborne estate to the S as their private residence and built the house largely to Albert's designs with Thomas Cubitt as architect from 1845–51. Osborne was strictly Victoria and Albert's private home, replacing the all too public Brighton Pavilion. Victoria said in 1845 'so snug and nice to have a place of *one's own*, quiet and retired, and free from all…departments who really are the plague of one's life'. Albert busied himself with remodelling the estate and laying out the terraces down to the Solent and it remained Victoria's favourite house after Albert's death in 1861, though as ever with Albert's memory, something of a shrine with rooms untouched as he left them. Italianate entrance lodge and cottages on the drive. The house itself is now very large, but there are three component parts, the central pavilion wing which was the private residence, Italianate like one of Cubitt's Belgravia houses but with an off-centre campanile, the much larger main wing at right angles with a first-floor loggia based on Palladio's basilica at Vicenza, containing official rooms on the N side and space for the Royal House-hold, then in 1890 the large Durbar Wing was added by J.L. Kipling (Rudyard Kipling's father). Everything was built to the highest tech-nical standards, with fireproof construction (even the skirting boards were cement), but, for a royal residence, relatively modest decoration. The facades are strictly symmetrical, cement rendered but given inte-rest by the two asymmetrical campanili, the second at the E end of the main wing marking the suite given over to Victoria's mother. The interiors are the most complete mid 19C scheme in the country, leaving aside their interest as showing Victoria and Albert's taste. Rooms in ornate late classical style, not exceptionally rich but well-planned about a central staircase. The staircase begins with Engel's 'Amazons and the Argonauts' marble group which Albert bought at the 1851 exhibition and rises between marbled walls to the landing with Wolff's statue of Albert as a Greek Warrior (1844). Throughout the pavilion and the main wing, sculptures bought by Albert or Vic-toria or commissioned groups of the royal children or even the royal dogs. Their taste was to the classical, of a sentimental kind. Albert himself sculpted a bronze greyhound on the terrace. On the terraces, fountains, one carrying John Bell's bronze nude 'Andromeda' which Victoria bought at the 1851 exhibition. In the grounds Swiss Cottages re-erected in 1853 and 1862 for the'children, a pretty landing house by the water (1855) and much splendid planting, directed by Albert in semaphore from the rooftop. S of the house, at **Whippingham**, the estate *church* (1854 and 1861; A. Humbert) in an odd Norman to EE style with big crossing tower. Monuments to the royal family, notably to Albert (1864; W. Theed) and Prince Henry of Battenberg with fine metal grille (1896; A. Gilbert). *Almshouses* (1880) for retired royal servants.

NEWPORT. A3020 5m S of Cowes. Set at the head of the navigable Medina river. Prominent parish *church* (1854; S.W. Daukes) in the manner of Pugin. Monument to the daughter of Charles I (1856; Maro-chetti) given by Queen Victoria and memorial to Prince Albert (1862; Marochetti) with white marble profile relief set on a dark ground. In High St, *Town Hall* (1816; J. Nash) with tower of 1887, in St. James' Square, *Guildhall* (1819; J. Nash) and ornate Gothic monument (1901), slightly Art Nouveau. To NW, *Parkhurst Prison*, a military hospital of 1799 taken over 1838 and much enlarged by Major Jebb, prison specialist. At **Carisbrooke**, 1½m SW, RC *priory* (1865; G. Blount), Gothic complex. At **Gatcombe**, 3m S, excellent early Morris glass (1865) in E window of the *church*. Gatcombe House has a museum of costume and collection of horse-drawn vehicles.

RYDE. A3054 7m NE of Newport. Seaside resort developed from the early 19C. The pier begun 1813 was the first piled passenger pier but much altered since. On the Esplanade some large 19C hotels. Union St has stucco terraces of c 1830 and the *Royal Victoria Arcade* (c 1840) glazed roofed shopping arcade with stucco street front. At foot of St. Thomas' St, *Royal Victoria Yacht Club* (1846; W. Huntley), handsome stucco Italianate building, purpose-built for the club, founded 1844. Around St. Thomas' Square some late Regency stucco survivals. In High St, *RC church* (1844; J.A. Hansom) with odd EE detail. Inland the tall steeple (1881) of *St. John's Church* (1868–72; G.G. Scott), Queens

Rd, ornately detailed and large. Further S, at Swanmore, *St. Michael's Church* (1861–63; the Rev. W. Grey and R.J. Jones), a serious Gothic work by an amateur architect with crossing tower and polychrome interior. Elaborate vaulted chancel with tile pavement and glass by Lavers and Westlake. Clergy house and schools complete the High Church group. 1m E, *Woodlands Vale Hotel*, complex building remodelled 1870 (S.S. Teulon) for the 5th Lord Calthorpe with bold entrance tower. 2m W, *Quarr Abbey*, a Benedictine Abbey founded from Solesmes in 1907. Extraordinary church (1911–12; Dom P. Bellot), the forms of early Cluniac churches rethought in a 20C way: brick built, uncompromising and sharp edged with an open tower over the E end of tremendous intersecting plain brick arches superbly constructed, the inner walls of the tower pierced with long lancet-like openings. 5m SE of Ryde, at **Bembridge**, *church* (1845) with broach spire and large *hotel* on the point (1882). *Bembridge School* has the important collection of Ruskin material amassed by J.H. Whitehouse, who founded the school on progressive principles in 1919 and edited Ruskin's diaries. Open by appointment. From St. Helen's, to N, can be seen the nearest of the four island *forts* built across the Solent as part of Lord Palmerston's defensive works of 1860.

SANDOWN. A3055 6m S of Ryde. Late Victorian seaside resort with *pier* of 1878 and 1895. Promenade built 1889 with hotels behind. To S, at **Lake**, *church* (1892; Temple Moore) of interesting double- nave plan and good detail. 1m further S is **Shanklin**, seaside resort on steep cliff side developed from the 1860s. *Pier* (1891). *Town Hall* (1879; E. Cooper), Steephill Rd, brick with French detail. On the hill, *St. Saviour's Church* (1869–87; T. Hellyer), Queens Rd, EE style, with tower turning octagonal. *Vicarage* (c 1870; Woodyer). 3m S, **Ventnor**, seaside resort developed from the 1840s. Modest esplanade with pier, much rebuilt, and terraces of houses some with ornate balconies stepping up the hill. Parish *church* (1837; R. Ebbels), Church St, dating from the very beginnings of the resort. Good stained glass of c 1895 (W. Reynolds-Stephens) rescued from the demolished Chest Hospital. 1m E, at **Bonchurch**, Dickens rented *Winterbourne* in 1849 and wrote part of 'David Copperfield' here. The poet Swinburne was brought up in Bonchurch at *East Dene*.

YARMOUTH. A3054 10m W of Newport. On the Quay, pretty *Yacht Club* (1897; Aston Webb). 3m S, *Farringford*, near **Freshwater**, Tennyson's home from 1853 to 1867 where many of his best works were written including 'The Idylls of the King'. Memorial Cross on Tennyson Down and commemorative stone in the church.

KENT

ASHFORD. A20 19m SE of Maidstone. Ashford had the railway works of the South Eastern Railway and plain brick railway houses survive SE of the station in Ashford New Town. 3m N, *Eastwell Park*, (1894; W. Wallace), rambling Tudor house, much romanticised in 1926, now a hotel. On the A251 a massive flint and stone square gatehouse (c 1843). 5m NE of Ashford, N of **Wye**, *Olantigh* (1904; Brown and Barrow), large red-brick and stone neo-Georgian mansion.

CANTERBURY. The principal 19C alteration to the *Cathedral* was the NW tower (1832–41; G. Austin) added to match the 15C SW tower. Some good monuments to archbishops, the best Archbishop Howley (c 1848; R. Westmacott Jr) in the N choir aisle under a Gothic canopy, Archbishop Sumner (1866; Weekes) and Archbishop Benson (c 1898, design by T.G. Jackson) in the N nave aisle and Bishop Broughton (1855; J.G. Lough) in the S nave aisle. W of the cathedral the *Archbishop's Palace* (mostly 1897; W. Caroe), picturesque Tudor. To the E, across the ring road, *St. Augustine's College*, Monastery St, a missionary college built 1844–48 for A. Beresford Hope by William Butterfield, the collaboration that later built All Saints' Church, Margaret St, London. This was Butterfield's first major commission, the rebuilding on its ancient site of the medieval monastery of St. Augustine. The rebuilding included the remaining medieval parts and was based on excavation though the result has the strong lines and lack of picturesque embellishments characteristic of Butterfield's approach to revived Gothic. Flint and stone buildings around an open quad with, on the S side, the refectory, a reconstruction of the abbot's guest hall, the chapel at right angles with a big traceried window, the warden's house of equal height and richer in detail than the fellows' lodgings beyond. Window details kept flush with the wall to emphasise height over decoration. At the E end, fine free-standing library, raised up on a vaulted basement with tall windows based on those at the medieval Archbishop's Palace at Mayfield, Sussex. Along the N side, the students' lodgings, two-storey with a cloister walk and small windows above lighting the bedrooms. Two thin turrets break up the length. In the centre, a stone conduit head. Off St. Dunstan's St, NW of the cathedral, *West station* (1846; S. Beazley), classical detail. On St. Thomas' Hill, *St. Edmund's School* (1854–55; P.C. Hardwick), big ragstone Gothic open quad with steep-roofed central hall.

At **Wickhambreux**, 4m E, in the *church*, spectacular American Art Nouveau E window (1896; A. Rosencrantz), an Annunciation over a field of lilies, an exceptional rarity in Britain. Off A2, 6m SE, at **Womenswold**, *Denne Hill* (1871; G. Devey), an early revival of Dutch gables and Kentish late 17C motifs. Lodge on A2. Much larger, by Devey, is *St. Albans Court*, **Nonington** to NE built from 1875, Elizabethan style in red brick with the picturesque device of having the bottom of the walls in stone that dies away irregularly into the brick as if the upper part were a reconstruction on ancient foundations. Balanced near symmetrical elevations with a massive off-centre circular bay on the garden front. This lights a lovely panelled two-storey hall with galleries and an open screen to the entrance passage. Devey half-timbered estate cottages in the village.

CRANBROOK. A229 13m E of Tunbridge Wells. Pretty Kentish town that became a minor artists' centre from c 1857 around the painters

F.D. Hardy and T. Webster, joined by J.C. Horsley and G.B. O'Neill to form the 'Cranbrook Colony'. Webster is commemorated in the parish *church* in a marble relief showing him in painter's smock (1889; H. Thornycroft). *Cranbrook School* has a handsome Queen Anne style main building (1883; T.G. Jackson) with moulded brickwork and a top cupola. On A229, 1m NE, at **Wilsley Green**, G.B. O'Neill rented Old Wilsley, a 15C hall house, while J.C. Horsley bought *Willesley*, now an hotel. The original house was early 18C but Horsley had R. Norman Shaw (1864) extend it at both ends and add a marine-looking belve dere on the rooftop. At **Goudhurst** to W, pretty Queen Anne *village hall* (c 1900) by the pond, and 1½m N, *Ballards House*, (1903; R. Blomfield) handsome early Georgian style. At **Beneden**, 3m SE of Cranbrook, *Benenden School* occupies an Elizabethan style mansion (1859–62; D. Brandon) built for Viscount Cranbrook, altered early 20C. The village is full of estate buildings of the Cranbrook estate, the best by George Devey including the *Primary School* (1861), *vicarage* and *Bull Inn*. The school is an early example, before Norman Shaw's work, of the move from Gothic to a lighter mixture of motifs partly vernacular. Later estate buildings by T.W. Cotman, the large gabled *village hall* by G. Crawley (1908). At **Rolvenden**, 2m SE, A28, *Great Maytham* (1909; Lutyens), one of his largest neo-Georgian works, grey brick with red-brick dressings, the lodge more lively than the house. At **Hawkhurst**, A268, 3m S of Cranbrook, *All Saints' Church* (1861), a good village church by Sir G.G. Scott, crisply detailed in local sandstone with spire set against the chancel. *Hall* (1875; A. Williams) in the Norman Shaw style nearby.

DOVER. Much battered during the war. The *Castle* was altered during the 1860s as part of the anti-French scare and Fort Burgoyne built to the N, gigantic earthworks but nothing compared to those on the *Western Heights* behind the Western Docks built between 1800 and 1862, where the whole hillside is excavated out over square miles of ground with underground batteries, ditches, redoubts. The central Citadel is now a Borstal, and little of the complex is accessible. In the Western Docks, former *Lord Warden Hotel* (1850; S. Beazley), white stucco Italianate, one of the largest early railway hotels, now offices. Along the seafront, *Waterloo Crescent* (1834–38; P. Hardwick), curved stucco terrace on a grand scale. In the town, *Town Hall*, Priory Rd, includes the early 14C Maison Dieu extended in matching flint (1881; W. Burges). Burges restored the old building (1859–62) with painted glass scenes of Dover history by E.J. Poynter. The new Town Hall was built to a cheaper plan after Burges's death by R.P. Pullan. S of Priory Rd, *Dover College*, founded 1863 and occupying the restored remains of the old Priory. Inland, at **Charlton**, St. Alphege Rd, *St. Peter and St. Paul Church* (1893; J. Brooks), a powerful work, tall ragstone exterior with big lancets over low aisles, inside, high boarded nave roof and lower chancel. Sparsely detailed stonework with blank arches framing the upper windows and the arcade arches dying into the main piers in a late Victorian way. A258, at **Walmer**, S of **Deal**, *Walmer Castle* was altered 1871 by G. Devey with picturesque touches, a curved gable, a tower with domed turret. 4m W of Deal, *Betteshanger House* (1856–82; G. Devey), a long drawn out remodelling of a Georgian villa into a complex and picturesque mansion. Devey and his artistic client, the Liberal politician Sir W. James, created a loosely connected composition suggesting a history of additions and altera- tions from the late Middle Ages to the 18C but mostly of that period in the 17C when Dutch gables were introduced to Kent. A subtle creation, let down only by the plate glass in the mullioned windows, it shows an appreciation for local materials and styles in advance of anything contemporary. The village *church* (1853; Salvin) also rebuilt for the James Family. 1m E, in **Northbourne** *church*, rich High Victorian stone and alabaster reredos (1865; J.F. Bentley).

FAVERSHAM. A2 6m NW of Canterbury, *Fremlin's Brewery* is the most prominent 19C monument. In Church Rd, large Gothic *schools* (1852; R. Hussey) around an enclosed courtyard, in South Rd, red-brick *almshouses* (1856–64; Hooker and Wheeler), spiky Gothic flanking a stone chapel. At **Ospringe**, 2m W, *church* rebuilt (1858–66; E.L. Blackburne) with High Victorian saddleback tower. At **Kingsdown**, 3m further W, ragstone *church* with spire (1865; E.W. Pugin), a complete mid Victorian estate church isolated but for the rectory.

FOLKESTONE. A20 6m W of Dover. A mid and late Victorian seaside resort more than a port town. The most memorable monument is the *Railway Viaduct* (1843; Sir W. Cubitt) crossing the valley at the back of the town on 19 arches up to 100ft high. By the harbour red-brick and terracotta *Royal Pavilion Hotel* (1898; R.W. Edis), behind, *Marine Parade* (1848; R. Tress), stucco terrace. In the town, the old *church*, top of the *Old High St*, has extensive 19C decoration, notably wall-paintings (c 1890–1900; A. Hemming) and good E and W windows by Kempe. In Guildhall St behind, *Town Hall* (1856; J. Messenger), stone Italianate, and *RC church* (1889; L. Stokes). Sandgate Rd leads W along the back of *The Leas*, a cliff-top resort with gardens in front of mid 19C villas and terraces running back to Sandgate Rd. At the end two large hotels of c 1900. At **Sandgate**, to the W, in Radnor Cliff Crescent, *Spade House*, H.G. Wells's house built for him by Voysey (1899; extended 1903). Here Wells wrote 'Kipps', 'Tono-Bungay' and 'The History of Mr Polly'. 5m NW at **Postling**, Joseph Conrad rented *Pent Farm* from 1898 to 1907, the period of 'Lord Jim', 'Typhoon' and 'Nostromo'. 5m W on B2067, *Lympne Castle*, highly picturesque 15C castle restored from ruin and given pretty stone forecourt buildings 1906–12 (Sir R. Lorimer). At **Elham**, B2065, 6m N of Hythe, *church* with exceptional early 20C fittings by F.C. Eden, the influence being the city churches of Wren.

GRAVESEND. A226 6m NW of Rochester. Thames-side port with two of the earliest surviving piers, really short landing stages, the *Town Pier* (1834) and *Royal Terrace Pier* (1842), classical detail in cast iron. Up the High St, Greek *Town Hall* (1836; A.H. Wilds). In the 1820s and 30s attempts were made to develop Gravesend and Northfleet as resorts, of which fragments remain behind Royal Terrace Pier. Terrace Gardens were planned by John Loudon and, by the *RC church* (1834: with tower 1872), Milton Road, Decimus Burton was to lay out an estate. The best 19C buildings now are the crown-spired *clock tower* (1887; J. Johnson) and the small waterfront *church* (1870; G.E. Street), Royal Pier Road. At **Northfleet**, the remnants of c 1835 development (H.E. Kendall) are in Burch Rd. In Perry St, *church* (1869; J. Brooks), severe plate-traceried early Gothic, Romanesque in the nave arcade. To W of Northfleet, on riverside, *Ingress Abbey* (1832; C. Moreing), now part of Merchant Navy College, Tudor Gothic all in Portland stone. S of A226 at **Galley Hill**, *RC church* (1894; R. Norman Shaw) in flint and stone with a low central tower, distinctly bleak. Good furnishings. At Stone, A2, 2m W, the former *Pauper Lunatic Asylum* (1862; J. Bunning), very extensive Tudor style brick complex.

LAMBERHURST. A21 5m E of Tunbridge Wells. To E, *Scotney Castle* (1837–44; A. Salvin), Tudor style house in yellow sandstone set above the glorious landscaped garden around the fragment of the original 14C castle in the valley below. This is one of the great achievements of picturesque landscaping in Britain, no longer the open views of the 18C but a cliff-like descent, well wooded with changing views of the old castle in its moat. (Gardens NT.) Salvin's house has an entrance tower with the unhistorical but picturesque effect of the battlements stepping upwards to a taller corner. 3m E, B2079, *Bedgebury Park*, a handsome classical house recased 1836–41 in sandstone for Viscount Beresford, general in the Peninsular War. It was given a French roof and a spire on the stable court in 1854 (R.C. Carpenter) for the Viscount's heir, Alexander Beresford Hope, the leading ecclesiological reformer. Beresford Hope's Gothic tastes had some rein at **Kilndown** *church* to the W where the plain box begun 1839 (A. Salvin) for the Viscount was taken over by his stepson in 1840 who attempted to create an interior closer to ecclesiological ideals. The chancel at Kilndown is, for all its half-achieved look by later standards, the first to be arranged as a ritual sanctuary divided by steps and screen from the nave and embellished with painted decoration and encaustic tiles. Stained glass from the Royal Works at Munich as none suitable could be found in Britain. Churchyard nicely enclosed with a sandstone lychgate (1860) and Tudor style schools (1846). Down the lane to NW, former *rectory* (1850; R.C. Carpenter), a handsome Gothic house with bold chimneys and narrow paired lancet windows. W of Lamberhurst, B2169, *Bayham Abbey* (1869; D. Brandon), large gabled stone house set on hillside overlooking the medieval ruins. Built for the Marquess Camden, now flats.

MAIDSTONE. The county town of Kent on the Medway. The parish *church* of c 1400 was restored 1885 (J.L. Pearson) who added the screen and large stone reredos (1896). Adjoining, Archbishop's Palace, heavily repaired in 1909. On the riverside big red-brick *Brewery* (1870). In the High St, *fountain* (c 1862; H. Blandford) with statue of Queen Victoria in a Gothic shrine and, on S side, iron-framed shopfront of c 1855. Off Week St, *Museum*, St. Faith's St, the 16C Chillington Manor overwhelmed by restoration 1875 and wings 1890 and 1897. Further N, on Chatham Rd, *Springfield*, the county offices around brick and terracotta mansion (1891; Waterhouse). At **Langley**, A274, 4m SE, *church* (1854; W. Butterfield) of powerfully simple lines, a sheer tower, with bell stage slightly set back and capped by a sturdy broach spire, set at the W end of a plainly detailed church. Excellent stonework. Painted chancel roof. *School* also by Butterfield. At **Linton**, A229, 3m SW, *Linton Park* (c 1829; W. Cubitt), a remodelling in stucco of a 1730s house, with portico and wings, imposing, like contemporary government buildings in India. In the *church* exceptional neo-classical monument (c 1835; E.H. Baily) to Viscount Brome, the young son of Earl Cornwallis. Another effigy, also in white marble, to Countess Cornwallis by Baily (c 1847). 2m NW of Maidstone, *Allington Castle*, beautiful 13C and 16C castle restored from ruin 1905–29 for the politician Lord Conway by W. Caroe. The hall and range to the gatehouse are new. Open to the public. At **Aylesford** to NW, *Preston Hall* (1850; J. Thomas), hefty Jacobean in yellow stone built for a partner of Sir M. Peto, the building contractor, for whom Thomas designed Somerleyton Hall, Suffolk.

MARGATE. A seaside resort from the mid 18C with early 19C terraces on Fort Hill going into the mid 19C at Cliftonville. In Shottendane Rd, *Convalescent Home* (1910; Thackeray Turner), large Arts and Crafts house, rendered and gabled. To the W, **Westgate on Sea**, cheerful late 19C resort all red brick and white windows. *Waterside Hotel* (1880; George and Peto), prettily tile-hung with a triple gable, marks the beginning of Westgate's fashionable period. Next door, *Exbury House*, built for the future Lord Redesdale with pretty slightly Japanese woodwork. To the S, on Canterbury Rd, *RC convent* (1905–10; F. Walters), roughcast and brick with tall chapel. At **Birchington**, to W, the first bungalows in England, built for seaside visitors in the 1880s. D.G. Rossetti came to one in 1881 and died here. He is buried in the parish churchyard under a beautifully carved Celtic cross by Ford Madox Brown, carved by Jane Patteson.

Estate cottages (1850; G. Devey), Penshurst

PENSHURST. B2176 5m SW of Tonbridge. Very much an estate village for Penshurst Place, and from c 1810 something of a centre for rural life painters around the collector William Wells. The *cottages* in the village combine romantic picturesque theory and acute observation of Kentish rural precedent, notably the half-timbered group at the entrance to the churchyard (1850) by the architect George Devey, pupil of the painter, J.S. Cotman. In the *church* a screen by Bodley and Garner (1895) and monument to Lord Hardinge, Governor-General of India 1844–48. Lord Hardinge's house, South Park, is now demolished and the statue that his family retrieved from Calcutta has also moved on. George Devey remodelled *Hammerfield* (1858), N of the village, in diapered brick and also *Swaylands* (1879–92), to SE, neither as successful as his cottages. At **Speldhurst**, to SE, *church* (1870; J.O. Scott) with excellent Morris glass of the 1870s in N aisle and S side of nave. W window by Kempe (1878). N of Penshurst, on B2027, **Chiddingstone Causeway** with *church* (1897; J.F. Bentley), Bath stone, broad in proportion with very large traceried windows each end. German stained glass (1906; von Glehn), deep coloured with heavy leading. At **Chiddingstone**, *Chiddingstone Castle*, castellated house mostly of c 1805 and 1835. To W, at **Hever**, *Hever Castle*, 14C moated castle bought by W.W. Astor in 1903 and restored to an Edwardian dream of the Middle Ages. Astor's American fortune made him as rich as any man in Britain. Cliveden, Buckinghamshire, was his main seat, Hever a country retreat. Under the architect F.L. Pearson the castle itself was restored, little altered externally and with the timber-framed inner courtyard rebuilt on the old lines. Inside, however, the rooms were decorated with the most luxuriant carved woodwork in an Elizabethan Renaissance style with lavish inlay and heavily moulded plasterwork. The kitchen court is wholly new, a romantic blend of stone and half-timber, convincingly Tudor. For his visitors Astor added across the moat a low picturesque 'Tudor village' allowing the castle to stand free against a romantic backcloth. The grounds were filled with Italian statuary of the highest quality with stone garden buildings and balustrades looking over a 45 acre lake that took 800 men two years to dig.

RAMSGATE. A254 4m SE of Margate. Seaport and resort with a late Georgian character. West of the harbour terraces from c 1800–30 on the cliff- top and at the W end *St. Augustine's Abbey*, the church and house that A.W.N. Pugin built for himself 1845–50. The *church is screened from the road by its cloister but open to the sea. Pugin's house, *The Grange*, abuts almost against the W end such that a tight complex of Gothic buildings results, the church buildings in black flint, the house in yellow brick. The church is severe, the walls patterned by bands of stone, without buttresses or other visual break except those that arise from the planning of the church. Short central tower, a spire was intended. Inside, Pugin's most accomplished church, the mouldings strong, fine stonework and timber roofs and exceptional fittings, glass by Hardman, typical Pugin timber screens, iron screen to the Lady Chapel by Hardman, towering stone high altar. The font with its tall wood cover was exhibited at the Crystal Palace as was the brass tabernacle. In the S transept Pugin's tomb (1853), recumbent medievalising effigy with Minton tile pavement around. Cloister chapel added 1857 by E.W. Pugin, who also built the abbey buildings across the road from the church (1860). *The Grange* (1844) has a battlemented tower balanced by a gable, tall roofs and a small oratory on the E side. The play of roofs, chimneys and such variety as there is of window detail all arise out of the plan and function of the various parts, as Pugin always advocated. W of the harbour, French-roofed *Pavilion* (1904; S. Adshead) and early 19C terraces on the cliff leading up to the large Gothic *Granville Hotel* (1869; E.W. Pugin). Further W, *East Court* (c 1880; E. George), Victoria Parade, tile-hung Queen Anne with well-handled play of levels and gables, the tiles green contrasting with the brick ground floor and big panelled chimneys. In the centre, W of High St, Guildhall Lawn, *Library* (1904; S. Adshead), scholarly and handsome neo-Adam.

At **Broadstairs**, 2m N, Charles Dickens spent the summers between 1836 and 1850. 'Nicholas Nickleby' was written at the *Royal Albion Hotel*, Albion St, 'Barnaby Rudge' at *Archway House* and 'David Copperfield' was finished at *Bleak House*, a castellated house then called The Fort, now a Dickens Museum. **Pegwell Bay**, 1½m S of Ramsgate, is, despite the hoverport, still as in W. Dyce's mysterious painting 'Pegwell Bay: A Recollection of October 5th 1858' now in the Tate Gallery. 4m S, A257, **Sandwich**. The *Guildhall* was heavily restored

(1910; E.J. May). At the foot of the High St, red-brick *Bell Hotel* (c 1885) by the Barbican. Upper Strand St leads up to *The Salutation* (1911; Lutyens), Lutyens' most perfect neo-Georgian house with great hipped roofs and excellent proportion of small-paned window to wall, simply but subtly handled. The entrance arch between two cottages is playfully bridged by a dormered roof on a big cornice. In Manwood Rd, *school* (1894; T.G. Jackson), red brick Queen Anne formally planned and prettily detailed. At **Sandwich Bay**, 2m E, large houses between the golf courses built from 1912 including a distinct heir of The Salutation.

ROCHESTER. Cathedral town on the Medway. The *Cathedral* suffered several restorations, but Pearson's refacing of the W front (1889) and C.H. Fowler's central tower (1904) were both based on archaeological evidence. Pearson also added the stone choir screen. In the S transept marble effigy of Dean Hole (1905; F.W. Pomeroy). *King's School*, beyond the Prior's Gate, has Tudor style main building (1842; L. Vulliamy) and spiky school house in red-brick and rubble-stone bands (1878) to rear on Maidstone Rd. In High St below, to E, *Eastgate House* (c 1590), now a museum with Dickens' Swiss chalet from Gad's Hill re-erected in the gardens behind. Rochester appears a great deal in Dickens' work. Back down the High St, lodges to *La Providence*, almshouses for French Protestants founded 1718 and rebuilt c 1840 and recently. Jacobean style *Medway Conservancy* offices (1909; G. Bond) beyond the Guildhall. 3m NW on A226 is *Gad's Hill Place*, the 18C house Dickens bought in 1856 and where he died in 1870. In the Swiss chalet in the gardens across the road he wrote 'Great Expectations' and 'Our Mutual Friend'. The *church* (1860) is lofty in ragstone and Bath stone with a spire. At **Strood**, across the river from Rochester, *St. Mary's Church* (1868; A. Blomfield), Vicarage Rd, High Victorian, stone outside, brick within.

2m SE of Rochester, **Chatham**. Naval dockyard town from the 17C, now battered and the naval docks likely to be redeveloped. Off High St, Medway St leads to the *Town Hall* (1898; G. Bond), stone with domed tower. On the corner of High St and Railway St, *bank* (1903; W.C. Jones) and *Post Office* (1901) both with Arts and Crafts details. In the High St, *Fountain* pub with c 1900 tiled front. In Dock Rd, *St. Mary's Church* (1884–1901; A.W. Blomfield), incorporating parts and monuments from the previous parish church. The statue of Lord Kitchener was returned from Khartoum in 1958. In Hills Terrace, strongly detailed brick *RC church* (1863; H. Clutton). The *Dockyard*, Dock Rd, had remarkable 18C and early 19C buildings, mostly not accessible, and also important early cast-iron roofed sheds (1845–47 and 1853). *Royal Naval Barracks* (c 1905), free Baroque style of A. Webb's Dartmouth College. On the hill above the main gate, in **Gillingham**, *Brompton Barracks*, Pasley Rd, a vast square of 1804–06 with Crimean War *arch* (1856; M.D. Wyatt), General Gordon *statue* (1900; Onslow Ford), *Institute* opposite (1872; Sir F. Ommanney), all this part of the Royal Engineers' headquarters.

SEVENOAKS. A21 7m N of Tonbridge. In the High St, small-scale *Market House* (1843). Off London Rd, *Lime Tree Walk* (1878–82; T.G. Jackson), a row of cottages in red brick with roughcast upper floors built by Jackson and his father as low-cost houses for working people. There was a coffee house opposite for recreation. The cottages are derived from Norman Shaw's houses at Bedford Park, London, in using Queen Anne elements, white-painted small-paned windows, tiled and shaped gables, but less elaborate than middle-class Bedford Park. They seem both in their high-minded intentions and in the simple and unselfconscious design the direct ancestors of the houses in the Garden Cities like Letchworth, Hertfordshire, after 1900. 3m NE at **Kemsing**, *church* with chancel decorated c 1900, wall-paintings, stained glass and Perp. style woodwork mostly by J.N. Comper, pulpit and screen by W.F. Unsworth. 2m W of Sevenoaks at **Sundridge**, A25, *Combe Bank*, 1761 Palladian villa with main saloon decorated (1880) by Walter Crane mixing Renaissance, Classical and Georgian motifs in a splendid ceiling with bronzed and silvered relief figures. The house later belonged to the chemical tycoon and art collector Mond, who added the tunnel-vaulted ballroom (c 1907; W. Cave) in the N wing, late 18C in style. At **Brasted**, just beyond, *White Hart Inn* (1885; E.T. Hall), cheery half-timber. Further W, at **Westerham**, in the *church*, rich S aisle window of the Six Acts of Mercy (1864; H. Holiday) and organ case (1871; J.F. Bentley). On the green, *statue* of General Wolfe (1910; D. Wood). In London Rd, picturesque half-timbered *almshouses* (1874).

SITTINGBOURNE. A2 7m SE of Chatham. To NE, by Milton Creek, **Murston** *church* (1873; W. Burges) flint and stone with incomplete tower. Punchy W rose window and boarded trefoil-section roof. On the Isle of Sheppey to N, **Sheerness**, formerly a naval dock town. The dockyard has been much battered since the navy left but the remarkable *•Boat Store* (1859; Colonel G. Greene) survives on the E side, an absolutely plain iron-framed building of four apparent storeys, the windows in bands divided by the iron uprights. It seems to be the earliest multi-storey iron-framed building, the storeys being storage levels each side of a full-height central area. Functional throughout, the same beams serve as columns and also as tracks for the travelling gantries. Without architectural features that would date it to the 19C, the building uses iron simply and unselfconsciously to enclose a working space and in doing so anticipates modern construction techniques. In the town, *RC church* (1863; E.W. Pugin), Broadway, High Victorian brick and stone, tall interior.

Dockyard Boat Store (1859; Col G. Greene), Sheerness

TONBRIDGE. At the N end of High St, *Tonbridge School*, complex of sandstone buildings, with at the centre old chapel (1859) and S end Tudoresque work of 1827. The most impressive buildings are of c 1894–1900 by W.C. Jones, the *Big School* to the rear, the front block with tower and the red-brick and stone *chapel*. Long roof lines and good Gothic detail. In the chapel, glass by C. Whall in the sanctuary, and in the ante-chapel superb war memorial *gateway (1918; H. Wilson), bronze and alabaster Arts and Crafts style. At the S end, on A26, *St. Stephen's church* (1851–54; E. Christian), ragstone with land-mark spire. 3m NE at **Hadlow**, *Hadlow Tower* (c 1838), 170ft Gothic folly dominating the Weald, in the implausible picturesque style of Beckford's Fonthill Abbey and built of rendered brick which adds to the insubstantial quality. The designer was W.B. May, the owner of the house attached, now mostly gone. 2m NW of Tonbridge, at **Hildenborough**, *church* (1843; E. Christian), sandstone with shingled spire and apsed chancel, the interior remarkable for the very wide arch-braced roof, the arches springing from corbels low on the walls. The transepts have a Morris window each. Opposite, *convent* (1866; G. Somers Clarke), French Gothic country house in red brick and stone. At **Leigh**, B2027, 2m SW, estate village of *Hall Place* (1872–76; G. Devey), large and rambling diapered red-brick mansion built for Samuel Morley, Liberal MP and hosiery millionaire. Tower, gables and generally Tudor detail, reduced in size after a fire. Lodge and gate by the church with picturesque half-timbered cottage. Beyond more estate cottages including a little square (1886; George and Peto), N of the green, and further cottages towards Penshurst. Diapered brick *Evangelical chapel* (1871; Devey), Morley was a Nonconformist.

TUNBRIDGE WELLS. A26 4m S of Tonbridge. Spa from the 17C that developed into a select resort town in the 19C and became Royal Tunbridge Wells under dispensation of Edward VII. *Central Station* (1911; R. Blomfield), brick and Portland stone screening at the back the original red- brick station (1845; R. Gardener). Mount Pleasant runs N with crude French-roofed *Public Hall* (1870; Wilson and Will-cox) on right. At the top, to left, *Holy Trinity Church* (1827–29; D. Burton), large Georgian Gothic, the church for Burton's *Calverley estate* (c 1828–40) on the other side of Mount Pleasant off Crescent Rd. *Calverley Park Crescent* (1830) and *Calverley Park*, a picturesque group of villas, already Italianate with deep eaved roofs, look over a steeply sloped park. The yellow-grey colour of the local sandstone makes this one of the most attractive early 19C suburban estates. Larger and later villas in Camden Park, Calverley Park Gardens and Pembury Rd. N of the Mount Pleasant crossroads, on left, former *Congregational church* with very handsome stone portico (1866). Further on, to right, *Opera House* (1902; J. Briggs), pompous red brick and stone with green domes, apparently large but the theatre only extends behind the centre. Attractive auditorium, sadly used only for bingo. In Monson Rd, *Technical College* (1901; H.T. Hare), free Jaco-bean in red brick and stone with large oriel windows. Late 19C cast-iron arcade in front of the shops opposite. S of the centre, A267, at **Broadwater Down**, spiky spired *church* (1864; R.L. Roumieu), expen-sively built for Lord Abergavenny of Eridge Castle, in detail rogue Gothic with colliding effects of scale. To W of the centre, the Common with large c 1870 hotels along the ridge, and at **Rusthall**, A264, 1m W, *church* (1849; H.I. and E.N. Stevens), central tower and large N aisle added 1864, good timber roofs, especially complex under the tower. At **Langton Green**, 1m further W, *church* (1862; G.G. Scott) with several early Morris windows (1865), notably the W window by Morris and S aisle W window with evangelists by Morris, Burne-Jones (St. Mark) and Ford Madox Brown. Rich E window (1904; C.E. Kempe). Further on, at **Groombridge**, *Hillside* (1870; R. Norman Shaw), tile-hung and half-timbered, with massive chimneys, Shaw's Old English style fully developed. Shaw's two larger houses in the area are just over the Sussex border S of Groombridge. E of Tunbridge Wells at **Pembury**, *The Tower House* (1904; C.E. Mallows), off A21 to W, rough-cast Arts and Crafts house in the manner of Voysey, much altered. On B2160, 3m E, **Matfield** *church* (1874; B. Champneys), prettily detailed sandstone with timber and shingle short tower and spire. N of Tunbridge Wells at **Southborough**, *Broom Hill* (1831–38; D. Burton), villa for Sir D. Salomons with outrageously grand Loire château style stables (1890–94; W.B. Hughes).

LANCASHIRE

BLACKBURN. A666 13m N of Bolton. In its day the greatest cotton-weaving town in the world. Mill buildings and mill chimneys still survive, notably along the Leeds–Liverpool Canal. In Exchange St the *Lewis Textile Museum* has working examples of textile machinery. Adjoining, in Library St, *Museum and Art Gallery* (1872–74; Woodgate and Collcutt) Gothic. In Victoria St, *Town Hall* (1852–56; J. Patterson) palazzo style and *Exchange* (1862; W.H. Brakspear) Gothic. In Blakey Moor, *King George's Hall* (1913; Briggs, Wolstenholme and Thornely), Imperial classical with law courts behind (1912–21), and *College of Technology*, (1888; Smith, Woodhouse and Willoughby) with much terracotta ornament, Gladstone *statue* (J. Adams-Acton) outside. In Church St, *Cathedral*, largely 20C, the W end the former parish church (1820–26). Adjoining, *Diocesan Offices* (1870; F. Robinson), the former church school and good ashlar classical building of 1860. The *station* (1888) is a late example of the Italianate style. Overall glazed roof.

9m SW of Blackburn, A6, **Chorley**, cotton town, the birthplace of H. Tate, sugar tycoon and founder of the Tate Gallery, London. *Talbot Mill* (1908) claimed to be the largest cotton mill built with 140,000 spindles. Of these late mills, steel-framed and clad in hard red brick, *Coppull Mills* (1906) to SW, B5251, is one of the most impressive with its two domed towers. SE of Chorley in Pennine foothills at **Rivington**, *reservoirs* (1847–57), part of the Liverpool water supply. Lord Lever-hulme, the soap king, bought Rivington Hall 1904 and laid out the E side of the reservoir as a public park, *Lever Park*, with terraced gardens (T.H. Mawson) and a replica of Liverpool Castle at the S end. Leverhulme's Moorland Garden is gradually being rescued from total decay. 3m S of Blackburn, A666, **Darwen**, mill town, the *India Mills* (1859–67), among the best surviving Lancashire cotton mills. Rock-faced stone with 300ft brick chimney. *Holy Trinity Church* (1827–29; T. Rickman), Commissioners' church in typical Perp. style. In Belgrave Square, *chapel* (1847; E. Walters) with fancy Gothic W front. On Blackburn Rd, *St. Cuthbert's Church* (1875–78; Paley and Austin).

5m E of Blackburn, A678, **Accrington**, cotton town associated with the family of Sir R. Peel, Prime Minister, the first from an industrial background, hence the multitude of Peel statues in northern towns. Across the W entry to the town, *railway viaduct* (1847). Beyond, *Town Hall* (1857; J. Green), Italianate with upper portico, built originally as the Peel Institute. Adjoining, *Old Market* (1868; J.F. Doyle) with sculpted centrepiece. In Manchester Rd, *Haworth Art Gallery* (1908; W. Brierley), housed in neo-Jacobean house of the cotton manufac-turer, W. Haworth. Exceptional collection of Tiffany glass. N of centre, on Whalley Road, *Dyke Nook* (c 1910; W. Brierley); another good early 20C Jacobean-style house. At **Whalley**, 5m N, A680, 28-arch railway *viaduct* (1850), made slightly Gothic where it crosses the road to the ruins of Whalley Abbey. 4m NW, *Stonyhurst College*, the principal Jesuit school in England, set up 1794 in the 16C mansion of the Shire-burn family. The original mansion was extended to surround a full quadrangle (1843–56) and a large church added (1832–35; J.J. Scoles) in the King's College, Cambridge, manner, but the dominant Victo-rian addition is the very long open court to S (1877–89; Dunn and Hansom) in late 16C style analogous to the original house, but richer in detail. The result is despite its size more cheerful than the usual Gothic.

BLACKPOOL. A583 16m W of Preston. Largest and one of the last developed of British seaside resorts, most of the building dating from the later 19C when Blackpool became the principal excursion town from the northern industrial cities. The Promenade runs nearly six miles along the seafront with three *piers*, North Pier (1862; E. Birch), *Central Pier* (1867) and *South Pier* (1892), the North Pier the least altered. The last remaining electric tramway in Britain runs the length. The *Blackpool Tower* (1891–94; Maxwell and Tuke) is the town's landmark, at 518ft a reduced version of the Eiffel Tower, rising from a complex of variety halls. Notably rich interiors to the circus, under the legs of the tower, and the ballroom (1899; F. Matcham). To E, *Winter Gardens*, begun 1875 (T. Mitchell), the original winter garden converted to a music-hall with good interior decoration (1897; Wylson and Long). In Church St, *Grand Theatre* (1894; F. Matcham) has a particularly lush auditorium with painted panels and lively plasterwork. In Corporation St, to N, *bank* (1881; Cooper and Tullis), high single-storey Italianate banking hall, and in Talbot Square, *Town Hall* (1895; Potts, Son and Hennings). In Abingdon St, *Christ Church* (1865; J.M. Taylor), spiky polychrome brick with the broad nave and fantastic complexity of timber to the roof that Taylor liked. In Talbot Rd, *Yates Wine Lodge*, built as the Assembly Rooms, and *RC church* (1857; E.W. Pugin), the interest the E end (1894; Pugin and Pugin) with octagonal crossing. On the seafront N of Town Hall, the largest hotels, notably the *Imperial Hotel* (1867; Clegg and Jones), built as the Hydro, much enlarged 1875 and 1904.

At **Rossall**, 4m N, *Rossall School*, founded 1844 with brick Gothic buildings of c 1850–90 (E.G. Paley, and Paley and Austin). Stone chapel (1861). Sir P.H. Fleetwood of Rossall Hall founder of the school, was the creator of **Fleetwood**, the first new town built for the railways, intended as a port at the N end of the line from Euston, London. The original grand plan by D. Burton (1836) came to little as the railway into Scotland ended a brief heyday as an embarkation port for Glasgow. *Queen's Terrace*, the *North Euston Hotel*, the two *lighthouses*, and the *church* were built to Burton's designs (1836–43). 12m NE of Blackpool, at **Pilling**, off A588, *church* (1886; Paley and Austin), handsome spired work with chequered stonework in beige and purple. 5m S of Blackpool, **Lytham St. Anne's**, Lytham developed in early 19C especially after 1846 when the railway came, St. Anne's created from 1875. Lytham has attractive buildings of c 1830–40 in Bath St and Queen St, *Market House* (1847; C. Reed) with tower added 1872. In *St. Cuthbert's Church* (1834) one Morris window (1874). St. Anne's has a *pier* (1885) and Victorian promenade *gardens* on the seafront and *Grand Hotel* (1906). The original *St. Anne's Hotel* (1875), St. George's Rd, is Tudor style. *Church* 1873 (Paley and Austin) with big W tower added 1887 (R.K. Freeman). In **Fairhaven**, *King Edward VII School* (1908; Briggs, Thornely and MacLaughlan) and *Congregational church* (1907–12; Briggs, Wolstenholme and Thornely), white glazed tile, Byzantine with stained glass scheme (C. Elliott) of notable heroes of Protestantism.

BURNLEY. A56 22m N of Manchester. Cotton town, the centre of Lancashire cotton weaving by the later 19C with over 100,000 looms at work. Still, despite the decline of the industry, Burnley remains one of the most impressive mill towns, with the best surviving area of mills in the 'Weavers Triangle', S of centre, off Manchester Rd, along the Leeds–Liverpool Canal. In Sandygate, *Clocktower Mill* (c 1840), stone with clocktower added 1863. Across the canal bridge, *Slater Terrace* (c

1851), mill housing built over a canal-side warehouse. On Manchester Rd, *Old Town Hall* (1885–88; Holtom and Fox), grandiose Renaissance style with copper dome. Adjoining, *Mechanics Institution* (1855; J. Green), ashlar-fronted palazzo, a distinguished work. In Yorkshire St, *RC church* (1846–49; Weightman and Hadfield), Puginian Gothic on a large scale. High altar by E.W. Pugin (c 1865), N, Towneley Chapel decorated 1879. NW of centre, Padiham Rd, *All Saints' Church* (1846–49; Weightman and Hadfield), another correctly detailed church, relatively early. Broach spire. W of centre, Accrington Rd, *Holy Trinity Church* (1835–36; L. Vulliamy), lancet Gothic in the Commissioners' manner with W tower. SE of centre, on Todmorden Rd, former *Methodist chapel* (1860), Corinthian classical front.

3m NW, at **Padiham**, *Jubilee Mill* (1887) still has a working engine of 1888. *Gawthorpe Hall* 1600 house of the Shuttleworth family, just outside Padiham, was altered by C. Barry (1849–51) who heightened the tower and remodelled the interior. 4m N of Burnley, A56, **Nelson**, cotton town developed up the valley to **Colne**. Just S of Nelson, *Brierfield Mill* (1868), unusually handsome, in stone. At **Barnoldswick**, 6m N of Colne, the compound engine that drove 1000 looms has been preserved with the engine house of the former *Bancroft Mill*. 6m S of Burnley, A56, **Rawtenstall**, mill town developed in the early 19C by the Whitehead family. Numerous large mills, *Newhallhey Mill* (c 1861), a woollen mill with tall Italianate chimney, and *Ilex Mill* (1856), one of the early iron-framed cotton mills. By the church, domed *Library* (1906; Crouch, Butler and Savage) and *Methodist church* (1841; J. Simpson), Ionic classical, built for the Whitehead family. The family also paid for the Corinthian porticoed *United Methodist chapel* (1855–57; Noble) in Oakley Rd nearby. *Rossendale Museum*, Whitaker St, is housed in a mid 19C mill-owner's house. 2m N, at **Crawshaw Booth**, handsome *church* (1890–92; Austin and Paley) built for the Brooks family of Crawshaw Hall, mill-owners. At **Helmshore**, W of Rawtenstall, some of the surviving relics of the 18C woollen industry. *Higher Mill* (1789), Holcombe Rd, is now a museum of the textile industry. At **Bacup**, 5m E of Rawtenstall, *Ross Mill*, large and typical early 20C cotton mill. In Yorkshire St, *Natural History Museum*, bulging late 19C collection of natural history, archaeology and industrial relics. On Burnley Rd, *church* (1882; J.M. Taylor), characteristic heavy-handed detail, and *Broadclough Mill* (1835).

LANCASTER. In the centre, Dalton Square, *Town Hall*, (1906–09; E.W. Mountford), part of the beneficence of H. Williamson, Lord Ashton, linoleum tycoon. Handsome early Georgian style with giant Ionic portico and central clock tower, the side elevations more Baroque. In front, *Victoria Memorial* (1907; H. Hampton), another Ashton gift, stone statue flanked by lions on a high base with thickly modelled bronze relief of the great figures of the Victorian age. Behind Town Hall, *Fire Station* (1909; Mountford) with copper-domed cupola. To NW, in Market St, *Museum* in Old Town Hall (1781), *Westminster Bank* (c 1860) palazzo style, and *King's Arms Hotel* (1879; Holtom and Connor). In Meeting House Lane, *Storey Institute* (1887; Paley and Austin), free Jacobean, now used for occasional exhibitions. To W, *Lancaster Castle Station* (1846; W. Tite), appropriately Gothic, extended in similar style to an end tower in 1858. S of Market St, Penny St runs towards the Infirmary. At S end, *Alexandra* and *White Cross Hotels*, early 20C, free Jacobean, and *Old Station*, now part of nurses' home of the infirmary, built 1840 as the terminus from Preston in dignified classical style. In South Rd, Storey's Works, including baronial former *Militia Armoury* (1857). The *Infirmary* is late 17C style (1894; Austin and Paley). To SW on Ashton Rd, A588, *Ripley School* (1856–64; J. Cunningham), Gothic orphanage with attractive chapel (1886; Paley and Austin). *Royal Albert Hospital* (1867–73; Paley and Austin), Lancaster's monumental but practical memorial to Prince Albert, originally the Royal Albert Asylum for Idiots. High Victorian Gothic with Venetian touches and tall pavilion roof over the entrance tower. E of Dalton Square, Nelson St runs towards *RC Cathedral* (1857–59; E.G. Paley), tall, apsed with 240ft spire all in well-detailed c 1300 style. Apse glass by Hardman. To E, *Royal Grammar School* (1851–55; Sharpe and Paley), Gothic. Wyresdale Rd leads SE to Williamson Park, a gift of Lord Ashton 1881. On the crest of the hill, the most splendid memorial in Britain, the *Ashton Memorial* (1906–09; J. Belcher), Lord Ashton's temple to the memory of his wife, Italian Baroque style with English Baroque touches, a great domed lantern

The Ashton Memorial (1906–09; J. Belcher), Lancaster

rising over a square base with corner cupolas and columned porticoes. A monumental flight of stairs runs up to the W front. The material is best Portland stone and the dome is copper-clad, the whole 150ft mass a landmark not just from the city but also from the motorway to E. Inside, two chambers only, octagonal main hall and circular room above. Equally prominent from the motorway is *Lancaster Moor Hospital*, the long grim Gothic range an addition of 1882 (A. Kershaw) to the original county asylum of 1811–16. N of the centre, over the bridge, *Methodist church* (1901; ?A.G. Chant), Owen Rd, high quality free Gothic.

4m W of Lancaster, A589, **Morecambe**, holiday resort developed from 1848. On the seafront; two *piers*, West End (1893–96), much shortened, and Central (c 1872). On Marine Rd, *Winter Garden* 1878, much enlarged 1896 (Mangnall and Littlewood), the earlier part iron-roofed between two copper domes, the later part with scrolly gable and very large tunnel-vaulted auditorium. On Marine Rd West, *Alhambra* (1901; H. Howarth), elaborate free Jacobean front, missing its main gable since a fire. *Promenade Station* (1873), attractive Gothic symmetrical front with glazed roof to concourse behind. In Victoria St, *St. Lawrence's Church* (1876; Paley and Austin) distinguished Dec. with finely proportioned interior. By the same firm, *St. Barnabas' Church* (1898), Regent Rd, and *St. John's Church* (1899), St. John's Rd. 7m NE of Morecambe, A6, **Carnforth**, railway junction of three lines, Tudor style *station* (1846; W. Tite) surviving on northbound platform. 3m NE, *Capernwray Hall* (1844; E. Sharpe) impressive Tudor Gothic stone mansion, battlemented with near symmetrical main front and large tower set back. 3m N of Carnforth, at **Yealand Conyers**, *Leighton Hall*, Georgian Gothic house of the Gillow family, furniture makers, with wing and tower added to one side (1870; Paley and Austin) to create a picturesque asymmetrical composition. 8m NE of Lancaster, A683, at **Hornby**, *Hornby Castle*, romantic castellated house around a medieval tower, the main part 1849–52 (Sharpe and Paley) with central entrance tower. The *church* has 16C apse and tower, the rest mostly 1889 (Paley and Austin). 5m NE, at **Tunstall**, *Thurland Castle*, medieval origins but the extremely picturesque Gothic to Elizabethan outline is due to Paley and Austin (1879–85). Tunstall was the Brocklebridge of Charlotte Bronte's 'Jane Eyre'. At **Cowan Bridge**, A65, to N, was the school where the Bronte sisters were educated 1824–25, Lowood in 'Jane Eyre'.

2m S of Lancaster, at **Scotforth**, *church* (1874; E. Sharpe), neo-Norman, the style more common in the 1840s, saddleback-roofed tower over the crossing and details in terracotta. Free Gothic *Methodist church* (1908; A.G. Chant). 3m S at **Galgate**, *silk mill*, the oldest in England, founded 1792, additional buildings of 1830 and 1852. *Church* 1906 (Austin and Paley). Just SW, *Ellel Grange* (1857–59; J. Weightman), large stone Italianate villa built for W. Preston, Liverpool distiller, handsomely detailed with campanile tower. In the grounds, *church* (1873; W. and G. Audsley), unconventional detail, rich encaustic tiled floor. 4m SE, at beginning of Wyredale, **Dolphinholme** *church* (1897; Austin and Paley), attractive small work with crossing tower. At the head of the valley, *Abbeystead* (1886; Douglas and Fordham), a shooting lodge for the Earl of Sefton on the grandest scale, gabled Elizabethan style with tower behind, well set on the hillside. *Estate buildings* and *church* alterations by Douglas. 5m SW of Ellel, at **Cockerham**, *Crookhey Hall* (1874; A. Waterhouse), Gothic small country house with characteristic entrance tower and pavilion roof.

ORMSKIRK. A59 12m N of Liverpool. Parish *church* with curious
tower and spire side by side restored 1877–91 (Paley and Austin). 3m
NW, A570, *Scarisbrick Hall*, Gothic mansion remodelled from 1836
by A.W.N. Pugin for C. Scarisbrick, one of the rare commissions where
Pugin's Gothic designs were properly realised. The original house,
recased (1815; J. Foster Jr) in Regency Gothic, is still visible to N and
W sides, but Pugin's intention was to recreate a medieval manor house
complete with great hall, suitable for an old Catholic family. The S
front does achieve the Gothic dream with the roof of a convincing
medieval great hall rising over Perp. bay windows and porch in the
correct medieval position to one side, the Gothic detail rich with
carved inscriptions and heraldic shields. Battlemented ranges each
side link to projecting wings, the W wing of 1815 embellished by
Pugin, but the E wing, far more ornate, High Victorian Gothic, is quite
a different creation, rebuilt 1862–68 by E.W. Pugin for Anne, Lady
Scarisbrick. E.W. Pugin's work culminates in the clock tower, at 170ft
more appropriate to a town hall, but a magnificent creation in itself
and a landmark for miles over the flat landscape. Beyond, picturesque
octagonal kitchen, part of A.W.N. Pugin's work. Brick stable court
with most romantic entrance tower and corner tower, by E.W. Pugin.
The interior of the house is as much a monument to Charles Scarisbrick, reclusive collector, notably of medieval and Flemish 16C carved
woodwork, which being built into the house has survived. Carvings
decorate every doorcase and fireplace and cover the walls of the
panelled rooms. The rich colouring of the ceilings appears to date from
the 1860s (J.G. Crace) contrasting well with the dark carved woodwork. Of A.W.N. Pugin's designs the magnificent open roof of the hall
looks forward to the decoration of the Houses of Parliament as does the
decoration of the King's Room. *RC church*, N of the house, 1888 (Pugin
and Pugin).

PRESTON. A6 30m NW of Manchester. Cotton town still with many
large red-brick mills, also a centre of Catholicism like much of S Lancashire. In Church St, parish *church* (1853–55; E.H. Shellard) with fine
steeple and hammerbeam roofs. In the Market Place, *Harris Library
and Museum* (1882–93; J. Hibbert), late and extremely dignified neo-
classical work with echoes of Glasgow Greek work and also of St.
George's Hall, Liverpool. Foursquare and lifted on a high base with
Greek Ionic portico and neo-classical tympanum sculpture (E.R.
Mullins), the centre of the building raised up as a square lantern with
pilastrade in the Glasgow manner. Each side of the portico, square
piers with the ground-floor cornice threaded through but free-
standing above, a motif from St. George's Hall. *Post Office* (1903) and
Sessions Hall (1900–03; H. Littler), Edwardian Baroque with giant
columns and 170ft central steeple. In Lancaster Rd, to N, *Market*
(1875), a vast cast-iron roofed space, *Magistrates Court* (1857; J.H.
Pack), *Prison* behind in Earl St. Two early Victorian churches by J.
Latham, *St. Thomas'* (1837–39), neo-Norman with tower and spire
over the chancel, and *All Saints'* (1846–47), classical with Ionic portico. *RC church* (1833–36; J.J. Scoles), Meadow St, Gothic with flying
buttresses to the spire. In Watling St, ashlar classical *Barracks* (1842–
48) with fine entrance gateway. Quadrangle behind, one side demolished. On Garstang Rd, *RC church* (1863–67; E.W. Pugin), steeply
gabled front and tall interior. E end 1888 (Pugin and Pugin). S of
Market Place, in Fishergate, *Baptist church* (1857; Hibbert and
Rainford), Italian Romanesque to Gothic, well detailed. In Avenham
Lane, *College of Arts* (1846; J. Welch), ashlar classical with pediment,

built as the Institution for the Diffusion of Knowledge, and *St. James'*
Church (1870–81; Hibbert) apsed High Victorian Gothic.

S of Fishergate, the 18C area of Preston. In Winckley Square, Sir R.
Peel *statue* (1852; T. Duckett). In East Cliff, overlooking Avenham
Park, *Park Hotel* (1882; A. Mitchell), now County Offices, very large
red-brick railway hotel gabled in Norman Shaw manner and accen-
tuated with a pyramid-roofed sheer tower. In the Park, *statue* (1873;
M. Noble) of the 14th Earl of Derby, Prime Minister. In Chapel St, *St.*
Wilfrid's RC Church (1879–80; I. Scoles and S. Nicholl), fine brick and
terracotta early Renaissance style basilica, tunnel-vaulted with apse.
W of the centre, *St. Walburge's RC Church* (1850–54; J.A. Hansom),
Weston St, a landmark especially from the railway, the immensely tall
white stone tower and spire standing almost detached from the brown
stone church, a single vessel with apsed E end. The contrast is most
striking. Inside the church displays an elaborate hammerbeam roof
covering the entire space apart from the narrow apse which has tall
windows with glass by Hardman. In St. Mark's Rd, *St. Mark's Church*
(1863–66; E.G. Paley), EE style with strong tall tower at NE end by the
apse. E of centre, *St. Mary's Church* (1836–38; J. Latham), St. Mary's
St, large neo-Norman, the tower building up in an extraordinary way
with set-back stages to a short spire. In St. Austin's Place, *St.*
Augustine's RC Church, mostly of 1890 (Sinnott, Sinnott and Powell)
but incorporating the portico of the original church (1838; A. Tuach),
now the centrepiece of a Renaissance style front with twin towers and
cupolas, very Italian but with a neo-classical sharpness to the detail.
Tunnel-vaulted interior.

6m W of Preston, A583, at **Kirkham**, parish *church* with fine steeple
(1843–44; E. Sharpe). In The Willows, *RC church* (1842–45; A.W.N.
Pugin), quite plain with broach spire. W of the church, *Grammar*
School (1909–11; Greenaway and Newberry), long gabled domestic-
looking front in the manner of Voysey, roughcast with mullion windows, pleasingly informal.

LEICESTERSHIRE

LEICESTER. Predominantly red-brick town with distinguished later 19C buildings to the centre, its wealth built on the hosiery and shoe industries. Numerous warehouse and factory buildings still survive close to the centre. At the centre, stone Gothic *clock tower* (1868; J. Goddard), heavily carved with statues of leading Leicester figures. Overlooking the tower, at E end of High St, former *Coffee House* (1885; E. Burgess) with timber oriels in the Norman Shaw manner and half-timbered gables, but the brickwork unfortunately painted. Further W in High St, on S side, the sharp corner to Silver St is well filled by a c 1900 terracotta block with conical roof and cupola. Beyond, terracotta facade of the former *Arcadia Electric Theatre* (1910; Ward and Bell), a complete surviving early cinema, and the *Singer Building* (1904; A. Wakerley), almost all glass with a barrel vault reminiscent of the Crystal Palace rising over painted tile panels. Animals representing the different parts of the Empire decorate the terracotta piers. From Silver St, the *Silver Arcade* (1899; A. Hall) runs S, three galleries within. In St. Martin's St, S of Silver St, grandiose Portland stone *National Westminster Bank* (1900; Everard and Pick) with giant Ionic loggia and twin cupolas. In Greyfriars, adjoining, *No. 5* (1876; I. Barradale), Norman Shaw influenced office building with oriels and roughcast gables, very prettily handled. *Leicester Cathedral* is a medieval parish church, but its character is Victorian, due to the proud tower and broach spire (1861–67; R. Brandon). Much of the rest of the church was rebuilt by Brandon (1846–62), S porch 1896 (J.L. Pearson).

SE of the Cathedral, the Market Place with former *Corn Exchange* in centre, lower floor 1850 (W. Flint), upper floor, turret and grand outside stairs added 1855 (F. Ordish) in matching palazzo style. Statue of the Duke of Rutland (1851; E. Davis) in front. To S, Town Hall Square, with *Town Hall* (1873–76; F.J. Hames) on W side, the first important public building in the Queen Anne style pioneered by Nesfield and Shaw, and clearly derived from Nesfield's Kinmel Park, Clwyd. Elegant late 17C to early 18C detail with cheerful sash-windows, especially elongated for the stair lights, and an ample hipped roof over the centre with very tall stacks. Characteristic of Nesfield are the tiny asymmetrical touches, the off-centre ridge stack and the slightly varied lower floors under the stair lights. The main asymmetrical element, the great clock tower with cupola, is set right over to one side. In the gardens in front, fountain with winged lions (1879; Hames). On the N side of the square, *Sun Alliance Building* (1891; Goddard, Paget and Goddard), Flemish gabled with fine moulded brick friezes and carved Portland stone ground floor. On the S side, in Bishop St, *Reference Library* (1904; E. Burgess), matching the Town Hall, and, to left, *Alliance Building Society* (1885; Burgess), built as the Liberal Club. In Bowling Green St, to W, Gothic asymmetrical front of *Juvenile Court* (1865; Shenton and Baker) with good carved detail.

E of Town Hall Square is Granby St, continued N to the clock tower as Gallowtree Gate with the former *Thomas Cook Building* (1894; Goddard, Paget and Goddard), similar to the Sun Alliance building, but terracotta- fronted with relief panels depicting Thomas Cook's great railway excursions, the beginnings of the modern holiday industry. In Granby St, *National Westminster Bank* (1869; W. Millican) Italianate and *Midland Bank* (1872–74; J. Goddard), rich Ruskinian Gothic in red brick and stone with trio of two-storey windows to

Granby St and pavilion-roofed entry tower. Remarkable banking hall within, stained glass by Goddard, influenced by Owen Jones probably. Further on, *Yorkshire Bank* (1898; Goddard and Co.) encrusted with blocked columns in the Baroque style and *Grand Hotel* (1897; C. Ogden: 1898; A. Hall), gabled vaguely Flemish but the 1898 corner sprouts an early 18C style steeple. Opposite, exotic Moorish glazed front of the *Turkey Cafe* (1910), the tile work by W. Neatby of Doultons. Nearby, the former *Victoria Coffee House* (1887; E. Burgess), most splendid of Leicester's temperance drinking houses, three storeys on the street line, the next two cut back to a Loire château skyline topped by a conical roof. In Belvoir St, former *Baptist chapel* (1845; J.A. Hansom), known as the 'Pork Pie Chapel' from its bulging rounded front, curved to express the shape of the interior, a logical but unusual design. Beyond, two neo-classical buildings by W. Flint, *Lending Library* (1831) and the *Phoenix Assurance* (1844), very handsome with Greek Ionic centrepiece, and very prominent due to the vagaries of Leicester's ring road system. In Wellington St, behind the Library, good Ruskinian Gothic *warehouse* (c 1865).

S of Wellington St, the New Walk, laid out 1785 with villas and terraces of c 1820–50 up to the *Museum* (1836; J.A. Hansom), built as a Nonconformist school, with Tuscan portico in painted stucco. N of the Museum, Waterloo Way cuts through to the *Station* (1892; C. Trubshaw), brick and terracotta with a turret at one end and, originally, two separate forecourts for arriving and departing with ornate arches in the front screen wall. W of Waterloo Way, *St. John's Church* (1853; G.G. Scott), Dec. in Charnwood granite banded with sandstone, now much decayed, giving an interesting texture. Disused. S of New Walk, further stuccoed early 19C terraces in King St and Upper King St around *Holy Trinity Church*, (1871–72; S.S. Teulon), actually a ferocious remodelling of plain classical building of 1838. W end spire of the most complex outline flanked by pavilion-roofed outriders, themselves rising out of a seemingly random collection of porches and vestibules. Behind, on Welford Rd, *Leicester Prison* (1828; W. Parsons), a complete stone toy-fort for the entrance. To W, W of the Royal Infirmary, in Jarrom St, *St. Andrew's Church* (1860–62; G.G. Scott), unusual for Scott in its complete polychromy, a severe brick envelope, almost without mouldings but the walls treated to a display of coloured brickwork, rising in intensity to rich diapering over the window heads and concentrated banding in the gables, all more typical of Butterfield or W. White at this time. Dramatic pierced timber transverse arches to the nave. Gateway St runs N to *Leicester Polytechnic*, incorporating the Technical College (1898) and a good warehouse (1888) on Oxford St with corner dome and Gothic detail. To N, by the Castle, *St. Mary de Castro Church* much restored in 19C. Good E windows by Wailes (1862) and tall carved reredos by Bodley (1899).

Returning to the clock tower, to E, Humberstone Gate, E of the Haymarket Centre, has on N side *No. 44* (1863; J.F. Smith), palazzo style distillery offices, and the former *Girls' School* (1877; E. Burgess) in an accomplished Norman Shaw style. On S side, *Secular Hall* (1881; W.L. Sugden) mixing Queen Anne motifs wildly. Symbols of truth, justice and liberty under the main window and busts of Christ, Socrates, Voltaire, Paine and Owen on the ground-floor piers. The Secular Society promoted discussion of political and social ideas. William Morris gave his 'Art and Socialism' lecture here. In Rutland St, *Alexandra House* (1895–98; E. Burgess), splendid terracotta bootlace warehouse, strongly modelled with early Renaissance detail, corner entry with dome and the upper floor set back behind a rich cornice and balustrade. Further on, on corner of Colton St, *warehouse* (1875) in the mixed Gothic and Italianate manner more common in Leeds than in Leicester. Nice busts of Minerva holding a train and Mercury holding a sailing ship.

OUTER LEICESTER

To the N, on Belgrave Gate, A6, *St. Mark's Church* (1870–72; E. Christian), an emphatic composition of unbuttressed apse and SE tower with stair tower echoing the apse, all in dark slate but limestone banding breaking up the upper part of the tower before the limestone spire. Polychrome arches inside on granite piers. In the apse, painting of 'The Triumph and Apotheosis of Labour' (1910; J.E. Reid). W of Belgrave Gate, *Abbey Park*, laid out 1878–82 around the ruins of Leicester Abbey. Off Abbey Lane, *Museum of Technology*, housed in former Abbey Pumping Station (1891). Original beam-engines. E of the centre, S of Humberstone Rd, A47, *North Evington*, laid out from 1885 as an industrial community with factories, housing and central market place with public hall and coffee tavern. Factories in St. Saviour's Rd, including Smith, Faire and Co. (1894; E. Burgess), factories and housing mixed elsewhere, Asfordby St and Halstead St, surviving housing in East Park Rd, Mere Rd, and Gwendolen Rd, mostly by A. Wakerley, the promoter of the whole scheme. *St. Saviour's Church* (1875–77; G.G. Scott), at NW end of St. Saviour's Rd, has prominent broach spire and neo-Norman W front. High interior with round granite piers. At **Humberstone**, NE of Humberstone Rd, *church* rebuilt 1857–59 (R. Brandon), notable for the local alabaster much used inside.

SE from the station, London Rd, A6, runs out to Victoria Park with, on N side, set back up Prebend St, *College of Music* (1836; J.G. Weightman), built as the Collegiate School, Perp. central hall with wings. Further up, *St. James' Church* (1900; H.L. Goddard) with terracotta and brick basilican interior, based on Torcello Cathedral. To S, Victoria Park, laid out 1883, with Lutyens' War Memorial arch (1923) by London Rd. To SW, *Leicester University*, the principal building the plain brick classical former Lunatic Asylum (1836; W. Parsons). In University Rd, *De Montfort Hall* (1913; S. Harrison), intended as temporary, but an impressive design with broad eaves roof and colonnaded E front, all white-painted render. The top end of New Walk running from Waterloo Way to Victoria Park has villas of the 1850s and 1860s W of University Rd and of the 1880s to E. S of Victoria Park the wealthy suburban fringe of Leicester with large villas on both sides of London Rd, mostly c 1880–1900. In Clarendon Park Rd, *St. John's Church* (1884–85; Goddard and Paget), red brick with impressive tall interior based on Pearson's St. Augustine's, Kilburn, London. In Ratcliffe Rd, *No. 32* (1891; E. Gimson), Arts and Crafts simplicity in contrast to its neighbours, red brick with stone slates and casements. Further out, just into **Oadby**, early 20C large suburban houses in Stoughton Drive S, now University *Halls of Residence*.

To the W, off Glenfield Rd in Kirby Rd, *St. Paul's Church* (1870; Ordish and Traylen) with unusual simplified treatment, mouldings dispensed with, and sheer plate-traceried windows in the apse rising to a ring of gables finished abruptly. Polychrome arcade arches and short piers, raised high. To SW, off A46, at **Braunstone**, by the church, group of *cottages* (1858–59) by Butterfield, three pairs in Main St and a terrace, Cressida Place, on the green, no Gothic motifs, just hipped dormers, casements and sturdy chimneys, excellent examples of simple design. Another similar terrace 2m NW at **Kirby Muxlee**.

LOUGHBOROUGH. A6 11m N of Leicester. In the Market Place, former *Town Hall* (1855; W. Slater), ashlar, palazzo style but with an oddly Gothic bellcote over the centre. To left, *Midland Bank* (1896; Goddard, Paget and Goddard), Portland stone, French 16C style, one of a series of handsomely detailed banks built for the Leicestershire Bank. To right, *National Westminster Bank* (1884; W. Fothergill), inventive Gothic in red brick with picturesque entrance tower and details characteristic of Fothergill's work in Nottingham. Off Leicester Rd, A6, *Grammar School* (1849–52; Morris and Henson), diapered brick Tudor, set in an attractive park laid out at the same time. NE of centre, off Nottingham Rd, A60, the best surviving mill buildings, notably hosiery works in Clarence St.

4m E of Loughborough, off A60, at **Prestwold**, *Prestwold Hall*, 18C house recased (1842; W. Burn) in stone with heavier window mouldings, balustrade and columned porch, sober but decidedly more opulent than the original house. Painted decorated interiors in rich Italian style of contemporary London clubs. *Church* adjoining with Packe family monuments, notably effigy of the schoolboy C.H. Packe (died 1842; R. Westmacott Jr) in Eton clothes. 3m NE, at **Wymeswold**, *church* restored 1844–46 by Pugin, a rare example of a restoration where Pugin had enough funds. Painted chancel roof, E window by Wailes, sedilia, stalls, screen, pulpit and font by Pugin, and a hanging corona by Hardman, all restrained, not overwhelming the medieval original. Externally Pugin replaced the aisle windows and added the fine two-storey N porch and timber lychgate. The client was H. Alford, prominent later Victorian churchman, Dean of Canterbury from 1857. 6m SE of Loughborough, A46, *Ratcliffe College*, founded as a boys' school by A. Phillips (later A. Phillips de Lisle), the leading figure in the revival of Catholicism in Leicestershire. Gothic buildings begun 1843 to a grand plan by Pugin, but only the E side of the quad with entrance tower is Pugin's, N and S ranges in Puginian manner 1854–58 (C.F. Hansom) with W end additions. By E.W. Pugin, Big Study on S range (1863) and W side with central chapel (1866–72). Cloisters around the quad.

SW of Loughborough, the granite outcrop of Charnwood Forest. On the E side, at **Woodhouse**, B591, *Beaumanor Park* (1845–47; W. Railton), rich Jacobean style in red brick and stone with much curly strapwork, well above Railton's usual thin detail. At **Woodhouse Eaves**, to S, row of large late 19C houses built as country retreats for Leicester industrialists. 4m SW, off A50, at **Ulverscroft**, group of Arts and Crafts stone cottages built for his own family by E. Gimson. The best, *Stoneywell Cottage* (1897–99), is delightful, built into the side of a hill with all the appearance of being itself an outcrop. Massive end chimney and a zig-zag plan of only two rooms, everything carefully primitive with massive boulders incorporated in the walling, small wooden casements and never a right angle. No other cottage of its period so fully achieves the dream of the simple rural life central to the thinking of the followers of William Morris. Interior to match with whitewashed timbers and break-neck winding stair. Originally thatched but now slated. On the N edge of the Forest, *Mount Saint Bernard Abbey*, the first abbey built in England since the Reformation, founded 1835 for Cistercian monks by Ambrose Phillips de Lisle. The Earl of Shrewsbury, pre-eminent with Phillips in the revival of Catholic building in the early Victorian period, actually paid for the monastery, designed for nothing by A.W.N. Pugin and begun 1840. Original cloister S of the Abbey with guest-house to W in an attractively simple Gothic, lancet windows and a curved S stair tower. The W end of the church is Pugin's, the tower and E end added in similar style in 1935, simple severe lancets, appropriate to Cistercian principles. 2m NW is *Grace Dieu Manor*, de Lisle's own house (1833–34; W. Railton), stuccoed Tudor Gothic with tower and service range added by Pugin (1841). Chapel chancel by Railton (1835), nave by Fr Lithgoe SJ (1837), alterations by Pugin 1841 and 1848 (N aisle). The rood screen (1837) was the first in England since the Reformation. Pugin altar in NE chapel and glass in N aisle. S side glass 1856 (Hardman), W window by the Rev. F. Sutton. To NE, N of A512, **Shepshed**, small hosiery manufacturing town with improbably elaborate brick and terracotta *bank* (1903; A.E. King) in the centre, Baroque with Art Nouveau sculptural detail.

12m W of Loughborough, A512, **Ashby de la Zouch**, market town and from 1820 a spa. In Market St, Italianate stone *Town Hall* (1857) with cast-iron market and French 16C style *Midland Bank* (1891; Goddard, Paget and Goddard), the pair to the one at Loughborough and equally well detailed. Off Market St, parish *church*, much restored (1878; J.P. St. Aubyn) with rich alabaster font and pulpit by Earp. At the foot of Market St, prominent towers of *Holy Trinity Church* (1838; H.I. Stevens), lancet Gothic, and the ambitious neo-Norman *RC church* (1908–15; F.A. Walters). By the RC church, *Loudoun Memorial* (1879; G.G. Scott), high and ornate version of the medieval Eleanor crosses. Beyond, the *Royal Hotel* (1826; R. Chaplin) and terrace adjoining mark the survive of the spa founded by the 1st Marquess of Hastings. The Greek Revival Baths have gone. The former railway *station* (1849) is in matching Greek style. SW and SE of Ashby, the Leicestershire coalfield. **Coalville** to SE, A50, is the largest colliery settlement, founded c 1820 but mostly bleak late 19C. Just S, at **Hugglescote**, ambitious High Victorian *church* (1878–88; J.B. Everard), massive with crossing tower.

MARKET HARBOROUGH. A6 15m SE of Leicester. In the parish *church* good E window glass (1859; Hardman) and S chancel window of c 1878. At the top of High St, *Congregational church* (1844; W. Flint), handsome classical with Ionic loggia and Corinthian upper order. Behind the church, the *Council Offices* occupy a converted corset factory (1889; Everard and Pick) with corner tower, a nice re-use. E of centre, railway *station* (1884) in an unusual Queen Anne style. 4m W, A427, at **Theddingworth**, *church* restored 1858 (G.G. Scott) with painted decoration to chancel and organ case by Canon F.H. Sutton, marble and alabaster pulpit and E window by Clayton and Bell. Exceptionally elaborate font cover (1893; G.F. Bodley). At **Husbands Bosworth**, 2m W, church mostly rebuilt 1861 (E.F. Law), High Victorian carving and polychrome arches. W window by J. Powell and Sons. At **South Kilworth**, 3m SW, *church* with aisles and chancel rebuilt 1868 by Bodley, W window by Hardman. At **Lutterworth**, 12m W of Market Harborough, *Town Hall* (1836; J.A. Hansom), stuccoed Ionic classical with curved corners. In the centre much early to mid 19C stuccoed classical building, notably the *Manor House*, Market St, and *The Terrace* at S end of High St. 5m N of Market Harborough, at **Tur Langton**, B6047, *church* (1865; H. Goddard and Son), High Victorian red brick with brick spire, apse and plate-traceried windows, a strong work, most unexpected in a country village where its aloofness is accentuated by an ornate iron railing along the churchyard wall. Interior all brick, apart from the arcade columns, with black brick banding and moulded or notched edges. Glass by Heaton, Butler and Bayne.

OAKHAM. A606 10m W of Stamford. Former county town of Rutland. By the Market Place, *Oakham School* with Tudor style buildings dating from the years of expansion after 1858, notably School House (1858; S. Smirke) facing Market Place. In High St, to S, *Victoria Hall* (1838; J.W. Johnson) ashlar classical. Ashwell Rd leads N, past former *workhouse* (1836; Donthorn) to **Ashwell**, 3m N, with *church* restored 1850–51 (Butterfield) with painted chancel roof and good fittings, notably the font with its steep wooden cover. Some typical *cottages* by Butterfield in brick with half-hipped gables and sashes in Braeside and Croft Lane, and a half-timbered *almshouse* on Cottesmore Rd. 2m NW of Oakham, A606, at **Langham**, *Ruddle's Brewery*, home of the famous Rutland beer, with buildings from 1858.

11m NW, **Melton Mowbray**, Stilton cheese and pork pie centre since the mid 19C. Parish *church* restored by G.G. Scott (1865–69), E and W windows by Wailes, 1858 and 1849. In Nottingham St, N of High St, former *Corn Exchange* (1854) Italianate. On Burton St, to SE, *King Edward VII School* (1907–10; E. Shelbourn), Baroque with clock tower. *Melton Town station* (1846–48; W. Parsons and S. Wood) has an Italianate loggia. 9m NE of Melton Mowbray, *• Belvoir Castle* (open to public), one of the most thorough pre-Victorian romantic Gothic works, medievalised 1801–30 by J. Wyatt and the Rev. Sir J. Thoroton, the Duke of Rutland's chaplain. Splendid Gothic interiors, especially the two-storey entrance hall with stair opening off and the upstairs ballroom with plaster rib vault. Other main rooms have splendid decoration in the Louis XIV and neo-classical styles. In the grounds, neo-Norman mausoleum (1826–28), vaulted and heavily carved with altar position taken by the Baroque monument to the 5th Duchess (1826; M.C. Wyatt).

3m NE of Oakham, at Exton, *Exton Hall*, large Jacobean style house (1851–53; H. Roberts) with RC chapel (1868; C.A. Buckler) attached, built for the Earls of Gainsborough. E of Oakham, at the E end of Rutland Water, a huge reservoir, the upper half of **Normanton** *church*, preserved as a landmark but half-buried. Baroque tower (1826–29; T. Cundy Jr). S of the reservoir, SW of **North Luffenham**, *The Pastures* (1901; Voysey), one of Voysey's most picturesque houses, loosely grouped round a courtyard, designed to increase the scale of a relatively modest house. Roughcast walls with characteristic flush stone windows, and dormer gables. Pretty clock tower between the service ranges. 2m W, at **Lyndon**, *church* restored 1866 (T.G. Jackson) with rich chancel decoration and sgraffito pictures to reredos. W window by Powell's (1866). 6m S of Oakham, A6003, **Uppingham**, market town with *Uppingham School* dominating the centre. Chapel and schoolroom (1863–65; G.E. Street), altered 1964. Conical roofed turret to chapel, schoolroom in two storeys. W court largely by T.G. Jackson 1889 and 1894–97, 17C style with gate-tower. The handsome Elizabethan style hall dates from 1921–24 (E. Newton). In High St and London Road, boarding houses of 1860–70, notably *The Lodge* (1868), High St, French Gothic, and *Highfield* (1862; C. Barry Jr), London Rd. In Market Place, Jacobean *Midland Bank* (1900; Goddard and Co). 4m W of Uppingham, **Horninghold**, estate *village* mostly of 1882–1914 (Goddard and Co) for the Hardcastle family, the garden suburb influence clear in the planting and broad verges.

LINCOLNSHIRE

BOSTON. A16 36m NE of Peterborough. The parish *church*, one of the largest in England, was restored 1856 (G.G. Scott) with E window by O'Connor and font by Pugin (1853). In the Market Place, *Lloyds Bank* (1864), Italianate, and *statue* of H. Ingram (1862; A. Munro), founder of the 'Illustrated London News'. To N, *Sessions House* (1841–43; C. Kirk), Tudor style, and *Barclays Bank* (1836; H.F. Lockwood). To E, in Red Lion St, *Centenary Methodist Chapel* (c 1910; Gordon and Gunton), grand Baroque stone front to a chapel of 1839. To S, in South St, *Shodfriars Hall*, originally 16C but given an ornate trim in 1874 (J.O. Scott). W of Market Place, by the Bridge, *Assembly Rooms* (1822), Regency style stucco with tall upper windows. Over the bridge, High St, *White Hart* with heavily detailed Italianate extension. On London Rd, S of the centre, *St. Thomas' Church* (1912; T. Moore) with mullion windows of 17C type, E end added 1933.

5m SW, A16, at **Algarkirk**, *church* restored 1850–54 (R.C. Carpenter) with painted decorated chancel and painted organ case. Chancel and S transept glass by Hardman. *School* (1857; G.G. Scott). 8m SW, A16, at **Pinchbeck**, *church* restored 1855–64 (Butterfield) with W window by O'Connor. Butterfield built the small brick *church* to W at Pinchbeck Bars (1850), stone with W bellcote on a centre buttress, and the surprising parsonage (1850), stone below and roughcast above like a house of c 1900. Pinchbeck Marsh *pumping station* has a beam-engine of 1833. **Spalding**, to S, has been centre of the bulb industry since c 1900. In Market Place, former *Corn Exchange* (1854–56; Bellamy and Hardy) Jacobean. In Sheepmarket, *Sessions House* (1842; C. Kirk) Tudor style. Across the river, in Church Gate, *Ayscoughfee Hall* 15C to 16C, Tudorised 1845 (W. Todd). Parish *church* restored 1865–67 (G.G. Scott) with glass by Clayton and Bell and reredos of 1875 (J.O. Scott). In Church St, Tudor style *almshouses* (1843; W. Todd). To N, *St. Paul's Church*, Fulney (1880; G.G. Scott), large red-brick church with spire, harsh externally but imposing EE interior with arcade arches grouped in pairs under a blank arch. 2m W of Spalding, Pode Hole *pumping station* (1825) with original Boulton and Watt engines. 12m E of Spalding at **Fleet**, *Hovenden House* (c 1910; J. Dixon-Spain) brick neo-Georgian, and large *rectory* (1854; B. Ferrey).

7m N of Boston, B1183, at **New Bolingbroke**, a new settlement of 1824 around a weaving factory with crescent of original houses. *Church* and *rectory* 1854 (S.S. Teulon), church with spiky tower and spire but interior brickwork plastered over. At **Revesby**, 2m N, estate village of the Banks family of Revesby Abbey. Sir J. Banks (1743–1820), the naturalist who accompanied Cook to the Pacific, is commemorated in the lavish *church* (1891; C.H. Fowler). Expensive panelled sanctuary with gilded angels and mother-of-pearl inlay. Around the green, estate cottages, school (1858) and almshouses (1862), an attractive red-brick group. *Revesby Abbey* (1843; W. Burn) is Jacobean style in stone with shaped gables and ornate porte-cochère. 6m W, B1191, **Woodhall Spa**, improbable late 19C development with pinewoods and half-timbered hotels. 7m NE of Revesby, **Spilsby**, birthplace of Sir J. Franklin (1786–1847), the explorer lost in the search for the North West Passage. In the Market Place, Franklin *statue* (1861; C. Bacon). Beyond the church, Greek Doric portico of *Sessions House* (1824; H.E. Kendall). 18m NE of Boston, A52, **Skegness**, seaside resort laid out from c 1875 with *church* (1880; J. Fowler) in the centre of the grid of streets and large hotels along the seafront. Lumley Rd, running back to the station, has *Lumley Hotel* (1879–83) and *Hildred's Hotel* (1897; A. Coke Hill). *Links Hotel* (1902; Brewill and Bailey), *Seacroft Hotel* (1904; E.A. Robson). *Pier* (1881; Clarke and Pickwell). 7m W, off B1195 at **Firsby**, *church* (1856; G.E. Street), High Victorian with W rose and plate tracery. Tablet to Mary Walls (died 1877), gilded and inlaid with background flowers in the stylised manner of the Aesthetic Movement.

GAINSBOROUGH. A156 19m NW of Lincoln. Red-brick industrial town on the Trent. George Eliot's 'Mill on the Floss' was set here. In the Market Place, *Town Hall* (1891), and in Market St, *County Court* (1870). By the river, good surviving warehouses, though the reputed 'Mill on the Floss' has gone. In Beaumont St, *Marshall's Works* (1850) with Britannia over the entry. 3m E, A631, at **Corringham**, *church* with lovely interior decorated 1883–84 by Bodley, in combinations of deep matt colours with gilding. By Bodley the screen and organ case, fine examples of his delicate late Gothic style, also richly painted. E window by Wooldridge (1873) and S aisle E by Kempe (c 1880). 5m N of Gainsborough, off A159, at **Laughton**, *church* rebuilt by Bodley and Garner (1894–96) for Mrs Meynell-Ingram, Bodley's patron at Hoar Cross, Staffordshire, and Holbeck, Leeds. New tall chancel with long Dec. windows, nave clerestory and S porch. Fine interior with screen, organ case and reredos by Bodley. Effigy of Mr Meynell-Ingram (1874; T. Woolner). Glass by Burlison and Grylls.

GRANTHAM. A52 24m E of Nottingham. Market town, an engineering centre from the early 19C and much expanded after the arrival of the railway in the 1850s. In the centre, *Town Hall* (1867–69; W. Watkins), St. Peter's Hill, brick and stone, eclectic with fancy clock turret and French pavilion roofs. Isaac Newton *statue* (1859; Theed) in front. To N, Finkin St, *Savings Bank* (1841; Salvin), Jacobean style, and *Wesleyan chapel* (1840), twin-towered classical. Further N, the parish *church*, most magnificent of Lincolnshire medieval churches, restored 1866–75 by G.G. Scott. Rood screen by Scott (1868), reredos by Blomfield (1883), font cover (1899) and organ case (1909) by W. Tapper. In North Parade, *RC church* (1832; E.J. Willson), ashlar classical with cupola. In Market Place, former *Corn Exchange* (1852), stone-fronted classical. On London Rd, around the station, red-brick terraces reflecting 19C industrial development, engineering works established 1815.

3m SW, A607, at **Harlaxton**, *Harlaxton Manor* (1831–38; A. Salvin: 1838–53; W. Burn), the most unbelievable of Victorian houses, a Jacobean prodigy house of a scale and lavishness to rival the great houses of c 1600, but built by G. Gregory, a bachelor with a reasonable landed fortune, apparently to rival the Duke of Rutland's new works at Belvoir, Leicestershire. Everything is conceived on the grandest scale and executed in the finest ashlar with a vigour that has something of the Baroque in the main building and very much of the Baroque in the splendid screen walls that flank the forecourt at the head of the straight drive, just under a mile long. The Baroque of the screen walls, somewhere between Vanbrugh and S Italy, has little precedent in 19C architecture, Burn seemingly their designer. The house itself, building up through polygonal and curved bays and oriels to a skyline of turrets, curved gables, pierced balustrades and chimneys to the central tower and cupola, concentrates the drama of genuine houses in this style with a romantic genius of effect. Interiors run from Jacobean to

Harlaxton Manor (1831–38; A. Salvin: 1838–53; W. Burn), Harlaxton

Louis XV all excellently carried out but nothing prepares for the Cedar Staircase, an exercise in illusionist Baroque rising through three floors to a painted sky, the topmost level adorned with Father Time figures looking down from a vertiginous ledge. Bavarian Baroque in inspiration, wondrously successfully handled for a style otherwise unknown in Britain. In the village, estate cottages of c 1830–40 decked out with odd brick details and imported pieces of carving. Denton *church*, 1m W, has a handsome organ case by J.F. Bentley (1887). 5m S of Grantham, A1, at **Stoke Rochford**, *Stoke Rochford Hall* (1841; W. Burn), large and ornate ashlar Jacobean style house, a clear follower of Harlaxton in the symmetrical entrance front with curved oriel over the porch and lavish array of gables, cresting and chimneys. Rich interiors mostly Jacobean, but some, as at Harlaxton, Louis XV. Estate *village* by Burn (1840–45), Tudor style stone cottages. On the drive 60ft obelisk (c 1845; Burn) to Sir I. Newton. The *church* has monuments to the Turnor family of the Hall, one to C. Turnor (died 1886) with portrait roundels in N chapel. Reredos designed by Mrs Mary Watts, wife of the painter (cf. Compton, Surrey). *Easton Park*, across the A1, has derelict fragments of 19C gardens from a lost house. 2m SW, B676, at **Stainby**, *church* (1865; R. Coad) with prominent broach spire and all the interior fittings carved by the Rev. W. Thorold, after 1877. More carvings by this accomplished parson at Gunby *church*, just S.

3m N of Grantham, A607, **Belton**, the estate of the Brownlow family of Belton Hall (NT). Belton and Manthorpe, to S, are complete estate villages of the early to mid 19C. At Belton, *church* with Brownlow monuments from the 17C onwards. In the mortuary chapel (1816) tomb chest with effigy of the 1st Earl (died 1853; Marochetti). At **Manthorpe**, estate *church* (1847; G.G. Place) with central broach spire. 10m NE, A153, at **Sleaford**, market town with, in Market Place, *Sessions House* (1831; H.E. Kendall), Tudor Gothic, Gothic *Corn Exchange* (1857; C. Kirk), *bank* (1903; Watkins and Sons), and, on E side, medieval parish church with one of the Lincolnshire EE spires so much an inspiration to Victorian architects. 19C chancel glass by Holland (1857), S aisle E window by Hardman 1853 and one S aisle window by Morris. S of church, *almshouses* (1830 and 1841; Kendall) with centre chapel. In Eastgate, *Lafford Terrace* (1856; Kirk and Parry), Italianate range of centre, wings and end pavilions. Further out, former *workhouse* (1838; Donthorn) and *Gas Works*, both Tudor style. S of Market Place, *Handley Memorial* (1850; W. Boyle), Southgate, Gothic cross with figure of H. Handley MP. In Northgate, N of Market Place, *almshouses* (1857) and *Grammar School* (1834; C. Kirk), Tudor. *Sleaford Maltings* (c 1892–1905; H. Couchman) is one of the largest in the country, a sequence of eight separate six-storey blocks with central tower, some 1000ft overall. 2m W, A153, *Rauceby Asylum* (1897; G.T. Hine). At **South Rauceby**, to N, estate village of *Rauceby Hall* (1842; W. Burn), gabled Elizabethan mansion. At **Ruskington**, 4m NE of Sleaford, B1188, the *church* has one good Morris window (c 1874), S aisle E. At **Caythorpe**, 5m N of Belton, A607, *Caythorpe Court* (1899; R. Blomfield), 1¾m E, large stone-gabled house with mullioned windows in early 17C style. 5m NW, off A17, **Brant Broughton** *church* with a chancel of wonderful richness by G.F. Bodley (1874–77). Complete Bodley scheme with stencil decoration, organ case and reredos painted in deep colours with some gilding set off by fine stained glass, E window by Burlison and Grylls, the rest by the rector Canon Sutton, himself an authority on German Renaissance glass. Rood screen (1890) by Bodley and font cover 1889 by T. Garner. This is the finest example of Bodley's restoration work, every detail and effect of colour in harmony.

LINCOLN. The *Cathedral* has notable 19C fittings, especially stained glass. In the nave, W window and four at W end of S aisle of c 1861–62 by the Revs. A. and F.H. Sutton in strong 13C style. In adjoining bay to E, one by Hedgeland (c 1854), one by Clayton and Bell (c 1860). Effigy of Bishop Kaye (1857; R. Westmacott Jr). Over pulpitum Gothic organ case (1826; E.J. Willson). In S transept, Bishop King statue (1913; W.B. Richmond) powerful bronze. In the choir, pulpit (1863–64; G.G. Scott). In SE transept good glass of c 1850–60, S side by Hedgeland, chapel windows by Revs. A. and F.H. Sutton. At E end, great E window 1855 (Ward and Hughes) and effigy of Queen Eleanor, replica of that in Westminster Abbey. On N side, Bishop Wordsworth tomb (c 1885; Bodley and Garner) with effigy. On S side memorial to the painters P. de Wint and W. Hilton (1864; W. Blore) and alabaster effigy of Dean Butler (died 1894; Chavaillaud). Around the cathedral, to W, *Deanery* (1873; J.L. Pearson), to S, former *Bishop's Palace* rebuilt within the medieval buildings in 18C and 1886 (E. Christian). Fine tall chapel 1898 (Bodley and Garner). NE of the Cathedral, on the Green, Tennyson *statue* (1905; G.F. Watts), bronze with the long cloak and floppy hat familiar from photographs of the poet. N of the cathedral, *Cathedral School* (1847; W. Burn), built as the Deanery. In Eastgate, to E, *St. Peter's Church* (1870; Blomfield) with S aisle of 1914 (Temple Moore). Pretty chancel decoration by Bodley (1884). W of cathedral, the Castle, with former *Gaol* (1787) and a remarkably grim prison chapel (1845) where each convict had a cubicle to head-height, tiered so that only the preacher was visible and each cubicle self-locking. To W, *Assize Courts* (1823–26; R. Smirke), castellated Tudor. *Observatory Tower* has an early 19C observatory dome on top. Dominant, to N, *Water Tower* (1910; R. Blomfield), stone, massively square.

Bailgate leads N to Newport past *St. Mary Magdalene's Church* by Castle Hill, rebuilt 1882 (Bodley) with continuous wagon roof and good organ loft by Bodley. In Newport, *St. Nicholas' Church* (1838; G.G. Scott), Scott's first important church, still the lancet Gothic of

Commissioners' churches. Broach spire. In Burton Rd, to W, *Museum of Lincolnshire Life*. S of Castle Hill, to W, in Wordsworth St, *Bishop's Hostel*, former Infirmary (1776) with chapel of 1906 (Temple Moore). To E, on Christ's Hospital Terrace, *St. Michael's Church* (1853; S.S. Teulon). SE of the Cathedral, Greenstone Stairs leads down to Lindum Rd at *Girls' High School* (1893; W. Watkins), red brick and terracotta, one of a number such buildings by Watkins, the leading late 19C local architect. Adjoining, to W, *Usher Gallery* (1927; R. Blomfield). Pretty early 19C *temple* on the hill and early Victorian houses with verandahs looking S. Lindum Terrace, to E, is early Victorian. In Upper Lindum St, former *Grammar School* (1884; Watkins), free 17C mannerist style, after Norman Shaw. Further E, in Sewell Rd, *St. Anne's Bedehouses* (1847–60; A.W.N. Pugin), red-brick and stone almshouses around a court with brick chapel (1853; Butterfield), tall with flèche. Beyond, *County Hospital* (1878; A. Graham), Jacobean. To S, *Arboretum* (1872), park with pretty bandstand. On Monks Rd, to S, *All Saints' Church* (1903; C.H. Fowler), tall brick, Dec. style with buttressed W front, fittings by Comper. Monks Rd runs W to Broadgate.

S of Monks Rd, the 19C industrial terraces running down to the river. In Rosemary Lane, patterned brick *Wesleyan Schools* (1859; Bellamy and Hardy). In Silver St, *Constitutional Club* (1895; Watkins) with domed corner and terracotta decoration and, adjoining, former *Methodist church* (1864; Bellamy and Hardy), freely Italianate. On N side, Dutch gabled building by Watkins, on S side, *Royal Insurance* (1857; P. Bellamy), rich palazzo style. In High St, by the Stonebow, *National Westminster Bank* (1883; J. Gibson), severely handsome palazzo. Saltergate runs E from the Stonebow. In Free School Lane, to N, *Library* (1906; R. Blomfield), handsome stone building with domed centre, French 18C style. *St. Swithin's Church* (1869; J. Fowler) is the lower town's most prominent church, with high spire modelled on Louth, added 1888. W of High St, on Guildhall St, *bank* (1848), late Georgian with Jacobean ornament to ground floor, and *Post Office* (1906; W. Oldrieve), stone, free Tudor. To SW, S of Newland, *Brayford Pool* with early to mid 19C warehouses surrounding the water, the River Witham being navigable from here to Boston. Footpath runs E to the High Bridge. High St opens on E to Cornhill with Corinthian *Corn Exchange* (1847; W. Nicholson). *Barclays Bank* (1873; H. Gamble) on corner is Italian Gothic. In St. Mary's St, *Central Station* (1848; H. Goddard), Tudor style, in grey brick, surprisingly elaborate with tower, steep gables and oriel. Off High St, to SW, *St. Mark's Station* (1846), decayed classical front with Ionic portico, built for the Midland Railway. *Hannah Memorial Methodist Church* (1874; Bellamy and Hardy), grand Corinthian, nearly opposite *Central Methodist Church* (1906), brick and stone Baroque.

SE of centre, in Canwick Road, *St. Andrew's Church* (1876; J. Fowler) has chancel decoration by Bodley (1882). 2m S of centre, A15, at **Bracebridge**, *County Asylum* (1849; Hamilton), very large Italianate. 3m SE, B1188, at **Branston**, *Branston Hall* (1884; J.M. Anderson), brick Jacobean. *Stonefield* is a builder's folly in yellow brick and black stone, gabled and castellated. 3m SE, at **Nocton**, *Nocton Hall* (1841; W. Shearburn), gabled Tudor built for the 1st Earl of Ripon, briefly Prime Minister 1827–28. The *church* (1862; G.G. Scott) is exceptionally rich, built as a memorial to the Earl, with High Victorian naturalistic carving, plate tracery and rich marble fittings. Wall-paintings in red outline and stained glass by Clayton and Bell. Chancel *effigy* of the Earl (1862; M. Noble). 2m S, **Blankney**, estate *village* in stone (c

1830–50) of the Chaplin family of Blankney Hall, now demolished. In the *church*, marble memorial to Lady F. Chaplin (died 1881; Sir J.E. Boehm). Lychgate by Bodley.

NE of central Lincoln, Wragby Rd, A158, leads out past *Lincoln School* (1905; L. Stokes), long front in free 17C style, spare and elegant detail with artisan mannerist derived centrepiece and cupola. At **Langworth**, 7m E, the *church* of 1960 incorporates important Arts and Crafts material from H. Wilson's 1901 chapel at Walmsgate Hall, altar canopy, organ, font, chancel beam and memorial to T. Dallas-Yorke, fine sinuous bronze work and marble panelling. 2m W at **Sudbrooke**, neo-Norman *church* (1860; J. Dobson), based on Steetly, Derbyshire. Vaulted apse. 2m W, off A46, **Nettleham** *church* with chancel rebuilt 1882 (Bodley and Garner), stalls and screen by Bodley (1912). 3m N of Lincoln, A15, *Riseholme Hall*, rebuilt 1845 (W. Railton) for the Bishop of Lincoln, late Georgian style. *Church* (1851; S.S. Teulon) with deep coloured chancel glass by Gibbs. 4m N, off A15, at **Hackthorn**, estate *church* (1850; C. Mainwaring), the tower based on Magdalen Tower, Oxford. Mainwaring, an antiquarian and collector, designed all the carving and fittings. Good E window by Wailes and chancel S window by Holiday (c 1861). At **Cold Hanworth**, 3m E, extremely spiky *church* (1863; J. Croft), with rock-faced exterior and polychrome brick and stone interior. Fleshy leaf carving and hefty roof coming down to diagonally set square columns on brackets. Inventive tracery, especially the E window. Clayton and Bell glass. At **Spridlington**, 2m NW, *church* (1872; J. Fowler), unexpectedly grand with saddleback roofed tower and broad interior. At **Faldingworth**, 3m NE of Cold Hanworth, A46, *church* (1892; C.H. Fowler) in the manner of Bodley with painted decoration in sanctuary.

LOUTH. A157 26m NE of Lincoln. Market town dominated by the great 15C spire of the parish *church*. Heavily restored interior (J. Fowler). To S, *Vicarage* (1832; C. Carter), Tudor Gothic. In Eastgate, *Town Hall* (1854; P. Bellamy), handsome Italian palazzo of unusual grandeur with rusticated ground floor, heavy cornice and balustrade. Galleried hall inside. *Wesleyan chapel* (1835) has late Georgian brick front. S of Town Hall, *Market* (1866; Rogers and Marsden), iron and glass hall with tower to Market Place, tall and thin, Gothic with pyramid cap and flèche. The tower is recessed between two matching red-brick buildings. In Cornmarket, decayed Italianate front of former *Corn Exchange* (1853; P. Bellamy), narrow three storeys with columned first floor. Plain brick and stucco buildings of c 1840 here and in Mercer Row. Further out, on Eastgate, *Holy Trinity Church* (1866; Rogers and Marsden), hefty rock-faced exterior with octagonal top to tower, and former *station* (1848; Weightman and Hadfield), unusually palatial Jacobean, red brick and stone with shaped gables and central porte-cochère. In Church St, *St. Michael's Church* (1863; J. Fowler), High Victorian with polychrome brick interior.

3m S of Louth, A16, at **Haugham**, *church* (1840; W. Nicholson), stuccoed brick imitation of Louth parish church. Complete fittings and E window of c 1840. Similar *churches* with characteristic fittings at **Raithby**, A153, 3m NW, and **Biscathorpe**, 6m W of Louth, both by Nicholson. 13m S of Louth, A153, **Horncastle**, with 31ft *monument* in Market Place (1894; E. Lingen Barker) and Italianate *court house* (1865; C. Reeves) at head of North St. 6m NE, **Somersby**, birthplace of Alfred Tennyson, whose father was rector. At **Harrington**, 2m E, *Harrington Hall* garden is supposedly remembered in Tennyson's 'Come into the garden, Maud'. *Church* (1854; S.S. Teulon). 7m NW of

Louth, at **Binbrook**, *church* (1869; J. Fowler), surprisingly grand with broach spire and apse, in Fowler's most conventional early Dec. style. At **Tealby**, to W, was *Bayon's Manor*, romantic castellated house built by Tennyson's uncle, Charles Tennyson d'Eyncourt MP, c 1836–45. Tennyson's father had been disinherited in favour of Charles, who spent a fortune on this latter-day Fonthill, now almost entirely gone. 8m N, N of **Caistor**, B1361, *Pelham's Pillar* (1849; E.J. Willson), 128ft tower commemorating the twelve million trees planted by the 1st Earl of Yarborough, of Brocklesby Park, 5m N, on the county border. *Brocklesby Park* is early 18C with interiors of 1898 (R. Blomfield).

STAMFORD. A1 14m NW of Peterborough. In *St. Mary's Church*, altar front by J.D. Sedding (1890), Renaissance style, and, in Lady Chapel, E window (1890; C. Whall) in late Pre-Raphaelite manner, Whall's first important commission. One N side window by Whall (1893). Behind the church, *Stamford Hotel* (1810–29; J.L. Bond), a hotel of exceptional scale for the early 19C, reminder of Stamford's importance on the main road north. To left, *Nos 13 and 14 St. Mary's St* (1849), handsome classical pair with Ionic shopfronts, each side of a cul-de-sac. S of St. Mary's, *Town Bridge* (1849; B. and E. Browning) with Tudor style houses each side. On Wharf Rd, along the river, was Blashfield's Terracotta Works, one of the chief Victorian pioneers of ornamental terracotta. Over the bridge, in St. Martin's, *Burghley Estate Office* (1879; J. Corby) and *Burghley House*, the great Elizabethan house of the Cecil family (open to public). The 10th Earl of Exeter was 'the Lord of Burleigh' of Tennyson's poem. To W of St. Martin's High St, in Station Rd, *Stamford Town Station* (1846–48; S. Wood), stone Tudor style with octagonal turret. To E of St. Martin's High St, in Water Lane, former *Stamford East Station* (1856; W. Hurst), Jacobean style to complement Burghley House, the Marquis of Exeter being the main promoter of the line, and hence unusually elaborate and carefully detailed. N of St. Mary's St, in High St, *St. Michael's Church* (1835–36; J. Brown), lancet Gothic typical of the 1830s, but well executed in stone and an important feature on the High St. It has been converted to shops after years of disuse. N of High St, in Broad St, *Browne's Hospital*, 15C original building to the street with attractive court behind of 1870 (J. Fowler). W of All Saints' Church, in Scotgate, two early 19C almshouses, *Truesdale's Hospital* (1832; Basevi) and *Snowden's Hospital* (1822; T. Pierce). Beyond, *Rock House* and *Rock Terrace* (1841–42), a richly carved Italianate villa and its former stables. SW of All Saints', in St. Peter's St, former *Stamford Institution* (1842; B. and E. Browning), distinguished palazzo front, Grecian and Italianate elements combined, the ground floor particularly original in the relation of slightly recessed doorway and pediment to channelled piers framing the side windows. By Browning also, the refronting of *Barn Hill House* (1843), N of All Saints', in Greco-Roman manner, similarly sharply detailed. At **Bourne**, 9m NE, A6121, in the Market Place, *Town Hall* (1821; B. Browning), small but cleverly combining a horseshoe stair recessed within the front behind a screen of columns. Gothic *drinking fountain* (1860; E. Browning). In West St, *Baptist Church* (1835) and *Bourne Institute* (c 1865), High Victorian Gothic.

LONDON

CENTRAL LONDON

CITY OF LONDON

Bank

The Victorian period witnessed a decline in the City's residential population, and its expansion as the commercial centre of the empire. Railway lines were ruthlessly cut through the medieval street pattern, bringing commuters from the ever expanding suburbs. New streets, also cut through the City, and the surviving medieval streets were lined with proud banks and commercial buildings, usually classical (and when Gothic, invariably of an Italian variety), displaying the city fathers' identity with the bankers and merchants of late medieval and Renaissance Italy. Much of the Victorian City has been lost to bombing, even more to post-war redevelopment, which showed a capacity for ruthlessness equal to that of the Victorian period, but with none of the architectural and planning gains. Fortunately, many parts of the City retain a Victorian or Edwardian flavour, no better illustrated than at the point where seven major streets meet the Bank of England, 'the heart of the empire'.

Here a medieval street layout is overlaid by the 19C creations of King Edward St and Queen Victoria St. The symbolic centre of the City is the *Royal Exchange* (1841–44; Sir W. Tite), built, after a typically mismanaged competition, in a rich and heavy Italianate style, with an octostyle portico and a sculptured pediment. Like its 16C and 17C predecessors it originally had an internal courtyard open to the elements, but this was unfortunately roofed over in 1880. The walls of the cloister within the courtyard are covered with historical paintings of c 1900. Standing in front of the Royal Exchange, by the equestrian *statue of Wellington* (1844; F. Chantrey), observe, from right to left, Soane's *Bank of England*, almost entirely rebuilt by Herbert Baker in the 1920s, Edwin Cooper's *National Westminster Bank* (also 1920s), in Poultry, Lutyen's *Midland Bank*, the Gothic *Mappin and Webb* building (1875; J. and J. Belcher), occupying the prominent triangular site on the corner of Poultry and Queen Victoria St, George Dance's *Mansion House* with, in its Palladian Egyptian Hall, a fine collection of 1850s statues of English literary subjects, the *Scottish Provident Institution* (1908–1915; Dunn and Watson with W. Curtis Green), a good classical building, and the domed *Royal Insurance* (1905; J.M. Anderson). Stretching behind to the E are Cornhill, Lombard St and Threadneedle St, all retaining their medieval line, therefore narrow and curving, connected by little lanes. In Cornhill, especially noteworthy is the *Banco Nazionale de Lavoro*, Nos 33–5 (1857; H. and F. Francis), splendidly ornate classical. On the S side, Hawksmoor's tower for *St. Michael's Church*, which was remodelled and refitted by G.G. Scott in 1860, most of his work removed 1960. The Wren style woodwork is of the 1850s by W.G. Rogers. Also in Cornhill, on the S side, *No. 55* (1893; Ernest Runtz), in red terracotta, and, on the N, *No. 65*, plain Gothic by l'Anson, the Italianate *Nos 66–7* (1880; T.C. Clarke), and *No. 71* (1896; T. Cuthbert) with Grecian details. Lombard

St contains a number of classical and italianate buildings, Victorian, Edwardian and inter-war, *No. 39* (1868; H. and F. Francis), a richly decorated building on the corner with Gracechurch St and, *Nos 20–4*, Royal Insurance Buildings (1910; Gunton and Gunton). On the corner with King William St is Hawksmoor's magnificent *St. Mary Woolnoth*. King William St, laid out in the 1830s to connect the city with the new London Bridge, is characterised by large early 20C classical buildings. Most of the N side of Threadneedle St is taken up with the Bank of England and the *Stock Exchange*, but further E are *Nos 43–6*, mid Victorian by T.H. Smith, and *No. 38* Bank of Scotland (1902; J.M. Anderson). *Royal Exchange Buildings* (1907–10; George and Yeates) faces the E elevation of the Royal Exchange, with its fine Wren style tower, across a narrow square, with a statue of the housing philan- thropist *G. Peabody* (1868; W.W. Story) and two fountains, one by the influential French sculptor A.J. Dalou (1879).

Queen Victoria St was cut through between 1867 and 1871, con- necting the City to Blackfriars Bridge, the Embankment and the West End. The District Railway was constructed beneath at the same time. Its conjunction with narrow medieval streets presented a number of triangular sites, of which the Victorian architects took full advantage. Most prominent is the *Mappin and Webb* building on the corner, with its angle turret. On the S side, the *Bank of New Zealand* (1873; J. Whichcord), a fine Italianate building, also occupying a corner site, unfortunately its top storey has been mutilated. At the time of writing the buildings on the corner of Poultry and Queen Victoria St are threa- tened with demolition. Further up on the S side, *Nos 39–52*, Albert Buildings (1871; F.J. Ward), on the corner with Cannon St is a fine arcaded Gothic composition, with 20 bays towards Queen Victoria St, the centre eight raised. On the opposite side, noteworthy survivals are *Nos 68–70* and *No. 71a*, a stone-fronted bank of the 1870s. Look N up Queen St to admire the *Atlas Assurance* (1836; T. Hopper) in Cheap- side. Surrounding buildings have been rebuilt further back, so this stands proudly forward, with a pavement arcade running beneath. Beyond Mansion House tube station, Queen Victoria St has been mostly redeveloped and contains little of 19C interest. However, *No. 146* (1867; E. l'Anson), near the College of Arms, is a good Italianate palazzo built as the headquarters of the *British and Foreign Bible Society*.

Blackfriars, Embankment, Temple, Fleet St

Close to where the railway bridge crosses Queen Victoria St, is one of London's finest public houses, the *Black Friar*, a plain enough building of about 1875, its glory the refashioning of c 1905 by H. Fuller Clark, an Arts and Crafts Byzantine extravaganza of polished marble, mosaics and copper in celebration of monkish revelry. At the entrance to *Blackfriars Bridge* (1869; J. Cubitt) stands Queen Victoria (1893–96; C.B. Birch), looking southwards. The curving corner to Victoria Embankment is amply filled by *Unilever House*. Beyond, the *City of London School* (1881–82; Davis and Emmanuel), in a richly orna- mented Renaissance style. One really has to cross the road to appre- ciate this fine building. On the corner with Carmelite St, *Sion House* (1886; Sir A. Blomfield), in picturesque Tudor reddish brick. *Telephone House* (1908; A.N. Bromley), a building in free classical style, presents a fine face to the Embankment. N of the Embankment at this point is a series of regularly laid out contemporary streets, mostly still very Victorian in character. In Carmelite St, a good former *fire station* of the 1880s in a Dutch Gothic style and, on the corner of Tallis St, *Carmelite House* has a stair hall with paintings in cinque-cento manner (1898). Along the S side of *Tallis St* is a series of early newspaper buildings, still with their external gantries and loading bays. In John Carpenter St, the former *Guildhall School of Music* (1885–87; Horace Jones), its palazzo front to Tallis St an extension of 1896 (Andrew Murray). In Temple Avenue, *Temple Chambers* was built in 1894 to contain barristers overflowing from the Temple. Opposite, *Temple House*, also 1894, a red-brick office building with a nice corner clock turret. Tudor St to the N has several terracotta and stucco commercial buildings on its S side and, at its W end, the entrance to the Temple.

Back on the Embankment, the gabled Hamilton House (1899 onwards) is the last building before the green expanses which surround the *Temple*. The neo-Elizabethan building of brown brick glimpsed through the trees is an 1848 extension by Sydney Smirke to the more plain *Paper Buildings*, built by his elder brother Sir Robert ten years earlier. The *gate piers* and pretty little *entrance lodge* to the Temple date from 1880, but before turning into the Temple note the two griffins marking the City boundary on the Embankment. These come from J.B. Bunnings's magnificent Coal Exchange, formerly in Lower Thames St, disgracefully demolished in 1962 for a road widening. Barry's large and exuberant building in the style of a French château (1878) has an elaborate archway leading into Middle Temple Lane. With its medieval church, Elizabethan hall, and 17C and neo-Georgian 20C collegiate type layout, the Temple contains little for the single-minded Victorian enthusiast. In Middle Temple Lane, *Harcourt Buildings*, a yellow brick Tudor Gothic building of c 1830, with a larger extension in similar vein dating from 1896. To the W of Middle Temple Hall, *Garden Court* (1884–85; St. Aubyn), neo-Jacobean with gables and prominent brick chimneys. On the N side of *Brick Court*, another range by St. Aubyn, even earlier, this time Tudor and rather dull. More interesting are *Nos 2–3 Hare Court* (1893–94; T.G. Jackson), red-brick Norman Shaw style. Around the W side of the Temple church, further Victorian buildings, none of great interest.

The 17C brick gatehouse at the top of Middle Temple Lane gives access to Fleet St, the medieval link between Westminster and the City. *The Temple Bar Memorial* (1880; Horace Jones), with inset figures of Queen Victoria and the Prince of Wales, and surmounted by a large dragon, marks the site of the 17C gateway. This was dismantled in 1878 and taken to Hertfordshire, but it may soon find an unlikely new home on the N side of St. Paul's. On the N side of Fleet St, are Street's *Law Courts* (see Westminster below p. 238). Next comes the large former *Bank of England* (1886–88; Sir A. Blomfield and Son), cinquecento in style, with projecting outer bays and marble columns. Then, taking the corner with Chancery Lane, *No. 193* (1883; Archer and Green), a terracotta building. By the Temple Bar Memorial, on the S side of Fleet St, is *No. 1*, Childs Bank (1879; J. Gibson), excellent Italian palazzo. *No. 10* is a brick terracotta building by R.W. Edis (1885). *No. 16*, a narrow, stuccoed building of the mid 19C, has an elaborate first-floor Venetian window. *Nos 18–19* (1898–99; A. Blomfield and Son) is an interesting essay in a free Baroque manner and like the Blomfields' earlier Bank of England has projecting outer bays. This may be out of deference to *Hoare's Bank* (1829; Charles Parker), a noble and restrained building which is, after Soane's Bank of England, the earliest surviving purpose-built commercial building in the City. Opposite is *St. Dunstan in the West* (1829–33; J. Shaw), the only 19C

Anglican parish church in the City. Its octagonal tower is of vital importance in the townscape. Next, also by Shaw, is the *Australian Mutual Provident Society* building (1834), neo-Elizabethan, of yellow brick with stone dressings. On the S side, *No. 49* (1911; J.M. Brooks) is a fine Edwardian classical building with an arched entrance to Segeant's Inn flanked on the left by a niche containing a large sculpture. Continuing E along Fleet St are a number of 19C buildings, none special, until we reach *Nos 142–3*, Mary Queen of Scots House, on the N side, with Mary's figure in a Gothic niche, cusped Gothic arches to the windows and elaborate carved bargeboards in stone. Further E on the same side, *No. 132*, *Mersey House*, a single bay building of 1906–07, is an original Arts and Crafts inspired design. *No. 92*, *Bartholomew House* (1900; H.H. Gordon), on the S side, is free Tudor with good Art Nouveau carved details.

Ludgate Hill, St. Paul's, Holborn

The two N segments of Ludgate Circus (1864–70) survive, including the *King Lud*, a gin palace of 1870 (L.H. Isaacs). In Farringdon St, stretching away to the N, following the line of the old Fleet river, the only Victorian building of note is *No. 26* (1888), asymetrical in brick and stone on the E side. The view up Ludgate Hill towards St. Paul's is ruined by the bridge carrying the London, Chatham and Dover Railway, opened in 1866. There was a station at this point, of which a little remains. In Ludgate Hill, on the corner of Ludgate Court, the *Midland Bank* (1888; T. Collcutt), red brick and terracotta in 16C Flemish style. This is followed by a range of *classical buildings* of the mid 19C and, leading off in Ludgate Square, a number of Victorian *warehouses*. Further N in Ludgate Hill, and curling around the S side of St. Paul's, the scale increases with some grand stone buildings of the 1890s. On the N side of Ludgate Hill, *Nos 34–40*, a boldly stuccoed building of the 1850s.

The classical austerity of *St. Paul's* did not greatly appeal to the Victorians, and although they did not try to gothicise it, they did the next best thing, which was to 'byzantinise' it with mosaics. Those in the spandrels of the dome under the crossing are by A. Stevens (the four prophets), Watts (St. John and St. Matthew) and A. Brittain (St. Mark and St. Luke). The sculpture in the drum of the dome was designed by Kempe (1892–94) and executed by Farmer and Brindley. In the chancel, mosaics by Sir William Richmond (1891–1912), the large reredos by Bodley and Garner replaced after the last war by the present baldacchino. The greatest Victorian addition to the Cathedral was the *Wellington Monument, Alfred Stevens' masterpiece (1857–1912), in the nave. In the N aisle, the painter Lord Leighton (1902; T. Brock), the bronze sarcophagus raised high between figures of Painting and Sculpture, the latter recording Leighton's importance to the 'New Sculpture', the movement towards naturalism and realism that Leighton encouraged both as sculptor and as President of the Royal Academy. Also in the aisle, *General Gordon* (1833–85), the greatest of Victorian military heroes, effigy by J.E. Boehm, reliefs of his exploits behind. At the W end, the Prime minister *Melbourne* (c 1855; Marochetti), commemorated by two white angels before the black marble Gate of Death. In the S aisle, Holman Hunt's famous painting 'The Light of the World', in its second version, said to have been the most expensive Victorian picture ever commissioned, at 12,000 guineas. In the transepts, the overwhelming collection of monuments to late 18C and early 19C military and naval figures with only a few Victorian interlopers. In the N transept, the composers *Sullivan* and *Stainer* and the architect *C.R. Cockerell* are commemorated. In the S transept, *Sir H. Lawrence* (1862; J.G. Lough), killed at the siege of Lucknow, and the painter *Turner*. At the E end, late 19C Deans and Bishops of London, including *Bishop Creighton* (1905; H. Thornycroft), historian of the Papacy, and *Bishop Blomfield* (died 1857). The crypt is where the monuments are thickly clustered. In the S aisle, the Painters' Corner, monuments to *Landseer, Orchardson, Turner, Holman Hunt, Constable* and *J.S. Sargent*. In the nave, *Nelson* is under the dome in the great marble 16C sarcophagus made for Cardinal Wolsey, and, to the W, *Wellington* in a porphyry sarcophagus by F.C. Penrose. At the W end, the bronze gun-carriage (1852; G. Semper) used for Wellington's state funeral. In the S transept, a bust by Rodin of the writer *W.E. Henley*. Of sculptural interest, Woolner's *Landseer*, Frampton's *R.J. Seddon*, *E.V. Neale* and *Sir W. Besant*, and *Lord Lytton* by Gilbert.

S of the Cathedral, in Dean's Court, is F.C. Penrose's *Choir School* (1875), now a youth hostel, most striking with Italianate details and good sgraffito decoration. Its main frontage looks onto Carter Lane, a quiet enclave of considerable charm. In Church Entry, an architectural curiosity, *St. Anne's Vestry Hall* (1905; Sir B. Fletcher), a small and well-detailed Baroque building, empty and neglected at the time of writing. On the N side of St. Paul's, in Newgate St, Wren's *Christ Church* was damaged by bombing and subsequently mutilated, quite unnecessarily, for road widening. Between here and Giltspur St, all the buildings on the N side are Victorian or early 20C. The large *post office*, stone and slightly recessed, dates from 1902. *Nos 115–17* (1879; Ford and Hesketh) are red brick and *Nos 118–26* introduce the style of Holborn Viaduct. Leading S off Newgate St, Warwick Lane, with the *Cutlers' Hall* (1886–87; T. Taylor Smith), the terracotta frieze above the ground floor by Benjamin Creswick, a protégé of Ruskin. Also S, in Old Bailey, is the *Central Criminal Court* (1900–07; E.W. Mountford), one of the best examples of the Edwardian revival of English Baroque. Sculpture by Pomeroy and, inside, the mosaic and mural decoration by Joseph Moira. It is a thousand pities that this great building necessitated the demolition of Dance's *Newgate Gaol*. Opposite the Court, only the rather French-looking *Britannia House* (Nos 16–17) is notable. On the corner with Holborn Viaduct, a large building, built as an hotel in 1874.

Holborn Viaduct was laid out by the engineer William Heywood, City Surveyor, and was opened by the Queen in 1869. It required the demolition of many older properties and in its turn has been largely redeveloped in the last 20 years or so. The *Viaduct* itself is by Heywood, of cast iron supported on granite piers, which carry statues personifying Commerce, Agriculture, Science and Fine Art. At each corner four pavilions with steps led down to Farringdon St. Those on the N side were demolished in the 1960s, but the S two remain, dedicated respectively to Sir Thomas Gresham and Henry Fitz-Elwyn, the first Lord Mayor (in the 13C). Dating from the same time is Holborn Viaduct *Railway Station*, rebuilt in the 1960s, and the *City Temple*, the only Nonconformist church to be built in the City in the 19C (1873–74; H.F. Lockwood). Two Wren style towers were intended, but only one built. The church was rebuilt after bomb damage, but the facade remains. Further up, also on the S side, the turreted *rectory* (S.S. Teulon) of St. Andrew's Church is best seen from St. Andrew St. *Holborn Circus* has been insensitively redeveloped in recent years, although a *National Westminster Bank* of 1870 survives on the corner of Charterhouse St, and, in the middle of the circus, the bronze equestrian statue of *Prince Albert* (1874; C. Bacon), saluting the achievement of the Viaduct. The N side of Holborn is dominated by the red-brick and terracotta Gothic of Alfred Waterhouse's *Prudential Assurance Building*. The first part, on the corner of Brooke St, dates from 1879 and the rest from 1899–1906. S, in Fetter Lane, *No. 78–81* (1902; Treadwell and Martin), a Gothic with Flemish and Art Nouveau touches. *Dyers Buildings* is an attractive enclave with buildings of yellow brick with red-brick dressings. Between the two streets, tucked away behind a bank, is *Barnard's Inn*, a 14C hall facing a courtyard with, on the W side, *Nos 4–6*, a three-storey block in red brick with stone dressings, built in free Renaissance style for the Mercer's School in 1894, and threatened with demolition at the time of writing.

Smithfield to Liverpool St

The area of Smithfield Market has long been a public space, whether for the trade in cattle or for the witnessing of executions, and it retains an open character untypical of the City and all the more welcome for that. The main *Market* buildings (1866), by Sir Horace Jones, City Surveyor, who also built Leadenhall and Billingsgate Markets, are on the N side of West Smithfield and comprise a large, single-storey cast-iron structure with a classical envelope of red brick and Portland stone. Good decorative ironwork abounds. On the E and W sides of West Smithfield, an assortment of office buildings, mostly Victorian, although the much restored timber framed gateway on the E side is medieval and leads into the fine Norman priory church of *St. Bartholomew the Great*, by Aston Webb, who added the porch in 1893. Rahere, 12C founder of the church, also founded *St. Bartholomew's Hospital*, which occupies the S side of West Smithfield. The octagonal *church* (1823; T. Hardwick), joining the 15C hospital church of St. Bartholomew the Less, is charming, un-archaeologically Gothic. In 1834 P. Hardwick practically rebuilt Gibbs' early 18C *Gatehouse*, and the walls to the left and right, in 1842 he added the *Receiving Room* and a new block to the N of Gibbs' hall range, all very sympathetically. The hospital was further expanded at the end of the 19C along Giltspur St. Running S from the W side of West Smithfield is Little Britain, which starts off blandly, but where it changes direction E, becomes a delightful enclave of Victorian office and commercial buildings. On the N side, *Nos 9–10*, late 19C in Tudor style, and *No. 12* (1858; T. Young and Son), a red brick and stone warehouse, with arcading on every storey. Before this, in King Edward St, a large, grim *post office* (1907–11; Sir Henry Tanner), with a statue of *Sir Rowland Hill* (1881; E. Onslow Ford) in front. *Postman's Park*, the churchyard of the late 18C St. Botolph's, Aldersgate, contains an uplifting series of plaques recording examples of heroism.

Gresham St to E, was formed in 1845 by the joining together of two ancient lanes. The best buildings are at its E end, but, leading off to the S, in Foster Lane, the *Goldsmiths' Hall* (1835; P. Hardwick), rich classical with a very good interior. Further down Gresham St, on the corner of King St, opposite the *Guildhall*, *Nos 42–4*, (1850; Sancton Wood), very nicely detailed Italianate. The buildings to the E of this are stuccoed and more restrained, but, on the N side, on the corner of Basinghall St, is a prominent stone classical building, *Gresham College* (1912; D. Watney and S. Perks), with an elaborate doorway in Basinghall St. In Basinghall St, on the corner of Guildhall Buildings, the former *Guildhall Library* (1870–73; Sir. H. Jones), Perp. and very ecclesiastical in feel. *Guildhall Buildings* (1893; Andrew Murray) are also Perp. On the E side of Basinghall St, *Nos 13–14*, Library Chambers (c 1875), and, just to the N, an archway into *Mason's Avenue*, which has 1920s half-timbering all down the N side and a pub at the E end with convincing Grinling Gibbons style carving. Mason's Avenue emerges into Coleman St, its narrow, canyon-like character destroyed by new buildings on the W side but with, on the E side, a number of classical Victorian buildings including, at the N end, the *Armourer's and Brazier's Hall* (1840; J.H. Good), modest with an elaborate heraldic centrepiece. Running parallel with Coleman St, and despite its ancient name laid out only in the 1830s, is Moorgate. S of London Wall, worth noting are *Nos 1–5*, on the corner of Lothbury, a classical building of 1903 (Mountford and Grüning), *Nos 7–9*, Basildon House, late 19C Baroque but with Grecian detailing, and *Nos 13–15*, on the corner of King's Arms Yard, a striking Flemish Gothic stone building of 1890–93 (Aston Webb and Ingress Bell). E, in Great Swan Alley, the wonderfully picturesque, free Baroque *•Institute of Chartered Accountants* (1890–93; J. Belcher), with sculptural ornament by Hamo Thorneycroft and J.J. Stevenson, and a fine interior. Copthall Avenue, beyond, has late 19C buildings on its E side, including *Nos 19–27* (1890; Basil Champneys), red brick, with curious pediments.

No. 7 Lothbury (1866; G. Somers Clarke)

Gresham St continues into Lothbury, with the *Bank of England* (see above p. 201) occupying the S side. On the N side, next to Wren's St. Margaret's Church, the excellent Venetian Gothic of Somers Clarke's

*No. 7 (1868), with a longer return elevation in Tokenhouse Yard. After this the road narrows into Throgmorton St, the S side of which is taken up with the backside of the *Stock Exchange*. Further up on the N side, a good range of buildings dating from the mid 19C to the early 20C and displaying virtually the whole gamut of Victorian eclecticism. The most important is *Drapers' Hall*, of which the two bays furthest E, straightforwardly classical, and the three narrow Baroque bays next to them are by Herbert Williams (1868–69). The eight-bay W addition (1898–99; T.G. Jackson), with bearded caryatids around the entrance, is brick and stone Jacobean, the rear elevation in Throgmorton Avenue good neo-Wren. In the extreme W bay of Jackson's addition, an archway leads into Throgmorton Avenue, laid out by W.W. Pocock in 1874 with one really noteworthy building the *Carpenters' Hall* (1876; Pocock), at its N end, now facing on to London Wall. Beyond Drapers' Hall, in Throgmorton St, *No. 26*, its W part Italianate (1871; W. Burnet), built for the Ottoman Bank, the E part Gothic (1869; T.C. Clarke). At the bend of Old Broad St, an archway under the plain mid 19C Gothic *No. 123* leads into Austin Friars, which now consists mainly of Victorian and Edwardian buildings around three sides of the rebuilt Dutch church. Most notable are *No. 12*, a nice brick building in Queen Anne Style (1883; E. Grüning), *No. 23* (1888; A. Webb and I. Bell), an eccentric design, and *No. 28* (1894; Charles Reilly Sr), with brick and terracotta detailing. In Old Broad St, *No. 122* is a large, gently curving Italianate bank spoilt at ground-floor level. Opposite, on the E side, *Nos 13–17*, Royal Bank of Scotland (1861; E.N. Clifton), a regular stone-faced palazzo. Most important is *No. 19*, Philip Hardwick's City of London Club (1833–34), its austere frontage concealing an opulent interior. The E stretch of London Wall is largely post-war, but, on the S side, between Great Winchester St and Copthall St, is an uninterrupted row of Victorian buildings, including the Carpenters' Hall and a richly detailed *building* of 1879 on the other corner of Throgmorton Avenue. On the N side, a large Edwardian block, the front of which looks, with other large Edwardian and inter-war blocks, on to Finsbury Circus. In Blomfield St, the best Victorian building is *No. 23*, Finsbury House (1877; E.C. Robins), on the corner into Finsbury Circus, built in Palladian style as the London Mission House.

Blomfield St continues into Liverpool St, where one should pause at the site of *Broad St Station*, opened in 1865 and demolished in 1985 to make way for the Broadgate Centre. 9 years after Broad St Station came *Liverpool St Station*, serving the Great Eastern Railway. Its present appearance is the result of two building campaigns. The original station (1873–75; E. Wilson), with a stock brick Gothic facade lying at right angles to the street and magnificent cast-iron and glass shed, is best viewed from the corner of Old Broad St, in front of the *Railway Tavern* (1877) or the nice symmetrical Italianate building, *Nos 76–80*, next to it in Old Broad St. Alongside the station, Charles Barry Jr added the red-brick and terracotta *Great Eastern Hotel* (1884), extended (1894–95; R.W. Edis) in similar vein towards and along Bishopsgate, to include the *Abercorn Rooms*, the bar of which has some good fittings. At the same time, the less exciting *eastern train-shed* was built.

Bishopsgate, Queenhithe

Opposite Liverpool St Station, on the E side of Bishopsgate, between Devonshire Row and New St, there is a good group of Victorian and

Edwardian buildings, with narrow frontages and in various historical styles. Set back in the middle, and now a clothes shop, is a Gothic *fire station* of 1885. Further N, *Dirty Dicks*, a colourful pub with a Victorian front. Near the corner of Brushfield St is the City's most notable Art Nouveau building, the *Bishopsgate Institute* (1894; C.H. Townsend), with an elaborately moulded front of buff terracotta topped by turrets. Above its fine, wide main entrance, a frieze with a stylised tree motif. A generally plain interior, with the exception of the hall. To the N, a number of Victorian office buildings, especially on the E side, threatened by the City's determination to widen Bishopsgate at that point. To the S, on the W side, the 18C church of St. Botolph is an important landmark. In its churchyard, the charming neo-Wren *Fanmakers' Hall* (1861), formerly St. Botolph's Church School, with 18C figures in the niches. Also, just E of the churchyard, towards Old Broad St, the Turkish-looking *restaurant*, built as a Turkish bath, is a delightful architectural eccentricity. Further S, most of the E side of Bishopsgate has been redeveloped recently on a new alignment. On the W side, on the corner of Threadneedle St, *National Westminster Bank* (1864– 65; J. Gibson). Built, like Soane's Bank of England, of one storey, it has a richly moulded facade with Corinthian columns and statues along the parapet. Inside, a magnificent banking hall, top-lit by three glazed domes. The whole building was at one time threatened with demolition to make way for the new *Nat West Tower*, but was reprieved and now acts as a footstool to Seifert's tower. On the opposite corner with Threadneedle St, another bank, the first of a continuous row of stone-fronted Victorian buildings, which gradually increase in scale towards Cornhill. The best of these is the palatial *Royal Bank of Scotland*, Nos 1–3 (1877; T.C. Clarke). On the E side, just before St. Helen's Place, one Victorian survival is *No. 48*, a narrow and elaborately carved building with good ironwork. Running E is Leadenhall St, now dominated by the new *Lloyds Building*. Its most important Victorian building, Norman Shaw's *New Zealand Chambers* (1873), was destroyed by bombs in the war. Off Leadenhall St, to the N, in St. Mary Axe, *Baltic Exchange* (1900–03; Smith and Wimble), a grand classical building with a feebly small pediment. Further E, Creechurch Lane has a number of mid–late Victorian warehouses and offices on its E side, and, running off its W side, in Bury St, *No. 32* (1914) is a pioneering building by Dutch architect Berlage for a Dutch shipping company. A unique product of the continental avant-garde in the City.

Bishopsgate continues into Gracechurch St. Opposite the nicely modelled stone Baroque facade of *Nos 1–2*, on the E side, is the entrance to *Leadenhall Market* (1881; Horace Jones), laid out in a cross form, the market and shops being covered by a splendid canopy of decorative ironwork and glass. On the E side of the market, off Lime St, in Cullum St, *Bolton House* (1907) has a jolly frontage with green and blue majolica trimmings. In Lime St, the *Bunch of Grapes* has a vine frieze in the bar and, outside at first-floor level, a coat of arms bearing the appropriate legend 'vinum exhilarat animum'. Following the curve of the street to the S, the *Ship* was a fine Victorian pub until recently 'restored'. In Fenchurch St, on the N side, *Nos 150–2* is an attractive narrow building in Venetian Gothic style. *Fenchurch St Station* (1854; G. Berkeley), serving the former London, Tilbury and Southend Railway, lurks in Railway Place and has a curved pediment of excessive width, reflecting the train shed. The best building in Fenchurch St is *Lloyd's Register of Shipping* (1900–01), a brilliantly successful attempt by Thomas Collcutt to fuse Baroque form and Arts and Crafts detail. The external sculpture is by George Frampton and the magnificent interior contains more of his sculpture, as well as paintings by Brangwyn, Gerald Moira and E.J. Lambert. The building takes the corner of Lloyd's Avenue, laid out at the same time and described by David Lloyd as 'the most impressive turn of the century commercial street in the City'—unfortunately eaten into by mediocre new developments since he wrote in 1976. Collcutt supervised most of the building, thus giving the street architectural coherence. The restrained classical *No. 8* is Norman Shaw's last building (1908), and, innovative as ever, he used a reinforced concrete frame, one of the first in London. Lloyds Avenue connects Fenchurch St and Crutched Friars. At the bottom, in Crosswall, is an *office* (1881–83) built for Fenchurch St Station, a reticent and subtly asymmetrical Italianate design. Crutched Friars bends around into Jewry St, with *Sir John Cass College* (1895; A.W. Cooksey), William and Mary style. In Aldgate High St, Cooksey's *Sir John Cass School*, nine years later and more Baroque. Red brick and Portland stone. Also in Aldgate, the 18C *St. Botolph's Church*, given an extraordinary new Arts and Crafts Gothic ceiling (1889; Bentley).

Returning SW, Crutched Friars continues into Hart St, containing the *Ship*, a small pub of 1887 with elaborately carved and moulded decoration on the facade. Left into Mark Lane, where *Nos 59–61* (1864; George Aitchison), a powerful Italian Gothic building, is an important early example of iron construction. S, at the junction of Great Tower St and Byward St, is *Christ's Hospital* (1914; C.J. Blomfield), Queen Anne style. Byward St leads into Lower Thames St with, on the S side, beyond the long and monotonous Custom House of 1817, Sir Horace Jones' *Billingsgate Market* (1875), like his other market buildings, in a light, semi-classical idiom. It is now disused and awaiting conversion. As Lower Thames St has little else to offer, turn N up Lovat Lane. On the E side, Wren's church of *St. Mary at Hill* contains some neo-Wren fittings (1848–49; W. Gibbs Rogers), so convincing that this more than any other Wren church conforms most closely to the appearance his contemporaries would have known. Emerging into Eastcheap, one is confronted on the N side by *Nos 33–5* (1868; R.L. Roumieu), a crazy and dazzling Gothic building which breaks *all* the rules. *Nos 23–5* is also extraordinary, being a mid 19C Romanesque-Moorish concoction with polychrome brickwork and a cornice enlivened with beasts' heads. The S side of Eastcheap was widened in the 1870s, and most of the buildings date from the 1880s and 1890s. *No. 20*, Peel House (1884), by City Architect A.M. Peebles, has some interesting Egyptian style details, including a panel over the door with camels. On the corner of Fish Hill, the *Monument* pub, with a panel in the splayed corner at second-floor level showing the Monument in its late 19C setting. The present setting does not bear favourable comparison.

W of this is an area almost wholly the result of 1830s and 1840s replanning. London Bridge was rebuilt, and King William St laid out to join it to the heart of the City. Surviving from this time, on the approach to London Bridge, is Henry Roberts' fine Greek Revival *Fishmongers' Hall* (1834). Cannon St had existed in the Middle Ages, but in the 1840s it was widened and extended as far as St. Paul's, under the direction of J.B. Bunning. Noteworthy survivors from Bunning's original layout include the block on the S side between Dowgate Hill and College Hill. On the N side, *No. 103* (1886; F. Jameson), Venetian-Byzantine, and *Nos 123–7* (1895; A.H. Gordon), red brick and terra-cotta. *Cannon St Station*, built originally in 1865, was largely rebuilt

Nos 33–35 Eastcheap (1868; R.L. Roumieu)

exactly 100 years later by John Poulson. However, the *towers* (E.M. Barry) which flanked the river end of the train-shed, with their squat lanterns and spires, survive, and a fine view of one of these and the impressive retaining walls, with blank arcades, can be seen down Dowgate Hill. On the W side of Dowgate Hill, no less than three City livery company halls. *Dyers' Hall* (1839), appropriately enough by Charles Dyer of Bristol, is Palladian in character. *Skinners' Hall*, 17C with a Georgian facade, is entered through *No. 6*, a red-brick Venetian Gothic building. *Tallow Chandlers' Hall*, also 17C in origin, has a very attractive Italianate courtyard of 1870–71. To the W, in Cloak Lane, the Jacobean *College Hill Chambers*, and, in College St,

Innholders' Hall (1886), a building interesting only for the older features it incorporates. Upper Thames St is a hideous and dangerous thoroughfare which has to be crossed in order to get to Queen St Place, the approach to Southwark Bridge, dominated on the W side by *Thames House* (1911; Collcutt and Hamp), large and exuberant with plenty of sculpture. Just beyond, facing Vintners Place, on the W side of the 17C Vintners' Hall, a delightful Coade stone statue of a schoolboy, dating from 1840. The warehouses and wharves S of St. Paul's have now largely disappeared, leaving just a few reminders of the industrial character of the area, before it was sacrificed to office building and the convenience of motor traffic. In Garlick Hill survive a number of robust *warehouses* with gantries and loading bays, empty at the time of writing but suitable for conversion. S of Queen Victoria St is the Queenhithe area, destroyed by Upper Thames St. One or two riverside *warehouses* remain, such as that on the corner of Bull Wharf Lane and Upper Thames St. On the E side of Queenhithe is a pleasant group of buildings, in particular *Nos 20–1*, with attractive Arts and Crafts detailing. It is worth walking down to the bottom of Queenhithe for a tast of the old riverside and for a fine view of *Bankside Power Station*.

CITY OF WESTMINSTER

Hyde Park

19C improvements to the old Royal park began with the fine stone *bridge* (1826–28) and under D. Burton various small Greek Revival lodges were erected along the E side at the same time as the entrance screen at Hyde Park Corner. The Victorian gates to the Park are mostly of highly ornate ironwork along the S side (Queen's Gate 1858). At the N end of the Serpentine, *Italian Gardens* (1860–61) with stone terraces, pavilion and sculpture by J. Thomas replacing an open sewer. To the S, *Peter Pan statue* (1912; G. Frampton), in the gardens where the eternal boy landed nightly according to J.M. Barrie's 'The Little White Bird'. Nearby, *Physical Energy* by G.F. Watts (begun 1883, cast 1906), a most advanced work for its time, a man on horseback symbolising controlled energy, the modelling exaggerated and the surface deeply pitted to emphasise unity with the earth. An earlier casting stands over the tomb of Cecil Rhodes at Cape Town. By the bridge, *Serpentine Gallery* (1908; H. Tanner), well designed neo-Georgian. At the NE corner *Marble Arch* (1828; J. Nash), originally the front screen to Buckingham Palace, moved here in 1851 when the forecourt building of the Palace was added. Fine cast-iron gates, but the arch is dwarfed by roads and large buildings. At the SE corner a comically sentimental statue of *Byron* (1880; R.C. Belt) with his dog, Boatswain, gazing up.

Belgravia and Pimlico

Hyde Park Corner is a large space that despite all the efforts of the 19C fails to be imposingly monumental although individual buildings are handsome. *Apsley House* (1828–29; B. and P. Wyatt, recasing work by Adam 1771) was presented to the Duke of Wellington by the nation in 1820 and contains the Wellington Museum. The *screen* to Hyde Park dates from 1825 and the old *St. George's Hospital* from 1829 (W. Wilkins), the upper floor an unfortunate addition of 1859. In the centre, *Constitution Arch* (1828; D. Burton), originally marking the N approach to the Palace, on axis with the screen. The arch was removed to its present site in 1883 when the colossal equestrian statue of Wellington (1846) mounted on top was taken to Aldershot, Hampshire. It had much annoyed the Duke by appearing to point an imperious baton into his upper windows. The present Victory group dates from 1911 (A. Jones) and Wellington has a dull statue nearer ground level (1888; Boehm).

The W side of Hyde Park Corner is partly filled up by the N end of a big group of palatial stone houses with French Second Empire pavilion roofs (1863–70; T. Cundy III) that stretches from Grosvenor Crescent down Grosvenor Place to Grosvenor Gardens by Victoria Station. This marks the E edge of the *Belgravia estate* of the Dukes of Westminster. The estate was planned c 1822 and the principal square, *Belgrave Square*, was built from 1825 (G. Basevi), introducing the white stucco that unifies the whole estate. Belgrave Square is monumental, the centres of each side marked by giant columns. In the corners are smaller town houses. The biggest, in the SE corner, *Sefton House* (1842; P. Hardwick), has, inside, a most opulent onyx staircase of c 1900 done for Lord Howard de Walden. N of the Square, *Wilton Crescent* (1825), refaced in Portland stone (c 1910; Balfour and Turner) when the original stucco seemed too cheap. The brick church (1840; T. Cundy II) was the scene of disturbances over ritualistic practices under the first vicar, Bennett. It now has a High Church chancel (1892; Bodley). To the N, *Nos 15–17, Knightsbridge*, an ornate yellow brick pair of town houses (c 1860) at the E end. W of Wilton Place a whole block in a free Edwardian mixture of red brick and carved stone (1903–04; Caroe). On the opposite side, *Albert Gate* (1845; T. Cubitt), two very large stucco mansions, framing the entrance to Hyde Park, built to provide a formal N approach to the Belgravia estate for which Cubitt was chief developer. The E side mansion was owned by G. Hudson, 'the Napoleon of the railways', and became the French ambassador's house after Hudson's bankruptcy. Beyond the W side mansion a handsome stone fronted bank (1850; G. Porter) and then the *Hyde Park Hotel* (1888; Archer and Green), a real asset to the skyline from the Park with its great array of French pavilion roofs and cupolas. To the S, *Lowndes Square* (1837–46), developed by T. Cubitt, except for the S side (1837–39) where his brother Lewis Cubitt built a terrace of unusually strong detail, Italianate but with a hint of Elizabethan. S of Belgrave Square is the heart of Thomas Cubitt's building work for the Grosvenor estate, *Eaton Place* and *Eaton Square*. The E ends are earlier and a stylistic progression can be seen from the big columns and pilasters that ornament the houses of the late 1820s, set against stock brick, to the stucco slightly Greek detail of the 1830s, still with large pilasters, and finally to the Italianate of the 1850s, without pilasters but with grand cornices. The church at the E end (1824–27; Hakewill) has an interior made ecclesiastical to later Victorian taste (1875; A. Blomfield) by inserting Romanesque arcades within the original classical box. At the W end of the Square in *Eaton Gate*, a block of buildings of c 1900 (Balfour and Turner), most original in the combination of Portland stone lower floors and brown brick gabled upper parts. In the manner of Philip Webb, the detail is stylised to avoid period reference. The stucco district stretches on S to Ebury St. At the E end of Ebury St, another well designed later group, *Lygon Place* (1910; Balfour and Turner). At the W end, artisan flats (1871), with attractive iron balconies to the outside stairs.

On Pimlico Rd, *St. Barnabas' Church* (1847–50; T. Cundy II), the very model of a church built on the principles of the ecclesiologists, built for Bennett, the High Church vicar of Knightsbridge. The design is so carefully correct as to arouse suggestions that it may have been

Butterfield's. A ragstone group of church, schools and priest's house, around a courtyard, quite the antithesis of the large preaching churches of a few years earlier. The interior had all the elements of revived Anglican worship: raised altar and sanctuary, chancel screen, carved font and stained glass. The original stained glass was by Wailes, but much has been replaced. Succeeding High Church vicars introduced new fittings of great quality. The wall-painting, reredos and screen are by Bodley (1893 and 1906), the Lady Chapel by Comper (1900). In Buckingham Palace Rd, late 19C houses and, by Eccleston St, *Chantrey House* (1907), handsome block of flats in red brick with delicate ribbons carved in the gables. To N, *Grosvenor Hotel* (1860; J.T. Knowles), a railway hotel of exceptional splendour crowned by bulbous French roofs. Recent cleaning has revealed the quality of the stock brick and of the naturalistic leaf decoration. Portrait busts decorate the first and top floors. *Victoria Station*, behind, is an amalgam of parts, the far side the original station of 1860 with yellow brick buildings and iron train-shed (1862; J. Fowler) refronted in Portland stone (1908; A. Blomfield). The part nearer the hotel is all of 1898, also with a Portland stone front, for a different railway company.

S of the station, around Belgrave Rd is *Pimlico*, a further development by T. Cubitt, begun c 1836 (Eccleston Square) but mostly of the 1840s to 1860s. The scale is smaller and the set-piece squares less impressive than in Belgravia. Stucco is the prevailing material with large ragstone churches by T. Cundy II in Warwick Square and St. George's Square. The Warwick Square *church* has elaborate chancel decoration of the 1890s in alabaster and tile mosaic with high altar by J.F. Bentley. On Grosvenor Rd, along the river, by the railway bridge, *Pumping Station* (1875), decked out with a green French curved roof and the chimney disguised as a tall campanile. In Vauxhall Bridge Rd, *St. James the Less' Church* (1860–61; G.E. Street), a key High Victorian church in polychrome brick of great strength with an almost detached tower capped with a Rhenish type roof of short spire flanked by four spirelets. The interior is brick with circular granite piers to the arcade. Exceptional fittings, carved pulpit, low iron chancel rails on stone wall with inlaid decoration, and reredos, all by Street, stained glass by Clayton and Bell and a painted chancel arch by G.F. Watts. The quality of Street's ironwork, always vigorous, is unsurpassed in the external iron railings. Street also designed the *school* to complete the group (1863–66).

Westminster

Westminster Abbey is the principal national shrine, a role which threatened to flood the building with marble memorials by the end of the 19C. The Abbey itself went through drastic alterations, rebuildings or just damage from the 17C onwards. Equally drastic were the 19C attempts to recreate the original of which the most obvious is the N transept front, the work of G.G. Scott from 1875 and J.L. Pearson from 1878–90. Both Scott and Pearson researched carefully the previous form of the transept and analysed the carved stonework found as work proceeded. The finished front is a fine thing in itself, but the cost of achieving a homogeneous 13C look was the loss of historical authenticity. Scott's other major work was the restoration of the chapter house, giving it the tall pointed roof, completely rebuilding the vault and central pier and renewing the carving. A splendid 13C space has been recreated from what was quite battered, but the cost again was high. Inside, nearly every famous Victorian sculptor is represented and nearly every famous Victorian commemorated. From the W end, on the W wall, statue of the *7th Earl of Shaftesbury* (died 1885; Boehm). To the N side, splendid effigy in bronze on marble to the *3rd Marquess of Salisbury* (1909; W. Goscombe John, to design by G.F. Bodley). On the W wall busts to *Joseph Chamberlain* (died 1914; Tweed) and *General Gordon* (1892; O. Ford). In the N aisle, behind the choir stalls, are the musicians and scientists, the scientists with a group of five portrait medallions. Effigy of *Lord John Thynne* (1884; H.H. Armstead, designed J.L. Pearson) and splendid statue of *Wilberforce* (1838; S. Joseph), a memorable combination of kindliness and energy. In the nave itself, architects and explorers, *David Livingstone*, movingly inscribed, *Scott, Barry, Pearson* and *Street*, and the engineer *Stephenson*, all with fine brasses. The S side begins with the War Memorial chapel, earlier memorials to *Henry Fawcett* (1887; A. Gilbert) with fine metalwork, *General Booth, Charles Kingsley* (died 1875; Woolner) and *F.D. Maurice* (died 1872; Woolner), founder of the Working Men's College. In the aisle, the Indian mutiny soldiers, *Outram* (died 1863; Noble) and *Lord Lawrence* (1879; Woolner). Behind the choir stalls, a nice portrait pair to the *Wesley brothers* (1875; Adams-Acton). The choir screen, recently brilliantly repainted, is of 1828 (Blore) and carries handsome *organ cases* (1895–97; Pearson). Choir stalls beyond, also by Blore. The *high altar* and mosaic reredos are part of Scott's restoration. The N transept is the heaviest with Victorian statuary: the row of statesmen, *Peel* (1852; J. Gibson) in classical dress, *Gladstone* (1903; Brock) in academic dress, *Disraeli* (died 1881; Boehm) in Garter robes, *Sir John Malcolm* (1838; Chantrey), administrator in India, in military dress, and the three Cannings, the Prime Minister *George Canning* (1834; Chantrey), *Earl Canning* (died 1862; Foley), Governor General of India during the Mutiny, and *Lord Stratford de Redclyffe* (died 1880; Boehm), ambassador to Constantinople. Opposite, the enormous monument to the elder Pitt (1784), *Palmerston* (1870; Jackson), and *Castlereagh* (died 1822; J.E. Thomas). In the W aisle busts of Lord *Aberdeen*, Prime Minister (1874; Noble), *C. Buller*, reformist politician (died 1848; Weekes), *Sir H. Edwardes*, soldier (died 1868; Theed), and *Cobden*, radical and free-trader (died 1865; Woolner). In the closed off E aisle, monument to the explorer *Franklin* (1875; Noble), with inscription by Tennyson and statues of the lawyer *Sir W.W. Follett* (died 1845; Behnes) and the engineer *Telford* (1839; Baily). The S Transept became 'Poets' Corner' in the 18C and busts and plaques have proliferated ever since, some contemporary, many added years after. There is an almost contemporary bust of *Longfellow* (1884; Brock), one of *Tennyson* in middle age (1857; Woolner), strongly featured, *Southey* (1844; Weekes), also good, the epitaph by *Wordsworth*, who has a full statue (1854; Thrupp). *Coleridge* (T. Thornycroft) and *Burns* (1885; Steell) were commemorated long after their deaths. *Thomas Campbell* is buried near his statue (1848; W.C. Marshall). Also buried here, *Dickens, Browning, Macaulay, Tennyson, Hardy* and *Kipling. Ruskin* has a bronze plaque (c 1900; O. Ford) on the S wall, *Thackeray* an unflattering bust (c 1863; Marochetti) on the W wall where are also *John Keble* (1872; Woolner) and *George Grote* (1855; C. Bacon). The E parts of the Abbey, crowded with Elizabethan and Jacobean monuments already, have few 19C intruders save, to the rear of Henry VII's chapel, the fine marble monument to the *Duc de Montpensier* (1830; Westmacott) brother of Louis Philippe. Nearby is the effigy of *Dean Stanley* (1884; Boehm), liberal theologian and the Dean responsible for the major part of the restoration of the Abbey. In the S aisle, a select group of imperialists, Cromer, Curzon, Milner and Rhodes. To the rear of the cloisters in Little Dean's Yard, *Westminster School. No. 3* (1896; T.G. Jackson) ruins a continuous facade of 1790, though a pretty building in itself. *Dean's Yard* has mostly 19C W and N sides. The N side with the archway and stone fronts to Broad Sanctuary is a Gothic terrace (1854; G.G. Scott), like part of a college quadrangle but each side of the arch quite different. In front, Gothic Westminster School *Crimean War Memorial* (1859; Scott), with carving by J.B. Philip. Lord Raglan, the commander-in- chief, was an old boy of the school.

Victoria St runs W from the Abbey, constructed 1845–51 through densely populated slums. Most of the original buildings have since gone save the nicely ornate *Prince Albert* pub half-way up. N of Victoria St, facing the Abbey, *Central Hall* (1905–11; Lanchester and Rickards), French Beaux Arts in inspiration, an enormous square dome crowning the auditorium. The detail as well as the style suggests more a Continental or Latin American public building than the main assembly hall of the Wesleyan Church. Spectacular Baroque staircase inside. Further W, Caxton St, *St. Ermin's Hotel* (1887; E.T. Hall), large red brick and stone, the last of the big hotels that once filled this end of Victoria St. Buckingham Gate, beyond, has the *Westminster Chapel* (1864; W.F. Poulton), polychrome brick with a large oval interior, the principal London Congregational church boasting a history of dynamic ministers who could fill the space and more. At the end of Castle Lane, Palace St, with large utilitarian *school* block (1876; R.R. Arntz), in front a *statue* of Alderman Waterlow, pioneer of improved housing in London. Late 19C houses in Palace St but the best is back in Buckingham Gate, *No. 20* (1895; R. Blomfield), very elegant gabled red brick with a pretty oriel and delicate bronze ship. *No. 10*, facing Buckingham Palace, the Duchy of Cornwall offices (1854; J. Pennethorne), is Italianate in decorous stucco. *Nos 5–9* were a row of grand stucco houses, the closest a citizen might get to the Palace, and *No. 2* (1860–61; J. Murray) a large hotel in the Italian palazzo style, well handled. E of No. 10, Birdcage Walk with the stucco *Wellington Barracks* (1833–59). The *chapel*, bombed in 1944, has been rebuilt, keeping the splendid mosaic-covered apse (1877–79; G.E. Street) from the damaged building, also Street's font.

S of Westminster Abbey a tight area of late 17C streets interspersed since the late 19C with buildings associated with the Anglican Church whose administrative offices are in Dean's Yard. *St. Edward's House* (1905; Caroe), at the corner of Great College St, ecclesiastical Gothic in red brick, *Faith House* (1905; Lutyens), Tufton St, small scale and handsomely designed neo-Georgian, and, at the foot of Great College St, *No. 1 Millbank* (1903; Caroe), the offices of the Church Commissioners, brick and stone, very freely detailed with mullioned windows and the little scrolls that appear in other Caroe buildings—his assistants called them 'Caroe's worms'. On the corner of Cowley St, *The Corner House* (1911; Lutyens), large neo-Georgian pair of houses. In the gardens S of the Houses of Parliament, Rodin's *• Burghers of Calais* (1895), as powerful a sculptural group as will be found anywhere in Britain. At the other end, the *Buxton Fountain* (1865; C. Buxton with S.S. Teulon), charming octagonal stone building with painted enamel panels on the roof. Beyond Lambeth Bridge, on Millbank, *•Tate Gallery* (1897; S.R.J. Smith), cheerful Portland stone classical building with a dome, paid for by the sugar tycoon Sir Henry Tate. The National Gallery of British Art contains major 19C paintings, the collection steadily enhanced as works are brought out of store. The Modern Collection begins with outstanding Impressionist works. Behind, off

John Islip St, the *Millbank Estate* (1899–1903; LCC Architects Dept), the most famous of the pioneering housing estates of the new London County Council. Tall red-brick blocks detailed simply with sash windows and steep gables. The first blocks have white gables showing over blunt parapets, strong simple chimneys and splayed-off angles, all showing the influence of advanced Arts and Crafts architects like Webb and Lethaby. From *Vauxhall Bridge* (1904–06), with some sadly placed but good quality bronze sculpture against the piers, Vauxhall Bridge Rd leads N (for St. James' Church see above p. 214). On the E side, Rochester Row with *church* (1847–49; B. Ferrey), serious Dec., the spire sadly lopped. It was built in the midst of slums by Baroness Burdett Coutts as a memorial to her father. Further up, a courtyard group of *almshouses* (1881; M.B. Adams). Opposite the top of Vauxhall Bridge Rd, in Victoria St, the *Victoria Palace* (1911; F. Matcham), a white glazed front capped by a cupola, the style somewhere between Beaux Arts classical and English Baroque. Lush interior.

Westminster Cathedral (1895–1903; J.F. Bentley)

Further E, off Victoria St, *Westminster Cathedral* (1895–1903; J.F.

Bentley), the prime RC church in England and Wales, and the crown of Catholic aspirations in England since Catholic emancipation in 1829 and the restoration of the English hierarchy in 1850. Bentley's design replaced earlier Gothic schemes with one of cathedral scale and dignity that could suffer nothing from comparison to the medieval Gothic of Westminster Abbey, or indeed the classicism of St. Paul's. The roots of Bentley's design are Byzantine but yet in detail, combination of details and exterior form so original and personal that the issue of derivation seems minor. Bentley, like Webb, had a genius for detail, for simplifying decorative forms to complement the main lines of the architecture. Note the way that the red brick and Portland stone are combined such that the basic insistent horizontal rhythms are varied by closer spacing of the bands or interrupted for decorative treatment over arches. The exterior repays knowing well the interior grandeur overwhelms at first visit. Wider and higher than any Gothic cathedral in Britain, the central space is awesome, composed of four shallow saucer domes carried on plain brick transverse arches. The side arches are subdivided into two, also displaying the same massive plain brick. Light comes from small arched windows in the E dome and at the E end, also from side windows but diffused by the immense thickness of the side arches. All this darkness is contrasted with the marble facing of the lower part of the church which shows Bentley's mastery in the handling of colour. Carved detail and plain colour complement each other without distracting from the main lines. The marbles themselves are superb. At the E end, a lovely baldacchino and hanging cross focus the design. Over the apse arch is the one piece executed of the mosaic that was to have covered all the bare brickwork. Note also the hanging light fittings, proof that suitable designs for electric lights are possible in a cathedral. The *Stations of the Cross* (1913–18; Eric Gill) are most powerful relief sculpture. The chapels vary in the quality of the decoration, some being decorated by Bentley, some after his death by his partner Marshall. On the S side, the *Holy Souls Chapel* is most completely Bentley with exceptional coloured marble work. By the transept door, chantry to Cardinal Vaughan by Marshall with effigy by J. Adams-Acton. The SW *Blessed Sacrament Chapel* has very good marble and metal work by Marshall, the mosaics were added in 1953–61. On the N side, the Lady Chapel mosaics date from 1931. Behind are the stairs to the crypt, where Cardinals Wiseman and Manning are buried. Along the N aisle are the *Chapel of St. Andrew* (c 1912; R.W. Schulz) in a lovely blue grey marble with bold metal screen and wonderfully delicate inlaid stalls of ebony and ivory by Ernest Gimson, the *Chapel of St. Patrick* in green marble, and the *Chapel of SS. Gregory and Augustine* by Bentley with a fine altarpiece and rich mosaics. The baptistery attached is also by Bentley. Beyond the Cathedral is the *Archbishop's House* and *Clergy House* complex divided from the E end of the Cathedral by the *Diocesan Hall*, all by Bentley.

Whitehall

The Houses of Parliament (1839–60; Charles Barry). The Old Palace of Westminster was burnt, apart from the magnificent Westminster Hall (1394–1401) and the early 14C crypt of St. Stephen's Chapel. Barry won the 1835 competition that for historical reasons specified a Gothic or Elizabethan style, incidentally marking an important leap forward for the Gothic Revival. Barry's design was Perp. of c 1500 in style, closely and richly modelled in a regular rhythm of bay windows, buttresses and pinnacles. It is the antithesis between the regularity of detail and of major sections of the facades and the dramatic asymmetry of the range of towers and spires—beginning with Big Ben at the N end, continuing with the delicate lantern spire over the central lobby and terminated at the S end by the colossal bulk of the Victoria Tower—that makes the complex outstandingly satisfying visually. Essentially, a long and wholly symmetrical river front of two storeys punctuated by six three-storey towers gives the clue to the classical planning of the main spaces arranged along a central spine between the outer ranges. From the central lobby vaulted passages lead N to the House of Commons and S to the House of Lords. Beyond the House of Lords on the same central spine is the Royal Gallery, allowing the royal entrance to be at the S end under the Victoria Tower. The road

The Houses of Parliament, Victoria Tower (1839–60; Sir C. Barry), Whitehall

front is by contrast quite asymmetrical, the reason for this being the survival of the two medieval buildings towards the N end. The main entrance leads into the vaulted St. Stephen's Hall and hence to the central lobby, but the Hall is not at right angles to the main spine as it stands over the medieval crypt. The interior is of a wealth that baffles brief description for Barry had the assistance from 1836 to 1852 of A.W.N. Pugin for the metalwork, carving, furniture, wall-paintings and hangings, tiles, carpets and stained glass. Pugin's dedication to the Gothic Revival, his fantastic capacity for detailed design and his inventiveness are the reason that so massive a public building rarely sinks inside to arid grandiosity. The Houses of Parliament also encompass the story of the revival of public sculpture in Britain, the creation of a national school of historical painters, the rediscovery of fresco, all this the influence of Prince Albert, the other tireless figure in the history of the building. Albert saw the building as a vehicle for reviving the arts of public decoration, on the model of the Royal Palace at Munich, and the appropriate decoration of public buildings is a way to national improvement in taste and education.

Guided tours enter from the S end up the great stair to the *Queen's Robing Room*, where Pugin's pattern decoration first appears in its full splendour. The fireplace is particularly fine. On the walls are five frescoes by Dyce of virtues illustrated from the story of King Arthur, among the best early frescoes in the building. Carved wooden panels below by Armstead. The great *Royal Gallery* beyond is dominated by the two enormous and rather darkened paintings by D. Maclise of the Death of Nelson and of Wellington and Blucher after Waterloo (1861–65). Gilt statues (c 1865–69; J.B. Philip) ornament the doors and window. There are also royal portraits. Pugin's painting covers the ceiling, but here overwhelmed by his encaustic tile floor, made by Minton. The *Prince's Chamber* beyond has a white marble statue of Queen Victoria, stiffly flanked by Justice and Clemency (1856; J. Gibson), and bronze reliefs of Tudor scenes (1853–56; W. Theed). Two fine Pugin fireplaces. The *House of Lords* is Pugin's masterpiece, a double-cube space profusely decorated in Gothic carved woodwork, the panelled ceiling suspended (in a most un-Gothic way) from a metal frame above. The colour is dark and rich, obscuring the frescoes at each end and the 18 figures of the barons of Magna Carta (cast in zinc and copper coated). Everything is focused on the throne, a piece of revived Gothic woodwork of marvellous richness and subtle colouring, a huge canopy panelled with royal arms and insignia over the chair, itself a most pleasing piece raised on lions and topped by the crown, the lion and the unicorn. The *Peers' Lobby*, encaustic tiled, opens into a corridor frescoed with Stuart and Commonwealth period scenes (1856–66; C.W. Cope) which leads to the octagonal *Central Lobby* of the building. The sculpture here, as across the whole outside of the building is by John Thomas, whose role in the detail of the exterior statuary and stonework was analogous to that of Pugin inside. Four statues, including Gladstone (1900; Pomeroy), introduce the 'petrified lobbyists', the marble figures of statesmen that fill especially the main entrance and St. Stephen's Hall to the W. Beneath St. Stephen's Hall is the medieval crypt given a rich painted decoration all over the vault and fine marble fittings. E of the Central Lobby a corridor with frescoes of 1910 leads to the Lower Waiting Hall with more Pugin decoration and marble statues. Barry is commemorated (1865; Foley) with a seated statue on the stairs. N of the Central Lobby is the domain of the House of Commons with corridor frescoed (c 1855–65) by E.M. Ward leading to the Chamber of the House of Commons, all this side destroyed in 1941, and rebuilt to a more subdued design. Big Ben, technically the name of the 13½ ton main bell, has come to be the name for the clock tower, most effectively balancing with its slim outline the enormous mass of the Victoria Tower. The Victoria Tower, 330ft high, Big Ben, 302ft with 23ft clock faces, both rise sheer from the ground. Big Ben, terminating the view over Westminster Bridge, has become, like the dome of St. Paul's, a symbol of London. Note how well the sheer, windowless tower carries the broader clock stage and how delicate is the two-stage curved pyramid roof. In front of the Houses of Parliament, *Cromwell* (1899; H. Thorneycroft), a good pensive work, and *Richard I* (1860; Marochetti), ideally chivalric on a splendid horse.

Parliament Square has a further selection of statues, *Abraham Lincoln* (St. Gaudens) and *Canning* (Westmacott) on the W side. Within the Square, Prime Ministers *Palmerston* (1876; Woolner), *Derby* (1874; Noble), *Disraeli* (1883; Raggi) and *Peel* (1876; Noble). On the W side, the former *Middlesex Guildhall* (1906–13; J.S. Gibson), one of the very best public buildings of its date, and one of the last Gothic ones. The detail is a fanciful 15C French Gothic treated with Arts and Crafts verve, contrasting plain areas of wall with concentrated carving to the porch, parapet and central tower. Sculpture of high quality by H.C. Fehr, notice the figures over the hoodmoulds of the ground-floor windows. Adjoining, *Royal Institution of Chartered Surveyors* (1896; A. Waterhouse), red brick and terracotta, until recent cleaning a drab corner of the Square. The N side has *Government Offices* (1900–15; J.M. Brydon), very large Wren style block, Portland stone with a main portico between stone cupolas and short towers at the outer corners. Bland but suitably imposing. Bridge St leads down to *Westminster Bridge* (1862; T. Page) with iron Gothic detail. At the head, *Boadicea* (1856; T. Thorneycroft), bronze chariot group of the British queen and her daughters complete with murderous swords on the axle ends.

Victoria Embankment (1864–70; Sir J. Bazalgette) runs from Westminster Bridge to Blackfriars Bridge and is one of the major Victorian improvements to London, carrying both sewerage and the underground railway. Granite retaining wall with handsome bronze dolphin lights. On left, former *New Scotland Yard* central offices of the Metropolitan Police, but now parliamentary offices. The N block (1887–90) is Norman Shaw's most original contribution to the design of public buildings. A foursquare block, the lower part in granite supporting two storeys of brick banded in stone, the corners emphasised with circular tourelles. The long roof above carries powerful banded stone and brick chimneys. Many of the details are Queen Anne, but full-blooded Baroque appears in the porch and gable ends. Since cleaning, the colourful effect is particularly good from across the Thames. The S block was added to Shaw's design 1902–06, with Cannon Row Police Station behind. Further N, set back, *Whitehall Court* (1884; Archer and Green), Portland stone block of flats with a splendid variety of tall pavilion roofs that are the element of fantasy in the view over Whitehall from St. James's Park. The N corner with the sharp corner turret is the *National Liberal Club* (1885; A. Waterhouse), similar materials, the great rooms were all decorated in coloured tile. In the gardens in front, a collection of statuary, *General Gordon* (1888; H. Thornycroft) with nice reliefs of virtues on the base, *Sir Bartle Frere* (1887; Brock) in his uniform as High Commissioner in South Africa, *William Tyndale* (1884; Boehm), and a dull *Sir James Outram* (1871; Noble). Across the road, bronze relief of *Bazalgette* (1889;

Simonds) inscribed in Latin 'he put chains on the river'. Northumberland Avenue was opened in 1876 over the site of Northumberland House. The compulsory purchase and demolition of London's grandest Jacobean house, that could have been saved by a slight adjustment to the line of the street, has been regretted ever since. The street was built up with large hotels in the 1880s *Metropole Buildings* (1885) was the Metropole Hotel, *Northumberland House* (1882–85) the Hotel Victoria. In between, *Nigeria House* was the Society for Promoting Christian Knowledge (1876; J. Gibson), architecturally the best. At the top, facing Trafalgar Square, on right, *Grand Buildings* (1878–80; F. and H. Francis), built as an hotel, the large rounded front to the Square mutilated by having the sculptural detail chiselled off.

Trafalgar Square (1826–30) is London's principal public square, a space endearingly only half-way to being grand, this due to the irregular way that some eight or nine streets run in, the strong slope, only partly disguised by levelling the centre (1840; C. Barry), and the jumble of buildings along the S side. *Nelson's Column* (1839–42; W. Railton), 187ft to the hat, much criticised at the time for lack of imagination, a Corinthian column with Nelson on top (statue by E.H. Baily), seems admirable now in the way that the slim shape appears in the view up Whitehall. The long facade of the *National Gallery* (1832–38; Wilkins), never an imposing building for all its columns, pretty dome and elevated site would have been overwhelmed by anything more massive in the Square. Around the base of the column are four bronze reliefs (1849–52) of Nelson's battles, the Nile to N, Copenhagen to E, St. Vincent to W and Trafalgar to S. Around are the great bronze lions (1858–67) modelled by the painter Landseer from a lion provided by the zoo which died inconveniently soon. Around the square are statues, the best, the equestrian *George IV* (Chantrey; 1829–43), intended for the top of Marble Arch. Two standing generals, *Sir Charles Napier* (1856; G.G. Adams), conqueror of Sind, with leonine whiskers, and *Sir Henry Havelock* (1861; Behnes), reliever of Lucknow.

Whitehall, running S, begins unpretentiously. On the right, *Old Shades and Whitehall House* (1904; Treadwell and Martin), lively free Gothic. Further down, the first official building, *Crown Estate Office* (1909; J.W. Murray), classical. Beyond, much bigger, former *War Office* (1898–1907; W. Young), inflated Baroque disguising the first two floors as a rusticated basement and the next two with an Ionic order. At the corners, Baroque cupolas. Spectacular main staircase. Opposite, behind the Horse Guards, the large red brick and stone *Admiralty* (1894–95; Leeming and Leeming), better now that it is cleaned but confused in detail. Attached to Inigo Jones' Banqueting Hall, an eclectic stone-fronted building built for the *Royal United Services Institution* (1893; A. Webb and I. Bell), pretty detail but fussy next to Inigo Jones. On the W side, the *Cabinet Office*, originally the Board of Trade, given a fine Corinthian columned front (1844–45; C. Barry) nicely set against channelled rustication. To the S, the *Foreign Office* (1868–73; Sir G.G. Scott) on a much more massive scale, compare the floor heights with Barry's building. The complex stretches right back to St. James's Park, formal and symmetrical to Whitehall, picturesquely varied with a corner tower to the Park. The story of the competition is a typical Victorian muddle. In 1856 Scott did not win, the buildings were to have been two, by different architects, a Foreign Office and a War Office, Scott's design was Ruskinian Gothic and came third. In 1858 a change of government allowed Scott to gain the commission, another change in 1859 brought in Palmerston who disliked the Gothic. By this time an India Office had replaced the War Office and Scott was able to substitute a Renaissance style and keep the commission, working with the India Office architect, M.D. Wyatt. Wyatt seems to have suggested the picturesque Park front and designed the courtyard of the India Office, but the exterior detail was Scott's. All the principal rooms were in the Park front, from left to right, the Foreign Secretary's under the pavilion with superb staircase up from Downing St, his aides in the restrained block to the right, then the India Office begins at the big tower, the Council of India rooms in the curved section, and then the main offices in a Venetian palazzo that forms the corner by King Charles St. The Renaissance detail moves easily from Bramante to Sansovino. The Whitehall front has much fine sculpture by Armstead and J.B. Philip and the overall sculptural treatment offers a good comparison with the early Victorian classicism of Barry to the N and the late Victorian classicism of Brydon to the S, in neither of which does figure sculpture or contrasting colour play any part. The unhappiest piece of sculpture is Queen Victoria on the roof. On the other side of Parliament St, smaller scale buildings stretch to Parliament Square. Some 1890s red brick and terracotta (Nos 53 and 54), the Red Lion, a good pub of the same date, and, opposite the pub, No. 47, the former Whitehall Club (1864–66; C.O. Parnell), a splendid palazzo, in the rich Venetian mode which allows for generous carving, especially on the main entrance.

St. James's Park and St. James's

St. James's Park, dating from the 16C, was relandscaped by Nash (1828) as part of the improvements for George IV. The Buckingham Palace approach now has a wholly Edwardian air although The Mall, along the top of St. James's Park, was laid out c 1662 for Charles II. The Mall runs between the Palace and Trafalgar Square, its main elements part of a transformation of 1901–13 that make it the closest London equivalent to the Beaux Arts style avenues of Paris or Latin America. The E end is screened by Admiralty Arch (1911; A. Webb), a cunning building, really an office block of dumb-bell plan pierced by a triple archway, and disguising the change in axis from Trafalgar Square to the Mall. It is intended as a triumphal arch on a processional way but official parsimony prevented this being the sole function so perhaps happily it remains a low-key monument. The other end of the Mall is the *Queen Victoria Memorial (1901–11; A. Webb), the sculpture by T. Brock. The main memorial is very large, Portland stone, with Victoria facing up the Mall flanked on the sides by Truth and Justice and back-to-back with Motherhood, this last a lovely and unmonumental group. In bronze on top, Victory perched above Courage and Constancy. Bronze relief fountains surround the base with, at the four corners, bronze lions with figures of Peace, Progress, Agriculture and Industry. A very Victorian ensemble in its elaborate symbolism but characteristically turn of the century touches appear in the sculpture, Art Nouveau swirls, the realism of the poses. In a ring around, stone pillars with youths carrying symbols of the dominions and colonies. The fine gates to Buckingham Palace are part of the same scheme, as is the main front (1911–13; A. Webb), a Portland stone skin over the front range of 1847 that closed the originally open courtyard of Nash's palace of 1826–36. The range facing the garden and the side wings are essentially Nash. Queen Victoria was the first sovereign to live here, financial crises having overwhelmed Nash and George IV. Constitution Hill runs NW from the Palace with pretty iron lamps. Three

Queen Victoria Memorial (1901–11; A. Webb), The Mall

attempts were made on Queen Victoria's life in 1840 and 1842 (twice) on Constitution Hill and The Mall.

At the E end of Green Park, next to St. James's Palace, *Lancaster House*, (1825–27; B.D. and P. Wyatt), one of the grandest private houses in London, built for the Duke of York but sold incomplete to the Duke of Sutherland who added the top floor and completed the interior (1833–38). The splendid staircase is partly by Barry and the interiors (occasionally open) show the loosening of Greek Revival forms to something richer and more colourful in the manner of Versailles. Behind, in Cleveland Row, *Bridgewater House* (1846–51; C. Barry) for the 1st Earl of Ellesmere, a very grand palazzo, stone faced and fully Renaissance in detail. By contrast with Lancaster House the elements of Barry's new style are obvious, all the decoration confined to the main lines, corners, cornice, windows, door and porch. The classical columns and pilasters of the Regency do not appear, nor does any picturesque feature save perhaps Barry's favourite chimneys rising from the corners. It is a most rich design, massively insistent in its heavy moulding of the horizontal lines and of the corner rusticated blocks. The interior has a great two-storey central hall richly marbled and painted (against Barry's wishes) in the manner of Raphael's Vatican Logge (1858; J. Gotzenberger). In *St. James's Palace*, but inaccessible, are two state rooms decorated by William Morris (1866–67) where bold pattern design, mostly floral on dark backgrounds, covers the basically late 17C woodwork of the lower part of the walls and the doors. In Marlborough Rd, *Queen Alexandra Memorial* (1926–32; A. Gilbert), a last work by the greatest late Victorian sculptor begun when he was 72, twenty-five years after he had left the country a bankrupt. Swirling Art Nouveau figures against an extraordinary Gothic screen.

The Reform Club (1838–41; Sir C. Barry), Pall Mall

In Pall Mall, the W end has Norman Shaw's two buildings for the Alliance Assurance. Facing E down Pall Mall, *No. 88 St. James's St* (1904–05) is in Shaw's Baroque manner, Portland stone fronted because the Crown would not have red brick and stone on this site. The ground floor of three powerfully rusticated arches carries a calm five-window front above, but at the attic the centre three bays rise up a floor under an open pediment, a surprising but successful device that accentuates the height in the long view down Pall Mall. Opposite, *Nos 1–2 St. James's St* (1882–83) is quite different, red brick and stone towering to Dutch gables with a polygonal turret on the corner. Especially good are the broad ground-floor arches. On the S side, the first of the Pall Mall clubs, *Nos 71–76*, the *Oxford and Cambridge Club* (1836–38; R. and S. Smirke), neo-classical in an original way, dispensing with columns but suggesting a row of pilasters by setting the upper windows and carved reliefs above in tall recesses. Further on, the *Royal Automobile Club* (1908–11; Mewes and Davis), French late 18C on a grand scale, much larger than any earlier club and thought vulgar at the time (as indeed were the motor cars). Louis XVI style interiors and flashy neo-Grecian swimming pool. The *Reform Club* (1838–41; C. Barry) seems now the very model of a gentlemen's club, a stately palace presenting, like the palaces of Renaissance Rome, a stern front to the world. Barry really introduced this style to London at the smaller *Travellers Club* (1830–32) next door which by comparison has a prettiness and delicacy which should not disguise the sureness of Barry's design, every detail and moulding picking out a main element of the building. The Reform Club with its far larger scale, its stone front and splendid cornice was one of the potent models for the early Victorian period. Its dignity and sobriety struck a chord certainly, but also, by dispensing with the pilasters and classical trimmings of the Regency period, it provided a very flexible model that could be extended sideways or upwards without loss of proportion. The *Athenaeum Club* (1827–30; D. Burton) and the former *United Service Club* (1826–28; J. Nash) that flank Waterloo Place illustrate different approaches to club design. The Athenaeum distinguished with Grecian references, especially the frieze, on a building that like the Traveller's Club has abandoned the strict Greek Revival. Nash's building is mixed classical with a double height portico. A frieze to match the Athenaeum was added by D. Burton (1858). Between the two in Waterloo Place, the *Duke of York's column* (1831–34), the S end of Nash's street improvement that led from here to Regent's Park. To each side, facing St. James's Park, *Carlton House Terrace* (1827–33; J. Nash), giant stucco terraces, several given lavish Victorian interiors, notably *No. 6* (1889; E. George) and *No. 7* with paintings by G.F. Watts. *Nos 8–9* was the Prussian and later German embassy, *No. 11* Gladstone's house (1857–75). In Carlton Gardens, further W, Palmerston lived at *No. 4*. In Waterloo Place, a collection of statues, on the E side, the Indian Mutiny generals, *Campbell* (Marochetti; 1867) and *Lawrence* (Boehm; 1884) and *Scott* of the Antarctic by his wife (1915). On the W side, *Field Marshal Burgoyne* (1874; Boehm) who directed the siege of Sebastopol in 1854. Also *Sir John Franklin* (1856; Noble), the Arctic explorer who disappeared in 1847. Lady Franklin's long search for the vanished expedition (1848–59) and the pathetic cairn found telling the story was one of the heroic tales of Victorian England. In the middle, *Edward VII* (1912; B. Mackennal), equestrian statue on a plinth by Lutyens. N of Pall Mall, in a square rebuilt 1908–25 in grand classical manner, the *Guards' Crimea Monument* (1860; J. Bell) flanked by statues of those unlikely allies, *Lord Herbert* (1867; J.H. Foley), the Secretary at War, and *Florence Nightingale* (1915; A. Walker). She also appears in one of the reliefs on the Herbert monument. In Pall Mall to E, on S side, *No. 125* (c 1900), granite faced with copper dome and bronze ground-floor columns, the first of a series of c 1900 shipping offices around Cockspur St. On N, *Kinnaird House* (1915–22; R. Blomfield), large with corner towers in a French 18C style. On E side, *Oceanic House* (1906; H. Tanner), pompous stone, and on S, *Nos 14–16* (1907; A.T. Bolton) for the P & O line with ship motifs and bronze work round the door, *No. 18* (1907; Aston Webb) for Canadian Railways with Dominion shields, and *No. 20* (1901; W. Woodward), pretty Gothic facing E to Trafalgar Square. Beyond *Nos 26–7* (1888; W. Williams), red brick and terracotta. Across Spring Gardens, lavish stone *bank* (1871; F. Porter) with three layers of granite columns. E of Kinnaird House, *University Club* (1906 and 1924; R. Blomfield) with shallow recessed bows, generally French 18C in detail. In Haymarket, *Her Majesty's Theatre* (1897; C.J. Phipps), busy stone facade piling up to a square dome where Sir H. Beerbohm Tree had his acting academy. *Theatre Royal* (1821; J. Nash) has a fine portico, the interior 1905. Beyond, *Burberry's* (1912; W.F. Cave), bold two-storey front, columns below, big arches above.

To W, St. James's Square, *No. 5* (1854; T. Cubitt), refronted in stone, *No. 7* (1911; Lutyens), big and influential red-brick neo-Georgian house, and *No. 12* (1835; T. Cubitt), an early Italianate front. On the W side, *No. 14* (1896; J.O. Smith) is the London Library founded 1841 by

Carlyle, *No. 16* (1865; C. Lee), the East India and Sports Club, and, at the corner of King St, *No. 17* (1847; Johnson), rich stucco Italianate. In King St, the art dealers Christie's, established here 1823, with an early 20C stone front. St. James's St begins at the S end with Norman Shaw's two fine buildings for the Alliance Assurance, Nos 1–2 and 88 (see above p. 225). *No. 86* on the W side was the Thatched House Club (1862; J. Knowles), towering stone front with naturalistic foliage carving. Next door, • *No. 74* was the Conservative Club (1843–45; Basevi and S. Smirke), dignified neo-classical of the type made outdated by Barry's Reform Club. *Nos 69–70* was Arthur's Club (1826–27; T. Hopper), an early revival of Palladianism, now the Carlton Club. At the top end *No. 50*, Jamaican High Commission, formerly Crockford's, refronted in stone (1872; C.J. Phipps) with giant Corinthian columns. Crockford's was the leading London gaming house in the early and mid 19C. On the E side, *White's Club*, the oldest London club, the clubhouse 1787, refronted 1852 (J. Lockyer). Jermyn St, running E, has several good early 20C buildings. On the corner of Bury St, *Nos 70–7* (1902; R. Morphew), thoroughly Arts and Crafts, built as bachelors' lodgings, *No. 106* (1906; Treadwell and Martin), free Jacobean, and *No. 112* (1912; R. Morphew), plainer than his earlier Nos 70–2 but with the same strong detail and tall proportions. At the foot of Duke St, *No. 2* (1910–12; Harris and Moodie), a theme on the Italianate palazzo played extremely boldly, the two-and-a-half-storey front equivalent to a normal four and articulated with three stone rusticated arches below and three pedimented stone windows above, set against red brick. In Duke of York St, *Red Lion* pub, little altered interior with sparkling cut- glass mirrors.

Piccadilly and Mayfair

Piccadilly Circus lost its circular form at the end of the 19C and has never regained much shape. In the centre, *Eros*, the fountain memorial to Lord Shaftesbury (1886–93; A. Gilbert), swirly Art Nouveau forms topped by the winged youth, the first sculpture to be cast in aluminium. The major part of the Circus was rebuilt 1923–27 in a neo-French design of Sir R. Blomfield's after a long dispute over plans by Norman Shaw to continue the design of his Regent St front of the Piccadilly Hotel (1906) down to the Circus. On the S side, *Criterion Theatre* (1870–78; T. Verity) with big pavilion roofs. The theatre itself is in the basement and still retains, unaltered, the interior of 1884. Splendid tile decorations to the stairs and foyer. The old Long Bar with gilded ceiling is now a shop. Opposite, the *London Pavilion* (1885; Saunders and Worley) with painted classical facades, apparently stone under the paint. The interior has been gutted. In Piccadilly, on the N side, *Piccadilly Hotel* (1906–08; R. Norman Shaw), colossal Portland stone front, the centre set behind an open screen and the W end a great Dutch gable. Here Shaw, aged 75, gave the Baroque revival a formidable example of how to design the massive facades required for the new scale of buildings. Particularly influential were the giant ground-floor arches, actually two stories high, though the shopkeepers objected to the loss of valuable display space for the stone piers. Sadly the E wing was never built and a small scale Baroque front (1903) was allowed to be re-erected on the site in 1911. Opposite, *National Westminster Bank* (1892–94; A. Waterhouse), stone fronted with none of Waterhouse's colours or gables, just an odd indecision about the style. Beyond St. James's Church, former *Royal Society of Painters in Water Colours* (1883; E.R. Robson), handsome with two-

storey piers and, above, a blank wall ornamented with busts of artists
(O. Ford). Opposite, *Burlington House*, the complex of learned socie-
ties set up around the courtyard of Lord Burlington's c 1720 Palladian
mansion. The Piccadilly front with the archway was added 1868–73
(Banks and Barry), the most elaborately decorated of the 19C ranges,
good neo-Renaissance detail but heavy and crowded. The side wings
are simpler in the same style while Burlington House itself was remodelled for the *Royal Academy* (1872; S. Smirke) leaving the 18C house
beneath a new top storey with statues of artists in niches between
granite columns. The new exhibition galleries at the back were added
by Smirke (1867). Beyond, on Piccadilly, at the corner of Old Bond St.
No. 1 (1880; A. Waterhouse), brick and terracotta, and, opposite, a
nicely detailed stone building (1905). At the corner of Albemarle St,
former *Albemarle Hotel* (1887; George and Peto), in Doulton's terracotta, Flemish Renaissance style. The medallions in the window bays
were based on coins at the British Museum. Opposite, flanking the top
of St. James's St, two lavish marble-faced Edwardian offices, on E
side, *Norwich Union* (1907; Runtz and Ford), on W side, former *Royal
Insurance* (1907; Belcher and Joass), a most disquieting facade where
detail in some sense classical has been squeezed and stretched with
chunky pediments and stone tablets in an alternating rhythm high up.
Even higher, an open loggia above two attic floors above. The angularity and broken rhythms show how far Edwardian Baroque could go
towards its own mannerism. Beyond, the *Ritz Hotel* (1903–06;
Mewes and Davis), the most prominent of the French Beaux Arts
inspired buildings that came to London at the time of the Entente
Cordiale with France. Very French in design with tall ornamented
roofs and banded rustication. The ground floor is granite, very
smoothly handled. Sumptuous interiors. This was one of the first steel-
framed buildings in London. On N side of Piccadilly, *No. 94*, Lord
Palmerston's house from 1855–65. Beyond, facing Green Park, are
stone-fronted buildings, late 19C, *Nos 96–7* (1891; T. Verity), *Nos 98–
100* (1883; Edis), and *No. 101* (1890; Edis), marble-faced in a free
Renaissance style. *No. 105*, Hertford House, was refronted (1849; W.
Cubitt) in stone and given marble ground-floor trimmings in the late
19C, one of several 18C mansions refronted during the 19C and early
20C along Piccadilly. *No. 137* (1904; Collcutt and Hamp) stands out
with its green and white gable, and use of glazed brick.

N of Piccadilly, from the W, in Hamilton Place, several large stone
town houses, most notably *No. 5* (1880; W. Rogers), with ornate curved
bays. In Down St, ragstone *church* (1865; F. and H. Francis), the gable
to the street a nice contrast to the secular surroundings, inside a richly
coloured E window by Clayton and Bell over marble reredos. In
Stratton St, further E, *No. 8* (1871; George and Vaughan), an early
work by Ernest George, Gothic, and *No. 15* (c 1896; C.J. Cooper),
stone-gabled front. Berkeley St leads to Berkeley Square. *No. 47*
(1891; George and Peto), on the W, delicate Renaissance detail. On the
E side, *No. 3* (1896; Huntly-Gordon), gabled and artily detailed, on
the N, *Nos 25–6* (1904; Verity), flats in the French style. In Charles St,
to W, *No. 37* (1890; W. Alwright), English Speaking Union, built as a
town house with the most mixed Baroque to Georgian facade and
lavish ironwork. Iron of an earlier date opposite on *No. 20* (c 1860). To
the NW of Berkeley Square, off Hill St, *RC church*, Farm St, the
principal Jesuit church in London. Built 1844–49 (J.J. Scoles) as a
single vessel with large traceried windows each end. High altar by
Pugin in sanctuary, with marble and lapis lazuli chancel rail (1903).
Aisles were added on the right (1878; H. Clutton) and on the left

(1898–1903; W.H. Romaine Walker) giving complex and rich vistas. E of Berkeley St, in Albemarle St on E side, the cheerful *Royal Arcade* (1880), much the liveliest of London's arcades with stucco-decorated arches carried on two stories of columns. At the top end, *Royal Institution* (1838; L. Vulliamy), a screen of giant Corinthian columns thrown across what were 18C houses to give suitable academic solemnity. *No. 23* (1896), red brick and terracotta, *No. 24* (1911; George and Yeates), opposite, coolly classical. In Old Bond St, on E side, *No. 14* (1911; Lanchester and Rickards) for Colnaghi's gallery, *No. 22* (c 1900) with pale glazed terracotta and grey granite columns to the upper floors. On W, *No. 25* has a good 19C shop front, formerly Mappin and Webb. To the E in Burlington Gardens, *Museum of Mankind* (1866; J. Pennethorne), built for the University of London, Italian Renaissance with a facade varied by corner towers and broad porch. Pink granite shafts to contrast with the Portland stone. Crisply carved detail and statues of scientific and philosophical figures from Archimedes to Adam Smith. Facing W, down the street, *No. 1 Savile Row*, 19C shopfront (1870) refacing an 18C house.

Regent Street was mostly rebuilt after 1900 in Portland stone. The best building towards the S end is the rear of the *Piccadilly Hotel* (1905–06; R. Norman Shaw) which was to be the model for rebuilding the Quadrant. Powerful Baroque, much better than the Piccadilly front, the same rusticated arches below, but, above, three storeys contained behind an Ionic colonnade of paired columns, the lower third made ponderous with square blocks. This is overpowering architecture. With its huge chimneys it sits well in the middle of R. Blomfield's milder Quadrant, better as a centrepiece than extended to the full range. Most of the street dates from the 1920s, but at the top end, on the W side, *Nos 235–41* (1898; G.D. Martin) display a crowded late Victorian front capped by a green square dome. The notable feature is the Venetian mosaic work above the ground floor. In Conduit St, running W, on the S side, *Nos 61–5* (1865–66; J. Murray), large stone-faced palazzo built as a draper's store. *No. 20* (1907; Treadwell and Martin), good free Gothic. *Nos 26–7* (1896; A.H. Kearsey) has decorative terracotta by Doulton's. In Maddox St, to N, *Nos 46–58* (1844), a nice row of stucco houses with unusual round-arched detail, and *No. 47* (1892), all glazed yellow terracotta. In St. George's St, *Nos 6–7* (1904; Wimperis and East), the rear of Sotheby's, a crowded display of Edwardian motifs even including slim angle shafts with bedpost caps after Voysey. Off Hanover Square, *No. 2 Brook St*, National Westminster Bank (1860; F. Pownall), late Georgian in form but with Jacobean detail. In Hanover St, *No. 7*, another of Treadwell and Martin's lively commercial fronts (c 1900), also by them, *No. 7 Dering St* (1907), NW of Hanover Square. New Bond St has a wide variety of late 19C and early 20C commercial fronts, on E side, *No. 74* (1900; Treadwell and Martin), good free Gothic with twining grapes carved in relief, *Nos 67–8*, pink terracotta and red granite columns (the same design is repeated further down at the corner of Maddox St and at No. 22 Old Bond St in cream and grey), and *Nos 65–6* (1896; A. Keen), pretty Queen Anne in red brick with Venetian windows in stone bays. On W side, *Nos 131–4* (1914), smooth design of recessed bays, slightly Arts and Crafts influenced, set in a classical frame, *Nos 135–7* (1876; W. Sams), stucco eclectic detail, formerly the Grosvenor Gallery, the centre of avant-garde life in from 1876–90. This is where Ruskin saw the Whistler painting that outraged him and led to Whistler's disastrous libel case. *No. 139* contrasts an enormous granite arch with plain yellow brick above. *Nos 144–6* (1911; Lanchester and Rickards),

French 18C style with a pretty central window. *No. 148* (1876; E.W. Godwin) is the Fine Art Society, the first floor originally an open balcony. Further down, *Nos 165–9*, Asprey's, has a splendid two-storey plate-glass and iron shopfront.

W of New Bond St, the *Mayfair estate* of the Dukes of Westminster, stretching as far as Park Lane. During the 19C and early 20C the estate was much rebuilt with very large private houses, mostly in terraces on the sites of smaller 18C houses. There are three main types, associated with successive Grosvenor landlords. From c 1840–70, refrontings in an Italianate style in white brick and stone or stucco characterise the period of the 2nd Marquess and his architect T. Cundy II. From 1870–1900, the 1st Duke favoured the gabled red brick and stone or terracotta of the Queen Anne and Dutch styles. After 1900, under the 2nd Duke, neo-Georgian styles came to predominate.

In Grosvenor St, *Nos 21–2* (1898; Balfour and Turner), red brick and stone with strong details influenced by Philip Webb. Balfour was estate surveyor and there are a number of similar works in Mayfair, all of high quality. Across Davies St, *No. 46* (1910; Blow and Billerey), a grand Portland stone palazzo, built for the mogul of the London tram system, Speyer. In Brook St, parallel, *Nos 40–6* (1898; Balfour and Turner), the gables crowstepped as if with children's building blocks. *Nos 52–4* (1896; P.M. Horder), smooth fronted with mullioned windows like Voysey's houses in Hans Place. Opposite, *Claridge's* (1894–98; C.W. Stephens), London's most aristocratic hotel since the mid 19C. The building, red brick and red stone, is lumpish. The opposite side of Davies St, *Nos 39–49 and 59–61 Brook St* are Jacobean gabled with terracotta (1883–86; R.W. Edis). At the N end of Davies St, *No. 58*, former Boulding's Sanitary Ware showroom, is cheerfully terracotta-clad (1889; J. Wimperis and Arber). To W an area of artisan flats, the 1st Duke was a notable patron of the movement for improved housing, rehousing some 4000 people here and in Pimlico. Flats between Gilbert St and Balderton St largely 1886–92 except Clarendon Buildings, Balderton St (1871–72). In Duke St, the *Ukrainian Catholic Cathedral*, originally a Congregational chapel (1889–91; A. Waterhouse), brick and terracotta Romanesque, the oval interior expressed externally and strong spired corner tower. To N, *Nos 55–73* (1890–92; W. Caroe), a very handsome range, brick and finely carved stone with lively detail. To S, *Nos 75–83* (1894; W. Caroe), moulded brick, the S end particularly original with battered corner towers flanking a higher attic feature. Duke's Yard, to S, has pretty row of mews houses (1900; Balfour and Turner). *Brown Hart Gardens* (1905; C.S. Peach) is an electricity sub-station disguised under a raised terrace with Baroque pavilions. In Balderton St, Gothic *St. Mark's Mansions* (1872; R.J. Withers). In North Audley St, *St. Mark's Church* (1824; J.P. Gandy), Greek Revival, the interior made Romanesque (1872; A. Blomfield) with lavish fittings. *No. 14* (1887; T.H. Watson), prettily Dutch gabled, *Nos 24–9*; (1891; T. and F. Verity), richly terracotta ornamented. In Grosvenor Square, *No. 4* (1864; T. Cundy II) is a good survival of the Italianate favoured by the 2nd Marquess. In Upper Brook St, *Nos 16–18* (1907–13; E. Wimperis), stone faced and gabled in the taste of the 2nd Duke, as also several houses on the S side. In Park St, running N, *Nos 91–103* (1913–25; E. Wimperis and Simpson), red brick, early 18C style. Opposite, *Nos 98–104* (1896; H.O. Cresswell), gabled, banded brick and stone. In Green St, to E, *No. 10* (1893; Balfour and Turner) with prettily carved doorway and, at W end, *No. 32* (1897; S. Smith), dignified neo-Georgian with busier terrace houses by Smith at *Nos 16–19 Dunraven St*. In Park St to S of Upper Brook St, *Nos 37–53* (1908;

W. Caroe), freely Baroque, part stone faced. *Nos 44–50* (1911; Blow and Billerey) were given a stone porticoed front as the row then faced Hyde Park over Grosvenor House garden, since built over. At the S end of Park St, *Nos 14–22* (1896; Balfour and Turner) and *Nos 8– 12* (1897; A. Kersey), Tudor with broad bands of mullioned windows. On Mount St, *No. 54* (1896–97; F.B. Wade), very grand private house for the Earl of Plymouth, free version of Wren's style in brick and stone. Opposite, by Balfour and Turner, *Nos 68–9* (1896), *No. 78* (1896), *No. 79 Balfour Place* (1892), and E side of *Balfour Mews* (1898). Across South Audley St, on S side, a long range, *Nos 87–102* (1889–95; A. Bolton), richly terracotta trimmed. *Mount St* is the best area of Mayfair to see this late 19C extravagance. Opposite, *Nos 27–8 and 34–42 South Audley St* (1888; T. Verity), with the Audley pub at the corner, and *Nos 13–26* (1896; Read and Macdonald) with mullioned bays. Opposite the *Connaught Hotel* (1894), *Nos 104–13* (George and Peto 1886), two different late Gothic styles, two different shades of terracotta. *No. 114*, RC presbytery (1886; A. Purdie), faces Carlos Place with a long range by J. Trollope (1891) curving at the corner. *Nos 115– 21* (1886; J.T. Smith), opposite, are all terracotta faced, *Nos 125–9* (1886; W.H. Powell) banded brick and terracotta. Opposite, *Nos 4–5* (1888; George and Peto). In South Audley St more similar, but *Nos 17– 21* (1875; George and Peto, extended 1889), beyond the Grosvenor Chapel, are the first buildings in the Queen Anne style on the estate. The 1st Duke apparently suggested this break from the previous Italianate, and Messrs Goode and Co, suppliers of fashionable Japanese porcelain, gave themselves a building in the most up-to-date style. On Park Lane, to the SW, *No. 47* (1899; Romaine Walker), stonefronted Gothic mansion, almost the last of the Park Lane Victorian houses to survive.

Soho

Behind the National Gallery, *National Portrait Gallery* (1890–95; E. Christian), Florentine Renaissance style. Opposite, the curved front of the former Westminster City Hall (1890; R. Walker). Facing up Charing Cross Rd, the actor-manager *Henry Irving* (1910; Brock) in bronze. The *Garrick Theatre* (1889; C.J. Phipps) has a long stone front and original interior. Further up, *Wyndham's Theatre* (1899; W. Sprague), a busy classical front in stone and a Louis XVI style interior, unaltered, with painted ceiling. On the W side, the *London Hippodrome* (1900; F. Matcham), red sandstone and ornate, the corner open dome with chariot group on top. Cranbourne St leads into Leicester Square, mostly rebuilt. The N side has two former hotels of 1897–99. Off the SW corner, in Panton St, *Comedy Theatre* (1881; T. Verity), charming small stucco-fronted theatre, little altered inside. N of the Square, in Lisle St, *St. John's Hospital* (1897; Treadwell and Martin), a pretty Dutch Renaissance design facing down into the Square. On Charing Cross Rd, tall tenement buildings with bookshops below and *Welsh Church* (1888; J. Cubitt), interesting centralised plan, the exterior cheaply Romanesque with an octagonal lantern. At Cambridge Circus, *Palace Theatre* (1891; T.E. Collcutt), most unusually treated outside with bands of terracotta ornament and minaretlike turrets. Much damaged but the large auditorium remains. It was built as the home of English opera by D'Oyly Carte. To the W, Shaftesbury Avenue, opened 1886. On N side, *Queen's and Globe Theatres* (1906–08; Sprague), originally matching, but the Queen's refronted in 1959. Both have original interiors, the Globe especially good. The

Apollo Theatre (1901; L. Sharp) has a most exotic exterior with winged figures over the cornice at each side, Louis XIV style interior. The *Lyric Theatre* (1888; C.J. Phipps), a long facade like a terrace of houses, little altered interior. Opposite, the *Trocadero* (1897; Ansell), gabled in red brick and red stone, once London's most famous restaurant.

To the NW, tight network of streets behind Regent St. In Warwick St, *RC church* (1788) with marbled apse by Bentley (1874). In Beak St, at the top of Great Pulteney St, *Sun and 13 Cantons* pub (1882), red brick with moulded brick details, stands opposite a building clad in pale green glazed bricks with Portland stone details (c 1905). At the top of Carnaby St, *Shakespeare's Head*, well-detailed c 1900 pub. In Argyll St to N, *London Palladium* (1910; F. Matcham), the painted Corinthian front dates in part from the 1868 Corinthian Bazaar. Interior of 1910, very large and little altered, and still principally used as a variety theatre, for which it was built. The Argyll pub opposite has a snug interior of the 1890s. In Wardour St, to E, former *Novello's* offices facing W down D'Arblay St (1906; F.L. Pearson), a strong design of tall mullioned windows over a low shallow-arched ground floor. In Soho Square, *French Protestant church* (1893; A. Webb), decorated inside and out with Doulton's terracotta, the interior striped in buff and brown. *No. 3* (1903; R.J. Worley), plays elaborate games of concave and convex curves with stylised tree decoration. On the E side, *RC church* (1891–93; Kelly and Birchall), red-brick Italian style with campanile tower. Behind *No. 1*, in Manette St, small High Victorian stone *chapel* (1862; J. Clarke). On Charing Cross Rd, towards Cambridge Circus, large red-brick and red stone tenements (c 1890), and, opposite, *No. 1 Old Compton St* (1904; R.J. Worley), dark green glazed brick and stone, neo Baroque.

Oxford St and Marylebone

At the E end of Oxford St, N side, the *Tottenham Pub* (1892; Savile and Martin), cheerful striped front and original interior with engraved and coloured mirrors. *No. 62*, Evelyn House (1908–10; C. Holden), stone-faced free classical. *Nos 158–62* (1906–08; Belcher and Joass), highly mannered marble-faced building, playing with the classical vocabulary in an alarming and sculptural way. Tall columns support second-floor piers which in turn support third-floor paired columns, an order of things that is visually odd, the more so because there are no strong horizontals to play against this stack of different elements. Order is restored at the top by arched upper windows emphasising the vertical bay divisions. Within the bays window architraves float airily detached from surrounding wall. The new freedom allowed by a stéel frame structure is nowhere more boldly exploited. Beyond, *Nos 164–88* (1906; R.F. Atkinson), the former Waring and Gillow store, freedom of a more conventional but no less exuberant sort, red brick and stone in a lavish adaptation of Wren's Hampton Court building with added Baroque zest. Especially good stone carving.

In Margaret St to the N, *All Saints' Church* (1850–59; W. Butterfield), one of the key churches of the Gothic Revival, built as the model church of the Ecclesiological Society. The Society in its influential leaflets on church building called for churches with clearly divided naves and chancels, preferably separately roofed and differentiated by a grander scale of ornament in the chancel. Beyond this, recommendations were made on vestries, porches, towers and all fittings as to their appropriate placing and design. The principles are broadly those of Pugin and lead towards the characteristic Puginian

All Saints' Church (1850–59; W. Butterfield), Margaret Street

Dec. church. All Saints' is remarkable for how far it goes beyond these first principles, reinterpreting them for the needs of a church on a tight urban site. The church is set in a courtyard entered through a lychgate and flanked by school and clergy house. The building material is brick, red, striped and diapered in blue-black, with stone introduced for the church windows and porch. From a distance the powerful and plainly detailed tower and spire rises over the rooftops, pure three-dimensional design, square to pyramid to octagonal. Inside, polychrome richness of a sort never previously attempted, all the wall surfaces patterned in brick and coloured tile, brilliant but always subordinate to the strong stone forms of the arcades, chancel arch and clerestorey. There is no screen, but an inlaid marble wall focusing attention on the windowless E wall, panelled with Gothic arcading framing painted panels (originally by W. Dyce, replaced 1909 by J.N. Comper). Butterfield's felicity in design is overwhelming, the pattern design, the bold forms and rich marble work of the chancel wall, pulpit and font all introduce High Victorian Gothic fully grown at birth. Glass by A. Gibbs, mostly. Comper repainted the chancel vault and designed the Lady Chapel reredos (1911). W of the church *Nos 9–12*

(1907; Simpson and Ayrton), good Edwardian flats with a range of strong two- and four-storey stone oriel bays.

Around Mortimer St, buildings by A.B. Pite, inventive turn of the century architect. *No. 82* (1896), near Regent St, shows his interest in the mannerism of Michelangelo's architecture in the stone window detail to the first floor, supplemented by two Michelangelesque figures framing the window above. *Ames House* (1906), on the corner of Great Titchfield St and Mortimer St, and a warehouse at *No. 21 Little Portland St* show Pite's later interest in simple planes of brick intersecting and receding, a feature best seen nearby, Foley St, in the former *All Souls' School* (1906–08). In Riding House St, former Boulting's offices, *No. 59* (1903; H.F. Clark), free style brick and stone with squared-off projecting bays. In the *Middlesex Hospital*, Mortimer St, unexpectedly, a fine vaulted and marble-lined chapel (1890; J.L. Pearson). In Ogle St, N of Foley St, *RC church* (1862; S. Nicholl) with altar and reredos by J.F. Bentley. The Fitzroy Square area to the NE was an artistic quarter from the early 19C. *No. 7 Fitzroy Square* was the home of C.L. Eastlake 1843–65, the influential Director of the National Gallery, *No. 37* the home of Ford Madox Brown from 1865–81. In Hallam St, to W, *General Medical Council* (1915; E. Frere), suave neo-Grecian front with broad bow window and delicate detail. In Langham St, *Hospital* (1896), completely clad in black and white glazed tiles on a round-arched facade. Portland Place was much rebuilt c 1910. At the S end, the bulky brick Gothic *Langham Hotel* (1865; J. Giles), the big asymmetrical tower was destroyed by bombing. Further up, statue of *Quintin Hogg* (1906; Frampton), founder of the Regent St Polytechnic.

In Oxford St, W of Oxford Circus, older buildings survive on the S side, mostly of the later 19C. W of Harewood Place, a red-brick front with two incongruous pointing figures was once the *Noah's Ark* pub (1890; J.T. Alexander). *No. 441* (1907; Balfour and Turner), beyond North Audley St, has an interesting front of stone with grey granite columns to each floor. *Selfridge's* (1908–09; R.F. Atkinson), London's finest department store building, envelops its several storeys in a monumental stone colonnade, so large that the cornice can deftly accommodate a row of windows. N of Oxford St, in Bryanston St, *Church of the Annunciation* (1910–12; W. Tapper), a fine stone-vaulted interior within a plain red-brick shell. Painted decorated high altar by J.C.N. Bewsey. To E, N of Wigmore St, in Manchester Square, *Wallace Collection*, in Hertford House, 18C town mansion built for the Dukes of Manchester, but remodelled c 1872 for Sir Richard Wallace to house the art collection he had inherited from his natural father, the 4th Marquess of Hertford. The interiors have recently been returned to something like their Victorian glory. Behind, in George St, *St. James RC Church* (1885–90; E. Goldie), a fine EE design in pale stone with magnificent vaulted interior, based on Westminster Abbey. Apsed sanctuary with tile mosaic panels and Lady Chapel with reredos by J.F. Bentley. To E, *Nos 14–16 New Cavendish St* (1902) have distinctive Arts and Crafts carved decoration, including a stylised turkey. To E, N of Wigmore St, a grid plan of late 18C streets around Wimpole St and Harley St, the plain Georgian facades interspersed with turn of the century buildings, some terracotta clad in contrast, some subtle variations on Georgian styles, of which *No. 101 Harley St* (1904; W.H. White) with its shallow stone bow window is a good example. *No. 37 Harley St* (1899; Beresford Pite) is, unusually, of Bath stone, freely detailed with high quality Art Nouveau sculpture. On Wigmore St, much terracotta of the 1890s, the corner of Wimpole St (1891; F.L.

Pearson), *Nos 42–6* (1890; E. George) and the *Wigmore Hall* (1890; T.E. Collcutt). On the S side the large white-tile clad former *Debenham's store* (1907; Wallace and Gibson). In Cavendish Square, statue of Lord George Bentinck (1848; T. Campbell), leading opponent of Sir Robert Peel over the repeal of the Corn Laws. In Henrietta Place, to W, *Royal Society of Medicine* (1910–12; Belcher and Joass).

Regent's Park

Marylebone Rd, laid out in the 18C, was only gradually built up and is notable primarily for the large c 1900 blocks of flats, but, more significantly, it covers the world's first underground railway, the Metropolitan Line, from Paddington to Farringdon St, opened 1863. It was built by the 'cut-and-cover' method, here under one of the few London streets wide enough. *Baker St Station* has been restored to its original condition, with shallow yellow brick vault over the tracks. Opposite *Marylebone Church* (1813–17; T. Hardwick), where Robert and Elizabeth Browning were married in 1846, the red-brick *Royal Academy of Music* (1910; E. George and Yates). Further W, *Marylebone Town Hall* (1914; Sir E. Cooper), Imperial classical in Portland stone, a contrast to the modest red-brick and stucco *Court House* (1874). On the N side, *York House* (1899; R.W. Edis), bulky brick and terracotta former Hotel Grand Central, built in connection with *Marylebone Station* (1899) just behind, the last of the London main line railway termini. The Great Central Railway was an attempt to challenge the established railway companies through an amalgamation of various small lines, but the cost of building their extension into London itself near bankrupted the company. W of York House, diapered brick Gothic former *Grammar School* (1857; W. and E. Habershon). N of Marylebone Rd, in Glentworth St, *St. Cyprian's Church* (1902–03 J.N. Comper), a High Church shrine in memory of a dedicated High Church clergyman, Fr C. Gutch, and one of Comper's finest works. For shortage of funds, the exterior is quite plain, the interior a light and lofty Perp. receptacle for Comper's carved and painted woodwork, in the late Gothic manner of Bodley but more delicate and blended with Renaissance motifs. The painted timber roofs, the great rood screen (1924) and the altar canopy (1948) represent a slow process of embellishment to a unified scheme that has halted before the painting and gilding becomes overpowering and when the contrast of white and colour is most effective.

Regent's Park to E, the culmination of John Nash's great scheme for the Prince Regent, linking his palace on the Mall with a new landscaped park surrounded by terraces of mansions, is still substantially intact, as laid out from 1812–30. Around the outer edge the monumental terraces in stucco, with only one Victorian interloper, *Cambridge Gate* (1875; Archer and Green), at the SE corner, doing everything to reject the aura of Nash. Within the Park are the white stucco villas, of which eight were built c 1815–30, but most altered since. On the Inner Circle, *St. John's Lodge* (1818: extended 1847; C. Barry) has inside the remnant of some painted decoration by H.W. Lonsdale for the Marquess of Bute. At the NE corner of the Park the former *St. Katharine's Hospital* (1826; A. Poynter), a neat stock brick Gothic group of almshouses around a chapel. On the N side, *London Zoo*, founded here in 1827 by Sir Humphrey Davy and Sir Stamford Raffles. Modern improvements are gradually removing the older structures, but as yet the concrete mountain top of the Mappin Terraces (1913; Belcher and Joass) survives and also the giraffe house of 1836 (D. Burton), between the Outer Circle and the canal.

Covent Garden

New Oxford St is largely rebuilt, some of the early stucco buildings surviving E of Shaftesbury Avenue (c 1843–48), especially notable *No. 53*, Smith's umbrella shop, almost a last survivor of the overall advertising that was typical of 19C commercial premises. The *Shaftesbury Theatre* (1911; B. Crewe), cheerful orange terracotta with corner cupola. Opposite, *Central Baptist Church* (1848; J. Gibson), white brick, neo-Romanesque. On the corner of Endell St and High Holborn, former *schools* (1860; E.M. Barry), tough polychrome Gothic in brick, designed for 1500 children, an industrial school and soup kitchen for the poor of the Drury Lane slums. In High Holborn, the former *Holborn Town Hall* (1906; Hall and Warwick) and library (1894). The *Princess Louise* pub has a tiled and mirrored interior (1891) of exceptional splendour. On the N side, *Nos 127–9* (1904; C. Holden), sharply detailed classical.

Endell St runs S into the northern part of Covent Garden, a web of small streets with 18C houses and 19C workshops and warehouses interspersed with tenement blocks. On left, *Swiss Protestant Church* (1853; G. Vulliamy), on right, *No. 22* (1859; R.J. Withers), a fine Gothic block built for Lavers and Barraud, stained-glass makers, in diapered brick with roofline dormers. Long Acre is the main E–W road. The *Kemble* pub (1837; Collis), stucco classical, quite ornate, was described at the time as 'better than Palladio's house in Vicenza, though less well known', a breathtaking comment. Further W, Stanford's, *Nos 12–14* (c 1901; Read and Macdonald), a tall stone front. In Neal St and Shelton St, stock brick *warehouses*. In Mercer St, artisans' dwellings of c 1900 built for the Mercers' Company. In St. Martin's Lane, on W side, *Albery Theatre* (1903; Sprague), stone classical front and Louis XVI style interior. Further down, the *• Salisbury* (c 1899), a full-blown Victorian interior, behind the benches exotic bronze lamps, the bulbs fitted to flowers looming over half-dressed maidens with spaniels. Beyond, *Duke of York's Theatre* (1892; W. Emden) with a pretty loggia over the entrance. Decorative dome inside. Opposite, *London Coliseum* (1904; F. Matcham), an enormous variety theatre now revitalised for the English National Opera. Originally all terracotta, but now painted, a landmark with its Baroque cupola topped by a glass globe (which used to revolve). The interior is spectacular for its size, crude ornateness of the decor, and the games the architect has played with the curves and changing levels of the balconies and boxes. E of William IV St, former *Charing Cross Hospital* (1831–34; D. Burton), stucco, the main feature facing the Strand. It has been much altered since. Bedford St leads N, on right, the original Civil Service Stores (1876; Lockwood and Mawson), red brick and pretty terracotta detail. In Garrick St, on left, *No. 5* (1860; A. Allom), stucco with mixed detail and a band of inset tiles, further up, *Nos 15–17*, the Garrick Club (1860; F. Marrable), stucco palazzo on a very grand scale, the windows well spaced and the floor heights generous. Matching flanking buildings, *No. 9* with an original painted shopfront. Opposite, *No. 14* (1860; A. Blomfield), high Victorian Gothic in coloured brick, a corner block, and then a two-gabled range to Floral St. In Floral St, *dance studios*, built as a school (1860; C.G. Searle), with a little campanile. In King St, to S, at W end, a good complex of buildings for the Westminster Fire Office, *No. 26* (1860), facing Garrick St, big stucco block rounded to the corner. *Nos 27–8*, channelled stucco with very good shopfront, apparently a 18C house stuccoed 1808, altered and extended E (1857; T. Little). On S side *No.*

13 (c 1870) has pretty glazed ceramic plaques above the first-floor windows.

In Covent Garden, the NW corner (1877; H. Clutton) is an enlarged version of the 1630 piazza building by Inigo Jones, of which the last fragment was on this site. The *Market Hall* (1828–30; C. Fowler) was originally open between the two ranges of neo-classical buildings, the centre covered over with an iron roof in the later 19C. The fruit market moved away in 1974 and, since, everything has been cleaned up and restored with shops and restaurants replacing the fruit sellers. Market buildings along the S side, Jubilee Market (1903) and the Flower Market (1887–91), now the *London Transport Museum*. On the E side, Bow St and the *Royal Opera House* (1857–58; E.M. Barry), stucco classical with the best theatre interior in the country, richly modelled plaster especially good on the horseshoe fronts to the balconies. As part of the same development Barry built the *Floral Hall* (1858) on the S side, an iron and glass building, originally curved roofed and domed. Most of the fine ironwork of the walls survives but the roof and dome were burnt. *Bow St Magistrates Court* (1879; Sir J. Taylor), opposite, is the oldest police court in London. S of the market buildings, in Tavistock St, *Nos 2–10*, former Country Life offices (1904–05; E. Lutyens), in the manner of Wren, in red brick and stone topped by two magnificent chimneys. The treatment of the floor levels elevates the apparent main floor to second-floor level, while the first floor is a clever mezzanine threaded through the Baroque pediment of the entrance. To the W, Maiden Lane, with *RC church* (1873; F. Pownall) set flush with the street line. In Henrietta St, to N, *St. Peter's Hospital* (1881–82; J.M. Brydon), Queen Anne style, and, at NW corner, *No. 22* (1858; C. Gray), stucco palazzo style but the detail Gothic. S of Tavistock St, Burleigh St, with polychrome brick Gothic former *vicarage* (1859; Butterfield). At the E end of Exeter St, portico of former *Lyceum Theatre* (1834; S. Beazley) where Henry Irving and Ellen Terry worked. The interior of 1904 survives, battered, as a dance hall. Opposite, a corner building (1863; C.O. Parnell), richly modelled. In Tavistock St, early LCC flats (1903), on Drury Lane and Kemble St, *Bruce House* (1907), LCC lodging house for single men, the style of these a humane red brick with sash windows. In Wild St, *Peabody Buildings* (1881; A. Darbishire), the earlier style of artisan housing.

Lincoln's Inn and Law Courts

Kingsway, driven through (1900-05) from the Strand to Holborn, divides Covent Garden from the lawyers' London to the E. At the S end, Aldwych, a cresent aligning the new street with Waterloo Bridge. On NW corner, *Inveresk House* (1907; Mewes and Davis), Parisian style, but its quality much diminished when the corner dome and attic were removed for more storeys. Beyond, two similar theatres (1905; W. Sprague), the *Strand* and the *Aldwych*, flank the big pavilion-roofed *Waldorf Hotel* (1907; A.M. Mackenzie), typical of the Portland stone classical buildings of this area. *Bush House*, the formal endpiece of Kingsway, is of 1925 by the American architect H. Corbett, *India House* 1928–30 (Sir H. Baker) and, to E, *Australia House* (1912–18; A.M. Mackenzie), pile up figure sculpture. Opposite, *No. 99* (1911; J.J. Burnet), much more restrained. In Kingsway, on the W side, on corner of Keeley St, *No. 65* (1910–11; J.J. Burnet), the most famous of the early steel-frame buildings in London, not for its date, but for the functional way in which the exterior expresses the frame with plain four-storey piers over a squared-off ground floor and mezzanine.

Further up, *No. 42* (1906; Lutyens), mannered classical, and *No. 44* (c 1905), free Jacobean. Further up, *RC church* (1909; F.A. Walters), curved gable front and Flemish Renaissance interior. Opposite, *Holy Trinity Church* (1910–12; Belcher and Joass), Baroque play of opposite curves to a facade intended to rise to a huge tower. Tunnel-vaulted interior.

To the E, Lincoln's Inn Fields, with, on the N side, *Nos 17–18* (1871; A. Waterhouse), stone and Gothic, and *No. 19* (1868; P. Webb), early and very original synthesis of Gothic and sash windows of a 18C proportion, a tall stone bay flanked by brick, the motifs all strong with the feeling of having been rethought from first principles. On the S side, *Land Registry* (1906 and 1913; H. Tanner), big neo-Jacobean block. Further on, *Royal College of Surgeons* (1836; C. Barry), Barry refaced the building to bring the Ionic portico of 1806–13 more into harmony with the rest of the building. Previously it had been compared to the 'helmet of Pericles on the head of a Quaker'. Barry fluted the columns, stuccoed the front and raised it a storey. It was unfortunately raised and extended further in 1888. To the N, in High Holborn, *Pearl Assurance* (1912; Moncton and Newman), very large Edwardian Baroque. Further E, on S side, *No. 336*, Staple Inn Buildings (1903; A. Waterhouse), pink terracotta. In Lincoln's Inn, associated with lawyers since the 13C, the *hall and library* block (1842–45; P. and P.C. Hardwick), towards Lincoln's Inn Fields, is well-handled Tudor, all in diapered brick and of considerable size as the main floors are raised above ground and reached by outside stairs. The hall has G.F. Watt's fresco, 'The Lawgivers' (1859), at the far end. In Chancery Lane, on the E side, *No. 33* (1874; Giles and Gough), Gothic, on W, *No. 87* (1863; A. Blomfield), narrow Gothic front in polychrome brick. On the corner of Carey St, *No. 95a* (1865; F.W. Porter), stone Renaissance style bank. Opposite, *Public Record Office* (1851–96; J. Pennethorne), the range to Chancery Lane is the later part, repeated Gothic arches rising full height to a pinnacled and battlemented parapet with taller towers, all faced in Portland stone, the effect surprisingly grid-like and modern. The Record Office Museum is open to the public. The *Law Society*, on the S side of Carey St, has an Ionic porticoed hall (1831; Vulliamy) given side wings (1849 and 56) and extended to Carey St (1902; Adams and Holden) with a powerful square block cut back at the upper corners, the detail stripped and angular classical. Inside this part, a Common Room with marble and bronze Corinthian piers and a series of bright faience plaques by C. Dressler. Beyond, *No. 114* (1856; T. Bellamy), a very handsome palazzo front, the windows set against a rusticated wall face. The rear (1874) has delightful detail including firemen's helmets and picks, as this was a fire insurance office.

In the Strand, to W, *Royal Courts of Justice* (1873–82; G.E. Street), built on the site of a crowded slum from which over 4000 people were moved. Street's building is the most important High Victorian Gothic public building in Britain, begun just after the Houses of Parliament were finally completed. The contrast is in the far bolder 13C style Gothic with its rich play of projection and recession. The front would have been broadly symmetrical but the W quadrangle was never built. The material is crisply carved Portland stone with some red stone shafting. The main entrance is recessed and flanked by octagonal stair turrets with the tall gable of the central hall rising behind a deeply modelled Gothic archway capped by an open arcade. To the E, a long almost symmetrical range broken for the entrance to the side quadrangle, the entrance flanked by gables, the corners brought out as tourelles. At the E end, the main tower, bolder and harsher in detail, capped by a strong pyramid roof. A magnificent painted clock projects high over the street. As the building is always seen in the long side view, the tower, tourelles and octagonal stair turrets make a most picturesque group with the roof of the hall crowned by a flèche behind. The hall itself is one of the great Victorian interiors, stone clad, stone vaulted with tall grouped lancets high up leaving a generous area of plain wall above the richer arches and arcading at ground level. In the hall, monument to G.E. Street (1886; H.H. Armstead). The side elevation to Bell Yard is in red brick and stone with a further tower.

The Strand and Embankment

Opposite the Law Courts, *Lloyds Bank* (1883; G. Cuthbert) surprises as soon as entered: the whole entrance hall is clad in brightly coloured Doulton's tiles and the banking hall lined with tile pictures from the plays of Ben Jonson, remaining from when this building was the Palsgrave's Head Restaurant. Outside St. Clement Dane's church, finely modelled statue of *Gladstone* (1905; H. Thornycroft). Somerset House, the great complex of 18C government offices, fills the area between the Strand and the river, the E side extended for *King's College* of London University (1829–35; R. Smirke), the W facade, to Lancaster Place, added 1852–56 in harmonious but heavier style by J. Pennethorne. W of Lancaster Place, the *Savoy Hotel* (1903–04; T.E. Collcutt), clad in Doulton's Carraraware, an extension to the original hotel, facing the river, of 1884. This was the first London hotel to provide bathrooms for each bedroom. Built for R. D'Oyly Carte, promoter of the Gilbert and Sullivan Savoy operas and owner of the Savoy Theatre (1881) now embedded in the hotel extension. The Strand front of *Shell-Mex House* is the rear of the Hotel Cecil (1902), a mammoth hotel originally fronting the river built by the speculator Jabez Balfour who went bankrupt spectacularly for £8,000,000 in 1892. On N side of the Strand, smaller buildings including the *Vaudeville Theatre* (facade 1891; C.J. Phipps). At the corner of Agar St, *No. 429* (1907; C. Holden), Zimbabwe House, granite and Portland stone in a most mannered and sharp edged classical style. The first- floor tall windows play with a Venetian window theme, the windows above complicate the motif with Epstein's now battered sculptures in the side panels and a blank arch over, above the windows have pilaster sides like an architrave surround but with the top member simply removed. Beyond, Nash's stucco West Strand Improvements (1830–32) with the centrepiece missing and replaced by a recessed glass screen for Coutts Bank. Opposite, *Charing Cross Station*, the front an hotel (1864; E.M. Barry), with its roofline rebuilt. *Eleanor Cross* in the forecourt (1865; E.M. Barry) substitutes for the medieval cross marking the last point on the return of the body of Queen Eleanor to London (1291). The original site is where the statue of Charles I stands in Trafalgar Square. The station itself had an arched roof which collapsed in 1905 destroying the *Playhouse Theatre* in Craven St below. The theatre was rebuilt in 1907 (Blow and Billerey) retaining the 1882 exterior but substituting a pretty French style interior.

On Victoria Embankment, E of Villiers St, gardens with a series of statues, a seated *Robert Burns* (1884; Steell), standing *Sir W. Lawson* (1909; McGill), teetotaller and radical opponent of the Boer War and the House of Lords. Opposite, fountain to the blind economist *H. Fawcett* (1886; Mary Grant), then *R. Raikes* (1880; Brock), founder of the Sunday Schools, and *Arthur Sullivan* (1903; W. Goscombe John), his partner *W.S. Gilbert* commemorated across the road (1914; Frampton). *Cleopatra's Needle* was brought to London in 1878 from Heliopolis. Egyptian granite obelisks had been prestigious features of papal Rome and Napoleonic Paris, so Victorian London (and New York) could not be left behind. Beyond Waterloo Bridge and Somerset House more gardens, with statues of *Brunel* (Marochetti), *W.E. Forster* (1889; H. Pinker), the Yorkshire MP largely responsible for the 1870 Education Act which he stands holding, and *John Stuart Mill* (1876; Woolner). Behind, in Temple Place, *No. 2* (1892–95; J.L. Pearson), the former Astor Estate office, a miniature Elizabethan country house in Portland stone, most beautifully detailed, the carving a model of late 19C decoration, lively in design, clear and crisp in execution. The interior is palatial, marble floors, carved woodwork and a first-floor great hall with hammerbeam roof.

Bloomsbury and Euston (actually within the borough of Camden)

Tottenham Court Rd is the W edge. At the S end, E side, the *Horseshoe* (1877; E. Paraire), originally one of the grandest pubs in London with restaurant and café, the detail squared up in a manner very faintly suggestive of Glasgow. Doubled in size 1892 and the ground floor and interiors wrecked more recently. Further up, on W side, *Rising Sun* pub (1896; Treadwell and Martin), a delicate free Gothic front with charming Art Nouveau carving. Great Russell St leads E with late 19C hotels to the *British Museum* (1823–48; R. Smirke) with its splendid colonnaded S front. The forecourt is enclosed by ornate iron railings (1849; S. Smirke). This is the finest Greek Revival building in London. Instead of the grand square that such a building would have in most continental cities, mid Victorian commercial buildings (1855–62; Searle and Trehearne) line the streets immediately outside the gates. The *Museum Tavern* (1855), Museum St, has a good pub front. Off Coptic St, in Streatham St, the pioneering *Model Dwellings* (1849; H. Roberts), among the very first flats built to rescue the poor from the insanitary slums, and the earliest to survive. Plain brick exterior, the rear with open balconies giving access, a plan still used in British housing. Each flat had a lavatory. From Museum St, Bloomsbury Way leads E. Facing Bloomsbury Square, *No. 3* (1887; F. Pinches), red brick and curved gabled. On S side, *Sicilian Avenue* (1905; W.J. Wortley), red brick and cream terracotta pedestrian street, pretty shopfronts and columned screens each end. In Southampton Row, *Central School of Arts* (1907; A.H. Verstage), a building influenced by Lethaby, Principal of the school, which probably accounts for its avoidance of period detail and the elemental nature of such detail as there is. The general effect is oddly muddled, no single element of the building is strong enough to form a focus and the regularity of the facade features seems to ask for a formal symmetry that the internal plan and Arts and Crafts principles of functional external treatment do not allow. To the S, *Kingsgate House* (1901; A. Keen), mixed Edwardian detail.

Southampton Row runs N to Russell Square with the large terracotta faced *Russell Hotel* (1898; C.F. Doll), lavish French Renaissance detail and sculptures of four British Queens by H.C. Fehr. Some of the original early 19C houses were given terracotta details to cheer them up at the same time. To the N, Tavistock Square and Gordon Square, built up from c 1820–50 under T. Cubitt for the Bedford estate. In Gordon Square, on the corner, *University Church* (1853; R. Brandon), built as the cathedral church of Edward Irving's Catholic Apostolic Church.

Irving (1792–1834), a Scots minister of great eloquence and presence, turned to the subject of prophecy in the scriptures and was eventually excommunicated by the presbytery of London and ejected from his church. The Catholic Apostolic Church grew from his discussions with the rich banker Henry Drummond, but was not set up until 1835 when 12 guiding apostles were chosen. The ceremonial was elaborate, close to Roman Catholic practice, hence their splendid church, fully vaulted Dec. style stone, complete with Lady Chapel. The 300ft spire intended was never built, but otherwise the cathedral is remarkable for having been built to such a scale within a very short time. To the N in Gordon Square, *Dr Williams's Library* (1848; T.L. Donaldson), Tudor Style in deliberate contrast to the Square. SW of the church, a handsome block (c 1830; T. Cubitt) facing E, originally intended as three houses but completed as Coward College. To W, more extravagant terracotta to *Dillon's* (1907; C.F. Doll). To N, on Gower St, S of Euston Rd, *University College* (1827–29; W. Wilkins), founded to provide university education without religious bias, and the first college of London University. Neo-Grecian, the main interior space remodelled 1848 (T.L. Donaldson) to hold the plaster originals of Flaxman's sculptures. Opposite, *University College Hospital* (1897–1906; A. Waterhouse), contrasting in every respect, built to an innovative cross-plan set diagonally on the square ground floor. At the S end of Malet St, the *King Edward VII wing* of the British Museum (1904–14; J.J. Burnet), grandly neo-classical, but with personal touches, as in the window heads and the porch breaking through the podium.

E of Southampton Row, in Queen Square, *St. George's Church*, basically 18C, given a spiky overhaul 1867 (S.S. Teulon). On the S side, *Italian Hospital* (1900; T.W. Cutler), cheerful brick with a dome to one side. Other hospitals fill the Square and the E end of Great Ormond St, notably the *Hospital for Sick Children* (1872–76; E.M. Barry), the exterior battered and altered but a fine chapel inside. On the W of Queen Square, premises of the *Art Workers Guild*, founded 1884 to bring together architecture, painting, sculpture and the crafts. Nearly all the leading figures of the Arts and Crafts movement were members as can be seen from the portraits and roll of names in the lecture hall. Between Great Ormond St and Theobald's Rd, early 19C streets. *No. 48 Doughty St*, where Dickens wrote 'Oliver Twist' and 'Nicholas Nickleby' 1837–41, is the Dickens House Museum. Collection of manuscripts and relics. On the corner of Gray's Inn Rd and Theobald's Rd, the *Yorkshire Grey* pub (1877; J.W. Brooker), lively white brick front with naive carved cavalryman in the gable. *Gray's Inn*, to the S, one of the Inns of Court, is mostly of the 17C, the library of 1841 (Wigg and Pownall). Statue of Sir F. Bacon in South Square by Pomeroy (1912). To E, in Clerkenwell Rd, *St. Peter's RC Church* (1863 and c 1890), a delightful red-brick pedimented front, appropriately Italian for so Italian a district, though the detail is more English Queen Anne. The interior more thoroughly Italian. The *Bourne estate* (1901–02) is one of the first LCC housing estates. To S, just E of Gray's Inn Rd, in Brooke St, the polychrome brick tower of *St. Alban's Church* (1859–62; W. Butterfield), the W front a magnificently solid design stair tower between tall W windows and a saddleback roof. The rest was rebuilt within the old walls after bombing. The entry from Brooke Market is under the contemporary *Clergy House* by Butterfield. In the square, which has a nice secluded air, pleasant low c 1910 LCC housing. Gray's Inn Rd is almost all redeveloped though the little streets to the E, Ampton St and Frederick St, where the great builder Thomas Cubitt began his career in 1815 and had his workshops, have some surviving fragments, the early 19C developments around Regent Square have mostly gone. To W, at the W end of Tavistock Place, *Mary Ward House (1895–98; Smith and Brewer), a community building paid for by Passmore Edwards, millionaire philanthropist, designed in the advanced Arts and Crafts manner, suggestive of Mackintosh in Glasgow. Broadly symmetrical with wings flanking a recessed hall but the symmetry powerfully challenged by the strong stone porch of the hall. Red brick with a broad band of stucco under the deep eaves. The wings, slightly higher, have small paned windows set in opposing diagonals marking the stair on each side. In Cromer St, to NE, *Holy Cross Church* (1887; J. Peacock), tall brick with heavy font by Pearson.

The Midland Grand Hotel, St. Pancras Station (1868–74; Sir G.G. Scott), King's Cross

Euston Rd runs to N with three major railway stations. *King's Cross Station* (1851–52; L. Cubitt) was the Great Northern terminus. A massive yellow brick front expresses the two arches of the train-shed behind, the middle pier crowned by a clock turret. Severe and plain brickwork of high quality emphasising that this is a screen wall only, the booking offices were to the left and the railway offices to the right in plain late Georgian type ranges. Set behind to left, *Great Northern Hotel* (1854; L. Cubitt), a large curved brick and stucco block facing NE. Across the road, *St. Pancras Station*, built for the Midland Railway (1868–74). To the front, Sir G.G. Scott's magnificent Gothic hotel in red brick with stone and granite details, the most lavish of all railway hotels in Britain. The building rises four storeys and then is crowned by a steep roof with pinnacles and dormers between a massive square tower over the carriage entry and hotel entrance and a slimmer E end tower capped by a spiky lantern spire. The composition makes the most of the line of the tracks, which is not square on to

Euston Rd, allowing the building to slope back between the two towers and then be connected again to the street line by a big W end range that curves forward enclosing the triangular forecourt. From all angles the two towers and the pinnacled gable of the W range make a superbly romantic composition. Recent cleaning has revealed again the richness of the colour scheme. In the former hotel, Scott's staircase survives. The *train-shed behind (1863–65; W.H. Barlow and R. Ordish) is a single huge iron span of lattice girders rising curved to meet in a point 100ft up. The 243ft span was the widest in the world for many years. The Gothic detail of the hotel continues in the side walls and booking office and also in the impressive arcades down the streets to each side. To the N, on Battle Bridge Rd, *gasholders* (c 1865 and later), the earlier ones with three orders of superimposed cast-iron columns recently well repainted. On Euston Rd, the Greek Revival *St. Pancras' Church* (1819–22; W. and H.W. Inwood), the most thoroughgoing Regency adaptation of Greek forms to an Anglican church. Opposite, *Euston Fire Station* (1902; H.F. Cooper), one of the early LCC Arts and Crafts influenced buildings. Bold tall proportions, mainly brick, broken for the most complex pattern of stone oriels, bay windows and craggy gables with sheer brick chimneys. All this variety expresses the functions within and suggests the possibilities latent in the 'free style' of c 1900 before the classical styles, Georgian or Baroque, became standard for public buildings. Across Euston Square, *Nos 194–8 Euston Rd* (1907; A.B. Pite), interpreting the grand classical manner with all the freedom of the Arts and Crafts. Giant Ionic columns play in and out of the two principal floors in homage to C.R. Cockerell's Ashmolean building in Oxford, but placing a column in the centre of a two-storey paired window with no entablature above is a most mannered fancy. There is an apparent attic storey over the columns with a heavy cornice but the true attic is above that, treated with three gables over Venetian windows and flanked by open severe loggias. The entrance hall, clad in green and yellow matt tile with mosaic floor, is Greek rethought with wit and originality. Pite added the adjoining building to W in a plain style in 1912. *Euston Station* has been demolished, in the Square two pretty lodges (1869; Stansby) survive, and, among the new buildings, statue of *R. Stephenson* (Marochetti), engineer of the London–Birmingham line. N of the W end of Euston Rd, in Munster Square, *St. Mary Magdalene's Church* (1849–52; R.C. Carpenter), a model church of the Puginian type, in Kentish ragstone with Dec. details, all rather eroded. Nave and aisles separately roofed to give a three-gabled street front. Light and graceful interior.

Paddington

The area NW of Marble Arch was Tyburnia, the Bishop of London's rival development to the Grosvenor family's Belgravia on the other side of Hyde Park. Developed from 1825, when the Tyburn gallows were removed, it has fared less well, not surprisingly even the name never took hold, though the axial plan with crescents and squares was more imaginative. Post-war redevelopment cleared away most of the surroundings of *St. John's Church* (1829–31; C. Fowler), the focus of the diagonal axis, though part of Gloucester Square (c 1838–40; G.L. Taylor) and the big five-storey terraces fronting the Park survive to show the late Regency style of the estate into the 1840s. Sussex Gardens formed a main axis to the N, focused again on a church, *St. James'*, Lancaster Gate, where a cheap tower and spire of 1843

(Goldicutt and Gutch) fronts a flint-faced church by Street (1881), not of particular character. From the church, *Westbourne Terrace* runs N, developed from 1843–48 in more Italianate style by several architects, G.L. Taylor, G. Stokes, G. Alexander (*No. 28*) among them, consistent in the tall scale, overall stucco and heavy cornices. In the lesser streets around some attractive bow-fronted terraces. The centre of the area is now *Paddington Station*, Praed St, the London terminus of the Great Western Railway, the line to Bristol engineered by I.K. Brunel. The station itself lies behind the *Great Western Hotel* (1851–53; P.C. Hardwick), difficult to recognise today as the most luxurious hotel of its date, and notable for using, even before their appearance on the New Louvre in Paris, the bulbous pavilion roofs associated with the 'Second Empire' style. A 1933 modernisation swept away the features of the entrance and principal floor above. The *station* (1854; I.K. Brunel and Sir M.D. Wyatt) is a triple-arched iron shed crossed by two 'transepts', a reminiscence perhaps of the Crystal Palace, though considerable efforts were made to ornament with odd pendants under the main trusses, which themselves have tracery decoration, and the delightful iron oriels that look out over the transepts from Platform 1. The purpose of the transepts was to move rolling stock from platform to platform on gantries, an ingenious idea, never actually used. There was a royal waiting room on Platform 1, still distinguished by the royal arms, and a boardroom for the GWR behind one of the oriels. Further up Praed St, *St. Mary's Hospital*, with the 1892 Clarence Wing (W. Emerson) on the street and the plain brick and stucco original building (1845–48; T. Hopper) behind.

W of the Paddington area, large developments of mid 19C terraces, the largest, in stucco, fronting the Park, *Lancaster Gate* (1857; Sancton Wood), a formal composition centred on the square around the former *Christ Church* (1855), of which the spire only remains. Here the formal Italianate of Westbourne Terrace has been loosened to an eclectic Renaissance manner. In the streets behind and further W brick and stucco are as common as overall stucco. W of Queensway, Palace Court, built up c 1890 in red-brick Queen Anne style for fashionable aesthetes. On the E side, *No. 2* (1891; W. Flockhart), a complex and varied design swung round an octagonal corner tower, full, perhaps too full, of pretty touches. *Nos 8 and 10* (1889; J.M. Maclaren) are a very intriguing pair, decidedly asymmetrical but carefully balanced, with Norman Shaw motifs combined with stylised ornament of a slightly Byzantine character, very advanced for their date. Maclaren unfortunately died in 1890. On the W side, further down, *No. 47* (1889; L. Stokes), built for Wilfrid and Alice Meynell, displays an advanced taste, puritan by contrast with No. 2, red brick but with simple stone bands instead of the more usual pot-pourri of moulded brick ornament. Behind, in Moscow Rd, the *Greek Orthodox Cathedral* (1877; J.O. Scott), in suitably Greek-Byzantine style, the interior atmospheric with marble, mosaic and carved screens. On Queensway, at N end, former *Whiteley's store* (1910–12; Belcher and Joass), giant-columned with a curiously varied rhythm to the main colonnade, unrelated to the ground-floor spacing, and top dome and tower, scaled somewhere between ornament and feature.

The NW corner of the City of Westminster, cut off by railway and motorway flyover, includes the picturesque mid 19C villa development along the canal in Blomfield Rd, called *Little Venice*. Facing the canal, to S, in Maida Avenue, the *Catholic Apostolic Church* (1891–93; J.L. Pearson), the last of Pearson's great town churches, of which St. Augustine's, Kilburn (see Brent below p. 257), at the opposite end of

Randolph Avenue, is the outstanding example. Here, the familiar EE style brick and stone exterior has a cavernous recess for the W window from which advances like a tiny separate church an apsed baptistery. The interior is wholly stone, wholly vaulted, as serene as any by Pearson with characteristic complexities introduced in the baptistery and SE chapel vaults. In Formosa St, beyond Warwick Avenue station, the *Prince Alfred* pub has a particularly curvaceous timber front filled with etched glass. To W, S of the canal, the prominent banded brick and stone spirelet of *St. Mary Magdalene's Church* (1868–78; G.E. Street), Woodchester Square, originally designed for a built-up area, now standing prominent amid new housing. The clearance has unfortunately diminished the impact of the E apse and slim octagonal spire which soared up from a tightly angled street corner. Magnificent interior, the arcades varied to disguise the cramped space on the N side, focused on a richly marbled chancel with carved stone reredos (T. Earp) and glowing stained glass by H. Holiday (1869). In the crypt below, beautifully delicate painted decoration, reredos and organ case by J.N. Comper (1895).

St. John's Wood

From Marylebone Rd, Lisson Grove runs N to St. John's Wood Rd, past the yellow brick Gothic *RC church* (1836; J.J. Scoles) to *Lord's Cricket Ground*, in use since 1814. In the Cricket Museum, covering the history of the game, the original 'Ashes' urn. Grove End Rd curves up to St. John's Wood station through pleasant early 19C villas, here, and in Hamilton Terrace, to W. Numerous artists had their studios in the area, *No. 17 Grove End Rd* was owned successively by J. Tissot and Sir L. Alma-Tadema. On the corner of Abbey Rd, monument to the sculptor Onslow Ford. The *Hospital of St. John and St. Elizabeth* (1902; E. Goldie) has an impressive deep courtyard centred on a domed Italian Renaissance style chapel.

KENSINGTON AND CHELSEA

Brompton (between Sloane St, Brompton Rd, Kings Rd and Sydney St)

Sloane St is the E edge of a large area of late 19C development in the urban terrace version of Queen Anne, nicknamed 'Pont St Dutch', that is with red-brick fronts, tall shaped gables and much moulded decorative brickwork. On Sloane St itself, *Nos 63 and 64* (1894–96; F.B. Wade), an individual pair in Portland stone and brick, freely styled, slightly Art Nouveau. Further down, the *Cadogan Hotel* was where Oscar Wilde was arrested in 1895 immediately after the failure of his libel suit against Lord Queensberry. In Pont St the red brick of the *Cadogan estate* begins. Developed from 1877, this is a key area to see the change from the stucco Italianate to the more entertaining Queen Anne. The pioneers were R. Norman Shaw and J.J. Stevenson and the roots of their style were in the ornamented brickwork of late 17C England, Flanders and Holland. On the corner of Pont St some later striped brick houses (c 1888; H.B. Measures) and two early ranges, *Nos 42–58* (1877; J.J. Stevenson) and *60–6* (1877; W. Niven). The S side of Pont St and N and E sides of Cadogan Square behind have dull examples of Queen Anne (1876–86; G.T. Robinson) to contrast with the far more exuberant houses on the W side of Cadogan Square, including two pioneer and excellently detailed examples by Norman Shaw, *Nos 68 and 72* (1877–79), where the variety in fenestration and richness of brickwork show the new individualism that was to alter completely the even pattern of London terraces. The S side of the square is by J.J. Stevenson (1879 and 1884), much duller than Shaw, for all Stevenson's role in developing the style. Further up the W side, considerable variety, showing the progress of Queen Anne into more Flemish Gothic or Renaissance styles in the 1880s, particularly in the work of Ernest George, and also showing the introduction of terracotta and Portland stone in combinations with the red brick. *No. 62* (1881; R. Norman Shaw), *Nos 52 and 50* (1886; George and Peto), *Nos 28–36* (c 1885; G. Devey) and *Nos 22–6* (1888; E.T. Hall). At the NE corner, *No. 4* (1879; G.E. Street) is an oddity, the great Gothic architect showing that there might be a Gothic solution to the design of town houses, more serious than the cheerful eclecticism of the Queen Anne. Similar red-brick housing stretches N, W and S, across the Cadogan estate. To N, in Hans Rd, *Nos 14–16* (1892–94; C.F.A. Voysey), restrained red brick and stone, the windows in the unmoulded flush stone frames that Voysey used so often. The symmetry is delightfully disturbed by having three narrow semi-circular oriels over the porches where one would expect four. *No. 12* (1894; A.H. Mackmurdo) is a variation on Voysey's design. In Basil St, London County Council *Fire Station* (1907), good neo-Georgian, and Lincoln House (c 1910), eccentrically detailed flats.

Brompton Rd was largely redeveloped c 1900 with blocks of flats. *Harrods* (1901–05; C.W. Stephens) is a triumph of Doultons terracotta that covers the entire front and the dome. In the meat hall inside, good Art Nouveau tile decoration by W.J. Neatby. S of Brompton Rd, in Walton St, at the E end, *Walton House* (1882; R. Norman Shaw), brick and tile-hung studio house. Severe brick former *police station* opposite also by Shaw (1894). At W end, on corner of Sloane Avenue, *Michelin Building* (1909; F. Espinasse) with tile panels of the early days of motoring. W of Cadogan Square, in Moore St, *St. Simon Zelotes' Church* (1859; J. Peacock), the very model of 'spiky' Gothic, small in scale but all the external details elongated and acutely pointed, the interior displaying all kinds of tricks of plan and striking constructional polychromy. E window by Lavers and Barraud. To S, *St. Mary's RC Church* (1877–82; J.F. Bentley), Cadogan St, a model of sobriety by comparison, in stock brick and stone, the tall interior focused on an E wall elaborated by detached shafting in front of the windows. High altar and pulpit by Bentley (1864), from the previous church on the site, of which the Blessed Sacrament Chapel (1860; E.W. Pugin) also survives. To S, at the foot of Cadogan Gardens, *No. 25* (1893; A.H. Mackmurdo), unusual studio house with long oriel lights on the N front under a deep cornice. In Sloane Square, *Royal Court Theatre* (1888) and a ponderous Portland stone block on the S side (c 1900; A. Faulkner). At the S end of Sloane St, **Holy Trinity Church* (1889; J.D. Sedding), an incomplete shrine of late Victorian church design. The building, in brick and stone, free Perp. style, was intended to be decorated by the finest craftsmen of the day, but most of the sculptural and painted decoration was never begun. Fine interior, lit by broad traceried windows each end, the E glass by Burne-Jones. N aisle glass by Sir W. Richmond, S side glass by Christopher Whall. Excellent metalwork including the screen by Sedding with angels by F.W. Pomeroy, N chapel screen, light fittings and railings to the street by H. Wilson.

Chelsea (between Fulham Rd and the river)

S of Sloane Square, Cadogan estate red-brick houses of c 1880–90. Off

Royal Hospital Rd, to SW, Tite St, a little artistic centre for the avant-garde from the late 1870s. Oscar Wilde lived at *No. 34*, J.M. Whistler's famous White House was *No. 35* and J.S. Sargeant lived at *Nos 31–3*. Of the surviving houses, *No. 44* (1878; E.W. Godwin), built for the painter Frank Miles, is the best, the studio marked by a big Queen Anne gable. *No. 46* (1884; E.W. Godwin), a tower block of four superimposed studios, quite overwhelms the Miles house. On Chelsea Embankment, an important group of houses in the Queen Anne taste, larger and more expensive than Tite St, built for clients of artistic leanings with large fortunes. On the corner of Tite St, *No. 3* (1879; Bodley and Garner), a dignified symmetrical front of long windows outlined in red against the yellow brick of the walling, then *Nos 4–6* (1876–78; E.W. Godwin), *No. 7* (1878; R.P. Spiers) and *No. 8*, The Clock House (1878; R. Norman Shaw), symmetrical but for the clock, a complex front displaying Shaw's skill in handling varied elements. *Nos 9–11* (1878; R. Norman Shaw), a row of three houses, gabled with white sash windows and each with a projecting bay, upsetting neatly the regular rhythm of the upper floors, *No. 12* (1877; J.H. Pollen), *No. 13* (1877; E. l'Anson), *No. 15* (1877; R. Norman Shaw) with a single great gable from which originally a moulded brick chimney rose proudly, and *No. 16* (1877; A. Croft) show what varieties could be achieved within the Queen Anne. The finest house of the row, *ᐧNo. 17*, Old Swan House (1875; R. Norman Shaw), is restful by comparison, a subtle composition held in by a deep white cornice and neatly changing rhythm from the predominant glass of the three first-floor oriels to the brick of the overhanging upper floors. *No. 18*, Cheyne House (1875; R. Norman Shaw), was the first of the group, well planned on the corner site. Cheyne Walk beyond has buildings of the 1880s inserted in a 18C row. In the gardens, *memorial* to D.G. Rossetti with relief portrait by his fellow Pre- Raphaelite, Ford Maddox Brown. Rossetti lived at *No. 16 Cheyne Walk* from 1862 to his death in 1882, surrounded by his exotic pets. *Albert Bridge* (1873; R.M. Ordish) is the most festive of London bridges, especially since repainting. W of the bridge, *ᐧNos 38–9 Cheyne Walk* (1898–99; C.R. Ashbee), an Arts and Crafts pair of red-brick houses with long flush windows and white roughcast appearing in the upper floor and right-hand gable. All the pretty brickwork of the earlier Queen Anne style houses has been abandoned for stylish simplicity. Splendid iron railings. In the gardens, *statue* of Thomas Carlyle (1882; Boehm). Carlyle, the 'Sage of Chelsea', lived at *ᐧNo. 24 Cheyne Row* (open to public) from 1834 to 1881 and wrote his 'French Revolution' in the soundproofed study at the top of the house. Facing down Cheyne Row, *No. 35 Glebe Place* (1868; P. Webb), studio house for the painter G.P. Boyce and a building that shows clearly Webb as an originator of the Queen Anne style with its small-paned sashes and hipped roof. *Carlyle Mansions*, at the foot of Lawrence St, has decorative aesthetic movement plaques to an otherwise dull block. Here Henry James stayed the winters from 1912 and died 1916. *Battersea Bridge* (1890; Sir J. Bazalgette) replaces the one that appears in Whistler's 'Nocturne' paintings. Whistler lived at this, the cheaper, end of Cheyne Walk from 1862–78.

To the N, on Kings Rd, the *World's End*, one of the extravagent late 19C pubs built at the termini of horse-bus routes. Further E on Kings Rd, *Chelsea Town Hall*, the road front a handsome work in red brick and grey granite (1904–08; L. Stokes) and the rear, the original building (1885–87; J.M. Brydon), an important work in the return to English Baroque models, that is the architecture of the time of Wren. Up Manresa Rd, nearby, N of Kings Rd, *Chelsea College* occupies the former Public Library (1890) and technical college buildings (1891–95) also by Brydon and also English Baroque, the Library with a fine semicircular porch. In Sydney St, *St. Luke's Church* (1820–24; J. Savage), the first stone-vaulted church of the Gothic Revival. Dickens was married here in 1836 and Charles Kingsley's father was rector 1836–60.

Knightsbridge (between Hyde Park, Gloucester Rd and Cromwell Rd; largely in Westminster but for convenience included here)

N of Brompton Rd early 19C squares and terraces at the E corner give way to the ponderous stucco of the 1840s and 1850s in Ennismore Gardens and Princes Gate. The grandest houses are those fronting the Park in Princes Gate (c 1850–60) but Ennismore Gardens (c 1845; H.L. Elmes) is the more attractive ensemble. In the centre, the *Russian church* (1848; L. Vulliamy), a plain early Romanesque type church embellished with a campanile (1877) and then given Arts and Crafts ornament on the W end (1892; C.H. Townsend) and interior decoration in sgraffito plaster by Heywood Sumner, the reviver of this ancient technique. Sumner also designed the stained glass. *Prince of Wales Gate* into Hyde Park dates from 1847 (D. Burton). Across Exhibition Rd is the *Royal Geographical Society* occupying Lowther Lodge (1872–75; R. Norman Shaw), built on the scale of a country house for a wealthy MP. Here Shaw gave a major demonstration of the new style for domestic architecture that became the 'Queen Anne'. Wholly in red brick with sweeping roofs and bold chimneys, the windows white painted and framed in moulded brickwork and the attic gables highly decorated in aesthetic style with sunflowers, the house contrasts not just with contemporary stucco town houses but also with the country houses of the Gothic Revival. Shaw's roots in the Gothic Revival show in the restless asymmetry. Behind, facing Exhibition Rd, are a pair of Queen Anne houses, *Nos 1 and 2 Lowther Gardens* (1878; J.J. Stevenson), where the detailing of the moulded brickwork is particularly fine. Lowther Lodge is overwhelmed to the W by *Albert Hall Mansions* (1879–81; R. Norman Shaw), one of the first blocks of flats in London and one of the very few that are architecturally distinguished. Fine brickwork, Dutch gables and long sash windows disguise the size of the block. Shaw designed the plain blocks to the rear and other architects filled the remaining sites behind the Albert Hall confirming the quality of Shaw's first work. These last buildings are private or speculative intrusions onto the 83-acre site acquired from the proceeds of the Crystal Palace exhibition of 1851 for the building of centres of culture and education.

The 1851 exhibition in Joseph Paxton's great glass palace had been the triumph of Prince Albert, and his organising and educating spirit can be felt through all the chaotic jumble of museums and educational institutions in this area. Albert, hallowed and made universal guiding spirit, watches yet from the *Albert Memorial* (1863–72; G.G. Scott) in Hyde Park. The memorial is at once one of the finest achievements of the Gothic Revival, a N Italian Gothic shrine 175ft high in marble, granite, bronze and Portland stone, but also a museum of the best of British sculpture of the time. Albert himself in garter robes holds the catalogue of the 1851 exhibition, the bronze statue by J.H. Foley, above him the shrine of fantastic richness decorated with statues of the Sciences, the great spire ringed half-way by figures of the Virtues and at the top by mourning angels beneath exulting angels and the cross. Around Albert are Commerce, Engineering, Manufactures and Agriculture, four Portland stone groups, while, beneath, runs a stone frieze of artists (W and N sides by J.B. Philip, E and S by H.H. Armstead). Note among the architects, Pugin, Cockerell, Barry and Scott himself (the only artist portrayed who was then living). The most splendid sculptures are at the outer edge: Europe (P. MacDowell) around the bull of Europa; military France holds a sword, Germany, the home of literature, science and Albert, a book, and Italy, a lyre and palette; Asia (J.H. Foley) around a superb elephant (Foley is said to have contracted the pleurisy that killed him sitting on India's lap modelling her ample breasts in the first clay stage); Africa (W. Theed) around a camel; America (J. Bell) impassive on a buffalo. Opposite the memorial, the *Albert Hall* (1867–71; Lt-Col H. Scott), the perfect foil, a circular mass of red brick relieved by terracotta details of surprising delicacy. The encircling frieze depicts the triumph of the Arts. This combination of bold use of finely laid red brick with Renaissance style decoration in terracotta characterises all the early buildings on the S Kensington site and represents as much the taste of Prince Albert as of the two army engineers who designed most of them, Captain Fowke and Lt-Col Scott. Adjoining, *Royal College of Organists* (1875; Lt H.H. Cole), covered in sgraffito plaster decoration, an instance of the S Kensington emphasis on thoroughly practical combination of decorative art and architecture.

Queen's Gate, beyond, is one of the last streets of grand stucco-faced houses to be built in London, especially ponderous are the houses at the S end of the W side with colonnaded ground floors carrying first-floor porches. By the mid 1870s fashion was turning and at the NE end of the street is the clearest evidence with houses in the new red-brick Queen Anne style interspersed amid the stucco. *No. 196 Queen's Gate* (1875; R. Norman Shaw), the prototype Queen Anne town house, tall, gabled, full of variety especially in moulded brickwork, and generous in window space, a good example of the near symmetry, avoiding regularity, that Shaw and other leading Queen Anne architects learned from their Gothic Revival training. On the corner of Imperial Institute Rd, *No. 170* (1887; R. Norman Shaw) is a building that looks forward to the neo-Georgian of c 1900 in its plain facade, cornice and hipped roof. The inspiration for this very advanced design was the owner, F.A. White, cement manufacturer and collector (the cornice and corner stones are cement, not stone). *No. 167*, beyond, is of 1889 (M. Macartney), red brick and stone. Imperial College, which occupies most of the block between Imperial Institute Rd and Prince Consort Rd to the N, has, in the way of academic institutions, destroyed this central part of the S Kensington complex. Only the striped stone campanile remains of the magnificent *Imperial Institute* (1887–93; T.E. Collcutt). In Prince Consort Rd, *Royal College of Music* (1883; A. Blomfield), red-brick French château. Inside, c 1900 auditorium (S.R. Smith) and excellent historical collection of instruments and portraits of musical figures. Nearby, *Holy Trinity Church* (1902; G.F. Bodley), one of Bodley's last works, all elegant simplicity, good proportions and muted stained glass.

At the foot of Exhibition Rd, the *Henry Cole Wing* of the Victoria and Albert Museum (1867–71; Lt-Col H. Scott) in the S Kensington style with excellent terracotta decoration. Newly restored grand staircase inside. Facing Cromwell Rd, *Natural History Museum* (1873–81; A. Waterhouse), the finest 19C museum building in Britain and best example of that combination of didactic sculptural decoration with architecture that the Victorians thought appropriate to public buildings. The buildings are monumentally symmetrical in facade and

Natural History Museum, terracotta detail (1873–81; A. Waterhouse), Cromwell Road

plan. Based on German Romanesque precedent, cathedral-like towers flank the cavernous main portal and big steep-roofed corner pavilions balance the long facade. The outstanding feature is the complete covering in terracotta of a creamy brown colour, banded in slate blue. Throughout is the most lively decoration based on closely observed zoological and geological models. Animals and fossils appear at all points inside and outside, all based on Waterhouse's own drawings and modelled by Dujardin. The W half of the building is decorated with living, the E half with extinct creatures. Inside, the Great Hall combines cathedral-like space with great Baroque staircase and flying gallery. The roof is iron, prettily panelled with painted plant decoration. To the E, the *Victoria and Albert Museum*, a long red-brick and Portland stone facade (1899–1909; Sir A. Webb), an intriguing example of the stylistic eclecticism of the turn of the century, the conception grandly classical, the detail French late Gothic (the windows) to Renaissance and the skyline vaguely suggestive of Italy c 1500. The huge central octagon provides no useful space above the ground floor. This exterior range conceals the original *Quadrangle* (1859–72; Capt. F. Fowke) in the S Kensington red brick and terracotta. The terracotta detail by G. Sykes is exceptionally good. At the rear of this quad, restored *dining-rooms* decorated in tile by Sykes and Poynter next to the *Green Dining-Room*, one of the earliest decorative works of William Morris (1867). In the NW corner, elaborately tiled *staircase*. Recently restored to their original glory, the *Cast courts*, quintessentially Victorian collections of plaster casts of the great European works of sculpture (including Trajan's Column in two halves). The present Restaurant reveals only a fragment of exotic Victorian decoration excavated from a 1930s cover-up, but all the more tantalising for that. E of the Museum, *Brompton Oratory*, one of the leading Roman Catholic churches in Britain and intimately involved in the revival of Catholicism in England in the 19C. J.H. Newman left the Church of England and joined the Oratory in Rome in 1847. The London Oratory was founded in 1850. The original house (1854; J.J. Scoles), dignified and Roman looking, survives next to the present church (1878–96; H. Gribble) which is modelled on the Gesù church in Rome. It was to have had two front towers which would have altered the resemblance. The church is most stately if conventional, the best exterior feature the Baroque dome, an alteration to Gribble's design by G. Sherrin (1896). The interior, sumptuous in a thoroughly Italian way, includes much that was brought from Italy. Outside, W of the courtyard, statue of Cardinal Newman by Chavaillaud (1896). Behind the Oratory, like a country church, the rather meagre Anglican parish *church* (1829), in pleasing contrast.

South Kensington (between South Kensington and Earl's Court stations)

An area that shows the full range of Victorian housing of the wealthier sort within a small area. Just E of the underground station a nice Regency style development by G. Basevi including the stucco *Pelham Crescent* (1833) and the brick and stucco *Thurloe Square* (1839–45). S of the station this stock brick and stucco becomes grander in *Onslow Square* (1861; C.J. Freake). Stucco on a grand scale appears along Cromwell Rd and the S end of Queen's Gate. Individual mansions, albeit semi-detached, in the Italian palazzo manner, appear in *The Boltons* (c 1845–50), S of Brompton Rd. Late Victorian red brick of special exuberance appears N of The Boltons in *Harrington Gardens* and *Collingham Gardens* (1880–84; George and Peto), a complete development of exotic Dutch gabled houses decorated in moulded brick, stone and terracotta. *No. 39 Harrington Gdns*, the most spectacular, was built for W.S. Gilbert on the profits of 'Patience'. 'The Mikado' and 'The Yeomen of the Guard' were written here. On Cromwell Rd and Old Brompton Rd appear large blocks of late 19C flats, *Nos 200–22 Cromwell Rd* (1882; R. Norman Shaw) and *Coleherne Court* (1902; W.F. Cave), Old Brompton Rd, the former plain red brick, the latter freely eclectic. On Fulham Rd, *Brompton Hospital* (1844; Francis: 1880; T.H. Wyatt), red-brick Tudor hospital for consumptives, at the back a little ragstone chapel (1849; E.B. Lamb). In Queen's Gate, *St. Augustine's Church* (1871–76; W. Butterfield), the front angular and square shouldered, the interior splendidly polychrome and dominated by the low chancel arch above which a large traceried window gives a hint of the chancel roof. The multi-coloured interior is a brave recent restoration in paint of the structural colour obliterated in the 1920s. Off Old Brompton Rd, in The Boltons, *St. Mary's Church* (1849; G. Godwin), a ragstone suburban church distinguished by the central tower which goes octagonal under the spire.

Further W on Old Brompton Rd, *Brompton Cemetery* (1840; B. Baud), one of the finest London cemeteries. Baud's Bath stone circular classical chapel and colonnaded catacombs are quite exceptionally grandiose. The cemetery had had 155,000 burials by 1889 and is now no longer in use. The best tomb, by the W path, is the sarcophagus to F. Leyland (1902), patron of the Pre-Raphaelites and the man for whom Whistler painted the Peacock Room now in the National Gallery, Washington DC. The design is by Burne-Jones, a simple stone chest on stout columns wreathed in metal ornament. The painter Val Prinsep has a decayed Gothic sarcophagus raised on columns nearby (1904). Opposite, the recumbent lion guards the tomb of 'Gentleman' Jackson (died 1845), boxing champion of England 1795–1803, who later taught Byron to box. Also buried here are George Borrow (died 1861), Sir Henry Cole (died 1882), moving spirit behind the S Kensington museums, Sir John Fowler (died 1898), engineer of the Forth Bridge, Matthew Noble (died 1876), sculptor, and Samuel Smiles (died 1904), author of 'Self Help'. Off Warwick Rd, to N, *St. Cuthbert* (1884–87; H.R. Gough), Philbeach Gardens, a tall brick Gothic church with prominent green spirelet, notable for exceptional Arts and Crafts fittings. Dominant are the enormous wooden reredos (1914; Rev. E. Geldart) and the rood loft (1893), but the best work is by W. Bainbridge Reynolds (1855–1935). The lectern is the most exotic piece, all beaten copper and wrought iron, but most of the other metal-work, screens, altar rails, clock and Royal arms, is his too, sinuous in a controlled Art Nouveau way.

Kensington and North Kensington (between Queen's Gate and Ladbroke Grove station)

W of Queen's Gate, the stucco and brick of the 1860s and 1870s gives way to the red-brick Queen Anne styles of the later 19C. Hyde Park Gate has some battered stucco villas while *No. 18* (1871; R. Norman Shaw) is Shaw's first London town house, yellow brick and gabled, the motifs slightly Gothic, influenced by P. Webb. *No. 22* was the childhood home of Virginia Woolf. In Palace Gate, *No. 1A* is a late intruder (1898; C.J.H. Cooper), an Arts and Crafts stone front with very decorative railings. *No. 2* (1878; P.C. Hardwick), opposite, is the pompous house of the painter Millais illustrating how far Millais had gone from his Pre-Raphaelite days and how uninspired the later Victorian town house could be. *No. 8*, an early Queen Anne house (1873; J.J. Stevenson), demonstrates the alternative. Kensington Gate is a little stucco square (1847) charmingly finished with a pepperpot corner turret to Gloucester Rd. On Gloucester Rd, *No. 15* (c 1870; C.G. Searle), quite richly Gothic of the Ruskinian sort in white brick with yellow brick and stone details. Note the tiny windows up under the cornice. Further down on the W side, *St. Stephen's Church* (1866; J. Peacock), stone outside with spiky Gothic tracery and odd plan. The interior was whitened and very fine painted wood fittings were added c 1903 (G.F. Bodley), tall gilded reredos, organ galleries, one with charming red and white painted chapel beneath, rood beam and towering font canopy. To the N, Victoria Grove and Launceston Place are a pretty stucco villa and terrace development (1837–41; J. Bray), originally called Kensington New Town. Back on Kensington Rd, *Milestone*

Hotel (1883; T.G. Jackson), a Flemish Gothic red-brick front on the corner of *Kensington Court* (1883; J.J. Stevenson), a very large development of red-brick flats and houses built on the seven-acre site of the monster mansion built in 1873 for the speculator Albert Grant, who was bankrupt before he could enjoy the 100 rooms and marble terraces.

By the side of the Gardens, Palace Green is the S end of the grandest private road in London. *No. 1* (1868; Philip Webb) was built for the patron of the Pre-Raphaelites, George Howard, and decorated inside by Morris and Co. The exterior was controversial, the expanses of red brick, the seemingly haphazard placing of windows, the mixture of Gothic detail with moulded brick and sash windows reminiscent of the early 18C confused the eminent architects invited to assess the design. They could not see what style or period of architecture was intended, which Webb took as a compliment. *No. 2* is also of red brick, one of the first imitations of 18C brick architecture, built 1860–62 (F. Hering) for W.M. Thackeray, whose novels revived interest in the late Stuart and Georgian periods. Thackeray probably designed the house, the red brick quite exceptional at a time when stucco, stone or muted coloured brick were the usual materials except for the occasional work in Tudor Gothic style. Further up Palace Green, a grand series of brick houses of c 1900–10 in Queen Anne to neo-Georgian styles before Kensington Palace Gardens is reached. This is the original street, laid out 1843 (Wyatt and Brandon) and lined with detached or semi-detached houses, mostly Italianate but with Moorish and Gothic exceptions. All but one were built between 1844 and 1854. *No. 15* (1854; J.T. Knowles), a grand palazzo on the model of C. Barry's Reform Club, *No. 13* (1852; C.J. Richardson), the Gothic exception, missing its tower roof, *Nos 18–19* (c 1845; Sir C. Barry), palazzo style with corner towers, *No. 12A* (1863; J. Murray), stone fronted to contrast with the predominant stucco, *No. 12* (1845; R.R. Banks), a good example of the Barry palace style, by one of his pupils, and *No. 20* (1845; C. Barry), an odd design with the corners carried up as chimneys. The Moorish exception, *No. 24* (1845; O. Jones), is appropriately used by the Saudi Arabian embassy. At the top end, pretty lodge and gates (1845; Wyatt and Brandon). Back at Kensington High St, in Young St, to S, *No. 16*, where Thackeray lived from 1846 and wrote 'Vanity Fair'. In Kensington Square, beyond, sturdy Gothic *RC church* (1875; E. Goldie). On the corner of Church St, *St. Mary Abbots Church* (1870–72; G.G. Scott), the parish church of Kensington rebuilt for the energetic Archdeacon Sinclair, during whose time as vicar (1842–75) 21 churches were opened in the parish. Scott's church is very large, in conventional late 13C style without great personality, though the 278ft spire (1879) is handsome. The pretty cloistered walk (1888–93; Micklethwaite and Somers Clarke) and the diapered brick building adjoining help to give an ecclesiastical air to this tightly constrained site. Further W, on N side, Tudor style former Free School (1852; Broadbridge), now a bank. Behind the main road, the Phillimore estate laid out c 1860–75 with large stuccoed houses. *No. 18 Stafford Terrace* (open to the public) retains a complete late Victorian interior, an exceptional survival of aesthetic taste of that period, with rich wallpapers, blue-and-white china, crowded picture hanging and stained glass.

Further W, Holland Park, the park of Holland House, Jacobean mansion destroyed in the war. SW of Holland House was Little Holland House where a small artistic circle set up round Sara Prinsep and her two sisters, one of whom was the famous photographer Julia Margaret Cameron. The painter G.F. Watts 'came for three weeks and stayed thirty years' according to Mrs Prinsep. Most of the Pre-Raphaelites came regularly and when the Holland estate decided to raise money by redeveloping the site of the house in 1875 the two new roads, Holland Park Rd and Melbury Rd, were built up with artists' studio houses. Already built in Holland Park Rd was a studio (1864; Philip Webb) for Val Prinsep, Sara's son. This, since altered, is *No. 14*. Next door, the prodigious painter Frederick Leighton built himself the ultimate studio house, *Leighton House* (1865; G. Aitchison) (open to public), with a curious bleak exterior, supposedly classical in inspiration, like Leighton's paintings, and all red brick. In 1877 Aitchison added the Arab Hall, the glory of the house, designed to display Leighton's collection of Islamic pottery. Antique Saracenic tiles are incorporated in large numbers, the potter William de Morgan making up the deficiencies. The result is most successful, a great domed space, brilliantly coloured and screened by wooden lattices, the floor marble with a sunken pool. In 1875 Watts moved to a studio (now gone) in Melbury Rd, and studio houses followed quickly. *No. 8 Melbury Rd* (1875; Norman Shaw) was built for the painter Marcus Stone in the advanced Queen Anne style, the front dominated by three great oriel lights to the studio which occupies the whole upper floor. The central oriel was changed to increase the light some years later. Nearby, *No. 31* (1877; Norman Shaw), built for Luke Fildes, painter, a lovely front in early 18C style, the hipped roof with a crowning balcony or widow's walk. Quite different is *No. 9*, *The Tower House* (1875–81; W. Burges), the house of an architect who never wavered in his Gothic faith. A powerful simplified medieval design in red brick with minimal stone, the house is a demonstration of clear geometrical shapes, the stonework flush with the wall face to leave the lines unimpaired. The interiors, by contrast, were of a fantastic and luxuriant richness matched only by Burges' work for the Marquess of Bute at Cardiff Castle and Castell Coch, Glamorgan. The sculptor Hamo Thorneycroft lived at *No. 2* (1892; J. Belcher) and the painter Holman Hunt at *No. 18*. Across the road, *Nos 55–7* (1894; H. Ricardo) is robust neo-Georgian, notable for being faced in glazed brick, which Ricardo saw as a solution to the London atmosphere. In Addison Rd, *St. Barnabas' Church* (1828; L. Vulliamy), brick, Perp. style with a richly coloured W window by O'Connor (1852). Further up, *No. 8* (1906–07; Halsey Ricardo), one of the most remarkable houses of its time for the dazzling exterior colour, achieved by the use of glazed brick in brilliant green and blue for the walling, with the cornices, pilasters and main lines of the classical design in matt cream-coloured terracotta. A black engineering brick base and green pantiles on the roof and, to complete the picture, under the cornices are lovely painted tiles by the potter W. de Morgan, chiefly of fishes, a hint of the interior where de Morgan's work is used extensively, with work by other leading Arts and Crafts designers. W of Addison Rd, Holland Rd with, at the N end, *Church of St. John* (1872 and 1889; J. Brooks: and 1909), the front of 1909 disguising a noble vaulted interior, apse-ended with ornate carved stone screens and painted stone reredos.

Off Holland Park Avenue, to the N, the *Norland estate*, a pleasant early Victorian suburb (1839; R. Cantwell) with stucco Royal Crescent, villas in Addison Avenue leading to *St. James' Gardens* (1847; J. Barnett), a square of semi-detached houses around the estate *church* (1845), and Norland Square. On the opposite side, further up, Holland Park, a development of very large stucco houses of the 1860s, with ponderous detail in contrast to the Norland estate. To the N, off Portland Rd, *St. Francis'* (1859; H. Clutton), Pottery Lane, plain and severe small brick Catholic church in what was a notorious slum. Inside, fittings and Lady Chapel by J.F. Bentley, one of his earliest commissions, High Victorian Gothic altars in marble and alabaster with paintings by N. Westlake inset. The vaulted baptistery is all Bentley, over a fine granite and marble font. To the E, the Ladbroke *estate*, built over the site of an unsuccessful racecourse from 1841. The *church* (1844; Stevens and Alexander) on Ladbroke Grove marks the centre. Around are big stucco houses ingeniously planned with rear facades to long communal gardens. The most handsome group is *Stanley Crescent* and *Stanley Gardens* (1855; T. Allom) off Kensington Park Rd where Allom also designed a rare example of a classical style Victorian Anglican *church* (1855–57). Near Ladbroke Grove station, *library* (1891; H. Wilson), a pretty free Tudor design in red brick intended to be enriched with sculpture but built to a cheaper design. At the N end of Ladbroke Grove, entered from Harrow Rd, *Kensal Green Cemetery* (1832), the oldest of London's great cemeteries, set up as a private company by George Carden, the lawyer who began the campaign to reform burial practice in the 1820s. The chapels are Greek Revival (1837; J. Griffith) flanked by catacombs. This was the most successful of the early cemeteries, partly due to the royal Duke of Sussex being buried here in 1843, and is filled with distinguished mausolea standing out from the unkempt grass. Among the finest are the octagonal Gothic Molyneaux tomb (1864; J. Gibson), Gibson's own polychrome Gothic shrine (he died in 1892 but the monument is of c 1865), the extraordinary turbaned Indians supporting the canopy over General Casement (1845; F.M. Lander) and the fine canopied effigy of the painter W. Mulready (1863; G. Sykes). On a smaller scale is the extremely heavily carved Gothic shrine to Captain Ricketts (1868; W. Burges). Among those buried here are the architects D. Burton, J. Shaw, J.C. Loudoun, P. Hardwick, the sculptors W. Behnes and R. Sievier, the painters G. Cruikshank and T. Daniell, the novelists Thackeray, Trollope, Wilkie Collins, the engineers Sir Marc and Isambard Brunel, the tightrope walker Blondin, the writer on London's poor, Henry Mayhew, and the Chartist leader, F. O'Connor. In the Catholic cemetery to the W (1858; S. Nicholl), a domed Byzantinesque mausoleum (1904; C.H. Quennell). Francis Thompson, the poet, is buried here, also Cardinals Wiseman and Manning until their bodies were moved to the new Westminster Cathedral.

Returning to Notting Hill Gate, *Coronet Cinema* (1898; W.G. Sprague), complete small theatre surviving as a cinema. To the S, on Campden Hill, *No. 118* (1877; R. Norman Shaw), large studio house, yellow brick and tile hung, more Old English than Queen Anne in style, balancing a stepped gable in brick against a tiled one. To the E, off Kensington Church St, in Kensington Mall, *Mall Chambers* (1868; J. Murray), an early block of flats in yellow brick, well designed for the corner site.

OUTER LONDON

WEST LONDON

HAMMERSMITH AND FULHAM. **Fulham** is very largely red-brick housing of the late 19C, attractive in its completeness. At the Broadway, Portland stone *Town Hall* (1889; G. Edwards) and brick church of

1827. In Harwood Rd, to the S, *Board School* (1873; B. Champneys), one of the series of big well-lit buildings put up by the London School Board. In Fulham Rd, *Library* (1909; H.T. Hare), Baroque. By the parish church of Fulham, at the entrance to Fulham Palace, High Victorian Gothic *almshouses* (1869; J.P. Seddon), very picturesque with good carving. Off Dawes Rd, W of the Broadway, in Rylston Rd *RC church* (1847; A.W.N. Pugin), a complete work, rare for Pugin, but so placed that the tower and spire do not show from the street and of a dull Kentish ragstone. Off Fulham Palace Rd, *No. 17 St. Dunstan's Rd* (1891; C.F.A. Voysey), a pretty, low studio cottage in Voysey's favourite roughcast.

Hammersmith Rd leads into **Hammersmith** from the E. First, on the right comes *Olympia*, the 1930 front concealing an iron-roofed exhibition hall (1884; Coe and Goodwin). In Avonmore Rd, to the S *No. 22*, a very original Arts and Crafts studio house (1888; J.M. MacLaren). Further down Hammersmith Rd, on left, former Headmaster's house of *St. Paul's School* (1881–85; A. Waterhouse), showing the deep red brick and red terracotta that Waterhouse used for the school, now demolished. On the right, Brook Green, a pretty enclave with ragstone *RC church* (1851; W. Wardell: spire J.A. Hansom) and *St. Paul's School for Girls* (1900–04; G. Horsley), relaxed red brick and stone, the curved gables filled with good carved reliefs. On Hammersmith Rd, left, *Nazareth House* (c 1870; Goldie), utilitarian Gothic complex, on right, *Sacred Heart Convent* (1875–88; J.F. Bentley), an impressive array of sheer chimneys on the W block and the chapel with a big Perp. window to the street. Off Broadway, Shepherd's Bush Rd, *Library* (1904; H.T. Hare), cheerful Baroque, red brick and stone. Hammersmith *church* (1882; Roumieu, Gough and Seddon) is particularly harsh, rock-faced red sandstone with Bath stone lancets, but the tall proportions still have an impact despite the flyover behind. In King St, the *Salutation* pub with an unusual purple glazed tile front. In Glenthorne Rd, parallel, *St. John's Church* (1856; W. Butterfield), severe stock brick with saddleback tower, interior has been whitewashed but lovely organ case by J.F. Bentley survives. To the S, the pretty riverside of Upper Mall, where William Morris lived, in the 18C Kelmscott House, from 1878 until his death in 1896.

The northern part of the borough, N of Goldhawk Rd, has little to offer except in **East Acton**, N of Westway (A40), around Erconwald St, the *Old Oak Estate* (c 1910), one of the early public housing estates built by London County Council. Charming small-scale brick houses with small paned windows, sadly now much altered. For contrast, adjoining, *Wormwood Scrubs Prison* (1874; Gen. Sir E. Ducane), repetitive brick cell-blocks with a Gothic chapel in the middle, all built by convict labour.

HOUNSLOW. Riverside borough stretching from Chiswick out to suburban Middlesex. In **Chiswick**, *church* rebuilt 1883 (J.L. Pearson), incorporating chancel work by Burges (1861) with two fine windows by Lavers and Barraud. J.M. Whistler is buried in the cemetery behind, under a bronze table tomb. On Chiswick Mall, *Greenash* (1882; J. Belcher), gabled and tile-hung Norman Shaw style house. Behind, the bulk of Fuller's Brewery (late 19C). To the N, **Turnham Green**, with *church* (1843; Scott and Moffatt) and, in Barley Mow Passage, *factory* (1902; C.F.A. Voysey), glazed brick with curvy parapet between flat topped buttresses, built for Sandersons wallpaper. To W, *Gunnersbury Park* (1834; S. Smirke: and c 1850), stucco mansion, now museum, formerly belonging to the Rothschilds. On

Brentford High St, *Kew Bridge Pumping Station* (1867), now a museum with magnificent steam-powered beam-engines in operation. Next door, *church* (1887) houses a collection of mechanical musical instruments of fantastic ingenuity. In Windmill Rd, N of Brentford, *St. Faith's Church* (1907; G.F. Bodley), one of Bodley's long lean brick churches. At **Syon House**, to W, superb stone and glass domed *conservatory* (1830; C. Fowler).

EALING. Borough stretching from Acton towards the River Brent on the W. At the SE corner, by Turnham Green Station, *Bedford Park*, pioneer planned suburb, laid out 1875 in a fan shape radiating from the church. The suburb is architecturally important as being built entirely in the Queen Anne manner—red brick, white painted wood, generous roofs and tall chimneys—'quaint and pretty', said William Morris. Norman Shaw was the principal architect and his designs were adapted and repeated for some years. Queen Anne's Grove, Newton Grove, The Orchard, Priory Avenue and Woodstock Rd are the side residential streets. The three main roads meet at the *church* (1880; Norman Shaw) with its white cupola and green painted fittings. Opposite is the *Tabard* pub with tiles by W. de Morgan inside and, next door, the former shop, both buildings by Shaw with big gables. The *Vicarage*, E of the church, and *Victorian Society offices*, No. 1 Priory Gardens, are by Shaw followers, M.B. Adams and E.J. May. *Nos 1–2 The Avenue* were the first houses in the suburb (1875; E.W. Godwin), tighter designs than Shaw's, three storeys on a narrow plan giving a tall, sharp profile. *No. 14 South Parade* (1889; C.F.A. Voysey) is a conscious intruder, roughcast with a low hipped slate roof and small leaded windows in bands.

To the N, Uxbridge Rd leads through **Acton**, with pretty *Library* (1899; M.B. Adams) on left and large brick *church* (1865; F. and H. Francis). In **Ealing**, on the Broadway, *National Westminster Bank* (1874; C. Jones), ragstone Gothic, the first Town Hall, *Christ Church* (1852; G.G. Scott), big ragstone work with spire, and the *Town Hall* (1888; C. Jones), more ragstone Gothic. To S, High St leads to *St. Mary's Church* (1866–73; S.S. Teulon), a beefy brick tower and cast-iron interior added to a plain 18C brick church. To the N of Broadway Station, in Mount Park Rd, *St. Peter's Church* (1892; J.D. Sedding and H. Wilson), very good late 19C free Gothic, the W window elaborately traceried and filling most of the W wall. At **Hanwell**, to the W, *church* (1841; Scott and Moffatt), flint and brick set on a slight hill over the Brent valley, which the railway crosses on I.K. Brunel's superb shallow arched *Wharncliffe Viaduct* (1837).

HILLINGDON. Outer W London borough with little of Victorian interest. At **Uxbridge**, W of the new Civic Centre, *St. Andrew's Church* (1865; G.G. Scott), red brick and good spire.

NORTH-WEST LONDON

BRENT. **Kilburn**, the SE corner of the borough has *St. Augustine's Church* (1870–97; J.L. Pearson), Kilburn Park Rd, just on the boundary. This is Pearson's masterpiece, a soaring brick church, stone vaulted and crowned with a 254ft steeple based on St. Etienne, Caen. Pearson's handling of space is masterly, the interior an uninterrupted vessel, vaulted and framed by deep transverse arches rising almost as high as the main vault, setting back the long windows to deepen the perceived space. To the NW, **Willesden**, with *St. Andrew's Church* (1885; J. Brooks) one of Brooks' tall brick churches with spectacular high altar. To the E, off High Rd, *Jewish Cemetery* (1873), Glebe Rd, full of Rothschild memorials. To the SW, in **Harlesden**, *All Souls' Church* (1875; E.J. Tarver), a dull exterior but octagonal crossing with the most elaborate timber roof. To the N, N of Neasden, in Church Lane, **Kingsbury**, *St. Andrew's Church* (1844–47; S.W. Daukes), an important Tractarian church moved here from central London in 1933. Tall spired stone church with fittings by leading contemporary architects: E window by Pugin, Litany desk by Burges, lectern by Butterfield, font cover by Pearson, pulpit and reredos by Street. Benjamin Webb, editor of the 'Ecclesiologist', was vicar of the church 1862–85 and responsible for many of the fittings.

HARROW. NW of Brent, centred on **Harrow-on-the-hill**, where *Harrow School* has an imposing collection of red-brick Gothic buildings. *Chapel* (1854–57; G.G. Scott), flint and stone with much contemporary stained glass, *Library* (1861–63; Scott), red brick with coloured patterning, *Speech Room* (1872; W. Burges), two-towered severe front with broad rounded rear, not completed to Burges' original intentions. Various large boarding houses of the 1860s and 70s, especially on Peterborough Hill, with, at the top, near the main buildings, the *Butler Museum* (1886; B. Champneys), cheerful Queen Anne style in contrast to all the Gothic, and the *Music School* (1891; E.S. Prior). To the S of the school, London Rd and Mount Park Avenue, just off, have expensive late Victorian houses, notably Manor Lodge (1884) and The Orchard (1900), interspersed among the older villas, Harrow having been a popular country spot since the 18C. To the NW, **Pinner**, with a *church* restored 1880 by J.L. Pearson and in the graveyard the odd obelisk *tomb* with a sarcophagus halfway up by J.C. Loudon (1843) to his parents. The church was restored for Mr Tooke of Pinner Hill (Pinner Woods Golf Club) who also built for himself, on the E side of Pinner Woods, *Woodhall Towers* or *Tooke's Folly* (1864), a massive polychrome brick tower house. To the NE of Pinner, Hatch End and Harrow Weald. **Harrow Weald** has numerous Victorian houses up Brooks Hill, A409, towards Bushey. At the top, to the left, *Grims Dyke* (1872; Norman Shaw), a very good Norman Shaw house with big timbered gables and picturesque composition, built for the painter F. Goodall and from 1890 the home of W.S. Gilbert who died here in 1911 after rescuing a girl from the lake. Beyond, *Priory Close*, Common Rd, is by Waterhouse (1890). Gilbert is buried at *St. John's Church* (1849; H. Clutton I), Great Stanmore. In the church, effigy of the 1st Earl of Aberdeen by Boehm (1875). Off Stanmore Hill, the derelict *Stanmore Hall* (1847; J.M. Derick), Tudor Gothic, once all decorated by William Morris.

NORTH LONDON

CAMDEN (the borough from Camden Town northwards, for the S end of the borough see City of Westminster: Bloomsbury and Euston pp. 240–3). **Camden Town**, at the bottom of the High St, *Camden Theatre* (1901; Sprague), damaged but still with a good plaster interior. This end of Camden Town is associated with the Camden Town group of painters of c 1908–14 grouped around Walter Sickert who lived in Mornington Crescent. They specialised in real life depiction, generally of this area of London. To the N, at the foot of Camden Rd, parish *church* (1876–81; Bodley and Garner), long, tall, elegantly detailed stock brick and stone in the manner that Bodley used increasingly for town churches, the big upper windows giving a light interior despite the cramped site. At *Camden Lock*, street market occupying 19C warehouses on the Grand Union Canal which has a scenic industrial course around the back of Camden Town down towards the railway yards behind St. Pancras. To the N of Camden town, **Kentish Town**, with an elaborate pub, the *Assembly House* (1896), next to the station. Exceptional cut-glass work. SE of the station, Oseney Crescent, *St. Luke's* (1868–70; B. Champneys), a bold High Victorian church with saddleback tower, cross-gabled and the openings punched through in the plainest possible way. Good glass by H. Holiday. To the W of Camden Town, elegant stucco housing in **Primrose Hill**. The Yeats family lived at No. 22 Fitzroy Rd 1867–74. Jack Yeats was born here.

In Chalk Farm Rd, *The Roundhouse* (1847; R. Dockray), a vast circular engine house, 160ft wide, lately a theatre. To the W, each side of Haverstock Hill, mid–late 19C suburbs climbing the hills. Adelaide Rd, Eton Rd and Provost Rd were laid out in the 1840s on land owned by Eton College; the *church* in Eton Rd is of 1856 (E.M. Barry). S of Adelaide Rd, *St. Mary's Church* (1871; W. Manning), Primrose Hill, a long and tall brick vessel, the fine interior whitened during the incumbency of P. Dearmer (1901–15), the liturgical reformer. Steele's Rd, N of Eton Rd, has good studio houses of c 1870, No. 31 by J.M. Brydon. Eton Avenue to the W is largely of c 1900 with a very Arts and Crafts *fire station* (1912; C. Winmill) just off in Lancaster Grove. Belsize Park, to the N, is an attractive suburb developed from the 1840s, mostly c 1850–60. E of Haverstock Hill, houses of 1845–55 in Maitland Park with the *St. Pancras Almshouses* (1852) and, in Southampton Rd, *RC church* (1874–83; C.A. Buckler), long and dignified. NE of Maitland Park, Gospel Oak, with *St. Martin's Church* (1862–66; E.B. Lamb), in Vicars Rd, off Allcroft Rd, one of the best churches for studying the original Gothic church building of the 'rogue' architects, mostly Low Church for whom medieval precedent was of less significance than for their High Church colleagues. A tall tower with oddly detailed top looms over a broad, almost centrally planned nave with a narrower W section. An immensely complex hammerbeam roof. To the W, *Lismore Circus*, a grandly planned if plainly executed development of the 1860s. To the N *All Hallows* (1892; J. Brooks) Shirlock Rd, Brooks' last church and one of his best, ragstone with tall, long interior divided by high round piers intended to carry a full vault. Chancel (1913; Giles Scott), later but matching.

NE of Gospel Oak, Dartmouth Park and **Highgate**. Off Highgate Rd, Swain's Lane leads up to *Holly Village* (1865; H. Darbishire), a picturesque group of cottages built for her servants by Baroness Burdett Coutts, heiress and philanthropist. Gothic with lots of carved ornament and spiky detail. Beyond, *Highgate Cemetery*, the old cemetery (1839) on the left and the new cemetery (1854) on the right of Swain's Lane. The old cemetery, massively derelict, overgrown and recently partly reclaimed by dedicated volunteers, is one of the most atmospheric places in London, occasionally open. The buildings by S. Geary included Gothic chapels and lodges and the Egyptian style Cedar of Lebanon catacombs. The best mausoleum, that of Julius Beer, proprietor of the 'Observer', is N of the catacombs, a building (1880; J.O. Scott) intended to resemble the Mausoleum at Halicarnassus. The guidebook (1978) lists a fascinating variety of people buried here, among the best known, Karl Marx in the new cemetery, George Eliot, Christina Rossetti and Michael Faraday in the old cemetery. The old cemetery abuts *St. Michael's Church* (1831–32; L. Vulliamy) where S.T. Coleridge (died 1834) is buried. A.E. Housman wrote 'A Shropshire Lad' (1896) at *No. 17 North Rd*, N of the High St. W of Highgate, off The Grove, the grounds of *Witanhurst* (1913), a neo-Georgian house of considerable size. To the W stretches *Hampstead Heath*, preserved for London by public purchase in 1871 and extended by later acquisition.

Hampstead was a fashionable spot outside London in the 18C, during the 19C still detached from London. The area between Hampstead and London filled up between 1830 and 1870. The later 19C architecture is the most interesting when fashionable artists and followers of fashion built houses in the new Queen Anne style to the S, W and E of the village. Heath St is the main axis with the parish *church* (1745) in Church Row off the S end. The church was much extended 1843 and 1878 (F.P. Cockerell) with altar and reredos 1878 (T.G. Jackson), baptistery painting and W window 1884 (H. Wooldridge) and ceiling painting c 1880 (Alfred Bell), all being 'advanced' artists of the time, evidence of the influence of artistic Hampstead. Up Heath St, on the left, The Mount, scene of Ford Madox Brown's famous painting 'Work' (Manchester City Art Gallery) painted between 1852 and 1865. The big 19C houses start to the NW along West Heath Rd, mid to late Victorian with later Victorian and Edwardian houses on the area to the left (Redington Rd and Platt's Lane). In Platt's Lane, *Annesley Lodge* (1896; C.F.A. Voysey), built for Voysey's father to an L-plan, the upper windows in bands under the eaves, the door in the angle with typical Voysey ironwork. In Kidderpore Avenue, *St. Luke's Church* (1898; B. Champneys) and *Westfield College*, built around a stucco villa of 1844. More c 1900 housing in Redington Rd leading back to Frognal. *No. 39* (1884–85; Norman Shaw) was built for the illustrator Kate Greenaway, prettily tile-hung, with a top-floor studio set diagonally with a corner balcony to catch the NE light. Opposite is *University College School* (1906–07; A. Mitchell), good free neo-Georgian work in red brick with stone frontispiece. *Nos 49–51* (1892; R. Blomfield), early neo-Georgian pair with two big gables flanking two large hipped dormers, bold plain chimneys and small pane windows. *No. 42 Frognal Lane* (1881; B. Champneys), Champneys' own house, an exceptionally good Queen Anne design, square plan with hipped roof rising to four central chimneys. E of Frognal, in Ellerdale Rd, *No. 6* (1875–76; Norman Shaw), Norman Shaw's own house, very tall, the different window lengths and levels of the centre balanced by two tall, but different bays. The facade is more deliberately varied than in any of the similar town houses Shaw built for clients. On the E side of Heath St, small scale 19C housing giving over to good late Victorian houses by the Heath. *Gainsborough Gardens* (c 1885–95) is the best group. At the end of Well Rd, *The Logs* (1868; J. Nightingale), polychrome brick. Constable lived the last ten years of his life (1827–37) at *No. 40 Well Walk*. To the S of Heath St, Fitzjohn's Avenue, with some good late Victorian artists' houses, notably at the top end. *No. 61* (1878; Norman Shaw) was built for E. Long RA, who moved within six years as he grew richer to a much larger studio house in Netherall Gardens, also by Shaw, but now demolished. P.F. Poole RA owned *No. 75* (c 1880; T.K. Green). The most elaborate house is *The Tower House* (c 1870; J. Whichcord), French Gothic with a great pyramid-roofed tower. To the SE of Heath St, High St runs into Rosslyn Hill. Downshire Hill, on left, is a remainder of Regency Hampstead, leading up to *Keats's House* (now a museum), where the nightingale sang for the 'Ode to a Nightingale' (1819). *Hampstead Hill Gardens* (1877; Batterbury and Huxley), to the S, is a group of Queen Anne style artists' houses. At Hampstead Green, on the S side, *·St. Stephen's Church* (1869–72; S.S. Teulon), one of the boldest 19C Gothic churches, all in mottled red brick with a massive tower rising over the crossing, over-whelming the short chancel. The inside, now disused, is a riot of struc-tural colour set off by nogged brick and a superb timber roof. Across Rosslyn Hill, the former *Congregational church* (1883–84; A. Waterhouse), Lyndhurst Rd, in a round arched style, remarkable for its clever planning of the hexagonal interior space.

ISLINGTON. The S end of the borough touches the City at Finsbury Square, surrounded by high 20C office buildings, of which *Royal London House* (1904; J. Belcher) is most notable for its spired addition of 1930 by Belcher's partner, J.J. Joass, the earlier part in a restless Baroque. In City Rd, castellated *Barracks* (1857; J. Jennings). Old St runs W to **Clerkenwell**, one of the best areas for seeing the late 19C warehouses and commercial buildings that used to be common right around the City. Clerkenwell Rd, St. John St and Farringdon Rd still have tall brick and stone fronts, Gothic or Italianate. To S, Charter-house St follows the City boundary, with *Nos 109–13* (1900; A.H. Mackmurdo), quiet c 1700 style, and the *Fox and Anchor* (1898), covered in decorative tile work inside as well as out, to Charterhouse Square, where the medieval Charterhouse site housed Charterhouse School until it moved to Godalming in 1872 and the Merchant Taylors School until 1933. After bombing and restoration much of the 19C work has gone, but E. Blore's two Tudor style courts (1826–29) are N of the old buildings. N of Clerkenwell Green, in Seckforde St, handsome stucco front of the *Finsbury Savings Bank* (1840; A. Bartholomew), oddly out of place in this warehouse district. On St. John St, the former *Northampton Institute* (1893–96; E.W. Mountford), now part of the City University, brick and stone free mixture of N Renaissance and Baroque motifs, the corner tower happily intact, but the great curved gable and steep roof that topped the composition lost after bombing. To W, on Rosebery Avenue, large blocks of later 19C industrial dwell-ings and the old *Finsbury Town Hall* (1895; C.E. Vaughan) in free Elizabethan style. Off to the N, remnants of early 19C residential squares and terraces as far as Pentonville Rd which climbs up, with good views of St. Pancras Station, to the Angel. On the corner, the former *Angel pub* (1901–04; Eedle and Meyers), lavish terracotta with a corner dome, just right for its site. It was built so large because it was a terminus for horse buses from the centre of London. Further up on the right, brick former *electricity generating station* (c 1905; E.V. Harris), a small-scale neo-classical reminiscence of Newgate Prison, the famous 18C gaol demolished a few years earlier. On the W side of Upper St, the disused *Royal Agricultural Hall* (1861; Coe and Peck), a very large iron-roofed exhibition hall. On Islington Green, *statue* of Sir H. Myddelton (1862; J. Thomas). Further up Upper St, on the left, *Almeida Theatre* (1837; Roumieu and Gough), Almeida St, originally the Literary Institute, Greek Revival style. On the right, former *Congregational church* (1888; Paull and Bonella), Queen Anne style, unusual for a chapel, red brick with a big front oriel window. At the top end, set incongruously in a Regency terrace, the huge *Union Chapel* (1876; J. Cubitt), a massive front tower, pyramid-roofed, screening a large octagonal interior, the balconies fronted with inlaid marble.

To the W of Upper St is **Barnsbury**, an area of attractive streets and squares laid out from the 1820s to 1840s. S of Barnsbury St, *Milner Square* (c 1840; Roumieu and Gough), a powerful design with the main windows set between tall brick pilasters carrying a broad cornice with arched attic windows above. *Lonsdale Square*, across Liverpool Rd, is an early example of a complete square in the Tudor style (1843;

R.C. Carpenter). *Cloudesley Square* (c 1825), to the S, has as its centre-piece a *church* (1826–28) by Charles Barry in the Georgian Gothic vein. *Thornhill Square*, to the W, is c 1850, the end of the ample planning in this part of London. In the square, *Carnegie Library* (1906; A.B. Pite), an eccentric brick building with stone details, part Baroque (the window hoods), part Byzantine (the arcaded ground-floor windows). The *church* (1852) has fine E window (1880; W.M.Pepper). In Caledonian Rd, to the N, *Pentonville Prison* (1841–42), a model prison on the then new radiating plan, allowing surveillance of several wings from a central block. Plan by Major Jebb, arched frontispiece by Charles Barry. Further N Market Rd leads to the site of the *Caledonian Market* (1852–55; J. Bunning), a vast cattle market with central tower and pubs at each corner. The buildings survive though the market has been built over. NW of Caledonian Rd, Tufnell Park Rd, with a *church* (1868; G. Truefitt) on an octagonal plan, converted to a theatre.

Finsbury Park to the E has an estate at *Tollington Park* (1855–70; Roumieu and Gough) with rock-faced *church* (1856; A.D. Gough). Holloway Rd leads back S to **Highbury**, with, at the S end, *Central Library* (1906–08; H.T. Hare), monumental Edwardian Baroque on a small scale. E of Holloway Rd, off Highbury Grove, *Aberdeen Park*, a mid Victorian development of semi-detached houses, large but not special. In the centre, **church* (1859; W. White), now disused. A mildly polychrome exterior with pretty tiled octagonal tower conceals an exceptional interior with decorative brick work and inlaid tile. The E window is a rich design by N.H.J. Westlake (1865). Essex Rd, SE of Highbury, has a red-brick and stone early Georgian style *Library* (1916; M. Macartney). The area SE of Essex St was built up from the 1830s with small brick and stucco houses. In St. Peter's St, *church* (1834; C. Barry) with a needle sharp little spire added 1843 (Roumieu and Gough). In Duncan Terrace, to the W, *RC church* (1843; J.J. Scoles), neo-Romanesque with a later front. Broad interior.

BARNET (N London borough around the old centres of Hendon, Finchley and Barnet). N of Hampstead, Hampstead Way leads up to **Hampstead Garden Suburb**, pioneer suburb founded in 1906, planned by Parker and Unwin (see Letchworth, Hertfordshire p. 160) and intended for all classes, though now very much a wealthy dormitory for central London. Here the best of English house design of the early 20C, inspired by English vernacular architecture via architects such as Voysey, can be seen together with the more formal parallel strand of neo-Georgian. Central Square, formal and the crown of the suburb, is all by Lutyens (1909–11) in silver grey brick trimmed with red. Two churches flank the main axis to the *Institute. St. Jude's Church* and the *Free Church* are both classical in detail but in plan and massing the influence of the Gothic Revival and the Arts and Crafts movement is strongly present, illustrating Lutyens' own roots. Great roofs sweep down almost to the ground intersected by steep transepts. Early 18C, tall, arched windows light the main facades and tall dormers in similar style rise above the eaves to light the aisles. The Free Church is capped by an octagonal dome, St. Jude's by a tall spire on a brick tower of Romanesque boldness. The houses approaching the square from the N are also by Lutyens and other architects used similar early 18C forms on the S approach. Small gabled and rough-cast or brick houses predominate in the earlier parts of the suburb, Hampstead Way, Meadway, Willifield Way. On Hampstead Way *No. 22 and Nos 6–10 Meadway* (1908; Baillie Scott), *No. 20* by Guy

Dawber, and, in Heath Close, shops by Unwin and *Waterlow Court* (1909; Baillie Scott), a delightful collegiate quadrangle with arched ground floor, intended for single working women. By 1912 neo-Georgian formality had become the rule as in Parker and Unwin's open quadrangles facing each other across the E end of Corringham Way. To the W of the suburb, *Golders Green Crematorium* (1905; buildings by George and Yeates) pioneer and largest crematorium in Britain. The Jewish Cemetery (1895) across Hoop Lane has several elaborate mausolea.

To the W is **Hendon**. The old *church* on the hilltop in Church Rd was doubled in size (1914; Temple Moore) very well and has a fine N chapel screen by Bodley (1897) and high altar by Comper. To the SW, by Hendon station, *St. John's* (1895; Temple Moore), Algernon Rd, a plain, well designed brick church in the Bodley manner. To the N of Hendon is **Mill Hill**, well set on a wooded ridge. On the Ridgeway, *Mill Hill School* (1825–27; W. Tite), Greek Revival with pretty late 19C additions, chapel (1898; B. Champneys) and Library group (1907; T.E. Collcutt). E of this, *St. Vincent's Convent* with a tall chapel (1887; F. Tasker). W of Mill Hill School, *Drapers Cottage Homes* (1898; G. Hornblower), Hammer Lane, cottage homes spaciously laid out for retired linen and wool drapers. Beyond, on Lawrence St, the dominating campanile tower of *St. Joseph's College* (1866–71; E. Goldie). Highwood Hill leads into Totteridge Lane with, on the right, *Ellern Mede* (1876–77; Norman Shaw), a small country house, the main element a large Old English style timbered gable rising over a low porch. The rest of the house is tile-hung with tall chimneys well placed. **Totteridge** has a number of houses by T.E. Collcutt, who lived here, all gabled and roughcast with generous roofs, like Voysey but more varied. *The Lynch House* (1905), W of Ellern Mede, and a *lodge* to Totteridge Park (c 1907) are on Totteridge Lane. On Totteridge Green, *The Croft* (1895), Collcutt's own house, arranged on a courtyard plan with brick and roughcast set off by a pretty timber framed first-floor passage. Also on the Green, two cottages (1899). N of Totteridge is the old town of **Chipping Barnet**. The parish *church* has a new nave and aisle added to the medieval building (1871–75; W. Butterfield) in stone and chequered flint. Butterfield font and reredos of 1880, elaborate woodwork of 1890s and stained glass in aisles by Holiday (1888). At **Friern Barnet**, 3m SE, *Friern Hospital*, (1849; S.W. Daukes), originally Colney Hatch, the largest London lunatic asylum, the name a byword for lunacy as Bedlam had been in the 18C. *St. John's Church* (1889–1911; J.L. Pearson), Friern Barnet Rd, apsed stone church with flying buttresses, fully vaulted in stone, the effect particularly impressive at the E end where eight stone ribs join and an ambulatory behind the sanctuary extends the space around the altar through an arcade of paired columns. To the SW, off East Finchley High Rd, *St. Pancras and Islington Cemetery* (1854), very large with a spired *chapel* (Barnett and Birch) and in the centre *Mond Mausoleum* (c 1910; D. Bradell), a granite and stone Ionic temple to the chemical king and art collector Ludwig Mond (1839–1909). The painter Ford Madox Brown is buried here. *St. Marylebone Cemetery* (1854; Barnett and Birch), to the SW, off East End Rd, has some fine early 20C memorials, notably the Tate tomb (1909; F.L. Jenkins), Baroque with a youth arising on top. Edmund Gosse the author and Thomas Huxley the zoologist are buried here.

HARINGEY (N London borough around the old centres of Hornsey and Tottenham). On Archway Rd, *Highgate Archway* (1897) carries

Hornsey Lane over the Great North Rd. *St. Augustine's Church* (1885; J.D. Sedding) has a broad spacious interior and some Arts and Crafts fittings. The W front was added 1912–14 (J.H. Gibbons). Muswell Hill Rd leads up to *Alexandra Palace* (1875; J. Johnson), very large north London rival to the Crystal Palace, impressive from the E, Wood Green, where the elephantine central gable dominates the hilltop. The Great Hall behind was burnt out in 1980 but restoration is proposed. At **Wood Green**, E of the High Rd, *Noel Park*, a whole estate (1889) of small-scale workers' housing around the church of St. Mark (1889; R. Plumbe). In Tottenham Lane, to the SW, *Holy Innocents* Church (1877; A.W. Blomfield), craggy brick. At **Crouch End**, Broadway Parade, the *Queens* pub (1899; J.C. Hill) with Art Nouveau glass and rich woodwork. At **Harringay**, to the E, the *Salisbury* (1898; J.C. Hill), on the corner of Green Lanes and St. Ann's Rd, is similar and even larger, an example of the very large sums that were invested in pub building in the 1890s. Red brick and stone with polished granite ground-floor columns and Art Nouveau glass. To the NE is **Tottenham**, on the slopes above the Lea valley. The parish *church*, Church Lane, off Lordship Lane, was restored by Butterfield who is buried in Tottenham Cemetery adjoining. To the W, between Lordship Lane and White Hart Lane, *White Hart Lane Estate* (begun 1904), one of the pioneering London County Council cottage estates.

ENFIELD (Outer N London borough W of the river Lea, around the older centres of Enfield and Edmonton). At **Enfield**, to the W, in Windmill Hill, *St. Mary Magdalene's Church* (1883; W. Butterfield), a late work, but still richly coloured inside. Off London Rd, to S, *No. 8 Private Rd* (1887; A.H. Mackmurdo). Mackmurdo, founder of the Century Guild and key figure in the Arts and Crafts movement, designed little. This is his earliest surviving work, white painted roughcast, simple horizontals, without any of the gables, projections or prettiness of the Norman Shaw school, the inspiration being partly Whistler's house in Chelsea. In Village Rd, adjoining, *No. 13* (c 1875), Arts and Crafts. Further S, where Green Lanes meets Bourne Hill, *St. John's Church* (1904–09; J.O. Scott), flint and stone with handsome crossing tower. Further W, Waterfall Rd, **Southgate**, *Christ Church* (1862; G.G. Scott), an expensive church with spire, notable for the Morris glass, S aisle, W by Rossetti (1863) and N aisle by Burne-Jones. On the E side of the borough, on Hertford Rd, **Edmonton**, *St. Michael's Church* (1901; W.D. Caroe), red brick, free Gothic. To NE at **Ponders End**, *Pumping Station* (c 1900), Lea Valley Rd, arty brick.

EAST LONDON

HACKNEY. The S tip of the borough is really part of the City. Adjoining the site of Broad St Station, in Eldon St, *St. Mary Moorfields* (1899; G. Sherrin), replacing and re-using bits from one of the first important Catholic churches in London (1820). To N, an area still full of tall warehouses stretching up to Old St. In Worship St, *Nos 91–101* (1863; P. Webb), terrace of shops in the simplified Gothic that Webb used for his contemporary house for William Morris, the Red House, Bexleyheath; a rare example of design for commercial premises by an advanced Gothic architect. In Mark St, behind, the disused *St. Michael's Church* (1863–65; J. Brooks), once part of a whole complex of brick Gothic buildings but now a rather sad home for salvaged architectural fragments. On Old St, the former *Shoreditch Town Hall* (1866: extended in Baroque style 1902), the architect of the first part

Caesar Augustus Long according to the foundation stone. Red-brick and stone Police Court opposite (1903; J.D. Butler) in good neo-Georgian style. **Hoxton**, to the N, has largely been rebuilt. In Pitfield St, Arts and Crafts *Library* (1896; H.T. Hare). On Hoxton St, *Hoxton Hall*, a rare surviving London music hall (1863 and 1867) with two balconies. Recently restored. On Kingsland Rd, *St. Columba's Church* (1868–69; J. Brooks), now disused, a most important High Victorian church complex all in red brick. The church, E end on to the street, has a sturdy crossing tower, pyramid-roofed, and the whole has a massive scale, treated very simply. A compact group next to the church with picturesque dormers contained the vestry, vicarage, mission house and school. Brooks also designed *St. Chad's* (1868–69). Nichols Square, Hackney Rd, to the SE, again a magnificent plain brick vessel with apsed chancel and some stone vaulting. Vicarage by Brooks next door. Off Kingsland Rd, to the W, **De Beauvoir Town**, pleasant early Victorian suburb around De Beauvoir Square (Roumieu and Gough).

E of Kingsland Rd, Dalston Lane, **Dalston**, *Hackney Institute* (1902–03; A. Cooksey) and in St. Mark's Rise, *St. Mark's Church* (1862–67; C. Cheston Jr), 'London's largest parish church', a vast and ham-fisted building that achieves grandeur inside with a nave of great width, a complete set of contemporary stained glass including some stained roof lights, and fine metalwork. The tower (1877; E.L. Blackburne) matches the church in craggy vigour and has, on the S side, the only working turret barometer in Europe. In Shacklewell Row, to the N, *St. Barnabas' Church* (1909; C.H. Reilly), a complete contrast, a simple mission church in stock brick, the interior neo-classical or Byzantine in feeling, exploiting plain brick in a miniature reminiscence of Westminster Cathedral. As at the Cathedral the roofs are concrete, both barrel vaults and a shallow dome. A painted columned screen gives a touch of richness. Kingsland Rd runs into **Stoke Newington**, with Church St on left leading to the new parish *church* (1858; G.G. Scott: spire 1890) at the corner of *Albion Rd*, an early development (1822–40) by T. Cubitt, builder of Belgravia. Off the High St, *Abney Park Cemetery* (1840; W. Hosking), one of the early cemeteries on a large scale, with Egyptian style entrance gates and lodge. There is a fine statue to the hymn writer Isaac Watts (E.H. Baily) near the derelict chapel.

The centre of **Hackney** itself is to the SE, at the top of Mare St, with the *Hackney Empire Theatre* (1901; Matcham) the best building. The best Victorian area is to the SE around **Victoria Park**. In Victoria Park Rd, *French Hospital* (1865; Roumieu), heavy brick detail with a central rather French or Flemish tower. At the far end, beyond the railway, *St. Mary of Eton Church* (1880; Bodley and Garner), built for the Eton College Mission, a long red-brick and stone Gothic church with fine painted roof and strong square tower (1912). A gatehouse tower gives entry to the pleasant group of mission buildings. *Victoria Park* itself was laid out 1842–43 (J. Pennethorne) as the largest municipal park in London. Irregular plan with lakes and a large fountain (1861; H. Darbishire) given by the philanthropist Baroness Burdett Coutts.

WALTHAM FOREST (NE London borough around the old town of Walthamstow). The Lea valley marks the W side. On Lea Bridge Rd, *Pumping Station* (1891), just in Hackney, and 1m further on, at corner of Church Rd, *Library* (1903; W. Jacques), and beyond, on left, *Bakers Almshouses* (1857; T.E. Knightley). Hoe St leads N to **Walthamstow**. On High St, *Baths* (1900) and *Library* (1907). Church Hill, opposite, leads up to the old church and the *Vestry House Museum* with the first British motor car (1892; Bremer) and a local history collection. To the N, on Forest Rd, *Water House*, Lloyd Park, William Morris' home from 1848 to 1856, contains the William Morris Museum with much of Morris' work as well as paintings and works by contemporaries.

TOWER HAMLETS (E London borough adjoining City). Across the way from the Tower of London, *St. Katharine's Dock* (1825–28), **Wapping**, mostly now rebuilt, some in replica, but in the centre the attractive *Ivory Warehouse* (1861; G. Aitchison). St. Katharine's Dock is the nearest in the series of docks downstream of the Tower, the major part being the London Docks (1796–1820). Sadly the warehouses have all been demolished, massive retaining walls and the basins themselves remain. Bombs and planning have erased so much of inner E London, the London of sailors and dockers, Jews and Chinese, that the pages of Conan Doyle and Dickens come to life more from place-names than from surviving buildings. Along Wapping High St the riverside warehouses that survived are now becoming flats and studios. The railway tunnel from Wapping to Rotherhithe is the *Rotherhithe Tunnel*, built with heroic endeavour 1825–43 (Mark Brunel). E of Wapping are Shadwell, Ratcliff and Limehouse. *Narrow St*, **Limehouse**, has the most character, crossing the Thames exit of the Regent's Canal. The churchyard around Hawksmoor's St. Anne's Church (1712–30: interior mostly 1852) is cut off from the river by the old Blackwall railway line, one of the earliest in London (1839), built to connect the City with the East and West India Docks. Commercial Rd, on the N side of the churchyard, was built for similar purpose in 1810. Just E of the churchyard, *Sailors Hostel* (1901; Niven and Wigglesworth), Arts and Crafts Tudor.

Off Commercial Rd to the N is **Stepney**. White Horse Rd leads up to Stepney Green past pretty brick terraces of 1820–35 and the *Mico Almshouses* (1856). Stepney Green leads up to Mile End Rd. Between here and Whitechapel Jewish shops survive in some numbers. On left, *Sidney St* where *No. 100* was the scene of the bizarre 1911 siege where two armed robbers were besieged by police and army and finally burnt to death. The scale of the siege was largely due to contemporary fears of foreign anarchists setting up terrorist cells amid the immigrant E London population. Further on, behind the London Hospital, *St. Philip's* (1888–92; A. Cawston), Stepney Way, a fine red brick church in the manner of Pearson, vaulted and apsed. In the Lady Chapel a reredos by Bodley from St. Augustine's, Stepney. In Whitechapel High St, *Whitechapel Art Gallery* (1899–1901; C.H. Townsend), commissioned, with the library next door, by Passmore Edwards to bring the benefits of art to the East End. The gallery is one of those Arts and Crafts buildings that approach most closely continental Art Nouveau. Faced in tile, a great archway, off-centre, dominates the lower half, while above two side turrets with relief decoration and curvaceous tops (originally to have cupolas) frame a blank recessed space where Walter Crane's mosaic 'The Sphere and the Message' was to have gone. To the S, Leman St leads down to Cable St. In Graces Alley, off Ensign St, *Wilton's Music Hall* (1878), concealed behind a pub, the very rare survival of one of the larger Music Halls, often attached to pubs from the 1860s onwards. Disused but to be restored. N of Whitechapel, **Spitalfields**, around Commercial St. Wentworth St was said to be the heart of the Jewish East End. In Toynbee St, *Toynbee Hall* (1884; Hoole) was the famous centre set up by Oxford churchmen and graduates to help the poor and crowded population of the area. Brick

Lane, parallel, has Trumans Brewery, established here since the 18C. Between Bethnal Green Rd and Shoreditch High St, around Arnold Circus, is the LCC *Boundary St Estate* (1893–1900), the redevelopment of one of the most notorious slums in London, the Jago, commemorated in A. Morrison's 'A Child of the Jago' (1886). Tall well-lit redbrick blocks replaced narrow alleys, some 5500 people were rehoused, though apparently only eleven original inhabitants. Bethnal Green Rd leads to **Bethnal Green** where the *Bethnal Green Museum* (1875; J.W. Wild), an outstation of the Victoria and Albert Museum, is notable for the collection of sculptures by Rodin. In front, statue of the *Eagleslayer* (J. Bell), remarkably made in cast iron by the Coalbrookdale Iron Co for the 1851 exhibition. The roof structure of the museum is the iron roof of the first Museum of Science and Art (1855), built at S Kensington, the predecessor of the Victoria and Albert Museum. Next door, Edwardian Baroque *Town Hall* (1909). Old Ford Rd leads to the formal approach to Victoria Park (see Hackney above, p. 265) with large mid 19C houses each side. In Bonner Rd, *School* (1875; E.R. Robson), one of the best early Board Schools. Returning to Mile End Rd beyond Stepney Green is *Queen Mary College*, partly occupying the Peoples Palace (1885; E.R. Robson), an unsuccessful attempt to create a Crystal Palace for the East End. Beyond Mile End station pleasant early 19C houses around Tredegar Square on left and, on right, down Southern Grove, the spectacularly overgrown *Tower Hamlets Cemetery* (1848), the main East End cemetery. Bow Rd leads on to **Bromley** with the *Match Tax Fountain* (1872; R. Plumbe), testimonial erected by match manufacturers to the repeal of the tax and, beyond, statue of Gladstone (1881; A.B. Joy).

From Bromley, St. Leonard's Rd leads S to **Poplar**. In Brunswick Rd, *Library* (1904), stone fronted, and, at the end, entrance to *Blackwall Tunnel* (1892–97), road tunnel built by the LCC with handsome red stone gatehouse. Poplar *church*, Poplar High St, now in bad condition, is a chapel of 1776 encased in the most crustaceous and un-Georgian stone skin with candle-snuffer small spire (1867–70; W.M. Teulon). The original interior survives. In East India Dock Rd, *George Green's School* (1883; J. Sulman), Gothic with picturesque gables and tower, also Mr Green's *Sailors Home* (1841; Constable), a long stucco block, now offices, and the *statue* of George Green (1865; E. Wyon). Between East India Dock (1805) and the river was the terminus of the *Blackwall Railway* (1840; W. Tite) that ran on elevated tracks from here to Fenchurch St in the City. The area to the S, contained by a loop of the river, is the **Isle of Dogs** or Millwall, a narrow band of buildings following the line of the river, encircling the West India Docks (1799–1802: enlarged 1870) and the Millwall Docks (1864–68). **Cubitt Town** was a settlement created c 1850 by the contracting firm of William Cubitt for their works. At the S tip, a superb view of Greenwich. Nearby, in West Ferry Rd, *Fire Station* (1904), one of many built by the LCC, a neat design in brick in the late 17C style.

NEWHAM (E London borough stretching from dockland to West Ham). From Poplar, East India Dock Rd leads into **Canning Town**. To the S, Victoria Dock (1855) continued to E by Albert Dock (1880). Little of architectural interest save the three Queen Anne style *pubs* built by the dock company (1880–84; Vigers and Wagstaff), the *Ship*, Victoria Dock Rd, the *Connaught*, Connaught Rd, and most splendid but derelict, the *Galleons*, Woolwich Manor Way, E of Albert Dock. From Canning Town station Barking Rd leads E to **Plaistow** with, on right,

St. Andrew's Church (1870; J. Brooks), spacious tall church concentrated on apsed E end, the detail High Victorian and tough but as in other Brooks churches the plain space impresses most. Further on, at corner of Green St, the *Boleyn* pub (1899; Shoebridge and Rising), exuberant facade with all the current Flemish and Queen Anne motifs combined and lots of carving. At **East Ham**, small municipal complex on the corner of High St South, including brick and terracotta *Town Hall* (1903; H.A. Cheers).

The N part of the borough is **Stratford**, entered from Bromley. Off High St, to S, in the complex of waterways that make up the Lea river, *Three Mills*, group of mill buildings of 1776 and 1817, originally a distillery. Clock Mill has two drying cones has recently been restored. Further E, the long hump that covers the main sewage outfall for N London, running down to the river at Beckton, part of the huge undertaking of c 1864 by Sir J. Bazalgette. In Abbey Lane is the *Abbey Mills Pumping Station* (1865–68; J. Bazalgette), wonderfully exotic cruciform building in Italian Gothic style capped by a central cupola. The interior is a riot of ornamental ironwork, pierced and fretted, supported on a ring of columns. At Stratford Broadway, *Town Hall* (1868; L. Angell), round arched Italian with a domed tower, the obelisk (1861; J. Bell) to S. Gurney, Quaker philanthropist, opposite. Behind is the Court House (1881; L. Angell). To the SW, former Temperance Hotel (1901; S.B. Russell), now Housing Department, and altered remains of *Borough Theatre* (1895; F. Matcham) with a top cupola. In the centre, *church* (1832; E. Blore) with a good spire, and, in the churchyard, *Martyrs Memorial* (1879; J.T. Newman), Gothic and spired. On NE side, *bank* (1867; F. Chancellor), Italianate. Up Angel Lane to N, *Theatre Royal* (1884; J.G. Buckle), nondescript street front with attractive interior, the two balconies supported on iron columns. Along Romford Rd, E of Broadway, is *West Ham College* (1898–1900; Gibson and Russell), built as College, Library and Museum complex in the freest of late 19C Baroque styles with heavily blocked columns, curved and carved gables, ornate stone cupolas, and, over the museum, a broad shallow dome. Sculpture by W.B. Rhind. The College is now part of NE London Polytechnic. To NE, off Forest Lane and St. James Rd, *Jewish Cemetery* with the splendid stone mausoleum to Baroness E. de Rothschild (1866; Sir M.D. Wyatt), Portland stone, classical cum Renaissance and crowned by a stone dome. In the NE corner of the borough, off Romford Rd, *City of London Cemetery* (1856; W. Haywood), one of the best preserved Victorian cemeteries in London with good planting and layout.

REDBRIDGE (NE London borough around the old centre of Ilford). Leytonstone Rd leads N to **Wanstead**. From Snaresbrook Station, High St leads SE to the parish *church* (1861; G.G. Scott), ragstone suburban church with spire, and NW to Hollybush Hill where *Royal Wanstead School* (1843; Scott and Moffatt) stands at the edge of Epping Forest, a large Jacobean style stone asylum for orphans. To N of the station, on Hermon Hill, *Wanstead Hospital* (1861; G. Somers Clarke), a thoroughgoing polychrome Gothic work with Venetian Gothic windows and tracery to the tower openings. The roofs with triangular dormers and the tall slate roof to the tower are quite un-Italian, the building being essentially a synthesis of Italian Gothic and mid Victorian institutional planning, the next step on from imitation.

HAVERING (Outermost E London borough stretching from Rainham on the Thames to Romford and Upminster). At Romford, in the Market

Place, *church* (1850; J. Johnson), well placed with tall spire. Nearby, *Romford Brewery*, High St, on the little river Rom, mostly early 19C.

SOUTH LONDON: INNER BOROUGHS

WANDSWORTH. In the W of the borough **Roehampton** was in the 18C popular with the gentry on account of its proximity to Richmond Park. Several of the large mansions built at the time survive, their grounds to a greater or lesser extent developed with housing. The parish church of *Holy Trinity* (1896–98; G. Fellowes Prynne), Roehampton Lane, with its tall spire, is a major landmark. It replaced a church built only 50 years previously by B. Ferrey. The 19C *Vicarage* lies opposite, on the corner with Alton Rd. N is Thomas Archer's Roehampton House (1710), with lodges and wings by Lutyens (1911–13). To N, *Digby Stuart College and Convent* (c 1850–60; M. Hadfield and J.H. Pollen) plain brick Gothic. The E end of the *chapel* (1853; W. Wardell) survives incorporated in a new church. Adjacent *Lodge* also by Wardell. Peeping over the wall of the Froebel Institute (1777; J. Wyatt: 1851; W. Burn), Clarence Lane, is the neo-Romanesque *Mausoleum* (1862; W. Burn) built for the ballerina Pauline Duvernet. **Putney** lies to the E, its medieval *church* by the river mostly rebuilt by E. Lapidge (1836–37) and recently restored following a fire. The *Bridge* (1884; J. Bazalgette) is modelled on Rennie's London Bridge. The approach road, High St, was widened at the time of the Bridge's construction, and the *White Lion* dates from this time. On the corner with Upper Richmond Rd, the *Railway* is another good pub. To W, on edge of Barnes Common, *All Saints' Church* (1873–74; G.E. Street), Lower Common, brick with an extensive range of Morris and Co glass. In Putney Hill are a number of Italianate villas, notably No. 11, *The Pines*, part of a symmetrical pair of c 1870 and the scene of the rehabilitation of Swinburne at the hands of Theodore Watts-Dunton. Out to SW, on Kingston Rd, *Putney Vale Cemetery* was founded in 1891 and soon overtook Nunhead and W Norwood as the fashionable S London cemetery. Its best monument is the sublime Egyptian *mausoleum* to a brother of General Gordon. To E, in West Hill, the large Italianate *Royal Hospital* for *Incurables* (1864; W.P. Griffith). Off West Hill, in Sutherland Rd, the chapel of Giles Gilbert Scott's *Whitelands College* incorporates some fine Morris and Co. glass, mainly to designs by Burne-Jones, brought from the college's former premises in Chelsea. Further E, **Wandsworth** High St is dominated by the hideous Arndale Centre, but the old parish *church* has survived, mostly 18C, chancel 1899–1900 (E.W. Mountford). On the same side, the *Spread Eagle* is a late 19C pub with a splendid interior. Opposite, on the corner of York Rd, *Youngs Brewery* (1881). NW of the High St, in Oakhill Rd, Arts and Crafts cottages at *Nos 155–71* (1906; Edward G. Hunt) and, further W, *Nos 23–5* (1879 and 1880; William Young), for the architect and his sister respectively, the picturesque vernacular features of these houses in contrast to their Italianate and Gothic neighbours. S of the High St, a good *Board School* (1890; T.J. Bailey) in Merton Rd and, in Standen Rd, *Benham and Sons* (1904; W.T. Walker), a colourful Art Nouveau sweet factory. To E, in St. Ann's Hill, R. Smirke's *St. Ann's* has a chancel by Mountford, showing his later Baroque allegiance (1896). Nearby, off Wandsworth Common, broods *Wandsworth Prison*, with its fortified gatehouse (1849; D. Hill of

Birmingham). E, in Trinity Rd, the Gothic former *Royal Victoria Patriotic Asylum* (1857; Rhode Hawkins), built for the orphaned daughters of servicemen. NE, *Emmanuel School* (1872; Saxon Snell), built for the sons of servicemen, in a more restrained Gothic. S of the prison, in Lyford Rd, Edwardian houses, notably No. 68, *The White Cottage* (1903; Voysey). On the Common is a hexagonal weather-boarded *windpump* which has lost its sails (1837). In Beechcroft Rd, to SW, *Springfield Hospital* was the Surrey County Asylum (1840–42; E. Lapidge), Tudor style.

   Tooting lies to the S. On Trinity Rd, *Holy Trinity Church* (1854–55; Salvin), tower 1860 (B. Ferrey). Opposite, *Fire Station* (1907; W.E. Brooks) in the lively and eclectic style of the time. In Upper Tooting Rd, the *King's Head* (1896; W.M. Brunton), a florid symmetrical exterior and an interior brilliant with cut glass, patterned tiles and wrought iron. At the junction with Mitcham Rd, a *statue of Edward VII*. Off Mitcham Rd, in Franciscan Rd, **All Saints'* (1906; Temple Moore), a severe and excellently proportioned brick church with double aisles, filled with too many Italian furnishings collected by the first incumbent. The church lies at the heart of the pioneering LCC cottage estate of *Totterdown Fields* (1900–03). S, in Church Lane, the old parish *church* of Tooting was replaced in 1833 by the present Commissioners' Gothic church by T.W. Atkinson. Behind the former *St. Benedict's Hospital* (1887–88; W. Harvey), built as a RC college, neo-Georgian. Off Rectory Lane to the S, in Welham Rd, is *Furzedown School* (1910), a late LCC school, with Baroque centrepiece. *Furzedown Training College*, to N, incorporates a house of c 1800, bought in 1862 by Philip Flower, developer of the Park Town Estate in Battersea. James Knowles Sr altered it and added the fine conservatory at the back. The little *lodge* dates from c 1850. To the NE is Streatham Park, developed on the site of a house demolished 1863. Some late 19C villas survive. No. 2 West Drive, *Yew Tree Lodge*, is a smart neo-Georgian house by L. Stokes (1899) and No. 8 North Drive, *Dixcote*, is a Voysey design executed by W. Cave (1897) in characteristic roughcast, with mullion windows and prominent chimney stacks. W of Tooting Broadway, in Blackshaw Rd is *Lambeth Cemetery*, opened 1854, with brick Gothic lodges and chapels (F.K. Wehnert and J. Ashdown). In Garratt Lane to N, *St. Andrew's Church* (1889; E.W. Mountford), with one of G. Tinworth's terracotta fonts, and the extensive Tudor style *St. Clement Danes Almshouses* (1848; R. Hesketh). Leading NE from Tooting, **Balham** High Rd has some stucco houses of the early 19C. *St. Mary's Church* is a plain early 19C preaching box hidden behind a grand neo-Baroque W front (1903; William Newton Dunn). Apsed chancel (1882; A. Cawston), with marble and mosaic decoration of the 1890s, and glass by Clayton and Bell in the clerestory. In Ramsden Rd, the basilican church of *St. Luke* (1883; F.W. Hunt) has exceptionally rich furnishings, and striking electric light fittings of 1903, the *Library* (1898; S.R.J. Smith) is a pretty amalgam of Georgian and Tudor motifs. In Nightingale Square, *RC church* (1897; L. Stokes), economical, the interior space well handled.

   The N of the borough is **Battersea**. The old centre with church and High St, W of Battersea Bridge Rd, is now heavily redeveloped. In High St, *Sir Walter St. John School*, much extended from a diapered brick original by Butterfield (1858–59) which survives in the centre. Gothic great hall of 1913 (A.H. Ryan Tennison). In Trott St, impressive Norman *RC church* (1892; F.A. Walters). Further S, pretty free-style former *Library* (c 1900). In Battersea Park Rd, on the corner of Latchmere Rd, the *Latchmere* pub is prominent. Just E, in Reform St and

Freedom St, an early example (1903) of municipal *housing* by one of the London boroughs, the street names reflecting the colour of the local politics at the time. In Battersea Park Rd, the former *Battersea Polytechnic* (1890; E.W. Mountford), a key building of the revival of English Baroque formality, though still here an eclectic mix. Handsome Wren style library added 1909. *Battersea Park* is a Victorian creation, of 1854, built up with spoil from the docks down river. Typical layout of curving drives and boating lake. The riverside view of Albert Bridge, Chelsea Bridge and the 20C Japanese pagoda is a delight in the morning mist. E of the park, on corner of Queenstown Rd, *Battersea Park Station* (1867) impresses with the massiveness of its detailing, Italianate cum Gothic. Two-storey booking hall inside. The nearby bridge has cast-iron facing with the railway arms. Queenstown Rd continues S as the centre artery of the diamond shaped *Park Town Estate* (1863–64; J.T. Knowles Jr), grey brick houses with some carved ornament and a ragstone *church* (1869; Knowles) in St. Philip's Square, the centrepiece of the estate. On Queenstown Rd itself a bleak succession of red brick fronts. More cheerful is the *Shaftesbury Park Estate* (1872–77; R. Austin), just W around Sabine Rd, one of the first cottage estates, built by the Artisans, Labourers and General Dwellings Company, i.e. for a lower social class than Park Town, but prettily ornamented in coloured brick. To S is Lavender Hill, with one of S London's finest Victorian churches, *The Ascension* (1876–98; J. Brooks, completed Micklethwaite and Somers Clarke), a brick vessel of heroic scale and unbroken lines, utterly without extraneous ornament outside, the interior brick, even the arches, crushing down on sturdy round stone columns. Apse vaulted in wood, NE chapel in stone. Further W, *Battersea Town Hall* (1892; E.W. Mountford), handsome formal front in brick and stone, the detail Wrenian. Sculpture (P. Montford) of Battersea instructed by Labour, Progress, Literature and Art. Majestic stair hall inside, council chamber and public hall with ornate plasterwork. Further W, on S side, *Library* (1888; E.W. Mountford), showing Mountford in a pre-Baroque phase. On corner of Falcon Rd, the *Falcon* (1887), with good cut-glass decoration, and a grandiose department store, *Arding and Hobbs* (1910; J.S. Gibson) opposite. In St. John's Hill, the *Grand Theatre* (1900; E. Woodrow), brash and red outside, Chinese surprisingly inside, not helped by the ceiling being obscured. *No. 92* (1909; T.J. Bailey), neo-Georgian, was the LCC education office. At the top of St. John's Rd, in Battersea Rise, *St. Mark's Church* (1872–74; W. White), the best of several economical churches by White in the area, this one remarkably of concrete faced with brick. The picturesque shingled spire is a happy substitute for something grander intended. Other churches by White, St. Stephen's, Battersea Pk Rd, and St. Michael's, Chatham Rd, off Northcote Rd.

LAMBETH. Clapham was a country village around Old Town, NE of the Common. The significant 19C development was mostly away from Old Town, except for *Grafton Square* (1851). The 18C parish *church* has a chancel of 1903 by Beresford Pite, Pite's variations on classical themes as always interesting. On North Side, The Elms was the house of Sir C. Barry, and there are terraces at the top of Victoria Rise that may be by him or by E.M. Barry. Unexpectedly large and urban are *The Cedars* (1860; J. Knowles Jr), two five-storey terraces with French pavilion roofs, blood-brothers to the Knowles' Grosvenor Hotel, Victoria. They were so grand as the formal entry of a route N through the Park Town Estate (also by Knowles) in Battersea and over the river to central London (coincidentally Victoria). Further W, *No. 113* has a chapel behind by Philip Webb (1896) for William Morris's sister, quite plain. On the Common, a *bandstand* of 1862. At the E end, on the S side, *Alexandra Hotel* (1866), a particularly brash Gothic pub with a dome. *Crescent Grove* is a pretty villa estate of 1824. E of the hotel, *RC church* (1849–51; W. Wardell), Clapham Park Rd, one of the most successful Puginian Gothic churches in London, for once the Dec. fully achieved with enough money for a soaring spire. Cleaning has cheered up the normally depressing colour of the Kentish ragstone. Vaulted chancel. Fine additions and fittings by J.F. Bentley (Lady Chapel 1882), by Bentley also the *monastery* (1892) adjoining. To E, off Bedford Rd and Ferndale Rd, *housing* of c 1870 (T.E. Collcutt), lavishly terracotta ornamented. Acre Lane runs E into **Brixton**. At the junction with Brixton Rd and Coldharbour Lane is the Baroque *Town Hall*, marked by an angle corner tower (1906–08; Septimus Warwick and H. Austen Hall). Opposite, the free Renaissance *Library* (1893; S.R.J. Smith), the largest of several libraries built in the borough through the generosity of Sir Henry Tate, builder of the Tate Gallery, who lived in Streatham. E of the crossroads, the *viaducts* of the London Chatham and Dover and the S London Railways, the former brick and the latter iron. The *Railway Tavern* dates from 1880; polychrome brick with a corner turret. Nearby, Electric Avenue was one of the first London streets to be electrically illuminated. S of Brixton, in Brixton Hill, more early–mid 19C ribbon development and the Gothic RC church of *Corpus Christi*, begun 1886 by J.F. Bentley, the E end only completed. Off to W *Brixton Prison*, begun 1819. To the E, the large area of Tulse Hill and Brockwell Park is the former Brockwell Hall Estate, a Regency villa which survives in the middle of the park. E, in Rosendale Rd, *All Saints'* (1888–91; Fellowes-Prynne), a very tall Gothic church in red brick with stone dressings, given a rather French feel by the external ambulatory around the E end and the round tower with conical roof against the N aisle. Inside, a very tall stone screen. N, in Herne Hill, the *Railway Station* (1862) is an attractive polychrome brick building, Gothic. Ruskin lived at *No. 28 Herne Hill* with his parents, and in the area all his life. *Ruskin Park* (1907) off Denmark Hill is in his memory. (See also Southwark above, p. 275.)

Brixton Hill continues S into **Streatham Hill**. E, around Christchurch Rd and Palace Rd, was the Roupell Park Estate, developed between 1850 and 1880, with one or two of its grand classical villas still extant. In Christchurch Rd, *Christ Church* (1840–42; J. Wild) is perhaps the best example in this country of the *rundbogenstil*, a round-arched style that originated in Germany and combined Italian Romanesque and basilican forms. It enjoyed a vogue here in the 1840s. Christ Church is a simple and impressive brick church with a tall campanile at its E end. Inside there is an apse but no chancel, in the manner of the early Christian basilicas. In the aisles, windows by Walter Crane (1891). In Streatham High Rd at the corner of Mitcham Lane, the old parish church of *St. Leonard* (1830–31; J.T. Parkinson), with chancel extended 1863 to the designs of William Dyce, the Pre-Raphaelite painter. Dyce was a churchwarden and probably also designed the Gothic drinking fountain outside (1862). Unfortunately, Dyce's decoration in the chancel was lost in a recent fire. Opposite, *RC church* (1903; Purdie). The early 20C *Presbytery* is in Arts and Crafts cum Tudor style. Near Streatham Hill Station, Leigham Court Rd leads off to the SE. *St. Peter's Church* (1871) by R.W. Drew, a nephew of Butterfield, W end (1888) by Fellowes-Prynne, is impressive on a raised site. Off High Rd, in Pendennis Rd, *No. 5, Compton* (1872–73; Norman Shaw), built for G.H. Best the painter. Streatham Common lies to the S.

The N side was developed with large houses from the 1880s onwards. One earlier house survives as a convent, *Park House* (c 1830; Papworth), once the home of Sir Henry Tate, who added the porte-cochère 1880. Facing the W end of the Common, the *Pied Bull* pub, nearby, at No. 496 High Rd, the former *Beehive Coffee House* (1878–79; E. George and Peto), Queen Anne style, built to keep the workers from the nearby *India Rubber Works* belonging to Mr Cow of Cow Gum fame away from the alehouse. Ernest George lived in Streatham and built in the area, in his characteristic domestic style. Off the High Rd, in Guildersfield Rd to the S, is his and Peto's *St. Andrew Church* (1885–86), red-brick Perp. with terracotta dressings, also a gabled *Vicarage* (1886; George and Peto) and *Church Hall* (1898; George and Yeates). Streatham Common North leads E towards **West Norwood**, which saw some minor development in the early 19C and then boomed after the arrival of the Crystal Palace in 1856. In Crown Lane, the Tudor cum Jacobean *Royal Hospital for Incurables* (1894; Cawston: 1913; E.T. Hall). Knights Hill leads N to the parish church of *St. Luke* (1822; Bedford), a Commissioners' church given a new chancel and a Romanesque arcade in the nave by G.E. Street (1872–73). Nearby is *Norwood Cemetery, on a raised site like Highgate, laid out by Tite from 1837 for the South Metropolitan Cemetery Company. Tite designed the Gothic chapels and the fine iron gates. Beneath the chapels (now demolished) were catacombs, in which Tite himself was interred. The major monument in the Cemetery, to the banker J.W. Gilbart, is probably by Tite (1866), Gothic. Numerous other memorials make this the richest collection of Victorian funerary sculpture in the country. The best group is the Greek Orthodox Cemetery in the NE corner. The Greek Revival chapel to Augustus Ralli (1872) is attributed to J.O. Scott, architect of the Orthodox Cathedral in Bayswater. Mausolea to John Ralli (1863; Street) and, Renaissance style, to Eustratios Ralli (E.M. Barry and T.H. Vernon). Also by Barry, the fine Gothic memorial to Alexander Berens on the brow of the hill (1858). William Burges is buried here, with his mother, in a tomb designed by himself (1855). Mausolea to Sir Henry Tate (died 1890), by Smith, his trusted architect, and to Sir Henry Doulton (1897), appropriately adorned with Doulton ware, probably by R.S. Wilkinson, who built the Doulton works on the Albert Embankment.

N of Clapham, lie **Stockwell**, **South Lambeth**, **Kennington** and **Vauxhall**. Around Stockwell Park Rd, stucco villas and terraces of the 1830s and 40s. *Church* (1840; W. Rogers) in entertaining incorrect Gothic. N on Brixton Rd, *Christ Church* (1899–1902; Beresford Pite), remarkable domed neo-Byzantine design with external pulpit and an interior centralised plan quite unlike contemporary High Church interiors. To W, off Clapham Rd, *Albert Square* (1846–47; J. Glenn), a rare formal development on the scale more common N of the river. Further up, craggy and square-shouldered brick front to the *Belgrave Hospital for Children* (1900–03; H.P. Adams) showing clearly the work of C. Holden, then, aged 25, working for Adams. *Kennington Park* (1852–54) has, facing Kennington Rd, one of the model cottages (1851; H. Roberts) commissioned by Prince Albert for the Great Exhibition as a demonstration of improved industrial housing. To S, off Camberwell New Rd, in Vassall Rd, *St. John the Divine* (1870–89; G.E. Street), with handsome brick exterior and broach spire only a partial introduction to the beautifully proportioned interior with its bellying roof (painted by Bodley). The church was gutted in the war and restored with exemplary care by H. Goodhart-Rendel. W of Kennington Park, the *Oval* became a cricket ground in 1846. In Kennington Lane, the site of

Vauxhall pleasure gardens had by the mid 19C degenerated into slum quarters. Here the Rev. Robert Gregory commissioned Pearson to build *St. Peter's*, his first major town church (1863–64). Polychrome brickwork, austere. The interior entirely vaulted, with brick panels between the ribs. Good fittings, murals and glass at the E end by Clayton and Bell. A nearby late 18C house was altered by Pearson and made the *Vicarage*. Pearson also built *St. Peter's Schools* (1857–61), behind, alterations by J.T. Knowles Jr (1873), and *Herbert House* (1864), an orphanage. To the E, *Imperial Court*, the NAAFI headquarters, was built as a School for the Licensed Victuallers Co (1835–36; H. Rose), a monumental classical facade. At the junction with Kennington Rd, a subterranean *gents*, its c 1900 fittings intact. Nearby, in Cardigan St, Courtenay St and Courtenay Square, the Regency revival *Duchy of Cornwall Estate* (1913; Adshead and Ramsay) displays an elegance of design and humanity of conception sadly lacking in subsequent large housing developments in the borough.

Vauxhall Bridge, W of Kennington Lane, has good early 20C sculpture on the piers by A. Drury and F.W. Pomeroy. Opposite, the *Railway Station* (1838; Tite), much altered, so impressed a visiting delegation from Tsarist Russia that Vauxhall (BOKCAL) became the Russian word for a railway station. To the N, the *Albert Embankment* (1866–69; J. Bazalgette), accommodating, among other things, the sewer running from Putney. Its river-facing side has been developed in stupefyingly banal fashion in the last 30 years. Right, in Black Prince Rd, only one of the original buildings for the Lambeth Pottery of Messrs Doulton survives (1878; R. Stark Wilkinson), now called *Southbank House*. It is a wonderful example of the blending of the building and decorative arts, and a fine advertisement for the firm. The exterior is lavishly adorned with terracotta detail and, in the canted entrance on the corner, the pediment has a relief of potters at work by G. Tinworth, the most noted sculptor who worked for the firm. Also in Black Prince Rd, the annexe to *Beaufoy School* (1907; F.A. Powell), red brick Baroque, also has plentiful terracotta dressings. Further on, the almshouse type *Babies Hostel* (1913–14; Adshead and Ramsay), now part of St. Thomas's Hospital, but originally a nursery on the Duchy of Cornwall Estate. In Lambeth Rd, the former *Holy Trinity Infants School* (1880) forms a picturesque composition. Albert Embankment continues into Lambeth Palace Rd. *St. Thomas's Hospital* lies on the river-facing side. It was rebuilt on the present site 1868–71 by Henry Currey on the new principle of separate pavilions connected by a long corridor. Three of the original seven Italianate pavilions survive, as does the *chapel*, also Italianate, with Doulton relief panels in the reredos. Over Waterloo Rd to York Rd and the former *County Hall*, home of the LCC and the lately departed GLC. The winner of the competition held for the building in 1908 was Ralph Knott, an unknown quantity. His design, begun 1912, has a grand riverside frontage, an Edwardian realisation in stone of the architectural fantasies of Piranesi. The interior is more restrained, 18C in feel. A later, simpler block faces York Rd. Nearby, guarding the S side of *Westminster Bridge* (1854–62; T. Page), the large Coade stone *Lion* of 1837 came from the demolished Lion Brewery, Lambeth. To the E is *Waterloo Station* (1901–22; architect J.R. Scott, engineer J.W. Jacomb Hood). The constricted position does not show off the grand Edwardian Baroque facade to advantage. Flanking the E approach to Waterloo Bridge, in Waterloo Rd, the former *Royal Waterloo Hospital* (1903–05; M.S. Nicholson), red brick and terracotta, with tiers of arcading and Doulton panels. To E, in Aquinas St, *cottages* for the

Duchy of Cornwall Estate (1911; Adshead and Ramsay), and S, in Roupell St, *St. Andrew's and St. John's Primary School* (1868; Teulon), plain brick Gothic. Teulon's church of St. Andrew in nearby Coin St was bombed. In Waterloo Rd, S of the station, a former *Fire Station* (1910; LCC) on the W side, and S of The Cut, the *Old Vic Theatre*, originally the Royal Coburg Theatre (1818), charming galleried interior (1871; J.T. Robinson) still with a music-hall feel.

SOUTHWARK. Borough High St is the ancient heart of *Southwark*, and retains its medieval street pattern. Apart from the Cathedral, the only significant early survival is the legendary 17C *George* Inn, and even this was mostly demolished by the Great North Railway in 1889. The railway cut across this area ruthlessly in the middle decades of the 19C. *London Bridge Station* is the earliest London station, opened 1836 as the terminal of the London and Greenwich Railway, rebuilt several times since. From 1847 the station was divided between the SE and the London Brighton and S Coast Railways. In 1859–64 the SE railway was extended to Waterloo and Charing Cross, forcing St. Thomas's Hospital to move from Bermondsey to Lambeth, in 1866 it was extended to Cannon St (see City above, p. 210). Sandwiched between the railway and the river is the former priory church of *St. Saviour and St. Mary Overie*, raised to cathedral status 1905. Much restored in the 19C, first by George Gwilt Jr and R. Wallace, then by H. Rose, who rebuilt the nave in its entirety 1839–40, only for it to be rebuilt in turn by Arthur Blomfield (1890–97). N of the approach to the new London Bridge, (the old one is now in the Arizona desert), the Italianate *Hibernia Chambers* (1850; W. Cubitt). Also, No. 4, *Bridge House*, built 1834 (G. Allen) and one of the first grand railway hotels. Plain exterior, the rich interior destroyed 1971. In Clink St, by the river, to W, some tall brick warehouses give a hint of the old riverside atmosphere. Running W from Borough High St is *Southwark St*, cut through 1862 (J. Bazalgette), the first London street to be provided with a central duct carrying gas and water supplies and a telegraph service. Still lined predominantly with 19C industrial and commercial buildings. Grandest of these is the former *Hop Exchange* (1866; R.H. Moore), now Central Buildings, on the N side. Southwark was the centre of the London hop trade. Fine iron gates, scenes of hop picking in the pediment above. Inside, an exchange hall with decorative ironwork balconies, like the Coal Exchange in the City. Much rebuilt after a fire c 1920. On the S side, No. 99, *Kirkaldys Testing Works* (1877; T.R. Smith), in a plain round-arched style. Over the doorway, Kirkaldy's motto: 'facts, not opinions'. To S is Union St, with a *hop warehouse* of 1853 at No. 14 and the neo-Georgian *St. Saviour's Parochial and National Schools* (1908). To the S, the area around Marshalsea St was in the 19C a notorious area of crime and prostitution until developed by philanthropists at the end of the century. *Redcross Cottages* in Redcross Way and *Whitecross Cottages* in Ayres St (1887–90; Elijah Hoole) were built at the instigation of Lady Octavia Hill, founder of the National Trust, as humane and civilised housing for the poor. They form a picturesque group, which is completed by *Redcross Hall*, also by Hoole, its interior decorated by Walter Crane with 'deeds of heroism in the daily lives of working people'. Also commissioning good works, the Rev. T. Bastow, who financed cottages in Sudry St (1889; Hoole), and even the Ecclesiastical Commissioners who put up attractive almshouse-type housing in Copperfield St (1893–95; Clutton). To the NW, *Blackfriars Bridge* (1860–09; J. Cubitt and H. Carr) replaces the 18C structure, the disused railway bridge running alongside also by Cubitt and Carr.

The riverside area to the E of London Bridge was developed with warehouses in the 19C, culminating in the formation of the Surrey Commercial Docks (1864). The area is now being transformed as 'London Bridge City'. In Tooley St, E of Goodhart-Rendel's St. Olave House (1931), is *Chamberlain's Wharf*, a seven-storey warehouse of the 1860s. The charming *Denmark House*, No. 15 (1908; S.D. Adshead) was built for the Bennett Steamship Company. E of *Colonial House* (1903; C. Stanley Peach), a continuous row of warehouses of the 1850s and 1860s, the finest *Nos 47–9* (1860s; W. Snooke and H. Stock). *Hays Wharf* (1856), also by Snooke and Stock, was built around a dock, but had to be rebuilt only five years later after a great fire in Tooley St. Also in Tooley St, the *Police Station* and *Magistrates Court* (1904; J.D. Butler) have some dramatic Baroque effects. Near Tower Bridge, the handsome red-brick and Portland stone *South London College*, formerly St. Olave's School (1893; E.W. Mountford). Opposite, a *statue* of Bevington (c 1907; Sydney March), first Mayor of Bermondsey. Tower Bridge Rd was laid out 1902. *Tower Bridge* (1886–94; engineer Sir John Wolfe Barry, architect Sir Horace Jones) was given a Gothic uniform at the insistence of Parliament. A high-level footbridge connects the towers, for use when the bascules opened, which was very frequently in the days when the Pool of London thrived with commercial activity. E in *Shad Thames*, canyon-like giant 19C warehouses line the narrow street, connected at upper levels by iron bridges. Here the spirit of Doré's London lives on. More docks and wharves beyond, and an LCC pumping station (1906–08). What Southwark was to hops, **Bermondsey** was to leather. In Weston St, the stock brick *Leather Market* dates from 1833. Adjoining it, the *Leather, Hide and Wood Exchange* (1878; G. Elkington and Sons), with atlas figures in the porch and roundels depicting scenes from everyday life in the leather industry. Also in Weston St, the mid 19C brick and stucco offices of *Messrs Vos*, Leather Merchants, and, off in Leathermarket St, more mid 19C industrial buildings. Off Tower Bridge Rd, in Grange Rd, the *Alaska Factory*, its 1869 gateway surmounted by a seal, and, set back from the road, the picturesque *Boutcher School* (1871–72; J. Gale). NE, in Spa Rd, undistinguished municipal buildings and an early railway *viaduct* (1833–36) supported on cast-iron Doric columns. Grange Rd runs into Southwark Park Rd. The *Park* was laid out 1865–66 by A. Mackenzie, who was also responsible for Finsbury Park. S of Southwark Park Rd, in Lynton Rd, *St. Augustine's Church* (1875–78, 1882–83), the most notable product of Henry Jarvis and Son. Built cheaply of brick, with lancets, it has a lofty interior. Established to serve this poor parish and now threatened with demolition. The other major 19C church in Bermondsey, *St. Bartholomew's* (1866–67; E. Taprell Allen), lies S of Rotherhithe New Rd in Barkworth Rd. Also on an ambitious scale in brick and, as with St. Augustine's, the intended tower was never built. Along the river in **Rotherhithe**, a few remnants of the tall warehouses, the best around the church gradually being restored and found new uses, including the wonderfully named Hope Sufferance Wharf. Also restored is the *Engine House* to Sir Marc Brunel's Thames Tunnel of 1825–43, one of the heroic feats of early 19C engineering, with display of the fantastically dangerous construction process. The *Surrey Docks* beyond have been greatly diminished by infilling, and it is uncertain how much of this enormous complex will survive the redevelopment for industry and housing.

Way S of the riverside area the two traffic intersections of St.

George's Circus and the Elephant and Castle offer a depressing contrast between 18C and 20C urban planning. The Elephant is a nightmarish place, surrounded by tall blocks, the pedestrian forced to retreat below ground to the subways. The only architectural relief comes from the Corinthian portico of the *Metropolitan Tabernacle* (1859; W.W. Pocock), all that survives of the large building put up to house the large crowds who came to hear C.H. Spurgeon preaching. St. George's Circus and the roads leading off were laid out by Robert Mylne; unfortunately the surrounding buildings fail to take advantage of the architectural opportunities offered by the Circus. In Borough Rd, leading off to the E, the *Passmore Edwards Library* (1898; C.J. Phipps), Arts and Crafts. S of the Circus, set back in ample grounds, the *Imperial War Museum* (1812) is the former Bethlehem ('Bedlam') Hospital, enlarged by P. Hardwick and S. Smirke. Smirke's is the copper dome (1844–46). Opposite, the *RC Cathedral of St. George* (1841–48; A.W.N. Pugin), built as a parish church but made a cathedral after the restoration of the Catholic hierarchy in 1850. As so often with Pugin's RC commissions, the grand conception had to be tempered by financial stringencies. Furthermore, the church was badly bombed in the war, and is now to a great extent rebuilt, although sticking to Pugin's plan and retaining some original fabric and fittings. The church is in the approved 'middle pointed' style, and a great tower and spire were intended, but never built. The outside appearance does not impress. Inside, the most significant surviving original feature is the Petre Chapel in the S aisle (1848–49; Pugin), Perp. Also, in the N aisle, the Knill Chantry (1856–57; E.W. Pugin), to relatives of A.W.N. Pugin's third wife. Further original Pugin fittings in the Blessed Sacrament chapel. From the Elephant and Castle, **Kennington** Park Rd runs S, with good Georgian terraces and the Gothic *Vicarage* to St. Mary's Church. The church (1873; J. Fowler) was bombed but a fragment of the W front survives as a frontispiece to the new church. *Kennington Tube Station* (1890) is one of the earliest on the first true underground line (City and S London Railway). Its green dome contains lift equipment. To S, in Kennington Park Place, *No. 5* (1894; Norman Shaw) was built as Bishop's House for the Diocese of Rochester. In **Walworth** Rd, undistinguished 19C municipal buildings. To the S, around Liverpool Grove and Portland St, cottage type housing built by the Ecclesiastical Commissioners under Octavia Hill, who ran their estates in Walworth from 1884. New Kent Rd runs E from the Elephant. The ragstone Gothic church of *St. Matthew* (1885–87; H. Jarvis) has a tower and spire, its interior remodelled by Martin Travers in the 1920s. S, in Rodney Rd, the RC *English Martyrs* (1902–03; F.W. Tasker). In Old Kent Rd, on the left, the long, symmetrical *Bacon's School* (1896). Beyond, *Nos 215–31*, a 19C stucco terrace which includes the former premises of Carters the Hatters, now a tyre shop, with mural paintings and a bust wearing a hat. Old Kent Rd continues SE toward New Cross, crossing the derelict Surrey Canal. In Asylum Rd, off the SE end, the former *Licensed Victuallers Almshouses* (1827–33; H. Rose), among the largest groups of such buildings of the time, brick with Ionic classical centrepiece. In Glengall Rd, to W, a cranky Gothic *church* by the rogue architect Bassett Keeling (1864).

Walworth Rd runs S to **Camberwell**, the Green overlooked by a grandiloquent *bank* (1899; A. Williams). In Camberwell New Rd, the *Greek Orthodox Cathedral* occupies a large Gothic church built for the Catholic Apostolic Church (1873; J. and J. Belcher), the nave cut back after bombing. On Church St, by the Green, free styled *Police Station*

(1898), opposite, in Artichoke Lane, *Public Baths* (1891; Spalding and Cross) in striped brick and stone. Further E, the parish *church* (1841–44; Scott and Moffatt), a significant milestone in Scott's career, marking his conversion to archaeologically correct details and materials, and indeed significant in the history of Victorian church building as an early attempt at serious Gothic. Crossing spire. E window (Ward and Nixon) in deep colours partly designed by Ruskin. From Camberwell Green, Denmark Hill runs S. The *Railway Station* (1864–66) has been excellently restored as a pub, following a fire. Denmark Hill, developed with leafy suburban villas from c 1840, retains this character. S in Herne Hill, *St. Paul's* is a rebuilding by G.E. Street of a church destroyed by fire. The shell of the old church was kept, including the tower and spire. Street enlarged the chancel, the interior was embellished with lush carving by Earp and glass by Hardman. There is a tablet to Ruskin, who spent his early life in Denmark Hill and admired the church greatly. Gothic *vicarage* also by Street. (See also Lambeth above , p. 271) E of Camberwell Church St, Peckham Rd links the two old parishes of Camberwell and Peckham. On the corner of St. Giles Rd, *St. Giles' Hospital* (late 19C; W.S. Cross) has an unusual circular ward block and Arts and Crafts additions (1904; E.T. Hall). N, in Sedgemoor Place, the *Aged Pilgrims Home*, founded 1837 by William Peacock, quadrangular layout with an embattled gatehouse. Peacock also founded the plainer *Bethel Asylum for Aged Women* in Havil St. Back in Peckham Rd, the Baroque *Camberwell School of Arts and Crafts* and *Passmore Edwards South London Art Gallery* (1896–98; M. Adams). Left up Southampton Way and right into Wells Way. On the corner with St. George's Way, the now derelict 'Waterloo' church of *St. George*, apse by Champneys (1893) and traces of a redecoration of 1909. Also in Wells Way, the picturesque *Library* and *Swimming Baths* (1902; M. Adams), a stylistic hybrid, with elements of Gothic, Baroque and Queen Anne. In Rye Lane, **Peckham**, the ornate Italianate *Peckham Rye Station* (1866), London, Brighton and S Coast Railway, and a *Baptist chapel* (1863; Bland) with an impressive portico. Little remains of the old village of **Nunhead** to the SE. Nunhead Green is hardly worthy of the name and is surrounded by undistinguished buildings, except for the *Beer and Wine Homes* on the N side (1852–53; W.M. Webbe), gabled brick almshouses. Nearby, in Consort Rd, some earlier almshouses of the *Girdlers' Company* (1834), Tudor. Most of the older houses in Nunhead Lane have gone, but *St. Antholin's Church* survives (1877–78; E. Christian), red brick, EE. It contains the reredos from Wren's bombed church of St. Antholin. The most significant 19C contribution to the amenities of Nunhead was the *Cemetery*, laid out over 51 acres from 1840 by J. Bunning, later architect to the City of London Corporation, responsible for the Coal Exchange. His are the solemn neo-classical lodges and gates, the chapels by T. Little (1844), only the Anglican one surviving. People buried at Nunhead were generally less socially exalted than those who ended up at the more fashionable cemeteries, so the monuments are not particularly lavish or grand, although full of human interest. Most notable, the Romanesque mausoleum of the Stearne family, with Doulton terracotta detailing, and the so-called Martyrs Memorial of 1851, which commemorates the transportation in 1795 of five Scots nationalists who had advocated parliamentary reform.

From Nunhead Lane, East Dulwich Rd leads W, through the old hamlet of Goose Green, now part of Dulwich. Mainly late 19C suburban. *St. John's Church* (1863–65; C. Bailey), East Dulwich Rd, is

New College (1866–67; C. Barry Jr), Dulwich

ragstone Gothic with a tower and broach spire. In Lordship Lane, another ragstone Gothic church, *St. Peter's* (1873–74; C. Barry Jr), lavish interior. Opposite, large *United Reformed Church* (1890–91; W.D. Church), with a prominent spire, and an attractive *Library* (1856; C. Barry Jr). Barry was surveyor to Dulwich College and consequently built much in the area. His is the fine *North Dulwich Railway Station* (1866), red brick with stone dressings and a loggia in front. **Dulwich Village** retains its rural quality, thanks to the zealous husbandry of the college. Its centre is mainly Georgian or 20C Tudor, although the large and gabled *Crown and Greyhound* (c 1895) is a prominent exception. The old buildings of the *College*, at the N end of College Rd, date from the early 17C, though much altered and restored, first by Sir Charles Barry Sr who stuccoed them in 1831, then by Charles Barry Jr who added the cloister and rebuilt the tower 1866. The 17C Chapel was remodelled 1823 and in 1911 provided with a new reredos by Caroe. At the corner of Gallery Rd and Burbage Rd, the stuccoed *Old Grammar School* (1841–42; C. Barry Sr). In Gallery Rd is Sir John Soane's Picture Gallery, the first in the country. The old foundation of Dulwich College was reformed 1857 and this provided an opportunity for massive expansion further S in College Rd. The architect for the *New College* (1866–67) was Charles Barry Jr. Three large blocks connected by lower arcaded wings, in an overwhelming ornate N Italian Renaissance style, the centre a monumental Great Hall. To the N, Baroque *Library* (1902; E.T. Hall). S, in College Rd, *St. Stephen's Church* (1867–75; Banks and Barry). S of the College, the area between Sydenham Hill and Gypsy Hill Stations was laid out from c 1860 with large detached villas. Not much of this development remains apart from Nos *24–8 Dulwich Wood Avenue* (C. Barry Jr), *No. 22*, and the *Paxton*, an Italianate pub on the corner of Gypsy Hill. Off Kingswood Drive, in Bowen Drive, *Kingswood*, a large stone villa in Baronial style (1892; H.V. Lanchester), for the founder of Bovril.

LEWISHAM. In the N of the borough, what remains of **Deptford**'s former maritime glory has been swallowed by modern council housing. The finest Edwardian building is the *Town Hall* in New Cross Rd (1902–07; Lanchester, Stewart and Rickards). Liveliest Edwardian

Baroque, with maritime motifs. Also in New Cross Rd, *Haberdashers' Aske's School for Girls* (1891; Stock, Page and Stock), Queen Anne. The *School for Boys* is S in Pepys Rd, (1875; W. Snooke), a prominent and symmetrical brick Gothic building. The *statue of Robert Aske* in the forecourt (1836; Croggon) came from the School's previous premises in Shoreditch. Opposite, the large ragstone Gothic *St. Catherine's Church* (1893–94) by H. Stock, surveyor to the Haberdashers' Company. Lewisham Way leads SE to Lewisham and is lined with houses of the first half of the 19C. The *Library* (1914) by A. Brumwell Thomas, architect of Woolwich Town Hall, is a large Edwardian Baroque design. *Goldsmiths' College* (1843–45; John Shaw), simplified Italianate, close to the Queen Anne of the 1870s, the Baroque *chapel* also by Shaw, very surprising for its date (1853). Reginald Blomfield added a block 1907–08. To S, in Wickham Rd, *St. Peter's Church* (1866–70; F. Marrable), unusual with a lavishly treated polychrome interior. Lewisham Way continues SE into Loampit Hill. *Nos 60–8* are ornate mid Victorian villas. Just off, in Algernon Rd, *St. Barnabas'*, formerly The Transfiguration (1881; James Brooks), austere brick Gothic, the lofty interior now spoilt by horizontal subdivision. Loampit Vale continues S into **Lewisham** High St, at its N end the *Clock Tower*, erected to commemorate the jubilee of 1897. *St. Stephen's Church* (1863–64; G.G. Scott), ragstone Gothic, has a good painted reredos (1873) in the S chapel. *St. Saviour's RC Church* (1909; Kelly and Dickie) is red-brick Italianate, its campanile, surmounted by a statue, a local landmark (added 1925). On the corner of Ladywell Rd an LCC Fire Station (1899), now offices, and a group of municipal buildings, including the Gothic *swimming baths* (1884; Wilson, Son and Aldwinkle), the Perp. *Coroner's Court* (1894; J. Carline) and a Queen Anne *Police Station* (1900).

Ladywell Rd runs W towards Forest Hill and Brockley. The development of **Brockley** started about 1870, with large villas in ample gardens along wide tree-lined streets. Tresillian Rd is typical of this development. In Brockley Rd, the spire of the *United Reformed Church* (1882; J. McKissack and W.G. Rowan of Glasgow) is a landmark. Also in Brockley Rd, *Brockley Cemetery*, formed from the union of Deptford and Ladywell Cemeteries, separately founded 1858. The Dec. chapel in the Ladywell half survives (Morphew and Green). Brockley Rd continues S into Stondon Park, **Forest Hill**. On the right, *St. Hilda's Church* (1907; Greenaway and Newberry), with some idiosyncratic Art Nouveau touches. The development of Forest Hill came mainly after the arrival of the railway in 1839. Some mid 19C classical terraces remain on the S side of London Rd, and further Italianate villas of the same period in the streets to the N, e.g. Honor Oak Rd. An architectural curiosity in Liphook Crescent, W of Honor Oak Rd, is *No. 23*, a late 19C octagonal stone folly tower, formerly a garden building to the demolished Tewkesbury Lodge. S, in London Rd, is the *Horniman Museum* (1897–1901; Harrison Townsend), to house the collection of F.J. Horniman, tea merchant, naturalist and anthropologist. It is the most bold and original Art Nouveau building in London. It consists of a main block, with a large mosaic panel at its centre (Humanity in the House of Circumstance, by Anning Bell) and a curved gable above, the horizontality of which contrasts dramatically with the massive clock tower, topped by rounded turrets and a circular cornice. E of Forest Hill Station, in Church Rise, *Christchurch* (1852–62; E. Christian) is prominently situated on a hill with a stone tower and spire. S, in Perry Vale, a picturesque roughcast *Fire Station* (1901–02; LCC) with an octagonal tower. To the E, Woolstone Rd heads N towards **Catford**.

At the junction with Vancouver Rd, *St. George's Church* (1878–80; W.C. Banks), ragstone Gothic, with good stained glass in the W rose window (1899–1900; H. Holiday). Brick *vicarage* of 1855. At the top of Catford Hill, in Stanstead Rd, *St. Dunstan's College* was refounded in Catford (1883). Large buildings by E.N. Clifton, clearly under the influence of Waterhouse. In the centre of Catford, modern commercial and administrative buildings predominate. N, on Rushey Green, towards Lewisham, the attractive *Thackeray Almshouses* (1840), red and yellow brick, round-arched windows. In the S of the Borough, **Upper Sydenham** became fashionable after the arrival of the Crystal Palace. Paxton himself lived here. The large Victorian mansions have now mostly disappeared, but a noteworthy survival is *Sunnydene* at the corner of Sydenham Hill (1868–70; J.F. Bentley), in eclectic Queen Anne style. *Ellerslie*, next door, also by Bentley, but altered. From the smaller early 19C development of Sydenham is *St. Bartholomew's Church* (1827–32; Vulliamy), Westwood Hill, to the W, pre-ecclesiological Gothic, the chancel extended by Edwin Nash (1858), glass in W window by Clayton and Bell.

In the NE of the borough, **Blackheath** is predominantly Georgian. However, it did not become a parish until the 1850s, when *All Saints' Church* was built (1857–67; B. Ferrey), very Puginesque, offering a marked contrast to its neighbours in terms of style, scale and materials. More in keeping are the Italianate *Railway Station* (1849; George Smith, and c 1875–78) and *Blackheath Girls School* (1879; Robson), N in Wemyss St, an early piece of neo-Georgian. Lee Rd runs S from the village. The *Blackheath Conservatoire of Music* and *Concert Hall*, and the *Art Gallery* behind (1896; Edmeston and Gabriel), were set up by local cultural philanthropist William Webster. Webster also established the *Blackheath Art Club* (1896; Higgs and Rudkin) in Bennett Park, E of the village. Blackheath Park, to the E of Lee Rd, is in the borough of Greenwich, but may be dealt with here. It contains a good collection of late 19C houses, including *No. 1*, a late 19C Wren style Lodge, No. 2 *Windermere* (1896; Aston Webb) in Old English style, with plenty of half-timbering, No. 4, *The Gables*, also 1896 by Webb, half-timbered with some artisan mannerist touches. Further on, some Italianate villas of the 1830s. To the S, in Priory Park, the *Old Priory*, a castellated piece of 19C Gothic. The old hamlet of **Lee** was absorbed into Lewisham 1900. The old parish church survives as a ruin on the N side of Lee Terrace, W of Blackheath Station. On the opposite side is the new church (1839–41; John Brown of Norwich), a Commissioners' type church, its interior remodelled (1875; James Brooks) to make the Gothic more correct and at the same time refurnished, a reredos by Earp, glass by Clayton and Bell. N of Lee Terrace, the *Glebe* was laid out c 1849, some Gothic and Italianate villas remaining. S, in Lee High Rd, *Boone's Almshouses* (1875; E.B. l'Anson), with a brick Gothic chapel, and S, in Manor Lane, *Lochaber Hall* (1910; E. George), a simple former church hall. The area between Lee Terrace and Lee High Rd was developed with terraces and villas in the second quarter of the 19C.

GREENWICH. The architectural glories of **Greenwich** belong chiefly to the 17C and 18C, but there are nevertheless several Victorian plums to be picked. In Croom's Hill, which has the best Georgian houses in the borough, the RC *Our Lady Star of the Sea* (1851; W. Wardell) is a most satisfactory interloper. Contemporary with Wardell's church in Clapham (see Lambeth above, p. 271), also very Puginian, and also with a tower and spire. Pugin in fact decorated the chancel and the chapel of St. Joseph. The interior is very rich. W in Greenwich South St, neo-Tudor *Penn's Almshouses* (1884; G. Smith). In Greenwich High Rd, a small classical former *vestry hall* (1876; W. Wallen), now a community centre, a c 1700 style *Library* (1905–07; H.W. Willis and J. Anderson) with a cupola, and the *Railway Station*. The original 1840 station was re-erected here (1878) in slightly altered form. At the W end, Venetian style *grain silo* (1897; Aston Webb) by Deptford Creek. Also, in Norman Rd, *Pumping Station* (1859–62; J. Bazalgette) of the S London sewage system. S, in Blackheath Rd, the tall, gabled *Blackheath Road Schools* (1874; E.R. Robson and J.J. Stevenson), one of the first London Board Schools. E of the Royal Naval College, in Park Row, the *Trafalgar Tavern* is a charming riverside pub (1837; Joseph Kay). E, in Old Woolwich Rd, the monumental *Greenwich Power Station* (1902–10; LCC), and, further E, some fairly complete streets of early Victorian artisan housing, e.g. Pelton Rd, laid out from 1838 by George Smith for Morden College. Maze Hill, to S, has some good Georgian houses and *Vanbrugh Castle*. In Westcombe Park Rd, some mid 19C stucco houses and Queen Anne houses from 1876 onwards. In Mycenae Rd, *No. 99* (1881–82; E.R. Robson), a large brick and half-timbered house, and off in Kirkside Rd, *St. George's* (1890–91; Newman and Billing), a large brick church in the manner of James Brooks. Descending back down to earth and the more elusive charms of Woolwich Rd, which include *Greenwich Library* (1905; S.R.J. Smith), a cheerful stripy Baroque building, and, at the junction of Tunnel Avenue, a lively *Fire Station* (1901–02; LCC). Tunnel Avenue leads to the gloom of Blackwall Tunnel, its environs architecturally dismal. One pretty but derelict exception is *St. Andrew's and St. Michael's Church* (1900–02; B. Champneys). E of Tunnel Avenue, the remains of the huge *Greenwich Gasworks*, started 1883–86, complete with its own docks. Woolwich Rd runs E past the old village of **Charlton**, with *Charlton House*, the finest Jacobean house in Greater London. N, in Maryon Rd, *St. Thomas' Church* (1849–50; J. Gwilt; neo-Romanesque.

Like Deptford, **Woolwich** resounds with past maritime glories, and much of architectural interest in concentrated around the Dockyard and the Arsenal. The administrative centre is between Powis St and Wellington St. The *'Town Hall* (1903–06; A.B. Thomas), Wellington St, is one of the finest products of Edwardian municipal pride to be found in the capital. Florid Baroque in red brick and Portland stone, with an array of columns and pediments, three domes and an asymmetrically placed tower. In total contrast, the *Old Town Hall*, Calderwood St, is a modest little classical building of 1842. Also in Calderwood St, the *Public Library* (1901; Church, Quick and Whincop) and the *Woolwich Polytechnic Young Men's Christian Institute* (1890–91; H.H. Church), now part of Thames Polytechnic. Powis St is the main shopping street. Notable 19C buildings include the *William Shakespeare* pub (c 1900) and the *Royal Arsenal Co-operative Stores* (1903; F. Bethell), with a central dome, clearly influenced by Harrods. To the W, Woolwich Church St runs alongside the Royal Dockyard, closed since 1869. A prominent remnant of the dockyard is the *Steam Factory* (c 1838–44), with its 200ft chimney. On the riverside two dry docks of 1843 have been preserved for recreation. The hilly area to the S has mostly been redeveloped over the past 40 years, but in Borgard Rd, off Francis St, *St. Michael's Church* remains, chancel (1875) by J.W. Walters, nave (1887) by Butterfield. Woolwich *Arsenal* (1829, its upper part 1897) lies to the E of the town centre and is entered through the *gatehouse* in Beresford Square. The older buildings, some appallingly neglected, lie on the W of the site. The most significant buildings are 18C and early 19C but, behind James Wyatt's *Grand Store* (1806–13), is the *Armstrong Rifle Factory* (1858), with polychromatic brick detail. *Mallett's Mortar* (1857), in front of the Grand Store, was the largest ever made. The entrance to the *Shell Foundry* (1856–57; D. Murray) survives, with superimposed orders. S of this, a *statue of Wellington* (1848; T. Milnes). Running SW from Beresford Square is Woolwich New Rd and *St. Peter's RC Church* (1842; A.W.N. Pugin: chancel and side chapel 1887–89; F.A. Walters), Dec. and built on the cheap. The huge *Royal Artillery Barracks* (1775–1802) face S over Woolwich Common. *Crimean War Memorial* statue by John Bell (1860). In Grand Depot Rd, opposite the Barracks, is the garrison church of *St. George* (1863; T.H. Wyatt), bombed in the war and now preserved as a ruin. From Beresford Square Plumstead Rd runs E. The parish church of *St. Nicholas*, in **Plumstead** High St, has some medieval fabric. Restored 1867–68 by C.H. Cooke, enlarged 1907–08 (Greenaway and Newberry). The only other buildings of interest in the High St are municipal, the *Police Station* (1893), the *Library* (1904; F. Sumner) and the classical *Fire Station* (1913; LCC).

In the S of the borough is **Eltham**. The High St just about manages to keep a villagey feel. Three Victorian churches in the town centre, all minor works by major architects. The old parish *church* was replaced by the present church (1872; A. Blomfield). S, in Southend Crescent, *Holy Trinity* (1868–69; G.E. Street: additions 1909; A. Blomfield), with a reredos by Caroe, other fittings and glass by Kempe. N in Westmount Rd, *St. Luke's Church* (1906–07; Temple Moore). The most interesting 19C building in Eltham, however, is a house, though a college of education since early this century, *Avery Hill College* (1888; T.W. Cutler), Bexley Rd. Entered through a pretty frenchified Lodge in Bexley Rd, the house was a most luxuriously appointed Italianate villa, built around the bones of an older house for Col J.T. North, who had made his fortune in nitrate. Cutler massively overspent his budget, thereby incurring dismissal and a lawsuit. The Winter Garden with its domed centre is on a spectacular scale.

SOUTH LONDON: OUTER BOROUGHS

RICHMOND. In the N of the borough, **Barnes** consists mainly of late 19C and 20C development, although the area around the pond retains a pleasant rural feel. *Hammersmith Bridge*, which joins Barnes to the N bank of the river, was rebuilt 1887 by J. Bazalgette, using the piers of the 1827 bridge. A fine suspension bridge with cast-iron towers connected by arches at each end, the whole very decorative. Running S, *Castelnau* was developed, after the opening of the original bridge, from 1842 by William Laxton for the Boileau family of Castlenau House. On the corner with Lonsdale Rd, the former Boileau pub, now renamed the Old Rangoon, is prominently placed with a Tuscan porch. Otherwise, the early development of Castlenau consisted of the attractive yellow brick semi-detached villas which still line both sides. Rocks Lane continues S through the Common, in the midst of which is the *Railway Station* (1846; W. Tite), one of the earliest in London, attractive red-brick Tudor with tall chimney stacks. Station Rd leads back to the High St. By the pond is a former schoolhouse with barge-boards (1850). Opposite, in Church Rd, *St. Osmund's School*, 18C with charming Victorian Tudor Gothic additions. The Terrace follows the curve of the river after the High St and is lined with Georgian houses. Spanning the river is the cast-iron *railway bridge* (1846–49; J. Locke: doubled up 1891–95). Left, in Elm Bank Gardens, *St. Michael's Church*; (1891–93; C. Innes). In **Mortlake** High St, the parish church of *St. Mary* still has its 16C tower, but was otherwise mostly rebuilt by Sir A. Blomfield, chancel 1885, nave 1905. Behind, in North Worple Way, *St. Mary Magdalen's RC Church* (1852; G.R. Blount) with, in its nearby cemetery, the tent-shaped mausoleum to Sir Richard Burton (died 1890), scholar, explorer and translator of the *Arabian Nights*. Finally, near the Railway Station, the *Boot and Shoemakers Benevolent Institution*, red-brick Tudor almshouses of 1836.

Sheen Common was developed at the end of the 19C with large houses but many of these have gone. One survivor is *Oakdene*, No. 105 Christ Church Rd (1884; T.E. Collcutt) in Old English style. Nearby is *Christ Church* (1862–64; A. Blomfield). Off Christ Church Rd, the gabled *Longfield* (1879; Ingress Bell), and S, in Fife Rd, *The Halsteads* (1868; A. Blomfield), an early concrete house. The contractor was Joseph Tall. Also in Fife Rd, *The Angles* (early 20C) is named after the butterfly plan so fashionable in its time. Sheen Rd runs W towards **Richmond**. On the N side the neo-Norman *Richmond Church Estate Almshouses* (1843; W.C. Stow), in polychrome brick, and the grey brick Tudor *William Hickey's Almshouses* (1834; L. Vulliamy), arranged around an open courtyard, the central block containing the chapel. To the N, in Manor Grove, one of the first local authority housing schemes, a cottage estate built by the Borough of Richmond 1894–99). By Richmond Station, in Kew Rd, *St. John the Divine* (1836; L. Vulliamy), delightfully unarchaeological, with an eccentric W tower flanked by purely decorative flying buttresses. Chancel (1904; A. Grove), high quality with good Arts and Crafts fittings. George St curls around into Hill St. Off to the left is the parish *church*, its chancel rebuilt by Bodley (1903–04), and off to the right is The Green, mostly Georgian, with the remarkable exception of the *Theatre* (1899; F. Matcham), a terracotta confection which no planning committee would allow today. The old *Town Hall* (1893; W.J. Ansell), Hill St, is in a mixed Renaissance style. The area between here and the Italianate *Tower House* (1858; H. Laxton) in Bridge St is the site of Quinlan Terry's neo-classical riverside development. Then begins the long climb up Richmond Hill. Off, in The Vineyard, is a brick neo-Norman Nonconformist *chapel* (1831; J. Davies) and *St. Elizabeth of Portugal's RC Church* (1824), chancel, lantern tower and presbytery of 1903 (F.A. Walters). Further down are the neo-Jacobean *Bishop Duppa's Almshouses* (1850; T. Little). On Richmond Hill the large and confident *Petersham Hotel* (1865; J. Giles) and, at the top, the palatial *Star and Garter Home* (1921–24; Sir E. Cooper). In front, a fanciful cattle *fountain*, with a wrought-iron cage surmounted by dragons etc. (1891; T.E. Collcutt). Queen's Rd leads away to the left from here. Lying off the road is *Richmond College* (1841–43; A. Trimen), imposing neo-Tudor, in Bath stone, built as a Wesleyan theological college. To N, the dominant spire of *St. Matthias' Church* (1857–62; G.G. Scott). Good E and W glass by Wailes of the 1860s. Star and Garter Hill winds down to **Petersham**, replete with large and expensive Georgian houses. An extraordinary Victorian contribution is the idiosyncratically Lombard Romanesque *All Saints' Church* (1907–08; J. Kelly), Bute Avenue, red brick and terracotta, with a tall campanile and a lavish marbled interior including a baptistery for total immersion. The nearby *Church Room* (1900) combines Italianate and Queen Anne elements. In **Ham**, to S, the parish *church* (1830) is one of several plain brick works in the area by E. Lapidge.

Over Richmond Bridge to **Twickenham**, where the only Victorian building of note is the Commissioners' Gothic *Holy Trinity* (1840–41; G. Basevi) on The Green. To the W is the former hamlet of **Whitton**, now engulfed by Twickenham. *Kneller Hall*, Kneller Rd, the 17C house of Sir Godfrey Kneller, burnt down and replaced by the present neo-Jacobean pile (1848; G. Mair), is where military bands train. To the S, **Teddington** is most notable for Horace Walpole's *Strawberry Hill*. However, the later more serious and archaeological strain of Gothic is magnificently represented by *St. Alban's Church* (1889; W. Niven), Ferry Rd, now sadly empty and neglected but in its heyday a shrine of Anglo-Catholicism. Noel Coward sang in the choir. Built of cathedral proportions and scale, it was never finished and is now threatened with demolition, its rich fittings by A.H. Skipworth vandalised or dispersed. W, in Waldegrave Rd, is a cheerful little Baroque *library* of the type popular at the turn of the century (1906; H.A. Cheers). In Kingston Rd, the *Entertainments Hall* at Normansfield Hospital is of considerable interest as being a completely unaltered 19C theatre (1874; R. Plumbe). The fly door still works, the auditorium has a balcony with a cast-iron front and an elaborate proscenium with rich Gothic decoration. Much of the original painted scenery survives. The hospital and hall were built for Dr J.H. Langdon-Down, after whom Down's syndrome was named. Theatre was one of the remedial activities he encouraged. At the bottom of Kingston Rd, Hampton Court Rd leads W. In Church Grove, **Hampton Wick**, is the yellow brick lancet style *St. John's* (1829–30; E. Lapidge), with a picturesque *vicarage* by Teulon (1854). Beyond Hampton Court lies the village of **Hampton**. On the riverside in Hampton Court Rd is the delightfully incongruous boatyard building belonging to *Hucks and Co* , an elaborate wooden chalet imported from Switzerland c 1900. In Thames St, *St. Mary's Church* (1829–31), also by Lapidge and similar to the others, chancel by A. Blomfield (1888). In Upper Sunbury Rd, *Hampton Waterworks* consists of a series of buildings established at this point above Teddington Lock as a result of the Metropolis Water Act 1852, which sought to provide the capital with a purer water supply. Three companies moved here, the Southwark and Vauxhall, the Grand Junction and the West Middlesex, and all employed Joseph Quick the engineer to build them Italianate engine houses. Those belonging to the West Middlesex Co have gone, but the others survive, albeit deprived of their original machinery.

In the NW of the borough lies **Kew**, where the royal retreat of Kew Gardens was opened to the public by Queen Victoria in 1841 and developed as the Royal Botanic Gardens. From the 1840s to about 1880 under the directorship of Sir William and Sir Joseph Hooker the layout of the gardens was changed and the great museums and greenhouses added. The main *entrance gates* are from Kew Green (1845–46; Decimus Burton, the ironwork by Walker of Rotherham). However, the best 19C buildings are near the *Victoria Gates* in Kew Rd. Of these the greatest is the *Palm House* (1844–48; architect D. Burton, engineer Richard Turner of Dublin), a pioneering piece of iron and glass construction. It consists of a long central chamber with galleries and aisles, with a double curved roof, barrel-vaulted entrances in the centre of the long sides, and apsidal ends. To the N, the *Water-Lily House* (1852; D. Burton) was built to house the recently introduced

Kew Gardens, The Palm House (1844–48; D. Burton and R. Turner), Richmond

Victoria Regia water-lily. Cast iron and glass, slender iron columns and decorative scrollwork. Across the pond, Museum No. 1 (1856–57; D. Burton) is a utilitarian stock brick structure. S of the pond, the Italian Romanesque style *Campanile* (1847; D. Burton) was built to house water tanks and provide a chimney for the Palm House. The very large *Temperate House* (1859–62; D. Burton), unlike the Palm House, has straight wooden glazing divisions (now replaced in aluminium) and as a consequence is less impressive outside. Opposite its N end, the *North Gallery* (1882) was built by the architect and historian James Fergusson, as an illustration of his theory that Greek temples were lit by 'opaions and clerestories', to house a collection of flower paintings by Marianne North. S of this is a very early Queen Anne *Lodge* by Nesfield (1866), wonderfully exaggerated moulded brick chimney riding over a single-storey square cottage with hipped roof and over-sealed pedimented dormer, the whole designed with great verve. On Kew Green, the 18C parish church of *St. Anne* was adorned with an Italian Renaissance style *mausoleum* (1850–51; B. Ferrey) for the Duke and Duchess of Cambridge. The mausoleum lies to the E of Henry Stock's unusual E end (1884) with its octagonal cupola and curious tracery. Both the Hookers are commemorated inside with suitably botanic memorials.

KINGSTON. Kingston is the county town of Surrey and the coronation town of several Saxon kings. In the 19C the railway bypassed the town and went instead to Surbiton, which became a commuter town whereas Kingston did not. The 20C has witnessed the commercial growth of the town and the consequent loss of most of its historic character, but the medieval street plan and some timber-framed buildings survive in the Market Place. One side is dominated by the *Market House* (1838–40; Charles Henman Sr), an Italianate building which was formerly the Town Hall. In front, the *Shrubsole Memorial* (1882; F.J. Williamson). On the N side, *Boots* (1909), attributed to Dr William Finny, local antiquarian and seven times Mayor, an elaborate stucco and timber-framed facade with in the niches figures of monarchs crowned in Kingston. Nearby, the parish church of *All Saints'* was restored by Brandon (1862–66) and again by Pearson 20 years later. In Eden St, at its junction with the Market Place, is the classical *United Reformed Church* (1855–56; Barnett and Birch) and a Gothic *Post Office* (1875; R. Richardson). W, in London Road, the brick former *Police Station* (1864) and *Kingston Grammar School* (1877; J. Loxwood King), the latter a Gothic and Queen Anne hybrid in yellow stock brick with red-brick dressings. On the corner with Cambridge Rd is *St. Peter's Church* (1841), an early work by G.G. Scott, and noteworthy for being neo-Norman. Scott lived to regret having produced such an 'ignoble' design. N of London Rd, in Queen's Rd, the *vicarage* (c 1870; C.L. Luck) for the lofty Gothic *St. Paul's Church* (1874; F. Peck), nearby in Alexander Rd. W, in Kings Rd, the castellated former *Gatehouse* to E Surrey Barracks (1875; Major Seddon). S of the town centre, in Fairfield Rd, is the neo-Georgian *Library* (1903; A. Cox) and, around the corner, the handsome *Museum and Art Gallery* (1904; Cox). S, in Booner Hill Rd, *Kingston Cemetery*, its entrance marked by symmetrical Gothic *chapels*, one for the Anglicans and one for the Nonconformists (1855; Aickin and Capes). W, in Penrhyn Rd, is *Surrey County Hall* (1892–93; C.H. Howell: 1930s additions; Vincent Harris), Portland stone with a tall clock tower and an abundance of carved decoration. Kingston Hill leads E to Coombe, developed with large houses set in spacious gardens in the mid–late 19C. Many of the houses have gone, although some roadside lodges remain, notably the mid 19C classical lodge in Coombe Lane to the former *Coombe House*, and, from George Devey's *Coombe Warren* (1864), the picturesque gabled *Lodge* survives in Coombe Lane West, as does the *Orangery*, now incorporated in Soames House, a neo-Georgian house of the 1930s in Coombe Hill Rd. S, in Beverley Lane, are Devey's very attractive group of *Stables* and outbuildings to Coombe Cottage, which he built in 1863 for the banker E.C. Baring. Further large late 19C houses in George Rd and Warren Rd.

Surbiton lies to the S of Kingston, and is essentially part of it. When the railway arrived in 1840 the area was called Kingston New Town and even Kingston upon Railway. Odd pockets from the mid 19C development of the suburb survive, e.g. the stuccoed terrace of *Nos 2– 8 Victoria Rd* near the station, still very Regency in flavour. The station itself was rebuilt in the 1930s and is one of the best of that period. N, in

Claremont Rd, are more mid 19C houses and a Gothic *Clock Tower* (1905–06). Claremont Rd, The Crescent and Adelaide Rd were developed in the 1840s by a Thomas Pooley. To the S, in Ewell Rd, on the W side, are two symmetrical yellow stock brick terraces of about this time, and, opposite, *No. 85*, a mid 19C red-brick house. Also in Ewell Rd, and very much in contrast, is the robustly Baroque *Sessions House* (1894). N, in Surbiton Hill Rd, at the corner with Maple Rd, the terracotta *Assembly Rooms* (1882; A. Mason). In Maple Rd, *St. Andrew's Church* (1871), an early work of A.W. Blomfield, yellow and red brick Gothic. E, in King Charles Rd, *Christ Church* (1862–63; C.L. Luck) has a polychrome brick interior and good stained glass by Clayton and Bell and Lavers and Barraud, including the triple window at the W end of the N aisle, to a design by Burne-Jones (1871). Perhaps the most interesting church in Surbiton is *St. Raphael's RC Church* (1847–48; Charles Parker), Portsmouth Rd, a strikingly original Italianate design, paid for by Alexander Raphael, MP for St. Albans, hence presumably the dedication.

MERTON. On the W side of the borough the Victorian period bypassed the villages of Mitcham and Morden, only for them to be developed in the present century. In **Merton**, however, suburban expansion started in the late 19C with the creation from c 1870 of *Merton Park* by property developer and horticulturalist John Innes. He chose H.G. Quartermain as his estate architect, and the result can be seen around *Mostyn Rd, Dorset Rd* and *Sheridan Rd*, a proto garden suburb, with tile-hung and half-timbered detached houses. In the centre, the old parish *church* with Morris glass to Innes (1907). In Watery Lane is *Rutlish School*, rebuilt (c 1870–1900; H. Quartermain) as the home of Innes. *John Innes Park*, opposite, was the grounds of the house. The banks of the river Wandle witnessed South London's earliest industrial growth. In 1881 William Morris set up his printing works here but of these no trace remains. However, the *Liberty Printworks* survive, dating from 1910 onwards.

To the N the village of **Wimbledon** grew into an affluent suburb at the end of the 19C. Behind the large 1930s Town Hall, some municipal buildings of the turn of the century, *Magistrates' Court* (1895), *Police Station* (1900), *Fire Station* (1904). In The Broadway is *Wimbledon Theatre* (1910; C. Massey and R. Young), with good interior. In Pelham Rd, to S, *Schools* (1914; H.P.B. Downing), free baroque. The Broadway continues N into Wimbledon Hill Rd, with *Byron House*, stucco villa of c 1860. Leading off in Belvedere Drive, *No. 1* (1901; George and Yeates), Queen Anne, and, between St. Mary's Rd and Lake Rd, *Queen Alexandra's Court* (1904–12; George and Yeates), a brick neo-Georgian development around three sides of a quadrangle, with pavilion centrepiece to the fourth. Running SW from the junction with the High St is Ridgeway, with one or two large late 19C mansions and some smaller buildings of c 1900, e.g. *No. 54* (1908; T.G. Jackson) an unassuming Queen Anne building. Jackson lived in *Eagle House*, the fine 17C house in the High St, and built much around here. In Edge Hill, *Sacred Heart RC Church* (1886–1901; F.A. Walters), tall 14C style of flint and stone. Also in Edge Hill is *Wimbledon College*, founded 1860 as an Anglican Preparatory Military Academy. Teulon's picturesque brick Gothic building was burnt and replaced in 1980, but his schoolhouse and dormitories survive. In 1894 the house became a Jesuit school and F.A. Walters added the Perp. Chapel in 1910. Nearby, in Berkeley Place, *No. 13* (1894; J. Ransome) is an original building with nice detailing and, in Lauriston Rd, some fine houses of the late 19C and early 20C, include *No. 1*, a Queen Anne house by T.G. Jackson and *No. 9*, (1892–94; E. George) late 17C style. To NE, in The Grange, *No. 1* (c 1885; Aston Webb), *No. 4* (1908; Hubbard and Moore), roughcast and tile-hung, *No. 7* by Ernest Newton, and *No. 18* by A. Cawston. In Lingfield Rd, coloured brick *Village Club* (1858; S.S. Teulon). W of Ridgeway, in Copse Hill, S.S. Teulon's *Christ Church* (1859–60, W end 1881) with massive crossing tower and pyramid roof. Woodhayes Rd leads on to the Common. On West Side Common, *Cannizaro House* (c 1902), Baroque rebuilding of a Georgian house. Beyond, in Camp Rd, *Camp View* is a picturesque terrace, with oriels in the Norman Shaw manner. Parkside, the road to Putney, is lined with wealthy late 19C houses displaying a range of styles, with echoes of Ernest Newton, white gables over red brick, or the more thorough-going Arts and Crafts roughcast of Voysey, or varieties of Baroque to neo-Georgian formality.

SUTTON. Mainly characterless suburbia, especially in the N of the borough, but some villagey and semi-rural pockets survive. *St. Nicholas'*, the parish church of **Sutton**, hidden away in St. Nicholas Rd behind the new Civic Centre, was rebuilt by Edwin Nash (1862–64). On the corner with Cheam Rd is the much more prominent *United Reformed Church* (1907; Gordon and Gunton), ragstone with a 'crown' spire based on Newcastle and Edinburgh Cathedrals. On Brighton Rd, a *bank* (1902; F. Wheeler) with Art Nouveau curvilinear detailing. ¾m N, by Angel Hill, *All Saints' Church* (1863–66; S.S. Teulon) is a prominent landmark. W, the village of **Cheam** became surburbanised with the arrival of the railway. The parish *church* was rebuilt 1862–64 (F. Pownall) and has good glass by Clayton and Bell at W end.

E of Sutton, on St. Barnabas Rd, off Carshalton Rd, *Our Lady of the Rosary RC Church*, converted (1887; Ingress Bell) from a school and *St. Barnabas' Church* (1884–91; Carpenter and Ingelow), with a good late window by Morris and Co. in the E end. In **Carshalton**, behind high brick walls the 18C *Carshalton House* is now a convent school. The *Chapel* (1899–1900; I. Bell) has Byzantinesque mosaics inside. At the junction of Pound St and West St, a slab marks St. Margaret's Pool and commemorates its beautification and endowment by John Ruskin in 1876. Ruskin took a close interest in the waters of Carshalton, and in the cleaning up of the Wandle. The centre of Carshalton by the ponds remains a place of great charm. In a raised position on the S side of High St, the parish church of *All Saints'* was much added to (1893–1914) first by Sir Arthur and then by Reginald Blomfield. Inside, reredos (c 1900) and rood screen (c 1914) both by Bodley, embellished like much else in the church by J.N. Comper in the 1930s. Behind, in The Square, a little baroque *Library* (1908; R.F. Atkinson). SW of the village centre in Park Hill, *No. 19* (1868) is a rather plain house by Philip Webb for the novelist Mark Rutherford. S, in Beeches Avenue, No. 40, *Little Holland House*, was built 1903–04 by Frank Dickinson to his own design. The exterior is plain, but the interior richly fitted out in Arts and Crafts manner everything made by Dickinson (open to the public). E of Carshalton, at **Beddington**, in the medieval *St. Mary's Church*, Church Rd, is a delightful organ gallery by Morris and Co of 1869, and a reredos by Clayton and Bell of the same date, now rele-gated to the N aisle. The church was restored 1867–69 by Joseph Clarke, who also added the *lychgate* (now demolished), a second lych-gate over the road marking the entrance to an extension to the chur-chyard, and an ornamental timber-framed lodge terminating the view

N at the end of the road. On the E side of Church Rd he rebuilt *Carew Manor* (1865–66) as the Lambeth Female Orphan Asylum, red-brick institutional Gothic. Now a school, in the Middle Ages it was the famous home of the Carew family and retains its hammerbeam roofed *Hall* within Clarke's rebuilding.

CROYDON. S London borough around the older town of Croydon and including Surrey villages to the S now almost completely suburban. The centre of Croydon was almost wholly redeveloped in the 1960s, and is so nightmarish to behold that only the most dedicated Victorian enthusiast is recommended to visit it for the few plums it offers. The N of the borough is **Upper Norwood**. In Central Hill, *Virgo Fidelis* (1857; Wardell), RC convent, stock brick Gothic, with additions by the Goldies. Running SW from Crystal Palace in Church Rd, No. 128, *Rockmount*, is a large asymmetrical villa of c 1880. To the E, Sylvan Hill leads to *St. John's Church* (1881–87; Pearson), a noble brick church, vaulted, and with double aisles. On corner of Beulah Hill, *All Saints'* (1827–29; J. Savage), a Commissioners' church. In Grange Rd, running S from the foot of Church Rd, *St. Alban's Church* (1887–94; Bucknall and Comper), J.N. Comper's first church, red brick, Perp., without the lavish fittings for which he became renowned (see St. Cyprians, Glentworth St, Westminster, above, p. 235). Whitehorse Rd continues S, with *Baptist church* (1873; J.T. Barker), classical, red brick with stone dressings. E in Selhurst Rd, *Holy Innocents' Church* (1895; G.F. Bodley), a long, plain church in Bodley's simplified Perp. style. In Sydenham Rd, *No. 226* (1878; Norman Shaw) is old English in style and curious for being executed in concrete slab. At the bottom of Whitehorse Rd, St. James' Rd leads E towards **Addiscombe**. Here, *St. James'* (1827–29) is a Commissioners' church, and, as with All Saints', Beulah Hill, a chancel had to be added (1881; Charles Henman Jr) to bring it into line with Victorian liturgical demands. By the railway line, the *Freemason's Asylum* (1852; S.W. Daukes), Jacobean red-brick and stone almshouses and beyond, just opposite Addiscombe Station in Canning Rd, *St. Mary Magdalene's Church* (1868; E.B. Lamb), stone outside, low and spreading, the interior with a roof structure of maniacal complexity, quite unwarranted even for the broad internal space it covers. Large *Vicarage* (1870), also by Lamb.

Whitehorse Rd leads S to **Croydon**. By West Croydon Station, in Poplar Walk, is *St. Michael and All Angels'* (1880), the first of the series of later town churches by Pearson (see St. John's, Upper Norwood) where calm, high vaulted space dominates, complexity coming from the play of arcades and answering ribbed vaults, with the windows and mouldings subordinate. Apsidal end with passage aisle behind the altar. Sumptuous fittings by Bodley, Temple Moore, Comper, E windows by Clayton and Bell. At the point where North End becomes High St, the 16C *Whitgift Hospital* is a miraculous survival and an oasis of civilisation. Restored 1860 by Butterfield, his are the chimneystacks. Further on, the proud *Town Hall* and *Library* (1892–96; C. Henman Jr), Katharine St, brick and stone with a tall tower. Croydon had become a borough in 1883. S of the High St, *No. 4 South End* is a castellated brick building, erected 1860 as the *Steam Boot Factory*. To the E, in St. Peter's Road, *St. Peter's Church* (1850; G.G. Scott), flint with a prominent spire. The old Croydon lies to the W of the High St, its street pattern surviving beneath the flyover. The old parish church of *St. John the Baptist* was burnt down 1867 and rebuilt almost in replica by G.G. Scott. Exceptionally small, rich later 19C fittings. On the W side of the High St, is a good group of stone and terracotta commercial buildings of the 1890s.

E of the High Street in Coombe Rd, *Coombe Cliffe* (c 1860), villa built for John Horniman, tea merchant, father of the donor of the Horniman Museum (see Lewisham above, p. 280). Beyond, 100ft circular *Water Tower* of 1867. Coombe Lane continues into Gravel Hill, where the 18C *Addington Place* has a great hall within by Norman Shaw (1898–1900). S in Featherbed Lane, *Waterworks* (1888) with two beam pumping engines by Eastern, Anderson and Godden of Earith. S of Croydon, off the Brighton Rd, in St. Augustine's Avenue, the *St. Augustine's Church* (1881–84; J.O. Scott), Dec. To S, **Purley** is a 19C suburban development. Parish church of *Christ Church* (1877–78; J. Fowler), Brighton Rd. In Russell Hill, to NW, *St. Thomas More RC School* (1863; J.G. Bland), built as the Royal Warehousemen's, Clerks' and Drapers' School. Large Venetian Gothic building. W of Purley is the pretentious garden suburb of Woodcote Village, laid out 1901–20 by William Webb. Its parish church, *St. Mark's* (1910; G.H. Fellowes-Prynne), Edwardian Gothic.

BROMLEY. SE London borough of which Bromley and Chislehurst were expensive outer suburbs in the late 19C, the rest Kent villages, suburbanised in the 20C. The NW corner of the borough includes the Sydenham site of Sir Joseph Paxton's *Crystal Palace*, re-erected here after the Great Exhibition of 1851 and burnt down 1936. Of the lavish grounds all that survives are two terraces of the formal gardens and 27 educational models of dinosaurs. The *Railway Station* (c 1850), built for visitors to the Crystal Palace, does however survive. Off Anerley Hill, in Waldegrave Rd, the *Swedenborgian Church* (1883; Henley), Gothic and an early example of the use of concrete in church building. The effect is of melted toffee. Crystal Palace Rd runs SE towards Penge. In **Penge**, the *Watermen's Almshouses* (1840; G. Porter), High St, are the grandest survivor of the many almshouses built all over London for retired members of different trades or professions. Jacobean style, in brick. In St. John's Rd, *Royal Naval Asylum* (1847; P. Hardwick), more almshouses, this time Tudor and more modest. To the SE, **Beckenham** contains a number of Victorian churches, none worthy of special mention except *St. George's* (1885–87; W.G. Bartleet), High St. In Wickham Rd, Nos 72–6 (c 1884; F. Hooper) three houses in Norman Shaw's old English manner. In Bromley Rd, *Beckenham Public Hall* (1883; G. Vigers), cheerful Queen Anne under a big roof, and Nos *124–8*, (1884), an early but very confident work by Ernest Newton. E of Beckenham lies the old market town of **Bromley**. In the High St, more work by Newton, the *Bell Hotel* and *Bank* (1898), a pretty group with gables, bow windows and ornamental plaster. In Tweedy Rd, the *Town Hall* (1906; R.F. Atkinson), neo-Wren, with a neo-Georgian extension of the 1930s. Widmore Rd leads W to **Bickley** with late 19C and early 20C houses dotted between the later suburban houses. Here can be witnessed the transition of domestic architecture from the free style of the late 19C to the neo-Georgian of the early 20C, notably in the work of Ernest Newton, who built much here. Newton's earlier houses play with gables, chequerwork in brick and stone, and despite their asymmetry maintain a crispness and severity which comes through in his more regular neo-Georgian work. On Bickley Rd, No. 19 *Beechcroft* (c 1885), is one of his earliest houses, tile-hung and half-timbered in the manner of Norman Shaw. S in Bird in Hand Lane, No. 8 *Lyndhurst* (1883–84), built by Newton for himself and *Westwood* (1891). *Little Orchard* in Page Heath Lane dates from

1902 and is neo-Georgian. Nos 4–6 are an early pair by Norman Shaw (1866). N of Bickley Park Rd, past *St. George's Church* (1863; F. Barnes: spire 1905, Newton), St. George's Rd leads to Logs Hill. Off St. Nicholas Lane is *Bullers Wood*, Newton's first big house (1889), a varied facade tied together by a strong cornice. *Stables* also by Newton. In Chislehurst Rd, three neo-Georgian houses by Newton, in red brick, No. 35a *Ennore* (1903), *Bickley Court* (1904), a subtle work very far from 18C copyism, and *Cross Hand*, also 1904, but more 'correct'.

Bickley Park Rd leads into **Chislehurst**. On the left, *Camden Park* (18C and 1860) was the home of Napoleon III and Empress Eugénie during their exile. In 1890 the estate was acquired by William Willett, a builder and developer who in Mayfair and Hampstead popularised the Dutch Revival. He chose Newton as his architect for the development of the estate. Notable houses are No. 80 *The Cedars* (1893), Willett's own house; No. 68, *Derwent House* (1899); *Bonchester* (1898); No. 60, *Elm Bank* (1890); and No. 54, *Fairacre* (c 1890). Beyond, in Wilderness Rd, *Sunnymead* is a large and asymmetrical house of 1875. Chislehurst Common lies at the heart of the town. Along the SW side, in Bull Lane, *Easdens* was built by Sir Aston Webb c 1905 as a church hall and, at the end, Nos *1–5 Shepherds Green* (1907–08; E.J. May) a good group of gabled brick houses. To the N of the Common, in the High St, *Church of the Annunciation* (1869; James Brooks), a powerful stone building, tough in all its details. The fittings are mostly by Brooks, vast reredos, font, pulpit. Stained glass by Hardman. Also in the High St *Nos 46–54*, (1881; Manning and Anderson), a group of almshouses. N, in Kemnall Rd, *Foxbury* (1876; D. Brandon), a Jacobean style house. S, in Church Row, *Nos 16–19*, a group of Regency style Edwardian houses. In Hawkwood Lane, *St Mary's RC Church* (1854; Wardell) is a plain Gothic building with, on its S side, Clutton's 1874 *Mortuary*, designed to receive the remains of Napoleon III, but in the event they went to Hampshire. Off Hawkwood Lane to the W, in Morley Rd, *Yew Tree Cottage*, *Whin Cottage*, *Morley Cottage* and *Nant Gwyn*, a mini estate of 1878 by George and Peto introducing the characteristic late 19C Chislehurst style. Manor Park Rd leads to Manor Park and *Cookham Dene* (c 1882; Sir A. Webb) and, opposite, five Queen Anne houses of the 1870s by G. Somers Clarke Sr. In St. Paul's Cray Rd, *Crayfield*, *Cleeveland* and *Warren House* (1878), also by Somers Clarke and all virtually identical. Before this, his *Grange Cottage* (c 1880) is in a more Shavian manner. N of Chislehurst in Mottingham Rd, the *Ironmongers' Almshouses* (1912; G. Hubbard) in a neo-Wren style clearly influenced by Morden College. In Mottingham Lane, the yellow brick Victorian house, now the *Fairmont Ladies Rest Home*, notable only as the home of W.G. Grace, and *The Grange*, (c 1860), now Eltham College Junior School.

S of Bromley is **Hayes**. In Hayes St, *St. Mary's Church* was largely rebuilt in the 19C. N aisle 1856 (G.G. Scott), S aisle and vestry 1879 (J.O. Scott), chancel restored 1905 (T.G. Jackson). In Croydon Rd *Oast House* was built in the middle of the Common by Philip Webb (1873) for the eccentric Lord Sackville Cecil. A very assured design in ragstone and red brick. Also in Croydon Rd, to W, *The Warren*, a large red-brick mansion built in 17C Dutch style for Walter Maximilian de Zoete by G. Somers Clarke Sr. The *Lodge* is contemporary with the house. Croydon Rd leads into **West Wickham**. At the corner of the High St and Wickham Court Rd is *West Wickham House*, originally by W.M. Teulon but extended by Norman Shaw (1870–71) in full blooded Queen Anne style, and as such a pioneering building, though barely recognisable on the road side with shops cut into the ground floor. In the S of the borough, in **Downe**, *Downe House* was the home of Charles Darwin and where he wrote 'The Origin of Species'. Now a museum.

BEXLEY. A collection of Kent villages mostly homogenised by 20C suburbia. In **Belvedere**, in the N of the borough, *All Saints' Church* (1853–61; W.G. and E. Habershon), Nuxley Rd, built as a proprietory chapel for Sir Culling Eardley, soon became the parish church. Shingled broached W tower. The *vicarage* is contemporary. N, in Woolwich Rd, Nos 65 and 67, *Albion Villas*, are two of the earliest surviving concrete houses. Built 1856 by Joseph Tall, who patented his method of concrete shuttering in 1865. 2m NW, in Erith Marshes, *Crossness Power Station* (1862–65; J. Bazalgette), Belvedere Rd, yellow brick Romanesque, the engine house with good cast-iron architectural detail and four beam-engines by James Watt and Son. In **Erith**, 1m E of All Saints' Church, the *Station* of 1849 (S. Beazley) survives, also nearby *Christ Church* (1874; J.P. St. Aubyn), brick with a stone spire, the interior richly painted by Ward and Hughes (1906–09), and E window by Hardman (1875).

Crossness Sewage Works, Engine House (1862–65; J. Bazalgette), Bexley

Bexleyheath lies to the S. *Christchurch*, (1872–77; William Knight of Nottingham), Broadway, is a noble early French Gothic church, ragstone. Irregular Gothic *vicarage* (1868; E. Christian). Also in Broadway, the *United Reformed Church* (1868; Habershon and Pite), classical, and, at the W angle of the Market Place, the diminutive *Clock Tower* (1911; W. Epps). S, in Upton Rd, *No. 8* is a late (probably 1856) example of a *cottage orné*, yellow brick and thatched. In Red House Lane is *The Red House* (1859; Philip Webb), William Morris's house, though only for five years. Red brick and medievalising, but without the period copying of all but the most advanced Gothic of the time. Webb's picturesque arrangement is composed of basic elements, wall, window and roof, governed by the requirements of the plan. The windows are simple sashes, practical rather than Gothic, under curved heads. The strength of the house and much of the charm comes from the way that all the disparate elements are locked together by the steeply pitched roof, punctuated by sturdy chimneys. To the SE, in **Bexley**, *St. Mary's*, Manor Road, is the medieval parish church, much restored 1882–83 by Champneys, who designed the elaborate chancel screen. His presumably also is the Arts and Crafts wooden Gothic *lychgate*. W, in Park Hill Rd, *St. John the Evangelist's*, (1881–82; George Low), like Christ Church, Bexleyheath, the style Early French Gothic, but not of the same quality. At the junction with Parkhurst Rd, a *pillar box* of the 'Penfold', i.e. hexagonal, type favoured in the 1870s. Hurst Rd runs SW from the High St to Sidcup. In **Sidcup**, *St. John's Church* (1882–83; G. Fellowes-Prynne), Church Avenue, a big brick building with a tall stone screen within. In the churchyard an Art Nouveau *monument* to Mary Joan Sheffield (died 1899).

GREATER MANCHESTER

ALTRINCHAM. A56 7m SW of Manchester. In Market Place, half-timbered *bank* (c 1870; G. Truefitt), built for Brooks' Bank. *Town Hall* (1901; C. Hindle), Market St, free Elizabethan style. On Dunham Rd, to W, High Victorian Gothic *Unitarian chapel* (1872; T. Worthington) and, beyond, *St. Margaret's Church* (1853–55; W. Hayley) remarkable free Perp. detail more usually associated with the late 19C, the chancel especially dramatic, lofty and lit by a very large E window, in the manner of Bodley's later churches. **Bowden**, to S, was built up with wealthy villas after 1849, when the railway came. On Dunham Rd, *Denzells Hospital* (1874), very mixed in style, more villas along Green Walk running W to the grand parish *church* (1858; W.H. Brakspear) and in Langham Rd S of the church. To E, **Hale**, with notable series of early 20C houses by Edgar Wood 1m E of centre, on Hale Rd, A538. *Halecroft* (1891) is a substantial villa full of picturesque touches, gables, mullion windows, half-timbering, not exceptional. On the land around Wood built smaller houses (1901–07) in simple brick with white-painted windows, free from obvious period detail. The group includes No. 226 Hale Rd, Nos 116–21 Park Rd, and Nos 20 and 27 Planetree Rd. •*No. 224 Hale Rd* (1914–16) which Wood built for himself is quite different, flat-roofed with concave-curved front, simply detailed, but the whole centre bay decorated with the bright chevron-patterned glazed tiling, of Islamic derivation but in appearance Jazz-modern of the 1920s. Similar patterning to the door. 5m W of Altrincham, B5160, at **Warburton** by the ship canal, new *church* (1883), *Church House* (1889), *school* (1871), Post Office and cottages all by J. Douglas for R.E. Egerton-Warburton, the landowner.

BOLTON. A666 10m NW of Manchester. Textile manufacturing town from the 16C, the home town of both Crompton and Arkwright whose inventions in the late 18C made possible the cotton industry. By 1851 Bolton had some 65 cotton mills. In the centre, Victoria Square, with •*Town Hall* (1866–73; W. Hill), proudly classical after the model of Leeds with a giant Corinthian order, combined here with a fine portico and florid central clock tower rising to a domed cap. Pedimental sculpture by W.C. Marshall. Interior hall subdivided after a fire in 1981. In front, *statues* of Sir E. Chadwick (1871; Birch), whose report on the sanitary conditions of the new industrial towns (1842) shocked Victorian society into reform of public health, and of Sir B. Dobson (1900; J. Cassidy), Mayor of Bolton. On W side, *Exchange* (1825–29) Greek Ionic. Off Exchange St, in Mawdsley St, *County Court* (1869; T.C. Sorby) handsome Italianate palazzo. To E, Nelson Square, with seated *statue* of Crompton (1862; W.C. Marshall), one relief showing his spinning mule, *Education Offices* (1825; B. Hick) with Greek Doric porch, and at corner of Bradshawgate, *Prudential Assurance* (1889; Waterhouse) in the bright red house style. In Wood St, E of Bradshawgate, palazzo style *Halifax Building Society* (c 1849). Silverwell St, to S, leads to *St. Peter's Church* (1867–71; Paley), large Dec. with vaulted chancel. S of the centre, Trinity St *station* (1903) in hard red brick with a cupola tower. *Holy Trinity Church*, just W, is an expensive Commissioners' church (1823–25; P. Hardwick) in Perp. style. N of Victoria Square, in Knowsley St, *Market* (1853–55; G.T. Robinson) with pedimented portico and large iron and glass hall behind. In St. George's Rd, to N, *St. George's Church* (1794) with E end and interior of 1907 (J.L. Simpson). To E, off St. George's St, *All Saints' Church* (1869; G.E.

Street) plate-traceried High Victorian, now Ukranian church. *The Old Town Hall* (1825), St. George's St, is now a museum of local history.

Outer Bolton still has numerous cotton mills, the most prominent examples being of c 1900 in red brick with stone or terracotta decoration. N of St. George's Rd, in Davenport St, *Union Mill*, late 19C and early 20C. To W, Chorley New Rd (A673) leads out past *Queen's Park*, laid out 1866 to relieve unemployment, to surviving large industrialists' mansions on the outskirts, notably *Woodside* (1877–80). Chorley Old Rd, B6226, runs NW. To S, off Mornington Rd, *St. Margaret's Church* (1903; Austin and Paley), free Gothic stone church with tall arcades and continuous roof. N of Chorley Old Rd, Halliwell Rd, A6099, with *St. Paul's Church*, cottages and schools, a pretty Gothic group of 1847 and 1856 (J. Greenhalgh). To S, *St. Thomas's Church* (1875; Paley and Austin) Escrick St, a fine red-brick building with long roofline and EE detail. *Falcon Mill* (1903–04; G. Temperly) in Handel St, N of Halliwell Rd is six-storey in red brick, banded in yellow. Halliwell St continues beyond Moss Bank Way, A58, to *Smithills Hall* (open to public), Smithills Dean Rd, 15C hall house much extended in stone and half-timber (c 1875; G. Devey) to give a long gabled front to the terraced gardens. N from centre, Blackburn Rd, A666, leads out to Astley Bridge. In Astley St, to W, *All Souls' Church* (1880; Paley and Austin) brick with W tower. Impressive tall interior with apsed chancel flanked by side chapels. In Blackburn Rd, *Congregational church* (1895; J. Simpson), lavish Perp. style with tall spire, paid for by W.H. Lever of Lever Bros, later Lord Leverhulme. E of Astley Bridge, off A58, is *Hall i' th' Wood* (open to public), spectacular 15C to 17C black and white house restored c 1900 (J. Simpson) for W.H. Lever. SE of the centre of Bolton, Radcliffe Rd, B6209, leads to **Darcy Lever** with Leverhulme Park, given to the town by Lord Leverhulme 1917, between Radcliffe Rd and Bury Rd, A58. At **Lever Bridge**, *St. Stephen's Church* (1842–45; E. Sharpe), remarkable as one of the two churches built entirely, apart from wall infill, of terracotta, to demonstrate the versatility of the material (the other is at Fallowfield, Manchester). The tower and spire have gone but all the rest is intact, down to terracotta bench-ends and organ case, and the quality of the Gothic detail is indeed high. Contemporary opinion more than the limitations of the material meant that the 'pot churches' had no successors. SW of the centre, S of Derby St, A579, *Swan Lane Mills* (1904; Stott and Sons), seven-storey mill said to have been the largest under a single roof in the world.

3m SE of Bolton, A666, **Farnworth**, with *Library* (1910; W. Lomax) and *Town Hall* (1908; Lomax), brick and stone, late 17C Baroque style, in Market St. 5m SW of Bolton, A579, at **Atherton**, *Town Hall* (1898; J.C. Prestwick), Bolton Rd, 18C Baroque style. Four notable churches by the Lancaster firm of Paley and Austin, the parish *church* (1879) in the centre, grandly scaled, *St. Anne's Church* (1899–1901) Tyldesley Rd, with low tower clasped between chancel and transept, and *St. Michael's* (1875–77) at **Howe Bridge**, on A572 to SW. The fourth is at **Daisy Hill**, 2m NW, B5235, *St. James' Church* (1878–81), a most original work in brick and terracotta, broad aisleless nave and complex E end with N transept and equivalent S projection carrying a bellcote.

BURY. A56 8m N of Manchester. Cotton weaving and printing town, the leading calico-printing firm being that of R. Peel, father of the Prime Minister, who was born near Bury. *Statue* of Sir R. Peel (1852; Baily) in the Market Place with sheaves of corn at his feet, symbolising the repeal of the Corn Laws. *St. Mary's Church*, behind, has tower and spire of 1844, the rest of 1871–76 (J.S. Crowther), well-detailed Dec. with tall nave and apsed chancel. Apse glass by Hardman. In Silver St, to SW, *Art Gallery and Library* (1899; Woodhouse and Willoughby) free Renaissance. On corner of Bank St, *Lloyds Bank* (1868), built as the Bury Bank, ornate Italian palazzo style. In Market St, SW of Market Square, *Derby Hall and Athenaeum* (1850–51; S. Smirke), distinguished Italianate pair of buildings, the Derby Hall the original Town Hall and Court House, the Athenaeum with block rusticated porch and lower windows. At S end of Market St, domed *monument* to J. Kay, 18C inventor of the fly-shuttle. S of the centre, on Manchester Rd, *RC church* (1841; J. Harper) thin Perp. Further S, at Redvales, *St. Peter's Church* (1871: rebuilt 1899; J.M. Taylor), and to SW, *Estate Workshops* of the Earl of Derby's estates (1866; J. Green) with campanile-towered gatehouse.

2m W of Bury, at **Walshaw**, elaborate hillside *church* (1888; L. Booth) with landmark spire and High Victorian granite arcade piers. Built as a memorial to J. Haworth, cotton manufacturer. 3m E of Bury, A58, **Heywood**, cotton town, the industry built up by the Peel family. In the centre, parish *church* (1860–62; J. Clarke) with broach spire and stone free-style *Library* (1905). 3m SW of Bury, A665, **Radcliffe**, also a cotton centre. *St. Thomas' Church* (1864–69; W. Walker), Blackburn St, large Perp. style. To SE, *St. John's Church* (1866; J.M. and H. Taylor), Stand Lane, with spiky detail and octagonal central tower, characteristic of J.M. Taylor's style. The best mill near Bury is at **Summerseat**, 3m N of Bury, W of A56, *Brooksbottom Mill* (c 1875), unusually in stone with arched windows.

MANCHESTER. The heartland of the Industrial Revolution, built on the cotton industry, manufacture and trading. Already by the early 19C, visitors were amazed by the scale of the factories, the speed of urban expansion and the squalor of working conditions. By this time also Manchester's role in liberal and radical politics was well established, the emergence of militant trade unionism, seen as the seedbed of revolution (Peterloo Massacre of 1819), developing into the struggle for parliamentary reform in the 1830s. The conflict between capitalism and labour was more bitter in Manchester than in any other industrial town, and to visitors such as Engels violent social upheaval was self-evidently imminent. However, through the struggle for reform of the Corn Laws, led from Manchester by R. Cobden, an alliance of business interests and populism against the older landed interests was forged, with the Nonconformist churches important in providing a bond.

Symbol of the city is the *Town Hall (1868–77; A. Waterhouse), Albert Square, the outstanding 19C Town Hall in Britain, where the suitability of Gothic for public building is demonstrated in one of the masterly plans of the age. On a triangular site the main public civic rooms are grouped on the front elevation with offices down the two sides, the front range screening a parallel vaulted hall with curving stairs each end. In the centre of the triangle, axial to the front and stair hall, is the Great Hall. The Gothic style permits a fantastic skyline of gables, turrets and chimneys capped by the central tower and spire, and also a hierarchical treatment of window openings, the most ornate to the first-floor public rooms, the others suitably scaled to office use. Waterhouse's main front is symmetrical, the balance of centre, wings and angle blocks exemplarily handled. Vaulted entrance hall with the first of the series of statues and busts that are a feature of the building, where civic pride speaks in every aspect of the decoration. Chantrey's statue of J. Dalton (1837), discoverer of atomic theory, and A. Gilbert's

Town Hall (1868–77; A. Waterhouse), Albert Square, Manchester

statue of J.P. Joule (1893), physicist, are outstanding, the latter one of the masterpieces of late Victorian sculpture. At each end of the hall, the spatially dramatic effect of minor staircases in circular stone drums rising behind the vaulted main staircases. On the stairs, statue of J. Bright (1877; W. Theed), leader of the Anti-Corn-Law League. The Great Hall is a magnificent room, painted roof with hammerbeam trusses, apsed end containing the organ, and frescoes of Manchester history by Ford Madox Brown (1876–88). The principal rooms along the front, the Lord Mayor's suite, have panelled ceilings, carved fireplaces and decoration constantly repeating the honey-bee (Hive of Industry) motif. In Albert Square, recently restored *Albert Memorial* (1862–67; T. Worthington), canopied Gothic monument over statue (M. Noble), in form and in the programme of allegorical carving the clear prototype of the larger Albert Memorial in London. In the square, statues of Gladstone (1879; Raggi), Bright (1891; Theed), Alderman Heywood (1894; A. Bruce Joy) and Bishop Fraser (1887; Woolner), the finest of the group. On S side of the square, *St. Andrew's Chambers* (1874; G.T. Redmayne), *Bridgewater Buildings* (1872; Clegg and Knowles), once the Bridgewater Canal offices, both Gothic in the Waterhouse vein, *Albert Chambers*, Italianate, and *Memorial Hall*

(1864–66; Worthington), Venetian Gothic. On corner of Lloyd St, *Lloyd's House* (c 1875; Speakman and Charlesworth). The W side is mostly cleared, revealing *RC church* (1848; Weightman and Hadfield), Mulberry St, with Rhenish-helm top to the spire and Romanesque detail in red brick. On N side, Gothic corner building to Cross St (1877; Pennington and Brigden) and large Edwardian office to right (1902; Waddington, Son and Dunkerley).

S from Albert Square, Mount St leads past the fine extensions to the Town Hall (1925–38; E.V. Harris). *Lawrence Buildings* (1874; Pennington and Brigden) and *Friends Meeting House* (1828–30; Lane) opposite. Behind the Library, St. Peter's Square, with *cross* (1907; Temple Moore) on site of St. Peter's Church, *Cenotaph* (1924; Lutyens) and, on S side, *Midland Hotel* (1898; C. Trubshaw), vast brick and terracotta hotel built for the Midland Railway, much ornamented, screening the former *Central Station* (1880) across Windmill St. The station, refurbished as an exhibition hall, has a 210ft arched trainshed similar to that at St. Pancras, London, raised up on a brick-vaulted undercroft. W of Watson St, *Goods Warehouse* (1898), five-storeys with giant letters on all four sides proclaiming its identity. In Peter St, W of the hotel, *YMCA* (1911; Woodhouse, Corbett and Dean), terracotta faced. *Theatre Royal* (1845; Irwin and Chester) with fine stuccoed facade, a giant Venetian opening with Corinthian columns framing a statue of Shakespeare. Interior altered. To W, *Free Trade Hall (1856; E. Walters), Manchester's commemoration of the successful campaign against the Corn Laws, repealed 1846, appropriately on the site of the 1819 Peterloo Massacre when troops dispersed a demonstration, killing several people. A magnificent Italian palazzo style design, rich yet controlled with massive arcaded lower floor, upper windows contained in arches of coupled columns with carving in the tympana and crowning cornice with balustrade. Interior rebuilt after bombing. Opposite, good office and warehouse block, *Harvester House* (1868; Clegg and Knowles), stone fronted.

Mosley St runs NE to Piccadilly Gardens. On corner of Princess St, *City Art Gallery (1825; C. Barry), a neo-classical building of great quality, reminiscent of the work of Schinkel in Germany, built up in cubic masses, the centre portico and columned screens each side in effective contrast to the rusticated walling of the corner blocks. Over the portico a Grecian attic lights the stair well. The glory of the interior stair hall has recently been restored with the recreation of the painted decoration. Outstanding collections, notably of Pre-Raphaelites, including Madox Brown's 'Work', Millais' 'Autumn Leaves' and Holman Hunt's 'The Scapegoat', 'The Light of the World' and 'The Hireling Shepherd'. The Annexe, facing Princess St, is the former *Athenaeum* (1837–39; Barry), one of the first Italian palazzo style buildings outside London, a model for much later Manchester architecture. Further up Mosley St, on W, *Williams and Glyns Bank* (1860; E. Walters) palazzo style, the upper floors with top cornice and balustrade on a lower half of banded rusticated piers, massive and severe, actually disguising two floors as one. The matching S extension added c 1885. To N, *No. 16 Mosley St* (1839; E. Walters) warehouse built for Richard Cobden who had already established himself as a successful calico printer before his political career began. Across Marble St, facing Piccadilly Gardens, former *bank* (1836; R. Tattershall) with Corinthian frontispiece. In Piccadilly Gardens, *statues* of Peel (1853; W.C. Marshall), Wellington (1856; M. Noble), Watt (1857; W. Theed) and a magnificently imperious Queen Victoria (1901; E. Onslow Ford) back-to-back with a charming bronze of a nursing mother. On E side,

Portland St, three fine warehouse facades by E. Walters, c 1851–63, incorporated into a modern *hotel*, all Italian palazzo style, examples of the distinctive manner evolved in Manchester for these buildings that combined offices, showrooms and wholesale warehouses. On Aytoun St, *Grand Hotel*, built as a warehouse 1867 (Mills and Murgatroyd). Further warehouses survive in Piccadilly, Newton St and Dale St, N and E of the Gardens. On Piccadilly, towards Piccadilly Station, *No. 107*, Baroque style office in banded stone and brick (1898; C. Heathcote). In Ducie St, off Piccadilly, *London Warehouse* (1867) seven storeys in brick, built for the railway.

Britannia House, formerly Watts Warehouse (1851; Travis and Mangnall), Portland Street, Manchester

Portland St runs S from Piccadilly Gardens, past Britannia House, the former *Watts Warehouse* (1851; Travis and Mangnall), the most splendid of Manchester warehouses, stone fronted, 23 bays long, Italian Renaissance style, the continuous runs of repetitive detail interrupted by pilasters framing four sections that rise an additional storey to pavilions with pairs of rose windows, a quite unexpected departure from the chosen style. In Charlotte St, group of *warehouses* by E. Walters, No. 34 (1855), No. 12 (1860) and No. 10 (1857), Nos 10 and 12 more ornate but all in Walters' severely dignified palazzo manner. On corner of Princess St, *No. 101 Portland St* (1870; Clegg and Knowles), stone fronted well-detailed Gothic five-storey warehouse. In Princess St to E, *No. 101* Italianate warehouse and *No. 103* (1854; J. Gregan), former Mechanics Institute, palazzo style, on a skewed site. On opposite side, warehouses of the 1880s, notably *No. 74* (1880; Corson and Aitken) Scots baronial style. On Whitworth St, Edwardian Manchester warehouses and offices, glazed brick and terracotta cladding on steel frames extending NE to Piccadilly Station and SW to Oxford St. On corner of Princess St, *Lancaster House* (1912–15; H.S. Fairhurst and Son) with ornate corner turret. To NW, *UMIST* (1895–1902; Spalding and Cross), the Institute of Science and Technology, facing Sackville St, ornate gabled French Loire style. On N side of Whitworth St, *College of Higher Education* (1900; Potts, Son and Pickup). Behind, Canal St follows the canal to Minshull St with Venetian Gothic *Magistrates Court* (1871; T. Worthington), picturesque asymmetrical composition with corner tower answered by a pyramid roof on the shorter tower at the other end. Good carved detail. At E end of Whitworth St, *Fire Station* (1901–06; Woodhouse, Willoughby and Langham), terracotta and brick on a triangular site with tenement housing for police and firemen inside. At SW end of Whitworth St, *Bridgewater House* (1912; H.S. Fairhurst) stone below, white tile above and, on corner of Oxford St, *Refuge Assurance* (1891; A. Waterhouse) red brick and terracotta, very large, extended with 220ft clocktower (1910; P. Waterhouse). The tile and terracotta detail, by Doulton, is of high quality and is continued in the entrance halls and inner court. In Oxford St, W side, *the Oxford* pub (c 1900) with cheerful facade, then, *Tootal, Broadhurst, Lee* (1898; J.G. Sankey), red brick and terracotta with giant Corinthian columns. *The Palace Theatre* has a splendid auditorium (1913; B. Crewe), recently restored, disguised behind a dim exterior of 1953. On corner of Portland St, former *Behrens warehouse* (1860; P. Nunn) stone below, brick and stone above with giant arches. *Princes Buildings*, on W side of Oxford St, has attactive slightly Art Nouveau detail of c 1900.

Returning to Albert Square, Cross St leads N to King St. At the crossing, three c 1900 buildings by C. Heathcote, *Eagle Insurance* (1911) at SW corner, small-scale Edwardian Baroque, *Northern Rock Insurance* (1895) at SE corner, picturesquely gabled, and *Lloyds Bank* (1915) at NE corner, large-scale Baroque. To E, on S side, *Prudential Assurance* (1881; Waterhouse) in the usual bright red, but skyline and ground floor altered. Adjoining, **Bank of England* branch (1845–46; C.R. Cockerell), one of the series of outstanding classical buildings by Cockerell for the bank (cf. Liverpool and Bristol). Monumental though on a relatively small scale with the lower two floors contained in a giant Doric order and the upper floor with centre pediment, the base broken by the arched head of the centre window. Of all Victorian architects Cockerell's classicism is at once the most scholarly and the most original, here solving the problem of combining a temple front with a three-storey building by raising the pediment, and avoiding the conflict of two main cornices by reducing the upper one and breaking the centre with an arch that relates to the arches of the lower floor. *Nos 84–8 King St* (c 1840) are conventionally classical. On N side, corner of Brown St, *Reform Club* (1871; E. Salomons), lavish Venetian Gothic with Flemish touches. Symmetrical front with angle turrets and much carved decoration. Fine interior staircase and dining-room. To N, in Norfolk St, off Brown St, *bank* (1909; Briggs, Wolstenholme and Thornley) and *Stock Exchange* (1907; Bradshaw,

Gass and Hope). Opposite the Reform Club, *Midland Bank* (1929; Lutyens). In Brown St to S, *Lombard Chambers* (1868; G. Truefitt), Gothic bank with exotic corner and turret. In Booth St, *No. 10*, Savings Bank (1872; E. Salomons) ornate palazzo. In Spring Gardens, at the head of King St, fine late 19C group, *Commercial Union* (1881; C. Heathcote), former *Lancashire and Yorkshire Bank* (1890; Heathcote and Rawle) and former *National Provincial Bank* (1888–91; A. Waterhouse), curving round into York St with the former *Parrs Bank* (1902; C. Heathcote) exuberantly Baroque with a corner dome on the opposite side, marbled banking hall.

Bank of England (1845–46; C.R. Cockerell), King Street, Manchester

Returning to Cross St, on corner of St. Ann St, *Conservative Club* (1875; Horton and Bridgeford) and *Pearl Assurance* (1901). On corner of St. Ann's Square, *Williams and Glyns Bank* (1848; J.E. Gregan), finely detailed palazzo built as Sir B. Heywood's Bank, stone fronted with rusticated arches around Venetian windows below and first-floor Corinthian aedicules. One of the most distinguished buildings in this style. The house to E was the bank manager's house. *St. Ann's Church* (1709–12) was altered inside 1886–91 (A. Waterhouse). T. de Quincey was baptised here (1785). N of the Square, entrance to *Barton Arcade* (1871; Corbett, Raby and Sawyer), a delight, a glass-roofed winding street with two and three storeys of offices over the shops fronted by ornate iron balconies and two glass domes. (Main entry from Deansgate). Opposite, the *Royal Exchange* (1914–21; Bradshaw, Gass and Hope), the world's largest trading floor when completed, with some 11,000 members. Disused by 1960, a remarkable modern theatre has been deposited like a spaceship in the middle of the main hall. To N, Corporation St, dominated by the modern Arndale Centre. Beyond, on left, *Corn Exchange* (1892–1904; Ball and Elce), Hanging Ditch, florid gabled block with cupola at one corner. To rear, *Manchester Cathedral*, 15C collegiate church much altered in the 19C and after 1945. Tower heightened 1862–68 (J.P. Holden), restoration 1885 (J.S. Crowther) and attractive additions to W tower (1898) and to SE (1902) both by B. Champneys. In the N aisle, fine seated monument to H. Chetham (1853; W. Theed) with figure of schoolboy of Chetham's Hospital at the base. In S aisle, statue of T. Fleming (1851; E.H. Baily). At E end, effigy of Bishop Fraser (died 1885; J. Forsyth), bishop of Manchester from 1870, a popular promoter of causes religious, social and educational, known as 'the bishop of all denominations'. To N, *Chetham's Hospital*, 15C refounded as a school 1656 by H. Chetham and extended to E as Manchester Grammar School (1873–78; Waterhouse). Behind, *Manchester Victoria Station*, originally opened 1844 but the present frontage of 1909 (W. Dawes). By the corner of Victoria St, former *Palatine Hotel* (1842; Holden), one of the earliest railway hotels. S of Victoria St, *Victoria Bridge* (1837–39) crosses the Irwell into Salford.

On Deansgate, E side, entrance to *Barton Arcade* (see above) and, on corner of John Dalton St, *Queen's Chambers* (c 1875; Pennington and Brigden), Gothic with elaborate corner entry. On W side, *John Rylands Library* (1890–99; B. Champneys), built to house Rylands' collection of religious books and manuscripts. Rylands had the largest cotton business in Lancashire, with mills at Manchester, Bolton and Wigan, and was one of the promoters of the Manchester Ship Canal. Superbly detailed Gothic, Dec. style, but with a profusion and liveliness of carving almost Spanish on the main front. Subtle, near symmetrical street front with the main gable of the library set back, to allow more light, behind a two-storey porch between short towers with octagonal caps. Lovely interior with vaulted staircase rising to the reading-room, high and vaulted with galleried bays each side and great traceried end windows with stained glass by Kempe. Arts and Crafts metalwork of high quality throughout. Further down, Deansgate, on E side, on corner of Jackson's Row, former *School Board Office* (1878; Royle and Bennett), an early example of the Queen Anne style, the long windows, tall chimneys and moulded brickwork a cheerful alternative to classic or Gothic. In Quay St, to W, *Opera House* (1912; Richardson and Gill) with neo-classical facade influenced by Cockerell's Bank of England. Further S, *Liverpool Road Station* (1830), the world's oldest surviving railway station, built for the Liverpool and Manchester Railway and recently restored as the Museum of Science and Technology. Stuccoed entrance front in late Regency manner with the agent's house to left and a row of shops built for leasing to right. The scale is modest, most evocative of the earliest days of the railways. On N side of the tracks the original warehouse with access from the tracks at a floor higher than street level on the other side.

OUTER MANCHESTER

Behind Victoria Station, Ducie St, A56, leads NW to Bury New Rd. To E, *Strangeways Prison* (1866–68; Waterhouse) the octagonal centre prominent over the walls. On the main road, *Magistrates Court* (1867; Waterhouse). Waterloo Rd runs N past *St. Alban's Church* (1857–64; J.S. Crowther) tall, apsed church with tower at SE and the careful detail typical of Crowther's work. Further N, *St. John's Church* (1869–71; Paley and Austin), severe design with more of the High Victorian massiveness than in the firm's later works. Round apse and pyramid-roofed tower. N of Victoria Station, on Cheetham Hill Rd, A665, *St. Luke's Church* (1836–39; T.W. Atkinson) Perp. style with tower and

spire and unaltered galleried interior, *Town Hall* (1853–55; T. Bird)
brick and stone with offices addition to N (1861) and former *Library*
opposite (1877; Barber and Ellis). Cheetham Hill was an early 19C
development and the centre of Manchester's Jewish community. The
main *Synagogue*, opposite Town Hall (1857; T. Bird), stone fronted
with Corinthian central loggia. NE of centre, Rochdale Rd, A664, runs
to Collyhurst and Harpurhey. On W side, *Queen's Park*, Harpurhey
with *Art Gallery* (1883; Allison) containing collections of Victorian and
Edwardian paintings. *Christ Church*, Harpurhey (1838–41; E. Welch),
in Church Lane to N, is lancet Gothic with spire. Further N, Blackley
Library (1900; J. Gibbons), Rochdale Rd, free style, brick and
terracotta.

NE of Piccadilly Gardens, A62, Oldham St leads out to Ancoats, the
most important surviving industrial area close to the centre with factory buildings along the Rochdale and Ashton Canals. On Oldham Rd,
SE side, *Victoria Square* (1889; Spalding and Cross), Manchester's
first municipal housing with long red-brick gabled front to the main
road and utilitarian rear ranges with access to the inner court. Each flat
had a bedroom and living-room, sharing a sink and toilet with the
adjacent flat. There were no baths. To S, *St. Peter's Church* (1860; I.
and J. Holden), Blossom St, Romanesque with campanile and interior
remarkable for cast-iron columns, roof-trusses and even bench ends.
To NE, at **Miles Platting**, *St. John's Church* (1855; J.E. Gregan),
Oldham Rd, Romanesque in red brick with W rose window and
rounded apse. Built for Sir B. Heywood, banker. Off Varley St, to S, *St.
Mark's Rectory* (1892; Mackmurdo and Hornblower), Holland St,
advanced Arts and Crafts house, plain and square with coved cornice
and top-lit hall. E of the centre, Great Ancoats St runs SE. In Old Mill
St, to E, *Ancoats Hospital* (1873; Lewis and Crowcroft) patterned brick
Gothic. *Institute* adjoining 1890 (A. Darbishire). To S, A662, Ashton
New Rd leads out to **Clayton**. *St. Cross Church* (1862–66; Butterfield),
by Clayton Hall, is one of Butterfield's toughest town churches, in
patterned brick rising sheer to a continuous roof. Interior with diapered brick walls and E and W windows set high, at clerestory level,
emphasising the single space. Off Great Ancoats St, S of A662, in
Every St, *Ancoats Library* (1866; Waterhouse) Gothic with hipped
roof, small scale.

S of centre, A57, Hyde Rd runs past *Nicholls Hospital* (1879; T.
Worthington), brick Gothic with steep-roofed tower, to Gorton. In
Bennett St, W Gorton, N of A57, *St. Benedict's Church* (1880; J.S.
Crowther), very tall EE style brick church with W rose and pyramid-
roofed tower. In Gorton Lane, off Belle Vue St, to E, *St. Francis' RC
Church* (1866–72; E.W. Pugin), red brick and stone with the most
accentuated pointed W front of two long traceried windows divided by
three far-projecting buttresses, the centre buttress carrying a sharp
banded spirelet. Much carved detail and surface patterning. High
polygonal apse and ornate carved capitals inside. Built for the Franci-
scans. Hyde Rd continues E past *Unitarian church* (1869–71; T.
Worthington), fully ecclesiastical in the High Church vein, EE style
with steeple. Mausoleum to the founder, R. Peacock of Gorton Foundry, to W. SE of Hyde Rd, Stockport Rd, A6 runs out to Longsight. In St.
John's St, to W, *St. John's Church* (1845; J.E. Gregan) EE with broach
spire. To E, on Stanley Grove, *St. Cyprian's Church* (1908; Temple
Moore), chequered brick with plain tower. To S, on Slade Lane, A579,
St. Agnes' Church (1884; J.M. and H. Taylor) in angular High Victorian Gothic with very broad interior covered by a splendid timber roof,
braced with a complexity worthy of E.B. Lamb. On Stockport Rd,

Levenshulme, *St. Mark's Church* (1908; C.T. Barlow) free Gothic in brick and stone with broad brick interior and Arts and Crafts stained glass.

S of the centre, Oxford Rd runs SE from Whitworth St. At the top end large warehouses of the early 20C, as in Whitworth St. Beyond the Ring Road is Chorlton-on-Medlock, largely cleared of housing and taken over by the university. In Cavendish St, to W, former *Town Hall* (1830; R. Lane), Greek Doric pedimented portico, and *College of Art* (1880; G.T. Redmayne), Gothic with the studio windows each side of the centre functionally expressed. Extension 1897 (J.S. Gibbons). To S, *Manchester University*, the original buildings 1870–1902 (A. Waterhouse), built for Owens College, founded 1851, which became The Victoria University in 1880. The main range, to Oxford Rd (1883–87), has a high tower and asymmetrical front ending with the Whitworth Hall, completed 1902. Vaulted undercroft and stair up to the main hall similar to the Town Hall. The quadrangle, completed piecemeal, has the Manchester Museum, with collections of natural history, ethnology and Egyptology, on the E side, the Library on the S. N of the quadrangle, *Metallurgy Building* (1908; Heathcote and Son), Bridgeford St, attractive Edwardian Baroque. On E side of Oxford St, *RC Church of the Holy Name* (1869–72; J.A. Hansom), planned on the grandest scale with 240ft spire, but the tower capped with an octagon in 1928, much lower, but suited to the broad and looming outline of the church. French Gothic with flying buttresses and cross-gabled side chapels. The interior is exceptional, fully vaulted with terracotta infill between the ribs, high and so broad in the nave that the apse arch and ambulatory arches are contained within the span. The focus on the sanctuary is emphasised by canting in the walling from the last nave piers to the sanctuary arch. Rich reredos (1890; J.S. Hansom). To S, in Nelson St, *Nos 60–2*, late Georgian pair of villas. In No. 62 Mrs Pankhurst founded the 'Women's Social and Political Union' in 1903 to fight for votes for women. To be restored as a museum. To S, *Royal Infirmary* (1905–08; E.T. Hall) Baroque, opposite the *Whitworth Art Gallery* (1895; J.W. Beaumont) in Whitworth Park. Sir J. Whitworth, one of the leading mechanical engineers of the 19C, developing machine tools of an accuracy not previously achieved, devoted his fortune to educational and social philanthropy in Manchester. Exceptional fine art and textile collections. In Upper Brook St, E of the Infirmary, former *Welsh chapel* (1837–39; C. Barry), lancet Gothic single cell with W window and door recessed in a tall moulded and shafted arch, an impressive clarity to the design with even ranges of side buttresses and corner pinnacles. Interior now subdivided. *No. 84 Plymouth Grove*, a pretty stuccoed classical villa, was Mrs Gaskell's house, Charlotte Bronte, Dickens, Carlyle and Harriet Beecher Stowe among her visitors. In Hathersage Rd, between Plymouth Grove and Upper Brook St, ornate terracotta *Baths* (1905).

To S, flanking Anson Rd, A34, *Victoria Park*, the most attractive of Manchester's early suburbs, the earliest part, off Oxford Place, to W, laid out 1836, with stucco villas interspersed with later Gothic houses, the largest, in Lower Park Rd, now *Xaverian College* (1874–75; Waterhouse). E of Anson Rd, Daisy Bank Rd with *Addison Terrace*, stucco Tudor, and *First Church of Christ Scientist*, the major work of Edgar Wood (1903). Brick with white rendered church facade, a Y-plan group of buildings with low angled wings running back to the church front gable. The forms of the buildings are quite without period precedent, the sharp gable of the church has canted sides, a deep-arched doorway, cross-shaped upper window in stone frame and utterly plain stone shaft above rising through the gable apex. A stocky round tower links to the hall range to right and both canted ranges end in prominent chimney stacks. The acute angle of the church gable is echoed in the brick lychgate with a gable chequered in stone. The interior has been restored from near dereliction. W of Anson Rd and Victoria Park, Wilmslow Rd, A6010, with *Platt Hall* on W side, mansion of c 1764 containing Gallery of English Costume. Just W, in Platt Lane *Holy Trinity* (1845–46; E. Sharpe), the second of Sharpe's 'pot churches' (cf. Lever Bridge, Bolton) wholly clad in Fletcher's patent terracotta, even to the spire. The experiment was well in advance of its time and much criticised, even today the yellow interior is startling. Wilmslow Rd continues S to Didsbury. S of centre, *Didsbury College* (1842), handsome Greek Revival ashlar range with pedimented centre. Just SE, *Shirley Institute* (1865; T. Worthington), Wilmslow Rd, the most elaborate of Manchester suburban mansions, built for the editor and proprietor of the Manchester Guardian, J.E. Taylor. Loire chateau style in red brick and terracotta with off-centre entrance tower. W of Didsbury centre, Barlow Moor Rd, *Emmanuel Church* (1858) with a rich window (1889) by Morris and Co. in S transept.

S of central Manchester, A6144, Chorlton Rd runs into Withington Rd. To E, in Moss Side, *Alexandra Park*, laid out 1869. On W side, *St. Bede's College* (1877–80; Dunn and Hansom), red-brick and terracotta Florentine palazzo with ornate terracotta work by Doulton, enamelled panels by the entry and giant bees on the wall above. Chapel 1898. To S, *RC church* (1895; F.H. Oldham) and *Methodist College* (1879 and 1903–6). Just E, in Spring Bridge Rd, *Hulme Grammar School* (1886–87; A. Davies-Colley) tall red brick with shaped gable. W of Withington Rd, *Independent College* (1840–43; Irwin and Chester), College Rd, long ashlar-fronted Gothic range with centre tower and wings on an arcaded ground floor. Built for the Congregational Church.

OLDHAM. A62 7m NE of Manchester. Cotton manufacturing town, in the later 19C the most important of all, with some 260 mills taking in over a fifth of the total cotton imported. In the centre, parish *church* (1823–27; R. Lane) and *Town Hall* (1841; J. Butterworth), Greek revival, additions behind (1879–80; G. Woodhouse) with facades to Greaves St and Firth St in a larger-scale imposing classical style. By the church, brick and terracotta *County Court* (1894; H. Tanner). In Greaves St, small *solicitor's office* (1901; E. Wood), domestic in scale with dormers and casement windows, Art Nouveau stone lintel over the door. In Union St, *Library and Art Gallery* (1883) and *School of Art* (1855; N. Pennington) Italianate. Further W, *Prudential Assurance* (1901; Waterhouse) red brick with angle turrets. At the W end, in King St, Messrs Dronsfield's *offices* (1906–08; J.H. Sellers) advanced 20C style building, flat-roofed with recessed central tower, the angles chamfered in a manner more suggestive of the 1920s. Glazed green brick, grey granite surrounds to the big rectangular windows. Off King St, Park Rd runs SE from the A62 to *Alexandra Park* (1866) laid out to relieve unemployment after the cotton famine of the American Civil War. Off Abbey Hills Rd to SE, Manor Rd, Low Side, leads to *Low Side Manor* extended 1901 (J.H. Sellers) for one of the Dronsfield family. Imposing rusticated gatepiers. From Abbey Hills Rd, B6194, Holts Lane leads NE to **Lees**, past *St. Thomas' Church* (1848; E. Shellard), Perp. handled with some ecclesiological correctness. E of Oldham, A62 crosses the Pennines to Yorkshire. Under the summit, *Standedge Tunnels*, the first built (1811) for the Huddersfield Canal, followed by railway tunnels in 1849, 1871 and 1894, the tunnels about three miles long.

4m S of Oldham, A627, **Ashton-under-Lyne**. In the Market Square, *Town Hall* (1841; W. Young) classical with Corinthian columns extended to left 1878. Brick *Market Hall* on E side. Stamford St, to S, has *St. Peter's Church* (1821–24; F. Goodwin), Manchester St, closing the view W and the spire of *Albion Congregational church* (1890–95; J. Brooke) to the E. On the S side, *parish church*, rebuilt 1840–44 in a highly carved Perp. style, all the wall surfaces enriched with carved panelling, much carved woodwork, ceiling bosses, gallery fronts and pews. A crowded interior, not archaeologically correct at all but an outstanding example of the earlier phase of the Gothic revival, ornament on this scale normally being precluded by cost. The outstanding 15C stained glass was originally all in the E window. Off the W end of Stamford St, in Henry Sq, *Public Baths* (1870; Paull and Ayliffe), brick N Italian Romanesque to Gothic with a campanile tower. Converted to offices. SW of St. Peter's Church, by the canal, in Oxford St, *Oxford Mills* (1845 and 1851) with associated mill housing and Institute provided by the Mason family, leading Ashton industrialists. 1½m W of St. Peter's Church, off Manchester Rd, neo-Georgian *garden suburb* in Broadway (1913; Wood and Sellers) laid out as an extension to the 18C Moravian Settlement at **Fairfield**. 1½m W of Ashton, at **Droylsden**, A662, *Town Hall* (1858; Waterhouse) plain, in banded brick with segmental arched windows. 1m NE of Ashton, B6194, **Hurst**, built up around the *mills*, Queen's Rd, of the Whitaker family, founded 1808. In Queen's Rd, *Methodist church* (1846; W. Hayley) with fine monument to J. Whitaker (died 1840) by J.H. Foley. The parish *church* (1847; Shellard: tower and transepts 1862; G. Shaw), Kings Rd, was a Whitaker foundation. On A670, Mossley Rd, *Ladysmith Barracks* (1841–43), parade ground flanked by late Georgian style buildings, main entry aligned with a pedimented officers' mess. **Mossley**, to NE, A670, is a mill town on the steep valley sides of the Tame with large, mostly late 19C red brick mills in the valley.

1m N of Oldham, A671, **Royton**. At S end, in Broadway, A663, *St. Anne's Church* (1908–10; Temple Moore), fine work in late Gothic style with tall continuous roof and sheer S tower in the manner of Bodley. Wagon roof with passage aisles and simplified pointed arcading. School to N by Temple Moore (1916). 1m NW of Oldham, A669, at **Chadderton** *Town Hall* (1912; Taylor and Simister), red brick and stone 18C style with domed centre. 2m W, A669, **Middleton**, notable for the work of Edgar Wood, advanced Arts and Crafts architect of the turn of the century. In the Market Place, *Williams and Glyns Bank* (1893; E. Wood) faience-clad free Elizabethan. In Long St, *Methodist church* (1899–1901; E. Wood), Gothic group of church and schools, the church brick and red stone, schools rendered, relatively simple details but picturesquely arranged. Arts and Crafts furnishings, notably the pulpit, screen and font. Oak stalls and ceremonial chairs, the stalls emphasising plain construction in the Arts and Crafts way, the chairs with abstract inlaid decoration reminiscent of C.R. Mackintosh. To W, at end of Durnford St, *schools* (1908–10; Wood and Sellers), remarkably modern in design, flat-roofed with large centre block and towers terminating the wings, the centre block and wings marked by sheer unornamented stone stair bays emphatically contrasted with the red brick of the main buildings. Just N, *No. 36 Mellalieu St* (1910; E. Wood) brick house but with stripped modern detail and flat concrete roof. Further N, *Nos 33–5 Rochdale Rd* (1891; E. Wood) asymmetrical pair of houses with big canted bay balancing a gable. Unmoulded window details in the manner of Voysey. S of Long St, *Nos 33–7 Manchester New Rd* (1908; E. Wood) concrete roofed group, much altered but with original chevron patterned decoration in green and white tile, a prototype for inter-war architecture. To W, in Archer Park, Sefton Rd, *Westdeane* (1889; E. Wood), Wood's first large house, still conventional with half-timber and tile-hanging. Just N, in Sunny Brow Rd, *Dunarden* (1897–98; E. Wood), roughcast with hipped roof, tightly composed with two large five-sided bays. S of Oldham Rd, SE of centre, in Townley St, *St. Michael's Church* (1902; Austin and Paley) with fine NW tower. Off Oldham Rd, ½m E, in Elm St, *school* (1908–10; Wood and Sellers), the concrete roofs and brick decoration looking forward to the 1930s. Formal composition with arched-windowed hall rising over a low single-storey range, concave-curved enclosing a garden courtyard.

ROCHDALE. A627 6m N of Oldham. Cotton town from the late 18C, wool the main industry before that. It was at Rochdale that the British co-operative movement began when 28 poor labourers raised £28 to open a shop in Toad Lane in 1844. The co-operative movement was the foundation of British socialism, and the model of the Rochdale Equitable Pioneers was taken up all over Britain, providing cheaper goods, security against debt, a savings bank, libraries and educational opportunities for the members. Rochdale's most famous native was John Bright (1811–89), radical politician and the outstanding orator of his time. Bright joined Cobden to fight for the repeal of the Corn Laws and spoke for free trade, freedom of religion and electoral reform during a long career in parliament.

In the centre, *⋅Town Hall* (1866–71; W.H. Crossland), splendid Gothic building based on Flemish cloth halls, the great hall in the centre, parallel to the street, flanked in a near symmetrical composition by gable ranges at right angles, the gables stepped in the Flemish way. To left, almost independent, the 190ft clock tower. Its remarkable silhouette of stunted spire is due to A. Waterhouse who replaced the top stage (1883). Complete Gothic interiors with vaulted lower hall and stair hall. Great Hall with hammerbeam roof and vast wall-painting of the signing of Magna Carta (1870; H. Holiday). Painted decoration and fine carving throughout the main rooms. In the park behind, *statue* of Bright (1891; H. Thornycroft). Above the park, parish *church*, much restored with chancel 1883 (J.S. Crowther) and W window stained glass by Morris and Co (1872). Medieval stalls and screens much enriched in the 19C. The 18C vicarage next door is now *Rochdale Museum* with material relating to J. Bright. W of the Town Hall, *Library* (1883; J. Horsfall) linked to *Art Gallery* (1903–12). In Toad Lane, N of centre, *St. Mary's Church* (1740: 1909–11; J.N. Comper), the classical N wall of the 18C church retained with part of the arcade, to which Comper added a new nave in his late Perp. style achieving the fusion between classic and Gothic characteristic of Comper's later work, emphasised by the cupola over the nave. Fine light interior, stone faced with rood screen by Comper. The original shop of the Rochdale Pioneers is now the *Co-operative Museum*. NW of centre, off Spotland Rd, in Royds St, *St. Edmund's Church* (1873; J.M. and H. Taylor) expensively built for A.H. Royd with central crossing tower and roofs of outstanding complexity. Other churches by J.M. Taylor with his characteristic High Victorian angularity are *St. Peter's* (1868–71), to SE, off Moss St, S of Milnrow, in crazed rubble and red brick, *St. Mary's* (1871), Oldham Rd, Balderstone, 1½m SE, A671, with prominent spire and *All Saints'*, Foxholes Rd, off Park Rd,

N of Yorkshire St, A58. In Manchester Rd, to S, A58, *George and Dragon Hotel* (1897; E. Wood) free Tudor and *St. Aidan's Church* (1914; Temple Moore), further S, severe lancet Gothic with W tower, chancel higher than nave and the interior luminously white with severe square piers and unmoulded arches. Chancel with triforium and clerestory, differing treatment to each side. To W, on Bolton Rd, A58, at **Marland**, *Barcroft* (1894; E. Wood) farmhouse style Arts and Crafts house with stone-tiled roof and mullion windows.

3m N of Rochdale, A671, at **Healey**, *Healey Dell Viaduct* (1870; J. Hawkshaw), romantic 105ft rubble-stone viaduct on the disused line to Bacup. 5m NE of Rochdale, A6033, *Summit Tunnel* (1841; G. Stephenson), the longest tunnel in the world when built, with massive stone W portal. 2m E of Rochdale, A663, at **Milnrow**, *church* (1869; G.E. Street), with W tower and pyramid cap. Naturalistic carved capitals by T. Earp.

SALFORD. Twin city to Manchester, separated only by the River Irwell, but the centres otherwise continuous. Industrial town developed simultaneously with Manchester. The centre is Chapel St, cut up by the complex of railway lines running into Manchester Victoria. At corner of Irwell St, Gothic *bank* (c 1875). Opposite, in Bexley Square, *Town Hall* (1825; R. Lane) Greek Doric. To W, *Education Offices* (1895; Woodhouse and Willoughby) yellow terracotta, Northern Renaissance style, and *RC Cathedral* (1844–48; Weightman and Hadfield), fine Dec. work with central spire and vaulted choir, cathedral scale achieved by tall proportions. To W, St Philip's Place, aligned on *St. Philip's Church* (1825; R. Smirke) classical with round tower over Ionic semi-circular porch. In Encombe Place, behind, *Court House* (c 1865; C. Reeves) palazzo style, stone and brick. To W, N of The Crescent, *Library and Art Gallery*, Renaissance style in brick, partly 1850s (Travis and Mangnall), the first free municipal library in Britain. Statues of Victoria and Albert (1854 and 1864; M. Noble) in front. The oldest part of the *University of Salford* is the former Technical College (1896; H. Lord) next to the Art Gallery.

To NW, A6, at **Pendleton**, *Town Hall* (1865; A. Darbyshire) Venetian Gothic with steep slate roofs and *St. Thomas' Church* (1829–31; F. Goodwin and R. Lane) Perp. style Commissioners' church. To NW, in Eccles Old Rd, A576, *Buile Hill* (1825–27; C. Barry) one of Barry's first works, top storey and porte-cochère added 1860s. Now part of the *Museum of Mining*. NE of Pendleton, A576, in Gerald Rd, W of Cromwell Rd, *St. Sebastian's Church* (1900; Sinnott, Sinnott and Powell), severe lancet Gothic church in red brick with interesting interior, passage aisles and apse-narrow ambulatory of tall granite shafts. A576 continues NE to *Albert Park* (1877) and an area of villas of c 1840–50. On Great Cheetham St, E of A56, *St. James' Church* (1879; Paley and Austin) brick outside and inside, steep gabled. On Bury New Road, A56, *Greek Orthodox church* (1860; Clegg and Knowles) Corinthian classical with fine portico. SW of Salford, **Ordsall**, with docks of the *Manchester Ship Canal. Custom House* (1903), Trafford Rd. Off Ordsall Lane, St. Clement's Drive, *St. Clement's Church* (1877; Paley and Austin), brick, with tall interior and brick-vaulted chancel. To S, over the Irwell, **Stretford**. Over the bridge, in Chester Rd, Old Trafford, *Royal Deaf Schools* (1836–37; R. Lane) two Gothic ranges, originally joined by a chapel. Chester Rd, A56, runs SW, past *St. Anne's RC Church* (1862–67; E.W. Pugin), ornate with W rose window and NW spire, to the centre with old *Town Hall* (1879; Lofthouse) Gothic. John Rylands, industrialist and donor of the Rylands Library,

Manchester, lived at *Longford Hall* (1857) in Longford Park, Edge Lane.

2m W of Salford, A57, **Eccles**, cotton and silk manufacturing town. In the centre, *Town Hall* (1880; J. Lowe) and Baroque style *Library* (1907; E. Potts). To W, at **Patricroft**, Green Lane runs N to *Bridgwater Mill* (1836), now Royal Ordnance factory, built as the Britannia Iron Works for John Nasmyth, inventor of the steam hammer. The works are on the Bridgewater Canal. S of A57, Barton Rd follows the canal to the Manchester Ship Canal at **Barton upon Irwell**. A swing bridge carries the Bridgewater Canal over the Ship Canal. Just over the canal two churches side by side, *St. Catherine's* (1843; E. Welch) and *All Saints' RC* (1867–68; E.W. Pugin), highly elaborate church built for the de Trafford family, partly as their mausoleum. W rose window, polygonal apse and stone vaulting to the chancel and de Trafford chapel, the chapel vault springing from thin shafts free-standing just behind the thick arcade columns. Rich carving throughout and wall-painting over the chancel arch. At **Higher Irlam**, A57, 3m SW, *church* (1865; J.M. Taylor), High Victorian with W rose and elaborate roofs. 2m NW of Patricroft, B5211, **Worsley**, former seat of the Dukes of Bridgewater. The 3rd Duke built the Bridgewater Canal 1759–61. His successor, the 1st Earl of Ellesmere, built Worsley Hall, now demolished, and the *church* (1846; G.G. Scott) with richly carved spire, original bright stained glass in E and S chapel windows and effigy of the Earl of Ellesmere (died 1857) by M. Noble on tomb chest by Scott. 1½m N at **Walkden**, A575, *Ellesmere Memorial* (1868; T.G. Jackson), High Victorian Gothic tabernacle memorial to the Countess of Ellesmere. To NW, off Manchester Rd, A6, at **Peel**, *Peel Hall* (c 1850–60), red-brick and stone mansion, asymmetrical with Gothic to Jacobean detail. Now a hospital. 2m E, A6, at **Swinton**, *church* (1869; G.E. Street), stone with W tower, Dec. with finely traceried E window and arcade with carved capitals (T. Earp). Aisles and chancel chapels separately roofed giving a triple gabled outline. Built for the Rev H. Heywood of the Manchester banking family. 1m E, at **Pendlebury**, A666, *St. Augustine's Church* (1871–74; G.F. Bodley) built for E.S. Heywood, brother of the Rev. H. Heywood. One of the finest Victorian churches. Brick exterior, majestically tall, a single long vessel with a great E window in a wall elaborated with stone panelling, 10-bay sides, of finely traceried windows divided by shallow buttresses, the last bay to E canted inward. Masterly interior, a single space, wagon-roofed with internal buttressing and the aisles reduced to a mere passage through the piers. This gives an even rhythm of lofty arches each side framing the windows, culminating in the great E window, a wall of light set high above the painted reredos. Organ and screen by Bodley. Stained glass by Burlison and Grylls. *Gatehouse* and *school* by Bodley, originally also with parsonage to complete the group. At SE end of Bolton Rd, *St. John's Church* (1842) neo-Norman. ¾m NW of St. Augustine's, at **Clifton**, A666, *church* (1874; E.M. Barry) High Victorian with W rose window.

4m N of Salford, A56, at **Prestwich**, *St. Mary's Church*, Church Lane, medieval with tall E end of 1888 (Paley and Austin). *Philips Park*, to NW, reached from Stand, is the park of the demolished villa of the Philips family, leading Manchester merchants and politicians. **Stand** *church* at Church Lane, Whitefield, was Sir C. Barry's first work (1822), elaborate pinnacled and battlemented work with W tower, in the Georgian Gothic mode with plaster vaults.

STOCKPORT. A6 5m SE of Manchester. Cotton town, the centre steeply set on the S bank of the Mersey. *Stockport Viaduct* (1842; G.W. Buck) crosses the valley on 27 brick arches, the tallest 110ft high. The old centre is around Market Place with *Market Hall* of 1861. St. Peter's Gate runs SW crossing Little Underbank on an iron bridge (1868) to St. Peter's Church and the *Cobden Monument* (1862; G.G. Adams) to the radical MP and Free Trader. On Wellington Rd, A6, *Library* (1912; Bradshaw, Gass and Hope). Beyond, monumental Edwardian Baroque *˙Town Hall* (1904–08; A.B. Thomas), an astonishing display, presumably intended to emphasise Stockport's separate identity from Manchester. Two Baroque pedimented frontispieces flank the porch and act as launching pad for the central steeple, an encrusted variation on Wren, plain wings stretch each side, the whole faced in Portland stone. Marbled stair hall inside. The composition needs an avenue approach. Opposite, Greek revival *Infirmary* (1832; R. Lane). To S, *College of Technology* (1888; G. Sedger) and further down, to E, facing down St. Thomas' St, *St. Thomas' Church* (1822–25; G. Basevi), classical with cupola-capped tower and a portico at the E end. Further S, in Buxton Rd, *˙St. George's Church* (1896; Austin and Paley), beautifully detailed Perp. crowned by a 230ft spire over the crossing. A major work of the late Gothic Revival, sensitive and scholarly, every moulding precisely considered. Long interior vista to the broad E window. The church was built for G. Fearn, brewer, with the school and vicarage adjoining. His monument in the Corporation *cemetery* opposite is a model of the church spire.

2m W of Stockport, A560, **Cheadle**, the *Town Hall*, off Manchester Rd, is Abney Hall, the country villa of J. Watts, Manchester merchant, owner of Watts Warehouse. Brick, Tudor Gothic, originally of 1847 but much enlarged for Watts after 1849 (Travis and Mangnall) with further additions 1893 (G.F. Armitage). The remarkable feature of the house is the Gothic interior (1852–57), the earliest designs by A.W.N. Pugin, and the whole scheme executed and completed by J.G. Crace in the Pugin manner. Doorcases, fireplaces and ceilings panelled and painted, the stair hall crowned by an octagonal lantern, details of metalwork (Hardman) such as hinges especially good. One of the most complete surviving Puginian interiors. S of centre, off A5149, Wilmslow Rd, *Bruntwood Hall* (1861) large Elizabethan style manufacturer's house. 4m SE of Stockport, A626, **Marple**, at the junction of the Peak Forest and Macclesfield Canals. Cotton manufacture was begun at Marple in 1790 by S. Oldknow and the Peak Forest Canal (1800) was promoted by Oldknow to serve his mills. A canal *warehouse* survives in St. Martin's Rd with arches each end for boats to enter. By Marple Station, A626, *˙St. Martin's Church* (1869–70; J.D. Sedding), a simple stone building, possibly designed by Sedding's brother who died 1868, with handsome original fittings, screen, pulpit and reredos by Sedding and chancel glass by Morris and Co., the E window figures by Ford Madox Brown. Additions of outstanding quality by H. Wilson, N chapel (1895) and N aisle (c 1909), in Arts and Crafts to Art Nouveau taste. N chapel apsed and decorated with frieze of birds and trees in the vault. Inlaid altar rails and altar by Wilson, reredos by C. Whall. The oak and ebony font cover carrying a gilded iron open ball of Art Nouveau plant forms is exceptional. W and SW windows by C. Whall. By J.D. Sedding, the *school* (1869) behind, and *vicarage* (1873), St. Martin's Rd, the vicarage an advanced design leaving the Gothic for a free 17C style. 3m NW, at **Romiley**, B6104, *church* (1864–65; J.M. Taylor) wilfully blunt High Victorian. To S, *Oakwood Hall* (1844; E. Walters), Oakwood Road, stone Tudor style mill-owner's house set above the River Goyt.

2m N of Stockport, B6167, **Reddish**, mill town of the Houldsworth family whose magnificent brick *mill (1865) faces down Rupert St with giant arched bays flanked by Italianate towers. The Houldsworth family built some workers' housing by the mill at the W end of Leamington Rd and the outstanding group by A. Waterhouse of church, rectory, school and club nearby. The *church (1882–83) is Waterhouse's major ecclesiastical work, a powerful Romanesque design in brick and stone going early Gothic inside where height and width are quite spectacular, the arcade arches very wide and carried on massive granite columns with stylised foliage caps. The chancel, divided off by a marble Byzantinesque screen, is rib-vaulted and apsed with marble lining to the sanctuary. There are echoes of Butterfield's Keble College chapel, though the crisp detail of all the carving is typically Waterhouse. 5m NE of Stockport, A560, **Hyde**, cotton town. To S, on Stockport Rd, Gee Cross, *Unitarian chapel* (1846–48; Bowman and Crowther), fully ecclesiastical in the manner of contemporary Anglican churches, one of the first chapels to adopt ecclesiological strictures on correct Gothic style and planning. Just E, in Higham Lane, *Holy Trinity Church* (1873; J.M. Taylor), idiosyncratic Gothic, bargeboards to the roofs and inside complex roof timbering. Another Taylor work with similar harsh detail is *St. Thomas' Church* (1867–88), Lumn Rd, ¾m N, the walls of crazed rubble with brick.

WIGAN. A577 18m W of Manchester. Textile town from the 18C. Parish *church* rebuilt 1845–50 (Sharpe and Paley) reconstructing the medieval original. E and W windows by Wailes, encaustic tiling in the chancel by Minton and ornately carved stalls. One S aisle window by Morris (1868), three by Hardman (1855–66) and four N aisle windows by Clayton and Bell (1872–99). Gothic monuments in S chapel to the Lindsay family, Earls of Crawford, for whom the church was rebuilt. In Standishgate, two RC churches, *St. John's* (1819) classical, with Gothic cross in front (1852; Pugin), and *St. Mary's* (1818) Perp., testimony to the strength of Catholicism in Lancashire before Catholic Emancipation. *National Westminster Bank* (c 1870–75) French Loire style. In Church St, office front (c 1880) with oriel bays in the manner of Norman Shaw. In New Market, *Wigan Hall* (1875; G.E. Street), the rectory, in stone and half-timber with brick infill. Gatehouse to the street also half-timbered above. *School* opposite by Street (1867). In Rodney St, Gothic *Library* (1878; Waterhouse). SW of centre, A571, Billinge Rd, at **Highfield**, *St. Matthew's Church* (1894; Austin and Paley), refined EE with central tower and spire, all in superbly crafted red sandstone. S of centre, at **Poolstock**, *St. James' Church* (1866; E.G. Paley), large Dec. style with ornate chancel decoration of 1877.

1½m E of Wigan, A577, at **Lower Ince**, *St. Mary's Church*, (1887; Paley and Austin), large-scaled red-brick church with continuous roof and crowning flèche. Plain severe internal detail with passage aisles and vaulted chancel. At **Hindley**, 1½m E, *Library* (1886; T. Worthington) asymmetrical Elizabethan with tower. *St. Peter's Church* (1866; E.G. Paley), Atherton St, conventional Dec. with broach spire. At **Hindley Green**, 1m SE, *church* (c 1895; C.E. Deacon) free Gothic in brick. 1m SE, A578, at **Westleigh**, Firs Lane, *St. Peter's Church* (1880; Paley and Austin), brick church with crossing tower, Dec. with noble interior, high timbered roofs, hammerbeams to chancel, interrupted by a tall brick vault under the crossing. The detail, as always with Paley and Austin, spare. At **Leigh**, 2m SE, A577, mill town with typical Lancashire turn of the century red-brick mills, the largest,

Alder Mill, N of Chapel St, of 1907 with cupola over the tower. In the centre, Baroque *Town Hall* (1904–07; J.C. Prestwich), a handsome work in the manner of c 1700 with hipped roof and cupola. Parish *church* opposite rebuilt, except tower, 1869–73 (Paley and Austin) in Perp. style to match tower. 4m S of Wigan, A49, **Ashton-in-Makerfield**, with central *Library* (1905; J. and W. Thornely), red brick and stone with ogee-capped angle turrets. *St. Thomas' Church* (1891; F. Oldham) red sandstone, free Gothic.

MERSEYSIDE

BIRKENHEAD. 1m W of Liverpool, across Mersey. Port and ship-building town developed from 1824 by W. Laird, founder of the Laird shipbuilding firm, constructors of the first iron ship built in England (1829) and of the famous Confederate privateer 'Alabama' (1862). The *docks*, N of the centre along Wallasey Pool, originally a marshy creek, were begun 1844–47, but most of the present complex dates from after 1855 when Liverpool Corporation absorbed the potential rival. Laird's new town was laid out on a grid pattern parallel with the docks. The layout and the design of the main square, *Hamilton Square* (1825–44), echo the Edinburgh New Town, where J. Gillespie Graham, Laird's architect, designed the Moray Place area. Handsome late classical fragments are to be found around Hamilton Square, but Birkenhead's development was more piecemeal than consistent, Hamilton Square itself only complete on one side by 1839. In the Square, *Town Hall* (1883–87; C.O. Ellison), symmetrical porticoed front and tall central tower (heightened 1903), on the model of Bolton Town Hall. In Hamilton St, *Nos 24–8* (1844–47), palazzo style, the richer Renaissance manner that superseded Graham's classicism when building restarted in the 1840s. *Hamilton Square Station* (1886; G.E. Grayson) serves the railway under the Mersey, some 100ft below ground. Massive red-brick Romanesque style tower to hold water for the hydraulic lifts. In Chester St, behind Town Hall, *Sessions House* (1884–87; T.D. Barry) and, further S, *Assembly Rooms* (1846; E. Welch) on the edge of the original shopping area of *Market Cross* (1847; W. Scott), of which one of the two triangular blocks survives. Italian palazzo details. *Market Hall* (c 1843–45; Fox and Henderson), early iron interior by the engineers of the Crystal Palace. At S end of Hamilton St, former *N. and S. Wales Bank* (1880; J.P. Seddon), stone High Victorian Gothic, now Midland Bank.

Conway St runs W to *• Birkenhead Park*, laid out 1843–47 (J. Paxton) and, with Princes Park, Liverpool, influential in the design of public parks throughout Britain and abroad. Picturesque and irregular landscaping with thick planting concentrated around the two lakes, one crossed by a covered Swiss style timber bridge, and an encircling drive lined with villas and terraces to finance the scheme. The architectural styles of the houses are varied as also are the attractive stone lodges and gates at each main entry, the lodges a textbook of the architectural vocabulary available once classical restraint was abandoned. Villa suburbs were built outside the original grid, Clifton Park (c 1843; W. Scott), SW of Birkenhead Central Station, and around Devonshire Rd (c 1843; C. Reed) S of Birkenhead Park, both with attractive stone villas, and in Devonshire Rd, *Kenyon Terrace* (1844–48), a handsome terrace group. W of Devonshire Rd begin the larger villas of the manufacturers and bankers of Liverpool and Birkenhead, taking the higher ground looking W towards the sea. In Devonshire Place, *Redcourt* (1876–79; E. Kirby), built for G. Rae, banker and patron of the Pre-Raphaelites, now St. Anselm's Junior School. W of Grosvenor Rd, *St. Aidan's College* (1854–56; T.H. Wyatt and H. Cole), Tudor style theological college in brick. Chapel (1881; D. Walker). In Shrewsbury Rd, Bidston Rd and Noctorum Lane large villas of the later 19C. On Bidston Rd, *St. Saviour's Church* (1889–92; C.W. Harvey) with central tower and expensive fittings, some, including screen, by E. Rae, son of G. Rae. W window (1903; Morris and Co) to G. Rae. Reredos by Bodley (1906). 2½m SW of Birkenhead, **Prenton**, with early 20C wealthy suburb on Prenton Hill. *St. Stephen's Church* (1897–1909; C.E. Deacon), Prenton Lane, handsome freely detailed sandstone, brick inside. Simplified detail but the furnishings, by Deacon, exceptionally good, slightly Art Nouveau. The houses on Prenton Hill show the variety of early 20C domestic design, some brick, some rendered and some half-timbered. By A. Thorneley, *Manor House* (1909), *Pine Grove* (c 1910) and *The Homestead* (c 1909), all in Mountwood Rd, the last Thorneley's own house. The pinewoods, golf course and open views to W create the Edwardian suburban ideal.

S of Birkenhead, on the Mersey, **Rock Ferry**, the best part, *Rock Park*, a villa estate (1836–37; J. Bennison), where N. Hawthorne lived (1853–56) while American consul in Liverpool and finished writing 'Tanglewood Tales', has sadly been battered by a bypass but several early stuccoed and stone villas survive. Just S, between New Chester Rd and Greendale Rd, *Port Sunlight, the model community built by W.H. Lever, Lord Leverhulme, around his Sunlight soap factory. The factory moved here in 1888, and still survives in Wood St, and the village was largely completed by 1914, Lever insisting that every worker should have a house with proper garden and that the social life of the community should be provided for with recreation halls, social clubs, schools and technical college. The initial picturesque layout around sunken channels, former inlets off the Bromborough Pool, was formalised after 1910 so that the part N of Bolton Rd with avenues aligned on the Art Gallery has an Edwardian Imperial flavour absent in the earlier village by the factory. W. Owen was Lever's principal architect but for the housing many of the leading architects local and national were employed, the overall pattern being red brick and roughcast or half-timber, generally of the vernacular Tudor, but here and there much more elaborate. N of the factory the remaining channel is landscaped into an attractive garden, The Dell. Half-timbered houses overlooking from Park Rd (1892–94; W. and S. Owen: Nos 19–23 by Douglas and Fordham), more formal brick and terracotta in Cross St (*Nos 1–9* c 1896; Grayson and Ould), brick and stone Jacobean in Bath St (1896; J.J. Talbot). In Bridge St, *Lyceum* (1894; Douglas and Fordham) quite elaborate Jacobean, built as the school. In Bolton Rd, *Bridge Inn* (1900; Grayson and Ould), roughcast around a forecourt, originally temperance. The earliest houses of the estate are at the W end of Bolton Rd (1889; W. Owen). The main N–S axis intersects with The Causeway at the *War Memorial* (1919–21; W. Goscombe John), The Causeway aligned on the *church* (1902–04; W. and S. Owen), red sandstone, free Gothic. In the Lady Lever memorial loggia at the W end (1914), bronze effigies of Lord and Lady Lever. The *Lady Lever Art Gallery* (1914–22; W. and S. Owen) is monumental classical in Portland stone, long and low with domes over the wings and Ionic columned porticoes. Outstanding collection especially of 19C painting, including Holman Hunt's 'The Scapegoat' and Burne Jones' 'The Beguiling of Merlin'. The objects were all from Lord Lever's own collection. Behind, in Lower Rd, *Nos 15–27* (c 1906; C.H. Reilly), roughcast shallow crescent with full-length iron verandah and arched dormers. Other notable architects active in Port Sunlight include George and Yeates (Nos 25–9 and 33–9 Greendale Rd c 1901 and 178–90 New Chester Rd 1897), E. Newton (67–79 Bebington Rd 1897), E. Lutyens (17–23 Corniche Rd), J. Douglas (55–67 Pool Bank c 1899) and M.B. Adams (59–63 Greendale Rd c 1899). E of New Chester Rd, just S of Port Sunlight, Pool Lane leads to *Bromborough Pool Village*, an earlier industrial settlement begun 1853 for the Price's Candle Co., enlightened employers for the time, though by comparison with Lever's magnificence the three parallel streets are very modest. At **Bromborough**, to S, Merseyside industrialists had large villas. The *church* (1862–64; G.G. Scott) is appropriately scaled with broach spire, apse and well-composed S elevation of gabled aisle windows under circular clerestory openings. **Eastham Ferry**, to SE, was once important on the journey from Chester to Liverpool, the docks to S are the terminus of the Manchester Ship Canal.

On the W side of the Wirral peninsula the villages overlooking the sea became favourite retreats for wealthy industrialists. From S, **Thornton Hough**, B5136, 3m SW of Port Sunlight, is a complete *estate village, a recreation of old England with stone and timbered cottages, some set around a broad village green and almost all the creation of W.H. Lever who bought the Thornton Manor estate in 1891. J. Hirst, Yorkshire textile manufacturer, who had previously owned the estate, had built the Gothic *church*, *vicarage* and *school* (1866–68; Kirk and Sons) and *Wilshaw Terrace* (1870) with its turret. Lever bought Thornton Manor, his brother bought Hirst's house, Thornton House, their father built Hesketh Grange, and the rebuilding of the village followed. The cottages are very varied, the timber-framing becoming more archaeological in the later examples, the quality of detail exceptionally good. Lever built the neo-Norman *Congregational church* (1906–07; J. Lomax-Simpson), very handsome with crossing tower and apsed E end, the *Lever School* (1904; J. Simpson) and the *Village* (originally *Liberal*) *Club* (c 1904; Grayson and Ould), providing, as at Port Sunlight, for all his tenants' needs. *Thornton House*, originally built for J. Hirst, was rebuilt 1895 (Grayson and Ould) and extended 1906 (J. Lomax-Simpson) for J.D. Lever, stone and half-timber exceptionally sensitively done. On the way to Thornton Manor, *Hesketh Grange* (1894; Grayson and Ould), ornately plastered over a stone ground floor. Lever's own house, *Thornton Manor*, is the product of piecemeal expansion from the original early Victorian villa to the present monumental red sandstone Elizabethan style mansion, of which the severe S front (1913; J. Lomax-Simpson) was intended as the model for a final recasing interrupted by the 1914 war. The more picturesque entrance front (1896–97; Douglas and Fordham) was to have been replaced and a complete quadrangle formed linked to the half-timbered gatehouse (1910; Lomax-Simpson). Interiors in richly panelled 18C style and a vast barrel-vaulted Music Room (1902; J.J. Talbot) modelled on Norman Shaw's Dawpool. Terraced gardens (1905; T.H. Mawson), lake and avenues of trees complete the picture of a great country estate. To NW, A540, at **Thurstaston**, *Dawpool*, Norman Shaw's great house for the ship-owner T.H. Ismay has been demolished but the stables (1892) survive N of the church. The *church* (1883–86; J.L. Pearson) is a small-scale masterpiece with sturdy tower and spire between the nave and higher chancel. The interior is fully vaulted and stone-lined, quadripartite vaults springing low and the choir arch infilled with stone tracery on two slim shafts. To all this stone severity a carved reredos by Pearson and fine wooden organ case (1905; R. Norman Shaw) with painted side panels provide contrast. Stained glass by Clayton and Bell. In the churchyard, lychgate and stone chest tomb to T.H. Ismay of Dawpool by Norman Shaw.

1½m NW, at **Caldy**, *Caldy Manor Hospital*, Elizabethan-style mansion partly mid Victorian for R.W. Barton, Manchester merchant, partly early 20C for A.P. Eccles, Liverpool cotton broker. Pretty timbered tower on the road front, originally part of a chapel (1882; C.E. Kempe). *Church* adjoining, built as a school (1868; G.E. Street) but given a chancel and tower (1906–07; Douglas and Minshull) when converted. Reredos and some fittings by Kempe, originally in the chapel at Caldy Manor. Estate *cottages* (c 1832–45; R.B. Rampling) and *church hall* (1883) built for the Barton family. Early 20C villas on Caldy Rd, Croft Drive and King's Drive, up Caldy Hill. To E, across A540, *Hill Bark, Montgomery Hill, originally built at Bidston, Birkenhead (1891; Grayson and Ould) and re-erected here 1929–31, one of the finest recreations of timber-framed houses in the country. Little Moreton Hall, Cheshire, was the model for the spectacular patterned timber-work, the entrance court an array of irregularly placed gables, dormers and bay windows culminating in shaped and moulded brick chimneys. Unlike much earlier Victorian half-timber work this is pastiche done with knowledge, flair and sensitivity. Fine timbered great hall set across the depth of the house with Morris and Co stained glass, remnant of a complete scheme of decoration in Arts and Crafts style. *Hill Bark Farm* (1875; J. Douglas), just E, is a good stone and half-timber model farm group. **Frankby** *church* (1861; W. and J. Hay), to NE, has excellent Morris and Co. glass (1873) in N aisle. To W, at **West Kirby**, the parish *church*, Church Rd, has an extensive series of windows by C.E. Kempe (1870–1907). To N, on the road to Hoylake, *St. Andrew's Church* (1889–1909; J. Douglas), handsome free Perp. stone church with crossing spire, the roofs stepped up from transepts to nave to chancel. Meols Drive runs N to **Hoylake** at the NW corner of the peninsula, a resort mostly of the later 19C. In Stanley Rd, W of the station, *church* (1897; E. Kirby) in brick and terracotta, the interior brickwork particularly striking. Lavishly carved woodwork to the reredos and pulpit. At the NE tip of the peninsula, N of Birkenhead, **New Brighton**, developed as a resort from 1830. On Perch Rock, off Marine Promenade, *Lighthouse* (1827–30; J. Foster) and *Fort* (1826–29; J.S. Kitson RE) to defend the approach to Liverpool. Seabank Rd runs S towards **Wallasey** *Town Hall* (1914–20; Briggs, Wolstenholme and Thornely), Edwardian Imperial with central tower, proudly overlooking Liverpool. In Seabank Rd, to N, *Presbyterian church* (1907; Briggs, Wolstenholme and Thornely), impressive free Gothic, and *Aged Mariners' Home* (1882–91; D. Walker), composed around a central tower with turrets and spire.

LIVERPOOL. City built on the Atlantic trade. The great boom years from the late 18C to the early 20C, the import of cotton replacing the slave trade, saw the creation of one of the world's busiest ports. Bombing, catastrophic decline in the Atlantic trade and 20C road schemes have damaged much but Liverpool remains one of the great Victorian cities. Centre on a rough W–E axis between the pierhead on the Mersey and the group of civic buildings by Lime St Station. The centrepiece of the civic group, St. George's Plateau, is *St. George's Hall* (1841–56), a neo-classical building of outstanding merit designed by H.L. Elmes to contain a great hall, concert hall and assize courts, completed after Elmes' death by C.R. Cockerell. The building displays resourcefulness in using Greek detail on a monumental scale comparable with Schinkel's work in Germany. Giant Corinthian order, a full portico on the S end, apsed N end and, on the long E entrance front, a 14-column flat portico echoed each side by giant square pillars initially encased between sculptured panels but free-standing above as a deep loggia. The effect is heroic in scale, boldly modelled and made the more grand by the great flights of steps that act as a podium. Interiors by Cockerell of matching grandeur, great tunnel-vaulted main hall with granite columns, rich tiled floor and a fine collection of statuary including G. Stephenson (1851; J. Gibson), Sir R. Peel (1852; Noble) and Sir W. Brown (1858; MacDowell). Fittings and organ by Cockerell. The Concert Room at the N end is the richest in decoration, a circular space with undulating lattice-fronted balcony held up by classical maidens. Renaissance style wall and ceiling decoration.

The plateau outside acquired a full set of monumental *statuary* beginning with the *Wellington Column* (1863; G.A. Lawson) and Steble *fountain* (1879; W. Cunliffe) to N, equestrian statues of Victoria (1870) and Albert (1866) by T. Thornycroft to E, continuing with Disraeli (1883; C. Birch), on the steps, and Maj.-Gen. Earle (1883; Birch) at SE corner. W of the Hall, turn of the century memorials, Gladstone (1904; T. Brock), King's Liverpool Regiment (1905; Goscombe John), three statues by G. Frampton and one by F.W. Pomeroy. Along the N side, group of classical civic buildings beginning to E with *Sessions House* (1882; F. and G. Holme) with paired columned portico, then *Walker Art Gallery* (1874–77; H.H. Vale) with Corinthian portico flanked by statues of Raphael and Michelangelo. The gallery contains an exceptional collection of Victorian painting and sculpture. Adjoining, circular front of the *Picton Reading Room* (1875–79; C. Sherlock) neatly disguising a change in axis, Corinthian columns ringing an almost unbroken rusticated wall. Domed reading room inside, and library behind (1906). Stepping down the hill, *Library and Museum* (1857–60; T. Allom), porticoed again with wings each side and, beyond, Edwardian Baroque *Technical College* (1897–1902; E.W. Mountford) with convex front to Byrom St and giant window niches with blocked columns on the W front. E of St. George's Hall, *Lime Street Station*, the front hotel 1868–71 (A. Waterhouse), grandly symmetrical with tall facade articulated by pavilion-roofed towers. Strong round-arched detail to the main front, relatively sober until the roofline with its array of towers, dormers chimneys and steep roofs. Two arched train-sheds behind (1867 and 1874; W. Baker and F. Stevenson).

From the plateau Victoria St and Dale St run parallel towards the river. On N side of Dale St, *Magistrates Courts* (1857–59; J. Weightman), classical, with *Fire Station* (1898) and *Transport Offices* (1905–07) behind in Hatton Garden, both by T. Shelmerdine, one free Jacobean, the other Imperial classical. On S side, *Municipal Offices* (1860–66; J. Weightman), French Renaissance style, very large with central tower and pyramid spire, giant columns, and pavilion roofs over the wings. Adjoining, former *Conservative Club* (1882; F. and G. Holme), similarly French. Adjoining to W, two later 19C Gothic buildings before *Prudential Building* (1885; A. Waterhouse) makes a typical show in bright red brick and terracotta. Near symmetrical original building with neatly handled corner to Temple St, the tower with chimney sprouting through the pavilion roof and E end section added 1906. On N side, opposite Stanley St, *National Westminster Bank* (c 1860), ornate stucco classical. On S side, *The Temple* (1864–65; J.A. Picton), characteristic rich palazzo style offices by the best Liverpool practitioner of the style. Beyond, *Royal Insurance* (1896–1903; J.F. Doyle) with long front to North John St, very handsome Baroque, influenced by Norman Shaw, with whom Doyle worked, but interestingly the prototype for Shaw's monumental Baroque work in Regent St, London. Much blocked rustication of an early 18C type and off-centre tower and cupola. Sculpted friezes by C.J. Allen. In North John St beyond, *Solicitors Law Stationery Society* (1854), Italianate with curved pediment and pretty circular windows beneath. In Victoria St, to SE, *Fowler's Buildings* (1864; J.A. Picton), fine four-storey warehouse, closely glazed. In Cook St, to W, *No. 16* (1866; P. Ellis), the second surviving building by Ellis, Liverpool's unacclaimed pioneer of a functional aesthetic based on cast-iron framing and maximum glazing set in a thin grid of stone mullions. Ellis never had another architectural commission after this. In the courtyard behind even the minimal stone thought necessary for a formal front is replaced by thin iron mullions, most remarkable in the cantilevered spiral staircase. At S end of North John St, pilastered classical *Clarence Building* (c 1850). In Dale St, opposite North John St, *Rigby's Buildings* (c 1850), richly stuccoed, and *Union Marine* (c 1863; Picton), strong featured, round-arched office building. Opposite, *No. 14* (1906; W.A. Thomas), free Gothic, and *Nos 8–10* (1837–39; S. Rowland), the former Royal Bank with grand Corinthian order to the upper floors. Behind, in Queen Avenue, slightly earlier banking hall (S. Rowland) with Greek detail and very rich plasterwork. Opposite, *Liverpool, London and Globe* building (1855–57; C.R. and F.P. Cockerell), palazzo style handled with originality and the crisp detail combined with careful variation of the wall plane characteristic of Cockerell's work. Upper Corinthian order and full cornice, splendid doorway, the doorcase set in a giant arched recess with bold swags. On the High St side the staircase unexpectedly reveals itself. The *Town Hall* of 1749 with dome of 1802 and portico of 1811 has early 20C wall-painting in the entrance hall and 19C Minton tile floor.

Castle St, running S, has office and bank buildings, mostly in classical to Renaissance styles, stone fronted. *Midland Bank* (c 1875; E. Salomons) is brick with ornamental brick frieze, *Nos 3–5* (1889; Grayson and Ould) and the *National Westminster Bank* (c 1885) are typical of the ornate late 19C rebuilding in Castle St. Further down, on W, former *Parr's Bank* (1899–1900; R. Norman Shaw), striking use of colour in a large-scaled relatively sober front of 18C type. Granite lower floors, banded marble above with red terracotta window frames, all intended to be washable against the city grime. On corner of Brunswick St, *Co-operative Bank* (1892; W.D. Caroe), Northern Renaissance in granite and red stone with fine bronze doors by Stirling Lee. On corner of Brunswick St and Fenwick St, *Halifax House* (c 1850–60), palazzo style former bank. On E side of Castle St, *No. 22* (c 1830–40), with upper Corinthian portico, and former *•Bank of England* (1845–48; C.R. Cockerell), like the similar banks in Manchester and Bristol a remarkable fusion of the different strands of classical design. Monumental scale is achieved by a massive Doric colonnade across the lower floors, but this strong Greek frontispiece is the base to a great Renaissance open pediment, deeply projecting to achieve depth of shadow. On W side, *No. 44* (c 1900), introducing colour in bright green glazed tiles and gilded carving in the pediment, *Nos 48–50* (1864; J.A. Picton), and *Midland Bank* (1868; Lucy and Littler), richly ornamented. In Derby Square, Baroque *Victoria Monument* (1902; E.M. Simpson), the statue and fine bronze groups around by C.J. Allen. By Midland Bank, *Castle Moat House* (1841; E. Corbett), an intriguing attempt to fit three storeys into the frame of a Roman temple with Corinthian pilasters and pediment. At W end of James St, *White Star offices* (1895; R. Norman Shaw), banded red brick and stone with corner turrets, a neat variant on Shaw's New Scotland Yard, London.

Fenwick St runs N to Water St, the W continuation of Dale St. On NE corner of Fenwick St, *National Westminster Bank* (1850) with giant Doric order and, to E, Renaissance style *bank* (c 1860) prettily detailed. On N side, *•No. 14 Oriel Chambers* (1864; P. Ellis), Ellis's major iron-framed building, the slenderest stone mullions framing bays each of three iron oriels with an attic window over. Minimal Gothic detail to the frame. The rear wall is entirely glass in the 20C way, quite exceptional for the date. Up Covent Garden to N, *Mersey Chambers* (c 1860–70), the rear here with iron oriel windows, the main front faces Old Churchyard. Adjoining, No. 5 Chapel St, *Hargreaves Building* (1861; J.A. Picton), palazzo style. In Old Hall St, N of Chapel St, on E side, *Albany Buildings* (1856; J.K. Colling), office and warehouse building for the cotton trade, palazzo style, but quite un-Italian because Colling, author of a work on Gothic ornament, has given all the carved work a lively Gothic feel, based on carefully observed plant forms. Opposite, *Harley Chambers* (1860), palazzo style, and *City Buildings* (1906; F. Fraser), complete iron and glass recasing of an earlier warehouse. The former *Cotton Exchange* (1905; Matear and Simon), centre of Liverpool trading, has lost its monumental front, though iron-framed side elevations survive. In Tithebarn St, E of Chapel St, former *Exchange Station* (1884; H. Shelmerdine), Renaissance style hotel, the station behind gone. *The Lion* pub has good late 19C tiles and glass. At W end of Water St, overlooking The Strand, *Tower Building* (1908; W.A. Thomas) steel-framed and white-tiled, the slightly medieval top layer because it stands on the site of the medieval Tower of Liverpool. On the pierhead, the three mammoths of the Liverpool waterfront, *Royal Liver Building* (1908–10; W.A. Thomas), *Cunard Building* (1913; Mewes and Davis) and the *Mersey Docks Offices* (1903–07; A. Thornely), contemporaries but quite different, the Liver Building one of the early reinforced concrete buildings, clad in stone and granite with twin towers somewhere between Spain and New York, the Cunard a Florentine palazzo much enlarged, and the Docks Offices ponderous Baroque with the ever popular St. Paul's Cathedral dome on top. In front, Edward VII statue (1916; Goscombe John), Sir A. Jones memorial (1913; G. Frampton) and monument to the 'Engine Room Heroes' (1916; Goscombe John), intended as a memorial to the engineers on the Titanic.

Liverpool Docks stretch for miles each side of the pierhead, the 18C docks having been on the pierhead site and immediately upstream, but mostly reconstructed during the 19C expansion. The docks as they stand now are still in large part a memorial to Jesse Hartley, dock engineer 1824–60; whose works, be they riverside walls, dock walls, warehouses or watchman's huts, are characterised by massive strength, enduring materials, such as granite and cast-iron, and a functional clarity in design. N of the pierhead, *Princes Dock* (1816–21: reconstructed 1860), *Waterloo Docks* (1834) with splendid *corn stores* (1867; G.F. Lybster) in brick with paired arched windows and rusticated stone arcade at dock level. Numerous fine brick warehouses survive along Waterloo Rd and Great Howard St. From Dublin St N to Sandhills Lane, granite *Dock Wall* (1848; J. Hartley), some 18ft high with massively detailed entrances and lodges to the various docks. *Collingwood and Salisbury Docks* (1848) are by Hartley, the river entrance to Salisbury Dock exemplary in the scale of the stonework. *Victoria Tower* at the entrance is one of a series of hydraulic towers by Hartley, granite, octagonal and castellated, best seen from the river. Inland of Collingwood Dock, *Stanley Dock* (1848; Hartley) connected to the Leeds–Liverpool canal. Gates, walls, two massive warehouses and hydraulic tower by Hartley, the warehouses on the waters edge, the first floor carried on massive cast-iron Doric columns. The S warehouse now stands behind a vast *tobacco warehouse* (1900). *Bonded tea warehouse* (c 1885) to S, on Dublin St. The docks continue N into Bootle, the six up to Canada Dock all part of Hartley's work. S of the pierhead are Liverpool's finest docks, slowly being rescued from dereliction. *Canning Dock* (1829) and *Half-Tide Dock* (1844) occupy part of the site of the Pool of Liverpool, converted to docks in 18C. The *Maritime Museum* now occupies the docks and the Pilotage Building nearby. Three octagonal watchman's huts (1844; Hartley) by the river entrance. To S, *Albert Dock* (1841–45; J. Hartley), the crown of the Mersey docks, the water surrounded on all sides by Hartley's stern brick warehouses with cast-iron colonnades and broad elliptical arches along the ground floors. Some of the severity has been lost in cleaning, but the effect of brick, iron and granite reflected in water is unforgettable. Behind, at NE corner, *Dock Traffic Office* (1846–47; P.C. Hardwick) with a portico to Canning Place entirely of cast-iron, the size of the castings beyond belief. *Wapping Dock* (1855; Hartley) has a similar row of warehouses on the E side, battlemented hydraulic tower and extraordinary oval watchman's hut at the gates. Warehouses survive behind the docks and in Jamaica St inland, notably *Alfred Warehouses* (1867). Further S, King's and Queen's Docks, late 18C much reconstructed, and *Brunswick Dock* (1832; J. Hartley).

Albert Dock (1841–45; J. Hartley), Liverpool

E of St. George's Hall, Lime St runs S from Lime St Station. By the station, *The Crown* (1905), splendid Art Nouveau plasterwork outside, and in the bars full range of fittings to match. In Lime St, *The Vines* (1907), one of two wonderfully ornate pubs by W. Thomas, the exterior all curly gables and corner turret, the interior sumptuous classical to Baroque with panelling, marble, beaten copper and much carving, and the *Adelphi Hotel* (1912; R.F. Atkinson), built for the Midland Railway, Portland stone, neo-Grecian detail more typical of the 1920s. In Ranelagh St, *The Central* pub has good c 1900 interior. Bold St, running SE, is aligned on the tower of the bombed *St. Luke's Church* (1811–31; J. Foster). Stuccoed late classical buildings, *Nos 43–7* (c 1855), palazzo style in stone, and, at far end, former *Liverpool Savings Bank* (1861; Culshaw), stone, Italianate. To S at top of Great George St, *Congregational church* (1840; J. Franklin) with handsome semicircular Corinthian porch and dome over. On the hill to E, *Liverpool Cathedral* (1904–79; Giles G. Scott), the Gothic landmark of the Liverpool skyline and the largest church in Britain. Scott's design changed much from the initial plan of 1903 which had twin towers. The great central tower set between double transepts was a modification of 1910, not completed until 1942. The power of Scott's building derives from a massive and simple outline, the tower rising sheer over the centre, the roof running evenly both sides. Much of the walling is smooth and unbroken, but where detail occurs, in the windows, parapets and top stage of the great tower, it is of the most delicate filigree sort, this contrast most masterly in the tower. The interior plan is unusual, a single central space under the tower and including the transept crossings, rising to 107ft under the tower arches lit by high windows each side, one of the sublime creations of the Gothic revival. The choir extends for three high and wide bays to an enormous E window over an ornate sculpted reredos, Spanish Gothic in inspiration. The Lady Chapel, off to one side, the first part built, has fine, vaulted interior, after the manner of Bodley. Altarpiece by Bodley and Scott. In SE transept bronze effigy of 16th Earl of Derby (died 1908) designed by Scott, made by Farmer and Brindley. E of the cathedral, *St. James' Cemetery* (1825–29), laid out in an old quarry, especially dramatic with the cathedral rising above. Domed *rotunda* (1836; J. Foster) to W. Huskisson, the MP for Liverpool killed at the opening of the Liverpool–Manchester Railway. Mortuary chapel at NW corner (1829; J. Foster), Greek Doric temple with fine classical interior. Statue of Huskisson (1831–33; J. Gibson) moved from the rotunda. Around the cathedral attractive streets of late Georgian houses, especially in Percy St to E and Rodney St to NW. W.E. Gladstone was born at *No. 62 Rodney St* (1809).

In Hope St to N, on corner of Mount St, *College of Art* (1910; Willink and Thicknesse), neo-Grecian, the earlier building in Mount St 1882 (T. Cook). Also in Mount St, former *Mechanics Institution* (1835–37; A.H. Holme) with Ionic portico and wings. On corner of Hardman St, *•Philharmonic Hotel* (1898; W. Thomas), a pub of exceptional splendour, the decoration done by the University Schools of Art and Architecture in the liveliest Arts and Crafts vein, every corner decorated in mosaic, stained and embossed glass, beaten copper and carved woodwork. Most splendid is the wrought-iron gate across the main entry (H.B. Bare). In Hardman St, *Police HQ* former *Blind School* (1850; A.H. Holme). At the corner of Mount Pleasant, *Medical Institution* (1836–37; C. Rampling) with curved Ionic portico. Off to W, *YMCA* (1875; H.H. Vale), one of Liverpool's best Gothic public buildings, in the manner of Waterhouse. Mount Pleasant continues N past the RC Cathedral to the original buildings of *Liverpool University*, Brownlow Hill. Victoria Building (1887–92; A. Waterhouse), red brick and terracotta, Gothic with asymmetrical entrance tower. Early 20C buildings in Brownlow St to NW and Ashton St to E. On Mount Pleasant, *Students Union* (1910–13; Sir C. Reilly), a rare work by the influential head of the School of Architecture, Georgian to Beaux-Arts classical detail, quite different each end. N of the original university buildings, *Royal Infirmary* (1887–90; A. Waterhouse), yellow and red brick with sparse ornament except to the roofline, well planned with eight pavilions and four circular wards. Tiled chapel by Waterhouse. N of the Infirmary, on corner of Prescot St, rich Baroque *bank* (1905; J.F. Doyle) and curved fronted Gothic *Prince of Wales Hotel*. To N, N of Islington Sq, *Collegiate High School* (1840–43; H.L. Elmes), Shaw St, symmetrical Tudor Gothic front with giant entrance arch and octagonal hall behind. Just E, *St. Francis Xavier Church* (1845–49; J.J. Scoles), stone, apsed with thin granite columns and tall arcades. Rich fittings, especially the carved reredos, pulpit and altar rails. Lady Chapel (1885–87; E. Kirby) of the most complex plan, octagonal centre with nave and chancel. Purbeck marble shafts. *College High School*, to S, partly of 1856 (H. Clutton) partly of 1877 in brick and terracotta. In Islington, to W, on corner of Clare St, *office building* (c 1900) and, in St. Anne's St, *No. 26*, iron-fronted former coach works (c 1858) with three storeys of columned balconies, slightly New Orleans. Islington leads back to St. George's hall.

OUTER LIVERPOOL

The riverside docks (see pp. 320–1 above) run through N into Bootle. Inland, warehouses and industrial premises on Regent Rd, Derby Rd and Commercial Rd, the three parallel N arteries. On Commercial Rd and Boundary St, *Huskisson Goods Station* (1880). **Bootle** has a group of civic buildings E of Derby Rd, in Oriel Rd *Town Hall* (1882; J. Johnson), *Library* (1887), *Police Station* (1890), and *Post Office* (1905) on corner of Balliol Rd. In Balliol Rd, *Baths* (1888) and *Technical College* (1900; Best and Callon: 1909; Grayson and Ould). At **Seaforth**, to N, Sir J. Gladstone, father of W.E. Gladstone, had his country house. He paid for the parish church (1815), now demolished. Just N, **Waterloo**, resort founded (obviously) in 1815, with early 19C terraces facing the sea. At the N end of seafront, High Victorian Gothic house (1867) on corner of Harbord Rd. In Great George's Rd, *Town Hall* (1862) and, to SW, in Waterloo Rd, **Christ Church* (1891–94; Paley and Austin), handsome red stone church in the exceptionally well-detailed late Dec. to Perp. style favoured by Paley and Austin. Sturdy N tower with stair turret, the tower buttress appearing inside the church. N of Waterloo, A565, at **Great Crosby**, *Merchant Taylors' School* (1878; Lockwood and Mawson), brick Gothic with central tower, pyramid-roofed with lantern.

NE of St. George's Hall, **Everton** stretches N, once a wealthy suburb. The main artery is Everton Rd, A580, N of West Derby Rd. Just E of the former village green, in Aubrey St, monumental stone **Waterworks* (1853; T. Duncan) with circular Piranesian water tower of huge open arches, splendid stone retaining walls to the reservoir and Italianate pumping station. Everton Rd runs into Heyworth St with Everton parish *church* (1812–14; T. Rickman), interior entirely of cast iron, delicate and lacy, an outstanding achievement in the use of prefabricated materials. J. Cragg of the Mersey Iron Foundry was the promoter. Opposite, *Mere Public House* (c 1900), exaggerated half-timber, and *Library* (1895; T. Shelmerdine), good Arts and Crafts detail. In St. Domingo Rd, *RC church* (1856; E.W. Pugin), the E end of the first attempt at building the Catholic cathedral. To NE, *Stanley Park* (1867–70; E. Kemp), perfect example of Victorian park design, with romantic lake at N end crossed by a stone bridge and ornate Gothic terracing at the S end, screening the houses in Anfield Rd that helped to pay for the park. On the terrace Gothic pavilions (E.R. Robson) facing a little iron pavilion. By the Anfield Rd entrance, conservatory (1899) with Victorian statuary inside and pretty bandstand. To N, *Liverpool Cemetery* (1856–63), a grand example of Victorian cemetery design filled with memorials of all shapes and sizes. Grand-scale symmetrical plan with main axis running through from the highly Gothic entry on Walton Lane to a most sepulchral exit under the railway at Cherry Lane. Originally a central chapel interrupted this walk with two other chapels off to N and S, only the S chapel survives and gloomy catacombs each side of the site of the centre chapel.

Layout and architecture by Lucy and Littler. Further N, **Walton-on-the-Hill**. On County Rd, No. 195, *Glebe Hotel* (c 1870), unusually Gothic. Just N, Walton *church* (1828–32; J. Broadbent), Perp. style. To N, off Rice Lane, *Walton Prison* (1855; J. Weightman), Hornby Rd, the massive gatehouse much altered, but the long terraces of warders' housing surviving. Further up Rice Lane, cheerful red-brick and stone *Barclays Bank* (1898; Willink and Thicknesse) with domed turrets and Dutch gables. Longmoor Lane runs NE. Off to S, in Long Lane, *Hartley's Factory* (1866), massive red-brick castle complete with portcullis, not the expected image for jam-making. Interesting group of workers' houses just S. On Longmoor Lane, to E, *Cottage Homes* (1887), children's home on the then advanced plan of individual houses along an avenue, aligned on a central classical dining-hall with tower.

NE of centre, on West Derby Road, A5048, former *Olympia Theatre* (1905; F. Matcham), disused but with vast auditorium designed for circus and variety performances decorated in oriental style. S of the road, further out, *Newsham Park* (1868–70), one of the three municipal parks laid out on the outer fringes of the city, partly financed by releasing the fringes for expensive housing. On E side, Orphan Drive, *Park Hospital* (1871–74; Waterhouse), picturesquely planned but relatively plain Gothic orphanage. On West Derby Rd, **Tue Brook**, •*St. John's Church* (1868–70; G.F. Bodley), careful and unostentatious exterior in banded stone with tower and spire. Interior of exceptional splendour with complete painted and gilt fittings by Bodley, painted decoration by C.E. Kempe and chancel glass by Morris. Recent restoration has brought back the full glory of this loveliest of Victorian church interiors. *Vicarage* to S by Bodley. *Bank* opposite the church (c 1900; J.F. Doyle). To E, across ring road, Mill Lane leads to **West Derby**. At gates of Croxteth Hall, *St. Mary's Church* (1853–56; G.G. Scott), estate church built for Lord Sefton in best Dec. with apse and crossing tower. Lofty interior with round columns to arcade and stained glass by Hardman. *Schools* (1860), Gothic *cross* (1861; W.E. Nesfield), very elaborate and *cottages* (1861–70; Nesfield). *Croxteth Hall*, to NE, open to public, has 16C origins visible on S side, 1702 W front, 1874 E and part of S, in Tudor style, and N front 1902 (J.McV. Anderson) in the style of the W front. Picturesque *dairy* (1861–70; Nesfield), Gothic with tiled and painted interior. *Kennels and cottage* to E (c 1895; J. Douglas). S of the church, off Eaton Rd, *Sandfield Park*, mid 19c villa estate on winding roads.

E of St. George's Hall, London Rd leads to Kensington. *Library* (1890; T. Shelmerdine), free style with pretty glazed timber lantern. Adjoining, *Christ Church* (1870; W. and G. Audsley), hard polychrome brick with Romanesque detail. At corner of Deane Rd, *bank* (1898; J. Rhind), fanciful Baroque. In Deane Rd, Greek Doric entrance screen to *Jewish Cemetery* (1836–37). In this area early Victorian villas in Beech St and Holly Rd, E of Deane St, and N of main road in Elm Vale, Prospect Vale and Fairfield Crescent. On Prescot Rd to E, at corner of Derby Lane, *bank* (c 1890; Grayson and Ould). On Derby Lane, *St. Paul's Church* (1916; Giles G. Scott), impressive and individual brick church with broad pyramid-roofed central tower and windows projected under half-hipped roofs, marking cross-vaulted aisles. In St. Oswald's St, to S, *RC church* with tower and spire (1842) surviving from A.W.N. Pugin's original building. *Schools* (1855) to S. S of Kensington, in Edge Lane, *Botanic Gardens* (1836–37), founded 1800 by W. Roscoe, historian of the Italian Renaissance. Durning Rd leads S, past an exceptionally Gothic *fire station* (c 1870). At S end, *Edge Hill*

Station (1836; ?J. Cunningham), the most important relic of the Liverpool end of the Liverpool–Manchester railway. Two red stone classical buildings. On the platform level, engine house (1848), a reminder that for the first years of the railway trains were hauled from here through the tunnel to Crown St Station. Wavertree Rd leads E from Durning Rd to **Wavertree**. In Picton Rd, *Library* (1902) and *College of Art* (1898), both by T. Shelmerdine, characteristically freely detailed. To E, *Clock Tower* (1879) to Sir J.A. Picton, architect and historian of Liverpool. In Church Rd, to S, parish *church* (1794) with E end apse added 1911 (Sir C. Reilly), Reilly's work Beaux-Arts classical and spatially complex. Adjoining, *Blue Coat School* (1903–06; Briggs, Wolstenholme and Thornely), extensive buildings in early 18C Baroque style, the low entrance range crowned by an extremely bold tower, plain red brick with rusticated angles until the top stage which is stone with aedicule niches each side and concave-curved cap. Courtyard ranges behind. At S end, the chapel, domed Greek cross plan. Down Woolton Rd, to E, *St. Joseph's Home* (1845–47; A.W.N. Pugin), Gothic house enlarged 1866. Adjoining, *Bishop Eton Monastery* (1858; E.W. Pugin) with chapel (1851–58; A.W.N. Pugin).

S of centre, Princes Rd runs SE from Upper Parliament St. At top end, Berkley St, *Greek Orthodox church* (1865–70; H. Sumners), Byzantine style. In Princes Rd, E side, *St. Margaret's Church* (1868; G.E. Street), brick, quite modest but with much stencilled decoration. Glass by Clayton and Bell and good brass to the founder in chancel. *Vicarage* by Street, brick Gothic to N. To S, *No. 5* (c 1860), Gothic mansion with conical roofed turret, and *synagogue* (1874; W. and G. Audsley), Gothic with Moorish touches, rich marbled and gilded interior. Huskisson *statue* (1847; J. Gibson). Prominent beyond, fully ecclesiastical Gothic *Welsh Presbyterian Church* (1865–67; W. and G. Audsley) with landmark spire. *Prince's Park* (1842; J. Paxton) was one of the earliest Victorian public parks and Paxton's first. Characteristic winding drive and lake. Common to all the Liverpool parks, the outer fringes were developed for large villas to pay for the enterprise. Classical main entrance. Stuccoed terraces, generally Italianate, to NW and NE, notably *Prince's Park Mansions* (1843; W. Papworth). Ullet Rd divides Prince's Park from *Sefton Park* (1868–72), the largest of Liverpool's municipal parks, laid out by E. André of Paris to a pattern of curving drives in the same tradition as Prince's Park and with a large lake. In the centre, spectacular octagonal *Palm House* (1896; Mackenzie and Moncur), the very model of Victorian plant display down to the white marble statues on sentimental themes (Highland Mary, The Angel's Whisper). Eight statues around the outside (L. Chavalliaud). Very Gothic *lodges* each end of the Park. To N, in Ullet Rd, *St. Agnes' Church* (1883–85; J.L. Pearson), tall red brick in Pearson's favourite 13C style, apsed with E and W transepts. The interior fully vaulted and clad in stone throughout, the spatial effects intensified at the E end with ambulatory and Lady Chapel off the apse. Apse carving by N. Hitch, Lady Chapel screen and reredos 1903–04 (G.F. Bodley). Under the organ loft tiny octagonal space, vaulted. To E, *vicarage* (1887; Norman Shaw), an excellent composition in red brick with flush stone mullion windows, the detail kept minimal but effective use of canted bays and similar oriel. To E, *Unitarian church* (1896–99; P. Worthington), red-brick free Gothic group, attractively composed with hall (1902). Good Arts and Crafts fittings, Morris glass, and, in the library and vestry, frescoes by G. Moira in a Symbolist vein befitting the Unitarian subjects (Pursuit of Truth and Cardinal Virtues). To N, *St. Clare's RC Church* (1888–90; L. Stokes), in Arundel Avenue, free

Gothic, very advanced for this date. Long exterior in brick banded in stone with Perp. style windows set high. Inside, internal buttresses such that the windows are set deep with aisle and gallery pierced through the buttresses, the system of Pearson's Kilburn church, London, but here simplified with minimal moulding. Single roof running through to a high E window. *Presbytery* adjoining, also advanced for its date, horizontal emphasis with mullion windows in bands, the end windows actually on the corner. Art Nouveau carving to the doorway.

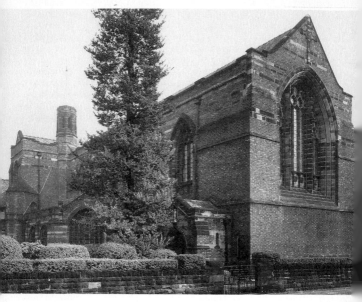

St. Clare's Roman Catholic Church (1888–90; L. Stokes), Sefton Park, Liverpool

SW of Ullet Rd, in Dingle Lane, *Turner Memorial Home* (1881; A. Waterhouse), picturesque and extensive stone Gothic buildings with chapel at one end. Inside, marble group of C. Turner and his son (1882; H. Thorneycroft), most informal, the two men seated, in everyday clothes, examining the plans of the building. To SE, off Aigburth Rd, at **St. Michael's Hamlet**, *church* (1814–15; T. Rickman) and five houses built for J. Cragg of the Mersey Iron Foundry, and hence using as much structural and decorative cast iron as possible. To SE, *Fulwood Park*, street of stucco Italianate villas (c 1840) running from Sefton Park to the river. Further SE at Grassendale, off Aigburth Rd, two similar riverside developments, *Grassendale Park* (c 1840) and *Cressington Park* (c 1850–60). At entrance to Cressington Park, handsome stone *lodge* and *St. Mary's Church* (1853; A.H. Holme). NE of Aigburth Rd, in Mossley Hill Rd, *Sudley Art Gallery* (c 1830), the picture collection of G. Holt, shipowner, mostly English 18C and 19C works. To N, *Mossley Hill* parish *church* (1870–75; Paley and Austin), splendid red stone work, the great crossing tower a landmark on the skyline from Sefton Park, the model of a rich suburban church. Fine interior, the crossing tower open to the bell-floor. To E, *vicarage* (1873). Rose

Lane runs E to N end of Allerton Rd, formerly the richest area of ship-owners' mansions. At N end of Allerton Rd, in Harthill Rd, *Quarry Bank* (1866), Gothic. *Hart Hill*, the mansion of J. Bibby, ship-owner, was to N. Elaborate *gatepiers*, with rescued statues from a demolished office building, opposite entry to *Calderstones* (1828). **Allerton** parish *church* (1872–76; G. Grayson) is a very grand memorial to Mrs Bibby, Perp. style with high W tower. Exceptional stained glass by Morris and Co. (1875–86). Mrs Bibby's monument is in the Italian cemetery style by F. Fabiani, who did monuments in the Staglieno cemetery, Genoa. Further S on Allerton Rd, *New Heys* (c 1865), and, in large grounds to E, *Allerton Priory* (1867–70; A. Waterhouse), fully Gothic with tower and vaulted porch, the grandest of the surviving Victorian mansions. To SW, on Woolton Rd, *Springwood* (1839), ashlar classical, and domed *lodge* (1847; H.L. Elmes) to the demolished Allerton Tower. *Allerton Hall* on S side (early 18C and 1810) was the house of the historian W. Roscoe. In **Woolton**, to NE, *Convalescent Home* (1873), Hillfoot Rd, Gothic, and, in Church Rd, parish *church* (1886; Grayson and Ould), Perp. style with expensive late 19C fittings. Early 19C villas in Church Rd and Beaconsfield Rd to N, *Knolle Park*, at junction, is classical of c 1840. Hillfoot Rd runs S to Speke Hall Avenue. *Speke Hall* (NT), the c 1600 house of the Norris family survives surrounded by the airport. F.R. Leyland, ship-owner and patron of J.M. Whistler, lived here in late 19C. Parish *church*, Speke Church Rd, a minor work by J.L. Pearson (1872–75).

ST. HELENS. A58 12m E of Liverpool. Glass manufacturing town, at the centre of the S Lancashire coalfield. In Victoria Square, Queen Victoria *statue* (1906; G. Frampton) and Gothic brick and stone *Town Hall* (1873–79; H. Sumners). N of centre, off City Rd, *Victoria Park* created from the grounds of an Italianate villa (c 1850) with campanile tower. 1m E of centre, A572, at **Parr**, *church* (1864; J.M. Taylor) with spire, characteristic polychrome walling and complicated timber roof inside. 3m E, A572, **Newton-le-Willows** and **Earlestown**. The Liverpool to Manchester railway passed through Earlestown, to W was the first large railway viaduct in Britain, the *Sankey Viaduct* (1831) and, to E, where A573 crosses the line, the scene of the first passenger train fatality when W. Huskisson, MP for Liverpool, was run down by 'The Rocket' on the ceremonial opening day. Marble *plaque*. Earlestown *station* (c 1840) is Tudor Gothic, the roof unfortunately lowered. In Market Place, Earlestown, *Town Hall* (1892; T. Beesley). At Newton, *St. Peter's Church* (1892–1901; Demaine and Brierley), free Perp. with strong W tower. 2m SE of St. Helens, at **Sutton**, N of St. Helens Junction Station, *church* (1893; Austin and Paley), red stone, well proportioned and detailed. SW of St. Helens, A58, at **Ravenhead**, the Pilkington Glass Works, and *Glass Museum*. N of **Prescot**, A58, the park of *Knowsley Hall*, mansion of the Earls of Derby, largely 18C but with parts dating to c 1500 and much 19C alteration. Some ornate interiors of c 1890–1910. The estate village is to NW of the park, B5194, with *church* rebuilt 1843–44 (Sharpe) and 1860 and 1871 (Paley). Fine broach spire. In Derby Chapel, Derby memorials including effigy of the 14th Earl (1872; M. Noble), leader of the Conservative party and three times Prime Minister between 1852 and 1868. At Prescot, *Museum*, 34 Church St, mainly of S Lancashire clock-making. 2m S of Prescot, at **Whiston**, Windy Arbor Rd, NE of M62 junction 6, *church* (1864–68; G.E. Street), severe yellow and red stone, without the intended spire. Clayton and Bell E window, late Morris glass in S chapel and W window (1897–98). 1m SE of Prescot, A57, **Rainhill**, where in 1829 the famous trial of steam locomotives was held resulting in victory for Stephenson's design. At Rainhill Stoops, to SE, *RC church* (1840) a fine stone Ionic temple with campanile tower, tunnel-vaulted interior with rich Corinthian scagliola columns. In Mill Lane, to W of A57, *The Tower* (c 1880), ornate Gothic mansion built for a Widnes industrialist, and other large later 19C houses. N of Rainhill vast *Mental Hospital* (1847–51; H.L. Elmes: 1886; G. Grayson), built as the Lancashire County Asylum.

SOUTHPORT. A565 19m N of Liverpool. Resort town developed from c 1800. On the seafront, *pier* (1859), the first in Britain built as a pleasure pier, rather than a landing stage. The Promenade was laid out 1834. At N end, the exotic Flemish Gothic silhouette of the *Hospital* (1882; Paull and Bonella) in red brick with slate octagonal spires. Lord St is the main centre, still with some Regency villas surviving at the S end; the street is laid out on an unusually generous scale, reminiscent of the Promenade at Cheltenham. The block from Nevill St contains a fine mixed late 19C and 20C group, beginning with the *National Westminster Bank* (1925), one of a number of good 20C classical buildings in Southport. *Barclays Bank* (1905) sober classical, *Nos 355–7* (1900) in curvaceous tiles, and *Albany Buildings* (1884), an improbable mixture of Gothic and half-timber, are followed by the exceptionally lavish granite-columned temple front of the *Midland Bank* (1888; E.W. Johnson) with high top-lit banking hall behind the windowless facade. A notable feature of Lord St is the range of iron verandahs in front of the shops, mostly late 19C. Overlooking London Square, on corner of London St, *National Westminster Bank* (1892; W. Owen), gabled Northern Renaissance style. On Lord St, stucco classical *Town Hall* (1852; T. Withnell), quite modest, and *Cambridge Hall* (1873; Maxwell and Tuke) in mixed Renaissance style, form a small civic group. NE of Lord St, on Manchester Rd, *Holy Trinity Church* (1903–13; H.A. Matear), expensive and grandly scaled church in Arts and Crafts influenced Gothic, the 137ft tower with octagonal crown especially inventive. Lofty interior with vaulted chancel. Southport runs into the suburb of Birkdale, mostly late Victorian area of large villas, though Birkdale Park, around Weld Rd, was developed from 1850 and some early villas survive.

NORFOLK

CROMER. A149 23m N of Norwich. Seaside resort developed in the late 19C when the railway came, with esplanade laid out 1894 and *pier* (1900). On the seafront a series of large red-brick hotels by G.J. Skipper who made his career here before moving to Norwich, *Grand Hotel* (1891), *Metropole* (1893) and *Hotel de Paris* (1895), all in the gabled N Renaissance style, ornamented in moulded brick. 2m SE, at **Overstrand**, two summer houses by Lutyens. *The Pleasaunce* (1897–99) is a remodelling of two villas, bearing the signs of gradual enlargement. Cloistered walks each side of the house, one centred on a pebbledashed pyramid-roofed clock tower, reminiscent of Voysey's work. The house itself more confused than picturesque with tilehanging and timbered oriels. *Overstrand Hall* (1899) is far more successful, a courtyard house in brick with some half-timber, sweeping roofs and a fine asymmetrical entrance composition with the main accent a big chimney-breast. Lutyens also designed the little *Methodist church* (1900) with lunette windows of neo-Georgian type lighting the clerestory. In the church tablet to Sir T.F. Buxton (1786–1845), leading figure in the anti-slavery movement. 5m SE, **Mundesley**, small-scale seaside resort mostly of 1890s. 7m SE, at **Happisburgh**, *Happisburgh Manor* (1900; D. Blow), large seaside villa built to Arts and Crafts principles entirely of local materials, beach shingle, flint and brick with an enormous reed thatch roof. Hectic patterning emphasises the materials, the manner of E.S. Prior's slightly later Home Place, Holt (see below). Most remarkable is the butterfly or X plan with central hall and radiating wings.

4m W of Cromer, **Sheringham**, another of the late 19C Norfolk resorts, developed after the arrival of the railway with the essential broad promenade and golf-course. *Grand Hotel* (1898; H.J. Green) in centre. On the Cromer road, *RC church* (1910; Giles G. Scott), red brick, tall spare proportions, the windows set high with rose window over the altar. 4m W, at **Kelling**, *Kelling Hall* (1912; E.B. Maufe), flint and brick butterfly-plan house, the centre here the substantial part of the house with great hipped roof and tall stacks each end, the wings canted away with slightly lower roofline. Vernacular details made formal with tall flat-topped bays and triple-gabled frontispiece. 2m SW, at **Holt**, in the Market Place, old *Schoolhouse* (1858; W. Suter), Tudor style. At W end of High St, polychrome High Victorian *Methodist church* (1859; T. Jeckyll), the full range of muscular Gothic effects, exceptional for a chapel, the interior to match. On the Cromer road, *Gresham's School*, moved out from the centre in 1900 to extensive Tudor style buildings (H.C. Clarke). Boldly scaled chapel of 1912–16 (M. Ayrton). Further E, **Home Place* (1903–05; E.S. Prior), most extreme product of the Arts and Crafts delight in using materials as found on the site, built to the then fashionable butterfly plan with 'suntrap' wings enclosing the garden front. Stylistically indefinable, the walls an undulating pattern of flint, lumps of brown stone and courses of thin tiles, laid flat to frame windows, but also in herringbone for decorative courses. The canting of the wings finds echoes in nearly every other junction of wall and roof, such that, although symmetrical, the building has a natural amorphous quality, as though weatherbeaten rather than planned into shape. Concrete, because available on site, used for most of the structure. 3m NW of Holt, **Glandford**, later 19C estate village for Jodrell family of Bayfield Hall. *Church* expensively rebuilt 1899–1906 (Hicks and Charlewood) in E

Anglian 15C style, the interior exceptionally lavish with hammerbeam roof, screens, marble font and stained glass by Kempe and H.W. Bryans. 2m N, E of **Blakeney**, *Wiveton Hall*, 17C gabled house extended in same style 1907 (G. Dawber). At **Langham**, 2½m SW of Blakeney, Captain Marryat, author of 'Children of the New Forest' and 'Masterman Ready' is buried in the churchyard. In the *church*, nave NE window by Morris and Co. 7m SW of Holt, off A148, at **Thursford**, *church* with High Victorian chancel (1862), itself a notable work with Ruskinian naturalistic capitals and columns doubled in depth but dominated by the glowing reds of the E window (1862), a superb design by the painter Albert Moore, made by J. Powell and Sons, Gothic figures but with an antique classicism in the faces and drapery. Side windows of 1873 by Wooldridge. 6m SW, A148, at **Sculthorpe**, *church* mostly rebuilt 1860 (T. Jeckyll) with excellent glass by Morris and Co in chancel S and S aisle E windows, also one very Gothic window in nave S by Heaton, Butler and Bayne (1862).

20m W of Cromer, A149, at **Holkham**, the estate of the Earls of Leicester, the great Palladian house set in its landscaped park, created from one of the bleakest parts of the Norfolk coast. Outside the house, column to 'Coke of Norfolk', the 1st Earl of Leicester (1754–1842), agricultural pioneer who created flourishing farmland from the marshes, introduced wheat, improved the breeding of livestock and was called 'the first farmer in England'. The *column* (1845; W.J. Donthorn) is appropriately flanked by cows and topped with a wheatsheaf. In the village, mid 19C estate housing. Off to W, *church* rebuilt 1870 (J.K. Colling), richly carved fittings and effigy of the Countess of Leicester (died 1870; J.E. Boehm).

GREAT YARMOUTH. A47 19m E of Norwich. Herring-fishing port that became a resort from the early Victorian period. The old town faced W to the Yare estuary while the resort, just across the narrow peninsula, faces the sea. Facing the Swing Bridge over the Yare, on Hall Quay, *Town Hall* (1882; J.B. Pearce), red brick and stone, asymmetrical with Queen Anne detail and tower. *Barclays Bank* (1854; A. Salvin) is palazzo style in brick and stone, built as Gurney's Bank. In Regent St, *Fastolff House* (1912; R.S. Cockrill) with pretty Arts and Crafts to Art Nouveau decoration. The broad Market Place runs up to the parish *church*, exceptionally large medieval building, much restored 1862 (J.P. Seddon) but gutted in 1942 and rebuilt inside. In Church Place, *Sewell House*, birthplace 1820 of author of 'Black Beauty'. To SE, in Regent Rd, *St. Mary's RC Church* (1848–50; J.J. Scoles), serious archaeological Gothic, in contrast to the same architect's *St. Peter's Church* (1831–33), St. Peter's Rd, in the late Georgian lancet style. Regent Rd runs to the seafront at the *Britannia Pier* (1900). Broad esplanades run N and S, the more interesting Victorian developments to S beginning with the Italianate *Coastguard Station* (1859), yellow brick ranges around an open court. Behind the Jetty, *Hippodrome Circus* (1903; R.S. Cockrill), long tripartite front with domed towers, freely detailed. To S, the Camperdown Estate, laid out in the 1840s with Yarmouth's grandest terraces in classical to Italianate style running down to the Wellington Pier. Behind the pier, *Masonic Lodge* (1863; H.H. Collins), built as Assembly Rooms. The *Wellington Pier* (1853) was mostly rebuilt 1900–03 with pier theatre. Dickens stayed at the *Royal Hotel* (1848) and the shore at Yarmouth was Peggoty's home in 'David Copperfield'. George Borrow, author and wanderer, lived at 37–9 Camperdown Place. S of *Kimberley Terrace* (1842; T.M. Nelson), King's Rd runs W to Queen's Rd and the handsome classical *Naval Hospital* (1809–11; E. Holl). *St. James' Church* (1870–78; J.P. Seddon) in flint and brick has High Victorian polychrome brick interior. Further S, *Nelson Column* (1817; W. Wilkins), high Greek Doric column with viewing gallery open to public under a gilt statue of Britannia. S of Great Yarmouth, A12, the resort of **Gorleston** and, 2m S, at **Hopton**, *church* (1866; S.S. Teulon) with polychrome brick interior and Morris and Co. stained glass. 8m NW of Yarmouth, off A149, at **Martham**, the *church* has most elaborate chancel (1855; P. Boyce), lavishly carved by T. Earp.

KING'S LYNN. A10 28m N of Ely. *St. Margaret's Church* in Saturday Market was restored by Scott (1872–75) when the remarkable E rose with three tiers of lights was reconstructed. Beneath, a high sculpted reredos by Bodley (1899). To NW, the 15C and 16C Guildhall in chequered flint, attractively extended to W in Arts and Crafts Gothic (1895; Tree and Price). Queen St runs N to King's Staithe Square with plain Italianate former *Gurney's Bank* (1869). In Tuesday Market, to N, *Corn Exchange* (1854) with giant columned front. *St. Nicholas' Church*, off to N, has lead spire by Scott (1869) and Italian Gothic style painted reredos (c 1880; Hardman) under the great E window. N of The Walks, the park E of centre, *St. John's Church* (1846; Salvin), EE style with stained glass by Wailes. NE of centre, on Gaywood Rd, *Grammar School* (1903; B. Champneys), excellent example of the relaxed Queen Anne style used by Champneys at Newnham College, Cambridge, symmetrical, generously windowed with Dutch gables and cupolas.

8m NE of King's Lynn, A149, the Sandringham estate, bought by Edward VII, when Prince of Wales, in 1861 and a royal residence ever since. *Sandringham House* (1870; A.J. Humbert) is a much gabled patterned brick Jacobean style house, expensive but not especially attractive. Extensive gardens (open to public) laid out around two lakes (W.B. Thomas), the original planting of dark evergreens, described as 'part of Scotland brought south', much lightened in this century. Splendid main entrance gates (1862; T. Jeckyll) in the most elaborate cast and wrought iron, exhibited at the 1862 exhibition. Estate cottages at West Newton to S, and estate *station* at Wolferton to W. Sandringham *church* was rebuilt 1857 (S.S. Teulon) and 1890 (A. Blomfield), notable for the extremely rich turn of the century fittings, silver altar (1911; Barkentin and Krall), lovely aluminium and ivory figure of St. George (1910; A. Gilbert) over the royal pew, and panelled baptistery with Italian marble font. 3m N, at **Snettisham**, *Ken Hill* (1879; J.J. Stevenson), medium-sized country house built for E. Green, Yorkshire industrialist, in the most up-to-date Queen Anne manner, in practice a free blend of late 17C and 18C details applied to a picturesque asymmetrical plan with steep roofs and prominent stacks, more medieval than 1700. The freedom of Gothic revival planning is here matched with a friendly, generously lit architectural style without the constraints of academic imitation, a loosening after the muscular seriousness of the High Victorians parallelled in the contemporary Aesthetic Movement in the other arts. 5m N, **Hunstanton**, seaside resort developed from 1861 by the Le Strange family of Hunstanton Hall. Styleman Le Strange (died 1862) was an accomplished artist in the Gothic revival tradition, painting the nave roof of Ely Cathedral. For the new resort he went to W. Butterfield for a plan and designs, intended to be irregular and picturesque, in contrast to the more common formality of seaside resorts. Butterfield probably designed only *St. Edmund's Terrace* on the Upper Green, but the brown stone Tudor style was followed in the surrounding houses and hotels. The centre has a character quite different from contemporary resorts, but the plan was not followed as the town developed. *Pier* of 1870. *Church* (1865) by F. Preedy, a pupil of Butterfield and related to the Le Strange family. At **Old Hunstanton**, *Hunstanton Hall*, c 1500 and 17C much rebuilt 1853 (?F. Preedy). In the *church* wonderfully rich E window (1863; F. Preedy) to Styleman Le Strange and S aisle E window by Le Strange.

6m E of King's Lynn, at **Roydon**, *church* rebuilt 1861–63 (G.E. Street) in severe neo-Norman style to match the surviving doorways. Fittings in Norman style by Street. 3m SE of King's Lynn, at **North Runcton**, *Runcton Hall* (1835 and 1853; A. Salvin), yellow brick Jacobean house for one of the Gurney banking family. 7m E, A47, at **Narford**, *Narford Hall*, c 1700 much remodelled in Renaissance style c 1860 (W. Burn). 11m S, **Downham Market**, in the Market Place cast-iron *clock tower* (1878; W. Cunliffe). *Town Hall* (1887; J. Johnson), Dutch-gabled *station* (1846). 2m N at **Stow Bardolph**, *Stow Hall* (1873; D. Brandon), brick Tudor style house replacing the medieval house of the Hare family.

NORWICH. The county town and one of England's major medieval cities. 19C Norwich was noted for its yarn industry, cattle market and the Norwich Union insurance company. Norwich *Cathedral* was restored by Salvin in the 1830s, when the W front and S transept were refaced, the W front altered again c 1900 (C.J. Ferguson). Interior: pictorial W window (1854; G. Hedgeland), stone pulpit (1889; Carpenter and Ingelow) and 15C screen, or pulpitum, extended 1833 (Salvin) to carry the organ. In N transept, W window by Morris and Co. (c 1901), Bishop Bathurst memorial (1841; Sir F. Chantrey) and Bishop Pelham effigy (1896; J. Forsyth). In the crossing, Bishop's Throne (1893–95; Pearson), choir pulpit (1889; J.D. Seddon), and in the choir, 15C stalls with canopies and front stalls by Salvin. Fine metal and marble altar rails by J.D. Sedding. Nurse Edith Cavell, shot in Brussels 1915, is buried in SE ambulatory. N of the Cathedral, *Bishop's Palace* (1858; E. Christian), red brick and flint Gothic. S of the Cathedral, in The Close, *No. 57* (1862; J.H. Brown), High Victorian polychrome Gothic. From the Great Gate, Tombland runs S to King St. At the junction with Prince of Wales Rd, *Royal Hotel* (1896; E. Boardman and Sons), red brick and terracotta, faces former *Crown Bank* (1866; P.C. Hardwick), now Anglia TV, stone classical with Ionic single-storey portico. Adjoining, former *Post Office* (1882; J.B. Pearce), red brick and red sandstone. To W, *Norwich Castle*, the magnificent keep of the Norman castle, now the Castle Museum. Externally refaced 1833–39 (A. Salvin), the interior later 19C (E. Boardman). Good collections of Norwich School painters. W of the Castle, in Castle St, *Royal Arcade* (1898; G.J. Skipper), with delightful Art Nouveau tile work (by W.J. Neatby of Doulton) to the facade and inside. The arcade runs through to Market Place. On S side, *St. Peter Mancroft* church with fine reredos by Comper. On N side, on corner of London St, *Jarrold's Store* (1903–05; G.J. Skipper), slightly Baroque with much glazing. Adjoining, in London St, G.J. Skipper's own *office* (1896), decorated in bright terracotta including a relief of the architect at work. The *Guildhall* on N side of the Market Place of 1407 and 1511 was much remodelled (1861; T.D. Barry) including the whole S front.

In St. Giles St, to W, *Nos 41–5* (1904–05; Skipper) in the rich Baroque style of Skipper's later buildings and *No. 47* (1907; A. Havers) also Baroque. *Borrow House*, Willow Lane, was the home of G. Borrow,

The Norwich Union Offices (1901–06; G.J. Skipper), Norwich

author of 'Lavengro'. Beyond St. Giles' Church, over the ring road, *RC Cathedral* (1884–1910; G.G. Scott Jr and J.O. Scott), fully cathedral scale, built for the Duke of Norfolk as a memorial to his wife in a serious and archaeologically correct EE style more characteristic of the mid Victorian era, and of the work of Scott Sr. Prominent and rich three-tier E end of shafted lancets with corner turrets and sturdy crossing tower. Interior stone vaulted and enriched with Purbeck marble shafting on the Salisbury Cathedral model. Rich 13C style glass by J.H. Powell of Hardman and Co. SW of the Castle, in Red Lion St, *Commercial Chambers* (1901–03; Skipper), small-scale Baroque, a prelude to Skipper's major work, the *Norwich Union* offices (1901–06) in Surrey St, to S, like a great late 18C country house with raised Ionic portico and heavily rusticated curving wings ending in statue niches, a building that outshines even its London contemporaries. Magnificent interiors, the marbled great hall with green columns supposedly originally intended for Westminster Cathedral, London, the board room in rich late 17C style with painted ceiling panels. E of the Castle, Prince of Wales Rd was cut through to *Norwich Station* (1886; J. Wilson and W.N. Ashbee), imposing red-brick and stone free Renaissance style building, the centre accentuated with a zinc-clad square dome, very prominent across the river. 19C villas along Thorpe Rd. Thorpe *church* was mostly rebuilt in High Victorian plate-traceried manner (1866; T. Jeckyll) with heavily naturalistic carving to capitals. NE of the Cathedral, in Cowgate, former *yarn mill* (c 1839; R. Parkinson) by the river, high five-storey mill in red brick distinguished by a domed circular stair tower at one end and impressively simple detailing.

5m NW of Norwich, off A1067, at **Taverham**, *Taverham Hall* (1860; D. Brandon), red-brick Tudor style mansion. 5m NW, at **Alderford**, *Great Witchingham Hall*, 16C origins with 1872 grand Tudor to Elizabethan style front. 3m N, at **Booton**, *church* built c 1875–91 to his own designs by the Rev. Whitwell Elwin, rector for over 50 years, editor of the 'Quarterly Review' and of the works of Pope. Elwin's design is a riotous assortment of Gothic details borrowed from illustrations, the scale almost always bizarre, nowhere more so than on the W front with its pair of diagonally set towers flanking a monster pinnacle. The proportions and outline of the church are characteristic of the 1820s, possibly because Elwin was recasing an earlier building. Inside, hammerbeam roof with enormous angels, the angelic theme echoed in the stained glass. 18m NW of Norwich, at **Guist**, *Sennowe Park*, country house rebuilt (1905–07; G.J. Skipper) for T.A. Cook, heir to the famous travel agency, in a rich late 17C style, far more exuberant however than any of the suggested models: red brick with profuse Bath stone details including a giant-columned curved bay with undulating top parapet over the attic, enriched with statues, and a porte-cochère with columns diagonally at the angles in the Baroque way. Palladian conservatory with curved roof and marbled interior attached at one end. Inside, carved woodwork and ornamental plasterwork in profusion, late 17C in style, outdoing again the originals, especially the carved panels of the staircase. Behind the house, a delightful water tower with octagonal stone top and copper spire, in the tradition of 18C follies. 13m N of Norwich, NW of Aylsham, at **Blickling**, *Blickling Hall* (NT), quintessential Jacobean house, built 1616–27. In the long gallery fascinating Pre-Raphaelite painted frieze (c 1860; J.H. Pollen), Celtic in inspiration, and bookcases also by Pollen, good examples of High Victorian woodwork, the decoration, simple notching, applied to the structural members, Gothic but without the paraphernalia of tracery and figure carving. The great canopied fireplace by Pollen was sadly a victim of changing tastes. Externally the lantern tower was replaced (c 1900; M.B. Adams) in suitable Jacobean style. Blickling *church* restored by Street (1876) with new W tower. E window by Hardman. Exceptional marble *effigy of the 8th Marquess of Lothian (1871–74; G.F. Watts), beautifully modelled with standing angels protecting. 8m NE of Norwich, at **Woodbastwick**, *Woodbastwick Hall* (1889; E. Christian), red brick Elizabethan style. *Church* restored 1878 (G.G. Scott).

4m SE of Norwich, off A146, at **Framingham Pigot**, *Manor House* (1862–64; J. Norton), gabled Elizabethan, and estate *church* in flint and stone (1859; R. Kerr). 9m S, B1332, at **Ditchingham**, Sir H. Rider Haggard, author of 'King Solomon's Mines', was squire and is commemorated by a window in the *church*. ½m E, *Community of All Hallows*, Anglican sisterhood established 1858 as a House of Mercy, or Training Centre for errant girls. Brick Gothic buildings (1858–64; H. Woodyer), cruciform plan with the steeply pointed dormers that Woodyer liked. Sisters' House (1876) and chapel adjoining. 4m S of Norwich, A140, at **Dunston**, Dunston Hall, elaborate later 19C Elizabethan style house (E. Boardman). 7m SW, off A140, at **Great Moulton**, *Old Rectory* (1832; W.J. Donthorn), early example of the Italianate villa with off-centre tower and arched lights, a form explored by John Nash c 1800–20 but not widely used until the 1840s. 5m SE, B1134, at **Pulham St. Mary**, in the *church* excellent fittings by Bodley (1886), organ case, font cover, upper part of screen and chancel decoration. 5m SW of Norwich, **Ketteringham**, scene of the stormy relationship between the squire and the parson, delightfully recorded from their letters and diaries by O. Chadwick in 'Victorian Miniature'. Sir J. Boileau, the autocratic squire, rebuilt the *Hall* (c 1840–52) and in the *church* are Boileau memorials and tablets to the family of Mr Andrew, the vicar. 4m W, at **Wymondham**, the *Abbey* church has the nave only intact, the blank E wall triumphantly filled by a great gold and blue

Gothic reredos by Comper, the contrast with the pale stone and plaster dramatic and successful.

THETFORD. A11 28m SW of Norwich. In the Market Place, *Guildhall* (1900; H.J. Green). 4m E, A1006, at **Shadwell**, *Shadwell Park* (1840–42; E. Blore: 1855–60; S.S. Teulon), Jacobean style house of the Buxton family, the earlier work in smooth ashlar with shaped gable, Teulon's additions far more Gothic in flint and stone ornamented with flushwork decoration. A splendid entrance tower with turret corbelled off one side balances Blore's gable to left with one of similar profile by Teulon to right linked by a range in white brick with sharply pointed dormer gables. Teulon's work on the main house, lavishly carved with Gothic figures and hefty foliage, is a riotous display, but the stable block to one side outshines even this. A full quadrangle in the most picturesque Gothic, the court is entered under a splendid clock tower with octagonal spire and lantern, the build up from square base to the top flourish of gablets, each stage stepped-back, masterly. The stable court within has further arrays of gables, turrets and varied rooflines. In the house, Teulon created a vast cruciform hall, the roofs a display of High Victorian woodwork, all exaggerated construction and heroic scale supported on richly carved corbels and well-shafts. For Lady Buxton, Teulon also rebuilt the *church* at **Brettenham** (1852), the interior richly fitted in marble and alabaster. Iron tower screen. Estate housing probably also by Teulon. Teulon restored the 14C *College* at **Rushford**, to SW, in 1855 as a rectory and built the bridge over the river, also for the Buxtons. 5m E of Shadwell, at **Garboldisham**, the *stables* (c 1870; G.G. Scott Jr) survive of the demolished Manor House, an early example of the move from Gothic to experimentation with 'impure' styles, here the Dutch-influenced artisan style of the later 17C. Banded brickwork and shaped gables, an elegant design.

N of Thetford much of the Breckland has become a Battle Area and inaccessible. The *church* at **West Tofts** in the middle has exceptional work by A.W.N. Pugin (1849–51), the chancel rebuilt, taller than the nave, with Hardman glass, painted screens and roof, and pretty painted organ loft. S chapel with fine encaustic tiles. To W, A134, at **Mundford**, *church* refitted 1911 by J.N. Comper, superb screen and organ, mixing Gothic and Renaissance forms. Chancel reredos, E window, stalls and painted roof by Comper. *Lynford Hall* (1856–61; W. Burn) is red brick and stone Jacobean style on an ambitious scale. *RC chapel* to S 1879 (H. Clutton). 5m W of Mundford, at **Methwold**, in the *church*, good early glass by H. Holiday (1866) in N aisle, deep colours, Pre-Raphaelite manner. Chancel glass c 1850. 6m N, at **Oxborough**, *Oxburgh Hall* (NT), 1482 moated house altered c 1835 (A.W.N. Pugin) who added the SE tower and the RC *chapel* by the gates. In the chapel, effigy of Sir H. Bedingfield (died 1862) on Gothic tomb chest. The Bedingfields remained Catholics from the Reformation. 6m NE of Mundford, B1077, at **South Pickenham**, in the church pretty painted Gothic organ case (c 1850; A.W.N. Pugin) salvaged from the church at West Tofts. *Pickenham Hall* (1902–05; R.W. Schultz) is neo-Georgian with Arts and Crafts touches. At **North Pickenham**, the *church* (1863) has fine W window (1864; Powell).

NORTHAMPTONSHIRE

BRACKLEY. A43 20m SW of Northampton. *Magdalen College School*, founded 1548 on the site of the Hospital of St. James and St. John, the chapel restored 1869 (C. Buckeridge) and the school buildings largely 19C. 1½m S, at **Evenley**, *church* (1864; H. Woodyer) with shingled spire and interior naturalistic carving. **Charlton**, 3m W of Brackley, was the home of F.E. Smith, Earl of Birkenhead, *The Cottage* (1912; A. James) being built for him. 8m NW of Brackley, A422, at **Middleton Cheney**, *church* restored 1865 (G.G. Scott), with exceptional early *stained glass by Morris and Co in the chancel E window (1864) and W window (1870) and later glass by the firm elsewhere. Gothic memorial in the churchyard (1866; W. Wilkinson) to the Horton family. 3m NE of Brackley, A43, at **Whitfield**, *church* (1870; H. Woodyer), severe lancet style with broach spire, late glass (c 1900–14) by Morris and Co.

DAVENTRY. A45 12m W of Northampton. 3m NW, A45, at **Braunston**, *church* (1849; R.C. Hussey), handsome Dec. with spire. Font (c 1875) by Butterfield in marble, an exercise in solid geometry. 4m N of **Daventry**, *Ashby St. Ledgers*, Jacobean manor house extended 1904–38 (E. Lutyens) for the 2nd Lord Wimborne of the Guest iron and steel family, including the addition of a 17C timber-framed house removed from Ipswich. Gardens by Lutyens and, in the village, a row of thatched *cottages* (1908; Lutyens). 2m N, at **Kilsby**, *Kilsby Tunnel* (1838; R. Stephenson), 1½m long, the longest tunnel ever built at that date, ventilated with 60ft wide shafts rising to castellated crowns. 5m SW of Daventry, at **Hellidon**, *church* restored 1845 (Butterfield) and extended 1867, with simple wooden furnishings of 1845. *School* by Butterfield (1867) with some half-timbering.

KETTERING. A43 14m NE of Northampton. In Market Place, former *Corn Exchange* (1853; E.F. Law). Behind, by the church, in Sheep St, Elizabethan style *Library* (1904; Goddard and Co); *Art Gallery* (1913; J.A. Gotch) with collection of works by Sir A. East RA (1849–1913). In Gold St, *Post Office Buildings* (1887; Gotch and Saunders) in terracotta. In Montagu St, Tudor style *School* (1892; Gotch and Saunders), with cross-gabled tower, and *Conservative Club* (1888; S. Perkins Pick), well detailed with a touch of half-timber in the main gable. 7m NW, off A427, at **East Carlton**, *East Carlton Hall* (1870; E.F. Law), Italianate with pavilion roofs, and *almshouses* (1866; E.F. Law). At **Ashley**, 3m NW, *church*, lavishly restored 1867 (G.G. Scott) with richly coloured chancel, painted decoration and glass by Clayton and Bell. By Scott also the *School* (1858) and *Master's House* (1865), all part of the works for the Rev. R. Pulteney, which included the remodelling of *Ashley Hall* (1865) and model *cottages* (1865–66) both by E.F. Law. 10m W of Kettering, A508, at **Lamport**, estate village of *Lamport Hall* (open to public), the Elizabethan, 17C and 18C house of the Isham family. N additions by W. Burn (1861). In the *church* richly coloured E window (1847; Warrington), pictorial Renaissance style to suit the 18C church. 4m N, at **Kelmarsh**, *church* lavishly refitted (1874; J.K. Colling) with luxuriant foliage carving, on which Colling was an expert, marble wall-panelling and floor, decoration by H.E. Wooldridge, E window by Westlake, side windows in chancel by W.M. Pepper. Colling was employed by the Naylor family of Liverpool, for whom he built the Albany Building, Old Hall St. 2m SW, at **Haselbech**, *church*, ornately altered (1859; W. Slater: and 1881) with much carved decoration by J. Forsyth.

NORTHAMPTON. The county town, noted for boot and shoe-making from the 16C, but the trade industrialised only in the later 19C. The centre has been savagely battered in recent years. In George Row, E of All Saints' Church, *County Hall*, an Italianate addition (1845; J. Milne) to the 1676 Sessions House. Altered 1890 (E. Law) and c 1900 (A. Webb). In St. Giles' Square, *• Town Hall* (1861–64; E.W. Godwin), one of the outstanding High Victorian public buildings, the influence of Ruskin pre-eminent in the Continental Gothic (French and Italian) forms, the structural polychromy, the full scheme of sculptural decoration (by T. Nicholls the reliefs, the statues and fine naturalistic capitals by R. Boulton) and in the overall resemblance to the Oxford Museum (via Scott's rejected Foreign Office design). Great Hall inside with cast-iron columns and brackets carrying a timber roof. Excellent stained glass by J.M. Allen on Arthurian themes. Old Council Chamber with heavily Gothic fireplaces and furniture by Godwin. W addition (1889–92; M. Holding and A.W. Jeffery) in similar style, the Gothic Council Chamber particularly good, the carving still in the Ruskinian vein. To left, Queen Anne style *office building* in moulded brick (1886; M. Holding). In Guildhall Rd, to S, *Museum and Art Gallery* altered from part of the former Gaol, collection relating to the shoe industry, *No. 9* (1872; E.F. Law) Gothic, and *Repertory Theatre* (1884–87; C.J. Phipps), narrow front to a delightful small auditorium with rococo dome. From All Saints', Drapery runs N, on E side, fine palazzo style *Bank* (1841; E.F. Law). The Parade, with former *Corn Exchange* (1850; Alexander and Hull), stucco classical, leads into the Market Square, with fragmentary remains of old buildings scattered around the perimeter. SE of Market Square, Abington St with *Library* (1910; H. Norman), Edwardian classical, and *Convent* (1871; W. Hull), plain Gothic range. In Abington Square *statue* of C. Bradlaugh MP (1894; G. Tinworth) in terracotta. To S, in St. Giles Terrace, *St. Giles' Church*, much renewed 1853–55 (E.F. Law), and Gothic *Schools* (1858; E.F. Law). In Spencer Parade, stuccoed villas (c 1840), Tudor and castellated, more in Cheyne Walk to S. In St. Giles St, running W, *Nos 81–7* (c 1885; M. Holding), brick Flemish Renaissance detail. In Gold St, W of All Saints', former *Brewery offices* (1881; S.J. Newman), brick and stone, and *Grand Hotel* (1890; C. Dorman).

N of centre, Sheep St leads N past *Holy Sepulchre Church*, Norman round church restored and extended 1860–68 (G.G. Scott). By Scott the roof of the circular part and the ornate font beneath, also the apsed E end with richly carved foliage capitals. Off Regent Square, to N, in Campbell St, the best Northampton shoe *warehouses*, one, Manfield's (1857), exceptionally grand, stucco Italianate with campanile tower, the other (1857; W. Hull) in brick with curved corner. To N, A508, early 19C terraces on Barrack Rd and *RC Cathedral*, the nave and aisles 1863 (E.W. Pugin), the tower and E end 1948–55, replacing the original church by A.W.N. Pugin (some Pugin glass reset in St. John's Church, Bridge St). Cathedral buildings 1876 (F.W. Tasker). E of Barrack Rd, in Duke St, *St. Lawrence's Church* (1877; Burder and Baker), tall brick in the EE style of J.L. Pearson. Adjoining, Clare St, heavily fortified *Drill Hall* (1859). E and NE of centre are the principal suburban extensions to the town, E of St. Giles St, in Billing Rd, the *Cliftonville* estate developed from 1845 with houses of the 1880s (M. Holding) in The Avenue, to S. *St. Martin's Villas* (1865; E.W. Godwin), Billing Rd, Gothic in brick and stone. *St. Andrew's Hospital* (1837; J.

Milne) was the county asylum in which the poet John Clare spent the years of his madness (1841–64). In Wellingborough Rd, running E from Abington Square, *St. Edmund's Hospital* (1837; G.G. Scott) built as the workhouse. To NE, off Kettering Rd, late 19C suburban houses on Abington Ave, Collingwood Rd and The Drive, Phippsville. The church of the area is *St. Matthew's* (1891–94; M. Holding), on Kettering Rd, the best of Holding's suburban churches in the style of J.L. Pearson, tall EE and stone vaulted in E end. Fine spire. The interior fully furnished with alabaster fittings by Aumonier, painted triptych by C.E. Buckeridge and apse glass by Clayton and Bell. 1m N, *Manfield Hospital* (1899; C. Dorman), the grand Jacobean mansion of Sir P. Manfield of the shoe firm.

4m NE of Northampton, off A43, *Overstone Park* (1860–62; W.M. Teulon), built for the banker Lord Overstone, one of the wealthiest men in Britain. Stone, encrusted with ornamental detail, presumably in emulation of the 'prodigy' houses of c 1600 such as Wollaton, except that the detail is more generally Italianate, where definable, for the line between Italian Renaissance and round-arched Italian Gothic blurs easily, as in the arched openings of the main towers. 5m NW of Northampton, A428, *Althorp*, seat of the Earls Spencer (open to public). Estate cottages at **Harlestone**, **Little Brington**, **Church Brampton** and **Chapel Brampton** of c 1850. Of the estate *church* at Little Brington (1856; P.C. Hardwick) only the tower and spire remain. NW of Church Brampton, at **Holdenby**, *Holdenby House* (gardens open to public), Elizabethan style (1873; R.H. Carpenter) on the site Sir C. Hatton's demolished 16C mansion. 3m N, at **Hollowell**, in the *church* (1840) good stained glass in apse by H. Holiday (1863). The church at **Guilsborough**, just NW, has interesting glass by Morris and Co (c 1880) in chancel with clear backgrounds to the figures. S of Northampton centre, at **Far Cotton**, A43, *church* (1885; M. Holding), apsed and stone vaulted in the style of Pearson. Landmark spire. 5m E of Northampton, off A428, *Castle Ashby* (open to public), great house of the Marquesses of Northampton. Hall, long gallery and chapel redecorated 1884 (T.G. Jackson). Italian style gardens with terracotta balustrading, lettered to match the 17C inscribed balustrades on the house. Grand orangery (1865; M.D. Wyatt) also terracotta ornamented. The *church* immediately E of the house, restored 1870 (G.E. Street), contains Compton family memorials including those to the 2nd Marquess and Marchioness by Tenerani of Rome, 1866 and 1836. *School* (1856; G.E. Street), good asymmetrical design, steep roofed. By E.W. Godwin, lodge (1869) to N and screen at end of S drive, on A428. In **Denton**, to SW, A428, *Compton House* (1893; F.B. Wade), free Jacobean in brick and stone, built for the Compton family.

OUNDLE. A605 13m SW of Peterborough. *Oundle School*, New St, founded in 16C, was expanded into a medium-sized public school in the later 19C. Tudor style buildings, The Cloisters (1880; J.S. Gwilt) and School House opposite (1887; H.C. Boyes), Hall and Library (1907; A.C. Blomfield) in Perp. 1m E, **Ashton**, late example of an estate village, built c 1900 (W. Huckvale) for C. Rothschild of the banking family. Stone cottages, all thatched, in 17C vernacular style, grouped around a village green, the late date showing in the convincingly old look. *Ashton Wold* (1900; Huckvale), Rothschild's house, has been reduced but model farm, boathouse and dovecotes survive. Rothschild, noted entomologist, is said to have been given the estate by his father because the rare Chequered Skipper butterfly was to be found in the area. 3m S of Oundle, at **Barnwell**, *Barnwell Castle*, 16C house in the castle ruins much altered and restored c 1890 and 1913 (Gotch and Saunders). Gotch was the leading authority on Elizabethan and Jacobean houses at the turn of the century. 3m W of Oundle, A427, at **Benefield**, *church* (1847; J.M. Derick), Dec. according to Puginian principles with broach spire and interior fitted for Tractarian worship, that is with screen, enriched chancel, carved stalls and encaustic tiles. E window by D. Evans. Reredos and rood loft added 1897 and 1904 by J.N. Comper. At **Brigstock**, 3m SW, in the *church*, marble effigy of the 1st Lord Lyveden (1876; M. Noble). 3m NW of Benefield, off A43, **Deene**, estate village of Deene Park, seat of the Earls of Cardigan. The notorious 7th Earl (died 1868), overbearing and choleric commander of cavalry, led the Light Brigade against the Russian guns at Balaclava. The *church* was mostly rebuilt in his memory 1868–69 (Sir M.D. Wyatt) with ornate E end, further embellished by Bodley (1890). E window by Westlake (c 1868). The glory of the church is the *monument to the 7th Earl (c 1870; J.E. Boehm), marble effigies of the Earl and Countess, he in full uniform asleep, she beside him watching, every detail of extreme naturalism. On the tomb chest bronze reliefs, one of Balaclava. 4m NW, at **Harringworth**, *Welland Viaduct* (1874–79), the longest viaduct in Britain, 82 red-brick arches carrying the railway over the Welland. 5m SW, *Rockingham Castle* (open to public), medieval to 17C castle altered 1839 and 1851 (A. Salvin), the model for the Dedlock family seat, Chesney Wold, in Dickens' 'Bleak House', though resemblances to that gloomy pile are not obvious.

WELLINGBOROUGH. A45 10m NE of Northampton. Railway engineering town. On E side, in Knox Rd, *St. Mary's Church* (1908–30), J.N. Comper's most complete church, the exterior a simplified Perp., the interior a glory of colour and light, more light and less colour than Comper intended as the plaster vault, modelled on Henry VII's chapel, Westminster Abbey, has never been fully coloured. Comper's architecture here is based on the very latest of pre-Reformation Gothic, already tinged with Renaissance influence, fan vaulting and pendants with the most intricate of lierne ribs, tall piers and Tudor arches, but the capitals, like those at Chelsea Old Church, early Renaissance. The painted decorated features, screens, organ case and baldacchine, take synthesis a stage further, overtly classical columns with Gothic detail, late 16C to 17C, but with a richness in colour that after the Reformation was restricted to funerary monuments. Comper perhaps suggests the development that might have occurred had England remained Catholic. Just E, *Wellingborough Station* (1857; C.H. Driver) with ridge and furrow platform glazing and contemporary goods shed, still with surviving hand cranes inside. 3m NE, A510, at **Finedon**, *Finedon Hall* rebuilt from 1830s to 1870s by W. Mackworth-Dolben in Gothic to Jacobean style with some polychromy. Notably massive tower on the stable range. In the village, Gothic estate cottages and pub. 4m NW of Wellingborough, at **Orlingbury**, *church* (1843; R.C. Hussey), good early example of archaeological Gothic design, Hussey was partner of T. Rickman. Estate cottages in the village. 3m W of Wellingborough, off A45, at **Mears Ashby**, *church* restored 1859 (C. Buckeridge) with E and W windows by Clayton and Bell, one chancel S window by A. Lusson of Paris. Gothic *vicarage* 1860 (Buckeridge).

NORTHUMBERLAND

ALNWICK. A1 34m N of Newcastle. *Alnwick Castle* (open to public), the 14C stronghold of the Percys, was rebuilt extensively for the 4th Duke of Northumberland from 1854 (A. Salvin), the work continuing into the 1880s, at a cost of some quarter of a million pounds. The result is one of the most romantic castellated silhouettes in Britain, the main keep flanked by the lower towers of the two baileys. The NW corner of the keep with the chapel apse is entirely Salvin's, as is the detail of the inner courtyard. The interiors, by contrast, are entirely Italian Renaissance, designed for the 4th Duke who thought the style more appropriate for the display of art works and consulted the leading Italian architect, L. Canina. Canina sent G. Montiroli as architect and a team of craftsmen to carry out the works and train local talent. The result is surprisingly successful, with scenes of Border martial history interpreted in the style of the Raphael Vatican logge and much Italian marble. Other examples of this particular taste are at Longleat, Wiltshire, and Hatfield House, Hertfordshire. In Percy St, early 19C town houses and *church* (1846; Salvin) with tower and very bright E window, made in Munich to designs by W. Dyce, hence more painterly than suited to stained glass. Effigy of the 3rd Duke of Northumberland (died 1847; Carew).

Cragside, the Drawing Room (1883–85; R.N. Shaw), near Rothbury

12m SW, B6341, *Cragside* (NT), near **Rothbury**, the country house of the Newcastle armaments king, Sir William Armstrong, built 1869–85 (R. Norman Shaw). Armstrong began with a small shooting lodge and progressively enlarged it to its present highly romantic silhouette on the rocky wooded hillside. The plan is most complex, arising from the problem of building around the old shooting lodge, the elevations are mostly of large mullioned and transomed windows at wildly varying levels with the main excitement reserved for the roofline where half-timbering and tiled roofs appear, particularly effective on the entrance side which is stopped against a heavy stone tower with pitched roof and cupola on top. The principal roofline feature is a larger tower, battlemented with a half-timbered top the size of a small house clustered about with massive chimney stacks. Fine interiors, newly restored, with much of the original furniture in aesthetic movement taste: William Morris glass, William de Morgan pottery and tiles, carved floral panels. In the drawing-room, colossal marble and alabaster inglenook. As befitted a great inventor and industrialist Cragside was equipped with the latest in modern technology, the first house in Britain fully equipped with electric light, telephones between rooms, hydraulic lifts and central heating.

BERWICK UPON TWEED. A1 29m N of Alnwick. The Tweed is crossed by the *Royal Border Bridge* (1850; R. Stephenson), 28 stone-faced arches riding high over the rooftops and the river, one of the finest railway structures in Britain. In Hide Hill, off Marygate, Italianate *Corn Exchange* (c 1860) with corner tower and palazzo style bank adjoining. 10m SW, A698, *Tillmouth Park* (1882; C. Barry Jr), Elizabethan style. 4m S at **Crookham**, *Pallinsburn Ho*, mostly neo-Jacobean of 1912. 2m SE, **Ford**, estate village of Ford Castle, where Louisa, Marchioness of Waterford, spent her widowhood improving the village on Ruskinian principles. The *School* (1860) has a set of murals by Lady Waterford of biblical scenes, the figures modelled from villagers and the landscapes Northumbrian. *Ford Castle* was remodelled for Lady Waterford (1860–65; D. Bryce) with a new tower and baronial alterations to the entrance front. 2m N, at **Etal**, *church* (1856–58; W. Butterfield) in mildly polychrome local stone with very steep roofs. 10m SE of Berwick, off A1, **Holy Island** is approached by a causeway over the sands. *Lindisfarne Castle* (NT) crowns the island, a 16C fort transformed (1902–06; E. Lutyens) into a romantic dream, still apparently more fort than private house with its sheer stone walls, keel-shaped at each end, and austere detail to the new work. The house was built for E. Hudson, owner of 'Country Life', and in best Arts and Crafts tradition few concessions were made to modern comforts, the lovely stone interiors have a monastic calm set off by whitewashed plaster and simple oak furniture. Further S, 5m E of Belford, B1342, *Bamburgh Castle* (open to public), the romantic silhouette visible on its rocky outcrop from miles around. The Castle is enormous and convincingly medieval, though in fact largely rebuilt (1894–1905; C.J. Ferguson) for Lord Armstrong, the Newcastle armaments and engineering tycoon. In the *churchyard*, monument to Grace Darling, heroic daughter of the Farne Islands lighthousekeeper who rescued nine survivors from the wrecked 'Forfarshire' in September 1838. Her boat is preserved in the memorial *museum*. There are attractive Tudor style stone railway *stations* (1847; B. Green) at **Belford** and **Chathill**, 6m S, built for the Newcastle to Berwick line.

BLYTH. A193 9m N of Tynemouth. Coal port for the Northumberland coalfield, also a resort town. *St. Cuthbert's Church* (1885–93; W.S. Hicks), good cruciform church with central tower, well detailed. *Presbyterian church* (1874; T. Oliver), Waterloo Rd, red brick with prominent brick spire. 4m SW, at **Cramlington**, mining town, *church* (1865; Austin and Johnson), High Victorian with bold W tower and fine N aisle window (c 1872; D. Cottier) with delicate Japanese-derived backgrounds. S aisle window by Cottier (1868) in harder colours. At **Stannington**, A1, 4m NW, *church* (1871; R.J. Johnson) with good tower and monument (1914; W. Reynolds Stephens) to Viscount Ridley of Blagdon Hall nearby. The Ridleys patronised the Newcastle sculptor J.G. Lough for many years and several of his monumental works survive in the grounds of the Hall.

HEXHAM. A68 20m W of Newcastle. *Hexham Priory* still has its magnificent 13C E part, the E front rebuilt (1858; J. Dobson) not successfully. The nave (1907–09; Temple Moore) replaces the original destroyed by the Scots, Dec. and unostentatious. *Town Hall* (1865; J. Johnstone). At E end of Battle Hill, *Midland Bank chambers* (1896;G.D. Oliver), free N Renaissance style with oriel and rounded rear, designed probably by J.H. Sellers. 5m N, B6318, *Chesters*, late 18C house of the Claytons who excavated the nearby Roman fort, much enlarged (1891–94; R. Norman Shaw) in an English Baroque style, pioneering in that the garden front wings are at an angle to the original house, the first example of the 20C favourite 'butterfly plan'. The W front is a giant curve with central Ionic columns, more Roman than English Baroque. 4m E of Hexham, **Corbridge**, with orieled *Town Hall* (1887; F. Emily) in Norman Shaw manner. 2m NW, *Beaufront Castle* (1837–41; J. Dobson), splendidly set over the Tyne Valley with an outline of strong castellated tower and varied lower ranges, the massing and stonework making it unusually impressive for the date. Built for a Newcastle merchant. 6m NE of Corbridge, at **Matfen**, *Matfen Hall* (1832–36; T. Rickman), an early Elizabethan revival house, the style suggested by the owner, Sir E. Blackett, who claimed later to have designed most of the building. Theatrical Gothic great hall with stained glass W window and hammerbeam roof, very impressive. Blackett designed the *church* (1841) in a heavy EE style, later spire. Along the Tyne valley runs the Newcastle–Carlisle railway, one of the earliest in the country, opened 1838. One early station survives at **Wylam**, 7m E of Corbridge, where, appropriately, George Stephenson, the first great railway engineer, was born in 1781. *Church* (1886; R.J. Johnson).

MORPETH. A1 15m N of Newcastle. In the Market Place, Vanbrugh's *Town Hall* of 1714 heavily rebuilt 1870 after a fire. In Newgate, *St. James' Church* (1843–46; B. Ferrey), grandly scaled neo-Norman set behind an arched screen. Crossing tower and apsed chancel with frescoes by Clayton and Bell. At **Whalton**, 5m SW, B6524; *Manor House* converted from a row of houses (1908; E. Lutyens) in Lutyens' classical manner. 12m W of Morpeth, B6343, **Cambo**, estate village of Wallington Hall with fine *church* tower (1883). *Wallington Hall* (NT), the late 17C mansion of the Blacketts, has a remarkable hall, the inner court roofed over in 1855 (J. Dobson) and given Italianate arcades wholly decorated with painted scenes of Northumbrian history by William Bell Scott, recommended by Ruskin, a friend of Lady Trevelyan, the owner. Ruskin and Lady Trevelyan assisted in painting the floral panels between the main scenes. The whole scheme is among the most complete of Victorian painted interiors surviving. In the hall the Pre-Raphaelite emphasis is taken further with Woolner's marble Mother and Child group and Munro's Paola and Francesca, both sculptors involved with the Pre-Raphaelites and with Ruskin, notably at the Oxford Museum. By Munro also the charming portrait of Lady Trevelyan inscribed 'She enclosed and decorated this hall on the advice of John Ruskin'. At **Otterburn**, 12m NW, A696, *Otterburn Tower*, a medieval tower house, altered in the late 18C and the 19C to a large picturesque castellated house.

NOTTINGHAMSHIRE

MANSFIELD. A60 14m N of Nottingham. In the centre, ample Market Place with classical *Town Hall* (1836; W.A. Nicholson) and former *Savings Bank* adjoining (1840). *Monument* to Lord G. Bentinck (1849; T.C. Hine). In St. John's St, *church* (1854–56; H.I. Stevens), good Dec. with spire. SE window of 1857, bright colours, possibly by Holland, W window c 1905. On Nottingham Rd, *Cattle Market* (1877; W. Fothergill), polychrome brick with Germanic circular tower, and, further S, *St. Mark's Church* (1897; T. Moore), a distinguished interior with broad nave and unmoulded square piers to passage aisles, severe by comparison with contemporaries like Bodley. Understated exterior with small tower at SE angle. NW of centre, off Chesterfield Rd, *Inisdoon* (1904–05; Parker and Unwin), Crow Hill Drive, Arts and Crafts house to a tight L-plan, roughcast with mullion windows. 4m S, *Newstead Abbey* (open to public), home of the Byron family from 1539 until sold by the poet in 1818 after an unequal struggle to rescue it from decay. Restored from 1820 (J. Shaw Sr) for Byron's friend Colonel Wildman in early 19C Gothic with a new Norman style tower to balance the medieval abbey front. Great Hall and staircase refitted c 1830. Chapel, in former Chapter House, has High Victorian polychrome decoration of c 1865. Across the lake, picturesque stables (1862; M.E. Hadfield). Byron collections in the house. 3m W, at **New Annesley**, A611, *church* (1874; T.G. Jackson), Dec. with broach spire, the delicate detail characteristic of the later Gothic Revivalists. At **Farnsfield**, 6m SE of Mansfield, *church* rebuilt 1859 (Hine and Evans) with contemporary glass in the apse by Wailes. One good Arts and Crafts window of 1904 (Mrs E. Everett).

NEWARK. A46 16m SW of Lincoln. The parish *church's* 237ft spire built in the 14C was a much used model for Victorian church designers, the distinctive 'eyebrow' over the bell-lights reappear in several 19C derivatives. Inside, SE nave window by Wailes (c 1860), adjoining window in the scholarly 13C style of A. Gerente of Paris (c 1868). E window by Hardman (1864) in memory of Prince Albert, richly coloured, reredos by Comper (1937). In Kirkgate, to W, former *bank* (1887; W. Fothergill) in characteristic polychrome Gothic, very lively, though the tower has been shortened. In Middle Gate, to S, *Market Hall* (1884; C. Bell), an addition to the 1774 Town Hall. By the Trent Bridge, former *Ossington Coffee Palace (1882; George and Peto), an exceptionally handsome work in the vernacular manner of Norman Shaw, that is with first-floor oriel windows of later 17C type and touches of half-timber, tile-hanging and ornamental plasterwork more loosely 17C, all strongly composed under a single roof, overhanging each end with the lower floor arcaded like a market hall. Viscountess Ossington was a leading supporter of the temperance pub movement and this is the grandest memorial to an unsuccessful attempt at drink reform. Up Northgate, *Northgate Brewery* (1882–90) with handsome Queen Anne style office building (1890; W.B. Sanders). On Castle Gate, to S of Trent Bridge, *Library* (1882; Heman and Beddoes), free Jacobean, and former *Corn Exchange* (1847; H. Duesbury), classical to Baroque. At E end of Lombard St, *Castle Brewery offices* (1882; W. Bradford) in heavily carved French Renaissance style with centre tower. In London Rd, former *Technical School* (1898; Mallows and Grocock), pretty Queen Anne style, and *Hospital* (1879; W.B. Sanders) in the more portentous version of Queen Anne, heavily detailed. Over Trent Bridge, *Newark Castle Station* (1846), modest but handsome Italianate in brick and stone. 1½m E of Newark, A17, at **Coddington**, *church rebuilt 1865–68 (G.F. Bodley) in strong Early French Gothic, outstanding for the decoration inside, lovely stencil painting of the roofs (the wall decoration has been painted out), painted and gilded woodwork and stained glass by Morris and Co , of 1865 in the chancel and 1881–82 in S aisle.

1½m NW of Newark, A617, at **Kelham**, *Kelham Hall* (1859–61; G.G. Scott), now Newark DC offices, red-brick and stone Gothic mansion, the fullest expression of Scott's ideas on domestic and secular Gothic, hence bearing a clear family resemblance to the major public buildings by Scott (the St. Pancras Hotel, the Leeds Infirmary and the rejected Gothic designs for the Foreign Office), most notably in the mixture of Italian and French Gothic forms and the large plate-glass windows that Scott thought essential to the modern house. Determinedly asymmetrical elevations, reflecting the internal planning, raised into towers at the main angles, and a high roofline adorned with clusters of stacks. The whole effect is more municipal than domestic, appropriate to its new use, and Scott's fertility in varying designs of Gothic windows overwhelms the broader lines of the design. Fully Gothic vaulted interiors, with luxurious naturalistic carving and painted decoration, the drawing-room vaulted like a chapter house with central column and the two-storey hall adjacent monumentally arcaded (intended to link to a grand stair never built). The client was ruined with the expense, hence the uncompleted interior. 5m W, at **Southwell**, the *Cathedral* provides the finest array of medieval naturalistic carving in Britain in the chapter house, to set beside the endless inventions of the Victorians on the same theme, Victorian naturalism, as at Kelham, typically more insistent, sculpture displayed with rather than as part of architecture. In the aisles, glass by O'Connor, some exhibited at the Great Exhibition. Fine bronze kneeling figure of Bishop Ridding (1907; F.W. Pomeroy), the design by W.D. Caroe. *Bishop's Palace* to S remodelled 1907–09 (Caroe) in rambling roughcast style.

Flintham Hall (1851–57; T.C. Hine), Flintham

3m N of Newark, W of A1, at **North Muskham**, *vicarage* (1863; G.E. Street). 6m N, W of A1 at **Moorhouse**, High Victorian *chapel* (1860; H. Clutton), small but massively detailed in Early French manner with vaulted chancel. 2m NW at **Egmanton**, *church* restored 1896–98 (J.N. Comper) in full Anglo-Catholic taste for the Duke of Newcastle. Comper's work is here late Gothic, influenced by German 15C work, the great screen with canopy over the rood set with gilded stars a masterpiece of late 19C church design. Painted organ case over the S door, pulpit based on a 15C example at Ghent, altar tabernacle and E window glass all by Comper. 7m SW of Newark, off A46, at **Flintham**, *Flintham Hall* (1851–57; T.C. Hine), fascinating remodelling of a 18C house in Hine's 'Anglo-Italian' style, the proportions of the older core apparent on the main seven-bay garden front, despite the addition of a narrow polygonal bay at one end to upset symmetry and of a high entrance tower on the side elevation. Hine's determination to bring novelty to conventional Renaissance details, such as window surrounds, illustrates one solution to the perennial problem of the antithesis between 'copyism' and 'bizarrerie', both to be condemned. Most remarkable is the enormous conservatory at one end, fronted by a stone grid clearly related to Paxton's Crystal Palace, a relationship made more obvious by the iron and glass barrel roof which brings the height of the structure up to the roofline of the main house, a scale completely unexpected in a private residence. Inside, this magnificent space is linked through to a two-storey library with viewing balcony reached from the gallery. The library fireplace is set in the most elaborate Renaissance style blank screen, made by Holland and Sons for the Great Exhibition. The whole interior remains almost as furnished in the 1850s. Open by written appointment.

NOTTINGHAM. Victorian Nottingham was built on the lace and knitting industries. Among the earliest towns to be industrialised, the Luddite riots (1811–16) against the introduction of machinery were most severe here. The Chartist leader Feargus O'Connor was MP for Nottingham 1847–48. The city centre is still notably Victorian with office buildings and warehouses signifying 19C prosperity. In the late 19C and early 20C bicycles (Raleigh), cigarettes (Player) and pharmaceuticals (Boots) became major industries. At the S edge of the central area, *Midland Station* (1904; A. Lambert), terracotta and stone, Baroque style, the ornamental part essentially a screen wall or outside porte-cochère (as at Leicester and Sheffield). To E, on London Rd, *Goods Station* (1857; T.C. Hine), previously the Great Northern Station, quite elaborate in mixed Jacobean style. N of Midland Station, over Nottingham Canal with 19C warehousing, one now the *Canal Museum*, Middle Hill climbs to the old centre. To E, High Pavement, with *Shire Hall* (1770), heavily remodelled and extended in Italianate style 1877 (T.C. Hine) on S. *St. Mary's Church* to N, the parish church, has chapter house (1890; Bodley) added in the hope of becoming a cathedral and SE chapel by Temple Moore (1912). Lovely bronze S door (1904; H. Wilson), Art Nouveau. Inside, screen and reredos by Bodley (1885), rich E window (1865; Hardman) to Prince Albert and bright strongly drawn S transept window (1867; Heaton, Butler and Bayne).

To the N, the Lace Market area with the finest surviving warehouses, notably those on Broadway (1853–55; T.C. Hine) and the *Adams and Page warehouse* (1855; T.C. Hine) at N end of Stoney St. The Broadway scheme is laid out on a curved street plan, lined with four-storey buildings in brick, loosely Italianate. The Adams and Page

W. Fothergill's offices No. 15 George Street (1894–95; W. Fothergill), Nottingham

building is far grander, stone-fronted with centrepiece set back and wings curving forward to the street, intended as model premises with library, dining-room, tea-room and chapel for the workforce. Hine's architecture is an eclectic blend of Renaissance elements, most distinctly personal the curious stone window tracery, like outsize Georgian glazing bars. In Plumptre Place, *Mills Building* (1906) with ornate Art Nouveau iron work, and, to N, on corner of Barker Gate, polychrome brick *warehouse* (1897; W. Fothergill) with picturesque treatment of the upper levels. N of Stoney St, Carlton St runs W, in George St to N, *No. 15* (1894–95; W. Fothergill), Fothergill's own office building, a statement of faith in the Gothic revival and its leading figures, the most delightful work of Nottingham's liveliest Victorian architect. True to his mentors, Pugin and Street, whose busts adorn the front, and Burges, Scott and Shaw, whose names are inscribed, Fothergill refers back to the heyday of the High Victorian Gothic in the brick polychromy and Gothic carved detail of the main front while the roofline shows the picturesque Germanic gables and timber-work that Fothergill adapted from Norman Shaw and the later 19C domestic revival school. In Pelham St, *Journal Chambers* (1860), polychrome Gothic. In Thurland St, to N, former *Corn Exchange* (1849; T.C. Hine), mixed Italian and Jacobean, and *National Westminster Bank* (1878–82; Fothergill), extravagant Gothic with carved decoration and central tower. Domed banking hall inside. Built as the head office of the Nottingham and Notts. Bank. In Victoria St, S of Pelham St, later 19C Italianate office buildings including former *Royal Exchange Insurance* (1872; Evans and Jolly). To W, Poultry runs into South Parade, the S side of the Market Place. Palazzo-style *National Westminster Bank* (1878; G.R. Isborn), stone fronted. *Yates's Wine Lodge* (1876) has a most atmospheric spit-and-sawdust interior with upper gallery surrounding the main floor. From Poultry, Bridlesmith Gate runs S, past heavily ornamented *Dog and Bear Hotel* (1876). In St. Peter's Gate, on N side, Gothic *Barclays Bank* (1874; T. Hawksley) and palazzo style *County Court* (c 1875; T.C. Sorby). *St. Peter's Church* has glass by Heaton, Butler and Bayne (c 1858 and c 1866) on S side and W window by J. Powell and Sons (c 1906). On Low Pavement, to S, *Savings Bank* (1836) classical, *No. 10* (1876; A. Smith) and *No. 16* (1910) High Victorian Gothic. Returning to Market Place, on N side at foot of King St, *Queen's Chambers* (1897; Fothergill), Gothic and determinedly picturesque with its stepped elevations and skyline of half-timbered gables and gargoyled brick turret. In King St, former *Jessops Store* (1895–97; Fothergill), equally lively, and *Prudential Assurance* (c 1890; A. Waterhouse) in the manner of the other offices for the firm, its hard red detail and well-composed S elevation effectively terminating the view up the street.

N of Upper Parliament St, *Theatre Royal* (1865; C.J. Phipps) with Corinthian portico facing down Market St, the auditorium of 1897 (F. Matcham) refurbished and altered 1976, one of the most notable modern renewals of a Victorian theatre. To N, complex of later 19C civic and educational buildings around Sherwood St, *Polytechnic* (1877; Lockwood and Mawson) and *Guildhall* (1887; Verity and Hunt) on either side, the college Gothic, the Guildhall French Second Empire style. To E, at S end of Mansfield Rd, Victoria Centre, on site of Victoria Station (1898; A.E. Lambert) of which the *clock tower* and *Victoria Hotel* (1901; R.W. Edis) remain. Just N, *The Yorker* pub (1898; W. Fothergill), curved to the corner, somewhat Germanic, like an illustration from Grimm. Shakespeare St runs W past Corinthian columned *Department of Adult Education* (c 1860) to Waverley St with former *College of Art* (1863–65; F. Bakewell), decorated with busts of famous artists and architects. Just N, *Arboretum* (1852) with statue of the Chartist F. O'Connor and pagoda (1863). Overlooking from N, *High School* (1866; T. Simpson), long castellated range with centre tower. The area up to Forest Rd to N, and to W of Waverley St, was laid out with villas, mostly of 1860s to 1870s. Off Waverley St, in Raleigh Rd, *All Saints' Church* (1863; Hine and Evans), High Victorian with prominent spire, gabled apse and good surrounding group of schools and vicarage. From College of Art, Clarendon St runs S past the *General Cemetery* (1837–40) with large terraced houses of 1860s, some ornately Gothic. To S, on Derby Rd, *RC Cathedral* (1841–44; A.W.N. Pugin), EE style, the parts clearly delineated and contributing to the well-scaled build-up to the crossing tower and broach spire. Relatively plainly detailed, for economy, but inside the chancel noticeably richer, though most of Pugin's fittings have gone. One chapel still has fine stencilled decoration to show Pugin's intentions. In College St, brick *Presbytery* (1844) and *Convent* (1845) by Pugin.

Wellington Circus marks the upper end of the large Victorian suburb laid out over the estate of Nottingham Castle for the 4th and 5th Dukes of Newcastle. T.C. Hine was the architect to the 5th Duke from 1854 and responsible for the layout and much of the building of The Park, W of the Castle. Wellington Circus dates from 1850–51. Just S in Regent St, *No. 25* (1846; T.C. Hine), Hine's own house, Gothic clearly influenced by Pugin. Hine also designed c 1852 the Jacobean terraces to W, *Nos 2–24* and *Nos 7–15*. *The Park* estate was laid out formally with two central circuses and the streets radiating out or curving around, the sloping site exploited through terracing, especially dramatic immediately under the Castle ridge. The first houses are here, in Castle Grove (1856; T.C. Hine), in white brick, mixed Elizabethan to Italianate, called by Hine 'Anglo-Italian'; the later ones within the formal layout are of the 1860s and 1870s, in red brick varying from Gothic to Elizabethan, 'Anglo-Italian' or Queen Anne. The Park is one of the most complete Victorian planned suburbs, formal in layout, uniform in its red brick but otherwise as varied as possible despite the role of Hine as architect and agent for the entire period of development. *Nottingham Castle*, the 17C mansion of the Dukes of Newcastle, was converted to Nottingham Museum (1876–78; T.C. Hine), the first municipal museum of art in England. 1m W, *Wollaton Hall*, Elizabethan mansion now Natural History Museum, *Industrial Museum* in stables covering all Nottingham industries and including working beam-engine.

N of centre, Mansfield Rd leads N, at the crest of the hill the Early French Gothic *St. Andrew's Church* (1869; W. Knight), determinedly muscular, an impressive landmark. Opposite, the Forest Recreation Ground, steeply below Forest Rd, with the crowded gravestones of *Church Cemetery* (1856) under Mansfield Rd. To NW of Mansfield Rd, Sherwood Rise, the S end laid out c 1845–50 with stucco villas, late 19C villas further N. E of St. Andrew's Church, Mapperley Rd, another area of rich manufacturers' houses (notably *No. 39*, Malvern House, 1874 by H. Sulley, in polychrome Gothic), running to Mapperley Park, mostly late 19C and Edwardian, on the estate of Mapperley Hall, Lucknow Avenue. On E side of Woodborough Rd, The Crescent is part of Alexandra Park, developed from 1855 (T.C. Hine). The scheme was intended to continue E to Hine's *County Asylum* (1857–59), now Coppice Hospital, Ransom Rd, a large Jacobean style symmetrical range with characteristic Hine detail. On Mansfield Rd, *No. 403* (1885; W. Fothergill) and *Nos 409–11* (1881–82; Fothergill), further N, outside the city boundary, at **Daybrook**, *Morley's Hosiery Factory* (1885) and *St. Paul's Church* (1890–96; J.L. Pearson), stone with fine tall spire, on the Normandy model that Pearson used at Truro and Kilburn. Effigy of the wife of the founder, Sir C. Seely, by T. Brock. Just NW, off B6004, Queen's Bower Drive runs N with drive to **Bestwood Lodge** (1862–65; S.S. Teulon) on right. Bestwood, built for the 10th Duke of St. Albans, is among the most acid of High Victorian Gothic houses, polychrome brick with sharply edged detail, some in stone, some in notched brick and a skyline of steep roofs interrupted by gables, dormers and turrets, the elements crashing together with all hint of symmetry avoided. The entrance porch is the tour de force of Teulon's design, the angles framed in a collision of buttresses, the Gothic entrance arch overhung by a stone oriel decorated with morose heads of Robin Hood and the Merrie Men and all capped by a pyramid spire. Two-storey great hall with galleries and massive fireplace. To W, *church* (1868; Teulon). On Mansfield Rd, to N, *Bestwood Pumping Station* (1871–74; T. Hawksley), Italian Gothic still in its landscaped grounds, the machinery unfortunately removed. For a working example, 3m N, off A60, *Papplewick Pumping Station* (1881–85; M.O. Tarbotton) (open to public) contains two beam-engines of 1884 in an interior temple to pure water, all ornamented with the most lavish cast-iron decoration, some lacquered gold, depicting water plants and birds. All this delicate ornament and the monumental engines contrast memorably. **Hucknall**, to W, 5m N of Nottingham, A611, is the burial place of the Byron family. Lord Byron's grave in the *church* is marked by a marble slab given in 1881 by the King of Greece. Unusually complete set of stained glass by C.E. Kempe, 1883–95, 25 windows in all. 4m W, off B600, **Beauvale House** (1871–73; E.W. Godwin), country retreat built for the 7th Earl Cowper on an isolated hill. Unusually romantic with steep hipped roofs clustered around a viewing tower with timber top lantern, all simply detailed with some half-timbering, the effect more N French or German than English vernacular, the close link between the Gothic revival and the vernacular manner of the school of Norman Shaw and Nesfield most obvious here. Three semi-detached cottages, lodge and manse at Moor Green also by Godwin. **Eastwood**, to SW, was the 'Bestwood' of 'Sons and Lovers'. D.H. Lawrence was born at *8a Victoria St* (1885), restored as it was in Lawrence's day. The surrounding streets of miners' houses have also been preserved.

4m S of Nottingham, off A60, at **Ruddington**, *Framework Knitters Museum*, Chapel St, restored workshops and cottages illustrating the early period of industrialisation of the knitting industry. 3m E, A606, at **Plumtree**, *church* restored 1874 (Bodley and Garner) with stencilled roof and screen. 4m S, off A606, at **Widmerpool**, *Widmerpool Hall* (1872; H. Clutton), stone Elizabethan-style gabled mansion with tall tower. *Church* by the hall elaborately rebuilt (1888–95) with marble effigy of Mrs Robertson (died 1891) of the Hall. 6m E of Nottingham, A52, at **Radcliffe-on-Trent**, heavy rock-faced *church* (1879; Goddard and Paget) with saddleback-roofed tower. 4m E, at **Bingham**, in the *church* S transept glass (c 1885) by the painter Frank Miles, his mother designed some attractive glass in the chancel (c 1873) and Frank Miles the lychgate outside (1881). Octagonal *Butter Cross* in Market Place (1861). At **Colston Bassett**, 5m S, *church* (1892; A.W. Brewill), an expensive work for the Knowles family of the Hall, elaborate Dec. with spire over the crossing. Marble angel memorial to Mrs Knowles (died 1892) inside. *The Hall* is Italianate (c 1860).

WORKSOP. A60 13m N of Mansfield. In the Market Place, *Corn Exchange* (1851; J.C. Gilbert), plain Jacobean. In Bridge St, *Trustee Savings Bank* (1843), stone-fronted classical. On the Chesterfield Canal, good early 19C yellow brick *warehouse* arched over the water. 1½m SE, *Worksop College*, one of the series of public schools linked to N. Woodard's Lancing College, Sussex, built (1890–95; R.H. Carpenter) to the plan established at the earlier schools of a quadrangular court flanked by open quads. Brick Tudor style with stepped gables. Chapel (1907; A. Webb), barrel-vaulted with E window by Kempe. N of the centre, *station* (1849; J. Drabble), stone Jacobean style, the unusual elaboration perhaps because this was the station for the ducal estates of Clumber and Welbeck.

S of Worksop, the cluster of great estates, called the 'Dukeries', carved out of Sherwood Forest. To SW, *Welbeck Abbey*, great house of the Dukes of Newcastle and later the Dukes of Portland. Extensive and plain 18C exteriors, the 19C interest is the work of the 5th and 6th Dukes of Portland. The 5th Duke (1800–79), a strange recluse at the end of his life, had a mania for plumbing and tunnelling, living in a few rooms but installing water-closets (unscreened) throughout the empty house and constructing miles of tunnels, one stretching 1¾m N towards Worksop wide enough for two carriages, others connecting the house with stables, lodges and the riding school. An underground suite built by the house included a vast ballroom, all well lit by circular skylights at ground level. The interiors are bleak and characterless, but the unsupported ceiling of the ballroom 63ft × 159ft was an engineering achievement. The Duke built the new Riding School (c 1860–69), the second largest in Europe with iron columns and glass roof, vast hothouses, a roller-skating rink and some 40 lodges around the estate. His works kept hundreds employed even if the end result leaves little to see. Inside the house some alterations of 1900 (George and Yeates) after a fire. The most interesting 19C work is in the old Riding School, converted to library and chapel 1889–96 (J.D. Sedding and H. Wilson), the furnishings by Wilson in Byzantine style with remarkable Art Nouveau metal and marble work, executed by F.W. Pomeroy, including lectern, font, altar cross, altar front and beaten bronze gates. In the library alabaster chimneypiece by Pomeroy of exceptional richness. Link to the house with good plasterwork in Arts and Crafts taste. SE of Worksop, *Clumber Park* (NT), the estate of the Dukes of Newcastle, the great house demolished in 1938 by the 9th Duke. By the lake *church* (1886–89; Bodley and Garner), built for the 7th Duke, one of the masterpieces of 19C church building, showing at its best the refined Gothic of the later Victorians after the hectic vigour of the High Victorian era. Red and white stone, late Dec. style, symmetrical about a central tower and spire rising 180ft, the spire delicately ringed by pierced stonework linked by flying buttresses to the tower pinnacles. Windows set high accentuating the internal height, varied only at the E end to increase the light on the altar. Interior fully vaulted, of noble proportions with excellent carved woodwork by the Rev. E. Geldart, stained glass by Kempe and alabaster high altar by Bodley. 3m S, *Thoresby Hall* (1865–75; A. Salvin), the third great house of the Dukeries, rebuilt for the 3rd Earl Manvers in monumental Elizabethan to Jacobean style. Near symmetrical main elevations to E and S with central tower features but the angles varied, all in an unsympathetic coursed rubble stone. The detail and materials make the outside bleak from close but the silhouette, with the two main features appearing asymmetrically, is impressive. Interiors on a magnificent scale, the hall rising three storeys, overlooked by upper galleries and linked to a monumental staircase. Estate housing and *church* (1876; A. Salvin) at **Perlethorpe** to E. 5m E, at **Milton**, W of A1, *Mausoleum* (1831–32; Sir R. Smirke), neo-classical, the W end intended as the parish church, the E end, entered from a Doric portico, the mausoleum of the Dukes of Newcastle, a rotunda flanked by tomb chambers. Severe Greek Doric detail, suitably funereal, the atmosphere enhanced by the isolated site. At **Bevercotes**, just W, *National Mining Museum*, Lound Hall.

9m E of Worksop, A620, **Retford**, market town on the old Great North Road. In the Market Place, *Town Hall* (1866–68; Bellamy and Hardy), with French pavilion roofs, and former *bank* (1887; Chorley and Connon) adjoining, bright red brick, Gothic. Parish *church* much restored 1854–55 (G.G. Place) and chancel refurnished 1873 (G.F. Bodley). Chancel glass 1858 by Wailes except E window (1874; Clayton and Bell). More mid 19C glass in the aisles. On London Rd, *Grammar School* (1855–57; D. Burton), Tudor style.

OXFORDSHIRE

ABINGDON. A34 8m S of Oxford. *St. Helen's Church* has chancel rebuilt 1873 (Woodyer) with reredos 1897 (Bodley). In Market Place, *Corn Exchange* (1886; C. Bell). To W, in The Square, stone-fronted *Congregational chapel* (1862; J.S. Dodd), classical. In Ock St, beyond, attractive *Baptist chapel* (1841) with painted Tuscan columned front. N of Ock St, *Albert Park*, a miniature suburb laid out c 1860 around semicircular gardens with Albert Memorial (1865), Gothic villas, some brick and half-timber, some stone, mostly by E. Dolby, large Gothic buildings for *Roysse's School* (1869–70; E. Dolby), and, central to the straight side, *St. Michael's Church* (1864–67; G.G. Scott), stone with bellcote.

3m NE of Abingdon, at **Radley**, *Radley College*, public school founded 1847, around the early 18C Radley Hall. Campanile tower (1847). Larger-scale later additions, brick Perp. chapel (1895) and dining-hall (1910) by T.G. Jackson, gate-tower and adjoining range 1904 (A.H. Ryan-Tenison). 2m SE of Abingdon, A415, at **Culham**, *Culham College* (1852; J. Clarke), teachers' training college founded by Bishop Wilberforce of Oxford, plain Gothic, the original buildings on three sides of a courtyard with cloister. Culham *station*, to E, is one of Brunel's small Tudor style stations (c 1845). To E, **Clifton Hampden**, Thames-side village with *bridge* (1864; G.G. Scott) and *church*, restored 1844 and 1864 by Scott, perched on a bluff over the river. Fittings mostly of 1864–67 including fine iron and bronze screen. Effigy of G.H. Gibbs (died 1842) in canopied tomb by Scott. Mosaic reredos (C. Buckeridge) and E window (Clayton and Bell) added 1873. H.H. Gibbs, Lord Aldenham, was patron of the church, the *vicarage* (1843 and 1865; Scott) and *school* (1844; J. Clarke) were built for the Gibbs family, the vicarage much extended (1905) to become the Manor House for Lord Aldenham. 3m E, A423, at **Dorchester**, *Dorchester Abbey*, a cathedral before the Norman Conquest, with magnificent 14C choir. Restoration for the Oxford Architectural Society from 1844. E window with its remarkable central buttress was restored by Butterfield (1846–47), glass in the rose by O'Connor. By Butterfield also the wagon roof, tile and alabaster E wall, nave benches, pulpit and lychgate (1852). In High St, *Church House* (1878; G.G. Scott), brick and half-timber with fish-scale tiles, built as a missionary college, partly incorporating older houses. In Martin's Lane, *School* (1872; Scott). In Bridge End, *RC church* (1849; W.W. Wardell), elaborate small chapel with richly decorated chancel, painted and gilt with much carved work. Glass by Ward and Nixon. 4m S of Abingdon, off A34, at **Steventon**, by the railway, former *Superintendent's House* (c 1840; I.K. Brunel), Tudor Gothic, of unusual scale because for a brief period 1842–43 the Great Western Railway's two committees, based respectively in London and Bristol, met here, half way between, for board meetings. *School* (1861–64; Street).

BANBURY. A423 23m N of Oxford. On the main crossing in Horsefair, *Banbury Cross* (1859; J. Gibbs), Gothic of the Eleanor Cross type with royal figures added 1914. *Church Hall* (1904; W.E. Mills), free Tudor in brown stone to N. Opposite, parish *church* (1790–1822; S.P. Cockerell), interior altered 1873 (A.W. Blomfield) with apsed chancel and imitation mosaic painting. Fine stained glass by Heaton, Butler and Bayne. In South Bar St, by the Cross, former *Poor Law Offices*

(1900; W.E. Mills), now Museum, Jacobean style, and to S, *RC church* (1838; Hickman and Derick), a nice group with presbytery and school. Chancel possibly by Pugin. E of the Cross, Market Place, with, on N side, ashlar classical facade of former *Corn Exchange* (1857; W. Hill), facing W. Adjoining, small palazzo style former *bank* (1840). Behind, *Nos 23–4 Cornhill* (1866; W. Wilkinson), virtuoso display of High Victorian polychrome brickwork, Gothic with the most varied facades possible on a cramped site. On W side of Market Place, *Midland Bank*, French-roofed front to another Corn Exchange (1857; J. Murray). To E, in High St, *Town Hall* (1854; E. Bruton), stone Gothic with pretty clock tower. W of the Cross, in West Bar St, High Victorian Gothic *terrace* of c 1870. To S, in Crouch St, entertaining stucco *villas* (c 1840) varying from Italianate to Gothic to suit all tastes. NW of centre, A41, *St. Paul's Church* (1853; B. Ferrey), Warwick Rd, EE style with good glass of 1850s.

2m NW, at **Wroxton**, *Wroxton Abbey*, 17C mansion restored and enlarged c 1840–60, the S wing added 1858 (J. Gibson) and the interior with much carved woodwork, partly new, partly reused 16C and 17C pieces. 3m SW of Banbury, A361, at **Bloxham**, *All Saints' School*, founded 1854 by an associate of N. Woodard of Lancing, Sussex, with the same Anglican ideals, but abandoned when only part of the N range had been built of a quadrangular design by G.E. Street. Refounded 1859 by the curate of Deddington, P. Egerton, who opened the school with no capital and one pupil but gradually built it up until, in 1896, it joined the group of Woodard schools. Egerton's buildings were also by Street, a schoolroom with dormitories over (1864), dining-hall (1869) and chapel (1871) raised up over classrooms to give it more prominence. Glass by Clayton and Bell. The parish *church* has splendid work by Street of 1865–66 and 1869–70, the chancel largely rebuilt with new reredos, stalls and E window filled with lovely early Morris glass, figures by Burne-Jones and the heavenly city above by P. Webb. Opposite, *vicarage* (1857; Street). At **Milton**, 2m E, *church* (1856; Butterfield), stone with heavily buttressed central tower, simple geometrical shapes powerfully handled. S porch and lychgate with good examples of Butterfield's wood construction. 2m E, at **Adderbury**, *church* restored 1831–34 (J.C. Buckler) and 1866–70 (G.G. Scott). Elaborate chancel fittings are mostly restorations of 1831–34, by Scott the recreated screen and stalls and new organ case. Gothic *schools* (1854; Buckler). The *Manor House*, S of church, is 16C restored from ruin 1887 (A. Webb). 2m S of Bloxham, at **Barford St. John**, *church* rebuilt 1860–61 (G.E. Street) with octagonal tower over S porch. At **Sibford Gower**, 7m W of Banbury, B4035, *church* (1840; H.J. Underwood), lancet Gothic, plain but impressive with Greek-cross plan. E window c 1840 by Willement. Mosaic, alabaster and marble wall monument to Mrs Stevens (died 1907). At **Sibford Ferris**, to SE, *Home Close* (1911; Baillie Scott), low gabled house in simplified Cotswold style.

BICESTER. A41 16m NW of Aylesbury. In the parish *church* splendid circular stone and marble pulpit by Street (1862) and one window by Morris in SE chapel (1866). *School* (1858; T. Nicholson). 1½m NE, A421, *Brashfield House* (1871–73; W. Wilkinson), gabled Tudor. 3m W of Bicester, B4030, at **Middleton Stoney**, *church* with tower rebuilt 1858 (S.S. Teulon) and mausoleum on N side of the Earls of Jersey, built 1805, made neo-Norman (S.S. Teulon) with dark romantic interior, red walls, gilt ceiling and marble floor. Jersey memorials including the 5th Earl (died 1859), altar tomb with portrait roundels,

and one to Princess Esterhazy and Lady C. Villiers (c 1860), heavily
sentimental. Chancel fittings and pulpit 1868 (G.E. Street). *Middleton
Park*, the Jersey house, was rebuilt by Lutyens (1938).

CHIPPING NORTON. A361 19m NW of Oxford. In the Market Place,
classical *Town Hall* (1842; G.S. Repton). W of the town, *Bliss Valley
Tweed Mill* (1872; G. Woodhouse), the only textile mill in Southern
England to rival the great Victorian mills of the North. Symmetrical
stone front with corner towers and absurd yet successful feature of a
dome from which rises a great columnar chimney stack. At **Churchill**,
3m SW, B4450, memorial *tower* (1870) to J. Langston and elaborate
Gothic *schools* (1870). William Smith (1769–1839), the 'father of
English geology', was born at Churchill. Monolith to his memory set
up 1891. 3m E of Chipping Norton, *Heythrop House*, monumental
Baroque house (1706–20; T. Archer) gutted by fire in 1831 and restored 1871–77 (A. Waterhouse) for A. Brassey, son of T. Brassey,
railway contractor. Top-lit great hall in the Baroque style with upper
stained glass by Morris. Lodge at **Enstone** by Waterhouse. Estate
church (1880; A.W. Blomfield) with carved angel supporters to the
roof. At **Little Tew**, to NE, *church* 1853 (Street) enlarged 1869 (C.
Buckeridge). To W, pretty group of brick *school*, *house* and
almshouses (1862; Buckeridge). Further on, *vicarage* c 1857 (Street)
enlarged 1868–69 (Buckeridge) and 1880, Gothic with grouped lancet
windows, wing with porch tower part of the later additions. 6m SE of
Chipping Norton, at **Kiddington**, *Kiddington Hall*, remodelled in Italianate style c 1850 (C. Barry) with formal terraced gardens. Stables by
Barry, the original design with low eaves roof and band of windows of
remarkable simplicity, but since altered. Pretty lodge, possibly by
Barry. At **Radford**, ½m N, small *chapel* (1841; A.W.N. Pugin), plain
and simple. 4m NE of Kiddington, at **Steeple Barton**, *Barton Abbey*,
16C to 17C with picturesque gabled front also lodge and gates of c
1840. In the village, *vicarage* (1856; S.S. Teulon) with arched-headed
sash-windows, showing Teulon an early experimenter with non-
Gothic forms in the design of simpler houses. At **Sandford St. Martin**,
2m NW, *church* with chancel rebuilt 1856 (G.E. Street). Lychgate by
Street (1863). 6m S of Chipping Norton, A361, at **Shipton-under-
Wychwood**, *church* restored 1858–59 (G.E. Street) with new chancel
fittings. E window by Hardman (1874), S aisle W window (1849) in 14C
style. *School* (1854; G.E. Street). Just W, at **Milton-under-
Wychwood**, fine pair of *church* and *school* (1853–54; G.E. Street), the
church with octagonal spirelet carried on a central buttress. *Vicarage*
(1898; T.G. Jackson) in Queen Anne style.

FARINGDON. A420 13m NE of Swindon. 3m NW, A417, **Buscot**,
estate village largely rebuilt c 1890 (George and Peto) for Sir A. Henderson of Buscot Park. Very pretty Cotswold stone group with village
hall, well in the centre, and numerous cottages, sensitively detailed
with mullioned windows and stone-tiled roofs. *Buscot Park* (NT) is late
18C altered 1889 (George and Peto). In the parlour on the garden
front, Burne-Jones' *Briar Rose sequence of paintings (1890) in early
Renaissance frames designed by Burne-Jones. Large mid 19C stable
block. In the parish *church*, NW of the village, chancel glass of the
1890s by Burne-Jones. N of the Thames, 3m E of Lechlade, at
Kelmscott, *Kelmscott Manor*, William Morris' home from 1871 until
his death in 1896, initially shared with Rossetti, an arrangement complicated by Rossetti's attachment to Jane Morris and gradual retreat
into laudanum. For Morris, Kelmscott was a rural ideal, Rossetti

shared little of this, he was 'all sorts of ways so unsympathetic with the sweet simple old place' wrote Morris in 1872, his own feelings for the house most beautifully expressed at the end of 'News from Nowhere' (1890). The house (open by appointment) contains Morris relics, furniture and textiles. Jane Morris built *Morris Cottages* (1902; P. Webb) in Morris' memory, two cottages adjoining built by May Morris (1915; Gimson). Morris's tomb (1897; P. Webb) is in the *churchyard*. 2m N of Lechlade, A361, at **Little Faringdon**, former *vicarage* (1867; Butterfield) in rock-faced stone with red tile roof and strong array of shouldered stone chimneys. 2m N, at Filkins, *church (1855–57; Street), one of Street's best small country churches, strong outline of steep roof and rounded apse with plate tracery. Chancel glass by Clayton and Bell (1868).

2m E of Faringdon, off A420, at **Littleworth**, *church* (1839; H. Underwood), one of the first built under the influence of the Oxford Tractarians, in this case E.B. Pusey, still typical of the Georgian or Commissioners' Gothic with none of the archaeological correctness soon to be thought essential for revived Anglican worship. 2m E, at **Buckland**, in the *church*, S transept completely decorated c 1890 in Powell's tile mosaic. *Buckland House* (1757; J. Wood Jr) was enlarged in matching style (1910; W. Romaine Walker), the original house now the centrepiece of a very large mansion still framed by Wood's octagonal roofed outer pavilions. In the village, Gothic *school* (1856; Street) and much mid to late 19C estate housing. 3m E, at **Longworth**, in the *church* remarkably modern looking E window of 1900 by Heywood Sumner over a painted reredos in beaten silver frame, typically Arts and Crafts. 4m SW of Faringdon, off A420, at **Watchfield**, small stone church by Street (1857–58) with neat W end composition of buttresses, nave, bellcote and door at W end of N aisle. At **Shrivenham**, A420, *Beckett Hall* (1831–34; T. Liddell), large Tudor Gothic house, symmetrical fronts picturesquely and not incorrectly detailed. Liddell was an amateur architect. Now library for Royal Military College of Science. In the village, Gothic *school* (1863), the gable and bellcote design a period piece, exaggerated roof pitch and determined asymmetry. To SW, **Bourton**, estate village of *Bourton House* (1845; W.F. Ordish) stone Tudor style.

HENLEY-ON-THAMES. A423 7m NE of Reading. On the riverside late 19C ornamental *boathouses* associated with the Regatta. The parish *church* is heavily Victorianised, enlarged 1853 (B. Ferrey) with much late Victorian glass, E window 1890, SE chapel and S aisle glass all by Lavers and Westlake. Fine glass of 1868 (Hardman) in NE chapel. *Almshouses* of 1830 and 1846 each side of churchyard. In the centre, very pretty early 18C style *Town Hall* (1900; H. Hare) with hipped roof and cupola. In Gravel Hill, beyond the Market Place, former *School* (1849), in flint and brick, and entry to *Friar Park* (1896), large brick and stone Flamboyant Gothic house designed for himself by Sir F. Crisp, solicitor. *Henley Brewery*, New St, has buildings and malthouses mostly of late 19C. On the riverside, each side of the bridge, the ornate half-timbered houses and hotels typical of this stretch of the Thames. *Little White Hart Hotel* N of bridge, *Imperia* and *Royal Hotels* to S, all of c 1890.

3m S, A4155, at **Shiplake**, *church* rebuilt 1869 (G.E. Street) wi' good marble and alabaster pulpit and reredos. *Shiplake Court* (18' George and Peto), E of the church, is Tudor to Renaissance style e rely in diapered brick with off-centre entrance tower and full-he great hall central to the garden front. Germanic water tower. 5m

Henley, W of B481, *Wyfold Court* (1872–76; G.S. Clarke), most elaborate French Gothic house, built for a Preston cotton magnate and MP, in diapered brick with much ornate stonework in Flamboyant style, the entrance front particularly spectacular with two steep-roofed and spiky towers. Vast interior rooms, originally designed for the owner's collection of paintings. Now Borocourt Hospital. At **Stoke Row**, just N, *church* (1846; R.C. Hussey) and exotic Indian style well with cast-iron columns holding an onion dome, given in 1863 by the Maharajah of Benares. To S, on the Thames, 3m NW of Reading, at **Mapledurham**, *church* altered 1863 (Butterfield) with chequered pattern to tower, new porch and timber piers inside dividing off a N aisle. Good Butterfield chancel fittings including pink marble panelling to E wall patterned with trefoils, quatrefoils and cinquefoils. 4m NW of Henley, A420, at **Nettlebed**, Arts and Crafts village *club* (1912; C. Mallows) opposite the church, courtyard plan with steep roofs. 6m W, **Wallingford**, by the Market Place, *St. Mary's Church*, rebuilt 1854 (D. Brandon) with elaborate marble and bronze pulpit by E. Onslow Ford (1889). Neo-Georgian *bank* (1915; F. Shann) on E side of Market Place. 1m SE, off A4074, *Carmel College*, **Mongewell**, built around a neo-Georgian Thames-side mansion (1890; R.S. Wornum).

OXFORD. Victorian Oxford grew principally with the University, nearly every college expanding or rebuilding during the period and North Oxford being laid out as a suburb for the families of dons. Most of the leading Victorian architectural schools left their mark on the town, but it is with the Gothic Revival and its High Victorian and High Church side that Oxford is most significantly associated. At Oxford, the High Church movement of the Anglican church had its origins, early theological debates and most bitter controversies. The Oxford Movement for the reform of the Anglican church through a re-emphasis on the church's roots in pre-Reformation theology, on ritual over evangelism and on the mysteries of faith, such as the Real Presence of Christ in the Eucharist, began at Oriel College with J.H. Newman (1801–90), E.B. Pusey (1800–82) and J. Keble (1792–1866), all fellows of the college in the 1820s. Keble's 1833 sermon on the 'National Apostasy', against state interference in the church, was followed by the sequence of 'Tracts for the Times' on doctrinal questions started by Newman and finally suppressed in 1841 by request of the Bishop of Oxford after Newman's Tract 90 came close to invalidating the doctrinal differences between the Anglican and Catholic churches. After Newman seceded to the Roman church in 1845, Pusey became the leader of the High Church party, with Keble, from his Hampshire parsonage, the continued inspiration. From Oxford, Tractarian inspired clergy and sons of landowning gentry spread revived Anglican practice to the furthest corners of Britain, building churches and schools to advanced Gothic patterns, arranged for ritual worship, in the expanding cities and in the remote countryside, while in Oxford, the argument between low church evangelicals and ritualists continued into the 1860s. Oxford was also the scene of controversy over Darwinian theory culminating in the debate between T.H. Huxley and Bishop Wilberforce of Oxford. The revived medievalism of the Pre-Raphaelites stemmed from Morris' and Burne-Jones' days as undergraduates at Exeter College. Ruskin's influence on generations of undergraduates began in the 1850s, the Oxford Museum (see below p. 358) enshrining his ideas on appropriate decoration and exemplifying the High Victorian Gothic outlined in the 'Seven Lamps of Architecture' and 'The Stones of Venice'. Ruskin's socialism influenced many, not least Morris, for whom Ruskin was the 'Master', focussing his discontent with industrial society and pointing the way to an ideal of creative labour, where the moral being of the labourer could escape the utilitarianism of capitalist manufacturing.

Carfax, at the centre of Oxford, is a commercial crossing, apart from the tower of St. Martin's Church. Ornate turn of the century stone buildings, *Tower House* and *Midland Bank* (c 1895; H. Hare) by the tower, *Lloyds Bank* (1900; S. Salter and R. Davey) on the NE corner with curvaceous gables and much mixed N Renaissance detail. From Carfax, the High St runs E. On N side, behind a late 18C front, the extensive covered *Market* with timber roofs and grid of shops within. On S side, Gothic *National Westminster Bank* (1866; F. and H. Francis). On N side, *Brasenose College*, the High St front 1886 and 1907 (T.G. Jackson) in a free 15C Gothic with gate-tower and delicate carving. In the 17C chapel, painting to vault (c 1890; Kempe), screen and organ case by Jackson (1892) and memorial to Walter Pater (died 1894; W.B. Richmond), fellow of the college from 1864. *St. Mary's Church* where Keble, Newman and Pusey preached, was much restored during the 19C, some notable Victorian stained glass, particularly the great W window (1891; Kempe). In the S aisle, E end, two windows by Pugin, made by Hardman, and one by Clayton and Bell to Keble. Choir screen 1827 (J. Plowman). Opposite, the High St front of *Oriel College*, the Rhodes Building (1908–11; B. Champneys), weighty mixture of 17C vernacular and classical motifs. In the front quad, entered from Oriel Square, hall, with decorative scheme of screen panelling and stained glass (1909–20; J.N. Comper), and chapel with stained glass by H. Wooldridge (1885), rich in colour. E of St. Mary's Church, *All Souls College*. Chapel restored 1872–76 (G.G. Scott) when figures were replaced in the great E reredos and the sanctuary refitted. Stained glass by Clayton and Bell of 1870s, imitating surviving 15C work, W window, Last Judgement, by Hardman (1861). On S side, *University College*, the W end New Building (1842; C. Barry) an instructive contrast with the Durham Building (1903; H.W. Moore) at the far E end of the High St front, Barry's work hard-edged and conventional, Moore's full of pretty detail, of an Arts and Crafts delicacy. In Front Quad, chapel remodelled 1862 (G.G. Scott) with new roof and choir decoration. E window glass (1862; O'Connor) in complete contrast to the 1641 van Linge glass elsewhere. W of front quad, *Shelley Memorial* in a domed, marble-lined chamber (1893; Champneys), the white marble corpse of the drowned poet (1892; E. Onslow Ford) on a dark marble and bronze plinth, the whole ensemble appropriately damp or submarine. On S side of the garden behind, *Library* (1861; G.G. Scott), like Exeter College Library a neat Gothic design, logical and original in its handling of Early Dec. motifs. On the E side of the college, Logic Lane, with the brick and half-timbered rear of the Durham Building, and, on W side, *Master's Lodgings* (1879; G.F. Bodley), tall, stone, Jacobean style. In *Queen's College*, on N side, in the dining-hall scheme of Renaissance style stained glass by Sir R. Blomfield (1909) in richly streaked and coloured glass by J. Powell and Sons. To E, *St. Edmund Hall*, excellent early *glass by Morris and Co (1865) in the chapel E window, side windows by Clayton and Bell. On the High St the college now includes a handsome roughcast gabled range (1901; E.P. Warren).

Opposite, the *Examination Schools* (1876–82; T.G. Jackson), the buildings that established a new style for Oxford in the late 19C, and Jackson as the leading practitioner, a style derived from the late Elizabethan and Jacobean, where Renaissance elements mingle with the native mullioned windows, gables and turrets. The design is an open quadrangle, facing E, and an entrance hall parallel to the N wing, facing the High St. This High St front has an ornate porch fronting a symmetrical range of mullion and transom windows, all under a steep roof and centre lantern. Inside a marbled and hammerbeam-roofed entrance hall. The courtyard front displays an array of great windows lighting the examination halls and a centrepiece that piles on motifs in three riotous storeys, marking, only indirectly, the position of the main stairs. Adjoining the High St front, *Ruskin School of Art* (1887; Jackson), a milder gabled front with delightful carved frieze. To E, *Eastgate Hotel* (1898; E.P. Warren), roughcast 18C style. Further E, *Magdalen College*, with, at W corner, Tudor Gothic library (1849–51; J.C. Buckler) built as a hall for Magdalen College School, and then the long front of *St. Swithun's Quad (1880–84; Bodley and Garner), scholarly 15C Gothic based on the original cloister, attractively detailed with row of oriels and fine chimneystacks. Gate-tower facing the original buildings to E. Only one and a half sides of the intended three were completed to the 1880 design. Entrance gateway (1885) and *President's Lodgings* opposite (1886) also by Bodley and Garner. The chapel was heavily restored 1829–34 (L. Cottingham) with tiers of figures on E wall and organ screen, correctly detailed but in a lifeless stone that suggests plaster. The interior with the 17C grisaille glass somehow achieves the atmosphere of an early 19C mezzotint. In the hall timbered roof of 1902 (Bodley and Garner).

S of High St, from the Examination Schools, Merton Lane curves W past *No. 12* (c 1885; Jackson) and former *Warden's Lodgings* (1908; Champneys) of Merton College, both in the Jackson manner, on N side. On S, *Merton College*, the entrance front altered 1836–38 (E. Blore). In Front Quad, S side, Hall, heavily remodelled 1872–74 (G.G. Scott), the E side part of St. Albans Quad (1904–10; Champneys) in prettily detailed free Tudor style. Merton chapel was restored in the 1840s, with all the 17C classical fittings removed. In 1849–53 Butterfield completed the alterations with the painted roof (painting by J.H. Pollen), stalls, tile and marble floor and font. Max Beerbohm, undergraduate 1891–94, is commemorated in the Beerbohm Room in Mob Quad. His hilarious 'Zuleika Dobson' (1911) is set in Oxford. Opposite, on corner of Magpie Lane, typical T.G. Jackson addition (1884) to *Corpus Christi College*. To W, *Christ Church*, main entry from St. Aldate's. Tom Quad was given battlements, NE corner tower and large SE tower 1876–79 (G.F. Bodley), the SE tower designed to hold the bells displaced from the *cathedral* in Scott's restoration. The cathedral approach from Tom Quad and W porch are also by Bodley. Scott's restoration (1870–76) included the neo-Norman E end, S transept vestry with gallery over, and choir paving and fittings. E windows by Clayton and Bell. Exceptional series of *windows by Burne-Jones. In the Latin Chapel, at NE corner, St. Frideswide window of 1859, one of Burne-Jones' first works, made for Powell's, vigorous crowded scenes and hot colours, full of energy; in the other E windows, series of 1874–78, elegant white robed female figures and rich foliage, among the best of Burne-Jones work for Morris and Co. One S aisle window of 1870. In N transept, glass by Clayton and Bell (1872) in 16C style. In the nave, floor slab to the Tractarian, E.B. Pusey (died 1882). S of the cloisters, facing Christ Church Meadow, *Meadow Buildings* (1862–66; T.N. Deane), High Victorian Gothic on a very large scale, a long front broken by tall staircase bays and a gate-tower with crow-stepped gable. Plate tracery and Venetian Gothic touches, themes from the Oxford Museum building, if bleak by comparison. Ruskin was an undergraduate at Christ Church 1837–39. Charles Dodgson, Lewis Carroll, undergraduate and later mathematics lecturer here, wrote the 'Alice' stories for Alice Liddell, daughter of the Dean. In the hall, portraits of Carroll by Herkomer, Dean Liddell by Watts, Gladstone by Millais. In St. Aldate's, N of Christ Church, on E side, *Town Hall* (1893–97; H.T. Hare), lavish stone building in the Jacobean manner of T.G. Jackson, ornately carved with interiors to match, especially the barrel-vaulted Great Hall. In the building, Museum of the development of Oxford with recreated interiors. Gothic *Post Office* (1880; E. Rivers) opposite. *St. Aldate's Church* is mostly of 1862 and 1873 (J.T. Christopher). To S, *Pembroke College*, the Old Quad remodelled 1829 (D. Evans). In Chapel Quad, to W, N side 1844–46 (J. Hayward) and Hall 1848 (Hayward), 15C style with hammerbeam roof. The 1732 chapel on the S side has interior painting and stained glass in Renaissance style by C.E. Kempe. At S end of St. Aldate's *Folly Bridge* (1825–27) with *toll-house* (1844) and *Isis House* (1849), a brick castellated folly. Good early 19C converted riverside *warehouse* to E. W of Pembroke College, *St. Ebbe's Church*, rebuilt 1814–17 and 1862–66 (Street). To SW, in Paradise Square, former St. Ebbe's *vicarage* (1852; Street).

N of High St and E of Cornmarket, runs Turl St. Behind All Saints' Church, now Lincoln College Library, *Lincoln College* with street front refaced 1824. Behind Front Quad, Grove Building (1880–03; T.G. Jackson), more Gothic than most of his works but with Renaissance motifs. Behind Chapel Quad, former Library (1906; Read and Macdonald), attractive late 17C style, bow-fronted. To NW, *Jesus College*, the front range refaced in 15C style 1854 (J.C. and C.A. Buckler). Chapel restored 1864 (Street) with rich reredos and sanctuary panelling. E window 1856 (G. Hedgeland). On E side of Turl St, *Exeter College*, the chapel roof and flèche soaring over the front range in the view down Ship St. Front range refronted 1833 (H.J. Underwood) in 15C style, though the building is of 1672 and 1701. The *chapel (1854–60; G.G. Scott) is overpowering, the emphatic height in contrast to the quad and to traditional Oxford college chapels. Proud array of buttresses with statues, apsed E end and sharp flèche on the ridge. Fully vaulted interior with stained glass by Clayton and Bell, sanctuary fittings by Scott and stalls by Bodley (1884). Burne-Jones tapestry (1890) of the Adoration of the Magi on S wall. (Burne-Jones, and William Morris, were undergraduates at Exeter 1853–57.) Behind E range, Library (1856; Scott), attractively handled c 1300 style Gothic with blank arcading, gables and steep roof, timber-vaulted inside. By Scott also the *Rector's Lodgings* and part of the N front to Broad St (1857), the E end of this front is of 1833 (H.J. Underwood).

Across Broad St, *Trinity College*, the old college buildings set back behind Front Quad, framed on N and E by ranges in T.G. Jackson's Elizabethan to Jacobean style (1883–87). In the chapel Renaissance style glass (1885; Powell's). J.H. Newman an undergraduate here. To W, *Balliol College*, the most heavily Victorianised of all the medieval colleges, appropriately in view of the leading position the college had in the later 19C, notably under B. Jowett, Master 1870–93. Plans were prepared by Pugin (1843) for a complete rebuilding but rejected and alterations were subsequently piecemeal. High St front and *Master's Lodgings* to W, 1867–68 (A. Waterhouse), asymmetrical High Victorian Gothic, harsh in detail but a subtle composition with varied floor levels each side of the tower and balance achieved by a big gable on the E end and round tourelle at the W. N front to the quad overwhelming in scale. Chapel (1856–57; W. Butterfield), immediately notable for its structural polychromy, a feature already by 1870 contentious enough to lose Butterfield the chance of building the front range, though such Ruskinian banding is exceptional in Butterfield's work. The polychrome interior was destroyed in 1937. Monument to Jowett (1897; E. Onslow Ford), miniature effigy on sarcophagus in bronze. At NW angle of front quad, tower (1853; Salvin), giving access to Garden Quad. On W side, Warren's Buildings (1910–12; E.P. Warren), free early 18C style, and Salvin's Buildings (1852; Salvin), Tudor Gothic with gate-tower. The Hall (1876–77; Waterhouse), at N end, is the one building successfully related to the shapeless quad, raised on a high basement with outside stairs, steep roof and flèche. NW corner block to St. Giles (1907; E.P. Warren), late 17C style.

At E end of Broad St, former *Indian Institute* (1883–96; Champneys), a very successful stop to the view in mixed 17C style, an array of curved oriels to the upper floor and round corner turret, elephants impinging into the otherwise conventional decoration as the only oriental suggestions. To S, *Hertford College*, the North Quad, adjoining the Indian Institute, of 1900 (T.G. Jackson), gabled with less of the ornate Jacobean than Jackson's other buildings, the banded brick and stone stacks unexpectedly festive. Bridge over New College Lane (1913; Jackson), a delightful fantasy, linking the new work to the main college. The main facade has plain ashlar wings of 1818–22 (E. Garbett) with a most successful centrepiece (1887–89; T.G. Jackson) playing novel games with Palladian themes. On the rear, stair tower to N, the diagonals of the stair providing further excuse for inventive juggling. N range by Jackson (1895). Chapel on S side (1908; Jackson) introducing Italian early Renaissance motifs, the E window of Palladian type but with an extra light each side. Good interior fittings by Jackson. To E, on New College Lane, *New College* with chapel restored 1877–79 (G.G. Scott). By Scott, the hammerbeam roof, screen, stalls and renewed sculpture of E reredos. Hall roof by Scott (1865). On N side of the college, facing Holywell St, long bleak four-storey range (1872; Scott) continued to E with tower (1896; Champneys), unsuccessfully attempting to link Scott's range to the much lower and prettily detailed range to E (1885; Champneys). N of Holywell St, in Mansfield Rd, on W side, *Manchester College*, founded as a Unitarian college in Manchester. Gothic buildings of 1891–93 (T. Worthington). In the chapel, complete scheme of stained glass by Burne-Jones (1893–98), richly coloured. Opposite, *Department of Geography* (1898; A.B. Jackson), built as a private house in gabled Cotswold style. Further up, *The King's Mound* (1892; T.G. Jackson), with Jacobean curved gables. In Savile Road, *New College School* (1904; Nicholson and Corlette).

Off Cornmarket, to W, *Oxford Union*, Union Passage, the original Debating Room (1857; B. Woodward) in red-brick Gothic with sawtooth notching around the openings, a form of decoration Woodward favoured as structural and economical. The glory of the building was the decoration by Morris, Burne-Jones, Rossetti, J.H. Pollen and others, painted in an atmosphere of wild enthusiasm and in a medium totally unsuited. The paintings all but disappeared though the remnant was restored in 1930. The roof decoration however was redone in 1875 by Morris and survives, different but delightful. Over the entry, panel designed by Rossetti, carved by A. Munro. Adjoining to E, matching library addition (1863; W. Wilkinson). Red-brick and terracotta new Debating Hall (1878; Waterhouse). To W, in New Inn Hall St, *Wesleyan Chapel* (1878; C. Bell) and *St. Peter's College*, the college chapel the former church of St. Peter-le-Bailey (1874; B. Champneys).

The college now incorporates the former Girls' Central School (1901; L. Stokes) to S, a free late 17C style range with cupola over the centre, excellently detailed in rubble stone and ashlar. To SW, on New Rd, *County Hall* (1840; J. Plowman), a relatively rare example of a neo-Norman public building, the style chosen because of the Castle mound adjoining. Opposite, Gothic *Probate Registry* (1863; C. Buckeridge). Behind the Castle mound, *Oxford Prison*, built around the medieval castle remains, partly late 18C, largely of 1850 (H.J. Underwood). Further W, on Park End St, remnant of former *LNWR Station* (1851; Fox and Henderson), of interest as built by the contractors for the Crystal Palace using the same prefabrication principles and roofing system. To S, off Hollybush Row, *St. Thomas's Church*, heavily restored in 19C, with painted chancel roof by Kempe. Pretty brick and stone *vicarage* to N (1893; C.C. Rolfe). In Osney Lane, tenement blocks, a rare example of university interest in city problems, E of Hollybush Row, *Christ Church Old Buildings* (1866; E. Bruton), 30 flats originally, around a drying-green, and W of Hollybush Row, *Christ Church New Buildings* (1893; E. Hoole) with domestic revival tile-hanging to impart some cheer. Hythe Bridge St runs E from the LNWR station to George St.

Ashmolean Museum and the Taylorian Institute (1841–45; C.R. Cockerell), Oxford. Photograph c 1885

On N side of George St, former *Fire Station and Corn Exchange* (1894; H.W. Moore), now Arts Centre, and on S side, former *Boys' High School* (1880; T.G. Jackson), Jacobean, attractively and expensively detailed with tall proportions. To N, on N side of Gloucester Green, the former *Boys Central School* (1900; L. Stokes), small picturesque Tudor Gothic front in stone with stone tiles screening main school rooms in brick arranged around a circular top-lit hall. *Worcester College*, beyond, has late 18C chapel and hall by J. Wyatt flanking the entry. The interiors were overhauled by W. Burges, chapel 1864, hall 1876–79, the hall has reverted to late 18C decoration, the *chapel survives, Burges's decoration in a highly coloured Renaissance style, a tour de force. Every surface is painted, statues, stained glass (by H. Holiday) and mosaic pavement added, all to a complex iconographical scheme that swamps Wyatt's work without altering it structurally. Remarkable fittings, carved and inlaid stalls, alabaster candelabra, all by Burges. At E end of Beaumont St, built

1828–37, Oxford's equivalent of St. Pancras, the *Randolph Hotel* (1864; W. Wilkinson), massive yellow brick Gothic pile with pavilion roofs, facing the *Ashmolean Museum* (1841–45; C.R. Cockerell). The museum occupies the centre and W wing, the Taylorian Institute the E wing, facing St. Giles. Cockerell's classicism went beyond the formalism of earlier neo-Grecian or neo-Roman architecture to an individual synthesis of classical and Renaissance forms based on a personal scholarship that began with his own study of the Temple of Apollo at Bassae, whence the unusual Ionic capital, and included such diverse influences as Vignola, Wren and French neo-classicism. Porticoed centre with wings raised a storey higher, the walling in Bath stone, the detail in excellently carved Portland stone. A broad frieze of interlaced carving unites the parts with a bracket cornice over the wings, which are given exceptional sculptural boldness by applied Ionic columns over which an arch breaks the frieze, creating a triumphal arch motif on the end walls and triple arcade on the sides. The side to St. Giles is emphasised as a facade by detaching the four columns, the projected entablatures becoming pedestals for four standing figures representing the main W European languages. Every detail shows unparalleled care in relationship of mouldings, treatment of wall surfaces and placing of sculptural decoration. The museum includes good collection of Pre-Raphaelite paintings. To SE, *St. Mary Magdalen Church* with N aisle added 1842 (G.G. Scott), correctly detailed Gothic, showing Scott already this early among the leading Gothicists. Much 19C glass, S chapel E by O'Connor 1864, bright coloured S wall E (c 1864; Wailes) and Lady Chapel E 1844 (Wailes). The N aisle was built in connection with the *Martyrs Memorial* (1841–43; G.G. Scott) to the three bishops burnt in Broad St in 1555–56, an enlarged version of the Eleanor Cross at Waltham Abbey, Essex.

On E side of St. Giles, *St. John's College*, the N end of the street front 1880–1900 (G.G. Scott Jr) a sensitive piece of late Gothic design, memorable for the lion's masks dotting the front. The chapel was restored 1843 (E. Blore). E window by Kempe (1892). On W side, *No. 66* (1869; G. Wyatt), High Victorian Gothic house, and *Pusey House* (1911–16; Temple Moore), founded as a 'house of sacred learning' in memory of Dr Pusey, housing his theological library. The last important Gothic work in Oxford, a distinguished quadrangular design, grey rubble stone with chapel along the N side, library on the W and rooms along the front and S, all in the refined spirit of the followers of G.F. Bodley. Fully vaulted chapel with windows set high over passage aisles, the choir and nave fully separated by a stone screen. Lavishly gilt altar canopy by Comper (1937). N of St. John's College, red-brick High Victorian *house* (c 1858; B. Woodward) with the notched brickwork of the Oxford Union. W of St. Giles, off Little Clarendon St, *Wellington Square* (c 1870), Oxford's one formal square, tall yellow brick houses on three sides. N of Little Clarendon St, facing Woodstock Rd, *Somerville College*, founded 1879, the second foundation for women in the University, some late Victorian red-brick buildings, by T.G. Jackson (1881) at NE corner of the main quad, by H.W. Moore (1886–94) at NW corner, with library range between (1902; B. Champneys). Neo-Georgian range with hall on E side (1910–13; E. Fisher). S of the Woodstock Rd entry, *St. Aloysius RC Church* (1873–75; J.A. Hansom), tall, apsed, yellow brick with front rose window. Ornate altar and reredos (1878). G.M. Hopkins was a curate here 1878–79. *Presbytery* 1877–78 (Wilkinson). N of Somerville College, *Radcliffe Hospital* (1759–70) much extended in similar style in 19C and 20C. Gothic chapel (1864; A. Blomfield) with fine deep-coloured

E window (c 1864; H. Holiday). W of Somerville College, in Walton St, *Oxford University Press* (1826–30; D. Robertson), monumental Roman classical front with triumphal arch entry linked to wings with giant columns. Opposite, *St. Paul's Church* (1836; H.J. Underwood), Greek Ionic temple front, now a theatre. To W, Jericho, an area of small brick terraces, largely built up for employees of the University Press. At end of Great Clarendon St, former *school* (1855–56; G.E. Street). In Cardigan St, *St. Barnabas Church* (1868–69; A.W. Blomfield), built for T. Combe, Superintendent of the University Press and patron of the Pre-Raphaelites, as a High Anglican establishment in this artisan part of the town. Lombard Romanesque, built cheaply of rendered rubble, brick and some concrete, Combe specifying that interior decoration was to be added gradually as funds were available. Inside richly gilded E end with Pantocrator in apse dome (1893) and fine tile mosaic decoration over the N arcade, based on Ravenna, by Powell's. Pulpit by Blomfield.

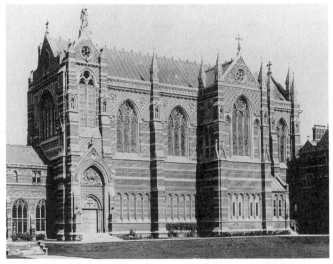

Keble College Chapel (1873–76; W. Butterfield), Oxford

E of St. Giles Church, Keble Rd leads to *Keble College* (1868–82; W. Butterfield), founded as a memorial to John Keble, built largely at the expense of the Gibbs family of Tyntesfield (cf. Avon), and a monument to Tractarian ideals. Wholly in contrast to earlier colleges, Keble is in red brick banded and chequered in yellow and black with much Bath stone, Gothic with long and varied front to Parks Rd culminating in the towering bulk of the chapel. Butterfield's composition is masterly, a formal quadrangle built up of asymmetric elements, a visual continuity achieved by horizontals of banding and rooflines, yet varied with gables, buttresses, massive chimneys and differing window elaboration. The structural colour breaks up the mass, red brick dominant in the lower levels, the banding and diapering increasing further up. The chapel's progress from severity at the lower levels to exuberant chequering, tracery, pinnacles and carved work above creates a dazzling effect in sunlight. Inside, a single vaulted vessel, high and broad with full iconographic scheme of decoration by Butterfield. Tile panels and stained glass by A. Gibbs. Richly marbled and tiled sanctuary. Lectern by Butterfield. In side chapel (1892; J.T. Micklethwaite) Holman Hunt's famous 'Light of the World'. Opposite the chapel, Library and Hall range under a single roof and reached by a single central stair. The hall is of magnificent scale, richly polychrome with painted roof. The library has excellent furnishings by Butterfield. To S, Pusey Quad, two ranges, to W and E, the E range intended to run through to the Warden's House, but instead the house was built free-standing (1876).

University Museum (1855–60; B. Woodward), Oxford.
Engraving 1860

Opposite, the *University Museum* (1855–60; B. Woodward), with Keble College, the outstanding Victorian monument of Oxford, designed under the influence and with the participation of Ruskin. Throughout the building and decoration of the museum the craftsmen were encouraged to seek inspiration for the carving in nature, this casket for the wonders of nature was itself to be a bible of natural forms and enriched with all the colour of British geology, instructive and beautiful. The outside is restrained in polychromy, mostly Bath stone, steep-roofed in patterned slate. The external carving by the O'Shea brothers of Ballyhooly, natural but unreliable geniuses, was never completed, nor was the great entrance portal begun by T. Woolner, to designs by J.H. Pollen, but enough was done to suggest the splendour intended. Inside, a galleried court roofed in iron and glass, the ironwork supremely Gothic (by Skidmore), naturalistic leaf forms abounding. Every capital of the arcades was to represent a different plant form, every shaft a different stone, though only the carving of the upper arcade on the W is original, the rest of 1905–14. Complete series of statues of eminent scientists by leading sculptors. Lovely medallion of the architect, Woodward (1861; A. Munro). Behind, Pitt-Rivers

Museum (1885; T.N. Deane), built to house General Pitt-Rivers' amazing ethnographic collection, all the items still arranged in the original way, crowded beyond belief and stimulating as few modern collections ever are. S of the Museums, former Chemistry Laboratory, based on the Abbot's Kitchen at Glastonbury Abbey, and, facing South Parks Rd, *Radcliffe Science Library* (1901; T.G. Jackson), extended W 1933. To N of the Museums, pretty *Lodge* (1888; H.W. Moore) and *Clarendon Laboratory* (1908–10; T.G. Jackson), red brick and stone formal late 17C style. Complex of late 19C and 20C university science buildings behind the Museums, N of South Parks Rd. At E end, *Observatory* (1874; C. Barry Jr). On S side of South Parks Rd, *Mansfield College* (1887–89; B. Champneys), Mansfield Rd, finely detailed three-sided Gothic quad with gate-tower (leading nowhere) on N. In the chapel, side windows stained glass (1909; Powell's), depicting a very catholic collection of notables of Nonconformity with the arms of the chief cities of Protestantism. The college was founded in Birmingham by the Congregational Church. At E end of South Parks Rd, *Linacre College*, large house of c 1890 with Queen Anne style additions (1907; B. Champneys).

OUTER OXFORD

From St. Giles Church, going N up Banbury Rd, the area of large suburban villas laid out from c 1850, the earliest classical or Italianate, stone or stucco, the later N Oxford style, recognisable in derivatives all over Britain, gabled and Gothic, tall and asymmetrical, generally red brick and stone, some yellow brick patterned in red or black. By the 1880s red brick triumphed, mostly with slightly Jacobean decoration in stone. The Queen Anne style is relatively rare. N of the church, 1850s villas and former *High School for Girls* (1879; T.G. Jackson), freshly Queen Anne with hipped roof, cupola and moulded terracotta first-floor columns. Beyond, *Nos 27 and 29* (1880; J.J. Stevenson), extremely pretty Queen Anne with white roof-top balconies, rubbed brick dressings, and sash windows, among the earliest villas of this style, so much in contrast to Gothic N Oxford, which begins immediately N and E. To E, Norham Manor Estate, laid out after 1860 (W. Wilkinson), with large Gothic villas (c 1865–70) in brick along Norham Gardens. On S side, *Nos 1–13* by Wilkinson, except *Nos 3 and 9* (C. Buckeridge). *Nos 15 and 17* by F. Codd and also N side and most of the houses in Bradmore Rd. *Lady Margaret Hall* at E end of Norham Gardens began in the end villa, the first Oxford establishment for women (1878). On E side of the front quad late 17C style brick and stone range (1896–1915; R. Blomfield). On Banbury Rd, N of Norham Gardens, the largest Gothic villas, *Nos 54, 56 and 58* heftily detailed (1865–67; J. Gibbs), *No. 60* (1865; Wilkinson), *No. 62* (1864; E. Bruton) with remarkable carved porch, very Gothic, carved animals and foliage in the manner of the Oxford Museum carving. The client was a follower of Ruskin, the sculpture may be by J.H. Pollen. Yellow brick houses opposite, mostly by Codd, Nos 43–5 by T.E. Collcutt (1868–70), Codd's work extending into Canterbury Rd. On W side, *Park Town* (1853–55; S.L. Seckham), Italianate villas flanking the entry to a pair of handsome stone-fronted classical crescents with further curved terrace, less elaborate, to E. Further N on Banbury Rd, in the streets E and W of Banbury Rd, on Woodstock Rd and W of Woodstock Rd, houses of 1880–1900, predominantly designed by H.W. Moore, characteristically red brick with mullioned windows, some ornament of a Jacobean sort, occasionally with tile-hanging or more elaborate stone detail.

Exceptions are *No. 121 Banbury Rd* (1902; H.T. Hare), free c 1700 style with neat arrangement of chimneys and dormers each end, *No. 2 Northmoor Rd* (1902; E. Allfrey), to E, handsome Queen Anne style, and *No. 7 Linton Rd* (1910; A.H. Moberly), neo-Georgian. On Woodstock Rd, *•St. Philip's and St. James' Church* (1860–66; G.E. Street), among Street's boldest works, a large church detailed with all the vigour of the best High Victorian work, lancets and plate tracery, Ruskinian banding of the stonework. What impresses immediately is the geometrical build-up of clearly defined shapes, the wall faces sheer, the gables and rooflines unbroken culminating in the central tower and spire, unusually of oblong plan with great buttresses spreading the load down to the transept walls. Short apsed E end, transepts and lean-to aisles to the nave. Interior with granite nave piers, the E end of the nave canted in to frame the chancel. Vaulted apse and transepts. Fine fittings by Street and glass by Clayton and Bell in apse and aisles. Further S, *St. Antony's College* occupying Gothic buildings of the Society of the Holy Trinity (1866–68; C. Buckeridge). Chapel added 1891–94 by J.L. Pearson, modifying the original design. Vaulted and apsed with vaulted undercroft. W of Woodstock Rd, in Kingston Rd, *Nos 114–38* and *149–64* (1870–73; C.C. Rolfe), four terraces of artisan cottages, very pretty in a simple Gothic manner. At N end of Woodstock Rd, *St. Edward's School*, red-brick Gothic buildings, begun 1873 (W. Wilkinson) around an open quad. On N side, large stone chapel (1876) with lancets and tower.

W of the station, *toll house* (1850; H. Underwood) on Botley Rd. Opposite, Osney Town, characterful area of small mid 19C terraces fronting on to the river to E. *St. Frideswide's Church* (1870–72; S.S. Teulon) is severe EE. Gothic with an octagonal central tower with pyramid roof instead of the intended spire. Apse with plate tracery. Doorway supposedly carved by Alice Liddell, the original Alice in Wonderland.

E of Magdalen Bridge, at The Plain, *Victoria Fountain* (1899; E.P. Warren). On S side, *Magdalen College School* (1893; A.W. Blomfield), rock-faced stone with Jacobean detail. To S, *St. Hilda's College*, founded 1893, around the c 1780 house of the botanist, Sibthorp. Extension to N (1862; Deane and Woodward), Gothic. The other 19C buildings to S around a former house of 1877 (Wilkinson). Iffley Rd runs SE. On N side, *•St. John's Church* (1894–96; G.F. Bodley), with W tower of beautiful simplicity, ashlar, a broad mid-buttress with carved rood between two Dec. style windows. Long, high roof with painted decoration, organ case, screen and pulpit by Bodley, glass by Kempe. Behind, the former Mission House of the Anglo-Catholic Cowley Fathers (1901; Bodley) with chapel and cloister link to the church. On S side, further E, *Greyfriars*, flint and stone Romanesque style church (1911; B. Williamson) with saddleback tower. Friary (1921). In Cowley Rd, E of The Plain, on N side, *Methodist church* (1903; S. Salter), curvaceous free Gothic, opposite, *Old Elm Tree* pub (c 1900; H.T. Hare), gabled stone and roughcast with canted front. Adjoining, early *cinema* (c 1910). To E, S of Cowley Rd, *St. John's Home*, Leopold St, founded by the Cowley Fathers as a home for the aged. Buildings 1873–75 by C. Buckeridge, Gothic, and 1882 (J.L. Pearson), Tudor. Addition and chapel 1906 (J.N. Comper) in stone, the chapel with painted roof and stone screen. From The Plain, St. Clement's St runs E. At the foot of Headington Hill, on N side, *St. Clement's Church* (1828; D. Robertson), plain neo-Norman with later tracery, J.H. Newman was the first curate in charge. On N side of Headington Hill, *Headington Hill Hall* (1861; J. Thomas), large yellow brick and stone

Italianate house with French roofs, built for the Oxford brewer, Morrell. N of the top of the hill, in Pullen's Lane, large late 19C houses, *Fairfield* (1879), *The Croft* (1880; A. Waterhouse), red-brick Gothic, and *Langley Lodge* (1895), tile-hung with timber work, like a Thames-side villa. On W side, *Pollock House* (1889; H.W. Moore), *High Wall* (c 1912; W. Cave), gabled 17C style, well detailed, and *Cotuit Hall* (1890; H.W. Moore). S of Oxford Polytechnic, in Warneford Lane, *Warneford Hospital*, founded 1813 as an asylum, refronted in eclectic style with French-roofed tower (1877; Wilkinson). Seated marble figure of Dr Warneford (1840; P. Hollins) in entrance hall.

5m E of Oxford, off A40, at **Wheatley**, *church* (1855–57; G.E. Street), the very fine tower and spire added 1868, an extreme example of Street's interest in the play and relationship of solids and planes, the ascending faces of the tower cut back with barely a projecting moulding, bell-openings in the cross gables of the top from which the spire rises with nothing but the clean edge to mark the transition from vertical to diagonal. Lancets to the body of the church. *School* (1858; Street), *vicarage* (1850 and 1866; E.B. Lamb). 3m S of Wheatley, at **Cuddesdon**, *church* restored 1849 (Ferrey) and 1851–53 (Street). W window by Street, made by Hardman. The former *Bishop's Palace* is a 20C ranch style house, incongruous next to *chapel* (1846; Ferrey), the original palace of 1679 was burnt. *Cuddesdon College* (1853–54; Street) was founded as a theological college by Bishop Wilberforce of Oxford. Fine stone Gothic range to the street with rose window of original chapel to right. Larger chapel added 1874–75 (Street), with hall below, giving considerable scale to the building. Fittings by Street, painted roof and stained glass by Clayton and Bell. *Vicarage* adjoining 1853 and 1859 (Street). Cottages for students by the church (1877). 4m N of Wheatley, at **Horton-cum-Studley**, *church* (1867; W. Butterfield), polychrome brick, yellow, banded in black, red and Bath stone. Strong simple forms, timber posts to the arcade and good font and reredos by Butterfield. Glass by A. Gibbs. 3m SE of Oxford, A423, at **Littlemore**, *church* (1835–36; H.J. Underwood) built for J.H. Newman in plain lancet style, chancel and tower added 1848 after Newman's time. Monument to Newman's mother (died 1836; R. Westmacott Jr) showing the church under construction. Newman planned a monastic retreat here and converted some stables N of the church into a group of cells. He was received into the Roman church here (1845).

WANTAGE. A338 15m SW of Oxford. Market town with *statue* of King Alfred (1877), born here 849, in Market Place. Parish *church* restored 1857 (G.E. Street) and lengthened to W (1877), E window by Hardman (1857). S chapel decorated 1895 (C.E. Kempe) in memory of the Rev. W.J. Butler, High Anglican vicar 1846–80, responsible for the foundation of the Wantage Sisterhood, the principal order of Anglican nuns. Handsome stone *vicarage* (1850), a very early work of G.E. Street, and *Church School* (1850; H. Woodyer). In Portway, *King Alfred School* (1849; J.B. Clacy), attractive asymmetrical stone Gothic with hall added 1872 (Butterfield). In Priory Rd, *St. Michael's* (1855; W. White), retreat house built for W.J. Butler, brown stone with brick tympana over the windows, long picturesque range. In Newbury St, *St. Mary's School*, with hall 1874 (Butterfield), heightened later, and picturesque free Gothic chapel (1898; C.E. Ponting). On Faringdon Rd, A417, *St. Mary's Convent* of the Wantage Sisterhood. Front range to the road 1855–56 (G.E. Street), stone, Gothic with steep roofs and simple window detail, extended by Street, chapel behind (1858–61), refectory (1866 and 1871). Novitiate behind added 1878 (Butterfield). New chapel (1887–89; J.L. Pearson), fully vaulted with complex E end of three tiny vaulted spaces framing the windows.

5m W, B4507, at **Kingston Lisle**, *Kingston Lisle House*, mid 18C, altered early 19C with very grand classical entrance hall, tunnel-vaulted with flying staircase leaping precipitately across. **Uffington**, to N, was the birthplace of T. Hughes (1822–96) and the setting for the early part of his 'Tom Brown's Schooldays'. Memorial in the *church*, restored 1850 (Street). 3m SW of Wantage, at **Letcombe Bassett**, *church*, mostly rebuilt in brick 1862 (Butterfield) with pink and white marble and tile reredos, tile floor and other Butterfield fittings. 2m E of Wantage, at **East Lockinge**, estate village of 1860s. 3m N of Wantage, at **Denchworth**, *church* restored 1852 (Street) and extremely attractive village *school* (1852; Street), in stone with prominent chimneys. Also by Street are the fine village schools nearby, at **Goosey** to W, **Stanford in the Vale** to NW, **Lyford** to N, all 1852. At **East Hanney**, to NE, A338, former *church* (1856; Street), small, gathered under a single sweeping roof.

WITNEY. A40 12m W of Oxford. Blanket manufacturing town with surviving mills of late 18C and 19C. In High St, *Methodist chapel* (1850; J. Wilson). Two elaborate iron shopfronts (c 1870) in High St and Market Square. *Corn Exchange* (1863). On Church Green, former *Police Station* (1860; W. Wilkinson), gabled Gothic, parish *church*, restored 1865–69 (G.E. Street) with chancel fittings by Street, W window by Wailes, and *almshouses* (1868; W. Wilkinson). 4m SW of Witney, A4095, at **Lew**, *church* (1841; W. Wilkinson), pre-ecclesiological Gothic, characteristic lancets and low-pitch roof, but charming octagonal turret over the porch. Nave NE window 1865 (Holiday). 3m W of Witney, off A40, **Charterville**, one of the Chartist settlements set up in 1847 by F. O'Connor to provide smallholdings for families from industrial towns. 78 single storey cottages and a school were built before the scheme collapsed in 1850. 2m N of Witney, B4022, at **Hailey**, *church* (1866; C.C. Rolfe) with most exaggerated High Victorian detail, curious bell turret and polychromy inside. 3m NW, at **Leafield**, *church* (1860; G.G. Scott), impressively simple EE style with octagonal crossing tower and spire (1874), the transition from square base to octagon neatly achieved with broaches and buttresses. *Vicarage* by Scott. 3m NE of Witney, *Eynsham Park* (1900–04; E. George), red-brick and stone Jacobean mansion with flat pierced parapets and ornate centre porch tower. Lodges survive of previous house (1843; Sir C. Barry). To E, at **Freeland**, *church, school* and *vicarage* (1869–71; J.L. Pearson), a remarkable picturesque High Victorian group built for relatives of the Raikes family, for whom Pearson designed Treberfydd, near Brecon, Powys. Church with saddleback-roofed tower, apsed chancel and lovely interior, the chancel vaulted with subtle painted decoration by Clayton and Bell, who also designed the glass. Vicarage, partly stone, partly half-timber, one of Pearson's best domestic works.

SHROPSHIRE

BRIDGNORTH. A458 20m SE of Shrewsbury. Market town on the Severn. In the centre, *Markets* (1855), very striking in black brick ornamented in red and yellow, round-arched Italian style. At N end *St. Leonard's Church*, mostly rebuilt 1860–62 (W. Slater), with medieval tower. In the churchyard half-timbered *almshouses* (1889).

LUDLOW. A49 30m S of Shrewsbury. The parish *church* was restored 1859–60 (G.G. Scott), W window by Willement. The poet A.E. Housman is buried in the churchyard to N. 4m S, B4361, at **Richards Castle**, *All Saints' Church* (1890–02; R. Norman Shaw), N of the village, a stately building with almost detached S tower, wall very much emphasised over window and the square outline only slightly modified by buttresses and parapet. Inside fine painted reredos (C.E. Buckeridge) in 15C Netherlandish style. Organ case by Shaw (1893). 8m SE of Ludlow, A456, at **Burford**, *church* restored 1889 (A. Webb), an excellent example of late 19C craftsmanship. Webb virtually rebuilt the tower. Inside, complete fittings, mahogany reredos carved by Aumonier with painted figures by H.W. Lonsdale, carved altar frontal, fine metalwork, especially the lectern by Starkie Gardner, stained glass by Powell's, oak screen and pulpit and marble chancel floor. 5m NW of Ludlow, A49, W of **Onibury**, *Stokesay Court* (1889; T. Harris), large gabled Elizabethan style house, one of the first equipped with electric light. Just SW, *Ferney Hall* (1856–60; J. Norton), hefty Jacobean. 6m W of Onibury, at **Bedstone**, B4385, *Bedstone Court* (1884; T. Harris), spreading mansion in overblown black and white half-timbering. 4m W at **Stow**, in the *church*, Arts and Crafts style reredos in copper and mother-of-pearl (c 1901; J. Powell and Sons). Late 19C stained glass, possibly also by Powells. 18m NW of Ludlow, A49, **Church Stretton**, developed as a resort in the late 19C with much half-timbering in the villas and hotels. Two good early 20C houses, *Woodcote* (1895; B. Parker), in stone and roughcast, and *Scotsman's Field* (1908; E. Newton), Burway Hill, roughcast with leaded bay windows. 13m N of Ludlow, B4368, *Millichope Park* (1840; E. Haycock Sr) with Ionic portico, a handsome late example of neo-classicism.

OSWESTRY. A4083 18m NW of Shrewsbury. Market town on the Welsh border, birthplace of the poet Wilfred Owen (1893–1918). 2m N, at **Gobowen**, station (1846), pretty stuccoed Italianate. To E, at **Hengoed**, *church* (1849–53; Rev. A. Lloyd) in lancet style. Dramatic N transept stained glass (1871; F. Ashwin) of sunrise on the Last Day. 6m SW, B4396, at **Llanyblodwel**, *church* (1847–50; Rev. J. Parker) in most eccentric Gothic with steeple of the oddest outline and rich interior fittings. *School* and *vicarage* by Parker. At **Llanymynech** to SE, A483, right on the border, *church* (1844; T. Penson), elaborate neo-Norman with detail in terracotta. 8m NE of Oswestry, A495, **Ellesmere**, with *Town Hall* (1833), classical and parish *church*, heavily restored 1849 (G.G. Scott) and in late 19C. Glass by Willement in S transept and S aisle, by O'Connor in N transept. Just SW, *Ellesmere College* (1879–83; Carpenter and Ingelow), one of the schools founded by N. Woodard, brick Tudor Gothic to Elizabethan, on a large scale with quadrangle and open quad to the playing fields, the plan of the other major Woodard schools. Incomplete chapel by A. Webb. At **Welshampton**, 2m E of Ellesmere, *church* (1863; G.G. Scott) with black marble arcade piers and good fittings by Scott. Contemporary glass. 2m SE, at **Lyneal**, *church* (1870; G.E. Street), small and pleasingly simple in stone banded with brick.

SHREWSBURY. The county town. In the centre, the Square with classical *Shire Hall* (1836–37; R. Smirke), *statue* of Lord Clive (1860; Marochetti) and Ionic porticoed *Music Hall* (1840; E. Haycock). To N, in Shoplatch, *Market* (1867; Griffiths) in red and yellow brick with 151ft tower. Pride Hill runs NE, *No. 14* has cast-iron decoration to the front. At the top of Castle St, outside the Library, *statue* of Darwin, born in Shrewsbury 1809. *Shrewsbury Station* (1848; T. Penson) is of remarkable scale, Tudor Gothic like a college or town hall, originally two-storey, raised to three by excavating out the forecourt (1903). Behind the station, in Howard St, *warehouse* (1835; Fallows and Hart) built for the canal company, with surprisingly grand Greek Doric front in stucco. SW of The Square, in College Hill, *No. 1*, stone-fronted former Savings Bank (c 1840). To S of Town Walls, *RC Cathedral* (1856; E.W. Pugin), tall and ornately traceried, the tower and spire never built. Over the Kingsland Toll Bridge, to SW, *Shrewsbury School*, moved out to this site 1882, the new school buildings (A.W. Blomfield) surrounding an original Georgian building of 1765. Tall chapel with stained glass by Kempe. E of the centre, immediately over the English Bridge, *Abbey Church*, the E end replaced 1886–87 (J.L. Pearson) with vaulted chancel and richly carved reredos. High Victorian Gothic *Congregational church* (1863; G. Bidlake) in Abbey Foregate. Off Coleham Head, to S, *Coleham Pumping Station* with two working beam-engines of 1900 preserved (open to public). Further SW, at **Meole Brace**, *church* (1867; E. Haycock) with excellent Morris glass in apse (1869–70). Mary Webb was married here. 4m S of Shrewsbury, at **Condover**, in the *church*, *monument to Sir T. Cholmondeley (1867; G.F. Watts), showing Watts, best known as a painter, to have been an exceptional sculptor. Kneeling free-standing figure, the hands clasped over a sword and leonine head turned upward, the very ideal of Victorian chivalry. 3m SW, at **Netley**, *Netley Hall* (1854–58; E. Haycock), late example of the Georgian tradition, classical in red brick and stone.

    4m NW of Shrewsbury, B5067, at **Leaton**, *church* (1859; S.P. Smith), spiky High Victorian Gothic, the W end particularly complicated. Tower and spire 1872. 2m NW, at **Yeaton**, *Yeaton Pevery* (1890–92; A. Webb), red sandstone picturesque Elizabethan style mansion with display of half-timber on the garden front. Just W, at **Little Ness**, *Adcote (1876–81; R. Norman Shaw), stone Elizabethan style mansion, Shaw's finest surviving house, an object lesson in asymmetrical design, whether the compact tall entrance front or the S front, where four separate elements each in a different plane are held together by the great chimneys of the outer bays while the buttressed gable end of the hall has strength enough to focus the whole composition. Sheer wall surfaces pierced by splendid mullioned windows, the moulded courses subtly accentuating the height and the brick chimneys melded into the stonework. The side of the hall is a single spectacular bay window of some 40 lights in a grid of mullions and transoms. Inside, full height hall spanned by stone transverse arches, the chimney-breast sloped back into the wall with exaggerated medieval panache. The planning of the house exploits this vainglorious space to the full with views under the screen from the entrance, the upper corridor running over the screen and even the attic floor having a timber-framed look-out from high in the hall gable. 8m N of Shrewsbury, A49, at **Grinshill**, *church* (1839; J. Carline Jr), neo-Romanesque, the tower improbably Italian looking. 3m E, at **Moreton Corbet**, in the *church* E window and reredos by Comper (1915). Monument in churchyard (1904; I. Furse), a bronze figure of a boy. 5m E of Shrewsbury, at **Withington**, *church* (1870; G.E. Street), High Victorian in red sandstone. Good fittings. By Street also (1864), the *Vicarage* at **Upton Magna**, 1½m W.

TELFORD. A5 11m E of Shrewsbury. New town based on the old industrial settlements of Dawley, Oakengates and Wellington. E of Oakengates, at **St. George's**, *St. George's Church* (1861; G.E. Street), High Victorian severity with plate tracery and lancets, richly polychrome interior. At **Donnington Wood**, to N, *church* (1843; G.G. Scott). S of Telford, historically famous coal-mining region. **Coalbrookdale**, where A. Darby began the smelting of iron with coke in 1709, where A. Darby II succeeded in making iron suitable not only for casting but for forging and where A. Darby III spanned the Severn with a single-arched *Iron Bridge* (1779), encapsulates the early story of the Industrial Revolution. The *Ironbridge Gorge Museum* has restored or recreated several major aspects of the industry of the region. In Coalbrookdale, the *Museum of Iron*, next to A. Darby II's blast furnace site, displays the history of iron-working and the increasingly ornate iron products of the Coalbrookdale works. At *Blists Hill Open Air Museum*, blast furnaces with restored engine house and engine for the blowing of air into the furnaces and numerous recreated industrial buildings, cottages and shops. **Coalport**, **Broseley** and **Jackfield** were pottery centres, Jackfield the works of Craven Dunnill and Maw and Co., leading manufacturers of tiles, and Coalport famous for china. At *Coalport China Works Museum*, restored factory buildings, a bottle kiln and displays of Coalport and Caughley china. The later 19C works of both Maw and Co. (1883) and Craven Dunnill survive at Jackfield; the Craven Dunnill works with faience decoration. The Maw works are to be reopened by the Ironbridge Gorge Museum. *Church* (1863; A. Blomfield), polychrome brick High Victorian. The *railway bridge* (1862; J. Fowler) is of Coalbrookdale manufacture, a single 200ft iron span. Good early Victorian *churches* of 1845 by H. Eginton at **Broseley** and **Dawley**, Perp. style.

8m NE of Telford, A518, at **Church Aston**, *church* (1866–67; G.E. Street), a small work with single roof and lead flèche. Good interior. 1m NW, **Newport**, the parish *church* rebuilt (1866–91; J. Norton) with one good Morris window in chancel (1872). In High St, *Town Hall* (1859; J. Cobb), Italianate. At **Chetwynd**, 2m N, A41, *church* (1865; B. Ferrey), ornate with broach spire and rich interior arcades. At **Edgmond**, 2m SW, the *church* has carved reredos (1889; Bodley and Garner) and chancel glass by Kempe.

WHITCHURCH. A49 20m N of Shrewsbury. In the High St, Gothic *Town Hall* (1872; T.M. Lockwood) and former *Market Hall* (c 1840), now bank with Tuscan columned front. In St. Mary St, classical *Savings Bank* (1846). 2m S, B5476, *Dearnford Hall* (c 1840), classical to Italianate house. 4m SE, **Calverhall**, estate village of *Cloverley Hall*, demolished house of 1864 by W.E. Nesfield, of which the stable block with its romantic pyramid-roofed tower, reminiscent of the work of Burges, survives. *Church* restored by Nesfield (1872–78) with stained glass by Morris and Powell's in chancel. By Nesfield also probably some of the estate cottages. 2m E, at **Tittenley**, *lodges* (1885; R. Norman Shaw) to the demolished Shavington Hall, stylish neo-

Georgian, unexpected at this date. 10m SE of Whitchurch, A442, at **Hodnet**, *Hodnet Hall* (1870; A. Salvin); Elizabethan to Jacobean style mansion built for the Heber family. (Gardens open to public.) Bishop Heber (1783–1826) hymn-writer, was author of 'From Greenland's icy mountains', his brother Richard (died 1833), friend of Walter Scott, a founder of the Athenaeum and above all a book-collector, who said 'No gentleman can be without three copies of a book, one for show, one for use, and one for borrowers'. Heber memorials in the *church* including effigy of Blanche Heber (1870; R. Cholmondeley).

SOMERSET

AXBRIDGE. A371 10m NW of Wells. In the Square, small classical *Town Hall* (1833). To N, parish *church*, restored 1879 with delicate carved screens (1888; J.D. Sedding). N of bypass, *St. Michael's Home* (1878; Butterfield), grey stone gabled sanatorium with central chapel, built for the Gibbs family of Tyntesfield (cf. Avon). 5m E, on top of the Mendips, at **Charterhouse**, small roughcast Arts and Crafts *church* (1908; W.D. Caroe). 5m SW, off A38, at **Brent Knoll** gabled stone *Manor House* (1862–64; J. Norton). To SW, B3140, **Burnham-on-Sea**, developed as a resort from the 1850s, stucco earlier buildings, red brick later, nothing on a grand scale.

BRIDGWATER. A38 11m N of Taunton. Port on the navigable river Parrett with surviving *docks* of 1841 N of the centre where Bridgwater–Taunton canal joins the river. In the centre, *Town Bridge* (1883) at foot of Fore St leading up to *Market Hall* (1826; J. Bowen), Cornhill, pretty neo-classical with flattened dome on an Ionic rotunda. To S, *Nos 8–10 Cornhill* (c 1860–70), four-storeyed Italianate office buildings. To N, *Royal Clarence Hotel* (1824), Regency style stucco, and *National Westminster Bank* (1904), restrained Baroque. In front of Market, Admiral Blake *statue* (1900; F.W. Pomeroy). In High St, *Town Hall*, stucco in style of c 1830, but apparently of 1865 (C. Knowles). The parish *church* has ornate timber roofs from a restoration of 1852. S of church, *Baptist chapel* (1837; E. Down), ashlar classical. By the river, S of Town Bridge, *Library* (1905; E.G. Page), pretty, with copper dome and lantern. Opposite, on east bank, *Infirmary* with Italianate front (1876). NE of Town Bridge, in Church St, Eastover, *St. John's Church* (1843–46; J. Brown), lancet Gothic church with W tower, all in Bath stone, built at considerable cost by the Rev. J.M. Capes, influenced by Newman and the Oxford Tractarians to build such a church in a poor district. Like many other Tractarians Capes went over to the Roman Catholic church, before this church was even completed. Tall interior with hammerbeam roofs. 5m NW of Bridgwater, at **Combwich**, by the Parrett, elaborately carved *church* (1870; C. Knowles) with spiky detail. 8m W of Bridgwater, S of A39, at **Over Stowey**, *Quantock Lodge* (1857; H. Clutton), large Jacobean style house built for the banker and Liberal politician Lord Taunton. More lively design in the outbuildings and the entrance lodge on the road to Aisholt. In the parish *church* some good Morris glass in the N aisle E and W windows, 1870 and 1875, and E window by Hardman 1857.

CASTLE CARY. A359 12m NE of Yeovil. In the centre, *Market Hall* (1855; F.C. Penrose), mixed Gothic and Jacobean detail. S of the centre, parish *church*, rebuilt 1855 (B. Ferrey) with ornate spire. 4m NE at **Bruton**, by the church, *King's School*, founded 1519 but the Gothic buildings mostly of 1870–72 and later. On the Yeovil Road, *Sexey's School* (1891; G.J. and J.W. Skipper), Jacobean style, built as a 'trade school' for the sons of farmers and tradesmen. 5m SE of Castle Cary, **Wincanton**, market town with red-brick *Town Hall* (1878; Wilson, Willcox and Wilson). Parish *church* rebuilt with original W tower now at W end of N aisle (1888; J.D. Sedding). 5m S of Wincanton, A357, N of **Henstridge**, *Inwood House* (c 1870), Jacobean style stone house, built for one of the Guest family, of Merthyr Tydfil iron fame. 2m W of Castle Cary, at **Alford**, B3153, *Alford House* (1877; F.C. Penrose), stone Elizabethan style on a late 18C core. 2m beyond, at **East**

Lydford, *church* (1866; B. Ferrey) with lavish spire and much carving,
built by the rector and patron of the living as a memorial to his wife. At
West Lydford, to NW, *church* (1846; B. Ferrey), archaeologically correct Somerset Perp. with W tower. 2m N, A37, at **Hornblotton**,
church (1872; T.G. Jackson), picturesque and sensitively designed,
the ecclesiastical equivalent of the Domestic Revival in secular
building with pretty wooden belfry and spire, originally clad in oak
shingles. There is none of the vigour or harshness of High Victorian
work, the interior glows with red and white sgraffito plaster decoration by Heywood Sumner. Reredos of alabaster with tile panels and
inlaid oak chancel fittings. Mosaic chancel pavement and stained
glass by Jackson, made by Powell's. The church was built for the
Thring family of Alford. 2m W at **Lottisham**, another pretty *church* by
Jackson (1876), smaller, with shingled bell turret over the chancel
arch. Good oak roof with chancel arch marked by curved oak braces to
the tie-beams.

CREWKERNE. A30 9m SW of Yeovil. In the Market Square, *Victoria
Hall* (1899), Jacobean. In Market St, *National Westminster Bank* (c
1845), Italianate. SE of the centre, *station* (1860; W. Tite), stone, Tudor
style. At Mount Pleasant, NE of centre, *Grammar School* (1880; G.R.
Crickmay), large stone Tudor style buildings with entrance tower set
high over the Yeovil road. At **Yeovil**, 9m NE, railway *station* (1853;
Tite), Tudor style, similar to Crewkerne, but in brick and stone. At Pen
Mill, E of centre, *St. Michael's Church* (1897; J.N. Johnston), Perp.
style with tower, all in Ham stone. At **Norton sub Hamdon**, 5m N of
Crewkerne, B3165, in the *church*, fine Arts and Crafts tower screen
and font (c 1904; H. Wilson). 8m W of Crewkerne, A30, **Chard**, market
town with central *Town Hall* (1834) ornamented with a projecting
two-storey portico. In Fore St, to E, *Lloyds Bank* (1849), Italianate,
built as an hotel. In High St, W of the Town Hall, *Harvey's Hospital*
(1841), gabled Tudor almshouses. The disused Chard Central *station*
(1866) has a late example of the wooden overall roof first used by
Brunel in some of his stations in the SW.

FROME. A361 15m S of Bath. Former weaving town on the river
Frome. In the Market Place, ornate *Lloyds Bank* (1874) with pink
marble *Boyle Cross* (1871; Hon. Mrs E. Boyle) outside. Over the
bridge, to N, *Museum*, former Literary and Scientific Institute (1870; J.
Hine), Italianate, exploiting a steep and acutely pointed site to great
effect, the entrance at the point of the site, in the tallest part of the
building, facing over the bridge. N of the Market Place, Bath St climbs
up to the *parish church*, the churchyard entered under a Gothic
screen (1814; J. Wyatville). The medieval church is wholly surprising
inside, as it was lavishly embellished from 1862 onwards for the Rev.
W. Bennett, High Church vicar, formerly of Knightsbridge, London,
where his ministry had provoked riots over ritual. Bennett and his
architect, C.E. Giles, reworked the whole interior, apart from the
chancel, already rebuilt (1844). Much sculptural decoration was introduced, mostly carved by J. Forsyth, notably the series of medallions
down the nave and the marble reredos. The chancel has a rich tile and
marble floor and the baptistery floor in incised marble depicts Virtues
and Vices. Later in the 19C the aisle windows were filled with glass by
Kempe, and a splendid carved rood screen (1892; Kempe) was added.
In the SE chapel, Minton tile pavement and E window by O'Connor,
both of c 1845, originally in the chancel. Outside, the S door has lively
carving by Forsyth, but, most surprising in an Anglican church, is the

Via Crucis, the sculpted Stations of the Cross (Forsyth) that line the steps up to the N door, over which is carved the Calvary. At the top of Bath St, on the corner of Christchurch St West, High Victorian *Wesleyan Schools* (1862; Wilson and Willcox), Gothic *Police Station* (1856; C.E. Davis) and, beyond, modest *Municipal Buildings* (1892; G. Halliday). To W, off Vallis Way, the Trinity, area of 17C weavers' cottages with *Holy Trinity Church* (1837; H.E. Goodridge) presenting a dramatic if incorrect Gothic front to Trinity St. Interior with extensive set of glass by Morris and Co. of late date, c 1900 to 1920. On the E side of the town, *Frome Station* (1850; J. Hannaford), a rare survivor, a timber station complete with timber roof spanning the tracks, a type favoured by Brunel and used on several stations in the south-west.

3m N of Frome, off A361, at **Lullington**, *Orchardleigh* (1856; T.H. Wyatt), Elizabethan style stone house with tall, rather French, slate roofs, built for the Duckworth family. One of the daughters married the poet Sir H. Newbolt who described the house as 'Gardenleigh' in his novel 'The Old Country' (1907). Newbolt is buried in the churchyard of the pretty 13C *church* (restored 1878; J.O. Scott), set on an island in the lake below the house. 3m NE, at **Rode**, off B3109, Rode Hill *church* (1824; H.E. Goodridge), powerful Georgian Gothic chapel with two outsize polygonal turrets flanking the entry and much internal detail, including the pew ends, in cast iron. 3m N, off A366, S of **Farleigh Hungerford**, *Farleigh House*, picturesque castellated house of c 1810–25. 3m W of Frome, **Mells**, former seat of the Horner family and later of the Asquiths, the son of Lord Asquith, the Prime Minister, having married into the Horner family. In the *church*, a delicate plaster relief of a peacock by Burne-Jones under the tower (c 1886), evidence of the artistic circle around Lady Horner, friend of Burne-Jones. Nearby memorial to Raymond Asquith, killed 1916, lettering by Eric Gill under bronze wreath by Lutyens, a family friend. In the NE chapel, equestrian monument (c 1920; Sir A. Munnings) to E. Horner, killed 1917. The church was restored in the 1850s with much stained glass by the local Horwood Bros, graduates of a proto-William Morris college set up by Prebendary Horner, the rector, in 1848 to train youths as schoolmasters and missionaries, but with much emphasis on craft work, particularly wood-carving and glass-painting. Further restoration 1880 (H. Woodyer) including pulpit, reredos, and E window by Hardman. In the churchyard is buried the poet Siegfried Sassoon. The village *War Memorial* and triangular shelter over the village pump are both by Lutyens. 3m N, at **Kilmersdon**, *Ammerdown House* (1788; J. Wyatt) with gardens redesigned from 1901 by Lutyens. In the grounds, tall glass domed *column* (c 1830) to T.S. Jolliffe (died 1824), for whom the house was built. In the village, by the church, a triangular lychgate by Lutyens (1900), like the shelter at Mells. 1m E of Mells, *Wadbury House* (1840; J. Wilson), large Italianate villa built for the Fussell family who had extensive ironworks in the narrow valley of the Mells Brook below the house. 2m S of Mells, at **Chantry**, delightful *church* (1844; G.G. Scott), remarkably well detailed for the date, with W end spirelet and most attractive interior, good E window by Wailes. Built for the Fussell family. 2m SW of Frome, A361, at **Marston Bigot**, *church* made neo-Norman in 1844 (E. Davis), the chancel, robustly detailed, looks rather later in date. *Marston House*, 18C seat of the Earls of Cork and Orrery, was rebuilt internally for the 9th Earl (1857; C.E. Davis). Below the church, *rectory* (c 1840; E. Davis) in the villa style of H.E. Goodridge, that is with an Italianate turret but the details very square-cut and more neo-Grecian. On the hilltop to the E, on the county border, **Gaer Hill** *church* (1857; W. Butterfield), magnificently sited small chapel with bellcote. Further N, on the ridge, at **East Woodlands**, a Longleat estate *church* rebuilt, except the tower, in 1872 and 1880 (J.L. Pearson) with a spire. Elaborate Gothic *vicarage* in High Victorian manner with fish-scale tiled roofs and nice arrangement of stepped stair lights in the stair tower. In the valley, SE of Marston Bigot, **Witham Friary** *church*, fragment of the first English Carthusian monastery, a small vaulted cell given an unadorned sheer W front and outside buttresses in 1876 (W. White) appropriate to the character of this remote spot.

GLASTONBURY. A39 5m SW of Wells. In the Market Place, *Market Cross* (1846; B. Ferrey). In the High St, by the George Hotel, *Lloyds Bank* (1885; G.M. Silley), gabled Gothic to harmonise with the medieval inn. 2m S, **Street**, company town of Messrs Clark, shoe-makers, whose factory occupies much of the W side of the High St. *Crispin Hall* (1885; G.J. Skipper) is a stone-fronted meeting room and institute, given by the Clark family. *The Shoe Museum* contains exhibits back to Roman times and traces the history of the company from the early 19C. 3m SE, at **Butleigh**, *Butleigh Court* (1845; J.C. Buckler), large castellated Tudor style house, now flats after years of dereliction. On the hill above the village, *Hood Monument* (1831; H.E. Goodridge), a tall column with glazed dome to Admiral Sir S. Hood, commander of the fleet in the East Indies, died 1814.

MINEHEAD. A39 25m W of Bridgwater. Port developed as a seaside resort mostly in the late 19C after the arrival of the railway. The railway, open part of the way to Taunton, is now run as a private line with steam trains. The sea-wall and 700ft pier were built in 1901. In Wellington Square, *St. Andrew's Church* (1880; G.E. Street), plain red sandstone church without its intended tower. Mid-buttress dividing the W windows and arcade with arches dying into the piers. In the Parade, *Market House* (1902; W.J. Tamlyn), Baroque. 4m W, **Porlock**, pretty village overlooking Porlock Bay. The *church*, restored 1892 (J.D. Sedding), has attractive Arts and Crafts leaded windows (1890) and choir stalls by Sedding (1895). Porlock was part of the estate of the Earls of Lovelace, of *Ashley Combe*, an Italianate Palazzo of 1866, above the village. Lady Lovelace was a friend of C.F.A. Voysey and designed some buildings in the Voysey manner, notably extensions to *Worthy Manor*, Porlock Weir, and *Gatehouse* at Culbone, to W. *Lilycombe*, on Porlock Hill, was built under Voysey's superintendence (1912). 2m E of Minehead, at **Dunster**, *Dunster Castle* (NT), seat of the Luttrell family from 1376 but much enlarged from 1867 (A. Salvin) for G.F. Luttrell. Salvin created the picturesque outline by raising the existing towers and adding the range that connects the c 1600 range with the gatehouse, the final effect most romantic with the battlemented towers rising over the village street. *Church* restored 1875 (G.E. Street) with E window by Clayton and Bell. 9m E of Dunster, A39, at **West Quantoxhead**, *St. Audries* (1870; J. Norton), large red sandstone Tudor style house built for Sir A. Acland-Hood, incorporating parts of an earlier Acland house. Elaborate estate *church* (1856; Norton) by the lodge, with tower, marble arcade columns and font, and other rich carving. E window by O'Connor (1857), brightly coloured.

SHEPTON MALLET. A371 5m E of Wells. In the centre, *Market Cross* restored 1841 (G.P. Manners). In the High St, *Lloyds Bank* (1877), Bath stone fronted. In Commercial Rd, Elizabethan style *Court House*

(1857; W.B. Gingell) and, further out, large stone former *Anglo-Bavarian Brewery* (1862). 4m E of Shepton Mallet, A361, at **East Cranmore**, *Cranmore Hall* (1866; T.H. Wyatt), stone Jacobean style house built for the Paget family. *Church* (1846; T.H. Wyatt) and, N of the main road, on a hilltop, *Paget Tower* (1862), tall thin Italianate folly. 3m N of Shepton Mallet, at **Oakhill**, small *church* (1861; J.L. Pearson) with bellcote and banded stonework. Off to the left, former *Congregational church* (1873; T.L. Banks), not large, but very elaborate spiky Gothic.

3m N of Oakhill, at **Stratton on the Fosse**, **Downside Abbey*, Benedictine Abbey and leading RC public school. The abbey church is built on a magnificent scale, begun 1872 and complete, bar the W front, by 1938, the several architects involved altering the style as each phase progressed, giving an effect of a Gothic church evolved over several centuries. The original part, by Dunn and Hansom, in an elaborately carved Dec. style, comprises the transepts and the tower attached to the S transept. The tower is the least successful part of the church; intended to support a spire over two tiers of bell-openings, it was given a third tier and the openings altered to suit a Somerset 15C style in 1938. It now stands 166ft high. A ring of E end chapels were built by Dunn and Hansom in the 1880s, with an apsidal ended choir on French Gothic lines in mind, for which the foundations were laid and outline is present in the ambulatory behind the high altar. When the great vaulted choir came to be built in 1901–05 the design was radically altered by Thomas Garner to a simpler Gothic, more characteristic of the late 14C, without the elaborate triforium and with a square E end rising on arches pierced through to reveal the arches of the ambulatory which follows the original plan. The effect at the E end is one of complex interpenetrating spaces enhanced by the consistent stone vaulting. The nave was added in 1923–25 by Giles Gilbert Scott, in a Perp. style slightly more severe than that used by Garner, continuing the main lines of the vaulting and reintroducing the triforium. The overall result is a great abbey church, harmonious in its overall white stone and stone vaulting, yet progressing and changing along its length, appropriately more complex and rich at the E end, but also with the complexity of side chapels that suggests a long history of addition and alteration. The fittings are many and variable in quality, much elaborate carved work in the earlier parts by Wall of Cheltenham, numerous carved tombs, notably that to Garner by his partner, G.F. Bodley; the furnishings of the Lady Chapel are entirely by J.N. Comper. Stained glass by Hardman in the N transept, by Westlake in the chapels of St. Laurence, St. Isidore and St. Benedict, and by Comper in the Lady Chapel and E window. S of the abbey church are monastic buildings around a partially complete cloister, all by Dunn and Hansom, large and over elaborate. Further S is the main school, a broad open quadrangle with the original c 1700 house extended to W by the first chapel and school range (1823; H.E. Goodridge) and then, in the angle, an attractive Puginian Gothic range (1853; C.F. Hansom). This was extended to the S with a further L-plan range in 1907–12 (L. Stokes) in an original free Gothic style with broad tower entrance and wide mullion and transom arched windows around the ground floor. The big roofline has attractive long dormers lighting the attic dormitories. The E end is an addition by Giles Scott of 1932 and 1939.

TAUNTON. A38 11m S of Bridgwater. The county town of Somerset. In the centre, *Municipal Buildings*, Corporation St, c 1500 Grammar School altered 1905 with *Library* (1904; Colbourne, Little and Goodson), free Tudor, and classical *School of Art* (1907; Samson and

Cottam) opposite. In Park St, to W, *St. Paul's House*, c 1800 extended in Gothic as a convent 1867–68 with tall chapel. Further on, *St. John's Church* (1863; G.G. Scott), lancet Gothic with tall spire, quite elaborate. S of Park St, facing Shuttern, *Shire Hall* (1855–58; W.B. Moffatt), large asymmetrical Tudor Gothic building with good entrance hall. At the centre of Taunton, Fore St, with to E, the tower of *St. Mary Magdalene's Church* framed down Hammett St. The 163ft tower of c 1500 was dismantled and rebuilt from the ground (1862; G.G. Scott and B. Ferrey). Interior with reredos of 1870 (G.E. Street) and W window of 1862 (A. Gibbs). In East St, stuccoed buildings of c 1835, and in Billet St, *RC church* (1861; B. Bucknall) terminating the street with a Somerset type tower. Good stained glass. On the outskirts of Taunton, three large 19C schools. To NW, off Greenway Rd, A361, *Taunton School* (1867–70; J. James), collegiate Gothic with 106ft porch tower. Chapel of 1906 (Sir F. Wills). To S, on South Rd, *King's College* (1867; C.E. Giles), High Victorian Gothic with pyramid-roofed entrance tower and plate-traceried windows. The school was bought in 1880 as one of the group of Anglican boarding schools linked to N. Woodard's original foundation at Lancing, Sussex. *Chapel* begun 1898 (W.E. Tower). To SW, *Queen's College* (1874; Giles and Gane), a Wesleyan foundation of 1843 with Tudor style buildings.

7m SW, A38, **Wellington**, with classical *Town Hall* (1833) in the centre. In Mantle St, to W, *RC church* occupying former Popham almshouses, Gothic in brick and stone (1833). 2½m S, on the Blackdown Hills, *Wellington Monument*, 175ft monumental pillar commemorating Waterloo. 11m W of Taunton, **Wiveliscombe**, with brick pedimented *Town Hall* (1840) and *bank* (1881), tile-hung with timber oriels in the Domestic Revival manner. Just W of the town, *Abbotsfield* (1872; Owen Jones), hefty design with pyramid-roofed tower, the intended second floor never built, disappointing as the only country house by the great Victorian designer. Built for L.C. Collard, piano manufacturer, friend of Wagner, who visited the house. 6m S of Taunton, off A303, at **Buckland St. Mary**, ornate *church* (1853–63; B. Ferrey) in flint and stone with pyramid-roofed tower. Lavish interior with much carved work in stone, marble and alabaster. Hammerbeam roofs and stained glass by O'Connor in chancel and Clayton and Bell W window (1857). Built by the Rev. J.E. Lance, partly as a memorial to his wife, whose altar tomb is in the chancel. 13m E of Taunton, **Langport**, birthplace of W. Bagehot (1826–77), political economist and lively writer on the Constitution. Bagehot's father was manager of Stuckey's Bank, now *National Westminster*, Cheapside (rebuilt c 1875). In the *church*, carved stone reredos (1887; J.D. Sedding) and lovely W window (1878; H.A. Kennedy) to Bagehot. Bagehot himself lived at *Herd's Hill*, just W of the town, A378.

WELLS. A39 21m S of Bristol. The Cathedral was restored during the 19C by B. Ferrey (Lady Chapel 1842, W front 1872) and A. Salvin (choir 1848–54). In the S chancel aisle, monument to Bishop Lord A. Hervey with recumbent effigy by T. Brock (1897). In the Lady Chapel E window by Willement 1843, rearranging ancient glass. *Bishop's Palace*, to S, heavily treated in 1846 (B. Ferrey). In the Market Place, *Post Office*, former Market Hall (1835; R. Carver), with Tuscan columns, originally open. W of the centre, Portway, *Blue School* (1898; H.D. Bryan). On the SW side of the town, Glastonbury Rd, former *workhouse* (1845; S.T. Welch), grey stone, Tudor style. On NE side of the town, in St. Thomas St, *St. Thomas's Church* (1856; S.S. Teulon), High Victorian with brick-banded stonework and sharply pointed outline of cross-gabled aisles and spire next to an apsed chancel. Excellent apse stained glass presented by Balliol College, the church being a memorial to Dean Jenkyns, a former Master of the college. Further E, B3139, *Mendip Hospital* (1848; G.G. Scott), vast red stone Elizabethan style County Asylum. At the back a big chapel with central octagonal tower and spire. 3m NW of Wells, at **Wookey Hole**, *Glencot* (c 1893; George and Peto), rock-faced Tudor to Elizabethan style house, built for the owner of the *Paper Mill*, now restored as part of the Wookey Hole caves complex.

STAFFORDSHIRE

BURTON-UPON-TRENT. A38 12m SW of Derby. The centre of English brewing vastly expanded during the 19C with some six major brewers, notably Bass, and vast complexes of malthouses ringing the town. Burton water extracted from deep wells into the Trent gravel beds was said to be distinctive for the high gypsum content. Recent changes in brewing have led to the clearance of much of the industrial architecture of quality in favour of the low buildings and open storage yards that characterise the centre now. From the *Trent Bridge* (1863–64), the long and modest High St follows the river with the late 19C Jacobean-style Bass offices the most prominent 19C group. In Horninglow St, *Magistrates Court* (1909; H. Beck), ceramic clad, Baroque style, and *Bass Museum of Brewing*, housed in the former joiners' shop (1866), the displays covering the history and technology of brewing over 200 years. Other buildings of the Bass Middle Brewery (1853) survive nearby, though the main building has gone. Bass *Maltings* in Wetmore Rd (c 1853–63) and Bass *Brewery* in Station St (1864) are notable close to the centre. Towards the station, *St. Paul's Church* (1874; J.M. Teale and Lord Grimthorpe), heavily detailed stone on a grand scale, the gift of M.T. Bass, the crossing tower the landmark of this part of town. S chapel, painted chancel decoration, lavish organ case and screens by G.F. Bodley. The Gothic *Town Hall* (1878), adjacent, was the Church Institute, built by M.T. Bass and extended (1894) for M.A. Bass, Lord Burton, whose *statue* stands outside (1911; F.W. Pomeroy). *Almshouse* courtyard (c 1875) nearby in Wellington St. On Shobnall Rd is the largest concentration of brewery buildings, the *Bass Maltings* (1873–75; W. Canning) a fragment of the largest in the world and the *Albion Brewery* (1875; W. and S.T. Martin) built for Mann's, with its associated workers' housing and church, most prominent. The first Lord Burton paid for *St. Chad's Church* (1903–11; G.F. Bodley), Hunter St, the architectural masterpiece of Burton, stone with almost detached sheer tower on the street, exceptionally grand, the bell-openings long and richly traceried in contrast to the lower parts. Dec. main body, the E end complex with side chapels and polygonal vestry, the N chapel end wall elaborated with panelling. In the N chapel handsome reredos by Bodley.

2m NE of Burton, A38, at **Stretton**, *church* (1895; Micklethwaite and Somers Clarke) built for one of the Bass partners, late Dec., strongly and sparely detailed with fine tower. E window by Sir W.B. Richmond. 4m W of Burton, S of B5234, at **Rangemore**, estate village of the Bass family, whose house, Byrkley Lodge, has been demolished. In the village *school* (1873), *club* (c 1887; R.W. Edis) and *Lodge* (1887; Edis). The stone *church* (1864–68; W. Butterfield) was transformed by additions of 1884–86, the S aisle, and 1895, the chancel, both by G.F. Bodley, for Lord Burton. The chancel is splendidly coloured with painted reredos, ceiling painting and marble flooring, and ornamented with carved figures. 4m W, at **Newborough**, *church* (1899; J.O. Scott), well detailed Dec., the curious spindly top to the tower and spire apparently not as intended. 2m S, at **Hoar Cross**, the *church* (1872–76; Bodley and Garner) is one of the glories of the Gothic Revival. The building is a memorial to H.F. Meynell Ingram of Hoar Cross Hall commissioned by his widow who devoted the rest of her life to embellishing it. Stately red stone exterior in late Dec. style, beautifully and sparingly detailed, crowned by a crossing tower of tremendous power, the sides a grid of deep-set panels and the top simply battlemented.

Holy Angels' Church (1872–76; G.F. Bodley), Hoar Cross

Bodley's model was the 15C tower at Ilminster, Somerset, but heightened and refined of extraneous detail such as pinnacles to emphasise height and mass. Inside the external emphasis on the chancel which is higher than the nave and much more richly treated is confirmed by a magnificent gradation of decoration through from the dark timber-roofed nave to the vaulted glory of the E end enriched with tiers of stone saints and paved in black and white marble. To one side a magnificent late Gothic style organ case designed by Canon F. Sutton, painted and gilded, to the other an ogee-arched opening magnificently sculpted over the effigy of H.F. Meynell-Ingram. In a corresponding position on the other side of the small chantry chapel the effigy of Mrs Meynell-Ingram under a painted and gilded canopy. Kneeling figure of F.G.L. Meynell (died 1910). Beyond, All Souls' Chapel, added 1900. On the other side of the chancel, Lady Chapel (1892). Complete furnishings by Bodley, including the rood screen and high font cover, all the stained glass by Burlison and Grylls. *Hoar Cross Hall* (open to public) (1862–71; H. Clutton) is red-brick and stone Jacobean with formal symmetrical garden front and more varied entrance side. Some details modelled after Temple Newsam, Mrs Meynell-Ingram's home outside Leeds. G.F. Bodley designed the Long Gallery panelling, plaster ceiling of the Banqueting Hall and the carved screen in the entrance hall. Most notable of his work is the chapel decoration (1897). 3m W, at **Abbots Bromley**, *church* handsomely rebuilt 1852–55 (G.E. Street) with chancel fittings by Street. *Abbots Bromley School* was founded under the auspices of N. Woodard's group of boarding schools for the 'middle classes', of which this (1874) was the second foundation for girls. Chapel (1875–81; R.H. Carpenter), brick, apsed with high sculpted reredos. 3m N, at **Marchington Woodlands**, craggy Gothic estate *church* (1858; A.D. Gough), particularly overworked on the spire. *Smallwood Manor* (1886; R.W. Edis), brick and terracotta, notable for being one of the first houses fitted with electric light. 3m S of Hoar Cross, A515, at **Yoxall**, the *church* was rebuilt 1865–68 (H. Woodyer) for H.F. Meynell-Ingram, and he was buried here before the church at Hoar Cross became his memorial. Effigy of Admiral Meynell (died 1865; C. Marochetti).

CHEADLE. A522 10m E of Stoke-on-Trent. *St. Giles RC Church* (1841–46; A.W.N. Pugin), built for the Earl of Shrewsbury, is the one parish church by Pugin where funds were sufficient to recreate truly the medieval glories to which all his writings aspired. Dark stone exterior, Dec., the body of the church an upward sequence of steep pitched roofs to the bellcote on the E end of the nave, solidly articulated with aisle buttressing and the tall vestry adjunct on the N side. The W tower and lovely crocketted spire are the finest Pugin built, delicate canopy work at the angles enriching the base of the spire. The interior is wholly decorated to Pugin's designs, with complete set of fittings. Painted decoration covers the walls, piers and roofs, apart from some modern alterations, the colours clear with simple stencilled patterns. Carved reredos, pulpit, font and screen, and fine metalwork, notably the Shrewsbury lions on the door. Brick *school* and *convent* adjoining by Pugin and *presbytery* in Chapel St.

5m E of Cheadle, at **Alton**, the estate of the Earls of Shrewsbury, romantically set over the Churnet valley. In the valley, the disused railway *station* (1849), Italianate style in contrast to the Gothic work on the crags above. *Alton Towers* (open to public), the Shrewsbury seat, is a romantic ruin now, still surrounded by its magnificent grounds. The castellated fantasy of towers and turrets was the result of work carried out over forty years, the bulk from 1811–27 for the 15th Earl including most of the garden buildings, but Pugin's patron, the 16th Earl, employed him from 1835 to build the now ruined Great Hall and decorate the chapel. Pugin's hall gable is the centrepiece of the silhouette. The immense length of the buildings, some 450ft, represents one of the last great sequences of formal state rooms built in England, that is public rooms quite separate from the domestic part of the house. In the grounds fantastic features appear at every turn, Greek to Gothic, including a seven-domed *conservatory*, pagoda-like Gothic *tower* and fully Chinese *pagoda* on the lake, mostly of c 1820–25. Across the ravine, the most spectacular of the landscape fantasies, *Alton Castle* (1845–51; A.W.N. Pugin) built for the 16th Earl to echo the castles of the Rhine. To the ravine, sheer walls between two high and thin towers, one against the exaggeratedly steep roof of the chapel. From the other side a third tower with leaded spire and, at the far end, the chapel apse rising to the height of the battlements of the main range such that the roof stands clear against the sky. The contrast of austere walling pierced by mullioned windows and the romantic display of the skyline is masterly. Pugin's creation, though not large, expresses the romantic medievalism of a patron who in his Catholicism and ancient lineage embodied the values of the Christian Middle Ages that Pugin advocated so fervently. Appropriately, the forebuildings of the castle are the *Hospital of St. John* (1840–47), on the model of medieval almshouses, incorporating a school, chapel, clergy lodgings, library and guildhall in attractive asymmetrical Gothic, the guildhall possibly added later by E.W. Pugin. In the chapel, Pugin decoration and reredos. Brasses to the 15th and 16th Earls. E window by Willement (1840).

St. John's Hospital (1840–47; A.W.N. Pugin), Alton

2½m SE of Alton, B5032, at **Denstone**, *church (1860–62; G.E. Street), a masterpiece in Street's most elemental geometrical manner, as if carved out of the solid. Three-sided apse, tower proceding from square to cone by variation of planes and windows set back from the wall face, which has subtle polychrome touches. Interior with black marble shafting in the chancel and exceptional fittings by Street, in stone and marble, carved by T. Earp. Superb stained glass by Clayton and Bell. By Street also the lychgate, *school* and *vicarage*, displaying in different ways his ability to compose mass to telling effect. The group was built for Sir P. Heywood of the Manchester banking family and he also gave the land for *Denstone College* (1868–73; Slater and Carpenter), the first of the offshoots of N. Woodard's 'middle-class' college at Lancing, Sussex, to be built in the Midlands, a development of the plan first established at Lancing with the buildings grouped in an H for maximum light and architectural effect. Schoolroom across the centre, dining-hall and chapel projecting each side to the front, classrooms and dormitories in the higher rear wings ending in steep-roofed pavilions, the style a spare and muscular Gothic. Chapel (1879–87; R.H. Carpenter), interior splendidly high, like Lancing. 2m SE, at **Rocester**, High Victorian *church* (1870–72; E. Christian) with marble arcade columns, squat with bold capitals in the muscular manner. E window glass by the potter W. de Morgan (1872). 3m W of Rocester, at **Hollington**, *church* (1859–61; G.E. Street), much more modest than Denstone but with the same characteristics of solid geometry. Single vessel with rounded apse broken by a gable over the E window. Street fittings and apse glass by Clayton and Bell (1861). 3m further W, A522, at **Tean**, the early 19C cloth *mills* of the Philips family, leading manufacturers from the 18C. *The Heath House* (1836–40; T. Johnson), to E, was built for J.B. Philips, Tudor Gothic and symmetrical with entrance tower. Earlier gardens with classical orangery (1831). At **Church Leigh**, 3m S of Tean, off A50, *church* (1846; T. Johnson), remarkably accurate Dec. for the date, the chancel even stone vaulted. E window by Wailes, W window by Morris (1874). The rich tiling of the chancel floor was designed by Pugin. The school was a good design by G.E. Street (1856–57) but much altered.

5m NE of Cheadle, B5417, at **Near Cotton**, *Cotton College*, founded 1846 by the 16th Earl of Shrewsbury and in 1848 the first home of the Oratorians of which J.H. Newman was Superior. Chapel (1846–48; A.W.N. Pugin) with broach spire, the first Gothic addition to the 18C house on the site. 6m E, A52, **Mayfield**, industrial settlement on the Dove valley with mills from the mid to later 19C in brick and stone. 2m N, at **Okeover**, *church* in the grounds of the Hall, remodelled 1856–58 (G.G. Scott) with ornate fittings. At **Ilam**, 3m N, in the Manifold valley, estate village of the Watts Russell family of *Ilam Hall* (1821–26; J. Shaw Sr), now a youth hostel and mostly demolished. The village is extremely picturesque with stone and tile-hung *cottages* (1857; G.G. Scott) and Eleanor *cross* (1840), memorial to Mrs Watts Russell. The *church*, restored 1855–56 (G.G. Scott), has the superb marble memorial (1831; F. Chantrey) to D.P. Watts in its own octagonal chapel, the old man recumbent on a Roman couch blessing his daughter and her children. Scott fittings in the main part of the church including fine iron screens.

LEEK. A53 9m NE of Stoke-on-Trent. Silk-manufacturing town on the edge of the Staffordshire uplands. William Morris learnt the art of vegetable dyeing from T. Wardle of Leek and the town was notable in the late 19C for the foundation of a number of organisations for artistic and social improvement on Morris lines, including the Leek Embroidery Society (1868), a temperance coffee tavern, co-operative workshops, a 'William Morris Labour Church' and an art school with library and institute. The leading figures were the local industrialists but late 19C Leek owes its architectural character to W.L. Sugden, local architect, Morrisian socialist and follower of Norman Shaw into Queen Anne styles. The parish *church* was restored 1865–67 (G.E. Street) with fittings by Street and chancel glass by Clayton and Bell. E of the Market Place, in Stockwell St, set back, *Nicholson Institute* (1881–84; W.L. Sugden), inventive Queen Anne mélange of late 17C details with cupola-capped tower over the entry balanced by a Dutch gable, the best of W.L. Sugden's works in Leek. Gothic *Memorial Hospital* (1870; W. Sugden Sr). In Derby St, former *bank* (1882; W.L.

Sugden) with plastered gable and oriels after Norman Shaw. In St. Edward St, *Spout Hall* (1871; R. Norman Shaw), half-timbered 16C style, the upper floors jettied over a stone ground floor. In Queen St, *St. Luke's Church* (1847; F. and H. Francis), extended 1873 (J.D. Sedding) with delicate screen and ornate reredos. Arts and Crafts style organ case (1903). In Mill St, the *Wardle and Davenport factory* (c 1860; W. Sugden Sr) and the restored 18C *Corn Mill*, now James Brindley Museum. At Compton, just outside the centre, *All Saints' Church* (1885–87; R. Norman Shaw), broad and spreading in proportions, the low gables and squat central tower quite different from the work of contemporary church architects. Shaw lights the nave and clerestory with small square-headed lights of late Gothic type, but in the tower these are reduced for the bell-openings to plain slatted oblongs as in a military fortification. At the E and W ends however broad traceried windows flood the church with light. Inside the constructional problems of a tower without transepts are daringly solved by broad arches across the nave buttressed by half-arches over the aisles. Interior fittings by W.R. Lethaby including the painted reredos, delicately panelled pulpit and massive black marble font, a splendid Arts and Crafts design. Later chancel and S aisle decoration by G. Horsley and glass by Morris and Co. Shaw also designed the *church* at **Meerbrook** (1868–73), 3m N, small with strong central tower in the High Victorian manner. Good fittings by Shaw and E window by Heaton, Butler and Bayne.

1m W of Leek, *Westwood Hall* (1850–53; Hadfield, Weightman and Goldie) stone-fronted Elizabethan style mansion with tower on the entrance front. 3m SW of Leek, A53, at **Longsdon**, *church* (1903–05; G. Horsley) by one of Shaw's pupils and with similarities to the church at Leek in the broad proportions. Fine square tower with traceried square-headed bell-openings and broadly splayed broach spire. 3m S of Leek, A520, at **Cheddleton**, canalside 18C *flint mill*, now a museum. Flints were powdered to whiten pottery. Cheddleton *church* was restored 1863–64 (G.G. Scott Jr) with delicate painted decoration to the chancel and outstanding early *glass by Morris and Co (1864–69). By Morris and Co also the painted wings to the reredos, a Flemish relief. Churchyard *cross, lychgate* and *school* by Scott Jr. 3m SE, at **Ipstones**, the *church* has fine Arts and Crafts screen and painted decoration of 1902 (G. Horsley). 10m E of Leek, off B5054, at **Sheen**, *church* rebuilt 1850 (G. Burleigh) for A. Beresford-Hope, patron of the ecclesiologists and leading figure in High Anglican church building. Beresford-Hope brought in W. Butterfield, the ecclesiologists' favoured architect, to complete the church and design the *vicarage* (1852). The co-founder of the Cambridge Camden Society, B. Webb, was given the living. The vicarage is sizeable, in stone, with most varied elevations and rooflines, Gothic in minor details, the complexities of the plan exploited to picturesque effect.

LICHFIELD. A5127 16m N of Birmingham. Lichfield *Cathedral* suffered badly in the civil war, was restored in the late 18C by J. Wyatt and then thoroughly reworked from 1857 by G.G. Scott when most of the tracery and the W front statues were renewed. Inside the outstanding feature of Scott's work is the metal *screen (1859–63) made by F. Skidmore, in painted iron, brass and copper, the last survivor of Skidmore's cathedral screens. In the nave, iron pulpit by Scott and lectern by Hardman. Richly carved font (1862; W. Slater). W window by Clayton and Bell (1869). The choir is wholly furnished by Scott, a splendid example of Victorian church decoration, the reredos and screens each side lavishly and delicately carved (J.B. Philip), inlaid with coloured marble, the marble pavement of matching splendour inset with roundel scenes. In the N choir aisle, alabaster effigy of Bishop Lonsdale (1869–71; G.F. Watts), the swirling drapery a tour de force of modelling, and kneeling statue of Bishop Ryder (1841; F. Chantrey). In the S choir aisle, monuments to Archdeacon Hodson (1856; G.E. Street) and to Major Hodson (1861–62; Street), particularly bold High Victorian forms, effigy of Archdeacon Moore (1879; H.H. Armstead) and of Dean Howard (1872; H.H. Armstead). The Chapel of St. Chad over the Consistory Court was refurbished in 1897 with reredos and glass by Kempe. In the Lady Chapel statues and reredos by Kempe (1895), off to S, effigy (1879; Nicholls) of Bishop Selwyn, Bishop of New Zealand (1841–68) and then Bishop of Lichfield, in whose memory Selwyn College, Cambridge, was founded. Beacon St leads from the Close to the *Library and Museum* (1857; Bidlake and Lovatt) and Museum Gardens with *statue* of Captain Smith (1910; Lady Scott) of the 'Titanic'. Off Bird St, in Friary, neo-Norman *clock tower* (1863; J. Potter). In the Market Place, *St. Mary's Church*, now Heritage centre, the spire by G.E. Street (1852–54) and the body of the church by J. Fowler (1868–70), the spire at 200ft measuring well against the cathedral spires. In the square, Samuel Johnson *statue* (1838; R.C. Lucas), a brooding figure with cartoon-like reliefs around the plinth. *Statue* of J. Boswell 1908 (P. Fitzgerald). In Bore St Gothic *Guildhall* (1846–48; J. Potter).

4m W of Lichfield, off B5012, at **Chasetown**, *church* (1865; E. Adams), Romanesque in harsh brick, even the decoration in cut brick, an unusual design. 6m NW of Lichfield, A51, at **Brereton**, the *church* (1837, enlarged G.G. Scott 1877) with sgraffito plaster frieze inside by H. Sumner (1897), fine Arts and Crafts work. **Rugeley**, to N, is on the edge of the Staffordshire coalfield. Gothic *Town Hall and Market* (1878; W.T. Foulkes) in brick with thin spirelet. In Heron St, prominent spired *RC church* (1849; C. Hansom) with E window glass by Pugin. William Palmer, the poisoner, executed 1856, is the most notorious native. At **Colton**, just NE, *church* rebuilt 1850–52 (G.E. Street) with complete fittings by Street. 3m SE of Rugeley, **Armitage**, on the Trent and Mersey Canal. *Spode House* is 18C Gothic refaced for the Mrs Spode of the pottery family c 1839 in stone. Large brick Perp. style chapel (c 1900; E. Goldie) added when the house became a Dominican priory. Neo-Norman parish *church* (1844–47; H. Ward). 7m SE of Lichfield, A51, **Tamworth**, market town, the parliamentary seat of three generations of the Peel family, including the Prime Minister, Sir R. Peel, whose *statue* (1853; M. Noble) stands in front of the Town Hall. The parish *church* was restored by G.G. Scott (1852) with carved reredos by J.B. Philip. Some excellent Morris glass in NE window (1874) and chancel clerestory (1873). Sir R. Peel is buried at **Drayton Bassett**, 3m S. Drayton Manor, built for his father, has been demolished. Just E of Tamworth, B5000, at **Glascote**, *church* (1880; B. Champneys), brick with inventively detailed gabled central tower. Morris and Co glass of 1903–05. Just NE, at **Amington**, *church* (1863–64; G.E. Street), the E window of 1864 exceptionally good early Morris and Co glass. 2m W of Tamworth, A51, at **Hopwas**, *church* (1881; J. Douglas), brick and half-timber, a hallmark of Douglas' churches in Cheshire. A central gabled roof is prettily raised slightly over the nave and chancel ridges and capped with a shingled spirelet, the effect slightly Germanic. 4m SW of Tamworth, at **Canwell**, in the grounds of the former Hall, dignified *church* (1911; Temple Moore), characteristically spare in detail with fine vaulted interior. 7m S of Lichfield, A454, at **Little Aston**, *Little Aston Hall* (1857–59; E.J. Payne), handsome stone palazzo style mansion, formally symmetrical with the heavy rustication and varied window shapes, characteristic of mid 19C classicism. Fine red stone estate *church* (1874; G.E. Street) with broach spire and ornate stone fittings by Street.

STAFFORD. A34 16m S of Stoke-on-Trent. The county town, shoemaking centre from the late 18C. The parish *church* was heavily restored from 1841–44 by G.G. Scott, who altered most of the 15C work for something closer to his preferred 13C to early 14C, thus removing the clerestorys from the chancel and S transept, the Perp. E and S transept windows, and renewing most of the arcade capitals. Such drastic work was partly justified by earlier damage, but mostly by the desire to return the building to its state at the 'best' period of medieval architecture, however conjectural some of the reconstruction might be. W window glass 1855 by A. Gerente of Paris. *School* by Scott (1856). In the Market Place, *Old W. Salt Library*, stone-fronted former bank (c 1860). In Eastgate St, *Borough Hall* (1875; H. Ward), Gothic, the hall marked by tall upper windows. In Martin St, *County Buildings* (1893–95; H.T. Hare), brick and stone, free late 17C style, not grand but prettily detailed. Nearly symmetrical, the larger Council Chamber at one end balanced by a smaller projection at the other, the Chamber made a major element by the sharp angle at which the building is seen. Good interior sequence along the length of hall, tunnel-vaulted stair and similar upper corridor to the domed square chamber decorated in Wrenian manner. In Foregate St, N of centre, · *General Hospital* (1892–97; Sir A. Webb), the same stylistic sources as the County Buildings but less lively. S of centre, on The Green, *Library* (1914; Briggs, Wolstenholme and Thornely). On Newport Rd, A518, to W, *Upmeads* (1908; E. Wood), suburban house built for a shoe-manufacturer, startling even today in its modernity. Flat concrete roof and brick elevations, square in outline and quite without period detail. Simple unmoulded stone window frames and full-height stone facing to the centre bay recessed between concave curves on the entrance side, slightly set back on the garden front. Such detail as there is, the subtle chamfering of the angles and the relation of projecting porches to the centre bays, is emphatically linear, looking forward to the 1920s. *Church* at **Castle Church** (1844; Scott and Moffatt), neo-Norman with medieval tower. S of centre, on Wolverhampton Rd, *RC church* (1861; E.W. Pugin), apsed, in brick and stone with characteristic angular detail. On the lane to Coppenhall, to S, *Burton Manor* (1855; E.W. Pugin) polychrome brick Gothic.

5m SE of Stafford, off A513, *Shugborough* (NT), 18C house and park of the Anson family, Earls of Lichfield. When the Trent Valley Railway wished to cross the park in 1847 the Earl of Lichfield secured a handsome castellated *tunnel entrance* below the Milford drive and arched *bridge* over the Lichfield drive, in classical style, worthy additions to the 18C monuments of the park. Part of the Jacobean style *station* at **Colwich** survives and a stone *bridge* at Trent Lane, **Great Haywood**, a Shugborough estate village. To NW, *Ingestre Hall*, 17C mansion of the Earls Talbot, Earls of Shrewsbury from 1856 in succession to the family of Alton Towers. N front in matching style by J. Nash (1808–10), interiors of 1882 (J. Birch) after a fire. In the *church* of 1676 family memorials, to J.C. Talbot and to Viscount Ingestre by F. Chantrey (1825 and 1826), marble effigy of the 18th Earl (died 1868; Sir J. Steell) and marble and bronze memorial to Viscount Ingestre (1918; Countess Gleichen). At **Hixon**, E of A51, *church* (1848; G.G. Scott), model example of the village church as approved by the ecclesiologists. To SE, *Blithfield Hall*, Bagot family property since the 14C, the house 17C and 18C, Tudorised 1820–24. *Church* restored by Pugin (1851) and Street (1860). Excellent Gothic *school* by Street (1857). At **Weston-upon-Trent**, A51, 5m NE of Stafford, the *church* has nave roof and clerestory by Butterfield (1872), the bold carpentry of the trusses and the diaper patterning of the E wall typical. E window by Gibbs. The former *rectory* opposite by G.G. Scott (1858), Jacobean style. 2m NW, A51, at **Sandon**, *Sandon Hall* (1852; W. Burn), neo-Jacobean stone mansion, built for the 2nd Earl of Harrowby, extensive, meticulously planned as Burn's houses were, with private wing distinct from the main apartments, but bleak in detail. Handsome conservatory (1864). In the gardens (occasionally open to public) the elaborate Italianate pavilion is the top of the belvedere tower from Trentham Park (1833–42; C. Barry), S of Stoke-on-Trent, the house of the Dukes of Sutherland demolished in 1910 (see below). Arts and Crafts *cottages* and pub by the lodge built c 1905 (G. Dawber) for the 5th Earl, a late example of such estate building. The former railway *station* (1849) is elaborately Jacobean, the house style of the North Staffordshire Railway, but with a large porte-cochère for the use of the Earl. 4m NW, at **Stone**, railway *station* (1849; H.A. Hunt), Jacobean three-gabled front, the next size up from Sandon but modest compared to Stoke, such is the hierarchy of the North Staffordshire line. In Margaret St, *RC church* 1852 (C. Hansom) with E end of 1861 (G. Blount). Effigy (1889; J.S. Hansom) of Bishop Ullathorne, first RC Bishop of Birmingham and leading figure in the re-establishment of Roman Catholicism in the Midlands after Catholic Emancipation. Gothic *convent* buildings attached (1852–58; C.F. Hansom: 1861: G. Blount), the convent chapel a very modest work of Pugin (1852). At **Oulton**, just NE of Stone, *St. Mary's Abbey* (1854; E.W. Pugin), church in restrained Dec., more typical of the elder Pugin, painted chancel roof and wrought-iron screen. Buildings attached partly of 1854, partly of 1892.

8m NW of Stafford, A5013, at **Eccleshall**, *church* restored 1866–69 (G.E. Street) with glass by Clayton and Bell. Lychgate (1892) and reredos (1898) by B. Champneys and fittings including organ case from the very end of the Gothic revival (1931; W. Caroe). 3m N, at **Slindon**, *church* (1894; B. Champneys), small and pretty, Dec. handled sensitively and freely. Squat crossing tower and vaulted E end. Built for the Salt family, bankers, of *Standon Hall*, 3m NW, large red stone Elizabethan mansion (1910; J.F. Doyle) influenced by Norman Shaw's work. 3m E of Standon, at **Swynnerton**, the *church* has very Gothic E window glass of 1864 (E. Sedding), richly coloured. By the Hall, *RC church* (1868; G. Blount). 1½m NW, off A51, at **Lower Hatton**, *pumping station* (1890 and 1898), red and yellow brick group, Italianate with corner tower. A similar *pumping station* (open to public) at **Mill Meece** (c 1905), N of Slindon, A519, has working horizontal rotary steam-engines. 5m W of Stafford, A518, at **Haughton**, *church* rebuilt 1887 (J.L. Pearson) with handsome EE style chancel and carved stone reredos and pulpit. 10m S of Stafford, S of A5, at **Brewood**, spired *RC church* (1843; A.W.N. Pugin) with presbytery and school in Pugin's simplest manner, windows functionally placed and elevations accordingly asymmetrical, the type of logical design that runs from Pugin through the major architects of the Gothic revival and was, for all its modesty, one of the most significant strands of Victorian design. 6m W, A5, at **Weston-under-Lizard**, *Weston Park* (open to public), 1671 mansion of the Earls of Bradford. *Church* by the house with family chapel (1876; E. Christian) and Bradford memorials. 1m N, at **Blymhill**, *church* mostly rebuilt 1856–59 (G.E. Street) in EE style. Excellent fittings by Street. *School* (1855–56; Street).

STOKE-ON-TRENT. Borough formed in 1910 from the six separate towns of the potteries, extending for some eight miles along the A50, from S to N, Longton, Fenton, Stoke, Hanley, Burslem and Tunstall. The heartland of the English ceramic industry from the 18C, the great names of Wedgwood, Davenport, Spode, Copeland and Minton established by the late 18C, Doulton a late arrival from London in 1877. The towns remained separate, each with its own centre and industries, none achieving predominance and all, until recently, characterised by the bottle-shaped kilns that gave distinction to the region. Arnold Bennett (1867–1931) in his novels depicts the potteries in their Edwardian heyday. In **Stoke** itself, the parish *church* (1826–29; Trubshaw and Johnson) has memorials to the leading pottery families including Josiah Wedgwood (died 1795) and Josiah Spode II (died 1827). E window 1829 (D. Evans). *Town Hall* (1834; H. Ward), Glebe St, built as the Market Hall with grander stone classical range added behind after the creation of the unified borough (1910; Wallis and Bowater). On London Rd, S of Church St, former *School of Science and Art* (1858–60; J. Murray), Gothic in brick and terracotta, and *Library* (1877; C. Lynam). Outside Minton's works, *statue* of C. Minton Campbell (1887; T. Brock). Herbert Minton's firm became the leading maker of encaustic floor tiles for the Gothic Revivalists. Associated with A.W.N. Pugin from the 1840s, it made some of the finest Victorian pavements, notably those of the Palace of Westminster and St. George's Hall, Liverpool. The *Minton Museum* shows the whole range of the firm's work. Off Church St, *Spode–Copeland Museum* displays the work of the other two great names of Stoke pottery. On Hartshill Rd, A52, to W, *RC Convent* (1857; C.F. Hansom) and *Holy Trinity Church* (1842; G.G. Scott), built for H. Minton with *school, vicarage* and *cottages* by Scott. The church is to correct ecclesiological standards, one of the first such in Scott's career, Minton's friendship with Pugin influencing the choice. Good display of Minton tiles. Just N of centre, Winton Square, laid out 1848 for the North Staffordshire Railway, one of the few examples of formal planning around a railway station in the country. Jacobean style buildings by H.A. Hunt, the most elaborate of his designs for the line, the *station* (1848) with columned loggia and stone bay window above, based on Charlton Park, Wiltshire, lighting the board-room. Railway housing each side and the *North Stafford Hotel* (1849) opposite. In the centre, statue of J. Wedgwood (1863; E. Davis).

SE of Stoke, **Fenton**, the smallest of the pottery towns, not one of the so-called 'five towns'. In Albert Square, Gothic *Town Hall* (1888; R. Scrivener) with Queen Anne *Court House* (1888; Scrivener) and *Library* (1905; F.R. Lawson) forming a small civic group with the large brick parish *church* (1890; C. Lynam). On corner of City Rd, former *Athenaeum* (1853; H. Ward and Son), palazzo style. King St runs SE to **Longton** with various surviving pottery buildings, the style generally late Georgian, the model of the *Boundary Works* (1819), King St, little altered for the *Aynsley Works* (1861), Sutherland Rd. In Times Square, *Town Hall* (1863; Burrell), stone-fronted classical, quite grand. SE of centre, on Uttoxeter Rd, *St. James' Church* (1832–34; T. Johnson), Commissioners' Gothic on a large scale and *Gladstone Pottery Museum*, the best surviving pottery works, not one of the largest but all the buildings of the manufacturing process complete around a huddled courtyard behind the office front. All the processes were separately housed and can be followed from mixing the clay to final despatch. 3m W of Longton, A34, at **Trentham**, *Trentham Park*, the remains of the great Italianate mansion (1833–42; C. Barry) of the Dukes of Sutherland. Of the mansion the principal surviving feature is the semicircular loggia and porte-cochère that screened the W front and the terraced parterres that step down to the lake, in their heyday one of the finest Italian gardens in Britain. Arcaded *sculpture gallery* attached to the *stable court* (Barry; 1841–50). *Church* remodelled by Barry (1844) with Leveson-Gower family memorials including statue of 1st Duke of Sutherland (1838; F. Chantrey) whose marriage to the last hereditary Countess of Sutherland brought vast and wild Scottish estates to a family already richly endowed, as Marquesses of Stafford, with lands made valuable in the first phase of the industrial revolution. Effigy of the 2nd Duchess (died 1868; W. Noble), close confidante of Queen Victoria, who nonetheless felt outdone by the splendour of the Duchess' London palace, Stafford House, and country seat, Cliveden, Buckinghamshire.

N of Stoke centre, divided by *Hanley Park*, laid out 1894 by T. Mawson, **Hanley**, the main commercial centre of the pottery towns. In Albion St *Town Hall* (1869; R. Scrivener), not grand, built as an hotel. To W, in Broad St, *City Museum and Art Gallery* with impressive collections of ceramics. In Market Square, palazzo style *Market* (1849). In Snow Hill, S of Broad St, *St. Mark's Church* (1831–33; J. Oates), Commissioners' Gothic with terracotta reredos (1896) by G. Tinworth, leading sculptor for Doulton. Arnold Bennett was born in Hanley and the house where his family lived from 1880, *205 Waterloo Road*, Cobridge, N of centre, is now the *Arnold Bennett Museum*. **Burslem**, to N, is called the 'mother of the potteries', J. Wedgwood was born here and had his first factory on the site of the *Wedgwood Institute* (1863–69; R. Edgar and J.L. Kipling), Queen St. The Institute housed the school where A. Bennett was educated. Splendid Venetian Gothic exterior in brick and terracotta, the upper blind arcade ornamented with sculpted reliefs. *School of Art* (1905; A.R. Wood). In Wedgwood St, *Town Hall* (1911; Russell and Cooper), classical in the Beaux Arts manner, mechanical compared to the *Old Town Hall* (1852–57; G.T. Robinson) with its curved Baroque portico and low dome. Good interior hall and staircase. In Nile St, the Burslem works of Doulton and Co , originally of Lambeth. Henry Doulton bought the Nile St Pottery in 1877, the first major outside firm to challenge the established manufacturers. Since 1956 Burslem has been the Doulton headquarters. The *Sir Henry Doulton Gallery* has examples of the firm's work from 1815. SW of Burslem, A527, at **Wolstanton**, by the church, Gothic *school* (1871–72; J. Brooks), an excellent design in brick on a sloping site with shafted windows and master's house attached. 3m NE of Burslem, B5051, at **Brown Edge**, the *church* (1844; J. Trubshaw: 1854; H. Ward and Son) has one excellent Morris window (1874). At **Tunstall**, just N of Burslem, in the centre, *Town Hall* (1883; A.R. Wood), Tower Square, and *clock tower* (1893). On the Boulevard, *Market* (1857; G.T. Robinson), the original Town Hall, much more modest than Burslem. W of centre, *Chatterley Whitfield Mining Museum*, coal mine with underground workings accessible to visitors. 6m N of Tunstall, A527, at **Biddulph**, *Biddulph Grange* (1896; T. Bower), notable for the gardens laid out from 1845 by John Bateman, a romantic combination of Early Victorian picturesque planting and follies in the Chinese taste of the late 18C. By the densely planted lake, a Chinese pavilion in elaborate fretwork looking out onto a Chinese bridge over the water, the bridge rebuilt simpler than the original. Also an Egyptian garden. Bateman paid for the rebuilding of the *church* (1848–51; R.C. Hussey) at **Knypersley** 2m S, with parsonage and school.

2m W of Stoke, **Newcastle-under-Lyme**, colliery and industrial town rather than a pottery centre. Parish *church* rebuilt 1873–76 (G.G. Scott) in handsome Dec. In Merrial St, *Ebenezer Methodist Church* (1857; J. Simpson), grand pedimented facade in brick and stone. In Queen St, *St. George's Church* (1828; F. Bedford), Perp. of late Georgian type with plaster vault. On London Rd, *RC church* (1833-34; Rev. J. Egan), an extraordinary facade completely covered in Gothic panelling, a single large traceried centre window but the similar aisle windows simply decorative blanks, a tour de force of brickwork. 3m W, A525, at **Keele**, * *Keele Hall* (1856–61; A. Salvin), now part of Keele University. Red stone Jacobean style mansion, the grandest Victorian country house in the county, built for Ralph Sneyd, whose family had owned Keele since the 16C and were suddenly wealthy from coal. Highly varied entrance court with stair tower in the angle and a profusion of shaped gables, not excessively ornamented but gaining effect from variation of masses, rooflines and window types. The garden fronts, by contrast, are calmer, more or less symmetrical and in part based on the previous house of c 1580. Inside, a full-height great hall galleried at both ends with monumental fireplace, galleried library and suite of state rooms decorated in mixed Renaissance style. Stable court in Tudor style (c 1835; E. Blore). Estate *church* to W (1868; J. Lewis). 3m W, A525, at **Madeley**, the *church* has an excellent S aisle W window by Morris and Co. (1873). E window by Clayton and Bell (1872). 6m SW of Newcastle, A53, at **Ashley**, *church* (1860; J. Ashdown), lavishly furnished in 1910 (C. Hare) in the manner of G.F. Bodley for F.G.L. Meynell of Hoar Cross (see above p. 381). Late Gothic style gilded reredos, screens and organ loft, marble paving and painted decoration. Marble memorials to two T. Kinnersleys, one of 1826 (F. Chantrey), reclining figure, the other a group of three angels about a rock (1861; M. Noble). 4m NW of Newcastle, at **Audley**, NW of the church, a row of *shops* (1855; W. White), rare example of commercial design by one of the advanced Gothicists. Brick, simply detailed with three gables, plain relieving arches over the first-floor windows and paired polychrome arches to the ground floors, broad for the shop-windows, narrow for the doors, the motif varied at the end for a carriage arch and footway.

SUFFOLK

BURY ST. EDMUNDS. A45 27m E of Cambridge. The *Cathedral*, since 1914, is the old parish church of St. James, 16C restored by G.G. Scott (1865–69) and enlarged to suitable scale from 1960. Some Scott fittings, W window by Hardman, aisle glass by Clayton and Bell. In Abbeygate St *Barclays Bank* (1856; H.F. Bacon), Italianate, enlarged to W 1880, *Alliance Assurance* (1891; J.S. Corder), Dutch gabled, and palazzo style *National Westminster Bank* (1868; J. Gibson). *Corn Exchange* (1861; Ellis and Woodard) with giant portico, *Library*, adjoining on Cornhill, (1836; B. Backhouse, and 1848), built as a Corn Exchange with Tuscan porticoes each end, and *Post Office* (1895; H. Tanner). Across the river, off Eastgate St, *Grammar School* (1883; A.W. Blomfield), brick and tile-hung. the *station*, N of centre, (1847; F. Barnes), Jacobean with shaped gables and two cupola-topped towers, one of a group of surprisingly ornate stations on the Ipswich–Bury line.

4m N of Bury, B1106, at **Culford**, *Culford Hall*, rebuilt 1894 (W. Young) for Earl Cadogan, London landowner and Viceroy of Ireland, in a style vaguely following the late 18C original. *Church* rebuilt 1857–65 (A. Blomfield) with marble effigy of Countess Cadogan (died 1907; F. Gleichen). 6m N, at **Elveden**, an equivalent but much larger house, *Elveden Hall* (1899–1903; W. and C. Young), rebuilt for Lord Iveagh, of the Guinness family, in bleak Italianate style, matching the existing house (1863–70; J. Norton) which is now the right wing. The scale is very large, befitting one of Edward VII's richest friends, and most of the 15,000 acre estate was devoted to raising pheasants, some 20,000 a year. The interior contains fascinating Indian style interiors, the older house having been built for Maharajah Duleep Singh of the Punjab, maintained here at safe distance from his country by the Imperial government. Lord Iveagh surpassed Duleep Singh's work with a monumental marbled Indian style great hall rising into the central dome, the design partly supervised by the director of the Indian section of the South Kensington Museum, London. Most of the village of Elveden was rebuilt by Lord Iveagh and the *church* lavishly enlarged (1904–22; W.D. Caroe) in a free Gothic based on East Anglian 15C models. Craftsmanship of exceptional quality, magnificent hammerbeam roof and alabaster reredos. The detached high tower connected by a cloister was finished in 1922. 2m E of Culford, at **Ampton**, *Ampton Hall* (1885–89; Balfour and Turner), careful neo-Jacobean. 3m SE of Bury, at **Rushbrooke**, *church* furnished c 1840 with much reused woodwork, characterful with the pews facing each other across the nave. 12m S of Bury, A134, at **Long Melford**, magnificent 15C church with tower by G.F. Bodley (1898–1903) successfully in keeping. 4m S, **Sudbury**, birthplace of T. Gainsborough, his statue (1913; B. Mackennal) in Market Hill. Town supposedly the 'Eatanswill' of 'Pickwick Papers'. *St. Peter's Church* was restored by Butterfield (1858) with stained glass by Hardman. Tall reredos by Bodley (1898). In Market Hill, former *Corn Exchange* (1841; H.E. Kendall), converted to a library, with columned front. Beyond, former *Institute* (1834), Greek Revival narrow front. By St. Gregory's Church, *RC church* (1893; L. Stokes), inventive free Gothic. 4m E, at **Edwardstone**, *church* with furnishings of c 1900 by Bodley, painted decoration, panelling, organ case, stained glass by Burlison and Grylls and fine iron light fittings. 7m W of Bury, A45, at **Higham**, *church* (1861; G.G. Scott) with round tower on East Anglian model. 7m W, **Newmarket**, horse-racing centre since the 17C. *Jockey Club* (1840) refronted in 1933. At top of High St, Cooper *fountain* (1910) with equestrian ornaments. On the outskirts large late Victorian and Edwardian brick houses associated with the racing.

IPSWICH. The county town and port on the river Orwell. Cornhill is the centre, with *Town Hall* (1867; Bellamy and Hardy) and *Corn Exchange* (1878–82; B. Binyon) outshone by *Lloyds Bank* (1889; T. Cotman), Gothic to Jacobean, in brick and stone. In Buttermarket, to E, *The Ancient House*, or Sparrowe's House, the highly ornamented pargetted front with overhanging oriels (c 1670) much imitated by Queen Anne style architects in the later 19C (cf. Norman Shaw's Swan House, Chelsea Embankment, London). *No. 11* (1899) is in the Norman Shaw style. *St. Lawrence's Church* has a fine flushwork tower (1882; F. Barnes). W of Cornhill, in Museum St, former *Museum* (1847; C. Fleury), stuccoed slightly Greek front. In Westgate St, to N, the *Crown and Anchor Hotel* (1840s and 1897). In High St, *Museum* (1881; H. Cheston), brick late 17C style, Dutch gabled. By Christchurch Park, to N, 19C terraces facing N on Fonnereau Rd and *Ipswich Hospital* (1836; W. Ribbans) in Anglesea Rd, gauche classical. In Henley Rd, *Ipswich School* (1850; C. Fleury), brick Elizabethan style with entrance tower. From Cornhill, Queen St runs S to the river. Albion Wharf runs E along the New Dock (1839–42) to the *Custom House* (1843–47; J.M. Clark), a most handsome Italianate building with Tuscan portico raised up and reached by balustraded steps. Deep bracketted eaves to the roof and pediment, hallmark of the change from Greek to Renaissance classicism. Off-centre campanile tower at the back. In Foundation St, to N, *Tooley Almshouses* (1846), gabled red-brick courtyard group with picturesque outside stairs in the gable ends. Gatehouse of 1861. To NE, in St. Helen's St, *County Hall* (1836; W.M. Brookes), brick Tudor style. *Ipswich Station*, SW of centre, over the river, has a long symmetrical Italianate front (1860; R. Sinclair).

  8m S of Ipswich, A137, at **Brantham**, *Brantham Court* (1850–52; P.C. Hardwick), gabled Elizabethan. By the *church* remarkable Arts and Crafts lychgate (c 1900; E.S. Prior). To W, around **East Bergholt**, the 'Constable country' of Constable's most famous paintings. Memorial window in East Bergholt *church* and fittings of c 1890 (T.G. Jackson). 2m W of Ipswich, A1100, at **Sproughton**, *Sproughton Court* (c 1864; W.E. Nesfield) in the manner of Philip Webb or the simpler works of Butterfield, asymmetrical with half-hipped gables and tall stacks, but no directly Gothic motifs. 4m N of Ipswich, A45, at **Claydon**, *church* remodelled 1862 by the Rev. G. Drury who apparently himself carved some of the detail of the ornate crossing and pulpit and designed the glass of the E window. 2m N, *Shrubland Hall*, originally of 1770, recased 1831–33 (J.P. Gandy-Deering), interestingly in more Italian than Greek classical manner, but made thoroughly Italian by Sir C. Barry (1849–52) with balustrade and a much emphasised belvedere tower. The Italian ˙garden, created by Barry, with balustraded stair descending the hillside from a top loggia to lower fountain, is quite the most successful transplant to Britain of the Villa D' Este type of semiformal landscape. Heavily Italianate lodges (c 1840–50). 2m N, at **Needham Market**, Elizabethan style *station* (1846; F. Barnes), a manor-house composition, far from ordinary. The *station* at **Stowmarket**, 3m NW, is also by Barnes (1849), Dutch gabled and equally ornamental. 11m NE, B1077, **Eye** *Town Hall* (1857; E.B. Lamb) is an idiosyncratic work, vaguely Jacobean with asymmetrical tower.

2m SW, at **Braiseworth**, small *church* (1857; E.B. Lamb), neo-Norman style but exaggeratedly notched and chamfered in detail.

8m E of Ipswich, A12, at **Woodbridge**, *Seckford Hospital* (1834; C.R. Cockerell), Seckford St, simple Tudor Gothic with almshouses (1869) attached. St. John St is an attractive early Victorian suburb, begun 1843, centred on *St. John's Church* (1844; A. Lockwood and J.M. Clark). In the Thoroughfare, *No. 40* (c 1845), palazzo style, well handled, effective in the curve of the street. E. FitzGerald (1809–83), translator of the Rubaiyat of Omar Khayyam, frequented Woodbridge, meeting his friends at *The Bull*, in Market Hill. He died at *Little Grange*, Pytches Rd, and is buried with his family at Boulge, just N, the rose over his grave a descendant of the rose over the tomb of Omar Khayyam. 12m N of Woodbridge, B1116, at **Framlingham**, *Framlingham College* (1863; F. Peck), the Suffolk memorial to Prince Albert, initially called the 'Albert Middle Class College'. Red-brick Gothic buildings, severe, with Prince Albert *statue* (1865; J. Durham) in front, all prominently set on a hillside. 6m NE of Woodbridge, A12, at **Little Glemham**, in the church, fine early 19C chapel to the North family with classical marble statue of D. North (1833; J. Gibson). 9m E, A1094, **Aldeburgh**, seaside resort where G. Crabbe (1752–1833) was born, remembered in his poem 'The Borough' (1810). Memorial (1847; Thurlow) in the *church*. Elizabeth Garrett Anderson, one of the first women doctors and first woman mayor in England, lived at *Alde House*. Her father owned the *Maltings* (1859–85) at **Snape**, 5m NW, now the centre of the Aldeburgh Festival. 4m N of Aldeburgh, **Leiston**, where the Garrett family had a locomotive *works*, built model *cottages* and the *church* (1853; E.B. Lamb), the church interior an amazing display of timber roofing, exceptionally wide in the evangelical way allowing the most complex structural solution over the crossing. Painted decoration in the chancel and E window by Kempe (1898). 2m N, at **Theberton**, C.M. Doughty, author of 'Travels in Arabia Deserta' (1888) is commemorated in the *church*. At **Knodishall**, just W of Leiston, *church* with painting by W. Dyce of Jacob and Rachel (1851). **Thorpeness**, 3m SE of Leiston, is a small resort laid out 1910–30 in weatherboarded vernacular style occasionally veering to the extremely whimsical, as in the *water tower* to S, disguised as a six-storey weatherboarded cottage.

11m SE of Ipswich, **Felixstowe**, the most Victorian of Suffolk resorts, mostly of the late 19C in red brick and half-timber. The *Felix Hotel* (1900–03; Hon. D. Tollemache and T.W. Cotman) on the cliff-top was a railway hotel, built for the LNER in gabled Jacobean style, and *Cranmer House* (c 1895; T.W. Cotman), Cobbold's Point, now part of Felixstowe College, was the grandest of the private houses, built for F. Cobbold of the brewing family. *Church* (1894; A. Blomfield), Orwell Rd, tall and broad in red brick with handsome spire. The *station* (1898; W.N. Ashbee) is Dutch gabled with much glazed roofing over the platforms.

LOWESTOFT. A12 10m S of Great Yarmouth. Fishing port and resort, the resort developed S of the estuary by Sir S.M. Peto of Somerleyton Hall after 1847 (when the railway arrived). Some 150 houses were built by 1850 with Peto's architect, J. Thomas, designing the station, fishmarket, hotel, reading room and 'ornamental works'. Much was demolished during the Second World War, one long terrace survives. N of the harbour, the old town, with *Town Hall* (1860; J. Clemence), notable for the stained glass in the council chamber (1855; J. Thomas) commemorating the 1855 Anglo-French treaty. At N end of High St, *lighthouse* (1855). **Oulton**, just NW of Lowestoft, was the home of G. Borrow from 1840, 'Lavengro' being written here. Memorial in the *church*. *Mancroft Towers* (1898; G.J. Skipper) is a very large Elizabethan style house.

5m NW of Lowestoft, **Somerleyton**, model village, church and great house built from 1844 for Sir S. Morton Peto (1809–89), building contractor. Nelson's Column, the London to Dover and Brighton railways, the Grand Trunk railway in Canada were Peto enterprises. The firm failed in 1866, shortly after Somerleyton had been sold to Sir F. Crossley, of the Halifax carpet family. Peto's architect was the sculptor J. Thomas, responsible for the carved work on the Houses of Parliament. The estate *village* is picturesque and thatched, on the early 19C model. *Somerleyton Hall* (open to public) is of brick and stone, Jacobean style, with lavish carved ornament, the Jacobean elements freely mixed with other Renaissance strands. Symmetrical garden front but with big belvedere tower behind to off-set the regularity. Heavily panelled and carved interiors, the entrance hall a period piece with glazed dome, tiled floor and marble statue (1865; J. Durham) of the Crossley heir as a barefoot boy in the centre. Stuffed polar bears in the corners. Terraced gardens with statuary by Thomas, greenhouses by Paxton and a maze. 2m NE, at **Lound**, the *church* interior is prettily painted and gilded (1914; J.N. Comper) with chancel glass by Holiday. 9m W of Lowestoft, A1116, at **Barsham**, in the *church*, E window (1874), an early work of C.E. Kempe. Lively painted rood canopy (1919). The extraordinary grid-work of the E end is the source for similar details in the Arts and Crafts churches by Lethaby at Brockhampton, Herefordshire, and R. Wells at Kempley, Gloucestershire. 6m W, B1062, at **Flixton**, in the *church*, fine marble monument to Lady Waveney (died 1871) by John Bell. Rhenish-helm roof to the tower (1856; A. Salvin).

SURREY

CAMBERLEY. A30 12m SW of Staines. Army town linked to the Royal Military College of Sandhurst, Berkshire, but mostly developed from 1862 when the *Staff College* (1861–63; J. Pennethorne) was established. Very large stock brick and stone complex with French roofs. Prince Albert died from a chill caught on the site. The town itself is leafy and late Victorian. On London Rd, Edwardian Baroque *Town Hall* (1906; H. and B. Poulter), further W, *St. Michael's Church* (1850; Woodyer) with dominant spire (1891). At **Bagshot**, 2m NE, *Bagshot Park* (1877; B. Ferrey), brick and stone Tudor, grim, built for the Duke of Connaught, Victoria's third son, who made his career in the army. 3m E of Bagshot, B386, at **Valley End**, E of Windlesham, *church* (1867; G.F. Bodley), a modest chapel in brick, well done. The *Old Vicarage* (1866; Bodley) is quite remarkable for its date, plain brickwork, hipped roofs and small-paned windows, a Georgian vernacular without a hint of Gothic.

CATERHAM. A22 9m S of Croydon. Suburb developed by the railway from 1856. On the hill to NW *Guards Depot* (1877) with polychrome chapel in stock brick with flint chequered gables (1885; W. Butterfield). Off A22 to SW, *Upwood Gorse* (1868 and later; P. Webb), Tupwood Lane, brick gabled house with bold chimneys, later parts tile-hung. To E, S of **Woldingham** station, *Marden Park* (1880; A. Cawston), large, polychrome brick house. 3m S of Caterham, at **Godstone**, by the church, very pretty *almshouse* group (1872; G.G. Scott) with a charming chapel, small scale, focused on a rich marble reredos. 3m E, A25, N of **Oxted** station, *Blunt House* (c 1890; J.O. Scott), handsome Wren style house, built by Scott for himself. Further E, towards Limpsfield, *Home Place* (1894; Douglas and Fordham). At **Limpsfield**, in the *church*, marble effigy of Lord Elphinstone (died 1860; M. Noble). On the hilltop to S, *St. Michael's School* (1886; J. Norton), a landmark from the M25, with a central Gothic tower more typical of the 1860s. At **The Chart**, on the ridge, *The Cearne* (1896; J.H. Cowlishaw), built for Edward and Constance Garnett. Life there c 1900 is enchantingly described in David Garnett's 'The Golden Echo'. N of Limpsfield, at **Titsey**, *church* (1860; J.L. Pearson), an important High Victorian work by Pearson. Shingled spire, polychrome stone interior and much carved work. particularly between the chancel and Leveson-Gower mortuary chapel. Glass by Clayton and Bell, Minton tiles. On the N side the vestry has vigorous Gothic detail, especially the door set in the corner behind an angle column, and a steep-hipped roof. *Lodges* to Titsey Place (1868; G. Devey).

CRANLEIGH. B2128 7m NW of Horsham. *Cranleigh School*, 1m N, begun 1863 (H. Woodyer) with Tudor style quadrangle and apsed chapel. N of **Ewhurst**, 3m E, on the slopes of the Hurtwood, *Coneyhurst* (1885; P. Webb), brick and tile hung, gabled with good chimneys. Behind, *Long Copse* (1897; A. Powell), Arts and Crafts stone house, hand-built and the effect, like Gimson's cottage at Ulverscroft, Leicestershire, of having grown from the hillside. To W, *Hurtwood* (1910; A.T. Bolton), quite remarkable, a large Tuscan towered farmhouse recreated in Surrey. To N, *Woolpit* (1885; George and Peto), brick and terracotta, free Tudor, built for Sir Henry Doulton, the head of the ceramic firm. To E, B2126, at **Holmbury St. Mary**, *Moxley* (1888; B. Champneys), tile-hung, *Holmdale* (1873; G.E.

Street), Street's own house with stone corner tower and Domestic Revival tile-hanging and half-timber, and *Hopedene* (1874; R. Norman Shaw), tile-hung and half-timbered with polygonal bay carried into the roofline. Later extensions. In the village, *church* (1879; G.E. Street) built at Street's expense and beautifully finished with marble pier shafts, Clayton and Bell glass to Street's design and wooden bellcote. E of the village, *Beatrice Webb House* (1893; W. Flockhart), half-timbered with pretty service end extension (1906; Lutyens).

DORKING. A24 5m S of Leatherhead. Dominating *church* (1868–77; H. Woodyer), Woodyer's grandest work, in flint and stone with soaring spire. Tall interior, accentuated by Woodyer's acutely pointed arches. The *station* (c 1865) has good platform ironwork. 1m N, A24, *Boxhill and West Humble Station* (1867; C.H. Driver), charmingly ornamental in Gothic with a little pyramid-roofed tower, all this to placate the local landowner. At **Pixham**, just N of Dorking station, small *church* (1903; Lutyens), brick with domed sanctuary, Byzantinesque. 2m NW of Dorking, at **Ranmore Common**, *church* (1859; G.G. Scott), estate church for Denbies, house of the great London builder T. Cubitt. Flint with central tower and spire, lavish interior carving and marbles. Glass by Clayton and Bell. *School* by Scott also. 1m W of Dorking, A25, *Milton Heath* (c 1870; P.C. Hardwick), red-brick Elizabethan style. On the slopes S of Dorking, off South St, estates of mid 19C villas on Rose Hill and Tower Hill. *Goodwyns Place* (c 1900; H.T. Turner), Tower Hill, free Tudor.

EPSOM. A24 4m NE of Leatherhead. In Church St, *church* with medieval tower, 1824 Gothic nave, and tall vaulted E end (1907; Nicholson and Corlette), free Gothic. In High St prominent *clock tower* (1847). *Epsom College*, to SE, has Gothic buildings (1853; T. Clifton). At **Banstead**, 3m E, *Banstead Wood* (1884–86; R. Norman Shaw) for the banker F.H. Baring, a large house, well composed with tile-hung gables and tall chimneys, the tile-hanging replacing original half-timber after a fire. 4m S, A217, at **Lower Kingswood**, remarkable Arts and Crafts *church* (1891; S. Barnsley), red brick and stone, freely Byzantine incorporating genuine Byzantine capitals. Mosaic and marble apse and fine inlaid woodwork by Barnsley, best known for his furniture.

ESHER. A3 13m NE of Guildford. Associations with Queen Victoria's uncle, Leopold I of Belgium, who lived at Claremont. In the parish *church*, triptych panel to his wife, Princess Charlotte (died 1817) with Leopold accepting the crown from Britannia. Leopold's effigy (1867; Susan Durant) is in **Esher Green** *church* (1853; B. Ferrey). Louis-Philippe of France died in exile at Claremont 1850. *Esher Place*, Esher Green, was rebuilt 1895–98 (A. Duchêne) in French 18C style for Sir E. Vincent, governor of the Imperial Ottoman Bank. At **Hersham** 1½m W, spired *church* (1885; J.L. Pearson), rock-faced stone. NE of **Cobham**, A3, *Benfleet Hall* (1860; P. Webb) for the painter S. Stanhope, red brick with minimal Gothic touches, more severe than the Red House, Webb's contemporary house for William Morris (see p. 294). *Cobham Park* (1870; E.M. Barry), S of Church Cobham, Loire château style for C.J. Combe, brewer. Beyond Cobham, to W of A3, *Foxwarren Park* (1856–60), designed by the owner, C. Buxton, brewery heir, in what was intended to be an East Anglian Tudor style, assisted by F. Barnes of Ipswich. Diapered brick with moulded brick details and crow-stepped gables. Estate buildings include model *farm*, between A245 and A3, in the same style but with sharply angular bargeboarded gables. 3m SE of Cobham, A245, *Woodlands Park Hotel* (c 1885; R. Plumbe), mixing most late Victorian motifs, mostly Norman Shaw's Old English, but a beefy porch and brick tower behind more High Victorian. Full-height balconied hall.

FARNHAM. A31 10m W of Guildford. In the parish *church*, E window by Pugin, exhibited at the Crystal Palace. At the foot of South St, *Liberal Club* (1894; Lutyens), an early work, pretty with late 17C artisan classical style windows. Adjoining, former *Council Offices* (1905; H.P. Watson), lively neo-Wren with cupola. 3m S, A287, *Frensham Place* (c 1880), stone, Jacobean. ½m S, *Pierrepont* (1876–78; R. Norman Shaw), one of Shaw's most lavish half-timbered houses, though still of medium size by 19C standards. Subtle entrance front, five gables, suggesting a symmetry where in fact the two left gables are quite different and canted at an angle. To right, massive projecting end gable of the hall with three sturdy buttresses. 1m W, *Frensham Heights* (1900; F.W. Waller), large brick and stone Tudor style house with great hall, remodelled from an earlier house for Mr Charrington, brewer. E of A287, in Sandy Lane, Frensham Common, *Lowicks* (1894; C.F.A. Voysey), one of Voysey's first mature houses, roughcast walls, deep hipped slate roof disguising two upper floors and battered angles and chimneys, extended several times by Voysey. 3m SE of Farnham, off B3001, *Crooksbury House*, a complex building by Lutyens, the first part 1890, tile-hung, extended to form a courtyard 1898, and again 1914. Stables with cupola 1890 and 1901. Garden by Gertrude Jekyll. Roughcast cottage on the drive (1889), Lutyens' first building.

GODALMING. A3100 4m S of Guildford. To N of the station, *Westbrook* (1899; H.T. Turner), good Arts and Crafts stone house, big roofs, unornamented walls with flush stone-mullioned windows. Further N, Frith Hill Road, *Red House* (1899; Lutyens), two-storey brick road front with parapet and big end chimneys conceals a towering three-and-a-half-storey garden side, rising sheer with tall plain bays topped by a parapet. *Charterhouse School* (1872; P.C. Hardwick), grandest of 19C public schools, crowns the hill. Stone, Gothic of a complex gabled and towered type, the main quad centred on a big tower but in fact asymmetrical, the wings balanced with smaller towers not actually matching. Cloistered quad to rear. Facing the chapel, range with tall corner towers capped with steep pyramid roofs, the whole effect picturesque if hard in detail.

2m NW at **Compton**, the shrine of the painter G.F. Watts, 'England's Michelangelo', who lived at *Limnerslease* (1890; E. George) from 1891 to 1904. The House is half-timbered, the name a coy play of archaic terms for painter and meadow, Burne-Jones called it 'Daubersden'. E of the house, the *Watts Gallery* (1903; C. Turnor), Mrs Watt's memorial to her husband, who laid the foundation stone aged 86. Fine collection of Watts' paintings and sculpture (open to public). Watts is buried in the churchyard in a cloister designed by Mary Watts. Between 1896 and 1906 Mary Watts and a team of villagers built the village *Cemetery Chapel*, quite unique in Britain, Celtic Revival blended with Art Nouveau and heavy with symbolic intent. Outside, brick and finely worked terracotta, bright red in colour, Celtic cross plan. Inside the entire surface covered in gesso reliefs of angels and cherubs linked by twining Art Nouveau ribbons, the effect the more overpowering from the deep lowering colours. Mary Watts designed the chapel, the decoration, organised the villagers into a Potters Art Guild, found the clay on the estate and modelled much of the decorative work herself—few disciples of Ruskin and Morris were so tireless. W of the church, *Eastbury Manor* (1874; E. Christian). NW of the chapel, towards Puttenham, *Prior's Field* (1900; Voysey), much extended as an experimental school by Voysey's pupil Muntzer. Further on, *Hurlands* (1898; P. Webb), brick and tile-hung. **Puttenham** *church* was rebuilt 1861 (H. Woodyer). SW of the village, *Lascombe* (1894; Lutyens), roughcast over brick base with massive chimney. 2m SW of Compton, at **Shackleford**, *church* (1865; G.G. Scott), apsed with central tower in stone. NW of church, *Norney* (1897; Voysey), an important early work, roughcast with flush stone-mullioned windows and slate roofs. Heavily emphatic stone central porch lined up with a central chimney carrying a bell. More typical garden side with curved bays each end under big overhanging plain gables. To SW, B3001, at *Oxenford Grange*, gatehouse and barn (1843; Pugin), powerful Gothic forms without carved trimmings. Pugin altered the church, to N, at **Peper Harow** (1844), designing the stained glass, the N aisle and arcade and chancel arch. Beyond Oxenford Grange, B3001, *Fulbrook* (1896; Lutyens), Tudor style entrance front, tile-hanging and half-timber to the garden sides. Good lodge (1897).

¾m SE of Godalming, B2130, at **Busbridge**, *church* (1865; G.G. Scott) with central shingled tower. Morris E and W windows (1899) and lovely iron screen (1899; Lutyens) topped by an Art Nouveau rood. Gertrude Jekyll, Lutyens' collaborator on so many gardens, is buried here with her family. *Busbridge Hall* (1906; George and Yeates), to S, big Jacobean style house with Dutch gables. **Munstead**, B2130, was the Jekyll estate where Lutyens built some of his first works and Gertrude Jekyll laid out her first gardens. N of the road, *Orchards* (1897–1900; Lutyens), one of his very best houses, Surrey vernacular, built around a courtyard entered under a great barn-like arch and approached past a stable wing, also barn-like and big-roofed with sloping buttresses. Beyond, *Munstead Grange* (1902; E.W. Mountford) and *Munstead House* (1877; J.J. Stevenson), the Jekylls' original house, since altered. To the N, Heath Lane, on E side, *Munstead Place* (1891; Lutyens), stone and half-timber, close to Norman Shaw's work, on W side, *Munstead Wood* (1896; Lutyens) for Gertrude Jekyll, Lutyens' first important house, stone with sweeping roofs and tall chimneys, vernacular inspired, Arts and Crafts care over the details. Lutyens outbuildings and cottages further N. On B2130, *Munstead Wood Hut* (1894; Lutyens), pretty tile-hung cottage built for Gertrude Jekyll. To N, *Little Munstead* (1895; Lutyens). Towards **Hascombe** several more houses designed by Lutyens or his contemporaries. On the ridge to W of B2130, *High Hascombe* (1896; Lutyens), two houses by R. Lorimer, *Whinfold* (1897) and *High Barn* (1901), and *Hascombe Court* (1907; J.D. Coleridge). Hascombe *church* (1864; H. Woodyer) is a model mid Victorian country church, stone with excellent play of roofs and shingled bell turret. Severe lancets to nave and chancel, the chancel apsed and an almost separate S chapel, more elaborately treated. Complete scheme of decoration in rich and sombre colours inside with glass by Hardman. 2m NE, A281, at **Grafham**, a small *chapel* by Woodyer (1861–64), built at his expense opposite the country house he built for himself, now a school.

GUILDFORD. On W side of river Wey, *St. Nicholas' Church* (1870–75;

S.S. Teulon), Bury St, High Victorian with central tower and almshouses (1840). On corner of Bury St and Portsmouth Rd, *Wycliffe Buildings* (1894; H.T. Turner), remarkable early flats, stone, building up on a steep site to a corner tower, the styleless simplicity of the best Domestic Revival architects applied to public housing. In Buryfields, off Bury St, *The Court* (1902), 15 houses around an open forecourt, also by Turner. W of Portsmouth Rd, The Mount leads up to the *cemetery* where Lewis Carroll is buried. To S, on Guildown, c 1900 houses, *The Grange* (1902; J. Belcher), Guildown Rd, and *Littleholme* (1907; C.F.A. Voysey), Upper Guildown Rd. On Portsmouth Rd, *1–4 Rectory Place* (1882; Norman Shaw), tile-hung cottages.

3m W of Guildford, A31, set below the Hogs Back ridge, *Greyfriars* (1896; Voysey), long roughcast house, roof sweeping down at the W gable, all the typical details of Voysey's work. 4m NE of Guildford, W of A3, by **Send** church, old *rectory* (1863; T.G. Jackson), Gothic house in the manner of Philip Webb, the first work of Jackson, and *Sendholme* (c 1865; G. Devey), Tudor style. At **Ockham**, 4m E, off A3, *estate cottages* of 1860s, polychrome brick, part of the works of the 1st Earl of Lovelace of Ockham Park and Horsley Towers. At **East Horsley**, A246, 3m S, many more cottages and *'Horsley Towers*, where the Earl acted as his own architect from c 1847–70 adding to the original flint Tudor style house (1834; C. Barry) increasingly dramatic extensions, in the 1850s turning to a Romanesque cum Moorish style in flint and patterned brick. The sunken drive tunnelling under the first range of buildings is quite eerie and the combination of brick and flint harsh and restless. Inside, the Earl was much taken with vaulting, being an amateur engineer, adding cloisters, passages, towers and chapel all vaulted in brick. S of Guildford, A281, at **Shalford**, pretty *schools* in flint and brick (1856; Woodyer), to S at **Bramley**, *Snowdenham Hall* (1868 and 1887) to W, diapered brick mansion extended in half-timber and tile-hanging. To E of Bramley, at **Wonersh**, B2128, *Barnett Hill* (c 1905; A. Mitchell), impressive c 1700 style mansion, built for one of the Cook, travel agents, family. Brick with excellent Baroque detail in stone outside and plaster inside. *Chinthurst Hill*, NW of the village, is an early work (1891) by Lutyens, stone, Tudor. 1½m E of Wonersh, at **Blackheath**, some modest buildings by C.H. Townsend, radical Arts and Crafts architect, including the *church* (1892), low and roughcast with a strong brick entrance arch, the tiny *Congregational chapel* (c 1893) with a broad curved head window in the gable, the *village hall* (1897) and several cottages. *Greyfriars* monastery (1895; F. Walters), simple stone Gothic buildings. 1m S, *The Hallams* (1894; R. Norman Shaw), splendid last work by Shaw in his tile-hung and half-timbered manner, by then commonplace all over southern England. A sweeping roof broken by a full-height half-timbered porch bay with, to right, a great hall window, projecting and rising from ground to eaves, and further right a bold chimney balancing the porch bay. 4m NE of Wonersh, A248, at **Albury**, estate village of *Albury Park*, remodelled 1848–57 by A.W.N. Pugin and his son for the banker Henry Drummond, notable for the array of Tudor style chimneys. There are three churches, the *old church* by the house which has a transept vividly decorated by Pugin (1839), the *new church* (1842; W.M. Brookes), brick, Romanesque, provided by Drummond for the village, and the *Irvingite church* (1840; W.M. Brookes), N of the house, elaborate Perp. Drummond was the earliest supporter of Edward Irving, evangelical preacher; conferences held at Albury before Irving's death in 1834 led to the foundation of the Holy Catholic Apostolic Church, with Drummond as one of the Apostles.

HASLEMERE. A286 14m SW of Guildford. Town developed largely in the late 19C rush to the Surrey hills, here led by Tennyson in 1868, whose description of the view from Blackdown, 1m SE, 'Long known and loved by me, Green Sussex fading into blue With one gray glimpse of sea', was known to all the later arrivals who included the scientist John Tyndall and the parents of G.M. Hopkins. In the parish *church*, window (1892; Burne-Jones) to Tennyson and another to Hopkins in N aisle. High Victorian marble font (1870). Tennyson's *Aldworth House* (1869; J. Knowles Jr), 1m SE, just in Sussex, is quite grand, but not romantic. Mullioned windows and tall dormers, between Elizabethan and Francois I. *Lythe Hill* (1868; F.P. Cockerell), to NW, was a large Tudor mansion, damaged by fire. In the town, *No. 72 High St*, good late 19C tile-hung facade. To S, off A286, *Broad Dene* (c 1900; W.F. Unsworth), Hill Rd, tile-hung on stone, and *Red Court* (1895; E. Newton), Scotland Lane, an important work by Newton, neo-Georgian but with a deliberate flatness of detail that shows the influence of Lethaby in avoiding direct period reference. W of the town, **Shottermill**, B2131, where George Eliot wrote part of 'Middlemarch' at *Brookbank* (1871). Towards Hindhead, A287, *Honeyhanger* and *Branksome Hilders* (c 1900; E.J. May) and, off Polecat Lane, *New Place* (1897; Voysey), built for the publisher Methuen, one of Voysey's most elaborate houses, roughcast with slate roof and flush stone-mullion windows as usual but with more carved stonework and complex three-gabled garden front. More c 1900 houses into **Hindhead**. Near the centre, *Undershaw* (1897; J.H. Ball), built for Sir Arthur Conan Doyle, now an hotel. 2m N, off A3, at

Tigbourne Court (1899; E. Lutyens), Wormley

Thursley, Lutyens was brought up in a house N of the church and his first work (1888) was to *The Corner. Prospect Cottage* was the village Institute (1900; Lutyens). *Warren Mere* (1896; Lutyens) to NE, tile-hung with much play of hipped roofs, extended by Lutyens (1909). 5m NE of Haslemere, A283, at **Wormley**, *ˈTigbourne Court* (1899–1901; Lutyens), one of Lutyens' best houses, the front with three gables set off by curved screen walls to the wings that end in strong paired chimneys. Lovely combination of golden stone with red brick and thin bands of ˈred tiles. By the station, *King Edward's School* (1867; S. Smirke), neo-Jacobean in diapered brick. George Eliot lived at *Roslyn Court*, Wormley, 1877–80. 3m S, SE of **Chiddingfold**, *Pickhurst* (1883; J.M. Brydon), Norman Shaw Old English style house with half-timber and tile-hanging, well handled.

LEATHERHEAD. A24 4m N of Dorking. 4m SW *ˈPolesden Lacy* (NT), quintessential Edwardian house, externally unostentatious neo-Georgian extension (1902–06) of a villa of 1834 into a low but extensive mansion. In 1906 it was bought by Mrs Greville, brewery heiress and political hostess, who remodelled the interiors including the hall, panelled with part of a Wren reredos, and the gilded drawing room, mostly an Italian 18C interior transported and cut to fit. At **Great Bookham**, *school* (1856), tall cottage pair and terrace (1864) on corner of Eastwick Lane, all by Butterfield.

REDHILL. A23 11m S of Croydon. Town developed alongside the Brighton railway from 1841. In the centre Jacobean *Market Hall* (1860). To S, *St. John's Church*, mostly 1889–95 by Pearson, but retaining the aisles of 1860, impressive transverse arches to nave and vaulted chancel, all stone, though the exterior is brick. 2m N, off A23, at **Gatton**, *church* (1834), a rare example of a rich collector's estate church, full of continental treasures, mostly woodwork, collected by Lord Monson and all jumbled together quite unaffected by notions of correct Gothic or of forming a coherent ensemble. Such collecting, widespread during the early 19C, was usually tidied up by later Victorians. *Gatton Park* was rebuilt in 1936 retaining a splendid temple front (1891; S. Dyball). 2m N, S of **Chipstead**, *Shabden Park* (1873; E.M. Barry), French Renaissance style, steep roofs and heavy stone dormers. 2m W of Redhill, A25, **Nutfield**, with estate cottages of c 1860–70. *Nutfield Priory* (1872–74; J. Gibson) was built for the Yorkshire textile heir, J. Fielden MP, stone Gothic with big tower to one end. At **Buckland**, A25, 3m W of Redhill, pretty *church* (1860; H. Woodyer) and *school* (1862).

STAINES. A30 11m SW of Brentford. In the centre, *Town Hall* (1871–80), Italianate. On Laleham Rd, *St. Peter's Church* (1893; Fellowes-Prynne), impressive late Victorian suburban church facing river, full-height stone chancel screen inside. At **Laleham**, B376, 3m SE, Matthew Arnold was born and is buried in the churchyard. At **Ashford**, B378, 2m NE, *Charity School* (1857; H. Clutton), High Victorian Gothic. 3m SW of Staines, A30, *ˈRoyal Holloway College* (1879–87; W.H. Crossland), unforgettable red-brick and stone ensemble around two courtyards of enormous scale. This, the first women's college of London University, is the monument of Thomas Holloway (1800–83), Cornish patent medicine vendor whose huge fortune was built by advertising on a scale unprecedented in Britain. By 1880 Holloway spent £50,000 a year promoting his pills. Despite prejudice against doctors, lawyers and priests he left over a million pounds for the college and nearby sanatorium. The college is based on Loire châteaux, the two side ranges with an exuberant skyline of tourelles, chimneys and dormers and the three cross ranges each with a stone centrepiece, Continental Late Gothic in inspiration. Holloway bought for the college a collection of the best modern paintings, on display in the picture gallery. 1m N, A328, at **Englefield Green**, *church* (1859; E.B. Lamb), well set on the green, very personal Gothic with spreading low proportions, odd top to the tower and splendid polychrome brick and stone interior under a complex timber roof. Several large 19C houses overlooking the Thames. To NW, *St. John's* (1888; J.F. Bentley), RC preparatory school for the defunct Jesuit Beaumont College, interesting Loire style building with canted wings. 1½m S of Egham, B389, at **Virginia Water**, *Holloway Sanatorium* (1871–84; W.H. Crossland), Holloway's other foundation, here Flemish Gothic with a tower behind a Great Hall, a magnificent painted interior, hammerbeam-roofed all deep red, green and gold. At **Lyne**, 1½m SE, *church* (1849; F. Francis).

Royal Holloway College (1879–86; W.H. Crossland), near Staines

WEYBRIDGE. A317 6m SE of Staines. *St. James' Church* (1846; J.L. Pearson), an early work following Puginian models, much extended by Pearson. Rich marble chancel decoration. Pretty iron *bridge* (1865) over the Wey. Near the station, *Brooklands* (1891; R. Blomfield), gabled Queen Anne style. To NE, *Oatlands Park*, mostly rebuilt 1856 (T.H. Wyatt) as an hotel. *Nos 1–3 Oatlands Drive* (1882; R. Norman Shaw), pair of houses of the type Shaw built in Bedford Park, London. To SE, B365, *Whiteley Village*, a planned village for old people built 1914–21 with the million pounds left by William Whiteley, department store owner, who died in 1907. Remarkable formal layout around a central circle with Whiteley's monument. Houses by leading architects of the day, a planned village of the highest quality.

WOKING. A320 5m N of Guildford. Developed around the railway from 1838, 2m from Old Woking. In Oriental Rd a centre for oriental studies was founded by G.W. Leitner (1840–99), Anglo-Hungarian orientalist, professor of Arabic at King's College, London, at the age of 21. Original building (1865; T.R. Smith) built as Royal Dramatic College, Leitner added the onion domed *mosque* (1889; W. Chambers) in a correctly Indian style. *Christ Church* (1889; W.F. Unsworth), impressive plain brick church. At Maybury Hill, SE of the station, *convent* (1883–1900; J.L. Pearson), red-brick and stone buildings, Tudor style, the *chapel wholly stone inside and fully vaulted, the E end particularly complex and dramatic, triple apsed, with rich marble baldacchino and altar. To E, on Old Woking Rd, Pyrford Common, *Little Court* (1902; Voysey), large roughcast house under a big tiled hipped roof, characteristic Voysey details, but the entrance front broken by a tall gabled stair tower to one side. 1m NE of Woking, A317, at **Woodham**, *church* (1893) and, Woodham Lane, *Woodhambury* (1889) both by W.F. Unsworth, the house in a pretty tile-hung style built for himself. 2m NE, *Ottershaw Park* (1910; Niven and Wigglesworth), very expensive Palladian style remodelling in stone of a 1761 house for a South African diamond tycoon. *Church* (1864; G.G. Scott), polychrome brick and stone. 3m W of Woking, *Brookwood Cemetery* (1854), laid out by the London Necropolis Company on a vast scale to bring the dead out from London, via the company's funereal railway platform at Waterloo Station. Acres of monuments set amid evergreen trees. At **Pirbright**, to S, the explorer H.M. Stanley is buried. At **Worplesdon**, A321, SE of Pirbright, *Merrist Wood* (1877; R. Norman Shaw), now an agricultural college, half-timber over stone to entrance front, a big porch gable balanced by a massive chimney. Tile-hung garden side.

SUSSEX (EAST AND WEST)

ARUNDEL. A27 8m NW of Worthing. Seat of the Dukes of Norfolk. The 15th Duke (1847–1917) created the romantic neo-medieval skyline, rebuilding *Arundel Castle* (1879–1900; C.A. Buckler) into the largest of Victorian castles, impressive from a distance, but bleak in detail and stonework. Fully vaulted chapel, shafted in Purbeck marble. When the 15th Duke came of age it was decided to build a Catholic church outside the castle walls worthy of the Duke's position as the leading Roman Catholic layman in England. This is now a *cathedral* (1869–73; J.A. Hansom), French Gothic in style and French in outline, rising well over the town, a great slate roof, apsed and crowned with a flèche. Lofty interior, stone vaulted with full-height stone piers and large upper windows all adding to the impression of height. Hardman stained glass. Cottages and school by Hansom nearby. The Dukes are buried in the Fitzalan chapel of the parish *church*, divided from the main part and approached from the castle. Monuments from the 15C, large effigies to the 14th and 15th Dukes.

BRIGHTON. The great interest of Victorian Brighton is the churches, particularly those associated with the High Church Father A.D. Wagner who built five in the poorer areas of the town. Wagner was constantly a centre of controversy over ritual but, as in the East End of London, High Church ceremonial and the dedication of Tractarian clergy succeeded in bringing the Anglican church to areas thought beyond redemption. Brighton is also the most consistent Regency seaside resort in the country, its stucco terraces of imposing scale. The *⁎Royal Pavilion* (1815–22; J. Nash), the Prince Regent's Indian fantasy, stands on the W edge of the old town facing over the Old Steine. In the stables and outbuildings behind, *Museum* with good Victorian collections. In New Rd, *Theatre Royal* with facade of 1894 (C. Clayton) in red brick and stone. In North St, red brick *Prudential Buildings* (1904; P. Waterhouse) at W end, Jubilee *clock tower* (1887). To N off Queens Rd, *St. Nicholas' Church*, the medieval parish church restored (1853) for H.M. Wagner, vicar of Brighton 1824–70. Inside, enormous Wellington Memorial font cover by J.B. Philip (1853), much later glass by Kempe and wall painting (1892). At top of Queen St, *Brighton Station*, the original stucco building (1841; D. Mocatta) survives behind later ironwork. At the rear, glass and iron train-shed (1883; H. Wallis). The illustrator Aubrey Beardsley was born at *No. 31 Buckingham St* to W in 1872 and educated at the old Grammar School, *No. 80*. S of Queens Rd, in West St, *St. Paul's Church* (1846–48; R.C. Carpenter), built by H.M. Wagner for his son Arthur, the Father Wagner of Brighton ritualism. Flint and stone with plain Puginian interior, including chancel screen. The chancel has glass by Pugin, painted roof by Bodley and painted retable by Burne-Jones 1861. *Lectern* (1888; Hardman) with bronze angels surrounding. A spire was intended but the present timber octagonal lantern (R.H. Carpenter) is most effective. E of West St, on the seafront, Old Ship Hotel, where Dickens stayed. In Middle St, *Hippodrome* (1900; F. Matcham), vast domed interior given over to bingo, up Market St, stucco *Town Hall* (1830), complex staircase of 1899 inside. At foot of Old Steine, *Palace Pier* (1891–1901; R. Moore), more central of the two piers that make the Brighton seafront so special. At the head of the pier, Theatre (1901) with Moorish arcades around.

Old Steine runs N to Victoria Gardens and *St. Peter's Church* (1824–

St. Bartholomew's Church (1872–74; E. Scott), Brighton

28; C. Barry), impressive Regency Gothic in stone, the two stages of the tower especially inventive. Chancel 1900–06. To NW, off London Rd, *St. Bartholomew's Church* (1872–74; E. Scott), Ann St, one of the most remarkable churches in Britain, known from the start as Noah's Ark for its immense ship-like presence. A Father Wagner foundation, it was intended as a landmark in a poor district and consists of a single brick vessel as tall as Westminster Abbey decorated at the W end by simple bands of stone, patterning in the brickwork and a great circular window unrelieved by any tracery. Inside the scale overwhelms, brick, patterned a little but almost without mouldings or stone work, the arcade arches sharply pointed and of great depth, the roof dark, boarded with king-post trusses. The E end was never built, instead the church was given part of an outstanding Arts and Crafts decorative scheme by Henry Wilson (1895–1910). Byzantinesque square baldacchino in coloured marbles with alabaster capitals, the vault of mosaic and mother-of-pearl, standing in a marble paved sanctuary. On the altar, tabernacle and six candlesticks by Wilson in Art Nouveau beaten metal. The original silver plated altar crucifix stands over the Lady altar now, above a most beautiful beaten silver altar frontal of the Adoration of the Magi. Wilson's metal work is not sinuous like continental Art Nouveau but sturdy and elemental reflecting Celtic and

Byzantine precedent. In front of the high altar, marble columns hold bulbous bronze candle holders (c 1908) with bronze and enamel altar rails below (1905). Wilson also designed the Byzantinesque pulpit (1906), reminiscent of Bentley's work in Westminster Cathedral, panelled green marble on red marble columns high enough to allow entry beneath to a tiny spiral staircase behind. Massive octagonal font by Wilson (1908). The E end mosaics are of 1911, not to Wilson's design. NE of St. Peter's church, in Lewes Rd, on left, *St. Martin's Church* (1874; G. Somers Clarke Jr), built by Father Wagner and his brothers to the memory of their father, the Rev. H.M. Wagner, lancet style in yellow and red brick, tall and wagon-roofed. Fittings by Clarke including the towering reredos painted by H.E. Wooldridge who also designed the E window. Other glass by J. Powell and Sons.

E of Old Steine, seafront terraces on Marine Parade, early 19C. Paston Place leads N past the *Bombay Bar* (1892), a little Indian style building originally a mausoleum to Sir Albert Sassoon, Jewish philanthropist from Baghdad who headed a Bombay banking and commerce empire, to the Royal *Sussex Hospital* (1828; C. Barry). W of the hospital, *Brighton College* (1848; G.G. Scott), flint and stone Gothic, chapel (1859), hall (1863). Brick and terracotta S range (1886; T.G. Jackson), more cheerful. E of Paston Place, the fringe of Kemp Town, Thomas Kemp's stucco development (1823–40). In Eastern Terrace, *No. 1* was the house of Sir A. Sassoon, his guests the Shah of Persia and Edward VII. *Chichester Terrace* begins the main Kemp Town development, Chichester House is supposedly the Dr Blimber's Academy of 'Dombey and Son'. *Lewes Crescent* and *Sussex Square* are the centrepiece of the estate, stucco terraces around a very large open space. Under an esplanade across the front, a tunnel to the sea. 3m E, on the coast, A259, **Rottingdean**, where Burne-Jones lived at *North End House* 1881–98. His nephew Kipling wrote 'Recessional' there, 'Stalky & Co ' and 'Just So Stories' at *The Elms*, opposite. Kipling Room in the library. In the *church* stained glass by Burne-Jones. *Roedean School* (1898; J.W. Simpson) is a well-planned but bleak cliff-top complex.

W of West St towards Hove, on the seafront, the two grand Victorian hotels, *The Grand* (1862; J. Whichcord), stuccoed Italianate, and *The Metropole* (1888; A. Waterhouse), brick and terracotta, the roofline spoilt by extra floors. Further up, the *West Pier* (1863–66; E. Birch), perhaps the best iron pier built in Britain, but sadly derelict. Original are the little octagonal kiosks and pretty lampstands, the big end pavilion theatre was added in 1893 and the concert hall in the middle in 1916. By the entrance an ornamental iron bandstand. The Bedford Hotel was the fashionable hotel of 19C Brighton, visited by French exiles like Louis-Philippe and Louis Napoleon. The slopes above have terraces from the 1820s to 1850s, many with the ammonite capital that Amon H. Wilds used in his developments. Off Montpelier Rd, to E, Victoria Rd and *St. Michael's Church*, St. Michael's Place. Red brick and stone bands, plate-traceried Gothic, but actually two churches, the S aisle an early work of G.F. Bodley (1861), the tall main church a posthumous work of W. Burges (1892), both of the highest quality. The Bodley church has the muscular feel of work by Street or Butterfield, short round arcade piers with big capitals, brick edging to the arches. Choir stalls by Burges, font by Bodley, E window by Clayton and Bell, but outstanding the work by Morris and Co , the painted roofs by Morris and Webb and the stained glass of the W rose and on the S side. The Burges nave, executed by J.S. Chapple, is soaring Early French Gothic, the style of Cork Cathedral and Burges's work of the 1860s, and was in fact designed c 1868. Complex Early French shafting and plate tracery, especially fine in the tracery screens in front of the clerestory windows, wood-ribbed vault. The E and W windows have glass by H.W. Lonsdale and the carved work is by T. Nicholls, long time Burges associates. Sanctuary decoration and reredos (c 1900; Romaine Walker), N aisle glass (Kempe) and high altar (1914; Temple Moore) more typical of their date.

On the seafront Brighton becomes Hove at the Edward VII memorial (1912) with further stucco terraces beyond in the Brunswick Square area (1825–28). In Waterloo St, *St. Andrew's Church* (1827; C. Barry), one of the first examples of a Florentine quattrocento style being used in the 19C, a stucco front with bell turret. To the N and W the estate developed by Sir Isaac Goldsmid after 1830, Brunswick Place (1850s) and on the seafront the great open space of *Adelaide Crescent* and *Palmeira Square*, the W end equivalent of Kemp Town. On the E side of Adelaide Crescent ten houses of 1833–36 (D. Burton), the rest were built 1850–60 and Palmeira Square 1855–70. Further W, grid-like pattern of avenues laid out by J. Knowles Jr and brick takes over from stucco, detached and semi-detached houses from terraces. In Church Rd, *Town Hall* (1882; A. Waterhouse), red brick and terracotta with central tower. Further W, *Hove Museum* with 19C furniture collection, housed in villa of 1876, and parish *church* (1833–36; Basevi), neo-Norman in flint. W of the Town Hall, The Drive runs N with large c 1890 scrolled-gabled villas (H.B. Measures) in red brick to *All Saints' Church* (1889–1901; J.L. Pearson), very large stone church in the 13C Gothic Pearson preferred, remarkable inside for the stone transverse arches that span the nave and the splendid scale. The sanctuary is stone vaulted, narrower and brighter lit than the rest of the church focusing on the great carved reredos and three windows above, the view down the church framed by the stone arches. Glass by Clayton and Bell.

CHICHESTER. *Chichester Cathedral* was not heavily restored during the 19C but the main tower and spire are replicas (1861–66; G.G. Scott) after the original collapsed and the NW tower was rebuilt to match the SW tower (1897–1901; J.L. Pearson). In the choir, S aisle, tomb of Dean Hook (c 1875; G.G. Scott), tomb chest in richly coloured inlaid marbles. In the Lady Chapel complete scheme of stained glass by Clayton and Bell. In the nave, monument to Bishop Dunford (c. 1895; Bodley and Garner). In West St, *St. Peter's Church* (1848–52; R.C. Carpenter), well proportioned and a foil to the Cathedral opposite. In East St, former *Corn Exchange* (1832), Greek. N of the walls, in College Lane, *Bishop Otter College* (1849; J. Butler), neo-Tudor brick. 6m NW, B2146, at **Stansted**, *Stansted House* (1903; A.C. Blomfield), red brick and stone early Georgian style mansion.

CRAWLEY. A23 25m N of Brighton. At **Lowfield Heath**, 2m N, A23, *church* (1867; W. Burges), a minor work, but with all Burges' punch in the W wheel window, with carved figures at the compass points and the pyramid-roofed tower. Massive detail within, especially to the chancel. To SE of Lowfield Heath, B2036, *Crabbet Park* (1873), designed for himself by W.S. Blunt, poet and Arabist, a successful very early example of neo-Georgian in brick and stone, more like 1900 than 1873. Elaborate real tennis court and orangery with Tuscan columns added c 1908 by Lady Anne Blunt, Arab scholar and breeder of Arab horses. At **Crawley Down**, E of Crawley, B2028, *Heatherwood* (1891; J.M. Maclaren), a tight composition of irregular forms swung around a corner chimney, brick and tile-hung, not large but inventive. 2m S of Crawley, W of A23, *Cottesmore House School*, originally Buchan Hill (1882–83; George and Peto), a most elaborate red-brick and stone house with tower and shaped gables, Pont Street Dutch in the country. Huge baronial fireplace in the hall. SE of **Worth**, B2110, *Worth Priory*, originally Paddockhurst (1869–72; A. Salvin), big Tudor style house, extended with a gatehouse range (1897; A. Webb), which contains an elaborately panelled and plastered room with lively plaster frieze by Walter Crane.

CROWBOROUGH. A26 6m SW of Tunbridge Wells. A scattering of good turn of the century houses including *Winscombe House* (1899; Baillie Scott), Beacon Rd, in the Voysey style with sweeping gables and long low window bands, and, ½m NW, *Angrove House* (1908; F.B. Wade), extensive brick and half-timbered house. At **Withyham**, B2110, 3m N, *Old Buckhurst*, to SW, is an early Tudor gatehouse restored and extended (c 1914; C. Brewer). To SE, *Buckhurst* (1830–35; J.A. Repton), neo-Tudor house for Earl de la Warr. On B2188, fragment of *Leyswood* (1869; R. Norman Shaw), dramatically sited Old English style house, one of three around Groombridge that launched Shaw's blend of 16C and vernacular elements into country house building. The stables and gate-tower survive. Just to NE, *Glen Andred* (1866–68; R. Norman Shaw), Shaw's first major house, built for the marine painter E.W. Cooke, with the Old English style fully fledged, tile-hung gables, tall chimneys, leaded mullioned windows, the entrance front a subtle near symmetrical composition of five advancing and receding gables. The third house, Hillside, is just in Kent. **New Groombridge** *church* (1884) is a minor work of Norman Shaw. 5m E of Crowborough, B2100, at **Mark Cross**, *St. Joseph's College* (1868; E.W. Pugin) with chapel c 1875 (E. Goldie). 4m S of Mark Cross, A267, at **Mayfield**, *Convent* in the former palace of the Archbishops of Canterbury, the hall, converted to a chapel (1863–66; E.W. Pugin), has the original spectacular transverse arches taken up by late Victorian church architects. Later convent buildings by P.P. Pugin (1890s). 4m E of Mark Cross, B2100, at **Wadhurst**, *Wadhurst College* (1888; A Croft), originally a private house, red brick with a prominent saddlebacked and dormered tower. *Houndsell Place* (1912; A. Ball), original neo-Georgian with long windows and generous hipped roof behind a parapet, the forecourt flanked by pyramid-roofed pavilions. At **Flimwell**, 5m E, A21, *Seacox Heath* (1862–72; Slater and Carpenter), stone French Gothic mansion built for the Liberal politician Viscount Goschen. Off A26, 5m SW of Crowborough, at **Heron's Ghyll**, *Oldlands* (1869; Sir M.D. Wyatt), stone, gabled, since altered. Opposite, *Temple Grove School* (1868; J.F. Bentley), built for the poet Coventry Patmore.

EASTBOURNE. Victorian Eastbourne developed after 1850 under the Dukes of Devonshire, landlords, with H. Currey as their architect. In Devonshire Place, *statue* of the 7th Duke (1901; Goscombe John), the houses around Italianate of the 1850s. Similar developments along the front, *Grand Parade* (1851–55) is stuccoed with giant columns, a late version of the Brighton type. Later houses go from the Italianate to French Second Empire by the 1870s, and then to the more jolly seaside style associated with Norman Shaw, gables, tile-hanging and half-timber, by the 1880s. One *pier* (1866–72; E. Birch) has attractive ironwork, and a theatre (1899) rebuilt inside. The *Town Hall* (1884; W.T. Foulkes) is most elaborate mixed Renaissance, with a tall tower. The *station* (1866 and 1886) is a brick Gothic building with an attractive lantern roof. On King Edward's Parade, Gothic *All Saints' Hospital* (1869; H. Woodyer). On Compton St, *Devonshire Park Theatre* (1884; H. Currey) with pretty plasterwork inside. Devonshire Park was laid out by Currey. In South St, *St. Saviour's Church* (1867–72; G.E. Street), a major work in red brick and stone with a tall spire. The brick is exposed within and the chancel is vaulted. The last part of the nave is canted in to focus on the chancel. Good carved work and fittings. At **Willingdon**, A22, to N, *The Hoo* (1902; E. Lutyens), opposite the church, combining motifs from the vernacular revival with a formally symmetrical garden front, the centre with weatherboarded gables. To NW, off A27, *Folkington Manor* (1843; W. Donthorn), large, flint Tudor style mansion.

EAST GRINSTEAD. A264 9m E of Crawley. From London Rd, prominent *RC church* (1898; F. Walters), neo-Romanesque. To N, Moat Road leads to former *St. Margaret's Convent* (1865–83; G.E. Street), one of Street's finest works, built for the Anglican Sisterhood of St. Margaret. The buildings are Gothic, grouped around a cloister, the style simple and uncluttered for the domestic parts, richer for the refectory and appropriately most elaborate for the *chapel (1879–83), one of the masterpieces of Victorian church building, tall under a long roof with strong saddleback tower to one side. Inside, stone-vaulted chancel, the ribs carried on black marble shafts, reredos carved by T. Earp, and low-vaulted and apsed E chapel. 1½m SW, B2110, *Standen (1891–94; P. Webb), Webb's best preserved house (NT). Webb and his clients, the Beales, took traditional Sussex elements to create a large house that is quite without the pomposity of more formal Victorian houses, loosely composed around a squat roughcast tower with generous roofs, tall plain chimneys and segment-headed Georgian sash windows. Tile-hanging, weatherboard, brick and stone suggest organic growth. Inside airy white-painted rooms, deliberately unselfconscious yet all with hallmarks of painstaking design, as in the fireplace and panelling details. SE of East Grinstead, A22, **Ashurstwood**, with several large houses on the slopes of Ashdown Forest. *Barton St. Mary* (1906; Lutyens), pebble-dashed free Tudor with tile-hung gatehouse, *Ashurstwood House* (c 1900; J. McV. Anderson), further on at **Forest Row**, *Village Hall* (1892; J.M. Brydon), prettily tile-hung with cupola. Off B2110, Chapel Lane leads to *Shalesbrooke* (c 1900; M. Macartney), stone and tile-hung Tudor. At **Coleman's Hatch**, 2m SE, *Hollyhill* (1885; J.O. Scott), brick Jacobean style.

HASTINGS. In the Old Town, off High St, *St. Clement's Church* where Rossetti married Lizzie Siddal, the Pre-Raphaelite beauty, in 1860. Coventry Patmore, the poet, lived in the High St from 1875 at Old Hastings House and paid for the handsome *RC church* (1882) by his friend and biographer B. Champneys. The seafront has good Regency stucco terraces, especially Pelham Crescent and its church (1828) under the Castle. To the W, the Victorian centre around the Albert Memorial *clock tower* (1863) and *Holy Trinity Church* (1851–59; S.S. Teulon), apse-ended and with cross-gabled aisles. On seafront, *Queen's Hotel* (1858; F.H. Fowler), Italianate, and terraces of c 1860 interrupted by former *Palace Hotel* (1886; A. Wells), large and very mixed in detail. *Hastings Pier* (1869–72; E. Birch) marks the edge of **St. Leonards**, the centre a planned resort laid out from 1828 by James Burton, terraces on the seafront, villas behind. In Church Rd, *St. Paul's*

Church (1868; J. Norton), expensive suburban church with hefty tracery and vaulted chancel. *Warrior Square Station* (1852; W. Tress), Italianate with broad eaves. Warrior Square dates from 1853–64. 3m W of St. Leonards, **Bexhill**, resort town developed by the Earls de la Warr from c 1880 with gabled and bargeboarded terraces and houses. *Nazareth House* (1893; L. Stokes), Royston Gardens, free late 17C style, a long front under a hipped roof with semicircular arched ground-floor windows and two pyramid-capped towers behind. Later buildings by Stokes to 1909. From Hastings, 3m inland, on A21, at **Baldslow**, *Claremont School* (1880; R. Norman Shaw), quite large Old English style house. At **Northiam**, 8m NE, A28, *Great Dixter*, the 15C house extended c 1910 by Lutyens incorporating another timber-framed house from Benenden, Kent. Famous Lutyens-designed garden open to the public. **Battle**. A2100 5m NW of Hastings. *Battle Abbey*, now a school, is the medieval abbey vowed by William the Conqueror, incorporated into a 16C house and rebuilt as a Gothic mansion (1857; H. Clutton). The Great Hall is Clutton's principal room. Battle railway *station* (1852; W. Tress) is remarkably Gothic, complete with bell turret and open timber roof to the waiting-room. At **Netherfield**, B2096, 4m NW, *church* (1859; S.S. Teulon), marble, mosaic and stone reredos. At **Etchingham** A265, 7m N, *station* (1851; W. Tress), Tudor style in stone. **Rye**. A259 11m NE of Hastings. Lamb House (NT), West Street, was the home of Henry James from 1898–1916, 'The Ambassadors' and 'The Golden Bowl' written here. Just N at Point Hill, a group of neo-Georgian houses designed by Sir R. Blomfield who lived at *Point Hill*. *Saltcote Place* (1900) is the largest, red brick with a pediment and top cupola. At **Rye Harbour**, 1½m SE, *church* (1848; S.S. Teulon), apsed with High Victorian touches in the tower and fittings.

Balcombe Viaduct (1840; J. Rastrick)

HAYWARDS HEATH. A272 11m N of Brighton. *Holy Cross Convent*, Bolnore Rd, Anglican Convent founded by Elizabeth Neale, sister of J.M. Neale, ecclesiologist and founder of the East Grinstead Convent. Brick buildings (1887–89) and chapel (1902–06; W. Tower), tall with vaulted apse and good fittings. Tower was pupil and partner of C.E.

Kempe which shows in the design of the rood screen and glass. Kempe lived at Lindfield, B2111, 1½m NE, at *Old Place*, 15C house, which he extended and gave elaborate gardens with an ornate pavilion. 3m N, B2028, at **Ardingly**, *Ardingly College*, like Lancing and Hurstpierpoint a foundation of Nathaniel Woodard. H-plan buildings in red brick begun 1864 (Slater and Carpenter) with the chapel and hall across the centre, the chapel, impressively tall, completed 1883. W of Ardingly, at **Balcombe**, *Balcombe Viaduct* (1840; J. Rastrick), 37 arches across the Ouse valley, balustraded with little end pavilions, one of the finest railway viaducts in England. Tremendous vista underneath through the main piers. *Balcombe Place* (1856), Tudor style, has fine additions (1899; G.C. Horsley), free Tudor with barrel-vaulted music room. 1½m SW, *Ditton Place* (1904; Smith and Brewer), free neo-Wren style with big curved open pediment and curved porch. Good interiors. W of Haywards Heath, at **Cuckfield**, *church* with ceiling painting (1865; Kempe) and screen (1880; Bodley). *Cuckfield Park*, 16C mansion, much restored 1848, is supposedly the 'Rookwood' of Harrison Ainsworth's novel. 3m W, off A23, at **Bolney**, *Wykehurst* (1871–74; E.M. Barry), a superbly built Loire château, the best example of the type in Britain, built for Henry Huth, banking heir and book-collector, and given modern devices unknown in most British country houses until the next century, hot water, central heating, cavity walls. 5m SW of Haywards Heath, at **Hurstpierpoint**, *College* (1851–53; R.C. Carpenter), the first school built by N. Woodard to bring education to the 'middle' or 'trades' classes. Severe flint Gothic, as at Lancing (see below p. 415), intentionally austere, impressively so. Large chapel and library range added 1861 (R.H. Carpenter). In the village, *church* (1843; C. Barry), the last church Barry built, large and competent, but without the flair of the Puginian Gothicists to whom Barry abandoned this field.

Wykehurst Park (1871–74; E.M. Barry), Bolney

HORSHAM. A24 14m S of Dorking. In the parish *church* much 19C glass including E window by O'Connor and bright SW and NW windows by C. Heaton. At Carfax, large *bank* (1897; F. Wheeler). To N, *St. Mark's Church* (1870; Habershon and Brock), rock faced and bold in detail. In West St, former *Corn Exchange* (1866; E. Burstow), Italianate, part of Black Horse hotel now. 2m SW, *Christ's Hospital School* (1893–1902; A. Webb), a huge complex, largest of the late 19C schools, all in red brick and stone, Elizabethan detail. Colonnaded main quad with statue of Edward VI surrounded by four famous old boys including Coleridge (c 1900; W.S. Frith). 9m SE, off A281, *St. Hugh's Monastery* (1875–83), a complete Carthusian monastery, designed by a Calais architect, Norman, on a very large scale. Male visitors only admitted.

LEWES. On Brighton Rd, *Prison* (1850–53) by D.R. Hill of Birmingham, a prison specialist. Grim flint and brick. In the High St, *Town Hall* (1893; S. Denman) and, further E, *No. 10*, red brick former library (1862; G.G. Scott), Gothic. At **Offham**, A275, 2m NW, *church* (1859; E. Christian) with apse and central tower. 3m E of Lewes, *Glyndebourne* (1876; E. Christian), Tudor style around a 16C core. **Uckfield**. A26 8m NE of Lewes. At **Little Horsted**, 2m S, A26, *Horsted Place* (1850; S.W. Daukes), Tudor style house in diapered brick with a corner entrance tower, the materials and details as Pugin might have designed, and the interior staircase actually by Pugin and exhibited at the Crystal Palace. 4m E of Uckfield, B2102, *Possingworth Manor* (1868; M.D. Wyatt), in the same style as Horsted Place, but larger, coarser and more complicated in plan. The W side was a large picture gallery for Louis Huth's collection, his brother built Wykehurst at Bolney (see above p. 412). 4m E, A265, *Heathfield Park*, 18C house greatly enlarged in a c 1700 style (1898–1910; R. Blomfield). 3m E, at **Burwash Common**, *church* (1867; Slater and Carpenter), High Victorian Gothic with vaulted chancel and apse. At Burwash, *Bateman's* (NT), Kipling's house from 1906. Pook's Hill is nearby. NW of the village, *St. Joseph's College* with impressive *chapel* (1887; B. Whelan) tunnel vaulted in brick in the nave, rib-vaulted chancel. At **Buxted**, A272, 3m NE of Uckfield, *St. Mary's Church* (1885; Scott and Cawthorn), built for Father Wagner of Brighton in flint and stone apparently using a system of sevens in the measurements. Glass by Kempe, altar canopy by Bodley. 7m NW, on A275, **Danehill** *church* (1892; Bodley and Garner), serious Dec. with strong tower. Long interior dominated by the screen carrying the organ. Font cover by Bodley. *Chelwood Manor* (1904; A. Prentice), large and half-timbered.

MIDHURST. A272 12m N of Chichester. St. Ann's Hill, the walk to Cowdray House, has estate *cottages* (c 1880; E.C. Lee), prettily tile-hung. More estate housing in **Easebourne** by the ruins. The modern Cowdray House is 1m E, late Victorian gabled and tile-hung. H.G. Wells was a chemist's apprentice in Midhurst and taught briefly at the grammar school. Midhurst is the Wimblehurst of 'Tono-Bungay'. 2m NW, *King Edward VII Sanatorium* (1903–06; Adams, Holden and Pearson), very large but not oppressive in a free gabled Tudor, stripped of period detail. Original L-plan chapel. 1m S of Midhurst, A286, *obelisk* to R. Cobden, radical politician and advocate of free trade, born here and buried (1865) in **West Lavington** church with Gladstone among the mourners. The *church* (1850; W. Butterfield) is strong and simple, stone with shingled turret. Inside, the font and chancel rail are Gothic reduced to basic forms with powerful effect while the chancel arch rises from corbels of exceptional naturalistic vigour. Rectory also by Butterfield with exemplary play of roofline and chimneys. Church and vicarage were built for Archdeacon Manning, who went over to Rome before they were finished and became Cardinal Archbishop of Westminster. 3m SE at **Graffham**, *church* rebuilt 1874–89 (G.E. Street) in flint with shingled spire. ½m N, *Woodside* (1905; H. Ricardo), roughcast and gabled Arts and Crafts house, built for Ricardo himself. On A286, 6m S of Midhurst, *West Dean Park* (1804; J. Wyatt), remodelled (1891–93; George and Peto) for Edward VII's friend, the big-game hunter W. James. Sumptuous oak hall, Jacobean style. In the *church*, bronze effigy of James (died 1912; Goscombe John). 7m E of Midhurst, A272, **Petworth**. *Petworth House* has additions by A. Salvin (1869–72) including the S end. In the Market Place, *bank* (1901; F. Wheeler), Edwardian Baroque, in North St, curly Gothic lampstand in iron by Sir Charles Barry (1851).

Lancing College Chapel (1868–1978; R.H. Carpenter) near Lancing

WORTHING. A259 10m W of Brighton. Seaside resort developed from 1800. The pier, originally of 1860, has later buildings. Behind some grand terraces in the Brighton manner, c 1830, and further back villas of the mid 19C. at **Broadwater**, just inland, *cemetery*, where Richard Jefferies and W.H. Hudson, two of the best writers on rural England, are buried. At **Findon**, 2m N, A24, the *church* has a tiled reredos (1867) by Morris and Co., an exceptional rarity in the firm's work. Font by

G.G. Scott. At **Sompting**, A27 to NE of Worthing, *Sompting Abbotts* (1856; P.C. Hardwick), flint, Tudor Gothic with a French roofed tower. 2m E, above **Lancing**, *Lancing College*, the crown of the fifteen schools founded between 1848 and 1891 by Nathaniel Woodard, curate of New Shoreham, to provide for the middle classes a system of Christian education, based on the existing upper class public schools. The school buildings were begun 1854 (R.C. Carpenter) in a severe flint and stone Gothic, the main court one of the best expressions of Puginian ideals, detailed without ostentation, generous in scale and proportion of roofs to wall, a 19C equivalent of medieval Carthusian simplicity. The central range is more elaborate with dormer gables and buttresses (the central gable a later alteration), hierarchically apt as it contained the library and original chapel. The present chapel (1868–1978; R.H. Carpenter) is truly heroic, standing sheer on the slope of the Downs, rising some 150ft at the apsed E end, built over a century, much of it built by hand labour under Woodard's son Billy, who raised the apse to its full height when funds for completion were more than uncertain, to ensure that the design could not be scaled down by later economies. French Gothic style with huge upper windows and flying buttresses, stone vaulted inside. The emphasis is all on sheer height. Great W rose added to the original design finally in 1977. 4m W of Worthing, A280, at **Angmering**, *church* rebuilt (1852; S.S. Teulon) with very naturalistic capitals and fittings by Teulon. At **Rustington**, 2m SW, *Knightscroft* (1879; R. Norman Shaw), Sea Lane, a good tile-hung house hemmed in a sea of bungalows. Built for the composer Sir Hubert Parry. *Rustington Manor* (c 1885; J.L. Pearson), red-brick and stone Tudor. On the seafront, *Convalescent Home* (1897; F. Wheeler), free Queen Anne style.

TYNE AND WEAR

GATESHEAD. Across the Tyne from Newcastle, battered by slum
clearance and road and rail approaches to Newcastle. In Hudson St,
under the end of the High Level Bridge, former *station hotel* (1844;
G.T. Andrews), stone classical, remains of one of the first station and
hotel groups built for the railways. To W, in Rabbit Banks Rd, remains
of North Eastern Railway workshops, standing high above the river. S
of the present station, in West St, *Town Hall* (1868; J. Johnstone), rich
Italianate palazzo. To the side, in Swinburne St, former *Free Library*
(1882; Johnstone), Jacobean, building society offices (c 1880), and
former National Provincial Bank (1873; J. Gibson), Italian palazzo,
absorbed into the Municipal Buildings. To SW, Prince Consort Rd,
with *Art Gallery* (1914–17), Corinthian classical, leads to Saltwell
Park, the area of grander suburban villas developed from 1850. The
park is the former grounds of *Saltwell Towers* (1860–71) built for himself by the stained glass manufacturer W. Wailes with a splendidly
romantic skyline of turrets and battlements, all in polychrome brick.
Other large villas to E in Durham Rd, and *church* (1894; S. Piper) with
bold SW tower. W of Prince Consort Rd, **Bensham**, with early 19C
villas and fine stone *church* (1900; W.S. Hicks), Rawling Rd, with
octagonal tower and rich carving and furnishings.

JARROW. A185 5m E of Gateshead. A shipbuilding town from 1852 to
the Depression of 1933 when the closure provoked the famous Jarrow
March of the unemployed. More recently battered by road construction. The *church* of St. Paul founded 684, the monastery of the Vene-
rable Bede, has a nave of 1866 (G.G. Scott). To W, Clayton St, *Christ
Church* (1868; Johnson and Hicks), rock faced with fine spire. In
Ellison St, *statue* of Sir Charles Palmer (1903; A. Toft), founder of the
shipyard. 2m S, *Boldon Colliery*, complete mining village with brick
houses in terraces, begun c 1865.

NEWCASTLE UPON TYNE. Major Victorian city enveloping the old
medieval town that spread down the steep riverbank from the
Cathedral and Castle above, ruthlessly overpowered by the railway
(1847–49) that cuts past the Castle and over the Tyne on the *High
Level Bridge* (1849; R. Stephenson). This is one of the most impressive
of early railway bridges, six spans on stone piers, cast-iron bows carrying the railway with road suspended below. The modern centre of
Newcastle was laid out in the 1830s by the entrepreneur Richard Grainger under his architect John Wardle, with important buildings by the
eminent local architects J. Dobson and J. and B. Green. The result is
the noblest and most consistent classical city centre in England. The
old town by the Tyne has bold brick and stone 19C warehouses interspersed with surviving older public buildings and houses. The *Swing
Bridge* (1876) replaces the original Tyne Bridge and was built by the
great armaments and shipbuilding king, W.G. Armstrong, to allow
passage to his works. Former *Fish Market* (1880; A. Fowler), red brick
and stone. From the Guildhall, Side, a steep street, climbs up under a
fine stone *railway arch* (1848 and 1894). On Quayside, *Custom House*,
refronted in stone (c 1840, S. Smirke). King St and Queen St were
rebuilt c 1860 with offices after the explosion of a chemical warehouse
over the river had burnt out the area. Returning up Side to St. Nicholas
St, with dignified classical *Post Office* (1871; M. Thompson) opposite
the *Cathedral*, a very large medieval church raised to cathedral

status 1882. Much Victorian glass by Wailes of Newcastle and towering Gothic reredos (1857; J.S. Westmacott). Other chancel fittings and pulpit of 1880s by R.J. Johnson. In S chancel aisle effigy of the antiquarian J.C. Bruce (1896; G. Simonds) and in N chancel aisle Bishop Lloyd (1908; F.W. Pomeroy). In St. Nicholas Square, *Queen Victoria* monument (1900; A. Gilbert), a major work, the Queen, imperious in flowing robes on a canopied chair of Art Nouveau extravagance. To E, Mosley St, *No. 42* (1855; B. Green), richly Italianate, overlooking St. Nicholas Square. On N side, *National Westminster Bank* (1870–72; J. Gibson), Italian palazzo. In Dean St, *Cathedral Buildings* (1900; Oliver, Leeson and Wood), cheerful gabled office building with decorative bay windows and carved work.

Grey St, the centrepiece of Grainger's part of the city, runs N to meet Grainger St at an acute angle marked by the *Grey Monument* (1838; B. Green), a big Roman Doric column carrying E.H. Baily's statue of Earl Grey (1764–1845), the Whig Prime Minister who carried the 1832 Reform Bill to law. *Grey St* (c 1835–38; J. Wardle) is exceptionally noble, stone classical facades with columned centrepieces breaking up the blocks. The central W side building was a branch of the *Bank of England* (1835). On the E side the range to Shakespeare St is by Dobson culminating at the Corinthian portico of the *Theatre Royal* (1837; B. Green), the most monumental theatre exterior in Britain. Auditorium rebuilt (1901; F. Matcham) after a fire. Shakespeare St and Market St are also part of Grainger's scheme. At the top of Grey St, handsome bank on right. On left, at junction of Grey St and Grainger St, *Exchange Buildings* (1838; J. Wardle) with domed and columned rotundas each end, one facing the Grey Monument. Through the centre of this block is *Central Arcade* (1905; J. Oswald), glass-roofed and glazed tile-clad Edwardian shopping arcade, quite unspoilt. Behind the monument, *Emerson Chambers* (1904; F. Simpson), office block with extremely ornate roofline, especially the corner turret with clock. To E, *Laing Art Gallery* (1904; Cackett, Burns Dick), New Bridge St, Baroque with excellent collections. In College St behind, *College of Commerce* (1882; R.J. Johnson) pretty Queen Anne style and *Dental Hospital* (1887–95; Dunn, Hansom and Dunn) late Gothic style in brick and terracotta. At S end of Northumberland St, *Pearl Assurance* (1904; F. Simpson) Art Nouveau inspired. Grainger St (1835–39; J. Wardle) is less elaborate than Grey St but still fine, completed only in 1870s. On W side, *Market* (1835; J. Dobson), one of the best covered markets in Britain, extending back to Clayton St, with fine facades all around. Off Grainger St, to E, Bigg Market with two good buildings of c 1900, *Half Moon Chambers* and *Sunlight Chambers* (1901; W. and S. Owen). The S end of Grainger St is more Victorian leading down to Central Station. In Grainger St, *Trustee Savings Bank* (1861; J. Watson). In Westgate Rd, *Tyne Theatre* (1867; W. Parnell), Italianate front with exceptional plastered interior of three balconies. Theatre interiors of the 1860s are rare survivals. At the junction with Collingwood St, on N side, former *Union Club* (1877; M.P. Manning), Loire style, and opposite, *Neville Hall* (1870; A.M. Dunn), Gothic with attached Wood Memorial Hall (1872), and *Literary and Philosophical Society* (1822–25; J. Green) where Sir J.W. Swan demonstrated his electric light bulb in 1879, a simultaneous discovery with Thomas Edison in the US. Good collection of Victorian sculpture. Further on *R. Stephenson monument* (1862; J.G. Lough), bronze statue of the engineer. In Collingwood St, to E, *Lloyds Bank* (1891; R.J. Johnson), rich Italianate in stone and red granite. Opposite, *Collingwood Buildings* (1899–1903; Oliver and Leeson). *Central*

Station (1848–63; J. Dobson) is one of the finest in Britain. The monumental stone entrance front was designed in Roman Doric grandeur by Dobson, the entire front a columned open carriage entry, but the railway decided to have offices and T. Prosser altered the design. The front screens a triple-arched curved train-shed by Dobson and R. Stephenson, the first of the arched roofed sheds. Rolled iron ribs on cast-iron columns, originally three arches with higher central arch, but expanded to five (1893). Flanking the station, *Royal Station Hotel* (1854). W of the station, *RC Cathedral* (1844; A.W.N. Pugin), Dec. with triple gabled E end. The fine 220ft spire was added 1860–73 (J.A. Hansom). E window by Wailes, possibly to Pugin's design. Low spreading interior. Further W, Westmorland Rd leads to Rye Hill, with large *RC church* (1891; Dunn and Hansom), central octagonal tower.

Central Station (1848–63; J. Dobson and T. Prosser), Newcastle upon Tyne

N of the centre, Northumberland St leads to *St. Thomas's Church* (1828–30; J. Dobson), Barras Bridge, bold if incorrect EE with plaster vault on iron columns. To W, *University*, College Ave, the earliest parts a courtyard (1887–92; R.J. Johnson) in red-brick Gothic originally, completed 1904–14 (W. Knowles). *Leazes Park* to W is landscaped from the Town Moor. On S side, *Leazes Terrace* (1829; T. Oliver), splendid stone late Georgian development. N of St. Thomas's church, *Hancock Museum* (1878), a late example of the Newcastle classical tradition with severe Doric pillars. Natural history collections. To E of Hancock Museum, Jesmond Rd runs NE, cut by the motorway. Behind *Jesmond Church* (1858–61; J. Dobson), neo-Georgian *Royal Grammar School* (1907; Sir E. Cooper). Jesmond Rd leads past the *General Cemetery* (1839) to Jesmond Dene, the wooded valley of the Ouseburn, presented to the City by Lord Armstrong in 1883. Jesmond was the suburb where Newcastle's industrialists lived, Armstrong himself, and his partners C.W. Mitchell at *Jesmond Towers*, mostly Gothic of c 1822 and 1833, and Sir A. Noble at *Jesmond Dene House*, mostly 1896 (F.W. Rich), neo-Tudor, reminiscent of Armstrong's house at Cragside, Northumberland (see above p. 341). Noble's real tennis court still exists. Mitchell built and partly designed *St. George's*

Church (1888; T. Spence), Osborne Rd, lofty interior, expensively finished with Byzantinesque mosaic and stained glass probably to Mitchell's design, influenced by Art Nouveau. E of central Newcastle, industrial areas of Byker and Walker, largely cleared since 1945. New Bridge St runs E to Byker Bridge with, to N, *Ouseburn Viaduct*, stone piers, seven spans, the lattice pattern of the arches reproducing in iron the original (1839) design which was built in wood and replaced in 1860. Similar *Wellington viaduct*, also rebuilt in iron, to E, by Hadrian Station, Wallsend. *St. Luke's Church*, **Wallsend** (1886; Oliver and Leeson), impressive EE style. Wallsend, originally a separate shipbuilding town, joins Newcastle.

NORTH SHIELDS. A193 7m E of Newcastle. Tyneside town developed c 1800 by the Duke of Northumberland, most of the rebuilding early 19C Georgian in style. The centre, Northumberland Square, c 1800, with Italian Renaissance style *Presbyterian church* (1850–57; J. Dobson). In Howard St, brick Italianate *Library* (1857; J. Johnstone), and in Saville St, *Town Hall* (1844; J. Dobson), Elizabethan style. To E, **Tynemouth**, developed as a resort from c 1800. In the centre, *Queen Victoria Monument* (1905), fine seated bronze. On Front St, Gothic *clock tower* (1861, Oliver and Lamb). Massive stone *monument* (1847; J. Dobson) to Admiral Lord Collingwood (1750–1810), who took command at the Battle of Trafalgar after Nelson's death, 50ft pedestal with 23ft statue (J.G. Lough). In Tynemouth Rd, *Tyne Master Mariners' Asylum* (1837; J. and B. Green), Tudor. Tynemouth *Station* (1882; W. Bell) has notably ornate ironwork. 2m N, **Cullercoats**, fishing village, with seafront *church* (1881–84; J.L. Pearson), splendidly severe in stone, with tall apsed chancel and, on the S side, tall and plain buttressed tower carrying a broach spire. The inside is fully stone vaulted, the effect enhanced by tall upper windows. The Duke of Northumberland commissioned the church. Further N, **Whitley Bay**, mostly later 19C seaside resort.

SOUTH SHIELDS. 6m N of Sunderland. Fishing village developed into coal port and resort during 19C. Tyne Dock opened 1858. Seafront parks created from 1890, previously the town had faced the Tyne. From Market Place, King St leads E with *Scotia Bar* (1903; H. Grieves), lively Edwardian pub at E end. In Barrington St, S of Keppel St, *Savings Bank* (1842; J. and B. Green), stone classical. By river, on Corporation Quay, former *Customs House* (1863; T. Clemence), white brick and stone debased classical. To E, in Ocean Rd, *Art Gallery* (1858–60; J. Wardle), built as Mechanics Institute, big Florentine arched upper windows. Opposite, *Technical College* (1867; T. Clemence), red brick and stone, Jacobean style. Protecting the mouth of the Tyne, *South Pier* (1854–95). In Pier Parade, *Jubilee Memorial* (1890; J.H. Morton), Baroque clock tower. In Westoe Rd, to S, *Municipal Buildings* (1905–10; E.E. Fetch), monumental Edwardian Baroque, in stone with open pedimented centrepiece, the pediment loaded with sculpture and set against a balustraded attic. To one end, a fancy topped tower, all this a considerable monument to South Shields civic pride. Further S, Westoe village was the prosperous Victorian suburb. On Westoe Rd, *Ingham Infirmary* (1871; R.J. Johnson), very early example of revived Queen Anne. In Westoe, enclave of advanced Queen Anne style houses, two for brothers of the architect J.J. Stevenson, a pioneer in the style. *Southgarth* (1874; J.J. Stevenson) the gable, oriel and big chimneystacks that Stevenson and Norman Shaw introduced into their London houses as 'Queen Anne' at this time. On the same side, *Winterbottom House* (1882; H. Grieves), prettily Dutch gabled, *Westoe Hall* (1864) one of J.J. Stevenson's first works, half-timbered centre with top lantern, and *Manor House* (1896; J.H. Morton). Opposite, *Normanhurst* (1885; W. Hanson) and, to W, lively semi-detached pair (1892–96; H. Grieves), *Ravensworth* and *The Briary*, with octagonal corner towers and playful moulded detail. *St. Michael's Church* (1881–1909, Johnson and Hicks), Mowbray Rd, up-to-date Gothic, well detailed in brick and stone. Off Sunderland Rd, *Harton Cemetery* (1888–91; H. Grieves) elaborate paired chapels with central spire, free Perp. style. In Sunniside Lane, Cleadon Park, *waterworks* (1860–62; T. Hawksley), Italianate with park-like grounds.

SUNDERLAND. Port at the mouth of the River Wear, greatly developed during the 19C with docks, shipbuilding and engineering works. The present centre of Sunderland, S of Wearmouth Bridge, was originally Bishopwearmouth, becoming the commercial centre after the railway station opened 1879, but with early 19C suburban terraces developed after the opening of Wearmouth Bridge (1796). Bridge St leads S into Fawcett St, on corner of High St West, *No. 103 High St West* (1850; G. Middlemiss), classical with Corinthian columns and dome. Opposite, former *Tea Rooms* (1873–77; F. Caws) with terracotta elephants along the roofline and Gothic cum Indian detail. Large late 19C banks and commercial buildings to S, *Barclays Bank* (c 1875), *Midland Bank* (1902; W. Brierley) and *Lloyds Bank* (c 1890), all classical and *Nos 21–2* (1890; F. Caws), lavishly terracotta ornamented. In Borough Rd, to E, *Library and Museum* (1877), mixed classical and French roofed design. In John St, to N, early 19C brick terraced houses with Doric doorcases, similar but smaller in Frederick St, Foyle St and West Sunniside. In High St West, to N, *National Westminster Bank* (1876; J. Gibson), handsome Italian palazzo. High St West beyond Bridge St leads to the old centre of Bishopwearmouth with, opposite the church, *Fire Station* (1907) and *Empire Theatre* (1907; W. and T. Milburn) with big Baroque corner entrance and intact interior, the boxes closest to the stage most ornate, curved with columns and balustraded roof. Behind the church, *almshouses* (1863; E.R. Robson). E of the present centre, along High St East, was old Sunderland, mostly cleared or given over to warehousing, a consequence of the construction of Hudson Dock 1850, to E of Barrack St, between the town and the sea. Some warehousing of c 1860 on Hudson Dock North. S of the Art Gallery, *Mowbray Park*, S end created 1854–57 out of the stone quarry of Bildon Hill. On the hill, *statue* of General Sir Henry Havelock (1861; Behnes), Indian Mutiny hero of the Relief of Cawnpore, son of a Sunderland shipbuilder. Around the park villas from early 19C, classical terraces at SW corner, Douro Terrace, Esplanade, Grange Crescent and S of Park Rd to Mowbray Rd. On Ryhope Rd, two large villas, part of the Polytechnic, on E side, *Langham Tower* (1889; W. Milburn), Norman Shaw style half-timber and brick, and *St. Bede Tower* (1854; B. Green), Italianate with campanile tower. *Christ Church* (1862–64; James Murray), Ryhope Rd, prosperous suburban church with spire. E window excellent early Morris glass (1864). E of Ryhope Rd, the suburb of Hendon with workers' terraces, some the single-storey 'Sunderland cottages' that are a local feature. In Suffolk St, handsome spired *church* (1889; C.H. Fowler). At **Ryhope**, further S, hefty *church* (1870; T. Edby) and *Pumping Station Museum* (1866; T. Hawksley), a lavishly built and landscaped Jacobean style waterworks with original engines, occasionally fired.

N of the River Wear is **Monkwearmouth**, the chief monument *Monkwearmouth Station* (1848; T. Moore), just over the bridge, most imposing Greek classical with Ionic portico and curved Doric columned wings. The reason for this unexpected grandeur is that George Hudson, the railway king and promoter of the Gateshead to Sunderland line, of which this was the terminus, was elected MP for Sunderland in 1845 and this is his celebration and reward to the electors. It became a suburban halt from 1879 when the *Wear Bridge* took the line across to Sunderland. Now an excellent railway museum. To W, Southwick Rd, leads to **Southwick** with large basilican *church* (1888; C.H. Fowler), Cornhill Ave. The old parish *church* dates from 1842 (G. Jackson), typical lancet Gothic of the period. To NE, Roker Avenue leads past former *Miners' Hall* (1894) to Roker, wealthy Edwardian seaside suburb around Roker Park. *St. Andrew's Church* (1906–07; E.S. Prior) is one of the most important churches of its time in Britain, Gothic in stone, but the forms and details rethought from first principles. Massive exterior with tower set to E end, slab-like strips of stone for mouldings and blunt profile. The window tracery reduced to unmoulded verticals and horizontals with triangular heads to the lights, Anglo-Saxon in feel, though the big end windows are of Perp. scale. The interior is stone faced, a series of parabolic arches rising from short paired piers leaving a passage for access along the wall. Above the windows, deep-set in splayed reveals, arched heads setting up a rhythm in counterpoint to the main transverse arches, an effect increased by canting in the arches over the transepts at their junction with the chancel. The construction of the arches, purlins and ridge is reinforced concrete. Excellent fittings, E window by H.A. Payne, inlaid wood lectern by Gimson, font by R. Wells and altar tapestry a Burne-Jones design.

5m W of Monkwearmouth, A1231, at **Washington**, *Washington Hall* (1854; A.B. Higham), Elizabethan in red brick with stone and terracotta ornament, built for the chemicals tycoon, I.L. Bell. Alterations 1865 by Philip Webb, whom Bell patronised early in his career, brick, Gothic but with the segment-headed small-paned windows that signal Webb's move away from Gothic detail. Gabled bay and massive brick chimney-stack. N of A1231, *Industrial Museum*, Albany Way, on site of closed colliery with engine house (c 1888). At **Birtley**, 3m W, neo-Norman *church* (1849; G. Pickering) with two N windows of 1872 in Pre-Raphaelite manner by M. Maris for the Glasgow firm of D. Cottier. 5m SW of Sunderland, A183, on Penshaw Hill, *monument* to 'Radical Jack' Lambton, 1st Earl of Durham (1792–1840), liberal politician whose part in the 1832 Reform Bill is commemorated in an austere hilltop Greek Doric temple (1844; J. and B. Green).

WARWICKSHIRE

ALCESTER. A422 8m W of Stratford-upon-Avon. Parish *church* (1729), heavily Gothicised 1870 (F. Preedy). Inside monument to 1st Marquess of Hertford (1828; F. Chantrey) and seated effigy of Sir H. Seymour (1882; Lord E. Gleichen). In the High Street stucco classical *Corn Exchange* (1857). 2m N, at **Coughton**, *RC church* (1857; J.A. Hansom), built for the old Catholic Throckmorton family of Coughton Court. E window by Hardman. 3m N, at **Studley**, *Studley Castle* (1834; S. Beazley), impressive neo-Norman to Gothic mock castle about a central keep, now an agricultural college. 2m N, at **Mappleborough Green**, *church* (1888; J.A. Chatwin) in rock-faced stone with vaulted S chapel, expensively detailed. 3m E, at **Ullenhall**, *church* (1875; J.P. Seddon), High Victorian, apsed with marble arcade columns and much shafting inside, fine wagon roofs. 2m NE of Alcester, at **Kinwarton**, *church* restored 1847 (Butterfield) with timber screen and excellent E window by O'Connor.

LEAMINGTON SPA. A425 2m E of Warwick. Spa town developed from the late 18C, the heyday between 1820 and 1840 when Dr Jephson ran the treatment. (Ruskin was sent to Dr Jephson in 1841.) In the centre, *Pump Room* (1813, altered) and Jephson Gardens laid out 1834 along the river. Parish *church* begun 1843 to designs by the vicar, J. Craig, ashlar on a grand scale with rich Flamboyant tracery, haphazardly arranged. High apse with deep coloured glass (1851; Chance Bros). The W end and fine tower were added 1898 (A. Blomfield). Opposite, *Victoria Terrace* (1836–38) introducing the stucco style of Leamington. The *Manor House Hotel*, to W, Gothic of c 1860, was the home of the world's first lawn tennis club (1872). To NW of Pump Room, *RC church* (1861–65; H. Clutton), Dormer Place, with prominent tower (1878), originally pyramid-roofed. Tall High Victorian interior apsed with paired columns and bold tracery details, especially the S rose window. N of the Pump Room, florid *Town Hall* (1883; J. Cundall) in brick and stone, Jacobean to Baroque with high domed tower, all much in contrast to the surrounding stucco. The heart of Leamington is *The Parade*, built up c 1820–35 with stuccoed terraces, now much replaced in replica. Similar terraces in the streets off before the formality breaks down into detached villas, classical and some Gothic. To NW, *•St. Mark's Church* (1879; G.G. Scott Jr), Rugby Rd, brick, Gothic loosened from High Victorian toughness, delicate surface decoration on the tower top; interior with strong vertical lines, the arcade piers of simple diamond section without capital mouldings. Fine boarded roofs, again in contrast to the stressed timberwork of the High Victorians. Chancel glass by Kempe and Gothic organ case. The former *vicarage* (1873; G.G. Scott Jr) is uncommonly stately in brick and stone, banded and detailed in the Queen Anne way with pedimented curved gables and sash windows. Scott Jr was an early pioneer of the move away from Gothic. In Binswood Avenue, off Kenilworth Rd, *Leamington College* (1847; D.G. Squirhill), diapered brick Tudor Gothic, quite grand symmetrical front with chapel behind. S of centre, on Tachbrook St, *St. John's Church* (1877; J. Cundall), brick, EE style with landmark steeple. SE of Leamington, at **Whitnash**, *church* rebuilt 1855–80 (G.G. Scott), richly carved altar and pulpit by Agnes Bonham. One chancel N window by A. Bell (1856) and E window by W. Holland. To S, at **Bishop's Tachbrook**, A452, *church* restored by T. Garner with NE window by Morris and Co (1863), the clear backgrounds, unusual in Morris work, due to Garner. At **Bishop's Itchington**, B4451, 5m SE, *The Cottage* (1888; C.F.A. Voysey), Station Rd, Voysey's first work, already with the hallmarks of his style, roughcast with simple leaded windows in strips. 5m NE of Leamington, B4453, prominent on a hilltop, *Princethorpe Priory*, founded 1833, the dominant building the bright red chapel (1897; P.P. Pugin) with massive tower and polygonal apse. Elaborate carved Gothic altar. The older buildings are plain brick (1833–35; Craven: 1837–50; J.A. Hansom). 2m N, at **Stretton-on-Dunsmore**, *church* (1835–37; T. Rickman), ashlar, in outline still early 19C but with tracery already correctly detailed. Cast-iron tracery to the W door.

NUNEATON. A444 9m N of Coventry. The town most associated with George Eliot. Her father was agent to the Newdegate family of *Arbury Hall* (open to public), 2m SW, and she was brought up at *Griff House* on A444, 2m S. *Arbury Mill* is suggested as the 'Mill on the Floss'. In Nuneaton, *St. Mary's Church*, Manor Court Rd, contains the remains of the Benedictine nunnery church, the nave of 1878 (C.C. Rolfe), the chancel and N transept more archaeologically recreated by H. Brakspear (1906 and 1930). At **Hartshill**, 3m W, off A47, the *church* (1843; T.L. Walker) is neo-Norman in stone and brick, crude but memorable W front with blue brick arched portal. 4m N, **Atherstone**, in Long St, *Midland Bank* (1837; J.A. Hansom), classical. At E end, *Dominican Priory* (1837–41; J.A. Hansom), Gothic to Elizabethan in red brick, the chapel added 1857. *Atherstone Station* (1847; J. Livock) has original gabled Jacobean buildings, no longer in use. Just W, on the hillside, *Merevale Hall* (1838–44; E. Blore), a romantic Jacobean silhouette of curved gables with off-centre tower, all in smooth ashlar in the early Victorian taste. A winding drive up the hill makes the most of the picturesque possibilities, though the main front is symmetrical. By the church, *gatehouse* (1848; H. Clutton), Gothic, a strong design with the severity of outline typical of the advanced Gothicists in contrast to Blore's lighter surface ornamentation. *Rectory* by Clutton, as also the chancel of the *church* (1848) at **Baddesley Ensor**, to NW. 4m S of Nuneaton, at **Bedworth**, *church* (1888–90; Bodley and Garner), red sandstone Perp. style, handsome interior with glass by Burlison and Grylls in E window. Tudor style *almshouse* courtyard to N (1840).

RUGBY. A428 11m E of Coventry. A railway junction and engineering town, architecturally notable for Rugby School, founded 1567, the first of the old grammar schools to be refashioned in the 19C as training grounds for the young not merely in learning but in moral, intellectual and religious discipline. Thomas Arnold, headmaster 1828–41, father of the poet Matthew Arnold, was the creator of the Victorian public school system, that rounded discipline summed up as 'Mens sana in corpore sano'. Thomas Hughes' 'Tom Brown's Schooldays' (1857) depicts Rugby under Arnold. W.S. Landor and Lewis Carroll were pupils. Rugby football was invented here in 1823. The *school* buildings begin with the Old Quad (1809–15; H. Hakewill) in grey brick Tudor Gothic and Arnold Library (1842), but the major work was begun in 1867 under Dr Temple with Butterfield as architect. Butterfield's work is in the full polychrome brick manner of Keble College, Oxford, the brick banded in stone, vertical emphasis imposed by arcaded tall recesses and projecting chimney on the New Schools (1867–70), the corner block of the New Quad. On the S side of the quad, the chapel, a tour de force of compressed strength, a monumental crossing tower, square, cut back to octagonal with squat stone spire, the diagonal thrust emphasised by buttresses and a short canted apse clamped against the E side. The transition from square to octagon is achieved by massive patterned stone haunches with the great windows rising between. Beyond the tower a broad congregational space created by double-gabled transepts. The nave, in quieter Butterfieldian style, replaces the original chapel and is by T.G. Jackson (1897). Inside, a spatial sequence of exceptional quality, the nave opening into the transeptal space marked by sheer banded stone columns, the walls banded and inlaid in stylised patterns. Then a transverse-vaulted narrowing under the tower with tall wall arcades and painted ceiling and finally the vaulted apse with mosaic decoration. Stained glass, 16C Dutch in E window, by Gibbs in the transepts N and S and by Hardman in nave NW and SW, the NW the unsuccessful outcome of an attempt by Butterfield to alter the Hardman style. Effigy of Dr Arnold (1844; J. Thomas). Other school buildings in Barby Rd include *Old Sanatorium* (1867; F.C. Penrose), *School Field* (1852; G.G. Scott), *Temple Reading Room* (1878; Butterfield), *Temple Speech Room* (1908; T.G. Jackson) and *New Big School* (1884; Butterfield), broad proportions with chequered gable and horizontal banding, less emphatically patterned than the earlier works. Rugby parish *church* (1877–79; Butterfield), with 180ft stone spire (1894–96), has a splendid polychrome interior, quieter than the chapel, banded piers in pink and cream, the roofs prettily painted and running through to the chancel over a chancel arch, the upper part left open as a rood loft. In Dunchurch Rd, *RC church* with tall steeple (1872) added to a church by A.W.N. Pugin (1846) much enlarged 1864–67 (E.W. Pugin). The church was built for Captain Hibbert, for whom Pugin built *Bilton Grange* (1841–46), at **Dunchurch**, to S, diapered brick Gothic house with entrance tower capped like Big Ben and, essential to Pugin's conception of the revived Gothic house, a great hall. Pugin's hall roof, chimneypieces and tiled floor survive inside. Large extensions 1889–91 each side including chapel.

1½m SW of Rugby, A427, at **Bilton**, *church* restored 1873 (G.F. Bodley) with pretty stencil decoration. At **Thurlaston**, 2m W of Dunchurch, A45, *church* (1849; Butterfield), designed as a school to be used as a church on Sundays, hence the pyramid-capped tower with lantern is actually the schoolmaster's house. Exemplary simplicity in red brick. 7m S of Dunchurch, A425, at **Lower Shuckburgh**, *church* (1864; J. Croft), spiky and inventive Gothic, the tower hexagonal with gablets and spire, the interior with notched brick arches and vaulted chancel, the cells between the ribs decorated in tile. To SE, *Shuckburgh Hall*, refronted 1844 (H.E. Kendall Jr) in mixed Italianate style, with highly decorated estate *church* (c 1860) in the grounds full of Shuckburgh memorials from the 16C onwards. 1½m N of Rugby, A426, at **Brownsover**, *Brownsover Hall* (c 1860; G.G. Scott), diapered brick Gothic, asymmetrical with steep-roofed entrance tower. *Church* remodelled by Scott (1877).

STRATFORD-UPON-AVON. A46 8m SW of Warwick. The main Victorian contribution to Shakespeare's town was the Memorial Theatre, sponsored by C.E. Flower, brewer, built 1877 and burnt 1926. The Library and Gallery attached to the present theatre are a survival (1881; Dodgshun and Unsworth). By the bridge, *Shakespeare Memorial* (1888; Lord R. Gower). Shakespearian scenes invade the *Midland Bank* (1883; Harris, Martin and Harris), Chapel St, in red terracotta, and the parish *church* received a 'Seven Ages of Man' window (1885) from Shakespeare's American admirers. The church was restored 1888 and 1898 (Bodley and Garner), organ case by Bodley. The 19C Shakespearian revival of Stratford began in 1847 with a national subscription to buy Shakespeare's *Birthplace* in Henley St as a memorial, Walter Scott, T. Carlyle and H. Irving scratched their names on the window panes of the bedroom upstairs.

2m N, off A46, *Welcombe Hotel* (1867; H. Clutton), Jacobean style mansion built for M. Philips, Manchester merchant. *Obelisk* (1876) to Philips. 3m NW, at **Wilmcote**, two of Butterfield's earliest works, *school* (1844), much rebuilt, and *vicarage* (1846), stone, simple Gothic detail. 4m E of Stratford, B4086, *Charlecote Park* (NT), mansion of the Lucy family from the 13C, the house begun 1558 was extensively remodelled from 1829 (T. Willement) and after 1847 (J. Gibson). Neo-Elizabethan interiors with much carved woodwork, stained glass by Willement. Estate *church* (1851; J. Gibson), stone vaulted. Just NW, at **Hampton Lucy**, *church* (1822–26; Rickman and Hutchinson) built for the Lucy family, one of the finest of Georgian Gothic churches, boldly scaled in ashlar, the details not skimped, the interior high and luminous with plaster vaulting. Sympathetic apse added 1856 (G.G. Scott) with E window by Willement (1837) reset. 2m E of Charlecote, B4087, at **Newbold Pacey**, *church* (1881; J.L. Pearson), simple EE style, carefully handled with saddleback-roofed tower. At **Wellesbourne**, 2m SW, the *church* has a richly decorated chancel (1873). 2m S of Wellesbourne, off B4086, *Walton Hall* (1858–62; G.G. Scott), stone Gothic mansion in Scott's favourite c 1300 style, quite severe, the entrance front grouped around a pyramid-roofed tower, the garden front with full-length arcade. Plate-glass sashes in straight-headed surrounds, more Scott than c 1300, practical rather than archaeological. Estate cottages of c 1860–70. Just E, over Fosse Way, **Combrook**, estate village for Compton Verney, *church* (1866; J. Gibson), heavily carved, *school* (Gibson) and estate cottages in stone with timber Gothic porches. 7m E, off A41, at **Avon Dassett**, *church* (1868; C.E. Buckeridge), fine work in the manner of G.G. Scott, broach spire and 13C detail. Handsome blue and grey reredos and glass probably by Clayton and Bell. Buckeridge also designed the *church* (1866) at **Radway**, 3m SE.

S of Stratford, off A34, Alscot Park estate cottages at Preston, Wimpstone and Alderminster, Tudor style. S of Alderminster, *Ettington Park* (1858–62; J. Prichard), the fullest application of Ruskinian ideals of structural colour and sculptural ornamentation in the country, a recasing of an earlier house in the richest Gothic, English 13C style but banded in stones shaded from grey to yellow to give a quite un-English effect and the slate roofs steeply pitched in the French way. The main facade is subtly near symmetrical, the turrets in the angles of varied height and shape and the ends of the wings treated differently. The surfaces shimmer with colour while the carved decoration of capitals and window heads is based on natural forms, following Ruskin. The facades are further ornamented with sculpted panels (H.H. Armstead) in Gothic style establishing the lineage of the owner, E.P. Shirley, back to medieval times. By Prichard also, *The Grange*, in **Newbold on Stour**, just S. 5m S, at **Shipton on Stour**, *church* rebuilt except tower 1854 (G.E. Street). 5m E, off B4035, at **Winderton**, High Victorian *church* (1878; W. Smith), well detailed with polychrome banding in chancel.

WARWICK. A46 8m NE of Stratford-upon-Avon. *Warwick Castle* (open to public) had extensive works carried out in 1872 (A. Salvin) after a fire, including the reconstruction of the Great Hall and the Renaissance style decoration (G.E. Fox) of the library. Off A445,

Emscote Rd, *All Saints' Church* (1854; J. Murray), enlarged 1868 (G.F. Bodley) with broach spire. Screen by Bodley, painted decoration and marble font by C.E. Buckeridge (1871). 4m NW of Warwick, A41, at **Haseley**, *Manor House* (1875; W. Young), large Tudor style mansion with high entrance tower behind a two-storey porte-cochère. 2m N, at **Wroxall**, Wroxall Abbey (1866; W. Scott), harsh Tudor Gothic brick mansion, heavily gabled with granite columns to the entrance. 4m W, off B4439, at **Lapworth**, the *church* has two excellent S chancel windows (1861; Clayton and Bell), designed for G.E. Street, E window 1872 (Powells). At **Hockley Heath**, 1½m NW, unusually churchy *Baptist chapel* (1877; G. Ingall), cruciform with apse and high spire, The *church* (1879; J. Cotton) to N is polychrome brick. 6m W of Warwick, at **Henley-in-Arden**, Beaudesert *church*, just E of A34, restored 1865 (T. Garner) with good glass by Morris, the clear backgrounds, required by Garner, unusual for the date. In New Rd, *Brooke End* (1909; C.F.A. Voysey), simple Voysey house roughcast with deep roof punctuated by a pair of dormers and high plain stacks. 3m S of Warwick, A429, at **Sherbourne**, *church* (1862–64; G.G. Scott), an expensive work in stone with tall spire and rich Dec. detail, carving, vaulted chapel to the donor, marble arcades and glass by Clayton and Bell. The pulpit has excellent metalwork by Skidmore and the font is encrusted with edible-looking half spheres of coloured marble.

WEST MIDLANDS

BIRMINGHAM. Birmingham in the later 19C was synonymous with enlightened municipal government and Liberalism. As a metal-working centre with an extremely broadly based economy and large skilled work-force it was less dependent than the other great manufacturing centres on single industries with their vulnerability to trade cycles, and less stratified between masters and workforce; from this arose the strong Birmingham voice for political reform and municipal self-sufficiency. The radical strain runs through from T. Attwood, founder of the Birmingham Political Union (1829) to J. Sturge and the Complete Suffrage Union of 1845, John Bright, radical MP for the city from 1857, to the Birmingham Liberal Association of 1865 which was the basis of the Liberal 'caucus' that ran Birmingham thereafter, the power base from which Joseph Chamberlain became Mayor in 1873. Under Chamberlain the various strands of Birmingham radicalism—reforming politics, Nonconformity in religion, civic pride and the belief in improvement through education—came together in a Town Council whose 'civic gospel' was the complete overhaul of the amenities and utilities of the town, bringing under municipal control education, health, sanitation, water, gas and public works.

Birmingham, despite the devastation of more recent municipal reformers, has a city centre of distinct character, the red brick and terracotta style of the late 19C has a Gothic, Ruskinian side going back to the 1860s, developed by the prominent local firm of Martin and Chamberlain. There is much good turn of the century Arts and Crafts style decoration, for which Birmingham, with its long craft tradition, was an important centre.

The civic centre is Chamberlain Square with the Gothic *memorial* to Joseph Chamberlain (1880; J.H. Chamberlain), erected to celebrate the achievements of Chamberlain's municipal career, just after his election to Parliament. Few politicians have had such a memorial built in their own lifetimes. Also in the Square, *statue* of G. Dawson (1880; T. Woolner), nonconformist preacher, called by C. Kingsley 'the greatest talker in England', and a key figure in the forming of the Birmingham ideal of civic responsibility. The ironwork around it comes from the original Reference Library, promoted by Dawson. In Victoria Square adjoining, the *Council House, Museum and Art Gallery* (1874–85; Y. Thomason), a crowded Renaissance design, lavishly decorated and capped by a dome uncertainly scaled to the rest of the building. Grand staircase inside with Victoria (1883; T. Woolner) and Albert (1868; J.H. Foley) statues. On the Museum corner, 'Big Brum', 160ft clock tower, unhappily perched next to the entrance portico. The Art Gallery has outstanding collections, especially of the Pre-Raphaelites. Over the main stair, fresco of 'Corporation St 1914' by J. Southall. N extension is solid Edwardian classical style (1910–19; Ashley and Newman). Across the square, *Town Hall* (1831–35; Hansom and Welch) a Roman Corinthian temple, columned all round and clad in Anglesey marble, stately and uncompromising. All that it lacks is a forum; the sloping site adds grandeur to the main front, but unfortunately the rest of the civic buildings are behind; the front overlooks a jumble of roads and buildings. Nearby, *Post Office* (1889; Sir H. Tanner), more festive than most such buildings, with steep pavilion roofs and domed turrets.

Colmore Row was remodelled from 1866 with stone-fronted business palazzi, the best survivors on the N Side between Newhall and

Church Sts: on corner of Newhall St, *Nos 85–9* (1870; Y. Thomason), the former Union Club, with skyline of urns. Further down, *No. 63* (1867; Y. Thomason), the front altered but with handsome domed banking hall. On the S side, on corner of Waterloo St, *No. 130* (1904; Goddard and Paget), Edwardian Baroque bank. In Waterloo St handsome stuccoed houses of c 1830. *Nos 122–4 Colmore Row* (1900; W.R. Lethaby), the Eagle Insurance Building, strikes a radically novel note among its neighbours; stone with detail outside period styles, the ground floor square grid of windows echoed on larger scale by the three upper floors, but with the upper square softened by an undulating pattern of pediments that brings the eye to the parapet chequered in brick and patterned with stone discs. The discs are sun symbols, reflecting Lethaby's desire to return ornament to first principles as set out in his influential book 'Architecture, Mysticism and Myth' (1891). *Nos 114–6* (c 1905), Baroque with raised portico, and *No. 110* (1902; Henman and Cooper) in granite, freely styled with domed turrets flanking the centre. In Bennett's Hill, *Nos 37 and 38* (c 1870) are richly Italianate. *Nos 1–6* (1827) are stuccoed Regency style. Burne-Jones was born in a house in Bennett's Hill, in 1833. On the corners of Waterloo St, *No. 7* (c 1860), stone Italianate; *No. 8* (1869; J. Gibson), the former National Provincial Bank, elaborately corniced, with domed corner entry and fine banking hall, and the *Midland Bank* (1830; T. Rickman), grandly Corinthian, porticoed to the front. On N side of Colmore Row, opposite the Cathedral, *No. 55* (c 1870), pavilion-roofed stone office building. On S side, in Temple Row W, *Lloyd's Bank* (1862; J.A. Chatwin), rich banking palazzo. The *Cathedral* (1709–25; T. Archer) is a major work of the 18C English Baroque, chancel of 1883. Outstanding deep coloured *stained glass at E end (1884–87) and under the tower (1897) by Burne-Jones. Outside, *statue* of Bishop Gore (1914; S. Lee), first Bishop of Birmingham (1905). E of the cathedral, *Great Western Arcade* (1875; W.H. Ward) glass-roofed through to Temple Row.

Church St runs N into the area N of Colmore Row, developed in the later 19C, where some of the best examples of Birmingham brick and terracotta architecture survive. In Church St, *Nos 37–43* (1898–1900; Newton and Cheattle); Nos 37–9 robustly arcaded, Nos 41–3 prettily detailed in the Arts and Crafts manner, and the *Old Royal* pub (c 1895), ornately treated with Dutch gables in brick and terracotta. *Nos 57–9* (1909) is in the more severe manner of the late Edwardian period, probably steel framed. Edmund St is part warehouses with, to the W end, a fine group of civic buildings. On the N Side, *No. 136* (c 1880) is in the Ruskin-inspired Venetian Gothic introduced by the firm of Martin and Chamberlain, while the Gothic of *No. 134* (1897) is Arts and Crafts inspired. Opposite, *Nos 125–31*) (c 1900) are gabled doctors' chambers with two-storey oriels.

On the corner of Newhall St, *Nos 17–19* (1896; W. and F. Martin), built for the Bell Edison telephone company, show the Birmingham style at its finest, strongly articulated with brick piers between tall arched bays, the piers carried up on the Edmund St front, through Dutch gables to splendid chimney stacks, and elsewhere topped with exotic turrets. Exceptionally fine decorative work in terracotta and cut brick. On the N side, the row of public buildings, on the corner, *Nos 100–2* (1883–84; W.H. Ward), stone, Renaissance style former offices of the Board of Guardians of the workhouse, then *No. 98* (1875; Martin and Chamberlain), elaborate Gothic former School Board offices, richly decorated in terracotta, *No. 96*, (c 1890), and finally the buttresses and dormers of the side wall of the *School of Art* (1881–85;

Martin and Chamberlain), the first municipal school of art in Britain. The main front, to Margaret St, is asymmetrically flanked by gables of different sizes, the high Edmund St Corner answered less elaborately at the other end by a gable with a magnificent terracotta roundel. Excellent interior craftsmanship.

On the opposite corner of Cornwall St, *Birmingham Midland Institute* (1899; Cossins, Peacock and Bewlay), brick and stone, richly decorated in mixed Renaissance style. In Cornwall St a fine Arts and Crafts group in brick and stone; *Nos 85–87* (1899; Henman and Cooper), Nos 89–91 (1904; C.E. Bateman) and *Nos 93 and 95* (1901–02; Newton and Cheatle). In Newhall St, *Nos 56–60* (c 1900), ornate terracotta and brick, *No. 61* (c 1900), with deep eaves on iron brackets. *No. 45 Great Charles St* (1895; A.S. Dixon) was built for the Birmingham Guild of Handicraft, the leading Arts and Crafts group outside London. Simple unadorned brick with gables, the windows stepped to the slope of the hill, a contrast to the rich commercial buildings to which the Guild members contributed so much decorative work. The inner ring road cuts off the artisan area to the N from the centre.

Newhall St and Bennett's Hill lead down to New St, the S fringe of the 19C centre. On corner of Bennett's Hill, *Nos 51–53 New St* (1908; Riley and Smith), domed, Edwardian Baroque. On S side, *Nos 80–93*, a mixed later 19C group; No. 80, at W end, Venetian Gothic, and *No. 128* (1867–69; E. Holmes), handsome palazzo style bank. In Cannon St, on N side, *Nos 39–43*) (c 1900; Essex, Goodman and Nicol), entirely faced in terracotta, and *No. 17* (1881; J.L. Ball), at N end, with delicate Queen Anne details in moulded brick. Off Union St, *City Arcade* (1898–1901; Newton and Cheatle) with excellent glazed tile and terracotta decoration by W.J. Neatby of Doulton.

The Victoria Law Courts (1887–91; A. Webb and I. Bell) Birmingham

Corporation St runs NE, laid out from 1878 as part of Joseph Chamberlain's Improvement Scheme under which some 93 acres were acquired for a new boulevard through a slum district. The S end is mostly rebuilt. Beyond the Old Square roundabout, *Nos 153–61* (c 1900; Crouch and Butler), Arts and Crafts brick and terracotta, and the palazzo style *County Court* (1882; J. Williams) in stone. Further on, the splendid red brick and terracotta *Law Courts* (1887–91; A. Webb and I. Bell), late Gothic to Renaissance in style, beautifully detailed by W. Aumonier. The Great Hall, parallel to the road front, is hammer-beam-roofed with magnificent chandeliers, the detail exceptionally rich. Only the Natural History Museum in London can equal the display and quality of the terracotta work. Opposite, *Methodist Central Hall* (1903; E. and J.A. Harper), taking its cue from the Law Courts in the brick and terracotta and adding the essential element to this civic group, a tall, slender tower. Coleridge Passage leads N towards the *General Hospital* (1894–97; W. Henman), another bright red terracotta work, much altered.

N of Centre. Across the inner ring road, by St. Chad's Circus, *RC Cathedral* (1839–41; A.W.N. Pugin), a battered survivor of 20C bombing and redevelopment, but still standing well in uncompromising red brick. Tall proportions, steep roofs and two thin W towers with spires, economical but effective in massing, North German in feeling. Inside, the effect is of extreme height, achieved by tall and slender arcade piers. Most of Pugin's painted decoration and his screen have gone, but Pugin glass, made by Warrington, survives in the chancel. N transept window by Hardman (1868). 16C pulpit and 15C woodwork in the stalls and Bishop's throne, adapted by Pugin. Romanesque-style crypt with monument to Bishop Ullathorne, first Bishop of Birmingham. The area around the Cathedral was the gun-makers' district of small workshops, typical of the specialist metal-working trades established around the Birmingham Canal. In Princip St (to the E) *Nos 16–18* is a small canalside factory of c 1850.

N of the Cathedral, facing down Snow Hill, *Nos 1–7 Constitution Hill* (1896; W. Doubleday), terracotta with Gothic rounded tower strikingly capped by an ogee-domed cupola. Good sculptural detail and lettering. Further up Constitution Hill, Henrietta St is flanked by a pub and offices (c 1880), in a colourful mix of brick, glazed tile and terracotta. The Birmingham Jewellery-quarter of small-scale workshops interspersed with larger factories extends SW from Constitution Hill and Great Hampton St. In Constitution Hill, *Nos 32–42* (c 1912) an engineering works on the larger scale, while *Nos 60–62* (c 1820–30), with painted Royal arms, was a lacquer and papier-mâché craft workshop. Great Hampton St begins with a well-placed Gothic *pub* (c 1875) and has notable early 20C Arts and Crafts style jewellery workshops; *Nos 16–18* (1912) in Portland stone-dressed brick; the *Lucas works* (c 1907), formerly three workshops, the centre terracotta, the blocks each side in brick; and, at the top left, *Nos 60–4* (c 1912), very large, with arcaded elevations. *Nos 80–2* (1872), The Great Hampton St Works are Venetian Gothic, while *No. 45* (c 1850), the Pelican Works, have an Italianate office front and long brick workshops in Hockley St behind. In Vyse St, at the end of Hockley St, some houses of c 1840–50 converted to workshops. *No. 9* is a Gothic works of c 1880. On Icknield St, to the W, the extensive premises of the *Birmingham Mint* (1860), Italianate, the crown of the Birmingham metalwork industries, founded 1794 and minting coins from 1851. The former *Icknield St School* (1883; Martin and Chamberlain) is one of the best of the Birmingham Board Schools, Birmingham being a leader in the provision of state education. Gothic gables grouped around a brick tower capped by a complex slated spire.

S of Vyse St, in Frederick St, Albion St and Vittoria St, the most complete surviving part of the jewellery quarter, early stucco and brick houses still interspersed with the later workshops, stucco surviving into the 1860s before giving way to patterned brick and later to terracotta. At the foot of Frederick St, the *Argent Works* (1862; J.G. Poland) in polychrome brick, Lombardic style, arcaded with corner towers. At the end of the 22-bay Frederick St front, the corner tower held Turkish Baths. In Legge Lane, *Nos 3–5* (1893; Essex, Nicol and Goodman) in terracotta with Dutch gable. In Albion St, *Nos 62–65* (1883; W.T. Foulkes) in brick with heavy cornice and *Fire Station* (1909; T. Price), Edwardian free style, mixing Wren and Arts and Crafts motifs. In Regent St, *No. 3* (c 1860) is heavily stuccoed like a bank of the period. On corner of Vittoria St, *Nos 54–58* (1905; Essex, Nicol and Goodman), red brick, curved to the corner, severely articulated with brick piers. Further down Vittoria St, *Nos 82–86*, the School of Jewellery, was a Gothic workshop of c 1865, raised a storey (1906) and extended (1911; Cossins, Peacock and Bewlay) for the school, founded 1890. On corner of Regent Place, *Standard Works* (1879; T.F. Williams), a flatted factory, built as 15 small workshops, each with its own entry. On W side, the *Unity Works* (c 1865), unadorned factory of dignified proportions capped by a stone cornice. In Regent Place, *Nos 12–14* (c 1883) is a gabled Gothic factory.

Caroline St runs S to St. Paul's Square, late 18C with its *church* (1776; steeple 1822; F. Goodwin); the square never as fashionable as hoped and by the late 19C invaded by workshops, most prominently on the Brook St corner. In Newhall St, *Museum of Science and Industry* displaying all aspects of Birmingham's industrial history in part of the Elkington's electro-plating works. In George St, the *New Hall Works* (c 1860). W on A457, at corner of Icknield St, *Spring Hill Library* (1893; W. and F. Martin), Gothic, compactly composed with spired clock tower over the entry, an excellent example of the inventive style of the firm. Recently saved from demolition for the road that has claimed everything around.

NW of centre: Handsworth. From Hockley Circus under A41 flyover, Hunter's Rd runs N into Lozells with early 19C villas and *Convent of Our Lady* (1840–41; A.W.N. Pugin), simple and functional Gothic in brick with steep roofs, the gables of the wings coming forward to the road to impressive effect, achieved without any of the flourishes of normal Gothic work of the period. Villa Rd runs W to the A41, Soho Road. Soho was the location of Matthew Boulton's Soho Manufactory, established 1761, a complete factory site in a rural setting, in contrast to the small workshops of the city centre. *Soho House*, refronted 1796 (J. Wyatt), Boulton's house, survives beside *St. Michael's Church* (1855), but the factory has gone. On Soho Rd, mid-19C villas and the former Handsworth *Town Hall* (1878; Alexander and Henman) in brick and terracotta with clock tower.

To S of A41, on Handsworth New Rd, A4040, *Bishop Latimer Church* (1903–04; W.H. Bidlake), finely detailed free Perp. in pale brick with high tower. Complex exterior play of buttresses with square-shouldered lines typical of the period. Tall interior with hammerbeam trusses to nave and vaulted chancel. Nearby *Schools* (1901; Buckland and Haywood-Farmer), brick, single-storey with large parabolic-arched windows in a range of five gables, notably advanced for the

date. N of Soho Rd, Grove Lane runs up to Handsworth Park.
Opposite, *St. Peter's Church* (1905; J.A. and P. Chatwin), unfinished at
W end, but with powerful composition of apse against a heavy
crossing tower. At N end of Grove Rd, on Oxhill Rd, *St. Andrew's
Church* (1907–09; W.H. Bidlake), free Dec. in brick with fine interior in
the manner of Bodley, tall arches embracing the side windows and the
low arcade of the passage aisles. Up College Rd, former *Handsworth
College* (1880–81; Goddard and Ball), Tudor style with high central
tower, built for the Methodist Church. To E, on Handsworth Wood Rd,
Nos 133–7 three Arts and Crafts houses (c 1900–05; Crouch and
Butler) at NE end of Somerset Rd, in varied vernacular materials,
prettily composed. To S, on Hamstead Rd, *St. Mary's Church*,
medieval but mostly rebuilt 1820 (W. Hollins) and 1876 (J.A. Chatwin),
notable as a shrine of the founders of Birmingham's manufacturing
industries. In the chancel, memorial to M. Boulton (died 1809; Flaxman) with an illustration of the Soho Works and bust of W. Murdock
(died 1839; Chantrey) who invented the system of gas lighting, first
used at Soho 1802, and contributed to the development of the steam
engine. In a side chapel (1825; T. Rickman), Chantrey's fine seated
* *monument* to Boulton's partner James Watt, the inventor of the steam
engine, patented 1769 and refined in the 1780s to become the work-
horse of the Industrial Revolution.

N and NE of centre. NE from High St, Albert St leads to * *Curzon Street
Station* (1838; P. Hardwick), the northern terminus of the London and
Birmingham Railway, with an imposing Ionic portico that contained
the booking office, smaller but echoing the triumphal Doric portico,
now gone, at London Euston station. The inconvenient site meant that
by 1854 the station was abandoned for one at New St and the splendid
monument survived as a goods terminus. N of centre, the A34 runs
through **Aston** High St past the *Barton Arms* pub (1900; J. and L. Lea),
the best Victorian pub in Birmingham, Jacobean outside and with a
fully appointed two-storey interior decorated in tiles, cut-glass and
rich woodwork. A splendid cast-iron staircase leads up to the upper
club room and billiard room. To N, on corner of Victoria Rd, polychrome Gothic *Christ Church Baptist Church* (1864; J. Cranston), vividly
coloured brick with almost detached steeple rising from a cluster of
pinnacles. To NE of Aston Park, on Witton Lane, Aston *Parish Church*,
mostly rebuilt 1879–80 (J.A. Chatwin) but with medieval spire. Arts
and Crafts plaque to J. Feeney (1901; G. Frampton).

1½m NE, A5127, on Sutton Rd, **Erdington**, former *Erdington
Abbey*, monastery built 1880 (A. Dempster) for German Benedictines
expelled by Bismarck. Plain stone Gothic with strong tower, added
1896 (H. Haigh). The abbey is linked to the spired *RC Church* (1848–
50; C.F. Hansom), lavishly sculpted. N of Erdington, at junction of
A452, Chester Rd and College Rd, * *St. Mary's College*, Oscott, RC
training college built 1835–38 (J. Potter) in Tudor style, notable for the
chapel fittings (1837–42; A.W.N. Pugin), including the exceptional E
window glass and polychrome painted decoration. Pugin and his
patron, Lord Shrewsbury, introduced the fine continental furnishings
incorporated into the reredos and the c 1500 brass lectern from Lou-
vain. Pugin designed much furniture for the college, where he was
Professor of Ecclesiastical Antiquities. In front of the college, canopied
statue of the Virgin, (c 1840; Pugin), the statue based on a 15C work
that Pugin gave to St. Chad's Cathedral, Birmingham.

SE of Centre. At the Bull Ring, *St. Martin's Church*, the original parish church of the city, almost entirely rebuilt 1873–75 (J.A. Chatwin). S transept window by Burne-Jones. Outside, *Nelson Monument* (1809; Sir R. Westmacott). To E, in High St, **Deritend**, a N Italian Lombard style *church* (c 1910) with campanile tower, intended as the chapel for a boys' hostel, but never used as a church: the Anglo-Catholic founder became Roman Catholic. In Milk St, one of the Birmingham *Board Schools* (1890), Gothic with characteristic ventilation tower. In Heath Mill Lane, former *church* (1910; A.S. Dixon), simple and dignified Romanesque basilica, apsed at both ends, the interior cool and light, with delicate colouring to the roof and screen, the E apse decorated in marble and mosaic. In Allcock St, *Board School* (c 1875–80; Martin and Chamberlain), gabled Gothic in brick with stone details.

On the main A34, *Holy Trinity Church*, Camp Hill (1820–22; F. Goodwin), Georgian Gothic with cast-iron window tracery, well-placed on the hill. In Ravenhurst St, to W, Jacobean style *almshouses* (1849; J. Hornblower) set around a lawn. At N end of Stratford Road, former *Board School* (1883; Martin and Chamberlain), Gothic with two timbered spirelets. Off Moseley Rd, to SW, *St. Alban's Church*, Conybere St (1879–81; J.L. Pearson), tall, spare, red brick exterior in EE style enclosing one of Pearson's noble interiors, fully vaulted in stone, lit by high clerestory windows, the vaulting harmoniously adapted at the E end to a rounded apse. The SE chapel displays Pearson's skills in miniature. Iron chancel screen. E window glass by H. Payne (1909). Arts and Crafts altar triptych in SE chapel (1919; K. and M. Bunce). *Almshouses* (1879; J.A. Chatwin) around a garden, Gothic, but with Queen Anne style moulded brick detail to the end houses and centre Warden's house. On Moseley Rd, stuccoed early to mid 19C villas, and, at **Balsall Heath**, *Library* (1895; Cossins and Peacock) with prominent corner tower, curved at the angles to give an advanced Arts and Crafts look, belied by the more conventional terracotta detail. Three Flemish-gabled great mullioned windows face the road. Adjoining *Baths* (1907; W. Hale and Son) in similar materials, more ornate but more conventional, with domed turrets. Opposite, former *College of Art* (1899; W.H. Bidlake), brick and stone Wren style, with finely detailed two-storey curved-pedimented porch. Baroque hall and staircase within.

To S, at **Moseley**, *The Fighting Cocks* pub (1899; Newton and Cheattle), St. Mary's Row, the late Victorian pub reinterpreted in Arts and Crafts details, the corner tower and Dutch gables familiar pub features, but here the tower contrasts sheer unadorned surfaces with delicate detailing to the entrance and top stage, and the oriels on the main gabled front have a simplicity far from the normal riot of terracotta. In Salisbury Rd, to W, *Nos 16 and 59* are Edwardian Arts and Crafts suburban houses. To S, in Yew Tree Rd, *·Highbury Hall* (1879; J.H. Chamberlain), built for Joseph Chamberlain M.P., now an old people's home. Very Gothic red brick and stone asymmetrical exterior, the stonework ornamented with naturalistic carving, but most remarkable for the surviving interiors lavishly decorated in the hard materials favoured by advanced Gothicists. A full-height Great Hall with timbered roof gives on to the stair hall, screened by a marble-shafted arcade, the walls embellished with tilework and carved stone, the fireplace massively Gothic. Similar decoration through the subsidiary rooms, especially fine in the Billiard Room. *Uffculme*, adjoining to E, is a Jacobean mansion of 1890. E of The Fighting Cocks, in Wake Green Road, large late Victorian villas, *Nos 8* and *10–12* give way to smaller Arts and Crafts houses, *Nos 31, 40 and 50*, also to be found in St. Agnes Rd to S. Off Wake Green Rd, *Moseley Grammar School*

(1854–56; J. James), collegiate Gothic, built as a Congregational training college in what was then a quite rural setting.

From the Grammar School, College Rd runs E to Stratford Road, A34. To N, on E side, *St. John's Church*, **Sparkhill** (1888; Martin and Chamberlain), red brick, remarkable for the very large interior space achieved by intersecting iron arches of impressive span, an evangelical, or low-church solution giving primacy to the preacher rather than ritual use of the chancel. N on Stratford Rd, *·St. Agatha's Church*, **Sparkbrook** (1899–1901; W.H. Bidlake), Arts and Crafts Gothic of the highest quality, one of the landmarks of the later Gothic revival. For the exterior, the W tower is everything, lofty, but treated in a wiry East Anglian Perp. manner, the deeply-set bell-openings and strong octagonal corner turrets emphasising the red brick mass, while the fine stone tracery and crown of pierced pinnacles superimpose a lively movement. The interior leaves medieval precedent further behind, pale brick lozenge-shaped piers are the basis of an impressively unified articulation, the leading edge of the piers carried up as wallshafts to the transverse timber trusses of the nave, while laterally the finely moulded stone arches of the lower arcade and brick arches across the upper windows die into the diagonal faces. In the chancel stone transverse arches and free Perp. tracery to the E window. The original fittings were lost in a fire. Further N, *Stratford Road Schools* (1885; Martin and Chamberlain), prettily mixing brick, terracotta and half-timber with cheerful spired bellcote. At the end of Walford Rd, S of St. Agatha's *Emmanuel Church* (1900; W.H. Bidlake), unfinished but with Arts and Crafts spirelet over the entry.

Golden Hillock Rd leads N to **Small Heath** past the Armoury Rd site of the Birmingham Small Arms *factory* where the need for rapid expansion in 1915 was met by a starkly functional exposed concrete-frame structure, one of the first in Britain. In Waverley Rd, by Small Heath Park, to N, *Board School* (1892; Martin and Chamberlain), one of the best of the Birmingham schools, with pinnacled and spired tower. On Coventry Rd, A45, opposite the park, *St. Oswald's Church* (1892–99; W.H. Bidlake), tall, red brick in the manner of G.F. Bodley. The *vicarage* (1899; Bidlake) in Dora Rd, to E, is a neat Arts and Crafts design under a hipped roof of Queen Anne type. Returning W on Coventry Rd, *Library and Baths* (1893; W. Martin) on a corner site to Green Lane, the corner library entry marked by monumental round tower turning octagonal for a ring of terracotta ornament under a short conical roof, the whole improbably exotic. Library behind with gable sculpture and plainer baths beyond, an ingeniously planned complex. In Herbert Rd, S of Coventry Rd, *St. Aidan's Church* (1893–98; T. Proud), brick and terracotta with notably lofty interior and fine late Gothic painted rood and screen (1912; F.B. Bond).

In **Bordesley Green**, at E end of Green Lane, *St. Benedict's Church* (1909; Nicol and Nicol), Byzantine style, the semi-domed apse to Hob Moor Rd impressive externally, but notable for the Byzantinesque painting inside by H. Holiday (1912–19).

SW of Centre. From Chamberlain Square, Broad St runs W beyond the ring road. On S side, on corner of Gas St, *No. 266* (c 1875; Martin and Chamberlain), Gothic asymmetrical front built over the canal. Behind is the *·Gas Street Basin*, terminal of the Worcester and Birmingham Canal which was cut through to join the earlier Birmingham Canal in the 1790s, now landscaped and the hub of the attractive and much-used Birmingham canal system. On N side of Broad St, *Barclay's Bank* (1898; C.E. Bateman), Wren style with banded brick and stone chim-

neys, the porch oddly diagonally-set on the end wall. At top of Sheep-
cote St behind, *City Engineers Depot* (c 1840), a former canal-railway
interchange built as a coal wharf for the London and North Western
Railway. Intriguing, split-level horseshoe plan of stores and stables. In
the street, early 19C canalside works.

Over the Five Ways interchange, on Hagley Rd, early to mid 19C
stuccoed villas and terraces. On N side, the *Birmingham Oratory*,
founded by J.H. Newman in 1847, the first English house of the Oratorians and a centre of English Catholicism ever since. Cardinal
Newman lived in the Priest's House (1850–51; T. Flanagan) from 1852
to his death in 1890. His rooms in the handsome Roman palazzo style
building are preserved. The entry to the church is through the school
block (1859–61; H. Clutton), a severe brick and stone range with
arched windows at upper level giving onto a cloistered court in Romanesque style, the back of the school block built out at first floor on
massive stone brackets. Newman's church was replaced (1903–09;
E.D. Webb) in grandiose domed Roman Renaissance style with a
broad tunnel vault on marble columns, and lavish coloured marble
and mosaic throughout. The Oratorians, and Newman in particular,
favoured the triumphant style of the Counter-Reformation Catholic
church over Gothic medievalism. Off Monument Rd, in Waterworks
Rd, *Pumping Station* (c 1880; Martin and Chamberlain), Gothic in
polychrome brick, the chimney suggesting a tower from an Italian
town hall. Attractive stucco *villas* in Monument Rd and Reservoir Rd.

N of Hagley Rd, further W, the Rotton Park estate, mid Victorian, the
church (1868–76; J.A. Chatwin) a model suburban church with prominent spire and expensive detail. In Rotton Park Rd, *Nos 17–19* (1896;
J.L. Ball) are a simple Arts and Crafts pair. In Norfolk Rd, S of Hagley
Rd, the *Calthorpe Estate Office* (1860 and c 1870), built for Lord Calthorpe, whose **Edgbaston** estate was developed from c 1810 as one of
the most extensive residential suburbs in Britain, carefully controlled
as to layout, spacing of houses and excluding commerce and industry.
Even the Wolverhampton canal runs a picturesquely rural course
through the estate. The house is Italianate in brick and stone, with rich
interior woodwork of c 1870. To W, on corner of Woodbourne Rd, *No.
20 Westfield Rd* (1893; J.L. Ball) late 17C Wren-style house, carefully
detailed. *No. 25 Woodbourne Rd* (1897; C.E. Bateman) is in the
advanced Arts and Crafts style of Voysey, deceptively simple vernacular, roughcast with bands of leaded windows and sheer brick stacks.

E of Norfolk Rd, off Harborne Rd, *Berrow Court*, Berrow Drive (c
1875; Martin and Chamberlain), asymmetrical Gothic villa in red
brick and stone, now an hotel. The stair hall and some interior Gothic
details survive. To S, in Yateley Rd, *Nos 15–21* (1899–1907; H.
Buckland), a group of four Arts and Crafts houses, the best, No. 21
(1899), with a Voysey-like play of simple geometrical shapes under a
broad hipped roof. In Harborne, to SW, *Board School*, High St (1885;
Martin and Chamberlain) with spired clock tower. N of High St, off
Ravenhurst Rd, *Harborne Tenants Estate* (1907–10; Martin and
Martin), garden suburb built as a co-partnership venture, with simple
brick and roughcast cottages spaciously laid out on tree-lined roads.
The centrepiece, The Circle, has modest shops and community buildings. On Ravenhurst Rd, *Nos 108–34* are two blocks of two-storey
flats, the upper flats reached by bridges from the road, Returning NE,
the main part of the Edgbaston Calthorpe estate lies between the
Harborne and Bristol roads with Calthorpe Rd the main axis. Despite
later infill and demolition along the principal roads this remains one of
the outstanding 19C villa suburbs, spanning the period from the

Regency to the 1860s with a consistent pattern of building, stucco predominating but red brick with stone or stucco dressings prominent by the 1850s. The styles are generally classical, progressing through varieties of the Greek to a consistent and rich Italianate by the 1840s, though there are occasional Tudor or Elizabethan houses and some bolder High Victorian Gothic statements. The names of architects are mostly not known, but the rich Italianate may be due to J.A. Chatwin, a pupil of Sir C. Barry, the progenitor of the style, as *Nos 38–9 Frederick Rd* (1848) are known to be a Chatwin design.

Off Harborne Rd, in Westbourne Rd, the *Botanical Gardens*, opened 1832, with *palm-house* (1871) and *glasshouse* (1865). At the entry to the polytechnic hostels, *lodge* (1879) in picturesque 'old English' style, the gables showing the sunflower hallmark of aesthetic taste. At E end, *St. George's Church* (1836) much enlarged 1884 (J.A. Chatwin). In Calthorpe Rd, some of the early villas, *Nos 35 and 36* (c 1835), particularly fine with Greek to Egyptian detail. From the N end, St. James's Rd crosses Frederick Rd, George Rd and Wheeley's Rd, all lined with villas. At corner of George Rd, *The Round House*, a Gothic folly of c 1810, extended c 1830. In Elvetham Rd, *St. James's Church* (1852; S.S. Teulon), spiky Gothic in pink stone, the roofs carried down low for a wide aisleless interior planned with low church emphasis on unobstructed space. Complicated roof timberwork. In Wellington Rd, at end of Charlotte St, Regency to early Victorian villas, as also in Carpenter Rd, except for *No. 50* (c 1870; Martin and Chamberlain), Gothic in polychrome brick. *No. 12 Ampton Rd* (1858; J.H. Chamberlain), introduced this Ruskinian Gothic to Birmingham, the boldness of the Gothic detail and careful polychromy can be contrasted with the conventional Tudor-Gothic of the contemporary *Nos 10 and 11*. Church Rd continues Calthorpe Rd S to the early 18C *Edgbaston Hall* and much rebuilt *parish church*. In Priory Rd, *No. 24* (1880; Martin and Chamberlain), substantial and richly treated Gothic house, built for the editor of the 'Birmingham Post'.

From Church Rd, Edgbaston Park Rd winds down to Birmingham University. At the S end, on W side, *°Garth House* (1901; W.H. Bidlake), one of the best of Birmingham Arts and Crafts houses, roughcast over brick with leaded timber windows, a simplified vernacular vocabulary from which an inventive composition of gables and tall brick stacks is achieved, varied yet held in balance, the relation of chimney to gables and window-bay on the garden front particularly neat. From the entrance the composition pivots on an unadorned square brick tower over the stair, a surprisingly strong and functional element at the core of the softer composition around, though without functional justification, (the upper part contains only a box-room). On the E side, further down, *Winterbourne* (1903; J.L. Ball), built for J.S. Nettlefold of the steel firm, in finely detailed brick, late 17C style. *King Edward's School*, moved here from New St in 1938, has chapel with Perp. stone-vaulted interior, originally the upper corridor of the New St Building (1833–37; Sir C. Barry). *°Birmingham University* began as Mason College (1870) in the city centre and moved here when the university charter was granted in 1900. The buildings designed to outshine the other 19C universities were begun to a grandiose semicircular plan (1901–09; A. Webb and I. Bell) to meet Joseph Chamberlain's vision of a building to match the great cathedrals of the Middle Ages. Like those cathedrals, Chamberlain intended that his generation would lay down the plan and future generations would complete the great scheme. Chamberlain's death, shortage of funds and the First World War, meant that the great vision was modified and diminished and the rigid symmetry of the first design shows up the poorer quality of the later additions. On the radius of the semi-circle, the Great Hall flanked by teaching blocks, of which three were to the original plan, presenting an array of Byzantine-domed pavilions to the inner court behind which radiate the more functional working spaces. The Byzantine style was quite new to university design and, characteristically for the date, fuses in detail with a variety of styles, most obviously the late Gothic of the traceried windows. Ceramic friezes by R.A. Bell and fine Renaissance style carving to the Great Hall entry. The hall is vast, tunnel-vaulted and filled with stained glass by T.R. Spence. Opposite the Great Hall, the Chamberlain Tower, a dramatic Italian Gothic campanile visible for miles around, the hard red brick emphasising the soaring lines. Sir E. Elgar was first Professor of Music (1905–08).

Below the university, the crowded suburb of **Selly Oak**. On Bristol Rd, set back, Gothic *Pumping Station* (c 1890; Martin and Chamberlain) and banded stone *parish church* (1861; E. Holmes). To SW, off Bristol Rd, at Westhill College, *The Close* (1911–13; Harvey and Wicks), picturesque quadrangle of 16C-style vernacular houses with good brickwork and half-timbering, built as Quaker almshouses in the grounds of one of the houses of the Cadbury family, Quaker chocolate manufacturers whose Bournville factory became the centre-piece of a pioneering garden suburb from 1894. On Bristol Rd, *Fircroft* (1902; W.A. Harvey) and *Woodbrooke* were Cadbury family houses.

The earliest part of ***Bournville** is to the E around Linden Rd and Bournville Green. The Cadbury family insisted on housing well provided with gardens, public open space and community buildings easily accessible to the works. A wide social mix was intended from the first, and, to ensure a balanced community, housing was not reserved to the Cadbury employees. In this, Bournville provided a model for the later garden suburbs and indeed for 20C town planning. W.A. Harvey was responsible for the layout and many of the buildings; though it is the planting and open spaces that most immediately catch the eye, the housing being in unpretentious cottage style. Around the Green, more self-conscious public buildings, the octagonal *Rest House* (1914), the *Quaker Meeting House* (1905), *Junior School* (1905), *Infants' School* (1910), *Ruskin Hall* (1902), parish *church* (1925) and *church hall* (1913), Arts and Crafts simplified detail, mostly Tudor, but Romanesque for the church and hall. The Junior School with its broad squat tower is the most striking. On Sycamore Rd, a half-timbered range of *shops* (1905; H.B. Tyler) and the reconstructed 15C *Selly Manor House* moved here in 1912–16 to add a genuine medieval flavour. *Minworth Greaves Manor*, a 14C cruck hall was another transplant of 1929. To S, on Bournville Lane, the Recreation Ground with *pavilion* (1902; H.B. Tyler) in picturesque half-timber, and beyond the factory, the Arts and Crafts towered *Baths* (1902; G.H. Lewin) with exotic buttressed cap to the tower and finely carved frieze below the main window. In Maryvale Rd, Tudor-style *almshouses* (1897; E. Harper) around a court.

½m E of Bournville, on Vicarage Rd, **Kings Heath**, a small group of Arts and Crafts houses of c 1895 at S end of Cartland Rd and in Stanley Rd by C.E. Bateman, with, on Vicarage Rd, the *Red Lion Inn* (1904; Bateman), a thoroughly and attractively medieval hostelry, drinking made acceptable for a middle-class 'cottage' estate. This was the fore-runner of the 'reformed' pub, a drinking place with the atmosphere of old English villages to banish the bright alcoholic glitter of contemporary city pubs.

SW of Bournville the Bristol Rd, A38, runs out towards Worcestershire.

At Longbridge, on the city boundary, *Pumping Station* (c 1876; Martin and Chamberlain), finest of the Birmingham water-supply buildings, reflecting the civic pride in publicly-owned utilities, Birmingham's most significant achievement in the years of Chamberlain and the Liberal caucus being the reform through public ownership of water, sewage and gas works. Chamberlain said 'the Water Works should never be a source of profit, as all profit should go in the reduction of the price of water'. The station is Gothic, a cathedral of sanitation, with proud octagonal tower rising above the body of the building. On the hill to NW, *Hollymoor Asylum* (1896–1905; Martin and Martin), the copper-domed water-tower a landmark.

COVENTRY. A45 15m E of Birmingham. Central Coventry is mostly rebuilt since wartime bombing. In Earl St, *Council House* (1912; Garrett and Simister), gabled Elizabethan with Lady Godiva among the statuary. In Bayley Lane, *Drapers Hall* (1832; Rickman and Hutchinson), neo-classical. Outside the centre, on London Rd, *Cemetery* laid out 1843 by Sir J. Paxton with chapels and lodge all in different styles, the Greek Ionic chapel particularly fine. Paxton was MP for Coventry (1854–65) and is commemorated by a Gothic column (1865; J. Goddard) by the N entry. S of the station, *Grammar School*, Warwick Rd (1884; E. Burgess), Tudor style with gatehouse tower.

DUDLEY. A433 7m W of Birmingham. Black Country iron and coal centre but with a history to the Middle Ages. In the Market Place, Baroque style *fountain* (1867; J. Forsyth), given by the Earl of Dudley, whose estates covered this part of the Black Country. In Priory St, handsome stone-fronted *County Court* (1858; C. Reeves), palazzo style. In St. James Rd, Baroque style *Library* (1909; G. Wenyon). N of the centre on Tipton Rd, *Black Country Industrial Museum* on a basin of the Birmingham Canal, just E of the Dudley Tunnel. Reconstructed chain-making and glass-cutting workshops, period house, shops and chapel.

To SW, at **Kingswinford**, *Broadfield House Glass Museum*, Barnett Lane, museum of the Stourbridge and Brierly Hill glass industry with collections of 19C glass. At **Stourbridge**, 5m SW of Dudley, glassmaking was introduced in the 16C. In Market St, *Town Hall* (1887; T. Robinson) and *Market* (1827). To N, on Lower High St, Gothic *Grammar School* (1862; T. Smith), and *St. John's Church* (1859; G.E. Street), severe and economical in brick with lancet windows. At S end of Market St on New Rd, *RC Church* (1864; E.W. Pugin), Dec., the spire added 1890. To E, on Hagley Rd, Edwardian free Tudor *Library* (1905; F. Woodward).

SE of Dudley, A457, at **Oldbury**, *Municipal Buildings* (1890; Wood and Kendrick), Dutch gabled in red brick. The complex of canals running NW from Birmingham through an industrialised, and more recently de-industrialised, landscape, deserves exploration. The original Birmingham Canal to Wolverhampton via the Dudley Tunnel (1768–72) was superseded by T. Telford's deep-cut direct canal (1826) and Oldbury lies between the two systems. To E, at **Smethwick**, *Galton Bridge* is the finest of the iron bridges over Telford's canal. In High St, Smethwick, *Council House* (1905; F.J. Gill) in late 17C style.

SOLIHULL. A41 8m SE of Birmingham. On Warwick Rd, *Grammar School* (1879–82; J.A. Chatwin), extensive Gothic range in brick with off-centre tower. Off Station Rd, to SW, *RC Church* (1838; A.W.N. Pugin), minor work, Perp. style, chancel added 1878. 3m E, B4102, **Hampton in Arden**, with *lodge* and *cottages* to the Manor House of 1868 (W.E. Nesfield), pretty examples of the revival of vernacular forms pioneered by Nesfield and Norman Shaw, brick and ornamental plasterwork with tile-hanging and heavily modelled chimneys. At the *Manor House*, octagonal Gothic clock-tower (c 1870; Nesfield), an exuberant High Victorian design, the roof with dormers on four sides and a top lantern, the walls with carved panels of Zodiac symbols. The house is plain neo-Tudor of c 1840.

SUTTON COLDFIELD. A5127 7m N of Birmingham. In the centre, *Barclay's Bank*, Mill St (1859; G. Bidlake), High Victorian Gothic, built as the Town Hall. The parish *church* to E has decoration in the Arts and Crafts taste (1914 and 1929; C.E. Bateman). To N, off High St, *Town Hall* (1905; A.R. Mayston), Edwardian Baroque but including a Gothic former hotel of 1863.

To N, off Lichfield Rd, **Four Oaks**, turn of the century suburb with good Arts and Crafts houses by leading Birmingham architects, in Barker Rd, *Withens* (1898; W.H. Bidlake) and in Hartopp Rd further N, *Redlands* (1904; C.E. Bateman) and *No. 37* (c 1900; W.H. Bidlake). *Methodist Church*, Lichfield Rd (1907; Crouch and Butler), free Gothic in stone with crossing tower and neat group of attendant buildings, well set at the angle of two main roads. In Mere Green Rd, to NE, *church* of 1834 with attractive Arts and Crafts Gothic additions of 1906 (C.E. Bateman).

S of Sutton Coldfield, on Birmingham Rd, **Wylde Green**, *Emmanuel Church* (1909–16; W.H. Bidlake) EE Gothic, freely handled, with tall clerestory over low aisles and polygonal apse. For Erdington and New Oscott, see Birmingham, NE of Centre (see p. 432).

WALSALL. A34 9m N of Birmingham. In the centre, on Lichfield St, *civic buildings* (1902–05; J.S. Gibson), monumental Baroque Town Hall crowned by a splendid tower, the entrance flanked by Michelangelesque sculpture; an outstanding example of Edwardian civic pride; Library and Museum adjoining. In Leicester St, to the side, Greek Doric porticoed *County Court* (1831). To E, *St. Paul's Church* (1892–93; J.L. Pearson), severe Dec. with sheer pair of apses at E end and tall interior. To S, High St, aligned on the *parish church* rebuilt 1820 (F. Goodwin) with iron tracery and Georgian Gothic interior. In High St, Italianate former *Guildhall* (1867; G.B. Nichols). To W, *Digbeth Arcade* (1895; J. Ellis) and, in Bradford Place, red-brick Gothic former *Science and Art Institute* (1888, Dunn and Hipkiss).

To S, A461, at **Wednesbury**, *Library*, Walsall Rd (1908; Crouch, Butler and Savage), and off to N, *parish church*, Church Hill, the nave of c 1827, Perp. style, the E end of 1890 (B. Champneys) apsed with painted decoration. To S, on Holyhead Rd, A41, *Art Gallery* (1890; Wood and Kendrick), characterful with crowded, vaguely Renaissance decoration and busts of artists on the upper floor.

WOLVERHAMPTON. A41 15m NW of Birmingham. Principal town of the Black Country, an iron-making centre from the 18C. In the centre, *parish church*, 15C with W front and E end 1852–65 (E. Christian). By the churchyard, Lichfield St, *Museum and Art Gallery* (1883; J.A. Chatwin), ornate Italianate with columned frontispiece to the front and side, Bath stone with red granite shafts to the street front centre. Blank upper floors and long carved reliefs (R. Boulton) of the arts and sciences. To W, Gothic *Barclays Bank* (1876), and, in Queen Square, Prince Albert *statue* (1865; T. Thornycroft), equestrian in military uniform. *Lloyd's Bank* (1878; Chatwin), Dudley St, has a handsome Italianate front of superimposed pilasters on four floors and carved panels over the ground floor. In North St, *RC Church* (1825–27; J. Ireland), Regency classical with good interior, a shallow dome over the altar at the end of a tunnel-vaulted nave. Fine domed S transept added 1901 (E. Goldie). *Town Hall* (1869–71; E. Bates), long Renaissance front with French roofs. E of the Museum, in Lichfield St, *Royal London Insurance* (1900–02; Essex, Nicol and Goodman), stone, Baroque; and *Grand Theatre* (1894; C.J. Phipps), brick and stone street front with upper loggia and fine auditorium, lavishly decorated with deeply curved balconies. On Railway St former *Chubb Lock Factory* (1899), large-scale five-storey works prominently sited. On the *station* approach former offices and carriage-entry (1852), Italianate, with corner turrets and stone arches, now blocked, for the roadway. In Queen St, *Athenaeum* (1835), *No. 46* (1826), the *Dispensary and County Court* (1813 and 1829), and the former *Library and Assembly Room*, similar neatly classical public buildings. On Garrick St, S of Market St, free-styled brick and terracotta *Library* (1900–02; H.T. Hare) cleverly fitted to the corner site. Off Snow Hill, to S, in George St, *House of Mercy* (1860; E.W. Pugin); Gothic street front and chapel behind added to a 18C house on St. John's Sq. NW of the Ring Road, *West Park* (1879–81), a classic Victorian public park with clock tower and conservatory (c 1900; D. Gibson). On Compton Rd, A454, W of centre, Tudor Gothic *Grammar School* (1875; Giles and Gough), asymmetrical with entrance tower.

Wightwick Manor, the Great Parlour (1893; E. Ould), near Wolverhampton

1½m W, A454, *Wightwick Manor (1887 and 1893; E. Ould), NT, the most complete example of late 19C artistic taste in the country. T. Mander, paint manufacturer, commissioned an old English house from a Liverpool and Chester architect specialising in timber-framing. The house, therefore, is black and white, half-timbered in the Cheshire manner, with much decorative framing, ornate carved bargeboards and delicate timber oriels. The entrance section of 1887 also has hard red brick and tile-hanging, like contemporary work in Chester; the later extension loses this Victorian signature for full timber-framing, excellently done. The interiors, augmented since with Pre-Raphaelite pictures and Morris furnishings and glass, are 17C style, informally arranged with bay-windows and inglenooks providing the intimate spaces beloved by late Victorians, the windows leaded with fine stained glass by C.E. Kempe, the panelling and moulded plasterwork richly and sensitively executed. The finest room is the Great Parlour, decorated by Kempe with painted panelled roof on broad trusses, the walls hung with Morris textiles under a plaster frieze of Orpheus and Eurydice. Typical of the 1890s is the collection of blue-and-white china displayed in cabinets. Inglenook fireplace with pretty rose frieze on the overmantel. Contemporary gardens. In Mount Rd, to NE, *The Mount Hotel* (c 1870, 1891 and 1908), brick and stone Jacobean, built for another member of the Mander family.

WILTSHIRE

AMESBURY. A303 7m N of Salisbury. *Church* restored (1853; W. Butterfield) with a new W front, NE turret on crossing tower and some fittings including the pulpit. *Amesbury Abbey* (1830; T. Hopper), to the W is neo-Palladian, in sympathy with the previous house on the site, but of a massiveness no earlier Palladian would have attempted. The stair hall is massive too but elementally simple like Vanbrugh. At **Cholderton**, 4m E, A338, *church* (1840–50; Wyatt and Brandon), the nave roof is genuine medieval, brought from a warehouse on the Quay at Ipswich by the rector, T. Mozley, Newman's brother-in-law. Mozley's 'Reminiscences' give much of the fervour of the Oxford Movement and of the great church building enthusiasm that followed. At **Wilsford**, 2m SW of Amesbury, *Wilsford House* (1904–06; D. Blow), 17C style, built in the Arts and Crafts way with local labour. Blow had restored (1898) *Lake House*, the c 1580 mansion nearby which has similar chequered flint and stone walls.

Abbey Mills (1875; R. Gane) Bradford on Avon

BRADFORD ON AVON. A363 8m SE of Bath. A wool-manufacturing town from the 16C to c 1900 with substantial mill buildings still left in the extremely pretty heart of the town which is largely 17C and 18C. *Town Hall* (1854; T. Fuller), heavy Jacobean, the main English work by the architect of the Houses of Parliament, Ottawa. *Abbey Mills* (1875; R. Gane), Church St, stone and Gothic, rising impressively sheer from the river edge. Now offices. The *Avon Rubber Co* factory by the bridge incorporates a mill of c 1845. After the failure of the wool industry Messrs Moulton set up the early British rubber industry here. In Silver St, three-storey plate-glass shopfront (c 1870), the *Old Bear* pub (c 1860), stripy Gothic, and a group of former brewery buildings, the office decorated with classical heads over the windows, 'Health' above, 'Merriment' below. Over the river *Station* (1848; I.K. Brunel), Tudor style. On Bath Rd, *Christ Church* (1841; G.P. Manners), prettily grouped with contemporary school and well set on the hilltop. Beyond, *Old Ride School* (1848; H. Clutton), Jacobean style small country house. At **Winsley**, 2m W, *Sutcliffe School* (1904; Silcock and Reay), gabled stone country house, and, 1m beyond, *Conkwell Grange* (1907; G. Dawber), handsome late 17C style house.

CHIPPENHAM. A4 4m W of Calne. In High St, *Town Hall* (1833 and 1850; J. Thomson), the gift of J. Neeld of Grittleton (see below), round-arched style. Opposite, elegant *National Westminster Bank* (1876; G.M. Silley). N of the river, *station* (c 1840; I.K. Brunel), still intact, and tall railway viaduct. To N, *St. Paul's Church* (1857; G.G. Scott), plain interior but fine spire. On Malmesbury Rd, *Greenways Hospital* (1897; H. Brakspear), country house in free Tudor style with tower on garden front. At **Foxham**, 4m NE, off B4279, *church* (1878; W. Butterfield), small with no external division between nave and chancel, but inside a large wood chancel screen with Butterfield's typical strong forms. At **Grittleton**, 7m NW of Chippenham, the estate of Joseph Neeld, who inherited a Regency silversmith's fortune in 1828. Between 1837 and his death in 1856 he had built the gargantuan *•Grittleton House*, the exterior a blend of Romanesque and Jacobean (the latter due to a change of architect midway), the interior quite spectacular, two inter-secting halls rising through two storeys and even higher under the central tower. This undomestic arrangement was designed for the display of sculpture. Neeld and his architect, James Thomson, built all around the estate: cottages at Grittleton, lodges, including two with eccentric towers, Fosse Lodge to N and Crowdown to SE. At **Alderton**, 2m NW, most of the village including the church, vicarage and school was rebuilt c 1845. At **Leigh Delamere**, 2m SE, the church, vicarage, almshouses and farm were rebuilt c 1846. The *•church* has a copy of its original 13C bell turret and a most atmospheric interior, the chancel lit by a small round window with a dove in golden clouds, Gothic reredos with quite un-Gothic statues by E.H. Baily, a fine tile floor and at the W end an apocalyptically coloured Crucifixion window (T. Wilmshurst). At **Sevington**, nearby, the original bell turret now sits on a village school by Thomson. Two picturesque farms, at **West Foscote**, visible from M4, and, some miles S, at **Lanhill** on A420, give a further taste of Thomson's architecture, a Victorian survival of the Regency 'cottage ornee'. At **Rodbourne**, off A429, 6m N of Chippenham, *church* with lovely E window (1863; Morris). 4m E of Chippenham, on A4, **Calne**. *Church* has fine organ case c 1905 by C.R. Ashbee, made by the Camden Guild (cf. Chipping Camden, Gloucestershire). *Town Hall* (1884; C.B. Oliver), Bath Rd, rock faced and grim. At **Derry Hill**, 2m W, A342, estate *village* of Bowood House with the superb *•Golden Gates* (1834–38; C. Barry), Italian style lodge and campanile tower. More estate housing of slightly earlier date at Sandy Lane, 1m S. Interesting prefabricated thatched *Church* (1892; J. Hopkins). At **Cherhill Down**, 3m E of Calne, off A4, *Lansdowne Obelisk* (1845; C. Barry), visible from miles around.

CORSHAM. A4 4m W of Chippenham. *Corsham Court*, 16C house of the Methuens, was given a ponderous N front (1845; T. Bellamy) to replace a prettier but gimcrack work by Nash. Bellamy's grand stair-case inside is impressive. The *church* has tower and spire by G.E. Street. At **Hartham**, 1m N, a very Victorian group of *church* (1862; P.C. Hardwick), lodge and iron gates belonging to Hartham Park, some distance away. W of Corsham, on A4, *Rudloe Park Hotel* and, 1m beyond, *Fogleigh House* (c 1880; J. Hicks), examples of the overblown Victorian villa, heavily carved and sporting porch towers of Gothic cum 19C French origins. At **Box** handsome stone portals to Brunel's *Box Tunnels* (1837–40), one of the major engineering feats of the London–Bristol line. Beyond Box, on A4, pretty *cemetery* (1857; Poulton and Woodman), the spiky chapel something of a virtuoso dis-play of the famous local stone. **Melksham**. A350 5m S of Chippenham. *Town Hall* (1847), stone, classical with the stretched proportions typical of the 1840s. 2m NW, A365, at **Shaw**, *church* lavishly trans-formed in 1905 (C.E. Ponting) in Arts and Crafts Gothic. The tower and flèche are ornamental but hardly prepare for the completely timbered interior with much carving by H. Hems. At **Lacock**, A350, 3m N of Melksham, the National Trust have converted a barn to a museum of photography in recognition of the pioneering photography in the 1840s of W. Fox Talbot of Lacock Abbey.

DEVIZES. A361 20m S of Swindon. Market Place with nice contrast of Gothic monuments, pretty cross of 1814 looking lightweight next to the Italian Gothic *fountain* (1879; H. Woodyer), a fine thing let down by the statue on top. *Corn Exchange* (1857; W. Hill), monumental classical. Opposite, *Lloyds Bank* (1892), lively red-brick front, the late Victorian reinterpretation of the Georgian town house. Next door, *No. 40* (1866) has Gothic ornament charmingly applied to a similar front in stone. In the corner, long covered *Butter Market* (1839). Off St. Johns St, on the original castle mound, *Devizes Castle* (1838; H. Goodridge: 1870–80; J. Randell), big castellated house, convincing from a dis-tance with two main towers. At the other end of the Market Place looms *Wadworth's Brewery* (1885; J. Randell). Beyond, *The Assize Court* (1835; T.H. Wyatt), with a pure Greek portico. On the outskirts, A361, Gothic *toll-house* (1814) and *St. Peter's Church* (1866; Slater and Carpenter), small with the tough simple forms of the 1860s. To S, on A360, at **Potterne**, the *Porch House* was restored (1876) for the portraitist G. Richmond. S of the village *Blounts Court* (1870), rock-faced castellated house built for a Trowbridge clothier. 4m S at **Littleton Pannell**, Market Lavington *Manor House* (1865; E. Christian), large diapered brick Tudor style country house, and *A'Becketts* (1904; E.P. Warren), red-brick late 17C style house. At **West Lavington**, *Dauntseys School* (1895; C.E. Ponting), pleasant low red-brick main block with cupola.

MARLBOROUGH. A345 11m S of Swindon. In the Market Place, *Town Hall* (1901; C.E. Ponting) in a free late 17C style, effectively placed. The *Bear Hotel* (c 1895; G.R. Crickmay), nearby, is an inven-tive blend of Queen Anne motifs. On London Rd, *school* (1905; Silcock and Reay), pretty neo-Georgian. On W side, *Marlborough College*, founded 1843 around a fine house of c 1700. On the E side of the court, lodge and gates (1877), Bradleian Building (1871) and Museum Block (1882), all by G.E. Street and none in his preferred Gothic but all paying reference to the late 17C. Next to the lodge, Tudor style N block (1893; T. Garner). Opposite, *Chapel (1883–86; Bodley and Garner), tall and elegant in Sarsen stone and Bath stone. One Burne-Jones window (1877) and ornate reredos (1866). On the W side, A

House (c 1845; E. Blore) in the style of the original house but with later white oriels. Blore also built the Master's Lodge, behind the original house, and B House to the E. The Bath Rd is crossed by an arched bridge, part of the Field House (1910; A. Webb). Further out, Barton Hill and Elmhurst (1862; W. White), Littlefield and Cotton House (1870–72; G.E. Street), both unusually built of concrete block, rendered and tile-hung. Further still, Upcot House (1885; Norman Shaw), prettily tile-hung in fishscale tiles. To the SE, off A346, **Savernake Forest**, part of the estate of the Marquesses of Ailesbury whose great house, *Tottenham Park* (1823–25; T. Cundy), stands in the SE corner of the forest. Estate *church*, to N, (1861; T.H. Wyatt), richly carved with spire and lovely Art Nouveau monument (c. 1893; A. Gilbert) of a young woman screened behind a frond of bronze flowers. At **Crofton**, to S, *pumping station* (1811) for the Kennet and Avon Canal with magnificent beam-engine of 1812, still working (occasionally open to public). At **Great Bedwyn**, to E, former *rectory* (1878; G.G. Scott Jr), accomplished Queen Anne style work in grey brick with red dressings. **Pewsey**. A345 6m SW of Marlborough. Diminutive statue of King Alfred (1911) in centre. The *church* has wood-carving and painting of c 1890 by the rector B. Pleydell Bouverie. Pulpit and stalls by G.E. Street (1861). On W side of town, *Cemetery Chapel* (1862; C.J. Phipps), a tiny High Victorian work pared down to geometric forms. Near the church, *school* (1861; G.E. Street), Gothic. Street also rebuilt the *church* (1861) at **Wootton Rivers**, 2m NE, pretty shingled spire and good fittings. At **East Grafton**, A338, 6m E of Pewsey, neo-Norman *church* (1844; B. Ferrey), the tower with a stone pyramid cap and lively corner figures. It was to have been vaulted but the vault fell in, killing the Rev. Montgomery, his memorial by Pugin at Bishopstone, Salisbury. 6m SE of Grafton in remote country is **Chute** where J.L. Pearson built two churches for T.E. Fowle of Chute Lodge. Chute *church* (1869–72) is an almost complete rebuilding with new spire of a 18C building. **Chute Forest** *church* (1875) is wholly new and has an impressive interior, all red brick with transverse arches carrying the roof timbers. Now preserved by the Redundant Churches Fund.

SALISBURY. The *Cathedral* was restored by G.G. Scott from 1863 to remedy the damage of Wyatt's 1789 restoration. Subsequent changes of taste have swept away most of Scott's fittings save the pulpit and bishop's throne. In the S choir aisle one window at W end by Burne-Jones (1878) and a good pair further E by Holiday (1881 and c 1892). In the N transept, monument to R.C. Hoare (1841) by R.C. Lucas, a Salisbury boy who became a successful sculptor and notorious over a bust bought by the royal museum in Berlin as a Leonardo but claimed by many to be the work of Lucas, though never proven. In the S transept tomb of Major J.H. Jacob (1863; G.E. Street), ornate alabaster and mosaic table tomb. The centre of the town is Market Place with *Library*, well converted from Market Hall (1859), and *Lloyds Bank* (1869), rich stone front of former Wiltshire and Dorset Bank. In Exeter St, E of the cathedral, *RC church* (1847; A.W. Pugin), a very minor work but with E and two S windows by Pugin, made by Hardman. In St. Nicholas Road, off Exeter St, *St. Nicholas' Hospital* (partly rebuilt by Butterfield), the Hiram's Hospital of Trollope's 'The Warden'. Trollope's Barchester is a blend of Salisbury and Winchester. From the Market Place to SW, High St, at N end, *County Hotel* (1874), stone, Italian Gothic, to S at W end of Crane St, *Church House* (15C and 1887; G.R. Crickmay), the 1887 river front all half-timber and tile, and, to E in New St, *College Chambers* (1871; A. Bothams), polychrome brick.

St. Mary's and St. Nicholas' Church (1841–45; T.H. Wyatt and D. Brandon), Wilton

To W, off A30, at **Bemerton**, *St. John's Church* (1860; T.H. Wyatt), a lavish estate church built for the Herberts of Wilton with good carved work and E and W windows of c 1860. A colourful reredos (c 1900) in the Arts and Crafts vein by Nellie Warre, the rector's daughter. At **Wilton**, beyond, one of the grandest estate churches in the country, *St. Mary's and St. Nicholas' Church* (1841–45; Wyatt and Brandon), built for Sidney Herbert, Secretary at War and Florence Nightingale's supporter during the Crimean War. The church is a North Italian Romanesque basilica translated to England and filled with genuine Italian marbles and Cosmati work as well as exceptionally good carving of c 1845 and E end mosaics of c 1900. Outstanding imported medieval glass. Tomb of Lord Herbert and his mother with effigies carved by J.B. Philip (c 1862). At **Bishopstone**, 4m S of Wilton, the *church* has in the S transept the memorial (1844; A.W.N. Pugin) to Rev. G. Montgomery (see above), Gothic tomb chest with Pugin stained glass above. 3m SE of Salisbury, off A36, at **Alderbury**, *church* (1858; S.S. Teulon), the spire rising from a four-gabled tower. 1m N, on the old Salisbury Rd, *St. Marie's Grange* (1835; A.W.N. Pugin), Pugin's own house, a statement of faith in the revived Gothic, built in diapered brick with towers and chapel, all on a small scale. It was enlarged c 1841 after Pugin had left but possibly to his design. Just W of Alderbury, *Longford Castle*, the extraordinary triangular 16C house of Sir Thomas Gorges, altered and partly restored 1870–80 (A. Salvin), who recreated the elaborate NW front and filled in the triangular central court.

SWINDON. Very much the largest town in Wiltshire, the creation of the Great Western Railway after 1839 and location of the railway's engineering works. All this is New Swindon. On the hill to the S is the old town with a prominent spired *church* (1851; G.G. Scott) and late Georgian style *Market Hall* (1853) with hefty tower (1866; Wilson and Willcox). New Swindon centres on the *works*, mostly later 19C, the last built the most attractive in contrasting red and blue brick. All this is best seen from the train. The station is only a fragment of the original. Also best seen from the train is the *church* (1843; G.G. Scott) where the tower and spire are set on the N side, the passengers' view being thought more important than that of the inhabitants. Between the station and the church is the *railway village* (c 1850–53), one of the few 19C attempts to give workers' housing architectural dignity and an overall plan. The plan a severe grid and the houses stone faced, mostly two-storey rising to three at the corners. The stone came from the excavation of the Box Tunnel further up the line. The *Railway Museum* is housed in a much larger building, originally a lodging house for 'navvies' or itinerant labourers. N of Swindon, off A419, at **Blunsdon St. Andrew**, *Blunsdon Abbey* (1860; E.J. Mantell), ruins of a castellated house, probably more dramatic ruined than it ever was complete. *Church* nearby rebuilt (1864–68; W. Butterfield) with good E window glass by Butterfield. Further N, 3m NE of Cricklade, **Marston Meysey** *church* (1874; J. Brooks), a rare country church by Brooks, very simple but with vaulted chancel. Brooks also built the vicarage and the school at Meysey Hampton (1872). S of Swindon, within the new town, **Coate**, on A345, was the boyhood home of Richard Jefferies whose 'Bevis' (1882) describes the area. Coate Farm is now a Jefferies museum.

TROWBRIDGE. A361 6m SW of Melksham. The county town but essentially a cloth-manufacturing centre from the 15C to early this century. In the centre, *Town Hall* (1887; A.S. Goodridge), quite lavish in the 'Northern Renaissance' style of Collcutt's Wakefield Town Hall, Yorkshire. Nice carved reliefs and 'visual aids' like the truncheon over the old police office. Next door, facade of *Market Hall* (1861; C.E. Davis), round arches with admonitory texts intertwined in foliage. Off Castle St in Court St the best series of early 19C mills surviving. In Fore St, *National Westminster Bank* (1851), palazzo style to compete with the magnificent early 18C merchants houses around. *No. 5* (former mill offices c 1864) has an Italian Gothic stone front. Similar mill office buildings in Stallard St over the river (1878; W. Smith). Messrs Bowyers' main offices are by the river in the converted *Studley Mill* (1860), red-brick Gothic with, actually over the river, a rare survival of a brick drying shed for the teasels used in knapping the cloth. At the top of Stallard St, *Holy Trinity Church* (1838; A.F. Livesay), very solid lancet Gothic with a plaster vault on iron columns. N of the parish church, Church St, *Tabernacle chapel* (1882; Paull and Bonella), handsome Perp. with an earlier chapel behind, the lancet windows very long and filled with iron lattice glazing. At the top of Union St a passage leads left to *St. Thomas' Church* (1868; W. Smith), an unusual Greek-cross plan in rock-faced Gothic, the interior quite splendid with four great stone ribs carrying the roof over the crossing space. Very shallow chancel (indicating Evangelical origins) with High Victorian Gothic fittings. On and N of the Hilperton Rd, A361, various large mid 19C houses of cloth magnates, notably *Highfield*, Hilperton Rd, and *Rodwell Hall*, Victoria Rd.

WARMINSTER. A36 7m S of Trowbridge. A long main street with, at the top of the hill, *Town Hall* (1832; E. Blore), the detail copied from

Longleat. The next building up, with Jacobean gables, was the *Literary and Scientific Institution* (1838; E. Blore). On A36, to the SE, **Boreham** *church* (1865; G.E. Street), a severe design with plain tall lancets. Good fittings and remarkable tile mosaic decoration to the walls (1911–15; C.E. Ponting, made by Powell's). At the roadside, school and handsome lychgate (1872–74; Street). Off A36, to S, at **Sutton Veny**, exceptional *church* (1866-68; J.L. Pearson), a most harmonious design based on English 14C precedent, crowned by a central tower and spire. An important church in Pearson's work, marking the return to English Gothic after his experiments with High Victorian polychromy and toughness. The chancel is vaulted with fine stained glass by Clayton and Bell and bands of painted decoration in deep red monochrome. Further E, on A36, **Heytesbury** *church*, a 13C church with very fine chancel details restored 1865–67 by Butterfield for Lord Heytesbury. Butterfield added the subtle coloured line decoration over the E wall and chancel side walls and the good bright glass by A. Gibbs. S of Warminster, A350, **Longbridge Deverill** *church* should be visited for the memorial font in the Thynne chapel by Alfred Gilbert (c 1900), a most improbably tall font in sinuous bronze supporting and surrounding an alabaster bowl. 6m S at **East Knoyle**, *Clouds* (1881 and 1889; Philip Webb), set above the village to W, was Webb's largest house, a personal synthesis of Queen Anne motifs, round arches over the windows and Gothic shafts between, all capped by big brick and stone striped gables, sadly now removed along with other details. To the E at **Fonthill Gifford**, estate *church* (1866; T.H. Wyatt) of the Marquess of Westminster's demolished Fonthill House. Rich carving and a picturesque spire. Fonthill is a graveyard of six important houses, including William Beckford's fantastic Fonthill Abbey (1796–1812), built on various sites between the 16C and 1904, all now gone. SW of Longbridge Deverill, B3095 leads through **Kingston Deverill**, with an attractive *church* (1846; Manners and Gill), to **Mere** where the *church* has good Pre-Raphaelite glass (1865; H. Holiday) in the aisle W windows. At **Zeals**, A303, 2m W, an early *church* by G.G. Scott (1845). Off A362, W of Warminster, *Longleat*, the great Elizabethan mansion of the Thynnes, later Marquesses of Bath. The Victorian interest is the series of lavish Italian style interiors through the state rooms carried out for the 4th Marquess in the 1870s. Heavy Venetian style ceilings with painted panels and painted friezes mostly by Italian artists under the firm of J.D. Crace give an extraordinary opulence. **Westbury**. A350 4m N of Warminster. Victorian Westbury was mostly the creation of A. Laverton, clothier of Angel Mill, Edward St, and his architect, W.J. Stent. From the S end of Edward St, in Bratton Rd, *schools* (1884), *Laverton Institute* (1872), Venetian Gothic well handled in red brick and stone, and *Prospect Square* (c 1869), a picturesque group of almshouses and cottages apparently built by Laverton after unsuccessfully standing for Parliament and discovering that his opponent had threatened eviction to tenants voting for Laverton. Further out, in the *cemetery* (1857; E. Bruton) splendid spired mausoleum (c 1870) with a tall vaulted octagonal chamber. At **Heywood**, A350, 2m N, *Heywood House* (1837; H. Eginton), early Jacobean revival, well detailed. 2m W of Westbury at **Dilton Marsh**, large neo-Norman *church* (1844; T.H. Wyatt), one of the more impressive works in this style, if bleak inside. To SW, A3098, at **Chapmanslade**, small *church* (1866–67; G.E. Street), simple design, the chancel marked from the nave by subtle changes in string course and ridge tiles. Good fittings.

NORTH YORKSHIRE

HARROGATE. A61 17m N of Leeds. Victorian spa town, the 'Cheltenham of the North', the waters known since the 16C but only really developed in the 19C. There were two centres, Low Harrogate, the modern centre, by the sulphur springs and gardens, and High Harrogate, ¾m E, with iron springs. High Harrogate developed first with *Granby Hotel* (c 1820, enlarged since) in Granby Rd, *County Hotel* (c 1830), Devonshire Place, and *Christ Church* (1831; J. Oates), built in solid lancet style with galleried interior. Numerous memorials to visitors whom the waters did not help. Low Harrogate developed slowly as the main centre. Byron stayed at the *Crown Hotel* in 1806. A *pump room* was built over the spring in 1842 (I. Shutt), now the Royal Pump Room Museum, and the handsome late classical *White Hart Hotel*, Valley Drive, was built in 1846. The Valley Gardens date from the 1880s, and later came the two principal public buildings of the spa, the over detailed *Royal Baths* (1893–97; Baggalay and Bristowe), designed to compete with continental rivals, and the *Royal Hall*, built as the Kursaal (1902–03; F. Matcham and R.J. Beale) with much cheerful exterior detail and a splendid auditorium with coved ceiling and unusual arrangement of six boxes each side of the stalls, rather than stacked vertically. The largest hotels came at the turn of the century, the *Hotel Majestic* (1900; G.D. Martin) particularly vast in brick and stone with domed centre. In Oxford St, *Opera House* (1900; J.P. Briggs) with octagonal corner feature and cupola, the auditorium intact and well refurbished. S of the station, Victoria Park, villa suburb of c 1860. The handsome Gothic *Congregational church* (1862; Lockwood and Mawson), Victoria Avenue, exemplifies the dominance of the Nonconformist churches among the Yorkshire manufacturers who had houses here. Sir Titus Salt, of Saltaire, was prominent on the building committee. The outstanding Anglican church is on the later 19C Duchy estate, N of Valley Gardens, *St. Wilfrid's Church* (1905–35; T. and L. Moore), Duchy Rd. A complex and monumental stone building in severe EE, reminiscent of a medieval abbey in the cluster of lower buildings rising up to the high main roof interrupted by a squat tower. Nave and chancel by Temple Moore (1905–14), the E end framed by plain towers, transepts added, to the original design but simplified, in 1924–28 by Leslie Moore, the N transept tower-like, the S apse-ended and scaled like a full chancel. In 1935 the low Lady Chapel was added and a partly cloistered court to SE. Inside the spatial effects are masterly, rib vaulting throughout, the altar set against a triple arch through which the much smaller scale shafts and vaults of the Lady Chapel are seen. The fittings harmonise with the purity of the interior, reticent glass by V. Milner, oak rood screen by Temple Moore (1919).

1m NE of centre, at **Bilton**, *church* (1855; G.G. Scott), EE style. 3m E of Harrogate, **Knaresborough**, where the steep gorge of the river Nidd is spanned by a stone railway *viaduct* (1848; T. Grainger) called, despite its evident picturesqueness, 'one of the most notable railway crimes of England' for the way in which it bisects the town. The parish *church*, much restored in 1870, has good Morris glass (c 1872) in chancel S and S aisle W windows. Among the Slingsby family monuments going back to the 17C, effigy of Sir C. Slingsby (died 1869; J.E. Boehm). 4m E, prominent from A1, *Allerton Hall* (1848–51; J. Firth), blackened stone Gothic to Jacobean mansion. 2½m SE of Harrogate, *Rudding Park* (gardens open to public), handsome Regency house

(1805–24) with exceptionally large Gothic *chapel* (1874; A.E. Purdie) in the grounds, High Victorian with naturalistic carving. Just W, the *Crimple Viaduct* (1848; J.C. Birkinshaw) crosses the valley on 31 stone arches, the tallest 110ft high. 3m SW of Harrogate, B6161, at **Beckwithshaw**, *Moor Park* (1859; Andrews and Delaunay), stone Jacobean style mansion. 4m N of Harrogate, A61, at **Ripley**, estate village rebuilt for the Ingilby family 1827–28 with terraced cottages, all quite modest, the centrepiece the *'Hotel de Ville'* (1854), proudly named Tudor Gothic village hall. *Ripley Castle* (open to public), the 15C to late 18C house of the Ingilby family, has landscaped grounds with picturesque lake created in 1844.

RICHMOND. A6108 31m N of Ripon. Market town at the entrance to Swaledale, dramatically set over the Swale. In the Market Place, *Market Hall* (1854). To NE, *Savings Bank* (1851), a dignified classical front. Station Rd leads out to the disused *station* (1846; G.T. Andrews), very Gothic with porte-cochère disguised as a short cloister. *Richmond School* (1849; G.T. Andrews) has Perp. buildings, the more elaborate part added 1867. 5m SE, off A6136, at Brough Hall, *RC church* (1834) designed by Sir W. Lawson, with the architect I. Bonomi, on the model of the 13C Chapter Library at York Minster. A two-storey building, incorporating a school below, the upper chapel tall and light, exceptionally carefully detailed for the date with shafted windows and carved capitals. E window by Willement (1837). 6m E of Richmond, B6271, at **Bolton-on-Swale**, the *church* has painted plaster decoration and wall tiling of 1877 by W.E. Nesfield in the aesthetic taste, something of a rarity in church decoration.

RIPON. A61 10m N of Harrogate. *Ripon Cathedral* was restored 1862–70 by Sir G.G. Scott, the towers being in danger of collapse. His restoration was criticised for the removal of the tracery in the splendid lancets of the W front, tracery that Scott saw as an unfortunate 14C alteration to the purity of the 13C original. Scott put in the timber vaults of the nave and chancel and restored the 15C choir stalls. In the nave remarkable Arts and Crafts bronze and marble pulpit (1913; H. Wilson), in the chancel high altar and reredos by J.N. Comper (1922). Much 19C glass, E window by Wailes (1854) altered 1896, choir aisle E windows c 1865 (Lavers and Barraud), W window 1886 (Burlison and Grylls). In Cottsgate Hill, N of Market Square, *RC church* (1860–62; J.A. Hansom and E.W. Pugin), remarkable for the tower-like roof of the octagonal chancel. High altar by E.W. Pugin and stained glass in nave by J.H. Pollen (1878) removed from the Marquess of Ripon's chapel at Studley Royal, whence came also the alabaster Lady altar. N of centre, *Training College* (1858; J.B. and W. Atkinson), College Rd, Italianate, and, to NW, former *Bishop's Palace* (1838–39; W. Railton), now Spring Hill Schools, Tudor style with Gothic chapel added 1848 (Railton).

W of the town, the *Studley Royal* estate, the great 18C landscape created 1720–70 by John and William Aislabie, successive owners of the great house, now demolished. The estate passed in 1859 to the 2nd Earl, later Marquess of Ripon, liberal politician, Governor-General of India 1880–84, whose wife decided to build the *church set axially on the great drive that aligns on the towers of Ripon Cathedral to E. Studley Royal church, like Skelton church (see below) E of Ripon built at the same time for Lady Ripon's mother, was designed by William Burges and is unequalled among Victorian estate churches, costing some £50,000 (Butterfield's Keble College Chapel, Oxford, cost

£40,000) and taking seven years to build, 1871–78. As other architects turned to less vigorous models, Burges remained faithful to his High Victorian blend of Early English and Early French models, powerful in detail and allowing the boldest effects of sculptural decoration. The church is conventionally planned with W spire and E end facing the long drive, such that from afar the spire rides over the body of the church, the forceful tracery of the E window already distinct, but, closer to, the full sculptural richness of the E end, with three groups of figures in tabernacles filling the gable, dominates. Inside, no other Victorian church can equal the glowing colour of stained glass, fresco, marble and mosaic, the entire scheme to the theme of 'Paradise Lost and Regained'. The nave is relatively calm, Purbeck marble shafted like Salisbury Cathedral with a fine boarded three-lobed roof. In the chancel, choir and sanctuary are two distinctive square spaces, the one with a pointed barrel roof painted with bands of gilded stars and processional figures of the Te Deum, the other quite beyond the conventions of English Gothic, covered by a gilded and painted wooden dome on pendentives, where cherubim and seraphim surround the gilded crown. The perfection of proportion is achieved by filling the window openings with a veil of tracery, identical on all three sides despite the larger E window. Alabaster wall panelling, mosaic floor representing the Garden of Eden and superb sculpture in the tracery each side, notably the magnificent lion that carries the central shaft on the S side, the use of coloured marbles for the shafts itself creating the vision of heavenly glory to which all the decoration aspires. The stained glass made by W.G. Saunders to designs by Burges, F. Weekes and H.W. Lonsdale is among the finest in Britain, superb in colour, the designs and leading perfectly suited to the medium, the chancel windows illustrating the Book of Revelation. The sculptural work by T. Nicholls perfectly counterpoints Burges' architecture, notably the monumental Tennessee marble font inset with four bronze figures of the Ages of Man. Metalwork too, especially the vestry door, given by Burges, is of startling vitality. The only addition is the marble memorial to Lord and Lady Ripon (1908). The *cottages* by the church (1873) are also by Burges.

4m SE of Ripon, the *Newby Hall* estate (open to public), owned from 1859 by Lady M. Vyner, cousin and mother-in-law of the Marquess of Ripon of Studley Royal. In 1870 Lady Vyner's son was kidnapped in Greece and murdered before the ransom could be paid. She decided to use the unspent ransom money to build two churches, the one at Studley Royal (see above), his sister's estate, the other in his memory at **Skelton** on the Newby estate, both designed by W. Burges. Skelton *church* (1871–76), dedicated to Christ the Consoler, lacks the overwhelming colour of Studley Royal, displaying instead a heavily modelled pale stone interior shafted in black marble in the nave and enriched with excellent sculpture by T. Nicholls. Colour comes from the outstanding stained glass by W.G. Saunders, designed by F. Weekes, and from the marble introduced in the chancel shafts. Exterior and interior details similar to Studley Royal, the emphatic tracery of the E and W windows, the sculpted E gable outside, and inside the veil-like inner tracery to the sanctuary windows, but quite different is the contrast between the high nave with its hefty shafts and massive corbels and the low rib-vaulted chancel, the wall over the chancel arch filled with sculpture of the Ascension by Nicholls. By Nicholls also the low reredos, the fearsome lions on the organ loft and the marble font with its shrine-like mahogany cover. Outside the E end, a tall Gothic octagonal shrine. Burges also added certain garden sculpture (1876) at Newby Hall, the forecourt piers, the sculpted feature at the end of the statue walk and part of the layout of the S parterre.

5m NE of Ripon, off A61, **Baldersby St. James**, *estate village* built for Viscount Downe of Baldersby Park by W. Butterfield (1855–59), church, rectory, agent's house, school, two pairs of cottages and a short terrace are the whole of it, loosely and informally grouped around the church spire. The buildings show a hierarchy of detail, materials and embellishment increasing up the social scale, though all have in common the half-hipped roofs and battered chimneys. The simplest houses show no ostensibly Gothic details at all, for medieval dress was not an inescapable necessity for Gothic Revival architects who looked to the Middle Ages as much for freedom in planning, asymmetrical design and picturesque massing. The cottages are in brick, the vicarage and school in stone with some half-timber, the church entirely stone outside, conventional Gothic window shapes appear only on the school and church where their use would be appropriate to study or worship. The interior of the church is fully polychrome, of red brick banded with stone and increasing in richness towards the chancel with its low stone screen, tiled floor and alabaster reredos, one of Butterfield's best coloured interiors. E window by O'Connor, W window by Wailes, aisle and clerestory glass by F. Preedy. 13m NW of Ripon, W of Masham, at **Healey**, *church* (1848; E.B. Lamb), one of the group built for the Frankland family of Thirkleby (see Thirsk below p. 456), with heavily timbered roofs and the crossing space dramatically left open right up into the spire.

SCARBOROUGH. A64 40m NE of York. Seaside resort from the 18C though famous for its medicinal waters even earlier. The old town is by the harbour under the castle spreading SW around the bay to the early 19C resort overlooking the steep *Valley Gardens*, a remarkable piece of romantic landscaping (c 1830; R. Sharp). Overlooking the valley, *The Crescent* and *Belvoir Terrace* (1833–57; R. Sharp), fine neoclassical designs, and in front, three (of a planned nine) classical villas, the *Natural History Museum* (1835), *Londesborough Lodge* (1837) and the *Art Gallery* (1847), the last more Italianate than neo-classical. In the valley, the circular *Rotunda Museum* (1828; R. Sharp), built to house the geological collections of William Smith (1769–1839), the galleried exhibition room inside still much as first designed. Overhead, the *Cliff Bridge* (1826–27) joins the old town to the South Cliff, 70ft above the valley bottom. To the N, the *Grand Hotel* (1863–67; C. Brodrick), larger and more vertiginous than the Scarborough cliffs, in yellow and red brick, the vast bulk of the main hotel set on top of a four-storey basement, itself on terraces above the sea. In its heyday this was one of the largest hotels in Britain, yet it was open only in July and August, when the wealthy West Yorkshire industrialists took their holidays. The style has loose affinities with the French Second Empire mode then fashionable for hotels all across Europe, but Brodrick's elongated domes at the four corners with their 'widow's walk' balconies on top strike a note of fantasy, especially when seen on a misty day. The *Town Hall* (1852; H. Wyatt) was built as a private villa and taken over in 1894. On the main E–W axis between the station and the old harbour, the larger late 19C commercial buildings appear in Newborough and Westborough. On Vernon Rd, to S, the *Public Library* (1840), neo-classical, built as the Odd Fellows Hall, and the much decayed tower of *Christ Church* (1826–28; Atkinson and Sharp). Scarborough *station* (1846; G.T. Andrews) has a stone front of pedimented centre and pavilions, but this dignified facade acts as the podium for most oddly proportioned Baroque clock tower, added 1884. The original train-shed survives, amid the later extensions. The *Pavilion Hotel* (1870; Stewart and Barry) overlooking the station was the largest of the rival hotels to the Grand, decked out with Second Empire pavilion roofs.

Valley Bridge Rd crosses the valley towards the southern part of the town, developed from the 1840s. The earliest part is the Esplanade on the South Cliff with stucco terraces (1845) overlooking the *Spa* (1877–80; Verity and Hunt), an entertainments complex with theatre, ballroom and bandstands, a French pavilion roof over the main entrance and square-domed pavilions each end of the terrace. Oval *bandstand* of 1913 (E. Cooper). The gardens climbing up the cliff were laid out for the previous Spa building of 1867 by Joseph Paxton. Behind, in Albion Rd, *St. Martin's Church* (1861–62; G.F. Bodley), severe High Victorian exterior with plate-traceried windows and saddleback-roofed tower, a strong silhouette without extraneous detail. The outside is no preparation for the interior, the stained glass, one of the first commissions of William Morris's firm, and the painted decoration, partly by Morris and Co , partly by Bodley, make this one of the outstanding examples of Pre-Raphaelite church decoration. The Morris glass dates from 1861 to 1873, to an overall theme, from the W end, Adam and Eve (F.M. Brown) and Annunciation (Burne-Jones), progressing to the E end, Crucifixion (F.M. Brown) and Parable of the Vineyard (D.G. Rossetti). The pulpit has ten painted panels, wholly Pre-Raphaelite in a simple wood framework decorated with child-like patterns. Other painted decoration has faded or been heavily repainted (E end) but the delicate linear quality of the early pattern designs is still discernible. Bodley added the W narthex in 1879, NE Lady Chapel in 1902 and fittings in the delicate style of his later years; typical the reredos and rood screen of c 1890. His organ case is a spectacular example of Victorian church woodwork. By the W front, the former *vicarage* (1867; G.F. Bodley), a very early example of moulded brick detail in a late 17C manner, a prototype of the Queen Anne style. The play of near symmetry in the gabled road front is subtly done. On Ramshill Rd, spired *Congregational church* (1864–68; Lockwood and Mawson), one of a number of impressive chapels in the town, built for the West Yorkshire visitors. Expansive mid to late Victorian suburbs lie on both sides of Ramshill Rd and Filey Rd, the Westbourne estate, to W, laid out from 1862 by Paxton with *Holy Trinity Church* (1880; E. Christian) displaying a blunt broad apse and banded slate roof to the slope of Westbourne Grove. On Filey Rd, *Scarborough College* (1900; Hall, Cooper and Davis), free Tudor.

N from the centre, Queen St leads up to Castle Rd, past the *RC convent* (1884; F. Walters). On Castle Rd, *RC church* (1858; E. Goldie) with good stained glass and apse painted decoration. The parish *church* was restored c 1850 (E. Christian) with some bright glass of that date. Anne Bronte is buried in the churchyard extension beyond the chancel ruins. By the castle, *Castle-by-the-Sea*, a castellated villa that was the home of the painter A. Grimshaw from 1876. Some development of the 1840s to the N, overlooking North Bay, always less fashionable than the South Cliff.

5m W of Scarborough, A170, at **Wykeham**, *church, vicarage* and *school* (1853–55) by W. Butterfield for Viscount Downe of Baldersby, grouped in relation to the tower of the old church, to which Butterfield added the spire, the vicarage an especially good example of interlocked geometrical shapes. 9m W, **Pickering**, market town at the foot of the moors. From here the *North Yorks Moors Railway* (1836) has been rescued as a private line, and runs excursions up to Goathland. In Potter Hill, fine free Tudor group of *RC church* and hall (1911; L. Stokes), in stone, L-plan on a sloping site. In the church, carved stone font by Eric Gill (c 1910) of superb quality. 6m W, at **Appleton-le-Moors**, powerful High Victorian *church (1863–64; J.L. Pearson), not large but massively detailed with a single roof covering nave and aisles, the tower and stone pyramid spire breaking through the roof slope. Inside, Early French detail is richly applied with a shafted arcade round the apse and a powerful cornice dividing wall from roof. Subtle stone polychromy and excellent sgraffito plaster decoration in red and white (Clayton and Bell). *Appleton Hotel* was the parsonage (1865; Pearson). In the village, the *school* (1865; Pearson) with plate tracery and some half-timber. 7m SE of Scarborough, **Filey**, seaside resort. The parish *church* has some good 19C glass. On the cliffs, *Northcliffe* (1891; W. Brierley), substantial stone mansion in the Yorkshire Jacobean style. 12m W, A64, at **East Heslerton**, *church* (1877; G.E. Street), the most northerly of the group of churches in the old East Riding built by Street for Sir Tatton Sykes of Sledmere, of which the others, though now divided between Humberside and North Yorkshire, are described with Sledmere (see Great Driffield, Humberside, pp. 162–3). East Heslerton is an excellent composition with apsed chancel roof rising above the nave, the chancel walls elaborated with buttresses, a hint of the vaulting within. N tower turning octagonal at the bell stage and capped with a stone spire. Glass by Clayton and Bell.

SELBY. A19 14m S of York. *Selby Abbey* was extensively but not harshly restored after a fire in 1906 by J.O. Scott, the crossing tower rebuilt 1908 and the S transept added in 1912, to replace one destroyed in 1690. Fittings mostly of 1908 and later, but fine W window and N aisle second window from W by Heaton, Butler and Bayne (c 1870). *RC church*, W of centre, quite ornate Dec. of 1856 (C. Hansom) with prominent spire.

7m S, A1041, at **Carlton**, *Carlton Towers (open to public), wildly impractical Gothic mansion created from an early 17C house with late 18C stable wing for the 9th Lord Beaumont, heir to an old Yorkshire Catholic family, who in a romantic short life fought for the Prussians, the Carlists in Spain and the British in Zululand, bankrupted the estate in building works and financial speculation and attempted at Carlton Towers to create a mansion suitable to a family with ancestry back to the time of Bannockburn. In 1873–74 E.W. Pugin began a reconstruction that recased the 17C house and stable wing for economy in grey cement with stone details, most extravagant in the almost Spanish Gothic main doorway. Three utterly different towers provide the romantic silhouette across the flat landscape, but this was only intended as a beginning, the house was to have been doubled in size by the addition of a chapel and great hall connected at right angles by a functionally useless grand stair in a monumental tower. Pugin however was dismissed and the decorative work inside the existing parts entrusted to J.F. Bentley (1875–77). The interiors are the outstanding feature of the house, three large staterooms in the former stable block with the bedrooms unceremoniously pushed behind. Bentley was a master of Gothic design, delicate and intricate in detail, fertile in invention. Painted decoration, carved woodwork and stonework, metalwork from door fittings to chandeliers, stained glass and hangings were all to his design. The principal interior is the drawing-room, the walls in plaster, moulded and gilded to look like stamped leather above dark Gothic panelling inset with painted scenes. Massively beamed but delicately coloured ceiling, the frieze set with gilded crowned Bs, and monumental fireplace, exquisitely coloured, displaying the 36 quarterings of Lord Beaumont's arms, the display of lineage an appropriate centrepiece for the whole redecoration. The chandeliers and door ironmongery are particularly fine metalwork designs. The adjoining card-room has complete stencilled decoration but the picture gallery beyond is unpainted, where money presumably ran out. In the village, opposite the gates, a row of *cottages* (1876; Bentley) in simple Domestic Revival style, an Anglican *church* (1861–66; J.B. Atkinson) built by the widow of the 8th Lord Beaumont, who had abandoned Catholicism, and a *RC church* (1840–42; Weightman and Hadfield) built by a relative of the 8th Lord who objected to his apostasy. 3m W, at **Hensall**, *church*, *vicarage* and *school* (1853–54; W. Butterfield), one of the three sets of simple brick buildings built for the 7th Viscount Downe in the area (for Cowick and Pollington see Scunthorpe, Humberside p. 167), good examples of Butterfield's most economical work. In the church, tiled reredos and font cover notably Butterfieldian.

SETTLE. A65 30m SE of Kendal. Pennine town, the departure point for the Midland Railway's *Settle–Carlisle line (1875), the most arduous railway construction in England, crossing 72 miles of wild country, and built entirely by pick-and-shovel labour. In the Market Square, *Town Hall* (1832; G. Webster), Elizabethan style. George Birkbeck (1776–1841), initiator of adult education for the working classes, founder of the Mechanics Institutes and of Birkbeck College, London, was born in Settle. His memorial is in **Giggleswick** *church* across the river. *Giggleswick School* was founded in 1512 with buildings from 1867 (Paley and Austin) in grey stone Elizabethan to Jacobean style. Splendid green-domed *chapel* (1897–1902; T.G. Jackson), Gothic intermingled with Romanesque in red and cream stone. Interior with good Arts and Crafts sgraffito work on the crossing arches and mosaic decoration in the dome. 10m NW, B6480, at **Lower Bentham**, *church* restored 1876–78 (R. Norman Shaw), almost completely rebuilt with fittings by Shaw, organ case (1886) and font (1890) by W.R. Lethaby, the font exceptionally fine Arts and Crafts work in alabaster, simple drum form with tendril frieze, the font cover most exotic, six fins carved with plant motifs carrying an openwork spire surmounted by a globe. *Rectory* (1884; R. Norman Shaw), stone and roughcast Tudor, now the school. 10m N of Settle, on the Settle–Carlisle line, *Ribblehead Viaduct* (1875; J.S. Crossley), the largest viaduct of the 23 on the line, 24 stone arches marching over the empty moor. Just N, the *Blea Moor Tunnel*, 1½m long.

SKIPTON. A65 25m NW of Leeds. Market town, centre of the Craven district. At top of the High St, *Town Hall* (1862), Italianate, and *Library* (1910). On Gargrave Rd, A65, *School* (1871; Paley and Austin), stone Tudor style buildings. 3m W of Skipton, A59, *Broughton Hall*, 18C house with entrance front of 1838–41 (G. Webster). A fine Italian garden survives with formal parterre of patterned box hedges (1855–57; W.A. Nesfield), statuary and pretty Italian pavilion (1855; Andrews and Delaunay). On S front a large colonnaded conservatory (1855; Andrews and Delaunay), triple-roofed, the taller centre fronted with a glass-domed rotunda. 3m W, N of A59, *Gledstone Hall* (1923–27; E. Lutyens), one of the last country houses, Ionic porticoed with steep roofs and long windows in the French manner, excellently proportioned if cooler and less inventive than Lutyens' earlier works. Formal forecourt and gardens with pavilions, the S front overlooking an axial water garden. 5m E of Skipton, B6160, *Bolton Abbey*, the priory church founded 1150 ruined in its E parts but the 13C nave intact, restored 1875–77 (G.E. Street). The estate belonged to the Dukes of Devonshire, the churchyard cross commemorates Lord Frederick Cavendish, assassinated in Dublin 1882. *Bolton Hall* is the former priory gatehouse extended in early and mid 19C.

THIRSK. A19 23m N of York. In the Market Place, stone-fronted *bank* (c 1900; Bedford and Kitson). To S, in Castlegate, Italianate *Savings Bank* (1849) and *RC church* in polychrome brick with good glass of c 1867 inside. **Sowerby** *church*, to S, has hefty neo-Norman work at the crossing, probably by E.B. Lamb (1840–41), the timber lantern added 1879 (C.H. Fowler). 4m NW of Thirsk, at **Kirby Wiske**, Sion Hill Hall (1912; W. Brierley), large and accomplished neo-Georgian house, reminiscent of the work of Lutyens. 5m SW of Thirsk, A168, at **Topcliffe**, the *church* (1855; G.T. Andrews) has one of Burne-Jones' earliest stained glass works (1860) in a S window of the chancel, made by Lavers and Barraud. Only the Annunciation panel is by Burne-Jones, in a vivid and strongly drawn manner more akin to Rossetti than to Burne-Jones' later work. 2m E, at **Dalton**, *church* (1868; W. Butterfield), built for Viscount Downe of Baldersby, stone outside, the interior polychrome, like Baldersby (see Ripon above p. 452) on a smaller scale, with timber screen marking the chancel arch and heavy carved and inlaid reredos. Outstanding series of windows by Morris and Co. (1868–69). 3m SE, at **Sessay**, estate village of Viscount Downe of Baldersby. W. Butterfield designed some plain brick cottages (c 1850), precursors of the estate village at Baldersby in their hipped roof shapes, battered chimneys and plain vernacular detail. The *church* was rebuilt by Butterfield (1847–49) in Dec. style with shingled spire and much play of different roof lines. 3m SE of Thirsk, two churches by E.B. Lamb, in complete contrast to Butterfield's work. **Bagby** *church* (1862), built for the Frankland family, has a central crossing roofed like a malthouse from which narrower transepts, chancel and nave extend, the intention being to achieve a large central preaching space. **Thirkleby** *church* (1850), also built for the Frankland family, is much larger, and Lamb's oddities of proportion loom larger, roofs overwhelming walls, spire overwhelming tower, and the junctions of parts like accidental collisions.

14m E of Thirsk, A170, **Helmsley**, market town at the gates of *Duncombe Park* (now a school), early 18C Baroque mansion with wings in matching style by Sir C. Barry (1843) for the 2nd Lord Feversham. The interior is Baroque reconstruction (1879; W. Young) after a fire. The lodge, by Helmsley Castle, also by Barry. In Helmsley Market Place, canopied *memorial* to Lord Feversham (1869; G.G. Scott) with statue by M. Noble. *Town Hall* (1901; Temple Moore) in late 17C style. Lord Feversham rebuilt the parish *church* (1866–67); Banks and Barry) in Norman to EE style, heavily detailed, the interior slightly lightened by Temple Moore c 1900, with high altar and painted N aisle roof. Helmsley had a vast parish stretching up into the moorland to the N, and the vicar from 1870–1913, the Rev. C.N. Gray, had built a series of delightful small and rugged stone churches by G.G. Scott Jr and his successor, Temple Moore. 2m N, **Carlton** *church* (1881; T. Moore), very simple lancet style with red and green painted woodwork inside. 3m further N, **Eastmoors** *church* (1876–82; G.G. Scott Jr), on a tiny scale, in a wild spot, cleverly planned with aisle designed to double as a schoolroom and pretty painted decoration. **Pockley** *church* (1876; G.G. Scott Jr), on the next lane N off A170, is more substantial, with fittings by Moore and painted chancel roof. NW of Helmsley, B1257, at **Rievaulx**, by the abbey ruins, Temple Moore rebuilt the chapel by the gatehouse as the parish *church* (1907). 7m further up Bilsdale, at **Cresset**, *church* (1896; Temple Moore). At **Sproxton**, 2m S of Helmsley, the *church* was a 17C chapel dismantled and re-erected (1878; G.G. Scott Jr) for Lord Feversham, with furnishings in 17C style by Temple Moore, an unusual fidelity to a period then not greatly appreciated. 3m SW, *Ampleforth Abbey*, monastery and school set up here in 1802 by the English Benedictines refuged in Lorraine in 1619 and displaced by the French Revolution. A confused group of buildings dominated by the tower of the *church* (1922–61; Giles G. Scott), a fine design, externally Gothic but with Romanesque shallow domes inside. The long period of building shows in the steady elimination of carved detail. The original late 18C house survives, much altered, though everything since has been Gothic. College buildings (1861; C.F. Hansom) and Monastery (1894–98; B. Smith).

9m N of Thirsk, A168, **Northallerton**, the county town, with handsome brick and stone Wren style *County Hall* (1904–15; W. Brierley). 7m N, A167, at **Great Smeaton**, *Smeaton Manor* (1877–79; Philip Webb) reinterprets Queen Anne themes in a memorably personal way, the main front in warm red brick dominated by a sweeping hipped roof, more Dutch than English in its scale. While symmetrical, the front rhythms of window spacing are more intricate than any Queen Anne original, the ground floor projected slightly under a tiled roof, like a very shallow loggia with two arches left open and three filled in and glazed. Stables by Webb also. The house was one of several works by Webb for members of the Bell family, chemical and steel manufacturers of Middlesbrough. Sir Lowthian Bell's house at **East Rounton**, 5m E, has been demolished, though Webb's *school* (1876) survives, a *village hall* (1906) by G. Jack, Webb's successor, and some estate cottages. In the *church* (1884; R.J. Johnson), memorial to Gertrude Bell (1868–1926), Lowthian Bell's granddaughter, traveller and diplomat, instrumental in founding the kingdom of Iraq in 1920. 3m N, A19, *Crathorne Hall* (1903–07; Sir E. George and Yeates), unexpectedly grandiose Edwardian stone mansion, now an hotel, the garden front with Palladian attached portico but the entrance front 17C style with cupola-capped stair towers in the angles. To SE, at the foot of the Cleveland Hills, **Carlton** *church* is by Temple Moore (1896) and **Kirby** *church*, 3m E, has a chancel by Moore (1900) added to a church of 1815.

WHITBY. A171 20m N of Scarborough. Fishing town and resort, fictionalised as 'Monkshaven' in Mrs Gaskell's 'Sylvia's Lovers' (1863) and the setting for part of Bram Stoker's 'Dracula'. The Victorian West Cliff (1848) was a speculation of G. Hudson, the railway tycoon, developed by others after his ruin. Whitby *Station* (1847; G.T. Andrews) was given a handsome arcaded front as an advertisement for the new resort. *East Terrace* (c 1850) by J. Dobson, Hudson's architect, was to be the model, but Hudson's financial troubles intervened, and the later terraces are less impressive. *St. Hilda's Church* (1884–86; R.J. Johnson) stands well at the end of Hudson St, large scale with centre tower and Dec. detail. Good fittings, including much Kempe glass. In the old town along the Esk, on Quay Rd, *Yorkshire Bank* (1841), stone, late classical front. Further S, *Midland Bank* (1891; Demaine and Brierley), gabled Elizabethan. Whitby parish church, up Church

Steps, is the outstanding example of a church that the Victorians did not restore, crowded with high pews and galleries. Just W of the town, the Esk valley is crossed by the 13-arch *Larpool Viaduct* (1885), carrying the disused line to Scarborough 125ft above the river. 5m SE, **Robin Hood's Bay**, picturesque fishing village steeply above the harbour. Parish *church* (1868–70; G.E. Street), severe and well-proportioned stone-apsed building with saddleback tower and vaulted chancel. Excellent stained glass by H. Holiday. 3m NE of Whitby, A174, *Mulgrave Castle*, 18C house castellated and made romantic c 1804–14 (W. Atkinson) for the 1st Earl of Mulgrave and set in an appropriately romantic landscape, from designs by Repton of 1792. The *church* at **Lythe**, sensitively rebuilt (1910; W. Tapper) with new tower, S aisle and vaulted S chapel.

YORK. *York Minster* has Victorian work by S. Smirke (the nave roof 1841), G.E. Street (transept restoration 1872–80) and G.F. Bodley (nave flying buttresses 1902), more significant are the 19C monuments, none outstanding. In the nave, effigies of Archbishops Vernon-Harcourt and Musgrave (1855 and 1863; M. Noble), in N transept, *Admiral Cradock* (died 1914; F.W. Pomeroy), alabaster and bronze, and in vestibule to Chapter House, effigy of Dr Beckwith (died 1843; J. Leyland). Chapter House vault with painted decoration by T. Willement (1844). The S transept, gutted by fire 1984, had effigies to Archbishop Thompson (1896; Bodley) and Dean Duncombe (1882; Street). In the choir, fittings and roof by Sir R. Smirke (1829–32) after a fire in 1829. At the E end, presbytery altar 1905 (G.F. Bodley) and N aisle altar with terracotta sculpture by G. Tinworth (1879). S of the W front, *Boer War Memorial* (1905; G.F. Bodley). Duncombe Place was cut through 1859–64, opening out the W front of the Minster, the *Dean Court Hotel* was three Gothic houses (c 1864), the *RC church* (1862–64; G. Goldie) is acidly High Victorian, Early French Gothic in rude contrast to the Minster, and the *York Dispensary*, on corner of Blake St (1899; E. Kirby), makes an equally startling contrast in bright red brick, Gothic, with much carved and moulded detail. *St. Leonard's Place* (1844; Robinson and Andrews), a stuccoed crescent with cast-iron balcony runs NW to Exhibition Square. *Theatre Royal* (1880; G. Styan), very Gothic to the front, hardly tasteful, but memorable. The interior (1902; F. Tugwell) has pretty Art Nouveau decoration to the balcony fronts. In Exhibition Square, *City Art Gallery* (1879; E. Taylor), Italianate with collection of paintings by W. Etty, born in York, whose *statue* (1910) is outside. Opposite, *De Grey Rooms* (1841–42), stuccoed Italianate, built as an Officer's Mess. A lane runs from the Square to Museum Gardens, laid out around the ruins of St. Mary's Abbey for the Yorkshire Philosophical Society after 1837. The Society's premises are now the *Yorkshire Museum* (1827–30; W. Wilkins), Greek Doric with Corinthian columned hall. Extension in matching Greek, but built of reinforced concrete (1912; E.R. Tate). Gothic *lodge* (1874; G.F. Jones) to the gardens. In Museum St, *Yorkshire Club* (1868; C.O. Parnell), mixed Jacobean.

Lendal Bridge (1861–63) by T. Page, designer of Westminster Bridge, London, has Gothic detail. From here, a view of the 15C *Guildhall* and its Gothic extension (1888; E.G. Mawbey). In Lendal, off Museum St, *Post Office* (c 1895; H. Tanner), and then St. Helen's Square, with, on W side, *Yorkshire Insurance* (1840; G.T. Andrews), stone-fronted palazzo, and *Savings Bank* (1829; Watson and Pritchett), curved Corinthian facade. Coney St runs SE to High Ousegate with palazzo style *Midland Bank* (c 1865; J.B. and W. Atkinson) at near end and bright red *Barclays Bank* (1901; E. Kirby), richly Gothic, by All Saints', at NE end. From Pavement, N of the church, Fossgate runs SE to the Foss Bridge, past the glazed tile front of the former *Electric Cinema*. From Foss Bridge, a view upstream of *Leetham's Mill* (1895–96; W.G. Penty), the best industrial building in the city, built between the river Foss and an inlet with battlemented tower facing downstream. From Pavement, Coppergate runs SW to Clifford St, a Victorian creation, with the *Law Courts* (1890–92; H.A. Matear) dominant, in red brick and stone, turretted and gabled with much carved detail. Marbled entrance hall. In York Castle, the *Castle Museum* occupies the old Debtors Prison (1705) and Female Prison (1773–77) with reconstructed street of shopfronts of the 18C and 19C in the Female Prison and an Edwardian street display in the Debtors Prison. Across Lendal Bridge, Station Rd runs up to the disused *Old Station* (1841; G.T. Andrews), for which the tracks came through medieval city wall. Large U-plan terminus with Italianate main front to Tanner Row, a long facade reflecting the departure side, the station *Hotel* at the head of the platform, and the arrival side being added in 1853. By the hotel, former *NE Railway Headquarters* (1906; H. Field), red brick and stone, steeply roofed and grandly scaled, late 17C style. The present *station* (1871–77; T. Prosser) is quite undistinguished outside, but spectacular inside with 800ft long curving *train-shed of four arched parallel roofs on iron Corinthian columns, the largest span some 80ft wide by 50ft high. The *Royal Station Hotel* (1877; W. Peachey) makes up for the external plainness of the station, very large in yellow brick, mixed style, the main interior lounge and stair rising through the building with vistas of cast ironwork. On Leeman Rd, *National Railway Museum*, the most extensive collection of railway exhibits in the country.

Station train-shed (1877; T. Prosser), York

SW of the station, A1036, The Mount, early 19C suburb. *The Mount*

School occupies a handsome stucco villa (c 1850). Beyond, *Elm Bank Hotel*, Mount Vale, has Art Nouveau interiors (1898; G. Walton), by one of the Glasgow contemporaries of C.R. Mackintosh, swirling floral friezes and stained glass, more conventional than Mackintosh or Walton could be. In St. George's Place, *No. 5* (1906; W. Brierley), brick, vernacular revival, built for the architect himself. In Scarcroft Rd, *school* (1896; W. Brierley) the finest of the four Board schools in York by Brierley; freely styled and generously lit, they are models of the type. Others are in Poppleton Rd (1904) and Haxby Rd (1904). SE of central York, at **Heslington**, York University occupies the estate of *Heslington Hall*, 16C brick mansion heavily renewed 1852–55 (P.C. Hardwick). NE from York Minster, in Monkgate, handsome Italianate *County Hospital* (1851; J.B. and W. Atkinson), and, on Heyworth Rd, prominent spired High Victorian *church* (1868; G.F. Jones). 2m N of centre, **New Earswick**, garden suburb (1902; Parker and Unwin), laid out by the Rowntree family, not only for employees of their chocolate factory, but as an attempt to provide pleasing, healthy housing for workers on middling incomes, while still returning a commercial profit. A complete village of pleasant vernacular revival houses on winding roads was built together with social centres (but no pub), the houses generally separated from the traffic roads, an early example of such planning. NW of centre, A19, the suburb of **Clifton** with *St. Peter's School* (1838; J. Harper) in quite ornate Gothic, ashlar fronted, and *church* (1866; G.F. Jones), heavily detailed in High Victorian manner. By the church, Gothic *school* and tile-hung domestic revival *vicarage*, both by J.L. Pearson (1877–79).

5m SW of York, off A64, at **Bilbrough**, *Bilbrough Manor* (1901; Temple Moore), careful Elizabethan. Neo-Norman *church* (1873; G.F. Jones), more notable for the tomb of General Fairfax (died 1671). **Tadcaster**, 4m SW, is well known for J. Smith's *brewery* (1883–85). In the parish *church*, E window with Morris glass (c 1875). 2m SE, *Grimston Park* (1840–50; D. Burton), Italianate remodelling of an earlier house, with a campanile tower to one side, to offset the otherwise symmetrical elevations, a synthesis of classical and picturesque traditions. Terraced Italian gardens laid out by W.A. Nesfield. 5m S of York, B1222, *Moreby Hall* (1828–33; A. Salvin), Tudor to Elizabethan style country house, an early example of the revival. 2m E, A19, at **Escrick**, estate village of Escrick Hall. Estate *church* (1856; F.C. Penrose), High Victorian with monuments to the Lawley family of the Hall including one to Lady Lawley (1828) by Thorwaldsen, the Danish neo-classical sculptor admired above all others in the 19C. Inscription to the Rev. S.W. Lawley by Eric Gill (1907). 7m SE of York, B1228, at **Elvington**, *church* (1877; W. White) with attractive Germanic timbered top to the tower. Unusually free carving to the arcade capitals. 9m NE of York, E of A64, at **Howsham**, *church* (1859–60; G.E. Street), a model of sturdy geometrical design, one of Street's best village churches. Street's handling of the mass seems based on the play of facets and planes in solid geometry, the spirelet turning from square to octagon without mouldings, the gable rising sheer over a lean-to porch and the E end a perfect curve subtly articulated by plinth and horizontal bands of pink stone. Inside, the curve of the apse is emphasised by a painted boarded roof and the windows ornamented with cusped arches, the cusping also on the chancel arch. Excellent carved stone reredos, pulpit and font inlaid with marble, and fine glass by Clayton and Bell. 3m NW, A64, at **Whitwell-on-the-Hill**, *church* (1858–60; G.E. Street) for Lady Lechmore of Whitwell Hall, the spire, a landmark from afar, placed against the chancel. Severe outline, as at Howsham, with

Church (1859–60; G.E. Street), Howsham

subtle polychrome banding. Excellent stone and marble fittings by
Street, E window by Clayton and Bell, chancel side windows and W
window by Wailes. Lychgate by Street. The *parsonage* (1860; Street)
has a complex roof form of gables and hips, some Gothic touches. 9m
NW of York, N of A59, at **Nun Monkton**, the *church* is the nave of a
12C nunnery chapel, the E end rebuilt 1873 with excellent stained
glass by Morris and Co.

SOUTH YORKSHIRE

BARNSLEY. A61 13m N of Sheffield. Centre of the South Yorkshire coalfield. Town centre benefitting from the steep rise up from the river and canal. In Pitt St, *Temperance Hall* (1836; W.J. Hindle), Greek classical. In Regent St, *County Court* (1871; T.C. Sorby), palazzo style, the previous court-house (1861) was reused as a railway station after this one was built. In Wellington St, disused *Theatre Royal* (1899; W. Emden), pedimented stone front, the auditorium still intact. In Brinckman St, *St. Peter's Church* (1894–1912; Temple Moore). 3m N, at **Carlton**, B6132, *church* (1874–79; G.E. Street), severely detailed with central saddleback-roofed tower and stone tunnel-vaulting in the chancel. *Vicarage* by Street (1878). At **Cawthorne**, 5m W of Barnsley, *church* much rebuilt 1875–80 (G.F. Bodley) for the family of the Pre-Raphaelite painter Spencer Stanhope, who designed the W window glass and painted the pulpit. One Morris window in N chapel.

DONCASTER. A630 19m NE of Sheffield. Industrial town noted for horse-racing since the 17C and railway engineering since the 19C, when the Great Northern Railway established its works here. Cathedral-scale parish *church* (1854–58; G.G. Scott) replacing a medieval building of similar scale burnt to the ground. Scott followed the outline of the earlier building, including the 170ft central tower, but otherwise the details are more unified Dec., Scott's favourite style. The superb tower is Perp. in outline but not in detail, interestingly Scott wished to reproduce the 15C predecessor exactly but was over-ruled. Lofty and well-proportioned interior focused on the E window (1862; Hardman) and rich chancel decoration (Scott). In the Forman chapel, splendid serpentine marble font (Scott) and glass by Wailes (1858). W window by Ward and Hughes (1874), aisle windows all of 1857–66, by a variety of makers, consistent in their bright colours but otherwise a good demonstration of the range of styles practised. In the town centre, *Corn Exchange* (1870–73; W. Watkins), mixed style with fine iron hall behind, and *Market Hall* (1847–49; J. Butterfield), classical. On corner of Baxter Gate and High St, *Midland Bank* (1898; Demaine and Brierley). In French Gate, former *Guildhall* (1848; J. Butterfield), Corinthian classical.

3m E of Doncaster, B1396, at **Cantley**, *church* altered 1892 and refitted 1903–06 by J.N. Comper, the first of Comper's colourful Gothic transformations of medieval churches. Painted rood screen and loft, side screens, altar tester, stencilling and stained glass, in delicate late Gothic style. 6m W of Doncaster, A635, in **Hickleton** *church*, memorials to the Wood family, Viscounts Halifax, of Hickleton Hall. The 2nd Viscount was leader of the High Church or Anglo-Catholic party in the Anglican church. Bust of the architect G.F. Bodley (died 1907). 3m NE, at **Brodsworth**, *Brodsworth Hall* (1861–70) by Casentini, an Italian architect from Lucca, stone late classical to Renaissance facades, not especially distinguished but the interiors a complete period piece of the mid Victorian era, painted decoration, marbled columns and tiled floors, the plan designed for the display of statuary, all white marble by Italian sculptors.

SHEFFIELD. Industrial city well set on a hilly site, noted for fine cutlery from the 16C and steel from the 18C. Centre surprisingly modest for so large a town, only the *Town Hall* (1890–97; E.W. Mountford) making an appropriate show, with tower rising 210ft to an ornate cupola-capped top stage, free 17C style combining shaped gables and mullion and transom windows with delicate Renaissance detail. Monumental marbled stair-hall with statue of 15th Duke of Norfolk (1879; Onslow Ford). In Surrey St, to one side, *Freemasons Hall* (c 1860), Italianate with Florentine tracery. In Norfolk St, *Upper Chapel* (1848; J. Frith), stone-fronted Italianate, and opposite, former *Hays and Son premises* (1876), now part of the Art Gallery, unusual combination of brick and stone on a flush facade, the stone with incised ornament. *St. Marie's RC Church* (1846–50; Weightman and Hadfield), archaeological Dec. with fine spire. Pugin designed reredos and W window (1850), organ case by J.F. Bentley (1875) and Lady Chapel added 1878 (Hadfield and Son). In George St, *No. 14* (c 1865), with Italian Gothic touches, and Italianate *National Westminster Bank* (c 1850). In Tudor St, by the Crucible Theatre, *Lyceum Theatre* (1897; W. Sprague) with domed corner entry and rococo plasterwork to the auditorium. George St runs up to High St, with Church St to W. In Church St, on S side, *Williams and Glyn's Bank* (1866; Flockton and Abbott), palazzo style with granite columns to each floor in the end bays, then Corinthian columned *Cutler's Hall* (1832; S. Worth and B. Taylor), a grand Greek facade, the interior remodelled 1867 (Flockton and Abbott) including the grand stair and main hall, *Midland Bank* (1838; S. Worth), also neo-Grecian with fine banking hall, and *National Westminster Bank* (c 1895), neo-Tudor. Opposite, the churchyard flanked by gabled offices of the 1880s. The *Cathedral* was the parish church, much confused in plan because the scheme to enlarge it after it became a cathedral in 1914 was abandoned. The original church was heavily remodelled 1880 (W. Flockton) when the nave was rebuilt and transepts added. E window by W.F. Dixon, the similar W window has been reset opposite the main entrance. Adjoining, in N aisle, good brightly coloured window of 1862. N of the Cathedral, off North Church St, in Bank St, *County Court* (c 1870; T.C. Sorby), palazzo style. E of High St, in Fitzalan Square, *Post Office* (1893; J. Williams), and in Commercial St, former *Gas Offices* (1875; C. Hadfield) with painted glass dome by J.F. Bentley in the main hall. S of Fitzalan Square, *Midland Station* (1905; C. Trubshaw), a large covered forecourt screened by a 12-bay arcade, the shallow gables reflecting the iron and glass roof behind.

W of the centre, on Western Bank, A57, Sheffield *University*, Tudor style brick buildings (1903–05; E.M. Gibbs), much extended since. Adjoining, in Weston Park, *Mappin Art Gallery* (1886; Flockton and Gibbs), Greek Ionic temple to the Arts, very pure for the date. Good collections of 19C painting and sculpture. By the Museum, terracotta *column* to G. Sykes, Sheffield born artist (died 1866), responsible for much of the ceramic decoration on the South Kensington Museum, London. Sykes designed the S gate to Weston Park in similar style, terracotta, Renaissance. Statue to E. Elliott 'the Corn Law Rhymer' (1854; N. Burnard). To SW, on Glossop Rd, *King Edward VII School* (1837–40; W. Flockton), Greek Corinthian on a monumental scale, eight-columned centre portico, lower wings and end pavilions, portico-fronted. Greek Revival schools on this scale are exceptional outside Scotland, this one was originally Wesleyan, the association of classicism rather than the Gothic with learning lasting longer among Nonconformists. Opposite, in Broomfield Rd, the spire (1871; W.H. Crossland) of *St. Mark's Church* survives attached to a modern building, now the university church. On Glossop Rd terraces and villas of c 1830–40, the grandest, *The Mount* (c 1835; W. Flockton), built for the poet J. Montgomery, owner and editor of the 'Sheffield Iris', Greek

Ionic style. SW of the School, on Clarkehouse Rd, *Botanical Gardens* (1836; B. Taylor) with classical entrance and handsome classical glasshouses. To W, an area of wealthy manufacturers' houses, *Endcliffe Hall* (1860), on Endcliffe Vale, and *Oakbrook* (c 1865), Fulwood Rd, both Italiante, the most notable. Beyond Oakbrook, *St. John's Church* (1887; Flockton and Gibbs), Ranmoor Park Rd, wealthy suburban church with prominent spire. To W, at Ranmoor, *Methodist College* (1863; W. Hill), Gothic, long asymmetrical front. In Nethergreen Rd, to SW, *almshouses* (1869), Gothic, built for M. Firth of Oakbrook, industrialist, and founder of Sheffield University. SE of the Botanical Gardens, *General Cemetery*, Cemetery Rd, laid out 1836 (S. Worth), densely packed memorials, including monument to J. Montgomery (1861; J. Bell). Greek Revival lodge and old chapel, though the gates are Egyptian. SW of central Sheffield, off A621, Abbeydale Rd South, *Abbeydale Industrial Hamlet*, museum based on a reconstructed late 18C scythe works, the setting rural but fully industrialised with crucible furnace for making the steel. Sheffield was notorious for the low life expectancy of the men involved in grinding fine steel tools, silicosis killing some 50% between the ages of 20 and 30 where, unlike Abbeydale, a dry process was used.

E of Sheffield Station, on Park Hill, *Shrewsbury Almshouses* (1825; Woodhead and Hurst), Norfolk Road, Tudor Gothic courtyard group in stone facing over Monument Park with *Cholera Monument* (1833) to the victims of the 1832 epidemic. S of Granville Rd, Norfolk Park was part of the estate of *Queen's Tower*, East Bank Rd, castellated house (1839) built for a manufacturer and enlarged 1855 for the 15th Duke of Norfolk, dominant landowner in the town. N of central Sheffield, the River Don provided the power for the cutlery industry, the area of Savile St and Attercliffe Rd having the works of Spear and Jackson, Firth and Brown. Across Wicker Lane, A57, *Wicker Bridge* (1848; J. Fowler), stone classical railway bridge. NW of centre, off Corporation St, in Alma St, *Kelham Island Industrial Museum*, with reconstructed workshops and working 12,000 hp steam-engine. In Green Lane, to W, *Green Lane Works*, originally 18C works of Hoole and Sons, firegrate manufacturers, with handsome classical gatehouse (1860), capped by a Wrenian cupola. 3m S of central Sheffield, at **Norton**, the sculptor, Sir F. Chantrey (1781–1841), is buried in the churchyard and commemorated by an obelisk. 4m NE of Sheffield, **Rotherham**, coal and iron town, the 15C parish *church* of exceptional size restored 1873–75 (G.G. Scott). E window by Clayton and Bell.

WEST YORKSHIRE

BRADFORD. City built on wool, in Bradford's case worsted, the yarn made from long-fibre wool with the fibres combed parallel, as opposed to the criss-crossed fibres of woollen yarn. Bradford became the international centre for trading in woollen cloth, notable for the number of foreign merchants, especially from Germany, the largest export market. Although the woollen industry in Bradford dates back to the 16C, the expansion came after the introduction of machinery in the late 18C. There were 20 mills in 1820 and some 300 by 1900. Bradford still has impressive groups of high stone warehouses, almost all in Italian palazzo style, built for the export trade.

Town Hall extension (1902–09; R.N. Shaw), Bradford

In the centre, the Florentine campanile of the *Town Hall* (1869–73; Lockwood and Mawson), an impressive High Victorian public building in the Gothic of William Burges and the 'muscular' school, in fact a close adaptation of Burges' design for the Law Courts, London, of 1866. The combination of N Italian and Early French Gothic gives a characteristic sharpness of detail, impressive on the long main front, not originally seen in so open a setting which accentuates the near symmetry about the campanile and orielled centre pavilion. The chief rooms are on the arcaded first floor. The main entrance hall was remodelled in Baroque style (1913; W. Williamson). In 1902–09 the Town Hall was extended down Town Hall St, one of the last and remarkable, designs of R. Norman Shaw, harmonious with the original, yet in detail an eclectic exhibition of motifs from Shaw's career, late Gothic in the dormers to 18C in the iron balconies, and, on the first floor, the High Victorian of the 1869 building. A demonstration of controlled licence by a masterly architect, the asymmetrical corner to Norfolk St with the great two-storey bay window inset on the angle shows a nerve that few architects could match. The Gothic dining-hall with sculpted fireplace is by Shaw, the fine cruciform Council Chamber with plasterwork by E. Gimson may not be. In Bridge St, behind the Town Hall, *St. George's Hall* (1851–53; Lockwood and Mawson), a concert hall built on the temple plan of Birmingham Town Hall, but interpreted in a florid Renaissance style with attached colonnades. Galleried interior with organ centrepiece of the apsed end wall. Further down, the *Victoria Hotel* (1867; Lockwood and Mawson). In Hall Ings, adjoining St. George's Hall, *Bradford Telegraph* offices (1852–53; Andrews and Delaunay), built as a wool warehouse, and one of the first to introduce the rich Italian palazzo style typical of the city. Five storeys with a skilful hierarchy of decoration, capped by a bold cornice. Market St runs NE from the Town Hall. At corner of Bank St, * *Wool Exchange* (1864–67; Lockwood and Mawson), the centre of Bradford's wool trade, and of appropriate scale, Ruskinian Gothic, based on the Doge's Palace, Venice, and with structural polychromy as advocated by Ruskin, though at the N end a Flemish Gothic spired tower crowns the entry. Ruskin, consulted on the building and disillusioned with the multitude of Venetian Gothic buildings spawned by his 'Stones of Venice', delivered his famous rebuke: 'I don't care about this Exchange ... you send for me, that I may tell you the leading fashion ... the newest and sweetest thing in pinnacles ... you cannot have good architecture merely by asking people's advice on occasion'. The portrait medallions are an instructive selection of heroes of industry, politics and exploration. Inside a trading-floor with open timber roof on granite columns. In Market St, *National Westminster Bank* (1872; Milnes and France). In Bank St, Gothic *National Westminster Bank* (1867; Andrews and Pepper). On corner of Bank St and Kirkgate, *Bradford Club* (1877; Lockwood and Mawson), Italianate, and, opposite, *Midland Bank* (1858; Andrews and Delaunay), Venetian palazzo style.

At end of Kirkgate, *Forster Square Station* (1890; C. Trubshaw), the station hotel more impressive than the low station with enclosed forecourt. The area between Forster Square and Bradford Exchange Station was the main warehouse district, called Little Germany from the numbers of German traders based here. Since the rebuilding of much of the centre, it is the part where Bradford's textile wealth can best be appreciated. In Forster Square, *Post Office* (1886; H. Tanner). Up Church Bank, the *Cathedral*, mainly 15C parish church that became a cathedral only in 1919 and was given a new E end after 1951. In the new Lady Chapel some excellent early Morris and Co glass (1862). In Vicar Lane, below, the entry from Leeds Rd is flanked by two fine buildings by Lockwood and Mawson, the former *Law, Russell warehouse* (1873–74), the sharp S angle given five storeys of coupled columns framing recessed windows topped by a small dome, and the former *American-Chinese Export warehouse* (1871) in rich Renaissance style, the corner doorcase embellished with a fierce American eagle. Behind the Law, Russell building, *No. 66* (1866; Milnes and France), four storeys with strongly modelled stone detail. *Nos 64*

(1867) and 72 (c 1860) are also Milnes designs, the firm having also designed the warehouses in Well St, *No. 39* (1867) and *Nos 43–5* (1864). Burnett St, Peckover St, Chapel St and East Parade all have warehouses, mostly of the boom period of 1860–73 when European markets were opened for trade. The *Delius warehouse* (1873; Milnes and France) in Peckover St belonged to the father of the composer. Leeds Rd was once entirely lined with warehouses, E. Milnes claiming to have built over 30 there in the 1850s. The *Schuster warehouse* (1869–73; Milnes and France) at corner of George St is notable.

From Forster Square, Cheapside and Manor Row run NW. In Manor Row, the harsh Gothic former *Grammar School* (1872–74; Andrews and Pepper), some tall *warehouses*, and the dignified palazzo style *Registry Office* (1876; Andrews and Pepper), built for the workhouse Board of Guardians. Manningham Lane runs N, gradually built up with villas and terraces, of the 1840s around the neo-Norman *St. Jude's Church* (1843; W. Rawsthorne), and of the 1860s and 1870s towards Manningham, as at *Blenheim Terrace* (1865; S. Jackson). Manningham *church* (1847–48; Mallinson and Healey), St. Paul's Rd, has a fine central spire. NW of Manningham, Heaton Rd, *Manningham Mill* (1871–73; Andrews and Pepper), the most splendid of Yorkshire mills, a vast stone Italianate building, five storeys, with round-arched detail judiciously applied to the corners and upper floor. The mill is so placed as to be visible from all over the west of Bradford, the 250ft chimney, disguised as an Italian campanile, crowns the hilltop, an unequalled display of manufacturing pride. The mill was built for S.C. Lister, later Lord Masham, and employed some 5000 people in its heyday. In *Lister Park* E of the mill, the *Cartwright Hall* (1900–03; J.W. Simpson), given by Lister, a combination of art gallery and public entertainment suite. The building is in the most grandiose Baroque style, lavishly sculpted and with an impressive, if functionally useless, two-storey porch crowned by a high cupola. The central hall is similarly ornate. Statue of the Rev. E. Cartwright, inventor of the power loom, by H.C. Fehr. In the park, Gothic memorial (1874; Lockwood and Mawson) to Sir Titus Salt of Saltaire (see below). N of the Park, *Heaton Mount* (1864; T. Fairbank), Emm Lane, manufacturer's mansion in lush Italianate style. None of the other Bradford mills approach Manningham Mill in grandeur, but *Lumb Lane Mill* (1858; Lockwood and Mawson), behind St. Jude's Church, and the groups W of the centre on Thornton Rd and Great Horton Rd are among the best. On Great Horton Rd, the *Alhambra* (1914; Chadwick and Watson) dramatically faces Princes Way with a domed rotunda entry and a pair of domed turrets behind. Fine interior. The *Alexandra Hotel* (1879; Andrews and Pepper), in mixed Renaissance style is now a students' hostel. Bradford University, founded 1966, took over as its most impressive building the former *Technical School* (1880; Hope and Jardine), monumental Italianate with giant Corinthian order and high central domed cupola, all apparently symmetrical but the giant order is of columns one side and pilasters the other, an oddity mitigated by the sharp perspective of most views. Between Great Horton Rd and Thornton Rd, at Lidget Green, *St. Wilfrid's Church* (1905; Temple Moore). S of the centre, at Little Horton Green, *All Saints' Church* (1861–64; T. and F. Healey), the most impressive of Bradford's Victorian churches, apsed with fine spire. NE of centre, on Barkerend Road, *St. Clement's Church* (1892–94; E.P. Warren), notable for painted chancel decoration by Morris and Co., the figures in the late style of Burne-Jones. To N, on Otley Rd, *Undercliffe Cemetery* (1854; W. Gay), much overgrown and vandalised but filled with memorials to the textile families of Bradford, the best along the central avenue that spectacularly overlooks the city. The Egyptian mausoleum to D. Illingworth (died 1854) of Providence Mills is perhaps the finest, but it is the ensemble of obelisk and sarcophagus, granite and marble that is memorable. To NW, off A658, the *Bradford Industrial Museum*, Moorside Rd, occupying the former Moorside Mill, has displays of the industries and transport of the area, and a fully furnished mill-owner's house.

3m NW of Bradford, A650, at **Shipley**, is *·Saltaire*, the outstanding model industrial settlement in Britain. Sir Titus Salt (1803–76) decided to transfer his extensive mills from central Bradford in 1850, choosing a green site by the river Aire for a single factory in which all the processes of making fine alpaca and mohair cloth would be concentrated. Salt had already made a huge fortune from Peruvian wool and the new factory was to be the finest in the world, covering two acres and containing 1200 looms, the interior a fireproof iron frame by the engineer Sir W. Fairbairn, the exterior given an Italianate gloss by Lockwood and Mawson, Salt's architects for the whole settlement. After the mill (1850–53) came the rest of Saltaire, ultimately a small town of some 900 houses with appropriate public buildings and park, but no pubs. The *mill* is on an island site between the railway and canal, shared only with the *Congregational church* (1858–59), industry and religion a separate nucleus. The church is the most splendid of Salt's buildings, an Italianate reinterpretation of the neo-classical church at Banbury, Oxfordshire, with a circular tower or lantern rising from a circular portico, columned in a rich Corinthian order, echoed inside down the side walls. Salt is buried in the attached mausoleum. Across the canal is the mill extension of 1868 with Italian Gothic tower, and beyond, over the river Aire, the public *park* given by Salt in 1871. The *town*, S of the mill, is laid out on a grid plan with streets of sober houses in terraces, two-storey generally, the centre and corner houses three-storey. By contemporary standards the accommodation was generous, though there were no gardens. Along Victoria Rd are the public buildings, the *Institute* (1872), Renaissance with a centre tower and French pavilion cap, facing the *Schools* (1868), with lawns between and four stone lions guarding. The Institute was for the recreation and education of the workforce, with library, reading-room and meeting hall for 800. The Schools were for 750, though there were only three classrooms. Further down are the *almshouses* (1865), the most attractive houses in Saltaire, picturesque Italianate around an open garden. Further up the Aire valley, mill towns and villages succeed each other, the views to open hills. In **Bingley** town centre, the *Damart Mill* is prominent. *Mechanics Institute* by A. Waterhouse (1864). Around Bingley, a number of mill-owners' houses, the largest, Milner Field (1871; T. Harris), built for T. Salt's son, was fully High Victorian in the manner of Burges. Only lodges survive. *Oakwood Court* (1864; Knowles and Wilcox), N of centre, has early Morris glass on the staircase and one splendid fireplace surviving from a scheme of decoration by Burges (1865).

3m NW is **Keighley**, a much larger mill town, the mills along the Worth valley, a tributary of the Aire. *Dalton Mill* (c 1865) is the best, Renaissance details and a chimney with viewing gallery. On North St, *RC church* (1840; A.W.N. Pugin), very simple originally, enlarged 1907, and *Public Library* (1904), Edwardian free style. N of the centre, *Cliffe Castle* (1875–78; G. Smith), mansion built for the worsted manufacturer H. Butterfield, now the town Museum and Art Gallery. Castellated Tudor style with towers, the detail simplified in early 20C, but the most spectacular feature is the domed Winter Garden (c 1885; W. Bailey). The Second Empire style interiors are slowly being restored. From Keighley the Worth valley ascends SW towards **Haworth**, home of the Brontë family from 1820. The *Parsonage* is now a museum, and its leaflets give supposed settings of the sisters' novels. Any walk on the moors brings 'Wuthering Heights' to life. At the *Black Bull*, in the village, the unfortunate Branwell Brontë drank. The *church*, where Patrick Brontë was vicar, Charlotte married and the family buried, contains Brontë memorials, but apart from the tower, is not the one they knew, having been rebuilt 1879–80 (T. and F. Healey). The old railway from Keighley to Haworth has steam locomotives, with a railway museum at Haworth. The line ends at **Oxenhope**, W of Haworth, where there is a well-detailed neo-Norman *church* (1849; Bonomi and Cory).

DEWSBURY. A653 7m S of Leeds. Centre of the 'heavy woollen' district noted for blanket making, and still very much a mill town. Neo-Jacobean *station* (1849) with large Italianate warehouses around. The largest central mill is *Spinkwell Mills*, Halifax Rd, later 19C. The *Town Hall* (1888; Holtom and Fox) has a high central cupola tower and French pavilion roofs, tightly composed on a steep site. On Huddersfield Rd, *St. Paulinus RC Church* (1867–72; E.W. Pugin), cramped on a slope, exceedingly tall proportions.

The heavy woollen district extends N into **Batley**, which has Gothic warehouses of c 1870–80 on Station Rd. At **Morley**, to N, notably proud *Town Hall* (1895; G.A. Fox) on the model of Bolton. At **Heckmondwike**, NW of Dewsbury, the *Upper Independent Chapel* (1890; A. Stott) with giant Corinthian portico and Baroque cupola is a chapel of quite unexpected grandeur, now disused in its crowded graveyard. **Liversedge** to NW has a substantial Georgian Gothic *church* (1812–16; T. Taylor) built for the dedicated church-builder, the Rev. H. Roberson, model for the Rev. Helstone, in C. Brontë's 'Shirley' which is set in this area. The Spen valley was notable for Nonconformity and radical politics, in general chapels are more prominent than churches. In **Cleckheaton**, to NW, the *Providence Place Chapel* (1857–59; Lockwood and Mawson) displays a splendid pedimented front of giant columns carrying arches in a rich Italianate version of the temple front. This very large Congregational chapel had an even larger Methodist rival of 1875–79, now demolished. The *Town Hall* (1890–92; Mawson and Hudson) is based on Wakefield Town Hall. 3m SW of Dewsbury, A644, at **Mirfield**, *church* rebuilt 1871 (G.G. Scott), a strong EE design. At **Battyford**, just W, above the Calder, the Anglican *College of the Order of the Resurrection* with dramatically sited neo-Norman chapel (1911; W. Tapper) in red sandstone, the brick nave added in 1937. The interior, simple and restful in detail, has complex spatial effects from the enclosing arcades around the central crossing.

HALIFAX. A58 13m SW of Leeds. Wool town from the middle ages, the centre of a weaving district that extended up into the hills around in the days of home manufacture. The *Piece Hall* (1776–78), where home-manufactured cloth was traded, is the outstanding Yorkshire monument of the pre-industrial phase. Halifax in the 19C had two dynasties of mill-owners, the Crossleys and the Akroyds. The Crossley fortune was in carpet manufacture, based on their 1851 patented steam loom, and their Dean Clough mills covered some 30 acres and employed nearly 6000 people. The three Crossley brothers,

John (died 1879), Joseph (died 1868) and Sir Frank (died 1872), Non-conformists in religion and radical Liberals in politics, contributed to or paid for most of the notable public buildings in the town, and dominated its political life, locally as councillors and mayors and nationally in parliament. The Akroyd family firm had mills manufacturing worsted just by Dean Clough at Haley Hill and S of the town at Copley. Edward Akroyd rivalled the Crossley brothers in his munificence.

On the E edge of the town, the parish *church*, mostly 15C, restored 1879 (J.O. Scott), the organ case the most notable 19C addition. The area between the church and the centre, apart from the restored Piece Hall, has been flattened. Behind the Piece Hall, the splendid 235ft spire of the *Square Congregational Chapel* (1855–57; J. James), given by the Crossley brothers, and now bereft of its church. The previous chapel of 1772 lies derelict next door. In Market St, to W, the *Borough Market* (1891–98; Leeming and Leeming), like the Kirkgate Market, Leeds, stone ornately French Renaissance outside buildings intersected by arcades into a large iron and glass hall. Octagonal centre with centrepiece clock cum lamp-bracket, an extravagant cast-iron confection, matching the detail of the columns and arches of the hall. N of the Market area, between Crown St and the Town Hall, is the civic heart of Halifax, a handsome area of tall stone Italianate buildings, the core, Princess St and Crossley St, rebuilt during the mayoralty of John Crossley (1850–51) at Crossley expense to provide a suitable setting for the intended new Town Hall. Lockwood and Mawson provided the handsome palazzo style designs for the area, of which the *White Swan Hotel* (1857–58) takes the appearance of the Crossleys private palazzo, on the model of the palaces of Rome, with the family arms (newly granted) adorning the front. The *Marlborough Hall* (1856), Crossley St, was the Mechanics' Institute, its high two storeys almost equalling the four of the adjoining *Halifax Building Society* original head office (1871; S. Jackson). The *Town Hall* (1859–63; Sir C. and E.M. Barry) was the culmination of the Crossley–Akroyd rivalry, expressed in munificent donations to the town. The Akroyd faction offered a Gothic design by G.G. Scott but the Crossleys won the day, and indeed the war for dominance in the town, and Barry provided a rich Venetian Renaissance design, arcaded on both floors, and designed, like Barry's London clubs, around a top-lit central hall. Where Venice fades from the design is in its most prominent feature, the extraordinary spired tower that fills the view up Princess St, a Gothic outline rethought in Renaissance terms, unquestionably Victorian in its sculptural richness.

Up Northgate, to North Bridge and the area of *mills* in the steep-sided Dean Clough. The Crossley *Dean Clough Mills* are largely of 1857–58 (R. Ives) and 1867 (F. Petty), high stone ranges filling the valley floor. The *Bowling Dyke Mill* at North Bridge was built for the Akroyd firm (1851) and high over the Crossley mills is the main Akroyd *Haley Hill Mill* (1837). On Haley Hill, Edward Akroyd laid out the model settlement of Akroydon, with its magnificent church whose spire from its hillside site so successfully overtops the Crossleys' spire in the town below. *All Souls' Church* (1856–59; G.G. Scott), despite the ravages of stone decay, caused by a poorly chosen limestone, is the very model of a full-scale Victorian town church, Dec., judiciously ornamented with carved work and statuary, the tower and spire properly the crowning glory. Inside, no expense was spared, especially fine is the carved detail with much naturalistic foliage on the capitals and a steady intensification of richness towards the altar with polished marble shafting and painted decoration. Carved marble and alabaster

Town Hall (1859–63; Sir C. Barry and E.M. Barry), Halifax

reredos, pulpit and font by J.B. Philip, who was responsible for all the carved work on the building. Low iron screen and gates by Skidmore. Almost all the stained glass is contemporary with the building, notable the great E and W windows by Hardman and the transept windows by Clayton and Bell. Outside the church, *statue* of Edward Akroyd (1875) holding a plan of Akroydon. Behind the church, the *vicarage*, by Scott.

Akroyd Park was the grounds of *Bankfield*, Akroyd's house, which overlooks the church, the mill and the workers' houses of Akroydon. The house, now a museum, was a plain villa recased and enlarged in 1867 (J.B. and W. Atkinson) in Florentine palazzo style. The model village, a little further up, was planned and partly designed by G.G. Scott in 1859 with gabled Gothic terraces, formally arranged around a village green (which substituted for gardens). The effect was deliberately rustic and pre-industrial, though the designs were modified by W.H. Crossland before work began in 1861 as the intended occupants, who were to be freeholders through a mortgage scheme guaranteed by Akroyd, apparently found the Gothic look too redolent of almshouses. Each house has the initials of the owner over the door. The community was socially mixed and not restricted to Akroyd employees, both ideas in advance of their time. On the green, a Gothic 'Eleanor cross' (W.S. Barber). The most prominent building, grander than any of the houses, however, is Col Akroyd's *stable block* (W.H. Crossland). Shroggs Park to the W, across the valley, was another Akroyd gift, laid out 1874.

The area of Crossley family benefactions was W of the centre on Gibbet St and Hopwood Lane. On Hopwood Lane, *Belle Vue* (1856–57; G.H. Stokes), the Louis XV style mansion of Sir Frank Crossley, actually the recasing of an earlier villa, looks across, like a small French town hall, at the *People's Park* (1856–57; Sir J. Paxton), given by Sir Frank and adorned with an arched pavilion (1856; G.H. Stokes) overlooking a lake. In the pavilion, statue of Sir Frank (1861; J. Durham). Sir Frank's benefactions also included the Margaret St *almshouses* (1855; R. Ives), E of Belle Vue. Although Belle Vue is an expensively finished house with grand marble staircase, the scale is modest, and the grounds cramped between the road and Lister Lane cemetery. (After being created a baronet in 1862, Sir Frank abandoned Halifax for 3000 acres of Suffolk at Somerleyton.) The *Park Chapel* (1869; R. Ives) to W, again a Crossley foundation. To N, the *West Hill Park estate* (1863–69; Paull and Ayliffe) of workers' housing built for freehold sale by John Crossley, much plainer than Akroydon, arranged in terraces at right angles to Gibbet St with the shops and larger houses fronting the main road. W of the People's Park, the *Technical College* (1895; Jackson and Fox). S of the park, in Arden Rd, very extensive group of Gothic *almshouses* (1863–70; R. Ives), built for Joseph Crossley. At SW end of Kings Cross Rd, on the hill over the Calder valley, the *·Wainhouse Tower* (1877), originally built by J.E. Wainhouse as a chimney to disperse smoke from his Washer Lane Dyeworks, but completed as a 'general astronomical and physical observatory' for Wainhouse after he had sold the dyeworks, hence the Indian-Moorish top viewing gallery, perched on 230ft of brickwork. On Skircoat Moor Rd, the *Crossley Orphanage* (1857–64; J. Hogg), now a school, a monumental pile with French pavilion roofs and centre lantern, designed for 270 children, quite one of the grandest orphanages of the age, sited on the ridge to be a landmark from all around.

In the Calder valley below, off the Wakefield road, **Copley**, Colonel Akroyd's first model industrial settlement. The mill of 1847 has gone but the terraces of neat Tudor style cottages (1849–53; G.G. Scott and W.H. Crossland) survive. Unlike the later cottages at Akroydon, these were built by the firm for rent, not for sale. The quality of design and construction was exceptional for the date, although these are still back-to-back cottages. School, library and *church* (1863–65; W.H. Crossland) were provided. Between Copley and Halifax, the 23-arch *viaduct* (1852) of the line to Halifax. Up the Calder valley, at **Sowerby**

Bridge, good early 19C warehouses and mills by the canal. Large Perp. parish *church* (1819; J. Oates). 2m W, on S side of the Calder, at **Boulder Clough**, former *Methodist church* (1898; Sutcliffe and Sutcliffe), a most unusual Arts and Crafts design with two round stair towers framing an arcaded loggia. S from central Halifax, there are mills along the Hebble most notably *Holdsworth's Mill* (c 1865), still in use, with a courtyard plan and high chimney. At **Elland**, A629, the *Gannex mills* are prominent.

HUDDERSFIELD. A62 11m SW of Leeds. Woollen town developed from the early 19C by the Ramsden family who gave the centre of the town its regular plan. Mills still fill the valley floor, especially to the W, where the hills come close. The central streets are broad with handsome stone classical to Italianate buildings. The best area is around the railway station. The Ramsden estate surveyor J. Kaye controlled the development but outside architects designed the more important buildings. Sir W. Tite was consultant in the 1850s. St. George's Square is the hub, with the *station (1847–48; J.P. Pritchett) its centrepiece. More like a town hall, and quite outshining Huddersfield's Town Hall, the station has a full Corinthian six-column portico to the main block, intended as an hotel, Corinthian colonnades each side and end pavilions. Flanking the square, *George Hotel* (1849–50; Wallen and Child) and *Huddersfield Building Society* (1856; W. Tite), one of the typical Ramsden estate warehouses, both handsomely Italianate. Opposite the station, *Lion Building* (1852–54; J.P. Pritchett). The warehouses extend into Railway St and surrounding area. In Railway St, the *Ramsden estate office* (1872; W.H. Crossland). In Westgate St, *Byram Arcade* (1880–81; W.H. Crossland), a Ramsden estate development with Flemish Gothic entrance building and glazed arcade behind. In Ramsden St, *Municipal Offices* (1878; J.H. Abbey), in Princess St, *Town Hall* (1878–81; J.H. Abbey), eclectic Italianate to French, in Queen St South, *Polytechnic* (1881–84; E. Hughes), symmetrical stone Flemish Gothic. From the station New North Rd runs NW through suburbs laid out in the early 19C with terraces and villas and the typical public buildings of the period, Gothic parish *church* (1816; T. Taylor), classical *Infirmary* (1829–31; J. Oates), Gothic *College* (1839; J.P. Pritchett) and Ionic *Congregational chapel* (1843; Perkin and Backhouse).

Further out, on Halifax Rd, **Edgerton**, *Banney Royd* (1900; Edgar Wood), large Tudor style stone mansion with strong Arts and Crafts to Art Nouveau touches. Good interior carved work. Edgar Wood had connections in **Lindley**, to W, and designed an extension to the *Methodist church*, East St, with a very Art Nouveau communion table (1895). His *Clock Tower* (1900–02), Lidgett Rd, is as remarkably modern as anything of its date, with strong vertical lines, symbolic sculpture (by Stirling Lee) integrated into the design and a conical roof held in place by corner pinnacles, echoing the work of C.H. Townsend in London. W from the centre of Huddersfield the A62 follows the Colne valley, parallel to canal and railway. On the railway, 20-arch *Longwood Viaduct* (1849; A.S. Jee). By the canal, at **Milnsbridge**, *Union Mills*, large scale, the earliest part dating from 1850s. Mill buildings line the valley right up to Marsden and the pass to Lancashire. S from central Huddersfield, the Holme valley runs back to Holmfirth, crossed just S of Huddersfield by the spectacular stone *Lockwood Viaduct* (1848; J. Hawkshaw). On Castle Hill to E, *Victoria Tower* (1897), visible from miles around. **Holmfirth** is an atmospheric stone town with former *Town Hall* of 1842. N of central Huddersfield, on St.

John's Rd, *St. John's Church* (1851; W. Butterfield), built for the Ramsden family, with spire and lofty interior, in relatively conventional Dec. 3m N of Huddersfield, A616, is **Brighouse**, textile town that specialised in making the wire carders for teasing the wool. The parish *church* (1830; L. Hammerton) has one good Morris window (1872) and there is Morris glass of 1871 in the chancel of *St. James' Church* (1870; Mallinson and Barber), Bradford Rd. On Bradford Rd, *Woodvale Mill* (1880), built as a silk mill. N of Brighouse, A641, at **Bailiff Bridge**, large complex of mid to late 19C *carpet mills*.

ILKLEY. A65 17m NW of Leeds. Victorian resort town in Wharfedale set on the slope beneath Ilkley Moor. The centre is the *station* (1865; J.H. Sanders) with *Town Hall* (1906; W. Bakewell) opposite, but the beginnings of the spa pre-date the railway, the first hydropathic establishment, the Ben Rhydding, E of the centre, dating from 1844. The hillside S of the station up to the moor was gradually built up with villas, the largest on Queens Drive and along the edge of the moor, the styles progressing from gabled Gothic and baronial in the 1860s and 1870s to more relaxed half-timbered 'old English' styles in the 1880s and 1890s. The *church* of the hillside area, St. Margaret's (1876–79; R. Norman Shaw), is a broad Perp. design, focused each end on full-width traceried windows, a design that was much imitated in the later Gothic revival. Fittings added from Shaw's designs over a long period, reredos by J.H. Gibbons. Among the Ilkley villas, *Heathcote (1906; E. Lutyens), King's Rd, is of quite another order, like one of the great villas of Renaissance Italy hemmed by English suburbia. Heathcote is not an exceptionally large house, but all the elements of the design have a monumental strength, and the formal symmetry, building up from single storey to three-storey centre in a progression of hipped roofs and bold stacks is that of a great country house. The stylistic elements refer both to the English Baroque and to the Italian Renaissance work of Sanmicheli, an unusual source in English classicism, though the daring play of planes both vertical and horizontal could only be by Lutyens. At the very summit of Ilkley, *College of Education* (1853–58; C. Brodrick), a hydropathic hotel originally called Wells House, a large and excellently detailed Italianate building, square with corner towers and central hall. 5m E of Ilkley, A660, at **Otley**, in the churchyard, the *Bramhope memorial* to the 23 men who died in the construction of the Bramhope tunnel on the Leeds–Thirsk railway. The memorial is a miniature replica of the castellated N portal of the *tunnel* (1845–49; T. Grainger), 3m E of Otley, A660.

LEEDS. The prosperity of Leeds, one of Britain's outstanding Victorian towns, was built on the merchandising of textiles, more than the manufacture, supplemented by engineering. The town became the principal West Yorkshire centre for service industries, shops, banks, insurance and for entertainment. From the station, Park Row bisects the centre, the principal commercial streets to E. To W, Victorian office buildings overlaying the Georgian 'West End' of Leeds, and to N, on Headrow, the principal civic buildings. Outside the station, on City Square, a cluster of *statuary* unhappily placed in the centre triangle, the centrepiece T. Brock's handsome equestrian bronze of the Black Prince (1899), no local connection but intended, improbably, to symbolise chivalry and democracy. Around eight bronze maidens (1899; A Drury), originally holding lamps on the surrounding balustrade, four represent 'Morning', four 'Evening'. Statues of James Watt (1898; H. Fehr), the engineer, Joseph Priestley (1899; A. Drury), discoverer of oxygen and minister at the Mill Hill Chapel, J. Harrison (1903; H. Fehr), 17C founder of St. John's Church, and Dr W.F. Hook (1902; F. Pomeroy), vicar of Leeds 1837–59. On W side, *Post Office* (1896; H. Tanner), on SE corner, former *bank* (1899; W.W. Gwyther), with domed giant-columned rotunda to the street, and on E side, *Mill Hill Unitarian Chapel* (1847; Bowman and Crowther), a notably early example of full ecclesiastical Gothic being used for a chapel, slightly outmoded Perp. style, but wholeheartedly done.

On Park Row, *Lloyds Bank* (1898; A. Waterhouse) on W side, smooth banded brick and terracotta over granite with unusual Renaissance details, further up on E side, *Cheltenham House* (1890), with sculpted frieze representing Trade, *Prudential Assurance* (1894; A. Waterhouse), Gothic facade of brick and terracotta well-set at the end of South Parade, and *Nos 21–2* (1869; G. Corson), rich palazzo style. Opposite, former *Bank of England* (1862–64; P.C. Hardwick), more staid palazzo manner. Early 20C tile-clad office buildings in South Parade and a mix from late Georgian to Victorian in East Parade. In Infirmary St, at S end of East Parade, the *Yorkshire Bank* (1894; Perkin and Bulmer), Leeds' most substantial commercial building, stone Gothic with corner tower. In King St, *Atlas Chambers* (1910; Perkin and Bulmer) in white tile, free Baroque, with lively cast detail. The *Metropole Hotel* (1897–99; Chorley and Connon) displays the Leeds terracotta over an ornate bulk. In the streets to the W, the 18C houses were gradually replaced from c 1860 with the characteristic brick and stone Gothic *warehouses* of Leeds with polychrome Ruskinian touches, notable examples at the corner of Wellington St (1861; G. Corson), in Wellington St opposite the Wellesley Hotel (1866; Hadfield and Son, upper floors altered) and scattered through the parallel streets N to Park Square, Nos 37–41 and 44 York Place by G. Corson (1870), Nos 1–2 York Place (c 1870; S.E. Smith) and No. 30 Park Place (1863; T. Ambler). In Park Square, *St. Paul's House* (1878; T. Ambler), the most exotic of Leeds warehouses, Italian Gothic with Moorish corner pinnacles, the detail in exceptionally fine terracotta, by Doulton, mostly buff coloured but blue and white around the main

Town Hall (1853–58; C. Brodrick), Leeds

doorway. Built for Sir J. Barran, the first ready-made clothing tycoon of Leeds. In the gardens, bronze *statue* (1905; A. Drury).

To N, the civic centre dominated by one of the outstanding municipal buildings in Britain, the *Town Hall* (1853–58; C. Brodrick), the first of the great northern town halls built to a scale that eclipses even government buildings in London of the same date. The design is monumental classical, a square plan ringed by giant Corinthian columns carrying a fine balustraded cornice uninterrupted by any pediment, a French classical motif. The building exploits the raised site with a high rusticated basement and imposing flight of steps up flanked by stone lions (W. Keyworth). The great tower, square, ringed by columns under a Baroque lantern was apparently not originally intended, but added at the suggestion of Sir C. Barry, the assessor of the competition. Carved tympanum over the door by J. Thomas and a high entrance hall to which the painted decoration has recently been restored. Victoria (1858) and Albert (1865) statues by M. Noble. The great hall behind is a splendidly rich tunnel-vaulted space, heavily modelled with giant columns, recently restored to bacon-pink colour and the apse filled with an enormous organ. Adjoining to E, *Municipal Buildings* (1876–84; G. Corson), mixed Italianate, the group including the *School Board Offices* (1878; G. Corson) to N and *Art Gallery* (1887; W. Thorp) to E. The opposite side of the street never achieved civic grandeur, a mixture of late 19C buildings, most prominent the grey stone *Pearl Buildings* (1911; W. Bakewell) in an unhappy mixture of Gothic and Baroque. W of the Town Hall the bright brick front of *Oxford Place Methodist Chapel* (1896–1903; Danby and Thorp) and the Gothic *Britannia Buildings* (1868). Great George St runs W to the *Infirmary* (1863–67; G.G. Scott), polychrome brick Gothic on the pavilion plan recommended by Florence Nightingale to inhibit the spread of infection. Scott's Gothic seems the inspiration for much of the later Leeds warehouse style, G. Corson, the leading local Gothic architect, indeed added the identical E pavilion and designed the former *Medical School* (1865) in Park St in similar style.

E, on Great George St, behind the Town Hall, Gothic *Victoria Hotel* (c 1861), adjacent building 1865 (G. Corson), Italianate former *carriage works* (1848), and, on corner of Cookridge St, Romanesque arched *printing works* (c 1870). Opposite, *RC Cathedral* (1902–04; J. Eastwood and S.K. Greenslade), Arts and Crafts Gothic with the advanced motifs of such architects as L. Stokes, windows set in broad-arched recesses, emphatic verticals bluntly capped at parapet level. Broad interior and shallow chancel, remarkably spacious and freely detailed. High reredos and triforium gallery in the chancel, Lady Chapel altar (1842; A.W.N. Pugin) and pulpit (c 1865; J.F. Bentley) removed from the previous cathedral. To N, *Mechanics Institute* (1865–68; C. Brodrick). A decade on from the Town Hall, Brodrick's architecture has moved from formal classicism to a muscular French Second Empire inspired manner, the massive stone details strikingly free and excellently wrought in the hard Leeds stone. Behind, *College of Art* (1903; Bedford and Kitson). Further up, Gothic facade of the former *Coliseum Theatre* (1885; W. Bakewell), more like a grand chapel, but Gothic in Leeds reappears on all types of building. In Great George St, *St. Anne's Presbytery* (c 1904; J. Eastwood), Edwardian free style, and the buildings of *City of Leeds School*, main building on corner of Woodhouse Lane (1889; Kelly and Birchall), designed for 2500 pupils, and former *Pupil Teachers' Centre* (1900; W. Braithwaite), intended for teacher training of the best secondary school pupils. Across Woodhouse Lane, S of Merrion St, *St. John's*

Church, remarkable late Gothic of 1638, a rare example of church building in Stuart times. Victorian taste had little time for the crowded woodwork of the interior and demolition was only just averted by the intervention of Sir G.G. Scott in 1865 but the restoration (1866–68; R. Norman Shaw) was nonetheless destructive. Changing taste led to a slow reversal of the worst effects, the cresting being restored to the screens and the pulpit reconstructed. In the chapel to the founder, J. Harrison, stained glass (1885; Burlison and Grylls) depicting Harrison's good works.

To E, in New Briggate, *Grand Theatre* (1877–78; G. Corson), Gothic outside which is rare, except in Leeds, the long front representing the theatre to the left and a concert hall over the shops to the right. The theatre auditorium, unaltered, is one of the finest in Britain, domed with a suggestion of fan vaulting and encrusted with ornamental plasterwork. On the Headrow, to S, by the *Horse and Trumpet* pub, *City Palace of Varieties* (1865; G. Smith), the best surviving Victorian music-hall in Britain, intimate interior with balconies on three sides, performances here still recapture the fervent immediacy of Victorian song and dance shows. In Briggate, *Thornton's Arcade* (1877; G. Smith), built for the music-hall proprietor, the first of the fine series of shopping arcades in this area, Gothic with high glazed roof on iron arches. Further down, *Queen's Arcade* (1888; G. Clark) and, on E side, the exuberant red-brick and terracotta facades of the development around the *County Arcade* (1898–1900; F. Matcham), two new streets and bisecting arcades between, the arcade interiors particularly splendidly embellished in glazed tile, mosaic and marble. The centrepiece, the theatre facing Briggate, has gone. Albion Place, on W side, leads into the pedestrianised commercial heart of Leeds with former *Church Institute* (1866–68; Adams and Kelly) prominent in polychrome brick Gothic, various late 19C terracotta facades, palazzo style *County Court* (1870; T.C. Sorby) on S side and similar *Leeds Club* (1863) on N. In Albion St, on corner of Commercial St, the finest office palazzo in Leeds, built for the *Leeds and Yorkshire Assurance* (1852–55; W.B. Gingell), the modelling of the ground floor from Florentine sources particularly imposing. In Commercial St, *No. 14* (1868; G. Corson), stone-fronted Italian Gothic, well detailed with craggy three-gabled skyline. To S, in Turk's Head Yard, between Briggate and Trinity St, *Whitelock's*, hidden-away pub worth finding for the late 19C polished brass, tiles and stained glass inside. Trinity St runs down to Boar Lane, at *Holy Trinity Church* (1721) with handsome Wrenian steeple of 1841 (R.D. Chantrell). Boar Lane was mostly rebuilt from 1866 with tall warehouse blocks, varying in style from Renaissance to Gothic, lined along the S side, still despite the decay an impressive streetscape.

Lower Briggate runs S to *Leeds Bridge* (1872; T.D. Steel) and the industrialised landscape along the River Aire. On Lower Briggate, *Dyson's Clock Shop*, late 19C remodelling of a 18C house, exterior and interior most striking. Call Lane runs under the railway NE to the *Corn Exchange* (1861–63; C. Brodrick), one of the great works of Victorian architecture, oval in form, reflecting the exchange floor within, the outside an even two-storey array of arched windows set in diamond-rusticated walling under a fine cornice. The effect is measured and severe, an amphitheatre rethought in Italian and French Renaissance terms. Inside, intersecting iron trusses carry the roof over a vast oval space surrounded by two floors of offices, the roof glazed at the top and on the N curve, the one exception to the regularity. All the interior fittings simple and functional, befitting the purpose of the

The Corn Exchange (1861–63), Leeds

building. Late 19C warehouses in Vicar Lane opposite. The *City Markets* (1903–04; Leeming and Leeming) are very ornate outside, gabled and turretted, while the interior is a breathtaking display of iron and glass around a central octagonal space, the ironwork including dragons recently brightly repainted. Kirkgate runs SE, past brick and terracotta *Yorkshire Bank* (1900), under the railway to the *parish church* (1838–41; R.D. Chantrell), the railway having effectively banished it from the city centre. The church was rebuilt for W.F. Hook, High Church vicar of Leeds, and intended for very large congregations. It therefore combines a serious approach to Gothic architecture and clearly defined chancel space with heavily ornamented galleries filling all the available room under the arcades. Plaster vaults at the E end and much 19C stained glass, the E window with imported continental glass, chancel side windows 1841–46 (T. Wilmshurst) and W window 1856 (D. Evans). In S aisle, for comparison, St. Peter window of 1811 (T. Wright), in the glaring tones of early 19C glass. Reredos 1872 (G.E. Street) with wall mosaics of 1876. In NE chapel, effigy of W.F. Hook (died 1875; W. Keyworth) on tomb chest by G.G. Scott. At SE end monument to W. Beckett, MP and banker (died 1863; C. Marochetti).

OUTER LEEDS

S of Leeds Station, *Victoria Bridge* (1837–39) crosses the Aire. Prominent by the canal to W, the two campanili of the *Tower Works*, Globe Rd, the Giotto Tower (1899; W. Bakewell) and the Verona Tower (1864; T. Shaw), both were chimneys, the taller Giotto tower for dust extraction from pin manufacture. In Marshall St, off Water Lane, *Temple Mill* (1838–40; I. Bonomi), linen mill built for John Marshall MP, remarkable fantasy in the Egyptian style, stone fronted with giant lotus columns. Early 19C red-brick mills adjoining. W of Leeds centre, Wellington St leads out to *Wellington Bridge* (1817; J. Rennie) over the Aire. S of the bridge, on Armley Rd, *Castleton Mill* (1838), red brick with curved end wall. S of Armley Rd, castellated *Prison* (1847) and, off to N, on Canal Rd, *Armley Mill* (c 1807), now Leeds Industrial Museum, built for B. Gott (1762–1840), leading Yorkshire wool manufacturer of c 1800, whose factories were among the first in the north to exploit machinery and steam power bringing all the processes under a single roof. Gott's own house was *The Mansion* (c 1818; R. Smirke) in Gotts Park to W. The crown of Armley, on the hilltop is, *St. Bartholomew's Church* (1872; Walker and Athron), stern EE style in blackened stone with splendid crossing tower and spire rising sheer over the apse and transepts. Stone-vaulted E end and magnificent organ by Schulze. Reclining effigy of B. Gott (died 1839; J. Gott).

N of centre, Woodhouse Lane leads to an area of early 19C suburbs, now dominated by Leeds University. Spired former *Blenheim Chapel* (1864; Paull and Ayliffe), now converted to offices. In Blackman Lane, to NE, *All Souls' Church* (1876–80; G.G. Scott), a noble EE work with handsome W tower and vaulted chancel, built to the memory of W.F. Hook, vicar of Leeds. *Leeds University* was established as the Yorkshire College of Science, for which the original buildings (1877–86; A. Waterhouse) were built. Red brick with centre tower and asymmetrical wings, the hall lights to right stepped under shallow Gothic arches. Extensions 1894–1908 (A. and P. Waterhouse). The *Concert Hall* with an eclectic Renaissance front and centre tower was formerly a Presbyterian church (1870; J.B. Fraser), happily reprieved from demolition. Overlooking Woodhouse Moor, to W, *Leeds Grammar*

School (1858; E.M. Barry), Moorland Rd, stone Gothic with entrance tower and chapel of 1863. In the park statues of Wellington (1855; Marochetti), Peel (1852; Behnes) and a 30ft monument to Queen Victoria flanked by figures of Peace and Industry (1905; G. Frampton), all three moved here from in front of the Town Hall. N of the Moor, on Hyde Park Rd, prominent spire of *St. Augustine's Church* (1870; J.B. Fraser). Headingley Lane runs NW with attractive early Victorian villas set back and on the streets to E. The former *Headingley Hill Chapel* (1864–66; C. Brodrick) is a rare Gothic work by the architect of the Town Hall, strongly detailed with rose window and spire to one side, made more imposing by the flight of steps up to the front. Now offices. Set back, on N side, *Wesleyan College* (1867; Wilson and Willcox), High Victorian Gothic, notable for the centre tower where a Romanesque conical turret has been inflated as the main accent, ringed with red columns. On S side, •*St. Michael's Church* (1884–85; J.L. Pearson), the tower and spire the finest in Leeds, Pearson's Normandy French model already used for Truro Cathedral here well-suited to the hard Yorkshire stone. Transverse arched interior with EE lights, stained glass by Powell's and reredos by Temple Moore (1905). Fine iron screen. Further N, on Otley Rd, *St. Chad's Church* (1868; Lord Grimthorpe), expensive suburban church built at the edge of Beckett Park, by the architect member of the Beckett family, EE style with tall spire. Chancel added 1910 (J.H. Gibbons), a good design with E windows set high over a huge painted reredos. Weetwood, N of Otley Rd, was built up with large villas from c 1860, of which *Spenfield* (1875–77; G. Corson), Otley Rd, is the best survivor, severely Gothic stone house with corner turret and good Gothic interiors. Dining-room in the aesthetic movement taste (1888; G.F. Armitage) with enamelled peacock over the fireplace and painted plaster frieze, the woodwork Gothic, but more delicate than the earlier High Victorian work. N of the Ring Road, off Otley Old Road, *Cookridge Hospital* (1868–69; R. Norman Shaw), an early vernacular revival design by Shaw, the vernacular not Yorkshire but Kentish tile-hanging and brick, combined oddly with Yorkshire stone below. Gaunt proportions but clearly intended to be more welcoming than contemporary Gothic hospitals such as Scott's Leeds Infirmary. E wing in similar style added 1893. Off the Ring Road, to W, in **Horsforth**, *St. Margaret's Church* (1877–83; J.L. Pearson), Church Rd, stone EE style similar to Headingley but more modest, the spire not to Pearson's design.

NE of Headingley, around Meanwood, further large 19C villas off Stonegate Rd, *Meanwood Park Hospital*, Parkside Rd, belonged to the Beckett banking family, for whom Meanwood parish *church* (1849; W. Railton) was built. Gothic Beckett mausoleum in the churchyard. N of Stonegate Rd, *The Towers* (1867; E.W. Pugin), Gothic, and S, *Carr Manor*, partly of 1881 by E.S. Prior. Stainbeck Rd runs E to Chapel Allerton. •*Parish church* (1897–98; G.F. Bodley), Wood Lane, secluded from the main centre, a perfect example of Bodley's refined late style, Dec. to Perp. in smooth ashlar, the tower, standing detached to one side, as rarified a design as any in late 19C Gothic architecture, sheer and square, shallow buttresses and the bell-openings the only relief. The interior is coolly logical, an even array of slim piers with tall aisle windows and wagon roof running through to the E window interrupted only by the screen and culminating in a high painted reredos (1911). SE of Chapel Allerton, Harehills Lane runs to Roundhay Rd past *Chapel Allerton Hospital* (c 1830; J. Clark), stone Greek Revival mansion. Harehills, on E side of Roundhay Rd, is one of the battered but surviving areas of back-to-back housing, characteristic of 19C

Leeds. On Roundhay Rd, *St. Aidan's Church* (1891–94; Johnson and
Hicks), basilica in red brick, Romanesque outside, Early Christian
inside, attractively simple but with rich furnishings (c 1900; A.C.
Hick). The glory of the church is the apse ⁕mosaic (1914–16; Sir F.
Brangwyn) of the life of St. Aidan, crowded figures under a portent-
ously streaky sky punctuated by gaunt leafless trees, reminiscent
of the work of Puvis de Chavannes. Roundhay Rd leads out to *Roundhay
Park*, the landscaped grounds of the 1826 classical *Mansion Hotel*,
bought as a public space against opposition from local wealthy residents in 1872 and described as 'the finest provincial park in England'.

Nineteenth century back-to-back housing in Leeds

E of centre, N of the York Rd, Burmantofts, once the centre of the
Leeds terracotta industry. The *church* (1886; Kelly and Birchall),
Stoney Rock Lane, has a faience memorial to J. Holroyd (died 1890) of
the Burmantofts Faience Works and reredos of. similar material.
Nearby, the Corporation *Cemetery* crowded with monuments to the
poor of east Leeds. On the E outskirts, off Selby Rd, *Temple Newsam*,
17C mansion of the Ingram family, now a museum. Late 19C alterations for Mrs Meynell-Ingram, who devoted her ample fortune to
church building, patron of G.F. Bodley at Hoar Cross, Staffordshire
(see above p. 381). Chapel, converted from Library 1877, and grand
carved staircase 1894 (C.E. Kempe). Bodley rebuilt the chancel of
Whitkirk *church* (1901), Selby Rd, for Mrs Meynell-Ingram.

SE of central Leeds, above East St on Richmond Hill, *St. Saviour's
Church* (1842–44; J.M. Derick), Ellerby Rd, the first church in the north
to introduce Tractarian liturgy and architectural principles. It was
built anonymously by Edward Pusey, founder wih J.H. Newman and
J. Keble of the Oxford Movement, and sited in an impoverished area of
tenements notorious for the 'foulest vice'. The introduction of such
features as a screened chancel, vestments and choral services aroused
fears of 'popery' exacerbated by Newman's conversion to Catholicism
just before the consecration of the church, but High Anglican worship
found a foothold and prospered here. The building was archaeologically correct Gothic, intended to be crowned by a great spire on the
model of the University Church, Oxford, but never built. Exaggeratedly tall interior with fine stained glass in the four main windows by

O'Connor, the N, S and W windows to designs by Pugin. Later decoration by G.F. Bodley, including the screens and stencilled roof-painting, Bodley also designed the Pusey Memorial Chapel. Morris glass of c 1875–80 in N aisle, W, S aisle and porch. Font by G.E. Street (1871) and reredos by Temple Moore (1902). *Parsonage* (1846). Nearby, Church Rd, *RC church*, begun 1852 (J.A. Hansom) after the vicar, curate and part of the congregation of St. Saviour's had been converted, and clearly intended to outshine the Anglicans. W parts completed by W.W. Wardell, the apsed E end added 1866 (E.W. Pugin). Ornate Gothic with large W window and continental touch of cross-gabled aisles. S of St. Saviour's, in Cross Green Lane, *St. Hilda's Church* (1876–81; J.T. Micklethwaite), simple brick vessel carefully detailed, the interior particularly fine with wagon roof running through.

8m N of Leeds, at **Harewood**, *Harewood House* 18C mansion of the Lascelles family with outstanding interiors by R. Adam. S front remodelled 1843–50 (Sir C. Barry) in the heavier Renaissance classicism that early Victorians preferred, that is the single main accent, a portico, was replaced by an even range of pilasters under a rich balustrade, the low wings and end pavilions similarly elaborated, the wings raised to compete with the main block. The result is sober, formally grand and much enhanced by the splendid terraced garden (W.A. Nesfield) in front. 7m E of Leeds, A1, *Bramham Park*, early 18C mansion and formal gardens in the Versailles manner. Interiors and garden front entry of 1907 (D. Blow) in successful early 18C manner. Just N of Bramham village, at **Clifford**, *RC church*, in proud Romanesque style (1845–48; J.A. Hansom) apparently to designs by an amateur, J. Ramsay, but the monumental W tower based on Angoulême Cathedral added 1859 (G. Goldie). Handsome stone interior, round-arched with E end arcaded through to a Lady Chapel behind an arched stone screen. Stained glass by Pugin (1848–51) and A. Lusson, one of the leading French glass makers. 4m S of Bramham, A1, at **Aberford**, Gothic *Gascoigne almshouses* (1844; G.F. Jones), gabled and pinnacled with centre tower. To SE, *Lotherton Hall*, 18C house extended each side c 1900 in plain Georgian style. Now a country house museum containing the collections of the Gascoigne family given to the City of Leeds.

PONTEFRACT. A639 11m SE of Leeds. Market town. In the Market Place, *Market Hall* (1859; J. Wilson), stone fronted with giant columns flanking the entry. Glazed market hall behind. *St. Giles' Church* has chancel of 1869 with E window glass by Kempe (1879). In Salter Row, *Library and Museum* (1905) in red brick and terracotta. Town Hall designed (1785) by the father of Jesse Hartley (1780–1860), surveyor to the Liverpool Docks, who was born in Pontefract. **Castleford**, just N, is centre of the coal-mining area.

TODMORDEN. A646 13m W of Halifax. The only Yorkshire mill town built on cotton, the Fielden family dominating the industry as their memorials do the town. John Fielden (1784–1849) and his sons were radicals in politics, John Sr active in bringing in the ten-hour working day and advocate of the eight-hour day, his *statue* (1863; J.H. Foley), in Centre Vale Park, records public gratitude for the 1847 Ten Hours Act. John Fielden Jr built the three most prominent buildings of the town, all designed by John Gibson, the *Town Hall* (1870), *Unitarian church* (1869) and his own house, *Dobroyd Castle* (1865). The Town Hall is particularly handsome, a Corinthian temple with Renaissance details, the pedimental sculpture aptly showing Lancashire embracing Yorkshire, as the building spanned the river Calder, then the county boundary, so that magistrates from both sides could hear cases in the court. The church, on the hillside, quite outshines the parish church, fully ecclesiastical Gothic with tall spire and interior lavishly finished in stone and polished granite. The castle, prominent on the hill, is a castellated villa looking from afar larger than it is. Inside, full-height in Romanesque style, square below, octagonal above under a shallow glazed dome, all the shafts in polished granite. *Robinwood Mill* (c 1840) on the Burnley road was a Fielden mill with Gothic workers' housing adjacent. *Mons Mill* (1914) is typical of the largest brick Lancashire cotton mills. 5m E, **Hebden Bridge** has early 19C mills in the valley bottom with terraces clinging to the valley sides, some with the upper floor a separate house, entered from the higher level behind. *Bridge Mill* (c 1820) by the centre is converted to restaurant and shops. The *Birchcliffe Baptist Chapel* (1898) is a particularly magnificent Renaissance classical stone building, pedimented with arcaded loggia in front, now converted to community use. **Heptonstall**, just NW, one of West Yorkshire's prettiest villages, was a hand-loom weaving centre, from which Hebden Bridge grew. Parish *church* (1850–54; Mallinson and Healy), Perp. style standing by the ruins of the old church.

WAKEFIELD. A61 9m S of Leeds. The county town of West Yorkshire, cloth centre before the industrial revolution, but not notably an industrial town. The most prominent building is the *·Town Hall* (1877–80; T.E. Collcutt), Wood St, an important landmark in the transition from Gothic Revival styles to the loose eclecticism of the 'Queen Anne' movement. Here the building has the steep proportions of the Gothic Revival, three gabled oriels against a high hipped roof and a soaring tower behind, but the detail is that mix of Dutch, French and English 16C to 17C elements that the 'Queen Anne' pioneers such as Norman Shaw and J.J. Stevenson favoured for urban facades. The facade is symmetrical, tightly composed with the oriels rising through the parapet to high pedimented dormers, while the tower, determinedly off-centre, is Gothic in all but detail. Wood St is fortunate in its collection of public buildings. The *Museum* (1820–22; Watson and Pritchett), built as the Library and News Room, has a sober classical front with first-floor Ionic order, while the *Court House* (1806; C. Watson) is more flamboyantly Greek with full portico. Reticent two-storey addition of 1849. Beyond is the *·County Hall* (1894–98; Gibson and Russell), an instructive contrast to the Town Hall, for where Collcutt combined the vigorous compression of the Gothic Revival with N Renaissance detail after Norman Shaw, the County Hall, in the same N Renaissance vein, is far more delicate and an excellent demonstration of asymmetrical composition held in balance by the corner entrance cupola. Good interiors with original fittings, notably the domed council chamber. At S end of Wood St, Westgate, running E to the *Cathedral*, a noble 15C outline with 250ft spire, heavily remodelled by G.G. Scott 1858–74. Scott added the crockets that bristle up the spire and tidied up the interior. The stone vaulted E end (1901–05; J.L. and F. Pearson) was added after the church became a cathedral. Extensive stained glass by Kempe from 1872. Further W on Westgate, *No. 30* was the chemist's shop where the novelist G. Gissing was born in 1857. The disused *Opera House* (1894; F. Matcham) conceals a fine auditorium behind a battered facade. SE from the cathedral, Kirkgate runs down to the river Calder, past the Italianate *Kirkgate Station* (1857).

Over the river, the *Bridge Chapel*, the only significant medieval bridge chapel surviving in England. The W front is wholly reproduction (1847; G.G. Scott) and unnecessarily replaced so that the original could become a garden ornament at Kettlethorpe Hall, 2½m S. N of the Cathedral, at N end of Northgate, *Grammar School* (1833; R. Lane), formal symmetrical Gothic front, the centrepiece based on King's College chapel, Cambridge.

3m SW of Wakefield, on either side of the Calder, three late 19C churches, minor works by notable architects. On N side, **Horbury Junction** *church* (1892; Bodley and Garner), SE of Horbury, and, at **Horbury Bridge**, SW of Horbury, *church* (1884) by J.T. Micklethwaite. Over the bridge, at **Netherton**, *church* (1881; J.D. Sedding), all examples of economical design, well handled. Far from economical is **Ossett** *church* (1865; W.H. Crossland), NW of Horbury, with its towering 226ft spire over the crossing and strong EE detail. 5m N of Wakefield, A642, at **Oulton**, in the grounds of *Oulton Hall*, a stone classical mansion of c 1822 (R. Smirke), rebuilt 1851 after a fire. Estate *church* (1827–29; T. Rickman) of unusually high quality, brick vaulted with the spire excellently placed in the park landscape.

ISLE OF MAN

CASTLETOWN. 9m SW of Douglas. Capital town of the island until 1869. Nearby, *King William's College* (1830–33; Hansom and Welch), rebuilt after a fire 1844. The poet T.E. Brown was pupil and later Vice-Principal (1858–61), also a pupil was F.W. Farrar whose 'Eric, or Little by Little' (1858) is a school story partly based on his time here. In the town, *St. Mary's Church* (1826; T. Brine).

DOUGLAS. Principal town, and port for steamers from Liverpool since 1830. Mostly late 19C resort with *Legislative Buildings* (1894) and *Town Hall* (1899). Fine promenade along seafront. In Victoria Rd, two early works by the Arts and Crafts architect M.H. Baillie Scott, *The Red House* (1892) and *Laurel Bank/Holly Bank* (1895). At **Kirk Braddon**, A1, to W, John Martin (1789–1854), the painter, is buried. 5m NW, *Greeba Castle*, home of the novelist Hall Caine, author of 'The Manxman' (1894). At **Onchan**, 2m N of Douglas, *church* (1833; Hansom and Welch) with pretty spire. *Village Hall* (1897; M.H. Baillie Scott). At **Laxey**, 6m NE, A2, *Big Wheel* (1854), colossal 72ft iron waterwheel of former lead mines.

RAMSEY. A2 16m N of Douglas. Coastal resort with long *Queens Pier* (1882) originally for steamer traffic. Above the town, *Albert Tower*, Mountain Rd. 8m W, A3, *Bishopscourt*, **Kirk Michael**, residence of the Bishop of Sodor and Man.

THE CHANNEL ISLANDS

GUERNSEY. St. Peter Port. Picturesque steep site over the harbour, enlarged 1853. The town is dominated by the *Victoria Tower* (1846), off Monument Rd, built to commemorate a visit of Queen Victoria. Behind the parish church, the *Market* (rebuilt 1882). To S, *Hauteville House*, Hauteville, Victor Hugo's home from 1856–71, the years of political exile from Napoleon III's France, where 'Les Misérables' and 'Les Travailleurs de la Mer' were written. Sumptuously furnished with old woodwork and tapestry cut up and reassembled to suit Hugo's decorative taste. 2m N, **St. Sampson**, an important loading point for granite for road building during the 19C. In the *church*, E window by Hardman, S chapel E window by Clayton and Bell.

ALDERNEY. St. Anne. Victoria St, so named for a visit of Queen Victoria in 1854. The *church* (1850; Sir G.G. Scott) is perhaps the best 19C building on the islands. Short, compact with a central tower and apse. Local sandstone and Caen stone details, the style EE close to Norman. Around the coast a series of 13 forts built from 1847, all massively refortified by the Nazis 1941–44.

JERSEY. St. Helier. The centre is Royal Square, with *St. Helier's Church* (rebuilt 1864–68) behind. In the Square, Italianate *Royal Court* (1866) and *Library* (1886). In Halkett Place, to the N, *New Markets* (1882), glass roof on iron pillars, central fountain. The *harbour* was extended 1841–53 with Victoria and Albert Piers. From 1852–55 Victor Hugo lived at the *Maison Victor Hugo*, St. Luke's, to the S. At **St. Saviour's**, ½m NW, *church* where Lily Langtry, actress friend of Edward VII, was married (twice) and is buried.

SCOTLAND

BORDERS

DUNS. A6105 15m W of Berwick. Former county town of Berwickshire. In Market Square, *Royal Bank* (1857; Peddie and Kinnear), Italianate. *Duns Castle* (1818–22; J.G. Graham), a successful and picturesque Regency castle built on to the medieval tower. The Gothic detail is surprisingly good, due to the owner William Hay, amateur artist. 2m E, *Manderston House* (open to public), the best surviving Edwardian grand country house in Britain. Rebuilt 1901–05 (J. Kinross) for Sir James Miller, heir to a Baltic merchant fortune, Manderston appears outwardly a late 18C mansion in the style of Robert Adam. The garden front is largely the original house of c 1790 and this dictated the style of the rebuilding. Fine Ionic portico on the entrance front. Lavish interiors mostly in the Adam vein, with Kedleston Hall, Derbyshire, the most obvious model, chosen because this was Lady Miller's family home. The staircase, ballroom and much of the furnishing are French late 18C in style. Fine neo-Georgian stables (1895) with quite magnificent rosewood and brass fittings. Sir James Miller was a noted racehorse owner. In the estate village of **Buxley**, *Home Farm* (1897; J. Kinross), picturesque Scots baronial. Gothic cloistered courtyard, corner tower with delightful model dairy, octagonal, stone-vaulted and marble-lined, set beneath an oak-panelled tea-room.

EYEMOUTH. A1107 8m N of Berwick. Fishing town, modest 19C buildings. In the graveyard, monument to the 189 east coast fisherman drowned in the terrible storm of October 1881. 2m SW, A1, at **Ayton**, *Ayton Castle* (1851; J.G. Graham), imposing red sandstone house with massive central baronial tower. *Church* (1867; Brown and Wardrop), toughly detailed with W rose window. At **Cockburnspath**, A1, 12m N, *Dunglass Viaduct* (1846; Grainger and Miller), very handsome stone railway viaduct N of the village.

Ayton Castle (1851; J.G. Graham) near Eyemouth

JEDBURGH. A68 12m SE of Melrose. Former county town of Rox-
burghshire. In the Market Place, *Jubilee Fountain*, topped with a unicorn. At corner to Exchange Place, curved crow-stepped block with
Burgh Offices adjoining, an Italian former bank (1860; D. Rhind).
Castlegate leads out past the early 19C Greek *County Buildings* to the
former *County Prison* (1820; A. Elliot, and 1832), battlemented toy fort,
and museum. Along the river early and mid 19C mills. *Jedburgh
Abbey* was used as the parish church until 1875 when the Marquess of
Lothian built a new church and took over the ruins of the abbey to
prevent further damage. Restoration by R.R. Anderson. Effigy of the
8th Marquess of Lothian (died 1870) by G.F. Watts in N transept. 12m
SW of Jedburgh, **Hawick**, 19C centre of the woollen industry, called
the 'Glasgow of the Borders'. Hosiery and wool mills survive along the
river. In High St, *Town Hall* (1855; J.C. Walker) with landmark Scots
tower, *No. 12* (1857; Peddie and Kinnear), handsome Italianate bank,
and *No. 7* (c 1860), former British Linen Bank. *Albert Bridge* over the
Teviot (1865). *St. Cuthbert's Church* (1858) is a minor work of Sir G.G.
Scott. On the W bank *Wilton Mills* (mid 19C), stone woollen mills.
Wilton Church (1862; J.T. Emmett). To SE of the town three impressive
Victorian mansions, baronial *Glenmayne* (1866; Peddie and Kinnear)
and *Kings Knowes* with domed conservatory (1868; W. Hay) and
Gothic *Netherby* (1868; J. Walker).

KELSO, A699 15m E of Melrose. In The Square, *Town Hall* (1816),
refronted in Edwardian classical style (1905; J. Swanston). At corner of
Bridge St, *Bank of Scotland* (mid 19C), severe Italianate. In Bridge St,
some Ionic columned cast-iron shopfronts. In Woodmarket, *No. 27*
(1860; J. Burnet Sr), former bank with fine Greek detail, and
Cornmarket (1855; D. Cousin), Elizabethan style. Kelso Abbey ruins
were rescued in the early 19C by the Duke of Roxburghe. Nearby,
episcopal church (1868; R.R. Anderson), High Victorian Gothic. In
Roxburghe St, *St. John's Church* (1865–67; F.T. Pilkington) in the
spiky Gothic that was Pilkington's speciality. W front windows deep-
set with cusping, like fretwork, around the openings. In Bowmont St,
parallel, elegant *library* (c 1890; Sir G.W. Browne). Roxburghe St leads
out to *Floors Castle* (open to public), seat of the Dukes of Roxburghe.
A big plain house of 1721 was given a luxuriant Jacobean skyline of
battlements, chimneys and ogee domed turrets (1837–45; W.H.
Playfair). The result is particularly successful for the relative plainness
of the walls. Interiors partly of c 1840, partly redone in French style c
1905. 3m SW of Kelso, at **Roxburgh**, *Teviot Bridge* (1850; Grainger and
Miller), splendid stone railway viaduct, built on a curve. An elegant
wrought-iron footbridge crosses the river attached to the piers of the
viaduct.

PEEBLES. A702 23m S of Edinburgh. Former county town of Peebless-
hire. Over the Tweed bridge, parish *church* (1885–87; W. Young) with
tall crown tower. Good late 19C stained glass by D. Cottier. Adjoining,
former *County Buildings* (1844; T. Brown), Tudor style. In High St,
small *episcopal church* (1833; W. Burn) and *Chambers Institution*,
town house of the Earls of March rebuilt as a library and museum
(1859) and given to the town by W. Chambers, the publisher. Set back
from High St, *Church of Scotland* (1875; Peddie and Kinnear), with a
spire that balances the parish church tower in distant views. To E,
Peebles Hydro (1906; J. Miller) like a beached seaside hotel, roughcast walls and red tile roof. To W, off A72, *Manor Bridge* (1883) over
Tweed and *Neidpath Viaduct* (1863), eight-span curved railway via-

duct over the Manor Water. 3m S of Manor Bridge, *Glenternie* (1864; Brown and Wardrop), smaller baronial house. On B712, SW of A72, *Stobo Castle* (1805–11; A. and J. Elliot), castellated mansion, and, beyond, *Dawyck House* (1832–37; W. Burn), rambling baronial house with two round towers, extended 1898 (J.A. Campbell). Gardens open to public. 4m N of Peebles, A703, at **Eddleston**, the *Old Smiddy* (1862) with horseshoe shaped windows. To NE, *Portmore House* (1850; D. Bryce, and 1883), baronial with substantial square entrance tower, and, to SW, *Cringletie Hotel* (1861; D. Bryce), smaller baronial house. 9m W of Peebles, A72, *Castlecraig*, house of 1798 lavishly remodelled c 1900 by Sir J. Burnet. 7m E of Peebles, A72, **Innerleithen**, mill town on the Tweed. *United Free church* (1865–67; F. Pilkington), striking angular Gothic, the W front with three roses over a row of spiky lancets. To the W, *St. Ronan's Well*, celebrated in Scott's novel of that name. Pretty timber pavilion (1896). Two good plate-girder railway viaducts over the Tweed, *Horsburgh Viaduct* (1864), 4m W, and *Haugh Head Viaduct* (1866), 1m E. 2m E, **Walkerburn**, created around the famous woollen mills of H. Ballantyne and Sons after 1854. The *Scottish Museum of Wool Textiles* is here. On the slopes to NW of the centre, *The Kirna* (1867; F.T. Pilkington), angular Gothic house with steep roofs and heavily carved detail. 6m SW, off B709, *The Glen* (1855; D. Bryce), massive baronial house built for the chemical-master, Sir Charles Tennant, and enlarged with a four-storey tower to garden front 1874 (Bryce). Interiors remodelled by Lorimer 1905.

SELKIRK. A7 11m N of Hawick. Former county town of Selkirkshire. Woollen mills along the Ettrick Water. In Market Place, Scott *memorial* (1839; A.H. Ritchie). At opposite end of High St, *statue* of Mungo Park (1859; A. Currie), the explorer who disappeared in Africa in 1802. On the hill, castellated *County Buildings* (1869; D. Rhind). 2m W, A708, *Bowhill (open to public), mostly early 19C mansion of the Dukes of Buccleuch. Magnificent collections. 2m N, A707, *Sunderland Hall* (1850; D. Bryce), baronial remodelling of an 18C house. Beyond, *Fairnalie* (1906; J.J. Burnet), a good late example of the baronial tradition, harled with Scots 17C detail more sensitively used than in the 19C baronial houses. 2½m NW, *Peel Hospital* (c 1910; J. Kinross), similar Edwardian baronial. 7m N of Selkirk, A7, **Galashiels**, mill town with cloth mills along the Gala Water. In High St, *Church of Scotland* (1868), mixed Gothic front, next door *Nos 46–8*, plain Italianate bank. The old parish *church*, (1878–81; G. Henderson), Scott Crescent, has fine High Victorian spire. In Market St, *RC church* (1857; W. Wardell), Puginian Gothic. 4m SE of Galashiels, **Melrose**, the heart of Sir Walter Scott's country. The ruins of Melrose Abbey appear in Scotts first important work 'The Lay of the Last Minstrel' (1805). In Market Square, *Bank of Scotland* (1897; Sir G.W. Browne), gabled with free Renaissance detail, and *Corn Exchange* (1863; D. Cousin), crow-stepped gable. To W, in High Cross Avenue, modest *episcopal church* (1846–50; B. Ferrey), with contemporary rectory, and large Romanesque *Church of Scotland* (1866–72; Peddie and Kinnear), polychrome stonework and strong spire. Sir David Brewster (1781–1868), natural scientist and biographer of Newton, lived at Allerly, opposite Melrose, on the N side of the Tweed. 2m E, at **Drygrange**, *Leaderfoot Viaduct* (1862–65; J. Bell), very tall and elegant 19-arch stone railway viaduct over the Tweed. *Drygrange House*, to N, is baronial (c 1870; Peddie and Kinnear). 3m SW, on N side of Tweed, *Dryburgh Abbey* ruins, once owned by the family of Sir Walter Scott but sold leaving the family only the right 'to stretch their bones' here. Scott himself is buried in the N transept. Also buried here, the Haigs of Bemersyde, among them, Field Marshal Earl Haig, the 1914–18 war commander. *Dryburgh Abbey Hotel*, late 19C baronial. 2m W of Melrose is *Abbotsford* (1816–23; W. Atkinson), Sir Walter Scott's home from 1812 to his death in 1832. The house, open to public, was the pioneer of the baronial revival in Scotland, taking up specifically Scottish rather than the usual castellated motifs. The choice of style was Scott's, aided by the architect Edward Blore. Inside, fine baronial interiors and furnishings collected by Scott as well as literary mementos.

CENTRAL

ALLOA. A907 6m E of Stirling. Inland port of the Forth noted for brewing and yarn. On Mar St, *Town Hall* (1888; A. Waterhouse), tall proportioned Jacobean, given by the Paton family, leading industrialists. On the corner of Drysdale St, *County Buildings* (1863; Brown and Wardrop), baronial with a slate-roofed tower. On the corner of Mill St, *bank* (1906; J.M.D. Peddie and G.W. Browne), gabled Jacobean, well detailed. On the corner of Mill St and High St, *No. 2 High St* (1874; A. Frame), with a second-floor row of close set pilasters reminiscent of 'Greek' Thomson's work. Opposite, baronial *bank* (1861; D. MacGibbon). On corner of Mill St and Bank St, *Chalmers Church* (1855; J.,W. and J.Hay). In Bank St, *Royal Bank* (c 1845), severe classical, and *No. 16* (1873), more richly Italianate. To the W, in Bedford Place, the 207ft spire of the parish *church* (1817–19; J.G. Graham). In Primrose St, the *Public Baths* (1895–98; J.J. Burnet), Scots Renaissance with tall entrance arch and good carved detail in red stone. Interior all in banded tiles, almost Art Deco. To NW, on Tulliboddy Rd, *Inglewood* (c 1900; Mitchell and Wilson), large stone mansion, free Jacobean with big tower and red tiled roofs. Other early 20C industrialists' houses in Claremont, notably *The Gean* (c 1912). At **Tillicoultry**, 3m NE, entertaining early Gothic *church* (1828; W. Stirling) and Grecian *Municipal Buildings* (c 1830) in High St. *J. and D. Paton's mills*, Lower Mill St, are a large early 19C stone complex. 3m E, A91, at **Dollar**, parish *church* (1841; W. Tite). *Dollar Academy* (1818; W.H. Playfair) is a major monument of the Greek Revival in Scotland, founded by the will of J. McNabb, poor boy of Dollar who made a fortune at sea.

CALLANDER. A84 13m NW of Stirling. Resort town from the late 19C, called the 'Gateway to the Highlands' which begin at the Pass of Leny. 2m NW, *Leny House* (1846; D. Bryce), an early baronial work by Bryce with conical roofed tower. Callander is also the gateway to the Trossachs to the W, made popular as a romantic landscape as early as 1810 through Scott's poem, 'The Lady of the Lake'. It was at Brig O' Turk, A821, in the Trossachs that the romantic affair between Ruskin's wife Effie and the young Pre-Raphaelite painter J.E. Millais began in 1853. Millais painted the famous portrait of Ruskin in Glen Finglas. Effie had been a childhood acquaintance of Ruskin's from Perth, but the marriage was unsuccessful, she and Millais were married in 1855. On the E side of Loch Venachar, massive classical *sluice house* of the Glasgow waterworks (1856–59), a prodigious engineering undertaking. Odd conical roofed towers used to clear debris from the tunnelling mark the course of the conduit towards Aberfoyle. The road, A821, from Aberfoyle to the Trossachs, was built 1885 to open up the area. 3m W of Aberfoyle, on Loch Ard, *Corrienessan* (1886; J.J. Burnet), house influenced by Norman Shaw's work and, interestingly, by the sweeping roofs of the contemporary American 'shingle style'. 9m S of Aberfoyle, 3m E of Killearn (A875), *Ballikinrain Castle* (1868; D. Bryce), one of Bryce's largest castles around a massive circular entrance tower, reduced in size 1915. *Auchinlert* (1906) near Killearn is a handsome stone Arts and Crafts style house, plain gables with massive chimneys. 2m S of Drymen *Dalnair House* (c 1870), heavily detailed baronial tower.

DUNBLANE. A9 7m N of Stirling. The *Cathedral* lay partly ruined, the choir only used as a parish church (restored 1872; G.G. Scott), until 1889–93 when the nave was reroofed (R.R. Anderson). Ruskin thought there 'nothing so perfect in its simplicity' as the leaf-shaped W window. Good 19C fittings including screen and pulpit, choir stalls and organ case of 1911 (Lorimer). Large former hydro, the *Dunblane Hotel* (1875; Peddie and Kinnear). To N, A9, *Queen Victoria School* (1907; J.A. Campbell), complex of tall harled buildings and chapel with central tower and spire. 3m W, A820, is **Doune**, estate town of the Earls of Moray of Doune Castle. *Doune Park Gardens*, laid out in the early 19C around the new house, built 1802 for the 10th Earl, are open to the public. Fine mid Victorian pinetum. *Doune Castle* was partly restored for the 14th Earl from 1883. *Episcopal church* (1877–78; J. Brooks), George St, a good small High Victorian work with vaulted chancel and original fittings by Brooks. *Nos 1–11 George St* (1894; T. MacLaren) is a harled terrace with simplified Scots detail suggestive of C.R. Mackintosh. T. MacLaren was brother of the architect J.M. MacLaren (cf. Stirling, below, and Fortingall, Tayside) but built little in Scotland, emigrating to Colorado. 1m W, **Deanston**, where J. Smith (died 1850), inventor of the mechanical reaping machine, was manager at the cotton mills. *Deanston House* was remodelled in Italianate style 1882, an early work of J.J. Burnet. 3m S of Doune, *Blair Drummond* (1873; J.C. Walker), large baronial mansion, now a school, the grounds a safari park. 2m S of Dunblane, A9, *Keir House* (18C altered 1850 and 1900), visited by Chopin during his British tour in 1848.

FALKIRK. A803 21m W of Edinburgh. Centre of a coal and iron district during the 19C, especially notable the ironworks at Carron, 2m N, founded 1760. In the High St, 140ft *Town Steeple* (1813). *Nos 138–40* (1832; J.G. Graham), Greek Ionic bank building facing down Cow Wynd. On the corner of Cow Wynd, *Savings Bank* (1896) with Corinthian pilasters and curved to the corner. On corner of Newmarket St, *Royal Bank* (1879; Peddie and Kinnear), baronial, in Newmarket St, Duke of Wellington *statue* (1851; Forrest) and old *Municipal Buildings* (1879; W. Black), baronial with corner tower. In Hope St, *Sherriff Court* (1867; T. Brown), gabled with circular turret, and *Library* (1901), free Gothic. 1½m E, *Callendar House* (1869–77; Brown and Wardrop), an old house given a Loire style overhaul with stone towers and tall pavilion roofs. 3m NE is **Grangemouth**, the port for Falkirk. 2m NW, A9, at **Larbert**, *Larbert Hospital* (1861–70; F.T. Pilkington), Gothic with massive Pilkington detail, rough masonry and corner entrance, the corner held on a sturdy circular pillar.

STIRLING. From the *station* (1912; J. Miller), baronial style, the town rises to NW towards the spectacular castle rock. The 19C commercial centre is between Murray Place and King St. In Murray Place, *Post Office* (1894; W. Robertson), free early Renaissance style, and, adjoining *Nos 80–2*, former National Bank (1854; J.D. Peddie), excellently detailed Italianate. Opposite, *Nos 77–9*, former Commercial Bank (1872; D. Rhind). From Murray Place, *Arcade* (1879–82; J. McLean) leads through to King St with French roofed hotel at each end and two-storey glazed arcade between. In King St, adjoining *Nos 34–6* (1861), cast-iron and plate-glass shopfront. To left, *Nos 22–4* (c 1840), classical bank building with twin Corinthian porches, and, to right, *Nos 50–2* (1833; W. Burn), plain classical Bank of Scotland. On W side, *Nos 21–5* (1863; Peddie and Kinnear), Royal Bank, a less elaborate palazzo than the National Bank but well detailed. At S end, *Nos 1–2* (1862; J., W. and J. Hay), richly treated Italianate bank on corner of Murray Place. Dominant in King St, *Nos 65–7* (1816; W. Stirling), the former Burgh Buildings with curved front and slender classical steeple. Statue of Wallace over the door (1859; A.H. Ritchie). To left, in Corn Exchange Rd, *Municipal Buildings* (1908; J.G. Gillespie), handsome Scots Renaissance with Arts and Crafts touches, especially to the big SW tower. It was not completed to the original design. On S corner of Corn Exchange Rd, *No. 61 King St* (1900; J. Thomson), curved fronted bank, richly carved. Opposite Municipal Buildings, *Library* (1904; H.R. Taylor), elaborate with crow-steps, conical corner turret and tall centre block. In Spittal St, *No. 33* (1825), Greek Doric bank converted to Infirmary 1874 (Peddie and Kinnear). Off Spittal St, in Academy St, former *Stirling High School* (1854; J., W. and J. Hay), rubble-stone Gothic, but of exceptional interest for the •extension to Spittal St (1887–90; J.M. MacLaren), one of the key works of Scottish late 19C architecture, combining Arts and Crafts sculptural decoration and careful use of stone with a massiveness and use of rounded forms that suggest comparison with the work of H.H. Richardson in the USA. The steep slope means that the main range is set over a basement steadily increasing in height until, at the corner tower, it is almost two storeys high, emphasised by a great sculptured doorway. Above this the tower is sheer, the leading edge rounded off, the rear stair turret also rounded but rising to a polygonal cap with Arts

The Wallace Monument (1862–69; J.T. Rochead) Stirling

and Crafts battlements and pretty cupola. The main tower is capped by an observatory dome. The long range, like the tower, is severe and unadorned until the roofline where three Scots Renaissance gables and a sculptured niche soften the outline. Spittal St continues into St. John St towards the Castle Esplanade. To left, Valley Cemetery with memorial to the Virgin Martyrs, drowned by the tide in Wigtown Bay in 1685 during persecution of the Covenanters. On the Esplanade, heroic stone *statue* of Robert Bruce (1877; A. Currie). In the *Castle* itself, the museum of the Argyll and Sutherland Highlanders. The main 19C residential area was S of Dumbarton Rd, with early 19C houses in Allan Park and Victoria Square and mid Victorian villas around King's Park. In King's Park Rd, off Port St, *St. Columba's Church* (1901; J.J. Stevenson), handsome Scots Gothic with tower. On Dumbarton Rd, *Smith Art Gallery* founded 1873 and *Episcopal church* (1875; R.R. Anderson), lancet Gothic.

2m NE of Stirling, at **Causewayhead**, *Wallace Monument* (1862–69; J.T. Rochead), Abbey Craig, crown spired Scots baronial tower, 220ft high with massive bronze statue of Wallace (1887), set on a hilltop. It was intended as a Scottish Pantheon, the interior Hall of Heroes was to contain busts of great Scots figures. 3m N of Stirling, **Bridge of Allan**, a spa town from the early 19C at the foot of the Ochil Hills. Victorian villas well laid out. In Henderson St, *Royal Hotel* (1842) with Jacobean touches, Romanesque style *Macfarlane Museum* (1886; E. Simpson), and a cast-iron clock on column by Macfarlane's of Glasgow. In Keir St, *Holy Trinity Church* (1860), fittings of 1904 by C.R. Mackintosh.

DUMFRIES AND GALLOWAY

ANNAN. A75 19m NW of Carlisle. *Town Hall* (1875; R. Smith) red sandstone with dominating Scots tower. Thomas Carlyle was educated at Annan Academy, which appears, disguised, in 'Sartor Resartus'. *River Annan Viaduct* (1848; Grainger and Miller), fine stone railway bridge with rusticated arches. Similar viaduct over Port St. *Annan Station* (1848) is Italianate and well preserved. Carlyle was born and is buried at **Ecclefechan**, A74, 6m N. *Carlyle Birthplace Museum* and *statue* (1882; Boehm), the same as the one in Chelsea, London, where Carlyle spent most of his life. 6m NW of Ecclefechan, A74, **Lockerbie**, with long main street dominated by the Scots tower of the *Town Hall* (1873–84; D. Bryce). 3m S, off A74, *Castlemilk House* (1865; D. Bryce), one of Bryce's best baronial houses, the main element a massive round tower with porte-cochère. Nearby, at St. Mungo, *church* (1876; D. Bryce).

DUMFRIES. A75 16m W of Annan. Former county town of Dumfriesshire associated with Robert Burns whose mausoleum (1815; T.F. Hunt) is in St. Michael's churchyard. In Church Place, *Greyfriars Church* (1867; J. Starforth), with tall spire and sharp detail, like Pilkington's churches, but less muscular. In the square, Burns *statue* (1882; Mrs D. Hill). *St. Mary's Church* (1837; J. Henderson), incorrect Gothic with central turret and swept-up parapet. In Church St, by the old observatory (1835), now the *museum*, statue of Scott's 'Old Mortality' and pony (1840; Currie) in a columned rotunda. *Dumfries Academy* (1890; F. Carruthers), neo-classical with portico and elaborate cupola, successor to the building where J.M. Barrie went to school. The *Ewart Library* (1903; A. Crombie) commemorates W. Ewart MP, early advocate of the abolition of capital punishment (he succeeded in abolishing it for cattle-theft in 1837) and most noted for the Free Libraries Act of 1850. In Buccleuch St, Ionic columned *chapel* (c 1820; T.F. Hunt), castellated *County Court* (1863; D. Rhind) and *County Buildings* (1912; J.M.D. Peddie). Among the distinctive *Mills*, Rosefield Mills (1886)—a forerunner of Templeton's Mill, Glasgow—and Nithsdale Mills (1857) Italianate. S of the town *Crichton Royal Hospital* (1834–39; W. Burn), vast asylum completed 1871 (W.L. Moffat). Cathedral-like chapel (1892; Sydney Mitchell). 3m SW, A711, *Goldilea Viaduct* (1859), ten-arch stone railway viaduct. 6m S, A710, at **New Abbey**, *Shambellie House* (1856; D. Bryce), costume museum, part of the Royal Scottish Museum, housed in a medium-sized baronial house. The guidebook describes the acrimony between architect and client and hints at the difficulties of building these substantial houses in countryside often more accessible from sea than land. 19m NW of Dumfries, 3m NW of **Thornhill**, *Drumlanrig Castle*, great 17C castle of dukes of Queensberry, and after 1810, of the dukes of Buccleuch. 19C estate buildings. 2m W of Thornhill, **Penpont**, *church* (1867; C. Howitt), and, to W, *Capenoch* (1855; D. Bryce) medium-sized baronial house, built around an earlier building. At **Keir**, S of Penpont, K. McMillan invented the first pedal driven bicycle 1839 at Courthill Smithy. At **Closeburn**, S of Thornhill, towered Gothic *church* (1878; J. Barbour). At **Moniave**, 8m SW of Thornhill, *Kilneiss* (1884; J.J. Burnet), built for the painter, J. Paterson and *Crawfordton* (1865; Peddie and Kinnear) baronial style house.

LANGHOLM. A7 20m N of Carlisle. Mill town on the Esk. Parish *church* (1842; Burn and Bryce), lancet Gothic but quite elaborate pinnacled front. *Erskine church* (1867) thickly detailed tower and broach spire. Neo-Jacobean *library* (1877; J. Burnet). On White Hill, *obelisk* (1835) to Sir J. Malcolm, local boy who joined the Indian Army aged 12, had a distinguished career as soldier, diplomat and administrator and wrote the 'History of Persia' (1815).

KIRKCUDBRIGHT. A711 29m SW of Dumfries. Former county town of Kirkcudbrightshire. *St. Cuthbert's Church* (1838; W. Burn) lancet Gothic with spire. Castellated *courthouse* (1868; D. Rhind) and classical *Town Hall* (1878; Kinnear and Peddie). In late 19C, E.A. Hornel, the Glasgow school painter settled at *Broughton House*, now a museum with some of his paintings and his Japanese garden. At **Gatehouse of Fleet**, 6m NW, a 75ft granite *clock tower* (1871) overwhelms the main street. At Anwoth, 1m W, large granite pyramid *monument* (1842) to Samuel Rutherford (1600–61) leading Calvinist divine and minister at Anwoth. At **Kirkandrews**, 5m SW of Kirkcudbright, extraordinary farm group of early Italian and castellated character, built in early 20C for J. Brown, a Manchester magnate.

MOFFAT. A701 16m N of Lockerbie. Formerly a spa town but the Hydro hotel has gone. Empress Eugenie of France was a frequent visitor. In the centre, *Colvin Fountain* (1875), a bronze ram on rocky base. J.L. Macadam (1756–1836) the pioneer road-builder is buried in the churchyard. Tall early Gothic *church* (1887; J. Starforth) with matching manse. At the other end of town *St. Mary's Church* (1892; D. Burnie), with tall spire.

STRANRAER. A75 68m W of Dumfries. Town that replaced Portpatrick, 7m W as the port for Northern Ireland during the 19C, partly as a result of the railway. Gothic *Courthouse* (1872; Brown and Wardrop). 2m E, *Lochinch Castle* (1867; Brown and Wardrop), baronial castle of the Earls of Stair set in gardens laid out in the early 18C. At **Ardwell**, 9m S, fine spired *church* (1888; P. Chalmers).

WIGTOWN. A714 50m SW of Dumfries. Former county town of Wigtownshire with modest Gothic *County Buildings* (1863; Brown and Wardrop) and *Jail*, in Harbour Rd (1848), now police station. On Windy Hill *obelisk* (1858) to the Wigtown martyrs, put to death in 1685 during the persecution of the Covenanters. At Mochrum, 7m SW, *The Old Place* carefully restored from ruin for the 3rd Marquess of Bute (c 1875–99; R. Park) with Arts and Crafts interiors (1903–09; R.W. Schultz). Iron wellhead in the court by E. Gimson.

FIFE

CUPAR. A91 10m W of St. Andrews. The centre around St. Catherine St laid out c 1817, the *Corn Exchange* (1862; Campbell Douglas and Stevenson) has a good High Victorian Gothic spire set back from the street, the *episcopal church* (1866; R.R. Anderson) a lancet Gothic front to the street, the two interruptions to a Regency plan. S of the Mercat Cross, in Crossgate, *Duncan Institute* (1870; J. Milne) with crude Gothic tower and short spire. W of the cross, in Bonnygate, *St. John's Church* (1877; J. Sellars), handsome early Gothic with an octagonal spire. Next door, *Bonnygate Church* (1866; Peddie and Kinnear), heavily detailed with slated spire. *Cupar Station* (1847; ?D. Bell) is a very attractive Italianate group of centre block and pavilion wings, the platform canopy carried on cast-iron lotus columns. S of the town, *Hill of Tarvit House* (1905–07; R. Lorimer), neo-Georgian remodelling of a 1690s house, harled with steep hipped roofs and long sashes.

DUNFERMLINE. A823 17m NW of Edinburgh. Linen-manufacturing town from the 18C and the birthplace in 1837 of the Pittsburgh steel king, Andrew Carnegie, who devoted much of his vast fortune to philanthropic works in Britain and the USA, notably the provision of public libraries. The town is the headquarters of the Carnegie Trust and benefitted much from Carnegie's generosity, especially in the laying out of the deep glen of the Lyne Burn as a public park, *Pittencrieff Glen* (1903). *Pittencrieff House* (1610, 1731 and 1911) is now a museum with costume collection. In the park, large Art Nouveau *fountain* (1908; R. Goulden) and bronze *statue* of Carnegie (1914; Goulden). The *cottage* in Priory Lane, near the abbey, where Carnegie was born, is now a museum. *Dunfermline Abbey*, burial place of kings of Scotland including Robert Bruce, has a nave of c 1150 and parish kirk (1818–21; W. Burn) with plaster vault added in place of the demolished choir. Pictorial W window by the painter Sir J.N. Paton, native of Dunfermline. Kirkgate leads N with, at corner of Bridge St, large French Gothic *City Chambers* (1876; J.C. Walker) with spired clock tower. From Bridge St, High St runs E, dominated by the former *County Buildings* (1809–11; A. Elliot) with Wrenian spire. NE of the abbey, in Abbot St, *Carnegie Library* (1881; J.C. Walker), the first funded by Carnegie, Gothic style. Carnegie also gave the *Carnegie Baths* (1902; H.J. Blanc), turretted and gabled with carved panels and Moorish interiors, and the *Carnegie Clinic* (1909–12; D. Barclay), N Renaissance style both in Pilmuir St. In Bothwell St, the best of the linen factories, *Erskine Beveridge Court* (c 1870), Italian palazzo front. 7m W of Dunfermline, A985, the picturesque town of **Culross** with the 13C *Abbey* remains carefully restored 1905 (P.M. Chalmers). Nearby *Dunimarle Castle* (1840; R. and R. Dickson), large castellated mansion with round tower and *Brankstone Grange* (1864; D. Bryce) baronial. At **Kincardine** to W, *Tulliallan Castle* (1818–20; W. Atkinson), Georgian Gothic with fine mid 19C gardens by G.P. Kennedy and excellent gateway of 1908 (Watson and Salmond) at Blackhall. At **Torryburn**, 3m E of Culross, *Craigflower House*, remodelled in baronial style (1860; D. Bryce) with corner turrets and conical roofs. Now a school. 5m S of Dunfermline, at **North Queensferry**, the *Forth Rail Bridge* (see below p. 521).

FALKLAND. A912 5m N of Glenrothes. *Falkland Palace* (NTS), the

16C palace of James V, was restored from 1893–96 (J. Kinross) for the 3rd Marquess of Bute who bought the site in 1887 and put his prodigious wealth into a careful repair of the S wing with good painted decoration and carved work. Statue outside of O. Tyndall Bruce (1865; Sir J. Steell) for whom *Falkland House* (1839–44; W. Burn), to the W of the town, was built. This is one of the most successful Jacobean revival houses in Scotland, excellent stonework, an asymmetrical entrance front with tower, ornate chimneys and strapwork decoration and symmetrical garden front. The interior was embellished after 1887 for the Marquess of Bute with painted decoration and inlaid panelling. Now a school. Tudor style *lodge* to the town. In the High St, spired *fountain* (1856; A. Roos) to O. Tyndall Bruce and parish *church* (1848; D. Bryce), lancet style. At **Ladybank**, 5m NE, and **Markinch**, 5m S, early *stations* (1847; D. Bell), Italianate with awnings on cast-iron columns, as at Cupar. The Leven valley at Markinch and up to Leslie was a flax and linen area, also with numerous paper mills. 6m NE of Falkland, at **Collessie**, B937, *Kinloch House* (1859; C. Kinnear), large baronial remodelling of an early 18C house.

KIRKCALDY. A92 26m N of Edinburgh. Linen-manufacturing town from the 18C, but renowned from 1847 for M. Nairn's mixture of cork fibre and linseed oil paint, first called oilcloth and later developed to linoleum. A long waterfront town stretching from Invertiel to Dysart. In the High St, *Nos 218–22* (1834) and *No. 226* (1833; W. Burn), pair of neo-classical banks. In Kirk Wynd, plaque on the burgh school site where Carlyle taught in 1816. *Museum* and *Industrial Museum* above the War Memorial Garden, the Museum with a good collection of 19C and early 20C Scottish painters. In St. Brycedale's Ave tall spired *church* (1878–81; J. Matthews). *The Feuars Arms*, 66–8 Commercial St, has an Art Nouveau interior with stained glass and tiles. In **Dysart**, beyond, *Tollbooth*, High St, 1576 tower with hall added 1888 (Campbell Douglas and Sellars). In Rectory Lane, the *McDouall Stuart Museum*, birthplace of the first explorer to cross Australia (1861–62). *Church of Scotland* (1874; Campbell Douglas and Sellars), West Port, High Victorian with central tower and short slate spire. S of the centre of Kirkcaldy, *Invertiel Viaduct* (1847; Bouch and Grainger), prominent nine-span rock-faced bridge over the Tiel. From **Kinghorn**, A92, 2m S, a view of *Inchkeith* island, fortified from the 16C but the surviving works are largely of 1878–81 when very large batteries were built to protect the port of Leith. At **Burntisland**, 2m W, by the present station, *old station* (1847; D. Bell), classical, the original terminus of the line from Edinburgh to Dundee. From here the carriages were ferried to Granton, by Edinburgh, the world's first railway ferry. *No. 17 Leven St* (1850–54; R.C. Carpenter), a parsonage house with an unusual steep stepped gable to the whole front and mullion and transom windows under Gothic arches. The inspiration seems to be N German merchants' houses. On the hill above the town *Nos 1–4 Broomhill Terrace* (1858; F. Pilkinton), polychrome Gothic.

ST. ANDREWS. A915 56m NE of Edinburgh. Cathedral, university and golfing town, all of the greatest antiquity. Three streets converge on the cathedral ruins. In South St, *Holy Trinity Church* (1412 and 1906; P.M. Chalmers), the body of the church rebuilt in the 15C style to undo the effects of a 1799 rebuilding. *Nos 109–21* (1844; W. Scott), neo-classical three-storey range. On S side, *Town Hall* (1858; J.A. Hamilton), baronial, and *St. Mary's College*, founded 1537 with buildings on two sides of the 17C quadrangle, rebuilt 1764 and 1828 and extended in Scots Renaissance style (1889; W. Robertson) and again in early Georgian style (1908; R. Lorimer). To W, S of South St, *Madras College* (1832; W. Burn), a neo-Jacobean range with shaped gables, originally an orphanage and school. In Market St, the central street, the prominent slate spire of *Hope Park Church* (1865; Peddie and Kinnear). On North Street, the third street, *United College*, Jacobean style quadrangle (1829–31; R. Reid: 1845–46; W. Nixon). To N, facing the sea, on The Scores and Gillespie Terrace, large 19C buildings, villas, hotels, university buildings and, to the W, The Links with the *Royal and Ancient Golf Club* founded 1754, clubhouse (1854; G. Rae, and 1880) like a large villa in the Italianate style. From here begins the Old Course, open to anyone on payment of a green fee. The area of generous villas and terraces stretches around the W of the old town, the larger Tudor and baronial houses in Doubledykes Rd and Kennedy Gardens. In Queens Terrace, *episcopal church* (1867–69; R.R. Anderson), High Victorian EE style. In Hebburn Gardens, *No. 96* (1902; R. Lorimer), stone Arts and Crafts house with sweeping slate roofs. *St. Leonard's Church* (1903; P.M. Chalmers), good neo-Norman with saddleback tower. 2m S, *Craigtoun Hospital*, originally Mount Melville (1903; P. Waterhouse), large pink stone gabled Scots Renaissance style house built for the Younger brewery family. Craigtoun Park with formal gardens of c 1910 is developed with model village, children's railway etc. A959 9m S of St. Andrews, **Anstruther**, principal port of the group of fishing villages of the East Neuk. The *Scottish Fisheries Museum*, Harbourhead, has well-displayed items from the 16C to the early 20C. 6m W, B941, *Balcarres House*, 16C tower house much enlarged 1836–43 (W. Burn) and 1863 (D. Bryce). Large rambling stone house with pretty *North Lodge* (1897) and *Estate Office* (1903) by Lorimer, harled with slate roofs.

GRAMPIAN

ABERDEEN. The present centre of Aberdeen is largely an early 19C creation, bisected by the impressive straight length of Union St. The E end of Union St is Castle St with the restored 17C *Mercat Cross*. On the N side, *•Tolbooth and Town House*, the 1615 Tolbooth steeple incorporated in the large Gothic municipal offices (1868–74; Peddie and Kinnear). The offices are the most prominent landmark of central Aberdeen, Franco-Scots Gothic with a magnificent main tower standing forward and capped by a steep pyramid roof rising to 210ft. Arcaded ground floor and round turrets at the angles of the main front. To right, on the corner of King St, *No. 5* (1839–42; A. Simpson), former head office of the North of Scotland Bank, distinguised neo-classical building with Corinthian columned curved front of imposing scale, suited to the prominent site. Rich interior. The S end of King St has a good series of early 19C buildings, on left, *Nos 1–5* (1839; A. Simpson) and *Nos 7–9* (1836; J.G. Graham), the former Commercial Bank with heavy Roman Doric portico. On right, *Episcopal Cathedral* (1816; A. Simpson), Perp. style, chancel added 1880 (G.E. Street), much redecorated in bright colours by Comper 1928–43. To left of the Town House, Broad St runs N to *•Marischal College* of Aberdeen University, the front building (1903–06; A.M. Mackenzie) in shining white granite linked to the rebuilt *Greyfriars church* (1903). Perp. style with the strong vertical emphasis culminating in a richly pinnacled roofline, the facade set off by the tower of the church at the S end. Behind, earlier quadrangle (1837–41; A. Simpson), Tudor Gothic, the central tower raised (1893–97; A.M. Mackenzie) as the Mitchell Tower, visible from all over the city, 250ft high to the top of the flèche, the elaborate pinnacles echoed on the main facade. The Mitchell Hall was built behind the tower for graduation ceremonies. Union St runs W from the Town House, mostly early 19C, *Nos 60–2*, Clydesdale Bank (1862; J. Matthews), ornate Italianate. A fine Greek Ionic *screen* (1830; D. Burton and J. Smith), like Burton's Hyde Park Corner screen, London, gives access to the *East and West Churches of St. Nicholas*, one long building but used as two churches, the W church 1741 by James Gibbs, the E church and central tower rebuilt after a fire (1875–80; W. Smith). In Schoolhill behind, *Aberdeen Academy*, new buildings 1901, the original severe Greek Doric building (1840; J. Smith) surviving in Little Belmont St. By the arch to Robert Gordon's College, *statue* (1884; T. Burnett) of General Gordon. *Art Gallery and Museum* (1885; A.M. Mackenzie), adjoining, Renaissance style extended by Mackenzie 1905 and 1923–25, the latter the Aberdeen War Memorial Hall of Memory.

The road then crosses the deep Denburn ravine, the W side laid out as gardens along Union Terrace. On the N side of the viaduct (1886), a good group of buildings, *His Majesty's Theatre* (1906; F. Matcham), free Baroque with off-centre dome, *South Church* (1892; A.M. Mackenzie), Italian Renaissance church with Corinthian portico and dome, scenically very effective, and *Public Library* (1891; G. Watt), Renaissance style with steep roofs and cupola, similar to the work of J. Sellars in Glasgow. On the corner of Union Terrace heroic bronze *statue* (1888; W. Stevenson) of William Wallace and seated *statue* of Prince Albert (1863; Marochetti) in Field Marshal's uniform. Queen Victoria's first public appearance after Albert's death was to unveil this statue, after nearly two years of seclusion. Along Union Terrace, late 19C offices, *No. 20* (1897; A.M. Mackenzie), *No. 22* (1896; A.M.

*Clydesdale Bank (1862; J. Matthews) and Municipal Offices
(1868–74; Peddie and Kinnear), Union Street, Aberdeen.
Photograph c 1880*

Mackenzie) and *No. 24* (1902; Sydney Mitchell and Wilson), Italianate
to Baroque in style. *Nos 1–3* (1885; A.M. Mackenzie) is a handsome
Renaissance style building on the corner of Union St overlooking
Edward VII *statue* (1914; A. Drury). Union St crosses the Denburn
Ravine on a single span bridge (1802). By the bridge, Tudor Gothic
Trinity Hall (1846; J. and W. Smith). To N side, *Music Hall* (1820;
A. Simpson) with Greek Ionic portico. In Golden Square, to N, granite
statue (1842; T. Campbell) of the 5th Duke of Gordon. In Huntly St, to
W, *RC Cathedral* (1860; A. Ellis), with tall and spiky spire, and *Nos 50–
6* (1841; J. Smith), former Blind Asylum, classical on open courtyard
plan. S of Union St, *27–35 Bon Accord St* (1908; L. Stokes), telephone
exchange with Stokes' characteristic arched ground floor and pared
detail. In Crown St, *Post Office* (1907; W. Oldrieve), Scots gables and
turrets, in Crown Terrace, *St. John's Church* (1849; T. Mackenzie),
Dec. style, as advocated by English ecclesiologists at the time, taken
up in Scotland only by the episcopal church. Further E, beyond the
station, disused *Tivoli Theatre* (1872; C.J. Phipps), Guild St, Italian
Gothic exterior and fine domed interior of 1909 (F. Matcham). In
Market St, to E, *Nos 13–15* (1845; A. Simpson), former Mechanics
Institute, dignified neo-classical buildings. Market St leads S over the
Dee by *Victoria Bridge* (1881), with the main harbour and docks to the
E.

   W of centre, Union St ends at *Christ's College* (1850; T. Mackenzie),
Tudor Gothic with tower to one side. Albyn Place runs W into the
prosperous 19C suburbs. On Albyn Place, *Girls' High School* (1837; A.
Simpson), Greek Revival, courtyard plan. At Queen's Cross, resited
Queen Victoria *statue* (1893; C. Birch). In the area, large ornate villas,
No. 1 Queen's Cross (1865; J.R. Mackenzie) with octagonal entrance
tower, *No. 50 Queen's Rd* (1886; Pirie and Clyne), bold rock-faced
Gothic, and grand suburban churches, *Queen's Cross Church* (1881;
Pirie and Clyne) with strongly detailed grey granite tower and spire in
the manner of Burges, *St. Mary's Church* (1862; Rev. F. Lee), Carden
Place, called the 'Tartan Kirk' for its enthusiastic display of different
coloured materials, and *Melville-Carden Place Church* (1882; Ellis

and Wilson), two-towered with saddleback roof to W tower and spire to E tower over rounded apse. In Beechgrove Ave *church* (1898; G. Watt) with spire in manner of J.L. Pearson.

King St leads N from the centre past *No. 352* (1869–71; W. Smith), former Boys' and Girls' Hospital, Italianate range with pair of towers to the centre. St. Machar Drive leads W to Old Aberdeen, Chanonry leading N to *St. Machar's Cathedral*, 14C and 15C, and High St leading S to *King's College. Chapel* (1500–05) with splendid carved woodwork. Outside, the Bishop Elphinstone *monument* (1912–26; H. Wilson), a masterpiece of Arts and Crafts sculpture, the bishop's effigy recumbent on an ornate bronze bier, the stone pedestal flanked by standing figures at the corners and smaller seated figures down the sides modelled with the exquisitely worked drapery and naturalistic poses characteristic of the best turn of the century sculpture. The *College* buildings are a Tudor Gothic W front (1825; J. Smith) with S and E ranges 1860–73 (R. Matheson) and Elphinstone Hall (1927; A.M. Mackenzie). In the High St, New Building (1912; A.M. Mackenzie), Gothic. To S, in Spittal *St. Margaret of Scotland convent* with tall chapel by J.N. Comper (1898). Vaulted apse.

SW of Aberdeen, the A93 and B9077 run each side of the Dee. On N bank, A93, at **Cults**, *Cults West Church* (1913; A.M. Mackenzie) with low tower and stone spire, further W, at **Bieldside**, *episcopal church* (1902; A. Clyne), incorporating the granite screen by Butterfield (1849) from St. Ninian's, Perth. On S bank, B9077, ruins of *Banchory House* (1839; J. Smith), large Tudor Gothic. 2m W, St. Mary's College, **Blairs**, RC college with buildings of 1897 and chapel 1901. 12m W of Aberdeen, A944, *Dunecht*, large estate with cottages and lodges S of A944. Dunecht is a large and complex house, Italianate in style, the core of 1820 (J. Smith) originally Greek Revival, enlarged 1859 (W. Smith) and then further enlarged for the 25th Earl of Crawford and Balcarres by G.E. Street (1870–81) with chapel and tall campanile tower, now the dominant accent. Fine interiors including vaulted entrance tower with stair, very large library with iron galleries and Long Gallery, all by Street. The chapel has a vaulted apse and wagon roof. Terraced gardens with loggia and gazebo added 1913–20 (Aston Webb) for Sir W.D. Pearson, later Lord Cowdray. Lodges to W 1913 (Webb). 5m NW, *Cluny Castle* (1836–40; J. Smith), a late example of the Georgian castle style, all sash windows and round towers, not at all archaeological but impressive. 8m NW, off B992, *Castle Forbes* (1815–21; A. Simpson and J. Smith), unadorned granite Georgian castle, seat of the chiefs of the clan Forbes. 2m W of **Alford**, A994, *Breda* (1894; A.M. Mackenzie), late example of the baronial house, red granite with conical roofed entrance tower.

BALLATER. A93 44m W of Aberdeen. Gateway to Royal Deeside, formerly the station for Balmoral. *Royal Bridge* over the Dee (1885). *Victoria Barracks* (1860) were built for the royal guard. Glen Muick running SW towards Lochnagar leads up to *The Hut*, Victoria and Albert's shooting lodge and *Glas-allt-Shiel* on Loch Muick, Queen Victoria's 'Widow's House', a retreat built for her in 1868. Balmoral is 9m W of Ballater, with, as precursors, *Abergeldie Castle*, on S side of the Dee, which was leased to Edward VII when Prince of Wales, *Crathie church* (1893; A.M. Mackenzie), parish church for Balmoral and I.K. Brunel's wrought-iron box-girder *bridge* (1857). *Balmoral Castle* was Victoria and Albert's favourite residence, chosen partly because the landscape reminded Albert of Thuringia. They leased the original house on the site from 1848 and the new castle was built 1853–

55 (W. Smith) in baronial style, the main feature a massive almost detached square tower linking the two main ranges. The white granite of the walls has resisted ageing and the building remains almost exactly as it was finished. Albert influenced the design and the furnishing of the house, 'his great taste, and the impress of his dear hand, have been stamped everywhere', wrote the Queen. It was always intended as a family house, not a royal palace, and the interiors were not grand, though overpoweringly decorated in tartan for which both Victoria and Albert had a romantic fondness. The grounds are open to the public during the summer. After Albert's death his private rooms were left unaltered and the Queen set up monuments to his memory, a colossal bronze *statue* (1867; W. Theed) and a cairn where he shot his last stag. The A93 continues W to Braemar, on right, *Invercauld House*, 1750 given big baronial trimmings 1874 (J.T. Wimperis). In **Braemar**, late 19C *Fife Arms Hotel* and *episcopal church* (1899–1907; J.N. Comper) with crossing tower. Attractive interior, vaulted roof under tower and pretty screen and pulpit. Broad W window with glass by Comper. 3m further W, *Mar Lodge* (1895; A.M. Mackenzie), large stone and half-timbered shooting lodge built for the Duke of Fife, married to Queen Victoria's eldest daughter.

20m N of Ballater, A97, *Kildrummy Castle Hotel* (1900; A.M. Mackenzie), Jacobean style. Elaborate gardens around the ruins of the c 1300 castle (open to the public). **Strathdon**, B973, W of A97, has a surprisingly elaborate *church* (1853; J. Matthews) and a baronial mansion of 1891 (Sydney Mitchell). 11m E of Ballater, A93, **Aboyne**, created largely in the 1880s by Sir Cunliffe Brooks of Glentanar. *Church* (1842; J. Smith). 7m E, **Kincardine O'Neil**, *Kincardine House* (1897; Niven and Wigglesworth), large harled baronial house with convincing 17C Scots detail in red sandstone, one of the last of the baronial houses, but here with the Arts and Crafts movement's sensitivity to the past. At **Tarland**, 4m N of Aboyne, polychrome Gothic *church* (1869; W. Smith).

BANFF. A947 46m NW of Aberdeen. Former county town of Banffshire. At the foot of the High St, parish *church*, 1780 with tower and spire 1846–49 (T. Mackenzie) in classical style. *Banff Old Academy* (1837; W. Robertson), opposite, Greek Revival school building with Ionic portico. In Low St, to E, *County Hall* (1870; J. Matthews), Italianate, and *No. 49* (1837), severe stone bank building. Opposite, *Fife Arms Hotel*, the centre section of 1843 with Roman Doric porch and top balustrade. High St runs N to Castle St. On left, *Trinity Church* (1844; J. Raeburn), plastered with stone Ionic portico and a stubby cupola, and *Nos 31–5* (1852; T. Mackenzie), built as a Masonic Hall, Italian palazzo style on a small scale. On the other side of Banff Bay, **Macduff**, fishing town, originally Doune, renamed by the 2nd Earl of Fife, of Duff House. *Church* rebuilt 1865 (J. Matthews), prominently set with harled tower rising to a square top stage and octagonal cupola. Along the coast W of Banff, A98, small fishing towns at Portsoy, Cullen and Buckie. At **Buckie**, *RC church* (1851–57; Rev. J. Kyle), St. Andrews Square, exotic, with twin-spired W front and much marble within. *Buckie Maritime Museum*, Cluny Place, has fishing and local history collections.

ELGIN. A96 67m NW of Aberdeen. Former county town of Moray. The ruins of the *Cathedral* were cleared single-handedly from 1824 by John Shanks, cobbler, to whom there is a plaque. The ancient *Greyfriars church*, Abbey St, was restored from ruin (1896; J. Kinross) for the 3rd Marquess of Bute. Facing up the High St, *St. Giles Church* (1825–28; A. Simpson), handsome Greek revival. On Lady Hill, at end of the High St, *Monument* (1839; Mackenzie and Matthews) to the 5th Duke of Gordon (1770–1836), a large Roman Doric column with statue (1855). *No. 1 High St* (1842; T. Mackenzie) was the Literary and Scientific Institution, Italianate with pyramid-roofed tower. On S side, *Sheriff Court* (1864; A. and W. Reid), Greek Ionic. *Nos 82–6* (1857; Matthews and Petrie), by E end of St. Giles', former Union Bank with paired shell-headed windows, *Nos 85–93* (c 1830), pilastered late Regency block, *Nos 128–36* (c 1840), palazzo style, *Nos 141–5*, the Royal Bank (1876; Peddie and Kinnear), in the richer Italian palazzo style of the later 19C, and *Nos 164–6* (1845; A. and W. Reid), classical former Caledonian Bank. In Commerce St, S of High St, *No. 10* (1869; A. and W. Reid), the Elgin Club, Italianate. In East Rd, *Anderson's Institution* (1830–33; A. Simpson), noble Greek Revival building with Ionic centre and domed cupola, endowed by Maj.-Gen. Anderson who made a fortune in the army in India. In Moray St, *Elgin Academy* (1885; A. and W. Reid), classical with portico. In Gordon St, *Victoria School of Science and Art* (1890; G. Sutherland), Romanesque, heavily detailed, in the manner of H.H. Richardson's work in the USA. In Moss St, *Nos 42–6*, cast-iron shopfronts, and on corner of Maisondieu Rd, former *Station Hotel* (1852; T. Mackenzie), Italianate, and baronial *Station* (1902). 5m N of Elgin, **Lossiemouth**, with the new town of Branderburgh to N, laid out c 1839 by Col Brander around a new port. Romanesque style *church* (1899–1903, J.J. Burnet), a prominent landmark on the hill. 9m E of Elgin, A96, **Fochabers**, mainly 18C estate village of Gordon Castle. *Milne's School* (1846; T. Mackenzie), Tudor quadrangle with central statue, founded with £20,000 from A. Milne, local boy who emigrated after refusing a haircut demanded by the Duke of Gordon.

ELLON. A92 17m N of Aberdeen. Episcopal *church* (1870; G.E. Street) with good High Victorian detail, broached spirelet and nave canted into apsed chancel. Fittings by Street, glass by Clayton and Bell. 2m W, *Esslemont House* (1865; J.R. Mackenzie), baronial, replacing the old castle, ruins by A920. 7m NW, *Haddo House* (1731), seat of the Earls and Marquesses of Aberdeen. *Interiors in neo-Adam style by J.M. Wardrop. Fine chapel (1876–81; G.E. Street) in contrasting austere Gothic. Vaulted antechapel, wooden barrel roof to nave and E window by Burne-Jones. In the house, collections relating to the Gordon family, notably the 4th Earl of Aberdeen, Prime Minister 1852–55 and a distinguished Foreign Secretary 1841–45. At Haddo he was model improving landlord, planting millions of trees, draining land and rebuilding estate cottages. S of the estate, the hilltop *Monument* (1861) to the 4th Earl. *Church* (1865; Brown and Wardrop) at **Methlick**, to N, with saddleback-roofed tower. 6m W, B9005, **Fyvie**, estate village of Fyvie Castle (NTS). In the *castle* Jacobean style interiors by J. Bryce. Parish *church* (1808) remodelled for the Leith family of Fyvie Castle in 1903 (A.M. Mackenzie). E window one of the rare examples in Britain of glass by Tiffany of New York. Red granite Leith memorial in churchyard (1902; A.M. Mackenzie).

FORRES. A96 11m W of Elgin. On Castle Hill, tall obelisk to Dr Thomson, who died caring for Russian wounded after the Battle of Alma (1854). Thomson was native of Cromarty, but the Burgh decided not to pay for a memorial. In the High St, *Tolbooth* (1839; W. Robertson), baronial with tall tower and octagonal lantern. Courthouse and Jail to rear in Tolbooth St. In Tolbooth St, *Falconer Museum* (1868; A. and W. Reid), Italianate, commemorating H. Falconer (1808–65) who investigated fossils in India and Britain and did important work for the East India Company, leading to the introduction of tea planting (1834). *Nos 3–11* (1847; T. Mackenzie) were the Market, pilastered with late 19C shopfronts. By the Tolbooth, Gothic *Market Cross* (1844; T. Mackenzie). In High St, *No. 57*, Royal Bank, (1843; T. Mackenzie), late classical, *No. 104* (1852–54; Mackenzie and Matthews), bank in the richer mid 19C manner, and *Nos 122–6* (1881; J. Rhind), crow-stepped with conical turrets. In Victoria Rd, *episcopal church* (c 1830–40), given an Italianate exterior with campanile tower (1844; T. Mackenzie). Apse paintings (1907; W. Hole). 4m W, A96, *Brodie Castle* (NTS), 16C tower house extended 1825–50 (W. Burn and J. Wylson), its present appearance an amusing barometer of taste as the 19C architects stripped the harling from the old house to match the stone extensions, more recently the entire building has been harled to match the original appearance of the old house. 1½m W of Forres, N of A96, *Findhorn Viaduct* (1858; J. Mitchell), stone piers carrying a wrought-iron box-girder bridge, a rare survival of a type made famous by R. Stephenson's Menai Bridge (1850) where the box girders were complete tubes.

FRASERBURGH. A92 43m N of Aberdeen. Fishing port with one of the largest harbours on the NE coast. *Town House* (1853–55; T. Mackenzie), Saltoun Square, Italianate with tall cupola. In Broad St, *Custom House* (c 1830), with curved corner and Ionic columned entry. *South Church* (1878; J.B. Pirie) is remarkable, polychrome granite. *St. Peter's Church* (1891; J. Kinross) is Romanesque with late Gothic style rectory, also by Kinross. Attractive fishing villages to W at Pittulie and Rosehearty. 11m SW, A950, at **New Pitsligo**, *episcopal church* (1870; G.E. Street), High Victorian, built of local granite accentuating Street's severe lines. Apsed chancel raised on an undercroft.

HUNTLY. A96 39m NW of Aberdeen. Estate town of the Earls and Dukes of Gordon, though Huntly Castle was derelict by the 18C. Axial main street aligned on the castle with the drive spanned by the *Gordon Schools* (1839–41; A. Simpson), Jacobean style with octagonal tower over the archway. In The Square, *statue* of the 5th Duke of Richmond (1862), who inherited the Gordon estates, noted opponent of Catholic emancipation and free trade. Heavy Gothic *fountain*. On the corner of Gordon St, *Clydesdale Bank* (1842; A. Simpson), classical. In Gordon St, *Town Hall* (1886; Matthews and Mackenzie) with Franco-Scottish tower. In Gladstone Rd *Scott's Hospital* (1901; A.M. Mackenzie) with tower in late Gothic style of Marischal College, Aberdeen. *RC church* (1834; Rev. J. Kyle), most unusual octagonal design, domed within and with a Baroque tower. 11m NW at **Keith**, A96, another individual *RC church* (1831; Rev. W. Lovi), this time in the Roman Baroque manner, massive scrolls framing the front and an octagonal dome. 14m W of Huntly, A920, at **Dufftown**, castellated *tower* in centre built 1847 as a gaol, later town hall, now a museum. 5m NW of Dufftown, A95, *Aberlour House* (1838; W. Robertson), Greek Revival house with portico raised over a porte-cochère. 4m NE of Dufftown, *Drummmuir House* (1844; T. Mackenzie) large constellated Tudor style house.

PETERHEAD. A952 31m N of Aberdeen. Pink granite town noted as a fishing port from the 18C, the main British whaling port, in the early

19C. Very large harbour. Broad St runs up to the 1788 town house with stone *statue* (1868) of Field Marshal Keith, exiled in 1714 and later commander of the Prussian army under Frederick the Great. Statue presented by Kaiser Wilhelm I. *No. 78* (1857; D. Rhind), an Italianate bank building with arched windows and low wings each side. 5m W, at **Longside** *episcopal church* (1853; W. Hay) with good sculpted reredos. Hay was clerk of the works for G.G. Scott's St. John's, Newfoundland.

STONEHAVEN. A92 15m S of Aberdeen. Former county town of Kincardineshire. The old town was S of the Carron and the regularly planned early 19C new town between the Carron and Cowie. In the Market Square, *Market Buildings* (1826; A. Fraser), with 130ft spire added 1856. Italian Gothic *Bank of Scotland* (c 1870; Peddie and Kinnear). In Arbuthnot Terrace *church* (1875; R.R. Anderson) ambitious neo-Norman, completed 1906 (A. Clyne). B966 17m SW of Stonehaven, **Fettercairn**, estate village with a most outlandish 60ft Romanesque *arch* (1864; J. Milne) commemorating the visit of Prince Albert in 1861. Victoria chose the design herself. *Fettercairn House* of 1670 was given a Jacobean overhaul in 1826 (W. Burn), the first house in north-east Scotland in the style. Just to the N, *Fasque* (c 1810), a handsome Georgian castellated house bought in 1829 by Sir J. Gladstone, father of the Prime Minister. Sir John, a Liverpool merchant, made a fortune from West Indian trade and plantations. The Victorian kitchens, laundry, dairy and other offices have been recreated and the house (open to the public) contains Gladstone family relics. To NE, *Drumtochty Castle* (1810–39; J.G. Graham) castellated fantasy. Rogue Gothic *church* (1885; J.B. Pirie) at Auchinblae.

HIGHLANDS

CROMARTY. A832 23m NE of Inverness. Small port at the head of Cromarty Firth. *Lighthouse* (1846; A. Stevenson), slightly Egyptian details to the keeper's house. Prominent *monument* with statue (1859; A. Ritchie) on a 50ft Doric column to Hugh Miller (1802–56), Cromarty born, self-taught man of letters and geologist. His 'The Old Red Sandstone' (1840), a milestone in the observation of fossil remains, is still most readable.

DINGWALL. A9 14m NW of Inverness. On High St, *Free Church* (1870; J. Rhind), Gothic with elongated cupola to tower, and *Hydro offices*, an early bank building (1835; W. Robertson). In Ferry Rd, Gothic *Sheriff Court* (1842; T. Brown). On Mitchell's Hill, *tower* (1905; J.S. Kay) to General Sir H. Macdonald, Dingwall boy who rose through the ranks to command the Highland Brigade in the Boer War. He earned the name 'Fighting Mac' at Omdurman (1898). At Conon Bridge, 3m S, fine *railway viaduct* (1862; J. Mitchell) of five skewed arches over the Conon. 4m W of Dingwall, A834, is **Strathpeffer**, the prime Victorian resort of the Highlands, developed from the 1860s with villas dotted around large hotels, gardens and promenades. It is said to have something of the atmosphere of hill-stations in British India. As at Simla, half-timber decoration is applied to buildings large or small. Giant *Ben Wyvis Hotel* (1879–84; W.C. Joass) still very atmospheric, *Pavilion* (1880; Joass), and *Pump Room* (1909). 6m SW, S of river Conon, *Fairburn House* (1877; Wardrop and Reid), baronial castle.

DORNOCH. A949 48m N of Inverness. The ruined nave of the *Cathedral* was rebuilt (1835–39; W. Burn) for the Duchess of Sutherland. Statue of 1st Duke by Chantrey. Dornoch was the county town of Sutherland. *County Buildings* (1849; T. Brown) and *Prison* (1843) in Castle St. 11m N at **Golspie**, *Dunrobin Castle* (open to public), the seat of the Dukes of Sutherland. In 1785 the last hereditary Countess of Sutherland married the immensely rich heir to the Stafford and Bridgewater estates in England in the heartland of the industrial revolution. Sutherland by contrast was feudal and of little rental value, so like so many other Highland landlords the Countess and her husband (made Duke in 1833, the year of his death) introduced profitable sheep-farming over the previously tenanted lands of the clansmen. The result was depopulation, starvation and emigration. The process, largely accomplished by the 1830s, was completed by famine in 1836 and 1846. The *castle* was massively enlarged for the 2nd Duke (1844–48; Sir C. Barry) with pointed towers and Jacobean window details, the entrance front roofs altered 1915 (Sir R. Lorimer). Splendid furnishings and terraced gardens. In the grounds, Sutherland tombs around a garden temple removed from the Sutherland seat at Trentham, Staffordshire. Estate buildings include a half-timbered private railway station (1902; L. Bisset). Above the town, colossal *monument* (1834; W. Burn and F. Chantrey) to the 1st Duke, paid for by the tenants. At Drummuir, just W, Scots Jacobean style *Technical School* (1903; J.M.D. Peddie and G.W. Browne). 6m W of Dornoch, *Skibo Castle* (1898; Ross and Macbeth), built for Andrew Carnegie, Scots-born Pittsburgh steel king and philanthropist, but so large that Carnegie built himself a smaller house to retreat to. Inside, stained glass showing Carnegie's humble beginnings and startling success (G.

Moira). The castle was lit by electric light and has a marble swimming pool that converted to a ballroom.

8m W, off A9, N of Ardgay, *Carbisdale Castle*, large with heavily embattled tower, remodelled 1907 for the Dowager Duchess of Sutherland, now a youth hostel. Nearby, *Oykel Viaduct* (1867; J. Mitchell), 230ft iron lattice truss over the Oykel.

FORT AUGUSTUS. A82 34m SW of Inverness. The 18C fort was sold in 1867 to Lord Lovat who gave it to the Benedictine order. *Abbey* buildings are picturesquely composed Gothic (1876–80; J.A. Hansom) with cloister (1889; P.P. Pugin). The abbey church was begun in 1914 (R. Fairlie). At **Invergarry**, 7m SW, once the centre of the Macdonell clan, largely evicted by the chief in the early 19C, *Invergarry House* (1868; D. Bryce and 1875; J.M. Anderson), built for a later landlord, gabled medium-sized baronial house, now an hotel.

FORT WILLIAM. A82 67m SW of Inverness. Town mainly developed after the arrival of the railway in 1864, the 18C fort was demolished for the station. Unaltered former station *hotel* (c 1890; D. Cameron). Gothic *episcopal church* (1880; A. Ross), expensively fitted and, to N, *Belford Hospital* (1863), Palladian classical. 2m N, *Inverlochy Castle* (1863; Hesketh), baronial, much extended 1891 (J.M. Anderson) for Lord Abinger, one of the wealthiest of the English Highland landlords. 8m NE, B8005, *Achnacarry House* (1802–37; J.G. Graham), seat of the Camerons of Lochiel, built for the 22nd Chief, responsible for the eviction of most of his clansmen, in the hope that sheep revenues would pay his debts. Unfinished at his death in 1832. 18m W of Fort William, A830, *Glenfinnan Viaduct* (1901; Simpson and Wilson), 21-span concrete viaduct in glorious isolation. *RC church* (1877; E.W. Pugin). Further W on the same line, E of Arisaig, are concrete bridges at the head of Loch Nan Uamh and across the Borrodale, the latter a single 127ft arch, the longest concrete arch in the world in 1901. At *Kinlochmoidart*, A861, 24m S of Arisaig, large whinstone and red sandstone baronial house (1884; W. Leiper). Further SW, large stone castles in even more remote settings. *Glenborrodale Castle*, 15m SW, B8007, built c 1900 (Sydney Mitchell) on the S side of Ardnamurchan, has a massive main tower and picturesque turretted outbuildings. On Morvern, by Loch Aline, A884, *Ardtornish Towers* (1884–94; A. Ross), large and rambling with three square towers. Good interiors by J. Kinross. Concrete estate buildings of 1880s (S. Barham).

GRANTOWN-ON-SPEY. A95 34m SE of Inverness. Pleasant 19C resort town. Queen Victoria stayed at the Grant Arms Hotel in 1860. At **Nethy Bridge**, 5m SW, B970, *Aultmore* (1911–14; C.H. Quennell), handsome early 18C style country house, with hipped roofs and tall chimneys, built for the Scots owner of a Moscow department store.

INVERNESS. Superbly set on the River Ness, the town has always been the capital of the Highlands. Dominant *Castle* (1834; W. Burn), built as County Hall and extended for Prison (1845; T. Brown), all in appropriate castellated style. Good largely 19C town centre on S bank of the Ness, with Bridge St and High St the main axis. Numerous handsome mid 19C commercial buildings in the Italianate style reflecting the importance of the city. In the High St, fine porticoed *Bank of Scotland*, Nos 9–11 (1847; T. Mackenzie), built as head-quarters for the Caledonian Bank, and elaborate Gothic *Town Hall* (1879; Matthews and Lawrie) with Forbes Memorial fountain (1880) in front. In Academy St, to N, impressive *station* complex, the headquaraters of the Highland Railway, with *Station Hotel* (1855; J. Mitchell: 1858; Matthews and Lawrie) and *Railway Offices* (1873; Matthews and Lawrie) forming an open square of Italianate buildings with Highlander statue in the centre. Good 19C frontages in Academy St and glazed-roofed *Market Arcade* (1869; Matthews and Lawrie). Neo-Norman former Wesleyan chapel prominently sited. Bank St runs along the river with a picturesque group of church spires. The river is crossed by elegant suspension foot bridges and a very handsome stone *railway bridge* (1862; J. Mitchell). On the W bank, the *Cathedral* (1864–70; A. Ross), scaled-down French Gothic but suitably cathedral like with tall proportions and two W towers.

Inverness Castle (1834; W. Burn). Photograph c 1900

5m E of Inverness, B9006, near Culloden, *Nairn Bridge* (1898), 29-arch masonry viaduct, the longest in Scotland. 3m S of Inverness, B861, *Leys Castle* (1833; S. Beazley), Tudor and Romanesque mixture. 6m SW of Inverness, B862, on the NE end of Lock Ness, *Aldourie Castle* (1861; D. Bryce, and 1876–84; J. Matthews), baronial with office wing of 1903 (Lorimer). On N side of the Ness, A82, *Dochfour House* (1839; W. Robertson) an early example of Italianate, admired by Prince Albert before he began designing Osborne. 12m W of Inverness, off A831, *Beaufront Castle*, picturesquely sited seat of the Frasers, Lords Lovat. Largely rebuilt 1880 (J.M. Wardrop). 4m SW, A431, *Eileanaigas House* on an island in the Beauly river. Here the Sobieski Stuart brothers, claimants to the throne, lived a harmless courtly life in the early Victorian years and wrote treatises on the tartans. *Aigas House* is baronial of 1877.

KINGUSSIE. A9 38m S of Inverness. Briefly a spa in the late 19C with *Sanatorium* (1902; A. Mackenzie) and *Duke of Gordon Hotel* (1906) to show for it. At Loch Laggan, 20m SW, A86, Queen Victoria was tempted to buy *Ardverikie*, the shooting lodge of the Marquess of Abercorn, but it rained on her visit in 1848 and she chose Balmoral. The house was rebuilt in towering baronial style 1871 (J. Rhind).

NAIRN. A96 16m E of Inverness. Former county town and resort. In the High St, late 19C hotels, Italianate banks, *No. 73* and *No. 88* (both 1874; W. Mackintosh), *Town and County Buildings* (1818, 1842 and 1868), castellated with a tower and *St. Ninians Church* (1880; A. Maitland). In Academy St, spiky Gothic parish *church* (1897; J. Starforth). *Nairn Station* (1885; W. Roberts) is in an attractive crow-stepped Scots style. Station *hotel* (1896; D. Cameron). Good stone *viaduct* (1857; J. Mitchell), to E over the river Nairn. 11m S, off B9007, *Glenferness House* (1844; A. Simpson) well-detailed Italianate.

RHUM. Inner Hebridean island S of Skye. The island was depopulated for sheep in the early 19C and became a shooting estate in the later 19C. Sir George Bullough, wealthy industrial heir, inherited the island and built *Kinloch Castle* (1901; Leeming and Leeming), an expensive but unconvincing castellated house with lavish interior fittings (now Nature Conservancy Council). Here the full absurdity of the Victorian love affair with the Highlands can be appreciated, a great stone house built for the heir to a Lancashire fortune on a Scottish island depopulated of native inhabitants but overrun with imported deer.

SKYE. In **Portree**, the main town, largely 19C buildings with classical *courthouse* (1865; Matthews and Lawrie) on The Square. Late 19C *Royal Hotel. Skeabost Hotel*, 5m NW, A850, is a typical later 19C shooting lodge (1878; A. Ross). At the S end of the island, A851, *Armadale Castle*, now much reduced, the main block recased 1855 (D. Bryce), the rest of 1820 (J.G. Graham). Former seat of the Macdonalds of Sleat. It now contains the Museum of the Isles. On the mainland, 6m N of **Kyle of Lochalsh**, *Duncraig Castle* (1866; A. Ross) large towered house superbly set.

TAIN. A9 25m NE of Dingwall. Unspoiled early to mid Victorian town with turretted Tudor *courthouse* of 1848, incorporating Tolbooth of 1703. Notable buildings by A. Maitland, *Royal Hotel* (1872), *Town Hall* (1874) and *Queen St Church* (1891) with tall Italian tower. 6m S, off A9, *Balnagown Castle*, part ancient, part of 1820, part late 19C. 5m SW **Invergordon** formerly a major naval base. Tall-spired *church* (1859; A. Ross). 6m NW, off A836, *Ardross Castle* (1880; A. Ross) enormous baronial pile, the largest such work by Ross, the most prolific 19C architect in the Highlands.

WICK. A9 125m N of Inverness. Chief town of Caithness, set on the Wick Water, crossed by bridge of 1877. On Bridge St, classical *Royal Bank* (c 1830), *Town Hall* (1828) and *Sheriff Court* (1862; D. Rhind), opposite, Venetian palazzo style *Clydesdale Bank* (1875; J.R. Mackenzie). 3m N, *Ackergill Tower*, dramatically sited old tower house extended in baronial style (1851; D. Bryce). 6m N, A9, *Keiss Castle*, old tower much enlarged (1862; D. Bryce) in baronial style for the Duke of Portland. 21m NW of Wick, A882, **Thurso**, the most northerly mainland town, developed largely by the Sinclair family in the 19C. Parish *church* (1832; W. Burn) with monuments to Sir John and Sir George Sinclair (1835 and 1874) in front. *Library* (1859) at end of Sinclair St, classical with portico and cupola, originally Miller's Academy. Gothic *Town Hall*, High St (1870; J.R. Mackenzie). Also by Mackenzie the Clydesdale Bank Traill St (1866) and St. Andrew's Church (1870). 17m SW of Wick, A9, *Latheronwheel House* (remodelled 1851; D. Bryce), Scots Jacobean style. 3m SW, *Dunbeath*

Castle remodelled c 1880; J. Bryce), well-sited medium-sized baronial house.

LOTHIAN

DALKEITH. A68 6m SE of Edinburgh. The town is set on a ridge running up to the gates of Dalkeith House, the 18C mansion of the Dukes of Buccleuch. Just within the gates, lancet Gothic *episcopal church* (1843; Burn and Bryce) with W rose window. Richly carved and furnished interior with marble effigy of the 5th Duke (died 1884; J.E. Boehm). In the High St, *St. Nicholas' Church* with ruined 15C choir and the rest heavily rebuilt (1851–54; D. Bryce). In Eskbank Rd, to SW, former *Royal Bank* (1911; Sydney Mitchell and Wilson), well-detailed Italian palazzo style, a late example of the type. On Old Edinburgh Rd, to N, prominent in views from N, *Buccleuch Church* (1840; W. Burn), Commissioners' Gothic with tower and spire. On A68, to N, monumental iron *gates* with stone piers and vases (1848; Burn and Bryce) to Dalkeith House. S of the town, between A68 and A7, the estate of *Newbattle Abbey*, medieval to 19C mansion of the Marquesses of Lothian. 4m SE of Dalkeith, A68, at *Ford*, *Oxenford Castle*, rebuilt 1780 by R. Adam and then heavily added to (1840; W. Burn). 2m S of Ford, *Vogrie House* (1875; A. Heiton Jr), baronial with High Victorian sheer surfaces and the small-paned windows, ornate bargeboards and big modelled chimneys that appear in contemporary work of Norman Shaw. The tower is cut back from octagonal to a circular top stage and conical roof. An interesting move away from the heavy carved detail of conventional baronial houses. 5m SW of Dalkeith, A6094, E of **Rosewell**, *Whitehill* (1844; Burn and Bryce), richly carved Jacobean style stone house with symmetrical fronts of gables, bays and towers, the entrance front characteristically varied by a single square tower beside the porch. Now St. Joseph's Hospital.

7m SW of Dalkeith, A701, **Penicuik**, estate town of the Clerks of Penicuik House. In Bridge St, *South Church* (1862; F.T. Pilkington), a small work with all the virtuoso crashing of different shaped parts and cyclopean stonework of Pilkington's best work. Front gable of massively textured stonework, rock-faced cut back to ashlar with a main rose window feature, a central sexfoil surrounded by satellite circular openings punched through textured stonework, all raised over four sharply pointed arches of a glazed gallery. An octagonal tower to one side, complicated by strange stone tabernacles, ends abruptly at a carved top band. A spire was intended. The work of Gaudi in Spain comes to mind. Interior with square plan centre and complex timber roofs. On E side of Bridge St, *Park End* (1862; Pilkington), three houses with luxuriant rock-faced stonework and naturalistic carving. In the High St, *Cowan Institute* (1893; Campbell Douglas), pink stone Scots Renaissance with crow-stepped gable to one side and central clock tower. The Cowan family owned the paper mills in the North Esk Valley. In Bog Rd, *Craigie House Hotel* (1885; Sir G.W. Browne), Domestic Revival villa with half-timbered and pargetted bay, the rest red stone with Gothic touches. *Penicuik House*, to SW, is Palladian of 1761 with matching pavilion blocks of 1857 (D. Bryce), burnt out 1899.

DUNBAR. A1087 30m E of Edinburgh. The S entry to the town is dominated by the parish *church* (1819; J.G. Graham), Georgian Gothic. At Belhaven, just W of the centre, *Brewery*, largely 19C, and, on the crest to right of main road, *Knockenhair House* (1907; R.W. Schultz), harled with slate roof, the two sides slightly canted to follow the line of the hill and a bell-shaped tower roof over the centre. 3m W off A198, *Tyninghame House* (1829; W. Burn), an early work in the baronial style, recasing an older house with turrets, conical roofs and crow-stepped gables. Built for the 9th Earl of Haddington, briefly Lord-Lieutenant of Ireland and a political ally of Sir Robert Peel. Small-scale estate village at the gates.

EDINBURGH. Victorian Edinburgh is quintessentially the Edinburgh of large terraces, tenements and villas W of the Georgian New Town and S of the Old Town, but it is woven right through the older parts of the town, often in the most prominent landscape features, church spires, public buildings, monuments and grandly sealed commercial buildings.

THE NEW TOWN

Victorian commercial pressures produced the greatest changes along Princes St and George St, commercial pressures that in the case of Princes St have ousted in their turn many of the Victorian buildings. Princes St begins at the E end with the great bulk of the *North British Hotel* (1896–1900; W.H. Beattie), a man-made outcrop that seems related to Calton Hill behind. Built for the North British Railway over their Waverley Station, the style is loosely N Renaissance, five storeys to the street, eight behind. To the E, *General Post Office* (1861–65; R. Matheson), Italianate, the proportions spoilt by an extra storey added later. In front of the 1774 Register House, Wellington *monument* (1852; Sir J. Steell), the Duke bareheaded on a rearing horse. Behind, the *New Register House* (1856–62; R. Matheson), distinguished Italian palazzo style building, sober with the rich overall modelling that the Victorians preferred kept carefully controlled. Domed cast-iron reading room behind. Adjoining, the *Cafe Royal* (1862; R. Paterson), the best Victorian pub interior in Scotland, refurbished c 1898 with ceramics by Doultons including tile pictures of inventors in the public bar and completely tiled Oyster Bar. Back on Princes St, *No. 30*, the former Forsyth's department store (1906; J.J. Burnet), Scotland's first fully steel framed building. Inventive stone cladding subdividing the six floors into apparent major ground and upper floors with mezzanine between and attic above. The giant upper bays and vertically shafted corner tower were favourite Burnet motifs. St. Andrew's St leads into St. Andrew's Square with, on the corner, *No. 2* (1892–95; A. Waterhouse), red sandstone with octagonal corner turret, the Prudential Building. On the N side, *No. 23* (1846; D. Bryce), palazzo style former bank, and No. 28 (1897; J.M.D. Peddie and G.W. Browne), elegant red sandstone neo-Jacobean. On the E side, *Nos 38–9* (1847–51; D. Bryce), built as the head office of the British Linen Bank in the richest Roman classical style, six Corinthian columns set over a high ground floor, the main entablature broken forward over each column and carrying six statues. Here and in the contemporary Commercial Bank, George St, the full Victorian reaction against the sobriety of early 19C Greek or neo-classical styles can be seen. Rich interior. St. David's St leads S to Princes St with *Jenner's* department store (1893–95; W.H. Beattie) facing the Scott Memorial, extremely rich neo-Jacobean carving and a full-height galleried light-well inside. The *Scott Monument* (1840–46; G.M. Kemp), 200ft open Gothic spire rising over the statue of Sir Walter Scott (1846; Steell) was the largest Gothic monument built in Britain, massive with a complex interplay of tall arches to the lower part and a 'lacy intricacy of carved detail to the octagonal spire. Kemp was self-taught but had studied the Gothic in Scotland, England and on the continent. The monument is still in the Georgian picturesque tradition, a mass of applied ornament disguising the structure, but the scale and care over detail are already Victorian. Below are the Princes Gardens, laid out E and W of The Mound to mitigate the effects of the railway driven through between Castle Hill and the New Town. Princes St further W has lost much of its Victorian character, though the front of the former *Conservative Club* (1882; R.R. Anderson) survives as Debenhams store, Renaissance style with an off-centre three-storey bay. On The Mound, W.H. Playfair's *Royal Scottish Academy* (1822–36) and *National Gallery* (1850–57), the two most prominent of the Greek Revival buildings that reflect Edinburgh's aspiration to be the 'modern Athens', the Academy severe Greek Doric, the Gallery a lighter Ionic with its main porticos facing out W across the gardens. In the gardens, statues along the upper side and a very large gilded iron fountain. From the Academy, Hanover St leads N with *Nos 20–2* (1865; D. Bryce Jr) on the W side, well-detailed Italianate.

George St, parallel to Princes St, has a fascinating mix of 19C commercial buildings, mostly for banks or insurance offices, and late 18C houses. From St. Andrew's Square, on N side, *Nos 1–7* (1897; J.M.D. Peddie), neo-Palladian with pediment by Steell reused from the earlier building, and *George Hotel* (1840; D. Bryce, and 1879), the original three-bays wide with upper Corinthian columns, doubled in size 1879. Opposite, *No. 14*, built as the head office of the Commercial Bank (1846; D. Rhind) with Roman Corinthian giant portico and sculptured pediment (A.H. Ritchie). The round-headed windows behind are typically early Victorian, as is the sculptural richness of the building. *Nos 22–4*, Royal Society (1843; Bryce), palazzo style with two Doric porches, *Nos 29–31*, former Edinburgh and Leith Bank (1841 and 1847; D. Bryce), on the corner of Hanover St, and *Nos 62–6*, former Union Bank (1874–76; Bryce), show Edinburgh's main Victorian architect moving from using giant columns (at Nos 29–31) in the neoclassical way to Renaissance style ornament concentrated on the main openings and roofline. *Nos 72–80* (1903–07; J.J. Burnet) breaks the scale of the street with massive Baroque detail, the lower and upper floors grouped vertically and the attic floor treated as a gallery framed by domed towers. On N side, *No. 93* (1833; T. Hamilton), Regency style with iron columns at first floor supporting a second-floor balcony, *No. 95* (1840; D. Bryce), attractive small-scale office building, *Nos 101–3*, Bank of Scotland (1884; J.M.D. Peddie), particularly finely detailed neo-Renaissance palazzo, and *Nos 117–24*, Church of Scotland offices (1911; Sydney Mitchell and Jamieson), unusual granite-faced block, massively rusticated in slightly Florentine way. Parallel with George St, to N, in Queen St, at E end, *Nos 9–10*, Royal College of Physicians (1845; T. Hamilton), inventive Greco-Roman front, superbly detailed showing how the classical vocabulary could be used without the usual temple formula of giant columns or pilasters. To E, *National Portrait Gallery* (1885–90; R.R. Anderson), a complete interloper in the New Town, a sandstone version of the Doge's Palace occupying a full block. Some of the detail needs restoration. Interior stair hall with historical mural paintings. The W end of George St is Charlotte Square with the Scottish national Albert Memorial *Statue* (1873–76; Sir J. Steell) in the central garden. Albert in Field Marshal's uniform rides on a pedestal with delightful relief scenes from his life while four admiring groups look up from the base, upper classes, lower classes, armed services and the arts with education.

W of Charlotte Square, the area is dominated by the three spires of *St. Mary's Cathedral* (1874–1917; Sir G.G. Scott), perhaps the most successful feature the Victorians added to the Edinburgh skyline.

From a distance the spires compose romantically, while from Melville St a great Gothic cathedral lowers down a neo-classical avenue in perfect alignment. The cathedral, built for the Episcopal Church, has Scottish medieval detail but English Gothic precedent for the outline and the shape of the spires. Three spires characterise all three major 19C Anglican or episcopal cathedrals, Edinburgh, Truro and Cork, being aptly symbolic as well as compensating for any smallness in the body of the building. Scott's cathedral is logical and unified, strongly detailed in the nave, more delicate in the vaulted chancel, the vaulting ribs suggesting an apsed E end, where actually there is a straight wall. Fine chancel fittings by J.O. Scott, who completed the building. To N of Melville St and W of the cathedral are the terraces of the Victorian West End of the New Town, solid houses with Italianate detail, sometimes of ponderous size as in Drumsheugh Gardens where the W side houses have particularly splendid bay windows. At the N end of Palmerston Place, *Belford Church* (1888; Sydney Mitchell), with attractive red stone octagonal tower and spire. S of Melville St, Shandwick Place and West Maitland St continue Princes St westward to *Haymarket Station* (1842; J. Miller), the first Edinburgh railway station, built for the Edinburgh and Glasgow Railway, and now the most important early railway station surviving in Scotland. Handsome stone front in late Georgian manner. Haymarket Terrace leads W with *Donaldson's School* (1842–54; W.H. Playfair) set back in large grounds to N. Grand neo-Jacobean quadrangular building with central entrance tower and corner towers, built as a school for the deaf and dumb by the will of the Edinburgh printer, James Donaldson, who left an endowment of £240,000. Returning from Haymarket Station to Princes St, on N, *Gladstone Memorial* (1910–17; P. McGillivray), Coates Crescent, moved here from George St, the statesman on a pink granite pedestal flanked by Eloquence and History sitting on fragments of a Baroque pediment while two youths draw out long ribbons inscribed in Greek from a wreath they hold over a classical tripod. Sculpture of high quality. Just beyond, the tall campanile (1879; R.R. Anderson) added to *St. George's West Church* (1867; D. Bryce). The church is a rich and heavy Italianate, the campanile elegantly sheer with a Venetian top lantern.

NW and N of the New Town. N of Palmerston Place, Belford Road, with *Scottish National Gallery of Modern Art* (1828; W. Burn), long Greek Revival building, built as John Watson's School. Opposite, *Dean Education Centre* (1833; T. Hamilton), grand and unusual in its revival of English Baroque at this time, porticoed with two towers reminiscent of Hawksmoor or Vanbrugh. Built as an orphanage. Behind, *Dean Cemetery* (1845; D. Cousin), crowded and well wooded with rich collection of memorials. To N, on Queensferry Rd, *Stewart's Melville College* (1849–55; D. Rhind), picturesque Jacobean style on a grand scale, E-plan with two towers in the inner angles. On the road front, Boarding House (1874; F.T. Pilkington), aggressively opulent villa with heavy Italianate detail and bow-fronted centre, crowded with plate-glass windows. To NE, Fettes Avenue is aligned on the astonishing chateau front of *Fettes College* (1862–70; D. Bryce), symmetrical with towering central slate spire set off by steep roofed end towers and a roofline of dormers, crow-stepped gables and circular turrets, a combination of French and Scottish motifs. The view from the high ground of Queensferry Rd down the avenue can be breathtaking when there is mist below and the spire breaking through. To E, Inverleith Park and *Royal Botanic Garden*, with glorious stone and glass *palm-house* (1858; R. Matheson), pilastered with arched win-

dows below and a delicate glass roof above. Earlier octagonal palm-
house (1834) with fine cast-iron staircases. Inverleith Row leads S to
Canonmills, in Glenogle Rd, to W, *The Colonies* (1861), unusual terraces of two-storey houses that turn out to be flats with ground-floor
entrances at the back and steps up to first-floor entrances at the front.

CENTRAL EDINBURGH

From The Mound, the picturesque N side of Castle Hill has several
dominant Victorian monuments. Behind the National Gallery, the
twin Tudor towers of the *New College* (1846–50; W.H. Playfair). Off
to the right, the picturesque cluster of white gables and red roofs of
Ramsay Gardens (1893; Sydney Mitchell and S.H. Capper), built as
flats for university lecturers. To the left, the towering rear of the *Bank
of Scotland* head office, the original building of 1802 much augmented
(1865–70; D. Bryce) with wings, S side main entry and copper-clad
dome in Baroque style. Behind the college, the lovely spire of
Tolbooth St. John's Church (1842–44; J.G. Graham), the church
actually the assembly hall of the established church, and the spire, like
so many monuments and memorials in Edinburgh, conceived as a
landscape feature aligned with the New Town streets below and
enhanced by the college built on axis so that the college towers frame
the spire. The spire is 241ft high, built in a correct, albeit English, Perp.
style, in marked contrast to the contemporary Scott Monument.
A.W.N. Pugin assisted Graham in the design. Galleried hall with
plaster roof and Gothic woodwork partly designed by Pugin.
Opposite, the *Outlook Tower*, 17C raised and castellated 1853 when
the Camera Obscura was added on top in a revolving iron cupola
(open to the public). *Edinburgh Castle* was much restored in the 19C
but the most significant modern addition is the *Scottish National War
Memorial* (1924–27; Sir R. Lorimer). Below the castle, to SE, a good
group of 19C buildings in Johnston Terrace and Victoria St on the
steep slope above the Grassmarket with theatrically successful levels
of terraces, steps and tall buildings. *India Buildings* (1864; D. Cousin),
Victoria St, is a large office building with the offices opening onto a
central galleried light-well. *George IV Bridge* (1829–34) spans the
valley, with, on S side, the *Central Library* (1887–91; G.W. Browne),
well-detailed N Renaissance style in pink stone, opposite, *church*
(1857–61; J., J.M. and W. Hay), mixing Romanesque and Renaissance
in a remarkable way with boldly carved ornament. N of the bridge,
view back to the dome of the Bank of Scotland, and, on right, Lothian
County Hall (1900–05; J.M. Henry), revived Palladian.
   In Parliament Square, *St. Giles' Cathedral*, damaged and battered
after the Reformation and heavily restored 1829–33 and 1870–83.
Much Victorian glass by the Edinburgh maker, Ballantine. W window
of the N aisle by Burne-Jones. The chapel of the Knights of the Thistle
(1910–11; R. Lorimer) was added at the SE end, elaborate carving,
stained glass by Louis Davis. Monuments to R.L. Stevenson by A. St.
Gaudens of Chicago, and a fine one (1895; S. Mitchell) to the 17C
Marquess of Argyll, beheaded 1661, in the Hammermen's Chapel.
Outside, *statue* of 5th Duke of Buccleuch (1887; Boehm). The Parliament House, originally of 1632–40, became the principal law court
after the 1707 Act of Union. The Great Hall has a large Munich glass
window (1868; W. von Kaulbach) of the inauguration of the College of
Justice by James V. On the N side of High St, City Chambers, open
courtyard (1753–61) with Steell's sculpture of *Alexander taming
Bucephalus* (1832). Cockburn St was cut through to Market St and
Waverley Station in 1860, baronial style buildings (Peddie and

Kinnear). North Bridge (1897) is flanked by very large late 19C buildings, *Nos 20–56* 'The Scotsman' offices (1899; Dunn and Findlay), especially well carved and detailed, and *Nos 3–31* (1898; Scott and Williamson). South Bridge crosses high over Cowgate with views of tenements and the very tall red stone *Solicitors Building* (1888; J.B. Dunn) to the W.

In Chambers St, on the S side, *Heriot-Watt University*, a confused front of 1873–77 and 1887, the main element a French pavilion roof. Opposite, * *Royal Scottish Museum* (1861; R. Matheson) in Matheson's dignified Italianate style (cf. GPO, Waterloo Place). The interior by Captain F. Fowke, architect for much of the museum building in South Kensington, London, 1853–65, is the finest surviving Victorian cast-iron exhibition space in Britain. A great central hall with glazed roof on iron arches is flanked by two tiers of tall balconies supported on the thin columns that carry the roof, the result a space of exceptional delicacy and light, all the more remarkable after the solidity of the exterior. In South College St, disused *church* (1856; P. Wilson), a strong pedimented front, Italianate with the sharp detail more typical of Glasgow classicism. S of Lothian St, the main 19C part of Edinburgh University. Looking over the new plaza, to the W, the *McEwan Hall* (1887–97; R.R. Anderson), delicate early Renaissance detail applied to a very large circular auditorium, the gift of the McEwan brewing family. The projecting buttresses and the round staircase towers seek to break down the single mass making the building, for all the high quality of the detail, seem overworked compared to the similar Albert Hall, London. On the S side, Scots Renaissance *Students' Union* (1887; Mitchell and Wilson) and, adjoining, *Music School* (1858; D. Cousin), plain well-proportioned Italian palazzo. W of the McEwan Hall, more very large early Renaissance style buildings, the *Medical School* (1875–88; R.R. Anderson), again with excellent detail overpowered by the scale. The best part is the courtyard, where in the right light the Italian effect succeeds. Beyond, the *Royal Infirmary* (1870; D. Bryce), round turrets and stepped gables around a deep courtyard with large entrance tower, all symmetrical. On the N side of Lauriston Place, *Fire Station* (1898; R. Morham), good combination of red granite and red stone in a free late 17C style.

Lady Lawson St runs N to Spittall St. In Grindlay St, the *Royal Lyceum Theatre* (1883; C.J. Phipps), stucco exterior, pretty three balcony interior. Beyond, in Lothian Rd, the *Usher Hall* (1910–14; S. Harrison), imposing Beaux Arts classical domed concert hall. At the corner of Spittal St and Castle Terrace, an extraordinary *terrace* (1868–70; Sir J. Gowans), all acute angles and sharply facetted masonry designed according to Gowans' system of modular proportions based on a two-foot unit. The detail has elements of the Gothic and the Italian but all rethought in Gowans' hard-edged way. Further down Castle Terrace, *Unitarian church* (1835; D. Bryce), lively chapel front, unusual in the clearly Baroque window detail at a time when conventional taste was for the more restrained Renaissance forms. On the N end of Lothian Rd, by Princes St Gardens, two churches, *St. Cuthbert's* (steeple 1789, rest 1894; H.J. Blanc), remarkable for the murals by Gerald Moira and a stained glass window by Tiffany of New York, a richly coloured landscape in the opaque layered glass that was the speciality of the firm. *St. John's Church* (1816; W. Burn) is an excellent example of Georgian Gothic, with tall fan-vaulted interior, the vault plaster but excellently done. Opposite, *Caledonian Hotel* (1898; J.M.D. Peddie and G.W. Browne), a large pink railway hotel with detail unusually good for the type, arcaded and columned bottom floors, three relatively plain floors above with strong cornice over which are big curly gables, the largest on the entrance front.

OUTER EDINBURGH

In **S Edinburgh**, the Meadows form the N edge of the area of Victorian tenements, tall red or grey stone blocks of flats generally with full-height bay windows. Marchmont, immediately S of the Meadows, is the most complete area with more to the W in Bruntsfield Place, e.g. Nos 131–51 (1887; Sir G.W. Browne) and Nos 155–95 (1882; H.J. Blanc). To the N, *Barclay Church* (1862–64; F.T. Pilkington), Pilkington's masterpiece, a Gothic church that seems to have been born of violent upheaval. The craggy spire is a landmark from far around. Close to, Pilkington's architecture has a titanic strength quite of its own. Massive rocks seem to have piled on gargantuan Gothic carved work, rocky projections break forward, the junctions more like collisions than neighbours. The profusion of gables and complex centralised plan make for a roof structure and outline gullied and ridged like crumpled paper. Further N, *King's Theatre* (1905; Swanston and Davidson), Leven St, stone fronted with good rococo plasterwork inside. Bruntsfield Place leads SW. Off to N, *Bruntsfield church* (c 1870), Leamington Terrace, strong Early French Gothic with good spire, and *Boroughmuir School* (1910–14; J.A. Carfrae), Viewforth, the most impressive of the early 20C secondary schools in Edinburgh, four storeys, contrasting stone lower floors with red brick above embellished with stone Ionic columns. To each side a sheer brick tower with bold rusticated stone-arched openings under the roof. Bruntsfield Place reaches **Morningside** at 'Holy Corner' with four churches, the best, *Christ Church* (1878; H.J. Blanc), with French Gothic spire and spiky apse. The *Baptist church* with another spire (1872) is by McGibbon and Ross, authors of 'The Castellated and Domestic Architecture of Scotland'. *Morningside North Church* (1879; D. Robertson), neo-Norman with fine stained glass. Further S, on left, Falcon Avenue leads to *St. Peter's RC Church* (1908; Sir R. Lorimer), original interpretation of the basilican church with slim pyramid-roofed tower. From Holy Corner, Colinton Rd runs SW to the suburbs of Craiglockhart and Colinton. At **Craiglockhart**, *Sacred Heart College of Education* (1878; Peddie and Kinnear), originally the Edinburgh Hydro, in 1917 a military hospital where Wilfred Owen met Siegfried Sassoon stood here. Sassoon's encouragement brought forth the best of Owen's war poems. In **Colinton** a number of turn of the century houses by R. Lorimer, roughcast with slate roofs, similar to the contemporary work of Voysey in England. On Colinton Rd, *Rustic Cottages* (1901; Lorimer), nearby, in Westgarth, *church* (1888–97; R.R. Anderson) with pretty tower. At the foot of Dreghorn Loan to W, *Laverockdale House* (1912–14; Lorimer), quite large late 17C Scots style house. To SW, *Bonaly Tower* (1836; W.H. Playfair), Bonaly Rd, baronial castle on the slopes of the Pentlands built for Lord Cockburn (1779–1854), judge and conversationalist. In Colinton, N of the Water of Leith, numerous Lorimer cottages in Gillespie Rd (Nos 14, 21, 26 and 32), Pentland Avenue, Spylaw Avenue and Spylaw Bank Rd. E of Morningside is **Grange**, an area of large later 19C villas, especially on Grange Loan and Blackford Rd. In Blackford Rd, *No. 35* (1900; G.W. Browne), roughcast and red stone. Beyond, in Dick Place, *Nos 48–50* and *38–40* (c 1864; F.T. Pilkington), the former a very rogueish double villa, rough and angular with triangular windows in the chimney-breasts, the latter (best seen from Grange Loan) a large round-arched house with polychrome details. To E of Grange Loan, **Mayfield** with fine spired *church* (1876–79; H.J. Blanc), Early French Gothic. To E, Dalkeith Rd. In the suburb of **Inch**, 1m SW, *Kingston Clinic* (1869; F.T. Pilkington), Kingston Avenue, one of Pilkington's largest houses, heavily Gothic with a splendid entrance tower with loggia around the base. At the N end of Dalkeith Rd, *Pollock Halls of Residence*, built around two large baronial houses (1860–70; J. Lessels). In Lutton Place to NW, *St. Peter's Church* (1857–67; W. Slater), English mid 19C Gothic with a good spire and granite piers inside.

Barclay Church (1862–64; F.T. Pilkington), Edinburgh

E of Princes St is Calton Hill, rocky crag with picturesque and fantastic assortment of early 19C monuments of which the unfinished Parthenon (1822), intended as the national monument to the Napoleonic Wars, is the most prominent. Leith Walk, running NE, connects Edinburgh with its port, the formerly separate town of **Leith**, the centre a battered mixture of imposing Georgian public buildings, Georgian and Victorian warehouses and Victorian tenements. The centre is Bernard St leading to the shore along the Water of Leith. The

Royal Bank (1871; Peddie and Kinnear), at the corner of Constitution St, is a well-detailed palazzo. *Nos 12–18*, a mid 19C Italianate warehouse. On the opposite side, the former *Corn Exchange* (1861; Peddie and Kinnear), round-arched Renaissance with a bulbous green dome. On Constitution St, W side, *RC church* (1853; E.W. Pugin and J.A. Hansom), plain Gothic, apsed to the street. Good stained glass of c 1880 in S aisle. On the E side, Links Lane leads to Wellington Place where *No 11* is an exceptionally good five-storey warehouse with rope mouldings to the doors (1862; J.A. Hamilton). The range continues in John's Place. W of Leith, Commercial St leads past the *Custom House* (1812) to **Granton**, an additional harbour constructed for the Duke of Buccleugh c 1838 with *Custom House* and other classical buildings on Granton Square (c 1838; J. Henderson). E of Leith is **Portobello**, a seaside resort from the late 18C. In High St, *Police Station*, former Municipal Buildings (1877; R. Paterson), small but heavily baronial. In Brighton Place, to S, *RC church* (1904; J.T. Walford), most original with blunt pinnacles and similar thin steeple to the tower, more Art Deco than turn of the century in feel. Prominent from the railway.

HADDINGTON. A1 15m E of Edinburgh. In Court St, the long triangular centre, crown-spired *monument* (1880; D. Rhind) to the 8th Marquess of Tweeddale and, on S side, Tudor style *County Buildings* (1832; W. Burn) and classical *Corn Exchange* (1853). At W end, *West Church* (1890; Sydney Mitchell and Wilson), free Gothic, and *monument* (1843; R. Forrest) to R. Ferguson MP, a figure on a Doric column with mourners around. In Knox Place, to S, *Knox Academy* (1877; J. Starforth), spiky Gothic with central tower. 4m NW, A6137, **Aberlady**, estate village of the Wemyss estate. In the *church*, marble effigy of Louisa Countess of Wemyss (died 1882; J. Rhind). The interior was rebuilt 1886 (W. Young) and the stained glass (E. Frampton) introduced 1889. *Gosford House*, to SW, was built 1790 by R. Adam and given grandiose wings for a later Earl of Wemyss (1886–90; W. Young). The Adam house is disused, one of the Young wings roofless, but the other, the present house, has an entrance hall of municipal proportions, all pale stone, white marble and pink marble columns to the gallery around. Hefty stone lodges (1854 and 1857; R.W. Billings) on A198 W and N of the house. 3m NE of Aberlady, **Gullane**, developed c 1900 as numerous villas were built close to the Muirfield Golf Links, notably on Hill Rd. *Grey Walls* (1901; Lutyens), E of the village, is a handsome rubble-stone villa with red pantiled roofs, the front of an interesting quadrant plan with parapet and roof lantern. Garden laid out in small compartments with Gertrude Jekyll. 4m NE, **North Berwick**, developed as a resort in the late 19C with large villas, notably *Carlekemp* (1898; J. Kinross), Abbotsford Rd, to W, gabled Cotswold style with lavish interiors, now a school, and, nearby, *Milton Lodge* (1896; J.M.D. Peddie and G.W. Browne), early Georgian style. In Old Abbey Rd, to SW, *Marly Knowe* (1902; Lorimer), harled with bell-cast gables. In Wishart Avenue, *The Grange* (1893 and 1904; Lorimer), harled with gables and a baronial tower, in Greenheads Avenue, *Glasclune* (1889; Kinnear and Peddie), Queen Anne style, and *Redholm* (1892; Kinnear and Peddie, extended 1903), Tudor to Elizabethan style.

LINLITHGOW. A803 7m E of Falkirk. In the centre, Kirkgate runs up to the parish church and palace past Peel Garden with *statue* of the first Marquess of Lothian (1911; Frampton). The splendid 15C to 16C parish *church* was restored 1894–96, apse glass by Clayton and Bell 1885 and one S aisle window by Morris and Co. 1899. 1½m N, *Grange* (1904; J.N. Scott and A.L. Campbell), dramatically sited baronial house, harled with four-storey tower. 3m N of Linlithgow, **Bo'ness**, former port, supplanted by Grangemouth. Battered centre with *Town Hall and Library* (1901; G.W. Browne), neatly combined in a single long building with domed turrets at the join. 6m S of Linlithgow, A89, **Bathgate**, former mining and iron town, the first place where paraffin was made commercially, extracted from shale. The area still is marked by the piles of shale waste, called bings. In George St, *St. David's Church* (1904; J.G. Fairley), free Gothic with a copper-clad dome to the tower. In Marjoribanks St, *Bathgate Academy* (1831; R. and R. Dickson), neo-classical school with Greek Doric centre capped by a big square lantern turret and flanked by columned wings with end pavilions. 3m NE, *Bangour Village Hospital* (1898–1906; H.J. Blanc), large self-contained asylum built for the City of Edinburgh to the then novel dispersed plan with patients housed in separate houses around the hospital and nurses' home. Church of 1924–30.

SOUTH QUEENSFERRY. A90 9m W of Edinburgh. * *Forth Rail Bridge* (1883–90; Fowler and Baker), the most spectacular rail bridge in Britain. Originally a suspension bridge was intended but abandoned after the collapse of the Tay Bridge ruined the reputation of Sir T. Bouch, who designed both. The bridge as built is a steel cantilever bridge of two main spans of 1700ft, three towers rising 360ft and a total length of over 1½m including the approach viaducts. The Admiralty insisted on the bridge not interfering with the movement of warships, hence the 150ft headroom under the two central trusses. This was the first large steel railway bridge, giving the railway 135 acres of metal to keep painted. The headland to the E is the park of *Dalmeny House* (1814–17; W. Wilkins), an early example of revived Tudor Gothic, built for the Earls of Rosebery. N of the house, *Barnbougle Castle* (1881; Wardrop and Reid), tower house rebuilt on the foundations of the original castle, abandoned when Dalmeny House was built and recreated as a library for the 5th Earl of Rosebery, leading Liberal politician and first chairman of the London County Council (1889).

ORKNEY AND SHETLAND

ORKNEY

HOY. At the S end, *Melsetter House*, built 1898 for a Birmingham merchant by W.R. Lethaby, the leading Arts and Crafts theorist. The house grew from an existing building and Lethaby kept the rough harled walls and plain sash windows of the original, expanding it in similar austere style, the emphasis on strong chimneys and roofline. The result is dignified without being pretentious, a tall house set off by ranges of earlier outbuildings which Lethaby altered giving the effect of organic growth that advanced architects of the period sought. Carved symbols, hearts, a moon and stars show Lethaby's interest in elemental mythology. The interiors are light, plainly detailed with one splendid hall fireplace. Chapel converted from an existing building.

MAINLAND. **Kirkwall**, the principal town, is dominated by the medieval *Cathedral*, well restored 1848 and after 1913. By the ruins of the Earl's House, *County Buildings* (1876; D. Bryce), with crow-stepped gables and a round stair tower. Bryce had intended to repair the Earl's House. *Town Hall* (c 1890; T.S. Place), modest baronial. 16m W, **Stromness**, fishing port with late 19C hotel on the harbour front and, in Victoria St, plain Italianate *Bank of Scotland* (1871; W. Henderson).

ROUSAY. *Trumland House* (1872; D.Bryce), plain baronial house, the stone now harled.

SHAPINSAY. *Balfour Castle* (1846–50; D. Bryce), Bryce's first large baronial house, full of incident, a main tower, crow-stepped gables and circular turrets.

SHETLAND

MAINLAND. The capital, **Lerwick**, is tightly packed around the harbour. On Hillhead, *Town Hall* (1882; A. Ross), quite elaborate Gothic with tower behind and a rose window. *County Buildings* (1875), King Erik St, simpler Scots style. In Commercial St, *Bank of Scotland* (1904; J.J. Burnet), a refined piece of Edwardian classicism, surprising here. *Episcopal church* (1864; A. Ellis), Greenfield Place, with plate tracery and saddleback tower. Inside, stained glass by Sir N. Comper moved here 1973.

STRATHCLYDE

ARDROSSAN. A78 16m N of Ayr. Planned town laid out 1805 for the 12th Earl of Eglinton. Facing the sea, *Barony Church* (1844; Black and Salmon), Arran Place, much pinnacled with a bellcote spire. On Princes St, *No. 10* (1839), a stuccoed classical former bank. In *St. Andrew's Church*, fine Ascension window (c 1896) by Harrington Mann of Glasgow.

ARRAN. Largest island in the Firth of Clyde. At **Brodick**, *Brodick Castle* (open to public), the 16C castle of the Dukes of Hamilton, has Victorian work of 1844 (J.G. Graham) and 1856 (W. Burn). In front of the school, seated statue of the 11th Duke. At **Corrie**, 4m N, small *church* (c 1900; J.J. Burnet) with impressive E end, a central buttress closely flanked by two small lancets.

AYR. Former county town and resort much associated with Burns. The *New Bridge* (1877) replaces one of 1788 that Burns prophesied would not last in his poem 'The Brigs of Ayr'. New Bridge St leads S, dominated by the steeple of the *Town Hall* (1827–32; T. Hamilton), extended to High St (1878; Campbell Douglas and Sellars). No. 34 is a neo-Grecian bank building of c 1830. In Sandgate, *Royal Bank* (1857; Peddie and Kinnear), handsome Italian palazzo, and *No. 34* (1863; D. Rhind), also palazzo style, contrasting rubble stone and smooth ashlar. In the High St, two more bank buildings, *Nos 128–30* (c 1845), classical with Doric porches, opposite, pedimented neo-Georgian *Bank of Scotland* (1901; J.M.D. Peddie and G.W. Browne). Further down, the 113ft *Wallace Tower* (1832; T. Hamilton), Tudor Gothic. Alloway St leads down to Burns Statue Square, the *statue* of 1892 (G. Lawson) in front of the big pavilion-roofed *Station Hotel* (1883–86; A. Galloway). W of Sandgate, *Ayr Academy* (1886; Clarke and Bell), Fort St, imposing Glasgow style classical building. To S, *County Buildings* (1818–22; R. Wallace), Wellington Square, Ionic classical with a dome. In front, *statues* of the 13th Earl of Eglinton (1865; M. Noble), Lord Lieutenant of Ireland, but most famous as the host and creator of the 1839 Eglinton Tournament near Irvine (see below p. 524), General Neill (1859; Noble), commander in the Indian Mutiny, killed in the assault of Lucknow, and Sir James Fergusson (1910; Goscombe John). Across Sandgate, *Holy Trinity Church* (1888–1900; J.L. Pearson), Fullarton St, a minor work of the great church architect, only the chancel complete in Pearson's lifetime. Further S, on Racecourse Rd and the streets off, especially Park Circus, an area of Victorian villas with good spired *church* (1893; J.B. Wilson). Further out, on Doonfoot Rd, *Seafield Hospital* (c 1859; Clarke and Bell), large seaside mansion of the industrialist Sir W. Arrol. N of the river Ayr, in Main St, *Carnegie Library* (1893; Campbell Douglas and Morrison) free Renaissance style in red stone. 5m N of Ayr, A759, **Troon**. Resort town. *Old Parish Church* (1894; H. Blanc), pink stone, grandly scaled French Gothic in the manner of Pearson. Tall flèche but no tower. *Marine Hotel* (1897 and 1901; J.G. Gillespie), well detailed free Scots 17C style by one of Mackintosh's leading Glasgow contemporaries. In St. Meddan's St, *RC church* (1911; R. Fairlie), scholarly Scots 15C style church, low and sturdy with broad W tower, all carefully detailed with Arts and Crafts care.

9m N of Ayr, A78, **Irvine**. Now enveloped in a modern new town. Above the river, *Trinity Church* (1863; F.T. Pilkington), unmistakably by the same hand as the Barclay Church, Edinburgh. Massive rocky walls, a great rose window, polychrome banding and a sharp spire. No longer a church. In High St, *Town Hall* (1859; J. Ingram), Italianate with attenuated spire. 2m N is the site of *Eglinton Castle* (country park) where, in 1839, in the full flush of revived medievalism, the Earl of Eglinton staged the famous Eglinton Tournament, a recreated medieval joust attended by the boldest young aristocrats complete with throngs of followers, all romantically dressed. They were to fight before a Queen of Beauty and a hundred thousand people came. Torrential rain washed the whole affair into an unromantic mixture of armour and umbrellas.

16m SW of Ayr, A77, **Girvan**. Coastal resort. On corner of Hamilton St and Bridge St, Italianate former *bank* (1856; Peddie and Kinnear). In Dalrymple St, baronial *MacKechnie Institute* (1887; J. McKissack) with octagonal corner tower. *North Church* (1883; W.G. Rowan), Montgomerie St, has a fine spire. At **Turnberry**, 6m N, very large railway *hotel* (1905; J. Miller), built for the golfers, the railway has long gone but the golf thrives. 12m SW of Girvan, A77, *Glenapp Castle* (1870; D. Bryce), large baronial house further enlarged with SW tower c 1900 for the shipping tycoon Lord Inchcape.

BUTE. Island in Firth of Clyde, reached from Wemyss Bay. **Rothesay**, the main town, is a Victorian resort of great charm. In Guildford Square, an ornamental cast-iron shelter by Macfarlane's of Glasgow. *West Church* (1845; C. Wilson) is neo-Norman with a spire. 6m S, *Mountstuart*, seat of the Marquesses of Bute, rebuilt by the prodigal 3rd Marquess (cf. Cardiff Castle and Castell Coch, Glamorgan) as the last of his colossal building projects, begun 1879. The architect was R.R. Anderson, not Burges, but the style is still Gothic of an Early French mixed with N Italian kind. The overall design is as strong as anything of Burges', each front an unbroken mass of red stone, pierced by Italian Gothic windows and lightened at roof level by a gallery under the eaves. No gables break the roofline. Chapel of heroic proportions, vaulted and marbled, with the Wagnerian touch of red stained glass in the central octagon casting a livid glow on the white marble below. The house interiors were painted and carved in the manner of Burges' work in Wales, using the same craftsmen. At **Scoulag**, to N, triangular *lodge* (1897; R.W. Schultz), Arts and Crafts influenced. At **Port Bannatyne**, 3m N of Rothesay, *Kames Castle* was restored from almost nothing (1895–1908; R.W. Schultz) for the Marquesses of Bute.

DUMBARTON. A814 13m NW of Glasgow. Former county town noted for shipbuilding from 1844. The 'Cutty Sark' was built at Denny's yard, Dumbarton. In Church St, the old *Academy* (1865; W. Leiper), Gothic with a projecting tower. The former *Denny Institute* (1881; J. Crawford) is free Renaissance in style. On the W side of the Leven, a number of large Clydeside villas, *Helenslee* (c 1870) with big pavilion-roofed tower, *Garmoyle* (c 1890; Burnet and Campbell), Helenslee Rd, 17C Scots with the red tile roofs popular at the turn of the century, and *Dunmore* (1866; W. Leiper) with an octagonal Gothic tower and spire. Further N, *Levenford House* (1853; J.T. Rochead), heavy castellated house, well sited. NE of the town, overlooking the Stirling road, *Overtown Castle* (1859; J. Smith), baronial with a square tower. At **Cardross**, 2m W, *Kilmahew* (1870; J. Burnet Sr), impressive baronial house built for a director of Cunard lines. 3m N of Dumbarton, **Alexandria**, one of the centres of the turkey-red dyeing industry that was a feature of the Leven towns, including Bonhill, Jamestown and Renton until the 1920s. The Argyll Motor Co built the largest of the early motor works in Britain at Alexandria in 1904. To N, the S end of Loch Lomond, studded with castellated or baronial houses. On the E bank, *Balloch Castle* (1809; R. Lugar) and *Boturich Castle* (1834; Lugar), Georgian castellated houses, picturesquely planned. On the W side, *Auchindennan* (c 1870), *Auchinheglish* (c 1875; Campbell Douglas and Sellars) and *Arden* (1868; J. Burnet Sr), Victorian romantic silhouettes.

GLASGOW. Despite years of decline this century, Glasgow remains the most important Victorian city in Britain outside London, and recent cleaning and restoration have brought back to life a centre that demonstrates an architectural vitality in the 19C quite different to anything in England in the period. Glasgow built its wealth on trade, principally with the Americas, the Clyde Navigation Trust being responsible during the early 19C for opening the river to shipping, and wharfs and docks followed. The great Glasgow industry was ironfounding, and from this developed the engineering industries, most notably shipbuilding, boiler-making and locomotive building. Glasgow had a textile industry from the 18C, but it was the bleaching and printing of cloth that was principally carried out in the 19C, due to the discovery of chlorine bleach exploited by the Tennant family at their St. Rollox works, in its day one of the largest chemical works in Europe. The city centre reflects this 19C prosperity, the earlier survivals, apart from the Cathedral, being few and modest.

City Chambers (1883–88; W. Young) Glasgow. Photograph c 1929

George Square is the civic centre, dominated by the grandiose *City Chambers* (1883–88; W. Young), splendidly ornate confection of Renaissance detail, sometimes uncomfortably crowded as in the three-storey centre portico but the side cupolas and splendid central tower successfully animate the whole building. Inside, a sequence of spaces of exceptional richness, the entrance hall granite-columned with mosaic vault and floor giving access to two staircases unsparingly decorated in marble, alabaster and mosaic. One stair leads to the

Council Chamber, dark mahogany-panelled in a Renaissance to 17C style, the other to a barrel-vaulted Banqueting Hall, neo-classical style, with murals by Glasgow School artists of c 1900. The centre of George Square is filled with a large selection of 19C *monuments*, most prominent Sir Walter Scott (1838; A.H. Ritchie) on an 80ft column. There are equestrian Victoria and Albert statues by Marochetti, a seated James Watt (1830; Chantrey) and standing figures of Sir J. Moore (1819; Flaxman), the Peninsular War hero, Burns (1876; G. Ewing), Sir R. Peel (1859; Mossman), Gladstone (1902; H. Thorneycroft), Field Marshal Lord Clyde (1868; Foley), commander during the Indian Mutiny, J. Oswald (1855; Marochetti), MP for Glasgow at the time of the Reform Bill, and the poet T. Campbell (1877; Mossman). On the S side of the square, *Post Office* (1875–76; R. Matheson), Italianate. On the W side, a long palazzo style range, the S end the *Bank of Scotland* (1869; J.T. Rochead), facing St. Vincent Place, extended (1874) to form a symmetrical front to George Square but the symmetry lost when the N end acquired extra floors and a dome (1907; J.J. Burnet). N of the square, *Queen St Station* with broad iron arched roof (1878; J. Carswell).

Queen St leads S from George Square, on right, *Nos 151–7* (c 1834; D. Hamilton), neo-classical, richly decorated cornice over giant pilasters. Beyond, Royal Exchange Square, laid out 1830 around the *Royal Exchange* (1827; D. Hamilton) with giant Corinthian portico and cupola closing the view down Ingram St. Behind, the more conventional Greek Ionic portico of the *Royal Bank* (1827; A. Elliott), the whole making an excellent late Georgian ensemble. In front of the exchange, Duke of Wellington *statue* (1844; Marochetti). In Ingram St, *No. 191*, former Union Bank (1876; J. Burnet I), a refronting in rich Renaissance style with massive upper cornice and uneven rhythm of granite columns and pilasters to the main floors. Next door, *No. 177, Savings Bank* (1896; J.J. Burnet), Roman Baroque banking hall with splendidly carved curved pediments and a central dome, added to the front of the original bank (1866; J. Burnet I) to which J.J. Burnet added a colonnaded attic (1900). N of Ingram St, in John St, *John St Church* (1859; J.T. Rochead), unusual Italianate design the upper colonnades direct glazed and the end bays with windows in frames more mannerist than the severe lines of the rest of the building. S of Ingram St, in Miller St, handsome series of mid Victorian warehouses in Italianate style, *No. 81* (1849; J. Salmon I) with particularly delicate early Renaissance details, *Nos 61–3* (1854; J. Burnet I), and, on the other side, *Nos 84–90* (c 1877) and *Nos 48–56* (1863–65; J. Smith), built as Stirling's Library, quietly distinguished in the manner of C. Barry's London clubs, with channelled ground floor framing arched windows and ashlar facing above articulated with corniced first-floor windows and small attic openings in architrave frames. Parallel with Ingram St, facing Wilson St, *City and County Buildings* (1844; Clarke and Bell), a long block running back to Ingram St, Greek Revival with a raised Ionic portico at the S end and a Corinthian upper colonnade in the centre of the W front. In Brunswick St, to E, *Nos 102–4* (1859; R.W. Billings), highly individual Gothic warehouse, by an architect distinguished as an antiquarian, so the extraordinary undulating hoodmoulds and harsh angularity must be seen as an attempt to rethink warehouse facade design in modern terms, using a vocabulary that has its roots in Gothic, but no more than that.

Returning to George Square, in St. Vincent Place, beyond the Bank of Scotland, *No. 24* (1889; T.L. Watson), elegantly Dutch gabled with pretty Renaissance carving on ground floor, this building preventing the completion of the richly Italianate *Clydesdale Bank* (1870–73; J. Burnet I) next door. Buchanan St, at right angles, is the principal commercial street, the beginning of a formally planned grid of streets extending westward, laid out in the early 19C. On the corner of St. Vincent St, ponderous five-storey Renaissance style *bank* (1900; J.M.D. Peddie). On the opposite corner, *Western Club* (1840–41; D. and J. Hamilton), palazzo style with individual detail, especially the big square-columned windows to the outer bays, echoing the centre porch. Unfortunately rendered in a sandy cement that loses the crispness of stone or stucco. Beyond, on the corner of St. George's Place, the *Stock Exchange* (1875; J. Burnet I), splendidly Venetian Gothic in the best High Victorian manner of Street or Burges, the strong cornice continuing the line of the club next door. Burnet's design derives from the Venetian Gothic competition designs for the London Law Courts of 1866, and was criticised at the time for plagiarising Burges. The building was extended in St. George's Place in 1894 and 1904 by J.J. Burnet. Behind St. George's Church, *Royal Faculty of Procurators* (1854; C. Wilson), Venetian Renaissance style palazzo in the opulent style set for gentlemen's clubs by the contemporary Carlton Club in London, the upper floor particularly rich with coupled columns and carved frieze. On the N side of St. George's Place, former *Athenaeum* (1886; J.J. Burnet), the Renaissance vocabulary used in a way that looks forward to the Edwardian Beaux Arts inspired classicism with smooth ashlar wall and much play of subtly varied planes in the wall face. High arched upper windows in an Ionic colonnade carrying statues against a blank parapet. On the corner, former *Liberal Club* (1909; A.N. Paterson), free Renaissance with much mannered variety in the details, especially the roofline of attic corners, modelled chimney-stacks and low balustrade between. Next door, *No. 179 Buchanan St* (1891–93; J.J. Burnet and J.A. Campbell), former Athenaeum Theatre, high and narrow, a Dutch gable with richly modelled bay paired with an emphatically vertical stair tower, ancestor of similar features on Burnet's later buildings. *Nos 164–8* (1898; J.A. Campbell) has similar bay window and arch features. Behind St. George's Place, in West George St, *No. 112* (1868; D. Bryce), much altered former Junior Conservative Club, originally similar to Bryce's severe Union Bank, George St, Edinburgh with balconied pedimented upper windows over a banded rusticated ground floor. Opposite, *Nos 117–21* (1892; W. Leiper), lavishly carved office block for the Sun Life Assurance, French Renaissance detail and a domed corner. To W, *Nos 144–6* (1879; J. Sellars), former New Club, heavy French Second Empire flavoured building with pavilion roofs, near symmetrical but a massive entrance to one side set off by a two-storey bay on the other. On the corner of Hope St, *Nos 157–67* (1902; J.A. Campbell), powerful eight-storey corner block, the top two storeys treated as an arcaded gallery, Spanish in feel, but set on a severe block articulated by tall bays each side and a wider central bay that seems to support the gallery balcony. Further N, *Nos 170–2 Hope St* (1905; Salmon and Gillespie), the first reinforced concrete building in Glasgow, a tall eight floors on a cramped site, the front treated with gable and corner turret familiar from turn of the century buildings in Glasgow, but the side wall three unornamented bays rising the full height, exploiting the material for maximum light where ornamental design was not required. At the N end of Hope St, and nearby, three 19C theatres of quality. On Hope St, the *Theatre Royal*, magnificently restored, the fine interior (1880 and 1895; C.J. Phipps) concealed behind a plain exterior. After years as a television studio the Theatre Royal was brought back to life as a home for the Scottish National Opera. In Bath St, the *King's Theatre* (1904; F. Matcham), Baroque exterior and lush curvacious auditorium. On the corner of Renfield St and Renfrew St, the *Pavilion Theatre* (1904; B. Crewe), terracotta facade and rococo style interior.

In Hope St, to S, *Nos 91–117* (1877; Peddie and Kinnear), originally the Central Station Hotel, grandly pilastered with a tall French roofed skyline. In St. Vincent St, W of Hope St, *No. 142* (1899; J. Salmon II), called the 'Hatrack', the most original of the remarkable series of Glasgow office buildings of the turn of the century, characteristically solving the problem of inserting office space into an early 19C house plot with a narrow soaring frontage, here of eight storeys and attic, only three bays wide. Salmon's front sets up a rippling movement between the centre and outer bays, more window than stone. There are Art Nouveau touches in the curved oriels each side of the ground-floor bay and the lively skyline of pointed dormers over the half-octagonal top floor, but the overall logic of the floor arrangements and their lighting requirements comes through as the principal determinant. Further E, *Nos 122–8* (1906; J.A. Campbell), pilastered centre framed by vertically emphasised outer bays rising to a complex attic. E again, *Nos 84–94* (1902; J.A. Campbell), articulated vertically with three full-height shallow bays, rising eight floors with a deep-eaved roof between creating a line of shadow. Rear expressing the steel frame in unornamented brick bays. Opposite, *Nos 81–91* (c 1860), handsome palazzo style stone front. Parallel to S, in Gordon St, *Nos 2–16* (1854; D. Rhind), built for the Commercial Bank, extremely refined Renaissance detail carried across a three-section facade, the centre rising to a columned attic floor, a stately front that needs a wider setting. Further W, on the opposite site, *Ca d'Oro* (1872; J. Honeyman), iron-fronted upper floors over a stone arcade. Delicate iron arches with roundels over, but unfortunately marred by a heavy top addition. Beyond, *Central Station Hotel* (1884; R.R. Anderson), carefully detailed Dutch gabled building with handsome tower set back from a rounded corner, the tower rising sheer and strong to a pyramid roof fronted with Baroque gables, more Scandinavian than Dutch. Opposite, *Grosvenor Building* (1860; A. Thomson), a warehouse block by 'Greek' Thomson, four storeys, the first and second treated as a giant pilastrade under a strong cornice, but made more complex by framing the first-floor windows in aedicules that stand forward of the pilasters setting up their own insistent horizontal. Over the cornice an eaves gallery under a minor cornice. Later top-floor additions. In Waterloo St, across Hope St, *Nos 15–23, Waterloo Chambers* (1899; J.J. Burnet), a complex and ponderous design where Burnet sought a new manner of articulating the large facades of office buildings, with varied and broken horizontal lines building up to a massive tower-framed centrepiece where the wall is recessed behind heavy paired columns standing overpoweringly over a row of decorated bay windows. At *Atlantic Chambers, Nos 43–7 Hope St* (1899; J.J. Burnet), the result is more harmonious, with three-storey bays rising from a second-floor balcony and strong horizontals repeated in an eaves gallery seven floors up.

Argyle St passes under Central Station from Hope St. In Union St, to N, *Nos 84–100*, the *Egyptian Halls* (1871–73; A. Thomson), 'Greek' Thomson's last great warehouse design, emphatically horizontally ordered with three upper storeys of 18 windows narrowly divided by pilaster piers or in the case of the upper gallery by fat columns of Egyptian derivation. The entire front appears carried not on wall but

The Egyptian Halls (1871–73; A. Thomson), Union Street, Glasgow

on these piers and columns separated by uninterrupted cornices. The upper cornice is of a corresponding boldness, relating to the scale of the main front, not to the thick columns that apparently support it. *Nos 54–76* (1855; W. Lochhead) is a cast-iron facade of broad spans between masonry piers with applied columns to each floor. S of Union St, Jamaica St, with a further series of warehouses, *Nos 24–30* (1864; J. Honeyman), with a Venetian Renaissance stone front, adjoining * *Gardner's* (1855; J. Baird), 'The Iron Building'. Iron fronts were developed in the United States and in Glasgow at much the same time, c 1850, the extent of the use of iron varying from complete iron-framing to structure and facade, as at Gardner's, to the use of iron in conjunction with masonry to achieve greater window areas. Gardner's is the finest such building in Britain, exploiting the lightness that the use of iron allows. The basic frame of four bays by three is expressed in uninterrupted vertical piers, the cross beams between the piers treated as cornices over panels of arched lights, the heads varying from a shallow curve on the first floor to a full arch on the top floor. The details, arches, panels below the windows, bracket cornices and sunk panels on the main piers exploit most delicately the decorative possibilities of cast iron. *Nos 60–6* (1857; Barclay and Watt) is a much altered iron-fronted warehouse with tall arched bays between pilaster piers and *No. 72* (1854; W. Spence) has the floors arranged in unbroken horizontal bands with iron columns between the windows, but stone cornices and angles disguise the iron frame. On Clyde St, the recent renewal of the river front has reclaimed a suitable setting for the fine neo-classical *Custom House* (1840; J. Taylor) and the lovely * *Suspension Bridge* (1851; A. Kirkland) with its Greek revival pylons. The next bridge visible upstream is *Victoria Bridge* (1851; J. Walker). Dixon St leads N into St. Enoch Square, site of the demolished St. Enoch Station. Pretty and toy-like baronial *Underground Station*

(1896; J. Miller). From here a dramatic view N up Buchanan St. *Nos 21–31 Buchanan St* (c 1879; W. Spence) is a good four-storey block with upper pilasters, the corner domed section to Argyle St added 1902. Further N, *No. 91* (1896; G.W. Browne), pretty gabled N Renaissance building originally one of Miss Cranston's tea-rooms with interior by G. Walton and C.R. Mackintosh. *Nos 63–9* (1879; J. Sellars), the 'Glasgow Herald', was extended to the rear in Mitchell St (1893; Keppie and Mackintosh), a fine six-storey building with octagonal corner tower and plain, strongly handled lower floors showing Mackintosh's unornamented style developing within the conventions of late 19C Glasgow gabled and turretted office building. On Argyle St, E of Buchanan St, *Nos 106–14* (1898; H. and D. Barclay), gabled office block, formerly with one of Mackintosh and Walton's tea-rooms inside. *No. 63*, on corner of Dunlop St, the Buck's Head building, is by A. Thomson (1863), added to a now demolished range of c 1859 from which it took the curious parapet line of piers with clay finials, some of which were chimney-pots. The two main floors are cast-iron, Thomson's only cast-iron front, not in fact structural at all but a decorative screen of thin columns supporting only the attic balcony. Masonry attic floor with piers of most curious shape.

OUTER GLASGOW

East of Centre

Well E of the present centre, lay the old centre of Glasgow, which has been entirely absorbed by warehousing, demolition associated with the railway and later road schemes. Argyle St leads E into Trongate and the foot of the High St at Glasgow Cross. Saltmarket leads S to the river and the *Justiciary Court House* (1807–14; W. Stark), Greek Revival, but mostly rebuilt 1910 preserving only the outline and portico of one of the early fully Greek public buildings in Britain. Further W, on Clyde St, *Fishmarket* (1873; Clarke and Bell), an elegant French classical front to a large cast-iron market hall. The Justiciary Court House overlooks the E end of Glasgow Green. On the Green, *Doulton Fountain* (1887), red terracotta monumental work made for the 1888 Glasgow Exhibition with life size statue of the Queen and figurative groups symbolising the peoples of the Empire by W.S. Frith, F.W. Pomeroy and others. Now decayed and in danger of removal. The *People's Palace* (1894; A. Macdonald), on the Green, built to bring entertainment to east Glasgow, now houses the Museum of Glasgow History. Across the Green, *Templeton's Carpet Factory* (1889; W. Leiper), one of the unexpected delights of Glasgow, a polychrome Italian Gothic building on a scale rivalling the front of the Doge's Palace, all carried out in bright glazed brick, red terracotta and faience, the company having decided that the quality of their carpets demanded a building of equal artistic aspirations. Returning to Glasgow Cross, Gallowgate runs E towards Tolcross, 2½m, where *Tolcross House* (1848; D. Bryce), a medium sized baronial country house in its own park is now a childrens' museum. From Glasgow Cross the old High St runs N to Castle St and the Cathedral. By the Cathedral, *Barony Church* (1886; J.J. Burnet), tall lancet Gothic in the manner of J.L. Pearson with severe exterior and interior to the 'Gerona plan' where the chancel arch and narrow openings to the chancel aisles are framed by a broad nave, itself aisled. The plan had been used by Pearson at his Red Lion Square church in London in the 1870s, and this and the early pointed style seem designed to appeal to Pearson who assessed the Barony Church competition. On the other side of the Cathedral Square, attractive Renaissance style *Barony North Church* (1878; J. Honeyman) with low square angles framing an Ionic columned centre and one angle tower rising to an octagonal cupola. *Glasgow Cathedral*, mostly built from late 12C to 14C with poor W front of 1848. The site, picturesque with the hill of the necropolis behind, is overwhelmed by the bulk of the Royal Infirmary, a sad replacement for the original Infirmary of 1792 by the Adam brothers. *Glasgow Necropolis*, laid out 1833, is undoubtedly the finest cemetery in Britain, the craggy hilltop crowned by an array of obelisks, columns and mausolea in beautifully kept park-like surroundings. Winding paths up to the summit lined with elaborate vaults pierced into the rock. The John Knox monument (1825) crowns the hilltop, surrounded by monumental masonry including the elaborate Romanesque circular *Menteith mausoleum* (1842; D. Cousin), the Moorish domed *W.R. Wilson mausoleum* (1849; J.A. Bell) and others in all the styles from Greek to Gothic. Up Castle St, to N of Barony Church, in Barony St, *Martyrs School* (1895; C.R. Mackintosh), plainest of Mackintosh's schools, rectangular with play of different levels only on the corner stair tower. Castle St leads N to Springburn Rd. In Springburn Park, 1½m N, *Mosesfield House* (1838; D. Hamilton), Elizabethan style small country house, absorbed into the city.

Templeton's Carpet Factory (1889; W. Leiper), Glasgow Green

West of Centre

W of Hope St the early 19C grid pattern of central Glasgow retains more of its early 19C scale, with one notable square, *Blythswood Square* of 1823–29. In St. Vincent St to S, *St. Vincent St Church* (1859; A. Thomson), a temple portico raised on a high Grecian substructure massively detailed with a band of heavily framed square openings around the sides and back and two doors framing massive short piers. The temple rises above flanked by 'aisles' with a sort of Egyptian window feature at each end and pilastered windows between. The shape arises from the square interior plan of which the temple is the upper part and the 'aisles' represent the upper galleries each side.

Thomson's eclectic ingenuity is nowhere more vivid than in the extraordinary tower to one side that develops into a dome of elongated shape, made up of Graeco-Egyptian elements but so exotic in appearance as to suggest something Hindu, wholly unexpected after the rigidly square lines of the main church. Further W, in Elmbank St, N of St. Vincent St, former *Glasgow Academy* (1846; C. Wilson), handsome 11-window Italianate block with rusticated piers carrying statues flanking the ground floor centre bays. To N, Bath St and Sauchiehall St run E–W. In Sauchiehall St, to E, *No. 199* (1904; C.R. Mackintosh), the famous Willow Tea-Rooms, severe white facade without concession to period style or decorative carving, the long first-floor window marking the former Room de Luxe, reached by a stair with balustrade of steel, iron and glass balls reminiscent of 20C abstract sculpture. The matching frieze in the main ground-floor room survives. The whole interior has been recently restored.

School of Art, the Library (1907; C.R. Mackintosh), Glasgow

Behind, on Renfrew St, *Glasgow School of Art* (1896–1909; C.R. Mackintosh), a building in isolation in its time, the product of an individual mind that cannot be easily linked to any contemporary architectural movement, Art Nouveau or Arts and Crafts without the differences becoming more apparent than the links. The N entrance front is an array of great studio windows, three and then four bays separated by the entrance bay, massive and asymmetrical, suggesting a castle front but softened by the curves of the door frame, first-floor window and parapet in front of the recessed upper window. There is a balanced strength about this front, the unadorned studio windows given a broad-eaved roof, this strong horizontal interrupted by the gatehouse tower effect of the entrance bay just as the lines of the studio windows are interrupted, but as the facade is always seen in perspective unity is maintained, enhanced by the stone front wall with iron railings, the extraordinary vegetal brackets that run against the upper studio windows and the delicate balcony across the entrance bay. The E end wall, in rougher rubble stone, has suggestions of Scots 16C castles, but only suggestions, an octagonal turret grows from the wall face to terminate in a cupola, but the arched-headed two-light window from the entrance front, quite without baronial parallels, reappears. The W end of the school, added in 1907, rises cliff-like from the steep hillside, punctuated by shallow oriels with tiny window panes, three on the left side under the blank side wall of the studios, while on the right the library end is marked by three oriels of almost 65ft, similar to those on the left, with the small-paned glass flush with the stonework but the glass on three levels, the first even with the windows to the left, then the main library windows, 25ft high, a cascade of uninterrupted glass with curious lobe-like stone framing down the sides, and finally a narrow band of glass, the oriels continued above in stone to parapet level with a gable above. Notable interiors especially the library, galleried with the most complex effects of space achieved by setting the galleries well back from the supporting piers that rise uninterrupted into the roof. Moulded ornament is almost completely absent, but there are notched balusters on the joists between the gallery fronts and the main piers and odd flattened oval panels to the galleries, pierced below the galleries like an organic fringe.

On Sauchiehall St, *Nos 336–56*, the Grecian Building, (1865; A. Thomson), the upper floor treated as a long-eaved gallery with Egyptian type columns free-standing in front of the windows, neatly substituted in the end bays and side walls by piers between the windows treated as broad pilasters. To W, overlooking the inner motorway, *Charing Cross Mansions* (1891; J.J. Burnet), large curved corner block riotously mixing bay windows, pavilion roofs, balconied upper floor and crowning cupola on a spire-like stalk. Right in the centre, most ornate three-storey sculpted feature around a clock face. Gabled range to E added by Burnet 1897. To N of Charing Cross, road schemes have altered the old street pattern, and streets of tenements survive in isolation around St. George's Cross and Maryhill Rd. In St. George's Rd, *St. George's in the Fields* (1886; H. Barclay), Greek Ionic temple with fully sculpted pediment, surprising in the midst of redevelopment, a strayed Madeleine. Maryhill Rd leads N to Garscube Rd, at Queens Cross. *Queens Cross Church* (1896–97; C.R. Mackintosh), Mackintosh's only church, is now owned by the C.R. Mackintosh Society. Free Gothic with a remarkable battered tower, the batter accentuated by a taller stair turret rising straight. A great deal of incident in the relatively short side elevation, paired transept-like gables, a recess with flying buttress and then a tower-like two-storey porch with Art Nouveau sculpted detail. Further NW, off Maryhill Rd, *Ruchill Church Hall* (1899; Mackintosh), Ruchill St, a small work, but obviously Mackintosh, emphatically sheer wall wrapped around a curved corner and intriguing play of planes in the gabled right-hand section.

W of the motorway begins the area of elegant 19C terraces of Woodlands Hill. Sauchiehall St runs S of the hill with pleasant terraces built from 1840 onwards. At the W end, *Royal Crescent* (1839; A. Taylor) with very mixed classical detail. Woodlands Hill to the N was built up from the 1830s, beginning parallel to Sauchiehall St in *Woodside Crescent* and *Terrace* (c 1830–40; G. Smith), continued to W in *Claremont Terrace* (1842–47; J. Baird). Further attractive terraces were built on the E side of the hill, e.g. *Lynedoch Crescent* (c 1845; G. Smith), before the layout of the summit and Kelvingrove Park to the W was put in hand under C. Wilson with Sir J. Paxton advising on the park. *Park Circus* (1855; C. Wilson) crowns the summit, still in scale close to late Georgian prototypes, while Park Terrace, on the W side, has French pavilion roofs. The drama of Woodlands Hill is provided by towers: the tower of the demolished *Park Parish Church* (1858; J. Rochead) standing as a Gothic sentinel to the cluster of three Italian towers on the former *Free Church College* (1856–61; C. Wilson), an inspired piece of landscape design, architecturally a most exotic, and on a gloomy day, eerie creation. Wilson's design combines, asymmetrically, Renaissance elements that seem to demand symmetry, a palazzo style main block and, to the left, the pedimented front of the former chapel flanked by the two lower towers, of tall thin profile at variance with the Wrenian frontispiece. At one corner of the main block rises the principal campanile, splendidly assured with the very long arched lights of the smaller towers, but here capped by a bold cornice and lantern turret. The view across the Park to Woodlands Hill from the University is one of the most attractive Victorian town landscapes in Britain. Behind Lynedoch Crescent, *Woodlands Parish Church* (1874; J. Burnet I), a High Victorian design with fine spire and handsome round turretted group of ancillary halls behind. W of the Park, on a high ridge, *Glasgow University* (1866–72; G.G. Scott), a long Gothic front, at two storeys too low for the length, but redeemed by the central feature, a small version of a Flemish cloth-hall behind an exaggeratedly large porch tower in six stages with heavy projecting top stage and delicate openwork spire, added 1887 (J.O. Scott). The spire is a landmark over West Glasgow. Two rear quadrangles are divided by the Bute Hall (1878–84; J.O. Scott), raised on a fine stone vaulted undercroft. The hall above is vaulted on slender iron columns. *John Macintyre Building* (1887 and 1895; J.J. Burnet) behind, built as the University Union, Tudor Gothic with squat flat-parapet tower. Across the road, *Wellington Church* (1883; T.L. Watson) with full Roman Corinthian portico and recessed side colonnade. To E, *Nos 41–53 Oakfield Avenue* (1865; A. Thomson), terrace contained by big pedimented end blocks with square piers dividing the windows. The treatment of the upper windows of the centre with linked window heads and sunk panels with honeysuckle motifs between is especially characteristic of Thomson, creating a three-dimensional effect by recession from the wall face. In Hillhead Gardens, *Hunterian Art Gallery*, belonging to the University, with the reconstructed interior of C.R. Mackintosh's house, complete with furnishings and an outstanding collection of paintings by Whistler. In University Gardens, *No. 12* (c 1900; J.G. Gillespie) with a bay rising up to an octagonal cupola, free style, reminiscent of Mackintosh in the treatment of cupola and plain parapet, and more Mackintosh influence in the interior. On the corner of University Avenue, *Gilmorehill Church* (1876; J. Sellars), Early French Gothic.

Bank St leads back down to Great Western Rd, the straight artery running NW from the city laid out in the 1830s and around which the handsome terraces of west Glasgow were built. The leafy residential areas of Woodside, Hillhead, Belmont and Kelvinside attractively follow the contours of the low hills. The grander terraces front on to Great Western Rd. E of Bank St, on Great Western Rd, two prominent spires, *Lansdowne Church* (1863; J. Honeyman), with tall slender spire, and *St. Mary's Episcopal Cathedral* (1871–93; G.G. Scott), also EE in style, but more elaborately modelled, especially the tower with intersecting diagonal panelling under the cornice and a Lincolnshire spire. The grandest sequence of terraces begins further NW, opposite the Royal Botanic Gardens, but in Belmont, N of Great Western Rd, *Belmont Crescent* (1869), Belmont St, is attractive and *Northpark Terrace* (1866; A Thomson), Hamilton Drive, a severe and handsome example of Thomson's terrace designs, probably part of an unexecuted larger scheme. On Great Western Rd, the first major terrace is *Buckingham Terrace* (1852; J.T. Rochead), on the N side, an original departure in terrace design in that the ground floor is advanced slightly with first-floor balcony broken for a regular sequence of tall, shallow bay windows, avoiding the disjointed look that full-height bays give to a facade. Beyond, the *Botanic Gardens*, laid out in the 1840s by Paxton with the main greenhouse the wonderfully atmospheric *Kibble Palace*, designed by Mr Kibble for his house at Coulport and transferred here in 1873. Kibble's greenhouse was in two sections, with his house between. Re-erected, the two are united with the main circular conservatory of spectacular width rising to a low glass dome, like a stranded flying saucer, and then a glazed tunnel linking to the smaller domed frontispiece with curved-ended transepts. Inside, the atmosphere is made more overpoweringly Victorian by a collection of marble statuary by leading sculptors dripping damply in the humid air. Across the road, *Grosvenor Terrace* (1855; J.T. Rochead) in palatial Venetian style with applied classical orders to each floor, the most richly modelled Glasgow terrace. Recently rebuilt after a disastrous fire. *Kelvinside Parish Church* (1862; Campbell Douglas and Stevenson) provides a fine Gothic accent at the E end, Italian Gothic in the manner of G.E. Street, and behind, in Saltoun St, is the Sainte-Chapelle derived *Belmont and Hillhead Church* (1875; J. Sellars). *Kew Terrace* (1849; J.T. Rochead) faces *Kirklee Terrace* (1845; C. Wilson), the earliest of the Great Western Rd terraces, Italianate, nicely varied between three-storey centre and end blocks and two-storey linking ranges. Behind *Belhaven Terrace* (1866; J. Thomson), to S, in Dundonald Rd, *Greek Orthodox Cathedral* (1877; J. Sellars) with powerful Early French front. Beyond Belhaven Terrace, *Great Western Terrace* (1867; A. Thomson), massively long, raised above the road, detailed with the utmost severity. Square Ionic porches are the main accent down the long length, but monotony is avoided by two three-storey blocks set slightly in from each end. The terrace is a lesson in the design of very long frontages, where the classical centrepiece has no value as the viewpoint is always in the long perspective. Behind, *Westbourne Church* (1880; J. Honeyman), Westbourne Gardens, delightful Renaissance classical church with two-storey portico and little cupolas set back each side.

On Hyndland Rd, *Westbourne Terrace* (1871; A. Thomson) with a ground and first floor similar to Rochead's Buckingham Terrace, the ground floor acting as a podium for upper bay windows. Further up, *St. Bride's Church* (1904; G.F. Bodley), like Bodley's English work of the time, a single long roof over nave and chancel, boarded and differentiated at the chancel by a rood beam and low sanctuary wall. W end and tower 1915. Hyndland Rd continues past *Hyndland Parish Church* (1886; W. Leiper), Crown Rd leading off on left to *Crown Circus* (1858; J. Thomson), an unusual convex crescent. Dowanhill and Partickhill, on the other side of Hyndland Rd, pleasant leafy suburbs of villas and terraces, culminate in spectacular views down to the Clyde at Partick. Hyndland St leads down, crowned by the 195ft spire of *Dowanhill Church* (1866; W. Leiper), Early French Gothic with the relation of tower to spire particularly well handled. Dumbarton Rd leads back towards the centre, past the *Glasgow Art Gallery* (1892–1900; Simpson and Milner Allen), an overblown eclectic structure, centre-piece of the 1901 Glasgow exhibition. Good painting collections, especially of turn of the century Glasgow artists. Argyle St runs SE with surviving tenement development to S in *Minerva St* and *St. Vincent Crescent* (1849–55; A. Kirkland), immensely long, double curved and of some grandeur, the curved entry from Argyle St with a giant order of pilasters, a type more common in Edinburgh.

South of the river

S of the river, Glasgow's inner city, notably the Gorbals area, has been the most thoroughly redeveloped part of the town, the old tenements giving way to roads, tower blocks and a great deal of ill-defined space, most obvious in the Gorbals, but extending downstream towards the shipyard area of Govan. Gorbals St is reached over Victoria Bridge. The *Citizens Theatre* (1878; Campbell Douglas) has lost its columned front, but retains a fine interior. At the foot of Gorbals St, *Caledonia Rd Church* (1856; A. Thomson), burnt-out shell of 'Greek' Thomson's most Greek church, an Ionic temple front set on a massive basement characterised by masonry banded in alternate thin courses. Unlike the St. Vincent St church the temple front is not carried right through the body of the church, the main part here is lower and wider with square pilastrades, giving the effect of a composition built up of massive building blocks, a rhythm perhaps intended as a stage-by-stage ascent that culminates in the magnificent sheer tower, stark mass set off by banded stonework and plain square openings high up divided by elemental square columns, nothing interrupting the sheer face. A recessed pyramid-roofed lantern, more decorated than any other element in the design, caps the tower, relieving the severity. Thomson's handling of mass and his reinterpretation of Greek elements are without parallel in British architecture. Caledonia Rd leads out SE towards Rutherglen past the *Southern Necropolis*, the main South Glasgow cemetery, laid out in the 1840s. Just S of the Caledonia Rd Church, *St. Ninian's Wynd Church* (1888; W.G. Rowan), Cathcart Rd, Romanesque with a massive W front, really a tower achieved by making three-dimensional a facade based on Normandy precedents.

Pollokshaws Rd runs SW from Gorbals St to *Queen's Park*, laid out by Paxton. On the N side, *Camphill Church* (1878; W. Leiper) with a Normandy Gothic spire of fine outline clearly influenced by J.L. Pearson. The spire behind, in Queen's Drive, is *Queen's Park High Church* (1872; Campbell Douglas and Stevenson), a more complex High Victorian design with curious low arches over the main tower lancets. At the SW corner of the Park, *Langside Hall* (1847; J. Gibson), the re-erected National Bank, originally in Queen St, and the first major work by the leading bank architect of the 19C, richly modelled with overall rustication and superimposed orders. S of the Park, *Langside Hill Church* (1895; A. Skirving), last of Glasgow's classical churches, raised on a high basement in the manner of Thomson, but more lushly detailed. In Mansionhouse Rd, to S, *No. 25* (1856; A. Thomson), pair of houses set high over the river Cart with deep eaved roofs and brilliantly designed. The two houses appear one large asymmetrical design, but in fact the plans are reversed so that the gabled frontispiece of one reappears on the rear of the other. Characteristic Thomson square piers to the windows, glazed behind leaving the structure and the glazing distinct, an effect compared to the work of Frank Lloyd Wright. Just S, in *Millbrae Crescent*, two terraces in the Thomson manner, diluted, built by his partner R. Turnbull 1876. Well to the SE, in Cathcart, is the other major Thomson villa, *Holmwood* (1857–58), Netherlee Rd, overlooking the river Cart and standing in its own grounds. Loosely composed with broad eaved roofs, the villa builds up in plan from a roughly rectangular ground floor to an L-shape upper floor. The various parts are separately expressed, so that the single-storey dining-room reads as a separately gabled range answering to the similar gable of the two-storey block, linked by a single-storey porch and hall from which the stair tower rises to the top lantern. The parlour is distinguished by a circular bay, with, as elsewhere, the glazing set behind the line of the columns, separating it from the load-bearing structure. While, in style, a development of the picturesque Italian villa with details in Thomson's angular Greek vein, Holmwood looks forward to compositional solutions more typical of the early 20C. The house is now a convent. NW from Queen's Park, Moray Place runs parallel to Pollokshaws Rd. *Nos 1–10* (1859; A. Thomson) is one of Thomson's finest terrace designs, pedimented end houses with a giant order of square columns, the upper windows glazed right up to the columns while the lower floor has a minor order of pilasters. The long central section repeats the window forms without the giant order, the upper floor appearing as a continuous square colonnade while masonry piers divide the lower openings. Thomson himself lived in No. 1. Nithsdale Rd leads NW into Pollokshields. Nos 200 and 202 are both villas by Thomson, *No. 202* (1870) a plain asymmetric villa but *No. 200* (1871) wholly different, a single-storey house, symmetrical and square in plan, with an Egyptian columned entrance flanked by a triple window each side divided by square columns with Grecian capitals, all the openings unmoulded deep recesses back from a single masonry wall face. This is a powerful, if theatrical, design enhanced by the crispness of the stone carving contrasting with the mottled surface of the main stone wall. Just N, in Albert Drive, *No. 301*, The Knowe (1852; A. Thomson), Thomson's earliest Glasgow villa, still in the round-arched Italianate manner with a short campanile tower in the angle. One odd feature is the inverted swelling of the porch columns, narrowest at the base. Villas in most Victorian styles survive in Pollokshields. Albert Drive leads back to Pollokshaws Rd, past the *Museum of Transport* with collections of locomotives, trams and cars.

From Pollokshaws Rd, Eglinton St runs N back towards Glasgow Bridge. *Nos 355–429*, Queens Park Terrace, is a long tenement block by A. Thomson (1857–58) running from Turiff St to Devon St in an unbroken row. Upper window details with all the motifs reused in Thomson's later works and a remarkable effect of receding wall face. First-floor windows in full aedicule surrounds, the next floor with a continuous stepped hood over the windows, flush with the wall below but forward of the wall above, which has sunk panels between the upper window heads establishing yet another layer of surface. Kilbirnie St, opposite, leads into West St and Scotland St. *Scotland St

School (1904; C.R. Mackintosh) is a board school made remarkable by framing the front in two great curved stair towers, almost wholly glazed, thin mullions of great height dividing the long leaded windows. Subtle details to the stonework of these towers, especially in the top floor, and the whole composition framed by a screen of tall railings in which a blockhouse row of lavatories plays a central part. Nearer the river, large warehouses still survive. In Tradeston St, parallel to West St, *No. 118* (1900; W. McGibbon) is Florentine Gothic with a tower and *No. 95 Morrison St* (1897; Bruce and Hay) an immensely overblown version of a French Second Empire town hall, built for the Co-operative Society. To W, on Paisley Rd West, *Walmer Crescent* (1857; A. Thomson), a shallow curved row of tenements with the first use of Thomson's undulating hood, over the first-floor windows, and an upper square colonnade. Five large two-storey projections break up the length. To W, Govan Rd leads N into **Govan** past the docks. Much redeveloped, the grand urban scale still shows a little. *Nos 640–6* (1897; W.J. Anderson) and *No. 816*, Bank of Scotland (1899; J. Salmon II), are good turn of the century works. At Govan Cross, the *Pearce Institute* (1903; R.R. Anderson), beautifully detailed gabled N Renaissance building, the gift of a leading shipbuilding family. Anderson also rebuilt *Govan Parish Church* (1884–88). Down Langlands Rd in Elder Park, another example of industrial munificence, the *Elder Library* (1902; J.J. Burnet), charming single-storey Baroque pavilion with curved portico and dome above. The Elder family also gave a *Cottage Hospital* (1902; J.J. Burnet), built in the style of c 1700, S of the park in Drumoyne Rd.

Around Glasgow

On the A81, 5m NW of Glasgow, **Bearsden**. Glasgow suburb with substantial late Victorian villas. On Drymen Rd, *Shaw Hospital* (1895; J. Thomson), Scots 16C style with central tower. At New Kilpatrick, to E, parish *church* with good Glasgow stained glass of c 1900, W window 1909 by S. Adam. 3m NE, *Mugdock Reservoir* (1855), with imposing stone buildings typical of the Glasgow water system, a municipal and engineering achievement that gave the city pure water from the Trossachs, channelled from Loch Venachar some 18m N to Mugdock and thence to Glasgow.

6m NE of Glasgow, A603, **Kirkintilloch**. Iron and coal town. At **Campsie**, 4m NW, *Lennox Castle* (1837–41; D. Hamilton), the most impressive neo-Norman style castle in Scotland with large keep and angle towers, very square and regular but for the keep rising to one side over a big porte-cochère.

4m W of Glasgow, A814, **Clydebank**. A shipbuilding town founded 1871 around the yard of J. and B. Thomson and later famous for the John Brown and Co. yard that built the 'Lusitania' (1906) and subsequent Cunard and White Star liners. Attractive free classical *Municipal Buildings* (1902; J. Miller), Dumbarton Rd, with clock tower and former *Clydebank Riverside Station* (c 1896), attractive Scots Renaissance red stone building.

4m W of Glasgow, A8, **Renfrew**. Former county town, the *County Buildings* (1878) prominent with pavilion-roofed and turreted tower. In High St, parish *church* (1861; J.T. Rochead) with stone spire. In Blythswood Rd, former *Grammar School* (1841; J. Stephen), cruciform Greek Revival building fronted by a Greek portico and tower, a smaller version of St. Pancras' Church, London. 5m NW, *Erskine House* (1828; R. Smirke), an early example of revived Elizabethan style. At **Bishopton**, to W, *Formakin House* (1912; R. Lorimer), handsome but never completed red stone Scots 17C style house. Good entrance lodges with tall bell-shaped roofs.

3m SE of Glasgow, A724, **Rutherglen**. Industrial town now attached to Glasgow. In Main St, *Town Hall* (1861; C. Wilson), baronial landmark with tower, and parish *church* (1900–02; J.J. Burnet). To S, **Cambuslang**, birthplace of J.C. Loudon (1783–1843), tireless writer on horticulture and estate improvement. Parish *church* (1841; D. Cousin) with tall spire.

11m E of Glasgow, A89, **Airdrie**, iron and coal town. In Bank St, Greek style *County Buildings* (1856; J. Thomson Sr) and *old Town Hall* (1825), replaced by the *new Town Hall* (1912; J. Thomson and Sons), Stirling St, Edwardian classical. Airdrie was the first place in Scotland to set up a free public library under the 1850 Free Libraries Act. 3m W is **Coatbridge**, the chief iron town in Scotland by the later 19C, developed by the ironmaster John Baird (1802–76). By 1864 there were nearly 50 blast furnaces and 10,000 employees at the Baird works.

14m SE of Glasgow, A721, **Motherwell**, heavily industrialised iron

The Cathedral of the Isles (1849–51; W. Butterfield), Millport, Great Cumbrae

and steel town, the iron works founded 1871 became the largest steel works in Britain by 1914. Now much post-industrial decay. Iron towns at Wishaw to SE, Cambusnethan and Newmains to E. At **Newmains**, *Coltness Memorial Church* (1878; Wallace), built for J. Houldsworth, iron-founder, with polychrome brick interior and contemporary stained glass.

GREAT CUMBRAE. Island in Firth of Clyde, reached from Largs. The town of **Millport** is a Victorian resort of stucco and stone terraces. On the seafront, *Garrison House* (1819 and later), Gothic house of the 6th Earl of Glasgow who was a leading figure in the revival of the episcopal church in Scotland. At Millport, Lord Glasgow founded the Community of the Holy Spirit, to be a monastic community in accordance with the ideas of the Oxford Tractarian movement with which Lord Glasgow had been much involved. The college and church, now the *Cathedral of the Isles*, were built from 1849 by W. Butterfield, one of his most attractive works. The church with a sharply pyramidal spire is set between two long stone ranges so that the roofs and chimneys compose with the taller church and spire. Excellent simple detailing to the chimneys, small-paned windows and hipped dormers. The church has a tall stone screen and tiled chancel decoration.

GREENOCK. A8 20m W of Glasgow. Clydeside shipbuilding centre with docks and repair yards along the shore, notably the 676ft long range of *warehouses* (1886) in James Watt Dock, East Hamilton St. In Hamilton St, *Municipal Buildings* (1881; H. and D. Barclay), testimony to the 19C wealth of the town, Renaissance style with 244ft slim banded tower and cupola. In Nelson St, *County Court* (1867; Peddie and Kinnear), solid baronial with pavilion-roofed central tower, and *Old Kirk* (1840 and 1854; D. Cousin), classical with a tall, thin version of a Wren steeple. In Union St, *Watt Institute, Museum and Library* (1837; E. Blore, and 1876), the Institute built by James Watt's son to hold his father's scientific library, and statue by Chantrey. The 1837 buildings are Elizabethan style and the Museum has a large top-lit hall with display cases. Opposite, *episcopal church* (1877; Paley and Austin) with a strong, severe pyramid-roofed tower. In Ardgowan Square, *Estate Office* (1886; R.R. Anderson), 17C style with hipped roof and asymmetrical entry, and palazzo style *Greenock Club* (1865; Wardrop, Anderson and Brown). The *Old West Kirk* of 1591 was moved in the 1920s to Campbell St, at the E end of the Esplanade, to make way for industrial development. Inside excellent early glass by Morris and Burne-Jones, the best in Scotland (c 1870), and one window by D. Cottier (c 1873), the leading Scottish glass painter. 4m W is **Gourock**, Clydeside resort and ferry port. On the seafront, Renaissance style *Gamble Institute* (1875). The open crown spire of *St. James Church* (1877; J., W. and J. Hay) is the chief landmark. 4m E of Greenock, A8, **Port Glasgow**, shipbuilding town on the Clyde. To W, *Broadfield Hospital* (1869; D. Bryce), Old Greenock Rd, baronial with square tower and a splendid octagonal domed conservatory to one side. 4m SE, A761, **Kilmacolm**, village with numerous c 1900 villas. *Church of Scotland* (c 1902; W. Leiper), Duchal Rd, late Gothic with tower. Among the villas, *Windyhill* (1899 and 1901; C.R. Mackintosh), Houston St, roughcast vernacular without picturesque trimmings, just battered chimneys and long slate roofs. Several villas by J. Salmon including *The Bishop's House* (1905), Porterfield Rd, stone with mullion windows, *Rowantreehill* (1898), stone and half-timber, and *Den o' Gryffe* (1903), Knockbuckle Rd. Off the Port Glasgow road,

Auchenbothie House (1898; W. Leiper), substantial harled baronial house with circular entrance tower. To N, W of Langbank, *Finlaystone House* (1900; J.J. Burnet), sumptuous baronial remodelling of an earlier house. Now a museum.

Municipal Buildings (1881–89; H. and D. Barclay), Greenock. Photograph c 1900

HAMILTON. A724 11m SE of Glasgow. The site of Hamilton Palace, the great mansion of the Dukes of Hamilton, is now a park but the *Hamilton Mausoleum* (1848–53; D. Bryce) survives, a splendid piece of funerary architecture, heavily rusticated classical with a dome and splendid bronze doors (J. Steell) modelled on Ghiberti's in Florence. In the town, by the bridge in Cadzow St, Edwardian group of *Municipal Buildings* (1906–14; A. Cullen). *No. 113* is a classical bank building (c 1840; D. Hamilton). On corner of Cadzow St and Muir St, *fountain* (1893), given by Mr Watson, colliery owner, with seated figure of Mrs

Watson and mining implements. In Almada St, Greek Ionic *Sheriff Court* (1870; W. Murray). 2m N, **Bothwell**, Clydeside suburb only partly industrialised. On the hill E of the river, *Greenbank*, 20 Geen St (1855; A. Thomson), the first of 'Greek' Thomson's villas fully in his mature style with the stripped classical detail, broad, low roofs and pyramid-roofed tower. W of Bothwell, coal-mining and cotton town of **Blantyre**. David Livingstone, missionary and explorer, was born here and worked in the Low Blantyre mills from the age of ten. His birthplace is now a *museum*. *Livingstone Memorial Church* (1882; McKissack and Rowan).

The Hamilton Mausoleum (1848–53; D. Bryce), Hamilton

HELENSBURGH. A814 7m NW of Dumbarton. Clydeside resort, a favourite site for villas during the late 19C, as was most of the shore of Gare Loch to the N. *Hill House (1902–04; C.R. Mackintosh), Upper Colquhoun St, is Mackintosh's finest house (open to public). The basic elements, sheer walls, steep roof and conical-roofed turret, recall Scots 16C houses but Mackintosh uses them simplified to the extreme. The angle of the L-plan is cut back to the circular tower while the main gable shows a battered chimney set between a box-like projection and a sloping roof edge, giving a play of geometrical planes. Inside, some of Mackintosh's most luminous interiors with white painted woodwork marked by long plant-stem verticals and chequerboard pierced holes. By contrast, two large houses by W. Leiper, *Cairndhu Hotel* (1872), in stone, François Ier style, the interiors with painted woodwork and glass by D. Cottier in advanced aesthetic movement taste, reminiscent of Morris and Co., but the figures more neoclassical, and *Dalmore* (1875), pink stone baronial. There are later villas by Leiper, more influenced by Domestic Revival work in England, with such unScottish features as half-timbering and red tile roofs. The *Red Tower* and *Tordarroch*, Douglas Drive, and *Brantewood*, Munro Drive West, are late works by Leiper. In Princes St, *episcopal church* (1867; R.R. Anderson), lancet Gothic with fine sheer tower. The coast road to the N is lined with villas, some large-scale baronial houses also, *Blairvadoch* (1848; J.T. Rochead) and *Shandon House* (1849; C. Wilson) are landmarks N of **Rhu**. Across Gare Loch, the Rosneath peninsula was similarly popular. At **Rosneath**, *The Ferry Inn* (1898; Lutyens), harled with a characteristic Lutyens corner window. On the W side, near **Cove**, *Craig Ailey* (1850; A. Thomson), Italianate with short campanile tower and round-arched detail. To N, baronial *Knockderry Castle* (1855).

Hill House (1902–04; C.R. Mackintosh), Helensburgh

INVERARAY. A83 44m NW of Dumbarton. Estate town of the Dukes of Argyll, and former county town of Argyllshire. 4m E, *Dunderave Castle*, carefully restored 1911 (R. Lorimer) for Sir A. Noble, owner of *Ardkinglas* (1906; R. Lorimer), near Kilmorich on the opposite shore of Loch Fyne. Noble was a partner in the armaments firm Armstrong, Whitworth and Co. The house is in the baronial style preferred by Lorimer, domesticated with long small-paned sash windows and carved dormer heads. A main tower with cap-house and turret, a round tower with conical roof varied to a slight wave outline and plain stepped gables build up to a picturesque composition inflating the apparent size of the house. 14m SW of Inveraray, A83, *Minard Castle Hotel* (1848), castellated house by Loch Fyne. 10m further, *Kilmory Castle*, Lochgilphead, castellated house of c 1820–30. 39m S of Inveraray, A815, **Dunoon**, Clydeside resort reached by ferry from Gourock. Seafront lined with villas of the 19C. Timber pier (1896) with clock tower and, on the front, *statue* (1898) of Burns' Highland Mary, Mary Campbell, who came from Dunoon. 7m S, on the tip of the peninsula, *Castle Toward* (1821; D. Hamilton), romantic castellated house. 7m N of Dunoon, *Younger Botanical Garden* (open to the public), a woodland garden laid out from 1891 by H.J. Younger around Benmore House (1862 and 1874), baronial.

39m SW of Inveraray, A83, **Tarbert**, fishing port on the narrow link between Knapdale and Kintyre. Prominent *church* (1886) with crown steeple. 3m N, *Stonefield Castle* (1836; W.H. Playfair), castellated mansion with tower and corner turrets, now an hotel. 12m N, **Ardrishaig**, harbour built 1837 at the E end of the Crinan Canal that cuts through to Loch Gilp on the W coast. 11m S of Tarbert, *Skipness House* (1881; J. Honeyman), baronial. 38m S of Tarbert, A83, **Campbeltown**, principal town of Kintyre and a late 19C resort. *Library and Museum* (1899 J.J. Burnet), free classical, long and low with a cupola. 10m S, E of **Southend**, *Macharioch* (1874); G. Devey), Scots style house with crowsteps and tower built for the Duke of Argyll, loosely and picturesquely planned as in Devey's English houses. 14m N of Campbeltown, B842, *Torrisdale Castle* (c 1815; J.G. Graham, and c 1900), picturesque castellated house. 3m N, B879, *Carradale House* (1844, D. Bryce), an early work of Bryce, harled with conical turrets, moderate sized baronial. 9m NW of Campbeltown, *Glenbarr Abbey* (1814 and 1844), castellated house. From **Tayinloan**, 5m N, boats go to **Gigha** where the gardens of *Achamore House* (1884, J. Honeyman) are open to the public. The house was a shooting lodge built for Lord Abinger.

KILMARNOCK. A77 8m NE of Ayr. Engineering town on the Kilmarnock Water, prominently crossed by a 23-arch railway viaduct (1848). Some good red stone commercial buildings, notably in John Finnie St, laid out 1864. *Nos 72–84* (1879) have a top-floor gallery like 'Greek' Thomson's work in Glasgow. In Portland St, *West High Church* (1844; D. Cousin). On London Rd, *Palace Theatre* (1862; J. Ingram), Green St, built as a Corn Exchange with an Albert Memorial corner tower. In Elmbank Avenue, *Dick Institute* (1878; R. Ingram), large pedimented classical museum and art gallery. In Kay Park, the *Burns Monument and Museum* (1879; J. Ingram), outlandish rock-faced Gothic tower over the museum with a statue of the poet. 4m N, E of **Kilmaurs**, B751, *Rowallan Castle* (1903–06; R. Lorimer), Scots later 17C style, baronial but with long sash windows and carved dormer heads, built for a Glasgow MP. Lorimer's first major house, built with the sensitivity to materials of the Arts and Crafts movement and an understanding of Scottish architectural tradition that avoids the ornate and often harsh stonework of much 19C baronial work. Fine interior plasterwork and a good towered gatehouse. 8m SE of Kilmarnock, W of A76, *Ballochmyle Viaduct* (1846; Grainger and Miller), stone railway viaduct over the river Ayr with 181ft central span. 3m NE, at **Sorn**, B743, *Sorn Castle*, picturesquely sited 16C tower enlarged 1863 (D. Bryce). 4m S at **Old Cummock** parish *church* (1863; J.M. Wardrop) and *RC church* (1878; W. Burges), both built for the Marquess of Bute who owned Dumfries House nearby. The RC church is a minor work of Burges with a W rose window, completed apparently by J.F. Bentley.

LANARK. A72 31m SE of Glasgow. Former county town on the upper Clyde. In the High St, *Royal Bank* (1876; Peddie and Kinnear), Italianate. In Hope St, pedimented classical *Council Offices* (1834–36). In St. Vincent Place, ornate Gothic *RC church* (1856–59; Goldie and Hadfield) with spire and granite arcade columns. 1m S, *New Lanark, the pioneering industrial settlement founded around David Dale's cotton mills. Robert Owen was manager from 1800–24, and with considerable success set out to create a model community where all the needs of the 1,800 inhabitants would be met. Much survives today of the original, the late 18C mills and tenements, Owen's *Institute* (1816) and *school* (1817), to give a good idea of the most practical and influential

British Utopian community. 1m S, W of the Clyde, *Corehouse* (1824–27; E. Blore), Elizabethan style country house. 13m E of Lanark, via the A72, **Biggar**. Market town, ancestral home of the Gladstone family. The *Gladstone Court Museum* has trade and craft exhibits set out in a reconstructed street. Baronial *Corn Exchange* (1860; D. McGibbon) in High St. 2½m SW, *Cornhill House* (1871; W. Leiper), High Victorian rebuilding of an earlier villa with pavilion-roofed tower and strong French Gothic detail. Entrance lodge in similar style.

LARGS. A78 12m SW of Greenock. Coastal resort. In Bath St, *Clark Memorial Church* (1890–93; Kerr and Abercrombie), good spired church in the manner of J.L. Pearson, built for the Paisley thread family. Fine contemporary stained glass by S. Adam and C. Whall. On the Greenock road, *Netherall House* (1876–92; Campbell Douglas and Sellars), turretted and towered house of the great physicist Lord Kelvin (1834–1907), electrical and submarine cable pioneer. The first house in Scotland to have electric light. Further N, *Knock Castle* (c 1855; J.T. Rochead), craggy, square baronial house. At **Wemyss Bay**, to N, coastal resort and ferry port. Festive railway *station* (c 1895; J. Millar), half timbered with a tower and connected directly to the pier.

MULL. The largest Inner Hebridean island. 4m NW of **Tobermory**, *Glengorm Castle* (1860; Peddie and Kinnear), baronial with square tower. 23m SE of Tobermory, at **Lochdonhead**, *Torosay Castle* (1856; D. Bryce), baronial.

OBAN. A85 39m NW of Inveraray. Fishing port and resort developed after the arrival of the railway in 1880. Half-timbered *station* with clock tower. Oban's most unexpected monument is *McCaig's Folly* (1897) on Battery Hill, an incomplete Coliseum built by J.S. McCaig, banker, as a museum and memorial to his family. 5m NE, at **Connel**, steel cantilever *bridge* (1903) and *church* (1888) with central tower. 8m E, A85, *Inverawe House*, 16C tower house restored 1913 (R. Lorimer).

PAISLEY. City made rich on thread under the two leading families of Coats and Clark. *Paisley Abbey*, damaged in the 16C, was slowly restored, the nave 1859, transepts c 1900, and the new choir and cloisters 1912–28 (P.M. Chalmers and R. Lorimer). Opposite, the *Town Hall* (1879; W.H. Lynn), classical with tall clock tower, a memorial to G.A. Clark, whose *monument* (1885) stands in front. In Dunn Square, *statues* to two of the Coats family. To N, in Gilmour St, *No. 3* (c 1855), curved cornered former bank, and *station* (1839; unk wn), castellated to match the now demolished County Buildings. N of the railway, *County Hall* (1891; G. Bell), St. James St, Glasgow classical with upper Ionic portico. Italianate *Sheriff Court* (1885; G. Bell) adjoining. To W, *St. James' Church* (1880–84; H.J. Blanc) with good French Gothic spire. In the High St, *No. 10* (1871; J. Honeyman), former bank with curved Italianate front. In New St, *The Bull Inn* (1901; W. McLennan), pub in the style of C.R. Mackintosh or the Vienna Secession, an exceptional survival. Shallow bays to the front of differing heights, a curved gable and candle-snuffer turret. Bar windows, stained glass and fittings all in Glasgow style Art Nouveau curves. At the W end of High St, *Museum and Library* (1871; J. Honeyman), Ionic classical, a gift of Sir P. Coats. In Oakshaw Rd, to N, *Neilson Institute* (1849; C. Wilson), imposing round-arched classical with a ribbed central dome. Nearby the very grand *Coats Memorial Church* (1886–94; H.J. Blanc), the size enhanced by an elevated site. Central tower and crown spire. *No. 56*

(1897; T. Abercrombie) was a nursing home founded by the Coats family and *No. 49* (1884; J.Honeyman) the Coats Observatory, massively detailed with copper dome.

The Bull Inn (1901; W. McLennan), New Street, Paisley

TAYSIDE

ARBROATH. A92 16m NE of Dundee. Fishing town and resort. *Old church* (1831; J. Henderson), Kirk Square, with thin 152ft spire, the rest rebuilt 1894 in tall lancet Gothic (J.J. Burnet). In the High St, *Town House* (1803 and 1844) and *Nos 115–17* (1860; D. Rhind), Italianate bank. In the Market Square, former *Corn Exchange* (1855; C. Edward) with pedimented front. Dominating the town, castellated *water tower* (1885; W.G. Lamond). In Cairniehill, *The Elms* (c 1869; W. Leiper). Lavish Gothic villa. Arbroath's two most remarkable Victorian buildings are by the artist and amateur architect Patrick Allan Fraser. In the Western Cemetery, *•Mortuary Chapel* (1875–84), more richly carved than the eye believes possible, a Scottish version of the Manueline architecture of Portugal, and *Hospitalfield House*, W of the town, Fraser's own house (1866), baronial of unusual form, L-plan with low ground floor under heavily modelled tall upper floor and tall tower at the angle. *Rosely House Hotel*, 2m N, A933, seems of similar family.

BRECHIN. A94 43m NE of Perth. Cathedral town on the South Esk River. *Cathedral*, founded 1150, was restored 1899–1902 (J. Honeyman), the choir reroofed, transepts rebuilt and a new N aisle added. Glass by H. Holiday and W. Wilson. *Brechin Castle*, next to the cathedral, has a main range of c 1700, altered 1854–63 (J. Henderson). In Church St, former *Mechanics Institute* (1838; J. Henderson), Tudor Gothic with a central tower. In Panmore St, *Baptist church* (1856; J., W. and J. Hay) with tall spire of unusual outline. In St. Ninian's Square, *Museum and Library* (1892; J.G. Fairley), an attractive asymmetrical building with broad entrance arch, tall roof and cupola. *Southesk Church* (1896–1906; J.J. Burnet), adjoining, is most original, long low proportions, the church and hall built up against a massive short tower of Romanesque type and enclosing a cloistered courtyard. *Fountain* (1876; Wardrop and Reid) to the 11th Earl of Dalhousie, Secretary of State for War during the Crimean War. In Bank St, High Victorian *RC church* (1875; W. Leiper), French Gothic with octagonal spirelet. In Witchden Rd, *Maisondieu Church* (1891; G.W. Browne), classical, two-storey Ionic portico and tower with octagonal cupola. 2½m SE, *Kinnaird Castle* (1789 and 1854; D. Bryce), a complete recasing of the original house in Franco-Scottish Gothic, all steep roofs and round turrets, but the fantastic roofline was lost in a fire in 1921. 4m NE of Brechin, *Stracathro House* (1827–30; A. Simpson) neo-classical with noble Roman portico.

DUNDEE. Scotland's third city, a port, shipbuilding and engineering town that exploded in population during the 19C, largely due to the textile industry, specifically jute. Central Dundee has been very battered, most recently by the approach roads for the Tay road bridge. In the High St, ponderous columned front of the *Caird Hall* (1914–22; J. Thomson). Opposite, Reform St, laid out 1832, handsome Regency fronts surviving. *No. 34* (1840; W. Burn) was built to a richer Italianate design for the Bank of Scotland. Reform St is aligned on the Greek Doric *High School* (1834; G. Angus). At E end of High St, wedge shaped *bank* (1876; W. Spence), richly detailed but too small for the site. To S, *Episcopal Cathedral* (1853; G.G. Scott), a 210ft landmark spire, austerely detailed Dec. with cross-gabled aisles, transepts and tall vaulted apse. To W, *Nos 3–4 High St* (1899; G.W. Browne), Royal Bank, impressive free Renaissance front, the upper floors a giant arcade with pilasters and a richly carved attic under the cornice but the palazzo style overall form varied with 17C style mullion and transom windows within the arched bays. At the foot of Castle St, *No. 15 Shore Terrace* (1828; G. Smith), Greek Revival former coffee house, Dundee's most elegant merchants' club. The docks area has mostly disappeared under modern roads, but to E the lavish stone *Custom House* (1842; J. Leslie and J. Taylor) on the scale of a town hall with Greek Ionic centre portico. In Victoria Dock, 'HMS Unicorn' (1824), frigate of 46 guns, the oldest wooden warship still floating in Britain. Late 19C offices and warehouses survive between the Custom House and Seagate. In Seagate, *Robertson's Bond* (1897; D. Baxter), tall warehouse with Jacobean gables flanked by turrets. Commercial St to W was driven through in the 1870s, prominent domed corner block opposite St. Paul's Cathedral and stretch N to Murraygate all of 1877 (A. Johnston). In Murraygate, *Bank of Scotland* (1868; D. Cousin), palazzo style. In Commercial St to N, another stretch of unified street frontage (1871; W. Mackison), running into Albert Square dominated by the *•Albert Institute* (1865–67; G.G. Scott), stone Gothic hall in Scott's favourite Dec. style with added Scots features and a fine central flèche. Splendid horseshoe stair up to the first-floor entry. Extended E 1873 and 1887 to accommodate the Museum and Art Gallery. The interior stencil decoration has recently been partly restored. Opposite, *The Courier Building* (1902; Niven and Wigglesworth), severe, American looking, stone-fronted steel-framed headquarters of the Thomson newspaper group. To N, *Royal Exchange* (1854; D. Bryce), Panmure St, Flemish Gothic with an array of dormer windows and a corner tower. Behind, *Pearl Assurance*, Meadowside (1898; W.G. Lamond) also Flemish style. On E side of the square, *Prudential Assurance* (1895; A. Waterhouse and Son), red brick and stone in the house style of the firm. Meadowside runs W below the High School to the *General Post Office* (1898; W.W. Robertson), large near symmetrical Renaissance styled building, the E end pavilion answered at the W end by a corner dome. Below is the old city burial ground, The Howff, crowded with monuments from the 16C to the 19C. To W, *Barrack St Museum and Library* (1911; J. Thomson), Edwardian Baroque. Constitution Rd runs N, on left, *No. 1a West Bell St* (1840; J. Black), pilastered neo-classical former church. Further W, grand Roman Doric portico (1863; W. Scott) of *Sheriff Court Building*, a belated execution of a design by G. Angus of 1833. To W, across the ring road, *Tay Carpet Works* (c 1838–65), giant pedimented factory building of Gilroy Bros, a leading Dundee industrial dynasty. S of the courthouse, Lindsay St leads S with factory buildings at NW end including former *Lindsay St Works* (1874; Maclaren and Aitken) with French Gothic gabled tower. Nethergate is the W end of the High St with the *Town's Churches*, 15C tower, the church reconstructed after a fire (1842–47; W. Burn), flamboyant Gothic tracery. Whitehall St and Whitehall Crescent, S of Nethergate, are a city improvement of c 1885–90 with the *Gilfillan Memorial Church* (1887; M. Stark) in free Baroque style terminating the view S down Whitehall St.

Nethergate continues W of the centre across the ring road with Perp. *RC Cathedral* (1835; G. Mathewson) and tall French roofs of the *Queen's Hotel* (1878; Young and Meldrum). The Hotel was built as a railway hotel on the incorrect assumption that the main station would be rebuilt next door. Further W, *Dundee University*, founded 1880, buildings mostly post 1900 apart from the former *Technical College* (1886; J.M. Robertson), Small's Wynd, with low relief detail and nice carved panels of crafts and industries over the entry. *Geddes*

Quadrangle (1909; R. Anderson and Paul) is part of an uncompleted grand scheme in late 17C style. Perth Rd continues W with 19C villas and churches overlooking the Tay. *St. Mark's Church* (1868; Pilkington and Bell), polychrome stone, craggily detailed with the colliding elements characteristic of Pilkington, and the *McCheyne Memorial Church* (1870; Pilkington and Bell), similar with hefty spirelet and jarring combination of large traceried window and rose window to the front, are the High Victorian ecclesiastical contribution. Seymour Lodge, *No. 259 Perth Rd* (1880; C. and L. Ower), bargeboarded Gothic on an alarming scale, and *No. 474*, St. Helens (1850; C. Wilson), are the grandest of the houses. Over the Tay below is the *Tay Railway Bridge* (1882–87; W.H. Barlow), the longest bridge in Britain, lattice girder trusses on tall piers. This is the replacement for the 1870–78 bridge by Sir T. Bouch where the girders were carried on cast-iron clustered columns to a height of 80ft in the centre 'high girders', a design that did not make allowance for the effects of high winds. On 28 December 1879 hurricane winds blew down the high girders while a train was passing over and 75 people were killed. The Dundee poet, W. McGonagall (1830–1903), widely acclaimed as the worst poet writing in English even during his lifetime and unforgotten since, wrote his best remembered poem on the Tay Bridge disaster.

The area immediately above the bridge, Magdalen Green, was laid out as a park c 1845 and the area around was one of the early suburbs of Dundee. *No. 43 Magdalen Yard Rd* (1836) is an exceptional Greek Revival single-storey villa, built as house and Art Gallery for the collector G. Duncan MP.

NW of centre, Marketgait leads N to Lochee Rd, A923, and Dudhope Park with the 16C Dudhope Castle overlooking the city. Just E, *Royal Infirmary* (1853–55; Coe and Goodwin), very large and bleak Tudor style building on an imposing site. Lochee Rd leads NW to **Lochee**, company town of the firm of Cox Bros. *Camperdown Works*, Methven St, was their factory, a linen works that employed some 6000 people. The works (1861–8; G. Cox), were once very extensive, mostly single storey but with a clock tower capped by a cast-iron cupola at one end and *Cox's Stack* (1865; J. MacLaren) rising behind. The 282ft chimney is an unequalled industrial monument, built in patterned polychrome brick, like the campanile of an Italian town hall. *Clement Park* (1854; J. MacLaren), Harefield Rd, behind the works, was the Cox family mansion, stone, mixed Gothic style. In Lochee High St, to W, *St. Mary's Church* (1865; J.A. Hansom), remarkable Gothic church with chancel treated as a tall octagonal tower, heavily buttressed and with long windows flooding light over the sanctuary, the effect enhanced by a very long nave lit only by small windows. Next door, handsome *Library and Baths* (1894; J.M. Robertson), Jacobean style curly gables, pale coloured, contrasting with red stone main walls. Coupar Angus Rd leads NW to *Camperdown House* (1824; W. Burn), a major monument of the Greek Revival, temple-fronted at the E end, now used as the Spalding Golf Museum.

Hilltown leads N of Dundee centre from Victoria Rd. On corner of Victoria Rd, *No. 20* (1877; Pilkington and Bell), strongly modelled block with incised decoration and heavily corbelled eaves. E of Hilltown, *St. Mary's Church*, Powrie Place, with a twin-towered facade 1900; W.G. Lamond) in advanced Art Nouveau manner, the towers curved at the corners rising to round pinnacles clasping an arched top stage and capped by a lantern turret. Church behind of 1850 (G. Mathewson), Romanesque. Further N, *St. Salvador's Church* (1868; G.F. Bodley), St. Salvador's St, High Victorian Gothic with austere details, the arcades continuously moulded and flush with the wall face which is broken only for slim shafts rising to the open timber roof. Arches enlivened with some polychrome stonework and outstanding stencil decoration, recently restored. Chancel, like Butterfield's All Saints', Margaret St, London, windowless to E, the E wall filled by a magnificent painted and gilded carved wooden reredos. Across the chancel arch, delicate gilded iron screen. Glass by Burlison and Grylls. To E, on Dens Rd, *Dens Road School* (1908; W.G. Lamond), large Board School with distinctive Arts and Crafts or Art Nouveau detail, two big stair towers with wavy parapets, window bands stepped to emphasise stair levels and a large lunette window marking the upper landing. *Stobswell Girls School* (1908; W.G. Lamond), Eliza St, to NE, has a similar originality.

NE of the centre, N of Seagate, is Cowgate, part of the ancient city, industrialised as the centre moved W. To N, *Dens Mills* (1830s and later), the factory of the leading Dundee industrial family, the Baxters, patrons of the Albert Institute, the University and many other civic projects. The Dens Mills were flax mills, employing some 5000 workers in 1871. Two main massive stone ranges, the lower mill with a domed cupola at one corner, the upper mill with a lantern spire. Victoria Rd, N of King St, was created in the 1870s. On N side, *No. 60* (1874), baronial style factory, and *No. 72*, next door, High Victorian former church (1877; J.G. Fairley). Arthurstone Terrace, to E, has *RC church* (1897; Cappon and Lamond), free Gothic with Lamond's hand showing in the pretty top to the tower. At the top of Albert St, *Morgan Academy* (1836–66; Peddie and Kinnear), Flemish Gothic school building with central tower, like a smaller version of Fettes College, Edinburgh, lavishly detailed. To E, *Baxter Park* (1863; Sir J. Paxton), given to the city by the Baxter family. Renaissance style loggia in the centre. Arbroath Rd runs along the S end of the park. To E, Gothic arched entry to the *Eastern Necropolis* (1863).

From Seagate, Blackscroft leads E, past former *St. Roque's Library* (1910; J. Thomson), French 18C style pavilion, to Broughty Ferry Rd and **West Ferry**, once the richest suburb in Scotland, still with numerous large villas the late 19C. Further E, **Broughty Ferry**, fishing village that became a resort in the 19C. The original village by the harbour laid out 1801. On the harbour, *Broughty Castle* (1861; R.R. Anderson), a rebuilding of the original castle in convincing tower-house style, built for the War Office as part of the Tay defences. Now a museum. In Brook St, *St. Stephen's Church* (1871; T.S. Robertson), stained glass by Morris and Co., and *St. Aidan's Church* (1824) with slated spire. In Beach Crescent, by the harbour, *Orchar Art Gallery*, closed at present, in a villa (1866; J. Maclaren) built for a shipbuilder but bought by Provost Orchar to house his collection of 19C Scottish painting. Queen St behind has a number of Victorian churches. *St. Luke's Church* (1884; H.J. Blanc) at W end, tall red stone work in the manner of Brooks or Pearson, has apse glass by Morris and Co. *St. Mary's Church* is a minor work of G.G. Scott (1858). Further E, *Eastern School* (1911; W.G. Lamond) with the characteristic Art Nouveau parapets and lunette windows to the stair towers of Lamond's other Dundee schools.

DUNKELD. A9 15m N of Perth. The *Cathedral* was ruined in the late 17C, but the choir continued in use, restored 1814–18, and more comprehensively in 1908 (Dunn and Watson). Dunkeld Palace of the Dukes of Atholl was demolished for a grand-scale rebuilding, abandoned on the death of the 4th Duke in 1830. The present *Dunkeld*

House (1900; J.M. Henry) is relatively plain. In the centre, Gothic *monument* (1866) to the 6th Duke, and Tudor style former *Schools* (1853; R. and R. Dickson). Just SE of Dunkeld, **Birnam**, developed as a resort from the 1850s when the railway arrived. Bargeboarded Tudor style *station* (1856; A. Heiton), hotel and numerous villas. The painter Millais was a regular visitor. 5m SE, at **Murthly** *chapel* (1846; J.G. Graham) of the demolished castle. Romanesque with frescoed interior. 5m N of Dunkeld, *Dalguise Viaduct* (1863; J. Mitchell) carries the railway across the Tay, a lattice girder bridge with castellated towers.

FORFAR. A929 13m N of Dundee. Former county town of Angus. In East High St, *Episcopal Church* (1879; R.R. Anderson), lancet Gothic with banded marble chancel decoration. At The Cross, former *British Linen Bank* (1895; Kinnear and Peddie) with big scrolled gable. In Castle St, *Municipal Buildings* (1824; D. Neave) in centre of street. In Market St, former *County Prison* (1842; D. Smith), battlemented, and *County Buildings* (c 1870; J.M. Wardrop) baronial. In Jamieson St, *Lowson Memorial Church* (1912–14; A.M. Mackenzie) Scots 15C style on a grand scale with centre spire. Excellent glass by D. Strachan. 5m NE, A94, *Finavon Castle* (1865; Carver and Symon), spiky Gothic cum baronial house. 5m NW, A926, **Kirriemuir**, jute manufacturing town where J.M. Barrie was born 1860 at *No. 9 Brechin Road* (open to the public). His father was a handloom weaver. The town appears as 'Thrums' in several of Barrie's novels and Barrie is buried with his parents in the cemetery. In High St, *Nos 45–7* (1841; G. Angus), severe classical bank building. The *Episcopal Church* (1903; J.N. Comper), West Hillbank, is particularly finely detailed with curvilinear tracery and battlemented tower. *Kinnordy House* (1881; J.M. Wardrop), 2m NW, was the estate of Sir Charles Lyell (1797–1875) whose pioneering work on geology, 'The Principles of Geology' (1830–33), first established the fundamental categories, Pliocene, Miocene etc. His museum is still intact. 6m N of Kirriemuir, B955, on Tulloch Hill, *Airlie Memorial Tower* (1901; W.G. Lamond) to the 9th Earl of Airlie, of Cortachy Castle, killed 1900 in the Boer War. *Cortachy Castle* is basically 16C altered 1820 (R. and R. Dickson). 4m SW of Forfar, B9127, *Kinnettles House* (1867; Kinnear and Peddie), large baronial mansion. At **Meigle**, 12m SW of Forfar, A94, Sir H. Campbell-Bannerman, Liberal Prime Minister 1905–08, is buried in the churchyard. He lived at *Belmont Castle* (1793; with elaborate French style interiors of c 1885). Just S of the village. To SE, E of Newtyle, *Kinpurnie Castle* (1908; Thoms and Wilkie) baronial but with Arts and Crafts inspired simplicity. 6m E of Forfar, A932, *Guthrie Castle*, 15C tower house extended 1848 (D. Bryce) in baronial style.

MONTROSE. A92 31m NE of Dundee. In the High St, *Old Church* (1791) with fine Lincolnshire type spire (1832–34; J.G. Graham) and *statues* of Sir R. Peel (1852) and Joseph Hume (1859). Hume, reforming politician and political economist, was born in Montrose, 1777. *Nos 63–5* (1863; Peddie and Kinnear), finely detailed Renaissance style bank, and *Nos 208–12* (c 1870; J. Souttar), Venetian Gothic bank with crenellated roofline. In Panmure Place, *Museum* (1837; J. Henderson: 1888; J. Sim), small neo-Grecian building. Local history and natural history collections. Burns *statue* (c 1870; J.B. Rhind). In Bridge St, Greek Doric *Royal Infirmary* (1839; J. Collie). 2m N of Montrose, A92, *Charleton* (1892; R.R. Anderson), early 18C style house, well detailed with hipped roof and tall dormers. By the North Water Bridge, 5m N, *railway viaduct* (1865) of eleven stone arches.

PERTH. Former county town on the W bank of the Tay, the birthplace of the novelist John Buchan (1875) and childhood home of John Ruskin's wife Effie. Ruskin's grandfather owned *Bowerswell*, Bowerswell Road, SE of the city, and killed himself there. The house was sold by Ruskin's parents to the father of Effie Gray, and rebuilt 1848. After she left Ruskin for Millais they lived at *Annat Lodge*, near Bowerswell, where Millais painted 'Autumn Leaves' and 'The Vale of Rest'. '*Chill October*', his famous painting of the Tay below Kinnoul Hill, is in the City Art Gallery. Perth is the medieval setting of Walter Scott's 'The Fair Maid of Perth' (1828).

Waterworks (1832; A. Anderson), Perth

The city has a fine 19C waterfront to the Tay along Tay St, between the two parks, North Inch and South Inch. At the N end, *Middle Church* (1887; H.J. Blanc), well detailed lancet Gothic with tall flèche and N rose window. Adjoining, *Municipal Buildings* (1877–79; A. Heiton), long Gothic front rising to a corner turret by High St, reminiscent of Waterhouse. Gothic interiors. On the opposite corner of High St, *General Accident building* (1899; G.P.K. Young), Baroque building with corner dome and set-back attic in the manner of J.J. Burnet, then, *No. 26*, the Savings Bank (c 1873–6; A. Heiton), Renaissance style with pavilion roofs, *St. Matthew's Church* (1871; J. Honeyman) with 212ft spire, *Nos 36–44*, Victoria Buildings (1872; A. Heiton), long block with Glasgow Greek detailing, and *Nos 46–52* (c 1865–70), French Gothic. At South St, *Sheriff Courts Offices* (1863–66; D. Smart), Renaissance style. Across the street, neo-classical *County Buildings* (1819; R

Smirke), and *Nos 56–72* (1887–96; J. Young), long Gothic range, coarsely detailed, built as Natural History Museum and Baptist church. At the S end, *Tourist Information Centre*, houses in a splendid neo-classical rotunda (1832; A. Anderson) designed for the city waterworks. Marshall Place runs W along the top of South Inch with *St. Leonard's Church* (1885; J.J. Stevenson), prominently capped with a crown spire. At the foot of King St, Scott *statue* (c 1860). On the S side of the South Inch, *Perth Prison* (1810–12), built for prisoners of war and remodelled 1839–42 (T. Brown) as the General Prison for Scotland. Marshall Place leads to *Perth Station* (1847; W. Tite), Tudor Gothic like Carlisle station, but much extended. *Station Hotel* (1888; A. Heiton), adjoining in Scots Gothic style. Leonard St leads back to the W end of South St. In King St, to S, *St. Leonard's Church* (1834; W.M. Mackenzie), neo-classical. In York Place, to W, *Nos 1–9* (1907; G.P.K. Young), Edwardian Baroque, and former *Infirmary* (1836; W.M. Mackenzie), neo-classical but with heavy arched detail suggestive of Vanbrugh. In South St, to E, *No. 38*, on corner of Princes St, former Commercial Bank (1858; D. Rhind), severe Cinquecento style palazzo. To N, in St. Johns St, former Head Office of the Central Bank, *Nos 48–50* (1846; D. Rhind), palazzo style but the earlier date showing in the quieter detail closer to the style of Barry. The 15C *St. John's Church* has much 19C stained glass but the more interesting later work is by Lorimer as a war memorial 1923–26. In King Edward St, to W, *City Hall* (1909–14; H.E. Clifford), Beaux Arts classical. Edwardian rebuilding around the corner to High St, *Nos 2–8 King Edward St* (1904; Menart and Jarvie) with domed corner, and, in High St, *Guildhall* (1907; A.G. Heiton), early 18C style with open pediment. On N side, *Perth Theatre* (1900; W. Alexander), a good auditorium entered through the ground floor of a tenement block. N of High St E end, in George St, *Nos 22–4*, former Union Bank (1857; A. Heiton and Son), loose Renaissance detail, and *Nos 26–34* (1836; W.M. Mackenzie), classical former Exchange Coffee Room. At the top, the *Art Gallery* (1824; D. Morison), domed rotunda built for the Literary and Antiquarian Society, and designed by the Secretary of the Society. In Mill St, to W, *North Church* (1880; T.L. Watson), Romanesque, and, in Kinnoul St, *Sandeman Library* (1898; Campbell Douglas and Morrison), free Renaissance by one of the leading Glasgow firms. *Pullar's works* is a long range of 1865. To W, Methven St leads N to Atholl St and *St. Ninian's Episcopal Cathedral* (1849 and 1887; W. Butterfield), built for the Oxford Movement—influenced Earl of Glasgow (cf. Great Cumbrae, Strathclyde, p. 539 above), the choir first, the nave with fine tall roof, tall arcade arches and transepts being completed only in 1890. Chancel extension and vaulted S chapel by J.L. Pearson (1899). Across the Tay, E of the centre, the area of villas around the base of Kinnoull Hill. In *Kinnoull Church* (1826; W. Burn), Dundee Rd, a W window based on drawings by Millais. On the hill, *Murray Royal Hospital* (1825–33; W. Burn) classical with central octagon and *St. Mary's Convent* (1868–70; A. Heiton), Hatton Rd with tall apsed chapel.

4m E of Perth, A85, *Kinfauns Castle* (1820–24; R. Smirke), Georgian Gothic castellated house well set above the Tay. 3m N of Perth, *Scone Palace* (1803–08; W. Atkinson), the important precursor of the castellated 19C houses of Scotland, good Georgian Gothic interiors. Open to the public. 10m NW of Perth, in **Glenalmond**, *Trinity College*, founded by W.E. Gladstone as an Episcopalian public school in 1843 and given buildings in the best collegiate Gothic style, as promoted by High Churchmen in England at that date (cf. Lancing College, Sussex, p. 415 above). Open quadrangular plan to designs by J. Henderson, the

W front range with tall gatehouse tower and corner towers opening
into the quadrangle, a generous space with hall (1861; G.G. Scott)
linked to a large chapel (1851; Henderson) on the E side. There were
to have been cloisters around but only the N wing (1848) has one.
Chapel interior with good E window by Powell's. 17m W of Perth, A85,
Crieff, popular resort town during the 19C with a large neo-Jacobean
hydro, *Strathearn House* (1867; R. Ewan), just N of the centre on the
slopes of the Knock of Crieff. In Hill St, *Morison's Academy* (1866;
Peddie and Kinnear), baronial school building. In Strathearn Terrace,
St. Andrew's Church (1883; T.L. Watson), lancet style with tall steeple,
and in Heathcote Rd *South Church* (1880; J.J. Stevenson), modelled
on Dunblane Cathedral. 3m S, *Drummond Castle*, 15C tower with
later mansion house, made baronial 1878 (G.T. Ewing), set in grandly
terraced gardens (open to public). 10m SE of Crieff, A9, **Auchterarder**,
notable as the parish where the issue of the right of church congregations freely to choose their minister came to a head with the decision of
the court of session in 1838 in favour of state patronage, the cause of
the 'Disruption' of 1843 when some 400 ministers seceded from the
Church of Scotland to found the Free Church. At far end of High St, *St.
Andrews Church* (1843; D. Cousin), plain Romanesque. Two notable
baronial houses by W. Leiper, *Coll-Earn Castle Hotel* (1869–70), High
St, built for the industrialist A. Mackintosh, red stone with round
corner tower, lively animal finials on the dormers and an aesthetic
movement interior by D. Cottier with stained glass in the manner of
Morris and Co., fireplaces by B. Talbert with tiles by W. de Morgan
and W.B. Simpson, and *Ruthven Towers Hotel* (1882) Abbey Hill, also
with interiors by Cottier. *Auchterarder House*, to NE, Jacobean style
by W. Burn (1832), was remodelled 1887 (Burnet Son and Campbell),
altering the profile of the tower and adding rich marbled interiors.

PITLOCHRY. A9 27m N of Dunkeld. Resort town with largely Victorian buildings, the largest of which was the colossal turretted *Hydro*
(1875; A. Heiton), now the Atholl Palace Hotel, SE of the centre, which
cost £100,000 to build. Tudor style *station* (1863 and c 1890), prelude to
the dramatic railway journey N through the Killiecrankie Pass. On the
line castellated *viaduct and tunnel* at **Killiecrankie** and castellated
lattice girder *bridge* over the Tilt at **Blair Atholl**, all of 1863 (J.
Mitchell). Blair Atholl is the estate village of *Blair Castle*, seat of the
Dukes of Atholl. Entrance lodge and gates to the castle by D. Bryce
(1869). The Castle, open to public, was returned to a castle-like
appearance 1870–72 (D. Bryce) after being partly dismantled in 1690
and rebuilt in the 18C. The entrance tower based on Fyvie Castle is
Bryce's main addition. NE of Pitlochry, A924 crosses into Strathardle.
4m S of **Kirkmichael**, on W side, *Blackcraig Castle* (1856; P. Allan
Fraser), another fantastic and elaborately decorated baronial house by
the artist and amateur architect (cf. Arbroath, p. 547 above). Four-
storey tower and rash of turrets. Across the river is a fortified *bridge*
(1870) worthy of Ludwig of Bavaria, certainly an apt setting for
Wagnerian scenes.

S of Pitlochry, A827 runs W along the Tay towards Loch Tay.
Grandtully Castle, 3m E of Aberfeldy, is late 16C given a large
towered addition (c 1890; T. Leadbetter). At **Aberfeldy**, small *Town
Hall* of 1889 by the Arts and Crafts architect J.M. MacLaren, harled
with three stone arches to the front and a pretty bell turret on the roof.
By the bridge, Black Watch *monument* (1887; J. and W.B. Rhind)
commemorating the raising of the regiment in 1739. 5m W of Aberfeldy, at **Kenmore**, *Taymouth Castle*, estate of the Campbell family,

Taymouth Castle, the Library (1838; J.G. Graham and A.W.N. Pugin), Kenmore

Earls and Marquesses of Breadalbane, the richest estate of the central Highlands in the late 18C and early 19C, the wealth coming from the sheep introduced during the highland clearances and from slate. The Castle was rebuilt for the 1st Marquess from 1806–08 (A. and J. Elliott) in spectacular castellated style intended to eclipse Inveraray Castle, which belonged to the senior Campbell line, the Dukes of Argyll. The massive stair tower is one of the glories of Georgian Gothic with superb plasterwork by F. Bernasconi. Low E wing added after 1818 by W. Atkinson. The 2nd Marquess inherited in 1834 and set about more expensive works, remodelling the 18C W wing in castellated style and adding interiors of a Gothic splendour reminiscent of the Houses of Parliament, hardly fortuitous for although J.G. Graham was the architect for the works in 1838–39 the interiors are by A.W.N. Pugin, carried out by John Crace. The principal new rooms, Banner Hall, Drawing Room and Library are in the full flush of romantic medievalism, Gothic with intricate stone and woodwork, much heraldic painted decoration, originally supplemented with all the appropriate trappings of banners, armour and weaponry. The estate has several charming early 19C rustic lodges with log porches and a *dairy* (c 1838; J. Skene) clad in white quartz.

5m NW of Kenmore, **Fortingall**, estate village of Glenlyon House, owned in the late 19C by Sir Donald Currie, wealthy shipowner (the Currie line, and, after 1900, Union Castle), who paid for the restoration of Dunkeld Cathedral and patronised the Arts and Crafts architect J.M. MacLaren. In the village, *church* (1900; Dunn and Watson) in late Gothic style and *Fortingall Hotel* (c 1895; Dunn and Watson), gabled with good Arts and Crafts style lettering. Watson had been MacLaren's assistant and the later work at Fortingall continues the influence of MacLaren, who died young in 1890. Beyond the hotel, *Kirkton Cottages* (1889; J.M. MacLaren), delightful Arts and Crafts group, harled walls and thatched roofs, more Devon than Perthshire. The cottages are L-plan, the angle articulated by a massive chimney picturesquely composed with the two end walls, all seemingly haphazard in the vernacular tradition. *Glenlyon House* itself is late 17C to 18C carefully enlarged from 1891 (Dunn and Watson). Adjoining is the *Farmhouse* (1889; J.M. MacLaren), the road front an original composition quite without period detail, a precursor of Arts and Crafts work in similar vein by Voysey in England. The *Farm buildings* (c 1889; MacLaren) are equally original, a harled courtyard block accentuated with an octagonal corner dovecote tower and sandstone Scots dormers.

WESTERN ISLES

The Hebrides were the last parts of Scotland to be cleared of population for sheep in the 19C, at first by bankrupt clan chiefs, later by mainland speculators. The 1846 famine was particularly severe and many thousands went or were sent to Canada and Australia.

LEWIS. Lewis was bought (1844) by the millionaire Sir James Matheson who, rare among Highland landlords, attempted to relieve famine and build a sound economy, but he was unable to stem the emigration. In Stornoway, *Lewis Castle* (c 1846; C. Wilson), built for Matheson in battlemented Tudor style. Matheson's memorial is in the grounds. The castle later belonged to Lord Leverhulme, the soap magnate who owned Lewis and Harris from 1918 and tried, unsuccessfully, to regenerate the economy.

HARRIS. On B887, W of Tarbert, *Amhuinnsuid Castle* (1864–67; D. Bryce), baronial house of the Earl of Dunmore, who owned South Harris

WALES

CLWYD

COLWYN BAY. A55 5m SE of Llandudno. Seaside resort developed after 1865 as a rival to Llandudno but the seafront unhappily cut-off by the railway. *Pier* (1900; extended 1922). Streets of bright red brick with glazed canopies in the shopping area. Two fine churches by John Douglas, *St. Paul's* (1888–1911) Abergele Rd, and *St. John's* (1899–1903), Old Colwyn, to E. *Council Offices* Abergele Rd (1911; P.S. Worthington) Arts and Crafts style former convalescent home. 2m S of Colwyn Bay, B5113, at **Bryn-y-maen**, *church* (1897–99; J. Douglas), known as the Cathedral of the Hills with central tower and fine woodwork. Vicarage by Douglas. 6m SE, A548, at **Llangernyw**, *Hafodunos* (1861–66; G.G. Scott), one of Scott's major country houses, red-brick and stone Gothic, the style of Kelham, Nottinghamshire, and the St. Pancras Hotel, but not so overwhelming. Picturesquely composed with gables, bay windows, octagonal billiard room and entrance tower, shorn of its spire. Now a college. 3m E of Colwyn Bay, A55, at **Llanddulas**, *church* (1867–69; Street), one of several works in the area by Street for R.B. Hesketh of *Gwyrch Castle*, the great bastioned and turretted castle built c 1820–22 by L.B. Hesketh, now an amusement park. Street altered the *church* and designed the *school* (1870) at Llysfaen to W and the *school* at **Abergele** to E. In Abergele *churchyard* monuments to lives lost in the sinking of the Ocean Monarch (1848) and the Irish Mail train disaster (1868). 2m NE of Abergele, A548, at **Towyn**, Street's finest work for Hesketh, *church (1871–73), with High Victorian saddleback central tower, E window by Hardman and fine fittings, grouped with Vicarage and school also by Street. 3m E, A548, **Rhyl**, seaside resort developed from the 1850s. *St. Thomas' Church* (1861–69; G.G. Scott), a handsome work in EE style with slated broach spire.

2m SE of Abergele, at **St. George**, *Kinmel Park* (1868–74; W.E. Nesfield), the major country house of the 'Queen Anne' revival, the turning from High Victorian seriousness to something lighter and more cheerful that Nesfield and Norman Shaw began. Nesfield's design at Kinmel, for H.R. Hughes, heir to a fortune from the Parys Mountain copper mine in Anglesey, starts at Wren's Hampton Court, enlivened with even greater contrast of red brick and white stone, but with steep roofs and details from Louis XIII's France, bold chimneys and subtle asymmetry from the Victorian Gothic. Few Victorian mansions are as attractive, the long windows with small-paned sashes, the tall white-painted dormers, the delicate stone carving and the colours give a lightness to what is a very large house. At right angles to front and raised up, *stable range* (1855; W. Burn) in an unusually convincing early 18C manner, the fine ashlar a good foil to the colour of the main house. The *lodge* (1868; Nesfield), on A55, is a delight, a concentration of the influences visible in the house, more French perhaps, but with that key motif of late 19C aestheticism, the sunflower making an early appearance. Opposite, *Plas Kinmel* (1866; Nesfield), the Home Farm, with the vigorous asymmetry of the Gothic Revival. Just E, A55, at **Bodelwyddan**, the estate of the Williams family of *Bodelwyddan Castle*, 16C to 18C house remodelled in castellated style (c 1830–40; Hansom and Welch). On the main road, *church* (1856–60; J. Gibson), called the Marble Church, exceptionally lavish memorial to Lord Willoughby de Broke, white stone with 202ft spire. Interior lavishly carved by T. Earp with marble arcades, marble font, ornate lectern (1882), E window by O'Connor. At **St. Asaph**, 2m E, *Cathedral*, restored 1868–75 (G.G. Scott) with reredos carved by T. Earp. Memorial tablet to the explorer H.M. Stanley, born in Denbigh as John Rowlands and brought up at the St. Asaph Workhouse from which he fled, aged 16, after assaulting its tyrannical schoolmaster. 3m NE, A5151, near Dyserth, *Bodrhyddan Hall* (open to public), c 1700 house of the Conwy family overhauled in Queen Anne style (1872–73; W.E. Nesfield), wings each end of the original, one wing with the new entrance facade to the side. Pretty white-painted woodwork against red brick and central curved gable with sundial. Main hall with deep inglenook fireplace, a feature revived by Nesfield and Norman Shaw.

The Golden Lodge, Kinmel Park (1868; W.E. Nesfield), Abergele

MOLD. A541 11m NW of Wrexham. Former county town of Flintshire. Parish *church* with chancel added 1856 (G.G. Scott), reredos 1878 (J. Douglas), glass by Wailes. Former *County Hall* (1833; T. Jones), Chester St, modest, Tudor style. To SW, on New St, *chapel* (1863; W.W. Gwyther) with grand portico. In Earl St Edwardian Baroque *Town Hall* (1911; F. Roberts). 8m SW, A494, at **Llanbedr Dyffryn Clwyd**, *church* (1863; Poundley and Walker), High Victorian vigour in an extreme form from polychrome rock-faced masonry to a spirelet,

banded, facetted and interrupted for the stumpiest columns around
the bell. To SW, **Ruthin**, entered past *Grammar School* (1889–92; J.
Douglas), Mold Rd. In the Square, *clock tower* (1883; J. Douglas) and
parish *church* with tall spire added 1856 (R.K. Penson). *Christ's
Hospital*, almshouses founded 1590, was rebuilt 1865. In Castle St,
High Victorian *Town Hall* (1863; Poundley and Walker), rock-faced
masonry with steep-roofed tower and carved decoration. *Ruthin
Castle* within the medieval remains is a castellated house of 1826
enlarged into a much more impressive red sandstone castle (1849–52;
H. Clutton) with octagonal main tower and clock tower on the 1826
range. 3m S of Ruthin, A525, at **Llanfair Dyffryn Clwyd**, *church* res-
tored 1872 (J.D. Sedding) with good S aisle window of 1893 by C.
Whall. 8m N of Ruthin, A525, **Denbigh**, birthplace of the explorer,
H.M. Stanley. S of the town, the *North Wales Mental Hospital* (1848; T.
Fulljames), one of the great asylum buildings built under the 1845
Lunacy Act, stone Jacobean style. 3m N, A525, at **Trefnant**, *church*
(1853–55; G.G. Scott), richly carved Dec. style. Naturalistic carving to
the capitals. Vicarage and school by Scott. 3m E of Trefnant, at
Tremeirchon, *St. Beuno's College* (1846; J.A. Hansom), Jesuit college
with Gothic buildings where G.M. Hopkins was a student 1874–77
and wrote 'The Wreck of the Deutschland'. Romantic chapel (1866) on
a crag over the valley.

3m NW of Mold, A541, at **Rhydymwyn**, *church* (1860–63; J.L.
Pearson), plate tracery, grey Welsh stone banded with Bath stone. Tall
interior with contrasted coloured stones in the chancel. Fine reredos
with incised Last Supper. 3m N, off A55, at **Halkyn**, *Halkyn Castle*
(1824–27; J. Buckler), Tudor Gothic house built for the Grosvenor
family, enlarged for 1st Duke of Westminster (1886; J. Douglas). Fine
church (1878; J. Douglas), beautifully detailed with pyramid-capped
tower. 3m NW, **Holywell** with *St. Winifride's Well*, a place of pil-
grimage since the seventh century, looked after by Jesuits since 1873.
G.M. Hopkins came and wrote a poem about the well. Fr Rolfe,
thwarted Catholic priest, author of 'Hadrian VII' and other works of
extraordinary richness and acerbity, lived at Holywell, 1895–98. His
career there is described in A.J.A. Symons' 'The Quest for Corvo'. The
banners which Rolfe painted for the RC parish priest, and which led to
a characteristic feud, are visible on request at the *RC church* (1833; J.J.
Scoles). 1½m SW of Holywell, at **Pantasaph**, *Franciscan Friary*, with
church begun 1849 (T.H. Wyatt) as an Anglican church for Lord Denbigh, who then converted to Rome. Font by Pugin, and elaborate
memorial to Lord Denbigh (1893). Friary (1858), school and orphanage. The religious poet Francis Thompson lived here 1893–97. 1½m
N of Holywell, at **Greenfield**, disused *Holywell Junction Station* (1848;
F. Thompson), best survivor of the Italianate stations on the Chester to
Holyhead line. 4m NW, A548, **Mostyn**, estate of the Mostyn family,
leading landowners in the area for centuries. At **Glanydon**, to SE,
church (1844–45; A. Poynter). 1m W, *Mostyn Dock*, developed by the
family for coal and iron trade, and *Mostyn Hall*, partly medieval
enlarged in Elizabethan style (c 1845; A. Poynter), either side of the
A55. **Whitford**, S of Mostyn, has a large estate *church* (1843–46; A.
Poynter), rebuilt for the Pennant family. W of Mostyn, *Point of Ayr
Colliery*, started 1873, with seams running out under the sea. At
Talacre, to W, *Talacre Abbey* (1824–27; T. Jones), Tudor style stone
mansion built for the Mostyns, a Benedictine nunnery since 1920.

6m E of Mold, A55, **Hawarden**, home of the Prime Minister W.E.
Gladstone. *Harwarden Castle*, 18C, castellated 1810, belonged to his
wife's family. Gladstone moved in in the 1860s and died here 1898, his

study remains unaltered (occasionally open to public). *Church* rebuilt 1857 (G.G. Scott) has *Gladstone Memorial Chapel* (1901; J. Douglas) with *marble effigies of Gladstone and his wife by Sir W. Richmond, who designed the glass. Superb W window of the main church by Burne-Jones (1898). W of the church, *St. Deiniol's Library* (1899–1906; J. Douglas), a Gladstone memorial; the idea of a residential library where scholars could come to study was Gladstone's and the collection, initially mainly of theological books, was his. Gothic to Jacobean stone building, suitably collegiate, and beautifully detailed, especially the library itself. N of Hawarden, the industrialised S side of the Dee estuary. At **Queensferry**, A550, just S of the Dee Bridge, between the river and the railway, *engineering works* (1901; H.B. Cresswell), functional without period detail, the bold sloping buttresses to the walls and tower that give flavour of Voysey were to spread the load on the marshy site. To NW, *railway bridge* (1887–89; F. Fox), three-span bow-string girder bridge with 287ft opening section, the longest then built. At **Shotton**, *church* (1898–1902; J. Douglas). 2m S of Hawarden, A550, at **Penymynydd**, *church* (1843; J.C. Buckler) with complete scheme of painted decoration and stained glass by the Rev. J. Troughton, curate-in-charge 1843–64. To NW, N of **Buckley**, A549, *St. Matthew's Church*, rebuilt 1897–1904 (J. Douglas), Gladstone's son-in-law was vicar. Elaborate half-timbering outside, painted decoration inside. Apse glass by H. Holiday (1900).

WREXHAM. A483 12m SW of Chester. Main market town of North Wales, industrialised in the later 18C and 19C. In the centre, on High St, complex of *markets*, the earliest, with Jacobean front to High St, 1848 (T. Penson). General market (1879), bright red brick and good iron roof. On opposite side of High St *Sun Alliance* (1860; R.K. Penson) handsome stone facade. In Hope St, palazzo style *bank* (1876; J. Gibson). Beyond, *RC Pro-Cathedral* (1857; E.W. Pugin), built as a parish church, but used as the cathedral for the Diocese of Menevia. 2m S, *Erddig* (NT), the 17C and 18C house of the Yorke family brought back from near dereliction. The 19C interest, and the most touching feature of the house, is the complete survival of the servants' area with all the paraphernalia of wood-yard, laundry, kitchen equipment and collections of bicycles, mementos, children's toys amassed by a family that seems never to have thrown anything away. 2m SW of Wrexham, off A483, at **Bersham**, elaborate neo-Norman estate *church* (1876; J. Gibson), with polychrome vaulted interior. 4m S, **Ruabon**, source of the hard bright red brick that is much a feature of late 19C North Wales. Small Tudor style *station* (1860; H. Robertson). To SE, *Wynnstay*, seat of the Williams-Wynn family. The house (1858–61; B. Ferrey), Loire château style with tall roofs and an entrance tower, is now a school. To S, A483, Vale of Llangollen, crossed by two spectacular bridges. To E, *Dee Viaduct* (1848; H. Robertson), stone, 19 arches, 148ft high, one of the finest railway viaducts in Britain. To W, *Pontcysyllteu* (1794–1805), T. Telford's staggering canal aqueduct, 127ft high with cast-iron arches carrying the canal trough. Further S, at **Chirk**, the railway *viaduct* (1848) and *aqueduct* (1794–1801) are side by side crossing the Ceiriog, both stone, the railway bridge higher than the canal bridge. In Chirk village, former *school* (1843–44; A.W.N. Pugin), neat Gothic, extended since. *Chirk Castle* (open to public), continuously occupied since 1300. Work by A.W.N. Pugin with the decorator J.G. Crace includes the entrance hall and colour schemes in the 18C state rooms. 7m NW of Chirk, A5, **Llangollen**, mostly Victorian town, centre for tourism in the romantic valley since

the late 18C. *Plas Newydd* (open to public), S of A5, was the Gothic
cottage of the Ladies of Llangollen, two well-born Irish ladies, a
calling point c 1780–1830 for literary figures visiting North Wales,
among them Scott, Wordsworth and Southey. The house was Gothicised, the interior filled with bits of antique carved woodwork in
overwhelming profusion and the grounds were laid out in the
romantic manner. 7m W of Llangollen, at **Carrog**, *church* (1852) with
fine chancel addition (1867; G.E. Street).

SE of Wrexham, A525, Maelor Saesneg, the arm of Wales that
extends E of the Dee. At **Hanmer**, A539, 12m SE of Wrexham, *church*
rebuilt (1890; Bodley and Garner) except tower and chancel. Good
roofs and fittings. S of Hanmer, *Bettisfield Park*, Victorianised mansion
of the Hanmer family with Italianate tower, the house much reduced
from its 19C size. Further S, **Bettisfield** *church* (1874; G.E. Street), built
for the Hanmer family, one of Street's finest country churches with
handsome spire and complete interior fittings.

DYFED

ABERYSTWYTH. Seaside resort developed from the late 18C and from 1872, the first home of the University of Wales. On the New Promenade, *University College*, a fantastical Gothic pile, all gables and undulating curved fronts. The building was begun as a great seaside hotel by the railway entrepreneur, Thomas Savin, when his line from Shrewsbury opened in 1864, with the remarkable offer of a week's stay free of charge for the purchase of a return ticket from London. Savin went bankrupt the next year and the unfinished building was bought cheaply by the new University of Wales. J.P. Seddon was the architect and, as completed, the building was spectacularly High Victorian with complex skyline and half-timbered gallery under the eaves, but a bad fire and later extensions have diluted the original character. The *pier* nearby is the truncated remains of a structure originally 800ft long, built like the hotel in 1864–65 for the expected holiday traffic. Victorian terraces line the seafront along Marine Terrace and Victoria Terrace, the two south houses of Victoria Terrace by J.P. Seddon (1870), originally polychrome brick. In Terrace Rd, N of the station, *Ceredigion Museum*, folk collections and local history, housed in the former Coliseum (1905; A. Jones) with an attractive music-hall type auditorium. E of the town, the modern University and the *National Library of Wales* (1911; S.K. Greenslade). From the station, the *Vale of Rheidol Railway* (1902) runs up to Devil's Bridge, the last narrow-gauge railway and the last steam railway operated by British Rail.

University College (1864–94; J.P. Seddon and C.J. Ferguson), Aberystwyth

2m NE of Aberystwyth, at **Llangorwen**, B4572, *church* (1841; H.J. Underwood) built for the theologian and poet I. Williams, friend of Keble and Newman, hence by the Oxford architect who built Newman's church at Littlemore, Oxford. Porch and bell turret 1848 by Butterfield. 4m N, **Borth**, another seaside resort that T. Savin intended to develop after the opening of his railway. 5m SE, SE of Talybont, at **Elerch**, *church* (1868; W. Butterfield) with a pyramid spire over the E end and handsome severe interior. 1m E of Aberystwyth, A44, at

Llanbadarn Fawr, lovely c 1200 church restored with good fittings (1868; J.P. Seddon). 4m SE of Aberystwyth, off B4340, *Nanteos* (open to public), early 18C house of the Powell family with portico and stables (c 1840; E. Haycock). George Powell (1842–82), friend of Rossetti, Aubrey Beardsley and Swinburne, was a poet and translator of Icelandic sagas. Wagner visited him at Nanteos. 5m SE, B4340, *Trawscoed*, much Victorianised 17C house of the Vaughan family, Earls of Lisburn, with well-planted grounds. Now Ministry of Agriculture. Estate *church* (1840 and 1862–67; Butterfield) at **Llanafan**, 1m SE. 4m SE of Aberystwyth, off A485, *Abermad* (1870–72; J.P. Seddon), High Victorian Gothic house with elaborate porte-cochère and splendid heavily modelled pine Gothic staircase. Drawing-room rose window representing Ruskin's 'Seven Lamps of Architecture'.

CARDIGAN. A487 38m SW of Aberystwyth. Former county town near the mouth of the Teifi. *Guildhall* with covered market beneath (1858); R.J. Withers), the slope of the site giving an extra storey. Polychrome Gothic with red brick brightening the grey and cream stone, especially effective on the more functional arcading of the market at the back. The front building is N Italian Gothic with a steep roof, very much in the Ruskinian manner. It combined economically Town Hall, Corn Exchange, Grammar School, Library and two storeys of markets. In William St, grand Greek Doric *Bethania chapel* (1848). 13m E, off A484, S of Henllan, at **Dre-Fach Felindre**, *Museum of the Woollen Industry*, branch of the National Museum of Wales occupying the former Cambrian Mill.

CARMARTHEN. A48 27m NW of Swansea. County town of Carmarthenshire, since 1974 of Dyfed. In Nott Square, statue of General Sir William Nott (1851; E. Davis), son of a Carmarthen innkeeper, who commanded the troops that retook Kabul in 1842 after the massacre of the retreating British garrison. In Lammas St, set back, handsome Corinthian fronted *English Baptist chapel* (1872; G. Morgan). Further W, *Trinity College* (1848; H. Clutton), Tudor Gothic teachers' training college. 15m E, A40, **Llandeilo**, market town with splendid single arch *bridge* (1848; E. Haycock) over the Tywi. Just W, A40, *Dynevor*, medieval castle with new house to N, 17C refaced 1856 (R.K. Penson). On the opposite side of the valley, B4300, *Gelli Aur* (1826–37; Sir J. Wyatville), stone Tudor Gothic house built for the 1st Earl of Cawdor, now an agricultural training centre. Tudor Gothic estate cottages and school. 5m S of Llandeilo, A483, N of **Llandybie**, massive *Lime Kilns* (1858; R.K. Penson), cliff-like, the main group made spectacular with N Italian Gothic arcading and parapet. 3m S, **Ammanford**, A474, and the group of former mining towns up the Amman valley, **Glanamman** and **Brynamman**, with characteristic terraces of houses up the hillsides.

LAMPETER. A485 23m NE of Carmarthen. *St. David's University College* was founded by a bishop of St. David's in 1822 principally to train young men for the Anglican Church in Wales and was the second university foundation in Britain after the medieval period. Simple Tudor style quadrangle (1827; C.R. Cockerell) with chapel altered c 1878 (T.G. Jackson). 11m NE, A485, **Tregaron**, small town at the head of the Teifi. In the centre, *statue* (1893; A. Toft) of Henry Richards (1812–88), minister, MP and powerful advocate of independent arbitration as a means of avoiding war. 15m SW of Lampeter, A40, **Llandovery**, market town on the Tywi. Early 19C *Market Hall*, with slightly Greek octagonal lantern, and larger *Town Hall* (1840; G. Clinton) on open arcades with an Italianate tower at the back. By the railway, *Llandovery College* (1848; Fuller and Gingell), Tudor Gothic public school, asymmetrical front with tower, economical but well composed.

LLANELLI. A484 11m NW of Swansea. Battered steel-manufacturing town with Italianate *Town Hall* (1895) surviving in the centre. The dome-topped clock tower still the chief civic monument. Parish *church*, Bridge St, restored by G.F. Bodley (1907). *All Saints' Church*, Goring Rd, to N, is by G.E. Street (1872–87), the tower never built. At **Dafen**, to E, off A484, attractive small *church* (1873–74; G.E. Street), with circular turret. N of the centre, *Parc Howard Art Gallery*, Felinfoel Rd, house of c 1885 (J.B. Wilson) in a large park, local historical collections. At **Felinfoel** celebrated Victorian *brewery* and *church* (1857; R.K. Penson). 5m N, A476, at **Llannon**, Gothic *vicarage* by G.E. Street (1868).

MILFORD HAVEN. A4076 38m W of Carmarthen. Late 18C foundation to take advantage of the superb harbour, but never as successful as the founders, the Greville family, hoped. The Victorian naval history of the area centres on **Pembroke Dock**, established 1814, on the other side of the estuary, and on the hugely expensive fortifications undertaken from 1860, part of the Palmerston defences against the French (cf. Portsmouth, Hampshire). The entrance to the estuary was defended by a series of forts: S of Dale Point, *Dale Fort* and *West Blockhouse Battery* and in the estuary *Thorn Island Battery*; second line stretched from *South Hook Point* to *Stack Rock* in the middle and *Chapel Bay*, near Angle on the S side. Closest to Milford Haven were *Hubberston Fort* on the N side and *Popton Point* opposite. A series of landward forts was intended, as at Portsmouth, of which only one was built, *Scoveston Fort*, 2m NE of Milford Haven. Stack Rock is the most impressive, but least accessible of the forts. Those on land have the combination of massive earthworks and half-buried stone-faced buildings, galleries, passages and gun emplacements found in the Portsmouth forts. At Pembroke Dock, 5m E of Milford Haven, the naval dockyard closed in 1920. On the hill above, the *Defensible Barracks* (1844) survive as the golf club, the late Georgian style buildings surrounded by a deep dry moat.

ST. DAVID'S. A487 47m W of Carmarthen. The *Cathedral* was restored by Butterfield in 1846 and by Sir G.G. Scott from 1860–70, Butterfield replacing tracery, notably to the N transept, Scott carrying out a full restoration, carefully handled. Scott's deep purple W front comes as a shock, it replaces a previous effort by John Nash of 1793 and supposedly follows drawings of the original W front. Inside, Scott's hand is most visible in the choir with mosaics by Salviati and Hardman glass. At the E end, the Lady Chapel with vaulting, rebuilt 1902 (J.O. Scott). 6m NE of St. David's, the two tiny ports of **Abereiddy** and **Porth-gain**, former slate-quarrying centres, Abereiddy with a tiny harbour quarried out of the cliffs, Porth-gain larger but dominated by the remains of a granite-crushing works, constructed after 1904 for road stone. In the heyday of the slate industry some 100 ships were based at Porth-gain.

TENBY. A478 13m E of Pembroke. Seaside resort developed from the late 18C, but basically a medieval walled town. On the point between the two bays, *St. Catherine's Fort* (1868–78), another of the series built to protect the naval installations at Pembroke Dock (see above), this one against a landward attack from the E. Pleasant stuccoed houses, one, *No. 3 High St*, unexpectedly in Bath stone, supposedly shipped and reassembled from Bath in the mid 19C. On Castle Hill, the grandly titled 'Welsh National Memorial to Prince Albert', erected 1865 with marble statue of 'Albert Dda' by J.E. Thomas. The Mayor of Tenby sought to emulate here the efforts of the cities of Edinburgh and Dublin, hence the surprising site for a 'national' memorial. 9m W of Tenby, at **Cheriton**, *Stackpole Elidor church* with charming Art Nouveau lychgate (1898) and memorial inside to the 1st Earl of Cawdor (1860; J. Forsyth). The Campbell family of Cawdor inherited Stackpole in the 18C, hence the unlikely Scottish connection. At **Narberth**, A478, 11m N of Tenby, parish *church* rebuilt by T.G. Jackson (1879).

GLAMORGAN

ABERDARE. A4059 10m N of Pontypridd. Coal town in the Cynon Valley, developed from 1811 when the Glamorgan canal opened to Aberdare, and from 1846 when the railway came. The population increased tenfold from 1800–50. Lord Aberdare (1815–95), Home secretary under Gladstone, who reformed the licensing laws 1872 and helped to establish the University of Wales, was born here. In Victoria Square, *statue* of 'Caradog', G. Rhys Jones, conductor of the South Wales Choral Union, winner of choral competitions at Crystal Palace 1872–73. In the valley, other iron and coal settlements with terraces, chapels and Miners' Institutes, **Mountain Ash** to S, **Abernant** to E, **Trecynon** and **Hirwaun** to N.

BRIDGEND. A48 20m W of Cardiff. Market town much expanded in 20C. *St. Mary's Church* (1885; J. Prichard), Nolton, has good spire (1897). 2m NE, at **Coity**, the *church* has E window (1863) with very early Morris glass, figures by P.P. Marshall, borders by P. Webb. 2m SW at **Merthyr Mawr**, early 19C estate *village* with thatched cottages. *Church* (1859; J. Prichard). 6m E, A48, **Cowbridge**, centre of the Vale of Glamorgan. *Grammar School* (1848; J. Prichard), Tudor style. In High St, *Town Hall* (1823–30) designed by the local antiquary and landowner, Rev. J.M. Traherne, in whose memory the *church* at **St. Hilary**, 1m SE, was richly restored (1860–62; G.G. Scott). 6m SW, B4270, beyond **Llantwit Major**, *St. Donat's Castle*, 13C to 16C stone castle restored c 1900–10 (T. Garner and G.F. Bodley) but much, much more after 1925 by W. Randolph Hearst, the original of Citizen Kane. Now Atlantic College and one of the most romantic castles in Britain, even if the splendid medieval interiors were all imported from elsewhere by Hearst. 10m E of Bridgend, **Llantrisant**, hill town, *church* at the top restored 1873 (J. Prichard) with fine Burne-Jones E window. 3m SE, A4119, by roadside W of **Capel Llanilltern**, *chapel* (1863; G.E. Street). To E, N of A4119, *Craig-y-parc* (1913; C.E. Mallows), fine Arts and Crafts house, with garden front set behind columned screen over steeply terraced gardens. Now Spastics Society school.

CARDIFF. Capital of Wales officially only since 1955 but the major town of South Wales since the Industrial Revolution, the population rising from less than 2000 in 1801 to 164,000 in 1901. Cardiff's 19C history is bound up with the 2nd and 3rd Marquesses of Bute, Scottish peers who had inherited by marriage much of Cardiff just at the outset of the iron and coal boom. The 2nd Marquess promoted the first dock at Cardiff, 1839, and the first railway in Wales, to Merthyr Tydfil, 1848. The later 19C was Cardiff's heyday as a coal port. Industrial Cardiff is a sad place now, the station marks the boundary between the commercial centre and Bute Town, the dock area to S. On the roundabout, *Custom House* (1845), formerly fronting onto the Glamorganshire Canal. To E, Bute St runs S with fragmentary remains of the stuccoed houses of c 1840. Grim neo-Norman *church* (1841; T. Foster and Son). Further S, former commercial centre of the docks, with new *Custom House* (1898; H. Tanner) and Mount Stuart Square, surrounded by large and run-down commercial buildings. In the centre, *Coal Exchange* (1883–86; James, Seward and Thomas), ornately carved with fine hall (1911). Once the most important commercial building in Wales, this was to have been the seat of the Welsh Assembly had recent devolution plans been approved. At S end of Bute St, *Welsh*

Industrial and Maritime Museum, opened 1977, with good collection, particularly of steam-engines. It looks out over the remains of the docks, dominated by the splendid *Bute Docks Offices* (1896; W. Frame), Gothic in bright red terracotta with tall clock tower.

Bute Docks Offices (1896; W. Frame), Cardiff

The modern centre of Cardiff is N of the station, with St. Mary St and High St the main axis. By the station, *statue* of the 2nd Marquess of Bute (1793–1848) by J.E. Thomas (1853). In St. Mary St late 19C commercial buildings, and, on E side, the series of covered *arcades* that are the most attractive feature of commercial Cardiff. *Morgan Arcade* (1896; E. Seward) is the finest with original shopfronts and a curved plan. Opposite, *Royal Hotel* (1866; C. Bernard, and 1890), *Prince of Wales Theatre* (1878; W. Blessley), much altered, and adjoining to S, former *Philharmonic Hall* (1877) with a rare surviving music-hall interior, now bingo. To N, on E side, *Market Hall* (1886–91; W. Harpur) and, in High St, W side, *National Westminster Bank* (1857; Gingell and Lysaght), rich stuccoed palazzo. Further up, *Castle Arcade* (1887), good balconied interior.

Opposite the top of High St, * *Cardiff Castle* (open to public), Roman fort, medieval castle, Georgian castellated house and, most spectacularly, Victorian medieval fantasy. This last was the life's work of the 3rd Marquess of Bute, who succeeded his father aged six months and, by the time he came of age, was heir to one of the greatest fortunes in Britain. The 3rd Marquess, like Ludwig II of Bavaria, was a man out of sympathy with his own times, a scholar, mystic and passionate medievalist. He became, to national disapproval, a Roman Catholic at university in 1868 and put his immense personal energy into studies of languages, sacred texts, heraldry and architecture. In 1865, aged 18, he commissioned William Burges to begin the transformation of the Georgian castellated W range of the castle. Burges' medievalism and inventive capacity were perfect to bring to life Bute's dreams. The castle is essentially the SW corner of the large square enclosure, the surrounding walls rebuilt by the 3rd and 4th Marquesses with mostly unromantic regularity. The best view of Burges' work is from the W, outside the walls, where the fantastic skyline runs N from the great corner Clock Tower with its bold corbelled top and double roof (1869–73), the Herbert Tower (16C and c 1880), square with a steeply hipped roof, the Beauchamp Tower (15C and 1877–84), octagonal crowned with a splendid wooden flèche, and finally the Bute Tower (1873–79), the topmost section a protected roof garden. On the entrance front, between the Clock and Herbert Towers, is the Guest Tower (c 1875–80). Burges' Gothic is always strong, and the outlines and fenestration of these towers are severe and unornamented, the effect coming from play of masses until at the roofline fantasy has free rein. The interiors are of an exuberance, luxuriance and complexity that defy description. Painted decoration, sculpture, tiles, inlaid and carved woods, wrought and gilded metals fill every room, most rooms decorated to a particular theme, historical or iconographical, devised by Bute.

Cardiff Castle, the Dining Room (1873; W. Burges)

Burges designed every item and the joyous fertility of his imagination sparkles everywhere. The interior decoration ranges from Gothic to Islamic in inspiration, always minutely detailed and brilliantly coloured, giving the impression of being inside a jewelled casket. This is particularly so in the smaller rooms, Lord Bute's bedroom in the Bute Tower, the Chaucer Room in the Beauchamp Tower, the Study and Arab Room in the Herbert Tower and the two smoking rooms in the Clock Tower. Each room has its theme picked out from the smallest details to the overall painted decoration, particularly splendid in the Winter Smoking Room where the zodiac theme runs from the tiled pavement to the crystal stars of the vault, all benevolently overlooked by the golden Apollo on the chandelier. The Banqueting Hall, much larger, is fully baronial with the exploits of Robert the Consul, 12C Lord of Glamorgan, commemorated in murals by H.W. Lonsdale, and, delightfully, in the castellated fireplace, depicting the lord riding off, his lady waving from the battlements and his uncle, Robert of Normandy, gazing sadly from a dungeon window. Outside the castle, Burges designed the short stretch of wall E of the Clock Tower and the *Animal Wall* W of the Clock Tower with lively carved beasts along the coping. To the N, also by Burges, relatively plain stone *stables* (1872–75).

E of the castle, Cathays Park, the formal Edwardian municipal centre of Cardiff, built up 1898–1928 with large Portland stone buildings, the finest along the S edge, facing out to the town. The first two built, the *Assize Courts* and the *City Hall* (1897–1906; Lanchester and Rickards), are flamboyant Baroque revival buildings, designed by E.A. Rickards, whose sources seem to lie in Austria or S Germany, neither of which he had visited. Lanchester provided the lucid plan. The City Hall centres on a domed council chamber, the great lead dome capped by the Welsh dragon, and the stone frontispiece richly carved. Wings and end pavilions in plainer style give a long symmetrical front but, characteristic of the period, this symmetry is broken in the long views by a tall tower over the W side entrance, plain below and splendidly rich and complex Baroque at the top. This entrance aligns with the main entry of the *Assize Courts*, with twin cupolas flanking a Doric portico. The interiors of the City Hall, approached by a stone stair hall with marble columns and sculpture of heroic figures from Welsh history (St. David by Goscombe John, Hywel Dda by F.W. Pomeroy, Llewellyn by H. Poole), are richly plastered and panelled with fine bronze light fittings. E of the City Hall, *National Museum of Wales* (1910–27; Smith and Brewer), altogether cooler classical building, indicating the changing taste of the later Edwardian period, influenced by American Beaux Arts classicism. The domed front groups well with the City Hall. Excellent collections, notable for the French Impressionist paintings given by the Misses Davies of Gregynog and turn of the century sculpture by Rodin, A. Gilbert and Goscombe John. Facing the park behind, on E side, *University College* (1903–09; W.D. Caroe), a mannerist classical building taking its elements from artisan 17C sources, to which many architects trained in the Gothic Revival turned when unwilling to embrace the formalities of full classicism. Opposite, on W side, behind the Assize Courts, *University Registry* (1901), small and classical, and the ponderous giant Corinthian columned *Glamorgan County Hall* (1907–10; E.V. Harris) with big sculptured groups of Navigation and Mining (A. Hodge). The rear is a fine Italian palazzo style design. Concrete domed council chamber. Beyond, former *Technical College* (1916; P. Thomas), heavy classical.

SE of the Museum, in Park Place, *No. 20* (1871–74; W. Burges), built for Lord Bute's Chief Engineer at the Bute Docks. Strong Early French Gothic house in grey Caerphilly stone and Bath stone dressings, massive in detail, especially the plate-traceried windows and three-arched loggia. To SE, *Windsor Place* (c 1860), with handsome red-brick terraces, and rock-faced *Presbyterian chapel* (1866; F.T. Pilkington), the effect not as spiky as Pilkington's Scottish works as the W end is an addition (1893). Centralised plan with sloping floor. To E, Newport Rd leads out ½m to **Roath**. Beyond Royal Infirmary, Orbit St leads S to *St. German's Church* (1882–84; Bodley and Garner), Star St, an ambitious church in a poor area, the interior lofty and elegant, the nave piers especially slim and the windows deep-set. Bodley designed the pulpit, font, organ case and rood beam. Bodley also designed, for the same rapidly growing parish of Roath, *St. Saviour's Church* (1888), Splott Rd, ½m SE, lower and darker. Bodley organ case, reredos and pulpit. This industrial part of Roath, S of Newport Rd, was developed on lands belonging to Lord Tredegar, with stone-faced terrace houses, and Splott is now the best surviving part of industrial Cardiff. The Tredegar estate N of Newport Rd was developed with villas, and known as Tredegarville, stretching towards the old centre of Roath, ½m NE of the Infirmary. *St. Margaret's Church* (1869–72; J. Prichard), Albany Rd, the parish church, has a fine polychrome interior of patterned brick inset with local stones and alabaster. Lord Bute commissioned the church and added a NE mortuary chapel (1882) where various members of his family are buried under great granite blocks. *Roath Park* running NW from the church along the Roath Brook was given by Lord Bute to the city in 1887.

W from the centre of Cardiff, Cathedral Road, lined with large later 19C houses, leads out to *Llandaff Cathedral*, built 1170–1280 with NW tower of 1485 but derelict by the early 18C. From 1847–69 it was restored under J. Prichard and J.P. Seddon, with much Pre-Raphaelite work, but was disastrously damaged by a bomb in 1941. Outside Prichard added the fine SW tower and spire that give Llandaff its cathedral-like outline and rebuilt the chapter-house roof, turning a square base neatly to an octagon. Inside the dominant features are post-1949. Fragments of Morris glass survive in the S aisle, and in the NW chapel are the paintings by Rossetti from the old high altar. On The Green, N side, two large Gothic houses (1861; E. Christian), one now the *Bishop's Palace*. On Cardiff Rd, opposite High St, *Theological College*, partly Prichard's own house (c 1880), and, opposite, *Probate Registry* (1857; J. Prichard), High Victorian Gothic, a handsome design. ½m W, S of Fairwater Rd, *Llandaff Court* (1873; E.J. Robinson: 1875; James, Seward and Thomas), large Gothic house of J. Insole, ship-owner, now a library and community centre. 1m W, *Glan Ely Hospital*, St. Fagan's Rd, incorporating, on N side of road, Ty-Bronna (1903; C.F.A. Voysey), roughcast and deep-roofed house in the typical Voysey style. ½m beyond, at **St. Fagan's**, *church* restored by G.E. Street (1859) with large Gothic former *rectory* (1858; Prichard and Seddon). The *Welsh Folk Museum*, at St. Fagan's Castle, is the finest of its kind in Britain especially for the re-erected buildings, but also for the agricultural, domestic and industrial exhibits.

Off A470, 5m NW of Cardiff, at **Tongwynlais**, *Castell Coch* (1875–91; W. Burges) rises, an improbable fairy-tale castle on the steep E slope of the Taff Valley. There was nothing but a heap of stone when Lord Bute decided to reconstruct the 13C castle in 1871. Burges provided a castle that more than any other 19C castle in Britain looks the part. Three round towers on battered bases rise sheer from the dry

Castell Coch (1875–91; W. Burges), Tongwynlais

moat, massive and almost windowless, but authentically complete with arrow-slits and putlog holes, and the front towers linked by the gate-tower complete with working drawbridge and portcullis. Burges' medieval military architecture was scholarly, his sense of dramatic composition unequalled, thus the towers are capped by steep conical roofs which Burges justified from manuscript illustration as a feature, now lost, of British medieval castles and exploited to the full by varying the heights of the towers, setting the E cone behind the battlements while the other two overhang, and providing splendid clusters of circular stacks. Inside, a romantic courtyard with open timber gallery curving between the E and N towers and chamber range between the N and S towers. As at Cardiff Castle, the interiors are magnificent, though there are only four principal rooms, a Banqueting Hall with carved stone chimney-breast, an octagonal Drawing-Room, two-storied with gallery, decorated with scenes from Aesop under a brilliant vault of birds, butterflies and stars, Lord Bute's bedroom, relatively plain, and Lady Bute's bedroom, a beautiful circular two-storey room with painted and gilded dome with Islamic touches, as at Cardiff, spectacular red and gold bed and castellated washstand. There were no visitors' rooms, Lord Bute visited the castle only rarely.

S of Cardiff, A4160, overlooking Cardiff Bay and the Bristol Channel is **Penarth**, once with its own docks to the N, *Dock Offices* (1865), also a resort town and suburb developed by the landowner, Lord Windsor, who laid out the Esplanade with gardens and *pier* (1894). Above, large late 19C villas in Plymouth Rd. On the headland, NE of the station, *St. Augustine's Church* (1865–66; W. Butterfield), one of Butterfield's most colourful interiors, wholly unexpected within the strong grey stone exterior with low saddleback tower. The walls are of red brick patterned in white brick with pale stone bands, arches and circular medallions and the arcade piers alternating pink and cream sandstone. Fine reredos. At **Lavernock Point**, 2m S, Marconi sent the first wireless message in 1897. **Barry**, 4m SW of Penarth, was created 1884–89, from nothing, as a coal port and what was the largest dock in the world, by David Davies, colliery owner, who quarrelled with Lord Bute over the facilities at Cardiff. In the centre imposing Wren style *Port Building* (1898; A.E. Bell) with *statue* of Davies (A. Gilbert) in front.

MERTHYR TYDFIL. A470 25m N of Cardiff. The heartland of the Industrial Revolution in Wales, Merthyr Tydfil's wealth was iron, exploited from the mid 18C, and later coal, but decline from the early 20C has wiped away much of the industrial historical interest together with the scars of industry, removed more recently, so that it is difficult to imagine this the greatest town in Wales in the early 19C and the place of marvels and incandescent nightmares recorded by early tourists. George Borrow described the great Cyfartha ironworks of the Crawshay family in 'Wild Wales', one building striking him as 'such as Bosch would have imagined had he wanted to paint the palace of Satan'. The chief ironworks were Cyfartha, founded 1765, Dowlais, the Guest family works, founded 1759, Plymouth, the Hill family works, founded c 1780, and Penydarren, founded 1784, of the Homfray family. At the entry to the town, *St. Tydfil's Church* (1895–1901; J.L. Pearson), impressive Romanesque style interior, the tower earlier. Outside, pretty iron fountain canopy (c 1890) made by Macfarlane of Glasgow. High St runs N, much redeveloped, with, especially off to N, terraces of characteristic stone houses and large chapels. At the top end, Dowlais, the works, S of High St, mostly cleared, but on High St former *Guest Reading Room and Library* (1863; Sir C. Barry) built for Lady Charlotte Guest, translator of the 'Mabinogion', art collector, philanthropist and diarist. Her husband, Sir J.J. Guest, the first MP for the town, she called Merthyr. To NW, the site of the Cyfartha works below A470, with *Cyfartha Castle* (1824–25; R. Lugar) standing above, now housing the town museum. 5m E in the parallel Rhymney valley, **Rhymney**, iron town developed by the 2nd Marquess of Bute. *Church* (1839; P. Hardwick), built by the iron company, classical late Regency style.

NEATH. A465 6m NE of Swansea. Prominent pyramid-spired tower to *St. David's church* (1864–66; J. Norton). Further N, off New St, *Mechanics Institution* (1847; A.R. Wallace), Italianate, notable in that Wallace is best known as the naturalist who, in Borneo in 1855, came upon the theory of natural selection at the same time as, but independently from, Darwin. His 'Contributions to the Theory of Natural Selection' (1871) stands with Darwin's 'Origin of Species' at the foundation of evolutionary theory. Iron and glass roofed *Market* (c 1900). 3m S, A48, at **Baglan**, fine spired *church* (1882; J. Prichard), the interior richly coloured in different stones with mosaic pavement and marble reredos (H.H. Armstead). E and S transept windows by Burne-Jones (1880).

PONTYPRIDD. A470 12m NW of Cardiff. Well-set industrial town at the junction of the Rhondda valley with the Taff valley. Late Victorian town centre with lively covered markets. Above, spired *church* (1866–69; J. Norton) with hefty plate tracery. Beyond, *Town Hall* (1904; H.T.

Hare), pretty stone building, free Renaissance style. In *Ynysangharad Park*, statues of Evan and James James (Goscombe John) author and composer of 'Land of My Fathers' (1856), the Welsh national anthem. The Rhondda valleys to NW were at the heart of the Welsh mining tradition, but almost all the collieries have now gone. What remains are the terraces of stone houses on the steep slopes contrasting with the bare hills above. From **Porth**, the smaller Rhondda Fach valley leads N to **Maerdy**, while the main valley continues past **Tonypandy**, notorious for the use of troops in 1910 to break up a miners' demonstration. At **Pentre**, a large *church* (1888; Kempson and Fowler). **Treorchy** is famous for its choir, called the Royal Male Voice Choir since performing to Queen Victoria in 1885. **Blaenrhondda**, beyond Treherbert, has the most dramatic setting, right at the head of the valley.

PORT TALBOT. A48 9m E of Swansea. Iron and steel town developed from 1837 when the Talbot family of Margam Castle built the port at the mouth of the Afan. Aberavon was the old village, *church* (1856; Prichard and Seddon) with elaborate carved reredos by H.H. Armstead. On old A48 to SE, *St. Theodore's Church* (1895; J.L. Pearson), built in memory of Theodore Talbot of Margam, grand scaled and stone vaulted except in the nave. To NE, the Afan Valley, once a mining valley, now reforested and a Scenic Route. At **Afan Argoed**, 6m up, *Welsh Miners Museum*. **Margam**, 4m SE, A48, the Talbot estate, is now a public park, and *Margam Castle* (1830–35; T. Hopper) stands derelict, a most elaborately towered and pinnacled Tudor style house in red stone. The parish *church* is the nave of the 12C Margam Abbey, rebuilt in Italianate style at the ends (1808) and reroofed (1873). Three W windows with Morris glass (1873) and in N aisle marble effigy of Theodore Talbot (1881; H.H. Armstead).

SWANSEA. Port town at the mouth of the Tawe, industrialised from the early 19C, mostly metal industries. The industrial area, along the river N and E of the town, is now a scene of post-industrial dereliction, slowly being reclaimed. The town centre, on the W side of the Tawe, is almost entirely rebuilt after bombing. The New Cut Bridge, A483, leads in past reclaimed 19C docks. In Somerset Place, left of roundabout, old *Town Hall* (1850–52; T. Taylor), classical. In Victoria Rd, *Royal Institution of South Wales Museum* (1838–41; F. Long), Greek Ionic, the main South Wales scientific institution in the early 19C, archaeological and historical collections. To S, the disused South Dock (1847–59) with *Industrial and Maritime Museum*, gradually building a good collection of historic ships. The old centre ran N from the roundabout, with High St parallel to Strand, the original waterfront. In High St, disused *Palace Theatre* (1888; Bucknall and Jennings), brick and stone on triangular site with tower to curved corner. To W, beyond the Market, *Grand Theatre* (1897; W. Hope), Singleton St, stucco fronted with good intact interior. W along the seafront, Oystermouth Rd leads past *Victoria Park*, where the Patti Pavilion is the re-erected Winter Garden from Craig-y-nos, Powys, the home of the soprano Madame Patti (1843–1919). Further W, *Singleton Park*, site of University College, the park being the grounds of *Singleton Abbey* (1823–31; P.F. Robinson), home of the Vivian family, industrial tycoons of the Swansea copper-smelting industry. H.H. Vivian (1821–94), made Lord Swansea in 1893, was himself a distinguished metallurgist. At the top of the park, *St. Paul's Church* (1849–52; H. Woodyer), built for the Vivian family, with shingled spire like Woodyer's Surrey churches. *Schools* (1853; Woodyer) opposite. N of Swansea, A4067, the industrialised valley runs up to **Morriston**, copper and coal town with enormous *Capel Tabernacle* (1870; J. Humphries), 1800 seater chapel, called the Cathedral of Welsh Nonconformity.

GWENT

ABERGAVENNY. 16m W of Monmouth. The centre is dominated by the pyramid-roofed tower of the *Market Hall* (1871; Wilson and Willcox), a strong High Victorian Gothic building influenced by Burges. In Park Road, N of the centre, *RC church* (1858; B. Bucknall), tall nave and chancel with ornate tracery. 4m up the A465 at Llanfihangel is the road (B4423) to **Llanthony** where the priory ruins were owned by the poet W. Savage Landor 1808–1813. Landor, romantically taken with the beauty of the valley, wanted to mend the ruins and set up as a model country landlord. The results were disastrous, the ruins were damaged by Landor's attempt to rebuild, he quarrelled with his neighbours, disliked the Welsh and left eventually to settle in less exacting Bath. The road leads on to **Capel-y-ffin**, site of an odd experiment in reviving monasticism within the Church of England. J.L. Lyne, known as Father Ignatius, built a monastery 1870 and part of a church from 1872 in this very remote spot. Services were most sumptuous and many came to visit, some to remain as monks and nuns. Miracles and visions occurred, but after the death of Ignatius in 1908 the community declined and the church fell in. The monastery became the site of another experiment in 1924 when Eric Gill, stonecutter and letterer, set up his Roman Catholic artistic community here. At **Oldcastle**, 3m N of Llanfihangel, up the Monnow valley, a prettily set *church* (1864; J.P. Seddon) with a lovely W window by Seddon.

EBBW VALE. 9m SW of Abergavenny. One of the most industrialised of the South Wales valleys. *Ebbw Vale* itself, B4486, was a town made by steel but steel-making ended in 1978. The church of 1861 with spire of 1881 is the main architectural landmark. As elsewhere in the valleys the tight rows of terraces interspersed with chapels are contrasted with the great bare hills above. Coal-mining all but ceased and the coal tips are slowly disappearing, either removed or under scrubby grass. **Abertillery** and **Blaina** are the chief towns of the parallel Ebbw Fach valley (A467).

MONMOUTH. The county town. In the centre *statue* of C. Rolls, aviator and motor pioneer (Rolls-Royce), by W. Goscombe John. The *Museum* occupies the remains of the *Market* (1837; G.V. Maddox), the upper storey was removed after a fire. *St. Mary's Church* was rebuilt 1880 (G.E. Street). 2m NW of Monmouth, B4233, **Rockfield**, estate village of the Rolls family of Rockfield House and, principally, of *The Hendre*, 1½m W, brick and stone Tudor style, early 19C, with alterations by T.H. Wyatt and Aston Webb. At Rockfield, good estate *church* (1859; Prichard and Seddon) with fine carving. N of The Hendre is *Llangattock Manor* (T.H. Wyatt), another Rolls House, with derelict *church* (1875; Wyatt) where C. Rolls is buried. 4m SW of Monmouth, off A40, *Dingestow Court*, refronted in the Elizabethan style (1845; L. Vulliamy). In the village, *church* (1846; T.H. Wyatt) with monuments to the Bosanquets of the Court. Between Monmouth and Chepstow runs the Wye valley, favourite romantic spot for writers and painters from the late 18C onwards. Samuel Palmer came to *Tintern Abbey*, the great 13C ruin, in 1835. His wonderful drawing in the Victoria and Albert Museum, London, shows the abbey still romantically overgrown and clad in ivy. 2m W of **Chepstow**, off A48, at **Mounton**, *Mounton House* (1912), an attractive stone and half-timber house, largely designed by H.A. Tipping, writer on country houses and gardens for 'Country Life'. Tipping had already restored *Mathern Palace*, 3m S of Chepstow, the 15C palace of the Bishops of Llandaff, and laid out the lovely gardens.

NEWPORT. The largest town in Gwent and the main port for south-east Wales. The High St is a battered Victorian commercial centre with lively *markets* (1887; Linton and Kirby) just off. At the junction of High St and Commercial St, outside the Westgate Hotel, 20 working men were massacred in 1839 during a Chartist demonstration. Stow Hill runs off to the left with *RC church* (1838–40; J.J. Scoles) on the left. Impressive five-stage tower and an interior with tall cast-iron columns. The most exciting monument of Newport is the *Transporter Bridge*, at the S end of Commercial St, built in 1906 to designs by F. Arnodin, designer of the Marseilles transporter bridge. Vehicles drive onto a small section of bridge which is then hauled across the river suspended from great height. From the railway, *St. Mark's Church*, N of the town on a hilltop, is a landmark with its Perp. style tower (1874; Habershon and Fawckner).

The Transporter Bridge (1906; F. Arnodin and R.H. Haynes), Newport

3m N, A4042, at **Malpas**, a small well-carved Romanesque style *church* in pink stone (1849; J. Prichard). Windows commemorate the grasping T. Prothero, agent for the Tredegar estates, which included Newport. He lived at *Malpas Court* (1838; T.H. Wyatt), Whittle Drive, a dull Gothic house now a club, the grounds built over. *Llantarnam Abbey*, 2m beyond, is also by T.H. Wyatt (1835) with a nice lodge to the road. 4m N, A4043, **Pontypool**, iron-making centre that grew from 1,500 people in 1801 to 27,000 in 1891, typical of industrial South Wales. The best building is the *English Baptist Chapel* (1846), Crane Street, Greek Doric. At **Pontnewynydd**, 1½m N, tall Lancet Gothic *church* (1873; C. Buckeridge). The road continues up to **Blaenavon**, another iron town, the works founded in 1789 and now partially preserved as an industrial monument. 4m E of Pontypool, A449, **Usk**. In the *church* a lavish organ case made for Llandaff Cathedral (1862;

Seddon). Sir Matthew Digby Wyatt (1820–77), architect and secretary to the 1851 exhibition, is buried in the NW corner of the churchyard. Maryport St runs S with the *Sessions House* (1875; T.H. Wyatt), low, Italianate and oddly suburban in its setting. *Gaol* (1840; T.H. Wyatt) adjoining. By the bridge, *Cardiff Arms* pub and shop in cheerful yellow and red brick of c 1890. 4m E, off B4235, at **Llangwm Uchaf**, *church* restored 1870 (J.P. Seddon) who recoloured the superb 15C rood screen and loft and added the tiled floor and stained glass E window. 6m NW of Usk, off A471, **Llanfair Cilgedin** *church*, rebuilt 1876 (J.D. Sedding) with good fittings but exceptional for the complete scheme of decoration in sgraffito plaster by Heywood Sumner (1888), leading Arts and Crafts designer and the specialist in this medium.

GWYNEDD

ANGLESEY. Island separated from the mainland by the Menai Strait, crossed from Bangor, A5, by the *Menai Bridge* (1818–26; Telford), magnificent suspension bridge, 579ft between the great stone piers and 100ft over the water. The bridge completed the stagecoach route from London to Holyhead. 1m W is the *Britannia Bridge* (1850; R. Stephenson), the railway bridge to Holyhead, originally a tubular bridge like that at Conwy with iron box-section tubes, 460ft high and 230ft long, between massive masonry piers, slightly Egyptian in shape like those on Brunel's Clifton Bridge at Bristol. Carved lions guard the entrances. The tubes were burnt in 1970 and have been replaced by steel arched spans carrying rail and road traffic. *Statue* of Nelson (1873) W of the bridge by the shore. By the A5, *Anglesey Column* (1816) to the 1st Marquess of Anglesey, who led the cavalry at Waterloo. Statue on top 1860 (M. Noble). *Plas Newydd* (NT), 18C and early 19C mansion of the Paget family, Earls of Uxbridge and Marquesses of Anglesey, is just S, A4080. 4m NE of Menai Bridge, **Beaumaris**, the chief town of Anglesey with attractive early 19C buildings, notably *Victoria Terrace* (1835; Hansom and Welch), stone fronted and surprisingly grand. NW of the town, *Bulkeley Monument* (1875), obelisk to the leading Anglesey family. 17m W of Menai Bridge, **Holyhead**, port for Dublin, terminus of the road and railway from London. The harbour was rebuilt from 1810 by John Rennie with Admiralty Pier, custom house and harbour office. *Memorial arch* (1824; T. Harrison) on the pier, commemorating the visit of George IV. When the railway came in 1848 this prompted the construction of a much larger breakwater, completed 1880, enclosing the New Harbour. *Station* and former hotel 1880. In the parish *church*, restored 1877-79 (G.G. Scott), fine Morris and Co. window and carved effigy of W.O. Stanley (1897; H. Thorneycroft).

BANGOR. A5 21m W of Llandudno. *Cathedral*, low lying and much restored 1868–70 (G.G. Scott) and 1880 (J.O. Scott). E window by Clayton and Bell, choir fittings and reredos by J.O. Scott. In the High St, *Lloyds Bank* (1859; Weightman, Hadfield and Goldie), Elizabethan style, and *Clock Tower* (1887). N of the Cathedral, *University, founded 1884 with fine quadrangular buildings (1907–11; H.T. Hare) in a free Jacobean style, simplified in the Arts and Crafts way with a handsome short tower and good carved decoration. Behind, in College Rd, is the *Normal College* (1858–62; J. Barnett), Tudor style teacher training college, and rendered free Tudor style *Hall of Residence* (1908–10; H.T. Hare). At the NE corner of the headland, *Bangor Pier* (1896), 1500ft long promenade pier and landing stage, closed since 1971. SW of the town, *Friars School* (1899; J. Douglas), Jacobean, and, at Glanadda, *St. David's Church* (1888; A. Blomfield). Just E of the town, *Penrhyn Castle* (NT) (1827–47; T. Hopper), the most spectacular neo-Norman house in Britain, built for the slate quarry owning Pennant family, Lords Penrhyn. The 1st Lord Penrhyn (died 1808) developed the enormous quarries at Bethesda (see below) and linked them to the sea at **Port Penrhyn**. The 2nd Lord Penrhyn rebuilt the house for some half million pounds with massive keep linked to towered and battlemented ranges. The interiors are as neo-Norman as the outside, even to the megalomaniac furniture such as the Slate Bed, the slate dining-room sideboards and the carved oak bed made for Queen Victoria. The staircase is a tour-de-force of carved slate, almost Arabic in its richness, the Great Hall is plaster vaulted on the model of Durham Cathedral. Industrial Railway Museum in the stables. Estate village at **Llandygai**, with *church* containing a neo-Norman organ from the castle and fine monument to the 1st Lord Penrhyn (1821; Westmacott). At **Bethesda**, 5m SE, A5, the Penrhyn quarries, the biggest opencast hole in the world, 1140ft deep. The town has a long tradition of Nonconformity in religion and active trade unionism. Numerous chapels, the finest, *Jerusalem* (1872), in Italian palazzo style. 1m N at **Llanllechid**, *church* (1846; H. Kennedy) in a most misunderstood Norman style.

University College (1907–11; H.T. Hare) Bangor

5m SW of Bangor, **Port Dinorwic**, built c 1800 by the Assheton-Smith family of *Vaynol*, late 18C to early 19C house to NE, as a port for their slate quarries at Dinorwic. 19C industrial housing round the port, estate cottages nearer the house. **Caernarfon**, 4m SW, has streets within its walls to the medieval grid pattern. Outside the castle, *County Hall* (1863), porticoed. In Market St, *Market Hall* (1832; J. Lloyd). In Castle Square, E of the Castle, *statue* of Lloyd George, Prime Minister, MP for Caernarfon for 55 years. 6m E of Caernarfon, A4086, *Dinorwic Quarries*, a whole mountainside cut away in precipitous terraces above Llyn Padarn. The *Welsh Slate Museum* is in the workshops (1870) where all the ironwork, woodwork and machine repair for the quarries was carried out. A short length of the quarry railway that ran to Port Dinorwic has been reopened with original steam locomotives.

DOLGELLAU. A470 34m N of Aberystwyth. Former county town of Merioneth with *Shire Hall* (1825; E. Haycock). 2m E, B4416, at **Brithdir**, remarkable *church* (1895–97; H. Wilson), built to Arts and Crafts principles in massive unornamented local granite with sweeping slate roof carried forward of the W gable on stone corbels. Small plain windows, all combining to give the feeling of a building built against the elements, simple and in harmony with the locality. Barrel-vaulted apsed chancel brightly painted. *Vicarage* adjoining (1888; J.D. Sedding). 18m NE of Dolgellau, A494, **Bala**, market town with *church* of 1856 (B. Ferrey) at the N end and *statue* of T.E. Ellis

(1902; Goscombe John) in the High St. Ellis, Liberal MP for Merioneth, campaigned for home rule, church disestablishment and land reform. Tegid St leads down to Lake Bala past *statue* of the Rev. T. Charles (1895), pioneer of Methodism in North Wales and founder of the British and Foreign Bible Society. The *Bala Lake Railway* runs steam trains along the lake to Llanuwchllyn. On A4212, NW of the town, former *Calvinist Methodist Theological College* (c 1870) founded 1837. 5m E of Bala, B4402, at **Llanderfel**, *Pale* (1875; S. Pountney Smith), stone Jacobean style mansion with spire over the service wing, built for H. Robertson, railway engineer and MP; *Church* rebuilt 1870 (S. Pountney Smith).

7m W of Dolgellau, A496, at **Caerdeon**, *church* (1862) designed by the influential writer on architecture, the Rev. J.L. Petit, quite exceptionally for the time as a plain stone structure like an Italian farm building with no ecclesiastical trimmings (bellcote and chancel added later). Further W, on the edge of the water, *Coes Faen* (1844; T. Jones), highly picturesque villa with a spired clock tower. To W, **Barmouth**, resort town on a narrow strip of land under cliffs. *St. John's Church* (1889–98; Douglas and Fordham), dominant at the N end, with fine central tower. Above *St. David's Church* (1838), *St. George's Cottages*, acquired by Ruskin 1875 for his Guild of St. George, a social experiment intended to fund the setting up of industries on co-operative lines. *Barmouth Viaduct* (1867) is the last large timber railway bridge in use. 10m S, A493, **Tywyn**, developed as a resort in the late 19C by J. Corbett, salt tycoon of Droitwich, Worcestershire. In the centre, the *Corbett Arms Hotel*, *Assembly Rooms* and *Market*. From Twywn the narrow-gauge *Talyllyn Railway* (1866) runs NE for 7m. Two of the steam-engines still working date from 1866.

LLANDUDNO. A546 46m W of Chester. Resort town created from almost nothing after 1848 by the Mostyn family. The earliest parts are stucco terraces built from the 1850s, probably to designs by Wehnert and Ashdown, and the most attractive feature of the central area, around Mostyn St, are the iron and glass canopies over the pavements. In Lloyd St, *Town Hall* (1895; T.B. Silcock). At the W end of the seafront, *Grand Hotel* (c 1890; J.F. Doyle), *Pavilion* (1883; B. Nelson) and very attractive *pier* (1876; Brunlees and McKerrow) with elegant octagonal kiosks and still in excellent condition. On the far side of the headland, *Gogarth Abbey Hotel*, incorporating the villa where Dean Liddell of Christ Church, Oxford, spent summers in the 1860s and Lewis Carroll first told Alice Liddell the stories that became 'Alice in Wonderland'. At **Degannwy**, to S, on the coast road, *church* (1898; J. Douglas) with attractive low spire. 1m SE of Llandudno, *Gloddaeth*, 16C house of the Mostyn family, altered 1875 (W.E. Nesfield) with patterned plasterwork. 10m S of Llandudno, A470, *Bodnant* (1881; W.J. Green), large gabled house famous for the gardens (NT) laid out from 1875 with outstanding tree collections. 6m S, **Llanrwst**, with *church* restored 1882–84 (Paley and Austin). 5m S, on A5, **Betws-y-Coed**, resort village for Snowdonia. The new *church* (1873; Paley and Austin) is EE style with central tower and vaulted chancel.

From Llandudno the Conwy estuary, 6m S, A55, is crossed by the *Conwy Railway Bridge* (1849; R. Stephenson), a revolutionary tubular bridge of prefabricated iron box-section, prototype for the much larger Britannia Bridge to Anglesey. Castellated entrances to blend with Conwy Castle. Next to the railway bridge, *suspension bridge* (1822; Telford), also with castellated piers. **Conwy** *church*, restored 1872 (G.G. Scott), has a memorial bust (1852; Theed) to the Victorian sculptor, John Gibson, born in Conwy. *Castle Hotel*, High St, refronted 1885 (J. Douglas) with Jacobean gables. *Council Offices*, NW of town, in Bodlondeb, large house of c 1890 (T.M. Lockwood). S of the centre, A5110, at **Gyffin**, Arts and Crafts style roughcast and slate-hung *school* (c 1910; H.L. North). 3m S at **Llangelynin**, *church* (1840; T. Jones) with attractive early 20C interior in white, blue and red by H.L. North. 3m S, B5106, at **Caerhun**, remains of a Roman fort in the grounds of Jacobean style stone and half-timbered house (1892; T.M. Lockwood). 3m S, **Trefriw Wells**, with *pump room* of 1873, recently restored. 5m W of Conwy, A55, **Penmaen-mawr**, coastal resort visited by Gladstone. *St. Seiriol's Church* (1868; A. Waterhouse) is High Victorian with saddleback tower and polychrome brick interior. 2m W, at **Llanfairfechan**, early 20C estate to N laid out from 1910 by H.L. North, in the manner of Voysey. Carefully designed roughcast houses with thick slate roofs and slate fencing.

PORTHMADOG. A498 24m S of Caernarfon. Centre of the estate developed by William Maddocks from c 1800. The intention was to build a new port for traffic to Ireland at Porth Dinlaen, 19m W, the main trunk road from London passing across the Traeth Mawr estuary on a great embankment with Tremadog, N of Porthmadog, as the coaching town. The embankment was built 1808–11, a massive engineering feat, but the trunk road and railway went to Holyhead. Instead Porthmadog was developed as a harbour for the slate quarries, the *Festiniog Railway* opening in 1836 with horse-drawn trains, bringing slate from Blaenau Ffestiniog. Steam trains came in 1863 on a narrow-gauge track of less than 2ft width. Slowly since 1954 the line has been reopened. *Railway museum* at Porthmadog Station. 2m W of Porthmadog, at **Penmorfa**, *church*, restored 1899, and *Wern*, house built 1892 (J. Douglas) for the owner of Llechwedd slate quarry, Blaenau Ffestiniog. 11m E of Porthmadog, A487, at **Maentwrog**, *Plas Tan-y-Bwlch*, castellated house of the Oakeley family, quarry owners. House altered 1890 (J. Douglas), now a study centre for the National Park. *Church* prettily rebuilt 1896 (J. Douglas), with inserted timber arcades, low slated tower and spire, and new tracery, disguising the plain original building of 1814. At **Ffestiniog**, on the E side of the valley, neo-Norman *church* (1844; H. Kennedy), eccentrically detailed. **Blaenau Ffestiniog**, to N, became the principal town of the valley during the 19C when vast quantities of slate were quarried here, leaving a landscape of spoil heaps and quarry faces. N of the town, *Llechwedd Slate Caverns*, one of the largest quarries, started in 1846 and mostly mined underground, is open to the public. Further on, *Gloddfa Ganol*, once the world's largest slate mine, has a museum of the industry and three refurnished miners' cottages. 7m W of Porthmadog, **Criccieth**, small 19C resort. *St. Deiniol's Church* (1887; J. Douglas). At **Llanystumdwy**, 2m W, *Lloyd George Memorial Museum* commemorates the Prime Minister who was brought up here and is buried by the river. *Gwynfryn*, N of the village, mid Victorian house castellated like a toy fort. **Pwllheli**, 6m W, is a late Victorian resort, the promenade opened 1890. 4m NW, A497, at **Bodfuan**, large neo-Norman church (1894; Kennedy and Gregory) with crossing tower, unexpectedly grand.

POWYS

BRECON. A40 36m W of Monmouth. Former county town of Breconshire. In the centre, *Shire Hall* (1842; T.H. Wyatt), handsome Greek Revival, now home of the Brecknock Museum. In The Bulwark, *statue* of Wellington (1852; J.E. Thomas). Over the bridge, *Christ College* (1861–64; Prichard and Seddon) with High Victorian Gothic main school buildings and chapel in the restored chancel of the 13C Dominican Friary. Fine E window by Seddon (1865).

6m E of Brecon, B4560, at **Llangasty Talyllyn**, estate of the Raikes family of Treberfydd. R. Raikes, influenced by the Tractarians at Oxford sought to bring revived Anglican worship to this part of Wales where Nonconformity had reduced the established church to almost nothing. Raikes' architect was J.L. Pearson and work continued over ten years (1848–58). Pearson rebuilt the *church* in a simple EE style, with square tower, gabled nave, and chancel with porch and organ chamber providing smaller gables at right angles, all severely geometrical. Pretty painted decoration in chancel. Adjoining, *school* (1848 50), exceptionally attractive asymmetrical design with the gable of the master's house answered by the chimney of the schoolroom. *Treberfydd* stands on the hill to W, picturesque gabled house with porch tower and smaller tower to one side, giving access to the stable court. The manner of the house is that of Pugin with principal rooms emphasised externally and complex pattern of roofs and chimneys but with a mellowness in the handling of the stone not found in Pugin's work. 9m SE, A40, at **Crickhowell**, *Town Hall* (1833; T.H. Wyatt), an early example of the Italianate supplanting Greek styles, attractively designed in contrasting grey stones. Parish *church*, to SW, with shingled spire (1861). 1½m W, A40, *Maes Celyn* (1873; J.L. Pearson), with lodges on road of 1888. To NW, A479, at **Tretower**, *church* (1877; J.L. Pearson) and parish *room* (1887; Pearson), modest but attractive pair of buildings built for the ironmaster Lord Glanusk. 11m NE of Brecon, A438, at **Three Cocks**, *Gwernyfed Park* (1877–80; W.E. Nesfield), stone three-gabled Elizabethan style front. Lodge on main road. 5m NE, **Hay-on-Wye**, with Cheese Market (1835) and Butter Market (1833) in the centre between the narrow streets of the upper town and the wider streets close to the river. At **Clyro**, A438, just across the Wye, Francis Kilvert was curate 1864–76 and wrote delightfully of the area in his diaries. *Clyro Court*, to SW, is stone-fronted neo-Jacobean (c 1850), built for T.M. Baskerville. Conan Doyle wrote 'The Hound of the Baskervilles' staying here. 4m NW of Three Cocks, A470, *Llangoed Castle* (1913–19; C. Williams-Ellis), handsome 17C style mansion with tall hipped roofs, rubble-stone walls and mullion windows contrasted with a fine ashlar porch bay with more formal classical detail. Attractive stable court to one side suggests the architect's later work at Portmeirion, North Wales.

3m NW of Brecon, at **Battle**, *Penoyre* (1846–48; A. Salvin), Italian palazzo style mansion in smooth ashlar, like a London club come to the country, but with the addition of a broad loggia around the front and sides and massive porch tower, almost free standing, with belvedere top, on the entrance side. Painted decoration in the stair hall. The *church* at **Llandefaelog Fach**, to NE, B4520, has unusually rich late 19C fittings. 19m SW of Brecon, A4067, *Craig-y-nos*, house of 1842 T.H. Wyatt), slightly baronial, much extended in pink stone (c 1891) for Adelina Patti, celebrated soprano. Exceptional private theatre 1891; Bucknall and Jennings), wholly intact, gilded and painted interior embellished with the names of opera composers and original painted backdrop showing Patti as Semiramide. The floor could tilt to change the room from ballroom to theatre.

LLANDRINDOD WELLS. A483 40m W of Hereford. Resort town mostly developed after 1865 when the railway came, though the springs were known from the early 18C. Bright red and yellow brick streets and public parks, quite unexpected in mid Wales. The springs are in *Rock Park*. The former *Pump House Hotel* (c 1886) is now Powys County Council offices. 7m S, **Builth Wells**, with *Market House* (1875; Haddon Bros) by the bridge, Italian Gothic in stone with terracotta details. 9m W, at **Beulah**, NW of village elaborate estate *church* (1867; J. Norton) with highly coloured interior and fine fittings. E and W windows with glass 1868 by Clayton and Bell. 4m SW, **Llanwrtyd Wells**, remains of a late Victorian and Edwardian spa. Sulphur springs up lane to NW. 3m E, **Llangammarch Wells**, with mineral springs at *Lake Hotel*, 1m E. *Church* (1913–16; W.D. Caroe), Arts and Crafts interpretation of 15C Welsh churches, broad and low with an attractive simplicity.

   16m W of Llandrindod Wells, SW of Rhayader, *Elan Valley*, the vast water storage scheme built by Birmingham Corporation from 1892–1904. Three great dams, the valve towers picturesquely treated, control some 70 square miles of water, then sent by 75 miles of pipe to Birmingham. Superb masonry construction. *Village* (1906; Buckland and Haywood Farmer) for maintenance staff. 5m SE of Rhayader, A470, *Doldowlod House*, c 1827 Elizabethan style, built for James Watt, son of the inventor and his successor in the firm of Boulton and Watt. Extended (1878; S.W. Williams) with off-centre tower. 10m NW of Rhayader, at **Llangurig**, A44, *church* rebuilt (1877; G.G. Scott and A. Baker) with a new spire, and fine chancel fittings by Baker. The screen is a reproduction from drawings of the original dismantled 1834. Glass by Burlison and Grylls. 5m NE, **Llanidloes**, important weaving town from c 1800–60, and with Newtown and Welshpool centre of industrial unrest during the 1830s, culminating in a local Chartist revolution in 1839 when briefly magistrates and police were ejected from the town by angry workers. Back-to-back early 19C weavers' houses by the bridge in Victoria Avenue. In Great Oak St stone Jacobean style *Town Hall* (1908; Shayler and Ridge) and *New Market* (1838). In Cambrian Place, *station* (1864; B. Piercy), elaborate red brick Italianate, headquarters of the mid Wales railway. The medieval church has E end addition of 1880–82 (G.E. Street). 2m NW at **Van**, remains of a lead-mining community, mostly late 19C with some mine buildings and terraces of houses. 4m N of Llanidloes, a' **Trefeglwys**, *church* rebuilt 1864 (Poundley and Walker) with High Victorian detail to chancel windows and arch. B. Piercy, engineer o' the railways of mid Wales and Sardinia, was born here.

   6m N of Llandrindod Wells, at **Abbey Cwmhir**, High Victorian pai' of *Abbey Cwmhir Hall* (1867) and *church* (1866) by Poundley an' Walker, the house with some structural polychromy, the church period piece of tough design in the Early French manner, the towe' over the porch shaved to octagonal under a bell turret carried o' stumpy columns. Exceptional chancel glass of 1866 by Heaton, Butle' and Bayne. 19m NE of Llandrindod Wells, A488, **Knighton**, mostly lat 19C in centre with *Clock Tower* (1872; Haddon Bros). Parish *churc* (1875; S.P. Smith) with medieval tower and chancel added 1896 (J.I Pearson), painted decoration survives. *Station* (1861) is romanti' Gothic with exaggerated pointed gables, pyramid-roofed tower an' fretted bargeboards. 3m NW, *Knucklas Viaduct* (1864; H. Robertson), castellated 13-arched stone railway bridge. Just W, at **Heyop**, *church* (1880–82; J.L. Pearson) with old tower given a shingled spire. Simple 15C style, following previous building. 5m S of Knighton, B4355, at **Norton**, *Norton Manor* (1858), large Jacobean style house. *Church* rebuilt 1868 (G.G. Scott). To S, **Presteigne**, former county town of Radnorshire with stuccoed Greek *Shire Hall* (1829) and polychrome brick *Market Hall* (1869; T. Nicholson), Italian Gothic with a side clock tower.

WELSHPOOL. A458 18m W of Shrewsbury. Parish *church*, N of centre, restored 1856 (J. Billing) and 1870 (G.E. Street), by Street the nave roof, pulpit and elaborate chancel fittings. Chancel monument to the 2nd Earl of Powis, alabaster effigy (1852; E. Richardson) in carved recess designed by G.G. Scott. In Church St, *Church House* (1892; T. Price) and *Powysland Museum* (1874; D. Walker), High Victorian Gothic in yellow brick, still very Victorian inside with the collections of the local archaeological society. In High St, large *Town Hall* (1873; B. Lay), stone with steep-roofed central clock tower. In Mount St, *Christ Church*, (1839–44; T. Penson), neo-Norman with interior details all in terracotta, including the font, an early use of the material. Built for the coming-of-age of Viscount Clive of Powis Castle. *Welshpool Station* (1860) is surprisingly large with French pavilion roofs and good platform ironwork. *Powis Castle* (NT), continuously occupied since the 13C and by the Herbert family since 1587, has spectacular interiors from the 17C to 19C. The main 19C works were from 1815–18 by Sir R. Smirke and c 1902–04 by G.F. Bodley. By Bodley, the ground-floor dining-room and first-floor Oak Drawing-Room, richly Elizabethan. 2m E of Welshpool, B4388, prominent from Powis Castle, **Leighton**, where J. Naylor, Liverpool banker, built the *church* (1851–53) and *Hall* (c 1850–56) to designs by W.H. Gee of Liverpool. The two are linked by a mile-long avenue. The church, designed as a landmark with very large tower and spire, is expensive to the last detail with flying buttresses, carved gargoyles and lush tracery. Inside, a complete period piece with lofty hammerbeam roof, Minton tiles, much carved work and strongly coloured windows by Forrest and Bromley. The estate was laid out with the latest modern technology, its own gasworks, turbine-driven water supply, and a liquid manure tank on the mountain above served by a funicular railway, the manure being pumped through pipes to the fields. Fine plantations, notably of redwoods. The house is Gothic with an immense octagonal tower. Over the entrance a clockwork carillon that played folk tunes or suitable national anthems to arriving guests. Interior with massive great hall and remarkable decoration by A.W.N. Pugin and J.G. Crace, fireplaces, tile floors and painted ceilings. In the gardens, stone bridges, pools and fountains, one pool with statue of Icarus at the moment of hitting the water in his fall from the skies.

8m NE of Welshpool, A483, at **Llandysilio**, *church* (1867; G.E. Street), a good example of Street's small country churches with circular tower and conical cap, excellent fittings by Street, including E window, made by Clayton and Bell. Richly coloured S window in nave by J. Powell and Sons (1879). At **Llanymynech**, to N, *church* (1844; T. Penson), just in Shropshire, fully neo-Norman, but like Christ Church, Welshpool, with the ornamental detail in terracotta. 3m N of Welshpool, B4392, at **Guilsfield**, splendid medieval church restored 1879 by Street who added the screen with most unusual wheel tracery, E window, altar, reredos and pulpit. Memorial to J. Jones by J.H. Foley

(1857). 9m NW of Welshpool, A490, at **Bwlch-y-cibiau**, small, apsed *church* (1862–64; G.G. Scott) with W rose. Interior with good roofs, carved pulpit, E window by Wailes (1873), W window by Powells (1877). 2m N at **Llanfechain**, *church*, late 12C, restored 1883 (J. Douglas) with pretty shingled spire, chancel woodwork and reredos. 8m W of Llanfyllin, B4393, **Lake Vyrnwy**, Liverpool Corporation's water reservoir, constructed 1881–88 (T. Hawksley and G.F. Deacon) with great stone dam and *straining tower* (G.F. Deacon), 1m N, a circular stone fortified tower with stair turret and conical copper roofs. 5m S of Welshpool, A483, at **Berriew**, estate village of Vaynor Park with picturesque timber-framed houses, mostly 17C but given a late 19C trim of bargeboards and ornate chimneys. *Vaynor Park* is 17C refronted in Jacobean style (1840–53; T. Penson). 5m W, B4390, at **Manafon**, *church* restored 1898 (J. Douglas) with characteristic woodwork. *Henllys Hall* (1898), Elizabethan style in grey stone with red stone windows, is probably by Douglas. 5m SE, A483, at **Abermule**, iron *bridge* (1852; T. Penson) over the Severn. 1½m NE, B4386, *Cefn Bryntalch* (1869; G.F. Bodley), small country house in red brick with white sash windows, a very early example of the revival of Georgian motifs, showing Bodley and Philip Webb, who collaborated on the design here, among the pioneers in the development of an alternative to the Gothic. The style is not Georgian, however, but a relaxed combination of vernacular elements from the 17C and early 18C, half-timbering on the porch bay, pedimented porch and near symmetrical three-gabled garden front. By the road, brick and half-timbered lodge. To E, B4386, **Montgomery**, former county town of Montgomeryshire. In the Square, handsome 18C town hall with upper floor of 1828. Behind, parish *church* with ornate reredos (c 1850; R.C. Carpenter) and pulpit by Street (c 1877). NE of centre, ruined *County Gaol* (c 1832; T. Penson) with classical gatehouse (1866; J. Poundley) in triumphal arch form.

5m SW of Abermule, A483, **Newtown**, weaving town called the 'Leeds of Wales' in the early 19C but in decline after 1850. A centre of early socialism, Chartism being a strong force here in the 1830s, and also the home town of the most famous pioneer of socialism, Robert Owen (1771–1858), though the scene of his experiments was New Lanark, Strathclyde, in Scotland. He is buried by the ruins of the old *church* by the river, E of Broad St, with memorial (1902; A. Toft) showing labourers receiving justice from his hands. Broad St runs S from *Long Bridge* (1826; T. Penson) to the pretty *Library* (1902; F. Shayler), freely styled with half-timbered upper floor and corner balcony, at the crossroads. *Barclays Bank* (1898; Wood and Kendrick), in the richest red and yellow terracotta with clock tower, and *Midland Bank*, on site of Owen's birthplace with museum upstairs, complete the group at The Cross. On S side of town, on A483, *church* (1843–47; T. Penson), lancet Gothic all in yellow brick with saddleback-roofed tower. Chancel 1874, the E window of 1902 showing Queen Victoria offering her crown to Christ. *Baptist church* (1881; G. Morgan), opposite, unusually grand in red brick and stone with portico and complete galleried interior. On Kerry Rd, by the station, *Royal Welsh Warehouse* (1872; D. Walker), red-brick warehouse and shop of the mail-order business of Sir Pryce Pryce-Jones, founded 1861, the first in the world. N of the Long Bridge, Penygloddfa, still with characteristic weavers' housing. 5m N, B4389, **Tregynon**, estate village of *Gregynog*, to SW, owned in 19C by the Hanbury-Tracy family of Toddington, Gloucestershire. H. Hanbury-Tracy spent a fortune on improving the estate and supporting the declining woollen industry of

Newtown. Most surprising was his use of concrete. The house itself, built c 1837, is encased in concrete imitation timber-framing of c 1860–70. In the grounds, two concrete bridges, in the village, the *school* (1872) and *Concrete Cottages* as well as several farmhouses in concrete. The material was mass concrete, rendered over, with roofs of concrete finished in slate. In the *church* elaborate reredos (1902) and stencilled E wall around E window by Clayton and Bell (1875). 8m W of Newtown, A470, **Llandinam**, birthplace of David Davies (1818–90), the great railway builder of South Wales, creator of Barry Docks. By the bridge, *statue* of Davies (c 1895; A. Gilbert), identical to the one at Barry. Davies' first contract was for the approaches to the *bridge*, a pretty iron single span of 1846 (T. Penson). Hefty Gothic *chapel* (1872; Szlumper and Aldwinkle) on the main road. Parish *church*, restored 1864–65 by Street, with new timber bell stage to the tower, arcade and E window by Clayton and Bell. Davies' house, *Broneiron* (1864; D. Walker), is W of the village, plain Italianate. N of the village, *Plas Dinam* (1873–74; W.E. Nesfield), bought by Davies in 1884. Picturesquely composed house in the 'Old English' style developed by Nesfield and Norman Shaw in the 1870s, half-timbered and pargetted porch bay the focal element of a front with all the elements of the Nesfield–Shaw style present, great hall to right with large stone-mullioned bay, leaded parapet and pretty small-paned hipped dormers above, slate-hung gable beyond and varied array of lower gables to left. Roofline accentuated with tall moulded brick stacks. 8m NW, A470, at **Carno**, small High Victorian *church* (1863; J.W. Poundley), polychrome stone with conical top to the tower.

INDEX OF PLACES

INDEX OF ARCHITECTS, ARTISTS AND CRAFTSMEN

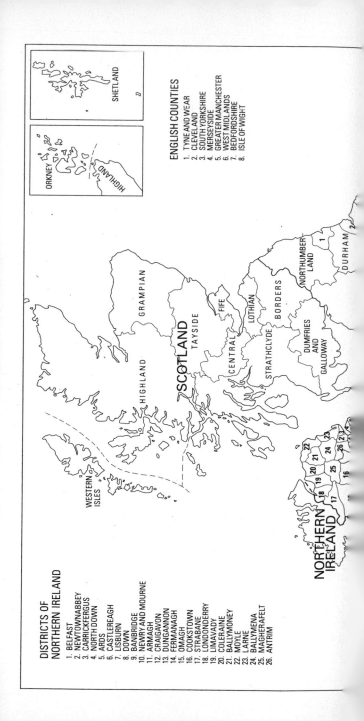

DISTRICTS OF
NORTHERN IRELAND

1. BELFAST
2. NEWTOWNABBEY
3. CARRICKFERGUS
4. NORTH DOWN
5. ARDS
6. CASTLEREAGH
7. LISBURN
8. DOWN
9. BANBRIDGE
10. NEWRY AND MOURNE
11. ARMAGH
12. CRAIGAVON
13. DUNGANNON
14. FERMANAGH
15. OMAGH
16. COOKSTOWN
17. STRABANE
18. LONDONDERRY
19. LIMAVADY
20. COLERAINE
21. BALLYMONEY
22. MOYLE
23. LARNE
24. BALLYMENA
25. MAGHERAFELT
26. ANTRIM

ENGLISH COUNTIES

1. TYNE AND WEAR
2. CLEVELAND
3. SOUTH YORKSHIRE
4. MERSEYSIDE
5. GREATER MANCHESTER
6. WEST MIDLANDS
7. BEDFORDSHIRE
8. ISLE OF WIGHT

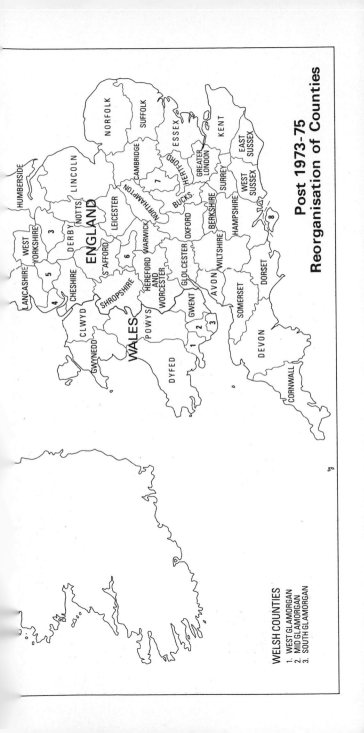

**Post 1973-75
Reorganisation of Counties**

WELSH COUNTIES
1. WEST GLAMORGAN
2. MID GLAMORGAN
3. SOUTH GLAMORGAN

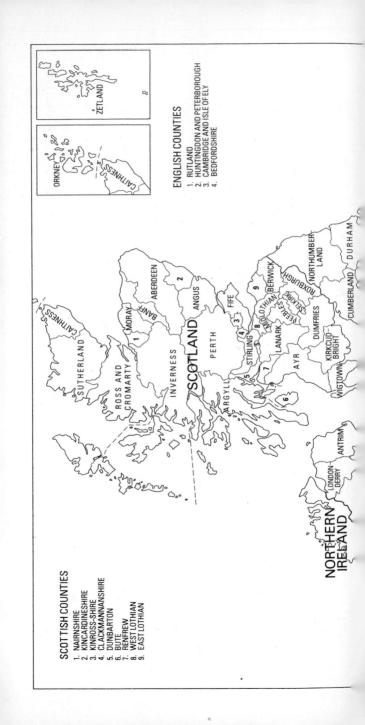

SCOTTISH COUNTIES

1. NAIRNSHIRE
2. KINCARDINESHIRE
3. KINROSS-SHIRE
4. CLACKMANNANSHIRE
5. DUNBARTON
6. BUTE
7. RENFREW
8. WEST LOTHIAN
9. EAST LOTHIAN

ENGLISH COUNTIES

1. RUTLAND
2. HUNTINGDON AND PETERBOROUGH
3. CAMBRIDGE AND ISLE OF ELY
4. BEDFORDSHIRE

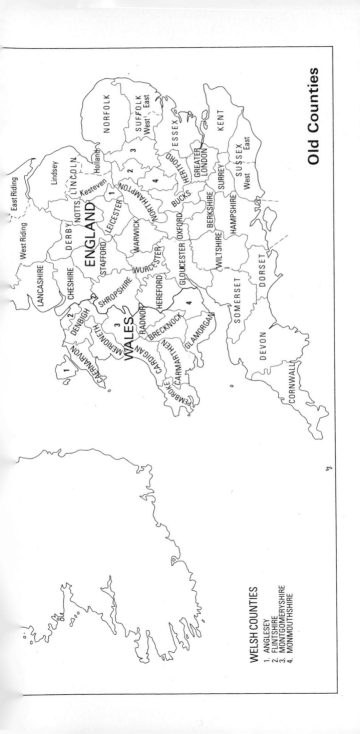

Old Counties

East Riding

West Riding

LANCASHIRE

CHESHIRE

DERBY

NOTTS

Lindsey

LINCOLN

Kesteven

Holland

NORFOLK

STAFFORD

LEICESTER

1

2

3

SUFFOLK
West¹ East

DENBIGH

SHROPSHIRE

2

WARWICK

NORTHAMPTON

4

HERTFORD

ESSEX

MERIONETH

WALES

3

RADNOR

WURCESTER

HEREFORD

BRECKNOCK

GLOUCESTER

4

OXFORD

BUCKS

GREATER
LONDON

KENT

CARDIGAN

CARMARTHEN

GLAMORGAN

BERKSHIRE

SURREY

SUSSEX
West East

PEMBROKE

WILTSHIRE

HAMPSHIRE

CAERNARVON

1

ENGLAND

SOMERSET

DORSET

DEVON

CORNWALL

WELSH COUNTIES
1. ANGLESEY
2. FLINTSHIRE
3. MONTGOMERYSHIRE
4. MONMOUTHSHIRE

NOTES

NOTES

NOTES